Introduction to CULINARY ARTS

Second Edition

THE CULINARY INSTITUTE OF AMERICA®

THE WORLD'S PREMIER CULINARY COLLEGE

PEARSON

Boston   Columbus   Indianapolis   New York   San Francisco   Upper Saddle River

Amsterdam   Cape Town   Dubai   London   Madrid   Milan   Munich   Paris   Montréal   Toronto

Delhi   Mexico City   São Paulo   Sydney   Hong Kong   Seoul   Singapore   Taipei   Tokyo

Acquiring Editor: Vernon Anthony
Program Manager: Alexis Duffy
Editorial Assistant: Lara Dimmick
Director of Marketing: David Gesell
Marketing Manager: Stacey Martinez
Assistant Marketing Manager: Alicia Wozniak
Senior Marketing Assistant: Les Roberts
Team Lead: JoEllen Gohr
Project Manager: Kris Roach
Operations Specialist: Deidra Skahill
Senior Art Director: Jayne Conte
Cover Art: Foodcollection RF/Getty Images, Inc.
Cover Designer: Jerilyn Bockorick
Interior Design: Penny Stamp
Media Project Manager: April Cleland
Full-Service Project Management: Amy Gehl, S4Carlisle
Publishing Services
The Culinary Institute of America President:
Dr. Tim Ryan '77
**The Culinary Institute of America Vice-President, Dean
of Culinary Education**: Mark Erickson '77
**The Culinary Institute of America Director
of Publishing**: Nathalie Fischer
**The Culinary Institute of America Editorial
Assistant**: Laura Monroe '12
Editor: Jerry Gleason
Composition: S4Carlisle Publishing Services
Printer/Binder: LSC Communications
Cover Printer: LSC Communications
Text Font: ITC Century Std Book

Credits and acknowledgments borrowed from other sources and reproduced, with permission, in this textbook appear on the appropriate page within text. Chef Knife: Yinghua/Dreamstime LLC; Ad: Anne Stahl/iStock Photo

Library of Congress Cataloging-in-Publication Data
Gleason, Jerry.
Introduction to culinary arts / Jerry Gleason, the Culinary Institute of America. — Second edition.
  pages cm
ISBN-13: 978-0-13-273744-9
ISBN-10: 0-13-273744-2
1. Cooking—Study and teaching. 2. Food—Safety measures. I. Culinary Institute of America. II. Title.
TX661.G54 2015
363.19'2—dc23
    2012047342

8

www.PearsonSchool.com/CTE

ISBN 10:   0-13-273744-2
ISBN 13: 978-0-13-273744-9

Foreword

The Culinary Institute of America has a strong commitment to culinary education. We have been in the forefront of culinary education since we first opened our doors in 1946. It is precisely because we feel so strongly about the benefits of a great education that we have partnered with Pearson Education to prepare the textbook you hold in your hands.

A culinary education offers you a clear path to a career—it does not just include culinary theory; it also provides practical knowledge and skills you can apply to your first job and throughout your professional life. As the foodservice and hospitality industries become more competitive, you need to have appropriate skills. This book reflects the areas we concentrate on in our associate and bachelor degree programs: product knowledge, sanitation and safety, nutrition and food science, and, of course, culinary and baking techniques.

There are many reasons to join the ranks of those who work with food for a living. Most people enter the culinary arts because they love food and cooking and because the want to make people happy. However, throughout your culinary career, you will find that what you offer to the industry, and what you can expect from it, will change. That is what a career is all about.

Keep your interest alive and your love for food and cooking fresh by trying new foods and new restaurants, taking classes or attending workshops, and perhaps even trying new types of work. Remember the spark that first urged you toward a culinary education. Do your best to nurture it, feed it, and keep it alive and growing. The rewards from this industry are among the greatest you could ever hope to achieve.

Source: Culinary Institute of America

Dr. Tim Ryan
President
The Culinary Institute of America

For Courses in Culinary Arts

Introduction to Culinary Arts, Second Edition, *covers everything from culinary theory and management to sanitation and safety to nutrition and food science to culinary and baking techniques, instilling practical knowledge and skills that students can apply throughout their career.*

Teaching and Learning Experience:

- From theory to application, provides a solid foundation in culinary arts
- Offers a wealth of features that spotlight key techniques and information
- Addresses culinary management and business

Web Description:

Your professional career in culinary arts begins here. *Introduction to Culinary Arts, Second Edition,* covers everything from culinary theory and management to sanitation and safety to nutrition and food science to culinary and baking techniques, instilling practical knowledge and skills that you can apply throughout your career.

Hallmark Features:

From theory to application, provides a solid foundation in culinary arts:

- Covers kitchen and culinary basics, including the HACCP System, fire safety, and foodservice equipment.
- Front matter includes the section *Culinary Education and Training* that walks students through the day in a life of a typical culinary arts student, outlines education requirements for various culinary degrees and professional development, covers a typical day working in a restaurant, and addresses the roles restaurants play in the economy.

Offers a wealth of features that spotlight important information:

- Boxed features throughout the text callout core topics and techniques. Topics include: *Culinary Science, Culinary History, Culinary Math, Culinary Diversity,* and *Basic Culinary Skills.*
- A *Reading Preview* opens each chapter and lists *Key Concepts* that students can expect to learn in the chapter.

Addresses culinary management and business:

- A separate chapter covers in depth the latest on nutrition and shows students how to build menus that offer healthy options for customers.

- A section dedicated to addressing customer complaints and other common problems associated with running a restaurant gives students tools to manage difficult situations when engaging the general public.
- A separate chapter details the steps involved in owning a restaurant, purchasing and tracking inventory, and the day-to-day details of managing a restaurant.

Table of Contents

UNIT ONE: KITCHEN BASICS
1. Food Safety
2. Kitchen Safety
3. Foodservice Equipment
4. Knives and Smallware

UNIT TWO: CULINARY BASICS
5. Using Standardized Recipes
6. Seasonings and Flavorings
7. Getting Ready to Cook
8. Cooking Methods

UNIT THREE: CULINARY APPLICATIONS
9. Breakfast Foods
10. Garde Manger
11. Sandwiches, Appetizers, and Hors d'Oeuvre
12. Fruit and Vegetables
13. Grains, Legumes, and Pasta
14. Stocks, Sauces, and Soups
15. Fish and Shellfish
16. Meat and Poultry

UNIT FOUR: BREADS AND DESSERTS
17. Yeast Breads, Rolls, and Pastries
18. Quick Breads
19. Desserts

UNIT FIVE: CULINARY MANAGEMENT
20. Working in a Restaurant
21. Menus
22. Nutrition
23. The Business of a Restaurant

Appendix
Glossary
Index

Introduction to Culinary Arts

Contents

Culinary Education and Training xii
- Culinary Education: A Day in the Life xii
- Becoming a Professional xviii
- Working in Restaurants xx
- Restaurant Industry Overview xxi

Unit 1 — Kitchen Basics   2

Chapter 1 Food Safety 2
- 1.1 Sanitary Food Handling .3
- 1.2 The Flow of Food 21
- 1.3 The HACCP System 30

Chapter 2 Kitchen Safety 38
- 2.1 Fire Safety 39
- 2.2 Accidents and Injuries 48

Chapter 3 Foodservice Equipment 68
- 3.1 Work Flow in the Kitchen 69
- 3.2 Receiving and Storage Equipment 75
- 3.3 Preparation and Cooking Equipment 81
- 3.4 Holding and Service Equipment 94

Chapter 4 Knives and Smallware 104
- 4.1 Using Knives 105
- 4.2 Using Smallware 124

Unit 2 — Culinary Basics   142

Chapter 5 Using Standardized Recipes 142
- 5.1 Understanding Standardized Recipes 143
- 5.2 Converting Recipes 154

Chapter 6 Seasonings and Flavorings **168**

6.1 Sensory Perception............................169

6.2 Herbs, Spices, and Aromatics 175

6.3 Condiments, Nuts, and Seeds 191

6.4 Seasoning and Flavoring Foods 196

Chapter 7 Getting Ready to Cook **208**

7.1 Mise en Place...............................209

7.2 Working in the Kitchen.......................217

7.3 Food Presentation 227

Chapter 8 Cooking Methods **236**

8.1 Dry-Heat Methods............................237

8.2 Moist-Heat Methods..........................252

Unit 3 Culinary Applications 266

Chapter 9 Breakfast Foods **266**

9.1 Eggs and Dairy..............................267

9.2 Breakfast Foods and Drinks 284

Chapter 10 Garde Manger.....................**295**

10.1 Dressings and Dips..........................296

10.2 Salads 305

10.3 Cheese.....................................320

10.4 Cold Food Presentation 332

Chapter 11 Sandwiches, Appetizers, and Hors d'Oeuvre **348**

11.1 Sandwiches 349

11.2 Appetizers and Hors d'Oeuvre 359

Chapter 12 Fruit and Vegetables **369**

12.1 Fruit.......................................370

12.2 Vegetables 389

Chapter 13 Grains, Legumes, and Pasta ...420
13.1 Rice and Other Grains 421
13.2 Beans and Other Legumes .434
13.3 Pasta 442

Chapter 14 Stocks, Sauces, and Soups 456
14.1 Stocks 457
14.2 Sauces 467
14.3 Soups 481

Chapter 15 Fish and Shellfish 497
15.1 Fish 498
15.2 Shellfish 518

Chapter 16 Meat and Poultry 533
16.1 Meat 534
16.2 Poultry 553

Unit 4 — Breads and Desserts — 565

Chapter 17 Yeast Breads, Rolls, and Pastries 565
17.1 Introduction to Baking 566
17.2 Yeast Dough 583
17.3 Breads, Rolls, and Pastries 592

Chapter 18 Quick Breads 604
18.1 Muffins and Quick Breads 605
18.2 Biscuits and Scones 611

Chapter 19 Desserts 622
19.1 Chocolate 623
19.2 Custards, Mousses, and Frozen Desserts 631
19.3 Cookies and Cakes 640
19.4 Pies, Tarts, Pastries, and Fruit Desserts 660

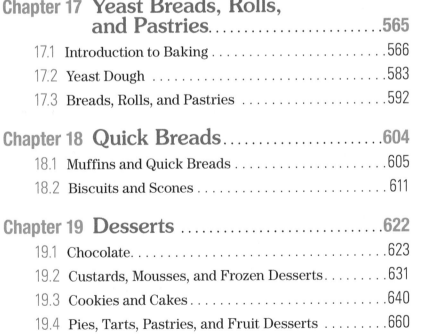

Unit 5 — Culinary Management 674

Chapter 20 Working in a Restaurant 674
  20.1 Restaurant Personnel 675
  20.2 Service Tools, Utensils, and Equipment 688
  20.3 Serving the Meal 700
  20.4 Handling Complaints and Problems 712

Chapter 21 Menus 723
  21.1 Planning the Menu 724
  21.2 Pricing Menu Items 740

Chapter 22 Nutrition 751
  22.1 Nutrition Basics 752
  22.2 Making Menus More Nutritious 772

Chapter 23 The Business of a Restaurant 787
  23.1 Owning Your Own Restaurant 788
  23.2 Purchasing and Inventorying 799
  23.3 Managing a Restaurant 807

Appendix 821

Glossary 832

Index 851

Feature Lists

CULINARY SCIENCE

The pH Scale 10

Chemical Hazard: Mercury in Fish 16

Flames of Different Colors 45

Calibrating a Thermometer 131

Recipes on the Internet 145

Osmosis 198

Why Do Egg Whites Cook before
the Yolks? 275

Steps in Making Cheese 327

Parts of a Grain 422

Dehydrating and Rehydrating Foods 437

Convection 462

Left- or Right-Eyed Fish? 504

Aquaculture 521

Home on the Range 548

History of Turkeys 555

Classes of Wheat 568

The 240 Factor 586

Baking Powder and Baking Soda 606

Where Does Chocolate Come From? . . .627

"Enriched with Essential Vitamins
and Minerals" 754

Colors and Nutrients 764

CULINARY HISTORY

Before the Refrigerator 28

Early Ovens and Stoves 59

The Oldest Tool Known to Man 116

Spice Routes 180

Professionalism: The Culinarian's
Code 225

Medieval Cuisine 242

The First Cookbook? 271

Caterina de Medici 310

Grana Padano 321

Pierre François de la Varenne 353

The Vatel Society 381

Travels of the Tomato 406

The Goddess of Grain 427

Soups and Sops 485

Antoine Carême 535

George Auguste Escoffier 612

Julia Child 641

Forks & Spaghetti 691

Nouvelle Cuisine 777

The Influence of Dieter Schorner 802

CULINARY MATH

Measuring Angles 120

Weight or Volume? 148

Converting Fractions 156

Multiplying Fractions 157

Personalizing a Timeline 213

Trim Loss 385

A Pint's a Pound? 575

Raw Food Cost 743

Basic Forecasting Technique 791

Balancing the Cash Register 809

CULINARY DIVERSITY

India 201

Italy 254

Vietnamese Breakfasts 287

Sweden 338

Spain 364

Thailand 443

France 473

Kosher Food 482

Russia 508

Caribbean 528

China 558

The Middle East 595

Mexico 615

Korea 634

Brazil 710

Greece 775

BASIC CULINARY SKILLS

Proper Hand Washing 13

Making a Chiffonade Cut 115

Making Julienne and Bâtonnet Cuts 115

Dicing 116

Making an Oblique Cut 117

Sharpening a Knife 121

Honing a Knife 122

Mirepoix 188

Sachet d'Épices 189

Toasting Nuts, Seeds, and Spices 194

Using Molds to Shape Foods 231

Grilling and Broiling 240-241

Roasting and Baking 243

Sautéing 244

Pan-Frying 247

Deep-Frying 250

Steaming 255

Poaching, Simmering, and Boiling 256

Braising and Stewing (with Initial
Searing) 258

Braising and Stewing (with Initial
Blanching) 259

Poaching Eggs 273

Frying Eggs 274

Scrambling Eggs 276

French Omelette 278

Clarified Butter 282

Cooking Pancakes and Waffles 285

Cooking Crêpes 286

Vinaigrette 298

Mayonnaise 301

Mixed Green Salad 312

Croutons 313

Making a Fan Cut 343

Making a Club Sandwich 356

Making a Wrap 357

Vegetable Tempura 361

Poaching Fruit 386

Puréeing Fruit 387

Trimming and Dicing Onions 407

Trimming and Mincing Garlic 408

Tomato Concassé 409

Glazing Vegetables (Classical Method) . . .411

Making Vegetable Braises or Stews 412

Deep-Frying Vegetables 414

Puréeing Potatoes 415

Boiled or Steamed Grains 428

Mush (Porridge) 429

Pilaf 430

Risotto 431

Cooking Dry Legumes 439

Fresh Egg Pasta 448

Boiling Pasta 449

Brown Stock 462

White Stock 463

Reducing Stock 465

Making a Glaze 465

Roux 470

Roux-Thickened Sauce 472

Pureé Sauce 474

Warm Emulsion Sauce 475

Broth 486

Consommé 487

Hearty Soup 488

Filleting Flat Fish (Quarter Fillets) 510

Filleting Round Fish 511

Sautéing Fish 514

Broiling Fish 515

Preparing Live Lobsters 522

Removing Meat from a Cooked
Lobster 523

Peeling and Deveining Shrimp 524

Opening Clams 525

Opening Oysters 526

Making Cutlets 549

Tying a Roast 551–552

Disjointing Poultry 556

Trussing Poultry 557

Boneless Breast Portions 559

Straight Dough-Mixing Method 587

Pizza Dough 589

Preshaping Dough into Rounds 594

Baguettes 596

Creaming Method for Blueberry
Muffins 609

Rubbed-Dough Method 614

Making Laminated Biscuits 617

Making a Ganache 629

Baked Custard 632

Stirred Custard 633

Boiled Custard 635

Frozen Soufflé 638

Creaming Method for Cookies 646

Foaming Method for Cookies 646

Cut-Out Cookies 649

Warm Foaming Method 655

Icing a Cake 658

Rubbed-Dough Method Pie Dough 661

Choux Paste 666

Service Sequence for Maître d' (Md),
Server (S), and Runner (R) 709

Batch Cooking for Vegetables 779

Replacing Oil with Stock in Vinaigrette . . .779

Culinary Education and Training

READING PREVIEW

Key Concepts

- Learning about a day in the life of a culinary arts student
- Understanding the different types of culinary education required to become a professional
- Learning about a typical day in a restaurant
- Understanding the role restaurants play in the economy

Culinary Education: A Day in the Life

A degree in culinary education, whether the traditional culinary arts or the baking and pastry arts, is an important first step toward becoming a professional. Culinary

Source: Culinary Institute of America

programs introduce some important topics, such as food safety, costing, and culinary history, along with such basic courses as writing and math. A well-rounded culinary education is a combination of classwork and hands-on work done directly in the kitchen or bakeshop. Real-world learning opportunities make theory into something much more concrete. Some programs require students to participate in an applied learning experience in a restaurant or hotel (known as either an internship or externship); some programs include restaurants staffed by students and open to the public.

The Culinary Institute of America offers two types of degrees. The associate's degree is a two-year program offering two areas of specialization: culinary arts or baking and pastry arts. The bachelor's degree is a four-year program. The freshman and sophomore years of the bachelor's degree cover the same coursework as the associate's degree. The junior and senior years focus on management topics, offer the chance to specialize in a specific cuisine, or focus on other areas such as culinary science. Here, you will meet two associate's degree candidates and two bachelor's degree candidates.

Culinary Arts: Associate's Degree Hi, I'm Stephen. I'm about nine weeks away from finishing my associate's degree. Here at school, I'm what we call an "a.m. student." That means a typical day of class starts at 6 or 6:30 in the morning and ends around 2 or 3 in the afternoon. The "p.m. students" start class at 2 and finish around

9:30 or 10. Those hours are pretty flexible, though. For a "Quantity Cooking" class last week, I started at 4 in the morning and finished by noon. The "Table Service" class I'm in now starts a little later, usually by 8, and I'm done around 4.

I've completed all of my hands-on kitchen classes; those are the classes where we spend the day in a kitchen cooking a specific type of cuisine or practicing a specific skill, such as butchering meat or filleting fish. At a community college, they might call kitchen classes "labs," but here at the school, we call them "kitchens" because students are making food that gets served to the rest of the school for lunch or dinner. Each class taught me a different set of skills, so now I'm able to prepare foods that weren't so familiar when I started. Boning a chicken is easy, and so is chopping onions. Right now, I'm in a class that actually "runs" a public restaurant. Half of my classmates work in the kitchen—what we call the "back of the house"—and others are in the dining room (the "front of the house"). I'm working the lunch shift, so by 7 in the morning, I'm gathering my things and putting on a tie to get to class by 8. As soon as I arrive in class, I do my side work to set up the dining room. "Side work" includes jobs like filling salt and pepper shakers or water pitchers, folding napkins, or assembling the menus. I'm assigned to the pantry, so I get coffee and tea ready, cut butter and lemons, and line baskets to hold breads and rolls. When the dining room is full of guests, the rest of the waiters rely on me to have those things ready for them. Once the dining room is ready, we sit for a lecture. The topics might include coffee service, apéritifs (pre-dinner drinks), or tableside preparation of salads or desserts.

The meal that the staff eats before service starts is called the "family meal." It is as much a learning experience as the lectures. We sample different dishes from the menu. That helps us describe the dishes to our guests. After that, we have our "line-up." That's when our professor, who is also the dining room manager (more commonly known as the *maître d'*), goes over the special drinks and other menu items for that day, tells us about any special events, and checks the room with us to be sure it's ready for our guests. We open the doors at 11:30 and stay open until 1 in the afternoon. We might have a number of responsibilities, depending on our schedule and the dining room position we are learning. Whether we are in the pantry, working as host, or as a server, our primary focus is learning and practicing professional table service.

After service, we clean up and reset the dining room for the evening class so they have all their tables prepared and ready to go. It is important to us that we have things ready for dinner service, because we all have to rely on each other. Teamwork is another one of the important skills we learn and practice. We end the class with a discussion on how the lunch service went and things that we could do to improve. We usually clean up between 1 and 3 in the afternoon. Cleanup is followed by the day's second lecture, and we are out of class between 3 and 4.

The rest of the day is mine, so I might go to the recreation center to work out before hitting the books or, if I have a research assignment, I might head to the library.

Dinner is usually around 6. It is nothing like a typical school cafeteria; I'll get my dinner from one or several kitchen classes. It might come from a kitchen class that's studying Asian or Mediterranean cuisine. I really enjoy the conversations at the table. Everyone critiques the food or thinks up ways to make it better. It's a great meal and also a great way to prepare for the classes that are coming up. Most nights, I use the hours between 7 and 11 to do my studying, unless I have a club meeting. Clubs usually meet around 9:30 or 10. If they met any earlier, half the student body would still be in class! Once in a while, I might go out for a bit of socializing or to the store with my roommate, Ben, when he gets home from his campus job at 11. That probably sounds late, but I've gotten used to the schedule. I hear it is a lot like the hours I'll be keeping when I get out in the industry. The last thing I do before I go to sleep is to get my table-service uniform ready so that when I wake up in the morning, I don't have to think about where I put everything.

Ben, my roommate, is just starting his bachelor's degree in culinary arts. I'll let him tell you about his typical day.

Chart 1 Associate's Degree, Culinary Arts: Freshman and Sophomore Years

Freshman Year First Semester	Freshman Year Second Semester	Externship	Sophomore Year First Semester	Sophomore Year Second Semester
Culinary Math	Introduction to Management	Applied Work Experience	Baking and Pastry	Introduction to Customer Service
Food Safety	Meat Identification, Fabrication, and Utilization		Skill Development	Wine Studies
Introduction to Gastronomy	Seafood Identification and Fabrication		Garde Manger	Contemporary Restaurant Cooking
Nutrition	Modern Banquet Cookery		Cuisines of the Americas	Contemporary Restaurant Service
Product Knowledge	Introduction to À la Carte Cooking		Controlling Costs and Purchasing Food	Formal Restaurant Cooking
Culinary Fundamentals	High-Volume Production Cookery		Cuisines of the Mediterranean	Formal Restaurant Service
	College Writing		Cuisines of Asia	
			Menu Development	
First-Year Seminar*	Culinary Practical Exam I*			Culinary Practical Exam II*
Externship Prep Seminar*	Externship Registration Seminar*			Costing Exam*
Total Credits: 15.0	**Total Credits: 16.5**	**Total Credits: 3**	**Total Credits: 18.0**	**Total Credits: 16.5**
	TOTAL CREDITS FOR AOS DEGREE: 69.0			

*Seminars and exams must be completed within these semesters.

Culinary Arts: Management Degree

I just completed my associate's degree requirements, and now I'm a junior in the bachelor's program. The schedule is a little different now. Most of my classes are lecture-style, instead of in a kitchen. It took a little while to get used to the additional reading and homework, but I know that if I want to move into a management position, I need to know about spreadsheets and accounting as well as psychology and marketing. So, when my alarm clock sounds at 6 in the morning, I get up and have a cup of coffee before heading to the recreation center to run a few laps on the indoor track. I find it helps me feel focused and alert all day. Then it's back to the dorm to iron my

Source: Culinary Institute of America

shirt. We are expected to wear "business casual" attire for our management classes, so ironing has become second nature after two years of school. Once I'm presentable, I head to the main dining room for some breakfast before class. I always think how glad I am that I don't have to get up at 2 like I did when it was my turn to be in "Breakfast Cookery" class, but I'm grateful for the experience. I can make eggs at least 60 different ways now!

I start with my "Accounting" class, where we are learning how to create profit-and-loss statements. My next classes, one in leadership and one in marketing, aren't for a

Chart 2 Bachelor's Degree, Culinary Arts Management: Junior and Senior Years

Junior Year First Semester	Junior Year Second Semester	Intersession	Senior Year First Semester	Senior Year Second Semester
Survey of Mathematics or Science Fundamentals	History and Cultures of Europe	Food, Wine, and (Agri) culture Trip	Principles of Macroeconomics or Principles of Microeconomics	Italian Renaissance and Baroque Art
Literature and Composition	Anthropology of Food I		History and Cultures of Asia	Advanced Wine Studies
Elementary [Foreign Language] II	Intermediate [Foreign Language]		Current Issues in Hospitality Technology	Marketing and Promoting Food
Financial Accounting	Foodservice Management		Human Resource Management	Leadership and Ethics
Women in Leadership	Advanced Cooking		Honors Thesis Seminar	Senior Thesis: Culinary Arts
Total Credits: 15.0	**Total Credits: 15.0**	**Total Credits: 3**	**Total Credits: 15.0**	**Total Credits: 15.0**
	TOTAL JUNIOR-/SENIOR-YEAR CREDITS: 63.0 (BPS)			
	TOTAL CREDITS FOR AOS AND BPS DEGREES: 132.0			

few hours, so I take a break for lunch and then study or do some reading to keep up with trends in the foodservice industry. Once my classes end, I have about 3 hours to finish up the rest of my homework before getting ready for my on-campus job working as server in one of the public restaurants. Most of the other servers are actually students, but when a class is small or there are lots of reservations, the restaurant hires student workers. I get a good dose of real-world experience waiting on guests for the rest of the evening. I'm back at my room by around 10 unless I have any club meetings. I'm part of the business club that plans and manages events such as guest speakers or special-event dinners. By midnight, I'm ready to hit the sack. Tomorrow is just a few hours away.

Source: Culinary Institute of America

Baking and Pastry: Associate's Degree

Hi! I'm Jessica, a baking and pastry associate's degree student attending a culinary college. My typical day starts around 8:30 or 9 in the morning as a tour guide for prospective students and their families. I show them the classrooms and the public restaurants, and then we go on to baking and pastry kitchens. That's what I'm studying, so I really enjoy explaining all the classes.

Around 11:30, I go to the dining hall for a cup of coffee to go or to meet with friends who are already in class and just sitting down for lunch. I go back to my room around noon to go over recipes for class or finish my piping homework. Piping homework involves filling a pastry bag with icing and practicing different borders on a cardboard cake circle instead of the real thing. The chef will check to make sure the piping is smooth and even. We also practice making petals and forming a flower from an almond paste also known as marzipan. It has about the same consistency as modeling clay, and you can add food colors to get some beautiful effects. Then at around 1:30, I leave for class where we are learning basic ratios for recipes, and techniques for making and assembling cakes. Each class begins with a lecture to go over a new method or find out what our production schedule is for that day.

Yesterday, we made 50 vanilla cakes, 12 chocolate cakes, and 8 gallons of icing. Usually, the chef-instructor gives us a short demo, and then it is our turn to practice hands-on. We work with a partner to finish our projects and assignments. We have a dinner break around 6, and then come back to the bakeshop to finish any last items and clean the kitchen before the last lecture of the day. Class is usually over by around 8:30, so after class I go back to my dorm. I usually have homework to do each night. It might be more piping or I might be doing some research or reading about the recipes I'll be preparing tomorrow.

My roommate, Hillary, is getting a degree in baking and pastry arts management. She's already finished the first two years toward her bachelor's degree. I'll let her take you through her day.

Chart 3 Associate's Degree, Baking and Pastry Arts—Freshman and Sophomore Years

Freshman Year First Semester	Freshman Year Second Semester	Externship	Sophomore Year First Semester	Sophomore Year Second Semester
Baking and Pastry Techniques*	Principles of Design		Controlling Costs and Purchasing Food	Introduction to Customer Service
Baking Ingredients and Equipment Technology	Café Savory Foods Production		Confectionery Art and Special-Occasion Cakes	Wine Studies
Culinary Math*	Introduction to Management		Chocolate and Confectionery Technology and Techniques	Café Operations
Food Safety	Basic and Classical Cakes		Contemporary Cakes and Desserts	Beverages and Customer Service
Introduction to Gastronomy	Individual and Production Pastries		Specialty Breads	Restaurant and Production Desserts
Nutrition	Hearth Breads and Rolls		Advanced Baking Principles	Restaurant Operations: Baking and Pastry
	College Writing			Menu Development
First-Year Seminar*	Baking and Pastry Practical Exam I*		Baking and Pastry Practical Exam II*	Costing Exam*
Externship Prep Seminar*	Externship Registration Seminar*			
Total Credits 15.0	**Total Credits 16.5**	**Total Credits 3.0**	**Total Credits 18.0**	**Total Credits 16.5**
		TOTAL CREDITS FOR AOS DEGREE: 69.0		

*Seminars and exams must be completed within these semesters.

Baking and Pastry: Management Degree I'm up by 6:30 to get ready for the day. My first class is psychology, followed by another in computers. In our computer class, we learn about point-of-sales systems and spreadsheets, skills that I know I'll be using when I get into the industry. I have a break in my classes until around 1:30. That leaves enough time for me to have lunch in the main dining hall. Students are lucky to have so many choices; we can visit one of several kitchen classes to try out different cuisines or cooking styles. My afternoon classes include a history course that focuses on Europe and a language class—I'm studying Italian to prepare for a seminar on food and wine between junior and senior year. We'll travel to Italy to learn about food, culture, and cuisine in Italy. We'll visit farms, vineyards, food manufacturers, and food artisans.

Source: Culinary Institute of America

There's usually a fair amount of homework to finish, but I can often fit some of it in between classes. That leaves me some time to

Chart 4 Bachelor's Degree, Baking and Pastry Arts Management: Junior and Senior Years

Junior Year First Semester	Junior Year Second Semester	Intersession	Senior Year First Semester	Senior Year Second Semester
Survey of Mathematics or Science Fundamentals	History and Cultures of Europe	Food, Wine, and (Agri) culture Trip	Principles of Macroeconomics or Principles of Microeconomics	Shakespeare: Play and Performance
Literature and Composition	Anthropology of Food I		Feasting and Fasting in Latin America	Consumer Behavior
Elementary [Foreign Language] II	Intermediate [Foreign Language]		Current Issues in Hospitality Technology	Marketing and Promoting Food
Financial Accounting	Foodservice Management		Beverage Operations Management	Leadership and Ethics
Introduction to Creative Writing	Advanced Pastry		Honors Thesis Seminar	Field Experience and Action Plan
Total Credits: 15.0	**Total Credits: 15.0**	**Total Credits: 3**	**Total Credits: 15.0**	**Total Credits: 15.0**
Total Required Business Management Credits 24.0		**Total Culinary Credits: 3.0**	Organizational Behavior	
TOTAL JUNIOR-/SENIOR-YEAR CREDITS: 63.0 (BPS)				
TOTAL CREDITS FOR AOS AND BPS DEGREES: 132.0				

get involved in campus activities and clubs. It's a great way to meet new students as well as lend a helping hand with questions about the school or the community. One club is all about international students, so we plan events that feature a specific cuisine. Right now we are planning a Jamaican feast. Last week, it was all about Indian curry. To prepare myself to tackle administrative and management jobs when I graduate, I also am part of the student government.

I don't get back to my room until 10 or 11 at night, so that is when I check my e-mails and finish my homework, and then it is time for bed. Tomorrow is right around the corner!

Becoming a Professional

The path toward achieving professional status involves:

- Formal education
- Certification
- Continuing education
- Professional development
- Establishment of a professional network

Formal Education A sound and thorough culinary education is a logical first step in the development of your culinary career. Increasingly, employers are looking for job applicants who have culinary degrees. There are more than 800 schools in the United States alone that offer some form of post-secondary culinary education. You can find information about schools by searching for "cooking schools" or "culinary programs" in a search engine. Some culinary arts programs are provided in schools and colleges that specialize in the culinary arts; others are part of either a technical or community college or university that offers programs in many disciplines. Schools may offer programs that result in a certificate or an associate or bachelor's degree. Master's programs with a strong emphasis on food, as well as degrees in related areas such as nutrition and food science, are also important to professional chefs. The best culinary schools incorporate plenty of hands-on application in their curriculum.

An apprenticeship is a way to achieve a formal education without attending culinary school. The apprenticeship program sponsored by the American Culinary Federation (ACF) combines on-the-job training with technical classroom instruction.

Continuing Education Once you have achieved your initial training, you need to keep your skills current. The culinary profession is constantly evolving, and you will need to attend classes, workshops, and seminars to hone your skills in specialized areas and to keep up with new methods and styles of cooking.

Professional Development and Certification As your career progresses, you should join professional organizations; read professional magazines, newsletters, and books; and participate in culinary competitions. Certification provides a way to prove that you have met certain standards in the culinary field. A certification is recognition of your skill level. Typically, a certification program involves a specific level of experience in the field, course work, and passing of a written and practical cooking examination. To maintain your certification, you will need to refresh your knowledge and provide documentation of continuing education and professional development on a regular basis. Some of the organizations listed here, including the American Culinary Federation and the International Association of Culinary Professionals, offer certificate programs in specific areas.

Culinary Associations

American Culinary Federation (ACF)
180 Center Place Way
St. Augustine, FL 32095
(800) 624-9458
www.acfchefs.org

The American Institute of Wine & Food (AIWF)
95 Prescott Avenue
Monterey, CA 93940
(800) 274-2493
www.aiwf.org

Chefs Collaborative
89 South Street
Boston, MA 02111
(617) 236-5200
www.chefscollaborative.org

The International Council on Hotel, Restaurant and Institutional Education (CHRIE)
2810 North Parham Road, Suite 230
Richmond, VA 23294
(804) 346-4800
www.chrie.org

International Association of Culinary Professionals (IACP)
1100 Johnson Ferry Road, Suite 300
Atlanta, GA 30342
(800)928-4227
www.iacp.com

The James Beard Foundation
167 West 12th Street
New York, NY 10011
(800) 36BEARD
www.jamesbeard.org

National Restaurant Association (NRA)
1200 17th Street, NW
Washington, DC 20036
(202) 331-5900
www.restaurant.org

Oldways Preservation Trust
266 Beacon Street
Boston, MA 02116
(617) 421-5500
www.oldwayspt.org

ProChef Certification
1946 Campus Drive
Hyde Park, NY 12538-1499
(845) 452-4600
www.prochef.com

Share Our Strength (SOS)
1730 M Street, NW, Suite 700
Washington, DC 20036
(800) 969-4767
www.strength.org

Women Chefs and Restaurateurs (WCR)
P.O. Box 1875
Madison, AL 35758
(877) 927-7787
www.womenchefs.org

Establishing a Network You will want to network with other professionals to gain insight, recommendations, or guidance. Perhaps you can find a mentor or coach to help you reach a new level in your career. You can also mentor others when appropriate.

Working in Restaurants

The staff in a restaurant's kitchen must be ready to prepare, at any moment, a great variety of dishes. This can only be accomplished if they all organize their work properly and complete tasks efficiently. They know the importance of doing all the backup work, taking as much care with it as with the final stages of cooking. Here's a preview of Saturday in a large restaurant that serves only dinner.

3–4:00 a.m.	The baker, the first to arrive in the kitchen, makes the breads and baked desserts for the day. After everything is baked, the baker finishes by scrubbing down all the work surfaces, tools, and equipment in the work area. Often the last thing the baker does is sweep the floor.
11:00 a.m.	Just as the baker finishes and tosses the morning's apron into the laundry bag, the pantry cook and prep cooks arrive. After checking the existing stock, the pantry chef reviews the list left by the chef from the night before and writes a list of tasks to accomplish. The pantry chef and the prep cooks are responsible for peeling, chopping, dicing, or grating a range of ingredients to be ready for the cooks when they arrive, as well as preparing stocks, salad dressings, and marinades. They check off their tasks as they are completed and, before they leave, they wipe down the cutting boards and work tables and hone the knives.
3:00 p.m.	The chefs and cooks arrive. They immediately want to know how many reservations there are. The line cooks are the ones who cook the foods ordered by the guests. They prepare any sauces, stuffings, side dishes, or garnishes for their section of the menu. One line cook might do all the sautéed dishes from the menu and another might handle all the grilled dishes. The sous chef and the chef decide on the nightly specials.

5:00 p.m.	One of the line chefs prepares the "family dinner," the meal served to the staff before service begins.
6:00 p.m.	Dinner service starts slowly, but begins to build rapidly as more guests arrive.
8:00 p.m.	Dinner service has built to a frenzied pitch. The chef is acting as an "expediter" to make sure the kitchen stays organized. That means he or she calls out the orders as they come in from the dining room. Each one of the line cooks repeats, or "echoes," the dishes that he or she is responsible for completing. The sous chef has stopped working on prep and begun helping the grill cook keep up with a rush of orders from that station. All the orders are coming in at the same time and all the line chefs are cooking dishes rapidly, but also with an eye toward maintaining quality.
10:00 p.m.	The restaurant's official closing time finally arrives. Things gradually begin to slow down. The staff is still working hard, but now their attention turns to cooling, wrapping, and storing food. Some of them begin to prepare for the next day. They all are responsible for cleaning their work areas from top to bottom. The chef talks to the dining room manager to get feedback on the night. The sous chef prepares an order for supplies the restaurant needs for the next day.
11:30 p.m.	Once the final counter is cleaned and polished and the last pots and pans are stored, it's time to turn out the lights and go home.

Source: Culinary Institute of America

Restaurant Industry Overview

- There are 976,000 restaurant locations in the United States, serving more than 70 billion meals and snacks.

Chart 5 2013 Industry Sales Projection by Segment

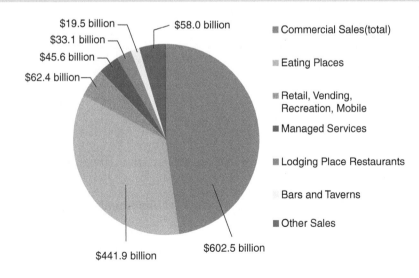

$19.5 billion
$33.1 billion
$45.6 billion
$62.4 billion
$58.0 billion

- Commercial Sales(total)
- Eating Places
- Retail, Vending, Recreation, Mobile
- Managed Services
- Lodging Place Restaurants
- Bars and Taverns
- Other Sales

$441.9 billion
$602.5 billion

- The restaurant industry employs an estimated 13 million people, making it the nation's largest employer outside of government.

Chart 6 Restaurant Industry Employment Projections, 2003–2025

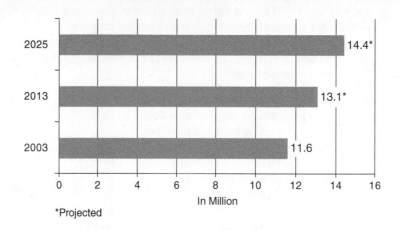

*Projected

- Latest restaurant sales forecasts show sales rising by nearly 3.5 percent annually.

Chart 7 Restaurant Industry Sales, 1970–2013

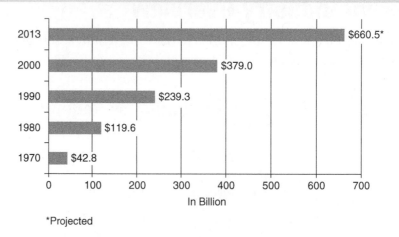

*Projected

- The restaurant industry provides work for more than 10 percent of those employed in the United States.
- More than 7 out of 10 eating and drinking establishments are single-unit operations.
- On any typical day in 2012, total industry sales were $1.7 billion dollars.

Source: National Restaurant Association, www.restaurant.org.

Introduction to
CULINARY ARTS

Second Edition

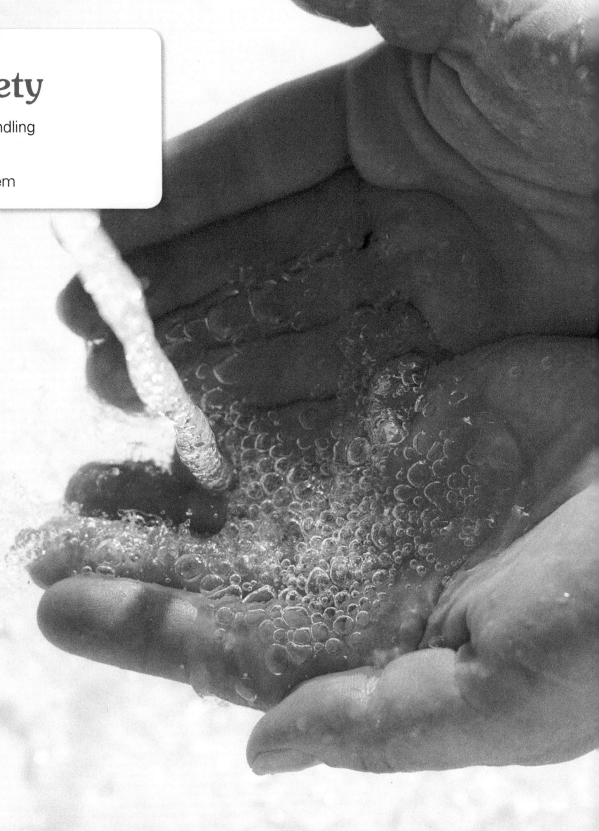

Food Safety

1.1 Sanitary Food Handling

1.2 The Flow of Food

1.3 The HACCP System

1.1

Sanitary Food Handling

Key Concepts

- Learning the importance of food safety
- Developing good grooming and personal hygiene habits
- Cleaning and sanitizing
- Disposing of waste and recycling
- Controlling pests

Vocabulary

- bacteria
- biological hazards
- chemical hazards
- cross-contamination
- direct contamination
- food-borne illness
- food-borne infection
- food-borne intoxication
- food contamination
- food safety
- food security
- fungi
- parasites
- pathogens
- pest infestation
- pest management
- physical hazards
- potentially hazardous foods
- safe foods
- sanitizing
- sanitizing solution
- temperature danger zone
- toxin-mediated infection
- viruses
- water activity (Aw)

Importance of Food Safety

Food safety and food security are two different but related concepts. **Food safety** involves the activities, standards, and procedures necessary to keep foods from becoming contaminated in such a way that they can make a person sick.

Food security refers to the availability of sufficient foods on a regular basis to maintain health. It means that individuals, communities, and nations have the economic resources necessary to provide the foods necessary for a nutritious diet to all members of a household or a community. Food security also means that there is adequate knowledge concerning nutrition and sanitation, as well as safe water, to maintain health.

Food security may also refer to keeping foods secure when they are in the restaurant to prevent intentional contamination. Many different procedures and actions can help keep your facility secure and safe, including specific procedures for requesting and receiving foods that are kept in locked storage areas, cameras to monitor receiving, storage and preparation areas, inventory control systems, and strict

BE SAFE

Food Allergies

People have allergies to a wide array of foods. Some have mild reactions; others can have severe, even fatal, reactions to certain foods. The following foods account for nearly 90 percent of allergic reactions:

- Milk
- Eggs
- Wheat
- Peanuts
- Soy
- Other nuts
- Fish and shellfish

adherence to the rules concerning the report of any theft, injury, or accident in the restaurant.

Safe foods are foods that won't make you sick or hurt you when you eat them. Unsafe foods, or foods that have been contaminated by various hazardous materials, can make you sick or injure you. **Food contamination** may be either biological or environmental. An example of biological contamination would be the presence of living organisms such as bacteria or viruses. Environmental contamination may be unintentional, as may happen if a bandage falls into a container or food, or intentional, as may be the case if a terrorist group were to introduce a deadly virus into a food-processing plant.

An illness that results from eating contaminated foods is referred to as a **food-borne illness.** Guests expect safe food when they come to a restaurant. They typically don't think about food safety. However, if a restaurant serves unsafe food and someone gets sick or hurt, the consequences can be enormous. Both the restaurant's profits and reputation can be hurt.

If customers can prove they got sick from eating unsafe food in a restaurant, they may sue. The incident could become public and the restaurant may be named in an unflattering news report. If a restaurant is found to have served unsafe food, it may be charged more for insurance. When people feel your food is unsafe, they talk about it. They may stop coming and the restaurant will lose customers. Eventually, the business could fail.

Foodservice establishments of all sorts, whether they are fine dining restaurants, diners, or cafeterias, have a responsibility to their customers and to themselves to serve safe foods. Cooks and chefs play a critical part in making sure the foods their customers get are as safe and wholesome as can be. They accomplish this goal by making sure that foods are purchased from a reliable source, that they are handled in a safe and sanitary way at each step of the way to the guest, and that they are not contaminated with substances that can make a person ill.

It is important to know the source of the foods purchased for a professional kitchen. This information is an important part of an overall food safety strategy, so that in case of any problems, you can find the ultimate source. Keeping our food supply secure is an important consideration. We know that our food supply may be vulnerable to bioterrorist attacks. This makes knowing the source of foods even more important, especially foods that are imported from foreign countries. Buying local foods may be an important component in protecting your customers from unsafe foods.

There are additional reasons to know more about the source of your food. Organic foods are less likely to have been treated with chemicals. Animals that are raised in a humane and safe manner are less likely to be contaminated with disease-causing organisms. Your establishment may also be interested in foods that are free of allergens such as peanuts and foods that do not have a negative impact on the environment.

All foods may contain a variety of organisms. Some of these are beneficial. For example, cheeses and yogurt cannot be produced without certain bacteria. Some are responsible for food spoilage, such as the molds you may see on foods that have been held too long or at the wrong temperature. Some organisms are capable of making humans sick. Destroying or reducing the levels of these disease-causing organisms, or **pathogens**, is the responsibility of all professional foodservice workers.

A food that contains disease-causing organisms may look, smell, and even taste fine. One that has spoiled generally looks, smells, and tastes unappetizing. Spoiled foods may affect foods stored near them, so it is important to clear them out of your food storage areas and dispose of them before they are used in cooking.

Some pathogens can cause a type of food-borne illness known as a **food-borne infection**. That means customers became sick because they consumed a food that contained a pathogen. The pathogen then takes up residence in the intestinal tract, where it continues to grow and reproduce, eventually causing a food-borne illness. A **food-borne intoxication** is the result of consuming the poisons, also known as *toxins*, produced by the pathogen and found in the food. Toxins may be present because of the activity of bacteria or as a result of chemical contamination, or they may be naturally present in the food. Examples of naturally occurring toxins include the green portion of a potato, which contains a toxin known as solanine, or those found in poisonous mushrooms such as the death cap. The word *toxin* is a part of the word *intoxication*. It is worth noting that alcohol, in sufficient amounts, is a poison that can cause serious illness and even death. In the case of a **toxin-mediated infection**, a person has eaten a food that contains harmful bacteria. The bacteria take up residence in the intestinal tract, where they produce toxins that make the individual sick.

Three potential hazards can contaminate food and produce food-borne illnesses:

- Biological hazards
- Physical hazards
- Chemical hazards

Biological Hazards Living organisms found in or on foods that can make us sick are called **biological hazards**. There are four basic types of biological hazards:

- Bacteria
- Viruses
- Parasites
- Fungi (including molds)

Bacteria are single-celled organisms that can live in food or water and also on our skin or clothing. Not all bacteria make you sick. If there is only

FIGURE 1–1

Bacteria

Magnified view of bacteria (rod shapes) on a cutting board.

DRAWING CONCLUSIONS *What would happen to food cut on this cutting board?*

Source: fusebulb/Fotolia

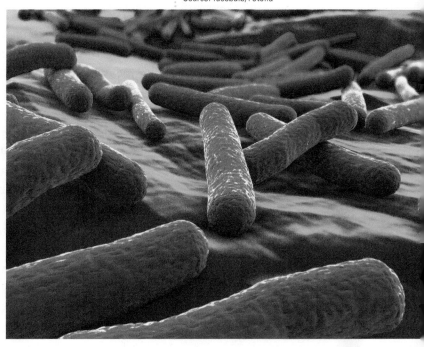

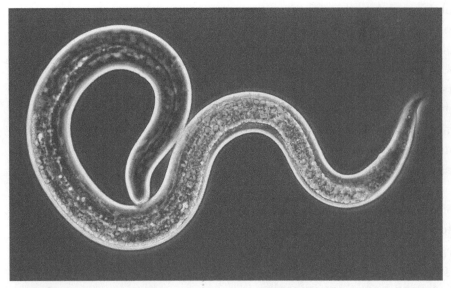

FIGURE 1–2

Roundworms (Parasite)
Pork and wild game meats are the most common vehicles for the food-borne roundworm *Trichinella spiralis*.

APPLYING CONCEPTS *Why should you make certain that pork and wild game meats are cooked to safe temperatures?*

Source: SINCLAIR STAMMERS/Photo Researchers, Inc.

Chef's Tip

Moldy Food

Moldy food may not make you sick, but it has certainly started to spoil. Because molds can penetrate deeply into food without being visible, it is best to throw moldy foods away.

a very small amount of bacteria in or on food, the bacteria may not make you sick. However, because of the rapid rate at which bacteria can reproduce, a food can become contaminated with a great many bacteria in a very short time. It is the volume of bacteria in a contaminated food that makes us sick.

Viruses invade living cells, including those in foods. Once a virus invades a cell, it tricks the host into making another virus, and the process continues. The living cell is known as the *host* for the virus. A virus needs a host in order to reproduce.

Parasites are multicelled organisms that are far larger than either bacteria or viruses. Some are actually large enough to see without a microscope. Similar to bacteria, they reproduce on their own. But similar to a virus, they need a host to provide a home and nourishment. Parasites include roundworms, tapeworms, and various insects. When we eat foods that contain parasites, the eggs or larvae take up residence in our bodies. As these parasites grow and reproduce, they make us ill.

Fungi can be single-celled or multicelled organisms. (*Fungi* is the plural of *fungus*.) A mold is an example of a fungus you can find in foods. Yeast is another example. We rely on some molds and yeasts to produce foods such as cheese or bread. However, harmful molds can contaminate foods. As a fungus grows and reproduces, it creates by-products, including various toxins that can result in either food-borne infection or food-borne intoxication.

Physical Hazards If you find a hair, a piece of a food's packaging, a bandage, or a piece of metal or glass in your food, you've found a physical hazard. **Physical hazards** are foreign objects, usually large enough to see or feel while you are eating. They are often responsible for injuries such as chipped teeth or cuts.

Chemical Hazards Cleaning compounds, bug sprays, food additives, and fertilizer are all examples of human-made **chemical hazards**. Any of these products, if not used properly, can contaminate food. Symptoms from eating chemically contaminated food can often be felt immediately and may include hives; swelling of the lips, tongue, and mouth; difficulty breathing or wheezing; and vomiting, diarrhea, and cramps.

Another chemical hazard involves toxic metals. Mercury and cadmium are toxic metals that have found their way into our food and water, often as a result of industrial pollution. The effects of these toxic metals can range from subtle symptoms to serious diseases.

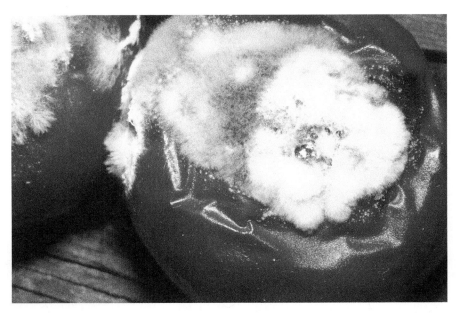

FIGURE 1–3
Moldy Tomato
Mold is a type of fungus found in spoiled food.

DRAWING CONCLUSIONS *Some kitchens cut off the moldy parts of food and use the remainder. Would you want to eat food from such a kitchen?*

Source: Sidney Moulds/Photo Researchers, Inc.

Food Safety and Sanitation Certification Courses in food safety, such as the ServSafe Essentials program from the Educational Foundation of the National Restaurant Association, teach food handlers safe practices. These practices include the following:

- Proper procedures for receiving and storing foods to keep them within safe temperature ranges

- Handling foods properly to destroy or remove pathogens by means of cleaning and cooking

- Holding foods safely to keep them out of the temperature ranges most pathogens prefer

- Keeping work surfaces and tools clean and sanitized to prevent pathogens from being transferred onto foods

- Cooking foods to safe temperatures within appropriate times

Getting a certificate in food safety is an important part of your culinary education. You can attend a class with a teacher who has been certified by ServSafe to provide the training you need. In some cases, the class you take in safety and sanitation as part of your culinary education may lead to a ServSafe certification. Your certification is typically valid for five years; however, requirements vary by individual states. To learn more about the requirements for the state in which you are working, contact the restaurant association for your state.

FOCUS ON Safety
ServSafe
For more information regarding ServSafe Certification see the ServSafe website.

Biological Hazards

BACTERIA			
Bacillus cereus	**Found in:** soil, foods	**Incubation*:** 8 to 16 hours	
Symptoms: cramps, diarrhea, nausea, vomiting	**Foods:** cereal products, cornstarch, rice, custards, sauces, meat loaf	**Prevention:** Cool hot foods quickly. Reheat foods evenly to 165°F. Don't store precooked foods in the refrigerator for too long.	

BACTERIA			
Campylobacter jejuni	**Found in:** animals	**Incubation*:** 3 to 5 days	
Symptoms: diarrhea, fever, nausea, abdominal pain, headache	**Foods:** unpasteurized milk and dairy products, poultry, beef, pork, lamb	**Prevention:** Thoroughly cook food. Avoid cross-contamination.	

BACTERIA			
Clostridium botulinum	**Found in:** animals, water, soil	**Incubation*:** 12 to 36 hours	
Disease: Botulism **Symptoms:** blurred vision, cramps, diarrhea, difficulty breathing, central nervous system damage; fatality rate up to 70%	**Foods:** refrigerated or improperly canned foods; low-acid foods (spinach, tuna, green beans, beets, fermented foods), smoked products	**Prevention:** Maintain a high temperature while canning food. Boil for 20 minutes before serving. Don't use food from swollen cans. Don't use home-canned food commercially.	

BACTERIA			
Clostridium perfringens	**Found in:** soil, dust, animals	**Incubation*:** 9 to 15 hours	
Symptoms: diarrhea, nausea, cramps, fever, vomiting	**Foods:** reheated meats, raw meat, raw vegetables, soups, gravies, stews	**Prevention:** Cool meat quickly. Reheat to 165°F. Avoid cross-contamination of raw meat and cooked meat.	

BACTERIA			
Escherichia coli (E. coli)	**Found in:** animals, humans	**Incubation*:** 12 to 72 hours	
Symptoms: nausea, vomiting, diarrhea	**Foods:** raw and undercooked ground beef and other meats, imported cheeses, unpasteurized milk	**Prevention:** Thoroughly cook ground beef. Avoid cross-contamination and fecal contamination. Practice strict personal hygiene.	

BACTERIA			
Listeria monocytogenes	**Found in:** soil, water, humans, animals	**Incubation*:** 1 day to 3 weeks	
Disease: Listeriosis **Symptoms:** nausea, vomiting, headache, fever, chills, backache, meningitis, miscarriage	**Foods:** unpasteurized milk and cheese, vegetables, poultry, meats, seafood, chilled ready-to-eat foods	**Prevention:** Use only pasteurized dairy products. Cook foods thoroughly. Avoid cross-contamination. Clean and disinfect surfaces. Avoid pooling of water.	

BACTERIA			
Salmonella	**Found in:** humans, animals, birds, insects	**Incubation*:** 6 to 48 hours	
Disease: Salmonellosis **Symptoms:** headache, diarrhea, cramps, fever. Can lead to arthritis, meningitis, typhoid. May be fatal.	**Foods:** eggs, poultry, shellfish, meat, soup, sauces, gravies, milk products, warmed-over food	**Prevention:** Cook to proper temperatures and reheat leftovers to 165°F. Eliminate rodents and flies. Practice strict personal hygiene. Avoid cross-contamination.	

BACTERIA			
Shigella	**Found in:** humans, food, water	**Incubation*:** 12 to 48 hours	
Disease: Shigellosis **Symptoms:** diarrhea, fever, cramps, dehydration	**Foods:** beans; contaminated milk; tuna, turkey, macaroni salads; apple cider; mixed moist foods	**Prevention:** Use safe water sources. Control insects and rodents. Practice strict personal hygiene.	

*Incubation *refers to the period between infection and onset of symptoms.*

Biological Hazards

BACTERIA	**Staphylococcus aureus (staph)**	**Found in:** humans	**Incubation*:** 2 to 4 hours
	Symptoms: vomiting, nausea, diarrhea, cramps	**Foods:** moist foods high in proteins, handled directly and left warm (milk, egg custards, turkey stuffing, chicken/tuna/potato salads, gravies, reheated foods)	**Prevention:** Store foods below 41°F and reheat thoroughly to 165°F. Do not allow people with infected cuts, burns, or respiratory illnesses to handle food.
BACTERIA	**Streptococcus pyogenes**	**Found in:** animals, humans	**Incubation*:** 1 to 4 days
	Symptoms: nausea, vomiting, diarrhea	**Foods:** milk, pudding, ice cream, eggs, meat pie, egg and potato salads, poultry	**Prevention:** Cook foods thoroughly and cool quickly. Practice strict personal hygiene. Use pasteurized dairy products.
VIRUS	**Hepatitis A**	**Found in:** humans, water	**Incubation*:** 10 to 50 days
	Symptoms: jaundice, fever, cramps, nausea, lethargy	**Foods:** shellfish from polluted water, milk, whipped cream, cold cuts, potato salad	**Prevention:** Cook shellfish thoroughly, to over 150°F. Heat-treat or otherwise disinfect suspected water and milk. Practice strict personal hygiene.
VIRUS	**Norwalk virus**	**Found in:** humans	**Incubation*:** 24 to 48 hours
	Symptoms: nausea, vomiting, diarrhea, abdominal pain, headache, low-grade fever	**Foods:** raw shellfish, raw vegetable salads, prepared salads, water with fecal contamination	**Prevention:** Obtain shellfish from approved certified sources. Practice strict personal hygiene. Thoroughly cook foods. Use chlorinated water.
PARASITE	**Anisakidae (roundworms)**	**Found in:** fish	**Incubation*:** 1 hour to 2 weeks
	Disease: Anisakiasis **Symptoms:** nausea, cramps, fever, abscesses	**Foods:** raw or undercooked seafood	**Prevention:** Cook fish to a minimum of 140°F. Freeze fish for 24 hours. Purchase fish from a reliable supplier.
PARASITE	**Giardia lamblia (protozoa)**	**Found in:** humans, animals, soil, water	**Incubation*:** 7 to 14 days
	Disease: Giardiasis **Symptoms:** diarrhea, cramps, nausea, weight loss	**Foods:** uncooked food, contaminated water or ice	**Prevention:** Practice strict personal hygiene. Use safe water sources. Wash raw fruits and vegetables well.
PARASITE	**Trichinella spiralis (roundworm)**	**Found in:** swine, wild game, rats	**Incubation*:** 4 to 28 days
	Disease: Trichinosis **Symptoms:** fever, diarrhea, sweating, muscle pain, vomiting, skin lesions	**Foods:** improperly cooked pork and wild game	**Prevention:** Cook meat to 145°F. Avoid cross-contamination of raw meats.
FUNGUS	**Mycotoxins**	**Found in:** molds and yeasts	**Incubation*:** varies
	Symptoms: hemorrhage, fluid buildup, cancer	**Foods:** moldy grains, corn, corn products, peanuts, pecans, walnuts, milk	**Prevention:** Keep grains and nuts dry.

*Incubation *refers to the period between infection and onset of symptoms.*

FAT TOM Pathogens grow rapidly when conditions are right. The length of time they are permitted to grow is a major factor in determining whether there are enough pathogens to make you sick.

Pathogens require certain environmental conditions in order to grow and reproduce. Some types of food offer a friendly environment for these disease-producing organisms. These foods are referred to as **potentially hazardous foods.** If these foods become contaminated, the pathogen will grow easily. When you know what a pathogen needs to grow, you can take steps to keep foods safe. "FAT TOM" stands for each of the conditions that pathogens need for growth.

FAT TOM
Food
Acidity
Temperature

Time
Oxygen
Moisture

Like humans, pathogens need a food source to grow and reproduce. Sugars and carbohydrates such as those in breads, cooked grains and cereals, starchy vegetables, and fruits are one type of food source. Proteins in foods are another. Meats, dairy, and eggs are all rich in protein.

Acidity levels in foods also play a role in determining how likely they are to become contaminated. Foods that are highly acidic, such as vinegar and lemon juice, as well as those that are alkaline, such as baking soda, are unfriendly to pathogens. That is why certain types of food preservation

---

The pH Scale

Some foods, such as vinegar and citrus juice, are highly acidic. Others, such as baking soda, are alkaline. The acidity or alkalinity of a food is measured on the pH scale. On that scale, 0 to 7 is acidic and 7 to 14 is alkaline. A pH of 7 is neutral; this is the pH of distilled water. The most favorable pH range for pathogens to grow is between 4.6 and 7.5, a range into which most foods fall. To measure the pH of a substance, scientists use strips of specially treated paper that change color depending on the acidity or alkalinity of the substance.

Lab Activity

1. Test the pH of various common foods and condiments.

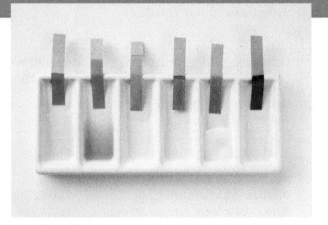

Source: Dorling Kindersley

Scientific Method

1. Create an experiment that allows you to test the hypothesis that pathogens are less likely to grow in highly acidic or alkaline foods.

strategies such as pickling foods are an effective way to keep them safe from contamination.

Pathogens also prefer to live in conditions that are warm, very similar to the conditions humans need to survive. They need foods that are at the right temperature. For most pathogens, a temperature close to our own body temperature of 98.6°F is desirable. However, pathogens can grow in temperatures from 41°F to 135°F. This range is known as the **temperature danger zone**. (Some states and counties have established slightly different ranges for the temperature danger zone. You are required to meet the standards of your state or county; for more information you may need to contact the local health department.)

Time plays a role, too. The longer a pathogen is in contact with the food, the more it can grow and reproduce. Bacteria, which reproduce by dividing in two once the cell becomes large enough, show the relationship between time and the development of a food-borne contamination clearly. One bacterium becomes two, two become four, four become eight, and so on. A single bacterium can become nearly 10 billion bacteria in just 10 hours.

Specific types of pathogens have specific oxygen requirements. Some pathogens need oxygen to stay alive, others do not, and others can live with or without oxygen.

Moisture is another requirement. **Water activity** (abbreviated as Aw) is a measurement of the amount of moisture available in a food. The scale runs from 0 to 1.0, with water having an Aw measurement of 1.0. Potentially hazardous foods have a measurement of .85 Aw or higher. Foods that are soft enough to chew easily often have enough moisture to support the growth of pathogens. Dried foods (dried pastas or beans, for example) are not considered potentially hazardous.

Certain groups of people may have a different level of risk if they consume foods that are contaminated with disease-causing organisms. A person who has a strong immune system may be able to eat unsafe foods and not risk becoming sick. Other groups, especially the very young, the very old, and those who are already sick, may become sick more easily. The very young have an immature immune system. The very old have a weakened immune system. Sick people have immune systems that are already under attack, making it more difficult for them to fend off an illness brought about by eating an unsafe food.

Sources of Contamination A food can become unsafe in two ways: by direct contamination or by cross-contamination. **Direct contamination** means that a disease-causing substance is introduced directly to a food. The

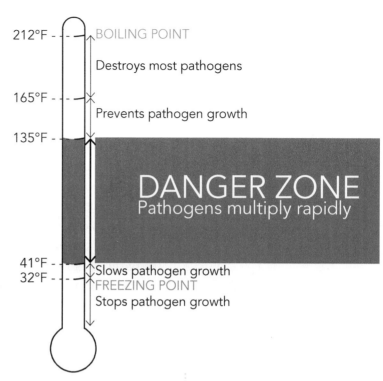

FIGURE 1–4
Temperature Danger Zone
Pathogens thrive and reproduce between 41°F and 135°F.

PREDICTING *Why do you think chefs rapidly cool food to below 41°F as a preparation for storing the food?*

food may be sprayed with an insecticide, for instance, or airborne toxins may settle on the food in the field or while it is being processed. In some cases, the pathogen is in the soil where foods are growing. When foods arrive at a restaurant or grocery store already affected by direct contamination, there may be a recall of the food if an outbreak of food-borne illness is traced to that specific food producer or processor. *Indirect contamination* means that the hazard is transferred from one source to the food by means of contact with something else. This type of contamination, known as **cross-contamination**, occurs when a food that is safe comes in contact with biological, physical, or chemical contaminants while it is being prepared, cooked, or served.

One of the most common causes of cross-contamination is the transfer of pathogens from raw foods to cooked or ready-to-eat foods through a chef's contaminated hands, equipment, or utensils. For example, bacteria from a raw chicken can be transferred to a ready-to-eat food such as lettuce or a tomato when the same cutting board is used without being washed and sanitized between foods.

Avoiding Cross-Contamination All culinary professionals need to be aware of the dangers of cross-contamination and take the steps necessary to avoid it. Cutting boards, knives, tools, and utensils must be cleaned and sanitized whenever you switch from one type of food to another. Some establishments require that cutting boards be color-coded and used for only one type of food. Food-handling gloves must be worn whenever necessary and replaced whenever they become soiled or torn. When you store foods, be certain that raw foods will not come in contact with or drip on cooked foods. Keep them in separate parts of the refrigerator or store them so that raw foods are never directly above cooked foods. Hold raw foods in containers that will prevent the raw food from dripping onto cooked foods. Follow safe procedures for tasting foods and never use the same tasting spoon to dip into a food more than once. Maintaining high standards of cleanliness for yourself, your workstation, and the entire facility is a key component of avoiding cross-contamination.

FIGURE 1–5

Cross-Contamination

Raw meat and raw vegetables on the same work surface.

 **DRAWING CONCLUSIONS**
What's wrong with this picture?

Source: David P. Smith/Shutterstock

IN THIS BOOK, *the symbol ⊘ means something is wrong with the picture.*

READING CHECKPOINT *What are the three types of hazards that can contaminate foods?*

Grooming and Hygiene

Everyone who works with food needs to make an effort to avoid cross-contaminating food. Keeping yourself clean, well groomed, and healthy is a vital part of keeping foods safe from contamination.

Your appearance and grooming is an indication of your overall hygiene and cleanliness. You are judged accordingly. So be certain that your hair is clean and controlled, that your hands are clean and your nails trimmed, and that your teeth are clean. Many restaurants have standards for their employees, especially when it comes to hair length, facial hair, piercings or tattoos, undershirts with logos or colors, style of footwear, and sock color. Your employers will expect that all of your clothing and uniform from socks to side towels are free of stains, rips, and tears and are clean when you start your shift. Be certain to follow these guidelines. They are meant to keep you and your customers safe as well as to help you present a professional appearance.

Hand Washing Washing your hands conscientiously and frequently is one of the most important elements in keeping foods safe. Every kitchen must have a proper hand washing station, outfitted with hot and cold running water, soap, a nail brush, and single-use paper towels.

You should wash your hands:

☑ When arriving at work or returning to the kitchen

☑ After using the bathroom

BASIC CULINARY SKILLS

Proper Hand Washing

① Wet hands, using hot running water.

② Apply soap and work it into a lather.

Source: Africa Studio/Fotolia

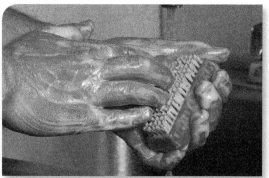

Source: Mike Gallitelli/Pearson Education PH College

③ Scrub hands, between fingers, and forearms for at least 20 seconds.

④ Scrub under your fingernails with a nail brush.

⑤ Rinse hands and forearms under warm running water.

⑥ Dry hands with clean single-use paper towels.

⑦ Turn off water, using towel.

⑧ Open door, using towel if necessary.

⑨ Discard towel in waste container.

Chef's Tip

Fits Like a Glove

Disposable gloves are available in various sizes. Choose a size that fits snugly, but without pinching.

FOCUS ON **Sanitation**

Latex Allergy

Some people are allergic to the latex used in most disposable gloves.

FIGURE 1–6

Disposable Gloves

Gloves act as a barrier between your hands and ready-to-eat foods.

APPLYING CONCEPTS *Why is it still important to wash your hands before putting on gloves?*

Source: Max Tactic/Fotolia

☑ After sneezing

☑ After touching your hair, face, or clothing

☑ After eating, drinking, or smoking

☑ After taking off gloves and before putting on a new pair

☑ Before handling food that will not be cooked again or ready-to-eat food, such as salads and sandwiches

☑ After handling garbage

☑ After handling dirty equipment, dishes, or utensils

☑ After touching raw meats, poultry, and fish

☑ After caring for or touching animals

☑ Any time you change from one task to another

Disposable Gloves In addition to washing your hands frequently, you should wear disposable gloves to prevent your bare hands from coming into contact with ready-to-serve foods. For instance, if you are cutting up an onion to cook in a stew, you don't need to wear gloves, because the onion will be cooked before being served to a guest. However, if you are slicing scallions to serve raw on a salad, you need to wear gloves.

Gloves act as a barrier to keep any microorganism on your hand from getting into the food. But gloves can become contaminated if they touch other foods or a dirty surface. If your hands aren't clean when you put the gloves on, contamination from your hands can get on the gloves. Once your gloves are contaminated, they can contaminate the foods you are preparing.

Wash your hands thoroughly before putting on gloves. Change your gloves whenever they become ripped or dirty. If you are handling raw meats, fish, poultry, or eggs, change your gloves after you are finished handling them and before you start working with cooked or ready-to-eat foods. Never handle money with gloved hands unless you immediately remove and discard the gloves. Money is highly contaminated from handling.

Treat disposable gloves as a second skin. Whatever can contaminate a human hand can also contaminate your gloves. Whenever your hands should be washed, you should put on a new pair of disposable gloves. Never reuse or wash disposable gloves.

Grooming Your uniform is a potential source of pathogens that can get into foods and cause food-borne illness. Start each shift in a clean uniform. Whenever possible, put your uniform on at work, rather than wearing it from your home to the workplace. Do not use aprons or towels hung on the apron string to dry or wipe down hands, tools, or equipment.

Control your hair (this includes beards) by wearing hairnets, hats, or beard restraints. Otherwise, your hair could fall into the food. Hairnets also reduce the need to touch your hair while on the job.

Jewelry that falls into the food you are preparing or serving is a physical hazard in the kitchen. It can also be a source of cross-contamination. Pathogens can contaminate jewelry and be transferred from the jewelry to food. In many kitchens, the only piece of jewelry that is allowed is a plain wedding band. Even watches are a potential source of contamination.

Personal Hygiene If you are sick with a contagious cold or disease, you should not come to work until the chance that you may infect others has passed. Keep your fingernails trimmed and do not wear polish. Keep makeup to a minimum, if you wear any at all.

Wear a bandage to cover any cuts or burns on your skin. Change bandages frequently so they don't become a breeding ground for bacteria. Wear gloves to prevent bandages on your hands from falling into food.

 **READING CHECKPOINT** *What are the steps in proper hand washing?*

 FIGURE 1–7
Good Grooming
Hairnets are required by most food establishments.

PREDICTING *How would you feel if you were in a restaurant and saw a kitchen worker without a hairnet?*

Source: Monty Rakusen/Getty Images

FIGURE 1–8
Bandaged Finger
Wear gloves to prevent bandages from falling into the food.

🚫 **CLASSIFYING** *What two types of hazards does this picture represent?*

Source: Vincent P. Walter/Pearson Education/ PH College

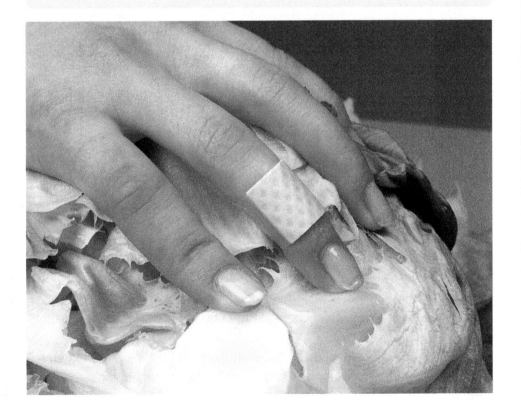

Chemical Hazard: Mercury in Fish

Mercury is released in the air through industrial pollution. Eventually it falls to earth, accumulating in streams and oceans. Bacteria in the water cause a chemical change that turns mercury into methylmercury. This type of mercury is a potent toxin that can damage the brain and nervous system, causing learning disabilities and other developmental problems in babies and children.

Source: Stephen Oliver/Getty Active, PS/Dorling Kindersley Media Library/ DK Images

Nearly all fish and shellfish contain traces of methylmercury. Large fish that have lived longer have the highest levels because they've had more time to accumulate the chemical. Methylmercury also builds up more in some types of fish and shellfish than in others.

Forty states have issued advisories warning residents to restrict their consumption of some types of fish because of this chemical hazard. Government findings show that 8 percent of all women of childbearing age in the United States have unsafe mercury levels. This translates to more than 300,000 babies who are born at risk each year.

The FDA and the Environmental Protection Agency (EPA) have issued the following recommendations for young children, nursing mothers, pregnant women, and women who may become pregnant:

- Do not eat shark, swordfish, king mackerel, or tilefish because they contain high levels of mercury.

- Eat up to 12 ounces (two average meals) a week of a variety of fish and shellfish that are lower in mercury, such as small ocean fish, shrimp, canned light tuna, salmon, pollock, and catfish. Be aware that albacore ("white") tuna has more mercury than canned light tuna.

- Check local advisories about the safety of fish caught by family and friends in your local lakes, rivers, and coastal areas.

Computation

Look up the mean values for mercury concentration, in parts per million (ppm) for nine different species of fish. (Use the information from the FDA website and search for *Mercury Levels in Commercial Fish and Shellfish*.) Compare these values to the mean value for canned tuna (albacore) and express the difference as a percentage. Based on these percentages, list three species of fish that you would choose to avoid consuming that is high in mercury.

Chef's Tip

Fill It Up

Some kitchens have "fill-to" lines in their three-compartment sinks. If your sink has fill-to lines, use them.

Cleaning and Sanitizing

In a professional kitchen, you must both clean and sanitize anything that comes in contact with foods. Cleaning and sanitizing your tools and work area is one of the most important ways to prevent cross-contamination. It is actually a three-step process. First, clean the surface by washing it. Then, rinse it thoroughly. Once it is rinsed, sanitize the surface.

Cleaning involves removing soil or food particles from surfaces such as cutting boards, knives, pots, pans, and other preparation and cooking equipment and utensils. It also involves sweeping the floor and removing grease and dirt from the stove's ventilation hoods, the walls, and the refrigerator doors.

Once an object is cleaned, it can be sanitized. In a professional kitchen, **sanitizing** means that you have used either heat or chemicals to reduce the number of pathogens on a surface to a safe level. You can sanitize surfaces

Types of Cleansing Agents

Type of Cleaner	Description
Detergent	Penetrates quickly and softens soil so the soil can be scrubbed and rinsed away.
Degreaser	Special type of detergent that contains a grease-dissolving agent. Also known as *solvent cleaner*.
Acid cleaner	Used to remove mineral buildup in coffee makers, steam tables, and dishwashing machines. Not for use on aluminum.
Abrasive cleaner	Used carefully to scour dirt or grease that has baked or burned onto pots and pans.

Source: Vincent P. Walter/Pearson Education/PH College

by using hot water (180°F) or a chemical sanitizer. Small tools and dishes can be submerged in hot water or a mixture of water and a sanitizer. Larger surfaces and appliances, such as meat slicers, can be sanitized after they are cleaned by wiping or spraying them with a **sanitizing solution**, a solution made by mixing water and a chemical sanitizer.

It is important to clean and sanitize all parts of the facility, not just hand tools and cutting boards. Walls, ceilings, and floors must also be cleaned and sanitized regularly to keep the entire facility safe. Refrigerators and freezers, ventilation systems, and garbage and recycling collection areas must be cleaned regularly. Follow the cleaning schedules established by your restaurant for all areas in your facility and use approved cleansers and sanitizers safely.

Sanitizing can be done manually. Small tools, containers, pots, and pans can be washed by hand in a three-compartment sink. The first compartment is filled with hot water and a detergent. The detergent helps to loosen food particles or grease so they can be rinsed away. The second compartment contains clean water to rinse away the dirt as well as the detergent. The third compartment contains either very hot water (at least 180°F) or a mixture

Types of Sanitizers

Sanitizer	Advantages	Disadvantages
Chlorine	Inexpensive; good for most sanitizing needs	Corrodes metal; irritates skin
Iodine	Moderate cost; less corrosive and irritating than chlorine	Can stain
Quaternary ammonium compounds	Stable at high temperatures (such as dishwashing machines)	Expensive; can leave a film when used with hard water

FIGURE 1-9

Three-Compartment Sink
Use cleansers and sanitizers properly.

PREDICTING *How might switching from one sanitizer to another change the amount of sanitizer you need to add to the third compartment of the sink?*

Source: Vincent P. Walter/Pearson Education/ PH College

of water and a chemical sanitizer. After sanitizing, equipment and tableware should be allowed to air-dry completely, because using paper or cloth toweling could result in cross-contamination.

Some kitchens have a four-compartment sink. The first compartment is used to scrape off remaining food from plates and cookware. It often has a garbage disposal unit. The remaining three sinks are set up for washing, rinsing, and sanitizing as described earlier.

The amount of sanitizer you add to the water depends on the type of sanitizer you are using. Leave the item you are sanitizing in the sanitizing sink long enough for the sanitizer to work. Be sure to read and follow the sanitizer's directions.

Dishwashing machines can be used to clean and sanitize tools and containers. Dishwashing machines use special detergents for cleaning. Some use very hot water to rinse and sanitize items, while others use chemical sanitizers. To keep these machines operating properly, be sure to scrape items before you put them into the machine.

Once tools and equipment are properly cleaned and sanitized, let them air-dry before putting them away. Do not use towels, as they may be a source of cross-contamination.

 **READING CHECKPOINT** *What is the difference between cleaning and sanitizing?*

Waste Disposal and Recycling

The garbage that accumulates as you work in the kitchen is not only unsightly. It is also a potential source of food contamination.

Source: barbaliss/Fotolia

Waste Disposal As you are cooking, you create a good deal of waste. Wrappers, packaging, bones, cans, and paper towels are all examples of the trash that you need to remove from the kitchen. Put all trash into a container as soon as possible so it can't get mixed with the food you are preparing.

Cover garbage cans and empty them every four hours or whenever they are full. Rinse out the container before you bring it back into your work area, and line it with a clean plastic liner.

Recycling Getting rid of garbage is expensive. Many restaurants use recycling to try to cut down on the amount of waste they produce. Depending on the community or state you live in, you may be able to recycle a variety of containers: cardboard boxes, glass jars or bottles, metal cans, and plastic containers. Notice the recycling symbol on recycling receptacles and some recyclable materials.

 **READING CHECKPOINT** *Typically, how often should garbage cans be emptied?*

Pest Control

Plenty of pests can come into a kitchen—mice, flies, cockroaches, and mosquitoes are just a few examples. No one likes to see pests, and for good reason. They can be the source of food-borne illness by carrying a pathogen. The pathogen may be found on the pest's skin or hair. Their droppings may also carry a potentially dangerous virus or bacteria.

Keeping pests out of the kitchen is an important part of keeping the kitchen sanitary. Most pests reproduce quickly. It takes only a short time for a couple of flies to go from being a nuisance to becoming a hazard.

Keeping Pests out of the Kitchen To keep pests out of the kitchen, you have to make it hard for them to get into the kitchen in the first place. They can arrive through any holes or gaps around doors or windows. They can come through almost any opening, including the roof or drains. All windows and doors need to shut tightly. Screens covering doors or windows should be free from rips or holes. Blocking any gaps along the foundation or in the roof also keeps pests out of the kitchen.

Pests look for food, so clean all areas and surfaces thoroughly. Wipe up spills immediately and sweep up crumbs. Storing foods properly also helps keep pests out of the kitchen. Keep foods covered or refrigerated.

Never store foods on the floor or touching the wall. Garbage cans should be lifted off the ground and must have tight-fitting lids. Don't pile bags of garbage over the rim of garbage cans or other trash containers. Cover recycling containers. Make sure cans and bottles for recycling are rinsed. Check all boxes and packaging for pests. Get rid of boxes as soon as you unpack the food. Some pests can hide in the packaging.

Pest Management A **pest infestation** means that there are large numbers of a species that is harmful to human health. There may be infestations of rodents such as rats or mice, of ants or cockroaches, and a variety of other species. Very often, the signs of the infestation will be easy to spot. Even if you don't actually see the pests, you may see evidence of the paths or trails they follow in the kitchen, foods or packages that have been gnawed on, or holes that they use to get into and out of the kitchen.

Sometimes, no matter how careful you have been, pests can invade the kitchen and become a real problem. Then you may need to rely on pesticides to control them. Pesticides are dangerous materials that must be stored well away from foods. They need to be applied properly to be effective. Local, county, and state regulations regarding the use of pesticides may differ, so many restaurants use a special service to control pests.

Ultimately **pest management** involves three steps:

- Maintaining the kitchen so pests can't get into it.
- Taking care of all waste properly, so pests can't find food.
- Using pesticides to eliminate any pests.

 **READING CHECKPOINT** *What is meant by pest management?*

1.1 ASSESSMENT

Reviewing Concepts

1. What is a food-borne illness?
2. What are the nine steps in proper hand washing?
3. What is the difference between cleaning and sanitizing?
4. Why is trash a problem in a kitchen?
5. What are the three steps involved in pest management?

Critical Thinking

6. **Predicting** Which do you think would have a higher Aw (water activity): a watermelon or a walnut?
7. **Inferring** Based on your knowledge of FAT TOM, why do chefs cool food quickly? (Explain your answer in terms of the conditions specified by FAT TOM.)
8. **Comparing/Contrasting** What is the difference between direct contamination and cross-contamination of food?

Test Kitchen

Gather food from the kitchen. Predict whether each item is acidic or alkaline, and then predict the pH of the items. Test the actual pH (for solid food, grind the food and mix with distilled water).

SCIENCE ———————————

Outbreaks of Food-Borne Illness

1. Describe a recent outbreak of a food-borne illness at a food establishment. Describe the specific cause, how many people were affected, and their symptoms. Discuss how the establishment could have avoided the outbreak.
2. Research how your state's department of health recommends that food establishments respond to an outbreak of a food-borne illness. Create a step-by-step procedure for a restaurant in the event of an outbreak.

The Flow of Food

READING PREVIEW

Key Concepts

- Describing the flow of food
- Receiving foods safely
- Storing foods safely
- Cooking foods safely
- Serving foods safely

Vocabulary

- dry goods
- First In, First Out (FIFO) system
- flow of food
- holding
- one-stage cooling method
- perishable goods
- time-temperature-abused food
- two-stage cooling method

The Flow of Food

Foodservice establishments of all sorts, whether they are fine dining restaurants, delis, or cafeterias, have a responsibility to their customers to serve safe foods. Cooks and chefs play a critical role in making sure the food the customer eats is as safe and wholesome as it can be.

Food can become contaminated between the time it arrives at the kitchen and the time it is served to customers. The **flow of food** is the route food takes from the time a kitchen receives it to the time it is served to the customer. Learning about the flow of food through a restaurant helps you learn not only when foods may become contaminated, but also how to reduce or eliminate the risk of contamination.

READING CHECKPOINT *What is the flow of food?*

Source: Culinary Institute of America

Receiving Foods

The foods that are purchased by a restaurant must come from a reputable source. The restaurant is responsible for being certain that the companies or individuals from whom it buys food meet all the necessary requirements for supplying and delivering safe foods. The source is responsible for providing the food in good condition.

The first step in the flow of food is receiving. When you receive food, there's a handoff of responsibility. You are now taking responsibility for the food your restaurant receives. You must always inspect any food you receive for damage. Different types of food have different potential problems.

Perishable goods, for example, are foods that must be properly wrapped and kept cold until they arrive at your restaurant. There are two types of

perishable goods—those stored in the refrigerator and those stored in the freezer. Examples of perishable goods requiring refrigerator storage are meats and milk. You are responsible for checking deliveries to be sure perishable goods are at safe temperatures when you receive them.

Perishable goods that require storage in the freezer should be completely frozen when you get them. The packaging should not have any rips or tears. If you see large ice crystals or drips, the food has started to thaw while it was on its way to you.

Foods such as flour, tea, sugar, rice, and pasta are known as **dry goods**. These foods should arrive at your restaurant well wrapped. Any packaging should be free from tears or rips. Canned goods should never have bulges, dents, signs of rust, or leaks.

You should reject any food that does not have clean, intact packaging or that is not at the appropriate temperature.

Nonfood items, including cleaning supplies, paper goods, and linens, must also be inspected when they are received. They should be in clean, intact packaging with no rips, tears, or leaks.

 **READING CHECKPOINT** *What is the first step in the flow of food?*

Storing Foods

Once you are certain food you just received is safe, make sure it is stored correctly. This is the second step in the flow of food. You need to avoid cross-contamination and spoilage, while storing foods efficiently. Store freshly delivered food behind food you already have on hand so the oldest food gets used first. Rotating the inventory in this way assures that there is less waste. This stock rotation technique is referred to as a **First In, First Out (FIFO) system**. It should be used for both perishable and nonperishable goods. Many food establishments write the date they received a food on the packaging, using an indelible marker.

All perishable goods requiring refrigeration must be transferred immediately to the refrigerator. If possible, store raw ingredients and prepared food separately. If raw ingredients and prepared food must be stored together, always store the raw food below any cooked or ready-to-eat foods to avoid cross-contamination. Foods that may drip or leak should be placed in clean, sanitized containers. Check the temperature of the refrigerator frequently with an appliance thermometer. Refrigerators should be kept between 36°F and 40°F. However, the ideal storage temperature for specific food items may require lower or higher temperatures than normally available in a refrigerator.

FOCUS ON Safety

The Ideal

The ideal storage temperature is the temperature that both is safe and ensures that the food item is at its optimal quality. It may be necessary to store food on ice in the refrigerator, for example, to achieve the ideal storage temperature.

Frozen food must immediately be transferred to the freezer. Never place hot food directly into the freezer. It will raise the freezer's temperature and could cause other frozen foods to thaw. Freezers should be kept between −10°F and 0°F.

Put dry goods away in a dry, clean, cool storage area well away from cleaning supplies or chemicals. If you need to transfer food from its original container, be sure the containers you use are clean and sanitized and have tight-fitting lids. Dry goods should be at least 6 inches off the floor and 6 inches away from the wall. Dry storage areas should be kept between 50°F and 70°F.

Store cleaning supplies and chemicals in the appropriate area, between 50°F and 70°F. They should be kept in a separate area of the storage room or, ideally, in a separate room or storage closet. Be sure that these items are clearly identifiable so that they cannot be mistaken for a food product. Linens and paper goods should also be stored separately to keep them from being contaminated or soiled during storage.

Ideal Storage Temperatures

Food Item	Ideal Storage Temperatures
Meat and poultry	32°F to 36°F
Fish and shellfish	30°F to 34°F
Eggs	33°F to 38°F
Dairy products	36°F to 41°F
Produce (refrigerated)	32°F to 50°F

 **READING CHECKPOINT** *What is meant by FIFO and why is it important to proper food storage?*

Cooking Foods Safely

When you cook foods, it is important to protect them from cross-contamination. Clean and sanitary work habits and proper food storage procedures are important parts of keeping foods safe from cross-contamination.

Preparing Foods Safely Store perishable foods in the refrigerator until you are ready to prepare them. Work with only what you need for about an hour. Don't let food sit on the counter. Return any unused portion to the refrigerator.

FIGURE 1–12
Colored Cutting Boards
Colored cutting boards are used for preparing specific types of food (yellow is used for poultry, red for raw meat, and so on).
RELATING CONCEPTS *How can colored cutting boards reduce cross-contamination?*
Source: Vincent P. Walter/Pearson Education/PH College

FIGURE 1–13

Checking the Temperature of Cooked Food

A thermometer indicates when the food comes to a safe temperature.

DRAWING CONCLUSIONS *The thermometer reads 145.7°F. Is this rotisserie chicken safe to serve?*

Source: Vincent P. Walter/Pearson Education/PH College

One of the biggest concerns when you are preparing food is cross-contamination. Be sure your hands and tools and any surface the food may touch are clean and sanitized. Prepare different types of food on separate cutting boards or in different areas.

Keep a container of sanitizing solution nearby. (It's important to use the correct proportion of sanitizer and water.) Also keep plenty of single-use towels on hand. Dip a single-use towel into the sanitizing solution and wring it out before you use it to wipe down cleaned cutting boards or knives. Spray the solution on tools that are difficult to wipe. You should also keep your hand tools (spoons, ladles, and whisks, for example) in a container of sanitizing solution between uses. Replace the solution when it gets dirty. Dirt in the sanitizing solution keeps it from working properly.

Monitoring Food Temperature You should expect raw foods, especially meats, fish, and poultry, to contain harmful microorganisms. Hazardous foods need to come to temperatures high enough to kill these pathogens.

Once you begin to cook, it is important to bring food to safe temperatures as quickly as possible. Since most foods are served at temperatures that fall within the temperature danger zone (between 41°F and 135°F), you need to minimize how long foods stay in that range.

Recommended Temperatures

Food Type	Recommended Internal Temperature	Minimum Time at Recommended Temperature before Serving	
Beef roasts (rare)	130°F	112 minutes	
	140°F	12 minutes	
Roasts (medium beef, pork), lamb, veal	145°F	4 minutes	
Fish, pork, and beef (other than roasts)	145°F	15 seconds	
Ground meats (beef, pork, and game), ham steak	155°F	15 seconds	
Poultry, stuffed meats	165°F	15 seconds	Source: Alexander Hoffmann/Shutterstock

Bring food up to a safe temperature and then hold the food at that temperature for an appropriate amount of time before it is served. The exact temperature varies according to the type of food you are preparing. Make sure your thermometers are accurate when checking temperatures.

Fully cook meats before adding them to other dishes. Casseroles and other foods that contain a combination of raw ingredients such as meat and poultry must be cooked to the final temperature of the food requiring the highest internal temperature. Don't mix leftover food with newly prepared food.

The distribution of heat in a microwave oven is often uneven. To distribute heat more evenly, stir and rotate the food frequently.

Cooling Foods Safely One of the leading causes of food-borne illness is improperly cooled foods. Cooked foods you plan to store for later use need to be cooled down to below 41°F as quickly as possible. There are two methods for cooling foods. Always depend on a thermometer reading to determine that the appropriate degree of coolness has been reached.

- **The One-Stage Cooling Method.** Using the one-stage cooling method, food should be cooled to below 41°F within four hours.

- **The Two-Stage Cooling Method.** The two-stage cooling method was approved by the Food and Drug Administration in its 1999 Model Food Code. In the first stage of this method, foods must be cooled down to 70°F within two hours. In the second stage, foods must cool down below 41°F within an additional four hours. The total amount of time elapsed during cooling the food is six hours.

Refrigerators are designed to keep foods cold, not to cool hot foods. They cool too slowly and food is at the temperature danger zone for too

FIGURE 1–14

Special Equipment for Cooling Cooked Foods

Using a chill wand to cool stock (left) and a blast chiller to cool pork (right).

SOLVING PROBLEMS *What cooling methods would you use if this equipment were not available?*

Sources: (left) Culinary Institute of America; (right) Vincent P. Walter/Pearson Education/ PH College

FOCUS ON Safety

Single Portions

Single portions of frozen food may be cooked from the frozen state, as long as the cooked item is at a safe temperature when served (examples: hamburger patties, french fries).

long a period. For example, it can take 72 hours or more for the center of a 5-gallon stockpot of steamed rice to cool down to below 41°F when taken directly from the stove and placed in a refrigerator. You need to cool food much more rapidly to ensure that it is safe.

Thawing Foods Safely Never thaw food by simply leaving it out at room temperature. Frozen food may be safely thawed in several ways:

- **In the Refrigerator.** The best—though slowest—method of thawing food is to allow the food to thaw under refrigeration. Place still-wrapped food in a shallow container on a bottom shelf of the refrigerator to prevent any drips from contaminating other items stored nearby or below. The time it takes to thaw a food in the refrigerator varies depending on the thickness and texture of the food.

- **Under Running Water.** Place covered or wrapped food in a container under running water of approximately 70°F or below. Use a stream of water strong enough to wash loose particles off the food, but do not allow the water to splash on other foods or surfaces. Clean and sanitize the sink before and after thawing foods under running water.

- **In the Microwave.** You can use a microwave oven to thaw some foods. This method is recommended primarily for individual portions that will be cooked immediately after thawing.

Once thawed, food should be used as soon as possible. For optimal quality and flavor, thawed food should not be refrozen.

 **READING CHECKPOINT** *What is the two-stage cooling method?*

LIQUID FOOD

- Pour liquid into a stainless-steel container before you begin cooling it.
- Place the container holding the liquid in an ice water bath. The bath should reach the same level as the liquid inside the container.
- Stir the liquid frequently.
- Set bricks or a rack under the container to allow the cold water to circulate.
- Use an overflow pipe to allow the water to run continuously as the food cools.
- Add ice directly to condensed food (this both cools it and dilutes the food).
- Use a chill wand.

Source: Culinary Institute of America

SOLID OR SEMISOLID FOOD

- Place the food in a stainless-steel container before you begin cooling it.
- Cut the food into smaller portions (true especially for meat).
- Spread the food in a single layer in a shallow container.
- Leave the food unwrapped until after it cools.
- Stir the food, if possible.
- Put the container of hot food in an ice water bath.
- Use a blast chiller.
- Wrap all cooled food before refrigerating.

Serving Foods Safely

Keeping food safe from the time you receive it and throughout the time you cook it is a good way to control most of the hazards that can cause illness or injury. Serving foods safely is the final step in making sure everything you serve your guests is not only delicious and attractive, but also safe.

Holding Some food is served as soon as it is cooked. Other food is prepared ahead of time and then kept hot in steam tables or cold in the refrigerator until you are ready to serve it. This is referred to as **holding** food. Holding food at the right temperature is an important part of keeping the flow of food safe.

Set the temperature controls on all food-holding equipment to the correct temperatures for food safety. Hold hot foods above 135°F (or higher, if the requirement is different for your state or county). Hold cold foods below 41°F.

Use a sanitized instant-read thermometer to check the temperature of the food you are holding. Discard food that has been in the danger zone longer than two hours. This type of food is referred to as **time-temperature-abused food**.

Reheating Improperly reheated food is a frequent culprit in food-borne illness. When food is prepared ahead and then reheated, it should move

Chef's Tip

Reheating Foods

A stew or soup will reheat more rapidly if you put a thin layer in a wide, shallow pan than if you put it in a tall, deep pot.

Before the Refrigerator

Before the refrigerator, people had to find other ways to store and preserve their food. In some cases, people used ice that was cut from ponds in the winter and stored in sawdust for use in the summer. But people also preserved food in many other ways.

Foods were often pickled—stored in salty water or vinegar with a mix of herbs and spices. Cucumbers, onions, green beans, tomatoes, cauliflower, broccoli, and many other vegetables were pickled so they could be enjoyed long after they were harvested. These pickled vegetables are still an important component of the Italian appetizer antipasto (ahn-tee-PAHS-toe). In other cuisines, nuts, fish, meat, and even eggs are sometimes pickled.

Green cabbage was pickled in a different way. In Germany, it was shredded, salted heavily, and then kept in a cool, dry place. The salt caused the cabbage to ferment and become sauerkraut. In Korea, cabbage is the major ingredient in kimchi (KIM-chee). In this spicy condiment, the cabbage is seasoned with garlic, chiles, onions, ginger, and other spices. It is stored in sealed jars in underground cellars or sheds for a month while it ferments.

Cod fish were salted heavily as a way of preserving them. This caused the cod to lose all its moisture, becoming as hard as a board. In this state it could be preserved almost indefinitely. To use the cod, which was called bacalao (bah-kah-LAH-oh) in Spanish and South American cuisines, it was necessary to soak it in water for a day, replacing the water three or four times as it dissolved the salt.

Research

Research any of the types of preserved food described here. Describe how the food was preserved and how it is used in the cuisine. Provide a recipe that uses the preserved food.

Source: David Murray/Dorling Kindersley Secondary Permissions/Dorling Kindersley

through the danger zone as rapidly as possible and be reheated to at least 165°F for at least 15 seconds within a two-hour time period.

A steam table will maintain reheated foods at safe holding temperatures (135°F or higher, depending on your local code) but will not bring foods out of the danger zone quickly enough. Bring food to the proper temperature over a source of direct heat such as a burner, flattop, grill, or oven. You may also use a microwave oven to reheat small batches of food or individual portions.

The greater the surface area of the food and the shallower the layer, the more rapidly the food will heat. Use a clean and sanitized instant-read thermometer to check temperature. Clean and sanitize the thermometer after you use it.

READING CHECKPOINT *What is the temperature for holding hot foods? Cold foods?*

FIGURE 1–15

Holding Food Safely
Check the temperature of chilled foods during service.

APPLYING CONCEPTS *Why is it important to check the temperature of this potato salad?*

Source: Vincent P. Walter/Pearson Education/ PH College

1.2 ASSESSMENT

Reviewing Concepts

1. What is meant by the *flow of food*?
2. What is the first step in the flow of food?
3. What is meant by *FIFO* and why is it important to proper food storage?
4. Cooked foods you plan to store for later use need to be cooled below what temperature?
5. What is the temperature for holding hot foods? Cold foods?

Critical Thinking

6. **Comparing/Contrasting** What is the difference between the one-stage cooling method and the two-stage cooling method?

7. **Relating Concepts** Some restaurant owners serve time-temperature-abused food, arguing that it is wasteful to discard food if it has been held for only an additional half hour. How would you respond?

8. **Inferring** Why is it a good idea to "expect raw foods, especially meat, fish, and poultry, to contain harmful microorganisms?"

Test Kitchen

Use two cans of commercially prepared soups. Empty each can in a separate pot and heat quickly to 165°F for at least 15 seconds. Empty each pot in identical stainless-steel storage containers. Place both containers into a separate ice water bath. Stir the soup in one container constantly, but don't stir the other. Record the temperature of the soups every five minutes. Evaluate the results over an hour's time.

SCIENCE
Thermometers

Prepare a report comparing five thermometers (including instant-read digital thermometers). Focus on their stated accuracy, features, and ease of use. Indicate whether some are better suited for some types of cooking situations than others. Include your final recommendation.

The HACCP System

Key Concepts

- Defining a food-safety system
- Using the seven steps of HACCP

Vocabulary

- corrective action
- critical control points (CCPs)
- critical limits (CLs)
- FDA Food Code
- food-safety audit
- food-safety system
- HACCP
- hazard analysis

Food-Safety System

A **food-safety system** is a system of precautionary steps that take into account all the ways foods can be exposed to biological, chemical, or physical hazards. A food-safety system's goal is to reduce or eliminate risks from those hazards.

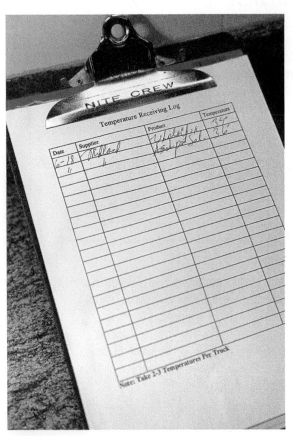

Source: Vincent P. Walter/Pearson Education/PH College

Standards and Inspections The Food and Drug Administration (FDA) has established sanitation standards that apply throughout the country. These standards are part of the **FDA Food Code**, a document that is updated frequently to reflect new findings about keeping foods safe. The FDA Food Code is not a federal law or regulation. It is simply a set of recommendations. It is up to state and local governments to establish their own laws and regulations. They can do this by adopting some or all of the FDA Food Code. They can also establish their own standards. However, the standards they develop must meet the national standards. Often, local standards call for more careful controls than the national standard.

Every foodservice establishment must be inspected by a representative of the local health department. The inspection is known as a **food-safety audit** (also called a *health inspection*). The number of times the establishment has to be inspected depends on a number of factors such as the number of meals served, the types of food on the menu, and the number of past violations. It is a good idea for a foodservice establishment to conduct self-inspections periodically to prepare for an official audit. That way, it can identify and correct any problems it may find.

When it is time for your establishment to be inspected, you should cooperate with the inspector. Whenever you can, you should accompany the inspector during the audit. You can learn a great deal during this inspection. The inspector will be looking carefully at foods and supplies; the grooming and hygiene of the staff; the temperatures for holding and serving foods; your procedures for cleaning and sanitizing; and your water supply, waste disposal, and pest control.

Once an inspection is complete, the foodservice establishment receives the results. If there are any violations, it must correct the situation. If it does not correct them, it may have to pay fines. Serious violations that remain uncorrected could mean the establishment is closed.

READING CHECKPOINT *What is a food-safety system?*

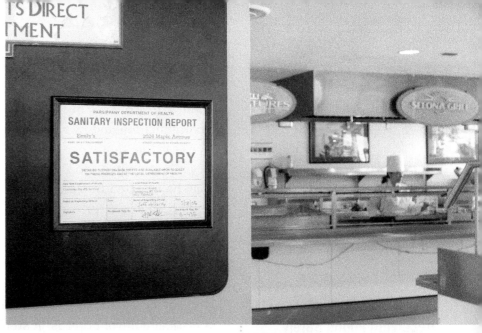
FIGURE 1–16
Health Inspection Report
The city health department gave this restaurant a satisfactory inspection.
DRAWING CONCLUSIONS *Do you think there is a connection between a restaurant's cleanliness and the quality of its food?*
Source: David Mager/Pearson Learning Photo Studio

The Seven Steps of HACCP

HACCP (Hazard Analysis Critical Control Point; pronounced "HASS-ip") is a scientific system for maintaining food safety that was originally developed for astronauts. It takes a systematic approach to controlling conditions that are responsible for most food-borne illnesses. It attempts to anticipate how and when food-safety problems are likely to occur and takes steps to prevent them.

The HACCP system has been adopted by both food processors and restaurants, as well as by the FDA and the U.S. Department of Agriculture (USDA). Although a foodservice establishment will need to make an initial investment of time and people to create a good HACCP plan, the system can ultimately save money and time, as well as improve the quality of food served to customers.

The heart of HACCP is contained in the following seven steps (each step is examined in more detail later in this section):

1. Conduct a hazard analysis.
2. Determine critical control points (CCPs).
3. Establish critical limits (CLs).
4. Establish monitoring procedures.
5. Identify corrective actions.
6. Establish procedures for record keeping and documentation.
7. Verify that the system works.

1. Conduct a Hazard Analysis A hazard analysis examines the flow of food from the moment you receive it until you serve it. As you know, there are two ways in which hazards are introduced into food: by direct contamination and by cross-contamination. You need to be aware of the points in that flow when conditions are most likely to encourage the growth of pathogens in a food. You also need to be aware of points when foods may be exposed to pathogens or other contaminants from other sources. Of particular concern are potentially hazardous foods: meats, fish, poultry, milk, eggs, and fresh produce.

2. Determine Critical Control Points Critical control points (CCPs) are specific points in the process of food handling where you can prevent, eliminate, or reduce a hazard. To quote the 2009 FDA Food Code, a critical control point is "a step at which control can be applied and is essential to prevent or eliminate a food safety hazard or reduce it to an acceptable level."

Receiving foods may be a critical control point. The cooking step in the flow of food is an example of a critical control point. By meeting safe temperatures for storing, holding, cooking, and serving foods, you can control hazards at various critical control points in the flow of food. Another way to do this would be to focus on how long a food is kept at a given temperature.

3. Establish Critical Limits Critical limits (CLs) indicate when foods are at unsafe temperatures. Critical limits also indicate how long food can be held at an unsafe temperature. These limits are established by local health departments and are typically based on the FDA's Food Code.

Your foodservice establishment may have even stricter limits in place, especially if you are cooking for people with special needs, such as elderly people, young children, or people who are sick. When you know the critical limits, you can make decisions about how to handle the food properly as you cook, serve, or store it.

4. Establish Monitoring Procedures Entering accurate measurements of time and temperature in a log book gives a foodservice establishment a record of how foods were handled. This record also alerts the establishment to any corrective steps they may need to take.

A good HACCP plan describes what measurements should be taken by a foodservice

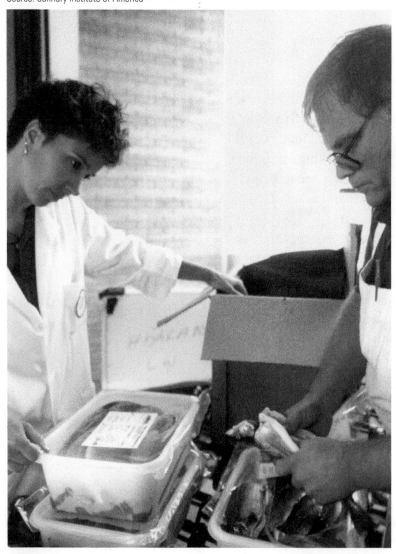

FIGURE 1–17

Receiving Foods Safely
Meat must be received at the proper temperature.

SOLVING PROBLEMS *What would you do if you received meat that was too warm?*

Source: Culinary Institute of America

establishment and how often. The plan also indicates the person responsible for taking and recording specific measurements.

5. Identify Corrective Actions

Whenever a measurement indicates that food is not at the right temperature or has been held in the danger zone for too long, a foodservice establishment must do something about it. This action is known as a **corrective action.**

For example, if food is held at an unsafe temperature for too long (such as 120°F for more than two hours), the corrective action would be to discard that food. If the food has fallen below the appropriate temperature but has not been at an unsafe temperature for too long a time, the corrective action would be to heat the food to a safe temperature.

FIGURE 1–18

Monitoring
Monitor the temperature of foods held in a steam table.

INFERRING *How do critical limits and monitoring procedures make the job of a foodservice worker easier?*

Source: Vincent P. Walter/Pearson Education/ PH College

6. Establish Procedures for Record Keeping and Documentation

Documentation for HACCP typically consists of time and temperature logs, checklists, and forms. It is important to record enough information so a foodservice establishment can be sure standards are being met. However, it is not a good idea to try to record so much information that foodservice workers can't keep up with it. Forms need be easy to understand and fill out.

7. Verify That the System Works

To be sure the system is working and the information being recorded is accurate, a foodservice establishment needs a system to double-check, or verify, the information recorded in the forms.

A supervisor, executive chef, or outside party should take time and temperature measurements to double-check the information. If their measurements don't match the measurements recorded in the log, it is likely that proper procedures are not being followed.

When the foodservice establishment looks into the situation, it may find that there are not enough thermometers or the thermometers are not working properly. It may find that the forms are too difficult to fill out and are untrustworthy. Or it may find that the person responsible for keeping the record is not doing the job correctly. If the establishment doesn't verify the system, however, it will never know it isn't working and, therefore, it will not be able to make the changes necessary to fix the problems.

READING CHECKPOINT *What are the seven steps of HACCP?*

Reviewing Concepts

1. What is a food-safety system?

2. What are the seven steps of HACCP?

Critical Thinking

3. Applying Concepts Why would the types of food on the menu be a factor in the number of times a food establishment is given a formal food-safety audit?

4. Comparing/Contrasting What are some advantages and disadvantages of food-safety systems such as HACCP for a foodservice establishment?

5. Inferring Why is it important for a foodservice establishment to develop its own verification system?

Test Kitchen

If your school has a cafeteria, research its HACCP program. Ask about each step in the program. If possible, watch a foodservice worker who is responsible for monitoring a critical control point. Pay attention to the worker's monitoring procedures and ask to review the logs for that particular critical control point for the previous week. Report on your findings.

SCIENCE

Lessons from the Space Program

Research the background of the HACCP program as it relates to the space program. Describe why the system was developed and how it was implemented in space. What relevance does its use in space have for earth-bound food establishments?

PROJECT 1

HACCP Procedures You are now ready to work on Project 1, "HACCP Procedures," which is available in "My Culinary Lab" or in your *Student's Lab Resources and Study Guide* manual.

Reviewing Content

Choose the letter that best answers the question or completes the statement.

1. Botulism is caused by
   a. bacteria.
   b. a virus.
   c. a parasite.
   d. fungi.

2. Freezers should be kept between
   a. 36°F and 41°F.
   b. 30°F and 32°F.
   c. 0°F and 10°F.
   d. −10°F and 0°F.

3. The first step in the HACCP system is to
   a. establish critical limits.
   b. establish monitoring procedures.
   c. conduct a hazard analysis.
   d. determine critical control points.

4. Hepatitis A is caused by
   a. bacteria.
   b. a virus.
   c. a parasite.
   d. fungi.

5. The ideal storage temperature for meat and poultry is between
   a. 32°F and 36°F.
   b. 30°F and 34°F.
   c. 38°F and 41°F.
   d. 41°F and 45°F.

6. A pathogen is
   a. a type of sanitizer.
   b. an organism that causes disease.
   c. a type of cleansing agent.
   d. a virus that causes salmonella poisoning.

7. The second compartment in a three-compartment sink is used for
   a. cleaning dirt.
   b. sanitizing.
   c. rinsing dirt and detergent.
   d. sterilizing.

Understanding Concepts

8. What is a food-borne illness?

9. What are the three types of potential hazards that can contaminate food and produce food-borne illnesses?

10. What is meant by the term *flow of food*?

11. What are the seven steps of the HACCP system?

12. What is FAT TOM? What does each letter stand for?

13. What is meant by the term *temperature danger zone*? What are the actual temperature limits for this danger zone?

14. What is the best, but slowest, method for thawing foods safely?

Critical Thinking

15. **COMPARING/CONTRASTING** What is the difference between direct contamination and cross-contamination?

16. **COMMUNICATING** Explain why the seventh step of the HACCP system is necessary.

Culinary Math

17. **APPLYING CONCEPTS** Is a food that has a pH of 8.5 a potentially hazardous food?

18. **APPLYING CONCEPTS** Is a food that has an Aw of .85 a potentially hazardous food?

On the Job

19. **APPLYING CONCEPTS** A customer asks the chef to cook a piece of beef very rare. Is the customer at risk? Is the restaurant at risk? Explain your answer.

20. **DRAWING CONCLUSIONS** How does the identification of corrective actions (the fifth HACCP procedure) make the job of the foodservice staff easier?

Food Processors and Manufacturers

Food processors and manufacturers play an important role in the foodservice industry. This job category includes a wide range of possibilities. Some processors and manufacturers work on a small scale; these companies may pride themselves on handcrafting items and on using traditional methods. They may sometimes be known as *artisans*.

Bakers Some people work as bakers who produce a wide range of goods to distribute through both wholesale and retail outlets. They measure, mix, bake, and decorate baked items including muffins, yeast breads, and pastries. Some operations are small-scale productions using wood-fired brick ovens; others are major companies that produce goods sold through retail chains on a national or global level. Some bakers work in specialty areas, including cake decoration and candy making.

Butchers Butchers process meats from initial butchering to fabrication into a wide range of wholesale and retail cuts. Some food processors work with meats to produce a variety of cured and processed meats, such as sausages, bacon, ham, and pâtés. Butchers may specialize in handling fish, shellfish, poultry, or game. They may

be found in large meat-packing plants, privately owned butcher shops or plants, or supermarkets.

Processors *Food processors*, also known as *food batchmakers*, commonly produce components that are used in professional and home kitchens. Examples of the items they produce include jams, jellies, sauces, pickles, condiments, preserves, marinades, and dressings. Large-scale commercial food-processing companies produce the boxed, canned, frozen, and prepared foods you see in grocery stores. Some processors provide their goods directly to retail outlets, while some specialize in products meant for foodservice.

Cheese makers Cheese, yogurt, and other items made from milk are made in both large and small operations. Depending on the type of operation, cheese processors may work within a farm operation, using the milk produced right at that site. Other operations are much larger, and the milk comes from a number of different farms to a central processor area.

Entry-Level Requirements

On-the-job training and apprenticeships are a common way to get a start in various food processing operations. Training in culinary or baking and pastry arts through a vocational or technical school is also common. Depending on the type of operation, a health certificate may be required.

Helpful for Advancement

To achieve higher levels within food processing, individuals often get degrees in areas related to their field. For instance, a bachelor's or master's degree in dairy management or food science would be important (and necessary, depending on the type of company and the position itself) to advance to a senior-level position, such as plant or team leader, research and development, executive, or manager. Experience, class work, and a degree in management, science, technology, or marketing are significant advantages.

Source: Laurentiu Iordache/Fotolia

MAYA KAIMAL

Maya Kaimal didn't plan to make a living from cooking. She started her career in publishing, working as a photo editor for *Saveur* among other magazines, but found herself drawn to her Indian culinary heritage, collecting recipes from her family there. She published two cookbooks that highlighted the cuisine of South India, where her father was raised: *Curried Favors: Family Recipes from South India,* and *Savoring the Spice Coast of India.* Sensing a growing appetite for Indian food in America, she left magazine publishing, and in 2003 she and her husband launched Maya Kaimal Fine Indian Foods. Her Indian simmer sauces reflect the authenticity of her cookbooks, and give busy people an easy way to prepare homemade tasting Indian food. Her all natural products are available nation wide.

Maya Kaimal

Source: Courtesy of Maya Kaimal

VITAL STATISTICS

Graduated: Pomona College

Profession: Owner of Maya Kaimal Fine Indian Foods

Interesting Items: Featured in *Bon Appetit, Food & Wine, Cooking Light, Food Arts,* and *The New York Times*

First-place winner for Best Cooking Sauce at the 2010 Fancy Food Show

Products received five-star rating on Amazon

Former photo editor of *Saveur* magazine

CAREER PROFILE

Salary Ranges

Entry: $20,000 to $40,000

Managers: $50,000 to $80,000 (or more)

Senior: Varies widely depending on the size of the operation

Owner/operator: Varies widely

Kitchen Safety

2.1 Fire Safety

2.2 Accidents and Injuries

INSTRUCTIONS

1. PULL PIN. HOLD UNIT UPRIGHT.

2. STAND BACK 6 FEET (2M) AIM AT BASE OF FIRE.

3. SQUEEZE LEVER AND SWEEP SIDE TO SIDE.

Fire Safety

Key Concepts

- Identifying fire hazards
- Controlling fires by using alarms and extinguishers
- Using a fire emergency plan

Vocabulary

- arson
- assembly points
- automatic fire control systems
- evacuation routes
- fire detectors
- fire emergency plan
- fire extinguishers
- hood suppression systems

Fire Hazards

An accidental fire can start in a kitchen for a variety of reasons. Open flames may set paper or cloth aflame, or a buildup of grease may ignite when it gets too hot. Water may splash into an outlet and create a spark that causes a fire. An accidental fire often results from someone's carelessness, but it is not caused by someone who intentionally starts a fire.

Arson, the act of deliberately setting a fire, is the opposite of an accidental fire. The best defense against arson is having a good fire-safety plan and keeping your building as secure as possible.

To avoid fires in the first place, you need to be aware of fire hazards. Some common types of fire hazards are gas, open flames and heat, grease, electrical wiring, and unsafe storage areas.

Gas Stoves, ranges, and other heating equipment often use natural gas or propane as fuel. Many of these larger appliances have a pilot light, which always stays lit. Unless you have been trained in lighting an appliance's pilot light, do not attempt to light it on your own. Alert someone who knows how to light the pilot light. If the pilot light is not lit, you could have a dangerous gas buildup that could lead to a fire, an explosion, or carbon monoxide poisoning.

Open Flames and Heat Open flames, such as gas burners or wood fires, can set paper, food, grease, clothing,

Source: Pakhnyushcha/Shutterstock

If You Smell Gas . . .

1. Alert your supervisor or boss immediately.
2. Switch off the gas at the main supply, if you know where it is. Otherwise, ask someone to do this for you.
3. Open all the windows and doors.
4. Don't use *any* electrical equipment. Don't turn the lights on or off; don't use your cell phone.
5. Leave the area.

and even metal on fire. Even things that are no longer flaming can be hot enough to catch something on fire. Metal cookware and wiring can get hot enough to start a fire if an easy-to-burn material gets close to them.

Items commonly found in the kitchen or the dining room may also produce a flame: matches, candles, or cigarettes and cigars. Throwing matches that are still glowing or hot into a wastebasket filled with papers may lead to a basket filled with flames.

The motors that run appliances and equipment—including mixers, grinders, refrigerators, and freezers—can get hot enough to start a fire.

Grease Grease fires are another common type of fire. A layer of dirt or grease is often the cause of a flare-up or fire in the kitchen. When equipment is kept clean, the kitchen is safer.

Follow a regular cleaning schedule for walls and work surfaces. Cooking appliances such as ranges, oven hoods, fryers, broilers, and ovens must also be kept clean. Also keep heating, air conditioning, and ventilation units, including hoods and filters, clean to avoid the risk of a grease fire.

Electrical Wiring More than 30 percent of all accidental fires in restaurants are caused by faulty electrical wiring, by electrical equipment, or by the improper use of electrical equipment.

Electrical plugs and outlets should always be used carefully. Never pull a plug from an outlet by the cord. If a cord looks frayed or a plug appears to be damaged, it should be replaced. The plugs on equipment may be either grounded (plugs with three prongs) or ungrounded (plugs with two prongs). Use the right kind of outlet for the plug you have. A grounded outlet has three holes to accommodate each of the prongs on a grounded plug. An ungrounded outlet has only two holes.

Overloaded outlets are a common cause of electrical fires. Be sure you don't have too many items plugged into a single outlet. The plate covering the outlet should be securely attached without any cracks or holes. Keep all outlets and plugs dry.

FIGURE 2–1

Overloaded Outlet

Never overload outlets.

🚫 **SOLVING PROBLEMS** *What possible solutions might there be for this overloaded outlet?*

Source: Thom Gourley/Flatbread Images, LLC/Alamy

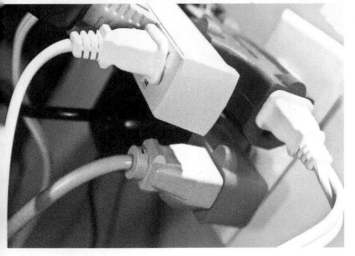

Unsafe Storage Areas Space for storage is limited in any kitchen. It is important that your storage areas are designed for fire safety. Store flammable items, such as paper supplies and linens, away from open flames or heating units. Keep cleaners or bleaches separated from flammable items as well. The combination can cause fires.

 **READING CHECKPOINT** *What are five common types of fire hazards?*

FOCUS ON Safety

Smothering Flames

If flames erupt in a pan, put a lid on the pan to smother the flames. Pull the pan off the heat until the fire is extinguished.

Fire Control

In case a fire starts in the kitchen or dining room, every foodservice establishment must have certain systems in place. Fire detectors, automatic sprinkler and hood systems, and portable fire extinguishers are necessary for fire safety.

Fire Detectors Fire detectors are devices that warn you about a fire so you can get out of the building safely. There are two basic types of fire detectors: smoke detectors and heat detectors.

- **Smoke detectors.** To detect the presence of smoke, smoke detectors work best when there is good airflow. If there is no way for the air to move—for example, at the end of a hallway—the smoke detector cannot function properly.
- **Heat detectors.** Activated by a sudden rise in temperature, heat detectors can sense a fire even when there is no smoke.

Fire detectors must be well maintained. If they are battery operated, it is important to replace the batteries on a regular schedule. Fire detectors must be installed and maintained by a fire-safety expert. They should be inspected monthly by a member of the kitchen staff and serviced yearly by a licensed professional.

Automatic Hood and Sprinkler Systems Automatic fire control systems include extinguishers, sprinklers, and alarms triggered by the heat of a fire. These systems work whether the building is occupied or not. Sprinkler systems release water to put out a fire. They are used in areas such as the dining room or the bathroom, but not in areas where food is prepared.

The National Fire Protection Association (NFPA) requires that special systems to put out fires be installed in areas over ranges, griddles, broilers, and deep-fat fryers. These systems, known as **hood suppression systems**, are located in the ventilation hood above the equipment. Instead of water, they release chemicals (in either a liquid or powder form), carbon dioxide, or gases (known as inert gases) that can smother a fire and put it out. Manufacturers have developed higher-efficiency heating systems, and restaurants have increasingly begun using vegetable oils, which heat to a higher temperature than animal fats. This has meant

Sprayers

FIGURE 2–2

Hood Suppression System
Hood suppression systems
release chemicals that blanket
the fire.

PREDICTING *If a restaurant's hood
suppression system went off during the
service and the food being cooked was
all discarded, would you recook all the
food and continue or refund customers'
money and close for the night?*

Source: Vincent P. Walter/Pearson Education/
PH College

FIGURE 2–3

Fire Extinguishers
The fire extinguisher on the left is
a water-based extinguisher. The
one on the right is a dry-chemical
extinguisher.

APPLYING CONCEPTS *On which
types of flammable materials should each
fire extinguisher be used?*

Source: Les Lougheed/Pearson Education/
PH College

that modern hood suppression systems have moved increasingly to more efficient wet chemicals that immediately stop flames and suppress fires. After a fire, the foamy wet chemical agent can be wiped up quickly with a damp cloth so the kitchen can resume normal operations quickly.

Fire Extinguishers Fire **extinguishers** are handheld devices you can use to put out a small fire.

A small fire is described as being no more than 3 feet wide or 3 feet tall. If the fire is larger than that, you should call the fire department immediately. If it is small enough to handle with a fire extinguisher, be sure to choose the right type of extinguisher.

Specific types of fire extinguishers are designed to handle specific types of fires. Fires are grouped into five classes, depending on the material involved in the fire.

Every fire extinguisher is marked with the class of fire it is meant to handle. Some fire extinguishers can be used for more than one class of fire, so there may be more than one letter on the extinguisher's label.

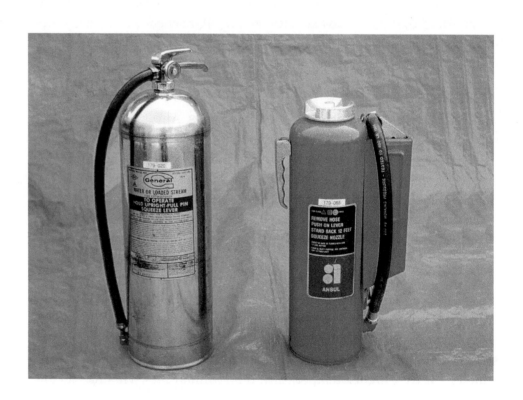

Fire Extinguishers and Classes of Fires

Class of Fire	Type of Flammable Material	Type of Fire Extinguishers to Use
Class A	Solids (paper, cloth, wood, plastic)	Class A / Class A/B
Class B	Flammable and combustible liquids (gasoline, alcohol, diesel oil, oil-based paints, and lacquers) and flammable gases	Class A/B / Class A/B/C
Class C	Energized electrical equipment (cords, outlets, circuits, motors, switches, or wiring)	Class A/C / Class B/C
Class D	Combustible metals (switches, wiring, and metals such as iron or copper)	Class D
Class K	Cooking oils and fats	Class K

Source: Icons from Pearson Education

- Water-based extinguishers work by dousing the fire with water. They are recharged with a clean water source. They can be used only on Class A fires.

- Foam extinguishers work by cooling the fire down and covering it in a blanket of foam that keeps air from getting to the fire. These extinguishers will not work if they freeze. Use foam extinguishers for Class A or B fires only.

- Dry-chemical extinguishers interrupt the chemical reactions that keep a fire burning. These extinguishers may be approved for use on Class A, B, or C fires or for Class B or C fires only.

You should know where extinguishers are located in the kitchen and what types of extinguishers they are. It is also important to learn how to use portable fire extinguishers safely—before you actually need to use one. A simple way to remember how to use a fire extinguisher is the PASS system.

PASS System for Using Fire Extinguishers

Pull the pin.

Aim low, at the base of the fire (stand 6 to 8 feet away from the fire).

Squeeze the trigger.

Sweep from side to side.

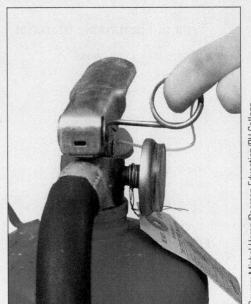

Source: Michal Heron/Pearson Education/PH College

All portable fire extinguishers need to be recharged on a regular basis as part of their maintenance. Recharging is done only by an approved fire extinguisher service company.

 **READING CHECKPOINT** *What are the five classes of fires and what types of flammable materials does each type include?*

FOCUS ON Safety

Boxed In

Foodservice establishments sometimes store empty boxes so they block escape routes. This is extremely unsafe. Boxes should be discarded or broken down and recycled.

Fire Emergency Plans

A well-designed **fire emergency plan** means you have an established plan of action in case of a fire. Such a plan requires that you post the numbers for the fire department and emergency rescue teams on every phone. It also requires that you post a diagram of the floor plan showing escape routes, fire exits, and assembly points.

Escape Routes Escape routes, or **evacuation routes**, give everyone in the building at least two ways to get out of the building. Fire exit doors need to be clearly marked and kept clear at all times. Fire doors open outward when you push on the door; they do not need to be opened with a key when you are exiting the building.

Having two routes means you can still get out even if a hallway, stairwell, or fire door is impossible to get through because of smoke or fire. Exit routes and fire doors should have some type of battery-powered lighting.

Flames of Different Colors

The color of a flame depends on two things: the amount of air that can get to the flame and the type of material that is burning.

Fire needs oxygen to keep burning. The less oxygen that mixes with the flame, the more yellow the flame looks. A candle or a campfire burns yellow because particles of the candle or wood are not being burned. These tiny unburned particles are carbon, left over from burning the candle or wood. Carbon glows bright yellow when it gets hot. Soot and smoke are nothing more than these unburned carbon particles.

If you look closely at a candle flame, you'll see that some of the flame is a different color. The center of the flame is blue, while the areas farther from the wick are yellow. That's because the area closest to the candle's wick burns at a much higher temperature; there are fewer unburned carbon particles in the blue area.

The flame on a gas stove is mainly blue because air is blended with the gas for a very hot flame that doesn't contain much unburned carbon. A blue flame burns at around 1700°C, while a yellow flame burns at only about 1000°C. The color of a flame also depends on the material being burned.

Lots of fuels produce blue flames when burned. The most commonly available fuels used in the household are natural gas and propane. Both burn with blue flames. Butane, found in lighters, also has blue flames. Other chemicals make flames of other colors. For instance, a mixture of copper and chlorine makes a greenish, turquoise, or bright blue flame. Lithium burns brilliant red. Carbon powder from graphite or charcoal dust burns bright yellow-orange, like a candle flame.

Lab Activity

Compare the efficiency of various fuels by evaluating the amount of unburned carbon produced by the fuel over an identical period. Use four fuel sources: a candle, sterno (or alcohol lamp), propane, and natural gas. Light each fuel's source and hold a small pan in the upper part of the flame for 10 seconds (making sure to hold the pan's handle with a pot holder or other appropriate heat protection). Compare the residue left on the knife. How would you rank the various fuels in terms of their efficiency in completely burning their available carbon? Does this have implications for cooking, holding, and serving food?

Source: Hector the Hero/Shutterstock

Natural gas burns with a blue flame

FIGURE 2–4

Evacuation Route

An evacuation route gives everyone in the building at least two ways to escape.

INFERRING *Why is it important to have more than one evacuation route out of a building?*

Source: Ron May/Pearson Education/PH College

Assembly Points Assembly points, or meeting points, are predetermined spots at a safe distance from the building. Everyone who has exited the building must come to one of the assembly points so it can be determined that everyone has left the building.

FIGURE 2–5

Exit Sign

An escape route is marked by an illuminated exit sign.

INFERRING *Why do you think exit signs and emergency lighting are often battery powered?*

Source: Vincent P. Walter/Pearson Education/ PH College

Fire Drills Drills give you a chance to practice escape routes. They also give you the opportunity to practice safe behaviors that may save lives during a real fire. Whether you are practicing in a fire drill or the fire is real, remember the following:

- ☑ Call the fire department immediately.
- ☑ Stay calm.
- ☑ Shut off any gas valves if you can.
- ☑ Start to get people out of the building as soon as possible. If there are guests or customers in the building, show them the best escape route. Tell them where to meet when they have come out of the building.
- ☑ Meet at the assembly point.
- ☑ Let a firefighter know immediately if someone is missing.

 **READING CHECKPOINT** *Why should there be two escape routes as part of a good fire emergency plan?*

2.1 ASSESSMENT

Reviewing Concepts

1. What are some common types of fire hazards?
2. What are the four steps in the PASS system for using fire extinguishers?
3. What is a fire emergency plan?

Critical Thinking

4. **Drawing Conclusions** How would a regular cleaning schedule minimize the risk of a fire?
5. **Analyzing Information** Which class(es) of fire extinguisher(s) is/are best suited for a fire involving electrical equipment?
6. **Applying Concepts** Which type of fire extinguisher (water-based, foam, or dry-chemical) would be best for a fire involving electrical equipment?

Test Kitchen

Examine the fire detectors, hood suppression systems, sprinkler systems, and fire extinguishers in your school's kitchen and dining area. Determine the class of fire for which each extinguisher is intended. Talk to the person at your school in charge of its fire emergency plan.

SCIENCE ———————————

Types of Fire Extinguishers

Research the way each of the most common types of fire extinguishers works (water-based, foam, and dry-chemical). Why are different types of extinguishers needed for different types of fires? How does each type put out a specific type of fire? Report on your findings.

Accidents and Injuries

READING PREVIEW

Key Concepts

- Identifying common accidents and injuries
- Using basic safety guidelines to prevent accidents and injuries
- Learning first aid and emergency procedures
- Understanding safety as an ongoing process

Vocabulary

- accident report
- anaphylactic shock
- automated external defibrillator (AED)
- carcinogenic
- cardiopulmonary resuscitation (CPR)
- corrosive
- Environmental Protection Agency (EPA)
- general safety audit
- hazard communication program
- Hazard Communication Standard (HCS)
- Heimlich maneuver
- Material Safety Data Sheet (MSDS)
- obstructed airway maneuver
- Occupational Safety and Health Administration (OSHA)
- toque
- worker's compensation

Types of Accidents and Injuries

An accident is any unplanned event that hurts someone or damages someone's property. Accidents and injuries are a constant concern in any work environment. When you know the most common types of injuries or accidents and how they happen, you can take steps to avoid or prevent them. The most common types of accidents in foodservice establishments are the following:

- Burns
- Cuts
- Sprains, strains, and falls

Burns Some burns are more serious than others, but all burns require immediate care. Burns are described as being first, second, or third degree. *Degree* refers to how severe the burn is.

Cuts It comes as no surprise that cuts are one of the most common injuries for cooks. You can get a cut from a knife or any sharp edge. Cleaning up broken glass can cause a cut, as can handling paper. There are different types of cuts.

- **Abrasion.** A minor cut, such as a rug burn, caused by rubbing the skin against something else.
- **Laceration.** A cut or tear in the skin, such as a knife cut. Lacerations can be quite deep. Deep lacerations or those in a place on the body that can open easily, such as your forehead, may require stitches.

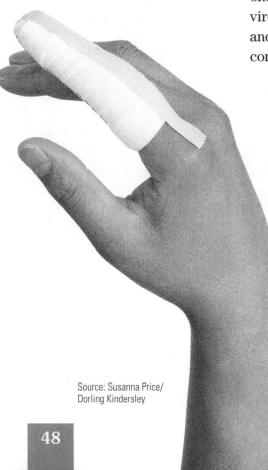

Source: Susanna Price/
Dorling Kindersley

Burns

Degree	Description	Treatment
First-degree burn	Skin turns red, feels sensitive, and may become swollen.	Treat with cool running water or by covering with towels soaked in cool water. Do not apply ice.
Second-degree burn	Burn is deeper and more painful than a first-degree burn. Blisters form. Blisters may ooze and are quite painful.	Cool the skin as directed for first-degree burns. Do not apply ointments or bandages. Seek medical attention.
Third-degree burn	Skin may turn white and become soft, or it may turn black and feel leathery or hard. Burned area does not have feeling because the burn has damaged the nerves.	Cover the burn with cool, moist, sterile gauze or clean cloth. Do not apply ointments, ice, or ice water. Seek immediate medical attention.

- **Avulsion.** A cut that removes a piece of skin or even a part of the body, such as a fingertip. Depending on severity, an avulsion may require immediate medical attention.
- **Puncture.** A wound resulting from a sharp object that pierces the skin and makes a deep hole in the skin. Depending on depth and location, a puncture wound may also require immediate medical attention.

Strains, Sprains, and Falls Sprains and strains are the result of twisting or wrenching your body out of its normal position. They are often caused by tripping or falling over something. If you step into a hole or onto something slippery, it is easy to sprain an ankle.

When you fall, you may try to stop yourself by grabbing something or putting your hands behind or in front of you. A sprained wrist or shoulder may then result.

You may suffer from strained muscles when you stand in the same position for too long, hold yourself in an awkward position (such as when you stretch or bend over to work), or make the same motion over and over again.

One of the most common types of strain is a back strain caused by lifting heavy things improperly.

FIGURE 2–6
Cutting with a Knife
Never underestimate the sharpness of a kitchen knife.
DRAWING CONCLUSIONS *Why is it important for a new chef to focus immediately on learning appropriate knife skills?*
Source: Dave King/Image Partners 2005 Active/Dorling Kindersley

READING CHECKLIST *What are the most common types of accidents in foodservice establishments?*

Preventing Accidents and Injuries

Preventing accidents and injuries is your responsibility. You can make yourself safer at work by observing safe work habits as described in this section. When you work safely, you help to create and maintain a safe environment for everyone.

Dressing for Safety You can protect your safety when you work in the kitchen by wearing the right kind of clothing, using the right tools and equipment, and learning to use all the tools and equipment in the kitchen properly and safely.

Large or dangling jewelry such as necklaces, earrings, bracelets, and rings can get caught in machinery. Take such items off before you start work.

The **toque** (toke) prevents hair from falling into the food. It also is open at the top for coolness.

Never wear loose or baggy clothing that could get caught on something or tangled in machinery or equipment. A chef's double-breasted jacket protects against burns and scalding on the arms. Be sure to keep your arms covered. You can rebutton a double-breasted jacket on the alternate side if one side becomes dirty.

The chef's apron adds another layer of protection. You can also change it easily if it becomes unduly soiled. The houndstooth pattern of the traditional chef's pants does not show dirt.

Wear slip-, grease-, and heat-resistant shoes to protect your feet. They should either lace up tightly or have no laces at all. Closed toes (and even steel-reinforced toes) in your shoes can protect you from being cut if a knife should fall. Closed toes also can help prevent bruises if something heavy falls on your foot and can protect against stubbed toes. The shoes' heels should be low to avoid twisted or sprained ankles.

Wear additional protective gear when appropriate, especially when you are working with chemicals such as those in cleaning compounds. You may need to wear goggles, a mask, and rubber gloves to protect yourself from chemicals or from the particles that may fly out of a meat grinder or mixer. Wear heavy leather gloves when you are opening crates or lifting heavy objects.

Handling Knives and Other Cutting Tools Safely

To avoid cutting yourself, keep your knives sharp as you work and keep your hands and your knives clean and dry. Keep your knives organized and safely stored at your workstation. Don't let your work area become so cluttered that it is difficult for you to work safely. If a knife falls, do not grab for it—just try to get out of its way.

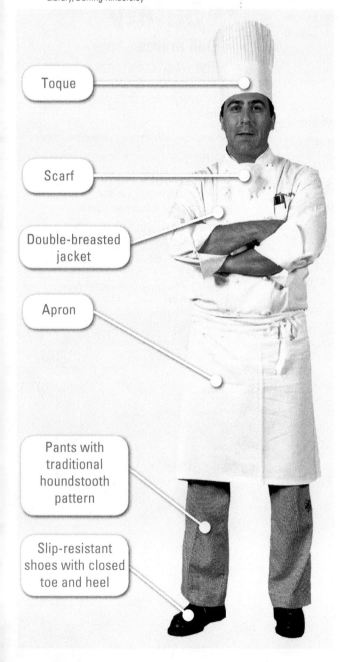

FIGURE 2–7

Uniform and Kitchen Safety
A complete uniform offers protection.

FORMING A MODEL *What parts of the uniform protect you from injury?*

Source: Max Alexander/Dorling Kindersley Media Library/Dorling Kindersley

- Toque
- Scarf
- Double-breasted jacket
- Apron
- Pants with traditional houndstooth pattern
- Slip-resistant shoes with closed toe and heel

To avoid cutting someone else with your knife, pass it to someone else safely by laying it down on a flat surface with the handle extending to the person receiving the knife. Let them pick the knife up from the table, rather than passing it in midair.

If you must carry a knife through a crowded kitchen, walk carefully with the blade pointed down and the knife held close to your side. Put the knife in a shield if possible.

Wear mesh cutting gloves to protect your hands, especially when you must exert pressure on the blade. Opening oysters and slicing meats are good examples of situations when a mesh cutting glove would help avoid accidents.

Take special precautions when you are working with machines or appliances that cut food (slicers, grinders, mandolines, graters, and so on). Most of these machines have guards that are meant to keep your fingers or hands away from the blade. Be sure you always use these guards properly. When you are cleaning any motorized equipment, be sure it is turned off and unplugged before you begin cleaning.

Other common sources of cuts in the kitchen are can openers, open metal cans, and the cutting bars on rolls of aluminum or plastic wrap. Keep your hands away from sharp and jagged edges.

Broken glass can cut an unwary person easily. Clean up broken glass right away with a broom. Ask people near the area to simply stay where they are until you finish cleaning up. Many establishments have a separate container to hold broken glass. It would be easy for broken glass to break through a plastic trashcan liner and cut you when you empty the can.

Preventing Burns An open flame, the handle of a hot pan, sputtering grease, and chemicals can all cause burns. The best way to prevent burns is to keep your skin away from hot or caustic materials.

Your uniform is one way you can protect yourself from burns. Wear long sleeves and keep them rolled down. When you need to move or carry a hot pot or pan, use oven mitts or dry side towels to protect your hands. Tell other workers that a hot pan or tray has been left to cool.

If you must walk through the kitchen with something hot, let people know you are walking near them. If possible, let them know before you start walking.

Putting hot pans or dishes into a sink full of water is not good for the utensils. It could cause them to buckle or even break. It is also dangerous for anyone who may unknowingly reach into the sink. Let hot pots and pans cool before washing them or putting them in the sink. Always keep a dry side towel on the handle of a hot pan to let other workers know that the pan and handle are hot.

The steam that is released when you lift the lid on a pot or pan can cause serious burns. To prevent steam burns, lift the lid so the side farthest from you opens up first. This directs the steam away from your face.

FIGURE 2–8
Carrying a Knife
Hold the knife properly to avoid hurting others.
DRAWING CONCLUSIONS *Why is this the best way to carry a knife in a crowded kitchen?*
Source: Culinary Institute of America

Chef's Tip

Dry Mitts or Towels

Replace your side towel if it gets wet. A wet side towel or oven mitt doesn't protect you from a hot pan or oven rack.

FIGURE 2–9
Preventing Burns
This chef thinks that because he is using a towel, he is preventing burns.

🚫 **PREDICTING** *What's wrong with this picture? Hint: What would happen if the hot liquid spattered from the pot?*

Source: Culinary Institute of America

FIGURE 2–10
Prevent Slipping
Let others know that the floor is wet or slippery.

APPLYING CONCEPTS *Why is using both a sign and a verbal warning the safest way to alert others that the floor is wet?*

Source: Michal Heron/Pearson Education/ PH College

A hot blast from an oven could be enough to cause burns on your face. If you wear glasses, the hot air could cause the lenses to fog up, temporarily obscuring your vision. Open oven doors carefully by opening them just enough for some of the hot air to escape before you open the door the rest of the way and then bend to look into the oven.

Hot oil and grease sputters when water is added to it. Moist food, frozen food, batter, and other liquids all contain enough water to cause oil to fly out of the pan or deep fryer. You should dry food as much as possible before adding it to hot oil. When you are adding food to the pan or the fryer, lower the food carefully into the oil. If possible, place food so the edge closest to you is placed in the hot oil first.

Avoiding Slips and Falls When you are walking, look where you are going. Be conscious of potential problems. Wet floors, uneven carpeting, broken pavement, loose steps, and objects that stick out into your path all can trip you. Keep floors and walkways clean, dry, and free from obstructions. Tell others about any hazards that may make them fall.

Walking in the dark makes it impossible to see hazards clearly, so turn on a light or use a flashlight. Replace lightbulbs or use a flashlight so you can see more easily.

Cleaning Up Spills Even a little spill on the floor can be enough to make someone slip and fall. Whenever you see liquid on the floor, clean it up immediately. Water is easy to lift up, but grease is more difficult to clean. Use mops or absorbent toweling to soak up the liquid. You may also need to scatter an absorbent material such as cornmeal on a spill, especially a grease spill, before scooping it up.

No matter what type of material is spilled on the floor, the first thing you should do is let the people in the immediate area know. Direct them to walk around the spill, or put up signs to indicate that the floor is wet or slippery.

Lifting and Moving Heavy Objects Safely You may need to move heavy or bulky objects into or out of storage, take a large pot off the stove, or lift a pan of food out of the oven. Moving heavy objects improperly can easily result in a strained or aching back.

Before you start to lift a heavy object on your own, take a minute to consider each of the following questions:

- Can you lift the weight on your own, or should you get some help?
- Is the load balanced?
- Could the contents splash or spill as you walk?

- Is your path clear of all obstacles?
- Is there somewhere for you to put the item down safely once you reach your destination?

When you have the help you need and have made sure the path is clear, you are ready to begin. To lift heavy items safely, use your legs and not your back. To do this, squat down, keeping your back straight, rather than bending over. Get a secure grip on the item you need to move. While you are holding the item firmly, lift yourself up with your legs.

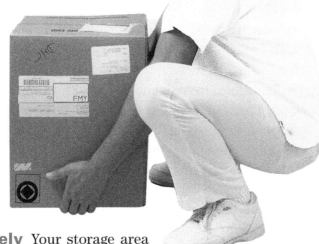

Using Ladders Safely Your storage area may have shelves that are above your head. To safely store or retrieve items higher than you can easily reach, you must use a ladder.

There are three basic types of ladders:

- Step stool
- Stepladder
- Straight ladder

A ladder is usually labeled with information about how much weight it can safely carry. Each part of the ladder should be in good condition. All of the steps (or rungs) should be intact. Ladders should have nonskid feet to keep them in place when you are using them. If your ladder is made of metal, make sure it is not touching anything electrical, such as wires, motors, or outlets.

The ladder you choose should be tall enough so you don't need to step on the top of a step stool or the top two rungs of a straight ladder. Make sure the ladder won't slip or move when you get on it. Step stools and folding ladders may have a brace that holds the legs of the ladder open. Be sure the braces are completely locked in place.

If you are using a straight ladder, you need to lean it at an angle, with the bottom of the ladder 2 or 3 feet away from the shelf or wall. Lean the top of the ladder against the shelf or wall. Check the ladder to make sure it won't slide or slip. If something you are trying to reach is not close enough to reach without leaning, get down from the ladder and move the ladder closer to the item. You should never lean to one side.

Get help if you need it. Always have someone hold the bottom of a straight ladder steady as you climb it. If you can't carry the item you need

FIGURE 2–11

Prevent Back Strain
Lift a heavy object safely.

INFERRING *If a chef strained his or her back badly and was unable to cook, what would the consequences be for the restaurant?*

Source: Michal Heron/Pearson Education/ PH College

FOCUS ON Safety

Watch Your Back
A back brace provides support for your lower back when you are lifting heavy objects and helps avoid sprains or strains.

FIGURE 2–12

Stepladder
A ladder is typically labeled with information about how much weight it can safely carry.

COMMUNICATING *If you needed help retrieving an object from a high storage shelf, but everyone seemed busy, what would you do?*

Source: Matthew Ward/Dorling Kindersley

to move with one hand, get someone to stand by who can hand you things or hold the things you've retrieved.

After you finish using a ladder, be sure to put it away properly. Tall ladders can easily fall, so be sure they are secured.

Driving You may be called on to drive for a work-related activity. It is important that you observe all safe-driving procedures. Your license must be up to date. Employers may want you to complete a defensive driving program. They may also check your driving record.

The vehicle you are driving should be safe to drive. The brakes should work. All lights, including turn signals and brake lights, must work properly. Tires need to have enough tread for traction on the road. If a vehicle supplied by your employer is not safe, bring it to your employer's attention immediately.

Wet, windy, snowy, icy, and dark conditions all make driving more difficult. Take extra care when you must drive at these times and leave plenty of room between yourself and other cars so you can react to other drivers and stop safely.

Avoid distractions while you are driving. Anything that takes your attention away from traffic, such as changing the station on the radio, talking on a cell phone, or eating or drinking, could easily cause an accident.

Follow safe-driving procedures. Always observe the posted speed limit and other traffic signs. Never pass a stopped school bus, and wear your seatbelt at all times.

 **READING CHECKPOINT** *What is the right way to lift something heavy?*

First Aid and Emergency Procedures

First aid is the care you give in response to an accident. It is important to assist the injured person as quickly as possible. Every kitchen should have a properly stocked first-aid kit that can be used for a variety of injuries including cuts, burns, and sprains. If your establishment offers delivery service or uses trucks for catering, first-aid kits should be placed in these vehicles as well.

The kit should include materials and supplies such as bandages, ointments, tweezers, scissors, and some medications, such as aspirin. It should also include a first-aid manual with information about how to treat various injuries. Whenever there is an accident and someone gets hurt, follow these guidelines:

- Check the scene of the accident.
- Stay calm and keep the victim calm.
- Ask anyone who is not directly assisting the victim to stand back.
- Call for medical help, if appropriate, or ask someone to call for you.

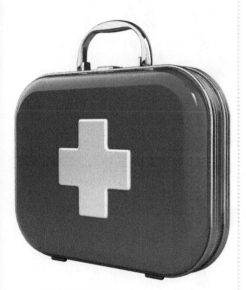

FIGURE 2–13
First-Aid Kit
This first-aid kit includes bandages, ointments, tweezers, and aspirin, along with a first-aid manual.

PREDICTING *Which supplies do you think will need to be replaced most frequently?*

Source: Sashkin/Shutterstock

- Administer first aid, using the information in your first-aid manual.
- Stay with the victim until medical help arrives.
- Complete an accident report.

The American Red Cross offers courses that teach the correct procedures in case of workplace accidents. You can contact your local office to find out when these courses are offered, and you can even take a course in first aid to become certified.

Burns Whenever someone is burned, the first step is to remove the heat source. This may involve removing clothing that is soaked with hot water or grease and moving the victim to a safe place. Keep the victim calm and still so he or she can rest while first aid is administered or until medical help arrives. Soak the burned area in cool water. If you can't easily get the burned area into a basin of cool water, soak a cloth in cool water and drape the cloth over the burn.

Cuts Clean the area well with soap and warm water. If the cut is bleeding heavily, cover the wound with sterile gauze pads and apply pressure until the flow stops. Cover the wound with a sterile dressing or bandage. The bandage should be changed frequently to keep it from becoming a potential site for cross-contamination. Anyone helping someone with a cut should wear disposable gloves and avoid coming in contact with blood.

Sprains, Strains, and Broken Bones Rest the injured part of the body. If possible, elevate the injured part so it is higher than the person's heart. This will help keep the swelling down. Apply ice to the injured area during the first 24 hours. Leave the ice in place for about 15 minutes each hour. Wrap or bandage the injured area to give it support. Serious sprains should be kept as still as possible. Some falls are strong enough to break, or fracture, a bone. Then, an x-ray and a visit to the emergency room or a medical professional is required.

Choking A guest or coworker can easily choke on a piece of food. When something gets lodged in a person's airway, that person is not able to talk or breathe. The **obstructed airway maneuver**, or **Heimlich (HIME-lick) maneuver**, is performed to remove the obstruction. Food-service establishments should have posters that show how to perform this maneuver.

CPR **Cardiopulmonary resuscitation (CPR)** (CARD-ee-oh-PULL-mohn-ayr-ee ree-suss-ih-TAY-shun) is a technique used to restore a person's breathing and heartbeat. CPR is called for if someone stops breathing because of shock, drowning, or other serious injury. It involves pressing the chest of the victim at a rate of about 100 times a minute in an effort to help circulate the blood artificially. Breathing into the mouth of the victim

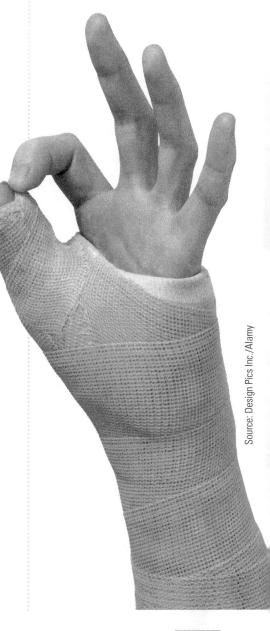

··FOCUS ON
·•Safety

Stitches
A deep cut or one that won't stop bleeding may need stitches. Waiting longer than six hours to get stitches increases the chance of developing an infection.

Obstructed Airway Maneuver (Heimlich Maneuver)

1. Make a fist and place the fist just above the victim's navel, with the thumb facing in.

2. Use a quick, upward thrust. Repeat this thrusting motion until the obstruction is coughed up.

Source: Andy Crawford/Dorling Kindersley Media Library/Dorling Kindersley

is no longer recommended for untrained rescuers. To become certified in CPR techniques, you need to complete a training program. Both the training and certification need to be renewed every year. Do not try CPR without appropriate training.

AED An **automated external defibrillator (AED)** is a device that shocks the heart into starting again. Using this device properly and quickly often means the difference between life and death when someone has a heart attack. If your establishment has an external defibrillator, learn its location. If you are not trained to use it, find out who on the staff does have the appropriate training so no time is lost when a real emergency occurs. Do not try to use an AED without appropriate training.

Anaphylactic Shock Some people have severe allergies to food, drugs, or insect bites or stings that affect their whole body. Some of the most common food allergies are fish, peanuts, shellfish, and tree nuts (walnuts, almonds, etc.). Such a reaction is called **anaphylactic** (an-ah-fil-ACK-tic) **shock**. Symptoms develop rapidly, often within seconds or minutes, from exposure to the substance. The symptoms may include hives, fainting, and nausea, but the most significant symptom is swelling in the throat severe enough to block the airway. A warning sign of severe throat swelling is a very hoarse or whispered voice or a loud wheezing sound.

Anaphylactic shock that affects the air passages is an emergency condition. Contact 911 immediately. Meanwhile, try to calm the person. If the allergic reaction is to a bee sting, scrape the stinger off the skin with something firm (such as a fingernail or a credit card). Don't use a tweezers. If the person has an emergency allergy medication, help the person take or inject it. Do not allow the person to try to swallow pills, however. It could lead to choking and worsen the condition. Have the person lie flat and raise the person's feet about 12 inches, but do not put a pillow under the head. Cover the person with a blanket or a coat.

Preparing for Emergencies There is no way to guarantee safety in every single situation. Natural disasters, including floods, earthquakes, blizzards, wind storms, and forest fires, are almost impossible to predict accurately. Losing power, no matter what the reason, is a serious safety concern as well. If someone shows up at your restaurant armed with a gun or explosives intent on either harming someone or robbing the establishment, more than one life could be put at risk.

The only way to protect yourself, your coworkers, and your guests against these situations is to use sensible safety precautions and to be prepared.

Different parts of the country experience different types of natural disasters. Blizzards are a danger in some parts of the country, hurricanes in others, and tornadoes and lightning strikes in others. To prepare for these situations, you should have bottled water, blankets, flashlights, and a battery-operated radio on hand. Make certain that all battery-powered devices have working batteries. Learn the best safety procedures for situations you are likely to encounter.

FIGURE 2–14

Emergency Preparedness
Some basic emergency items: first-aid poster for choking, emergency phone numbers, first-aid kit, and fire extinguisher.
FORMING A MODEL *What other emergency items might you include for your part of the country?*
Source: Culinary Institute of America

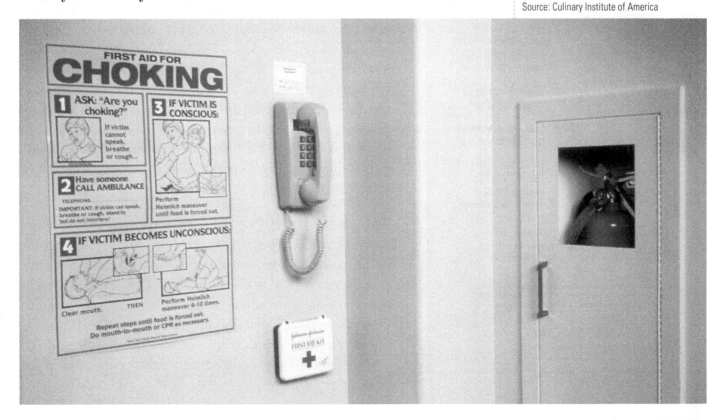

To protect your establishment from intruders, keep doors locked when the restaurant is not open. Try to have at least two people on hand whenever you must open or close the establishment. Turn on lights in parking lots and alleys when it is dark. Make sure alarms and other security devices are turned on to warn of a break-in.

 **READING CHECKPOINT** *How do you perform the obstructed airway maneuver (the Heimlich maneuver)?*

Safety as an Ongoing Process

Keeping yourself and your establishment safe from fire, accidents, and injuries is a job that is never complete. Safety is the result of staying alert, using safe procedures, and monitoring safety procedures on a daily basis to be sure they are being followed. Because safety is such an important concern, there are several federal regulations all employers and managers must know about and follow carefully.

Occupational Safety and Health Administration (OSHA) In 1970 Congress created the **Occupational Safety and Health Administration (OSHA)**. The mission of OSHA is to ensure that workers have a safe and healthful working environment. OSHA sets and enforces standards that employers must follow. OSHA regulations require employers to post safety and health information in the workplace. OSHA also requires that all employees follow these regulations for workplace safety.

The safety of every employee and every customer is the legal responsibility of the foodservice establishment. Any foodservice establishment that does not meet this responsibility is legally responsible for any accidents, injuries, illnesses, or deaths that may result. This responsibility extends through the entire premises, including the kitchen, dining room, bathroom, parking lot, and any area in or surrounding the building.

Environmental Protection Agency (EPA) Also formed in 1970, the **Environmental Protection Agency (EPA)** has a more general mission than OSHA, one that isn't specifically related to the workplace. The EPA's mission is to protect human health by safeguarding the air we breathe, the water we drink, and the land on which we live. However, the EPA plays a part in regulating workplace safety by requiring foodservice operations to track any chemicals that pose a risk to health.

Teen Workers!
You have a right to a safe and healthy workplace.

- Know your workplace rights.
- Talk to your employer about safety and health issues at work.
- Stay alert and work safely.
- Get safety and health training.
- Visit the OSHA Teen Workers website at www.osha.gov/teens

OSHA Occupational Safety and Health Administration
U.S. Department of Labor

OSHA is the federal agency that helps assure the safety and health of all workers, including teens, on the job. OSHA provides information, resources and guidance to employers and employees.

For more information, talk to your employer or call:
1-800-321-OSHA
www.osha.gov/teens
(TTY) 1-877-889-5627

Source: OSHA

Early Ovens and Stoves

It's 29,000 B.C.E. in central Europe and you've just killed a mammoth. Would you eat it raw or would you cook it? According to archaeologists, ovens are one of the key indicators of civilization and showed that a particular society stayed in one place, rather than roaming in the search for food. You would have cooked your mammoth in a roasting pit within a hut. The oven was simply a large hole, with hot coals in the bottom, covered with ashes. The mammoth would have been butchered and pieces of meat would have been wrapped in leaves, set on top the ashes, and covered with earth.

By 3200 B.C.E. civilizations in what are now India and Egypt had developed ovens made from hardened mud. The ancient Greeks and Romans continued to refine their ovens, even creating attractive portable ceramic ovens. In time this led to larger brick ovens for both commercial and private use. Instead of earth, ceramic, or brick ovens, people in the Middle Ages typically used fireplaces and large cauldrons for cooking.

The first written historical record of an oven actually being built from scratch was found in Alsace, France, in 1490. The oven was made entirely of brick and tile. The biggest problem with wood-burning ovens continued to be the smoke from the fire. This led to the development of fire chambers that completely contained the fire. Pots would go on top of the fire chamber, which eventually was vented through a chimney.

By the early 1700s, cast-iron wood-burning stoves began to be made in quantity. These were large and intended primarily for commercial use. A more energy-efficient wood-burning iron stove was invented by Benjamin Franklin in 1741. In 1834 Stewart Oberlin designed a compact cast-iron stove suitable for home use. At around this time, other types of fuel—kerosene, coal, and, eventually gas—began to be used. Gas stoves became common once gas lines were available in most urban settings. Electric ovens were invented in the late 19th century but were not in common use until electricity was widely available.

Source: Denis Barbulat/Shutterstock

Research

Research one of these early versions of an oven: early hardened mud/ceramic ovens, Greek/Roman brick ovens, early wood-burning cast-iron ovens, the first coal-burning oven, the first electric oven, or the first gas oven. Prepare a report describing your findings for the class.

Source: ppart/Shutterstock

Modern electric stove

Source: Pearson Education

Hazard Communication Standard Chemicals, such as cleaning agents, dishwashing compounds, sanitizers, or bleach, are often found in the kitchen. You may also find pesticides, metal polishes, and materials to control mildew and fungus. OSHA's **Hazard Communication Standard (HCS),** also known as *Right-to-Know* or *HAZCOM,* makes sure the employer tells all employees about the chemical hazards present on the job. This standard also requires employers to train employees in the safe use of any products containing chemical hazards.

Chemicals that are a hazard to your safety are those that can irritate or eat away your skin or the lining of your nose and throat or (if they are ingested) damage your entire digestive system. These irritating substances are referred to as **corrosive** (core-OH-siv) materials. The most common type of hazard associated with chemicals is burns, either from direct contact between the material and your unprotected skin or from a fire caused by the chemicals. Some chemicals can burst into flame easily, and some can ignite if exposed to air, moisture, or other chemicals.

The chemicals that pose a risk to your health are those that are toxic, poisonous, or cancer-causing, or **carcinogenic** (car-sin-oh-JEN-ik). Health hazards from chemicals include long- and short-term injuries or illnesses. Short-term illnesses may be relatively minor and last only a few days or weeks. However, long-term illnesses can last for months, years, or your entire life. Cancers that result from chemical exposure in the workplace can be life-threatening.

Material Safety Data Sheet (MSDS) A **Material Safety Data Sheet (MSDS)** describes the specific hazards posed by a chemical. There must be an MSDS for each product that contains chemicals. These sheets are usually supplied by the chemical manufacturer or supplier. Everyone working in the establishment must have access to this information.

Hazard Communication Program A **hazard communication program** is part of an effective safety program. It includes several important documents that can be used as evidence that reasonable care was taken if someone is injured. It includes the following:

- A written policy, stating that the establishment has the intention of complying with OSHA requirements for job safety.

- An up-to-date list, known as a hazardous chemical inventory, of every hazardous chemical product used or stored in the establishment, including the name, the amount on hand, and where it can be found in the establishment.

- An MSDS for every hazardous chemical included on the inventory. These sheets must be stored in a central location that is always accessible to every employee.

Sample Material Safety Data Sheet (MSDS)

Section 1:
Product and Company Identification
- Product name
- Company contact information (including emergency response numbers)

Section 2:
Composition/Information on Ingredients
- The chemical and common name of the ingredients that pose either a physical or a chemical hazard

Section 3:
Hazards Identification
- Emergency overview
- Acute effects
- Chronic overexposure effects

Section 4:
First Aid Measures
- Eye contact
- Skin contact
- Inhalation
- Ingestion

Section 5:
Firefighting Measures
- Flash point
- Lower and upper explosive limits
- Extinguishing media

Section 6:
Accidental Release Measures
- Steps to be taken in case of accidental spillage or release

Section 7:
Handling and Storage
- Handling
- Storage

Section 8:
Exposure Controls/Personal Protection
- Engineering controls
- Respiratory protection
- Skin protection
- Eye protection
- Chronic overexposure effects

Section 9:
Physical and Chemical Properties
- Physical description of the product, including appearance, odor, boiling point, pH, and any other characteristics that may help identify it

Section 10:
Stability Hazards Identification
- Stability
- Conditions to avoid
- Incompatibility

Section 11:
Toxicological Properties
- Components known to be toxic

Section 12:
Ecological Information
- Known effects on the environment

Section 13:
Disposal Conditions
- Disposal methods

Section 14:
Transportation Information
- Hazard class
- Dept. of Transportation shipping name

Section 15:
Regulatory Information
- OSHA warnings
- Toxic Substance Control Act
- Right-to-Know

- Labels for each chemical-containing product, including its name, its hazards, and the name and address of the manufacturer.
- A written copy of the training program for employees.
- A written copy of the hazard communication plan.

OSHA's Form 300 (Rev. 01/2004)

Log of Work-Related Injuries and Illnesses

You must record information about every work-related death and about every work-related injury or illness that involves loss of consciousness, restric days away from work, or medical treatment beyond first aid. You must also record significant work-related injuries and illnesses that are diagnosed b care professional. You must also record work-related injuries and illnesses that meet any of the specific recording criteria listed in 29 CFR Part 1904. use two lines for a single case if you need to. You must complete an Injury and Illness Incident Report (OSHA Form 301) or equivalent form for each form. If you're not sure whether a case is recordable, call your local OSHA office for help.

Identify the person			Describe the case		
(A) Case no.	(B) Employee's name	(C) Job title (e.g., Welder)	(D) Date of injury or onset of illness	(E) Where the event occurred (e.g., Loading dock north end)	(F) Describe injury or illness, part and object/substance that direc or made person ill (e.g., Second right forearm from acetylene torch)
			___/___ month/day		
			___/___ month/day		
			___/___ month/day		
			___/___ month/day		
			___/___ month/day		
			___/___ month/day		
			___/___ month/day		
			___/___ month/day		
			___/___ month/day		
			___/___ month/day		
			___/___ month/day		
			___/___ month/day		

Public reporting burden for this collection of information is estimated to average 14 minutes per response, including time to review the instructions, search and gather the data needed, and complete and review the collection of information. Persons are not required to respond to the collection of information unless it displays a currently valid OMB control number. If you have any comments about these estimates or any other aspects of this data collection, contact: US Department of Labor, OSHA Office of Statistical Analysis, Room N-3644, 200 Constitution Avenue, NW, Washington, DC 20210. Do not send the completed forms to this office.

Source: OSHA

Accident/Illness Reports and Records Accidents can cause injuries and illnesses that may result in time lost from work. Too many accidents indicates that proper safety practices are not being followed.

It is important to report accidents properly. If an accident at your establishment results in a death, you must report it to OSHA within eight hours, using a standard **accident report** form. If three or more employees are hospitalized because of an accident, you must report it to OSHA within eight hours as well. Other employee injuries and accidents must be reported within six working days.

All establishments are also required to keep a log of accidents and injuries that happen in the workplace for one year (OSHA Form 300). A specific form is filled in with the information from that log. The report must be posted where all employees can read it throughout the month of February of the following year.

Worker's Compensation Worker's **compensation** is a program run by each state that provides help for employees who are hurt or who become sick because of an accident on the job. It supplies money to replace earnings that the employee loses because he or she can't come to work and also pays for medical treatments, rehabilitation programs, and, if necessary, retraining for the employee.

General Safety Audit A **general safety audit** is a review of the level of safety in an establishment. Generally, audits are set up like a checklist, with a checkbox for yes or no. Any items that are checked "no" must be taken care of as soon as possible to keep the restaurant, its employees, and its guests safe.

The four areas of review are the following:

- Building
- Equipment

General Safety Audit

OK = None or minor discrepancy, **S** = Serious, **IN** = Improvement Needed, **U** = Unsatisfactory

#	Operational Methods and Personnel Practices (Cont'd)	OK	S	IN	U
377	Production facilities, equipment, and/or accessories were designed or provided to facilitate minimum hand contact with raw materials, work in progress, or finished product.				
378	Foods or raw materials capable of supporting the rapid growth of pathogenic microgorganisms were held below 41°F or above 135°F to whatever degree as appropriate and necessary to maintain internal temperatures below 40°F or above 140°F.				
379	Effective measures were undertaken to prevent cross-contamination between raw materials, refuse, and finished foods. These measures included limiting the movement of personnel between these areas.				
380	Equipment, containers, and utensils used to convey, process, hold, or store raw materials, work in process, rework, or finished foods were constructed, handled, and maintained during processing or storage in a manner that prevented the contamination of raw materials, rework, or finished foods.				

FIGURE 2–15

General Safety Audit

This is a small portion of a much larger general safety audit. The items in this portion of the form address concerns about pathogens and cross-contamination.

PREDICTING *If your restaurant received any marks indicating that improvement was needed, what would probably happen?*

- Employee practices
- Management practices

The audit reviews the condition of interior and exterior walls and floors, the roof, the foundation, the electrical wiring, and the plumbing. Parking lots, storage areas, and outside seating are also reviewed. Depending on the location of the restaurant, the audit may include such items as floodwater drainage, snow and ice removal, and meeting any necessary standards to withstand earthquakes, tornadoes, or hurricanes.

All equipment and vehicles must be kept in working condition. The audit reviews the condition of the furniture and rugs. Fixtures, including lighting and bathroom fixtures, must function safely and properly. Fire extinguishers must be installed and maintained properly.

Employees are also part of the general safety audit. It is required that employees be trained in safe procedures. Once trained, they are responsible for following those procedures.

The review is also concerned with the employer's hazard communication program, including its training program for employees and proper record-keeping procedures for accidents and illnesses.

READING CHECKPOINT *What kinds of information are included on an MSDS?*

Reviewing Concepts

1. What are the three classes of burns? Describe each and indicate its treatment.
2. What is the right way to lift something heavy?
3. How do you perform the obstructed airway maneuver (the Heimlich maneuver)?
4. What kinds of information are included on a Material Safety Data Sheet (MSDS)?

Critical Thinking

5. **Drawing Conclusions** Why should an employee review the MSDS for any products that he or she may be required to use?
6. **Predicting** What does a foodservice establishment's annual log of accidents and injuries tell you about that establishment?
7. **Comparing/Contrasting** For whom do you think the hazard communication program is more important: employers or employees? Why?

Test Kitchen

Check your school's hazard communication program. Review the MSDS for three common kitchen cleaners (such as oven cleaners, grease cleaners, or floor wax). Evaluate how you would deal with the variety of emergencies each product could cause.

SOCIAL STUDIES ———●
OSHA

Research the history of OSHA in the United States. Find out what rights workers had before OSHA. Why was OSHA created? How have OSHA regulations changed over time? Create a time chart that shows your findings and present it to the class.

PROJECT ② **Hazard Communication Program** You are now ready to work on Project 2, "Hazard Communication Program," which is available in "My Culinary Lab" or in your *Student's Lab Resources and Study Guide* manual.

Review and Assessment

Reviewing Content

Choose the letter that best answers the question or completes the statement.

1. A Class A/B fire extinguisher is used for which type of flammable material?
   a. paper, cloth, wood, and plastic
   b. electrical equipment, cords, and outlets
   c. combustible metals
   d. cooking oils and fats

2. The best way to put out a stovetop grease fire is
   a. to spray it with water.
   b. to use a lid to cover the flames.
   c. to sprinkle it with salt.
   d. to smother it with a damp cloth.

3. The best way to carry a knife in a kitchen is
   a. to hold the blade pointing outward and close to your side.
   b. to hold the blade pointing upward and above your head.
   c. to hold the blade pointing downward and close to your side.
   d. to hold the blade pointing forward and above your head.

4. A carcinogenic material
   a. causes cancer.
   b. irritates or eats away other materials.
   c. causes burns.
   d. causes blindness.

5. A toque is
   a. the name for a chef's jacket.
   b. the name for a chef's hat.
   c. a hot object from the oven.
   d. a dry mitt used to handle a hot object.

6. Foam extinguishers are used for
   a. Class A fires.
   b. Class B fires.
   c. Class A and B fires.
   d. Class B and C fires.

7. In the Heimlich maneuver, the fist is placed
   a. just below the victim's throat.
   b. high on the victim's chest.
   c. at the midpoint of the victim's chest.
   d. just above the victim's navel.

Understanding Concepts

8. What are the five classes of fires?

9. What are the four steps for the PASS system?

10. What are the steps in the Heimlich maneuver?

11. What is an automated external defibrillator?

12. What types of information are included on a Material Safety Data Sheet (MSDS)?

13. What is included in a hazard communication program?

14. What is the best way to lift heavy objects?

Critical Thinking

15. **ANALYZING INFORMATION** What information contained in a Material Safety Data Sheet would you consider most important as an employee?

16. **COMPARING/CONTRASTING** Compare the responsibilities of employees and management in relation to a general safety audit.

Culinary Math

17. **APPLYING CONCEPTS** If more than 30 percent of all accidental fires in restaurants are caused by faulty electrical wiring, and a restaurant needs 15 fire extinguishers, about how many Class C fire extinguishers should the restaurant have?

18. **ANALYZING DATA** A large restaurant/catering establishment has 317 employees. Last year 63 separate employees were injured on the job. What percentage of employees were injured last year?

On the Job

19. **COMMUNICATING** You work at a restaurant that offers voluntary safety training classes. However, employees are not paid for attending these classes. Would you attend? Explain your answer.

20. **COMMUNICATING** Why is the ability to deal with health emergencies part of a culinary professional's job?

Commercial Kitchen Consultant or Designer

A number of factors go into the operation of a successful restaurant, hotel, or catering operation. The design and functionality of the kitchen is one of the most important aspects. Designers and consultants who work on commercial kitchens need to be well versed in a number of topics: equipment selection, fire and safety codes, space requirements for storage, building codes and zoning, and more. The designer or consultant may often work as part of a team that includes architects, engineers, and construction crews.

Kitchen consultants may be involved in new construction, or they may be asked to assist in the remodeling or reconfiguring of an existing kitchen. Both activities have some specific challenges.

Consultants advise on a variety of issues including concept development, interior design, development assistance, financial information systems and real estate. Their product, or deliverable, can take the form of a written report or a hands-on approach. The term *restaurant consultant* encompasses a wide variety of disciplines and areas of expertise, including areas such as real estate, design, litigation, accounting, and operations.

Entry-Level Requirements

While there are no absolute requirements to call yourself a design consultant for a commercial kitchen, most successful designers have studied design and construction, through either class work or hands-on experience working with other designers or as part of the crews who do the actual work of installing equipment. Experience in the kitchen provides the designer with the kind of insight that they may not otherwise have.

Helpful for Advancement

A degree in design or architecture is an important way to indicate your level of professionalism and expertise. Working as part of a team that consulted on the design or overhaul of a commercial kitchen is another, especially when there is tangible evidence of the success of the design. This evidence may be in the form of recommendations or testimonials from clients, or in the form of awards and recognition that the restaurant receives.

Professional training in the proper use of design software (AutoCAD, for example) and the skills necessary to produce proposals, timelines, schedules, and task lists shows that you have the ability to work with other experts, including engineers, electricians, construction crews, architects, and designers. It also means that your clients can be confident that you are aware of the permits necessary for new construction or remodeling and that the work is properly inspected to meet all the relevant health, safety, and fire codes.

Project management is another area that consultants often look to for additional training in order to advance their careers.

Source: Culinary Institute of America

Designing a kitchen often includes major construction

VICTOR CARDAMONE

Victor Cardamone has brought together some unique and impressive qualifications as design consultant and owner of Mise Design Group, LLC. The mission of the company is to "bring cost-efficient, sustainable and effective operating designs to an industry dominated by the cookie cutter approach to hotel and restaurant kitchen development."* He believes that the same concept that gets cooks and chefs through the day and propels them toward success is the notion of mise en place, which means thinking through your work and getting everything ready so that you can be productive and produce quality work.

Victor Cardamone

VITAL STATISTICS

Graduated: The Culinary Institute of America, 1997

Profession: Sole proprietor, kitchen design and consultation company

Interesting items: Member of the American Architects Association, the American Culinary Federation, and the National Restaurant Association

Acquired the contract for food and beverage restaurant kitchen design services of the new $100 million Hilton Hotel to be located in Kampala, Uganda

Design firm working in the United States, the United Kingdom, the United Arab Emirates, and India

CAREER PROFILE

Salary Ranges

Entry level: $25,000 to $60,000

Senior: $60,000 to $120,000 (or more)

Hourly rates (entry level): $30 to $60

Hourly rates (senior consultant): $60 to $150

*Reprinted with the permission of Mise Design Group, LLC

Foodservice Equipment

3.1 Work Flow in the Kitchen

3.2 Receiving and Storage Equipment

3.3 Preparation and Cooking Equipment

3.4 Holding and Service Equipment

Work Flow in the Kitchen

READING PREVIEW

Key Concepts

- Understanding workstations and work lines
- Understanding kitchen work flow

Vocabulary

- mise en place
- work flow
- work lines
- work sections
- workstation

Workstations and Work Lines

A restaurant or banquet hall is a business that serves the public. Its kitchen is like a factory that converts raw materials into products. The kitchen is organized for efficiency, turning raw ingredients into satisfying and nourishing meals.

Workstations One of the most important ways a commercial kitchen increases its efficiency is by using workstations. A **workstation** is a work area containing equipment and tools needed for accomplishing a specific set of culinary tasks. Chefs often refer to workstations as simply *stations*. This means a chef may talk about the *fry station* or the *grill station*. The fry station, for example, prepares all the fried food for the entire kitchen. The grill station prepares all the grilled items for the entire kitchen.

Each station includes the necessary equipment for the function performed at that workstation. Each also may include an appropriate work surface. Each station would ideally include some type of small cold storage or freezer that may contain only enough ingredients for one night's service. Carts may be parked nearby so a chef can use them to transfer raw ingredients from the kitchen's main cold storage or freezers. Trash bins would also be necessary for efficient waste disposal. The workstation would have everything within easy reach. For efficiency,

Source: Kzenon/Fotolia

Chef's Tip

Parking Carts

Many work lines include special parking spaces for carts. To avoid accidents, you need to be aware of a cart's location. Store unused carts out of the flow of traffic.

the staff at a particular workstation should not have to leave it to accomplish their tasks.

Work Sections and Work Lines Workstations are the building blocks of a kitchen. Workstations are combined into larger work areas called **work sections**. For example, the fry workstation may be combined with the grill workstation.

To create work sections, workstations are positioned in different **work lines**, or geometric arrangements of equipment. Work lines are designed to fit the available space and to improve the efficiency of staff. Work lines determine how equipment, cooking, preparation, and storage areas are placed. There are five common arrangements of work lines:

- **Straight-Line.** The straight-line arrangement is usually considered the most efficient work line.
- **L-Shaped.** The L-shaped arrangement uses a limited amount of space but is still able to provide a large amount of work space.
- **Back-to-Back.** The back-to-back arrangement is efficient but requires a large amount of space.
- **U-Shaped.** The U-shaped arrangement offers the maximum work surface.
- **Parallel (or Face-to-Face).** In this arrangement, two work lines are arranged face-to-face, with one common work aisle.

 **READING CHECKPOINT** *What are workstations and work lines?*

Work Flow

The layout of the kitchen, including the types of work lines within the kitchen, directly contributes to the efficiency of the kitchen. So does the kitchen's work flow. **Work flow** is the planned movement of food and kitchen staff as food is prepared.

To ensure customer satisfaction and restaurant profitability, the work flow in the kitchen must be efficient. An efficient kitchen produces higher-quality food at a lower cost and in less time. Diners do not become impatient. The restaurant is able to sell more meals. The cost of food and labor is controllable. Good work flow reduces worker fatigue while also reducing the risk of accidents or food poisoning that can threaten the restaurant's existence. A good work flow in the kitchen requires the following:

- Planning
- Timing
- Communication

Work Lines

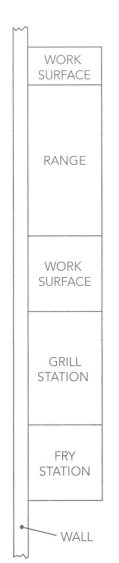

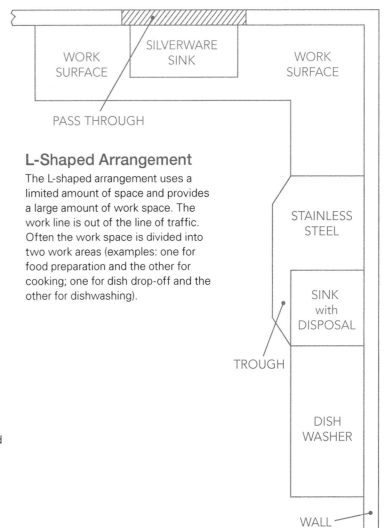

L-Shaped Arrangement

The L-shaped arrangement uses a limited amount of space and provides a large amount of work space. The work line is out of the line of traffic. Often the work space is divided into two work areas (examples: one for food preparation and the other for cooking; one for dish drop-off and the other for dishwashing).

Straight-Line Arrangement

The straight-line arrangement is usually considered the most efficient work-line arrangement. Equipment is typically placed along a wall.

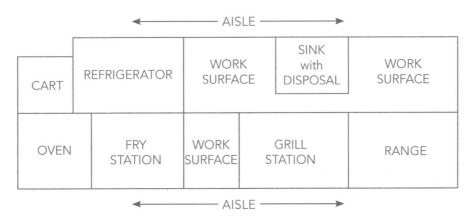

Back-to-Back Arrangement

The back-to-back arrangement is efficient but requires a large amount of space. A shelf or wall may separate the two tables. The back-to-back arrangement is often used in larger restaurants.

Work Lines

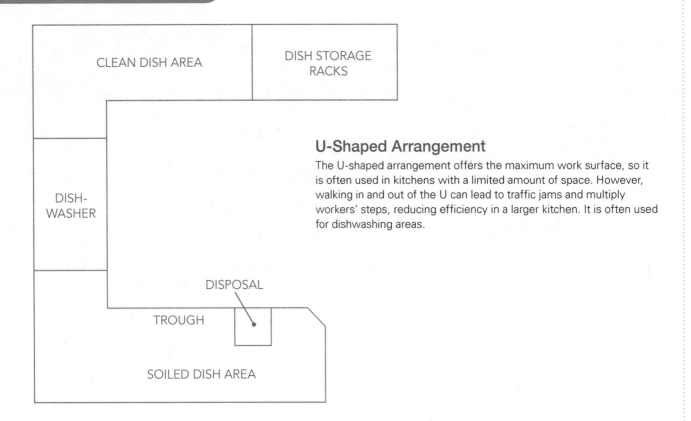

U-Shaped Arrangement

The U-shaped arrangement offers the maximum work surface, so it is often used in kitchens with a limited amount of space. However, walking in and out of the U can lead to traffic jams and multiply workers' steps, reducing efficiency in a larger kitchen. It is often used for dishwashing areas.

Parallel (or Face-to-Face) Arrangement

In this arrangement, two work lines are arranged face-to-face, with one common work aisle. The parallel arrangement also requires a large amount of space but is quite efficient (particularly when communication between workstations is required).

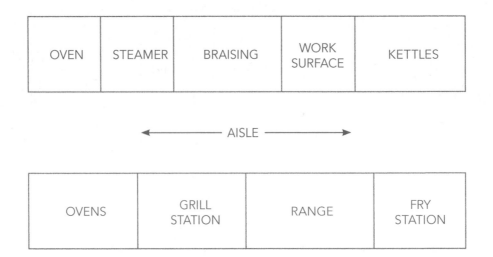

Planning One of the most important aspects of any workstation's work flow is the concept of **mise en place** (MEEZ uhn PLAHS). This French term means "to put in place." Mise en place includes gathering all the raw materials required for your station (doing whatever is necessary to make them ready to be used) and making sure you have all the equipment and tools required for your culinary operation. For efficient work flow, you don't want to stop what you are doing to prepare more raw ingredients or locate a missing tool or piece of equipment.

Other important types of planning that could apply to each workstation would be estimating the number of individual dishes that will be required by that workstation on a particular night or knowing each dish for which the workstation is responsible so you can prepare it consistently.

Timing The staff of every workstation needs to be aware of the role they play in making each diner's experience a pleasant one. That is why timing is a critical component of the culinary work flow. One of the most important aspects of a diner's eating experience has to do with the timing of the various dishes. In a restaurant, diners typically move through successive courses and order different items, each of which can take different times to prepare. A group of diners would have an unpleasant dining experience if

FIGURE 3–1

Importance of Timing
All the food for a large group must be ready at the same time.
DRAWING CONCLUSIONS *Why would a group be upset if their food was not ready at the same time?*
Source: Culinary Institute of America

Chef's Tip

"Echoing"

Always acknowledge an order from the chef. Say, "Yes, Chef," and then repeat the order. This is called *echoing*.

everyone did not receive appetizers at the same time or if one diner's main meal was delayed until the other diners were eating their desserts.

Communication In most foodservice establishments, communication between workstations is critically important. Additionally, as you will learn in later chapters, there is typically an individual who is in charge of making sure that each workstation does its job when it is needed. For example, preparing a dish too early can sometimes be just as much a problem as preparing it too late. In other cases, creating a dish requires the direct assistance of another workstation. The only way to make sure everything is prepared when it should be, and as it should be, is through communication.

READING CHECKPOINT *What is mise en place?*

3.1 ASSESSMENT

Reviewing Concepts

1. What is a workstation?

2. What does the term *mise en place* mean?

Critical Thinking

3. Inferring Why could a U-shaped work line be inefficient?

4. Comparing/Contrasting What is the difference between a workstation, a work section, and a work line?

5. Predicting Suppose the mise en place for a workstation was not completed before a restaurant began serving dinner. What would the person working at that station be required to do?

Test Kitchen

Working in teams, roughly sketch your school's kitchen. Identify workstations, work sections, and work lines. Point out the most efficient and least efficient aspects of your kitchen's work flow.

MATH

Using a Scale Drawing

Convert your sketch of your school's kitchen from the Test Kitchen exercise to a scale drawing. Measure the actual work area and equipment. Use grid paper with ¼-inch grids. Use a scale of ¼ inch to 1 foot (1 square represents 1 square foot).

3.2

Receiving and Storage Equipment

READING PREVIEW

Key Concepts

- Understanding receiving equipment
- Understanding refrigeration equipment
- Understanding storage equipment

Vocabulary

- blast-chill refrigerator
- cold storage area
- cook-chill technique
- counter scale
- dry storage area
- even-thaw refrigerator
- floor scale
- hanging scale
- ice cream freezer
- infrared thermometer
- low boy
- platform scale
- portable refrigeration cart
- quick-chill refrigerator
- reach-in
- refrigerated drawer
- undercounter reach-in
- walk-in

Receiving Equipment

As you know from Chapter 1, the flow of food starts in the receiving area. The receiving staff is responsible for the inspection and acceptance of incoming food, equipment, and supplies. They make sure the foodservice establishment gets what it ordered and that ingredients are safe, at the proper temperature, and not damaged or contaminated. After the food has been received and checked, it is stored.

A foodservice establishment typically inspects incoming goods in the receiving area at a receiving counter. This counter may have a low surface for inspecting packages and a high surface for paperwork. The receiving area is equipped with box cutters, scales, and a thermometer. Hand trucks and dollies are also stored at the receiving area for moving accepted goods from the receiving area to a storage area.

To check prepacked goods, such as cases of canned goods or bottles, the receiving staff can just count items and read labels. For other items, they must check quantity and quality. They check the look and smell of fresh produce, meat, and fish. They weigh bulk items. They also check the temperature of hot and cold items.

The receiving staff often uses an **infrared thermometer** to scan the temperature of foods without actually touching the food. These thermometers read surface temperatures instantly

Source: Elenathewise/Fotolia

by measuring invisible infrared radiation. Infrared thermometers come in several styles. They are also used in kitchens to check the temperatures of foods that are being held.

Receiving areas may have several kinds of scales: counter scales, platform scales, floor scales, and hanging scales. Modern scales show weights electronically. A **counter scale** sits on a counter and weighs moderate-sized packages. In some foodservice businesses, a **platform scale** on the receiving platform weighs bulky or heavy packages. Other businesses use a **floor scale** inside, in the receiving area, for such purposes. Both platform scales and floor scales may be equipped with rollers and are typically installed flush with the floor. A **hanging scale** weighs large items that can be lifted on a hook, like a side of beef.

READING CHECKPOINT *How do you check temperature without actually touching food?*

FIGURE 3–2

Infrared Thermometer

An infrared thermometer "gun" reads the temperature of objects at which it is pointed.

APPLYING CONCEPTS *Why would it be important to determine the temperature of certain incoming foods?*

Source: Vincent P. Walter/Pearson Education PH College

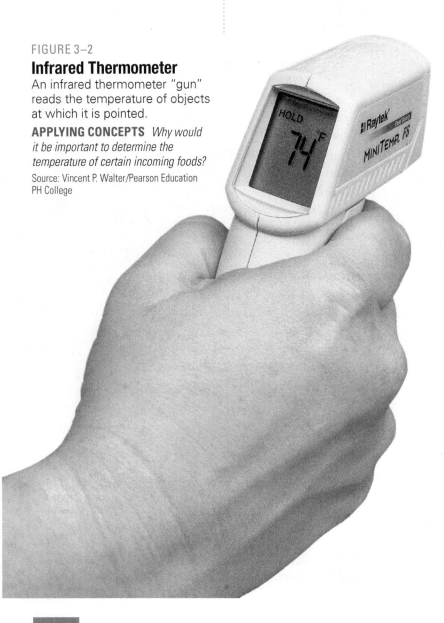

Refrigeration Equipment

Proper refrigeration keeps foods fresh and ensures food safety. This improves quality and reduces costs caused by spoilage. Well-planned refrigeration also reduces labor costs by improving the work flow. Refrigerated storage is often referred to as *cold storage.*

Types of Refrigeration Equipment

Large kitchens often have a few different types of refrigeration units. Kitchens keep most of the stored food in large units, transferring only enough food for a few hours to smaller units located at specific workstations.

- **Walk-Ins.** The largest refrigeration or freezing unit is called a **walk-in**. These units usually have shelves that are arranged around the walls and a door (sometimes with a plastic air curtain to keep the cold air in the walk-in). Walk-in units may be in the kitchen or even outside the building with an indoor entrance. Large walk-in refrigeration units allow for the storage of refrigerated items on carts as well as storage on the shelves.

- **Reach-Ins.** Similar to the refrigerators we are all used to, a **reach-in** may be a single unit or part of a bank of units. Reach-ins come in many sizes. Some reach-ins have pass-through doors that allow both wait staff and kitchen staff to access them. Reach-ins with glass doors let staff see items without opening the doors. This saves time finding ingredients. It also reduces electrical costs, because opening the doors lets warm air in.

- **Refrigerated Drawers and Undercounter Reach-Ins.** At individual workstations, a **refrigerated drawer** or an **undercounter reach-in** (often called a **low boy**) lets kitchen staff store a small amount of ingredients (typically enough for a few hours or a single night) within easy reach, thus increasing efficiency. This eliminates trips to the larger reach-ins or walk-ins during busy service hours. Typically, a drawer holds less than an undercounter unit, but drawers are often more efficient.

- **Portable Refrigeration Carts.** When a foodservice establishment needs temporary refrigeration units or does off-site catering, it uses a **portable refrigeration cart**.

- **Specialized Types of Refrigerators.** Specialized types of refrigerators are often used when a kitchen performs specialized types of operations. For example, kitchens that make large quantities of food for use later often use a **quick-chill refrigerator** or **blast-chill refrigerator** to quickly cool prepared food through the danger zone down to the safe storage temperatures. This type of cooking is called the **cook-chill technique.** Kitchens use an **even-thaw refrigerator** to thaw large amounts of food quickly and safely. These refrigerators add small amounts of heat to rapidly circulating cold air and never exceed 41°F. An **ice cream freezer** operates at colder temperatures than normal freezers, typically around 15°F.

FIGURE 3–3
Reach-In Refrigerator
Kitchens often have a bank of reach-in refrigerators.

INFERRING *Why is it important to store food correctly in a reach-in refrigerator?*

Source: Culinary Institute of America

Cleaning Refrigerators and Freezers As you learned in Chapter 1, it is important to keep foodservice equipment clean and sanitary. Maintain a regular cleaning and sanitation schedule for all refrigeration equipment. Before beginning any cleaning process, consult the person responsible for your establishment's refrigeration equipment.

FIGURE 3–4

Ice Cream Freezer
Commercial ice cream freezers need to operate at lower temperatures than normal freezers because they are often being opened, especially in hot weather.

PREDICTING *The manager of an ice cream shop that depends primarily on the walk-in summer tourist business insisted on buying the highest quality ice cream freezer possible. Why?*

Source: ferrerilavarialiotti/Fotolia

Chef's Tip

Order, Order

Most kitchens specify where different types of ingredients (vegetables, dairy, meat, and so on) go in the walk-in.

Follow these general guidelines for cleaning reach-in and portable refrigerators and freezers (clean walk-in refrigerators as instructed by your supervisor). Clean refrigerators every day. Freezers can be cleaned less often.

1. Turn off the unit, if instructed to do so by your supervisor.
2. Remove the food. Place it in a cold storage area.
3. Wash the interior with warm soapy water.
4. Rinse the interior with a clean damp cloth.
5. Sanitize the interior with a sanitizing solution.
6. Dry the interior with a single-use paper towel.
7. Turn on the unit and refill it with food.
8. On a daily basis, wash, rinse, and sanitize the outside.

READING CHECKPOINT *How do small versions of refrigeration equipment improve a kitchen's performance?*

Storage Equipment

Storage equipment should have four important qualities. It should be strong, durable, easily cleaned, and easily accessed. These qualities apply equally to storage containers and to shelves and shelving units.

Shelves Goods such as flour, dry pasta, canned goods, and supplies can be stored safely on shelves at room temperature in what is commonly called the **dry storage area**. Goods are also stored on shelves in walk-in refrigeration units in a **cold storage area**.

Stored goods must be easy to reach. The storage area may open to the kitchen or be in a separate room. Aisles in storage areas are usually 3 to 4 feet wide to accommodate carts. Shelves come in many sizes, but the maximum height is usually 6 feet, the maximum depth is usually 24 inches, and they stand at least 6 inches off the ground. With these dimensions, almost all staff can store and access goods without strain.

Kitchen shelves are generally made of stainless steel, galvanized steel, aluminum, or high-impact plastic. Wooden shelves are less common because they are harder to keep clean. Some departments of health prohibit wooden shelving.

Solid shelves have easy-to-clean rounded edges. Shelves made of mesh, wire, rods, or tubes are more common, though. These shelves hold goods securely but let dirt fall through to the floor and allow air to circulate. Shelving units usually stand at least 6 inches from the floor, on legs. This makes cleaning floors easy and keeps food dry and away from dirt and pests.

FIGURE 3–5
Shelves
These stainless-steel shelves are made of rods so food or dirt will fall through the shelves to the floor.
DRAWING CONCLUSIONS *Why is stainless steel typically used for kitchen shelves?*
Source: Steve Gorton/Dorling Kindersley

Shelves are also used in work areas to hold pots, plates, and spices. Dishes and silverware are often stored on specially designed carts for easy movement to serving areas.

Storage Containers Storage containers hold food and protect it from contamination. They also help staff move food between storage, preparation, and service areas. Foods in the kitchen may be stored raw, partially prepared, or cooked. Storage containers include insulated containers, bins, and a variety of bowls, pans, and canisters. Stainless steel, glass, and plastic containers are easiest to clean. Using glass containers can be a problem in the kitchen. If they break, they can cause physical contamination. Insulated containers can keep foods hot or cold. They are used for extra storage or for carrying meals off-site. Liquids can be served in insulated containers with spigots.

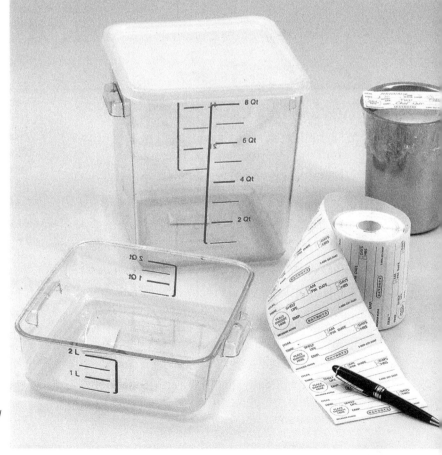

FIGURE 3–6
Storage Containers
It is important to label and date each storage container.
APPLYING CONCEPTS *If you were a chef and you saw a stored item in the refrigerator that wasn't dated, would you serve it?*
Source: Culinary Institute of America

Before placing any foods in a storage container, clean and sanitize the container. Bring hot foods to the right temperature before refrigerating them. Always cover containers with tight-fitting lids or with heavy plastic wrap or foil. Finally, label and date the container and indicate its contents. That way you can identify the contents at a glance and know what is too old to use. (Remember to use the FIFO [First In, First Out] system with all stored food.)

Wire bins are often used to hold packaged items. Plastic bins can hold dry goods such as rice, beans, and flour. Bins with wheels are easy to move to and from work areas.

Cleaning Shelves and Storage Containers Follow these general guidelines to clean shelves and storage containers:

1. Remove all food from shelves and storage containers.
2. Clean dry storage shelves and storage containers with hot, soapy water.
3. Rinse with a clean damp cloth or clean water.
4. Sanitize the shelves and storage containers.
5. Dry the shelves with a single-use paper towel. Let storage containers air-dry.
6. Refill the shelves and storage containers with food. (Remember to use the FIFO system.)

 **READING CHECKLIST** *How does refrigeration equipment improve kitchen performance?*

3.2 ASSESSMENT

Reviewing Concepts

1. Name four kinds of scales used by receiving staff.
2. Name five types of refrigeration equipment you might find in a kitchen.
3. Name four important qualities of storage equipment.

Critical Thinking

4. **Inferring** Why would receiving staff need to weigh incoming goods and check their temperature?
5. **Drawing Conclusions** Why should the aisle in a walk-in be wide enough to allow a cart?
6. **Comparing/Contrasting** Why are some foods held in walk-in refrigeration, while others are held in undercounter refrigerated drawers?

Test Kitchen

Work in teams to fill three different kinds of containers with water. Close and label the containers, testing the closed containers to make sure there are no leaks. Store in a refrigerator for two days. Describe each container based on the ease of (a) transferring water into the container, (b) sealing, (c) labeling, (d) storing/stacking, and (e) taste after refrigeration.

LANGUAGE ARTS
Compare/Contrast

Research three different types of refrigeration equipment. Write a description of each type (including prices), pointing out their similarities and differences. Focus on details you think would be appreciated by chefs and food preparation staff.

3.3

Preparation and Cooking Equipment

Key Concepts

- Understanding food preparation equipment
- Understanding cooking equipment

Vocabulary

- anti-griddle
- blender
- blending
- broiler
- buffalo chopper
- centrifuge
- combination steamer/oven
- convection oven
- convection steamer
- countertop blender
- countertop mixer
- deck ovens
- deep-fat fryers
- flattop range
- food chopper
- food dehydrator
- food processor
- freestanding mixer
- griddle
- immersion blender
- meat grinder
- meat slicer
- mixer
- mixing
- molecular gastronomy
- open-burner range
- planetary mixer
- pressure steamer
- range
- ring-top range
- salamander
- smoker
- sous vide machine
- spiral mixer
- steam-jacketed kettle
- Swiss brasier
- vertical chopping machine (VCM)

Food Preparation Equipment

Food preparation equipment is potentially the most dangerous equipment in the kitchen. When working with equipment for chopping, slicing, and grinding:

✔ **Learn to use a machine safely.** Ask an experienced operator to show you how to use the machine. Read the manufacturer's instructions. Do not use the machine if you haven't been trained in its use.

✔ **Use all safety features.** Always use blade guards, food plungers, and food holders. Wear wire mesh gloves or eye protection whenever appropriate.

✔ **Maintain and clean equipment properly.** Keep large equipment in good working order. Clean and sanitize the equipment thoroughly after each use.

✔ **Turn off and unplug the machine for cleaning.** Remember to turn off and unplug electrical equipment before cleaning and before you take it apart or put it back together. Leave equipment unplugged between uses.

Source: Oleg Zhukov/Fotolia

FOCUS ON Safety

Cutting Safely

Most cutting equipment is designed with safety features. Always use blade guards and food holders as you pass food across a cutting tool. Always secure lids and covers. Whenever appropriate, wear eye protection.

Food processor

Food chopper

Meat slicer

☑ **Be sure equipment is complete and stable.** Properly reassemble all pieces of equipment. Ensure that lids are secure. The machine should be on a firm surface and not tilted.

☑ **Promptly report any problems.** Tell your manager about any problems or malfunctions regarding the equipment. Also be sure to alert coworkers about any problems.

Chopping, Slicing, and Grinding Equipment With specialized cutting, blending, and mixing equipment, large volumes of food can be prepared rapidly. You may need this equipment to be efficient, but remember that this equipment can be extremely dangerous if it is used incorrectly or without appropriate attention. Review the guidelines in the preceding section concerning safe and proper use of equipment. A typical kitchen includes many of the chopping, slicing, and grinding pieces of equipment described in this chapter.

- **Food Processor.** The motor in a **food processor** is separate from the bowl, blades, and lid. With different attachments, a food processor can slice, grind, mix, blend, and crush foods.

- **Vertical Chopping Machine (VCM).** A motor at the base of a **vertical chopping machine (VCM)** is attached to blades in a permanently attached bowl. The VCM (also referred to as a *vertical cutter/mixer*) is used to grind, whip, blend, purée, or crush large quantities of foods. As a safety precaution, the hinged lid must be locked in place before the unit will operate.

- **Food Chopper.** Available in floor and tabletop models, a **food chopper** (also called a **buffalo chopper**) is obviously used to chop food. The food is placed in a rotating bowl that passes under a hood, where blades chop the food. Some units have hoppers or feed tubes and interchangeable disks for slicing and grating.

- **Meat Slicer.** Used to slice foods to even thicknesses, a **meat slicer** is especially useful for slicing cooked meats and cheeses. A carrier moves the food back and forth against a circular blade, which is generally high-carbon stainless steel.

- **Meat Grinder.** A **meat grinder** grinds various cuts of meat. Restaurants can use either a dedicated machine or a meat grinder attachment for a mixer or a food chopper. Meat is dropped through a tube and pushed through the machine, where it is cut by a blade, and the meat is then forced out. Sausage casings can be attached to some meat grinders so the meat is pushed into the casing as the meat is ground. A meat grinder typically has disks of varying sizes to create a range of textures.

Mixing and Blending Equipment Although the terms *mixing* and *blending* are similar, chefs don't usually use them in exactly the same way. **Mixing** is the process of combining ingredients so they are evenly spread

FIGURE 3–7
Meat Grinders
A dedicated meat grinder (left) produces large quantities of ground meat. A planetary mixer with a meat grinder attachment (right) produces smaller quantities of ground meat.

PREDICTING *What would influence a restaurant's choice between using a dedicated machine or a mixer attachment?*

Sources: (left) Ryan McVay/Photodisc/Getty Images; (right) Vincent P. Walter/Pearson Education PH College

throughout the mixture. **Blending** is a type of mixing in which the ingredients are chopped so the overall mixture has a uniform consistency. In addition to combining ingredients, blenders and mixers introduce air into the food.

Here's an example that illustrates the difference between mixing and blending: When chocolate chip cookie dough is mixed, the chocolate chips are mixed evenly throughout the dough, without being broken up. If the cookie dough were blended, the chocolate chips would all be chopped up and the dough would turn into chocolate cookie dough (without any chocolate chips).

A **mixer** is a machine consisting of a bowl and mixing tool for combining ingredients, primarily for batter and dough. Compared to blenders, mixers operate more gently and slowly. They are used primarily by bakers. Some mixers are used only for bread dough. Others can create several types of mixtures.

There are two sizes of mixers: countertop mixers and the larger freestanding mixers. A **countertop mixer** is typically used when the kitchen is not a commercial bakery. Larger countertop models stand about 2 feet high and can weigh more than 100 pounds. Countertop mixers come in sizes ranging from 5 quarts to 20 quarts. A **freestanding mixer** sits on the floor and is typically used in commercial bakeries. These large mixers stand about 5 feet high and weigh 3000 pounds (the weight of a minivan). They can process more than 500 pounds of dough in one batch.

There are two basic types of mixers:

- **Planetary Mixer.** The mixing bowl doesn't move in a **planetary mixer**. The mixing tool moves within the bowl, like a planet

FIGURE 3–8
Countertop Planetary Mixer
This mixer is using a whip attachment.

PREDICTING *Why might a small restaurant have many attachments for its planetary mixer?*

Source: Vincent P. Walter/Pearson Education PH College

orbiting the sun. These mixers can use bowls in various capacities. Planetary mixers (also known as *vertical mixers*) typically have three standard attachments for different uses: a paddle, a whip, and a dough hook. However, multipurpose attachments can transform a planetary mixer into a food processor. You can add a vegetable slicer, a shredder/grater, or a meat grinder. A large restaurant that does a lot of baking can get several uses from its investment in a planetary mixer.

• **Spiral Mixer.** On a **spiral mixer**, the bowl turns instead of the mixing tool (which is typically a spiral-shaped hook). Spiral mixers are used for mixing bread dough because they work gently. A special type of spiral mixer called a *French fork spiral mixer* or *oblique mixer* is used to make French-style bread dough. It has a forklike attachment.

A **blender** can make coarse or fine mixtures and frozen drinks by using a rotating blade. Blenders operate at relatively high speeds and typically chop ingredients so they are all the same size. There are two basic types of blenders:

• **Countertop Blender.** A motor at the base of a **countertop blender** (or bar blender) turns a propeller-like blade in its bottom. A removable glass, plastic, or metal container on top holds ingredients. The container has a removable lid. Speed settings for the motor are in the base.

• **Immersion Blender.** Also known as a *hand blender*, *stick blender*, or *burr mixer*, an **immersion blender** is a long, stick-shaped machine that houses a motor on one end and a blade on the other end. Its advantage is that foods can be blended directly in the cooking vessel. Most kitchens use handheld immersion blenders.

FIGURE 3–9
Blenders
One of the countertop blenders has a glass container, and the other has a stainless-steel container. An immersion blender is lying on the counter in front of the two countertop blenders.

APPLYING CONCEPTS *Which type of blender do you think you would find most useful for your home cooking?*

Source: Culinary Institute of America

Other Food Preparation Equipment Specialized types of food preparation often require specialized types of food preparation equipment. For example, raw food restaurants often require the use of a commercial **food dehydrator** which dries food so that it can be stored for later use either directly from the dry state, or partially rehydrated (that is, with some or all of the water added back to the food). Fruits, vegetables, or other food are placed on racks in the dehydrator, which is set to a warm, but not hot, temperature. Typically a fan blows warm, dry air through the racks, drying the food.

Molecular gastronomy (mo-LECK-u-lar gas-TRON-o-mee) is a specialized type of food preparation. It focuses on the physical and chemical processes that can occur in food preparation. For example, liquid nitrogen is used to freeze food instantly. Carbon dioxide is added to food to create bubbles and make foams. Scientific instruments, such as a **centrifuge** (a machine for separating substances of different densities), are often used in this type of food preparation.

Cleaning Food Preparation Equipment Always follow safety precautions when using electric food preparation equipment such as chopping, slicing, and grinding equipment or mixers and blenders. Water conducts electricity, so make sure to turn off and unplug equipment to avoid shocks. Sharp blades can easily cut you. Use special caution when cleaning sharp blades and wear wire mesh gloves.

The following procedures do not replace instruction manuals or your supervisor's directions. They offer general guidelines for safe and effective cleaning of all electric food preparation equipment.

1. Turn off and unplug the equipment.
2. Remove any attachments or bowls. Use blade guards, if necessary.
3. If necessary, take apart any processing assemblies to reach the parts that touch food. Lay out the parts on a counter for easy reassembly.
4. Wash each part with hot, soapy water. Wash blades by using motions that avoid the sharp edge.
5. Dry with a clean cloth.
6. Sanitize.
7. Wipe the equipment base and frame with a soapy cloth and then rinse with a damp cloth. Dry with a clean cloth and then sanitize.
8. Reassemble the clean, dry, sanitized parts.
9. Immediately replace any blade guards.
10. Lubricate with oil as specified by the manufacturer.

READING CHECKPOINT *What are five pieces of equipment that are used for slicing, chopping, or grinding food?*

FIGURE 3–10

Steam-Jacketed Kettle

This steam-jacketed kettle tilts so a chef can pour out the contents of the kettle easily.

COMPARING/CONTRASTING *When would a steam-jacketed kettle with a spigot be more useful than a tilting steam-jacketed kettle? When would a tilting kettle be preferable?*

Source: Culinary Institute of America

FIGURE 3–11

Swiss Brasier

A chef can prepare large amounts of meats or vegetables quickly and efficiently by using a Swiss brasier.

ANALYZING INFORMATION *Would a small restaurant be likely to use a Swiss brasier?*

Source: Culinary Institute of America

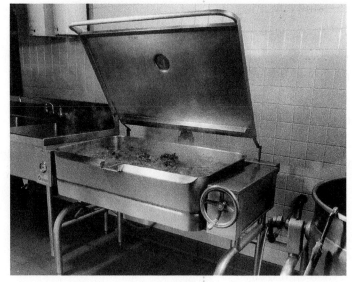

Cooking Equipment

Large restaurants and hotels often require specialized types of cooking equipment.

Kettles, Steamers, and Sous Vide Machines With kettles and steamers, chefs can prepare large amounts of food efficiently. Covered kettles and steamers use moist heat that is applied over a much larger area than is possible by using a single burner.

- **Steam-Jacketed Kettle.** Available in both freestanding and tabletop models, a **steam-jacketed kettle** is a kettle that provides even heat by circulating steam through its walls. Units may tilt and may have spigots or lids. Available in a range of sizes, these kettles are excellent for producing stocks, soups, and sauces.

- **Swiss Brasier.** Large, relatively shallow, and freestanding, the **Swiss brasier** (also known as a *tilting skillet* or *tilting fry pan*) is used to cook large quantities of meats or vegetables at one time. Swiss brasiers are versatile and can be used to perform many types of cooking.

- **Pressure Steamer.** In a **pressure steamer**, water is heated under pressure in a sealed compartment, allowing it to reach temperatures above the boiling point, 212°F. The cooking time is controlled by automatic timers, which open the exhaust valves after a specified amount of time. This releases steam pressure so the unit can be opened safely.

- **Convection Steamer.** Pressure does not build up in a **convection steamer**. The steam is generated in a boiler and then piped to the cooking chamber, where it is vented over the food. It is continuously exhausted. This means the door may be opened at any time. However, you need to wait for the steam to clear away before reaching into the convection oven. Otherwise, you could receive a serious burn.

- **Sous Vide Machine.** A **sous vide** (SU veed) **machine** cooks food in a sealed airtight plastic bag in a water bath, often for a long time. The machine maintains the temperature of the water precisely. The temperature is usually much lower than normally used in cooking (typically around 140°F). This keeps in juices and aromas and maintains the integrity of the item being cooked. At higher temperatures, the cell walls of the food burst, affecting the texture of the food.

Ranges, Ovens, Broilers, Fryers, Grills, and Griddles Stoves with which you are familiar probably have a stovetop (typically called a **range**) and an oven. The oven is often below the range. However, in a professional kitchen, this standard arrangement has many variations. Gas or electric ranges are available in many sizes and with various combinations of heating surfaces. Most ovens cook foods by surrounding them with hot air. This is a gentler and more even source of heat than the direct heat from the range.

- **Open-Burner Range.** Using electric elements or gas burners, an **open-burner range** lets you quickly adjust the heat level. Each element or burner has individual controls. Gas burners have a grid to hold the pot slightly above the flame. Pots and pans are set directly on an electric element.

- **Flattop and Ring-Top Range.** Consisting of a thick solid plate of cast iron or steel set over the heat source, the plate on a **flattop range** takes a while to be heated. After that, it provides an indirect, less intense heat than an open burner. The heat cannot be quickly adjusted. Pots and pans are set directly on a flattop. Flattop ranges (also called *French-top ranges*) are ideal for items that require long, slow cooking. A **ring-top range** is similar to a flattop range but has

··FOCUS ON
··Safety

Finding the Fire Extinguisher

Any heat source can get out of control. Know where the nearest fire extinguisher is in the kitchen and in the service area.

FIGURE 3–12
Restaurant Kitchen
Many common pieces of equipment are used in this kitchen.

INTERPRETING ILLUSTRATIONS
Would you classify this kitchen's work flow as a straight-line arrangement or a parallel one?

Source: Vincent P. Walter/Pearson Education PH College

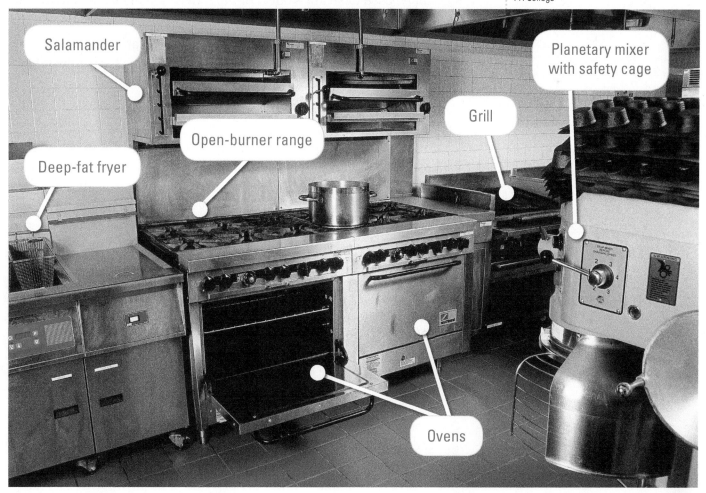

Salamander

Planetary mixer with safety cage

Open-burner range

Grill

Deep-fat fryer

Ovens

concentric plates, or rings, that can be lifted from the surface to provide more intense direct heat.

- **Conventional Oven.** The heat source in a conventional oven is under the bottom of the inside of the oven, which is also called its *deck*. Heat is conducted through the deck to the cooking space. Conventional ovens can be located below a range top. Food is generally placed in pans on wire racks.

- **Deck Oven.** Ovens can be stacked like shelves, one above another, like pizza ovens. These are called **deck ovens**, and the food is placed directly on the deck rather than on wire racks. Deck ovens normally consist of two to four decks, although single-deck models are available.

- **Convection Oven.** Fans force hot air to circulate around the food in a **convection oven**, cooking the food evenly and quickly. Some convection ovens have the capacity to introduce moisture. Special features may include infrared and a convection-microwave combination.

- **Combination Steamer/Oven.** Capable of using a combination of cooking methods, the **combination steamer/oven** (also referred to as a *combi oven*) can be powered by either gas or electricity. It can be used in steam mode, hot-air convection mode, or heat/steam (combi) mode.

- **Broiler.** With an intense radiant heat source located directly above the food, a **broiler** cooks food quickly. Some units have adjustable racks that can be raised or lowered to control cooking speed. A **salamander** is a small broiler used primarily for browning or melting foods.

- **Smoker.** Used for smoking and slow-cooking foods, a true **smoker** treats foods with smoke and can be operated at either cool or hot temperatures. Smokers generally have racks or hooks, allowing foods to smoke evenly.

Comparison of Microwave Ovens to Conventional Ovens

Microwave Ovens	Conventional Ovens
Heat very quickly	Heat more slowly
Cook by a combination of friction and heat transfer	Cook by conduction from the outer layer to the interior
Do not brown foods	Brown foods
Do not dry out food	Can dry out food
Cannot use metal pans	Can use metal pans

- **Microwave Oven.** By using electricity to generate microwave radiation, a microwave oven is able to cook, reheat, or thaw foods quickly. Microwave ovens do not brown foods effectively, however. This is why some models offer convection heating as well.

- **Deep-Fat Fryer.** Floor and countertop **deep-fat fryers** hold frying oil in a stainless-steel reservoir. A heating element, controlled by a thermostat, raises the oil to the desired temperature and maintains it at that temperature. Stainless-steel wire baskets are used to lower foods into the hot oil and lift them out.

- **Grill.** Grills have a radiant heat source below a rack on which food is cooked. Some grills may burn wood or charcoal; however, their fires require tending and special ventilation. Units in restaurants usually use gas or electric sources of heat.

- **Griddle.** Similar to a flattop range, a **griddle** has a heat source located beneath a thick plate of metal. Foods are cooked directly on this surface, which is usually designed with edges to contain the foods and a drain to collect used oil and waste. The **anti-griddle** is similar to a regular griddle except that instead of heating the surface of food, it freezes the surface instantly. This allows the creation of foods that are crunchy and frozen on the outside, but cool and creamy on the inside.

Selecting Equipment and Making Do with Limited Facilities

Restaurants must make careful choices about the equipment they use. Few restaurants can afford to spend money on equipment that they will use infrequently. Additionally, many restaurants, especially those in urban settings or historic buildings, may not have large kitchen spaces. Kitchen planners often must choose general-purpose equipment or equipment that can be used in multiple ways. If the type of food being planned requires specialized equipment, of course, then the space and resources must be found—perhaps at the expense of other, less important equipment.

Cleaning Cooking Equipment

Kettles, Steamers, and Sous Vide Machines

1. Turn off the equipment and allow to cool.
2. Loosen burned food with a scraper, if necessary.
3. Wash inside and out with hot, soapy water.
4. Rinse and dry.
5. Polish the outside with a clean cloth.

FIGURE 3–13
Griddle
Griddles are often used to make hot sandwiches.

PREDICTING *What would happen during a busy lunch hour if you ran out of space on a griddle for hot sandwiches?*

Source: Kim Steele/Digital Vision/Getty Images

•• FOCUS ON
•• Nutrition

Keep Oil Fresh
Clean deep-fat fryers on a regular schedule, and filter and replace the oil. Cooking causes oil to change into unhealthy saturated and trans fats. Also, old and dirty oil cannot fry as hot. This means foods absorb more oil and become soggy, fatty, and unappetizing.

The Microwave Oven

Radar, which uses short-wavelength signals to locate objects, helped win World War II. In 1946, Percy Spencer, a famed inventor at the Raytheon Company, stopped in front of a magnetron, the power tube that drives a radar set. To his surprise, Spencer noticed that the chocolate bar in his pocket was melting.

Spencer was curious and asked for some popping corn. Holding the bag of corn next to the magnetron, Spencer watched as the kernels exploded. Later Spencer put the magnetron tube near an egg. When the egg exploded, Spencer reasoned that if an egg can be cooked by microwaves, why not other foods?

Spencer and Raytheon went on to develop the microwave oven. In 1947, the first microwave oven weighed 750 pounds and was 5½ feet high. The first ones were used to cook large quantities of food quickly—in restaurants and on railroad cars and ocean liners.

Source: Alex Segre/Alamy

An early version of the microwave oven

Microwave ovens use microwaves to heat food. These are radio waves with a frequency of about 2500 megahertz (2.5 gigahertz). Radio waves in this frequency are absorbed by water, fats, and sugars. They are then converted directly into atomic motion—heat. Microwaves in this frequency are not absorbed by most plastics, glass, or ceramics, making them good cooking vessels for microwaved food. Metals, on the other hand, reflect microwaves, so they are not useful for cooking in a microwave.

The home microwave oven appeared in 1967 when Amana, a division of Raytheon, introduced its domestic Radarange. Other companies soon joined the countertop microwave oven market. By the end of 1971, the price of countertop units began to fall and their abilities grew. By 1975, sales of microwave ovens exceeded those of gas ranges.

Lab Activity

As a small group, research how a microwave oven works. Then generate a hypothesis describing how you think different types of foods will cook in a microwave. Test your hypothesis by cooking the foods. Prepare a presentation that summarizes your work.

Open-Burner Ranges

1. Turn off the range and allow to cool. Remove the grids (and the drip pan, if necessary).
2. Soak the grids (and drip pan) in hot, soapy water.
3. Wash the rest of the range with hot, soapy water.
4. Rinse and dry the range.
5. Wash, rinse, and dry the grids (and drip pan).
6. Replace the grids (and drip pan).

Flattop and Ring-Top Ranges

1. Turn off the range and allow to cool. Loosen burned food with a scraper.
2. Clean with hot, soapy water.
3. Rinse and dry.

Microwave, Conventional, and Convection Ovens

1. Turn off the oven and allow to cool. Unplug microwaves when possible.
2. Remove the racks (shelves and turntables).
3. Clean the racks in hot, soapy water. Rinse.
4. Dry the turntables. Air-dry the shelves.
5. Clean the oven inside and out with warm soapy cloth.
6. Rinse with a clean wet cloth and dry.
7. Polish the outside with a clean cloth.

Broilers

1. Turn off the broiler and allow the unit to cool completely.
2. Take out the rack.
3. Soak the rack in hot, soapy water, removing caked-on food with a scraper or wire brush.
4. Rinse with a clean, wet cloth.
5. Dry with a clean cloth.
6. Scrape caked-on food from the inside of the broiler.
7. Remove the drip pan.
8. Wash the drip pan with hot, soapy water.
9. Rinse the drip pan with a clean, wet cloth.
10. Dry the drip pan with a clean, dry cloth.
11. Replace the drip pan and racks.

Deep-Fat Fryers (Daily)

1. Turn off the fryer and allow to cool.
2. Wash all removable parts with hot, soapy water.

3. Clean all exterior surfaces of the fryer with hot, soapy water. Do not use cleansers, steel wool, or any other abrasives on the stainless steel.

4. Follow the manufacturer's directions to filter the cooking oil, and replace if necessary. Filter oil more often under heavy conditions.

Deep-Fat Fryers (Weekly)

1. Turn off the fryer and allow to cool. Completely drain the fryer vessel into either the filter or a steel container. Do not use a plastic bucket or glass container.

2. Clean the vessel with a good grade of cleaner or with hot water and a strong detergent.

3. Close the drain valve and refill with either the cleaning solution or water and detergent.

4. Using protective gloves and a brush, scrub the interior above the oil line until gummy deposits and carbon spots are eliminated.

5. Drain the vessel and rinse several times with clear water.

6. Rinse with a vinegar-and-water solution.

7. Rinse again with clear water to eliminate the vinegar-and-water solution.

8. Dry thoroughly with a single-use paper towel, paying close attention to drain area and heating elements.

Grills

1. Turn off the grill and allow to cool.

2. Clean the rack thoroughly with a wire brush and scraper, removing any burned food particles.

3. Oil the rack as specified by the manufacturer.

Griddles*

1. Turn off the griddle. (Unplug electric units.) Let the griddle come to room temperature.

2. Polish the top with a special griddle stone or griddle cloth. Work in the direction of the grain of the metal.

3. Recondition the top by coating it lightly with oil as specified by the manufacturer.

___

*For anti-griddles, follow the manufacturer's instructions for maintaining the griddle.

FIGURE 3–14

Cleaning Grill with a Wire Brush
Use a wire brush to clean dried particles from a grill, then follow the manufacturer's specifications for oiling it.

PREDICTING *Why do you think grills are oiled after cleaning with a wire brush?*

Source: Culinary Institute of America

4. Heat the griddle to 400°F and wipe clean.

5. Repeat if necessary. The clean griddle should shine.

6. Wash the rest of the griddle with warm soapy water. Rinse and dry.

 **READING CHECKPOINT** *What is the difference between an open-burner range and a flattop range?*

3.3 ASSESSMENT

Reviewing Concepts

1. Name five kinds of slicing, chopping, and grinding equipment used for food preparation.

2. Name two types of mixers and two types of blenders.

3. What is the difference between an open-burner range and a flattop range?

Critical Thinking

4. Comparing/Contrasting What is the difference between a pressure steamer and a convection steamer?

5. Predicting Which do you think would heat up faster, an open-burner range or a flattop range?

6. Inferring Why might a foodservice business want to use a single piece of equipment in several ways? Why might a foodservice business want to use specialized equipment?

Test Kitchen

List the equipment in your school kitchen in the categories used in this section: (1) chopping, slicing, and grinding equipment; (2) mixing and blending equipment; (3) kettles, steamers, and sous vide machines; and (4) ranges, ovens, broilers, fryers, grills and griddles. Ask the kitchen personnel which items are used most often and least often. Which items serve multiple purposes?

LANGUAGE ARTS ────●
Cooking Technology

Research a type of equipment used for cooking. Focus on comparing equivalent models of the same type of equipment available today (example: compare existing open-burner ranges).

PROJECT 3 **Cleaning Preparation and Cooking Equipment** You are now ready to work on Project 3, "Cleaning Preparation and Cooking Equipment," which is available in "My Culinary Lab" or in your *Student's Lab Resources and Study Guide* manual.

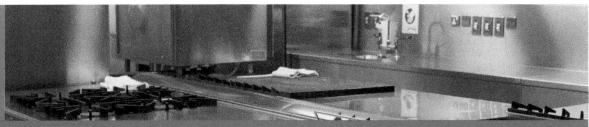

3.4

Holding and Service Equipment

READING PREVIEW

Key Concepts

- Understanding equipment for holding food
- Understanding equipment for serving food

Vocabulary

- chafing dish
- heat lamp
- holding cabinets
- hot plate
- hotel pans
- plate cover
- service carts
- sneeze guards
- steam table
- tray stands

Holding Equipment

The look, taste, temperature, and texture of food when it is presented can delight customers or disappoint them. Restaurants and other foodservice businesses use special equipment to hold food at the appropriate temperatures for customers. These businesses also use special equipment to make it easier for the staff to deliver and present food to customers.

A restaurant must select the holding equipment based on what type of food is served, how customers are served, and how quickly the food is served. For example, in a fast-food restaurant, food is prepared and packaged. It is

Source: © Goran Bogicevic/Fotolia

typically held under special lamps to keep it warm or in refrigerated cases to keep it cold. No special equipment is required to serve the food. The counter person assembles the food on a tray or in a bag. The customer is satisfied when food is up to standards and served in a quick and friendly way.

In a cafeteria, buffet restaurant, or banquet hall, the equipment for holding food also provides a way to display the food for diners to make their selections. A customer is satisfied by the look, variety, and quality of the food and by the convenience of choosing it directly.

With buffet or cafeteria service, **sneeze guards** protect foods. These see-through barriers allow customers to see food but eliminate the possibility of cross-contamination caused by a sneeze. Customers select food by reaching under the guard.

Foodservice establishments use holding equipment to hold food at safe temperatures. As you know from Chapter 1, the temperature danger zone is

Ahhhh–Choo!

What happens when you are standing in front of a salad bar and the inside of your nose gets a tickle? Something—maybe a strong odor, pepper, or that nasty cold of yours—is irritating your nose. A message is sent to a special part of your brain called the sneeze center, which then sends a message to all your muscles involved in the amazingly complicated process called sternutation (stern-you-TAY-shun), or sneezing.

Sneezing is actually an attempt by the body to expel irritating particles from the nose. And the body does a good job, indeed! Sneezing can send tiny particles, including germs, speeding out of your nose at up to 100 miles an hour!

So in the 1950s, when restaurants began developing salad bars and other types of quick-serve dining, companies developed sneeze guards. Originally, sneeze guards were just straight glass panels held by a wooden structure at head height. But soon sneeze guards were being made of decorative stained glass, leaving less and less room for customers to reach for food. Today, sneeze guards come in many sizes, but all must adhere to strict standards established by the National Sanitation Foundation and enforced by state and county Health Departments.

Sternutation

Source: Adam Hart-Davis/Photo Researchers, Inc.

Computation

As a group, research the range of height for people today. Then, based on data from your group, calculate the location of the nostrils relative to the height of a person. Based on your research and observations, what would you recommend as the highest and lowest edge of a sneeze guard? Compare your recommendation with that of the National Sanitation Foundation.

FIGURE 3–15

Salad Bar in a Cafeteria

A refrigerated unit keeps salad bar items cold.

INTERPRETING ILLUSTRATIONS
Why would a cafeteria with a sneeze guard need service staff to move food forward more often than in a setting without a sneeze guard?
Source: Fotosearch/SuperStock

between 41°F and 135°F, so hot foods must be held above 135°F and cold foods must be held below 41°F. Chafing dishes, steam tables, and hold lamps are used to keep food hot.

- **Chafing Dish.** Used to hold just one or two food items, a **chafing** (CHAYF-ing) **dish** is typically a stand, a water pan, an insert pan, and a lid. Most chafing dishes use Sterno (or other fuel) to heat water in the water pan. When the water is heated, it keeps the food in the insert pan at an even temperature. Because they are often used by customers to serve themselves, chafing dishes are usually decorative.

Chafing dish

Source: Bernard Prost/Alamy

- **Hot Plate.** Typically used to hold coffee and water, a **hot plate** uses an electrical heating element to keep beverages at the appropriate temperature.

- **Holding Cabinets and Covered Racks.** Available in a variety of sizes, **holding cabinets** and covered racks can hold trays of food or trays containing plates. While both holding cabinets and covered racks move easily on wheels, holding cabinets are usually completely enclosed and insulated to maintain a stable internal temperature. Some holding cabinets are specifically for hot or cold food and plug into an electric outlet to maintain their temperature.

- **Heat Lamp.** Another way to keep food hot is to use a **heat lamp**. These lamps use special bulbs and are placed directly above the area where food is held.

FIGURE 3–16

Covered Rack

This covered rack contains trays that can hold plates of food awaiting service.

INFERRING *What advantage does a covered rack offer when you are serving a large group?*
Source: Culinary Institute of America

- **Steam Table.** Resembling a large table with a deep, hollow top, a **steam table** is used to keep food hot. Hot water is placed in the top and heated. A grid above the steam accommodates a number of pans of different sizes. The steam from the water keeps food hot for service. Large steam tables usually have a thermostat to control the heating elements that maintain the desired temperature.

- **Refrigerated Holding and Display Units.** Ice-filled cases or refrigerated holding and display units are used to keep food cold. In buffets, areas serving cold items may include salad bars, sandwich bars, or dessert bars. The refrigerated unit holding these food items is similar to a steam table except that the unit uses refrigeration rather than steam. Some restaurants use containers or units filled with ice. Bowls can be placed in the ice. In some restaurants, fish or seafood is placed directly on mounded or carved ice.

Hotel pans are stainless steel or plastic containers typically used for holding and storing food. Hotel pans come in various standard sizes that can be combined easily in steam tables and other serving equipment that is designed to be used with hotel pans.

The full-size hotel pan is the largest, measuring $20\frac{3}{4}$ inches long by $12\frac{3}{4}$ inches wide. A steam table may be able to hold three, four, or more full-size hotel pans.

Other hotel pans are named as fractions of the full-size pan. A full-size hotel pan that is 6 inches deep holds 20 quarts. Most hotel pans are available in three depths: $2\frac{1}{2}$ inches, 4 inches, and 6 inches. The smallest hotel

FIGURE 3–17
Steam Table
This steam table with heat lamps and a sneeze guard keeps food warm for buffet dining.
DRAWING CONCLUSIONS *Why would a heat lamp be placed over pans of food in a steam table?*
Source: Vincent P. Walter/Pearson Education PH College

FIGURE 3–18
Hotel Pans
A full-size hotel pan is on the left; a two-thirds-size pan and a one-third-size pan are on the right.
RECOGNIZING PATTERNS *Why would the foodservice industry tend to use standard sizes for hotel pans?*
Source: Culinary Institute of America

Hotel Pans

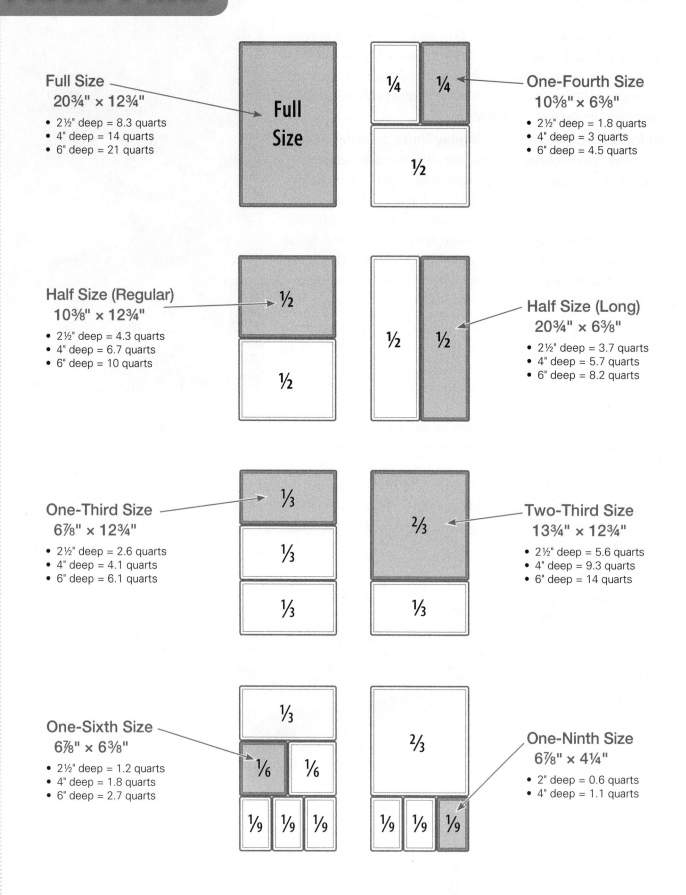

Full Size
20¾" × 12¾"

- 2½" deep = 8.3 quarts
- 4" deep = 14 quarts
- 6" deep = 21 quarts

Full Size

One-Fourth Size
10⅜" × 6⅜"

- 2½" deep = 1.8 quarts
- 4" deep = 3 quarts
- 6" deep = 4.5 quarts

¼ ¼

½

Half Size (Regular)
10⅜" × 12¾"

- 2½" deep = 4.3 quarts
- 4" deep = 6.7 quarts
- 6" deep = 10 quarts

½

½

Half Size (Long)
20¾" × 6⅜"

- 2½" deep = 3.7 quarts
- 4" deep = 5.7 quarts
- 6" deep = 8.2 quarts

½ ½

One-Third Size
6⅞" × 12¾"

- 2½" deep = 2.6 quarts
- 4" deep = 4.1 quarts
- 6" deep = 6.1 quarts

⅓

⅓

⅓

Two-Third Size
13¾" × 12¾"

- 2½" deep = 5.6 quarts
- 4" deep = 9.3 quarts
- 6" deep = 14 quarts

⅔

⅓

One-Sixth Size
6⅞" × 6⅜"

- 2½" deep = 1.2 quarts
- 4" deep = 1.8 quarts
- 6" deep = 2.7 quarts

⅓

⅙ ⅙

⅑ ⅑ ⅑

One-Ninth Size
6⅞" × 4¼"

- 2" deep = 0.6 quarts
- 4" deep = 1.1 quarts

⅔

⅑ ⅑ ⅑

pan is one-ninth the size of the full-size pan, is 2½ inches deep, and holds a little over half a quart.

Clean holding equipment according to the manufacturer's instructions. Silver or copper chafing dishes may require special cleaning.

Service Equipment

Just as with holding equipment, a restaurant selects service equipment based on what type of food is served, how customers are served, and how quickly the food is served. Fast-food restaurants may not require special service equipment other than trays for the customers. In a cafeteria, buffet restaurant, or banquet hall, the equipment for holding food is located in the dining area and customers often serve themselves.

In a full-service restaurant, most equipment for holding food is located in the kitchen. Food is prepared and orders are assembled in the kitchen. The finished food is artfully displayed on plates. The wait staff then must bring the plates to the diners. Ultimately, a restaurant meal is an orchestrated performance that allows guests to appreciate the food at the right temperature, with all the food on the plate arranged exactly as the kitchen intended.

Common types of tableside serving equipment are trays, tray stands, plate covers, and service carts.

- **Trays.** To transport dishes from the kitchen to the dining area, the serving staff may use trays. Plates on trays can be covered or uncovered.

- **Tray Stands.** Also called *jack stands*, **tray stands** allow serving staff to place a tray containing multiple dishes close to the table where the dishes will be served. Tray stands are usually made of wood or metal and can be folded when not in use. Some stands have a shelf to hold a tray of dirty dishes.

- **Plate Covers.** When serving staff must travel a significant distance to bring food to the customer, a plate may be covered with a **plate cover** to keep the food warm. When the plate has been set on the table, the plate cover will be removed.

- **Service Carts.** There are various types of **service carts**. Generally a service cart is used in the dining area to carry food or provide a work surface for carving, plating, or assembling dishes beside a table. A *flambé cart* (also called a *guéridon*) is a

Plate cover

Source: Rob Porazinski/Getty Images, Inc.—Artville LLC

Chef's Tip

Quality Service

When working in a service line, wear a clean uniform and use the right utensils. Greet diners, invite their requests, and serve their food carefully.

specialized type of service cart that holds an open burner for finishing a dish with a flaming sauce or cooking an omelette. A *pastry cart* displays a selection of desserts. A *chafer cart* holds a chafing dish with food that is kept warm. A *salad cart* lets wait staff prepare a salad as diners look on.

Clean service equipment according to the manufacturer's instructions. Silver or copper service equipment may require special cleaning.

 **READING CHECKPOINT** *Name four types of tableside serving equipment.*

3.4 ASSESSMENT

Reviewing Concepts

1. What is a steam table?

2. Name four common types of tableside serving equipment.

Critical Thinking

3. Solving Problems List as many combinations of different size hotel pans as possible that occupy the space of one full-size pan (examples: two half-size [long] pans; one half-size [regular] pan and two one-fourth-size pans).

4. Drawing Conclusions Why would a restaurant try to keep the lids of chafing dishes closed as much as possible when serving?

5. Applying Concepts A sneeze guard obviously benefits the customer, but does it benefit the food establishment? Explain your answer.

Test Kitchen

Divide into two teams. Have one team role-play serving food from hot and cold holding equipment in a buffet dining situation. Have the other team role-play customers in a rush. Switch roles after ten minutes. Record your observations as both servers and customers.

SCIENCE
Steam Tables

Research steam tables (including prices). Some questions you may consider: Why does a steam table heat evenly? How is the heat maintained at a constant temperature? What happens if the water in the steam table evaporates? What precautions are built in to avoid water evaporation? What sizes are available? When were steam tables invented? Do all steam tables use standard-sized hotel pans?

Reviewing Content

Choose the letter that best answers the question or completes the statement.

1. An arrangement of equipment and tools for accomplishing a specific set of culinary tasks is a
   a. work line.
   b. workstation.
   c. work flow.
   d. work section.

2. A small broiler used primarily for browning and melting foods is called a
   a. convection oven.
   b. griddle.
   c. salamander.
   d. deck oven.

3. Which of the following cooks food with a heat source from above?
   a. deck oven
   b. oven
   c. broiler
   d. flattop range

4. How is a chafing dish used?
   a. to cook hot food items
   b. to transport dishes from the kitchen
   c. to hold one or two hot food items
   d. to hold food in a steam table

5. Which of the following is the first step for cleaning electrical food preparation equipment?
   a. Soak the machine in hot soapy water.
   b. Disassemble the machine according to the directions in the manual.
   c. Carefully wash the blade.
   d. Turn off and unplug the machine.

6. What is the primary difference between a planetary mixer and a spiral mixer?
   a. A planetary mixer is smaller and sits on a countertop.
   b. A planetary mixer is larger and sits on the floor.
   c. The mixing bowl of a planetary mixer does not move; only the mixing tool moves.
   d. The mixing bowl of a planetary mixer moves; the mixing tool does not move.

Understanding Concepts

7. What is involved in mise en place and why is it important for efficient work flow?

8. How do workstations use refrigerated drawers and undercounter reach-ins to increase efficiency?

9. What is the difference between mixing and blending? Provide an example.

Critical Thinking

10. **APPLYING CONCEPTS** Review the safety guidelines for food temperatures in Chapter 1. Explain how holding equipment helps maintain these guidelines.

11. **FORMING A MODEL** Identify the work line arrangement of your home's kitchen (or a kitchen with which you are familiar). Provide a sketch of the kitchen with storage, preparation, and cooking equipment labeled.

Culinary Math

12. **SOLVING PROBLEMS** A restaurant's meat grinder can grind 6 pounds of meat in two minutes. A single serving of ground meat at the restaurant is 6 ounces. About how long will it take to grind enough meat for one night's service, which is 200 servings?

13. **FORMING A MODEL** A steam table has room for three full-size hotel pans. How many combinations of hotel pans can you put together if the restaurant wants the first space to use two half-size pans and the third space to be a full-size pan? The restaurant does not have any one-ninth- or one-sixth-size pans.

On the Job

14. **PREDICTING** A chef working on the grilling station always arrives at work late and doesn't have time to complete mise en place for his workstation before customers start arriving. What are the consequences of the chef's late arrival for customers? For the restaurant? For the chef?

15. **APPLYING CONCEPTS** Your restaurant received a load of beef that is intended for use for tonight's dinner. Your infrared thermometer indicates that the temperature of the beef when it was received was 43°F. Would you accept this delivery? Explain your answer.

Foodservice Equipment Manufacturers and Developers

Foodservice equipment manufacturers produce a wide array of tools and equipment, small and large, from ladles to large refrigeration equipment. Tools for cooking, storing, packaging, presenting, and serving foods are produced by a variety of companies, from small, boutique companies to large multinational corporations. Every professional kitchen relies heavily on its equipment. Some companies follow traditional methods of construction, while others are on the cutting edge. No matter what kind of materials they produce, they must meet exacting standards for safety and effectiveness if they are to become part of any professional kitchen. The background and training of the individuals who work in these companies are varied. Some are experts in metals, others in electronics, and still others in computers.

Thermal circulators, vacuum packers, and blast chillers are just a few of the pieces of equipment that have made their way from the laboratory to the kitchen. If you watch cooking programs, you've undoubtedly heard of these tools. Chefs who work in the area of molecular gastronomy are using tools such as cryo-guns that quickly chill foods to produce a range of textures and culinary effects. Traditional tools such as griddles are be-

Source: Dja65/Shutterstock

Food service manufacturers build large machines such as this industrial conveyor making cookies with a cherry on top

ing produced using new materials, such as ceramics. Finding culinary applications for these tools is one of the most exciting areas in the world of cooking.

As new or newly refined tools and equipment become available, manufacturers look to chefs and other culinary experts to help develop training materials and recipes. These materials are used by chefs to learn the basics of using the equipment. Research-and-development chefs may work on recipes for a new style of microwave. They may work with others to develop applications for ingredients and products that produce unique effects. For example, research-and-development chefs have developed a new technique for turning a high-fat liquid like olive oil into a powder. Edible paper made from soy and potatoes can be used, in combination with inks and dyes made from fruits and vegetables, to create edible wrappers, even menus that are "good enough to eat." Liquid nitrogen is used to flash-freeze or shatter foods instantly. Rotary evaporators are capable of creating and distilling a wide array of flavors never before dreamed of.

Entry-Level Requirements

While there is no single path one follows to get started in the area of experimentation and application of various industrial and scientific tools in the kitchen, a number of personality traits are useful: curiosity, interest in science, willingness to experiment, and a passion for new ideas.

Helpful for Advancement

Studies in the areas of food science, including a specialty known as *culinology*, give people the introduction and experience they need to excel. To succeed in the area of production and manufacture, studies in business management, microbiology, engineering, science, and technology may be helpful. Some companies, such as Electrolux, sponsor competitions and various programs to fund research and experimentation in the area of design.

CHRIS YOUNG

Although Chris Young completed degrees in theoretical mathematics and biochemistry, he found that he had a real knack for combining technology and math in the kitchen. He was the founding chef of Heston Blumenthal's Fat Duck Experimental Kitchen, the secret culinary laboratory behind the innovative dishes served in one of the best restaurants in the world. He was also a principal coauthor, with Nathan Myhrvold, of the acclaimed six-volume work *Modernist Cuisine: The Art and Science of Cooking,* which was named both the 2012 Cookbook of the Year and Best Professional Cookbook of the Year by the renowned James Beard Foundation. The book was a worldwide best seller. Chris went on to found ChefSteps.com, a free-to-learn online culinary school, of which he is the managing director.

Chris Young

VITAL STATISTICS

Graduated: University of Washington, with degrees in theoretical mathematics and biochemistry

Profession: Chef, author, researcher scientist, inventor

Interesting Item: Founded the Fat Duck Experimental Kitchen for Heston Blumenthal

Coauthored *Modernist Cuisine: The Art and Science of Cooking*

Inventor for the Global Good Fund at Intellectual Ventures

Invited speaker at the Culinary Institute of American, Johnson and Wales University, TEDx, The EG, and the Jet Propulsion Laboratory

CAREER PROFILE

Salary Ranges
Varies widely

Knives and Smallware

4.1   Using Knives

4.2   Using Smallware

Using Knives

Key Concepts

- Identifying parts of a knife
- Selecting the appropriate knife
- Using a knife properly
- Making the cut
- Maintaining knives

Vocabulary

- bâtonnet
- bolster
- boning knife
- brunoise
- chef's knife
- chiffonade
- cube
- diagonal cut
- dice
- fermière
- filleting knife
- flat edge
- forged blade
- gaufrette
- granton edge
- grit
- heel (of blade)
- hollow-ground edge
- honing
- julienne
- lozenge cut
- mandoline
- meat cleaver
- oblique cut
- paring knife
- paysanne
- rivets
- rondelles
- santoku knife
- scimitar
- serrated edge
- slicer
- spine (of blade)
- stamped blade
- steel
- tang
- taper-ground edge
- tempering
- tournée knife
- trueing
- utility knife
- vegetable cleaver
- whetstone

Identifying Parts of a Knife

Probably no other kitchen tool is as important to a chef as a knife. To use this important tool well, a chef must know how each knife is constructed as well as how to use the knife properly. A chef must know about the wide variety of knives, each designed for a specific task. A chef must know how to make the cuts that are required for particular dishes. Finally, a chef has to know how to maintain a knife.

A knife has several parts—each of which determines how the knife feels in the chef's hand, how it is best used, and how long the knife will last.

The Blade The blade is the cutting surface of the knife. The blade of a high-quality professional knife is made of a single piece of metal that has been forged or stamped into its desired shape. A **forged blade** is made from a single piece of heated metal that is dropped into a mold and then pounded and cut into shape. A

Source: Culinary Institute of America

stamped blade is made by cutting blade-shaped pieces from sheets of previously milled steel.

After a steel knife blade is shaped, it is put through a procedure known as tempering. The **tempering** procedure calls for the blade to be heated and then cooled several times. Tempering is done to ensure that the blade will be properly hardened and will not become brittle. If a knife blade becomes very hot (for instance, if it is left in a flame or in a very hot oven) the blade is said to have *come out of temper*. A blade that has come out of temper may be brittle and may shatter.

Blades are usually made of stainless-steel or high-carbon stainless steel, but modern knives sometimes use ceramic material or titanium. Stainless-steel blades are very hard and durable. They are made of chromium and carbon steel. They don't rust or discolor but are hard to sharpen. High-carbon stainless-steel blades are a mix of iron, carbon, chromium, and other metals. Ceramic blades are produced by heating ceramic powder until the particles adhere to each other to form a solid blade. Ceramic blades are harder than steel blades. This means that they will hold their edge longer than steel blades, but because they are so hard, they may need to be returned to the manufacturer for sharpening when they become dull. It is difficult if not impossible to properly sharpen them using a typical sharpening stone.

The blade of the chef's knife has several distinct parts:

- **Tip.** Used for fine work, paring, trimming, and peeling. The tip can also be used to core fruits and vegetables or to score items so they will marinate or cook more evenly.
- **Cutting Edge.** Used for slicing, carving, and making precision cuts. The most common type of cutting edge for general use is a **taper-ground edge**, in which both sides of the blade taper smoothly to a narrow V shape. A **hollow-ground edge** has a thinner, sharper blade with more metal removed. The edges are less durable than taper-ground blades. If the angle is on only one side of the blade it is known as a **flat edge**. This type of edge is typical of many Japanese-style knives.
- **Heel.** Used for cutting tasks that require some force, such as chopping through the joints of a chicken. The **heel** of the blade is the widest and thickest point of the blade.
- **Bolster.** Located at the heel of the blade, at the point where the blade and handle come together. The **bolster** gives the blade greater strength and durability.
- **Spine.** The noncutting edge of the blade is called the **spine** of the knife.
- **Flat Side of the Blade.** Used to crush ingredients such as garlic or spices.

Hollow-ground edge   Taper-ground edge

Flat edge

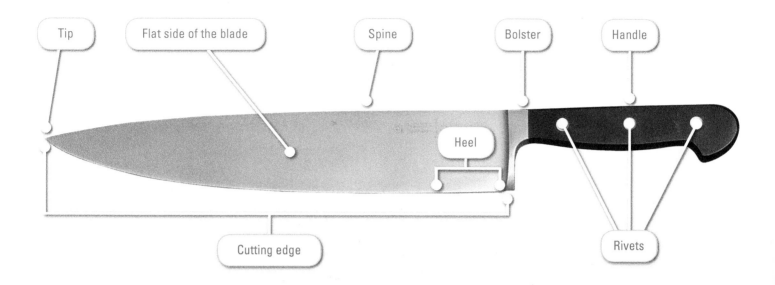

Tip | Flat side of the blade | Spine | Bolster | Handle | Heel | Cutting edge | Rivets

The Tang
The **tang** is the continuation of the blade into the knife's handle. Tangs can be either full or partial. A full tang is as long as the whole knife handle and is considered the most durable. Knives used for heavy work, such as chef's knives and cleavers, should have a full tang. Knives used for lighter work may have a partial tang that does not run the entire length of the handle. A *rat-tail tang* is long and narrow. Rat-tail tangs are completely covered by the handle and are not secured to it with rivets.

The Handle
Knife handles are made of various materials, including hard woods with very tight grain, such as walnut and rosewood; textured metal; and composite materials. Some are cushioned to make long hours of work less fatiguing.

Wooden handles are attached to the blades with **rivets**. If rivets are visible on the handle (they aren't always), they should lie flush with the surface of the handle to prevent irritation to the hand and to avoid creating pockets where microorganisms could gather. Composition handles are molded onto the tang.

Because you will be holding your knife for extended periods, be sure the material and the shape of the handle feel comfortable in your hand. Many manufacturers offer a range of handle sizes.

READING CHECKPOINT *What are the main parts of a knife?*

FIGURE 4-1
Different Types of Tangs
The knife on the left has a partial tang; the knife on the right has a full tang.
DRAWING CONCLUSIONS *Why would a knife with a full tang be used for heavy work?*
Source: Culinary Institute of America

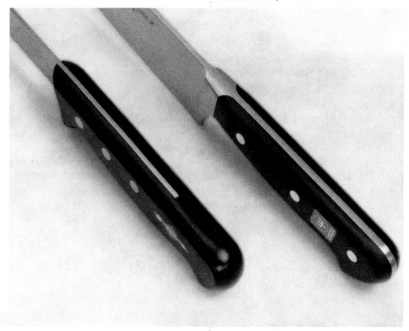

Types of Knives

All-Purpose Knives

A **chef's knife** (also known as a *French knife*) is the most-used knife. This all-purpose knife, with an 8- to 12-inch triangular blade, can be used for peeling, trimming, slicing, chopping, and dicing. A skilled chef can also use this knife to cut large foods into smaller pieces. A good quality chef's knife should be well balanced, with the weight of the blade equal to the weight of the handle.
Source: Culinary Institute of America

A **santoku** (san-TOE-koo) **knife** is a general-purpose knife that originated in Japan. It has become popular in kitchens around the world. Unlike a chef's knife, the edge of the blade curves down toward the tip. It may be ground with a flat edge, rather than taper-ground like many European-style knives. Santoku knives are used for slicing, chopping, and mincing foods.
Source: Pell Studio/Shutterstock

Utility Knife

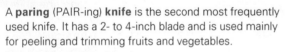

A **utility knife** is a smaller and lighter version of a chef's knife, with a 5- to 7-inch blade. It is used for light cutting, slicing, and peeling.
Source: Culinary Institute of America

Paring Knives

A **paring** (PAIR-ing) **knife** is the second most frequently used knife. It has a 2- to 4-inch blade and is used mainly for peeling and trimming fruits and vegetables.
Source: Culinary Institute of America

A **tournée** (TOUR-nay) **knife** is a type of paring knife with a curved blade, making cutting rounded surfaces easier. It is also known as a *bird's-beak knife*.
Source: Culinary Institute of America

Boning Knife

A **boning knife** is used to separate raw meat from the bone. The blade is usually about 6 inches long and is thinner than the blade of a chef's knife. The narrow blade allows you to work around bones, between muscles, and under gristle. Some boning knives have an upward curve; others are straight.
Source: Culinary Institute of America

Filleting Knife

A **filleting** (fill-AY-ing) **knife** is specially designed for filleting fish. It has a very flexible blade.
Source: Culinary Institute of America

Selecting the Appropriate Knife

There are almost as many types of knives as there are types of food. Each aspect of a knife—the length and flexibility of the blade, the type of cutting edge, the strength of construction—is designed for a specific task.

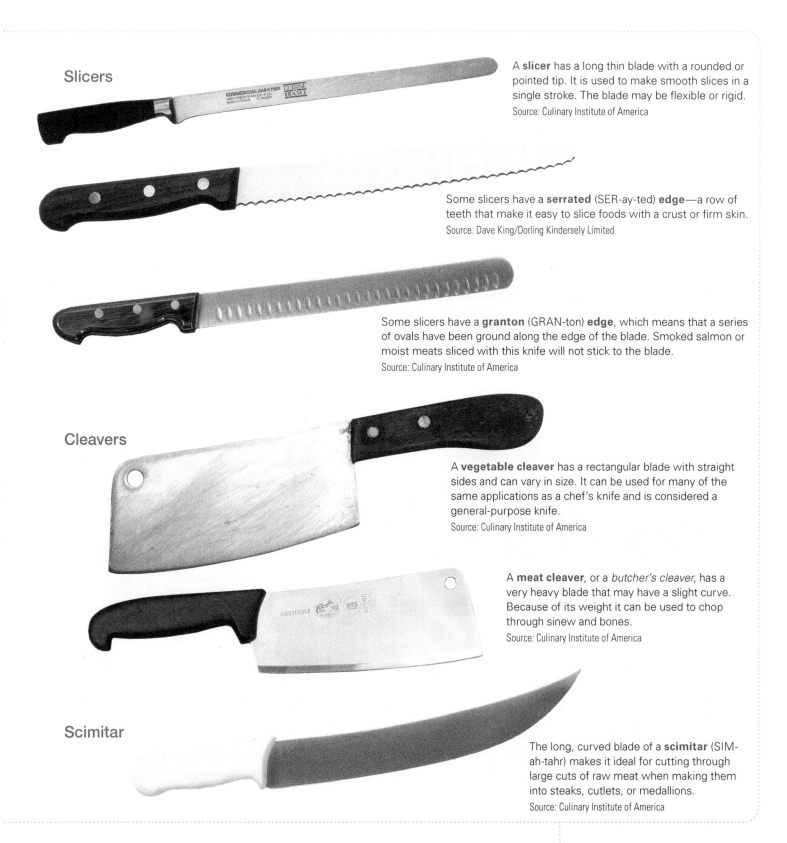

Slicers

A **slicer** has a long thin blade with a rounded or pointed tip. It is used to make smooth slices in a single stroke. The blade may be flexible or rigid.
Source: Culinary Institute of America

Some slicers have a **serrated** (SER-ay-ted) **edge**—a row of teeth that make it easy to slice foods with a crust or firm skin.
Source: Dave King/Dorling Kindersely Limited

Some slicers have a **granton** (GRAN-ton) **edge**, which means that a series of ovals have been ground along the edge of the blade. Smoked salmon or moist meats sliced with this knife will not stick to the blade.
Source: Culinary Institute of America

Cleavers

A **vegetable cleaver** has a rectangular blade with straight sides and can vary in size. It can be used for many of the same applications as a chef's knife and is considered a general-purpose knife.
Source: Culinary Institute of America

A **meat cleaver**, or a *butcher's cleaver*, has a very heavy blade that may have a slight curve. Because of its weight it can be used to chop through sinew and bones.
Source: Culinary Institute of America

Scimitar

The long, curved blade of a **scimitar** (SIM-ah-tahr) makes it ideal for cutting through large cuts of raw meat when making them into steaks, cutlets, or medallions.
Source: Culinary Institute of America

READING CHECKPOINT *What are the eight basic types of knives?*

Using Knives Properly

Remember when you first learned how to write? First you had to concentrate on holding the pencil and shaping each letter. With practice, writing became automatic and you developed your own unique signature. That is just like learning to use a knife properly. First you have to concentrate on holding the knife properly and shaping each item. Before long, using your knife becomes automatic and you develop your own unique style.

Holding the Knife

Method 1:

Grip the handle with four fingers and hold the thumb firmly against the blade's spine. This method gives you more power.

Source: George Doyle/Stockbyte/Getty Images

Method 2:

Grip the handle with all four fingers and hold the thumb against the side of the blade. This method gives you more control.

Source: David Murray and Jules Selmes/Image Partners 2005/Dorling Kindersley Media Library/Dorling Kindersley

Method 3:

Grip the handle with three fingers, resting the index finger flat against the blade on one side and holding the thumb on the opposite side. This method gives you most control.

Source: Culinary Institute of America

The Guiding Hand

When cutting an object on the cutting board, tuck the fingers under the knuckles slightly and hold the object, with the thumb held back from the fingertips. The knife blade rests against the knuckles, making it impossible to cut the fingertips.
Source: Culinary Institute of America

When cutting into a food horizontally, as you would do to butterfly fish or meat, or to cut bagels or cakes into layers, the guiding hand can be placed on top of the food to keep it from slipping. Hold your hand flat on the upper surface of the food and exert a little pressure.
Source: Culinary Institute of America

Sometimes while peeling or trimming, you may find yourself holding the food in the air, above the cutting surface. The guiding hand will hold and turn the food against the blade. Make sure the food, your hands, and the knife handle are all dry.
Source: Culinary Institute of America

The guiding hand is also used to hold a carving or kitchen fork when disjointing or carving cooked meats and poultry. The tines of the fork can be either laid across the surface or inserted directly into the food to hold it in place.
Source: David Murray and Jules Selmes/Image Partners 2005/Dorling Kindersley Media Library/Dorling Kindersley

Your choice of knife grip depends on the particular task, the specific knife, and your personal preferences. There are the three basic grips. While one hand holds the knife and makes the cuts, the other hand controls the food you are cutting.

READING CHECKPOINT *What are four ways the guiding hand is used in cutting with a knife?*

Knife Safety

1. Always hold a knife by its handle.
2. Never try to catch a falling knife.
3. When passing a knife to someone else, lay the knife down on a work surface and allow the other person to pick it up.
4. If you must carry an unsheathed knife in the kitchen, hold it straight down at your side with the sharp edge facing behind you.
5. Never borrow a knife without asking permission, and always return it promptly after using it.
6. Do not allow the blade of a knife to hang over the edge of a table or cutting board.
7. Do not use a knife as a tool to open bottles, loosen drawers, and so on.
8. Do not leave knives loose in areas where they cannot easily be seen or wouldn't be found normally (in a filled sink, under tables, on shelves).
9. Never store or use a knife above waist level.
10. Always cut away from your body.

Source: Culinary Institute of America

Chef's Tip

Safe Slicing

To slice safely, place the flat side of the food down so it won't slip. For rounded or irregular food, cut off a piece to create a flat surface.

Making the Cut

The purpose of using a knife is to make a food smaller and to shape a food. Small, uniform pieces will cook evenly; large, irregularly shaped pieces won't. A uniform size also makes the finished product visually attractive.

Sometimes preliminary trimming, peeling, or squaring off is necessary to make the actual cuts easier. Foods with a uniform texture once they are peeled and trimmed (such as potatoes, carrots, celery, and turnips) can be cut by using the techniques described here. Foods that grow in layers (such as onions) or have pits, cores, or seeds (such as avocados or apples) all require special variations of these techniques. Meat, fish, and poultry that are still on the bone also call for special cutting and carving techniques. Special cutting techniques for these foods are covered in other chapters.

The following are the four basic types of cuts:

- Slicing
- Chopping and mincing
- Precision cuts
- Decorative cuts

Slicing Slicing cleanly through food should be no problem if a knife is properly sharpened. Simply guide the knife through the food, keeping the knife straight and even and letting the knife do the work. Adjust the length of your stroke and the pressure you exert on the food to suit the texture of the food you are slicing.

When you make clean, even slices, you can cut a wide range of foods from fruits and vegetables to meat and fish. Choose your knife carefully. Longer, thinner blades are best for very fine cuts or slices. Smaller blades are easier to manage with smaller foods.

Other food preparation equipment, such as meat slicers or specialty disks for food processors, can be used for slicing. These are especially helpful when a large number of uniform slices are required. A special slicing tool called a **mandoline** (MAHN-duh-lihn) is sometimes used for very precise slicing. It has extremely sharp blades that can be adjusted to achieve precise cuts and thicknesses.

Source: Culinary Institute of America

Mandoline

Chopping and Mincing Chopping usually refers to cutting food into pieces that are roughly but not exactly the same size. Although *chopping* is sometimes used interchangeably with the word *mincing*, minced food is generally smaller than chopped food. To chop or mince, keep the tip of the knife in contact with the board and lower the knife firmly and rapidly, making repeated small cuts until you get the desired fineness.

Precision Cuts Precision cuts are used when nearly perfect uniformity is required. The ability to produce neat, even cuts shows your skill and craftsmanship. More importantly, it means food cooks evenly and retains the best possible flavor, nutrition, color, and appearance as it cooks. The following are some precision cuts:

- **Rondelles.** Pronounced rahn-DELLS, **rondelles** is a French term meaning "rounds." The round shape is the result of cutting through any cylindrically shaped vegetable, such as a carrot or cucumber. To make rondelles, first trim and peel the vegetable. Then slice through the vegetable to make round pieces, or rondelles. Make sure each rondelle is the same thickness.

- **Variations of Rondelles.** Rather than cutting straight down to make a rondelle, you can cut down diagonally to make a **diagonal cut**. This exposes a greater surface area of the vegetable and is often used for Asian-style dishes. Some variations on the rondelle cut, such as *ripple* and **gaufrette** (go-FRET) cuts, require special blades on a mandoline, food processor, or slicer.

FIGURE 4-4
Rondelles
Slice through the vegetable to
produce a rondelle.

APPLYING CONCEPTS *Why should
each rondelle be the same thickness?*
Source: Culinary Institute of America

FIGURE 4-5
**Using a Mandoline to Make
a Gaufrette Cut**
"Gaufrette" is French for
"waffle."

PREDICTING *How do you think the
taste and texture of a fried gaufrette
potato would differ from that of a
French fry?*
Source: Culinary Institute of America

- **Chiffonade.** Used primarily to cut leafy greens and other ingredients into very fine shreds, the **chiffonade** (shiff-en-ODD) cut is done by hand. Chiffonade is different from shredding. The cuts are much finer and more uniform.

Making a Chiffonade Cut

① **Remove stems,** if stems are tough.

② **Stack** several leaves on top of each other.

③ **Roll** tightly.

④ **Slice** the rolled leaves, using narrow parallel cuts to produce fine shreds. Hold the rolled leaves tightly.

Source: Culinary Institute of America

Source: Culinary Institute of America

- **Julienne and Bâtonnet.** Both the **julienne** (ju-lee-EHN) and **bâtonnet** (bah-tow-NAY) cuts are long, rectangular cuts that both showcase a chef's cutting skills and allow the vegetables to cook evenly. French fries are a type of julienne cut. Fine julienne cuts are about $\frac{1}{16}$ inch thick, julienne cuts are about $\frac{1}{8}$ inch thick, and bâtonnet cuts are about $\frac{1}{4}$ inch thick.

Making Julienne and Bâtonnet Cuts

① **Trim vegetables** so their sides are straight. This makes it easier to make even cuts.

② **Slice vegetables lengthwise,** using parallel cuts of the proper thickness ($\frac{1}{8}$ inch for julienne, $\frac{1}{4}$ inch for bâtonnet).

③ **Stack the slices,** aligning the edges.

④ **Make parallel slices** through the stack ($\frac{1}{8}$ inch apart for julienne, $\frac{1}{4}$ inch for bâtonnet).

Source: Culinary Institute of America

The Oldest Tool Known to Man

Stone cutting tools unearthed in Kenya are believed to be nearly 3 million years old. They are considered the oldest human-made tools. The first knives were made mainly from flint, a particularly hard stone. Once humans learned mining skills, soft metals such as copper, lead, and gold were extracted from ore. Unfortunately, these soft metals did not make strong knives.

By about 3500 B.C.E., copper was being melted with tin to form bronze. Iron was blended with the other metals to give items more strength and to resist rusting. Eventually, carbon was added and a metal known as carbon steel was developed. It resembled modern wrought iron.

At first, steel was used mainly for weapons. But by about 1500 C.E., steel knives, forks, and spoons were used by wealthy people as cutlery. By the end of the 1800s, carbon steel of a consistent quality could be produced on a large scale. In the early 1900s, advancements in steel manufacturing made knives more durable and flexible—able to withstand the rigorous use of professional chefs today.

Research

Research the history of metals, paying particular attention to the development of carbon steel.

Stone Age knife
with serrated edge

Source: Culinary Institute of America

- **Dice.** When you cut a **dice**, you produce a cube-shaped piece of food. First, the food is cut into either julienne or bâtonnet, as described earlier. The smallest dice is called a **brunoise** (brewn-WHAZ), which

BASIC CULINARY SKILLS

Dicing

1. **Trim and peel** the food, if necessary.
2. **Cut into slices.** Make slices the thickness you want the finished dice to be.
3. **Stack the slices** on top of each other.
4. **Make parallel cuts** of the same thickness as you used in step 2. This produces sticks.
5. **Place the sticks side by side.**
6. **Make parallel cuts** across the sticks, holding them in place by using your guiding hand.

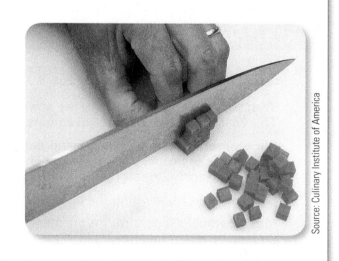

Source: Culinary Institute of America

means "to brown" in French. A brunoise is also known as a *fine dice* and is about ⅛ inch square. A fine brunoise is even smaller, only about ⅟₁₆ inch square. A medium dice is about ½ inch square, and a large dice, also called a **cube**, is at least ¾ inch square but can be larger. To make large dice or cubes, the bâtonnet cuts may range from ½ inch thick to 1 inch thick or more.

- **Paysanne and Fermière.** These cuts are generally used in older, more traditional dishes, as can be seen in their names. **Paysanne** (pahy-SAHN) means "peasant" in French, and **fermière** (FURM-ee-air) means "farmer." A paysanne cut starts with a bâtonnet that is ½ inch thick. Cut the bâtonnet at ⅛-inch intervals so you have a flat ½-inch square that is only ⅛ inch thick. A fermière has a bit more rustic look. To make this cut, start with a bâtonnet that shows the curved or uneven edges of the vegetable. Cut the bâtonnet into pieces that are ⅛ to ½ inch thick.

- **Lozenge.** The **lozenge** (LOZ-enj) **cut** is a diamond-shaped cut that is most often used in garnishes. To make this cut, start with slices that are about ¼ inch thick. Cut the slices into strips about ½ inch wide. Holding your knife at an angle to the strip, make parallel cuts to produce a diamond shape.

- **Oblique Cut.** The **oblique** (o-BLEEK) **cut**, or *roll cut*, creates a piece in which the cut sides of a vegetable are neither parallel (side by side) nor perpendicular (at right angles). This effect is achieved by rolling the vegetable after each cut (which is why the cut is some-times called a roll cut). This cut is used for long, cylindrical vegetables such as carrots. There are no specific dimensions for the oblique cut—the angle at which you choose to make the cuts is up to you, but the angle should be consistent with each piece.

Making an Oblique Cut

1. **Make a diagonal cut** to remove the stem end of the peeled vegetable.

2. **Roll** the vegetable 90 degrees (a quarter turn).

3. **Slice** the vegetable, using the same diagonal cut as you used in step 1, forming a piece with two angled edges.

4. **Roll** the vegetable 90 degrees and repeat the diagonal cut. Continue until the entire vegetable has been cut.

Source: Culinary Institute of America

Sample Cuts

Brunoise (Fine Dice)
⅛ × ⅛ × ⅛ inch
Source: Culinary Institute of America

Rondelles
Thickness varies
Source: Culinary Institute of America

Small Dice
¼ × ¼ × ¼ inch
Source: Culinary Institute of America

Diagonal Cut
Thickness varies
Source: Culinary Institute of America

Medium Dice
½ × ½ × ½ inch
Source: Culinary Institute of America

Oblique Cut
Size varies
Source: Culinary Institute of America

Large Dice (Cube)
¾ × ¾ × ¾ inch
Source: Culinary Institute of America

Lozenge
½ × ½ × ¼ inch
Source: Culinary Institute of America

Fine Julienne
1/16 × 1/16 × 1 to 2 inches
Source: Culinary Institute of America

Paysanne
½ × ½ × ⅛ inch
Source: Culinary Institute of America

Julienne
⅛ × ⅛ × 1 to 2 inches
Source: Culinary Institute of America

Fermière
⅛ to ½ inch
Source: Culinary Institute of America

Bâtonnet
¼ × ¼ × 2 to 2½ inches
Source: Culinary Institute of America

Decorative Cuts There are a few special cuts that a chef can use to produce a dish with a special look. These fine cuts are usually produced with a paring knife or a tournée knife.

- **Turned.** The turned cut is one of the most time-consuming cuts. It requires a series of precise cuts. The turned cut comes from the French verb *tourner*, meaning "to turn." Vegetables are cut into 2-inch pieces and are turned and cut so the end result is a football-like shape. Classic turned vegetables have seven sides, but the number of sides depends on the vegetables used. Turned vegetables can also have a flat bottom and only three or four curved sides.

- **Fluted.** To make fluted mushrooms, the mushroom cap is turned against the blade of a paring knife. This removes small strips from the cap, creating a ridged design.

- **Fans.** If you make slices through relatively soft foods, such as pickles or strawberries, without cutting all the way through one end, you can spread the sliced end of the food into a fan.

READING CHECKPOINT *What are the four basic types of cuts?*

FIGURE 4-6
Sharpening Stones
A three-faced stone is mounted on a rotating frame. Other sharpening stones have different grits on each side.

APPLYING CONCEPTS *When would a triple-faced stone be preferable to a two-faced stone?*

Source: Culinary Institute of America

Maintaining Knives

The mark of professional chefs is the attention they give to their tools. They keep knife edges in top condition by honing the knives frequently as they work, sharpening them when needed, taking them to a knifesmith when an edge needs to be rebuilt, and storing them properly. No professional chef would ever drop a knife into a sink of dishwater or put a knife away dirty.

Sharpening Knives with a Stone You give a knife an edge by using a sharpening stone (also called a **whetstone**). Stones are used to sharpen the edge once it has grown dull through ordinary use.

Sharpening stones are available in a variety of sizes, textures, and materials—both natural and manufactured. The relative coarseness or fineness of the stone's material is referred to as its **grit**. Large stones—some with several sides and a well for lubricating oil—can accommodate large or heavy blades. Smaller stones are more difficult to use on longer knives but are easier to transport.

Some chefs believe a knife blade should be run over a stone from the heel to the tip; others believe it should be run over the stone from the tip to the heel. Similarly, some

Measuring Angles

Angles are measured in degrees. Here's an easy way to remember an angle: think of a clock.

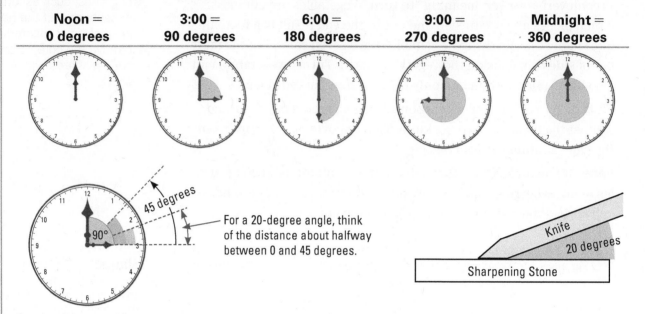

| **Noon =** 0 degrees | **3:00 =** 90 degrees | **6:00 =** 180 degrees | **9:00 =** 270 degrees | **Midnight =** 360 degrees |

45 degrees

90°

For a 20-degree angle, think of the distance about halfway between 0 and 45 degrees.

Knife

20 degrees

Sharpening Stone

Real-World Skills

Hold a knife blade at a 20-degree angle to a sharpening stone or a work surface.

chefs prefer to use a lubricant such as mineral oil on their stones, while others swear by water. Whichever way you prefer to run the blade over the stone, it is important to be consistent in the direction of the stroke. Water or mineral oil helps reduce friction as you sharpen your knife. Be consistent in the type of lubricant you use.

When using a sharpening stone, use a 20-degree angle for chef's knives and knives with similar blades. You may need to adjust the angle slightly to properly sharpen thinner blades, such as slicers, or thicker blades, such as cleavers.

Honing Knives with a Steel Between sharpenings, you maintain a knife's edge with a steel. A **steel** is a textured steel or ceramic rod used to keep the blade straight and to smooth out irregularities. A steel is also known as a *butcher's steel* or a *straightening steel*. Steels are not used to sharpen a knife's edge. They are used to straighten the edge, because with use, the knife's edge starts to roll over to one side. The process of straightening the knife's edge is called **honing** or **trueing**. Good chefs are in the habit of using a steel before they start any cutting task, as they work, and again before they store their knives.

Sharpening a Knife

1. **Position the stone** to keep it from slipping.

2. **Lubricate the stone** with mineral oil or water. The duller the blade, the coarser the grit of the stone you will need to start.

3. **Run the entire edge over the stone gently.** Use the coarsest grit you think you will need. Keep the pressure on the knife even and hold the knife at the correct angle (about 20 degrees). Use your guiding hand to maintain constant pressure.

4. **Make an equal number of strokes** on both sides of the blade. Use about 10 strokes.

5. **Switch stones.** Use an equal number of strokes on the stone with the next finer grit.

6. **Finish sharpening.** Use an equal number of strokes on the finest stone.

Source: Culinary Institute of America

7. **Hone the knife** to remove any burrs.

8. **Clean and sanitize** the knife and clean the stone before use or storage.

There are several honing techniques. The Basic Culinary Skill shown on page 122 is a method that is particularly suited to a beginning chef. Whichever method you use, always work in the same direction on each side of the blade. Always use a light touch, stroking evenly and consistently. Lay the blade against the steel; don't slap it. You should hear a light ringing sound. A heavy grinding sound means you are using too much pressure.

Keeping Knives Cleaned and Sanitized To keep your knives safe and in good condition, you must clean and sanitize them. Knives can harbor pathogens, which means that they are a potential source of cross-contamination. Regular and thorough cleaning and sanitizing removes pathogens before they can affect foods.

Clean knives in hot soapy water and dry them thoroughly between cutting tasks as well as after use and before storage. Sanitize the knife by wiping down the handle and blade with a sanitizing solution so the knife does not become a site for cross-contamination.

Don't clean knives in a dishwasher. Wooden handles can warp or split. Edges can be damaged by jostling. The high water temperatures of some dishwashers could make the blade come out of temper and more likely to break or shatter. Never drop a knife into a sink when cleaning pots. The knife could be dented or nicked by a heavy pot.

Storing Knives Proper knife storage prevents damage to the blade and harm to unwary individuals. There are a number of safe, practical ways to store knives: in knife kits or cases and in wall- or tabletop-mounted racks.

Source: cretolamna/Shutterstock

Steel

••FOCUS ON
••Safety

Washing Knives
Never put a knife in a sink when cleaning dishes. Someone reaching into the sink could be injured by the knife's blade.

Honing a Knife

1 **Hold the steel in a vertical position** with the tip resting on a nonslippery surface.

2 **Position the heel of the knife** against one side of the steel, near the handle.

3 **Draw the knife down the shaft** of the steel and out from the steel so the entire knife blade, including the tip, is honed. Maintain light pressure and use an arm action, not a wrist action, to draw the knife smoothly down the steel.

4 **Repeat** a few times for the first side of the knife.

5 **Repeat steps 2, 3, and 4 with the other side of the knife.** Use the same number of strokes as you used on the first side.

6 **Clean and sanitize** the knife.

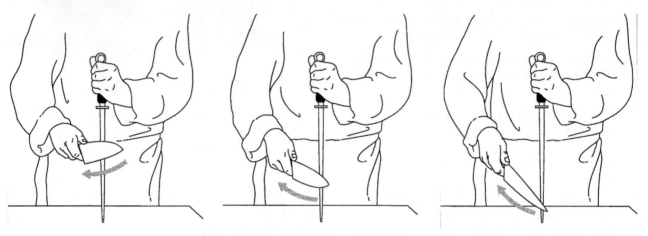

Draw the knife down the shaft while moving it out from the steel

- Knife guards or sheaths add an extra level of protection, especially when knives are stored loose in drawers.

- Choose a knife kit constructed of materials that are easy to clean and sanitize.

- Steel- and rubber-slotted holders are sanitary and can be washed and sanitized in the dishwasher.

- Mount slotted hangers on the wall, not on the side of a table where an exposed blade may be a safety hazard.

- Clean and sanitize sheaths, knife cases, and slotted knife holders often.

Maintaining the Cutting Surface Cutting boards should always be used when cutting foods. Cutting boards should be flat, with a smooth surface. If they become chipped or gouged, they should be either resurfaced or replaced. Wipe the board frequently as you work to remove peels, trim, and other debris.

There are safety standards concerning cutting surfaces. Fine-grain woods such as maple or oak are acceptable for use as a cutting surface, as long as they are properly cleaned and sanitized, according to the USDA Food Code. Porous

••FOCUS ON•• Safety

Cutting Board Safety

To keep the board from slipping or rocking as you work, lay it on a clean, dampened towel or rubber mat. Working on a warped cutting board is dangerous because it cannot be kept stable.

or softer woods such as pine are not acceptable, however. Composition cutting surfaces are also acceptable, and may be preferred in some operations because they can be washed and sanitized in warewashing machines.

When you switch from one type of food to another (from chicken to lettuce, for example), you should clean, rinse, and sanitize the board. Today, many kitchens use color-coded boards to help prevent cross-contamination. (These were discussed in Section 1.2 of this text.)

If the cutting surface is a butcher-block top or other large surface, first wipe down the entire surface with a scrub brush or scrubbing pad and a container of clean, soapy water. Using a scraper, lift away any residue. Wipe down the board carefully with a clean, damp cloth to remove any traces of soap. Finally, wipe down the entire surface with a clean cloth that has been wrung out in a sanitizing solution. To prevent sanitizing solution from becoming dirty too quickly, wipe down the board with a damp, clean cloth before swabbing with sanitizing solution.

READING CHECKPOINT *When is a sharpening stone used to maintain a knife?*

FIGURE 4-7
Knife Kit
A knife kit is a safe and practical way to store and transport your knives.

DRAWING CONCLUSIONS *Why might a chef be interested in transporting his or her knives?*

Source: Culinary Institute of America

4.1 ASSESSMENT

Reviewing Concepts

1. What are the main parts of a knife?

2. What are the eight basic types of knives and how are they used?

3. What are four ways the guiding hand is used in cutting with a knife?

4. What are the four basic types of cuts? Describe each.

5. When is a sharpening stone used to maintain a knife? When is a steel used?

Critical Thinking

6. Drawing Conclusions Why do you think chefs tend to use a chef's knife more than any other kind of knife?

7. Comparing and Contrasting What is the difference between a julienne cut and a bâtonnet cut?

8. Inferring Do you think a professional chef would tend to own a triple-faced sharpening stone?

Test Kitchen

Slice, chop, and dice a carrot, using a chef's knife. Now cut the same size pieces by using a paring knife. What are the differences?

LANGUAGE ARTS
Pronouncing French Terms

Many terms in the culinary world are French. Team up with a student who knows French, if possible. Practice your pronunciation of the French terms from this section: chiffonade, rondelles, julienne, bâtonnet, paysanne, tournée, gaufrette, fermière, and brunoise. When you are satisfied with your pronunciation, define each term.

4.2

Using Smallware

Key Concepts

- Selecting hand tools for specific tasks
- Selecting cookware for specific tasks
- Cleaning and sanitizing smallware

Vocabulary

- bain marie
- balance scale
- bimetallic-coil thermometer
- box grater
- braising pan
- casserole
- channel knife
- colander
- conical sieve
- conveyor belt dishwasher
- cookware
- corer
- crêpe pan
- custard cup
- double boiler
- drum sieve
- fish poacher
- food mill
- gauge
- gratin dish
- heat transfer
- kitchen shears
- liquid-filled thermometer
- melon baller
- microplane
- omelet pan
- palette knife
- Parisienne scoop
- pâté mold
- portion scale
- purée
- ramekin
- ricer
- roasting pan
- rubber spatula
- saucepan
- saucepot
- sauté pan
- sauteuse
- sautoir
- sheet pan
- single-rack dishwasher
- skimmer
- smallware
- soufflé dish
- spring scale
- steamer
- stockpot
- tare weight
- terrine mold
- thermistor thermometer
- thermocouple thermometer
- tongs
- turner
- undercounter dishwasher
- warewashing station
- whip
- whisk
- wok
- zest
- zester

READING PREVIEW

Source: Maksim Shebeko/Fotolia

Hand Tools

Hand tools, pots, and pans are often called **smallware**. The type of smallware used by a chef depends on the types of tasks the chef performs in the kitchen.

Culinary hand tools come in a huge variety. Although some hand tools are used in a home kitchen, others are more specialized and are not often seen outside a professional kitchen. Overall, hand tools can be broadly broken down into five general categories (specialized tools for baking and pastry are discussed in Section 17.1):

- Trimming and prep tools
- Shredding and grating tools
- Mixing and cooking tools
- Straining, draining, and processing tools
- Measuring tools

Selecting the smallware for any kitchen is an important task. The types of smallware needed in any kitchen will depend on the foods that are being prepared. It is important to have enough hand tools and other smallware to make it possible to complete the preparation of foods, from trimming and prep to cooking the dish either on the stovetop or in the oven. The materials used to make these tools help determine their durability. A kitchen often requires smallware in various sizes, depending on the size of the recipe that is being prepared. Be sure that all smallware items are properly maintained and that they meet all the appropriate safety requirements. Electric items should be easy to use and clean.

Trimming and Prep Tools There are many specialized hand tools for cutting and slicing food. Often the food served by a food establishment influences the types of specialized hand tools the establishment uses. For example, an Italian restaurant may require an olive pitter. A restaurant that specializes in apple-based products may require a specialized apple peeler, an apple corer, and an apple cutter.

Box grater

Shredding and Grating Tools Some foods can easily be shredded with a chef's knife. However, other more specialized tools, including slicers, mandolines, and mixers or food processors (with attachments) can also be used, particularly if a large amount of shredded food is required.

Grating is often done with the grater attachments on food processors and mixers. You could also use a **box grater**, a special hand tool for grating. A **microplane** is another general-purpose tool for grating food. Different types of graters and microplanes, whether specialized or general purpose, produce different types of results—from a coarse grate to a fine grate. Smaller openings in a grater are best for harder foods and make smaller, finer pieces. Larger openings are best for making large pieces and shreds. Specialized graters are available for specific tasks, such as grating nutmeg, cheese, or ginger. *Zesters* are handheld tools used to remove fine shreds of skin from lemons, oranges, and limes.

Mixing and Cooking Tools Chefs use mixers, blenders, and food processors to mix or blend food. They also use individual hand tools for mixing ingredients, including spoons and whips. When food is cooking, chefs use hand tools to stir the food to make sure that it is properly cooked. They also use hand tools such as ladles, skimmers, and turners for removing cooked food from the cookware in which it was cooked. Most of the mixing and cooking tools serve multiple purposes.

FIGURE 4-8

Microplane
A microplane being used to grate a lemon for lemon zest.

COMPARING/CONTRASTING *When would you use a microplane with small openings and when would you choose one with larger openings?*

Source: FoodPhotography Eisin/AGE Fotostock America Inc.

Trimming and Prep Tools

Peeler

A peeler cuts a thin layer from vegetables and fruits more efficiently than a paring knife. Peelers have a swiveling blade that moves easily over contours of food. If the blade is sharpened on both sides, it peels when moved in both an upward and a downward motion. Peelers are also used to make delicate garnishes, such as carrot or chocolate curls.

Source: Philip Wilkins/Image Partners 2005/Dorling Kindersley Media Library/Dorling Kindersley

Melon Baller

A **melon baller** scoops out smooth balls from melons, cheese, and butter. A melon baller with a scoop at each end, one larger than the other, is called a **Parisienne** (pah-REE-see-ehn) **scoop**.

Source: Culinary Institute of America

Olive Pitter

Olive pitters remove the olive pit by plunging a small rod through the olive. An olive pitter can also be used for pitting cherries.

Source: David Murray/Image Partners 2005/Dorling Kindersley Media Library/Dorling Kindersley

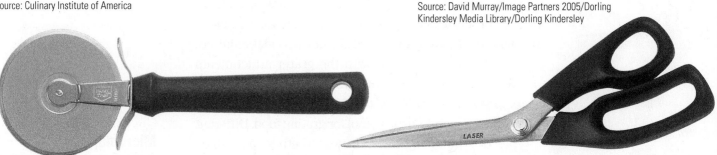

Pizza Cutter/Pastry Wheel

This handy tool is used to cut pizzas and pastry. Some cutters have plain edges and some are fluted to make decorative edges.

Source: Clive Streeter/Image Partners 2005/Dorling Kindersley Media Library/Dorling Kindersley

Kitchen Shears

Kitchen shears are handy for many kitchen chores, such as cutting string and butcher's twine, trimming artichoke leaves, cutting grapes into clusters, and trimming herbs. Poultry shears, a heavy-duty type of kitchen shears, can cut through the tight joints and ligaments of poultry.

Source: Dave King/Image Partners 2005/Dorling Kindersley Media Library/Dorling Kindersley

Channel Knife

A **channel knife** is used to cut grooves lengthwise in a vegetable such as a cucumber or carrot. A rondelle cut from the grooved vegetable has decorative edges that resemble a flower.

Source: Culinary Institute of America

Corer

A **corer** is used to remove the core of an apple or pear in one long, round piece. Corers are available in various sizes to use with small fruits like apples or larger fruits like pineapples. Some corers also cut the fruit into wedges or spears as they remove the core.

Source: ayedmoeed/Fotolia

Zester

A **zester** cuts away thin strips of the zest of citrus fruit peels. The **zest** is the colored outer layer of the peel.

Source: Neil Fletcher and Matthew Ward/Image Partners 2005/Dorling Kindersley Media Library/Dorling Kindersley

Fish Scaler

A fish scaler is used to remove the scales from a fish.

Source: Culinary Institute of America

Mixing and Cooking Tools

Mixing Bowls

Mixing bowls are usually made of a nonreactive material such as stainless steel. Glass, ceramic, or earthenware bowls may not be sturdy enough to use in a professional kitchen. (They can be used to serve prepared food.)

Source: Culinary Institute of America

Whisk

A **whisk** is a hand tool with thin wires in a sphere or an oval shape. It is used to add air to mixtures. Very round whisks add a large amount of air and are sometimes called *balloon whisks*. A narrower whisk is often referred to as a **whip**. Whips often have thicker wires and are used to blend sauces or batters without adding too much air.

Source: Dave King/Image Partners 2005/Dorling Kindersley Media Library/ Dorling Kindersley

Palette Knife

A **palette** (PAL-et) **knife** (also called a *straight spatula* or *flat spatula*) has a long, flexible blade with a rounded end. It is used for turning cooked or grilled foods and spreading fillings or glazes. (It is also used in baking.)

Source: Culinary Institute of America

Turners

A **turner** (also called an *offset spatula* or a *flipper*) has a broad blade and a short handle that is bent to keep the user's hands off hot surfaces. The blade can be perforated or unperforated. It is used to turn or lift hot foods.

Source: Culinary Institute of America

Rubber Spatula

A **rubber spatula** (SPAT-chew-la) has a broad, flexible blade. It is sometimes called a *scraper* and is used to scrape food from the inside of bowls and pans. Some have a blade made of silicone that can withstand high temperatures.

Source: Dave King/Image Partners 2005/Dorling Kindersley Media Library/ Dorling Kindersley

Skimmers

A **skimmer** has a perforated surface and is used to skim impurities from liquids. It is also used to remove cooked food or pasta from a hot liquid. Skimmers are sometimes referred to as *spiders*.

Source: Culinary Institute of America

Spoons

Spoons are used for mixing, stirring, scooping, and serving foods. They may be wooden or stainless steel and may be solid, perforated, or slotted.

Source: Culinary Institute of America

Tongs

Tongs are useful for picking up hot items such as meats or large vegetables. They are also used for the sanitary serving of such items as cookies or ice cubes.

Source: Culinary Institute of America

Kitchen Fork

A kitchen fork is used to move small pieces of meat from a grill or a broiler and to hold larger pieces of meat when cutting them.

Source: David Murray/Image Partners 2005/Dorling Kindersley Media Library/Dorling Kindersley

Straining, Draining, and Processing Tools

Food Mill

A **food mill** strains and purées foods at the same time. (To **purée** (pyur-AY) is to process the food until it has a soft, smooth consistency.) A food mill has a flat, curving blade that is rotated over a disk by a hand-operated crank. Professional models have interchangeable disks with holes of varying sizes.

Source: Culinary Institute of America

Drum Sieve

A **drum sieve** (SIV) is a tinned-steel, nylon, plastic, or stainless-steel screen stretched on an aluminum or wood frame. A drum sieve (also called a *tamis*) is used to sift dry ingredients or purée very soft foods.

Source: Culinary Institute of America

Conical Sieve

A **conical** (CON-i-cal) **sieve** (also called a *chinois*, *china cap*, or *bouillon strainer*) is also used to strain or purée foods. It is a very fine mesh sieve shaped like a cone.

Source: Culinary Institute of America

Colander

A **colander** (COL-un-der) is a large, perforated stainless steel or aluminum bowl, with or without a base, that is used to strain or drain foods.

Source: Culinary Institute of America

Ricer

A **ricer** is a device in which cooked food, typically potatoes, is pushed through a pierced container, resulting in rice-like pieces.

Source: Culinary Institute of America

Funnel

A funnel is used to pour liquid from a larger to a smaller container. Funnels come in various sizes and materials.

Source: Clive Streeter/Image Partners 2005/Dorling Kindersley Media Library/Dorling Kindersley

Straining, Draining, and Processing Tools There are many specialized hand tools for straining and draining foods. These tools are used with dry or liquid ingredients as well as with food that is in liquid. The delicate mesh of some strainers can be easily damaged. Never drop them into a sink, where they could be crushed or torn.

Chefs use mixers, blenders, and food processors to process foods, but they also use specialized hand tools for food processing, including sieves, food mills, and ricers. In some cases, the texture produced by these hand tools may be more desirable. Fine sieves are better at removing small fibers, while food mills and ricers may produce a more interesting, slightly coarser texture than food processors or blenders.

Measuring Tools Measuring is essential in every recipe, not only so a dish is prepared correctly, but also to help control the size and cost of a single portion. Measuring tools measure one of the following:

- Weight
- Volume
- Temperature

Hand Tools Measuring Weight

Portion Scale

A nondigital **portion scale** measures the weight of a small amount of food or an ingredient (typically a portion). Portion scales can typically be reset to zero so you can allow for the weight of a container or weigh more than one ingredient at a time. These scales have a spring and the amount of pressure on the spring is what causes the dial to move. That is why a portion scale may also be known as a **spring scale**.

Source: Paul Bricknell/Dorling Kindersley Media Library/Dorling Kindersley

Digital Scale

A digital scale (also called an *electronic scale*) provides a readout of the weight. Digital scales are usually considered more accurate than other types of scales. A small digital scale is often used as a portion scale.

Source: Culinary Institute of America

Balance Scale

A **balance scale** is typically used for weighing baking ingredients. The ingredients are placed on the left side and weights are placed on the right side. When the sides balance, the ingredients weigh the same as the weights.

Source: Clive Streeter/Getty Active/Dorling Kindersley Media Library/Dorling Kindersley

Hand Tools Measuring Volume

Measuring Cups and Spoons

Small stainless-steel measuring cups range from ¼ cup to 1 cup. Stainless-steel measuring spoons range from ¼ teaspoon to 1 tablespoon. Both the measuring cups and the spoons can be used to measure the volume of dry or liquid ingredients.

Source: Culinary Institute of America

Volume and Liquid Measures

Volume measures are typically made from metal and marked to show fractions. Volume measures are made in 8-, 16-, 32-, 64-, and 128-ounce sizes and are often marked every 4 or 8 ounces. Liquid measures also measure volume but usually have a pouring lip to make pouring liquids easier. They are usually transparent glass or plastic and come in 1-cup, 1-pint, 1-quart, 2-quart, and 3-quart sizes.

Source: Culinary Institute of America

Ladle

A ladle is used to portion liquids, such as sauces and soups. Ladles hold 1 to 16 ounces, depending on their size. Look for the measurement on the handle.

Source: Culinary Institute of America

Measuring Temperature

Thermistor Thermometer

A **thermistor** (therm-IS-tor) **thermometer** uses a resistor (a type of electronic semiconductor) to measure temperature. Thermistor thermometers give a fast reading (about 10 seconds) and can measure the temperature of thin and thick foods. They are not designed to stay in the food while cooking.

Source: Culinary Institute of America

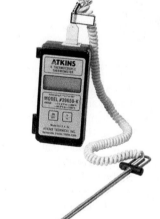

Thermocouple Thermometer

A **thermocouple** (THER-mo-cup-ul) **thermometer** uses two fine wires within the probe to measure temperature. Thermocouple thermometers give the fastest readings (2 to 5 seconds) and can measure the temperature in thin and thick foods. They are not designed to stay in the food while cooking.

Source: Culinary Institute of America

Bimetallic-Coil Thermometer

A **bimetallic-coil thermometer** uses a metal coil in the probe to measure temperature. Bimetallic-coil thermometers are available in an oven-safe version that can stay in food while cooking. They give slower readings (1 to 2 minutes) and should be used for food that is at least 2 to 2½ inches thick. An instant-read version is not oven-safe and gives a reading in 15 to 20 seconds.

Source: Culinary Institute of America

Liquid-Filled Thermometer

Liquid-filled thermometers are the oldest type of thermometer. They have either a glass or metal stem filled with a colored liquid. They are designed to stay in the food while cooking. Because they can present a safety hazard, glass-stemmed thermometers are less commonly seen in professional kitchens.

Source: Culinary Institute of America

Calibrating a Thermometer

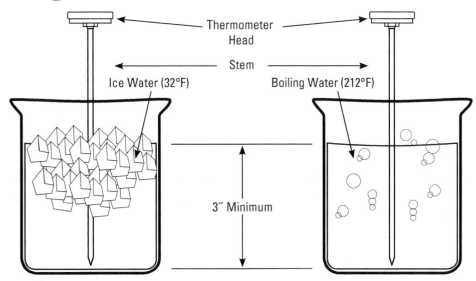

Thermometer Head

Stem

Ice Water (32°F)

Boiling Water (212°F)

3″ Minimum

Most professional bimetallic thermometers are calibrated by using a wrench and the adjusting nut under the dial. Calibration involves making sure the thermometer actually records the temperature accurately.

In the following Lab Activity, for true accuracy, distilled water should be used. The presence of substances other than water has the effect of raising the boiling point of water and lowering the freezing point. The boiling point is also affected by how far you are above sea level. The boiling point is the point at which vapor pressure (the steam rising from the surface of the water) equals the atmospheric pressure (the pressure from the atmosphere above the water). The higher you go, the less atmosphere there is to push down against the water. That means that at higher elevations, the boiling point of water will be less than 212°F above sea level.

Calibrate a thermometer before its first use, if it is dropped, or at regular intervals whenever its accuracy is in question. For specific calibration instructions on all thermometers, consult the manufacturer's instructions.

Lab Activity

1. Check with the local cooperative extension service or health department for the exact temperature of boiling water for your area's atmospheric pressure.

2. Fill a glass with crushed ice. Add distilled water until you have at least 3 inches of water. Stir well. Insert the thermometer and wait until the temperature stops dropping and becomes steady (this depends on the type of thermometer you are testing). Without removing the thermometer, adjust it until the dial reads 32°F.

3. Fill a pot with at least 3 inches of distilled water. Heat to boiling. Using tongs and an oven mitt, hold the thermometer in the boiling water. Be careful not to scald your hand. If possible, adjust the thermometer while it is in the boiling water until the dial reads 212°F. It may be necessary to take the thermometer out of the water, adjust, and test again until the thermometer is calibrated.

If you use a container to hold the food as you weigh it, you must adjust for the weight of the container. This is known as the **tare weight**. To do this, place the empty container on the scale and then adjust the weight to zero. On digital scales, you will simply press the button for tare. For balance scales, you will place counterweights on the right side until the balance is set to zero. For portion scales, you reset the dial to zero.

What are the five general categories of hand tools used in the kitchen?

Chef's Tip

Avoiding Warps

To keep pots, pans, and oven cookware from warping, never subject them to temperature extremes (leaving them over direct heat for long periods) or rapid temperature changes (plunging a hot pot into water).

Cookware

Pots and pans are often referred to as **cookware**. Pans usually have flat bottoms, one long handle, and low sides that may be curved or straight. Pots are usually taller than pans and have straight sides. They usually have two handles.

Choosing the correct cookware for a dish is an important skill. For any cooking task, a chef must first consider the size of the cookware. Foods should fit the pan comfortably. The depth of the pan will determine whether it is appropriate. Tall pots and pans are best for dishes that require a lot of liquid, such as soups and deep-fried dishes, while shorter pans are best to get a crisp surface when a dish is cooked in a small amount of oil or for foods that need to be turned as they cook.

In addition to considering cookware's size, a chef must also keep in mind the rate of **heat transfer**, or how efficiently heat passes from the cookware to the food inside it. Some pans are made of materials that react to changes in temperature quickly, and others are capable of holding the heat for a more consistent cooking temperature. This is determined partially by the cookware's material and partially by its **gauge** (GAGE), or the thickness of the material. The thinner the gauge, the faster the cookware heats, but the faster it cools off. For quick cooking, choose a pan that transmits heat quickly and is sensitive to temperature changes. Moderate gauge works well. For slow cooking, choose a pan that holds heat well and transmits heat evenly. Heavy gauge is best.

Pans used in ovens are produced from the same basic materials used to make stovetop pots and pans. However, because the oven's heat is indirect, it is also possible to use glass and ceramic pans and molds without risk of cracking and shattering them.

For every cooking task, a chef must choose cookware that is an appropriate size, made from appropriate material, and in an appropriate gauge. Another consideration for chefs is that some cookware is made from materials that react with food. Commonly used materials for cookware include the following:

- **Copper.** Copper transfers heat rapidly and evenly. Because copper can react with high-acid food to create toxic substances, most copper pans are lined with a nonreactive metal. Copper discolors quickly. Proper upkeep requires a lot of time and labor.
- **Cast Iron.** Cast iron holds heat well and transmits it very evenly. Cast iron is brittle, however, and must be treated carefully to avoid pitting, scarring, and rusting. Cast iron is sometimes coated with enamel to increase its life and make cleaning easier.

Cast-iron skillet

Cookware Stovetop Cooking

Stockpot

A **stockpot** is a large pot that is taller than it is wide and has straight sides. Some stockpots have a spigot at the base so the liquid can be drained off without lifting the heavy pot.

Source: Culinary Institute of America

Saucepot

A **saucepot** is similar in shape to a stockpot, although it is not as large. Saucepots have straight sides and two loop-style handles to ease lifting.

Source: Culinary Institute of America

Saucepan

A **saucepan** has straight or slightly flared sides and a single long handle.

Source: Culinary Institute of America

Sauté Pans

A **sauté pan** is a shallow, general-purpose pan that comes in two types. A **sauteuse** (SAW-toose) is a wide shallow pan with sloping sides and a single long handle. A **sautoir** (SAW-twahr) has straight sides and a long handle and is often referred to as a *skillet*.

Sources: (top) Culinary Institute of America; (bottom) Dorling Kindersley/Image Partners 2005/Dorling Kindersley Media Library/Dorling Kindersley

Wok

A **wok** has high, sloped sides, which make it great for quick stir-frying. Once one ingredient cooks, you can push it up the sides, leaving the hot center free for another ingredient.

Source: Dorling Kindersley/Image Partners 2005/Dorling Kindersley Media Library/Dorling Kindersley

Omelet Pan or Crêpe Pan

An **omelet pan** or **crêpe** (KRAYP) **pan** is a shallow skillet with very short, sloping sides. A nonstick coating is often used in these pans.

Source: Culinary Institute of America

Double Boiler

A **double boiler** is actually a pair of nesting pots. The bottom pot is filled with water and heated, providing steady, even heat for the top pot. A double boiler is often referred to as a **bain marie** (BANE ma-REE).

Source: Roger Phillips/Image Partners 2005/Dorling Kindersley Media Library/Dorling Kindersley

Steamers

A **steamer** is a set of stacked pots or bamboo baskets with a tight-fitting lid. The upper pots or baskets have perforated bottoms so steam can gently cook or warm the contents of the pots or baskets. In a metal steamer, water is placed in the bottom pot and it is placed on the range.

Sources: (top) David Murray and Jules Selmes/Image Partners 2005/Dorling Kindersley Media Library/Dorling Kindersley; (bottom) C Squared Studios/Photodisc/Getty Images

Fish Poacher

A **fish poacher** is a long, narrow, metal pan with a perforated rack used to raise or lower the fish so it doesn't break apart.

Source: Roger Phillips/Image Partners 2005/Dorling Kindersley Media Library/Dorling Kindersley

Oven Cooking*

Roasting Pan

A **roasting pan** is used for roasting and baking. Roasting pans have low sides and are made in various sizes. Roasting racks are placed inside the pan to hold foods as they cook so the bottom, sides, and top of the food all are cooked evenly.

Source: Dave King/Image Partners 2005/Dorling Kindersley Media Library/Dorling Kindersley

Sheet Pan

A **sheet pan** is an all-purpose baking pan. Sheet pans are shallow, rectangular pans with sides that are generally no higher than 1 inch. They may be full, half, or quarter size.

Source: Culinary Institute of America

Terrine Mold

A **terrine** (teh-REEN) **mold** is traditionally made of pottery but can also be made of metal, enameled cast iron, or ceramic. Terrines are produced in a wide range of sizes and shapes; some have lids.

Source: Culinary Institute of America

Soufflé Dish, Ramekin, and Custard Cup

A **soufflé** (soo-FLAY) **dish**, **ramekin** (RAM-i-kin), or **custard cup** is round and straight-edged. All three come in various sizes. Disposable versions made of aluminum are common.

Source: Roger Phillips/Image Partners 2005/Dorling Kindersley Media Library/Dorling Kindersley

Braising Pans and Casseroles

A **braising** (BRAYZ-ing) **pan** and a **casserole** (CASS-a-roll) typically have medium-high walls and lids to keep the moisture in. They may be made of various materials.

Source: David Murray/Image Partners 2005/Dorling Kindersley Media Library/Dorling Kindersley

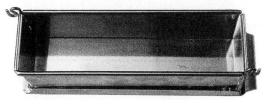

Pâté Mold

A **pâté** (pa-TAY) **mold** is a deep, rectangular metal mold. Some pâté molds have hinged sides.

Source: Culinary Institute of America

Gratin Dish

A **gratin** (GRAH-ten) **dish** is a shallow ceramic, enameled cast iron, or enameled steel baking dish.

Source: Tim Ridley/Image Partners 2005/Dorling Kindersley Media Library/Dorling Kindersley

*Baking pans used in making bread, pastries, and desserts are discussed in Chapter 17.

- **Stainless Steel.** Although a poor and uneven heat conductor, stainless steel is often used for cookware because it is easy to clean. Sometimes copper or aluminum is sandwiched in the bottom of the pan or pot to improve heat conductivity. Stainless steel will not react with foods.

- **Steel.** Other types of steel (blue steel, black steel, pressed steel, and rolled steel) transmit heat rapidly and are preferred when food must be heated quickly. These pans are generally thin and are prone to discoloration.

- **Aluminum.** An excellent heat conductor, aluminum is a soft metal that wears down quickly. It also reacts with foods. When a metal spoon or whip is used to stir a white or light-colored sauce, soup, or stock in an aluminum pot, the food may turn gray. Treated aluminum (often referred to as *anodized aluminum*) tends not to react with foods and is popular.

- **Nonstick Coatings.** A final consideration for chefs is the use of nonstick coatings in cookware. Nonstick coatings can be useful in cookware but require the use of wooden, plastic, or silicone utensils to protect the surface and extend the pan's life.

Source: Antonio Gravante/Fotolia

Pan with nonstick coating

 **READING CHECKPOINT** *What are some types of cookware used for stovetop cooking? For oven cooking?*

Cleaning and Sanitizing Smallware

Some foodservice establishments clean smallware by hand. Other establishments use a dishwasher to clean smallware.

Washing by Hand Even though smallware can be cleaned by hand, it is still important to thoroughly clean and sanitize it to prevent cross-contamination. A three-compartment sink is required for thorough cleaning and sanitizing. Some sinks may have four compartments instead of three. In that case, the first sink is used to scrape and pre-rinse dishes and smallware. This sink often has a garbage disposal unit. Some sinks with counter space provide holding areas for dirty and clean dishes. Dish carts often double as holding areas.

First, scrape food waste into a lined garbage can. Then rinse dishes and smallware in a sink. Some sinks have disposals mounted in sink drains, which may run in batches or continuous mode. They grind up food from rinsed dishes and smallware. Manufacturers recommend against grinding solid bones, fruit pits, and other large, hard objects. Be careful to keep silverware out of disposals.

When using a three-compartment sink, follow these general steps to clean and sanitize most smallware:

1. Clean and sanitize the sink area.

2. Scrape and pre-rinse smallware.

FIGURE 4-9

Three-Compartment Sink
A three-compartment sink is used for scrubbing pots and pans.

APPLYING CONCEPTS *Why is it important to replace the sanitizing solution according to the manufacturer's instructions?*

Source: Vincent P. Walter/Pearson Education/ PH College

3. Fill the first sink with 110°F water and detergent. Wash the smallware thoroughly with a brush. Drain and refill the water as needed.

4. Fill the second sink with water that is also about 110°F. Rinse the smallware to remove all traces of detergent.

5. Fill the third sink with water at the temperature specified by the manufacturer of your sanitizing agent. Add the recommended amount of sanitizing agent (chlorine or iodine). Submerge the smallware in the third sink for about 30 seconds.

6. Remove and air-dry smallware in a clean area. (Do not towel-dry. This can recontaminate smallware.)

Dishwashers A foodservice business needs to clean a flow of dirty tools, pots and pans, and dishes every day. The business usually establishes a **warewashing station** (also called a *scullery*) that provides rinsing, washing, and holding areas. The station also includes trash cans, sinks, garbage disposals, and professional dishwashing equipment. The dishwashing staff scrape and rinse plates and load the dishwasher. The equipment uses water at a high temperature to sanitize smallware and dishes. Clean dishes are then held on carts or shelves, ready for the wait staff.

Typically, three types of dishwashing equipment may be used in a professional kitchen:

- **Undercounter Dishwashers.** An **undercounter dishwasher** holds portable dish racks that allow for the easy transfer of clean and dirty dishes. Specialized glass washers are available.

- **Single-Rack Dishwashers.** A **single-rack dishwasher** processes small loads of dishes quickly. Scraped and rinsed dishes are placed in the upper compartment. The washer begins when the door is closed. Clean dishes are ready in minutes.

- **Conveyor Belt Dishwashers.** A **conveyor belt dishwasher** can process a high volume of dishes in a continuous flow.

Some dishwashers have the option of various cycles, depending on what you are washing. These cycles determine the water temperature as well as the length of the cycle. Choose the right cycle for your needs, if that is an

FIGURE 4-10
Conveyor Belt Dishwasher
These dishes are emerging from a conveyor belt dishwasher.

APPLYING CONCEPTS *Why is it important for the dishwasher to use water at high temperatures in the process of washing smallware and dishes?*

Source: Vincent P. Walter/Pearson Education/ PH College

option. Be sure that items going into the dishwasher are scraped. It is a good idea to rinse them with water. Some dishwashing setups include an area to load a rack that is over a sink along with a hand sprayer.

Load dishwashers properly. If items are stacked too tightly or piled up on top of each other, the water will not be able to reach all the surfaces. Make sure that any small items or sharp items are securely loaded so they will not fall out of the rack and into the washing unit. Load light plastic items so they cannot drop down onto the heating element. They will melt in contact with the unit.

Even though dishwashers are usually hot enough to clean and sanitize dishes, it is important to clean and sanitize the dishwasher itself. Keep all surfaces clean of debris. Wipe down the inside and outside surfaces of the dishwasher with a sanitizing solution. If hard water starts to build up, use a product that removes this scale and follow the manufacturer's instructions.

READING CHECKPOINT *What is the general method for cleaning and sanitizing smallware?*

4.2 ASSESSMENT

Reviewing Concepts

1. Identify the five general categories of hand tools.
2. List at least six types of cookware used for stovetop cooking.
3. What is a warewashing station?

Critical Thinking

4. **Applying Concepts** Explain the concept of heat transfer and gauge as it applies to cookware.
5. **Comparing/Contrasting** List the pros and cons of aluminum, stainless-steel, copper, and cast-iron cookware.
6. **Inferring** Why is a ladle regarded as a measuring tool?

Test Kitchen

Slice 2 ounces of Cheddar, using a chef's knife. Shred the same amount of cheese, using a mandoline. Grate the same amount of cheese, using a box grater (or the disks on a food processor). Compare the results and the amount of effort required to produce those results.

SCIENCE
Heat Transfer

Gather three 12-inch skillets: a cast-iron skillet, an aluminum skillet, and a stainless-steel skillet. Turn the stove burner to high. Place 1 tablespoon of water in each skillet. Use a stopwatch to record the amount of time it takes for the water to begin to sizzle after you place each skillet on the burner. Place only one skillet on the burner at a time and make sure to use an oven mitt when handling hot skillets. Analyze your data to rank the skillets' ability to transfer heat.

PROJECT 4 **Knife Skills** You are now ready to work on Project 4, "Knife Skills," which is available in "My Culinary Lab" or in your *Student's Lab Resources and Study Guide* manual.

Reviewing Content

Choose the letter that best answers the question or completes the statement.

1. Professional-quality knife blades are most often made from
   a. steel.
   b. pure iron.
   c. stainless steel.
   d. high-carbon stainless steel.

2. Which one of these is not found on a knife?
   a. stirrup
   b. tang
   c. rivets
   d. bolster

3. Which one of these knives has a long, thin blade?
   a. chef's knife
   b. slicer
   c. scimitar
   d. cleaver

4. Which one of these cuts is most time-consuming to execute?
   a. julienne
   b. bâtonnet
   c. turned cut
   d. rondelle

5. Which material is the poorest conductor of heat?
   a. aluminum
   b. copper
   c. cast iron
   d. stainless steel

6. Which utensil is used to make melon balls?
   a. zester
   b. Parisienne scoop
   c. palette knife
   d. mandoline

7. Which cookware has straight or slightly flared sides and a single long handle?
   a. stockpot
   b. wok
   c. saucepan
   d. saucepot

Understanding Concepts

8. What are the basic parts of a knife?

9. List at least seven knife safety points.

10. What are the four basic types of cuts?

11. Name and describe at least five precision cuts.

12. What is the difference between sharpening and honing a knife? When is it appropriate to sharpen knives? To hone them?

13. List the five general categories of hand tools and provide an example of each.

14. List five examples of cookware for stovetop cooking and five examples of cookware for oven cooking.

Critical Thinking

15. **COMPARING/CONTRASTING** If you could choose only two types of knives for your use in the kitchen, what would they be? Why?

16. **COMPARING/CONTRASTING** Of the five general categories of hand tools, which do you think is the most important? Why?

On the Job

17. **APPLYING CONCEPTS** You are cooking roast beef in an oven and want to make sure that it is cooked perfectly. What type of thermometer would you use? Describe how you would use the thermometer and what advantages your choice would have compared to other thermometers.

Culinary Math

18. **SOLVING PROBLEMS** A carrot has been squared off. It is now 4 inches long and 1 inch thick. You need to cut it in a medium dice. About how many individual diced squares will the carrot produce?

Cutlery, Restaurant Supplies, and Culinary Rentals

For many culinary professionals, a trip to a cutlery shop or a restaurant supply company is like a trip to the candy shop.

Cutlery and kitchen tools shops You may find long rows of gleaming knives hanging on the shelves featuring the products from famous knife manufacturers from around the world, such as Wusthof-Trident from Germany, Sabatier from France, Shun from Japan, and Victorinox from Switzerland. In addition to knives, these shops also carry a wide array of products from aprons to terrine molds that appeal to professional chefs as well as cooking enthusiasts. These shops offer services such as knife sharpening and repair.

Restaurant supply houses Restaurant supply houses carry almost anything that may be important in a restaurant, including refrigeration units, worktables, glassware, and china. Some of these stores are open to the general public; others are geared exclusively toward restaurants, hotels, and large-volume cooking operations such as cafeterias.

Source: Culinary Institute of America

Cutlery section of a kitchen tools store

Culinary rentals

Caterers often face special challenges when it is time to produce an event that includes food and drink for large numbers. Even if the operation has a dedicated banquet room, a caterer may be stretched and need to acquire additional glassware, flatware, or service ware. Caterers that produce events outside a banquet hall or banquet room, such as those who cater weddings at a client's home, have even greater needs. They may need tents, portable refrigeration, dance floors, tables and chairs, and more.

Entry-Level Requirements

While there are no absolute requirements to succeed in culinary retail and rental jobs, your customers may well have sophisticated tastes and exacting requirements. A basic understanding of kitchen operations and quality standards for the preparation and presentation of foods is a good start. You will be expected to know about the materials and construction of tools including knives and coffeemakers. Your customers will rely on you to help them find the right tool for the job. Outfitting a kitchen, whether a home kitchen or a volume operation, represents a big investment on the part of the client. Your abilities in knife sharpening, modification, or construction often depend on an apprenticeship with a knifesmith or metalworker.

Helpful for Advancement

Your goal may be to open your own business, manage a restaurant supply store, or establish a chain of rental operations. Studying business management, marketing, and advertising is a good idea. Attending trade shows related to the restaurant industry is a valuable way to learn about trends in kitchenware, catering, and restaurant operations that could have an impact on the goods and services you offer your customers. A master's degree in business management is not mandatory, but it is helpful for those who want to make their companies thrive and grow.

Source: Courtesy of Sean B. Nutley and Gregory Triana

Sean B. Nutley and Gregory Triana are the owners and operators of blue-cashew Kitchen Pharmacy in Rhine-beck, New York. Frequented by both culinary professionals and home enthusiasts, their shop is stocked with specialty kitchen equipment, service ware, and gadgets. Nutley and Triana carefully select merchandise to represent their brand and to provide a unique experience for their customers, regardless of culinary expertise or budget.

Sean B. Nutley
and Gregory Triana

Though neither Nutley nor Triana come from a professional culinary background, both have combined their love of food with strong professional backgrounds. With focuses in public relations and marketing, both Nutley and Triana worked in fashion and merchandizing, and they use their combined experiences to present sleek, stylized products to their customers.

Nutley and Triana opened bluecashew Kitchen Pharmacy in 2004, and it quickly doubled in size. Now a thriving community staple, the two credit their passion and drive for their success. As Triana said, "Listen to the path as it comes to you," and follow your interests to see where they will lead.

VITAL **STATISTICS**

Education: Sean B. Nutley: Degree in Public Relations from St. John's University; Gregory Triana: Degree in Marketing from Florida International University

Profession: Owners and operators, bluecashew Kitchen Pharmacy

Interesting Items: Considered opening a Cuban restaurant, but decided to open their store instead

Frequently host book signings and chef events at their shop, including Ted Allen, Gianni Scappin, and the Lee Brothers

Their shop is well-known for its music soundtracks, mixed by Triana

CAREER **PROFILE**

Salary Ranges

Entry Level: $25,000 to $35,000

Midlevel: $30,000 to $60,500 (or more)

Owner/Operator: Varies widely depending on the size of the store and the number of outlets you have for your goods

Using Standardized Recipes

5.1   Understanding Standardized Recipes

5.2   Converting Recipes

Source: John Davis/Dorling Kindersley

5.1

Understanding Standardized Recipes

Key Concepts

- Learning how kitchens find recipes
- Organizing recipes
- Understanding the sections of a standardized recipe
- Reading recipes
- Understanding measurement conventions and systems
- Understanding measuring techniques

Vocabulary

- household units
- portion
- recipe
- standardized ingredients
- standardized recipe
- tare weight
- volume
- yield

Finding Recipes

A **recipe** is a written record of the ingredients and preparation steps needed to make a particular dish.

Chefs collect and adapt recipes from a number of sources (including collecting them from other chefs and restaurants). The following are five common sources of recipes:

- **Cookbooks.** Among the best sellers in publishing, cookbooks are available in bookstores and libraries. Cookbooks may be written for use in professional kitchens or for home cooks. Some are considered general purpose. Others may feature a specific cuisine, ingredient, or cooking style.

- **Periodicals.** Newspapers and magazines that target the general public often feature recipes. Trade magazines and journals meant for caterers, chefs, bakers, and other foodservice professionals also publish recipes.

- **Food Producers and Manufacturers.** It makes sense that the producers of

Source: Stockbyte/Getty Images

Source: Andy Crawford/Dorling Kindersley Limited

food and the manufacturers of foodservice equipment would offer recipes to encourage the use of their products. They may be published as part of a newspaper or magazine advertisement, in a booklet, or through a website.

- **Cooking Contests.** A variety of organizations sponsor cooking contests. They generally publish winning recipes in cookbooks, in periodicals, and on the Internet. Reality shows like *Top Chef* are also a form of contest, and recipes are often reproduced in articles, cookbooks, and on websites.

- **The Internet.** The Internet contains many free recipes and recipe databases as well as a growing number of subscription services. You may be able to create and organize your own recipe collection on these sites. Cooking-related websites are produced by organizations such as the Food Network, cookbook authors including Mark Bittman, and bloggers such as Amanda Hesser at Food52.

 **READING CHECKPOINT** *What are some common sources for recipes?*

Organizing Recipes

Chefs often have large recipe collections that come from a number of different sources. To get the most out of their collections, they need ways to organize recipes so that they can find them quickly and use them to create or update their menus. There are several ways to organize recipes. Some are as simple as putting printouts or copies of recipes into a notebook with tabbed dividers or using folders. Software applications that provide recipe management tools are another good option.

A recipe collection that is organized into groups is an important tool for any cook or chef. If a collection is properly organized, it is easy to find the recipe you need quickly.

Common Recipe Categories

Organizing Idea	Possible Recipe Categories
Regional or ethnic recipes	Mediterranean, Texas, Russian
Historic recipes	Medieval England, colonial America
Recipes using a specific main ingredient	Fish, chicken, broccoli, mushrooms
Recipes for specific parts of a menu	Starters, main dishes, side dishes, desserts
Recipes for specific types of meals	Breakfasts, brunches, lunches, dinners, receptions, buffets
Recipes using a specific cooking method	Roast, stir-fry, barbecue, braise, sauté
Recipes for specific types of dietary needs	Gluten-free, diabetic, vegetarian, vegan

Recipes can be grouped for easy retrieval in a recipe category. Kitchens, magazines, cookbooks, and chefs create their own categories. Recipe categories can be based on regional dishes, ethnic dishes, dishes based on the main ingredient, and the part of a menu for which the dish is suited.

READING CHECKPOINT *What are the benefits of organizing recipes into categories?*

Standardized Recipes

A **standardized recipe** is a recipe designed to suit the needs of an individual kitchen. Using and writing standardized recipes is a big part of a professional chef's work. This type of recipe is different from recipes you might

---

CULINARY SCIENCE

Recipes on the Internet

The Internet is such a big source of cooking information that a person hardly knows where to begin. Of course, typing keywords into a search engine will produce a host of suggestions. (Try entering "tomato soup" in a search program such as Google or Yahoo. You'll find more than 1 million references!) You can limit the number of results from a basic Internet search by adding more terms. For instance, you could search for "tomato basil soup," or "creamy tomato soup," or "tomato soup with rice." You will see that the results from your search are likely to point you to a number of different websites.

A well-established website organizes its recipes and other information in a number of ways. The larger the collection, the more ways it can be organized. That allows the users to find what they need quickly. One such site is Epicurious, a site affiliated with Condé Nast, the publisher of the food-oriented magazines *Gourmet* and *Bon Appétit*. Epicurious, which bills itself as "the world's best recipe collection," started building its database of recipes in 1994. The name *Epicurious* is partially drawn from Epicurus, the Greek philosopher. The term *epicure*, someone who enjoys the finest things, comes directly from his name, as does the term *epicurean*.

Some sites specialize in large-volume recipes meant for the professional kitchen. Unichef and

Source: NetPhotos/Alamy

StarChefs are two sites that are interesting to explore, but there are many, many more. No matter what the source of your recipe, it is important that it be rewritten so that it is based on the ingredients, equipment, and serving standards used in your restaurant.

Research

Visit Epicurious. Investigate its recipe categories. Print out three recipes, each from a different recipe category. Describe the standardized recipe format used by Epicurious.

---

find in a consumer publication, such as a book or magazine. It is customized to meet the needs of an individual kitchen and can be used to manage food purchasing, food production, food safety, and food cost more effectively.

Purpose of Standardized Recipes Standardized recipes help food-service businesses because standardized recipes do the following:

- Support consistent quality and quantity.
- Encourage efficient purchasing and preparation.
- Reduce costs by eliminating waste.
- Improve customer satisfaction by producing a consistent dining experience.
- Enable the wait staff to answer guests' questions accurately and honestly. (For example, the type of oil used in a dish may matter very much to a guest with allergies.)
- Provide accurate information that can be used to determine the costs of a recipe as well as of an individual portion.

Sections of a Standardized Recipe Standardized recipes may include a number of sections. *The red sections listed below appear in almost all standardized recipes.*

- **Title.** The title of the recipe identifies the food item or dish.
- **Recipe Categories.** By identifying possible recipe categories, you can group and organize recipes in a way that makes retrieval easier. Sometimes recipes for simple items or items used in other recipes are classified as basic recipes. For example, a restaurant may have a basic recipe for boiled rice, baked potatoes, or a sauce.
- **Yield.** The **yield** of a recipe describes the measured output, expressed as one or more of the following: the total weight, the total volume, or the total number of portions. A **portion** is the serving size for one person expressed in pieces, weight, or volume.
- **Ingredients List.** This is one of the most important elements of a recipe. Ingredients are listed in the order in which they are needed. The ingredients list contains the name and amount of the ingredients you need. It may include advance preparation required (for example, trimming, peeling, dicing, melting, or cooling). It may also indicate a specific variety or brand. A standardized recipe shows the measurements as required for a recipe, however, so there may be additional work required in order to determine how much of an ingredient to purchase.
- **Equipment.** A recipe may list the equipment required for preparing, cooking, storing, holding, and serving an item. This information may be a separate list or may be indicated in other parts of the recipe. Often a recipe does not specify any particular equipment, and you will need to use your understanding of basic kitchen procedures to pick appropriate equipment.

•••FOCUS ON
•••**Nutrition**

Learning from Recipes
Recipes often list nutritional information about each dish. You can see how ingredients translate into calories, fat, carbohydrates, protein, vitamins, and minerals.

Blueberry Muffins

YIELD: 1 Dozen Muffins   **SERVING SIZE: 1 Muffin**

Ingredients

16 oz (3¾ cups)	All-purpose flour (plus 2 Tbsp to coat berries)
1½ tsp	Double-acting baking powder
½ tsp	Salt
¼ tsp	Nutmeg, ground
4 oz (½ cup)	Butter at room temperature
8 oz (1 cup)	Sugar
1	Egg, large
6 fl oz	Milk
½ tsp	Vanilla extract
1 cup	Blueberries, washed and patted dry
Optional	Cooking spray

Equipment

- **Appliances:** Oven, standing mixer with paddle attachment
- **Cookware:** Muffin tins, paper muffin tin liners, cooling rack
- **Hand Tools:** Scale *(optional),* measuring cups and spoons, sifter, mixing bowls, whisk, rubber spatula, 2-oz scoop

Method

1. Preheat the oven to 400°F.
2. Line muffin tins with paper liners or spray them lightly with cooking spray.
3. Sift together 16 oz flour with the baking powder, salt, and nutmeg.
4. Blend the milk, egg, and vanilla extract in a separate bowl.
5. In a standing mixer with a paddle attachment, cream together the butter and sugar until very light and smooth, about 2 minutes.
6. Add the flour mixture in three additions, alternating with the liquid ingredients, mixing on low speed and scraping down the bowl to blend the batter evenly.
7. Increase the speed to medium and mix until the batter is very smooth, another 2 minutes.
8. Mix 2 Tbsp flour with berries to coat them evenly.
9. Fold the blueberries into the batter, distributing them evenly.
10. Fill each muffin cup ⅔ full with batter using the 2-oz scoop.
11. Bake until the top of the muffin springs back when lightly pressed, 18 to 20 minutes.
12. Cool the muffins in the muffin pan on cooling racks for 5 minutes. Then remove them from the muffin pan and finish cooling them on the rack.

Serve warm or at room temperature. If desired, remove paper liner from muffin before serving. Store in an air-tight container with lid.

Recipe Categories

Muffins, Breakfast Foods, Blueberries

Chef's Tip

1. Coating blueberries with flour keeps them suspended in the batter so they don't all fall to the bottom of the muffin.
2. Shake baking powder before using. Ingredients can separate and need to be mixed for muffins to rise properly.

Potentially Hazardous Foods

- Egg
- Milk

HACCP

- Keep cold ingredients chilled below 41°F.

Nutrition	
Calories	195
Protein	3 g
Fat	9 g
Carbohydrates	26 g
Cholesterol	39 mg

Weight or Volume?

In the Blueberry Muffin recipe on the previous page, did you notice that there are two amounts shown for the flour, butter, and sugar? That's because the first measurement is for weight and the second measurement is for volume. But how do you know when a measurement is a weight and when it is a volume?

In a standardized recipe, dry ingredients that are more than a few tablespoons are usually shown by weight, not by volume. So, for example, the 16 oz of flour in the blueberry muffin recipe on the previous page is 1 lb of flour (16 oz = 1 lb; see "Weight Measurements" on page 151). However, the blueberry muffin recipe also shows the equivalent volume measurement of 3¾ cups. The rule is: When a measurement for a dry ingredient is in ounces, it's a weight measurement. If you don't have a scale, you need to convert the weight into volume (and this will differ for every ingredient).

Lab Activity

Weigh 16 oz of flour and 16 oz of puffed rice. Measure the volume of these equal weights. Can you see why it is important not to confuse a weight measure with a volume measure?

Chef's Tip

Service information is often included in the Method section, but may not appear in the Ingredient List. Read all recipes completely so that you are prepared with the appropriate accompaniment or garnish.

••FOCUS ON
•• Safety

Critical Control Points

Before you begin preparation, check the Method section for critical control points where specific temperatures or careful handling is essential to food safety.

- **Method.** This portion of a recipe includes the detailed steps required to make the dish. It may also list appropriate equipment and critical control points for safe food handling.

- **Service.** A recipe may include portioning information (if this information is not already listed in the Yield section of the menu), finishing and plating instructions, appropriate accompaniments (side dishes, sauces, and garnishes), and proper service temperatures.

- **HACCP.** As you learned in Section 1.3 of this book, Hazard Analysis Critical Control Point (HACCP) requires identification of critical control points (CCPs), or specific points in the process of food handling where you can prevent, eliminate, or reduce a hazard. A recipe may list the CCPs separately, or they may be included in the Method or Service sections. CCPs sometimes occur in the list of ingredients when potentially hazardous foods such as eggs or milk are used. Often when the recipe mentions temperatures and times for preparation, holding, storage, and reheating, a CCP is involved.

 **READING CHECKPOINT** *What elements appear in almost all standardized recipes?*

Reading Recipes

It is important to read a recipe before you begin preparation. This helps you work efficiently. You can plan your work and prepare the dish correctly. To understand and apply standardized recipes, use the PRN method for reading recipes.

PRN Method for Reading Recipes

Preview To get the big picture.

Read To focus carefully on the specifics of the recipe.

Note Write any adjustments and plans for preparation.

The following are some of the questions you may need to ask yourself as you read through a recipe:

- **Yield.** Does the recipe make enough or too much? (See the next section of this chapter to change the yield of a recipe.)

- **Ingredients.** Are you familiar with all the ingredients? Do you have all the ingredients? If not, can substitutes be used? Are you familiar with the appropriate preparation of all the ingredients? Some recipes may not list all the preparation steps; they rely on your knowledge to make appropriate choices.

- **Method.** Are you familiar with the techniques listed in the Methods section? Do you have all the necessary equipment? If not, is there an alternative method and will further adjustments be required in timing? (Chapter 8 describes most cooking methods called for in standardized recipes.)

- **Timing.** Do you have to adjust the recipe's timing? Which ingredients have to be prepared in advance? Do you need to preheat equipment?

- **Serving and Holding.** What do you do with the finished product? Do you have the appropriate accompaniment or garnish? Check any service and critical control point instructions.

If any of the questions you asked during your preview and read-through

FIGURE 5-1

Writing Notes
A chef writes notes about recipe adjustments or plans for preparation.

INFERRING *Why would a chef write down notes about adjustments to a recipe rather than just remembering the changes?*

Source: Doug Menuez/Getty Images

make you adjust the recipe in any way, jot down the changes you will make in the recipe.

 **READING CHECKPOINT** *Describe the PRN method for understanding a recipe.*

Measurement Conventions and Systems

Measurement Conventions Recipe ingredients are listed in a recipe according to one of three measuring conventions: count, volume, or weight. In addition to recipe measurements, there are measurements used when you buy ingredients. These measurements are referred to as *purchase units*.

- **Count.** When an ingredient is listed in the recipe based on the number of whole items, it is measured by count. Count is good for measuring **standardized ingredients**, which are ingredients that have been processed, graded, or packaged according to established standards. Eggs, shrimp, and butter, for instance, are standardized ingredients. For nonstandardized ingredients, count is less accurate. The weight of a peeled and cored apple, for example, depends on the size of the apple and the amount of waste. Similarly, one chef's small garlic clove might be another chef's medium garlic clove.

- **Volume.** The measurement of the space occupied by a solid, liquid, or gas is its **volume**. Volume measurements are best for measuring liquids and small amounts of dry ingredients such as spices or baking powder. Hand tools such as measuring cups, measuring spoons, ladles, and scoops are used to measure the volume of an ingredient.

- **Weight.** The weight of an ingredient is the measurement of its mass, or heaviness. Scales can weigh any ingredient, liquid or dry. Weight measures are typically preferred to volume measures because weight can be measured with greater accuracy.

Measurement Systems Weight and volume may be measured by using either the U.S. system or the metric system.

In the U.S. system, volume is measured in terms of fluid ounces (fl oz), pints (pt), quarts (qt), and gallons (gal). Recipes often use what are referred to as **household units** including teaspoons (tsp), tablespoons

FIGURE 5-2

Reading a Clear Measuring Cup

Read a glass measuring cup on a flat surface. Read with the mark at eye level.

DRAWING CONCLUSIONS *Why do you think volume measurements may be less accurate than weight measurements?*

Source: Pearson Education

Volume Measurements

Volume Measure	Metric Equivalent*	U.S. Equivalent*
U.S. SYSTEM		
1 teaspoon (tsp)	5 mL	⅙ fl oz
1 tablespoon (Tbsp)	15 mL	½ fl oz *or* 3 tsp
1 fluid ounce (fl oz)	30 mL	2 Tbsp *or* 6 tsp
1 cup	< ¼ L	8 fl oz *or* 16 Tbsp
1 pint (pt)	< ½ L	2 cups *or* 16 fl oz
1 quart (qt)	< 1 L	2 pt *or* 32 fl oz
1 gallon (gal)	> 3¾ L	4 qt *or* 128 fl oz
METRIC SYSTEM		
1 milliliter (mL)	1 mL	⅕ tsp *or* 0.0338 fl oz
¼ liter	250 mL	8.5 fl oz *or* > 1 cup
1 liter (L)	1000 mL	1.1 qt

U.S./metric conversions are approximate. 1 fl oz = 29.58 mL.

Weight Measurements

Weight Measure	Metric Equivalent*	U.S. Equivalent*
U.S. SYSTEM		
1 ounce (oz)	28 g	
¼ pound	112 g	4 oz
½ pound	224 g	8 oz
¾ pound	336 g	12 oz
1 pound (lb)	454 g	16 oz
METRIC SYSTEM		
1 milligram (mg)	0.001 g	
1 gram (g)	1 g	
⅛ kilogram	125 g	4.4 oz *or* > ¼ lb
¼ kilogram	250 g	8.8 oz *or* > ½ lb
½ kilogram	500 g	17.6 oz *or* > 1 lb
1 kilogram (kg)	1000 g	2.2 lb

U.S./metric conversions are approximate. 1 oz = 28.35 g.

In the U.S. system, weight is measured in terms of ounces (oz) and pounds (lb). In the metric system, weight is measured in terms of milligrams (mg), grams (g), and kilograms (kg).

Some recipes indicate quantities with simplistic abbreviations. For example, 1 teaspoon may appear as 1 tsp or simply 1 t. One tablespoon may appear as 1 Tbsp or 1 T. One cup may appear as 1 c. One gallon may appear as 1 gal or 1 G.

READING CHECKPOINT *About how many grams are in a ¼-pound hamburger patty? About what fraction of a kilogram is a 1-pound loaf of bread?*

Measuring Techniques

Use these techniques when measuring to ensure accuracy.

- **Dry Volume.** Overfill the measuring container and scrape off any excess. Some recipes call for packing (compressing) ingredients such as brown sugar or leafy greens.

- **Liquid Volume.** Set a clear measuring cup or other clear container on a flat surface. Reading with your eye at the level of the mark, fill to the mark.

- **Weight.** Choose a scale that suits the size of your food. Some scales are best for measuring ounces, others for pounds.

When using a food scale, be sure to account for the **tare weight**, the weight of the container holding the food. Place the container on the scale and reset the scale to zero. If your scale cannot be reset, note the tare and subtract it after weighing the food.

FIGURE 5-3

Using Scales

Scales usually display weight by using the U.S. system or the metric system.

PREDICTING *When might it be helpful to be able to display both weight systems?*

Source: Andy Crawford/Dorling Kindersley

Focus On Sanitation

Measuring Up

To avoid cross-contamination, clean and sanitize measuring tools between uses. Never let food come in direct contact with the scale. Always use a food tray, a container, a paper barrier, or plastic wrap on the scale.

Measuring Techniques

Measurement	Technique	Tools
Dry volume	1. Overfill container. 2. Scrape off excess.	Measuring cups, measuring spoons
Liquid volume	1. Set container on flat surface. 2. Fill to correct mark. 3. Inspect with eye level at mark. 4. Adjust as needed.	Graduated containers, measuring cups, measuring spoons
Weight	1. Set the tare. 2. Place food in container on scale. 3. Read weight and add or remove food.	Scale, food trays or containers to hold food on scale

Source: Ian O'Leary/Dorling Kindersley

READING CHECKPOINT *How would you measure ½ cup of flour? ½ pound of flour?*

5.1 ASSESSMENT

Reviewing Concepts

1. What is a recipe category? Give three examples of recipe categories.

2. What are the benefits of organizing recipes into categories?

3. What sections appear in most standardized recipes?

4. What are the steps in the PRN method for reading recipes?

5. How many quarts are in a gallon? Pints in a quart? Cups in a pint? Fluid ounces in a cup?

6. What is tare weight and why is it important in weighing ingredients for a standardized recipe?

Critical Thinking

7. Classifying List two foods that fit in more than one recipe category, and list the categories.

8. Inferring Explain how standardized recipes encourage efficient purchasing and preparation.

9. Solving Problems About how many liters are in a gallon?

Test Kitchen

Working in groups, record both the metric and U.S. weights of ¼ cup of each of the following: flour, white sugar, peanuts, popcorn, cooked white rice, dry white rice, water, fruit juice, and honey. Discuss the differences in weight between identical volume measurements. Discuss any differences in recorded weights by different groups.

LANGUAGE ARTS
Writing a Standardized Recipe

Write a standardized recipe for a simple dish you know how to prepare. Include all the sections that typically are used in a standardized recipe and as many other sections as you can.

5.2

Converting Recipes

Key Concepts

- Scaling recipes based on portion size
- Scaling recipes based on available ingredients
- Finding recipe yield based on available ingredients
- Using scaled recipes
- Finding the raw food cost
- Converting between professional and consumer versions of recipes

Vocabulary

- denominator
- edible quantity
- numerator
- purchase quantity
- purchase unit
- raw food cost
- recipe conversion factor (RCF)
- scale (a recipe)
- yield percentage

Source: Culinary Institute of America

Scaling Recipes Up or Down

Some days you may need to make more than your recipe calls for. Other days, you may need to make less. What do you do when your recipe's yield doesn't match your needs?

You can scale the recipe. To **scale** a recipe means you change the amount of ingredients to get the yield you need. You can scale up to increase the yield or scale down to decrease it.

Scaling a Recipe Up or Down

To scale a recipe up or down:

1. Find the **recipe conversion factor (RCF)**.

$$RC = \frac{\text{yield you want}}{\text{yield of original recipe}} = \frac{\text{new yield}}{\text{old yield}}$$

2. Multiply each ingredient amount by the RCF.

Try scaling a recipe now. First, you will scale up a basic recipe for boiled white rice. Then you will scale the recipe down.

RECIPE 125 CARD

Boiled White Rice

YIELD: 10 Serving   **SERVING SIZE: 1 Cup**

Ingredients

2½ cups	White rice
1 tsp	Salt
64 fl oz	Water

Recipe Categories
Boiled White Rice

Scaling Up Your kitchen's basic recipe calls for for boiling 2½ cups of rice, which yields 10 servings (each serving is 1 cup). However, you need 40 servings. How much of each ingredient do you need?

Scaling Up

To scale the recipe up:

1. Find the RCF.

$$\text{RCF} = \frac{\text{new yield}}{\text{old yield}} = \frac{40}{10} = 4$$

2. Multiply the amount of each ingredient by the RCF (as shown in the following table).

Scaling Up

Ingredient	Old Amount	RCF	New Amount
White rice	2½ cups	× 4	= 10 cups
Salt	1 tsp	× 4	= 4 tsp
Water	64 fl oz	× 4	= 256 fl oz

To make 40 servings, you will need 10 cups of rice, 4 tsp of salt, and 256 fl oz (2 gal) of water.

Converting Fractions

When we scaled a recipe up, the RCF was 40/20. You can change the form of this fraction to make multiplication easier.

You can either convert the fraction to a decimal, or you can simplify the fraction. Both methods give the same results.

Converting a Fraction into a Decimal

Divide the **numerator** (top number) by the **denominator** (bottom number).

$$\text{Numerator} \rightarrow \frac{40}{20} = 2 \leftarrow \text{Denominator}$$

Simplifying a Fraction

Divide both the numerator and denominator by the same factor.

$$\frac{40 \div 10 = 4}{20 \div 10 = 2}$$

Continue dividing until the fraction is in a convenient form. You can use a different factor, provided you divide both the numerator and the denominator by the same factor. This time, divide the numerator and denominator by 2.

$$\frac{4 \div 2 = 2}{2 \div 2 = 1} = 2$$

Computation

1. Convert the following fractions to decimals (you may have to round off): $5/20$, $30/15$, $25/5$, $16/32$, $15/12$, $8/40$, $4/9$, $5/27$.

2. Simplify the following fractions: $5/15$, $4/20$, $6/36$, $45/7$, $16/32$, $100/5$, $3/9$, $17/9$.

Scaling Down You will again use the basic recipe that yields 10 servings of boiled white rice. However, this time you need only 5 servings of boiled white rice. How much of each ingredient do you need?

Scaling Down

To scale the recipe down:

1. Find the RCF.

$$RCF = \frac{\text{new yield}}{\text{old yield}} = \frac{5}{10} = \frac{1}{2} = 0.5$$

2. Multiply the amount of each ingredient by the RCF (as shown in the following table).

Scaling Down

Ingredient	Old Amount	RCF	New Amount
White rice	2½ cups	× 0.5	= 1¼ cups
Salt	1 tsp	× 0.5	= ½ tsp
Water	64 fl oz	× 0.5	= 32 fl oz

Multiplying Fractions

When you scaled down the recipe, you had to multiply a fraction (2½) by the RCF, which can be shown as a fraction or as a decimal.

Multiplying Fractions

Convert whole numbers and fractions into one single fraction.

$$2\tfrac{1}{2}\ \text{tsp} = \frac{2}{1} + \frac{1}{2} = \frac{4}{2} + \frac{1}{2} = \frac{5}{2}\ \text{tsp}$$

Multiply this fraction by the RCF expressed as a fraction. Multiply the numerators and then the denominators.

$$\text{Numerator} \rightarrow 5 \times 3 = 15$$
$$\text{Denominator} \rightarrow 2 \times 10 = 20$$

Then simplify the fraction.

$$\frac{15 \div 5 = 3}{20 \div 5 = 4}$$

Multiplying a Fraction by a Decimal

Convert the fraction to a decimal. (Convert whole numbers and fractions into one single fraction. Then divide the numerator by the denominator.)

$$2\tfrac{1}{2}\ \text{tsp} = \frac{2}{1} + \frac{1}{2} = \frac{4}{2} + \frac{1}{2} = \frac{5}{2} = 2.5\ \text{tsp}$$

Multiply the amount of the ingredient by the RCF.

$$2.5\ \text{tsp} \times 0.3 = 0.75\ \text{tsp}$$

Convert the decimal to a fraction, using 100 as the denominator.

$$0.75 = \frac{75}{100}\ \text{tsp}$$

Then simplify the fraction. In this case, you can divide both the numerator and the denominator by 25.

$$\frac{75 \div 25 = 3}{100 \div 25 = 4}$$

Computation

1. Multiply the following fractions: ¾ by ½, ½ by ½, ⅔ by ½, ⅗ by ½, ⅘ by ⅔.

2. Multiply the following fractions by the specified decimal: ¾ × 0.5, 12 × 0.25, ⅔ × 0.5, ⅗ × 0.25, ⅘ × 0.60.

To scale down the recipe to make only 5 servings, you will need 1¼ cups of rice, ½ tsp of salt, and 32 fl oz (1 qt) of water.

READING CHECKPOINT *What is the formula for the recipe conversion factor (RCF)?*

Scaling Recipes Based on Portion Size

A foodservice establishment may decide to change its portion size. Perhaps it is offering a main dish as an appetizer and wants to reduce the portion. Perhaps the kitchen wants to increase the size of a portion because customers have complained that the portion is too small.

FIGURE 5-4

Different Portion Sizes
Different rice-based dishes require different-sized portions of rice.

CLASSIFYING *Can you think of dishes that might require large portions of rice? Small portions of rice?*

Source: Ian O'Leary/ Dorling Kindersley

Chef's Tip

Scaling Errors

Be careful when scaling. An error can dramatically change your results. For example, if you scale the amount of salt incorrectly, the dish may be inedible.

When you scale a recipe by changing the portion size, you always work with the recipe's yield. Remember that a recipe's yield can be expressed as the number of portions multiplied by the size of a portion.

Finding RCF when Scaling by Portion

To find the RCF when changing the portion size:

1. Find the old yield.

> Old yield = old number of servings × old portion size

2. Find the new yield.

> New yield = new number of servings × new portion size

3. Find the RCF.

$$\text{RCF} = \frac{\text{new yield}}{\text{old yield}}$$

4. Multiply each ingredient amount by the RCF.

Your kitchen's basic recipe for boiled white rice yields 10 servings of 1-cup portions. But you need 40 servings of ¾-cup portions. How much of each ingredient do you need?

Scaling a Recipe Based on Portion Size

To scale the recipe based on the new portion size:

1. Find the old yield.

> Old yield = number of portions × size
> Old yield = 10 servings × 1 cup = 10 cups

2. Find the new yield.

> New yield = number of portions × size
> New yield = 40 servings × $\frac{3}{4}$ cup = 30 cups

3. Find the RCF.

$$\text{RCF} = \frac{\text{new yield}}{\text{old yield}}$$

$$\text{RCF} = \frac{30}{10} = \frac{3}{1} = 3$$

4. Multiply the amount of each ingredient by the RCF.

(Continued)

Scaling to Change Portion Size

Ingredient	Old Amount	RCF	New Amount
White rice	2½ cups	× 3	= 7½ cups
Salt	1 tsp	× 3	= 3 tsp
Water	64 fl oz	× 3	= 192 fl oz

For 40 servings, with each portion measuring ¾ cup, you need 7½ cups of rice, 3 tsp of salt, and 192 fl oz (6 qt) of water.

READING CHECKPOINT *What are the steps for scaling a recipe when the portion size is changed?*

Scaling Recipes Based on an Available Ingredient

Occasionally a restaurant may need to scale a recipe to match the amount of a key ingredient available. This may happen because the restaurant purchased a large amount of an ingredient that is in season, for example, or because the restaurant receives a last-minute reservation and needs to plan the menu.

Scaling a Recipe Based on an Ingredient

To scale a recipe based on an ingredient:

1. Express the ingredient amount in the recipe and the ingredient amount that is available in the same measure.

2. Find the RCF.

$$RCF = \frac{\text{available ingredient amount}}{\text{ingredient amount in recipe}}$$

3. Find the new yield.

$$\text{New yield} = \text{old yield} \times RCF$$

4. Find the new amounts of each ingredient.

$$\text{New amount} = \text{old amount} \times RCF$$

Chef's Tip

Calculate Yield First

When scaling a recipe based on an ingredient, determine the new yield before you calculate the new amounts for the remaining ingredients. Once the yield works, you can calculate the new amounts for the remaining ingredients.

Your restaurant has just rented its banquet room at the last minute. You have 5 pounds of organic, skinless, boneless chicken breasts available. Will that be enough to serve 40 portions of your restaurant's special chicken dish? The recipe calls for 18 ounces of chicken breast and yields 12 cups of the dish. Portions are 1½ cups, so this recipe yields 8 servings.

Finding RCF when Scaling By Ingredient

To scale the recipe based on the available chicken:

1. Express the old and new ingredient amounts in the same measure.

> Old (recipe) amount of chicken = 18 oz
> New (available) amount of chicken = 5 lb
> There are 16 oz per lb, so 5 lb = 80 oz.

2. Find the RCF.

> $$RCF = \frac{new\ amount}{old\ amount} = \frac{80}{18} = \frac{40}{9} \ or\ 4.44$$

3. Find the new yield.

> New yield = old yield × RCF
> New yield = 8 servings × 4.44 = 35.52 servings

Using only the 5 pounds of chicken you have on hand, you will have only about 35 servings—not enough for the 40 guests. After you made this recipe-scaling calculation, you could decide to purchase enough chicken for five more servings or you could reduce the portion size.

READING CHECKPOINT *How do you scale a recipe based on an available ingredient?*

Using Scaled Recipes

When you make a recipe larger or smaller, preparation factors can change. You may need to cook the dish at a different temperature or for a different time. You may need a pan of a different size. You also may need to adjust the seasonings.

Cooking Temperature and Time Use the original cooking temperature and time as starting points. Watch closely for the results you

Changing Measurement Units

A magazine recipe for a shrimp dish serves 3. You want to scale down the recipe for a single serving, so your RCF is ⅓.

$$RCF = \frac{new\ yield}{old\ yield} = \frac{1}{3}$$

Your next step is to multiply each ingredient amount by the RCF.

The new amounts that are shown in the table are not very convenient. There is no measuring tool for ⅑ or ¹⁄₁₂ of a cup. And most measuring spoons do not include ⅓ or ⅔ of a tablespoon.

To convert these inconvenient measurements to ones that are easier to use, you will need to find equivalent units. (In the previous section of this book, measurement equivalents are listed in the two tables titled "Volume Measurements" and "Weight Measurements.")

Scaling a Recipe Based on an Ingredient

Ingredients	Old Amount	RCF	New Amount
Shrimp, large, cleaned	1½ lb	× ⅓	= ½ lb
Butter	⅓ cup	× ⅓	= ⅑ cup
Garlic, minced	4 Tbsp	× ⅓	= 1⅓ Tbsp
Green onions, thinly sliced	6	× ⅓	= 2
Fish stock	¼ cup	× ⅓	= ¹⁄₁₂ cup
Lemon juice	2 Tbsp	× ⅓	= ⅔ Tbsp
Parsley, fresh, chopped	2 Tbsp	× ⅓	= ⅔ Tbsp

To convert ⅑ cup to a convenient equivalent:

Find equivalents for 1 cup.

$$1\ cup = 16\ Tbsp$$
$$1\ Tbsp = 3\ tsp$$
$$so,\ 1\ cup = 16 \times 3 = 48\ tsp$$

You could find the equivalent in tablespoons, but because ⅑ cup is a small amount, you should find the equivalent in teaspoons.

Find the equivalents for ⅑ of a cup in teaspoons.

$$1\ cup = 48\ tsp$$
$$\tfrac{1}{9}\ cup = \tfrac{48}{9}\ tsp$$
$$\tfrac{1}{9}\ cup = 5\ tsp$$

Computation

1. A recipe serves 8. You want to scale it down to serve 2. Scale down the amounts required for your recipe. The amounts from the original recipe are: 2 lb, 3 cups, 1 cup, ½ cup, ¼ cup, 1 Tbsp, and 2 tsp.

2. A recipe serves 6. You want to scale it down to serve 1. Scale down the amounts required for your recipe. The amounts are: 1½ lb, 1 lb, 2 cups, 1 cup, ¼ cup, 4 Tbsp, 2 tsp, and ½ tsp.

want. Check for the correct internal temperature of food. When cooking several dishes in an oven together, expect a longer cooking time. (You could also try raising the temperature about 25°F.) When baking a half recipe of bread, cakes, or pies, the cooking time may be about ⅔ to ¾ of the original time.

Pan Size Choose a pan that comes closest to keeping the ingredients at the same depth as the original. If you are doubling a recipe, use a pan that has double the volume.

Sometimes your pot will not maintain the original ingredient depth. When this happens, you may need to adjust the time, temperature, and amount of liquid.

Seasonings When adjusting seasonings, especially salt, start with less than you expect to need. Season to taste, a little at a time. Taste after adding more. For example, when doubling a recipe, start with about 1½ times the original amount of seasonings. Then adjust to taste. If you record the amounts you add, you can revise the recipe for use again.

Limits on Scaling Recipes Some recipes do not scale well. For instance, delicate foods (such as soufflés) or baked items that use yeast (such as breads) do not scale well. In general, do not scale recipes that prepare a single large item, such as cakes, pies, or breads. For these recipes, scale to get a preparation list, but cook several batches to meet your needs.

Recipes cannot be scaled indefinitely. Some chefs recommend never scaling up or down beyond a factor of 4. More cautious chefs stay within a factor of 2. Large-scale changes require adjustments to equipment and method for the recipe.

Source: C Squared Studios/Getty Images

Baked items do not scale well

READING CHECKPOINT *How can scaling a recipe change preparation methods?*

Raw Food Cost

One benefit of writing recipes in a standard format and scaling them to the appropriate yield is that the chef can use the recipe to accurately determine how much food to purchase.

Some additional measuring conversions must be completed, because kitchens often purchase an ingredient that is measured in a different way than the ingredient is measured for a recipe. The quantities called for in your recipe must be converted to a purchase unit. A **purchase unit** describes the way the ingredient is sold, whether in pounds, bags, cans, cases, bunches, or by the piece.

Certain ingredients, especially fruits, vegetables, meats, fish, and poultry, have to be trimmed, boned, skinned, cored, or peeled before they can be used in a recipe. The adjustment that accounts for this loss is known as the **yield percentage**. If you need 2 cups of chopped parsley for a sauce, for instance, you must first convert the cups into ounces. Then if you know that you lose about 60 percent of the parsley when you remove the stems, you can determine how much parsley to buy. The amount you need to purchase for a recipe is called the **purchase quantity**. The amount that you use in the recipe and serve to guests is the **edible quantity**.

The money spent on the ingredients purchased for a recipe is known as **raw food cost**. You can look at the raw food cost in two ways. You can calculate the *total raw food cost* for a recipe by adding up the cost of all the raw ingredients. You can determine the *cost of a single portion* by dividing the total raw food cost by the number of portions the recipe makes.

Chefs consider the cost of the foods they buy, and they also consider the quality of the food. Being able to compare the raw food cost of a recipe using different types of ingredients can help the chef decide whether it is best to buy foods that are already trimmed and portioned. The higher cost may be justified if the product is of a higher quality and more consistent in size. Another factor the chef may consider is whether the kitchen staff has the appropriate time, equipment, and skill to transform whole birds or fish into breast portions or fish fillets.

Accurate information about what a recipe costs to prepare, as well as what a single portion costs, is critical to a successful restaurant. It can be used to set menu prices, as will be discussed in Chapter 21.

READING CHECKPOINT *How would you use the total raw food cost to determine the cost of a single portion?*

FIGURE 5-5

Purchased Quantity and Edible Quantity

The raw food cost for a recipe must be recorded properly to take into account any inedible parts of the food.

PREDICTING *When might it a good idea to buy pre-trimmed and pre-portioned meats or fish?*

Source: Culinary Institute of America

Converting Between Professional and Consumer Versions of Recipes

Standardized recipes, as we have already learned, are meant for use in a professional kitchen. They are customized to produce the right number of servings. They are based on the types of ingredients that are purchased in professional kitchens as well. In order to turn these standardized recipes into a recipe that could appear in a local newspaper, on a general-interest blog, or in a cookbook, you must modify the recipe. There are five things to consider:

- Level of difficulty
- Number of servings
- Ingredients
- Equipment used
- Use of professional terms

First, you must read through the recipe and decide whether it is easy, moderately difficult, or complex. An easy recipe has a short list of ingredients and a short method and does not call for unusual or expensive ingredients and equipment. A moderately difficult recipe may call for a longer list of ingredients and some advance steps (such as making a sauce or marinating an ingredient) and may include a subrecipe such as a stuffing. A complex recipe usually involves several subrecipes—for instance, a dough, a filling, a sauce, and a garnish—and may need to be completed over the course of a few days.

If a recipe is complex, you can make it simpler by using prepared or convenience foods where appropriate or by eliminating a subrecipe or two. If it is moderately difficult, you can help the reader by describing steps carefully and suggesting places to find unfamiliar ingredients or tools.

Next, you must adjust the number of servings the recipe makes. Most home cooks prefer recipes that make four to six servings, so you may need to scale large recipes down.

After you make that change, you will also need to think about the types of pots and pans that the home cook has. You may need to make some adjustments to the cooking times and temperatures, since home ovens may not be able to reach the same temperatures as restaurant equipment.

The terms used in standardized recipes may not be familiar to a home cook. It may be necessary to rewrite the recipe in language that is easy to understand. The best way to be certain that you have done a good job of converting a professional recipe for home use is to ask a nonprofessional friend or family member to prepare the recipe and ask them for their feedback.

READING CHECKPOINT *What are five things to consider when you convert a professional recipe for home use?*

FIGURE 5-6

Subrecipes
This pie has at least two subrecipes: the crust and the filling.
ANALYZING *What type of food do you think would tend to have the most subrecipes?*
Source: Culinary Institute of America

5.2 ASSESSMENT

Reviewing Concepts

1. How do you scale a recipe up?
2. How do you scale a recipe by changing the portion size?
3. How do you scale a recipe based on an available ingredient?
4. Can all recipes be scaled up or down?
5. How would you use the total raw food cost to determine the cost of a single portion?
6. What are five things to consider when you convert a professional recipe for home use?

Critical Thinking

7. **Solving Problems** A recipe yields 10 servings. You want to serve 15. If you keep the serving size the same, what is the RCF?
8. **Relating Concepts** If you increase the number of servings but decrease the serving size, what will happen to the total yield? Explain your answer and include an example.

9. **Inferring** Why might you need to increase oven temperature and cooking time when baking several items at once?

Test Kitchen

Bring in a recipe you like. Scale up the ingredients list as though you were going to make enough for the class. Compare the amount of the main ingredient you need to the amount your school kitchen has on hand. Would the school kitchen have enough of the ingredient to allow you to make the recipe? If not, scale the recipe based on the amount of the main ingredient that is currently available.

SOCIAL STUDIES
Origin of American Measurements

Research the history of the American system for measuring weights, liquid volume, and dry volume. Compare and contrast the American system and the English system. Describe your findings.

PROJECT 5

Scaling a Recipe You are now ready to work on Project 5, "Scaling a Recipe," which is available in "My Culinary Lab" or in your *Student's Lab Resources and Study Guide* manual.

Reviewing Content

Choose the letter that best answers the question or completes the statement.

1. What is a standardized recipe?
   a. a recipe that makes one portion
   b. a recipe that is the same in every cookbook
   c. a recipe that makes four portions
   d. a recipe tailored to the needs of an individual kitchen

2. A standardized recipe yields 10 servings and requires ¼ cup of beaten egg. You want to serve 30. How much egg should you use?
   a. ¾ cup
   b. 1⅓ cups
   c. 3 cups
   d. 12 cups

3. Which is an optional part of a standardized recipe?
   a. Recipe Categories
   b. Yield
   c. Ingredient List
   d. Method

4. A standardized recipe yields 2 qt. You want to serve 10 servings of 2 cups each. What RCF should you use to scale the recipe?
   a. ¼
   b. ⅖
   c. 2½
   d. 10

5. Which of the following are not equivalent measures?
   a. 1 cup = 8 ounces
   b. 1 cup = 10 tablespoons
   c. 1 quart = 2 pint
   d. 1 tablespoon = 3 teaspoons

6. A standardized recipe uses ½ cup of minced garlic to make 20 servings of ¾ cup each. How much minced garlic should you use to make 15 servings of ½ cup each?
   a. 2 tablespoons
   b. 4 tablespoons
   c. ½ cup
   d. 1 cup

Understanding Concepts

7. Explain the PRN method for reading a recipe.

8. Describe a situation that would require you to scale a recipe by the number of portions. Explain how to do this.

9. What is the purpose of recipe categories? Name two or more categories that could fit a recipe for egg salad.

10. Explain how and why you might adjust a recipe after scaling it.

11. If the total raw food cost for a recipe is $66 and the recipe creates 8 portions, what is the raw food cost of a portion?

Critical Thinking

12. **DRAWING CONCLUSIONS** Why is it necessary to read the mark in a clear measuring cup at eye level?

13. **PREDICTING** A recipe is scaled up by a factor of 1.5. What is the RCF to scale the larger recipe back to its original size? If the larger recipe served 24, how many did the smaller recipe serve? Show your work and explain your answers.

Culinary Math

14. **SOLVING PROBLEMS** The food tray on a kitchen's meat scale weighs 8 ounces. An assistant weighs 2 pounds of beef for stew, but forgets to set the tare. How much beef (measured in ounces) will go into the stew? If the stew must serve 8, how much beef will go into each serving? How much smaller is the beef serving than expected? Explain the consequences to the restaurant for the assistant's mistake.

On the Job

15. **APPLYING CONCEPTS** Your supervisor scales up a stew recipe so that it will serve 10, instead of 4, as in the original. She hands you a copy of the recipe with the scaled amounts written in pencil next to the original amounts. You notice that the original recipe called for 1 pound of beef, and the new recipe calls for 3 pounds of beef. Does this seem right? Are you sure? What should you do?

Food Communications

Food communications is the coverage of culinary topics in newspapers, magazines, and books, and on radio, television, and the Internet. People in this field have found careers as varied as food writer and TV chef. Have you ever picked up a magazine or a book simply because the food on the front cover looked so appealing that you wanted to eat it? This is the work of food photographers and stylists. Food communications includes writing, editing, copywriting (or advertising), scriptwriting, restaurant and book reviews, photography, television, and lecturing.

Food writers are communicators with a good basic knowledge of food and cooking. Some food writers edit or write books. There is a huge market for food books on every imaginable subject. Food writers also submit articles to magazines and newspapers. To write these articles, you need to be well read in the culinary arts and proficient in the kitchen. Food bloggers also write on a wide range of food-related topics. Some use their blogs as a way to generate income, while others use their blogs primarily as a way to promote themselves and to gain credibility that they can use to find work in more traditional areas, such as publishing, journalism, and advertising. Articles could range from a simple discussion of how to brew a pot of tea to an informational piece on nutritional cooking. A food writer with good presentation skills might be featured on a local radio program or might even become part of a television food show.

Editors are critical to the food communications business. Many food writers are also food editors. Publishers, magazines, websites, and advertising agencies rely on editors with in-depth knowledge of food, recipes, cooking techniques, and the culinary arts in general to be certain that recipes and text are accurate, reliable, and in a form that is appropriate for the audience.

Restaurant critics are food writers who understand what good food, good cooking, and good service is all about. They are able to discuss the style of a restaurant and trends in the restaurant business. Restaurant critics are important to restaurants, especially when their good reviews increase business.

Food photographers have the talent of making food look visually appealing in print. You see their work in ad campaigns and magazines and on book jackets. Their challenge is to photograph food so the viewer can almost taste it. What's required is an understanding of photography and lighting.

Food stylists work with food photographers. They are responsible for preparing and placing the food just right on the plate. Their culinary knowledge is critical—how to select the best product, apply the right technique, and cut the item expertly. It is up to the stylist to make sure that the lettuce leaves are perfect, with not a single blemish, and the entire presentation is picture-perfect.

Entry-Level Requirements

Culinary and writing skills (food writers and critics), culinary skills and knowledge of photography and design (food photographers and stylists).

Helpful for Advancement

Broad knowledge of the food industry and all food media outlets. Working as an apprentice (food photography and styling).

Source: Everett Collection Inc/Alamy

Martha Stewart has built a career based on writing about food and entertainment

JENNIFER ARMENTROUT

Jennifer Armentrout is the Editor of *Fine Cooking* magazine. She began her career at the magazine in 2000 as an Assistant Editor and rose through the ranks, becoming Test Kitchen Manager and then Senior Food Editor. In that position, she was responsible for making sure that every recipe published in *Fine Cooking* lived up to its billing and was 100 percent reliable, clearly written, and delicious. She also directed the test kitchen staff, wrote the test kitchen column in the magazine, and worked to ensure that all the technique coverage in the magazine was correct and easy to understand for the home cook. As Editor, she oversees all content for the print and digital editions of the magazine as well as its website, books, and special projects.

Jennifer Armentrout

VITAL STATISTICS

Graduated: Received a BA in anthropology from James Madison University, 1993

Received an A.O.S. in Culinary Arts with High Honors, The Culinary Institute of America, 1997

Profession: Editor of *Fine Cooking* magazine

Interesting Items: Began career in food as a prep cook in a Washington, D.C., restaurant before attending culinary school

Worked as an editor and writer on *The Professional Chef* after graduating from the CIA in 1997

Named Senior Food Editor in 2007

Named Editor in 2011

CAREER PROFILE

Salary Ranges

Entry-Level Staff Positions: $25,000 to $55,000

Midlevel Staff Positions: $30,000 to $60,500 (or more)

Senior Staff Positions: $60,000 to $90,000 (or more)

Freelance: Varies widely, depending on level of experience and type of work done

Chapter

6

Seasonings and Flavorings

6.1 Sensory Perception

6.2 Herbs, Spices, and Aromatics

6.3 Condiments, Nuts, and Seeds

6.4 Seasoning and Flavoring Foods

6.1

Sensory Perception

Key Concepts

- Explaining the role of the five senses in tasting food
- Identifying the ways a food's flavor can change
- Describing the flavor of foods

Vocabulary

- aromatic
- flavor
- opaque
- savory
- taste
- translucent
- umami

The Five Senses

Human beings have five senses: taste, sight, smell, touch, and hearing. Each of our senses plays a role in helping us taste our food. Not only do our senses help us identify the food we are eating, but they also help us decide whether food is ripe or a dish is properly cooked.

The Sense of Taste Our sense of taste depends on food coming in contact with our tongue as we chew or swallow. The taste buds covering our tongue allow us to distinguish among five tastes:

- Sweet
- Sour
- Salty
- Bitter
- Umami

You may not be familiar with the taste of **umami** (oo-MAM-ee). It is also referred to as the taste of **savory** (SAY-va-ree). This flavor, which is best thought of as meaty or brothy, was discovered in the early 20th century by a Japanese professor. The most common example of umami is the food additive MSG (monosodium glutamate). Umami is often found in protein, some vegetables, and fermented foods, such as soy sauce.

Source: Corbis Super RF/Alamy

FIGURE 6-1

Sense of Taste

Specific areas of the tongue are most sensitive to sweet, sour, salty, and bitter tastes. Umami doesn't have a specific location on the tongue.

APPLYING CONCEPTS *Which part of your tongue might be most affected when you taste a grapefruit?*

Source: Dorling Kindersley

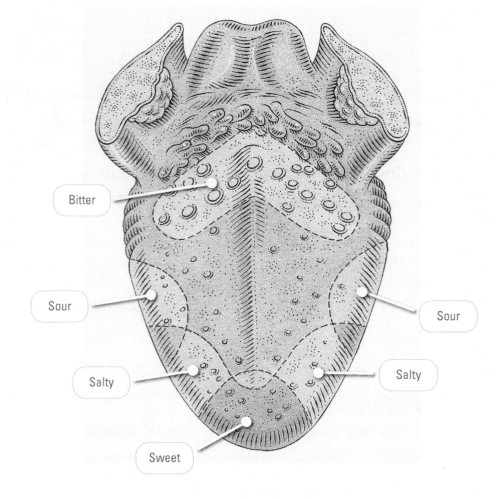

Bitter

Sour

Sour

Salty

Salty

Sweet

The Sense of Sight Typically, our first experience of food uses our sense of sight. We tend to prefer foods that look good. Foods that are ripe have the most appealing colors. Foods that are neatly cut and beautifully arranged are more appealing than foods that are not. That is why you hear chefs say, "People eat with their eyes," and talk about "feeding the eye." If something doesn't look good, people may not want to try it.

The Sense of Smell When it comes to food, smell is an extremely powerful sense. We check foods for ripeness by smelling them. We monitor how quickly foods are cooking by the smell coming from the stove or the oven.

We can distinguish among thousands of different smells or aromas. Foods with especially strong smells are referred to as **aromatic** (air-o-MAT-ic). Have you noticed that if you have a cold and can't smell things, it is very hard to tell what you are eating? That's because what we think of as the taste of a food is often strongly influenced by our sense of smell. The aroma of a particular food is one of the ways we tell the difference between foods that are similar in appearance and taste. For example, an orange and a tangerine are similar in appearance but different in smell.

The Sense of Touch Touch is the way we experience a food's texture and its temperature. We use our sense of touch, along with sight and smell, to help identify when foods are fully ripe or properly cooked. Some foods soften as they ripen or cook, while others become more firm.

The texture of food plays an important role in determining how food tastes to us. Thick or chewy foods stay in our mouths longer than foods that are thin and swallowed quickly. That means we have more time to taste and smell the thicker food. Fatty, oily, or rich foods also coat our mouths. These foods seem to have a fuller flavor than lean or watery foods.

Our sense of touch is also the way we experience such sensations as the burn of hot peppers, the cooling effect of mint, the drying or puckering effect tea has on the inside of our mouth, the numbing sensation of cloves, and the fizz of carbonated beverages—to name only a few of the ways food feels when we eat it.

The Sense of Hearing Hearing is also an important aspect of our food experience. For example, crisp foods make a loud crunch as we cut or bite them. When a food sizzles on a platter, we expect it to be very hot.

Chefs use their sense of hearing to help them keep track of how quickly foods are cooking. They can distinguish the sounds of a fast boil or a lazy simmer. They can also tell when the sounds of food cooking in the oven means the oven is too hot or too cool.

FIGURE 6-2
Food Texture
Think of the combination of textures in this fried chicken.
APPLYING CONCEPTS *What can a crisp, crunchy crust on chicken tell you about its flavor?*
Source: Nitr/Fotolia

READING CHECKPOINT *What five tastes can our taste buds distinguish?*

Changing a Food's Flavor

Taste is a word we can use in more than one way. As we just learned, *taste* refers to the sensation we experience through our taste buds when we put foods in our mouth. *Taste* is also the word we use when we mean the taste of the food in addition to its smell. **Flavor** refers to the way a food tastes, as well as its texture, appearance, doneness, and temperature. In practical terms, taste and flavor are used almost interchangeably.

Ripening or Aging The flavor of any food changes as it ripens or ages. Food that is not fully ripe may have a bitter or bland taste because it has not developed completely. When it is ripe, it will have the richest flavor. As food ages, the flavor continues to change until it reaches a point at which we consider the food spoiled or rotten. The natural aging and ripening process of any food changes the way it tastes to us. For example, a green tomato has a tart taste, a ripe tomato tastes sweet, and an overripe tomato tastes fermented.

Temperature The temperature of a food also plays a part in how it tastes to us. Very cold food seems less flavorful than warm or hot food. As foods get warmer, it is easier for us to taste and smell. A tomato that you take right out of the refrigerator doesn't have as intense a flavor as one that has been sitting on the counter at room temperature.

Preparation and Cooking When we prepare or cook food, we change it from its original state. The change may be quite simple. For instance, a ripe tomato may simply be sliced. Cutting the tomato changes the way it tastes, even though it is not a big change.

If we take the same tomato and cook it in a pan until it turns a deep brown, we've made a more significant change to the way the tomato tastes. If we chop the tomato and cook it until it is soft but not brown, it has an entirely different taste.

As you learn more about the different ways you can cook food, you will find that each cooking technique produces its own characteristic taste. Cooking is one of the most significant ways we can change the taste of food. We can improve the flavor of food when we cook it, but we can also ruin its flavor.

Source: Steve Gorton/Dorling Kindersley

 **READING CHECKPOINT** *What are three ways you can change the flavor of food?*

Describing Flavor

In a literal sense, if we wanted to describe how a food tastes, we would be limited to describing the degree of sweetness, sourness, bitterness, saltiness, or umami. That is all that we can actually taste. However, when we talk about the way food tastes, we are usually talking in broader terms. Typically, we are also considering the way the food appeals to all of our other senses as well. When we talk about a food or a dish in this way, we are talking about its flavor.

The Way Flavor Looks When you look at food, you can make some predictions about its flavor. Food that looks fresh and unblemished or has good color usually has the best flavor. We look for a good shape, one that is appropriate for the food. Additionally, the look of food is usually changed

FIGURE 6-3

Cooking Onions
Onions change from opaque to translucent to brown as they cook.

COMPARING *Do you have a sense of how these onions will taste at each of these stages of cooking?*
Source: Culinary Institute of America

during cooking. Here are some descriptive words we might use to describe the way food looks:

- **Opaque** (o-PAKE), meaning light does not pass through it
- **Translucent** (trans-LU-cent), meaning some light will pass through it
- Transparent or clear
- Colors, such as red, yellow, green, brown, white, ivory, or orange

The Way Flavor Smells There are hundreds, perhaps thousands, of words you might use to describe the way food smells. The way food smells before you eat it is sometimes quite different from the way it smells once you put it in your mouth.

One of the most obvious ways to describe a smell is to describe a similar smell. For example, you might say a food item smells like a lemon, like vanilla, like toast, or like mushrooms. The following are some other descriptive words relating to the way food smells:

Source: Ian O'Leary/Dorling Kindersley Limited

- Perfumed
- Pungent
- Earthy
- Stale
- Musty
- Fresh
- Strong
- Intense

The Way Flavor Feels Texture is the way food feels when we touch it, cut it, or bite into it.

Source: Ian O'Leary/Dorling Kindersley

The following are some descriptive words for a food's texture:

- Firm, hard
- Soft, yielding, melting
- Crisp, crunchy, crumbly
- Airy, frothy, foamy
- Thick, heavy, dense
- Watery, thin
- Warm, hot
- Cool, cold

The Way Flavor Sounds The sounds food makes gives you a clue about its flavor, too. Here are some descriptive words for the way a food sounds:

- Snap
- Sizzle
- Pop
- Crackle
- Crunch
- Fizz

Source: Dorling Kindersley

 **READING CHECKPOINT** *List several words you can use to describe how a food looks, smells, feels, and sounds.*

6.1 ASSESSMENT

Reviewing Concepts

1. What are the five tastes our taste buds allow us to distinguish?
2. What are three ways the flavor of food can be changed?
3. List several words you could use to describe *flavor* as it applies to each of the five senses.

Critical Thinking

4. **Classifying** Think about your favorite food. Which tastes are included in it?
5. **Comparing/Contrasting** Name a food that is more attractive to you hot and less attractive cold. Name one that is more attractive cold than hot.
6. **Classifying** Which of the senses, other than taste and smell, is most important to you in considering flavor? Explain your answer.

Test Kitchen

Cut an apple, an onion, and a radish each into a small dice. Divide into groups of two. While one person is blindfolded and holding his or her nose, the other person should feed the blindfolded person a small amount of each of the foods, asking the blindfolded person to identify the food. Reverse roles. Record the results.

SCIENCE ————————————●

Umami

Research the discovery of the taste of umami. Who discovered the taste? When was the discovery made? What does the name mean in Japanese? What foods are considered to have a strong umami taste?

6.2

Herbs, Spices, and Aromatics

READING PREVIEW

Key Concepts

- Identifying and using herbs
- Identifying and using spices
- Identifying and using additional aromatic ingredients
- Preparing and using aromatic combinations

Vocabulary

- battuto
- bouquet garni
- Cajun trinity
- capers
- cured foods
- herbs
- matignon
- mirepoix
- sachet d'épices
- spice blends
- spices
- standard mirepoix
- tamarind
- white mirepoix

Herbs

Herbs are the leaves and stems of certain plants. They are used to flavor a wide variety of foods. Some are considered sweet; others are thought of as savory.

Certain herbs, or combinations of herbs, are associated with particular cuisines. The taste and smell of basil and oregano, for example, may make you think of Italian foods. Tarragon and chives are often used in French cooking. Cilantro and parsley are important herbs in Chinese cooking. Oregano and mint are key flavors in Greek cooking.

Selecting and Storing Herbs Fresh herbs have intense flavors. When you select a fresh herb, smell it to check for a good aroma. As a fresh herb ages, its flavor gets weaker. Fresh herbs should also have a good color. The leaves should be intact. Bruised or wilted leaves and leaves that have become pale or turned yellow will not have the best flavor. Stems should be firm and not split. If the roots are still intact, as they may be on herbs such as cilantro or dill, they should be dry, not soft or wet.

Store fresh herbs in the refrigerator, wrapped loosely in a damp paper towel in a loosely closed plastic bag. Use fresh herbs within a few days for the best flavor.

Source: LiliGraphie/Fotolia

Herbs

Anise

Both the leaves and the seeds of anise (AN-ihss) have a sweet licorice flavor. It's the flavor of black licorice and black jelly beans. Anise seeds are also used in cookies and to flavor a variety of spirits. The seeds are chewed after a meal in India to aid digestion and sweeten the breath.

Source: photocrew/Fotolia

Bay Leaf

Bay leaves are smooth and rigid. They may be available fresh but are typically used dry. Bay leaves retain their flavor even after drying. Bay leaves are used to flavor soups, stews, stocks, sauces, and grain dishes. Remove bay leaves from the prepared food at the end of the cooking process. Even after cooking they are too rigid to eat and could cause choking.

Source: Dave King/Dorling Kindersley

Basil

Basil (BAY-zill) has pointed green leaves. Purple varieties and large- or small-leafed varieties are available. Some varieties have the aroma of cinnamon, clove, lemon, or other flavors. Thai basil has a licorice flavor and is widely used in Asian food. Uses include flavoring sauces (including pesto sauce), salad dressings, chicken, fish, and pasta. Basil is also used to flavor oils and vinegars. Dried basil typically has less flavor than fresh.

Source: Dorling Kindersley

Chervil

Chervil (CHER-vil), a member of the parsley family, has dark green, curly leaves. Dried chervil has far less flavor than fresh. Chervil has a flavor similar to parsley with a hint of licorice. It is one of the herbs typically used in the French blend of herbs referred to as *fines herbes* (FEEN erb).

Source: Roger Phillips/Dorling Kindersley

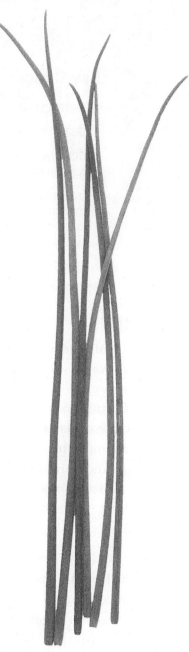

Chives

Chives belong to the onion family and have a subtle but savory flavor. Chives grow as long, hollow stems. The flowers or buds have a more intense flavor and are sometimes used to flavor or garnish a salad. Dried chives have far less flavor than fresh chives. Chives are typically minced or snipped before they are added to a dish.

Source: Dave King/Dorling Kindersley

Cilantro

Cilantro (se-LAHN-troh) is similar in shape to flat-leaf parsley. The leaves have scalloped edges. The flavor is fresh, tangy, sharp, and distinctive. It is used in many Asian, South American, and Central American dishes. It is also known as *Chinese parsley*.

Source: Dorling Kindersley Limited

Lemongrass

Lemongrass is a tropical grass with a long greenish stalk and serrated leaves. The inner stalks have a strong lemony flavor and aroma. Lemongrass is widely used in Asian dishes. It remains tough even after cooking and is removed before eating.

Source: Richard Embery/Pearson Education/PH College

Dill

Dill leaves have a feathery shape with a strong aroma and a tart flavor. Dill is used to flavor sauces and stews (especially in Central and Eastern European dishes). Dill seeds are flat, oval, and brown, with a caraway-like flavor. Dill pickles are flavored with dill seeds.

Source: Dave King/Dorling Kindersley

Curry Leaf

Curry leaf, with its pungent curry fragrance, is essential in many Indian foods. The fresh leaves are small and shiny and are available fresh in Indian markets. Dried curry leaves are also available, but they lack the flavor of the fresh leaves.

Source: fkruger/Fotolia

Marjoram

Marjoram (MAHR-juhr-uhm) is a member of the mint family. It has short, oval, pale green leaves, a sweet flavor, and a strong aroma. It's most commonly used in Mediterranean dishes.

Source: Dorling Kindersley Media Library

Mint

Almost everyone has tasted mint at some point. The leaves are typically textured and deep green. Different varieties of mint, such as spearmint or peppermint, have different flavors and aromas. Mint is used in many cuisines for both sweet and savory dishes.

Source: Clive Streeter/Dorling Kindersley

Epazote

Epazote (eh-pah-ZOH-teh) is a strong-tasting, pungent wild herb with flat, pointed leaves. It is usually available dried and is widely used in Latin American bean dishes because of its ability to reduce gas.

Source: Dustin Dennis/Shutterstock

Rosemary

Rosemary has needle-shaped leaves. It has a pungent, resinous flavor, similar to pine needles. Rosemary stems, also known as *branches*, are sometimes used as skewers for grilled or broiled foods. Dried rosemary is almost as pungent as fresh rosemary.

Source: Clive Streeter/Dorling Kindersley

Tarragon

Tarragon (TAHR-uh-gon) has narrow, pointed, dark green leaves with a strong licorice flavor. The stems are often added as a flavoring for simmered dishes and sauces. The leaves are typically chopped before they are added as a final flavoring ingredient. Tarragon is often used with chicken, fish, veal, and egg dishes. It is typical in many French-style dishes. Although dried tarragon does not have as strong a flavor as fresh tarragon, it has a potent aroma.

Source: Dorling Kindersley Limited

Oregano

Oregano (oh-REHG-uh-no) has small oval leaves with a pungent, peppery taste. Widely used in Italian and Greek dishes, the stems and leaves are used to flavor fish, meats, poultry, and tomatoes. Marjoram is similar in appearance and aroma to oregano, although it is milder.

Source: Ian O'Leary/Dorling Kindersley

Savory

Savory has small, narrow, gray-green leaves and a bitter, pungent flavor that resembles thyme and rosemary. It is available fresh and dried.

Source: Peter Anderson/Dorling Kindersley

Parsley

Parsley may have curly leaves with ruffled edges or flat leaves with scalloped edges. Flat-leaf parsley (shown here) is also known as *Italian parsley* and has a spicy flavor with a bit of licorice. Leaves and whole stems of parsley are often added to simmered dishes. The leaves may be added as a final flavoring ingredient or used in sprigs as a garnish.

Source: Philip Wilkins/Dorling Kindersley

Sage

Fresh sage leaves are oval and are covered with soft threads, giving the leaf a silvery, furry appearance. It has a pungent, slightly bitter, musty mint flavor and is often added whole to stews and soups. It is also used to flavor roast meats or poultry. Dried sage is often referred to as *rubbed sage*.

Source: Dorling Kindersley Limited

Thyme

Thyme (TIME) has small gray-green oval leaves. It has a lemony, minty flavor with overtones of rosemary. Some varieties have special flavors such as nutmeg, mint, or lemon. Thyme is used to flavor soups and stews. Whole sprigs or chopped leaves may be used. Dried thyme retains much of the flavor of fresh thyme and is widely available.

Source: David Murray/Dorling Kindersley

Many herbs are sold as either dried or ground leaves. Some are sold as a powder. Drying the herbs drives out the moisture in the herb, concentrating the herb's flavor. Be sure to smell dried herbs before you use them. They should have a pleasant smell. If they smell musty or have practically no aroma, they are probably too old to be of any use in cooking.

Buy just enough dried herbs to last six months. Store them in tightly sealed containers, away from heat, moisture, and direct sunlight.

Using Fresh and Dried Herbs Review your recipe to find out when to add fresh herbs. Some recipes call for whole sprigs, some for leaves, and some for only stems. Rinse and dry fresh herbs before chopping them or adding them to a dish. If your recipe requires cut herbs, cut them as close as possible to the time you need them. Once you cut a fresh herb, it starts to lose some of its flavor.

Whole sprigs and stems are usually added to a dish at the start of cooking so the herb can gently flavor the entire dish. For a more intense flavor, chopped or whole fresh leaves are added to a dish at the end of cooking.

Dried herbs often have a more intense flavor than fresh ones because they contain less water. (There are some exceptions. Dried chives, chervil, basil, and parsley have a less intense flavor than the fresh herb.) In general, you can substitute 1 teaspoon of a dried herb for every tablespoon of fresh herbs called for in a recipe. Most dry herbs need to be added to the dish early on as you cook so the liquid in the dish rehydrates them and the herbs can flavor the dish.

FIGURE 6-4
Adding Basil to Tomato Sauce
Fresh basil or oregano is often added to tomato sauce.
COMPARING/CONTRASTING *Why might adding fresh basil to a finished sauce give a different flavor than adding dried basil when you start to cook the sauce?*
Source: Culinary Institute of America

READING CHECKPOINT *What are herbs? Give five examples.*

Be sure to check spices before you use them. Rub them between your fingertips and then smell them. If the flavor is strong and pleasant, they are still fresh enough to use.

Spices

Spices are aromatic ingredients added in small amounts to foods to give them a specific flavor. They are the seeds, bark, roots, stalks, or fruits of a wide range of plants. Many of the spices we take for granted today, such as cinnamon or pepper, were once so costly that only rich people could afford them.

Although not all spices can be purchased whole, you should try to purchase whole spices whenever you can. Whole spices last longer than spices that are already ground. Ground spices lose their aroma or fragrance more quickly. Whole peppercorns, for instance, can last for several years in dry storage, but ground black pepper starts to lose its flavor after about six months. You can always grind whole spices as you need them.

Spices are sometimes added to a dish whole and then strained out. In other dishes, spices are ground and then cooked in a little oil or other fat to

CULINARY **HISTORY**

Spice Routes

Spices such as cloves, saffron, and cinnamon have been highly prized as both medicines and for cooking since about 3000 BCE. In the Middle Ages, using spices was a show of wealth. But why were spices so valuable just a few hundred years ago? It all has to do with transportation and trade.

First, the Chinese established a trade route, known as the Silk Road, that linked the East with the Middle East. Merchants traveled in caravans along a number of routes, carrying spices, silks, and gems.

Merchants along the way purchased goods and carried them farther west. By the time a spice such as cinnamon had traveled from China or the Spice Islands to Europe, it had changed hands many times. Of course, the price went up each time.

The locations where the spices were grown were jealously guarded secrets. Outlandish stories were often told to Europeans to keep them from getting their hands on the spices. For example, Romans, anxious to find a less expensive source for cinnamon, were told by Chinese merchants that

Caravan on the Silk Road

Source: PRISMA ARCHIVO/Alamy

the sweet spice had to be harvested from remote caves that were guarded by fierce bats.

Research

Research which spices were transported on the Silk Road in the Middle Ages. Provide a detailed description of (or the recipe for) a dish from the Middle Ages that would have used one or more of these spices.

Spices

Allspice

The small brown berries of allspice are ground for use as a spice. Allspice lives up to its name. It has a flavor and aroma that is a mixture of cinnamon, clove, nutmeg, ginger, and pepper. Allspice is typically available cracked or ground. Also known as *Jamaican pepper*, allspice is typically used in spicy, fragrant Jamaican jerked chicken.

Source: Culinary Institute of America

Caraway Seeds

A member of the parsley family, the caraway plant is actually an herb. However, the plant is best known as the source for caraway seeds. These small crescent-shaped seeds have a nutty, peppery, licorice taste. They are widely used in baked goods and savory dishes.

Source: Dorling Kindersley Media Library

Cardamom

These long, light green or brown pods contain a seed that has a pungent, musty, lemony flavor. Cardamom (CARD-uh-mom) is available in whole pods or ground. It is used widely used in Indian dishes.

Source: Dave King/Dorling Kindersley

Cinnamon

Cinnamon is the inner bark of a small evergreen tree that originally came from India and other eastern countries. It has a sweet flavor and aroma. It is sold ground or in rolled-up sticks. It is used in a number of desserts. It is also an important flavoring in many savory dishes.

Source: Culinary Institute of America

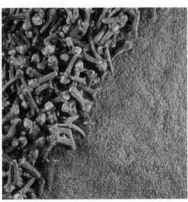

Cloves

Cloves (CLOVS) are the unopened bud of a tropical evergreen tree. Individual cloves are brown and are shaped like nails (which is why the Romans gave them the name *clavus*, the Latin word for "nail"). Cloves are extremely aromatic, with a sweet, astringent flavor. Like cinnamon, cloves are considered a sweet spice. Cloves are sold whole or ground.

Source: Culinary Institute of America

Coriander

Coriander (KOR-ee-an-der) is the seed of the cilantro plant (see "Herbs"). The flavor of the seeds and the leaves bear no resemblance to each other. The tiny tan seeds have an aroma that is a combination of lemon, sage, and caraway. Whole seeds are used in pickling and special drinks. Ground seeds are used in baking, curry blends, soups. Both forms are commonly available in supermarkets.

Source: areif/Fotolia

Cumin

Cumin (COO-min) is the crescent-shaped seed of a plant in the parsley family. It has a strong, distinctive earthy flavor and aroma that is often associated with Mexican cooking. Cumin is available whole or ground and is also used in Middle Eastern and Indian dishes.

Source: Culinary Institute of America

Spices

Fenugreek

Fenugreek (FEHN-yoo-greek) is an aromatic plant with bitter, strong-smelling leaves. Some cultures eat the leaves fresh, but they are not widely available in the United States. Dried leaves are also used as a flavoring agent. The yellow-brown fenugreek seeds are used, especially in Indian food, for curry powders, spice blends, and teas. They have an aroma and flavor similar to maple syrup. The seeds are widely available whole or ground.

Source: Roger Phillips/Dorling Kindersley

Fennel

With its feathery foliage, fennel looks like dill. It has a pronounced licorice flavor and is used fresh or dried. The oval seeds are used in Italian and central European cuisines for baked goods and savory dishes. Fennel seeds are usually sold as whole seeds.

Source: Culinary Institute of America

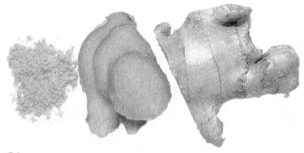

Ginger

Ginger is a tall tropical plant, but only the gnarled root is used as a spice. Ginger must be peeled to be used. Fresh ginger has a distinctive peppery, sweet flavor with hints of lemon and rosemary and a strong, spicy aroma. Powdered or ground ginger is made by drying fresh ginger and then pulverizing it. Ginger is used in Asian and Indian cuisines for both sweet and savory dishes.

Source: Martin Cameron/Dorling Kindersley

Juniper Berries

Juniper berries are the blue-black berries from juniper trees native to both Europe and America. The berries are too bitter to eat raw and are generally crushed before using to release their flavor. They are used to flavor meats (particularly wild game or strong-tasting meats), sauces, and stuffings. Juniper berries are the primary taste of gin. They are typically available in a dried berry form from specialty spice markets.

Source: Dave King/Dorling Kindersley

Mustard

Mustard is a member of the cabbage family, and its leaves are eaten as a vegetable. However, its seeds have an earthy hot flavor and a pungent smell. There are yellow, red, and black varieties of mustard seeds. Each has a distinctive taste. Mustard is sold as whole seeds or as a powder. The whole seeds are used in Indian cuisine.

Source: Culinary Institute of America

Nutmeg and Mace

The seed of the nutmeg tree, nutmeg is oval and has a smooth texture. Mace is the lacy coating that surrounds the seed. Both have a sweet flavor and are highly fragrant. Nutmeg tastes best when it is freshly ground, using a special grater. Both nutmeg and mace are available ground as well. They are used in both sweet and savory dishes.

Source: Culinary Institute of America

Peppercorns

Peppercorns are the berry of the pepper vine, which originally came from India and Indonesia. Besides black and white peppercorns, there are also green and pink peppercorns. Green peppercorns are unripened peppercorns that are pickled or freeze-dried. They have a soft texture and a sour taste. Pink peppercorns, which are available dried or pickled, are actually not peppercorns. They are the dried berries of a South American rose and have a bitter, piney flavor.

Source: Dave King/Dorling Kindersley

Peppers

Native to the Americas, peppers are vegetables. They have a wide range of colors and flavors ranging from sweet to extremely hot. Hot peppers are often referred to as chile peppers or chiles. Both sweet and hot peppers are dried and then ground to create a variety of sweet or hot spices. Paprika, for example, is a blend of dried red chiles with a flavor that can range from sweet to hot. Ground peppers are used as a spice in Central Europe, Spain, Italy, and the Americas.

Source: Dorling Kindersley

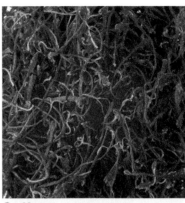

Saffron

Saffron is produced by drying the inner part of the crocus, a small purple flower. Saffron has a distinctive spicy, honeyed, but slightly bitter flavor and a strong, pungent aroma. Saffron not only flavors foods, it also gives them a deep yellow color. Saffron threads are usually crushed before they are added to a dish. Powdered saffron is also available.

Source: Culinary Institute of America

Sumac

Sumac (SOO-mac) is the berry from a bush that grows wild throughout the Middle East and Italy. The berries range in color from red-orange to purple-red and have a pleasantly fruity, astringent taste. It complements a wide variety of foods, including fish, meat, and vegetables. Sumac can be found in Middle Eastern markets in both a ground form and in its dried berry form.

Source: ninell/Fotolia

Star Anise

Shaped like a star, this dark brown pod from an evergreen tree contains a small seed in each of its eight segments. It has a distinctive sweet licorice flavor that is a bit more bitter than regular anise. It's widely used in Asian foods. It is available whole in Asian markets and is ground in Chinese five-spice powder.

Source: Unclesam/Fotolia

Turmeric

Turmeric (TER-muh-rihk) is the root of a tropical plant related to ginger. It has a perfumed aroma, a bitter, pungent flavor, and an intense yellow-orange color. It is used to add both flavor and color to food. Turmeric is a common addition to curry powder and is widely used in Indian cooking. It is also what gives American-style mustard its bright yellow color. Powdered turmeric is widely available in supermarkets.

Source: jeehyun/Fotolia

FIGURE 6-5

Curry Powder
Curry powder is a blend of up to 20 herbs and spices.

DRAWING CONCLUSIONS *What do you achieve when you combine many herbs and spices (including cinnamon, chiles, fennel seeds, ginger, coriander, fenugreek, turmeric, and cumin) into a spice blend such as curry powder?*
Source: Culinary Institute of America

distribute the flavor evenly through the dish. Often, spices are added directly to the dish as it cooks. Sometimes, spices such as mustard seeds or cumin are toasted before being added to a dish. This toasting subtly changes their flavor. Recipes usually indicate when and how to add spices to a dish. Spices are also used to flavor oils or vinegars, which are themselves used to flavor dishes.

Curry powder, chili powder, and pumpkin pie spice are all examples of **spice blends**, made by combining a variety of spices (and often herbs as well). Dry rubs for seasoning meats or poultry before they roast are another type of spice blend. Many spice blends are prepared and packaged for sale. Some chefs prefer to make their own spice blends so they can control the amount and type of spices in the blend. Spice blends are typically ground for an even texture, but some include whole spices and seeds.

 **READING CHECKPOINT** *What are spices? Give five examples of spices.*

Additional Aromatic Ingredients

Herbs and spices usually have strong and distinctive aromas. However, chefs sometimes use additional aromatic ingredients to add more flavor and aromas to a dish. The following are the three basic types of additional aromatic ingredients used in cooking:

- Aromatic vegetables and fruits
- Aromatic liquids
- Cured and smoked foods

Source: Jay Penni/Prentice Hall School Division

Aromatic Vegetables and Fruits You can add aromatic vegetables to a dish for additional flavor and aroma. Plants in the onion family, including garlic, green onions, and leeks, are the most common aromatic vegetables. Other vegetables prized for their aromas include mushrooms and celery. Tomatoes can be used for their aroma. They may be simply chopped and added to the dish or, to intensify their flavor, they can be cooked in the oven or in a pan over direct heat.

Fruits—especially citrus fruits such as lemons, limes, and oranges—are often used to add flavor and aroma to a dish. You can add just the zest (the outer peel) or the juice. In the Middle East, Asia, and India, the pulp of the **tamarind** (TAM-uh-rihnd) fruit is widely used to provide a sour-sweet taste, much the same way that lemons are used in Western culture. You can also use dried fruits such as raisins or apricots to add flavor and aroma to a dish.

Aromatic Liquids Chefs use a variety of liquids in cooking foods as varied as soup, vegetables, and grains. Broths and stocks (concentrated brothlike liquids) add aroma to a dish. Other aromatic liquids a chef may use are wines, spirits such as brandies, and liqueurs. Usually, these are heated to evaporate the alcohol and concentrate the taste.

Flavorful oils, including flavored olive oil, sesame oil, and walnut oil, can also be added to a dish to increase flavor and aroma. These oils are usually not allowed to cook for long in a dish. Getting them too hot for too long cooks away their delicate aroma.

Extracts are made by soaking aromatic ingredients such as vanilla or lemon in alcohol. Extracts can also be added in small amounts to a dish to increase flavor and aroma.

Cured Foods **Cured foods** are foods that are preserved by drying, salting, pickling, or smoking (such as ham, bacon, olives, or salted anchovies). They add a savory flavor and aroma to a dish, and they may also add

FIGURE 6-6
Pork and Beans
Smoked ham and vegetable stock are added to beans.

PREDICTING *How will the ham change the flavor of the beans? The vegetable stock? The combination of the two?*

Source: David Murray and Jules Selmes/Dorling Kindersley

Global Flavor Profiles: Spices, Herbs, and Aromatics

Asian

Cuisine	Herbs	Spices	Aromatics (Vegetables, Fruits, Liquids, Cured Foods)
Chinese	Chives	Chiles, cinnamon, ginger, star anise	Garlic, oranges, scallions, sesame oil, tangerines, rice vinegar, rice wine
Indian	Anise, cilantro, curry leaf, mint, sage	Allspice, anise, cardamom, chiles, cinnamon, cloves, coriander, cumin, fenugreek, ginger, mustard, nutmeg, paprika, saffron, turmeric	Garlic, onions, tamarind, tomatoes
Japanese		Chiles, ginger	Dried fish flakes, scallions, sesame oil, stock, rice vinegar, rice wine
Thai	Basil (Thai), cilantro, lemongrass, mint	Chiles, coriander, cumin, ginger, turmeric	Garlic, onions, scallions
Vietnamese	Basil (Thai), cilantro, lemongrass, mint	Chiles, ginger, star anise	Garlic, lemons, limes, onions, scallions, shallots

Latin American

Cuisine	Herbs	Spices	Aromatics (Vegetables, Fruits, Liquids, Cured Foods)
Brazilian	Cilantro, parsley, saffron, thyme	Cardamom, chiles, cloves, ginger, nutmeg	Cured meats, garlic, onions, oranges
Chilean	Oregano	Chiles, cumin, paprika	Garlic, olives, raisins
Latin American (general)	Cilantro, oregano, rosemary, tarragon, thyme	Chiles, cinnamon, cloves, cumin	Garlic, limes, onions, oranges
Mexican	Cilantro, epazote, oregano, saffron	Chiles, cinnamon, cumin	Garlic, lemons, limes, onions, oranges, tomatoes

Mediterranean

Cuisine	Herbs	Spices	Aromatics (Vegetables, Fruits, Liquids, Cured Foods)
French	Anise, basil, chervil, chives, lavender, marjoram, parsley, rosemary, sage, tarragon, thyme	Mustard, nutmeg	Anchovies, bacon, capers, carrots, celery, garlic, ham, leeks, mushrooms, olive oil, tomatoes, shallots, spirits, stock, vinegar, wine
Greek	Anise, basil, bay leaf, mint, oregano, rosemary, thyme	Allspice, cinnamon, cloves, dill, nutmeg	Garlic, lemons, olive oil, onions, raisins, tomatoes, spirits, stock, vinegar, wine

Global Flavor Profiles: Spices, Herbs, and Aromatics

Mediterranean *continued*

Cuisine	Herbs	Spices	Aromatics (Vegetables, Fruits, Liquids, Cured Foods)
Italian	Basil, marjoram, oregano, parsley, rosemary, sage, thyme	Chiles, cinnamon, fennel, nutmeg, red pepper flakes, saffron	Anchovies, capers, garlic, lemons, mushrooms, olive oil, onions, pancetta prosciutto, raisins, spirits, stock, tomatoes, vinegar, wine
Middle Eastern (general)	Marjoram, mint, oregano, parsley	Cinnamon, cloves, coriander, cumin, dill, ginger, nutmeg, sumac	Garlic, lemons, olive oil, olives, onions, raisins, sesame oil, tomatoes
Moroccan	Cilantro	Chiles, cinnamon, coriander, cumin, ginger, paprika, saffron, sumac, turmeric	Lemons, olive oil, olives, onions, raisins, tomatoes
Spanish	Bay leaf, parsley, thyme	Paprika, saffron	Anchovies, capers, chorizo, garlic, ham, lemons, olive oil, olives, onions, oranges, spirits, stock, tomatoes, vinegar, wine

Additional Cuisines

Cuisine	Herbs	Spices	Aromatics (Vegetables, Fruits, Liquids, Cured Foods)
African	Mint, parsley	Chiles, cinnamon, cloves, cumin, fenugreek, ginger, turmeric	Garlic, onions, tomatoes
Caribbean	Bay leaf, cilantro, oregano, parsley, thyme	Allspice, chiles, cinnamon, cloves, dill, ginger, mace, nutmeg	Garlic, limes, onions, oranges, spirits, tamarind
Eastern European	Dill, marjoram	Allspice, caraway seeds, cinnamon, cloves, ginger, juniper berries, mustard, paprika	Bacon, carrots, celery, garlic, mushrooms, onions, spirits, tomatoes, vinegar, wines
Scandinavian	Bay leaf, dill	Allspice, cardamom, cinnamon, cloves, ginger, juniper berries, mustard, nutmeg	Mushrooms, onions, spirits

saltiness. Cured foods are strongly flavored. They are usually added when you begin cooking a dish so they can flavor the dish evenly.

Capers (KAY-pers), the dried flower bud of a bush native to the Mediterranean and parts of Asia, are pickled in a vinegar-and-salt solution. They are widely used in Mediterranean countries to add a pungent taste to meat and vegetable dishes.

READING CHECKPOINT *What are the three types of additional aromatic ingredients commonly used in cooking?*

Aromatic Combinations

Any time you use more than one flavoring or aromatic ingredient in a dish, you've made an aromatic combination. Some specific combinations are used frequently in the kitchen. The three most common are the following:

- Mirepoix
- Sachet d'épices
- Bouquet garni

Mirepoix Mirepoix (MEER-uh-pwah) is a combination of vegetables used as an aromatic flavoring ingredient in many dishes. You can cut the vegetables in mirepoix into large or small pieces. To determine how big the pieces should be, read the recipe to find out how long the mirepoix will cook in the dish. Long-cooking dishes call for large pieces of mirepoix. Dishes that cook quickly need mirepoix that is cut into small pieces or thin slices.

By making a few changes to the ingredients in a mirepoix, you can produce a variety of aromatic combinations. The following are the most common types of mirepoix or mirepoix-like aromatic combinations:

- **Standard Mirepoix.** Used for a variety of stocks and soups, a **standard mirepoix** typically includes the following ingredients (by weight): 2 parts onion, 1 part carrot, and 1 part celery. For brown stock, soup, gravy, or stews, a tomato paste or tomato purée is often included in the mirepoix.

- **White Mirepoix.** A **white mirepoix** is used to flavor white stocks and soups that should have a pale ivory or white color. Parsnips replace the carrots. Leeks may replace some of the onions.

- **Cajun Trinity.** Used in many Creole (KREE-ol) and Cajun (CAGE-uhn) dishes such as gumbo, a **Cajun trinity** is a combination of onion, celery, and green pepper.

Source: Culinary Institute of America

Standard mirepoix ingredients: onion, carrot, and celery

- **Matignon.** A mirepoix-like aromatic combination, **matignon** (mah-tee-YOHN) contains onions, carrots, celery, and ham. The ham is not strained from the dish, so it is important to cut it into a dice that is edible. Mushrooms, herbs, and spices may also be required by your recipe.

- **Battuto.** Used in Italian soups, sauces, stews, and meat dishes, **battuto** (bah-TOOT-oh) includes a cooking fat (olive oil, chopped lard, pancetta, or fatback) with garlic, onions, parsley, carrots, and celery. Green peppers are also commonly added.

Sachet d'Épices and Bouquet Garni Sachet d'épices and bouquet garni are two classic aromatic combinations used in many dishes.

- **Sachet d'Épices.** A **sachet d'épices** (SAH-shay day-PEES) is a mixture of fresh and dried herbs and dried spices that is tied up in a piece of cheesecloth to make a small bag. *Sachet d'épices* means "bag of spices" in French. A standard sachet d'épices includes peppercorns, dried thyme leaves, and fresh parsley stems.

Sachet d'Épices

① **Measure** peppercorns, thyme, parsley, and any other ingredients.

② **Wrap** the sachet d'épices ingredients in a square of cheesecloth.

③ **Tie** the cheesecloth with string to make a bag.

Source: Culinary Institute of America

④ **Add** to the dish.

⑤ **Simmer** until the dish is aromatic. (Consult your recipe.)

⑥ **Remove** and discard.

Recipe Card

2. Sachet d'Épices

Source: Ian O'Leary/
Dorling Kindersley

Bouquet garni

• **Bouquet Garni.** Another combination of aromatics, a **bouquet garni** (boo-KAY GAR-nee) uses fresh herbs rather than dried herbs. It also usually includes an aromatic vegetable such as leeks, garlic, or scallions. The ingredients in a bouquet garni may also include sprigs of fresh thyme, fresh parsley stems, rosemary, and citrus peels. Leek leaves or a citrus peel may be used as a wrapper instead of cheesecloth. The ingredients are then tied up.

Recipe Card

3. Bouquet Garni

 **READING CHECKPOINT** *What are the three most common types of aromatic combinations?*

6.2 ASSESSMENT

Reviewing Concepts

1. What are herbs? Give five examples.
2. What are spices? Give five examples.
3. Aside from herbs and spices, what are the three additional types of aromatic ingredients commonly used in cooking?
4. What are the three most common types of aromatic combinations?

Critical Thinking

5. **Comparing/Contrasting** Using fennel as an example, describe when you would consider it an herb and when you would consider it a spice.
6. **Communicating** Of the herbs and spices listed in this section, which is your favorite? Describe the flavor of your selection.
7. **Comparing/Contrasting** How does a Cajun trinity differ from a standard mirepoix?

Test Kitchen

Divide into four teams. Each team will finely mince a different herb, either chives, oregano, tarragon, or rosemary. Mix the herb with 2 Tbsp of salted butter at room temperature. Spread on toast. Cut into enough squares for the class to sample. Rank the taste from most favorite to least favorite. Tally the results for the class.

SOCIAL STUDIES
Myths about Herbs and Spices

Research a particular herb or spice. Write a description of any myths or legends related to the herb or spice you chose. Research how the herb or spice acquired its name and whether it has historically been associated with any medical or health benefits.

PROJECT 6

Aromatic Combinations You are now ready to work on Project 6, "Aromatic Combinations," which is available in "My Culinary Lab" or in your *Student's Lab Resources and Study Guide* manual.

Condiments, Nuts, and Seeds

Key Concepts

- Identifying and using condiments
- Identifying and using nuts and seeds

Vocabulary

- condiments
- nuts
- seed
- tahini

Condiments

Condiments (CON-di-ments) are prepared mixtures we use to season and flavor foods. A condiment is something extra, served on the side and added by the individual diner to suit his or her own preferences. (Condiments can also be used as ingredients in a preparation.) A condiment can change the flavor of a dish by adding spicy, savory, sweet, sour, salty, or umami tastes to food. Condiments may also add color, texture, or even a temperature contrast, to further enhance the way a dish looks and tastes.

Sometimes condiments are selected just to add a new taste to a familiar favorite. For example, a pineapple salsa condiment may be served with a grilled chicken breast.

However, many dishes are served with a traditional condiment (for example, mustard with hot dogs). Mustard, ketchup (also called *catsup*), hot sauce, Worcestershire (WUSS-ta-shur) sauce, and steak sauce are all examples of traditional condiments you may choose to serve with meats, fish, or poultry dishes. Dressings, dips, and spreads can also be used as traditional condiments. For example, blue cheese dressing is often the traditional condiment served with Buffalo-style chicken wings, and salsa is traditionally served with chips.

Think of these traditional condiments. For a taco, you usually choose from a variety of traditional condiments including taco sauce, sour cream, shredded lettuce, sliced green onions, chopped tomatoes, grated cheese, and pickled jalapeños. For sushi, you usually can pick pickled ginger, wasabi, and soy sauce as condiments.

Source: Clive Streeter/Dorling Kindersley

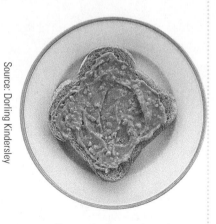
Selecting and Storing Condiments You can purchase fresh or perishable condiments or make them from scratch. When purchasing bottled, jarred, or canned condiments, be sure the container is intact and there are no leaks, bulges, or dents. Be sure perishable condiments are kept in the refrigerator.

Using Condiments Some condiments have extremely pungent or hot flavors. They are typically served in very small amounts. Others have sweet or mellow tastes. The portion size for any condiment can vary greatly from one dish to another and from one restaurant to another. The basic rule of thumb is to offer enough of the condiment so the guest can enjoy it with each bite of the main dish.

Before using a condiment, check it carefully and taste it. This gives you a chance to add more seasonings or flavorings, if necessary. It also allows you to detect any sour or off odors that may mean the condiment is past its prime.

READING CHECKPOINT *What is a condiment?*

Nuts and Seeds

Nuts are the fruit of various trees. The only exception is the peanut, which grows underground in the root system of a beanlike plant. Nuts are available in the shell or shelled. They are available uncooked, roasted, or blanched (cooked quickly in boiling water and then quickly cooled). Shelled nuts are available whole, halved, sliced, slivered, or chopped. Nuts and seeds are also used to produce butters, such as peanut butter or sesame paste, which is also called **tahini** (ta-HEE-nee).

A **seed** is the part of a plant that can grow into a new plant. Seeds come from a variety of plants, including herbs, flowers, and vegetables. The way a seed is used determines how we classify it. For example, some seeds are used in the same way you use a nut—in larger quantities, for their nutty taste and crunchy texture. Sesame seeds and poppy seeds are two examples. Other seeds are used the same way you use a spice—in smaller quantities, as a flavoring. Mustard seeds, cumin, nutmeg, and fennel seeds are some examples.

Storing Nuts and Seeds Nuts and seeds are best stored in a cool, dry, dark storage area. If nuts and seeds are received in vacuum packaging, they will last almost indefinitely. Loose nuts and seeds or opened packages, however, can become rancid quickly. You may be able to keep nuts still in the shell for up to six months. Unroasted nuts, sometimes referred to as *raw nuts*, can last up to three months in dry storage. Roasted nuts start to lose their quality after about a month. Sliced or chopped nuts have the shortest

Nuts and Seeds

Cashew

A cashew (CA-shoo) is kidney-shaped, sweet, and butter-flavored, with a high fat content. It is always sold shelled, because its skin contains irritating oils similar to those in poison ivy. Cashews are often used for snacking.

Source: Steve Gorton/Dorling Kindersley

Almond

Pale tan with a pitted, woody shell, an almond is teardrop-shaped. Bitter and sweet types are available. Bitter almonds must be cooked. Sweet almonds have a distinctive taste and smell and can be used raw or cooked.

Source: David Murray/Dorling Kindersley

Macadamia

The macadamia (mac-a-DAME-ee-ah) nut is nearly round. It has a very hard shell and is usually available shelled. It has a rich, buttery flavor and a high fat content.

Source: Matthew Ward/Dorling Kindersley

Chestnut

A chestnut is a fairly large nut that is round to teardrop-shaped. Chestnuts must be cooked. They have a high starch content and are used in both sweet and savory dishes.

Source: Roger Philips/Dorling Kindersley

Hazelnut

This small, nearly round nut has a distinctive rich, somewhat sweet taste. It is widely used in desserts because it complements chocolate and coffee.

Source: Matthew Ward/Dorling Kindersley

Peanut

Although the peanut is a seed that grows underground in a pod, it is usually treated as a nut. Peanuts are available in their shell or shelled, raw or roasted. Peanuts are often used for snacking, and peanut butter has made many of us familiar with the nutty taste of a roasted peanut.

Source: Dorling Kindersley

Pecan

Pecans are often sold whole in their smooth, thin, hard, tan shells. The golden-brown kernel has a high fat content and a nutty, sweet taste. It is often used in sweet dishes, such as pecan pie.

Source: Dorling Kindersley Limited

Nuts and Seeds

Pine Nut

These small, cream-colored, elongated nuts are the seeds from a Mediterranean pine. They have a distinctive, rich, slightly piney flavor and a high fat content. They are used in both sweet and savory dishes.

Source: Martin Cameron/Dorling Kindersley

Pistachio

The pale green color of the pistachio nut distinguishes it from other nuts. It is typically available whole, shelled and unshelled. The hard tan shell is sometimes dyed red when sold whole. The delicate but distinctive taste of pistachio is used in many desserts. It is also a favorite snacking nut.

Source: Martin Cameron/Dorling Kindersley

Poppy Seeds

Poppy seeds are the tiny, round, black seeds of the poppy flower. They have a sweet, nutty flavor and are used primarily in baked goods.

Source: Roger Phillips/Dorling Kindersley

Sesame Seeds

These small, flat, oval seeds may be black or tan. Sesame seeds have a rich, nutty flavor and are widely used in baking.

Source: Roger Phillips/Dorling Kindersley

Walnut

A walnut has a hard, wrinkled shell enclosing a nut with two tender sections. Walnuts are oily, with a mild, sweet flavor. They are used in sweet and savory dishes and are also used in snacking. White walnuts, or butternuts, and black walnuts are North American varieties. Butternuts are richer tasting, and black walnuts are stronger tasting.

Source: David Murray/Dorling Kindersley

BASIC CULINARY SKILLS

Toasting Nuts, Seeds, and Spices

1. **Shell** nuts or seeds.
2. **Add** to a dry, hot sauté pan.
3. **Stir** constantly.
4. **Toast** until aromatic and slightly brown.
5. **Transfer** to a cool bowl.

Source: Culinary Institute of America

shelf life, usually no more than three to four weeks. To keep them for longer periods, store them in sealed containers in the freezer.

Pastes made from nuts and seeds (such as almond paste, nut butter, tahini, and poppy seed paste) will keep in an unopened container for several months. Once the container is open, you can store them in dry storage for up to six weeks. Some butters or pastes can be kept in the refrigerator for up to two months or in a freezer for up to three months. Check them for fresh, pleasant aromas before using.

Using Nuts and Seeds Nuts and seeds are often roasted or toasted to bring out more flavor. It is easy to overcook or scorch nuts if you aren't paying close attention. When toasting nuts, keep them in motion by stirring them or swirling the pan. As soon as nuts or seeds start to turn color or become fragrant, remove them from the heat. Immediately pour them into a cool container. Otherwise, the heat held by the pan will overcook them. Overcooked nuts and seeds become too bitter to use in cooking.

 **READING CHECKPOINT** *How do you toast nuts, seeds, or spices?*

6.3 ASSESSMENT

Reviewing Concepts

1. What is a condiment? Give three examples.

2. How do you toast nuts, seeds, and spices?

Critical Thinking

3. Communicating Do you have a favorite condiment? Describe what flavor it adds to the dishes with which you normally use it.

4. Comparing/Contrasting Compare and contrast two nuts with which you are familiar in terms of their taste, texture, smell, and appearance.

5. Recognizing Patterns Explain why poppy seeds are discussed under the nuts category, fennel seeds are discussed under the spices category, and dill is discussed under the herb category.

Test Kitchen

Divide into four teams. Each team will use a small amount of one of the following untoasted nuts:

almonds, pine nuts, sesame seeds, and pecans. Set aside half of the nuts and toast the remaining half. Compare the untoasted nuts with the toasted nuts. Taste the nuts from other teams. Individually evaluate each of the nuts (both toasted and untoasted), ranking them from most favorite to least favorite. Tally the results for the class.

SCIENCE

George Washington Carver

Research some of the culinary uses for peanuts suggested by George Washington Carver. Did he invent peanut butter? Were some of Carver's culinary uses of peanuts later produced commercially? How many of these culinary uses were patented by Carver? Write a report describing your findings.

6.4

Seasoning and Flavoring Foods

READING PREVIEW

Key Concepts

- Understanding why foods are seasoned
- Identifying and using common seasoning ingredients
- Differentiating between seasoning and flavoring food
- Understanding the relationship of cuisines and flavor

Vocabulary

- black pepper
- cuisine
- high-sodium food
- iodized salt
- kosher salt
- monosodium glutamate (MSG)
- national cuisine
- regional cuisine
- rock salt
- sea salt
- seasonings
- sodium chloride
- table salt
- white pepper

Seasoning Foods

Seasonings are ingredients you add to a food to improve its flavor. Seasoning ingredients are added in such small quantities that you usually cannot taste the individual seasoning ingredients. If you add just enough seasoning, however, you will notice an improvement in the flavor of the food. Chefs season food to improve its flavor in one of the following ways:

- **Enhancing Natural Taste.** Sometimes, you add a seasoning to make the natural taste of the food more intense or noticeable. In other words, you are enhancing the food's taste. For example, if you cook pasta in plain water without any salt, the pasta won't have much flavor. But if you add just a little salt to the water, the pasta tastes more like pasta.

- **Balancing Tastes.** Sometimes, a seasoning helps to overcome strong tastes, especially sour, sweet, or bitter tastes. This is sometimes referred to as *balancing* the tastes in a dish. Vegetables that are bitter taste less bitter when you add some salt to them. Sour foods such as lemon juice taste less sour if you add a bit of sugar. Sweet foods taste less sweet if you add a bit of salt. Once the strong taste is reduced a little, it is easier to taste other ingredients or flavors in the dish.

Source: ILYA AKINSHIN/Fotolia

Chef's Tip

A Pinch of Salt?

Learn the size of your pinch. Take a three- or four-finger pinch of salt. Measure it on a scale or in measuring spoons. That is the size of one of your pinches.

- **Cutting Richness.** Seasonings can also change the way a rich or fatty food tastes. A little lemon juice or vinegar improves the taste of mayonnaise by making it taste less rich or oily. You may hear this referred to as *cutting* the richness or oiliness of a dish.

READING CHECKPOINT *Why do chefs season food?*

Types of Seasoning Ingredients

Seasoning starts with some basic ingredients. There are four basic types of seasoning ingredients:

- Salt
- Pepper
- Sugar and light-flavored sweeteners
- Acids

When you season a food, you add just enough of one or more of these ingredients to change the food's basic taste, but not enough to add a whole new taste.

Salt Salt is an important seasoning. Its chemical name is **sodium chloride**. It is used in all cuisines and in all countries. You can add it to foods before you cook them, as you cook them, or at the table. When salt is used in small amounts, it enhances the flavor of a food. In addition to salt, you can also use salty food, or **high-sodium food**, as a seasoning in a dish. Some high-sodium foods commonly used in the kitchen are soy sauce, Parmesan, bacon, and olives.

Salt can be found underground, where it is mined. Some mines dissolve the salt with water and then pump the salt-saturated water out of the ground. The water is allowed to evaporate and the salt remains. Salt is also found in sea water. The water is allowed to evaporate, leaving behind grains or flakes of salt.

Salt lasts almost indefinitely in dry storage. The only real concern is that the salt may become damp and turn into a hard cake. To keep this from happening, store salt in a cool, dry place in a sealed container.

- **Table Salt.** Salt that is refined to remove other minerals or impurities is referred to as **table salt**. This type of salt is processed to give it a fine, even grain. A small amount of a starch is added to keep the salt from turning into clumps. Iodine may be added to table salt as a nutritional supplement. The salt is then called **iodized** (EYE-oh-dized) **salt**.
- **Sea Salt.** Made by evaporating seawater, **sea salt** is usually not significantly refined, which means it contains additional minerals and other elements found in seawater.

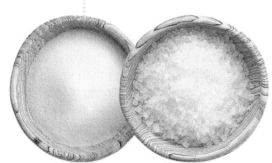

Source: David Murray/Dorling Kindersley

Table salt and sea salt

Rock salt

This often gives sea salt a slight color. Sea salt is available in grains of varying sizes, from extremely coarse crystals to flakes to a fine grain.

- **Kosher Salt.** A salt made without any additives, **kosher** (KOH-shure) **salt** is sold in coarse or fine grain styles. Kosher salt is typically flakier than table salt. Many chefs like to use kosher salt for general cooking purposes because it is additive-free. To substitute kosher salt for table salt, use twice the volume of kosher salt that is called for in the recipe.

- **Rock Salt.** Less refined than table salt, **rock salt** is generally not used for consumption. Its most common use in the kitchen is in ice cream makers or as a bed for certain items, especially oysters or clams that are served on their shells.

CULINARY **SCIENCE**

Osmosis

Salt changes food. It draws out water, blood, and other impurities, and it kills pathogens. This preserves food by drying it out and makes it less susceptible to spoilage. To keep foods safe to eat when there was no refrigeration, our ancestors used salt to remove as much water as possible.

The process by which salt accomplishes these changes is known as osmosis. *Osmosis is the movement of water through a cell wall to equalize the concentration of salt on both sides of the wall.* For example, when you salt a piece of meat, the fluid inside the meat travels through the meat's cell wall in an effort to dilute the salt on the other side of the cell wall. So the meat loses fluid.

However, osmosis occurs in both directions. First it draws fluid out of the cell. But when there is more fluid outside the cell than inside it, the fluid flows back into the cell, taking along the dissolved salt. Getting the salt inside the cell, where it can kill harmful pathogens, is the essence of salt-curing foods. That is how foods such as ham, bacon, and dry sausages are preserved. Because of osmosis,

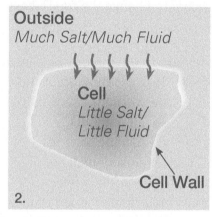

1. Fluid moves through the cell wall, diluting salt outside the cell.
2. Fluid, with dissolved salt, moves back into the cell, equalizing fluid on both sides of the wall.

salt often meant the difference between life and death for our ancestors.

Lab Activity

Form a team and locate a recipe for preserving a specific type of food (meat, fish, or a vegetable) using salt. Evaluate with your instructor whether it is possible for you to follow the recipe. If it is possible, follow the recipe to preserve the food you have chosen. If it is not possible for you to follow the recipe, write out the detailed steps for preserving the food of your choice as if you were preparing to actually do it.

- **Monosodium Glutamate (MSG).** Although not actually a salt, **monosodium glutamate** (mon-oh-SO-dee-um GLUTE-ah-mate), abbreviated as MSG, is used in much the same way as salt. MSG provides the umami taste rather than the salty taste and is often associated with Chinese or Japanese food. MSG enhances the meaty or brothy flavor in meat, poultry, fish, and vegetables. The source of MSG is seaweed.

Pepper In most people's mind, salt and pepper go together. They are the most widely used seasonings in the world. Pepper is actually a spice that is often used in small amounts as a seasoning. Typically only black pepper and white pepper are used as seasonings. (Other types of pepper are discussed in Section 6.2, "Herbs, Spices, and Aromatics.") Pepper is slightly hot and brings out the flavor in food.

- **Black Pepper.** From the dried, unripe berries of the pepper vine, **black pepper** is available as whole berries, cracked, or ground. Grinding pepper as it is needed is preferable because the taste is fresher and more aromatic.
- **White Pepper.** When the ripe pepper berries are allowed to dry and their husks are removed, you have **white pepper.** Usually, white pepper is used for light-colored sauces. White pepper is available in the same forms as black pepper, and, just as with black pepper, grinding pepper fresh is always preferred.

Sugar and Light-Flavored Sweeteners Sugar enhances the flavor of dishes—salad dressings, tomato sauce, vegetables, and even meat. When using sugar as a seasoning, you should add only a small amount of it to a dish. Sugar with distinctive flavor (such as brown sugar) is used as a flavoring agent, not as a seasoning. Sometimes a light-flavored liquid sweetener, such as light corn syrup, light honey, or light maple syrup, is used rather than sugar.

Acids Lemon or orange juice, vinegar, and wine are all examples of acids you can use to season food. Acids have a sour or tart flavor. In addition to seasoning food, acids can also improve the appearance and texture of food. For example, adding lemon juice when you cook an artichoke keeps it from turning brown. Adding vinegar to the water when you poach an egg gives the egg a better shape.

READING CHECKPOINT *Name four types of seasonings.*

Chef's Tip

Adding Salt

Be careful when adding salt. You can always add more salt, but you can't remove it.

Source: Culinary Institute of America

Black pepper
Whole, cracked, and ground

Source: Culinary Institute of America

White pepper
Whole and ground

Salting Water
Adding salt to water before cooking pasta.

APPLYING CONCEPTS *How can adding salt to water change the flavor of pasta?*

Source: David Murray and Jules Selmes/Dorling Kindersley

Flavoring Foods

When you *season* a food, you try to improve the food's unique flavor without changing it significantly. When you *flavor* a food, you change the food's flavor. You add other flavors—herbs, spices, aromatics, or condiments, for example—to the food's original flavor. Some chefs refer to the process of flavoring foods as *layering flavors*, adding flavor on top of other flavors to create a new pleasing combination of flavors.

Here's an example that demonstrates the difference between seasoning and flavoring. If you add a small amount of salt to the water you use to cook rice, the cooked rice will simply taste like cooked rice. That means it has been properly seasoned. However, if you add a lot of salt, the cooked rice will take on the distinct and easy-to-identify flavor of salt. Salt has become a flavoring in the dish, not a seasoning. In this case, the difference between an ingredient used as a seasoning and one used as a flavoring is a question of how much you use.

Many ingredients or combinations of ingredients can be used to flavor foods. Each flavoring ingredient is added to a dish at a specific time and in a specific manner to develop a desired flavor in the dish.

 **READING CHECKPOINT** *What is the difference between seasoning a food and flavoring a food?*

Relationship of Cuisine and Flavor

As you saw in Section 6.2, each region uses different combinations of herbs, spices, and aromatics to flavor food. These differences are often based on a region's **cuisine** (kwih-ZEEN), the characteristic style of foods, flavors, and cooking practices associated with a specific area.

The areas considered for a cuisine can vary widely. For example, you could focus on a **regional cuisine**, the cuisine shared by a specific region. These regions can be large and include many nations. Examples of this type of regional cuisine are Mediterranean cuisine, Latin American cuisine, and Asian cuisine. You could also look at a **national cuisine**, the cuisine shared by a nation. French cuisine and Chinese cuisine are examples of national cuisines.

India

India is an Asian country with cultural and culinary ties to China and Southeast Asian countries. Some of India's most important culinary influences came from Persia (modern-day Iran and Iraq) and Indonesia (the famous Spice Islands Christopher Columbus set out to find).

Northern India is a noted agricultural area, growing many types of grains. These are featured in an amazing diversity of breads, which are a significant part of any Indian meal. The southern part of India is famous for its fragrant basmati (bahs-MAH-tee) rice, which is a perfect accompaniment to the spicy and often hot southern food. In fact, the farther south you travel in India, the hotter the food becomes.

Vegetables are important in Indian cuisine. There is a strong vegetarian tradition, especially in areas where the primary religion discourages meat-eating. Condiments, including pickled vegetables, chutneys, and other relishes, are indispensable in a typical Indian meal.

Dairy foods are common in Indian cooking, making this cuisine different from that of most other parts of Asia. Ghee (GEE), a form of butter, is widely used to cook foods. Mustard seed oil and coconut oil are also important cooking fats. Yogurt and buttermilk are used on their own and as ingredients in other dishes. Indian cuisine also features a fresh cheese known as paneer (pah-NEER).

Curries and roasts are important Indian cooking techniques. A curry is a stew that may feature meat, fish, or chicken, or a combination of vegetables. It is flavored with a combination of spices and often finished with yogurt. Roasts are prepared in special ovens known as tandoors (tan-DOERS), which reach extremely high temperatures.

Above all, Indian cooking is noted for its use of herbs and spices. Spice blends known as masalas (ma-SAH-las) may contain a dozen or more herbs and spices, including

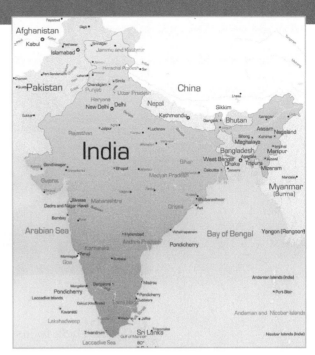

Source: Iryna Volina/Fotolia

mustard seeds, chiles, cinnamon, cloves, ginger, saffron, nutmeg, and bay leaves. Different types of curries are seasoned by different styles of masalas. Throughout India, the selection of spices for a masala is a personal matter. Each family may have its own formula, one that distinguishes their food from the food of their neighbors.

Source: Dave King/Image Partners 2005/Dorling Kindersley Media Library/Dorling Kindersley

Indian spices

FIGURE 6-8

Barbequed Ribs
Based on the descriptions of the regional differences in barbequed foods, what region might these ribs be from?

PREDICTING *What would be the first thing you would use in your analysis of these ribs?*

Source: fudio/Fotolia

Often chefs focus on specific regional cuisines. Some experts, for example, categorize Chinese cuisine into nearly thirty regional cuisines. Others focus on just four regional cuisines (Cantonese, Sichuan, Shandong, and Huaiyang).

Barbecued foods in America are another example of just how specific a regional cuisine can be. While barbecued foods are primarily a Southern/Midwest specialty, there are subtle differences between regions:

- In Eastern North Carolina, the whole hog is typically used, the meat is chopped up and mixed together, and a thin sauce made of spices and vinegar is used.
- Western North Carolina uses the pork shoulder and a thicker, sweeter, tomato-based sauce.
- Western South Carolina uses a peppery tomato- or ketchup-based sauce on pork.
- People in central South Carolina use a yellow sauce made from a mixture of mustard, vinegar, brown sugar, and spices.
- In coastal South Carolina, a spicy, vinegar-and-pepper sauce is popular.
- Memphis focuses on ribs, served "wet" (cooked with sauce) or "dry" (cooked without sauce and only dry seasonings).
- Kansas City smokes a wide variety of meat using only dry seasonings but serves a thick, sweet tomato-and-molasses sauce on the side.
- Texas has many varieties of barbecues, but they are usually focused on beef.
- Kentucky is unusual in that its preferred meat is mutton.

Sometimes you will hear a resident of a particular region talking about "home-cooked food" or a dish remembered from childhood. That food had

Examples of American Regional Cuisines

Regional Cuisine	Characteristic Ingredients	Characteristic Herbs, Spices, and Aromatics	Characteristic Dishes
New England	Seafood, dairy, beans, turkey, maple syrup, cranberries, potato, Cheddar cheese	Parsley, sage, nutmeg	Baked beans, clam chowder, clam bakes, lobster, crab cakes, blueberry pie, apple pie, rhubarb pie, pancakes, cranberry sauce
Midwestern	Wheat, corn, soybeans, wild rice, sugar beets, beef, pork, chicken, eggs, walleye, pike, cheese, morel mushrooms, apples, cherries, peaches	Sage, dill, caraway, mustard	Prime rib, pork sausages, meat loaf, hamburgers, corn on the cob, corn dogs, breaded pork tenderloin sandwich, deep-dish pizza, sugar cream pie, persimmon pudding, doughnuts
Southern	Chicken, pork, catfish, black-eyed peas, collard greens, mustard greens, turnip greens, okra, butter beans, peanuts, grits, rice	Black pepper, bacon	Fried chicken, country ham, chicken-fried steak, buttermilk biscuits, fried green tomatoes, succotash, cornbread, sweet potato pie, pecan pie, cobbler
Creole/Cajun	Crawfish, crabs, oysters, shrimp, fish, peppers, frogs, onions, celery, figs, okra, plums, grapes, pecans, peanuts	Cayenne pepper, Tabasco pepper, parsley, bay leaf, oregano, sassafras leaves, thyme, garlic, green onions	Pork sausages, crawfish boil, jambalaya, gumbo, crawfish étouffée, fried frog's legs, blackened redfish, dirty rice, red beans and rice, pecan pralines, beignets
Southwestern/ Tex-Mex	Beef, pork, chicken, beans, cheese, tomatoes, avocados, corn, limes, pine nuts	Chiles, cumin, garlic, onions, oregano, cinnamon	Guacamole, burritos, chili, fajitas, enchiladas, tacos, refried beans, salsa, tortillas, sopapillas, flans
Hawaiian	Pork, beef, fish, shellfish, taro, sweet potatoes, yams, breadfruit, bananas, coconuts, sugarcane, pineapples, guavas, candle nuts, jicama, winged beans	Green onions, chiles, teriyaki, five-spice powder, wasabi, soy sauce, chile water	Pit-roasted pig, stir-fried pork, fried spam, pipikaula (beef jerky), pork lau lau, poke (raw fish preserved with salt and seasonings), grilled tuna, swordfish steaks, poi

the authentic flavor of the region because specific products from the regions were used, with specific cooking practices (often using specific cookware) and specific condiments. Specific herbs, spices, and aromatics were used in that food's preparation, and specific condiments when it is served. All of these contribute to that region's particular cuisine.

READING CHECKPOINT *What is a cuisine?*

Reviewing Concepts

1. What are three reasons chefs season foods?
2. What are the four basic types of seasoning ingredients?
3. What is the difference between seasoning a food and flavoring a food?
4. What is a cuisine?

Critical Thinking

5. **Comparing/Contrasting** Describe the differences between table salt, kosher salt, and sea salt.
6. **Inferring** Why would only light-flavored sweeteners be used as seasonings?
7. **Classifying** Which type of pepper would you typically use for a light-colored sauce? Why?
8. **Predicting** Will there be times when a chef may want an unbalanced taste or very rich dish? Explain your answer.

Test Kitchen

Divide into four teams. Teams will make a salsa of a medium dice of tomatoes and a fine dice of onions, with three times as much tomato as onion. Then they will divide the salsa into two portions. Teams will focus on only one type of seasoning ingredient. For the first portion, use the seasoning ingredient only to *season* the portion. For the second portion, use the ingredient to *flavor* the portion. Evaluate the amount of the ingredient required for seasoning versus flavoring.

SCIENCE

Iodized Salt

Research the history of iodized salt. When was iodine first added to salt? Why was this done? Are there any problems associated with the use of iodized salt?

Reviewing Content

Choose the letter that best answers the question or completes the statement.

1. What is umami?
   a. an herb
   b. a flavor
   c. a nut
   d. a spice

2. Which of the following is not included in a standard mirepoix?
   a. onions
   b. carrots
   c. green pepper
   d. celery

3. A condiment is
   a. a flavoring served on the side and added by the individual diner.
   b. a spice combination used in Italian soups and sauces.
   c. a spice combination used in Cajun cooking.
   d. a type of seasoning ingredient.

4. When you say a cooked onion is translucent, you are saying that
   a. flavor from the onion has blended with other ingredients in a dish.
   b. aroma from the onion has blended with other ingredients in a dish.
   c. light passes through the cooked onion.
   d. light does not pass through the cooked onion.

5. Which of the following is not a reason why chefs season foods?
   a. to change the food's flavor
   b. to cut richness
   c. to balance taste
   d. to enhance natural taste

6. In general, you can substitute how much of a dried herb for every tablespoon of fresh herbs called for in a recipe?
   a. 2 tablespoons
   b. 2 teaspoons
   c. 1 teaspoon
   d. ½ teaspoon

Understanding Concepts

7. What are the five tastes our tongue can distinguish?

8. What are the three reasons why chefs season food?

9. What are the four basic types of seasoning ingredients?

10. What is a cuisine?

11. How does a sachet d'épices differ from a bouquet garni?

12. What is a condiment?

Critical Thinking

13. **COMPARING/CONTRASTING** What is the difference between seasoning and flavoring?

14. **COMPARING/CONTRASTING** What is the difference between a standard mirepoix and a white mirepoix?

Culinary Math

15. **RELATING CONCEPTS** A recipe that yields 10 servings calls for 3 tablespoons of fresh rosemary. You are scaling the recipe up to serve 40 people and you don't have any fresh rosemary. How much dried rosemary should you use?

16. **RELATING CONCEPTS** You are making a standard mirepoix for a large quantity of soup. The mirepoix will be cooked in the soup for a long time. The recipe calls for 40 ounces of onions. What other ingredients are required? How much of those ingredients will be needed? How should you cut the mirepoix ingredients?

On the Job

17. **FORMING A MODEL** You are making a light, white-colored soup. The recipe calls for the addition of a mirepoix. What ingredients would you use in the mirepoix?

18. **COMMUNICATING** You cooked a well-seasoned and flavorful dish. It was presented to a diner who immediately requested ketchup to put on it. What should you do?

Food Flavoring: Research, Development, and Manufacture

Food flavorists are playing an increasing role in the foodservice industry. Their work is similar to the work that goes into creating a perfume. They often play a critical role in the development of new food products. Some individuals and companies concentrate specifically on the flavors, colors, and textures of these foods. It may be surprising to learn that many processed foods appeal to us because of the unique flavor combinations they contain. These combinations are often the result of careful research and product development, rather than the qualities of the food in its "natural" state.

In some cases, the flavors that are developed bear little resemblance to an actual food product. They may be produced as a gel, a powder, or a liquid that is added to foods as they are processed by large manufacturers and food producers in order to make products that have a consistent flavor. That means that, no matter how foods like potatoes or apples may vary from season to season or from region to region, the manufactured goods that are sold to the public taste the same from week to week and year to year.

Source: Janet Worne KRT/Newscom

Food flavorists are playing an increasing role in the foodservice industry

Some of the items that are made in these labs do end up in the hands of chefs, giving them the flexibility to produce brand-new creations, such as those featured in restaurants that specialize in *molecular gastronomy* (also known as *modernist cuisine*). Others find their way to pharmaceutical companies that produce medicines to make them more palatable for patients. Still others end up at cosmetics companies.

Tasters are responsible for evaluating the quality of foods in their unfinished state. There are experts in such specific types of food as chocolate, olive oil, cheese, wine, beer, and spices. Still others are responsible for quality assurance. They rely not only on their natural ability to detect tastes, flavors, and textures in foods, but also on years of experience and constant study. In the case of foods such as wine and cheese that must age, the taster must be able to evaluate the immature or unripened food and, from that, be able to predict the final flavors of the food. These tasters are employed by a variety of companies, such as food importers and food processors. They may be responsible for finding producers or growers for specialty products and often travel to the site of production.

Entry-Level Requirements

At entry level, a bachelor of science degree with coursework in chemistry, food and nutrient analysis, food engineering, and microbiology is typical. Although many individuals entering the area of food flavoring have a predominantly science background, an increasing number arrive with culinary arts degrees or experience, as well as degrees related specifically to food science and technology.

Helpful for Advancement

To move up into areas of research and development as a manager, you will need advanced degrees (either a master of science or a PhD in food science or related areas such as biology, chemistry, or nutrition). Expert tasters typically enhance their skills in flavor detection and evaluation by taking workshops and undertaking an apprenticeship with a master in the field.

CHRIS LOSS

Chris Loss, Ph.D., is the Director of Menu Research and Development at The Culinary Institute of America, and a Professor in the Department of Culinary Science. Professor Loss received his culinary degree from the Culinary Institute of America (CIA), followed by bachelor's, masters, and Ph.D. degrees in Food Science from Cornell University, with concentrations in Microbiology and Nutrition. He manages and teaches online courses such as "Food Science and Technology Applications for Menu Research and Development." He has taught Introduction to Gastronomy, Food Safety, and Skills Theory as part of the A.O.S degree program at the CIA. Dr. Loss is responsible for fostering research at the CIA and developing and teaching new curriculum in the Culinary Science Department. His research program focuses on areas such as culinary strategies for reducing sodium in foods with a focus on herbs and spices, the effects of nutritional information in the food-service environment on consumer behavior, and development and evaluation of sustainable culinary practices.

Professor Chris Loss, Ph.D.

Source: Courtesy of Christopher Loss & Culinary Institute of America

VITAL STATISTICS

Graduated: The Culinary Institute of America, A.O.S. degree in Culinary Arts, 1993

Cornell University, BS in Food Science, 1996

Cornell University, Ph.D. in Food Science, 2006

Profession: Professor, Researcher, CulinaryScientist

Interesting Items: Worked with faculty and students at the CIA's California campus to open a garden; sold produce at St. Helena Friday Farm's Farmers Market

Interviewed Vice President of McCormick & Co. about chef/scientist collaborations to speed product development

Collaborated with Prof. Howard Schutz to determine flavor preferences of seniors

CAREER PROFILE

Salary Ranges

Food Scientist: $30,000 to $60,000

Manager, Research and Development Team: $60,000 to $80,500

Getting Ready to Cook

7.1 Mise en Place

7.2 Working in the Kitchen

7.3 Food Presentation

Mise en Place

Key Concepts

- Understanding mise en place
- Organizing your work
- Sequencing and simplifying work
- Setting up a workstation

Vocabulary

- assignment
- deadline
- mise en place
- setting priorities
- strategies
- tasks
- timeline
- work flow
- work sequencing
- work simplification

Understanding Mise en Place

Mise en place (MEEZ AHN PLAHS) is a French phrase that means "to put in place." Professional cooks and chefs use it to represent the activities they might perform to get themselves, their ingredients, and their equip-

ment ready so that they can start cooking. Mise en place can easily be thought of as a to-do list, but for a true professional, it is much more than that. A complete mise en place helps you determine not just what ingredients you need and what you need to do, but also when you need to do specific tasks, where you need to do the work (for instance, on the stove or at a worktable), and how to go about getting everything done for a deadline.

Chefs consider a thorough and complete mise en place vital to their success. You can think of mise en place as a collection of good work habits. Developing good work habits takes concentration, effort, and practice. Once these good habits are established, however, mise en place has several important benefits. You'll be more organized and efficient. You'll be more confident about your work. Your work will have better quality.

Basic mise en place skills also include the cutting techniques necessary to prepare a variety of ingredients; the preparation of certain mixtures to season, flavor, or thicken foods; and some common cooking and mixing methods. More advanced mise en place skills include the ability to prioritize work so you are doing the right things at the right time.

 **READING CHECKLIST** *What is the translation of the French phrase* mise en place?

Organizing Your Work

Mise en place is ultimately a way to organize your work. When your work is organized, you make better use of your time. But the only way to be organized is to plan your work.

Planning Your Work Planning your work involves three initial steps:

1. **Determine your assignment.** To make a good plan, you first need to know your **assignment**, the food for which you will be responsible. For example, if you are the grill cook in a restaurant, you know you need to prepare all the grilled foods on the menu. This may include appetizers, main dishes, side dishes, and sometimes even desserts. Your assignment may be to prepare specific menu items. Or, your assignment may be to prepare basic ingredients used in different menu items. After receiving your assignment, read over the recipes for the items on which you will be working. You need to gain a basic idea of the recipes. (Use the PRN [Preview, Read, Note] Method for Reading Recipes from Section 5.1.) Pay attention to how long food needs to cook or cool and whether you need special equipment, such as a food processor or a slicer.

2. **Prepare an inventory.** After you are familiar with your assignment, your next step is to prepare a written inventory of what you have on hand. Then prepare a written inventory of the things you do not have on hand. The inventory should include ingredients, smallware, and equipment. The sooner you know about a missing ingredient or tool, the sooner you can get it and the less your work will be interrupted.

3. **Break your assignment into tasks.** Your next step is to break your assignment into written **tasks**, smaller jobs that lead to completion of your assignment. Tasks can be further broken down into smaller tasks.

FIGURE 7–1

Planning Your Work

Taking the time to plan your mise en place is critical.

APPLYING CONCEPTS *Would it be difficult for you to take the time in a busy kitchen to plan adequately?*

Source: Culinary Institute of America

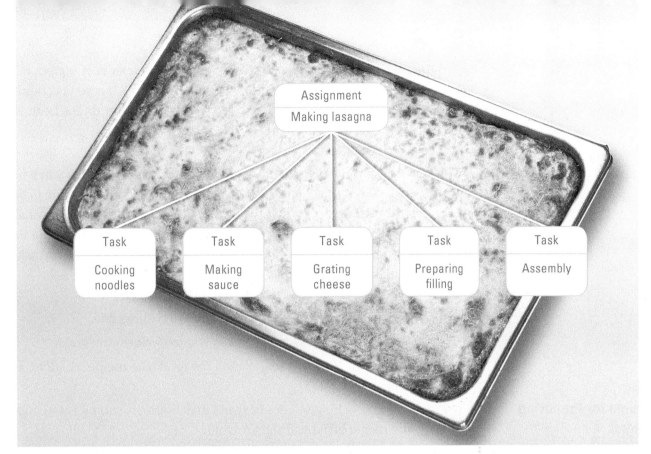

FIGURE 7–2

Breaking Down Tasks
A list of tasks for making lasagna.
APPLYING CONCEPTS *What task would you complete first?*
Source: Richard Embery/Pearson Education/ PH College

Here's an example of the relationship of tasks to an assignment. Imagine you are catering a party. Making the lasagna is your assignment. Your major tasks include cooking the lasagna noodles, making tomato sauce, grating mozzarella cheese, preparing a ricotta cheese filling, and assembling the lasagna. You can break some of these major tasks into smaller tasks so you can organize your work more efficiently. For instance, to make the tomato sauce, you accomplish the minor tasks of chopping onions, garlic, and tomatoes.

Breaking your assignment into tasks also helps you fine-tune the list of equipment you need for each task. For example, to boil lasagna noodles, you'll need a big pot as well as a colander to drain the noodles. To make the tomato sauce, you'll need a chef's knife, a cutting board, a saucepan or saucepot, and a mixing spoon. To make the filling, you'll need a bowl, measuring equipment, and a mixing spoon. To cook the lasagna, you'll need a baking dish and some aluminum foil. To serve the lasagna, you'll need a knife, plates, and a spatula.

Reviewing Your Lists One of the important benefits of good mise en place is that it allows you to work on more than one task at the same time. As you look over your major and minor tasks, you may notice that several recipes call for the same ingredient. If you add up what you need for all the recipes, you may find you can take one trip to the storeroom or refrigerator instead of making a separate trip for each task.

As you review your list of tasks, you may notice that some tasks can be grouped together, but certain activities need to take place at certain times. Sometimes you need to pay close attention to something as it cooks.

Other times, you can leave things to cook on their own. A big pot of water, for example, can take a long time to come to a boil, but you certainly don't need to watch it until it boils. Once you have the water on the heat, you can start another task.

Making a Timeline A **timeline** is a schedule that tells you when certain tasks have to be completed. The beginning of your timeline is the time you start working. The end of your timeline is the time your work has to be completed. The completion time is your **deadline.** You fill in the timeline by working backward from your deadline to decide when other tasks need to be finished.

A timeline requires you to do the following:

- Create a list of tasks for which you are responsible.
- Know roughly how long it takes you to perform the tasks.
- Know how long it takes to cook the food (the recipe usually provides this).
- Know how long to cool or rest a dish before it can be eaten (again, the recipe often will tell you this).
- Know how long you can hold food or a prepared item before it begins to lose quality.

To determine a timeline, follow these steps:

1. **Review your recipes.** Make a list of all the steps involved in preparing a complete mise en place. Jot down your time estimate for each task, including time to collect ingredients and equipment and to clean.

2. **Combine tasks.** Look for every recipe that calls for chopped garlic and add together the amounts you need.

3. **Assign a deadline for each task.** If you are a lunch cook, all the items you are responsible for preparing must be finished before the dining room opens its doors at 11:30. You can work backward from your deadline to determine your work schedule. Certain tasks must be finished before you can start certain other tasks.

4. **Prioritize the work.** Once you know when something must be completed, you can begin to prioritize tasks so you do them in the most efficient sequence.

Let's say it is 2:00 in the afternoon. You are serving lasagna at 7:00 this evening. Your recipe says it takes 1½ hours to bake the lasagna. It also says you should let the lasagna sit

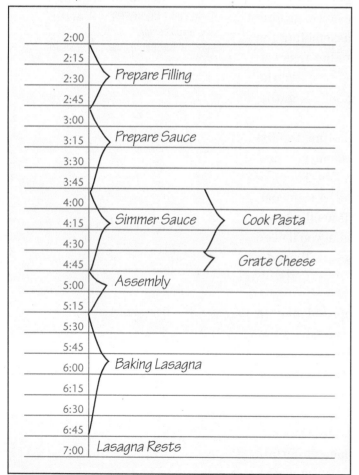

FIGURE 7–3

Timeline for Preparing Lasagna

Your deadline is 7:00.

SOLVING PROBLEMS *If the lasagna has to bake for 1½ hours, when do you need to put it in the oven?*

Personalizing a Timeline

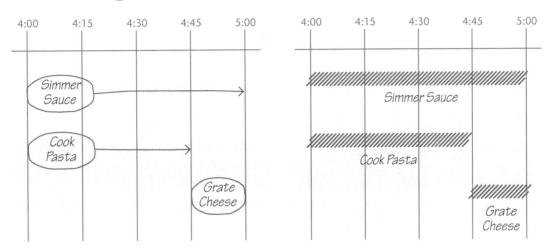

Portions of two sample timelines

Not everyone interprets information in the same way. This is true with timelines. Figure 7–3 shows a timeline charted against a table that is broken down in 15-minute time periods. Does this make the most sense to you? Does it adequately show the starting and ending times for the various major and minor tasks involved in the preparation of this dish? Does it show which tasks are going on at the same time?

Experiment with Timelines

Using the data in Figure 7–3, construct a timeline that shows all the major and minor tasks for the lasagna being prepared. Try to make the timeline as useful for yourself as you possibly can. You don't have to use the table format shown in Figure 7–3. You can use multiple colors, brackets, balloons—anything that makes your timeline helpful and understandable for you. Compare your timeline with classmates' timelines.

for 15 minutes before you serve it. That means on your timeline, the lasagna comes out of the oven at 6:45. It goes into the oven at 5:15. Assume it takes you 30 minutes to fill the pans. That means the noodles, sauce, filling, and cheese must be ready to use by 4:45. So you have 2½ hours to get all those items ready.

Setting Priorities Mise en place means that you work efficiently so everything is done at the right time. To accomplish this goal, you need to decide which tasks are the most important. This is referred to as **setting priorities**. Important tasks are given a higher priority; less important tasks have a lower priority. You need to think about your timeline as you set priorities.

One type of high-priority task is any task you need to get finished before you can start another task. Another type of high-priority task is one that takes a long time to finish. A low-priority task is one that does not have a relationship to another task and that does not involve a great deal of time. You could do this type of task at any point in your timeline and still make your deadline.

FIGURE 7–4

Last-Minute Preparation

Fresh ingredients, such as parsley, stay flavorful for only a short period of time.

DRAWING CONCLUSIONS *Should your timeline reflect the time needed to prepare fresh ingredients at the last minute?*

Source: Culinary Institute of America

Here's how to think about priorities. You need to make the lasagna sauce and filling, grate the cheese, and cook the noodles in 2½ hours. For your first priority, you decide to start the task that takes the longest time—making the sauce. Short tasks, such as grating the cheese, can be done last, or you can fit them in while the sauce simmers or the pasta water comes to a boil.

Problem-Solving Strategies A good mise en place is one that includes **strategies**, the skills and techniques you will use to get the job done. One of the most basic of all strategies is having a written plan. If you write down your plan, you can use it throughout the day as a reminder. A strategy for getting everything ready on time is to make a timeline. A strategy for working on more than one thing at a time is to prioritize tasks.

A strategy for coping with the unexpected is equally important. Just like the other strategies, problem-solving strategies are something you can learn with practice. No matter how good your written plan, however, there is a good chance something unexpected will happen. There may be a power outage. Someone may fail to show up for work. The delivery truck may be delayed. The pan you like to use for your tomato sauce may be in use somewhere else in the kitchen. When you are faced with these kinds of problems, you need to adjust your plan. Coping with the unexpected can be the best way to learn a new skill or lead to a better way to do something.

READING CHECKPOINT *How do you prepare a timeline?*

Sequencing and Simplifying Work

Work Sequencing An important aspect of mise en place is work sequencing. **Work sequencing** means doing the right thing at the right time. When you make a timeline and set priorities for individual tasks, you can use that information to create a work sequence. If your work is properly organized, or sequenced, you don't have to stop and wait for something while you are in the middle of preparing a recipe or serving a dish. As you think about your work sequence, look for the following:

- Dishes that can cook without being watched constantly
- Dishes that need a long time to prepare
- Tasks that can be interrupted or completed in a short time
- Tasks that cannot be interrupted or dishes that require constant attention as they cook

Foods that need a long time to chill, brown, come to a boil, or marinate need to be taken care of early in the day. While they are chilling, cooking, or marinating, you can do something else. You could perform tasks that take a short time or that can be interrupted while you take a few minutes to do something else. Ingredients that stay fresh or flavorful for only a short period, such as minced herbs or sliced tomatoes, should be cut or prepared as close as possible to the time you plan to serve the dish containing that ingredient.

Simplifying Work **Work simplification** means that you get things done in the fewest steps, in the shortest amount of time, and with the least amount of waste. Chopping all the garlic you need at once, rather than chopping garlic for each individual recipe, is an example of work simplification. One of the most important ways you can simplify your work is by learning which tool can do a specific task most easily.

You can find plenty of ways to save time as you work, if you look for them. The less time you have to spend walking from one place to another, the more time you'll have to get your work done. For example, if you need to get a pot to cook some potatoes, remembering to pick up a colander to drain the potatoes at the same time will save you steps. Try to get as many things accomplished on a single trip as you safely can.

READING CHECKPOINT *What is work sequencing?*

Setting Up a Workstation

Your workstation is the place in the kitchen where you gather together the tools and ingredients you need to prepare your mise en place and cook or serve foods. When you set up your workstation properly, you should not have to leave the area while you work. You should use your mise en place lists as reminders so you don't have to make several trips to get what you need or retrieve something you forgot.

The way you set up a workstation depends on the type of work you need to do. You need different tools and ingredients while you are preparing your mise en place than you do when you are preparing foods to serve. You need holding containers when you are preparing foods, pots and pans while you cook, and plates when you serve. You may also need a variety of hand tools, such as spoons, whisks, spatulas, peelers, or ladles.

Chef's Tip

Think Before You Walk

Never walk through the kitchen empty-handed. Take pots and pans to the sink when you are on the way to the refrigerator. Bring supplies back to your workstation after you've made a run to the dish room.

FIGURE 7–5

Work Flow

Arrange your work in an orderly sequence.

PREDICTING *How can organizing your work logically help you work faster?*

Source: Culinary Institute of America

Once you have all the ingredients, tools, and equipment you need, take the time to arrange them so they are easy to reach as you work. You should also try to put them into a logical order. This order is known as the **work flow** for a specific task. For example, if you are peeling and chopping onions, you might put all the unpeeled onions in a bucket on the left side of your workstation. Next to the bucket, you might place a cutting board. You might put a container to hold the peels directly in front of you, next to your cutting board, and a container to hold the peeled onions to the right of the board.

READING CHECKPOINT *How do you set up a work flow for a specific task?*

7.1 ASSESSMENT

Reviewing Concepts

1. What is mise en place?

2. What are the three initial steps involved in planning kitchen work?

3. What is work sequencing?

4. How do you set up a work flow for a specific task?

Critical Thinking

5. Drawing Conclusions Why would chefs think that a thorough and complete mise en place is vital to their success?

6. Inferring One of the benefits of good mise en place is that it allows you to work on more than one task at a time. Why is that important?

7. Solving Problems You have a number of small tasks that all have to be done at the same time. How would you indicate them on your timeline?

Test Kitchen

Pick a recipe that uses at least six ingredients and can be completed in less than eight hours. Prepare an inventory based on the ingredients available in your school's kitchen, break your recipe into major and minor tasks, and then construct a timeline to plan your cooking.

SCIENCE

The Critical Path

In the 1950s, various companies and the federal government developed the *critical path method*, a method for managing projects. It shows which activities are critical to maintaining a schedule. Research the critical path method. Describe who developed it and when, and how it relates to preparing a timeline.

PROJECT 7 **Mise en Place** You are now ready to work on Project 7, "Mise en Place," which is available in "My Culinary Lab" or in your *Student's Lab Resources and Study Guide* manual.

Working in the Kitchen

Key Concepts

- Learning to communicate
- Developing good work habits
- Learning how to deal with stress
- Becoming a professional

Vocabulary

- collaborate
- effective criticism
- initiative
- nonverbal feedback
- verbal feedback

Learning to Communicate

No matter how small a restaurant's staff may be, it is crucial for everyone to be able to share information. In the kitchen you will need to be able to:

- Communicate effectively
- Receive and give criticism
- Use feedback
- Resolve conflicts

Communicating Effectively When information comes from others to you and goes from you to others, you are communicating. It always goes both ways. However, in a kitchen you need to do more than just talk. You need to communicate effectively. There are four rules for effective communication in the kitchen.

Rules for Effective Communication

1. Listen with your full attention.
2. Ask questions.
3. Use the language of the kitchen.
4. Resolve conflicts with patience and respect.

The first rule of effective communication is to listen to what others are saying to you. When you listen to someone in the

Source: WavebreakmediaMicro/Fotolia

FIGURE 7–6

Listening Skills
Give your full attention when listening.

INFERRING *Is the waitstaff in the picture giving the chef their complete attention?*

Source: Culinary Institute of America

Chef's Tip

Write Clearly

You never know when other people may need to read something you have written. Always write clearly. Use correct spelling and grammar.

kitchen, you need to give that person your full attention. Look directly at the person as he or she talks. To be sure you correctly heard what was said, repeat what you heard. Many kitchens have a policy of "echoing" or "parroting." This means that you always acknowledge an order from the chef by saying, "Yes, chef," and repeating the order.

The second rule of effective communication is to ask questions. Always ask for more information or an explanation if you are not completely sure what you've been asked to do. When you ask a question, be as specific as you can. Pay close attention to the answer and be certain you understand it. If you hear words you don't understand or if you aren't sure about where something is located or when something needs to be done, ask for more information. A good way to make sure you remember the answers to your questions is to jot down a few notes to remind yourself about them. Keep a small notebook and a pen or pencil with you so you can write notes or look back over old notes you've already written.

The third rule of effective communication is to use the language of the culinary profession. Throughout this book, you will be introduced to the terms professionals use, including the proper names for techniques, preparations, and equipment. Using these terms properly helps you communicate with others effectively and efficiently. Remember that communication in the kitchen is professional communication. It is not personal communication. Avoid swearing or other inappropriate language.

The fourth rule of effective communication is to resolve conflicts with patience and respect. Imagine yourself involved in the conflict as "the other party." How would you want to be treated? Whether the conflict is with a coworker, a vendor, or a customer, you need to be patient and respectful, practice your listening skills, and resolve the conflict in a way that you would wish it to be resolved if you were involved in *both* sides of the conflict. Everyone deserves your patience and respect.

Receiving and Giving Criticism No matter how much experience you have or how long you have been working in a professional kitchen, you can learn a great deal from a specific type of communication known as criticism. Criticism, in this sense, is not used in the standard way we often see it used—as a type of personal attack. **Effective criticism** not only points out what went wrong or where things could be better, but also indicates how you can improve.

When you are on the receiving end of criticism, you may feel uncomfortable or even angry, regardless of how carefully the person criticizing you is speaking. Keep in mind that the point of criticism in the workplace is to make your work better.

Remember to listen carefully to criticism you receive. Use basic listening skills when you are receiving criticism. Ask questions if you are not sure what the criticism means or why it is directed at you. Give yourself a chance to think about the criticism before you respond.

Giving effective criticism to someone else is an important part of working with others. For criticism to be effective, you need to give it carefully. Try not to criticize someone when you are feeling angry or frustrated. Find a quiet time and place where you won't be disturbed. Stay calm and keep your voice and your temper even. Avoid using negative terms or using words that may sound as though you are making a personal attack on someone.

Keep your criticism focused on specifics. One way to be sure your criticism doesn't turn into a personal attack is to think about the exact changes you want to see and then to clearly state improvements that need to be made.

Effective Criticism

Receiving Criticism	Giving Criticism
Remember that the purpose of criticism is to make your work better.	Stay calm; don't criticize when angry or frustrated.
Listen carefully.	Avoid negative terms.
Ask questions if you don't understand.	Focus on specifics.
Think before you respond.	Clearly state what improvements are required.

Using Feedback Feedback is a type of review of your work. You can get feedback from many different sources and in many different ways. Your coworkers, your boss, and your customers all give you feedback.

Some forms of feedback are spoken; this is referred to as **verbal feedback**. Other forms of feedback are not spoken; this is referred to as **nonverbal feedback**. Just because feedback isn't said out loud doesn't mean it is not important. Be aware of things around you, such as the facial expressions and body posture of your coworkers, your customers, or your boss and whether plates are empty or full when they come back from the dining room.

One form of feedback comes in the form of compliments or complaints. A compliment tells you that you are doing something correctly. A complaint tells you that you are doing something incorrectly. Both complaints and compliments are personal opinions, of course, but that does not mean you shouldn't pay attention to them.

When you receive either a compliment or a complaint, you can use it to improve the quality of your work. A compliment is always pleasant, but you can do more with it than simply feel good about yourself. Think about what you did to earn the compliment so you can repeat it. Beyond that, you should also consider the ways you could make your work even better.

Feedback

This communication features both verbal and nonverbal feedback.

INTERPRETING ILLUSTRATIONS

What kinds of nonverbal feedback do you see in this picture?

Source: Erik Snyder/Getty Images

Chef's Tip

Finding Your Mentor

A mentor is someone whom you can turn to with questions about your career. A good mentor will provide honest feedback and criticism as well as pointing out ways that you can improve your work and become more successful.

A complaint should rarely be ignored. Be honest with yourself about why someone may have made the complaint. Then you can make a change and improve.

Resolving Conflicts There may be times when two people, or two groups, have a conflict, a disagreement about what should be done. Often each group or person views the other's position as a threat. Conflicts require respect for all positions, calm patience, and skillful listening. The solution to a conflict is often found in analyzing the cause of the conflict, finding out what the threat is, and discussing the threat directly. Each side must be flexible and willing to compromise in some respects without sacrificing their integrity or feeling threatened. Both sides need to work patiently for a resolution that works for all parties.

 READING CHECKPOINT *What are the four rules for effective communication?*

Good Work Habits

Thomas Jefferson believed that nothing can stop a person with the right mental attitude from achieving his or her goal. However, he also believed that nothing can help a person with the wrong mental attitude.

To be successful in the kitchen you need to develop the right mental attitudes and personal values. You also need to eliminate any traces of attitudes and personal values that will jeopardize your success. Doing this will develop your character in ways that will contribute to your ultimate success in the culinary profession.

Attendance/Punctuality You could be the best chef in the world, but it wouldn't matter if you weren't in the kitchen cooking. A kitchen depends on its chefs to arrive on time. The kitchen needs to be able to depend on you. The whole kitchen will suffer if just one chef is late. It is usually a good idea to be a bit early so you can begin your preparation and make sure you are ready when service begins. If you are not able to come to work or if you are going to be late, it is important that you notify your supervisor. If you know in advance that you will be late, discuss the possibility of trading a time shift with someone else so the kitchen will not be shorthanded.

Personal Integrity Ultimately in a kitchen you are responsible for managing yourself. You will always need to be fully aware of what is happening at each moment and take full responsibility for doing the right thing. What is the right thing? With time and experience, you will gain a sense of what should be done in a kitchen, what others expect of you. In the beginning, if you are unsure of what to do, it is important to ask a reliable source or your mentor what to do. If that isn't possible, ask yourself, "What is the best thing I can do in this situation?" Don't be satisfied with doing anything less than the best you can, but make sure that the answer balances quality and the time it takes to accomplish the task.

Productivity/Organizational Skills Let's say that you're on time and you want to do your best, but you are completely disorganized. Will you be able to contribute to the overall success of the kitchen? Probably not. Not everyone is good at being organized, but you will need to develop your organizational skills to be effective. You will also need to be productive, to make the best use of the time you have. Time is always limited in the kitchen. You need to accomplish a task to the best of your ability in the time you have.

Problem Solving/Decision Making When you work in a kitchen, you will always be solving problems and making decisions: Is the food cooked properly? Am I on time? Is this the way it is supposed to look? These moment-to-moment issues may not require sophisticated problem-solving or decision-making skills. In other cases, however, they become important. For example, if you are deciding whether it is worthwhile to include a particular dish on the menu or how to solve a problem in your workflow, you may need to focus on how you can make the best decision and arrive at the best solution to your problem.

Typically, experts talk about a five-step approach to decision making and problem solving, as listed in the box at the bottom of this page.

Initiative/Creativity You can do everything you are told to do—and it still may not be enough. As a professional, you are expected to go above and beyond. That means you are expected to take **initiative** (i-NISH-ee-ah-tiv),

FIGURE 7–8

Punctuality
It's usually a good idea to be a bit early.

PREDICTING *What would happen if a chef were late and he or she was unprepared for the beginning of service?*
Source: auremar/Fotolia

Five-Step Approach to Decision Making and Problem Solving

1. **State the problem clearly.** This makes sense. How can you solve a problem if you don't know what problem you are solving?

2. **Identify alternatives.** Sometimes there are no alternatives. For an important decision, try to list every feasible alternative you can think of, without worrying about how good that alternative may be.

3. **Evaluate alternatives.** You now begin your analysis. Rank the alternatives you listed in step 2. You can use a number scale, with a score of 1 for the least likely and 5 the most likely. This will to help you evaluate the alternatives in terms of how successful you think they might be.

4. **Make your decision.** Eliminate the low-ranked alternatives. Choose between the highest-ranking alternatives. Some people "sleep on their decision," allowing time to pass before they make their decision. Often, their subconscious will identify the right decision.

5. **Implement your decision.** Ultimately, you need to act! Once you act on your decision, don't forget to evaluate whether the decision is working as you anticipated. Some experts advise a follow-up step to evaluate the decision and then tweaking or changing it, if necessary.

to perform work without prompting or direction from someone else. Initially, this may not be possible because you don't know what is expected in the kitchen. But as you gain experience, you will be able—and expected—to take more initiative. One aspect of taking initiative is allowing yourself to be creative. You may see a new way of doing something. Before trying something new, however, it's usually wise to check with a manager to see if your creative idea is something that may be helpful or capable of being performed.

 **READING CHECKPOINT** *What are the five steps for decision making and problem solving?*

Dealing with Stress

Working in the culinary profession can be stressful in many ways. The pace can be exhausting. The kitchen may be loud. There are pressures to get a lot of work done quickly. Your work schedule may be prevent you from spending time socializing with family and friends. Stress can lead to a downward spiral. It can result in an unhealthy lifestyle, which can lead to more stress, which leads to reduced job performance, which leads to more stress—and can even jeopardize your job.

Use three steps to deal with your stress:

1. Think carefully about what is causing you stress.
2. Reduce your stress as much as possible.
3. Manage any remaining stress in healthy ways.

Causes of Stress Stress occurs when you have to handle more than you are used to. Stress can certainly be bad. It can be so overwhelming that you feel incapable of doing your job. But stress can also be good. It can be the result of challenging work—of learning a new job or taking on new responsibilities. The first aspect of determining your causes of stress is to figure out whether the stress is too much for you to handle right now, or whether it is temporary and will be reduced as you become more familiar with a new job or a faster pace.

If you feel the stress is bad, you need to determine why you are feeling stressed. Is it the result of your job or does it relate to something external (spouse, family, friends, an unhealthy lifestyle)? Are the hours you are working too much for you and causing you to feel constant fatigue? Are you anxious about your job performance? Are you having trouble with a supervisor? With a fellow employee? You must be honest with yourself. It may help to discuss the problem with your significant other, a family member, or a trusted friend. You must know what is causing your stress before you can find ways to reduce it.

Reducing Stress Once you know what is causing you stress, the next step is reduce the cause of your stress as much as possible. For example,

FIGURE 7–9

Not All Stress Is Bad
Working in a kitchen is often stressful.

COMPARING/CONTRASTING *When would stress be good? When would it be bad?*

Source: WavebreakmediaMicro/Fotolia

Tips for Managing Stress

- ✓ Get enough sleep. Avoid going to work fatigued.
- ✓ Get enough exercise. Working is *not* enough exercise.
- ✓ Develop healthy nutritional dietary habits.
- ✓ Don't smoke.
- ✓ Don't use drugs.
- ✓ If you drink, drink in moderation.
- ✓ Work on your personal time management.
- ✓ Work on communication skills. Learn to speak up and be assertive.

- ✓ Set boundaries. Learn to say no to unhealthy things or things that cause you unnecessary stress.
- ✓ Learn how to relax when you aren't working. This could involve breathing exercises, hobbies, sports, working out, spending time with family and friends, meditations—whatever works for you.
- ✓ Work on the things you can change, but don't worry about the things you can't change.
- ✓ Reduce your anxiety by focusing on the present.

if you are having problems with the hours that you are working, you may need to see if you can change them or cut them back. If you are having a problem with a supervisor or fellow employee, you may need to schedule a time when you can sit down with them and talk about your stress calmly and professionally. If you are uncomfortable doing your job, you may need to come early for special training. If you are not working efficiently, you may need to work on your time management. Ultimately, if the stress is too much for you to handle and you cannot find a way to reduce it, you may need to change jobs.

Managing Stress Most jobs in most professions involve a certain amount of stress. This is the good stress that challenges you and makes you feel that you've accomplished something at the end of the day. However, even this "good" stress can be overwhelming if you are leading an unhealthy lifestyle. The best way to manage stress is to focus on living a healthy lifestyle. Many of the tips on this page apply to your life on and off the job. Tests have shown that managing stress effectively influences job performance and leads to success and personal achievement.

READING CHECKPOINT *What are the three steps to use for dealing with stress?*

FIGURE 7–10

Get Enough Sleep
Try to schedule eight hours of sleep every day.

PREDICTING *What would happen if you were tired and the restaurant got very busy? How likely is it that you could keep up?*

Source: Ana Blazic Pavlovic/Fotolia

Professionalism

Professionalism involves maintaining the high quality of work expected of a professional. A culinary professional earns his or her living in a culinary field that requires a high level of culinary expertise. Culinary professionals desire to become masters of their profession. They strive to become experts in the skills and tools of their profession. They always give their best. By maintaining high standards for their work and their behavior, culinary professionals achieve a sense of professional self-esteem.

Technical Skills As a culinary professional, you must always strive to develop and increase your technical skills. If you are unfamiliar with a particular technique, practice it. If you need additional help, ask for it. Many restaurants require the use of computers. You will need to learn how to use any particular software required for your job and stay up to date as new versions of software are released. You may also need to read and comprehend technical manuals, articles, or culinary procedures in order to keep current with the latest culinary techniques, equipment, products, and trends.

Ethics A culinary professional must always act in an ethical manner. Wasting time amounts to stealing money from your employer and is unethical. It is also unethical to use unsafe food products, waste food, or use food of an inferior quality to that expected by management. Failure to act in accordance with employer expectations and organizational policies is also unethical. For instance, if your employer regards a certain recipe as confidential, then you would be acting unethically if you provided that recipe to a friend.

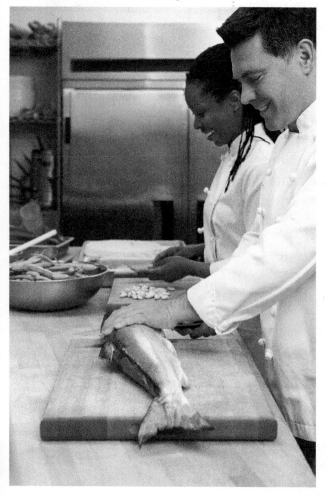

FIGURE 7–11
Value Diversity
Culinary professionals judge each other on the basis of their skills, knowledge, and effort.

INFERRING *Why is the kitchen no place for prejudice or stereotyping?*

Source: Noel Hendrickson/Glow Images

Diversity Professional kitchens are traditionally staffed by people of varying race, gender, color, nationality, and religion. Discriminating on the basis of any of these factors is unprofessional. Culinary professionals judge each other on the basis of their skills, knowledge, and effort. They respect the rights of others and appreciate the differences in each other's background. The kitchen is simply no place for prejudice or stereotyping. Both of these actions involve making judgments about a person's ability without any knowledge of that person's actual ability (often based on their race, gender, color, nationality, or religion).

Courtesy The kitchen is a busy and dangerous place to work. The respect you show to others is one of the ways to make your work easier and more efficient. Some simple acts of courtesy include making eye contact, cleaning up after yourself, and offering help to others when they need it. Courteous behavior is usually repaid by courteous behavior. If you treat your coworkers with respect, you can expect similar behavior in return.

Teamwork/Collaboration Typically you are working with other kitchen staff as a team to prepare food for customers. Team members have different responsibilities. You need to be aware of others' responsibilities as well as your own. The culinary staff is interdependent. This means that in order for the kitchen to function and produce the food that is required, you all depend on one another to do the jobs that have been assigned by managers.

Professionalism: The Culinarian's Code

Founded in 1929, the American Culinary Federation (ACF) is an organization that promotes the professional image of American chefs worldwide through education and certification programs. Due in large part to the efforts of the ACF, high-level American chefs are recognized as professionals.

The ACF has defined what it means to be professional in this field in the Culinarian's Code.

The Culinarian's Code

As a proud member of the American Culinary Federation, I pledge to share my professional knowledge and skill with all culinarians. I will place honor, fairness, cooperation and consideration first when dealing with my colleagues. I will keep all comments professional and respectful when dealing with my colleagues. I will protect all members from the use of unfair means, unnecessary risks and unethical behavior when used against them for another's personal gain. I will support the success, growth, and future of my colleagues and this great federation.

Source: Bravo TV/Courtesy/Everett Collection

Judges in Top Chef

The judges on a program like *Top Chef* contribute to the success, growth, and future of the contestants.

Research

Form a team to construct a rating system based on the Culinarian's Code. Use your rating system to rate contestants on culinary television shows where individuals compete for positions. Rate the contestants individually, not as a group. Compare your evaluations.

These jobs, the roles of the various team members, should be clearly defined. To be a good team member you need to be honest, supportive of your team members, and clear in your communication. You need to attend and participate in all staff meetings. Ultimately, you need to **collaborate** (ko-LA-bo-rate), to work together, with your team members for the good of the kitchen. Good teamwork leads to a total output that is greater than the sum of the individual input.

Leadership Even before you take on a leadership position in the kitchen, you can practice the skills of leadership when you lead by example. Do your job to the best of your ability. Speak up if something goes wrong or if someone is causing a problem. Share ideas you have about ways to improve work or reduce costs.

READING CHECKPOINT *Why is good teamwork important for a culinary professional?*

Reviewing Concepts

1. What are the four rules for effective communication?
2. What are the five steps for decision making and problem solving?
3. What are the three steps to use for dealing with stress?
4. Why is good teamwork important for a culinary professional?

Critical Thinking

5. **Drawing Conclusions** Why should criticism be focused on specifics?
6. **Predicting** Why is initiative important for someone who wants to make a career in the culinary arts?
7. **Inferring** Why would anxiety lead to stress?
8. **Inferring** Why is wasting time stealing money from your employer?

Test Kitchen

Have a class volunteer write down an order for eight main courses, with special instructions, and eight sides (an example: a hamburger, medium rare, with ketchup and pickle, no mayonnaise, and coleslaw). In a separate room, or out of hearing from the rest of the class, have a class member listen to the order by using effective listening skills. Continue passing the order from one class member to the next, always out of hearing from the remainder of the class. Compare the order as heard by the last class member to the order as it was originally given. Were there differences?

LANGUAGE ARTS ——————•
The Language of the Kitchen

Where would you look for unfamiliar words you encountered in the kitchen? The best approach is to use a dictionary or encyclopedia for culinary arts, cooking, or food. Write a report on the available culinary dictionaries or encyclopedias.

Food Presentation

Key Concepts

- Presenting foods
- Portioning foods
- Controlling temperature for effective presentation
- Using textures, colors, and shapes for effective presentation

Vocabulary

- asymmetrical
- plate presentation
- portioning foods
- presentation side
- symmetrical

Presenting Foods

Just as you need a good mise en place to get ready to prepare and cook foods, you also need a good mise en place before you can serve foods to guests. Presenting foods beautifully is a way to entice guests before they even take a single bite.

Basic Guidelines When guests sit down in a restaurant for a meal, they expect that the food will arrive in a reasonable amount of time, that it will be the food they ordered, that it will be at the right temperature, and that it will taste good. The way you put food into a dish or on a plate is referred to as your **plate presentation**. It is one way you can be sure the food gets to the table tasting and looking the way it should. There are three basic rules for plate presentation:

- Hot foods hot, cold foods cold.
- Plates neat, with no drips or smudges.
- Food attractive and appealing.

Basic Mise en Place for Service To prepare your mise en place for service, think about how food will arrive at the table. Then gather the items you need and arrange them in the area where you will be serving food. Everything should be clean, neatly organized, and within easy reach.

You need plates to serve most entrées and appetizers. You need bowls or cups to serve a soup, stew, or chili. To serve foods on a buffet line, you need hotel pans. For a reception,

Source: Culinary Institute of America

Chef's Tip

Cleaning Plates

Wring a paper towel out in hot water so it is only moist. Dripping wet towels will drip onto the plate and spoil the presentation.

you may need platters or trays. Some dishes call for a sauce or condiments served in a cup or bowl. All this smallware needs to be on hand and in easy reach.

You usually need hand tools to lift food onto a plate. Ladles or spoons are used for liquid food such as sauces. Salads are often served with tongs or scoops. Sandwiches and other foods that are put together by hand call for food-handling gloves. Gather enough hand tools to last until you are finished serving food.

Some foods are ready to serve as they come from the pan. Others may need to be sliced, cut, scooped, or arranged. You may use a variety of hand tools in addition to spoons and tongs. Carving knives (as well as carving forks, cutting boards, and a steel) should be part of your mise en place if you need to cut slices of food. Learning to use any specialized tools for presentation is a fundamental part of your mise en place for food presentation.

Use only edible food products on a plate to increase the attractiveness of your food presentation. For example, use only edible flowers. Don't use a flower that is inedible because customers will assume that anything on the plate may be eaten.

Finally, place a container of hot water and paper toweling at your workstation so you can clean the rims of plates, if necessary. Use towels once, then throw them away.

READING CHECKLIST *What are the three basic rules for plate presentation?*

Source: Culinary Institute of America

Portioning Foods

Portioning foods properly means serving the correct amount of a particular food. A portion of food is the same thing as a serving of food when it comes to putting food on a plate to serve a guest. Portion sizes can vary from one restaurant to another and from one food to another. Portion sizes for the same food should never vary at the same restaurant, however. This is especially true when the same food is being served to more than one guest sitting at the same table.

Importance of Portioning One of the complaints you may hear about a restaurant is that the portion size changes from day to day. This may make guests feel they are being overcharged. Consistent portioning makes your guests feel confident they are paying a fair price.

Serving the right amount of food every time you serve it is important for several reasons. Proper portioning makes it easier to plan your work. You can also reduce the amount of food that is wasted. The key to portioning food is measuring the portion accurately by using the appropriate tools.

Chef's Tip

Portions and Servings

A *serving* is the amount recommended by dietary plans such as MyPlate, while a *portion* is the amount of food you choose to serve or eat at any one time—and that may be more or less than a serving.

Tools for Portioning As you assemble your mise en place for service, remember to include the appropriate tools for portioning food. Ladles and scoops have already been mentioned as part of your mise en place for presenting food. They are also used to measure out portions. With a portion scale, you can measure out consistent portions of sliced meats or poultry. To select the right tool for a portioning job, you need to know what you are serving and what the proper portion size is for that food.

You can also think of the plates, bowls, cups, or hotel pans you use to serve food as a kind of portioning tool. To select the right serving pieces for a dish, you need to know how the correct portion ought to look when it is served on your plates. For instance, your kitchen may serve eight ounces of soup instead of six because six ounces of soup looks skimpy in your restaurant's soup bowls.

 **READING CHECKLIST** *Name several portioning tools you can use during service.*

FIGURE 7–12
Portioning Ice Cream
Each scoop of ice cream should be close to the same size.
PREDICTING *How would you feel as a customer if your scoops were different sizes?*
Source: Dorling Kindersley

Temperature

You need to cook and cool food to safe temperatures. You also need to serve food at the temperature that lets your guests most fully enjoy it. Chefs use a number of techniques and tools to get foods to the best temperature for service.

Keeping Foods at the Best Temperature Hot foods should be at least 135°F. If you are serving a food as soon as it comes from the oven, grill, or pan, it will already be hot enough. If you prepare a food ahead of time, you may keep it warm in a steam table. Some foods are kept warm in a low oven. Set the temperature of the oven or steam table to at least 135° and keep an instant-read thermometer on hand to check the food's temperature periodically.

Cold foods should be below 41°F, frozen foods below 32°F. Some foods, such as cheese, are most enjoyable when they are only slightly chilled or are at room temperature. These foods are held in the refrigerator, but before they are served, they should sit at room temperature long enough to lose their chill. Frozen foods, such as ice cream or sherbet, can be transferred to the refrigerator to soften slightly so they have a better consistency and a fuller flavor.

·•FOCUS ON
•·• Safety

Check the Temperature
Even though equipment such as steam tables and soup warmers often have dials to control temperature, the dials are not always accurate. Don't rely on the equipment's temperature setting. Use an accurate instant-read thermometer to check food.

Plates If you put hot soup in a cold soup bowl, the bowl will warm up and the soup will cool down. If you put a cold salad on a hot plate, the plate will cool down and the salad will warm up. To keep foods at the best temperature for service on their way from the kitchen to the table, warm or chill the plates before putting food on them.

Heat plates by arranging them in a place where they will be warm, such as near the stove or under a heat lamp. Have clean side towels on hand to hold the hot plates safely. Chill plates for cold dishes by stacking them in a refrigerator or other cool place.

READING CHECKLIST *How does the temperature of a plate affect the temperature of the food served on it?*

Textures, Colors, and Shapes

When you cook food, you change not only its flavor but also its texture, color, and shape. Some cooking techniques make food firm or crunchy. Others make food soft and tender. Some techniques change food from a pale color to a deep brown. Some food takes on a distinct and recognizable shape. You can highlight all these changes when you present a plate to a guest.

Texture Keeping hot food crisp generally means keeping it dry by holding it in uncovered pans. A rack keeps even the bottom of each piece dry and properly crunchy. Keep the food warm, but not so hot it starts to dry out. Usually a temperature of around 160°F is best. Another way to be sure that foods are hot and crispy when you serve them is to prepare smaller batches and cook them more frequently throughout the meal period.

The way you combine food on a plate is another way you can maintain or even improve its texture. A few crackers add a crunchy texture to a bowl of soup. Serving smooth sauces over food makes it more tender. Putting a sauce under crispy food keeps it from becoming soggy.

To keep cold food crisp, hold it in covered containers or well wrapped in the refrigerator. The covering keeps moisture in the food so it doesn't wilt, soften, or dry out. The cold temperature keeps it firm.

Food such as soups, sauces, or stews can develop a skin on the surface. To prevent a skin from forming,

FIGURE 7–13

Keeping Foods Crisp
Putting a sauce under these lamb chops keeps them crispy.

PREDICTING *What would happen had you poured the sauce over this dish?*

Source: John Rizzo/Getty Images

keep the food covered or topped with a little butter or oil. Skim off the skin or any fat that rises to the surface before you serve the food.

Colors To get the right color in a food, you need to cook it properly. Recipes instruct you to cook foods until they change color. Each dish has a color that tells you it is properly cooked. Once you've achieved that color, you need to serve the dish before the color starts to change.

When every food on the plate is the same color, the plate can look boring. Adding a few bright colors makes the plate more interesting and attractive. If everything on a plate is brown or white, you could add a vegetable with a bright green color for contrast.

Shapes and Arrangements The purpose of shaping and arranging foods before you serve them is to make them look more appealing. In some cases, the size and shape of the food you are putting on the plate can even help you determine what size and shape your plate should be. In other cases, the size and shape of your plate may determine the size and shape of the food you are serving. The color of the plate, the size of the border or rim on the plate, and any design or texture on the plate is part of your presentation.

To give shape to semisoft foods, you can use a pastry bag, scoop, or spoon them. Another option is to use a mold.

When you cut foods into a particular size or shape, your tools must be sharp so you make neat, straight cuts. This is as important when you are cutting foods before you cook them as it is when you slice or carve cooked foods to serve to the guest. Foods cook more evenly and have a better texture when you cut them properly, and they also look much more attractive.

Some foods look more attractive on one side than they do on the other. The good-looking side, referred to as the **presentation side**, should always be facing up so guests see it.

··FOCUS ON
··Nutrition

Color on the Plate

Including colorful green, white, yellow, orange, and red vegetables adds more than color to a plate. It improves the nutritional value of the dish and adds additional textures and shapes to the plate.

BASIC CULINARY SKILLS

Using Molds to Shape Foods

1. **Fill the mold.**
2. **Press food into the mold** lightly, using the back of a spoon.
3. **Put a plate on top of the mold.** The plate should be upside down.
4. **Turn the mold and plate over.** The plate should be right side up and the mold should be upside down on the plate.
5. **Tap the mold and lift it** from the food.

Source: Jerry Young/Dorling Kindersley

FIGURE 7–14

Symmetrical Arrangement
Limes arranged symmetrically around a lime caramel cream.

CLASSIFYING *Would an asymmetrical arrangement be as pleasing to the eye?*

Source: David Murray/Dorling Kindersley

Arrange food neatly on the plate. A little open space around food allows guests to see and taste food separately. Putting foods right next to each other or on top of each other blends them together (which, of course, is desirable for some dishes).

By arranging foods in different ways, you can also create different effects. For example, to make a piece of meat or fish look larger, you can slice it and spread the slices in a fan shape. When the food covers more of the plate, it looks like a bigger portion. You can also put something under a food to lift it up. Height is another way to change the appearance of a food.

Plates can be arranged so they are either symmetrical or asymmetrical. To make a symmetrical arrangement, imagine a line running through the center of the plate. If you have equal numbers of items placed on both sides of the plate, the arrangement is **symmetrical** (sym-MET-rih-cull). If you have unequal numbers of items on either side of the plate, the arrangement is **asymmetrical** (AY-sym-met-rih-cull).

READING CHECKLIST

What is a symmetrical arrangement? An asymmetrical arrangement?

7.3 ASSESSMENT

Reviewing Concepts

1. What are the three basic rules for plate presentation?
2. Name two types of portioning tools you can use during service.
3. How does the temperature of a plate affect the temperature of the food served on it?
4. What is a symmetrical plate arrangement?

Critical Thinking

5. **Drawing Conclusions** Why is it important to be concerned with the way food is presented?
6. **Inferring** Why might a kitchen choose to avoid putting sauce over the presentation side, choosing instead to put the sauce under the item?
7. **Relating Concepts** What kinds of plated food might be most suitable for a symmetrical arrangement? What kinds of food might be more suited for an asymmetrical arrangement?

Test Kitchen

Divide into groups of two. Using the same main course, each group will create a plate presentation. Groups can use different sides, sauces, garnishes, or anything available in the kitchen and available to the other groups. When all plates have been presented, discuss the presentations and vote on the most appealing one.

SOCIAL STUDIES

China Dishware

Research the origins of the word *china* as it applies to china dishware. How long has it been made? How is it made? Are there differences in quality in this type of dishware? Is dishware of this sort made today?

7 Review and Assessment

Reviewing Content

Choose the letter that best answers the question or completes the statement.

1. Which of the following is *not* true about mise en place?
   a. It can be thought of as a to-do list.
   b. It is a French phrase meaning "to work quickly."
   c. It represents the activity of getting ready to cook.
   d. It helps you determine what to do and when to do it.

2. Work sequencing means
   a. doing the right thing at the right time.
   b. doing all cooking at one time.
   c. arranging tools in a logical order.
   d. getting things done in as few steps as possible.

3. Which of the following is *not* true about receiving criticism?
   a. You should remember the purpose of criticism.
   b. You should ask questions.
   c. You should listen carefully.
   d. You should respond immediately.

4. What is the first step in the five-step approach to decision making?
   a. identify alternatives
   b. evaluate alternatives
   c. consult with experts
   d. state the problem clearly

5. Which of the following is *not* a tool used for portioning?
   a. ladles
   b. knives
   c. scoops
   d. portion scale

6. Hot foods should be at least what temperature?
   a. 115°F
   b. 125°F
   c. 135°F
   d. 145°F

Understanding Concepts

7. What is an asymmetrical plate arrangement?

8. What are the five steps in the five-step decision-making process?

9. What does it mean to portion food?

10. What is the presentation side of a prepared food?

11. What are the four rules for effective communication?

Critical Thinking

12. **APPLYING CONCEPTS** Why is it important to prepare an inventory of both the ingredients you have and the ingredients you do not have?

13. **DRAWING CONCLUSIONS** Why are timelines, setting priorities, and sequencing work important concepts for everyone working in a kitchen?

Culinary Math

14. **SOLVING PROBLEMS** You are using a 4-oz ladle for portioning chili. You have 1½ gallons of chili. How many portions do you have?

15. **APPLYING CONCEPTS** One of your dishes requires 2 oz of an ingredient; another of your dishes requires 4 oz of the same ingredient. You expect to prepare about 45 portions of the first dish but only 25 portions of the second dish. To simplify your work, you want to make only one trip to cold storage, where the ingredient is kept. How much of the ingredient should you take from cold storage?

On the Job

16. **COMMUNICATING** You have just made a mistake in the kitchen. The immediate supervisor, who is under a great deal of stress, immediately criticizes you, beginning with the phrase, "You always . . ." Is this effective criticism? Why or why not?

17. **APPLYING CONCEPTS** Can you apply the concept of mise en place to everyday living? Explain your answer.

18. **COMMUNICATING** A dish wasn't ready when it should have been and caused a problem. It wasn't your fault, but the chef was frustrated and criticized you. What should you do?

Culinary Instructor

Becoming a culinary instructor is a natural progression for many working cooks and chefs. In fact, any chef typically spends a good amount of time teaching others. Taking that basic skill and turning it into a career path seems like a logical choice. You may see a number of television programs or videos that teach cooking skills ranging from basic to experimental.

The best teachers not only have firsthand experience and expertise in the culinary techniques they are teaching, they also have the ability to explain the process logically and answer questions about why and when things are done in the kitchen or bakeshop. They create lesson plans, tests, and projects that allow students to demonstrate their mastery of the subject, grade papers, order foods and other materials for the classroom, and maintain a safe and sanitary work environment.

Demonstrators and private instruction

Culinary demonstrators are hired by companies and businesses to showcase new products or tools. The demonstrators give presentations in places such as department stores, shopping clubs, fairs, and festivals. While demonstrators are more likely to be focused on making a sale, private instructors offer a different service. They may teach classes as part of a school's adult education program, or they may be hired by individuals or stores to provide lessons in basic and advanced cooking and baking, menu planning, or special-needs cooking, such as cooking healthy foods for people with diabetes.

Lynn Gigliotti instructing a student at the Culinary Institute of America

High school or vocational teacher

Teachers in high schools or vocational schools teach students basic culinary techniques. They may also run an in-house café or restaurant that is open to the public. Teachers at this level often provide instruction in many areas, including sanitation, product knowledge, culinary techniques, and baking and pastry.

Instructor at a two-year or community college

At a community college or specialized culinary school, instructors teach in more defined areas. For instance, instead of teaching all types of cooking, an instructor may specialize in teaching a specific type of cuisine (Italian or Chinese, for instance) or specific techniques (bread baking or cake decoration).

Professor in a bachelor's or master's degree program

Some colleges and universities offer four-year programs and even master's degrees or Ph.D. programs in disciplines related to the culinary arts: food science, nutrition, hotel management, event planning, and culinary history. These individuals typically have specific areas of expertise and may have one or more degrees in related areas.

Entry-Level Requirements

Culinary demonstrators usually do not have a specific degree, but they are generally required to show that they have the skills necessary to properly showcase the product or tool.

Teachers in high schools and vocational schools must meet specific requirements that are set up by each state. Some states call for at least an associate's degree as well as a teaching certificate. Teachers must also pass background checks.

Culinary instructors in community colleges and two-year cooking schools often need at least an associate's degree in a culinary field. Many schools require a bachelor's degree. Instructors must meet minimum requirements for working and teaching experience.

Professors will have at least a master's degree and often must have a doctorate in a related field.

Helpful for Advancement

To advance as a culinary instructor, you will need three or more years of experience working in the culinary arts and at least one year of experience teaching at the post-secondary level. You should also have the ability to use technology in the classroom. Membership in professional culinary and education organizations such as the American Culinary Federation is helpful. Publishing articles or books in areas related to the culinary arts and the hospitality industry will assist you in your efforts to advance in the field and will probably be a continuing requirement as a culinary instructor.

LYNN GIGLIOTTI

Born in Philadelphia, Lynn Gigliotti spent a great deal of time learning her craft in restaurants around the country before joining the faculty of The Culinary Institute of America. One of her first jobs after graduating was as a cooking instructor at the Cook's Warehouse in Atlanta. She single-handedly built her catering and consulting business from her first event, a party for ten people, into a half-million-dollar upscale, off-premise catering business. She worked for famous chefs, including Jean-Louis Palladin and Gunther Seeger. Her own restaurant, Grappa, was featured in *Atlanta Magazine*'s "Best of 1999" and was named an Outstanding Restaurant in the 2001 *Zagat Guide Atlanta*.

Lynn Gigliotti

VITAL STATISTICS

Graduated: The Culinary Institute of America, 1988

Profession: Chef-instructor at The Culinary Institute of America

Interesting Items: Teaches Cuisines of the Mediterranean

Interested in sustainable agriculture and seafood

Appeared on the seventh season of *Top Chef* in 2010

CAREER PROFILE

Salary Ranges

Demonstrator or Private Instruction: $25,000 to $35,000 (or more)

Full-Time Faculty, Two-Year or Community College: $40,000 to $80,500 (or more)

Adjunct (Part-Time Faculty), Two-year or Community College: $2,000 to $3,000 per four-hour course

Professor: Varies widely depending on rank and type of institution, from $50,000 for lecturing professors to more than $100,000 for full professors

Chapter

8

Cooking Methods

8.1 Dry-Heat Methods

8.2 Moist-Heat Methods

Source: Ricardo Elkind/Getty Images

Dry-Heat Methods

READING PREVIEW

Key Concepts

- Understanding how dry heat affects food
- Identifying and using a variety of dry-heat methods
- Determining doneness in foods prepared by dry-heat methods

Vocabulary

- baking
- batter
- broiling
- caramelize
- carryover cooking
- conditioning the pan
- deep-frying
- dry-sautéing
- grilling
- Maillard reaction
- nutritional value
- nutritive value
- pan-broiling
- pan-frying
- radiant heat
- recovery time
- roasting
- sautéing
- searing
- smothering
- standard breading
- stir-frying
- sweating
- water bath

How Dry Heat Affects Foods

Any cooking method changes the way food looks and tastes. It also changes the nutrition food provides when we eat it.

Methods of Heat Transfer In the dry-heat methods, heat is transferred, or conducted, to the food in one of the following ways:

- By rays that come from a glowing, or red-hot, heat source such as burning coals, flames, or a hot electric element; this type of heat transfer is called **radiant** (RAY-dee-uhnt) **heat**
- By metal that conducts heat from a burner to the food
- By oil that is heated when a pan transfers heat from the burner to the oil

Changes to Food When you cook food by using a dry-heat cooking method, you can see, feel, and taste the changes in food. Another important change is not so easy to detect. These are changes to the food's nutritional value. These four changes—to the food's color, texture, flavor, and nutritional value—may be minimal or dramatic, depending on the food you are preparing and the technique you choose.

The heat source in these methods causes the outside of the food to dry out as it cooks. When the surface is dry, it changes color. Often foods prepared by using dry-heat methods have a golden or deep brown color. As foods brown, the flavor on the outside becomes

Source: Dave King/Dorling Kindersley

Chef's Tip

Dry-Heat Cooking

The higher the heat and the longer you cook, the more noticeable will be the changes in flavor, color, and texture when you are using a dry-heat method.

FIGURE 8–1

Caramelized Onion

This onion has been cut in half and roasted to caramelize it, turning it golden brown, soft, and sweet.

PREDICTING *If the onions are caramelized on the outside, does that mean their insides are cooked?*

Source: jabiru/Shutterstock

more intense. The color on the inside of the food also changes as you cook, although not as dramatically as the outside.

Food that contains sugar changes colors when sugars on the surface start to turn brown, or **caramelize** (CAR-muh-lyze), when they get hot enough. Protein-rich foods, such as meats, also become brown as they cook. When proteins turn brown as they cook, it is referred to as the **Maillard** (MY-yard) **reaction**.

When the heat comes into contact with the surface of food, the outer layer of the food stiffens. Sometimes you can see and feel a distinct crust. The crispy skin on a roasted chicken, the crunchy breading on a piece of deep-fried fish, and the crisp outer layer of a french fry are all examples of how dry-heat methods change the texture of a food. Eggs, meats, fish, and poultry all become firm as they cook. Other foods may become softer. Onions, for instance, change from a crisp texture to a soft, almost melting texture.

Maintaining Moisture in Food When you prepare food for dry cooking, you can take steps to combat the drying effect of the heat. For example, you could dust food with flour to help it stay dry as it cooks. Food such as meat or vegetables that you plan to grill or broil could be soaked in oil, flavorful liquids, aromatics, herbs, and spices before cooking to add moisture. You could also coat food in a batter or breading before frying it. One of the best ways to maintain moisture in food is to avoid overcooking it.

Nutritional Value The carbohydrates, proteins, and fats in food supply us with energy. However, food also provides other things, such as vitamins and minerals, that we need to stay healthy. When you consider all the benefits food may have for our bodies, you are talking about food's **nutritional value**, which is also referred to as its **nutritive** (NEW-tri-tiv) **value**.

Applying heat to any food can make it lose some of its nutritional value. The longer a food cooks, the more nutritive value it loses. Food cooked quickly with one of the dry-heat methods loses relatively few vitamins and minerals. Although cooking can take away some of a food's nutritional value, it can also add something to food that was not there before cooking.

One of the most significant ways that some dry-heat cooking methods change the nutritional value of food is requiring fat to be added to the food as part of the cooking process. Fats and oils added during the cooking process typically increase the calories and the fat in the food when we eat it.

Prepared, Convenience, and Partially Cooked Foods Professional kitchens can use a number of different products that are meant for dry-heat methods. These prepared and convenience foods include meats that have been trimmed, brined or marinated, stuffed, or breaded. Frozen foods such as shrimp and fish may be suitable for preparing directly from their frozen state. It is also possible to partially prepare foods by a dry-heat method, cool and store them safely, and then finish cooking them just before they are to be served. This is a common strategy when you must prepare and serve foods quickly to a large number of guests, such as at a banquet. It helps you use your equipment and your time effectively. It also means that you can cook foods far enough to be sure that everything is done on time and served at its best. For example, you might parcook steaks by broiling or grilling them to give them a good color on the outside but not cook them all the way through. They are cooled and then ready to finish in a short amount of time in the oven. French fries have the best texture if you partially cook them at a lower temperature, a step known as *blanching*. They can be cooled after blanching and finished at a higher temperature in a few minutes, to be ready when the guest orders them.

FIGURE 8–2
Fried Fish with French Fries
Fried foods develop a crisp crust.
APPLYING CONCEPTS *How is the nutritional value of potatoes changed by frying them?*
Source: David Murray and Jules Selmes/Dorling Kindersley

 **READING CHECKPOINT** *How does caramelizing differ from the Maillard reaction?*

Dry-Heat Methods

There are eight basic dry-heat methods of cooking. As an aid to memory, these methods are often grouped into four related pairs.

Grilling and Broiling Grilling is a dry-heat method in which food is placed on a rack for cooking. Grilled foods have a robust, smoky taste. The heat source is located below the rack holding the food. The heat source could be charcoal, gas, wood (in the form of chunks or logs), or an electric or infrared heating element. The radiant heat from the heat source heats up the metal in the rack enough to cook the food (creating the dark grill marks that are the sign that food was cooked on a grill rack). The radiant heat also cooks the parts of the food that are not in direct contact with the rack.

A griddle is sometimes used to prepare grilled food. However, rather than having an open rack over the heat source, a griddle uses a solid, flat metal plate above the heat source. Food that is cooked on a griddle may be referred to on a menu as *grilled* or *griddled*.

Dry-Heat Methods

- Grilling and broiling
- Roasting and baking
- Sautéing and stir-frying
- Pan-frying and deep-frying

FIGURE 8–3

Perfect Grill Marks

To create perfect crosshatch grill marks: (1) Place meat diagonally, presentation side down. (2) Pick up meat halfway through cooking the presentation side and reposition it in the opposite direction. (3) Turn over. It may not be necessary to crosshatch the other side.

APPLYING CONCEPTS *What does a crosshatch design on a grilled steak contribute to the customer's enjoyment?*

Source: Richard Embery/Pearson Education/ PH College

Broiling is similar to grilling, except the heat source is located above the food. When you put food into a broiler, it cooks from the heat of the broiler rack as well as from the radiant heat given off by the heat source above the rack. The heat in a broiler is typically a gas flame or an electric or infrared heating element.

Roasting and Baking Roasting and baking are dry-heat techniques in which food is cooked by hot air trapped inside an oven. As the hot air comes in contact with the food, the surface of the food begins to heat up and dry out. Eventually the surface starts to take on a deeper color. The food's texture changes as it goes from raw to cooked. Meats, fish, and poultry tend to become firmer as they cook, while vegetables and fruits become softer.

BASIC CULINARY SKILLS

Grilling and Broiling

① **Oil the grill** or rack by using an oil-soaked cloth.

② **Heat the grill** or broiler.

③ **Place the food on the grill or rack,** with the presentation side facing down. Brush with sauces or glazes if your recipe calls for them.

Source: Culinary Institute of America

(Continued)

Grilling and Broiling *Continued*

4 **Turn** the food.

Source: Culinary Institute of America

5 **Cook the food on the second side** until it is properly cooked.

6 **Serve** very hot directly from the grill on heated plates.

Source: Culinary Institute of America

Recipe Card

4. Grilled Sirloin Steak

In terms of the basic method of heat transfer, there is no significant difference between baking and roasting. We eat "baked" potatoes, although it would be just as accurate to call them "roasted" potatoes.

The difference between roasting and baking has more to do with the size of the food we are preparing. Generally, roasting indicates you are preparing a whole item or large piece of food. Baking typically means you are preparing smaller pieces of a larger food. A chicken you cook whole in the oven is referred to as a *roasted chicken*. But the same chicken cut into pieces and cooked in the oven is referred to as *baked chicken*. An exception is in the case of potatoes. A whole potato is considered "baked," while "oven-roasted" potatoes are generally cut into pieces instead of being left whole.

When meats are roasted or baked, they are sometimes seared before being placed in the oven. *Searing* is a type of sautéing and is discussed later in this chapter.

Baking also includes dishes that are mixtures and cooked in the oven. Examples of this type of baking include scalloped potatoes and pasta dishes such as lasagna. Baking also includes items produced in the bakeshop, such as cakes, cookies, pies, and breads. These foods cook in part by being exposed directly to the heated air trapped in the oven. They also cook in part from contact with the pan that holds them. The material in the pan transfers the heat from the air to the food inside the pan.

Medieval Cuisine

Medieval cuisine evolved during the Middle Ages, a period of time in Europe from the 5th to the 16th century. The way that food was selected and prepared in the Middle Ages, as well as the way that it was served, set the stage for modern European cuisine. Some of the cookbooks from that time feature a wide array of foods that may seem exotic to us. The dishes often included what appears to be large quantities of spices.

Grains, usually cooked into porridges and gruels, shaped into pasta, or baked into bread, were by far the most important foods for everyone living at this time. The type of grain varied depending by location. Wheat was grown widely, but in some areas, especially in northern Europe, rye, buckwheat, millet, oats, and barley were more common.

Medieval cuisine was influenced by religion in two important ways. The Catholic Church required several fasting days when meat could not be served. This fact inspired chefs and cooks to develop numerous dishes featuring fish and vegetables. Another way that the Church made an impact on cuisine was a result of the pilgrimages that knights made to the Holy Land. They returned with a wide array of culinary influences from the Arab world.

If you were part of the nobility or belonged to a religious order, you had many more options than a peasant. Serving meat at a banquet showed your high rank in society. Spices and sugar were used lavishly in wealthy households. In fact, medieval scholars believed that there were physical differences between the classes. They said that members of the upper classes would become ill if they ate the coarse, unrefined foods that sustained the peasants, while peasants would also become ill if they were to eat the highly refined, elegant foods meant for the upper class.

Banquets were an opportunity for a wealthy host to show off. Meals started with an aperitif in order to "open the stomach." The courses of the meal progressed from light to heavy. First came something considered very easy to digest, such as apples. This was followed by vegetables and salads, "light" meats such as poultry and goat, and soups. Next came the heavy meats such as pork and beef.

Source: INTERFOTO/History/Alamy

These meats were also accompanied by vegetables and nuts. Each course might include as many as thirty different dishes. The feast was concluded with a course meant to "close the stomach" that included aged cheese and spirits such as brandy.

No matter what type of food was being prepared, however, it was prepared directly over a live fire, often found in the main hall where it could provide warmth as well as cook foods. It wasn't until the later stages of the Middle Ages that a separate area was designated as the kitchen. Even without the sophisticated kitchen equipment we have today, medieval chefs were able to produce elegant and elaborate foods. Many recipes that we prepare today have their roots in medieval cuisine.

Research

Spices were extremely popular in medieval cuisine. Form a group to research the spice trade to Europe in the Middle Ages. Prepare a presentation to the class that identifies the most popular spices, where they came from, what they cost, and how they were used in the cuisine. If you have access to a kitchen, prepare a medieval dish that uses spices that would have been brought to Europe via the spice trade.

The heat in an oven is not as intense as the heat generated by a grill, a broiler, or even a burner on the stovetop. At times, however, it still may be too intense for delicate food. Chefs control oven heat by putting food in a pan or baking dish and then setting that pan in a larger pan. Then they add enough water to the larger pan to come up around the sides of the smaller pan. This is known as baking foods in a **water bath**. Because the water can only come up to 212°F, it insulates and protects the food. A water bath is often used when a chef wants the finished item to have a creamy, smooth consistency.

The type of oven you use will have an effect on the outcome of any roasted or baked dish. A conventional oven typically produces foods that are deeply colored on the exterior with a distinct crust. A convection oven results in a similar effect; because the air is kept in motion inside the oven, some foods cook more quickly than they might in a conventional oven. However, a microwave oven does not heat up the air inside. Instead, the food cooks by means of the energy that is transferred from magnetic waves. This makes microwaves useful for tasks such as defrosting and reheating foods. However, in the absence of the heated air, there is little to no browning. The

Roasting and Baking

1 Heat the oven.

Source: Culinary Institute of America

2 Sear the food in a hot pan on the stovetop or in a very hot oven, if your recipe calls for it. (Searing is a variation of sautéing and is discussed later in this section.)

3 Roast or bake the food, uncovered, until it is properly cooked.

4 Baste the food as it roasts or bakes.

Source: Culinary Institute of America

5 Rest the food before slicing or carving.

 Recipe Card

5. Roast Chicken with Pan Gravy

The word *sauté* comes from a French verb that means "to jump." Sautéed food cooks so quickly that you can imagine it simply jumping into the pan and then out of it, on to a plate.

waves affect different substances differently, so foods such as meats and poultry that include lean meat, fat, skin, or bones are difficult to prepare to an even doneness in a microwave.

Sautéing and Stir Frying Sautéing (SAW-tay-ing) is a cooking technique that cooks food quickly, often uncovered, in a very small amount of fat in a pan over high heat. Food that is suitable for sautéing is typically quite tender and thin enough to cook in a short time. Food is often coated with seasoned flour before sautéing. Sautéed foods are cooked primarily by contact with the pan. The fat you use helps to keep the food from sticking to the pan. It can also add some flavor to the food if you choose a flavorful fat such as butter or olive oil.

BASIC CULINARY SKILLS

Sautéing

1 **Coat the food** with flour, if indicated in your recipe. Otherwise, blot the food dry and season it.

Source: Culinary Institute of America

2 **Heat the pan** over direct heat.

3 **Add oil** or cooking fat. Use only a small amount.

Source: Culinary Institute of America

4 **Add food to the hot pan.** Do not crowd food.

Source: Culinary Institute of America

5 **Cook the first side.** Do not disturb until the food is halfway cooked.

6 **Turn** the food once.

Source: Culinary Institute of America

7 **Complete cooking** on the second side until properly cooked.

Recipe Card

6. Sautéed Chicken with Herb Sauce

When you sauté food in a pan on a burner, you should let the pan heat up first, even before adding any oil. Chefs refer to this step as **conditioning the pan**. Once the pan is hot, you can add oil. The oil will heat up very quickly, so you can start cooking right away. If you add food to a cold pan with cold oil, it will stick to the pan and your food will absorb more oil, altering its taste.

When you add food to a sauté pan, the pan cools off. The more food you add, the longer the pan takes to get hot again. The time it takes for the pan to heat up again is called the **recovery time**. The success of a sauté has a direct relationship to the recovery time. A short recovery time means foods will develop good color and flavor.

Turn sautéed food halfway through cooking. Resist the temptation to move food around unless it is cooking too quickly or starting to get too dark.

You can vary the steps in sautéing to produce different effects. There are four important variations of sautéing:

- Stir-frying
- Searing
- Pan-broiling
- Sweating and smothering

Stir-frying is similar to sautéing, but there are some basic differences. One of the most obvious differences is the pan you use. Stir fries are made in *woks*, pans with round bottoms and high sides. Foods for a stir fry are usually cut into small strips so they can cook quickly. You turn sautéed food only once, but when stir-frying you constantly stir and toss food as it is cooking to make sure it cooks quickly and evenly. Stir-frying is an important cooking method for Asian dishes.

Searing (SERE-ing) is cooking food, usually uncovered, in a small amount of hot fat just long enough to color the outside of the food. This can be done to give food, such as a cut of meat, a rich brown color (often before roasting it). Another application for searing occurs when you are preparing a large amount of food, as for a banquet. Food is seared to give it good color on the outside, and then it is put in the oven to finish cooking. Food is turned often to avoid burning.

Pan-broiling is very much like sautéing except that you use no fat. The food is uncovered and cooked over high heat. This method is used for foods that have a high fat content, such as bacon. Fat that is released by the food is poured off as it forms. This is sometimes referred to as **dry-sautéing**.

FIGURE 8–4
Stir-Frying Peppers
Stir-frying is an important cooking method for Asian dishes.
APPLYING CONCEPTS *How does stir-frying differ from sautéing?*
Source: Dave King/Dorling Kindersley

Recipe Card

7. Stir-Fried Scallops

FIGURE 8–5

Veal Cutlets
The standard breading should cover the entire surface of the food.

PREDICTING *What might happen if the breading is not applied evenly?*

Source: Culinary Institute of America

Sweating calls for lower heat than you would use for sautéing, searing, or pan-broiling. Food, typically vegetables, is cooked uncovered over a low heat in a small amount of fat. The food softens, releases moisture, and cooks in its own juices but is not allowed to brown. Another difference between sweating and sautéing is that you should stir foods more often when you sweat them. **Smothering** is a variation of sweating in which the pan is covered. This increases the amount of juices that are retained in the pan.

Pan-Frying and Deep-Frying In **pan-frying**, food is cooked in hot oil in a pan. The amount of oil you use in pan-frying is more than you use for sautéing. The oil should be deep enough to come halfway up the sides of the food you are cooking. So, for example, if the food is one inch thick, you need half an inch of oil in the pan. As with sautéing, you turn foods only once as they pan-fry to finish cooking.

You can partially cook thick or dense foods by pan-frying them on both sides until golden and crisp. They can finish cooking, uncovered, in the oven. If you cook them entirely in the pan on the top of the stove, the outside may overcook before the food cooks all the way through.

In pan-frying, you must heat the oil to the temperature specified in the recipe. Use a thermometer to check the temperature. Most foods are pan fried at about 350°F. If you add food to oil that is not hot enough, the cooked food will be pale and absorb the oil, making it greasy. If the oil is properly heated, food will turn out crisp and golden on the outside and the moisture and juice will be sealed on the inside.

Foods that are most often pan-fried are naturally tender and moist. Vegetables, fish, chicken, veal, and pork are common choices.

Pan-fried foods are usually coated before you add them to the oil. There are three basic coating options:

- **Seasoned Flour.** The simplest coating is simply flour that has been seasoned with salt and pepper. To coat the food, you add the food to the flour, turn it until the flour covers the entire surface, and shake gently so any extra flour falls off.

- **Standard Breading.** When a recipe calls for a **standard breading**, it means you dust the food with seasoned flour, dip it in beaten eggs, and then cover it in breadcrumbs (or another crumb mixture). You can add a standard breading to food several hours before you pan-fry it if you keep the food in the refrigerator until you are ready to cook it.

- **Batters.** There are many different types of batters, but a **batter** is typically made by blending a type of flour and a liquid. To coat a food with batter, first you coat the food with flour (or cornstarch) and shake off any excess. Then dip the food into the batter until the food is entirely covered.

Pan-Frying

1 **Coat the food,** if required by your recipe.

2 **Heat the oil** or cooking fat in a pan. It should be half the thickness of the food.

Source: Culinary Institute of America

3 **Add the food to the hot oil carefully.** Do not allow pieces to touch.

Source: Culinary Institute of America

4 **Pan-fry the first side** until a golden crust forms.

5 **Turn and finish cooking.** Thick foods can finish cooking, uncovered, on a rack in a 350°F oven.

Source: Culinary Institute of America

6 **Drain** the excess oil. Blot with a paper towel before serving.

Source: Culinary Institute of America

Recipe Card
8. Pan-Fried Veal Cutlets

Batter-dipped foods need to go into the pan immediately, so be sure the oil is hot and you are ready to cook before you start dipping food into the batter. Different recipes for batters can produce different textures, such as a beer batter or a tempura batter.

Foods are also cooked in hot oil when you are **deep-frying**, but with deep frying, the oil completely covers the food. Typically the oil is about

Dry-Heat Cooking Methods

Method	Food Category	Specific Applications
Grilling and broiling	Meat	Beef steaks (strip, tenderloin, Porterhouse, London broil, skirt, hanger, flank) Veal chops, cutlets Lamb chops, steaks Pork chops, tenderloin, cutlets Ground (beef, veal, lamb, pork)
	Poultry	Whole (including rotisserie) Halves Cuts (drumsticks, wings, thighs, breasts) Pieces Cutlets Ground
	Fish and seafood	Whole fish Steaks and fillets Lobsters, shrimp, octopus, scallops, oysters, clams, and mussels
	Vegetables, grains, and fruit	Whole vegetables (mushrooms, carrots, asparagus, corn on the cob) Sliced vegetables (squash, mushrooms, eggplant, beets, asparagus) Sliced fruit (apples, pineapples, peaches) Polenta
Roasting and baking	Meat	Beef roasts (rib, whole and portioned tenderloin, top round, sirloin, steamship round) Veal roasts from leg (may be known as "round"), loin, shoulder Lamb roasts from leg, loin, and rib Pork roasts from leg and loin; ham
	Poultry	Whole poultry Halves Cuts (drumsticks, wings, thighs, breasts) Pieces
	Fish and seafood	Whole fish Fillets and pieces Lobsters and clams
	Eggs	Custards Soufflés Shirred eggs
	Vegetables, grains, and fruits	Whole vegetables (peppers, carrots, mushrooms, potatoes) Sliced vegetables (root vegetables, squash, eggplant, carrots, beets, potatoes) Pilafs (rice, bulgur, barley) Whole fruits (apples, pears)

350°F to 375°F. Deep-fried foods are typically coated with standard breading or a batter. Foods that are coated with breading are usually lowered into hot oil with a basket. Foods coated in a batter are generally lowered into the oil carefully with a pair of tongs.

Dry-Heat Cooking Methods

Method	Food Category	Specific Applications
Sautéing and stir-frying	Meat	Beef steaks (strip, tenderloin, Porterhouse, London broil, skirt, hanger) Veal chops and cutlets Lamb chops and steaks Pork chops, tenderloin, cutlets Ground (beef, veal, lamb, pork)
	Poultry	Halves Cuts (drumsticks, wings, thighs, breasts) Cutlets Pieces Ground
	Fish and seafood	Whole small fish Steaks and fillets Lobster, shrimp, scallops, and calamari
	Eggs	Whole, fried Scrambled Omelettes
	Vegetables, grains, and fruit	Raw vegetables (tomatoes, mushrooms, eggplant, leafy greens) Blanched or parcooked vegetables (peas, green beans, cabbage, potatoes) Rice, stir-fried
Pan-frying and deep-frying	Meats	Beef (chicken-fried steak) Veal chops and cutlets Lamb chops and cutlets Pork chops, tenderloins, and cutlets
	Poultry	Halves Cutlets Cuts Pieces
	Fish and seafood	Whole small fish Steaks and fillets Calamari, shrimp, clams, and oysters Cakes and croquettes (crab, salmon) Tempura
	Eggs	Fried eggs (sunnyside up, over)
	Vegetables, grains, and fruit	Fritters and pancakes (typically calls for vegetables to be cooked separately and combined with a batter) Tempura Potatoes and sweet potatoes (cut into french fries or chips)

When you add food to the hot oil, the temperature of the oil drops. The time it takes to come back to the correct temperature, the recovery time, has an effect on the flavor, color, and texture of food. That is why you should add foods in small batches when pan-frying or deep-frying.

Deep-Frying

1 **Heat the oil** in a deep-fat fryer or a pot with tall sides.

2 **Blot the food** dry.

3 **Coat the food,** if your recipe calls for it.

Source: Culinary Institute of America

4 **Add the food to the hot oil** by using a frying basket or tongs.

Source: Culinary Institute of America

5 **Deep-fry** until the food is an even golden brown and is fully cooked.

6 **Remove the food.**

Source: Culinary Institute of America

7 **Drain** the excess oil. Blot the food on a paper towel before serving.

Recipe Card

9. Deep-Fried Breaded Shrimp

READING CHECKPOINT *What are the eight basic dry-heat cooking methods?*

Chef's Tip

Smoke Point

Fry with oils that can handle high heat without reaching the point where they begin to smoke. Corn, peanut, canola, and safflower oils are all suitable for frying at high heat.

Determining Doneness

Knowing when a food is done can be one of the biggest challenges in any of the dry-heat methods. Some foods can be prepared to more than one degree of doneness. Steaks, for instance, can be prepared to any doneness the customer requests, from rare to well done. Two important considerations in determining doneness are carryover cooking and resting food after it is cooked.

Carryover Cooking All foods continue to cook after you take them out of the pan, off the grill, or out of the oven. That is because the food holds heat. The remaining heat is enough to continue to cook the food. This process is known as **carryover cooking**.

The amount of carryover cooking depends on the size of the food. Big cuts of meat can hold more heat, so they continue to cook for a longer period. If you measure the temperature of the food at the center as it rests, you would see that it rises 2 or 3 degrees or as much as 10 or 15 degrees.

You can't stop carryover cooking, so you need to plan for it as part of the total cooking process. This means taking food from the pan, oven, or broiler before it is completely cooked. Then the carryover cooking finishes the cooking. If you wait until the food is completely cooked, carryover cooking will overcook the food by the time you serve it to your guests.

Resting Food Chefs allow food to rest after it is cooked, for three important reasons:

- Food cooks properly without overcooking. A resting period gives carryover cooking enough time for the food to reach its proper doneness.

- Food is moister. When food is being cooked, the heat outside the food drives the food's natural juices toward the center. Letting food rest allows the juices to redistribute, moving back to the outer parts of the food.

- It allows time for proper plating and presentation. Letting the food rest gives you a chance to finish any sauce or side dishes you plan to serve with it.

FIGURE 8–6

Carryover Cooking
Remove food from the heat before it reaches the temperature the customer requested.
DRAWING CONCLUSIONS *Which will have the greater amount of carryover cooking, a roast or a steak?*
Source: Swetlana Wall/Fotolia

 **READING CHECKPOINT** *What is carryover cooking?*

8.1 ASSESSMENT

Reviewing Concepts

1. How does caramelizing differ from the Maillard reaction?
2. What are the eight basic dry-heat cooking methods?
3. What is carryover cooking?

Critical Thinking

4. **Comparing/Contrasting** What is the difference between grilling and broiling?
5. **Comparing/Contrasting** What is the difference between sweating and smothering?
6. **Applying Concepts** What is the relationship between recovery time and a food's flavor, color, and texture when deep-frying?

Test Kitchen

Divide into two groups. Both groups will deep-fry three batches of french fries. The first group will allow a normal recovery time between batches. The second group will ignore recovery time and cook one batch immediately after the other. Evaluate the results.

SOCIAL STUDIES ●
Woks

Research woks. Describe the materials from which they are constructed, the sizes available, how they are used for cooking, how they should be maintained, and what types of dishes are typically cooked in a wok.

READING PREVIEW

Key Concepts

- Understanding how moist heat affects foods
- Identifying and using a variety of moist-heat cooking methods
- Identifying and using a variety of combination cooking methods
- Determining doneness in foods prepared by moist-heat and combination cooking methods

Vocabulary

- blanching
- boiling
- braising
- fork-tender
- fully cooked
- parboiled
- parcooked
- poaching
- rolling boil
- simmering
- steaming
- stewing

How Moist Heat Affects Foods

Moist-heat techniques have a built-in temperature control. Foods are cooked in a liquid. Most liquids will not rise much above 212°F, the boiling point of water. This means that food cooked by using a moist-heat method will have a different appearance, flavor, and texture than food prepared by a dry-heat method.

Heat Transfer When you cook food with one of the moist-heat methods, the food is cooked either through direct contact with a hot liquid or with steam that rises from the hot liquid. The heat is conducted from a heat source (usually a burner) through a pan and then from the pan to the liquid. When the food is added to the liquid, the heat is transferred from the liquid to the food. If the cooking method relies on steam heat, the food is cooked when the heat from the steam is transferred to the food.

Changes to Food Because moist heat is lower than the temperatures you can produce in a hot pan, in hot oil, or on a hot grill, the changes to a food's color on the surface are not as dramatic. The color on the outside of the food is often the same as the color on the inside. This plays a role in the way the food tastes. Instead of developing a roasted or caramelized flavor, foods are often said to have a clean taste.

Source: evgenyb/Fotolia

Foods such as meat, fish, poultry, or eggs become firmer as you cook them. Vegetables, fruits, and grains become softer. A chef uses these changes in texture as a way of determining when food has finished cooking.

Nutritional Value When food comes in direct contact with a hot liquid or steam, the water draws some of the nutritive elements out of the food. You can keep this to a minimum by cutting food as close as possible to the time you need to cook it and cooking it for as short a time as possible.

Prepared, Convenience, and Partially Cooked Foods Chefs use moist-heat methods as a way to either fully prepare or partially cook a variety of foods that they will finish or reheat later. When foods are prepared in advance, it is much easier for cooks to produce a completed dish at the moment that a guest orders the meal, rather than holding foods in a steam table. Foods that have been partially or fully prepared can be chilled and packaged. They may finish cooking in a hot water bath or be reheated in a microwave. Convenience foods such as sauces or stocks are generally simmered or boiled before they are used.

 **READING CHECKPOINT** *How is heat transferred to food in a moist-heat method?*

Moist-Heat Cooking Methods

The moist-heat cooking methods have many similarities. The major distinctions between them have to do with the foods you choose and the temperatures of the liquid in which the food is steamed or cooked. There are four basic moist-heat cooking methods.

Moist-Heat Methods

- Steaming
- Poaching
- Simmering
- Boiling

Steaming When **steaming**, you cook food in a closed pot or a large steamer. The steam trapped in the pot or steamer circulates around the food. The heat in the steam is transferred to the food. The food does not come in direct contact with the steaming liquid. Steaming is a gentle, moist-heat technique.

Steaming is a good way to retain as many of the food's nutrients as possible. It is a popular technique for preparing many vegetables, but it is also

Boiling Water

Cover pots of water, stock, or broth as you heat them. They come to a boil faster because the lid traps the heat in the pan instead of releasing it into the air.

··FOCUS ON
··Nutrition

Colors and Nutrition
The colors in food are often a clue to its nutritional value. Typically, the deeper the color, the greater the nutritional value. If the color is drawn out of the food and into the cooking liquid, nutrients are lost unless the liquid is served as part of the dish.

Italy

Italy is a long narrow country, surrounded by water, with mountains up and down its length. Before modern roads and transportation were available, these mountains made travel extremely difficult. That is why there are so many distinct cooking styles throughout the country today.

Most countries have a basic grain that is the foundation of their cuisine. Historically, wheat has filled that spot throughout most of Italy. Northern Italy often features the famous rice dishes from Venice, especially *risotto*, a creamy rice dish made with broth, butter, and cheese. Polenta, a dish made from cornmeal, is also favored in the north.

Pasta is made from a particular type of wheat known as *durum wheat* no matter where you are in Italy, but the accompanying sauces show regional differences. Tomato- and meat-based sauces are common in the south. Sauces made with cream and cheese are typical in the north. Pasta dishes may feature fresh pasta made into long ribbons like fettuccine, or filled and folded into ravioli or tortellini. Dry pasta is produced in hundreds of different shapes and sizes from tiny rice-shaped orzo to wide lasagna noodles. Dumplings, known as gnocchi, are popular too and can be made from potatoes, bread, or even semolina (a type of wheat cereal).

Another ingredient that gives a clue as to what part of the country a dish originated is the type of cooking fat it calls for. Olive oil is common throughout southern Italy, where the climate makes it easy for

Source: T33kid/Shutterstock

olive trees to flourish. Butter and cream are more common in the north, since it is too cold for olives.

Garlic, basil, olives, and capers are common flavors in Italian dishes, but each region takes its own spin on using them. Pesto, a sauce made with basil, olive oil, garlic, pine nuts, and cheese, comes from a region in northern Italy known as Liguria. Arrabbiata sauce, made in the central part of Italy, includes garlic, hot chiles, and tomatoes. A sauce from the south, puttanesca, features garlic, olives, anchovies, and tomatoes.

Many of the world's most famous cheeses come from Italy. Some of them are so important to Italy that they have been given legal protection. The real parmesan, known as Parmigiano-Reggiano, comes from a specific part of Italy and is labeled D.O.P., which stands for *denominazione di origine protetta*, as an assurance that it is the authentic product. Other foods may bear the letters D.O.P., including the famous Italian ham prosciutto.

Italian cooking as we know it today is based on ancient traditions, but it has also been transformed by foods from the New World, brought back by one of the most famous of all Italians, Christopher Columbus. He brought tomatoes, chiles, and corn. Until then, a dish of spaghetti or a pizza topped with tomato sauce would not have been possible.

Research

1. Research where in Italy pizza originated. How does a typical Italian pizza differ from those sold in pizzerias in this country?

2. Research the procedure used to make prosciutto di Parma.

3. What is the classic order of courses in an Italian meal?

Source: Africa Studio/Fotolia

Typical Italian food

used to prepare more tender, delicate meats and fish, including chicken breasts, whole fish, and shellfish such as clams or lobsters.

To add more flavor to foods as they steam, you can add seasonings, flavorings, and aromatics to the steaming liquid. As the liquid heats up, those flavors are released into the liquid and the steam it produces. The flavor is then transferred to the food.

Poaching, Simmering, and Boiling

Food prepared by poaching, simmering, or boiling is completely covered by hot liquid. **Poaching** is used for tender foods (eggs, fish, poultry breasts, and fruits, for instance) and requires a cooking temperature of 160°F to 170°F. **Simmering** is used for tougher cuts of meat, such as corned beef. The temperature of the liquid should be between 170°F and 185°F. **Boiling** is suitable for pasta and certain vegetables. The temperature of the liquid is boiling, 212°F.

Some foods that are actually simmered are referred to as boiled. Don't be misled by the name of a dish. Check the recipe to see what the correct temperature of the cooking liquid is supposed to be for a particular food.

Of course, the most accurate way to check the temperature of the liquid is with a thermometer. Chefs, however, can often tell how hot the liquid is by looking at the size of the bubbles and the rate at which they rise to the surface. When a liquid is boiling rapidly, it is referred to as a **rolling boil**.

FIGURE 8–7
Steaming Asparagus
Asparagus do not come in direct contact with the steaming liquid when steaming.
DRAWING CONCLUSIONS *Why would contact with the steaming liquid tend to reduce nutrients in the steamed food?*
Source: Richard Embery/Pearson Education/PH College

BASIC CULINARY SKILLS

Steaming

① **Heat water** in a steamer or pot until it is steaming.

② **Place food in the steamer pan** or rack, leaving enough room for the steam to circulate around all sides of the food.

③ **Place the steamer pan in the steamer** over the steaming water and cover.

Source: Culinary Institute of America

④ **Steam** until food is properly cooked. Open the steamer as few times as possible.

Recipe Card

10. Steamed Broccoli

How Hot Is the Liquid?

Stage	Description
Poaching	Many bubbles cling to the sides and bottom of the pan. Some motion is visible on top of the liquid, but it seems to be barely moving. **160°F–170°F**
Simmering	The size of the bubbles increases and they rise to the surface more rapidly and more frequently. The surface shows more obvious signs of motion. **170°F–185°F**
Boiling	The bubbles are very large and rise very quickly to the surface. There is very much motion on the surface. **212°F**

Poaching, Simmering, and Boiling

① **Bring the liquid to the correct temperature.**

- Poaching: 160°F–170°F
- Simmering: 170°F–185°F
- Boiling: 212°F

② **Add the food.** Add additional liquid, if necessary, to keep the food completely covered.

Source: Culinary Institute of America

③ **Add seasonings and aromatics,** if your recipe calls for them.

Source: Culinary Institute of America

④ **Cook the food** at a consistent, even temperature to the proper doneness.

⑤ **Lift or strain the food** from the cooking liquid.

Source: Culinary Institute of America

Recipe Cards

11. Poule au Pot

12. Corned Beef with Winter Vegetables

13. New England Shore Dinner

Moist-Heat Cooking Methods

Method	Food Category	Specific Applications
Steaming	Meat	Sausages (beef, veal, lamb, pork)
	Poultry	Breasts
	Fish and seafood	Whole fish Fillets Lobster, shrimp, crab, crayfish, and clams
	Eggs	
	Vegetables, grains, and fruits	Vegetables (leafy greens, peas, asparagus, corn) Grains, especially rice
Poaching	Meat	Tenderloins (beef, veal, pork)
	Poultry	Whole Cuts Pieces
	Fish and seafood	Whole fish Fillets Lobster
	Eggs	Eggs, whole but no shell
	Vegetables, grains, and fruits	Fruits, especially pears and apples
Simmering	Meat	Beef (shanks, short ribs, bottom round, corned beef, brisket, eye of the round) Veal (shanks and breast) Lamb (shanks and breast) Pork (ham)
	Poultry	Whole Halves Cutlets Cuts Pieces
	Fish and seafood	Lobster
	Eggs	—
	Vegetables, grains, and fruits	—
Boiling	Meat	—
	Poultry	Whole Halves Cutlets Cuts Pieces
	Fish and seafood	Lobster, crab, shrimp, crayfish, clams, mussels, and oysters
	Eggs	Eggs, hard-boiled or soft-boiled, in shell
	Vegetables, grains, and fruits	Most vegetables Dried beans and peas Most grains and hot cereals Pasta

 **READING CHECKPOINT** *How is heat transferred to food in a moist-heat method?*

Combination Cooking Methods

Combination cooking methods call for a two-stage process. The first stage of cooking calls for the food to be seared in hot oil. This is done to help food keep its shape as it cooks. It also provides the dish with the rich flavor that develops when food is seared in hot oil. In some cases, the searing step is replaced by briefly blanching the food in a boiling water or stock. The blanching step also helps foods keep their shape as they cook and gives the dish a specific flavor and color. After searing or blanching, the food is gently cooked in a flavorful liquid or sauce. There are two basic combination cooking methods.

BASIC CULINARY SKILLS

Braising and Stewing (with Initial Searing)

① **Heat a small amount of fat** or oil in a pan.

② **Add the food** to the pan.

③ **Sear the food** until it is evenly colored.

Source: Culinary Institute of America

④ **Remove the seared food** from the pan.

⑤ **Add mirepoix** or other aromatic ingredients and cook in the hot fat or oil.

Source: Culinary Institute of America

Recipe Cards

14. Braised Lamb Shanks
15. Yankee Pot Roast

⑥ **Return the food to the pan,** setting it on top of the cooked aromatics.

⑦ **Add cooking liquid** to the pan, enough to properly cover the food (about one-third for braises and completely covered for stews) and bring to a simmer. Cover the pan.

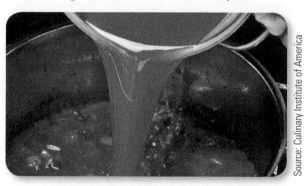

Source: Culinary Institute of America

⑧ **Cook at a low simmer** until very tender. Turn braised food as it cooks. Stir stews. Add more liquid, if necessary, to keep the food appropriately covered.

Source: Culinary Institute of America

⑨ **Skim** grease and other impurities from the cooking liquid.

Braising Braising (BRAYZ-ing) usually indicates that the food is left whole or in large pieces, with enough liquid to partially cover it.

Stewing Stewing indicates that food is cut into smaller pieces and then cooked in enough liquid to completely cover the ingredients.

Braises and stews are usually made from tougher cuts of meat, whole poultry, and firm-fleshed fish or seafood. You can also braise vegetables and beans. Food that is braised must be able to stand up to the long, gentle cooking process without completely falling apart.

Perfectly braised or stewed foods have a rich flavor and a tender texture. The sauce for a braise or a stew is actually nothing more than its cooking

Braising and Stewing (with Initial Blanching)

1. **Heat stock or water** in a deep pot.

2. **Add the food** to the simmering liquid.

3. **Blanch** until the food has lost its raw appearance. The exterior of meats, poultry, and seafood will firm up.

4. **Lift the blanched food** from the liquid.

5. **Cook mirepoix** or other aromatic ingredients in hot fat or oil in a separate pan.

6. **Add the blanched food** and enough cooking liquid to properly cover the food (about one-third for braises and completely covered for stews).

7. **Bring the cooking liquid** to a simmer, stir well, and cover the pan.

8. **Cook at a low simmer** until very tender. Turn braised food as it cooks. Stir stews. Add more liquid, if necessary, to keep food appropriately covered.

9. **Skim** grease and other impurities from the cooking liquid.

Recipe Card

16. Veal Blanquette

Source: Michael Nivelet/Fotolia

Combination Cooking Methods

Method	Food Category	Specific Applications
Braising	Meat	Beef (shanks, brisket, chuck, short ribs, spare ribs) Veal (shanks, roasts from leg and shoulder) Lamb (shanks, breast) Pork (roasts from leg and shoulder)
	Poultry	Whole Cuts
	Fish and seafood	—
	Eggs	—
	Vegetables, grains, and fruits	Vegetables (cabbage, celery, fennel, onions, carrots, eggplant, squash, potatoes)
Stewing	Meat	Beef (pieces from leg, shank, and chuck) Veal (pieces from leg, shank, and chuck) Lamb (pieces from leg, shank, and shoulder) Pork (pieces from leg and shoulder)
	Poultry	Cuts (drumsticks, wings, thighs) Pieces
	Fish and seafood	Pieces Lobsters, shrimp, scallops, and clams
	Eggs	—
	Vegetables, grains, and fruits	Vegetables (tomatoes, cabbage, celery, fennel, onions, carrots, eggplant, squash, potatoes) Beans and grains (typically fully cooked or parcooked before stewing) Fruits (prunes, apricots)

liquid. By the time the food is properly braised or stewed, it has released a significant amount of flavor and body into liquid, along with nutrients that may have been drawn out of the food and into the liquid. The result is an intensely flavored, complex sauce.

 **READING CHECKPOINT** *What are the two basic combination cooking methods?*

Determining Doneness

When using one of the moist-heat methods or the first stage in the combination cooking method, how do you determine when a food is properly cooked? The answer depends on how that food will be used. For example, if you are cooking the food and serving it right away, you will almost always cook the food all the way through. One exception is eggs, which can be cooked to a range of doneness if the customer makes a specific request. However, if you are using a moist-heat method to prepare an ingredient for use in another dish or for a specific type of presentation such as in a crudité platter, you won't cook it all the way through. The remainder of the cooking will be done when the final dish is cooked. You need to be able to judge when foods are partially cooked.

Proper Doneness The names for doneness in moist-heat and combination cooking methods include the following:

- Blanched
- Parcooked (or parboiled)
- Fully cooked
- Fork tender

Blanching foods involves cooking in a liquid or with steam just long enough to cook the outer portion of the food. When you blanch food, you may see a color change; for instance, blanched broccoli or peas become a bright green. When you use these blanched vegetables, they keep their brilliant colors. Blanching also draws out strong flavors or aromas that might overpower the finished dish. For instance, you might blanch a piece of country-cured ham to make it less salty. Blanching loosens the skin of foods such as tomatoes, chestnuts, peaches, and almonds so they are easier to peel.

To blanch food, bring water or other liquid to a full boil in a pot or a steamer. Add food directly to the liquid or the steamer. Let the food cook just long enough for the change you want. When that happens, lift the food out of the liquid or the steamer. Immediately put the food in a container of ice water. This stops the carryover cooking. Drain the food before you store it or use it in another dish.

Parcooked stands for *partially cooked*. Parcooked food is typically prepared in the same way as blanched food, using either liquid or steam. The food just cooks a bit longer. Parcooking helps you be more efficient, especially during service, because you only need to cook the parcooked food the remainder of the time required for fully cooked food. For example, if it takes 15 minutes to fully cook a food, and you parcooked it for 10 minutes, you would only need to cook it another 5 minutes for it to be fully cooked. Parcooking is actually a general word for partially cooking a food by any cooking method. Another technique, **parboiled**, refers exclusively to partially boiling a food.

Fully cooked food is cooked all the way through, or to the doneness your customer has requested. Be sure to observe the correct temperatures for doneness and remember to allow for carryover cooking.

Fork-tender foods are cooked to the point at which the food is just at the point of falling apart into shreds or flakes. This is the usual doneness specified for braised and stewed foods. Unlike fully

FIGURE 8–8
Blanching Tomatoes
Blanching loosens the outer layer of tomatoes so they are easier to peel after being dropped into ice water.

WRITING *Describe how blanching vegetables such as green beans or carrots might help make your work more efficient.*

Source: Richard Embery/Pearson Education/ PH College

FIGURE 8–9

Testing Broccoli for Doneness

Use a paring knife to test broccoli for doneness

PREDICTING *What would happen if you tested for doneness very often?*

Source: Culinary Institute of America

cooked foods that may require a knife in order to eat them, fork-tender foods can literally be "cut with a fork."

Test for Doneness Appearance is one of the doneness tests you can use, but it is almost always used in combination with another test. When you are only partially cooking food, the tool you use to test doneness is one of the following: a paring knife, a table fork, or a skewer. A parcooked food may be easy to pierce on the outside, but as you continue to push to the center of the food, there is more resistance. When foods are fully cooked, the knife or skewer should slide all the way into the food easily. Fork-tender foods are tested by picking up larger foods with the tines of a kitchen fork. They should slide easily from the fork without any resistance. Smaller pieces, such as those in stews, should be tested by either biting into a piece or cutting it with the side of a table fork; again, there should be no resistance.

 **READING CHECKPOINT** *How do you blanch food?*

8.2 ASSESSMENT

Reviewing Concepts

1. How is heat transferred to food in a moist-heat method?
2. What are the four basic moist-heat cooking methods?
3. Why are braising and stewing considered combination cooking methods?
4. How do you blanch food?

Critical Thinking

5. **Comparing/Contrasting** What are the differences among poaching, simmering, and boiling?
6. **Comparing/Contrasting** What is the difference between braising and stewing?
7. **Inferring** How would parcooking food increase the efficiency of a restaurant kitchen?
8. **Applying Concepts** Which type of cooking would take longer, poaching or simmering? Why?

Test Kitchen

Time how long it takes to cook a batch of green beans completely. Stop carryover cooking. Parcook the same amount of green beans half that time. Stop carryover cooking. Cook the parcooked green beans for half the time it took to cook the beans completely. Are these beans cooked completely?

SCIENCE

Healthy Steaming

Research the health benefits of steaming food. Why is it often called the healthiest method of cooking? How does steaming compare with other methods of cooking in terms of maintaining nutritive value?

 **PROJECT 8**

Moist-Heat Cooking Methods You are now ready to work on Project 8, "Moist-Heat Cooking Methods," which is available in "My Culinary Lab" or in your *Student's Lab Resources and Study Guide* manual.

Review and Assessment

Reviewing Content

Choose the letter that best answers the question or completes the statement.

1. The Maillard reaction occurs when
   a. food that is green turns bright green as it boils.
   b. food containing sugar turns brown as it cooks.
   c. food containing protein turns brown as it cooks.
   d. food that is hard turns soft as it cooks.

2. Which of the following is not a method of heat transfer for a dry-heat method?
   a. steam
   b. radiant heat
   c. the metal of the pan
   d. oil in the pan

3. Which cooking method cooks food quickly, often uncovered, in a very small amount of oil over high heat?
   a. pan-frying
   b. simmering
   c. stewing
   d. sautéing

4. Which of the following is not a dry-heat cooking method?
   a. pan-frying
   b. simmering
   c. pan-broiling
   d. sautéing

5. Which of the following is not a moist-heat cooking method?
   a. sweating
   b. simmering
   c. poaching
   d. steaming

6. What is typically the first step in stewing?
   a. pan-frying
   b. searing
   c. grilling
   d. deep-frying

Understanding Concepts

7. What is the difference between grilling and broiling?

8. What is the difference between roasting and baking?

9. How do searing, pan-broiling, and sweating differ from sautéing?

10. What is the difference between braising and stewing?

Critical Thinking

11. **RECOGNIZING PATTERNS** How are roasting and braising similar? How are baking and stewing similar?

12. **APPLYING CONCEPTS** For which type of cooking would you need to be more concerned about carryover cooking, roasting or baking?

Culinary Math

13. **SOLVING PROBLEMS** A recipe for a stew requires 3 cups of carrots with a turned cut. The recipe serves 8 people. You need to serve 50 people. How many cups of carrots should you cut?

14. **PREDICTING** The internal temperature of a 20-lb roasted turkey increases by about 15°F in the first 10 minutes after it leaves the oven. The internal temperature of a 12-lb turkey increases by about 7°F in the first 10 minutes after it leaves the oven. You are cooking a 16-lb turkey. You want the turkey to reach a fully cooked internal temperature of 165°F. Allowing for carryover cooking, at what internal temperature should you take the turkey out of the oven?

On the Job

15. **APPLYING A CONCEPT** You are in a hurry and need to sauté a large number of ingredients with different textures for one dish. Would you sauté them all at once to save time, add them one at a time to the sauté pan based on the amount of time they each needed, or sauté them individually at the same time in different pans, adding each to the final dish when it is ready? Explain your answer.

Cooks and Chefs

Chefs and cooks can determine the reputation and success of a restaurant. Chefs typically supervise cooks. Both must work independently and as a team, often under a great deal of pressure in tight quarters, but always with the aim of pleasing the customer. There are three management positions in the kitchen:

- *Executive chefs* are in charge of large kitchens, even chains of kitchens. They must have a diploma or certificate from a school or organization that can grant the title Certified Executive Chef (indicated by the initials CEC following the chef's name).
- *Head chefs* are chefs with professional cooks working for them. In kitchens without an executive chef, the head chef is in charge.
- *Sous-chefs* (SU-chefs) are second in command, reporting to the chef who in is charge of the kitchen. This is the lowest administrative position in the kitchen.

The next level of work in the kitchen is done by cooks working on specific types of food. Some examples are:

- *Sauté cooks* are responsible for sautéed items and their sauces. This is often considered the most glamorous of the various cooks' jobs. This job demands experience, stamina, split-second timing, an excellent memory, and the ability to multitask.
- *Grill cooks* are responsible for the preparation of all grilled or broiled items. Grill cooks have the same job requirements as sauté cooks.
- *Fish cooks* must know the various types of fish and shellfish and understand their anatomy.

At the lower level of the kitchen staff, employees often start with an apprentice or intern program. Most people begin their culinary careers as *apprentices* or *prep cooks*. The work is not highly skilled, but it is very important. Apprentices generally clean, trim, and prepare vegetables for stocks, soups, and salads. They also may be responsible for preparing the salads, salad dressings, and other simple menu items.

Source: Tyler Olson/Fotolia

Entry-Level Requirements

Cooks and chefs generally require a culinary degree for upper-level positions and some foodservice experience for entry-level positions.

Helpful for Advancement

To advance as a chef typically requires professional certification at increasing levels, as well as a knowledge of nutrition, accounting, and business management for upper-level positions.

GRANT ACHATZ

Grant Achatz is known as one of the leaders in *molecular gastronomy* or *progressive cuisine*, a style of cooking that has shaken up the culinary world by introducing to the restaurant scene new flavors, new techniques, new ingredients, new equipment, and even a new way of making reservations and ordering your meal.

Achatz got his start in his parents' restaurant in Michigan and then attended The Culinary Institute of America. After he graduated, he moved to California to work at the French Laundry, one of the country's most highly regarded restaurants; over the course of three years, he rose to the position of sous chef.

Grant Achatz

Source: Courtesy of Grant Achatz

In 2001, his next move was to the Chicago area, where he worked at Trio, a restaurant in Evanston, Illinois. Within three years, the restaurant was awarded a fifth star by the *Forbes Travel Guide*, making it one of an elite group of only 13 restaurants to be so honored.

Achatz has opened successful restaurants of his own, including Alinea and Next, and remains passionate and committed to his career, even when cancer of the tongue threatened to end it.

VITAL **STATISTICS**

Graduated: The Culinary Institute of America, 1994

Profession: Chef/Owner

Interesting Items: James Beard Foundation's Outstanding Chef of the Year, 2008

Alinea named one of the six best restaurants in the world, 2011

A famous early Alinea dish involved a peeled grape wrapped in peanut butter and a thin piece of toasted brioche, his reinvention of a peanut butter and jelly sandwich as part of progressive cuisine

CAREER **PROFILE**

Salary Ranges

Executive Chef: $45,000–$100,000+

Chef: $30,000–$60,000+

Sous Chef: $26,000–$45,000+

Cook: $14,000–$27,000+

Salaries can be higher depending on region, years of experience, or the size of the company

Chapter

9

Breakfast Foods

9.1 Eggs and Dairy

9.2 Breakfast Foods and Drinks

Eggs and Dairy

Key Concepts

- Selecting and storing eggs
- Preparing and serving egg dishes
- Identifying and storing dairy products

Vocabulary

- albumen
- butterfat
- clarified butter
- coddled eggs
- crème fraîche
- cultured dairy products
- custard
- flat omelette
- frittata
- homogenized
- lecithin
- milkfat
- omelette
- over egg
- pasteurized
- quiche
- rolled omelette
- scrambled eggs
- shirred eggs
- soufflé
- sunny-side-up egg

Selecting and Storing Eggs

Eggs have been part of our diets since long before humans domesticated animals. Centuries ago, we ate eggs from a wide variety of birds, including ducks, geese, quail, swans, and ostriches. Once we domesticated chickens, though, their eggs became the standard by which we cooked and a staple of our diet. This section is devoted specifically to chicken eggs—how to select the appropriate egg for the dish you are preparing and how to store your eggs to maintain their quality for the greatest length of time possible.

Egg Anatomy Eggs have three main parts:

- **Shell.** The shell is the hard outer casing that protects the egg inside. Eggshells are porous enough to allow air in and moisture out. The color of the shell doesn't have anything to do with the egg's quality, nutritional value, or flavor. Brown eggs and white eggs simply come from different types of chickens.

- **White.** The egg white, also called the **albumen** (al-BYOO-men), is made up of protein and water. The white appears clear and has a liquid quality in its raw state, but as it cooks, it turns white and hard. Looking closely at the white, you can actually see two separate parts: a runny, nearly flat outer ring and a higher, inner ring.

- **Yolk.** The yolk is the yellow center of an egg. It contains protein, fat, and a substance called **lecithin** (LES-i-thin), which serves as a natural emulsifier. The color of a yolk can vary from a pale yellow to a deep golden, depending on the diet of the bird.

Source: Stephen Hayward/Image Partners 2005/Dorling Kindersley Media Library/Dorling Kindersley

FIGURE 9–1

Parts of an Egg
Eggs are a popular breakfast food and an inexpensive source of protein.

INTERPRETING ILLUSTRATIONS
Can you distinguish the two parts of the white?

Source: ddsign_stock/Getty Images

Egg Inspecting and Grading Egg grading is done on a voluntary basis. When a farm calls for an inspection, a grader from the USDA (United States Department of Agriculture) gives a portion of the eggs a good once-over. The shell is the first thing the grader checks. It should be clean and free from cracks or holes. Some of the eggs are broken out of their shells onto plates so the grader can see how firm and high the white is and how much it spreads out on the plate. The grader also notes whether the yolk sits in the center of the white, slides to one side, or flattens out. As an egg ages, the white gets runny and the yolks flatten.

A grader can assign three grades to eggs: AA, A, or B. Once graded, the egg cartons can be marked with the official USDA grading shield.

- **Grade AA.** These are the freshest eggs, with compact whites and yolks that sit high in the center of the whites. Grade AA eggs (also known as *special*) have the best appearance in fried or poached egg dishes. The yolks are less likely to break when you separate the eggs into whites and yolks or while you are cooking or turning them.

- **Grade A.** These eggs have a slightly runny white. The yolk is not as high as AA and it is not as centered. Grade A eggs (also known as *extra*) are good for dishes where the eggs are blended or whisked and for preparing in the shell. The yolks break more easily than the yolks of Grade AA eggs.

- **Grade B.** Eggs that are Grade B (also known as *standard*) have a runny white and a flat, off-center yolk. They can be used in baking and batters and are used commercially to make liquid, frozen, and dried egg products.

Egg Sizes Egg sizing is also part of the USDA inspection process. There are standard names for egg sizes, and those names indicate the particular weight of the egg. No matter what size egg you are using, the white accounts for two-thirds of the egg's weight and the yolk accounts for the other third. The shell accounts for a little more than 10 percent of the total weight of the egg. The weights in the table on the next page include the weight of the shell. Remember to subtract that out when factoring what you need for a recipe or conversion.

Buying and Storing Eggs Eggs are sold in a variety of forms. The type of eggs your kitchen stocks depends on several factors: how many people you are cooking for, cost concerns, the way you intend to prepare or use the eggs, and the specific needs of your guests. Eggs are purchased in one of four basic forms:

- **Shell Eggs.** These are fresh eggs, sold in the shell and packed in cartons that contain 6, 12, or 18 eggs. They are also sold in cases; each case contains 12 flats, with 30 eggs on each flat, or 360 eggs

Egg Sizes and Weights

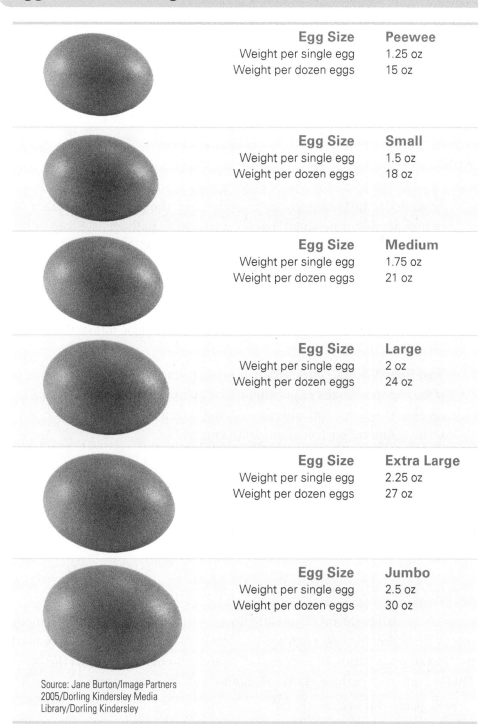

Egg Size	Peewee
Weight per single egg	1.25 oz
Weight per dozen eggs	15 oz

Egg Size	Small
Weight per single egg	1.5 oz
Weight per dozen eggs	18 oz

Egg Size	Medium
Weight per single egg	1.75 oz
Weight per dozen eggs	21 oz

Egg Size	Large
Weight per single egg	2 oz
Weight per dozen eggs	24 oz

Egg Size	Extra Large
Weight per single egg	2.25 oz
Weight per dozen eggs	27 oz

Egg Size	Jumbo
Weight per single egg	2.5 oz
Weight per dozen eggs	30 oz

Source: Jane Burton/Image Partners 2005/Dorling Kindersley Media Library/Dorling Kindersley

per case. If you are checking a delivery of eggs, open the cartons or cases and look at the shells. Remove and discard any eggs that are cracked or broken. Keep shell eggs refrigerated in their original containers. Avoid storing eggs with foods that have strong odors—eggs absorb odors easily.

- **Bulk Eggs.** These eggs are out of their shells and sold in cartons or tubs. You can purchase bulk eggs in different forms: whole eggs

Storage Times and Temperatures for Eggs

Type of Egg Product	Storage Time	Temperature
Shell eggs	5–7 days	33°–38°F
Bulk eggs	2–3 days	29°–32°F
Frozen bulk eggs	1–2 months	−10°–0°F
Dried eggs	1–2 months	40°F

Source: Culinary Institute of America

Flat of shell eggs

(blended yolks and whites), whole eggs with added yolks, yolks only, or whites only. Bulk eggs are **pasteurized**, the process of heating at high temperature to kill bacteria and other pathogens. Store bulk eggs in the refrigerator; store frozen bulk eggs at 0°F. Thaw them under refrigeration to keep them safe.

- **Dried Eggs.** Also known as *powdered eggs*, these eggs are stored on shelves in the dry storage area of your kitchen. Refrigerate dried eggs after opening the container. To use dried eggs, follow the instructions on the label.

- **Egg Substitutes.** Made either from egg whites or soy-based products, egg substitutes approximate the color, texture, and flavor of an egg. They are used when a customer has a dietary restriction preventing him or her from consuming egg yolks.

READING CHECKPOINT *What are the four forms in which eggs can be purchased?*

Cooking Eggs

Eggs are probably the most versatile food in the kitchen. Beyond the methods in the following list, eggs are used heavily in baking and pastry work and in the preparation of sauces and soups, all covered later in the book. This section covers the eight basic methods of cooking eggs:

- Eggs cooked in their shells
- Poached eggs
- Fried eggs
- Scrambled eggs
- Omelettes
- Shirred eggs
- Quiches
- Soufflés

The First Cookbook?

Have you ever wondered who wrote the first cookbook? Culinary historians believe that it may have been Guillaume Tirel, who went by the nickname of Taillevent (French for "slice wind"). Taillevent was born around 1310 and started his culinary career as a kitchen boy turning huge roasting spits before an open fire in the French royal court. By 1346 he had risen to head chef to Philip VI and he continued in service to wealthy families, including Charles VI, until his death in 1395.

One of the earliest collections of recipes, called *Le Viandier* (or *Le Viandier de Taillevent*), is often attributed to Taillevent, although the earliest version of it has been dated to around 1300. Taillevent, like many other medieval chefs, put together existing recipes, modified them, added new recipes, and presented the collection as his own cookbook.

The cookbook contains many recipes for stews, fish, roasted meat, and desserts. It even had a section on foods for invalids. Not all the recipes would suit modern tastes or meet contemporary sanitary regulations. For example, one recipe calls for removing a swan from its skin, roasting the carcass, and inserting the cooled roasted swan back in its skin, with all the feathers, using little wooden skewers to hold up the swan's neck up as if it were alive.

Recipes at the time of *Le Viandier* were not written in the way that standardized recipes today are written. Here's an example:

Green Egg and Cheese Soup

Take parsley, a bit of sage, just a bit of saffron in the greens, and soaked bread and steep in purée [of peas] or boiled water. Add ginger steeped in wine, and boil. Add the cheese and eggs when they have been poached in water. It should be thick and bright green. Some do not add bread, but add almond milk.

From *Le Viandier de Taillevent*, translated by James Prescott

Lab Activity

Form a team to reconstruct one of Taillevent's recipes. First, research *Le Viandier de Taillevent* and locate a recipe that seems like it might be appetizing to modern tastes. Make sure you research and understand all the ingredients and cooking methods. Serve your class the dish and ask for their feedback. Based on their response, consider whether this recipe would work today in a restaurant. What kinds of changes would be required (if any)?

Source: LeitnerR/Fotolia

One of the oldest collections of recipes is attributed to Taillevent, a French chef.

Eggs Cooked in Their Shells Eggs can be cooked in their shells, producing a variety of results:

- **Coddled.** An ingredient in a modern Caesar salad, **coddled eggs** have warm, thickened whites that are semi-opaque, and the yolk is warm but still very runny.

- **Soft-Cooked.** Also called *soft-boiled*, these eggs have whites that are barely set and very moist. The yolk is hot but still liquid. They are typically served in the shell in an egg cup. Special spoons may be provided to scoop the egg from the shell.

FIGURE 9–2

Soft-Cooked Egg

A soft-cooked egg is often served for breakfast directly in the shell.

DRAWING CONCLUSIONS *Why do you think an egg cup is used to serve a soft-cooked egg?*

Source: Culinary Institute of America

- **Medium-Cooked.** These eggs have fully set whites. The yolks are thickened and hot. They are served the same way soft-cooked eggs are.
- **Hard-Cooked.** Also known as *hard-boiled*, these eggs have whites that are completely set and firm. The yolks are also fully cooked and break apart easily when you push on them. Hard-cooked eggs are served as a hot dish at breakfast. They are also served in the form of deviled eggs and egg salad. Cut them into wedges or chop them to use as a garnish for a salad or a vegetable dish.

Eggs are cooked in their shells in simmering water. The shell protects the egg as it cooks. Eggs that are cooked until they are firm keep the shape of the shell even after they are peeled. Hard- and soft-boiled eggs should always be cooked at a steady, gentle simmer. A rapid boil shakes up the egg and can crack the shell. Once that happens, the whites overcook more easily and get tough. The yolk can turn grainy instead of creamy.

To cook eggs in their shells, lower the eggs into a pot holding enough simmering water to cover them by at least an inch. Cooking times in the following table are counted from the time the water returns to a simmer after you add the eggs.

Hard-boiled egg
Source: Richard Griffin/Fotolia

Cooking Eggs in Their Shells

Doneness	Time (Large Eggs)
Coddled	30 seconds
Soft	3–4 minutes
Medium	5–7 minutes
Hard	14–15 minutes

 Recipe Card

17. Hard-Cooked Eggs

Poached Eggs A poached egg is removed from the shell and then cooked in hot water until the white is set but still tender and the yolk is slightly thickened. Poaching, as you remember from Chapter 8, occurs when the liquid is kept at a steady temperature of 160°F to 170°F. Temperatures higher than that could produce rubbery whites. Add a small amount of vinegar to the water to keep the egg whites neat and compact.

Poaching Eggs

1 **Bring a pot of water to 165°F** and add a small amount of vinegar.

2 **Slide the eggs** into the water.

Source: Dave King/Image Partners 2005 Active/Dorling Kindersley/Dorling Kindersley Media Library

3 **Poach the eggs** until the whites are set, 3–4 minutes.

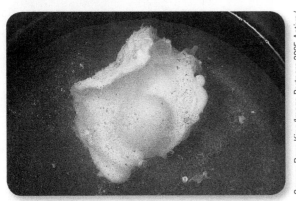

Source: Dave King/Image Partners 2005 Active/Dorling Kindersley/Dorling Kindersley Media Library

4 **Lift the eggs** from the water with a slotted spoon or spatula.

Source: Dave King/Image Partners 2005 Active/Dorling Kindersley/Dorling Kindersley Media Library

5 **Blot the eggs** on a paper towel.

6 **Serve** at once.

 Recipe Card

18. Poached Eggs

Use very fresh Grade AA eggs. If you crack the eggs directly into the poaching water, you might break the yolk and spoil the dish. Instead, crack the eggs into cups (one per cup). If the yolks break in the cup, you can still save them for use in another dish.

Slide the eggs out of the cups into the water. The eggs will drop to the bottom of the pan. As they drop, the whites will wrap around the yolks and form an attractive shape.

You can poach eggs to any doneness your customer requests. To prepare poached eggs ahead of time, partially cook them until the white just sets, and then hold them in cold water until needed. When you need the eggs, add them into the cooking water for a minute or two to bring them up to

Chef's Tip

Sour Eggs

Vinegar added to the egg-poaching water encourages the whites to set, but too much vinegar will flavor the eggs. Use no more than 2 tablespoons per gallon of water.

heat and finish the cooking process. They should be served immediately on heated plates.

Fried Eggs A perfectly fried egg is made with a very fresh egg that is cooked quickly in hot oil or butter. The white should be tender and fully cooked. The yolk, no matter how well done, should not break until the guest bursts it with a fork.

You can use just a thin film of oil if you are frying eggs in a nonstick skillet. Keep the heat at about medium high, just hot enough to cook the eggs quickly without scorching them.

There are two types of fried eggs. A **sunny-side-up egg** is cooked in the pan and not flipped. An **over egg** is flipped part way through the cooking process. The pan is then covered, resulting in a sunny-side-up egg that is fried and steamed. Fried eggs are cooked to three levels of doneness:

BASIC CULINARY SKILLS

Frying Eggs

① **Heat the pan** and the cooking fat over moderate heat.

② **Break the eggs** into a cup, slide them into the hot fat, and season them.

Source: Dave King/Image Partners 2005/ Dorling Kindersley Media Library/Dorling Kindersley

③ **Baste the eggs,** if desired.

Source: Dave King/Image Partners 2005/Dorling Kindersley Media Library/Dorling Kindersley

④ **Turn the eggs,** if desired.

⑤ **Cook the eggs** to the desired doneness.

Source: Dave King/Image Partners 2005/Dorling Kindersley Media Library/Dorling Kindersley

⑥ **Serve** at once.

Recipe Card

19. Fried Eggs

FIGURE 9–3

Two Types of Fried Eggs
One sunny-side-up egg served on ham and toast, and two eggs over easy served with bacon, hash brown potatoes, and toast.

COMMUNICATION *Which type of fried egg do you prefer? Why?*

Sources: (left) Clive Streeter/Image Partners 2005 Active/Dorling Kindersley Media Library/Dorling Kindersley; (right) Dave King/Image Partners 2005/ Dorling Kindersley Media Library/Dorling Kindersley

- **Easy.** The yolk is warm, runny, and totally unset.
- **Medium.** The yolk is partially set but its center is still slightly runny.
- **Hard.** The yolk is totally set, cooked all the way through.

Over eggs can be cooked over easy, over medium, and over hard.

CULINARY SCIENCE

Why Do Egg Whites Cook before the Yolks?

Eggs are made up of long strings of protein molecules. Weak magnetic bonds cause these strings to become tangled into knots. However, a little heat causes these magnetic bonds to break and the knots to become untangled. This allows the protein molecules to form their own new, stronger bonds. Eventually, they form a solid mass. This process is called *coagulation*.

The white portion of an egg is made up of only proteins and water, so it coagulates at a low temperature, around 145°F–160°F. Yolks contain more fat and other compounds that have stronger bonds and require more heat to break down. That's why the egg yolk remains raw after the egg whites are cooked.

Source: Jerry Young, Dorling Kindersley

Lab Activity

Fry three eggs, producing a different degree of doneness for each. Cook one until the whites are solid but the yolk is completely runny. Cook the next until the yolk is half done, cooked on the outside and runny on the inside. Cook the final egg so the white and the yolk are both completely solid. If you fry the eggs over low heat, you can actually watch as the white coagulates.

Scrambling Eggs

1. **Break the eggs** into a bowl. Add water or milk, if desired.

2. **Season** to taste with salt and pepper.

3. **Beat the eggs** with a fork or whisk until evenly blended.

4. **Heat the pan** and the cooking fat over moderate heat.

5. **Add the eggs and stir frequently.** Cook over low heat until they are soft and creamy.

Source: Culinary Institute of America

Source: Culinary Institute of America

6. **Serve** at once.

Recipe Card

20. Scrambled Eggs

Scrambled eggs with chives garnish, ham, asparagus, and toast

Source: Dorling Kindersley/Image Partners 2005/ Dorling Kindersley Media Library/Dorling Kindersley

Scrambled Eggs Scrambled eggs are a popular breakfast dish made by mixing the whites and yolks and then stirring them as they cook in a sauté pan or double boiler over low to medium heat. If you stir some water or milk into the eggs before they go into the pan, your scrambled eggs will be fluffier and moister after they cook.

Some garnishes need to be cooked before being added to the egg mixture. Others may be added directly. If you add a garnish, do it while cooking the eggs, not before. The eggs may be broken and scrambled beforehand and then reserved, covered, in the refrigerator until needed. They should not be held more than a day. When serving scrambled eggs, they should be fluffy and moist, but not runny. They should be plated on a warm plate and served immediately.

Omelettes An **omelette** is a popular egg dish served at breakfast or brunch. It can be filled or topped with a number of ingredients. Omelettes are made by first blending eggs as you do for scrambled eggs. There are two types of omelettes: a **rolled omelette**, which you make by stirring the eggs as they cook to keep them tender enough to roll or fold, and a **flat omelette**, which you do not stir but cook slowly for a firmer texture. Flat omelettes are not rolled or folded.

The two basic rolled omelette styles are the following:

- **French Omelette.** Swirl the egg mixture by moving the pan while also stirring the mixture with a fork until small soft moist curds

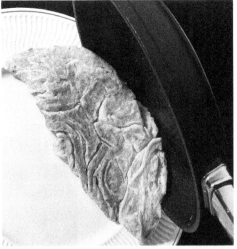

FIGURE 9–4

Two Types of Rolled Omelettes

French omelette on the left; American omelette on the right.

COMPARING/CONTRASTING
Describe the differences in these two omelettes.

Sources: (left) Culinary Institute of America; (right) Dave King/Dorling Kindersley Limited

form. Spread the curds in an even layer. The pan's heat sets the eggs on the bottom to make a smooth skin with no large cracks. The omelette is rolled out of the pan onto the plate. Fillings and garnishes are folded into the eggs, stuffed in the middle, or placed on top.

- **American Omelette.** The American omelette is practical for kitchens that use griddles to prepare most of their egg dishes, but they can also be prepared in an omelete pan. Instead of stirring constantly, the eggs are pushed away from the bottom and sides from time to time. This stirring technique results in larger curds, deep wrinkles, and a bit of browning on the outer layer.

Chef's Tip

Pans for Eggs

Nonstick pans are the easiest to use and clean. They require little if any cooking fat. They are excellent for making omelettes.

Egg Safety

The risk of getting a food-borne illness from eggs is very low. However, the bacterium *Salmonella*, serotype *Enteritidis* (often referred to as *SE*) has been found in a small number of eggs—in 1 out of every 20,000 on average across the United States. Most reported salmonellosis outbreaks involving eggs were the result of inadequate refrigeration, improper handling, and insufficient cooking. To ensure that your eggs maintain their high quality and safety, use the following precautions:

Source: Pearson Education Corporate Digital Archive/ Silver Burdett Ginn

1. Wash your hands before and after handling eggs and foods that contain eggs.

2. Wash, rinse, and sanitize equipment and work surfaces after handling eggs and foods that contain eggs.

3. Do not use eggs that are broken or cracked, have a slimy feel (may indicate bacterial growth), or have powdery spots that come off on your hand (may indicate mold).

4. Avoid dropping eggshell pieces into a raw egg.

5. Don't keep eggs out of the refrigerator more than two hours.

6. Defrost frozen eggs, egg products, and cooked egg dishes safely: in the refrigerator overnight or under running cold water. Use promptly.

7. Cook casseroles and other egg dishes to 160°F. Promptly serve after cooking.

8. Use hard-cooked eggs within one week. Use leftover yolks and whites within three days. Use cooked egg dishes within three or four days.

9. Some authorities warn against eating any egg preparation that is not fully cooked.

French Omelette

① **Blend the eggs** and add seasonings and garnishes.

② **Heat a pan** with enough fat to keep the eggs from sticking.

③ **Pour the eggs** into the pan.

④ **Stir the eggs** as they cook until small soft curds form.

Source: Culinary Institute of America

⑤ **Spread the eggs** into an even layer and add any filling, if desired.

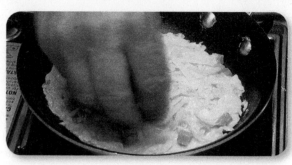

Source: Culinary Institute of America

⑥ **Remove the pan** from the heat and let the eggs rest in the pan.

⑦ **Shake the pan** to loosen the omelette.

Source: Culinary Institute of America

Recipe Card

21. Plain Rolled Omelette

⑧ **Roll the omelette** out of the pan on to a hot plate.

⑨ **Serve** at once.

An American omelette cooked on a griddle is usually folded in half on the griddle, removed with a spatula, and plated.

The basic flat omelette style is the **frittata** (free-TAH-ta). Also known as a farmer-style omelette (or a tortilla in Spain), a frittata is a round, open-face omelette made by pouring beaten eggs into a pan you've preheated over the burner. Once the eggs have cooked and set along the bottom and sides of the pan, you finish cooking the omelette in a hot oven and then cut it in wedges.

Shirred Eggs **Shirred** (SHURD) **eggs** are baked eggs, made by cracking a whole egg into a cup and then

Frittata with mushrooms and asparagus

Source: Clive Streeter/Image Partners 2005/Dorling Kindersley Media Library/ Dorling Kindersley

cooking it in the oven. They are typically covered with a little cream and topped with bread crumbs before they are baked. Shirred eggs have firm whites and soft yolks.

Ceramic dishes are the traditional choice for baked eggs because they help cook the eggs evenly and gently. As further insurance that your eggs will have the best texture, set the filled dishes in a large baking pan and add enough hot water to come up the sides of the dish at least halfway to make a hot water bath.

Quiches A **quiche** (KEESH) is another type of baked egg dish. Eggs are blended with cream or milk, a mixture known as **custard**. The custard is poured into a crust and baked in an oven until the custard is fully cooked. Most quiche recipes include a filling such as cheese, sautéed potatoes or onions, vegetables, or ham.

To check when a quiche is properly baked, insert the tip of a paring knife into the center. If it comes away clean, the eggs are fully cooked and the quiche is ready. Serve hot or at room temperature, as desired.

Soufflés A **soufflé** (soo-FLAY) is a light, puffed egg dish baked in a ceramic mold. The straight sides of the mold help the soufflé rise as it bakes. To make a soufflé, begin by preparing the molds. Rub or brush them liberally with butter to keep the eggs from sticking when the soufflé is served. Next, scatter bread crumbs or grated cheese over the butter to give the soufflé mixture something to help it rise properly.

The next step is separating the eggs. The yolks are stirred into a base, usually a thick sauce made with milk. The whites are beaten into a thick foam. You combine the base mixture with the beaten whites gently, using a stirring technique known as *folding*. Folding helps keep air in the egg whites.

Recipe Card
22. Shirred Eggs

Chef's Tip

Baked Egg Variations

You can bake an egg in a hollowed-out roll (brioche rolls are a good size and shape). Or you can make a hole in a serving of hash, top with an egg, and bake until the whites are set.

FIGURE 9–5
Baked Egg Dishes
Spinach quiche and shirred eggs.
COMPARING/CONTRASTING
Describe the differences in these two baked egg dishes.
Source: Culinary Institute of America

Recipe Card
23. Quiche Lorraine

Soufflés

Source: Culinary Institute of America

Recipe Card
24. Spinach Soufflé

Eggs separate most easily when cold. Use an egg separator or a funnel. Passing the yolk between two halves of a broken shell can introduce bacteria.

As soon as the soufflé is folded together, spoon or ladle it into the prepared dishes and bake in a hot oven.

READING CHECKLIST *What are the eight basic methods for cooking eggs?*

Identifying and Storing Dairy Products

Dairy products come in a variety of forms, with a variety of flavors and textures. Each form of dairy product is made up of water, solid particles, and fat, referred to as **milkfat** or **butterfat**. Dairy products are labeled according to the percentage of milkfat they contain. Milk and cream are pasteurized and then **homogenized**—a process that evenly distributes and emulsifies the fat particles.

Source: Culinary Institute of America

Milk containers

Milk Milk is served as a beverage and also used as an ingredient. There are several forms of milk, from skim milk to whole milk. A number of products are made from milk, including creams, butter, and yogurt. An important type of dairy product, cheese, is discussed in greater detail in Chapter 10.

Milk from cows is the basis of most dairy products, although you may also find goat's milk and sheep's milk dairy products. Milk is mostly water, with some protein, sugar, and fat.

The production of milk is closely regulated. Milk is inspected regularly to be sure it is kept sanitary. Milk and dairy products made from milk are pasteurized to kill harmful bacteria and then rapidly chilled. Homogenized dairy products are forced through fine screens to break up the butterfat so it won't separate and rise to the top.

Types of Milk

Form	Description	Type of Container
Whole	Contains no less than 3 percent milkfat.	Bulk, gallon, half-gallon, quart, pint, half pint
Low-fat	Usually contains 1 or 2 percent milkfat and is generally labeled accordingly.	Same as whole milk
Skim (nonfat)	Contains less than 0.1 percent milkfat.	Same as whole milk
Dry (powdered)	Milk from which water is completely removed. Made from either whole or skim milk.	50 lb bulk; 24 oz bulk
Evaporated	Milk that has been heated in a vacuum to remove 60 percent of its water. May be made from whole, low-fat, or skim milk, with milkfat content as high as 8 percent or as low as 0.5 percent.	14.5-oz, 10-oz, or 6-oz cans
Condensed	Evaporated milk that has been sweetened.	Same as evaporated milk

Cream and Cultured Dairy Products Cream is thicker, is richer tasting, and has a higher milkfat content than milk. It is homogenized and pasteurized and available in different varieties.

Cultured dairy products such as buttermilk, sour cream, and yogurt are made by adding a specific type of beneficial bacteria to milk or cream. As the bacteria grow, they thicken the milk or cream and give it a tart taste. **Crème fraîche** (krehm fraysh), French for "fresh cream," is similar in flavor and texture to sour cream, but because it contains so much butterfat, it will not curdle in hot soups and sauces the way sour cream and yogurt can.

Butter Butter is made by churning cream until the fat clumps together, squeezing out the water. The best-quality butter, grade AA or A, has a delicate, creamy flavor. Salt is often added as a preservative, but it should not be a strong flavor. Lower grades of butter are made from lesser-quality cream and may smell a little like cheese.

Butter is served as a spread for rolls, breads, and toast and as a topping for pancakes and waffles. You can introduce more flavor and color by blending butter with fruits, herbs, or other ingredients.

Whole butter is made up of mostly butterfat with milk solids and some water. When whole butter gets hot, the milk solids can burn and the butter will start to smoke. To use butter as a cooking fat at high temperatures, you need to remove the milk solids and water, leaving you with what is called **clarified butter**.

Margarine is a butter substitute. For the most part, margarine can be substituted for butter, although butter is typically more flavorful than margarine. However, some margarines are artificially flavored to make them better resemble butter, and some are blended with olive oil or canola oil to improve their taste.

Types of Cream and Cultured Dairy Products

Form	Description	Type of Container
Cream, heavy or whipping	Contains at least 36 percent milkfat. Light whipping cream is occasionally available, containing 30 to 35 percent fat.	Quart, pint, half pint
Cream, light	Contains between 18 and 30 percent milkfat.	Same as heavy cream
Half-and-half	Equal parts milk and cream. Contains between 10.5 and 18 percent milkfat. Used as a lightener for coffee.	Same as heavy cream and in portion sizes
Buttermilk	Thickened, cultured, tangy nonfat or low-fat milk. Used in baking.	Quart, pint
Sour cream	Thickened, cultured sweet cream. Contains between 16 and 22 percent milkfat.	Variety of sizes, starting with half pint
Yogurt	Thickened, cultured milk. Can be whole, low-fat, or nonfat; flavored or plain.	Variety of sizes, starting with half pint
Crème fraîche	Thickened, cultured, heavy cream with a nutty flavor. Contains 30 percent milkfat.	Variety of sizes, starting with half pint

Clarified Butter

1. **Place the butter into a cold pot** or pan.

2. **Heat the pan** over a moderate flame.

3. **Melt the butter** and bring it to a sizzling boil.

4. **Boil off most of the water** without burning the milk solids.

5. **Skim off the foam.**

6. **Ladle or pour out** the clarified butter to remove it, leaving the milk solids at the bottom of the pan.

Source: Culinary Institute of America

Source: Culinary Institute of America

Chef's Tip

Which Margarine?

Stick margarine usually contains the most trans fats, while soft margarine and whipped margarine contain less.

Some people regard margarine as a healthier alternative to butter, especially if the margarine does not contain trans fatty acids (also called *hydrogenated* or *partially hydrogenated fats*). Cholesterol, saturated fats, and trans fatty acids have all been linked to coronary heart disease. Typically the more solid the margarine, the more likely that it will contain trans fats.

Margarine is a good option for vegetarian and meatless cooking and baking. It is also used in kosher cooking for nondairy meals.

Characteristics of Margarine vs. Butter

Characteristics	Margarine	Butter
Made from	Vegetable oils	Animal fat
Cholesterol	Contains no cholesterol	Contains cholesterol
Good fats (poly- and monosaturated fats)	Higher	Lower
Bad fats (saturated fats)	Lower	Higher
Bad fats (trans fats)	Can contain trans fats	Contains no trans fats

Storing Dairy Products Like eggs, dairy products are highly perishable. Most dairy containers are dated to indicate how long the contents will remain fresh. Store dairy products away from foods with strong odors.

Storage Times and Temperatures for Dairy Products

Product	Storage Time*	Temperature
Pasteurized milk: whole, low-fat, skim	1 week	35°–40°F
Powdered milk	Unopened: 3 months Reconstituted: 1 week	60°–70°F 35°–40°F
Evaporated milk	Unopened: 6 months Opened: 3–5 days	60°–70°F 35°–40°F
Condensed milk	Unopened: 2–3 months Opened: 3–5 days	60°–70°F 35°–40°F
Buttermilk	2–3 weeks	35°–40°F
Yogurt	3–6 weeks	35°–40°F
Heavy or whipping cream	1 week	35°–40°F
Light cream or half-and-half	Opened: 1 week Unopened: 4 weeks	35°–40°F
Butter	3–5 months	35°–40°F
Clarified butter	3 weeks	35°–40°F

*Check expiration dates on products

 **READING CHECKPOINT** *What is the difference between milk and cream?*

9.1 ASSESSMENT

Reviewing Concepts

1. What are the four forms in which eggs can be purchased?
2. What are the eight basic methods for cooking eggs?
3. Describe the difference between milk and cream.

Critical Thinking

4. **Analyzing Information** You're making poached eggs. They keep coming out tasting acidic, and the whites are rubbery. What's going wrong?
5. **Predicting** When butter is not properly clarified, it has solid particles in it. What will happen to this butter when it is used to fry eggs, and how will it affect the flavor of the eggs?
6. **Classifying** You slide an egg into a pan to fry it. The egg white is compact; the yolk sits high in the center of the whites. What grade of egg is it?

Test Kitchen

Divide into teams and make omelettes. Half of the teams should use a griddle and make an American-style omelette, and the other half should use a pan and make a French-style omelette. What differences do you observe between the American and French omelettes? Considering the equipment, length of time needed, and the final product, which method would you use in a restaurant kitchen?

SOCIAL STUDIES ————————●
Dairy In Asia

Traditionally, dairy products are not part of the diet in East and South Asia. Research dairy consumption in that part of the world and try to come up with a theory as to why dairy is unpopular there.

Breakfast Foods and Drinks

READING PREVIEW

Key Concepts

- Preparing pancakes, waffles, and French toast
- Identifying breakfast breads and cereals
- Identifying breakfast meats and potatoes
- Identifying hot and cold breakfast beverages

Vocabulary

- batter
- caffeine
- Canadian bacon
- chicken-fried steak
- continental breakfast
- crêpe
- croissants
- French toast
- hash
- hash browns
- home fries
- muesli
- scone
- smoothie

Pancakes, Waffles, and French Toast

Pancakes, waffles, and French toast are popular, specially cooked breakfast foods.

Pancakes and waffles are made from batters. A **batter** is a very wet form of dough made from flour, oil or melted butter, eggs, milk or other liquids, salt, and usually baking powder. Varying the proportions of these ingredients will yield different results, and this is why waffles are fluffy and pancakes are cakey. Pancakes and waffles are served with a variety of toppings, including butter, syrup, fruit toppings, and whipped cream.

French toast is a piece of bread that is dipped in a mixture of milk and eggs and then fried until golden brown on both sides. The mixture often contains sugar, cinnamon, and nutmeg. French toast can be made with different types of bread and is typically served with syrup, fruit toppings, or powdered sugar.

Recipe Card

25. French Toast

Cooking Pancakes and Waffles

1. **Sift the dry ingredients** together.
2. **Combine all the liquid ingredients** in a bowl.
3. **Add the combined liquid ingredients** to the combined dry ingredients. Do not overmix.
4. **Coat a griddle or waffle iron** with fat and preheat.
5. **Ladle the batter** onto the cooking surface.

Source: Culinary Institute of America

6. **Cook the batter** until it takes on a golden color and is totally cooked. For pancakes, turn once when bubbles appear on top of the pancake and the edges begin to dry. The second side takes half as much time as the first to cook.

Source: Culinary Institute of America

7. **Serve** immediately.

Recipe Cards

26. Buttermilk Pancakes

27. Waffles

A **crêpe** (KRAYP) is a French pancake. It is created from an extremely thin batter that contains no baking powder, and it is cooked in a special pan over moderate heat. The result is a paper-thin, wrapper-like pancake. Breakfast crêpes are often spread with jam or a fruit mixture and then folded or rolled.

 **READING CHECKPOINT** *What are the basic ingredients of a pancake or waffle batter?*

Source: Neil Mersh/Image Partners 2005/Dorling Kindersley Media Library/Dorling Kindersley

Crêpes

Cooking Crêpes

1. **Combine** the eggs, milk, melted butter, and beat until just blended.

2. **Sift together** the flour, sugar, and salt and place in a mixing bowl.

3. **Add the wet ingredients** and mix until smooth, scraping down the bowl as you go.

4. **Add flavoring ingredients** and stir until blended and the batter is smooth.

5. **Rest the batter** under refrigeration for up to 12 hours; strain if necessary.

6. **Preheat and butter** a crêpe pan over moderate to high heat.

Source: Culinary Institute of America

Recipe Card

28. Crêpes Suzette

7. **Add the batter** to the pan, swirling the pan to coat it evenly with the crêpe batter.

Source: Culinary Institute of America

8. **Cook over moderate heat.** When set, turn over and finish the other side.

Source: Culinary Institute of America

9. **Cool crêpes,** if desired. Place on parchment paper and hold cold.

Source: Culinary Institute of America

Breakfast Breads and Cereals

A variety of breads are served at breakfast. They can be served as an accompaniment to eggs for a hearty breakfast or with coffee (or tea) and juice as a **continental breakfast**. Baking bread is discussed in Chapters 17

Vietnamese Breakfasts

The country of Vietnam is located in Southeast Asia and has a tropical climate. It is entirely exposed to water on its eastern border, so Vietnamese cuisine uses a lot of fresh seafood. Rice plays an integral role in the Vietnamese diet, as it does in almost all Asian countries. Because France occupied the country for many years, the cuisine has also developed a more Western style than most other Asian countries. There is prolific use of fresh herbs, citrus, galangal root (a sour, pungent form of ginger), lemongrass, and fish sauce.

A typical Sunday breakfast in Vietnam is quite different from what we are accustomed to. A savory, complex beef soup called *pho* (FUH), made with thin vermicelli rice noodles, is found everywhere, from large restaurants to street vendors. It has certain variations depending on locale, but the most popular form is dark and rich, has hints of roasted anise and clove, and is garnished with fresh cilantro, lime, bean sprouts, pieces of thinly sliced rare beef, and sometimes chili sauce. Slurping loudly, with one's head held just above the bowl, is considered the proper way to consume the dish.

Vietnamese breakfast: Pho
Source: David Murray and Jules Selmes/Dorling Kindersley

Research

Research the different varieties of pho. Describe how they are made. List the different kinds of ingredients used.

and 18. Foodservice establishments often use ready-made breakfast breads, including the following:

- Toasted bread, such as rye, white, or whole-wheat bread (sometimes with whole grains, nuts, seeds, or even dried fruits added)
- English muffins
- Bagels, made plain or with sesame seeds, raisins, or other ingredients
- **Croissants** (kwah-SAHNTs), which are buttery-rich, crescent-shaped yeast rolls
- Pastries, which are often filled with almond paste, fruit, or cream
- Doughnuts, which are deep-fried and often ring-shaped
- Muffins, such as corn, blueberry, or bran muffins
- Loaf-style breads, such as banana bread and cranberry nut bread

Continental breakfast with croissant

Source: BlueOrange Studio/Fotolia

Cereal and fruit are a popular
breakfast choice

Source: Ariwasabi/Fotolia

Chef's Tip

Don't Burn Your Bacon

If you are cooking bacon,
especially in the oven,
and you actually smell the
bacon cooking, you may
have overcooked it. Bacon
can be served crisp or
tender, but never burned.

- Biscuits, which are light and flaky. A **scone** is a rich biscuit that sometimes contains raisins and is served with butter, jam, or thick cream.

Cereal is a breakfast staple for both children and adults. It is also a breakfast choice in restaurants. Preparation of hot cereals, such as those made from oats or wheat, is discussed in Chapter 13. Cold cereals require no preparation. They are generally eaten with milk and topped with fresh fruit such as bananas or berries. Granola is often eaten with yogurt instead of milk. The Swiss version of granola is **muesli** (MYOOS-lee), a mixture of cereal (such as oats and wheat), dried fruit, nuts, bran, and sugar. It is eaten with milk or yogurt.

READING CHECKPOINT *What is a continental breakfast?*

Breakfast Meats and Potatoes

Meat plays a huge part in the American diet, and breakfast is no exception to that rule. A wide variety of meats are served at breakfast, often with both eggs and potatoes. The three most common breakfast meats are bacon, sausage, and ham.

- **Bacon.** Salted and smoked meat from the belly of a pig, bacon is available in many forms, such as sliced, thin or thick, or sold in one chunk as slab bacon. Bacon is usually highly fatty and shrinks during cooking. **Canadian bacon** is made from a much leaner portion of the pig. More similar to ham than to regular bacon, it comes in chunks or slices. Bacon is usually cooked in an oven to produce large volumes but may also be cooked in a pan on low heat.

FIGURE 9–6

Hearty Breakfast

Bacon, eggs, and potatoes.

CLASSIFYING *What are some other breakfast food combinations that can be served together on one plate?*

Source: Barbro Bergfeldt/Fotolia

- **Sausages.** A combination of ground meat, fat, liquid, and salt, with a variety of flavorings added, sausages are available as both patties and links. Links are wrapped in a casing, which is usually the intestinal membrane of an animal. The standard breakfast link sausage comes uncooked. Before cooking it for service, you may want to poach it so it stays together if you plan to slice or dice it. To poach the sausage, prick it with a needle anywhere you see an air bubble. Then submerge it in 165°F water until totally cooked (check this with an instant-read thermometer). After poaching, you can sauté the sausage in a pan or on a griddle.

- **Ham.** Common all over the country and available in many forms, ham used for breakfast is typically smoked, precooked, and presliced. Heat it under a broiler or on a griddle before serving.

- **Chicken-Fried Steak.** Popular in the South and Midwest, **chicken-fried steak** is a thin steak dipped into a mixture of egg, milk, and seasonings and then fried like chicken until crisp. It's topped with country gravy and served with eggs and biscuits.

- **Hash.** A tasty breakfast combination of chopped meat (typically corned beef), potatoes, and seasonings, **hash** is pan-fried and often served with a poached or fried egg on top.

- **Hash Browns.** A popular side dish, **hash browns** are finely chopped or grated potatoes, pressed down in a pan or on a griddle to brown on one side and then flipped to brown on the other side. **Home fries** are sliced potatoes that are pan-fried, often with chopped peppers and onions.

 **READING CHECKPOINT** *What are the three most common breakfast meats?*

Breakfast Beverages

For many people, breakfast is not complete without their beverage of choice. Breakfast beverages either provide additional nutrients or offer **caffeine**, a chemical found in coffee, tea, chocolate, and sodas that stimulates your body and mind.

- **Coffee.** Coffee is a dark brown liquid produced from running water through roasted, ground coffee beans. Coffee starts as a small, green bean grown in tropical climates. The beans are harvested by hand and then subjected to a long roasting process. Different flavors are related to the environment where the bean originates, as well as to the roasting process it undergoes. The more a bean is roasted, the "darker" the flavor and the less acidity and caffeine it has. To produce the best possible coffee, you want to start with a whole bean, grind it yourself, and immediately brew coffee from the grind. Also,

Source: Ivan Kmit/Fotolia

Sausage and eggs are a popular breakfast choice

 Recipe Card
29. Hash

··FOCUS ON
·· Nutrition

Nitrates and Nitrites

Nitrates and nitrites, types of preservatives, are sometimes added to sausages and bacon. Although not directly harmful, they break down into nitrosamines at high heat. These are one of the carcinogens found in cigarettes. The point? Cook your breakfast meats at lower temperatures, and don't eat too much. Or look for meats without nitrates and nitrites.

FIGURE 9–7
Coffee
Coffee goes through many stages
before it makes it into your cup.
DRAWING CONCLUSIONS *What
gives coffee its familiar dark color?*
Source: Kellis/Fotolia

you should keep coffee for only 20 minutes and then brew a new
batch. As the coffee sits, the acidity level builds and the flavor of the
coffee becomes unpleasant.

- **Tea.** Compared to coffee, tea is lighter in color, contains less caffeine
  and less acidity, and is actually made quite differently. Tea is made
  by allowing leaves to steep in hot water, where they release their essential oils slowly, flavoring the liquid. Many ingredients can be used
  to make tea. In Asian cultures, tea can be composed of fruit zest,
  spices, flowers, or even bark. Teas made from herbs such as peppermint leaves or chamomile flowers contain no caffeine.

- **Juice.** Available in a variety of market forms, juices are a popular breakfast accompaniment. Juices may be purchased as freshly
  squeezed, as reconstituted juice concentrates, or as frozen concentrates that are combined with water and stirred to produce juice.

- **Smoothie.** A **smoothie** is a cold drink made by mixing fresh fruit
  (such as bananas and strawberries), juice, and ice in a blender until
  thick and smooth. Smoothies can also contain milk or yogurt. The
  nutritional value of a smoothie can make it a breakfast substitute—a
  meal in a glass.

Papaya, berry, and coconut smoothies

Source: Simon Smith/Image Partners 2005/Dorling
Kindersley Media Library/Dorling Kindersley

 **READING
CHECKPOINT** *Which breakfast beverages contain caffeine?*

Reviewing Concepts

1. List the ingredients common to most breakfast batters.
2. What is a continental breakfast?
3. What are the three most common breakfast meats?
4. List breakfast drinks that do not contain caffeine.

Critical Thinking

5. **Classifying** What types of cooked eggs have a completely cooked white and yolk?
6. **Comparing/Contrasting** Describe the similarities and differences between pancake batter and the liquid mixture used to make French toast.
7. **Comparing/Contrasting** Describe the similarities and differences between bacon and Canadian bacon.

Test Kitchen

Split up into groups. One-third of the groups should make pancakes, one-third waffles, and one-third French toast. Start at the same time and produce three servings. Compare cooking times. As a chef in a restaurant kitchen, which would you prefer having on the menu?

MATH

Making Pancakes

You need to make pancakes for 20 people. Each person will eat two pancakes; each pancake is made from 4 oz of batter. A single recipe yields 1 qt of batter. How much batter do you need? How many times do you have to scale up the recipe (what is your RCF)?

PROJECT 9

Preparing Breakfasts You are now ready to work on Project 9, "Preparing Breakfasts," which is available in "My Culinary Lab" or in your *Student's Lab Resources and Study Guide* manual.

Reviewing Content

Choose the letter that best answers the question or completes the statement.

1. Grade A eggs are
   a. the freshest grade of egg, with a high, centered yolk and tight whites.
   b. good for blended egg dishes.
   c. used in commercial egg preparations.
   d. best for fried egg dishes.

2. A French omelette can be described as
   a. flat.
   b. coddled.
   c. rolled.
   d. baked.

3. The biggest difference between cream and milk is that
   a. milk has a higher milkfat content than cream.
   b. cream is lighter than milk.
   c. milk has a slightly more yellow color than cream.
   d. cream has a higher milkfat content than milk.

4. To make crêpes, you
   a. pour batter into the center of a pan and then cook over medium heat.
   b. ladle batter on to a griddle and then cook over low heat.
   c. pour batter into the center of a pan and then cook over high heat.
   d. swirl batter to coat the bottom of a pan and then cook over medium heat.

5. Hash can best be described as a combination of
   a. potatoes and corned beef.
   b. ground meats.
   c. meat and peppers.
   d. potatoes and onions.

6. You do not use batter to make
   a. pancakes.
   b. waffles.
   c. French toast.
   d. any of the above

Understanding Concepts

7. Describe the structure of an egg.

8. Compare and contrast poaching eggs and cooking eggs in the shell.

9. Explain how clarified butter is made.

10. What is a continental breakfast?

Critical Thinking

11. **COMPARING/CONTRASTING** What would you do differently if you were preparing an egg over hard versus a sunny-side-up egg, easy?

12. **CLASSIFYING** List breakfast options that use ready-made products and fresh ingredients and that require no cooking.

13. **APPLYING CONCEPTS** What is the best hand tool for pouring batter onto a griddle?

Culinary Math

14. **RELATING CONCEPTS** You're preparing scrambled eggs for ten people. Each person will eat 6 oz of eggs. How many large eggs are needed to feed everyone?

15. **RELATING CONCEPTS** A pancake calls for 2 oz of syrup for each pancake. The batter recipe yields 2 gal, and there are 4 fl oz (½ cup) of batter to a pancake. Based on the total number of pancakes made from the recipe, how much syrup is needed?

On the Job

16. **APPLYING CONCEPTS** You have only a griddle for cooking eggs. What types of egg dishes can you prepare?

17. **PROBLEM SOLVING** You're trying to poach eggs, but the yolks keep breaking when they hit the water. How might this be avoided?

Private and Personal Chefs

Private and personal chefs are considered "cooks for hire" because they work for individual clients, rather than a restaurant, hotel, or other foodservice organization. Both types of chefs plan and prepare meals according to clients' tastes or dietary needs.

No matter whether the chef works in the home or provides a delivery service, he or she must be keenly aware of the clients' needs. This can include their personal likes and dislikes, food intolerances or allergies, and diet-related health conditions such as diabetes or heart disease. Some chefs specialize in specific styles of cooking, such as vegetarian cooking, kosher cooking, macrobiotic cooking, heart-healthy cooking, or even cooking for weight loss (also known as *spa cuisine*).

Chefs who work for individuals develop menus for regular meals as well as for special events and parties that their clients may host in their homes. In some cases, they are responsible for coordinating any additional staff that may be required.

It is critically important to be diligent about all food safety standards and practices. The client's kitchen should be left immaculate when the work is completed. All foods must be handled with care to keep them safe and wholesome. This is especially important when foods are delivered to the client from another site.

Personal and private chefs may be self-employed or work for an agency. There are professional organizations dedicated to the needs of personal and private chefs that offer training materials as well as a forum and job listing service.

Although the terms *private chef* and *personal chef* are sometimes used interchangeably, there are some differences.

Personal chef A personal chef usually prepares meals for a few days or a week and leaves them for the client to reheat. Some personal chefs prepare meals at a separate site and deliver the food. Others bring the ingredients, tools, and packaging materials to the client's house and do the work there. Personal chefs generally work for more than one client, although they typically work for only one client in any given day. It is becoming quite common for personal chefs to provide cooking classes for their clients.

Private chef A private chef works exclusively for one household. Some private chefs provide all three meals for the household. In some cases, their duties may also include cooking for the client's household staff. They may be required to serve in some cases. Often, when clients entertain, they determine not only the menu but also the décor of the dining room and the table setting. They may also assume household management duties outside the kitchen. They may be considered *live-in*, which means that the client provides them with living quarters, or they may live elsewhere. Private chefs may also work for clients that are vacationing in rented villas or on yachts. They still work for just one client at a time, but the assignment may last from a weekend to a few months.

Entry-Level Requirements

There are no specific requirements in order to become a private or personal chef, but it is common to have a few years of experience working in professional kitchens. Many have completed

The client's kitchen should be left immaculate when work is completed

some culinary training at the postsecondary level. Most have completed ServSafe training and other health certifications as required by individual states.

Helpful for Advancement

In addition to culinary and baking and pastry skills, personal and private chefs should be skilled at menu planning and development, purchasing, basic and advanced culinary skills, management, and communication. The ability to speak more than one language is helpful. Knowledge of a variety of cooking styles such as ethnic cuisines as well as nutrition, financial management, and culinary trends is also helpful. This type of work can be competitive, so developing a strong network is a key. Self-promotion and marketing are important as well. Certification is available through some professional organizations, including the American Personal & Private Chef Association and the American Culinary Federation.

JEWELS QUELLY

Jewels Quelly started AngelFood Personal Chef Service and Catering Company in 1996 and is a Certified Personal Chef. Backed by over 25 years of experience in the food-service industry, Chef Quelly uses the freshest ingredients to provide her clients with exceptional flavor and memorable dishes.

Chef Quelly graduated from The Culinary Institute of America, where she was the Editor-in-Chief of the on-campus newspaper. In addition to owning her own company and being a private chef, she is also a published journalist, and has food columns in several newspapers. Chef Quelly was also the creator, producer, and host of a food and beverage radio program called Dig In with Jewels Quelly.

Jewels Quelly

VITAL STATISTICS

Graduated: The Culinary Institute of America, 1987

Profession: Owner of AngelFood Personal Chef Service

Interesting Items: Serves as a Subject Matter Expert on the National Restaurant Association's ServSafe test committee

As a student, she received The Culinary Institute of America Service Award for her work as Editor-in-Chief of the campus newspaper, *La Papillote*

Built a fully licensed professional kitchen in her home to prepare client meals

CAREER PROFILE

Salary Ranges

Entry Level: $25,000 to $35,000

Experienced: $30,000 to $75,000 (or more)

Garde Manger

10.1 Dressings and Dips

10.2 Salads

10.3 Cheese

10.4 Cold Food Presentation

Dressings and Dips

READING PREVIEW

Key Concepts

- Understanding the garde manger station
- Identifying and preparing dressings and dips

Vocabulary

- baba ghanoush
- balsamic vinegar
- basic vinaigrette
- dip
- emulsified vinaigrette
- emulsifier
- emulsion
- extra-virgin olive oil
- garde manger
- guacamole
- herbes de Provence
- mayonnaise
- salad dressing
- salsa
- tapenade
- vinaigrette

Garde Manger

The **garde manger** (GAHRD mohn-ZHAY), also known as the *pantry chef*, is the person (or persons) responsible for cold food preparations. In professional kitchens, the term *garde manger* is typically extended to include all the types of food for which the garde manger is responsible. Today, with diners becoming increasingly familiar with ethnic and imported foods, the garde manger is usually responsible for the foods discussed in this chapter:

- Salad dressings and dips
- Salads
- Cheeses
- Cold food presentations and garnishes

Source: Eric Limon/Fotolia

However, kitchens may have different requirements for their particular garde manger station. For example, if a salad requires a grilled chicken breast that is presented sliced and cold on the salad, the grill station would first grill the chicken and then deliver it to the garde manger to cool and use in the salad. Within a particular kitchen, the work flow determines which responsibilities are assigned to the garde manger. Cold sandwiches, cold hors d'Oeuvre and appetizers, and preserved meats (all of which are discussed in the next chapter) are often assigned to the garde manger as well.

Salad Dressings and Dips

A **salad dressing** is used primarily to flavor salads and, sometimes, to hold a salad together. Many salad dressings are also used as dips. A **dip** is a sauce or condiment served with raw vegetables, crackers, bread, potato chips, or other snack foods. Typically these foods are eaten as appetizers, often while the diner is standing.

Salad dressings and dips fall into five main categories:

- Vinaigrettes (both basic and emulsified vinaigrettes)
- Mayonnaise
- Dairy-based dressings and dips
- Cooked dressings and dips
- Vegetable- or fruit-based dressings and dips

Vinaigrettes A **vinaigrette** (vin-eh-GRETT) is a salad dressing made by combining oil and vinegar into an emulsion. An **emulsion** (e-MULL-shon) is a mixture of uniform consistency made with two ingredients that would otherwise not combine together.

There are two types of vinaigrettes:

- Basic vinaigrette
- Emulsified vinaigrette

A **basic vinaigrette** is a temporary emulsion, typically of some type of oil and some type of vinegar. The process of stirring or vigorously mixing the vinaigrette permits the vinegar and oil to mix together. However, over time, the individual ingredients will separate.

To make an emulsion permanent, an **emulsifier** (e-MULL-si-fy-er) is added, resulting in an **emulsified vinaigrette.** Examples of emulsifiers used for salad dressings are egg yolks, mustard, cornstarch, potato starch, and arrowroot. These substances attract both the oil and vinegar in the vinaigrette, thus binding the two ingredients together.

The standard proportion of oil to vinegar in a vinaigrette is three parts oil mixed with one part vinegar. Using an electric blender or mixer forms a basic vinaigrette more quickly and helps it stay emulsified

FIGURE 10–1

Mise en Place for Vinaigrette
It's important to achieve a balance of textures and flavors in a vinaigrette.

DRAWING CONCLUSIONS *Why should you try to use the best ingredients possible for a vinaigrette?*

Source: Culinary Institute of America

Vinaigrette

1 **Combine seasonings,** such as mustard and salt.

Source: Culinary Institute of America

2 **Add vinegar** and whisk to blend.

Source: Culinary Institute of America

3 **Whisk in the oil** gradually, in a fine steady stream.

Source: Culinary Institute of America

4 **Continue blending** ingredients until the mixture has a uniform consistency.

5 **Adjust seasonings,** if necessary.

Recipe Card

30. Red-Wine Vinaigrette

FOCUS ON Nutrition

Reduced-Fat Vinaigrette

For a lower-fat, lower-calorie vinaigrette, substitute up to half of the oil called for by the recipe with a lightly thickened vegetable juice, such as tomato.

longer than if blended by hand. To keep a basic vinaigrette well blended, mix it before each use.

The principle behind making a good vinaigrette is to achieve a balance between the mouth-coating texture and rich flavor of the oil and the sharp acidity of the vinegar. Because it can be a simple combination of just a few ingredients, a vinaigrette is only as good as its ingredients.

Although a vinaigrette can be nothing more than oil and vinegar that enhance the flavor of perfect salad greens, a vinaigrette can also be a complex mixture of unusual oils, fruit juices, herbs, and other components that provide a unique flavor experience on their own. The following are some of the ingredients you can use in creating vinaigrettes:

- **Olive oil.** The classic oil used in a vinaigrette is a flavorful olive oil. Olive oil is produced in many grades. Some chefs use a grade designated **extra-virgin olive oil**. This is the finest grade of olive oil, produced by pressing olives once without using any heat. It has a fruity, grassy, or peppery taste with a pale yellow to bright green color and a very low acid content. Other chefs feel that extra-virgin olive oil, because of its expense, is wasted in a vinaigrette where its delicate taste is masked by other ingredients.

The shelf life of extra-virgin olive oil is one year if stored in a cool, dark place, but the fresher it is, the better. For the best flavor, keep olive oil in a dark bottle, capped or corked, and away from direct heat. If pouring from a large can or bottle, pour off as much as you need for the day or the week into a smaller bottle. Keep the larger can or bottle capped, in a cool pantry or cellar.

- **Other oils.** Although olive oil is a traditional choice for vinaigrettes, many other types of oils can be used. Some that are often used are walnut oil, hazelnut oil, and sunflower oil. Olive oil and another type of oil are also sometimes mixed together. Oils that are flavored with herbs and aromatics are also available. Oils should be of high quality for the best flavor and nutritional value.

- **Vinegar.** A wide variety of vinegars can be used in vinaigrettes. Some of the most common types of vinegars used are red-wine vinegar, white-wine vinegar, cider vinegar, or commercial balsamic vinegar. Commercial **balsamic** (bal-SAH-mihk) **vinegar** is dark brown and has a sweet-sour taste. Vinegars flavored with herbs and aromatics are also available. Most vinegars used in a vinaigrette have a mellow taste.

  A vinaigrette is typically named for the acid used in making it. So, for example, if red-wine vinegar is used, the vinaigrette would be referred to as a red-wine vinaigrette.

- **Other acids.** Citrus juice, such as lemon, lime, or orange juice, is sometimes substituted for vinegar in a salad dressing. While each type of citrus juice adds acidity, it also adds fruit flavor to the vinaigrette.

- **Mustard.** Of all types of mustards, Dijon (DEE-jhan) mustard is the most commonly used mustard in vinaigrettes. Mustards are the most common type of emulsifier used in creating emulsified vinaigrettes. Prepared mustard can be added to a vinaigrette, but a dry, powdered mustard works just as effectively as an emulsifier. While it makes the emulsion more permanent, mustard, both prepared or dry, also adds a savory, spicy flavor component to the vinaigrette.

- **Herbs.** Fresh herbs can provide another dimension to a vinaigrette. However, herbs discolor and change flavor when added too far in advance. For this reason, add herbs at the last minute.

  Herbs suitable for use in a vinaigrettes include tarragon, thyme, dill, chives, chervil, mint, basil, or **herbes de Provence** (AIRBS duh

Source: David Murray/PM, Getty Active, PS/Dorling Kindersley Media Library/Dorling Kindersley

📁 Recipe Card

31. Basil Oil

Chef's Tip

Too Creative?

Although creativity is the mark of a distinguished garde manger, too many seasonings and conflicting ingredients can mask the taste of fine olive oil and good vinegar.

proh-VAWNS), a dried herb mixture traditionally associated with France's Provence region that can include such herbs as basil, thyme, marjoram, rosemary, sage, fennel seeds, and lavender.

- **Salt and pepper.** Salt is important in maintaining the balance of flavor in a vinaigrette. Without adequate salt, a vinaigrette often tastes too harsh. Because it has no additives, kosher salt is often used in vinaigrettes. White or black pepper may also be added to a vinaigrette. Even though salt and pepper were added in making the vinaigrette, it is still necessary to taste the salad with the vinaigrette to see if additional salt and pepper are needed.

- **Sugar.** Vinaigrettes sometimes contain a small pinch of honey or sugar (or other sweetener) to temper the acidity of the vinegar. Honey is also a common component in an emulsified vinaigrette where the honey and mustard combination produce a combination of savory, spicy, sweet, and sour flavors.

Although vinaigrettes are usually thought of as salad dressings, they have many other uses. Depending on the composition of the vinaigrette, it can be used for such things as the following:

- Adding flavor and moisture when grilling meat or fish
- Dressing cooked vegetables
- Dipping raw or cooked vegetables
  - Dressing bean, grain, or rice salads
  - Enhancing the flavor of sandwiches

Mayonnaise Mayonnaise (MAY-oh-nayz) is a cold, thick, creamy emulsion of oil and egg yolks. Mayonnaise has many uses in the pantry, either on its own or in combination with other ingredients. For example, combined with vinaigrette, it makes a creamy dressing for salads and other cold foods. Combined with canned tuna, it is used to make tuna salad. Combined with hard-boiled eggs, it is used to make egg salad.

Commercial mayonnaise is convenient and has a long shelf life. It suits many purposes but does not compare in flavor or consistency to properly made, fresh mayonnaise. Freshly made mayonnaise is often more richly flavored and looser in consistency than the commercial variety.

Although the recipe for mayonnaise involves only a few ingredients, care is necessary when combining the oil with the egg yolk. Initially, you need to whisk in the oil a drop at a time. The oil must be worked vigorously into the egg to create very small droplets that begin to form the foundation of the emulsion. If the oil is added too quickly and the droplets are too large, an emulsion

FIGURE 10–2

Mise en Place for Mayonnaise

Making mayonnaise results in a looser, more richly flavored product than most commercial mayonnaise.

APPLYING CONCEPTS *When might it make sense for a kitchen to use commercially prepared mayonnaise?*

Source: Culinary Institute of America

will not form and the mayonnaise will separate. When about one-fourth of the oil has been incorporated properly, you can add the remaining oil in a steady stream while whisking continually. Whether working by hand with a whisk or using an electric mixer or food processor, you should add the oil very gradually in the beginning and more steadily at the end.

Liquids such as lemon juice, vinegar, or water may be added to adjust for taste and consistency. Be sure to add these liquids before the oil is added, to ensure the stability of the emulsion. The mayonnaise is finished when soft peaks form. It may be thinned further by beating in additional water if a dressing consistency is desired. Any additional flavorings, such as chopped herbs, pickles, or capers, can be added to the finished mayonnaise.

Because the egg yolk is raw, mayonnaise must be made and stored with care to prevent contamination. Commercial kitchens typically use pasteurized eggs to prevent the possibility of rapid deterioration and the possibility of salmonella poisoning.

Chef's Tip

Oils for Mayonnaise

When making mayonnaise for use as a base sauce, use a relatively flavorless oil such as vegetable oil, so the oil's flavor will not conflict with flavorings added later.

BASIC CULINARY SKILLS

Mayonnaise

① **Blend egg yolks** with a little water.

Source: Culinary Institute of America

② **Whisk in one-fourth of the oil** a little at a time until a creamy and consistent texture forms.

Source: Culinary Institute of America

③ **Mix in additional flavoring ingredients** (such as vinegar, lemon juice, mustard), if using.

④ **Add the remaining oil** gradually, beating continually until soft peaks form.

Source: Culinary Institute of America

⑤ **Store** in the refrigerator.

Recipe Card

32. Mayonnaise

Common Mayonnaise Dressings and Dips

Dressing or Dip	Description	Use
Aïoli (aye-YOH-lee)	Garlic mayonnaise, possibly with flavoring such as herbs or sun-dried tomatoes	Cold poached fish, snails, fish soup, boiled meats or cooked vegetables, hard-cooked eggs, salads, or cold meats
Green Goddess	Mayonnaise mixed with tarragon vinegar and anchovies; flavored with parsley, chives, tarragon, scallions, and garlic	Salads, fish, shellfish
Russian dressing	Mayonnaise mixed with ketchup and possibly relish or pickles	Salads, sandwiches, hard-cooked eggs, cooked meats and vegetables
Tartar (TAR-ter) sauce	Mayonnaise mixed with dill pickles, capers, onions, lemon juice, or vinegar	Fried fish

Recipe Cards

33. Russian Dressing

34. Tartar Sauce

If the mayonnaise begins to separate (chefs refer to this as *breaking*), the problem can be corrected by gradually incorporating beaten pasteurized egg yolk into the mixture. Introduce the egg yolk slowly, whisking continually until the mixture becomes thick and homogeneous.

Dairy-Based Dressings and Dips Dairy products are sometimes used as the basis for salad dressings and dips. For a dip, you could start with a soft cheese such as cream cheese. (You will learn more about cheeses in

••FOCUS ON
••Safety

Pasteurized Eggs

Eggs used for making mayonnaise in an institutional setting should be processed and pasteurized in USDA-inspected plants to ensure against the possibility of salmonella.

FIGURE 10–3

Yogurt and Mint Dip

This refreshing dip is served with raw vegetables.

APPLYING CONCEPTS *Should you consider whether your guests are sitting or standing when you think about the consistency of a dip?*

Source: David Murray/PM, Getty Active, PS/ Dorling Kindersley Media Library/Dorling Kindersley

Section 10.3.) To obtain a thinner consistency, you could use cultured milks such as sour cream, crème fraîche, buttermilk, or yogurt.

Dairy-based salad dressings or dips can be flavored with lemons, pepper, poppy seeds, herbs, shallots or other members of the onion family, capers, olives, truffles, nuts, pimiento, pickles, or artichokes. Fruit or vegetable purées are sometimes added to change the color of the dressing or dip, while also adding flavor.

Cooked Dressings and Dips Some cold dishes call for hot dressings. A category of cooked dressings is the type that evolved in America to moisten coleslaw and potato salad. This type of cooked dressing has become popular because it contains little or no oil. Instead, it relies on milk, flour or cornstarch, vinegar, and eggs or mayonnaise. Cooked dressings may include mustard, bacon, or other flavoring ingredients, but they usually have a more acidic flavor than a mayonnaise-based dressing.

A separate category of dips is the light-bodied, warmed Asian dipping sauce served with dumplings. This type of sauce is often based on soy sauce, seaweed, or vegetable stock and may contain vinegar or some type of wine.

Wilted salads also use cooked dressings. Wilted salads are typically made by pouring a hot vinaigrette on a cold salad so the salad greens become wilted. They often feature other heated components, such as bacon or roasted vegetables. Cooked broccoli, which may be served at room temperature, can be topped with a sizzling dressing made of hot olive oil and garlic. A radicchio (rah-DEEK-kee-oh) salad is traditionally topped with a hot dressing made with olive oil, vinegar, and bacon.

Chef's Tip

Dips That Drip

For finger foods served to standing guests, thick dairy dips that don't drip are best.

Recipe Card

35. Blue Cheese Dressing

FIGURE 10–4

Wilted Spinach Salad

In a wilted spinach salad, do not allow the greens to lose their texture.

COMPARING/CONTRASTING *How would this salad differ in texture without the bacon? Would it be as appealing?*

Source: Clive Streeter/Dorling Kindersley

FIGURE 10–5

Three Dips

(Clockwise from top) Aïoli, tapenade, and guacamole.

PREDICTING *Why would you serve three different types of dip at once?*

Source: Culinary Institute of America

Recipe Card

36. Salsa Fresca

Vegetable- or Fruit-Based Dressings and Dips

Vegetable- or fruit-based dressings or dips may be cooked or uncooked. They may be puréed or chunky. In many cases, these dressings and dips can also be used as sauces as well.

- **Salsa.** Usually uncooked, a **salsa** is based on tomatoes or other fruits or vegetables with some tartness or acidity that is heightened by the addition of an acid (vinegar, citrus, or wine). Salsas are flavor-packed and typically also include hot peppers, spices, and herbs.

- **Guacamole.** A Mexican dip, **guacamole** (gwa-kah-MOH-lee) is made from mashed avocado typically seasoned with a combination of lemon or lime juice, tomatoes, cilantro, onions, and chiles.

- **Tapenade.** A dip made from black olives, capers, anchovies, garlic, herbs, lemon juice, and olive oil, **tapenade** (top-en-ODD) is originally from France's Provence region.

- **Baba ghanoush.** Made from roasted eggplant that has been puréed and seasoned with olive oil, tahini, lemon juice, and garlic, **baba ghanoush** (BAH-bah gha-NOOSH) originated in the Middle East, where it is served as a dip or a spread.

READING CHECKPOINT *What are the five main categories of salad dressings or dips?*

10.1 ASSESSMENT

Reviewing Concepts

1. What is the garde manger?

2. What are the five main categories of salad dressings or dips?

Critical Thinking

3. Forming a Model What are the steps in making a vinaigrette?

4. Communicating What is an emulsion?

5. Comparing/Contrasting What is the difference between a basic vinaigrette and an emulsified vinaigrette?

6. Forming a Model What are the basic steps in making mayonnaise?

7. Comparing/Contrasting How does a dip differ from a salad dressing?

Test Kitchen

Prepare a vinaigrette, using extra-virgin olive oil and red-wine vinegar. Compare it with the flavor of purchased red-wine vinaigrette. Evaluate the differences. Prepare mayonnaise. Compare it with the flavor and texture of purchased mayonnaise. Evaluate the differences.

LANGUAGE ARTS

Descriptive Writing

Research the process used for pasteurizing eggs. Describe what is done to ensure that harmful bacteria cannot grow.

Salads

Key Concepts

- Understanding the purpose of salads
- Preparing green salads
- Using other ingredients in salads
- Preparing composed salads

Vocabulary

- appetizer salad
- aspic
- bound salad
- composed salad
- dessert salad
- main-course salad
- mesclun
- molded salad
- salad
- separate-course salad
- side salad
- tossed salad

Purpose of Salads

A **salad** is a combination of raw or cooked ingredients, served cold or warm and coated with a salad dressing. Although salads are usually savory, they may also be sweet (as in the case of a fruit salad), or they can contain both savory and sweet elements.

In the course of a meal, depending on its ingredients and size, a salad can fall into one of the six following categories:

- **Appetizer salad.** An **appetizer salad** is designed to whet the appetite before the main course. It could be nothing more than a variety of attractive greens with an extra-virgin olive oil and red-wine vinaigrette. But it also could be a more elaborate salad featuring other foods from the garde manger such as cold meat, fish, seafood, or cheese. In America, green salads are often served as appetizer salads.

- **Side salad.** In informal meals, a **side salad** is served to accompany the main dish. If the main dish is heavy, a light crispy green salad might be an ideal side salad. If the main dish is light, a heavier side salad such as a pasta salad or grain salad would be a good choice. In a banquet situation, the side salad should not use ingredients included in the main dish, nor should it use ingredients from an earlier appetizer salad.

- **Bound salad.** A **bound salad** is made from a combination of ingredients that are held together by a thick, creamy dressing such as mayonnaise. Common examples include shrimp, potato, tuna, and

Source: Ian O'Leary/Image Partners 2005/Dorling Kindersley Media Library/Dorling Kindersley

FIGURE 10–6
Side Salad
A salad can contain many ingredients.

APPLYING CONCEPTS *Is it possible to add too many ingredients?*

Source: Culinary Institute of America

Recipe Card

37. Potato Salad

FIGURE 10–7
Bound Salad
This mayonnaise-based bound salad includes shrimp, potatoes, peas, carrots, red pepper, and egg.

DRAWING CONCLUSIONS *When would you serve this type of salad?*

Source: Neil Mersh/Image Partners 2005/Dorling Kindersley Media Library/Dorling Kindersley

egg salad. These salads may be served alone or in combination with other salads as part of an appetizer or a main-course salad. They may also be used as a sandwich filling (for more about sandwiches, refer to Chapter 11). And they may also be served as a side salad to accompany a main dish. Bound salads can also be held together by mixing the ingredients into a gelatin-thickened liquid, referred to as **aspic**. Another term for this type of bound salad is a **molded salad**.

- **Main-course salad.** In some cases, the main course is a salad. When constructing a **main-course salad**, it is important to provide a balanced meal with a protein source (meat, poultry, fish, beans, or eggs) and a variety of vegetables. In America, substantial main-course salads, often with chicken, fish, or meat, have become popular. The concept of a salad as a main course is not as common in Italy or France.

- **Separate-course salad.** In Italy, a green salad often follows the meat or fish course, especially if another type of salad, such as a seafood salad or a salad of preserved meats and pickled vegetables, was used as an appetizer salad. In France, a green salad usually appears as a separate course, after the main course. These **separate-course salads** are usually light, green salads with a simple vinaigrette or a single vegetable such as asparagus, to refresh the appetite and provide a break before dessert. In a banquet situation, a separate-course salad should not use the same ingredients as were used in an appetizer salad or a side salad.

- **Dessert salad.** Often featuring fruits, nuts, or gelatin, a **dessert salad** is usually served with a sweetened dressing, a citrus-based dressing, or whipped cream.

READING CHECKPOINT   *What are the six categories of salads?*

Green Salads

A green salad can be used as an appetizer salad, a side salad, a main-course salad, or a separate-course salad. Depending on its purpose, a green salad can consist of just one type of green or many different types of greens. Usually a green salad is a **tossed salad**, which means all the ingredients are combined with dressing.

Types of Salad Greens In terms of flavor, salad greens can be divided into three basic types:

- Mild greens
- Spicy greens
- Bitter greens

Basic Types of Salad Greens

Mild Greens	Spicy Greens	Bitter Greens
Bibb lettuce, Boston lettuce, iceberg lettuce, leaf lettuce, mâche, romaine lettuce, spinach	Arugula, mizuna, mustard leaves, watercress	Belgian endive, dandelion, escarole, frisée, radicchio

The type of greens you use depends on the purpose of the salad in the meal. For example, a side salad might best be kept simple so it refreshes the palate and aids in digestion by providing fiber. On the other hand, a green salad that is an appetizer salad is meant to stimulate the appetite. It may include a variety of greens chosen for flavor, color, and texture attributes.

When constructing an appetizer salad, you should aim for a balance of flavors and texture. For example, if using radicchio, which is crispy and bitter, you could mix in mild but crispy greens such as Bibb lettuce or Boston lettuce. Then you could add softer, mild greens such as mâche and complete the salad with a little watercress to add a soft, spicy component.

Some kitchens use prepared mixes of salad greens. Sometimes these mixes have a theme, but each has a slightly different taste and texture. For example, **mesclun** (MEHS-kluhn) is a French-style mix that often includes baby red romaine, endive, mâche, radicchio, and arugula. An Asian mixture might include tatsoi, bok choy, baby spinach, mustard, mizuna, and other salad greens.

FOCUS ON Nutrition

Healthy Greens
Some salad greens have greater nutritive value than others. Iceberg lettuce contains a great deal of water but relatively few vitamins and minerals. Spinach and other salad greens that are a deep green usually have more nutritive value.

Bibb Lettuce

Bibb lettuce is sometimes referred to as *limestone lettuce*. It is a heading lettuce with loose, tender leaves and a distinctive flavor. Bibb lettuce tends to be expensive. Boston lettuce is often substituted.

Source: Roger Phillips/Image Partners 2005/Dorling Kindersley Media Library/Dorling Kindersley

Boston Lettuce

Boston lettuce, or butterhead lettuce, is a heading lettuce with soft, tender leaves. It has a mild, delicate flavor.

Source: David Murray/Image Partners 2005/Dorling Kindersley Media Library/Dorling Kindersley

Iceberg Lettuce

Iceberg lettuce is a heading lettuce. The leaves are quite tight to make a compact, heavy head and are pale-green in color. It has a very mild flavor and a crisp texture.

Source: Philip Dowell/Image Partners 2005/Dorling Kindersley Media Library/Dorling Kindersley

Leaf Lettuce

Leaf lettuces may be green or red-tipped. They are a loose heading lettuce with tender leaves that are frilled on the edges. They are usually mild in flavor, but can become bitter if they are overmature when harvested.

Source: Richard Embery/Pearson Education/PH College

Mâche (MAHSH)

Mâche, also known as *corn salad* or *lamb's lettuce*, is grown in loose bunches and has rounded leaves. The leaves are very tender with a delicate flavor.

Source: Richard Embery/Pearson Education/ PH College

Romaine (roh-MAIN) Lettuce

Romaine lettuce may also be known as *cos* lettuce. Cos is the name of the island where romaine is said to have originated. It is a bunching lettuce with long, dark green leaves that are darker at the tips. It has a mild flavor and a good crunch and is the lettuce of choice for a Caesar salad.

Source: Richard Embery/Pearson Education/PH College

Spinach

Spinach grows in bunches and has deep green rounded leaves. Some varieties are smooth while other varieties of spinach have a more pronounced texture. Fresh young spinach (called *baby spinach*) is quite tender with a mild flavor.

Source: Dave King/Image Partners 2005/Dorling Kindersley Media Library/Dorling Kindersley

Spicy Greens

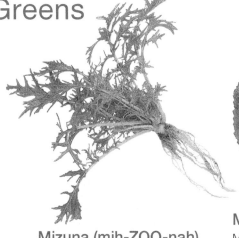

Watercress

Watercress is a bunching green with rounded, scalloped leaves and a pungent, peppery flavor.

Source: Stephen Oliver/ Image Partners 2005/ Dorling Kindersley Media Library/Dorling Kindersley

Arugula (ah-ROO-guh-lah)

Arugula, which is also known as *rocket*, has tender leaves with scalloped edges. Its flavor is pungent and peppery, becoming very biting as it ages.

Source: Richard Embery/ Pearson Education/PH College

Mizuna (mih-ZOO-nah)

Mizuna is a bunching green with long, sharply notched leaves. It has a slightly peppery flavor and a tender texture. It is often associated with Japanese cuisine.

Source: Neil Fletcher and Matthew Ward/ Getty Active/Dorling Kindersley Media Library/Dorling Kindersley

Mustard Greens

Mustard greens grow in bunches. The leaves are a slightly rounded with a serrated edge on a thin stem. It is slightly to very bitter as well as pungent in taste. Large, more mature mustard greens are typically served as cooked greens, in soups, or in stews.

Source: Neil Fletcher/Image Partners 2005/ Dorling Kindersley Media Library/Dorling Kindersley

Bitter Greens

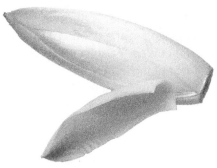

Escarole (ES-kah-roll)

Escarole is a loose heading green, with scalloped edges on leaves that are deep green at the tip and pale green or nearly white near the stem end. It is slightly to very bitter in taste. Large, more mature escarole is typically served as cooked greens, in soups, or in stews.

Source: Clive Streeter/Image Partners 2005/Dorling Kindersley Media Library/Dorling Kindersley

Belgian Endive (EHN-deeve)

Belgian endive has a tight, oblong head with white leaves with some yellow or green at the tips. Its flavor is slightly bitter. It is often prepared as a braised vegetable, in addition to being used as a salad item.

Source: Roger Phillips/Image Partners 2005/Dorling Kindersley Media Library/Dorling Kindersley

Dandelion (DAN-dee-li-on) Greens

Dandelion greens grow in bunches, with long, spear-shaped leaves that have distinct notches along the edges. They are used in salads when they are small and have a hot, somewhat bitter taste. Large, more mature dandelion greens are typically served as cooked greens, in soups, or in stews.

Source: Dorling Kindersley/Image Partners 2005/ Dorling Kindersley Media Library/Dorling Kindersley

Frisée (free-ZAY)

Frisée, or *curly endive*, is a bunching lettuce with sharp "teeth" on curly leaves. The interior leaves are light yellow. Its flavor is slightly to very bitter.

Source: Richard Embery/Pearson Education/PH College

Radicchio (rah-DEE-kee-oh)

Radicchio is a heading form of endive. It has leaves that are deep-red to purple with white veining and a somewhat bitter flavor.

Source: Richard Embery/Pearson Education/PH College

Caterina de Medici

Caterina de Medici was born in Florence on April 13, 1519. When she was just 14 years old, she was married to the son of the king and queen of France. In 1547, her husband became King Henry II. Legend has it that she when she arrived in Paris, she brought with her a number of chefs, cooks, and pastry chefs. Some people have argued that she was responsible for the changes in French cuisine that led to the development of what we know today as *haute cuisine* (high cooking). This has led some to claim that French haute cuisine developed from Italian cuisine. In truth, there is no accurate record of how many cooks and chefs she brought with her, what kinds of chefs they were, or what their effect was on the cooking done in the French court.

Many have credited her with a general improvement in table manners and etiquette. She was certainly responsible for a more elegant dining experience. It is quite likely that Caterina was responsible for some significant changes in the way that banquets were organized and served. Most historians agree that she did manage to separate sweet and savory dishes into separate courses. Florence,

the city where she grew up, was an important center for both trade and banking. She was fond of beautiful china, linens, and glassware. Some have suggested that she introduced the fork to the French court; however, it took nearly 100 years for forks to be generally accepted.

She also brought some foods with her from Florence that might have been new to the French, most notably spinach, artichokes, truffles, and peas. To this day, you may hear the term *Florentine* used in the name of dish when it contains spinach.

The foods, manners, and customs that Caterina introduced to France played a role in moving medieval French cooking toward the elegance and refinement of French haute cuisine.

Caterina de Medici

Source: lynea/Shutterstock

Research

There are many myths and stories about the role that Caterina de Medici played in the development of haute cuisine. Research her role in introducing and popularizing ice cream in France. Does the evidence you can find support a claim that she is the person who introduced it to France?

Fresh herbs such as parsley, basil, chives, sorrel, dill, tarragon, cilantro, mint, and chervil are often added to salads as additional flavorings. Certain herbs can serve as the main body of a salad. For example, a Middle Eastern salad uses only parsley as its salad green. Diced tomatoes and green onions are added, and the salad is dressed with olive oil and lemon juice.

Edible flowers are sometimes strewn on top of a salad to provide an interesting visual feature. Edible garden flowers include nasturtiums (nash-TUR-shums), pansies, calendula (cal-EN-dyu-lah), bachelor's buttons, carnations, fuchsia (FEW-scha), geraniums, Johnny jump-ups, primroses, roses, sunflowers, and violets.

Edible flowers from herbs are used in the same way as the edible garden flowers. Edible herb flowers include arugula, borage (BORE-age), chives, lavender, mustard, oregano, rosemary, sage, and thyme. Sprouts from beans, grasses, and salad greens are often used in salads as well.

Preparing Greens Because greens have a short storage life, they should be used as soon as possible after they are procured, usually within two or three days. They will keep best if washed and dried shortly before use. Once greens are cut or torn, their cut edges oxidize and discolor quickly. Some salad greens, such as spinach or arugula, may need to be washed several times to eliminate the sandy earth in which these ground-hugging greens are grown. You can store dried greens loosely in a clean container covered with a light, damp towel.

Greens should be fresh and perky when served. Keep them cool as long as possible before use. Salads should never include wilted leaves or tired sprouts. Dressing should be added at the last minute to ensure that the salad remains crisp.

Matching dressings to green salads is a matter of judgment. Of course, the dressing and the green salad should be compatible, but green salads generally go well with most types of dressings.

Gloved hands are the best utensils for mixing salad components well, but you can also use tongs or large spoons. The dressing should coat the salad ingredients with a light film. A thick or creamy dressing will require more tossing than a vinaigrette. If dressing collects on the bottom of the bowl, there is too much.

FIGURE 10–8
Salad with Edible Flowers
Edible flowers add visual appeal to a salad.

INFERRING *Should you ever put inedible flowers on a salad just for effect, planning to take them off before the salad is actually served?*

Source: Ian O'Leary/Image Partners 2005/Dorling Kindersley Media Library/Dorling Kindersley

FIGURE 10–9
Covering Salad Greens
Cover the cleaned, dried salad greens by placing a damp towel over them before placing them in the refrigerator.

DRAWING CONCLUSIONS *Why would a restaurant need to have frequent deliveries of salad greens?*

Source: Culinary Institute of America

Mixed Green Salad

1 **Rinse greens** thoroughly in cold running water.

Source: Lucky Dragon/Fotolia

2 **Dry** completely in a salad spinner.

Source: Culinary Institute of America

3 **Tear or cut** greens into bite-sized pieces.

4 **Dress** and toss well.

Source: Stephen Hayward/Image Partners 2005/Dorling Kindersley Media Library/Dorling Kindersley

5 **Garnish** with ingredients of choice.

Recipe Card

38. Mixed Green Salad

Chef's Tip

Dry Salad Leaves

After rinsing, salad greens should be spun or shaken dry. Excess water in the leaves dilutes the dressing and makes the salad soggy.

Good garnishes make green salads more appealing. Favorite additions to green salads are tomatoes, sprouts, fresh herbs, olives, thinly sliced onions, shredded carrots, cucumbers, mushrooms, and radishes. They should be fresh and cut into pieces that can be eaten in one bite. Other options are nuts and seeds, shavings of Parmesan cheese, crumbled feta cheese, or sliced hard-cooked eggs. Crisp garnishes such as crumbled bacon or croutons give a boost to green salads. You can make tasty croutons by frying bread cubes in olive oil or by baking seasoned bread cubes in an oven.

READING CHECKPOINT *What are the three types of salad greens?*

Croutons

1. **Preheat** oven to 300°F.
2. **Remove crusts** from stale sliced bread.
3. **Cut** into large dice.
4. **Toss lightly** with olive oil or melted butter.
5. **Sprinkle salt and dried herbs** (if desired) lightly on the bread.
6. **Place on baking sheet.**
7. **Bake** until lightly browned, about 12 minutes.
8. **Remove from oven** and cool.

Source: Richard Embery/Pearson Education/ PH College

9. **Store** in an airtight container at room temperature.

Other Salad Ingredients

Many ingredients other than greens can be used in a salad. The choice of other ingredients depends on the purpose of the salad and the other dishes in the meal or on the menu.

For example, it is important to consider the connection of a side salad to the main dish. If the main dish is a protein (meat, poultry, or seafood, for example), you may want to use a side salad that focuses on vegetables or starches. If the main dish is a starch, a side salad might focus on vegetables or proteins.

When thinking through a menu, it is also important to have appetizer salads, side salads, and main salads that appeal to a variety of tastes. A diner who orders a substantial main course, such as pot roast, that focuses on protein may be looking for a light appetizer salad. On the other hand, for someone who wants to eat light but desires some protein, a main-course salad with some protein would be ideal.

You can consider four other types of ingredients when constructing salads:

- Vegetables
- Starches
- Proteins
- Fruits and nuts

Vegetables The predominant ingredient in a salad can be raw or cooked vegetables, such as fennel or beets. Raw or cooked vegetables can also be added to green salads. Popular raw vegetable salads include tomato salad, coleslaw, carrot salad, cucumber salad, artichoke heart salad, fennel salad,

·FOCUS ON Nutrition

Low Calorie?

Salad is not necessarily a diet food. A large amount of a rich dressing or high-calorie additions to a salad can turn even a low-calorie green appetizer salad into a very high-calorie meal.

Chef's Tip

Salad Tomatoes

Some tomato varieties with thick skins and few seeds (plum tomato types) are best in sauces. Large slicing tomatoes or thin-skinned tomatoes, such as cherry or grape tomatoes, are best used raw in salads.

FIGURE 10–10

**Cooked Vegetables
in a Salad**
Grilled eggplant makes a good
addition to a tossed green salad.
PREDICTING *What other grilled
vegetables could be substituted for the
eggplant?*
Source: Rob MacDougall/Getty Images

Recipe Cards

39. Pesto

40. Pasta Salad with Pesto
Vinaigrette

and mushroom salad. Popular cooked vegetable salads include boiled or roasted beets, roasted peppers, steamed sugar snap peas, blanched green beans, boiled cauliflower, steamed zucchini, boiled turnips, and boiled potatoes.

Depending on the type of the vegetable and the final desired texture, cooked vegetables for salads are typically roasted, grilled, boiled, blanched, or steamed. Some vegetables, such as cabbage, peas, or sugar snap peas, are simply blanched for a cooked vegetable salad. Other vegetables may be cooked through. In some cooked vegetable salads, such as German potato salad, the vegetables should still be warm when dressed so the flavors combine. Other vegetables, such as zucchini and eggplant, should be dressed at the last minute to avoid sogginess. A chef needs to be aware of the flavor and final texture required by the recipe.

Some cooked salads combine more than one vegetable. Russian salad, called *insalata russa* (een-sah-LAH-tah roos-ah) in Italian and or *salade russe* (sah-LAHD rooss) in French, is a combination of boiled potatoes, beets, eggs, capers, and often turnips, carrots, peas, and other vegetables. A Russian salad is dressed with mayonnaise.

Starches Salads can feature starchy components, including bread, grains, pasta, and beans.

- **Bread.** Leftover bread is the basis of a number of traditional salads, including *panzanella* (pahn-zahn-EL-la), from Italy's Tuscany region, which is made from the region's saltless bread and tomatoes. *Fattoush* (faht-TOOSH), a Middle Eastern salad, is a combination of bread, lettuce, spinach, cucumbers, tomatoes, bell peppers, green onions, cilantro, and mint, dressed with lemon juice, olive oil, and garlic.

- **Grains.** Many kinds of grains, including cracked wheat, rice, and barley, can be used for salads. Grain salads are best made shortly before they are used, because they absorb the salad dressing easily and can become soggy. They also absorb other flavorings quickly. *Tabouli* (tah-BOO-leh) is an example of a Middle Eastern grain-based salad. It features cracked wheat.

- **Pasta.** Pasta salads are quite popular. A pasta salad could be the traditional macaroni salad; a couscous salad with lemon, mint, onions, and peppers; or even a Japanese salad made with buckwheat pasta and a peanut-based sauce. A pasta salad often becomes bland in storage. Before serving a pasta salad that has been stored, check its seasoning carefully.

- **Beans.** Beans and lentils make delicious and nutritious salads. They are cooked and served cold or at room temperature. Because beans don't become soggy, they are ideal when advance preparation is necessary. Virtually any kind of bean can be used individually in salads or combined with other beans (as, for example, a traditional three-bean salad). Beans must be cooked until very tender. They should be dressed close to service time because the acid in a dressing can toughen the beans.

Protein Protein sources, such as meat, poultry, seafood, and cheese, make excellent additions to warm or cold salads. In some cases, they are the primary focus of the salad. Meat could be roasted, chicken could be grilled, or shrimp could be boiled. No matter how the protein source is cooked, it should be freshly made.

Because seafood is highly perishable and delicate, it should be freshly cooked for use in a salad. If the protein source is cooked in advance and chilled, the dressing should be added no more than three or four hours before serving. This prevents excessive absorption of the dressing. Ideally, meats, poultry, and seafood used for salads should be moist and tender to the fork. Dressings add flavor; they should not be relied on to return moisture to overcooked food.

Meat, poultry, and seafood salads are served as an appetizer salad or, in a larger portion, as a main-course salad. Because such salads are substantial, they are not typically used as side salads or separate-course salads.

Traditional American-style chicken and seafood salads use a mayonnaise-based dressing. However, other types of protein-based salads, such as grilled chicken salad with Caesar dressing, are becoming more common.

 Recipe Card
41. Mixed Grain and Bean Salad

 Recipe Card
42. Caesar Salad

There are endless variations on meat, poultry, and seafood salads. Here are some examples:

- Taco salad
- Steak and barley salad
- Cajun-style shrimp salad
- Thai-style beef salad
- Curried chicken salad
- Lobster salad
- Grilled salmon salad
- Greek lamb salad with mint
- Seared scallop salad

Fruits and Nuts With the selection of fruits and nuts available today from all over the world, chefs can be highly creative with salads. Once thought of only for dessert salads, fruits are now often featured in appetizer salads and even in main-course salads. An example of an appetizer salad using fruit might be one consisting of pears, blue cheese, a spicy green such as arugula, walnuts, and a rich olive oil without any vinegar. Main-course salads often feature apples or pears. Fruit salads are also sometimes offered on breakfast or brunch menus.

Once cut, fruit deteriorates rapidly. Fruit should be cut close to the salad's serving time. Fruits that turn brown, such as apples and pears, can be placed in a bath of water and lemon juice to prevent discoloration for up to several hours. Lemon juice may create a distraction from the flavors desired in the final salad, however.

  **READING CHECKPOINT** *What are the four other types of ingredients to consider when constructing a salad?*

Composed Salads

A **composed salad** is a salad with any combination of ingredients (greens, vegetables, proteins, starches, fruits, or garnishes) that are arranged carefully and artfully on a plate or in a bowl. The entire composed salad can be dressed with one style of dressing, or individual components can be separately dressed with different dressings. The dressing for some or all of the components of a composed salad can be served *on the side*—that is, in a separate container to be applied by the customer.

A composed salad with greens is typically presented as an appetizer salad, a main-course salad, or a separate-course salad. A composed fruit salad can be a dessert course or a main course for breakfast or brunch.

Recipe Card

43. Tropical Fruit Salad

FIGURE 10–12

Fruit in a Salad

The slices of orange are an unexpected complement to the endive, watercress, red onion, and fennel.

ANALYZING INFORMATION *Describe the flavors in this salad and how they balance each other.*

Source: Dorling Kindersley/Image Partners 2005/Dorling Kindersley Media Library/Dorling Kindersley

Composed salads present a terrific opportunity for creativity in the garde manger station. Ingredients and garnishes are typically arranged beautifully on a plate or in a bowl, rather than being tossed.

Preparation of a Composed Salad A composed salad often has four component parts:

- **Main ingredients.** A composed salad often has one or more main ingredients as its centerpiece. The main ingredient could be roasted vegetables, a grilled chicken breast, sliced grilled steak, sautéed shrimp, or a grilled salmon fillet.

- **Supporting ingredients.** The main ingredients are often placed on a bed of greens or shredded vegetables. These supporting ingredients can form a base for the main ingredients. For example, the lettuce in a chef's salad carries the main ingredients of hard-cooked eggs, ham, turkey, and cheese strips. Some composed salads include many supporting ingredients artfully arranged on a plate around the main ingredients.

- **Garnish.** The visual appeal of a composed salad is important. The salad should be attractively garnished with ingredients that are appetizing as well as decorative. Consider what ingredients can help balance or enhance the other ingredients. Choose garnishes with an eye for texture as well as for flavor and color. Garnishes are discussed in section 10.4.

- **Dressing.** The dressing should balance the various flavors in the composed salad and be compatible with all the ingredients. It may be served on the side or placed attractively in an individual container as part of the composition. Alternatively, salads may be dressed immediately before service.

FIGURE 10–13

Composed Salads
French niçoise (nee-SWAHZ) salad (left) includes tuna, olives, egg, and green beans; Italian caprese (cah-PREHY-zay) salad (right) includes tomato, mozzarella, and basil.

COMPARING/CONTRASTING
Describe the differences between these two composed salad presentations.

Sources: (left) Dave King/Image Partners 2005/ Dorling Kindersley Media Library/Dorling Kindersley; (right) David Murray and Jules Selmes/Image Partners 2005/Dorling Kindersley Media Library/Dorling Kindersley

Recipe Card

44. Chef Salad

Chef's Tip

Garnishes

The quality of the salad in a restaurant usually provides a little preview of what can be expected from the meal to follow. Garnishes should not be an afterthought.

When preparing composed salads, focus on balance and contrasts. Ingredients in a composed salad should be arranged with an eye to design. Think of the balance of forms and shapes as you compose and garnish the salad. Of course, nothing can substitute for the freshness and good flavor of the food on the plate, but making the plate interesting and appetizing adds to the pleasure of the dish. Keep these guidelines in mind:

- **Flavors.** Put together various flavors, but make sure they are compatible. Flavors that fight each other are not usually put together on the same plate.

- **Textures.** Combinations of textures make salads appetizing. Crisply cooked crumbled bacon; soft, creamy goat cheese; mild, crisp Bibb lettuce; and a tangy vinaigrette, for example, have texture appeal as well as flavor appeal.

- **Colors.** Use color, such as vibrant yellow bell peppers, the purple of radicchio, or the white of endive, to add interest and appeal.

- **Height.** You can create interest by using height as a design element. Sliced vegetables, for example, can be stacked or layered for visual appeal.

Examples of Composed Salads Some composed salads, such as Niçoise salad, and caprese salad, are so well established that they have their own unique names and are among the most popular salads ordered at restaurants. Other composed salads depend on seasonal ingredients or special components for which the kitchen is known. For example, a rustic restaurant might serve a composed salad consisting of tuna, white beans, and roasted red peppers with a mustardy dressing. A restaurant well known for its curried chicken salad might choose to feature it in a composed salad with green beans dressed with a minty yogurt-based dressing, walnuts, grapes, and pickled watermelon.

Four Popular Composed Salads

Salad Name	Dressing	Ingredients
Chef salad	Vinaigrette	Tossed greens; julienned ham, chicken, or turkey; cheese; sliced vegetables; and hard-cooked eggs.
Cobb salad	Cobb dressing (olive oil, red-wine vinegar, lemon juice, mustard, garlic)	Lettuce (base) with sliced turkey or chicken breast, avocado slices, cheese strips, hard-cooked eggs, tomato, and bacon. Often garnished with blue cheese.
Caesar salad, with grilled chicken	Caesar dressing (olive oil, wine vinegar, egg yolk, garlic, mustard, sometimes anchovies)	Romaine lettuce (base), sliced grilled chicken (main ingredient), and grated Parmesan cheese. Often garnished with croutons.
Niçoise (nee-SWAHZ) salad	Red-wine vinaigrette	Tuna (main ingredient), with boiled sliced potatoes, tomato slices, hard-cooked eggs, black olives, anchovies, cooked green beans, and sliced bell peppers.

10.2 ASSESSMENT

Reviewing Concepts

1. What are the six categories of salads?
2. What are three types of salad greens?
3. Other than greens, what are four types of ingredients to consider when constructing a salad?
4. What is a composed salad?

Critical Thinking

5. **Comparing/Contrasting** What is the difference between a tossed salad and a composed salad?
6. **Inferring** Why would a dressing for a composed salad often be served separately?
7. **Predicting** In your opinion, does height add interest and appeal to a salad?

Test Kitchen

Assemble a collection of as many types of salad greens as you can. Prepare a red-wine vinaigrette. Sample each of the salad greens individually and together, with and without the vinaigrette. Write down your notes about the taste of the various salad greens. Compare your results with classmates.

LANGUAGE ARTS ———

Descriptive Writing

Research salads from three different countries. Write a standard recipe for your favorite one. Make your recipe and then write a review of your dish.

READING PREVIEW

Key Concepts

- Understanding types of cheese
- Buying, handling, and storing cheese
- Serving cheese
- Cooking with cheese

Vocabulary

- blue-vein cheeses
- cheese board
- cheese cart
- flight of cheeses
- fresh cheeses
- grating cheeses
- hard cheeses
- processed cheese
- rind
- semisoft cheeses
- soft, rind-ripened cheeses

Types of Cheese

Cheese is an important part of the garde manger tradition. With thousands of types of cheeses, a garde manger has a broad spectrum of cheeses from which to choose.

Although cheese can be made from the milk of cows, sheep, goats, or water buffalo, there are seven basic types of cheese, based on texture, taste, appearance, and aging:

- Fresh cheeses
- Soft, rind-ripened cheeses
- Semisoft cheeses
- Hard cheeses
- Blue-vein cheeses
- Grating cheeses
- Processed cheeses

Fresh Cheeses **Fresh cheeses** are moist, soft cheeses that typically have not ripened or significantly aged. These cheeses are used as spreads, eaten with fruits, or used in cooking and baking.

Examples of fresh, unripened cheeses include cottage cheese, cream cheese, farmer cheese, fresh goat cheese (called *chèvre*, SHEHV-ruh), mascarpone (mas-cahr-POHN-ay), fresh mozzarella (moh-tza-REL-lah), feta (FEH-tah), and fresh ricotta (rih-COH-tah).

Because they are fresh, soft cheeses are highly perishable. They should be used as soon as possible after they are purchased.

Source: Barry Gregg/Corbis

Grana Padano

Local cheese makers in northeastern Italy will tell you that their ancestors were making Grana Padano (GRA-nah pa-DAHN-oh), a grating cheese similar to Parmigiano-Reggiano, since before Roman times. These early versions of Grana Padano, called "Grana" for short, were probably made from a mixture of goat's, sheep's, and cow's milk. Cow's milk, which has a high butterfat content and makes a richer cheese, eventually became used almost exclusively to make Grana.

The Romans had a gift for recognizing a good thing when they saw it. They did nothing to stop the tradition of making Grana. But after the Roman civilization fell to successive waves of barbarians, the cheese makers went to the mountains while the barbarians laid waste to the countryside. Eventually, the green valleys grew wild and marshy, and malaria and famine were rampant.

The monks of the Po Valley, specifically Bernardo di Chiaravalle, are given credit for reviving Grana Padano in 1135. Under Bernardo's direction, the monks redirected water flow, using oxen to both re-cultivate the land and provide milk for cheese. They perfected and standardized their cheese-making method. Surplus milk was transformed into Grana Padano, a delicious and nutritious food that could be stored for relatively long periods of time without spoiling. The monks called it *caseus vetus*, old cheese.

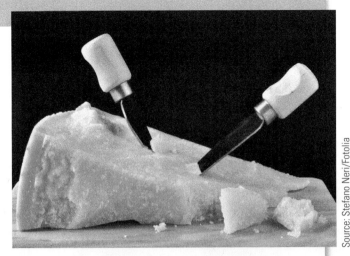

Sampling a piece of Grana Padano cheese

Source: Stefano Neri/Fotolia

Today, Grana Padano is made in the same areas of Italy, using the same recipe the monks used. Some of the dairy barns have given way to factories where Grana Padano is produced in huge rooms by workers wearing white lab coats and where technicians examine the finished cheeses for unwanted holes by using x-ray machines. But still, Grana Padana looks, and probably tastes, the same as it did way back when the monks were making it in the 12th century.

Research

Research the history of a particular type of traditional cheese, such as Cheddar, Gruyère, or Parmigiano-Reggiano. Describe where it originated, what milk is used, how it is made, how production has changed over time, and how it tastes.

Soft, Rind-Ripened Cheeses Soft, rind-ripened cheeses are soft cheeses that have been ripened by being exposed to a spray or dusting of "friendly" mold. These cheeses are aged until the **rind** (RYND), the surface, develops a soft, downy consistency. The rind, which is edible, provides a delightful contrast in texture and flavor to the interior of the cheese. When fully ripe, a soft cheese should be nearly runny.

Examples of soft, rind-ripened cheeses are Brie (BREE), Camembert (cam-em-BEHR), and Pont l'Évêque (PONT leh-VECK). Many soft ripened cheeses are named after the city or region making the cheese. However, because the names Camembert and Brie are not protected by French law, they are widely used for cheeses produced elsewhere. As a result, the flavor and quality of "brie" or "camembert" vary widely.

•••FOCUS ON
••• Nutrition

Nutritional Value

Most cheeses contain an average of 60 percent water. They contain fat but are also high in protein and calcium.

FIGURE 10–14

Soft, Rind-Ripened Cheese
When fully ripe, a soft, rind-ripened cheese should be nearly runny.

PREDICTING *How would you eat a soft cheese that has become runny?*

Source: lidante/Fotolia

Chef's Tip

Raw-Milk Cheeses

Cheeses made from nonpasteurized milk are called raw-milk cheeses and often have distinctive flavors. Typically made by small cheese producers who follow traditional methods, they are rare in the United States.

Semisoft Cheeses Semisoft cheeses are more solid than soft cheeses and retain their shape. They may be mild or strongly flavored as a result of the particular process used to make them. There are three types of semisoft cheeses:

- **Rind-ripened.** These are semisoft cheeses whose rinds are washed with a liquid such as grape juice, beer, brandy, wine, cider, or olive oil. The washing produces beneficial bacteria that penetrate and flavor the cheese from the rind to the inside. Examples of rind-ripened, semisoft cheeses are Muenster (MUHN-stuhr) and Port Salut (port sahl-OO).

- **Dry-rind.** These are cheeses in which the rind is permitted to harden naturally through exposure to air. The rind becomes firm, but the interior of the cheese remains tender. Examples of dry-rind semisoft cheeses are Bel Paese (bel pah-AYZ-eh), Monterey Jack (MONT-ter-ay JACK), Morbier (MOR-bee-ay), and Havarti (hah-VAHR-tee).

- **Waxed-rind.** In these cheeses, wax is applied to form a solid shell around the cheese as it ripens. The interior of the cheese remains consistently soft. Examples of waxed-rind semisoft cheeses are the Dutch cheese Edam (EE-duhm) and the Italian cheese Fontina (fon-TEEN-nah).

Blue-Vein Cheeses To make **blue-vein cheeses**, needles are injected into the cheese to form holes in which mold spores multiply. The cheese is salted and ripened in a cave. Roquefort (ROWK-fort) is often called the king of cheeses. It has been made since Roman times and was the favorite of Charlemagne. Other blue-vein cheeses include Gorgonzola (gore-gon-ZO-la), an Italian cheese; Stilton, from England; and Maytag blue, from America. Young blue-vein cheeses are mild in comparison to the aged versions.

Hard Cheeses **Hard cheeses** have a drier texture than semisoft cheeses and a firmer consistency. They slice and grate easily. The best-known hard cheeses are probably Cheddar cheese and Swiss-style cheeses such as Emmenthaler (EM-en-tah-ler) and Gruyère (gree-YAIR), which have many uses in cooking. Other popular hard cheeses include Colby, Jarlsberg (YAHRLZ-behrg), provolone (pro-vah-LONE), and Manchego (man-CHE-go).

Grating Cheeses **Grating cheeses** are solid, dry cheeses that have a grainy consistency, making them ideal for grating. They are often grated or shaved onto food rather than cut into slices because of their crumbly texture. However, chunks are also broken off the larger cheese to create bite-size chunks for cheese platters. Grating cheeses are often produced in 75- to 80-pound wheels. Some examples of grating cheeses are Parmigiano-Reggiano (parm-muh-ZHAH-noh reh-zhee-AH-noh), Pecorino-Romano (peh-kuh-REE-noh ro-MON-oh), and the greenish Sapsago (sap-SAY-go) from Switzerland.

Source: Neil Mersh/Image Partners 2005/Dorling Kindersley Media Library/Dorling Kindersley

FIGURE 10–15

Blue-Vein Cheese

The blue veins in a blue cheese are actually types of a beneficial mold.

ANALYZING INFORMATION *Does the idea of eating a moldy cheese cause you concern?*

Chef's Tip

Aging Cheese

The longer cheese is aged, the stronger its flavor will be.

Cheese Fresh Cheeses

Chèvre (Goat Cheese)

Chèvre (goat cheese) is made from goat's milk. It is produced in various shapes: block, pyramid, button, wheel, or log. When fresh, it has a tangy flavor and soft texture.

Source: Dorling Kindersley/Image Partners 2005/Dorling Kindersley Media Library/Dorling Kindersley

Feta

Feta is made from sheep's, goat's, or cow's milk. It is produced as a block. The cheese is white, with a tangy, salty flavor and a soft, crumbly texture.

Source: Roger Phillips/Image Partners 2005/Dorling Kindersley Media Library/Dorling Kindersley

Mascarpone

Mascarpone is made from whole cow's milk with added cream. It is sold in tubs. Mascarpone has an ivory or cream color; a buttery, slightly tangy flavor, and a soft, smooth, spoonable texture.

Source: Dorling Kindersley/Image Partners 2005/Dorling Kindersley Media Library/Dorling Kindersley

Mozzarella

Mozzarella is made from whole or skim cow's or buffalo's milk. It is produced as spheres or logs. The cheese is off white and has a mild flavor; it is sometimes smoked, and has a tender to slightly elastic texture (depending on age).

Source: Richard Embery/Pearson Education/PH College

Ricotta

Ricotta is made from whole, skim, or low-fat cow's milk whey. It is sold in tubs. The cheese is white, with a mild flavor; soft, moist to slightly dry, small curds; and a grainy texture.

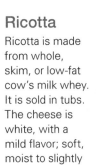

Source: David Murray/Image Partners 2005/Dorling Kindersley Media Library/Dorling Kindersley

Cheese

Soft, Rind-Ripened Cheeses

Brie

Brie is made from pasteurized, whole, or skim cow's or goat's milk, sometimes with the addition of cream. It is produced as a disk with a soft, white, velvety coating on the exterior. The cheese is light yellow, with a buttery to pungent flavor; it is soft and smooth with an edible rind.

Source: Philip Dowell/Image Partners 2005/Dorling Kindersley Media Library/Dorling Kindersley

Camembert

Camembert is made from raw or pasteurized whole cow's or goat's milk. It is produced as a disk with a soft, white, velvety coating on the exterior. The cheese is light yellow or a light cream color, with a slightly tangy flavor; a soft, creamy texture; and an edible rind.

Source: Roger Phillips/Image Partners 2005/Dorling Kindersley Media Library/Dorling Kindersley

Pont l'Évêque

Pont l'Évêque is made from whole cow's milk. It is produced as a square block. The cheese is light yellow, with a piquant flavor and a strong aroma. It has a soft, supple texture, with small holes and an edible golden-yellow crust.

Source: Roger Phillips/Image Partners 2005/Dorling Kindersley Media Library/Dorling Kindersley

Semisoft Cheeses

Edam

Edam is made from whole or part-skim cow's milk. It is produced as a loaf or sphere and may be coated with wax. Edam has a mild to tangy flavor (depending on age) with a firm texture and tiny holes.

Source: Philip Dowell/Image Partners 2005/Dorling Kindersley Media Library/Dorling Kindersley

Fontina

Fontina is made from whole cow's or sheep's milk. It is produced as a wheel and the cheese is a medium yellow color, with a nutty flavor and strong aroma. Fontina is semisoft and waxy.

Source: Philip Dowell/Dorling Kindersley Media Library/Dorling Kindersley

Monterey Jack

Monterey Jack is made from whole cow's milk. It is produced as a wheel or block, with a light yellow color and a mild to pungent flavor (it may be flavored with chiles, herbs, or sundried tomatoes). The cheese has a semisoft to very hard texture (depending on age).

Source: Philip Dowell/Dorling Kindersley Media Library/Dorling Kindersley

Muenster

Muenster is made from whole cow's milk. It is produced as either a wheel or a block. The cheese is light yellow; the rind may be orange. It has a mild to pungent flavor (depending on age) and is semisoft with a smooth, waxy texture with small holes.

Source: Philip Dowell/Image Partners 2005/Dorling Kindersley Media Library/Dorling Kindersley

Port Salut

Port Salut is made from whole or low-fat cow's milk. It is produced as either a wheel or a cylinder. The cheese is off-white with a russet exterior. It has a buttery, mellow to sharp flavor and a semisoft, smooth texture.

Source:Philip Dowell/Image Partners 2005/Dorling Kindersley Media Library/Dorling Kindersley

Hard Cheeses

Gruyère

Gruyère is made from raw or pasteurized cow's milk. It is produced as a wheel. The cheese is a light yellow color, with a mild, nutty flavor and a hard, smooth texture; it is shiny with small holes or cracks that develop as the cheese ages.

Source: Richard Embery/Pearson Education/PH College

Jarlsberg

Jarlsberg is made from whole cow's milk. It is produced as a wheel. The cheese is a light yellow color and is sharp, nutty, and hard with large holes.

Source: Philip Dowell/Image Partners 2005/Dorling Kindersley Media Library/Dorling Kindersley

Cheddar

Cheddar is made from whole cow's milk. It is produced as a wheel. The cheese is light or medium yellow, with a mild to sharp flavor (depending on age) and a hard texture.

Source: James Jackson/Image Partners 2005/Dorling Kindersley Media Library/Dorling Kindersley

Manchego

Manchego is made from whole sheep's milk. It is produced as a cylinder and is light yellow with a full, mellow flavor. The cheese has a semisoft to firm texture (depending on age) with holes.

Source: Roger Phillips/Image Partners 2005/Dorling Kindersley Media Library/Dorling Kindersley

Provolone

Provolone is made from whole cow's milk. It is produced in various shapes: pear, sausage, round, or cylinder. The cheese is light yellow to golden brown, with a mild to sharp flavor (depending on age) and a hard, elastic texture. It may be smoked.

Source: Richard Embery/Pearson Education/PH College

Blue-Vein Cheeses

Gorgonzola

Gorgonzola is made from whole cow's and/ or goat's milk. It is produced as a wheel. The cheese is medium yellow with blue marbling and a tangy, piquant flavor. It has a semisoft texture; some are creamy, others are crumbly.

Source: Dorling Kindersley

Stilton

Stilton is made from whole cow's milk. It is produced as a cylinder. The cheese is medium yellow with blue-green marbling; a piquant flavor, but mild for blue; and a firm, crumbly texture.

Source: David Murray, Dorling Kindersley

Roquefort

Roquefort is made from raw sheep's milk. It is produced as a cylinder. The cheese is white with blue-green marbling; a sharp, pungent flavor; and a semisoft, crumbly texture.

Source: Richard Embery/Pearson Education/PH College

Parmigiano-Reggiano

Parmigiano-Reggiano/Parmesan is made from part-skim cow's milk. It is produced as a wheel. The cheese is light yellow with a sharp, nutty flavor and a very hard, dry, crumbly texture.

Source: Culinary Institute of America

Pecorino-Romano

Pecorino-Romano is made from whole sheep's, goat's, or cow's milk. It is produced as a cylinder and has a very sharp, salty flavor and a very hard, dry, crumbly texture.

Source: Stefano Neri/Fotolia

Sapsago

Sapsago is made from buttermilk, whey, and skim cow's milk. It is produced as a flattened cone. The cheese is light green and piquant, flavored with clover leaves. It has a very hard, granular texture.

Source: Philip Dowell, Dorling Kindersley

Chef's Tip

Grating Cheeses

Use salty Pecorino with rustic-style dishes; use complex Parmigiano for more refined dishes and sauces.

Processed Cheeses Processed cheese is made from one or more cheeses that have been finely ground, mixed together with other nondairy ingredients, heated, and poured into a mold. Processed cheese food is like processed cheese except that it also includes other dairy products. At least 51 percent of the material in processed cheese food must be cheese. Additional moisture can be added to processed cheese food to make it spreadable.

READING CHECKPOINT *What are the seven basic types of cheese?*

Buying, Handling, and Storing Cheeses

Buying Cheeses A good way to learn about cheeses is from the experts: knowledgeable vendors and the cheese producers themselves. Buy only as

Steps in Making Cheese

Cheese making relies on science. Making pasteurized cheese involves the following basic steps:

- **Heating milk.** Milk is heated to destroy all bacteria (both pathogens and "friendly" bacteria).
- **Adding starter (acidification).** A starter is added to the milk, causing it to sour. The starter contains either an acid (such as lemon juice or vinegar) or *rennet*, an acid-producing substance produced from animal or vegetable sources.
- **Forming curds.** As the milk sours, the solid matter in the milk forms into solid clumps, or curds. This is called coagulation (co-AG-yew-la-shun).
- **Separating the curds and whey.** When the milk has coagulated, it has separated into curds and whey, the remaining liquid from the milk. The whey is drained off, leaving only the curds.
- **Draining and shaping curds.** Curds may be placed in bags, baskets, or molds before being placed on racks or hung to drain and dry. Soft cheese is drained and shaped at the same time. Hard cheeses, such as Cheddar, are shaped, drained, and then dried and shaped by pressing.
- **Aging.** Fresh cheeses are not aged. For other cheeses, aging can run from a few days up to several years. Cheeses undergo changes in flavor, texture, and color during ripening. Cheeses may be aged in wax rind, ashes, or leaves. They

Adding starter to the milk

may be rubbed, washed, or soaked. They may be injected with friendly molds.

Lab Activity

In two separate saucepans, heat 2 cups of milk until it is almost boiling. Add the juice of ½ lemon to one pan. Add 1 Tbsp of vinegar to the other. Continue to cook, stirring frequently, until the milk separates into white clumps or strings and a thin watery liquid (known as whey). Drain the curds through a colander lined with a clean cloth or a coffee filter. Taste the curds. Can you taste a difference between the curds made with lemon and the ones made with vinegar? Are there differences in the size or texture of the curds?

much as you need. Once they are cut, cheeses begin to lose quality and should be eaten quickly. This ensures freshness when the cheese is used.

When buying cheeses you should do the following:

- **Examine the label.** Labels provide information about the type of cheese and its origin, authenticity, ingredients, and date of production.
- **Examine the rind.** The color of the rind should be natural. Often, the more artificial the color and the more perfect the appearance, the less authentic the cheese may be.
- **Examine the interior.** The interior should not show any holes or coloring that is not meant to be there. For grating cheeses, be certain they are a healthy straw color and not dried out or powdery.
- **Taste the cheese.** You should taste the cheese before buying it, if possible. Make sure it is what you expected.

Source: Hemeroskopion/Fotolia

FIGURE 10–16

Buying Cheeses
The best way to learn about cheese is to ask your supplier.

INFERRING *Why would your supplier be interested in educating you about their products?*

Source: Ryan McVay/Photodisc/Getty Images

Handling Cheeses Cut off only as much cheese as you need at a time if you have a large chunk. Store the remainder properly in the refrigerator.

The mold on cheese, unlike mold on most foods, does not contaminate the entire cheese. You can remove any unwanted mold that forms on cheese by trimming it away from the contaminated area. To prevent mold spores from spreading to other parts of the cheese during handling, take care not to bring the moldy area into contact with the rest of the cheese.

Grate cheese only when you need it. Pre-grating cheese causes it to dry out and to lose a great deal of its distinct flavor. You can use box graters or a food processor fitted with a metal blade to grate cheeses.

You can cut fresh and soft cheeses with a cleaned and sanitized wire. Semisoft, blue, and hard cheeses can be cut with a chef's knife. Traditionally, grating cheeses are not sliced with a knife. Once you cut into a grating cheese, you can use a special cheese chipper with a wooden handle and triangular blade to chip or flake the cheese.

Cheeses must be handled hygienically to prevent potential hazards. Follow these sanitation guidelines when handling cheese:

- Use clean foodservice gloves or clean utensils to avoid transferring bacteria from your hands.

- Clean and sanitize work surfaces and other food-contact areas at the end of the day.

- Clean and sanitize equipment used to slice, cut, or otherwise work with cheeses at the end of the day.

Storing Cheeses Proper storage ensures freshness for the life of the cheese. Whole cheeses continue to age as long as they are uncut and stored properly. Cut cheeses begin to deteriorate as soon as the inside is exposed to air. Fresh cheeses spoil rapidly, while hard cheeses keep longer because of their low moisture content.

Plastic wrap does not allow cheese to breathe. It is best to wrap cheese in waxed paper or butcher paper and store it in a cool place. Be sure there are no tears or openings in the wrap. Alternatively, the cheese can be placed in a container with a tight-fitting lid. Don't reuse storage wrappings; they have been handled and exposed to the air and counter surfaces. Discard them and use fresh wrap.

 **READING CHECKLIST** *What is the best way to store cheeses?*

Serving Cheese

Fresh cheeses such as mozzarella should be eaten as soon as possible after they are made because they lose their flavor and creaminess as their moisture evaporates. It is best to purchase them on the same day they are to be used.

Cheeses typically should be served at room temperature. If cheeses have been stored in the refrigerator, they should be left for an hour at room temperature before serving. Set out only as much as you will use. If left out longer than several hours, hard cheeses become oily. Soft cheeses may dry out. Once cheeses are brought to the proper temperature for eating, they should be served immediately and not left out to sit. Individual cheeses are typically served as a separate course in either of two locations within a formal meal:

- **Appetizer course.** Offering fine cheeses for the appetizer course, or as part of a composed appetizer salad before the meal, provides an opportunity to make a good first impression on a guest.

- **Following a meal.** In the European tradition, cheeses often follow a meal and are served alongside fruit before a dessert course.

There are three basic ways to serve cheese as a separate course:

- **Individual cheese.** The advantage of serving a single cheese is that the guest can focus on the appearance, flavor, and texture of a single cheese without being distracted by other offerings on the plate.

- **Multiple cheeses.** Often, a number of different cheeses are offered at the same time (this is sometimes referred to as a **flight of cheeses**). Sometimes a flight of cheeses includes cheeses of the same variety, thus offering guests the opportunity to sample a range of cheeses from the same base ingredient (for example, goat cheeses). However, an assortment of different types of cheeses is more typical for a flight of cheeses.

- **Cheese cart.** Some restaurants offer an assortment of cheeses on a **cheese cart**, a cart that is wheeled to the guests' table to give them an opportunity to choose cheeses of different kinds. They can then see them as they make their choice. Typically, a guest orders cheeses and the server arranges them on a plate from the tableside. Bread, crackers, and fruit often accompany the cheeses.

Cheeses are often served on flat marble, china, or wooden platters, sometimes covered with non-toxic leaves (such as grape leaves). No matter which material is used in its construction, the flat platter is typically called a **cheese board**. When serving several cheeses at once, you can place each on separate cheese boards or you can serve

FIGURE 10–17

Cheese Board

This cheese board features eight types of cheese, with red and green grapes.

COMPARING/CONTRASTING *What are the advantages and disadvantages of serving so many cheeses at one time?*

Source: Martin Brigdale/Dorling Kindersley

them on a single cheese board, leaving plenty of room around each cheese to prevent soft cheeses from running into other cheeses. Provide a separate knife for each different kind of cheese.

Bread or crackers and fruit are often served with cheeses. Other foods that pair well with cheeses include cured meats (such as salami or prosciutto), roasted peppers, and cut-up raw vegetables.

 **READING CHECKLIST** *At what temperature should cheeses typically be served?*

Cooking with Cheeses

Although cheese is often used in cooking, heat alters its unique flavor. High heat causes cheeses to become tough and rubbery. As a general rule, use low heat when cooking cheeses. Here are three ways cheeses can be used in cooking:

- **In a dish.** Semisoft cheeses are ideal for integrating in a dish because they don't leach excess water the way fresh cheeses can. They should be shredded rather than sliced for easier and more even melting. Some cheeses that are particularly suitable for melting include

FIGURE 10–18

Fondue

Vegetables and bread are dipped in cheese fondue.

PREDICTING *Why would the texture of melted cheese be an important consideration for this dish?*

Source: Bernd Jürgens/Fotolia

Cheddar, Gruyère, and Fontina. *Fondue* (fon-DUE) is one of the best-known cheese dishes. Made with Emmenthaler or Gruyère cheese, it has a thick, creamy texture and is typically used for dipping cooked or raw vegetables and bread.

- **In a sauce.** Cheeses can add both body and flavor to sauces. In sauces that call for using aged, complex cheeses such as Parmigiano-Reggiano, use as little heat as possible. Cheese should be stirred into sauces at the last minute.

- **As a topping or garnish.** Cheese makes an excellent topping or garnish that complements or offsets the flavors and textures of other ingredients. You can use soft or hard cheeses, or a combination, for topping baked dishes. The properties of soft cheeses such as mozzarella make them excellent for melting. Grating cheeses, such as Parmigiano-Reggiano, provide a flavor boost. They can also be shaved for topping or garnish on salads and meat or vegetable appetizers.

Chef's Tip

Save Rinds

Save rinds from Parmigiano-Reggiano and Pecorino-Romano. Add small portions to soups and cooked tomato sauces for added flavor and texture.

READING CHECKLIST *What are three ways cheese is used in cooking?*

10.3 ASSESSMENT

Reviewing Concepts

1. What are the seven basic types of cheese?
2. What is the best way to store cheese?
3. At what temperature should cheese typically be served?
4. What are the three ways cheese is used in cooking?

Critical Thinking

5. **Classifying** Of the seven types of cheeses, which type are you most familiar with?
6. **Comparing/Contrasting** What is the difference between a fresh cheese and a soft, rind-ripened cheese?
7. **Applying Concepts** Describe three ways of serving cheese during the course of a meal.

Test Kitchen

Assemble a collection of as many cheeses as you can, making sure you have a representative of each of the seven types of cheeses. Sample each type of cheese (accompanied by bread, if you wish). Write down your notes about the taste of the various cheeses. Did you have a favorite? Compare your results with classmates.

SOCIAL STUDIES ———

History of Cheese

Research the history of cheese. What role has it played in history? Who is credited with inventing cheese?

PROJECT **10** **Tasting Cheese** You are now ready to work on Project 10, "Tasting Cheese," which is available in "My Culinary Lab" or in your *Student's Lab Resources and Study Guide* manual.

Cold Food Presentation

Key Concepts

- Identifying types of cold food presentations
- Identifying elements in cold food presentation
- Preparing centerpieces and garnishes

Vocabulary

- antipasto platter
- blinis
- braesola
- caviar
- charcuterie
- cocktail sauce
- cold food presentation
- depurated
- garni
- garniture
- grosse pièce
- on the half shell
- pâtés
- prosciutto
- raw bar
- sequencing
- sturgeon
- terrines

Source: Andrea1971/Fotolia

Types of Cold Food Presentations

A **cold food presentation** is a collection of cold foods that are presented in an artful manner, often in a buffet setting. Guests choose for themselves from among the foods, or they indicate their choices to wait staff, who assemble individual plates of food.

Cold food preparations present the garde manger with an opportunity for creative work and artistry. Because cold food presentations must be prepared ahead, the chef has greater control and flexibility than is possible with typical cooking. Cold food presentations may be simple or complex, focusing on one type of food or providing a wide variety of foods. The following are some examples of cold food presentations:

- Platters
- Trays
- Raw bars
- Caviar presentations
- Smoked fish presentations
- Charcuterie presentations

Platters The garde manger often uses a single large platter of cold food as an opportunity to provide a sampling of cold meats, cheeses, vegetables, fruits, and, perhaps, breads and crackers. A popular choice is the Italian **antipasto**

(an-tee-PAHS-toh) **platter**, an assortment of cured meats (such as prosciutto and salami), cheeses, and pickled vegetables.

Fruits are often presented on a platter. Because fruits oxidize and discolor when cut, platters often include fruit that can be eaten whole, such as grapes and strawberries. Cheese platters should offer a variety of types, flavors, and textures of cheeses. Cheeses should be offered on cheese boards for easy cutting. Fruits, crackers, and breads often accompany a cheese platter. An assortment of different kinds of salads presents another possibility for creativity.

Trays The garde manger may assemble a cold food presentation on a tray, which is then passed by wait staff or by diners at the table. A tray is smaller than a platter and usually holds less variety. When assembling a cold food presentation on a tray, take into consideration that the tray will be moving, so the food must be stable and not fall off the tray.

Raw Bars A **raw bar** is a bar or counter at which raw shellfish is served. It is an elegant and luxurious type of cold food presentation. It usually includes oysters, and sometimes clams, along with cooked mussels, scallops, shrimp, and lobster. The oysters and clams can be served **on the half shell** (meaning they are opened and served on one of their shells). Other raw seafood that can be served includes shrimp and crab. Fresh lemon, **cocktail sauce** (a dipping sauce of ketchup, horseradish, and possibly Tabasco sauce), and other accompanying sauces are included on the raw bar as well.

Throughout the world, shellfish is commonly eaten raw. However, raw bars or any service of raw shellfish and other seafood comes with a risk. The restaurant must be aware of possible associated health hazards. By law, all raw shellfish must come from suppliers with a tag detailing the place of origin, the date of harvest, and the wholesale grower and seller. These regulations make it possible to trace any shellfish sold to restaurants in the event of an outbreak of disease. When purchasing shellfish, follow these guidelines:

- Buy only cultivated shellfish that is raised in clean, controlled environments.
- Buy only depurated oysters, clams, and mussels. **Depurated** (DEP-yew-rate-ed) shellfish have been placed in tanks of fresh water to purge them of their impurities and sand.
- Get to know your suppliers and make sure they sell impeccably fresh shellfish.

FIGURE 10–19
Antipasto Platter
An antipasto platter consists of cured meats, cheeses, and pickled vegetables.

PREDICTING *Do you think you would like the combination of flavors and textures in an antipasto platter?*
Source: DreamPictures/Getty Images

Chef's Tip

High-Risk Eating

Individuals with certain health conditions—such as liver disease, diabetes, cancer, stomach disorders, blood disorders, or immune disorders—who consume raw shellfish or other seafood are at a higher risk than others.

FIGURE 10–20

Oysters on the Half Shell
A raw bar usually includes oysters on the half shell placed on ice to keep them at the appropriate temperature.

PREDICTING *Have you ever had raw oysters? If not, do you think you'd like them?*

Source: Clive Streeter/Image Partners 2005/ Dorling Kindersley Media Library/Dorling Kindersley

Beluga caviar

Source: Richard Embery/Pearson Education/PH College

Caviar Presentations Caviar is a type of salted fish eggs. In France and the United States, only the eggs from a large fish called a **sturgeon** (STURH-jen) are classified as caviar. Fresh sturgeon caviar should be plump and moist, with a nutty and mildly briny flavor. There are three types of European sturgeon: beluga, osetra, and sevruga. Each provides caviar, and each type of caviar has a different flavor and texture.

- **Beluga caviar.** The beluga sturgeon is the largest type of sturgeon, reaching its maturity at about 20 years, when it may weigh as much as a ton. This long growth period makes beluga eggs very expensive. Beluga caviar has the largest eggs, which vary in color from light steel gray to dark gray. Beluga caviar is always sold in blue tins or jars.

- **Osetra caviar.** Brownish with golden highlights, osetra caviar has a nutty flavor that distinguishes it from other caviars. The osetra sturgeon reaches a weight of 500 pounds and matures at between 12 and 15 years. Osetra caviar is always sold in yellow tins or jars.

Osetra caviar

Source: Richard Embery/Pearson Education/PH College

- **Sevruga caviar.** The smallest of the three true caviars, sevruga caviar is dark brown, with an assertive flavor. Mature sevruga sturgeon weigh about 150 pounds and mature in 8 to 10 years. Sevruga caviar is less expensive than the other two true caviars and is always sold in red tins or jars.

Sevruga caviar

Source: Richard Embery/Pearson Education/PH College

In America, the black sturgeon provides caviar that is commonly referred to as American caviar. Eggs from fish such as the hackleback, gray paddlefish, white fish, salmon, and lumpfish are also eaten like caviar.

Pressed caviar is made from mature, broken, or overripe eggs. The salted eggs are collected in a linen sack and pressed to release liquid. The result is a spread, which is often used on slices of black bread. It is also included as an ingredient in dishes and in sauces rather than using the more expensive caviar. Pressed caviar is very strongly flavored, with a different texture than other caviar.

Because of the high cost of and luxury associated with caviar, it is typically served on very special occasions. There are time-honored rituals and etiquette associated with serving and eating it. If caviar is served by a restaurant, the garde manger needs to be well informed about buying, handling, and serving it, because of its cost and rarity. Here are some guidelines to handling and serving caviar:

- Don't use metal utensils when handling caviar. Metal reacts with caviar, producing an off flavor.

- Chill caviar to 32°F. Because most refrigerators are not this cold, it is usually necessary to keep caviar on ice in the coldest part of the refrigerator. Replenish the ice when it begins to melt.

- Do not open a jar of caviar until you're ready to use it. Once the jar is opened, the caviar should be served within two to three days.

FIGURE 10–21

Caviar Service
Caviar must be kept cold.

PREDICTING *Have you ever had caviar? If not, do you think you'd like it?*
Source: Culinary Institute of America

- Serve caviar in its original container or in a nonmetallic serving bowl. Because it is highly perishable, the container or bowl should be placed on a bed of ice. The best serving platters or plates for caviar are nonmetallic and nonabsorbent, preferably of china.

- Handle caviar carefully to prevent the eggs from breaking.

- Serve caviar in dishes set over ice to keep it very cold.

- Use special mother-of-pearl, bone, or tortoiseshell spoons that are made for handling caviar.

- Traditional accompaniments for caviar service include chopped hard-cooked egg whites, chopped egg yolks (served separately from the whites), lemons, and sour cream.

- Serve caviar with lightly buttered white-bread toast or **blinis** (BLEE-nees), very thin Russian crêpes.

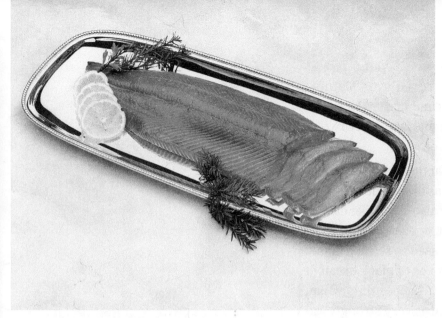

FIGURE 10–22

Smoked Salmon Platter
Salmon is often served with black bread, minced onions, and capers.

PREDICTING *Have you ever had smoked salmon? If not, do you think you'd like it?*

Source: C Squared Studios/Photodisc/Getty Images

Lesser quality, nonsturgeon fish eggs are not typically served by themselves. It is much more typical for nonsturgeon fish eggs to be used as ingredients or garnishes for other dishes.

Smoked Fish Presentations Smoked salmon and other smoked fishes are often used for cold food presentations. Their natural oils keep their flesh tender and moist. Thinly sliced salmon can be served on toast, black or whole grain breads, or other bread products. Classic combinations include the following:

- Smoked salmon, minced onion, and capers
- Smoked salmon, chopped hard-cooked eggs, capers, and parsley
- Smoked salmon with caviar-, mustard-, or horseradish-flavored sour cream
- Smoked trout with horseradish sauce
- Smoked sturgeon with caviar

Charcuterie Presentations Charcuterie (shahr-KOO-tuhr-ee) is a French term used in professional kitchens to refer to cured meats, sausages, pâtés, and terrines. These foods were traditionally prepared as a way to preserve foods successfully in an era when refrigeration was not available.

Cured meats include such items as hams like **prosciutto** (pro-SHU-tow), Italian country-style ham, and **braesola** (bray-SO-lah), Italian-style dried beef. These meats are brined with salt and a mixture of spices. They may also be smoked and dried, or simply air-dried.

Sausages are made by grinding meats along with salt, spices, and fat. Some sausages are more typically served hot at breakfast (see Chapter 9). Sausages may also be cured, smoked, or dried. These sausages can be sliced and served on a charcuterie platter. Examples include salami, pepperoni, summer sausage, mortadella, and Spanish-style chorizo.

Pâtés (pah-TAYS) and **terrines** (teh-REENS) are made by grinding meats together with spices, salt, and additional fat. They are placed in molds and gently baked. After they have baked and cooled, pâtés and terrines are sliced and served with a variety of accompanying sauces, such as mustard or chutney.

Pâtés are often baked in a crust-lined hinged mold. The mold makes it easy to remove the pâté from the mold without damaging the crust. Terrines are baked in special molds that are lined with thinly sliced bacon or even vegetables. Terrine molds were originally made from earthenware materials such as clay or ceramics. The term *terrine* is derived from the French term for earthenware. Examples of terrine and pâté molds can be found in Chapter 4.

Elements in Cold Food Presentation

The garde manger can use cold food presentation as a way to showcase the talents of staff, but design and decoration aren't everything. The food must be tasty and, ideally, healthful—as well as visually appealing. Serving tools should be both useful and attractive. In addition, thought should be put into creating an attractive and functional table arrangement.

Design Elements for Food Arrangements Although any of the following design elements can be used as a focal point in any sort of plating or food arranging, these design elements should be combined to create energy and interest. Too much repetition, regardless of the element used, is monotonous.

- **Balance.** Balance creates a sense of calm. Use symmetry and evenness in the composition when it comes to shape, color, and texture. Balance the colors, shapes, heights, and textures.

- **Color.** Nothing communicates excitement and vitality like color. Use natural colors, never artificial elements, to stimulate interest. When natural colors are used, you have no need for concern about colors clashing. Use colorful garnishes if the food is dull in color (as meats often are). However, using too much of the same color in an arrangement can be monotonous.

- **Texture.** Glossy surfaces add sparkle. Rough surfaces, such as homemade breads, for example, can reflect a rustic quality. Velvety textures, such as that of fresh mozzarella cheese or the creamy textures of soft cheeses, are seductive. Combining textures is important when you are designing cold food presentations.

- **Cooking technique.** Unlike hot foods, cold foods lack the advantage of any significant aroma to entice guests. Certain cooking techniques create enhanced visual appeal suggestive of an aroma. For example, charring or searing meats used for cold salads, or roasting vegetables to give them a warm cast, suggests an aroma, a taste, to your guests. Remember the chef's saying, "People eat with their eyes"? This is a case of fooling people's noses so they smell with their eyes.

- **Shape and height.** To communicate abundance and excitement, you can adjust the shape and height of your cold food presentations. You can roll flat foods such as sliced meats and thin breads. You can stack food in interesting arrangements, such as raw or blanched vegetables cut into long, thin strips and formed into haystacks, teepee shapes, or other artistic designs. Grated granular cheeses can be melted in a circular shape on a pan surface and then pinched into

Chef's Tip

Make It Easy

Arrange platters and dishes of food on a long table or sideboard so they are easy to see, easy to reach, and easy to serve.

Sweden

One of Sweden's most famous dishes, cured salmon, or gravlax (GRAHV-lox), has become a favorite salmon dish for the garde manger. It has a clear, delicate flavor and is easy to prepare.

Like most cured and smoked fish products, gravlax was born of necessity. Fishermen in Sweden and surrounding Scandinavian countries long ago devised this recipe as a way of preserving fish. After filleting the salmon, they covered it with salt and sugar and buried it along a cool, shaded stream while they continued their salmon fishing upstream. Prepared this way, the fish took on a delicate flavor and remained moist and fresh for up to a week. When the fish was cured, the fishermen returned to collect it.

The popularity of gravlax spread to bordering Norway, Finland, and Denmark. Today, it is found on the menus of fine restaurants and hotels all over the world.

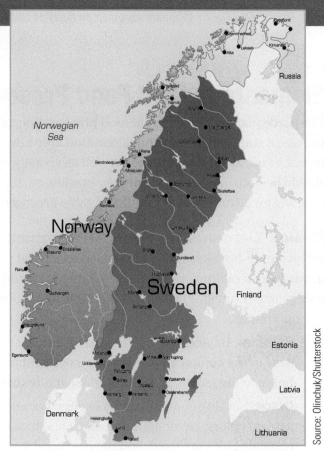

Source: Olinchuk/Shutterstock

Gravlax

Source: David Murray/Image Partners 2005/Dorling Kindersley Media Library/ Dorling Kindersley

Gravlax is still prepared by using sugar and salt, flavored with dill and white pepper, and topped with a weight that acts as a press. After preparation, it is eaten uncooked, accompanied by a sweet-and-sour mustard-dill sauce. Gravlax is an ideal dish for the garde manger station because it is prepared well in advance of serving.

Research

Research the method used for making gravlax. List the ingredients and describe the procedure. Research the traditional sauces that are served alongside it in three Scandinavian countries. Describe each sauce, list the ingredients, and explain the method of presentation.

little basket shapes for nesting greens or other foods. Pencil-thin breadsticks can jut out of an arrangement of silky prosciutto slices draped over each other on a platter.

- **Focal point.** You need to provide a center of interest for your presentation. It can be a single item or a combination of items.

- **Strong, clean lines.** Whether you use straight rows, angles, or curves, strong uninterrupted lines can be effective design elements. For example, you can create rows of vegetables rather than just placing them randomly or in a jumble. You can arrange sliced foods to form long overlapping lines.

Buffet Table Design The arrangement of items on a buffet table is just as important as the arrangement of food on your platters. Here are some tips for buffet table design:

- Guests should be able to reach food easily.

- Serving utensils and table utensils should be plentiful and within easy reach.

- Table design and layout must allow for any equipment necessary to keep foods cold as necessary.

- Larger or higher items should be placed behind smaller or lower items on the table surface.

FIGURE 10-24
Grosse Pièce
A large portion of this ham has not been cut.

PREDICTING *Do you see any design elements that have not been addressed in this presentation?*

Source: David Smith/Fotolia

FOCUS ON Sanitation

Cross-Contamination

Use gloves, tongs, and other tools when you're setting up or serving a buffet to prevent contaminating food as you work.

Serving Main Items There are typically two ways to serve the main item in a cold food presentation or a buffet:

- **Slicing and sequencing.** Slice foods with irregular or tapered shapes to create definite lines when the slices are arranged in a sequence. Arranging slices to overlap one another in the order they were cut is referred to as **sequencing**. When a tapered turkey breast is sliced and sequenced, for example, a regular design with clean lines results.

- **Grosse pièce.** Serving the main item **grosse pièce** (GROHSS pee-YES) means that a large part of the main item is left unsliced. *Grosse pièce* means "large piece" in French. A main item can be presented grosse pièce, but the slices cut from the main item can be sequenced.

Serving Tools Serving tools are important for cold food presentations. Although these are functional items, they are set on the table and therefore become part of the presentation. For this reason, you should use dining room tools for a cold food presentation rather than kitchen tools, which may be too large for serving and are certainly not designed for food presentation. Dining room serving tools include ladles, tongs, serving spoons, serving forks, serving spatulas, and serving scoops.

 **READING CHECKPOINT** *What are the two ways that main items are typically served in a cold food presentation or a buffet?*

Centerpieces and Garnishes

Two other considerations remain for cold food presentations and for buffets. These are centerpieces and garnishes. They help bring the presentation or buffet together.

Centerpieces A beautiful centerpiece can be a great attraction, communicating excitement and reflecting the artistry in the food presented on the table. Centerpieces reinforce or magnify the buffet's theme or concept. They help the guests understand the function or meaning of any presentation.

Tall or very large centerpieces must be carefully located. They should never block a guest's view of or access to the food. Stabilize top-heavy centerpieces so they don't wobble or fall over. Be certain that all elements of the display are safe when used with food. For example, toxic flowers (such as lilies of the valley) should not be used in a centerpiece where they could drop onto food and someone could accidentally eat them.

One of the most spectacular, but expensive, centerpieces is an ice sculpture. Ice carvings can be purely decorative or they can function as receptacles for food such as cooked shrimp or seafood salads. Individual ice sculptures in the form of decorative cups can hold frozen dishes, fruits, or vegetables.

Ice carving is a highly specialized skill, with the additional challenge that ice melts. However, some ice sculptures can be made easily from molds and assembled into larger pieces.

To make an ice carving, you need a large block of ice and a place to do the carving. Once the ice is carved, it should be stored in a walk-in freezer until it is ready to be set up as a centerpiece. To make a carving from a block of ice, prepare a pattern that you can use as a guide. A number of tools are used for ice carving, including ice picks, chisels, combs, and handheld or power saws. Large pieces are cut away from the ice using a saw. Finer cuts are made using chisels. Some chisels have grooved heads to produce special effects. Remember that ice carvings will melt as they are on display. Legs and other supporting parts of the sculpture should be thick enough to last for a few hours without cracking or snapping. If you were making a swan, for example, the neck should be thick enough to hold the head up. Otherwise, the head could snap off and the beautiful effect would be ruined.

When assembling ice sculptures, plan to use a sturdy base. Set the sculpture in a pan connected to a drain or valve that can capture water from the melting ice and transfer it to a tub. The base can be camouflaged with cloth, edible flowers, plants, or other safe decorations.

Ice sculpture centerpiece

Source: Gary Ombler/Dorling Kindersley

Garnishes The purpose of a garnish is to add flavor, color, and texture to individual items, individual dishes, composed platters and trays, and buffets in general. A garnish is meant to draw attention to the food, not to overwhelm the food or detract from it in any way.

You may hear the terms *garni* and *garniture* when garnishes are being discussed. **Garni** is a French term that simply means a garnished food or plate. The **garniture** is the item that is used as a garnish.

It used to be that all kinds of things with little eating appeal were used for garnishes simply for color effect. However, because well-trained culinary professionals know the importance of quality in food preparation and presentation, the garde manger thinks of garnishes as food, not simply decoration.

Garnishes cannot be an afterthought. The garde manger needs to put thought into the selection and preparation of garnishes because they must be an integrated part of the dish or presentation. Garnishes should not be boring or overused, like the ho-hum scrap of tired parsley tossed on top of every dish.

Here are additional guidelines for garnishing.

- **Function.** Garnishes should be used to create a visual impression and also to add a taste experience.

- **Flavor.** Garnishes should taste fresh and complement the taste of the item they garnish.

- **Color/visual appeal.** Garnishes should be visually attractive as well as good to eat. Typically, they add a different color to the main theme of the dish or presentation. The color of a garnish adds a new effect to the overall dish or presentation (see the table titled "Common Garnishes").

- **Textural appeal.** Typically, garnishes add a different texture than the dish or presentation with which they are used.

- **Appropriate size.** Keep scale in mind in designing garnishes. If they are too small in proportion to the food presented, they will look lost on the plate. If they are too large, they compete with the food that should be the focus of the dish or presentation.

- **Special effects.** Use fanning cuts (on pickles or strawberries, for example), sequencing, julienne or matchstick shapes, spiral cutting

Common Garnishes

	Color	Effect	Food Garnish
Source: David Murray and Jules Selmes, Dorling Kindersley	Green	Freshness and vitality	Chives, parsley, fresh herbs, green sprouts, scallions, greens, limes, green peppers
Source: Dorling Kindersley	Browns and golds	Warmth, comfort, richness	Lemons, bread sticks, bread products, hard-cooked egg wedges, butter curls, yellow peppers, miniature yellow tomatoes
Source: Neil Fletcher and Matthew Ward/Dorling Kindersley	Oranges and reds	Intensity, desire, hunger	Tomatoes, radishes, radicchio, carrots, red or orange peppers, edible nasturtium flowers

Making a Fan Cut

1. **Place item on its side on a work surface.**

2. **Cut in paper-thin slices** from tip to stem, leaving the flesh at the base of the stem still attached.

3. **Spread the slices out, using your fingers.** It should be spread like a fan.

4. **Lift the fan carefully** onto the plate or platter you are garnishing. Use a knife, spatula, or palette knife. Fruits such as strawberries can also be fanned.

Source: Culinary Institute of America

(using a spiral cutter), crinkle cuts, rosettes (such as radish "roses"), curls, paper-thin cuts, food sculpting, ice sculpting, and molds for soft foods such as aspic or butter.

The garnishes you add to your platters can do much more than make them look attractive. The most effective garnishes are eye-catching, neatly cut, and carefully arranged. They should have a specific relationship to the main items on the platter. If you look at some of the photographs in this chapter you will see that they employ both traditional and innovative garnishes.

Chefs use special tools to create some garnishes. Spiral cutters, zesters, channel knives, special cutters to produce ripple-cut or waffle-cut fruits and vegetables, melon ballers of various sizes, and tourné (bird's-beak) knives are commonly used to carve fruits and vegetables. (See Chapter 4 for more information about these knives and other small tools.)

- Citrus fruits can be sliced or carved into baskets. The colorful skin can be cut into long strips or grated to scatter over foods.

- Apples and pears can be cut into thin slices and then arranged in overlapping patterns.

- Herbs can be left in whole sprigs, or they may be chopped fine and scattered over the platter.

- Hard-cooked eggs can be sliced, cut into wedges, or chopped.

- Edible flowers and leaves can be scattered decoratively on a dish.

- Small balls (rounds or ovals) of fruits and vegetables can be used to soften a presentation.

- Cucumbers cut into slices or spirals or made into baskets or cups add freshness and coolness to a presentation.

- Strips and curls of carrots and celery add fresh color.

- Brushes made from leeks can be used to apply a dipping sauce or a glaze.
- Roses made from radishes add intensity and elegance.

 **READING CHECKLIST** *What are the purposes of centerpieces and garnishes?*

10.4 ASSESSMENT

Reviewing Concepts

1. Name at least five common types of cold food presentations?

2. What are the two ways main items are typically served in a cold food presentation or a buffet?

3. What is the purpose of a garnish?

Critical Thinking

4. Drawing Conclusions Why are only pressed (versus whole) caviar and other types of fish eggs used in cooking?

5. Compare and Contrast What design element for food arrangements do you think is most important? Why?

6. Predicting How is the appeal of a meat dish improved by the use of a garnish?

7. Drawing Conclusions Any service of raw shellfish or other seafood comes with a risk. Why would a restaurant take on that risk?

8. Predicting If you make an ice carving of a large goblet, what might happen if you made the stem of the goblet very thin?

Test Kitchen

Divide into four teams. Each team will create a small platter as a cold food presentation, complete with garnishes. Evaluate other teams' efforts based on the design elements for food arrangements. Tally the results.

SCIENCE

Smoked Fish

Research how fish, such as salmon and trout, are smoked. Focus on such questions as the following: How long does the process take? At what temperature are they smoked? Is any special type of wood used to produce the smoke? Are herbs or spices used in the smoking process to add flavor? Are there regional or national differences in how fish are smoked?

Review and Assessment

Reviewing Content

Choose the letter that best answers the question or completes the statement.

1. Mayonnaise is
   a. a vinaigrette.
   b. an emulsion.
   c. a cooked dressing.
   d. all of the above

2. The three types of salad greens are
   a. sweet, sour, and bitter.
   b. mild, spicy, and bitter.
   c. mild, strong, and sweet.
   d. sweet, spicy, and sour.

3. Parmigiano-Reggiano is a
   a. soft, rind-ripened cheese.
   b. hard cheese.
   c. grating cheese.
   d. blue-vein cheese.

4. Caviar is
   a. salted eggs from a sturgeon.
   b. a type of smoked fish.
   c. raw fish.
   d. a shellfish, usually eaten raw on the half shell.

5. Frisée is
   a. a slightly to very bitter salad green.
   b. a type of blue cheese.
   c. a mayonnaise-based dressing.
   d. a type of sturgeon that produces caviar.

6. Mesclun is
   a. a French-style mix of salad greens.
   b. a type of soft, rind-ripened cheese.
   c. a style of vinaigrette.
   d. a type of smoked fish.

7. Which of the following is not a fresh cheese?
   a. mascarpone
   b. Brie
   c. ricotta
   d. feta

Understanding Concepts

8. What is a vinaigrette?

9. What is a side salad?

10. What is the difference between fresh cheese and a soft, rind-ripened cheese?

11. What is caviar?

12. What is the garde manger?

13. What is the difference between a tossed salad and a composed salad?

14. What are the two methods of serving a main course in a cold food presentation or a buffet?

Critical Thinking

15. **RECOGNIZING PATTERNS** What is the difference between a hard cheese and a grating cheese?

16. **PREDICTING** How would you describe the taste of a salad containing radicchio, escarole, endive, and arugula? Based on the taste of the salad, what type of ingredients might you include in a dressing?

Culinary Math

17. **SOLVING PROBLEMS** A recipe for shrimp salad uses 32 oz of mayonnaise, 8 oz of lemon juice, and 2 heads of celery for 12 lb of shrimp. You have only 6 lb of shrimp. How much of each of the other ingredients is required to make this salad?

18. **APPLYING CONCEPTS** If the ratio of ketchup to prepared horseradish for cocktail sauce is 7 to 1, how many quarts of ketchup are necessary to make 1 gal of cocktail sauce? How many quarts of horseradish are necessary?

On the Job

19. **COMMUNICATING** A customer indicates that she is a vegetarian. She orders a niçoise salad. Is there a problem? If so, what should you do?

Garde Manger, Charcutières, and Butchers

The area of culinary arts referred to in a general way as garde manger is more diverse than you might imagine. Garde manger includes such traditional work as the preparation and presentation of cold foods as well as jobs that have recently become more popular: butcher and sausage maker (charcutière [shahr-KOO-tee-air]). One reason that this area of culinary specialization has seen increased interest has to do with a great culinary awareness on the part of the guests coming to restaurants. They are more likely to be familiar with the traditional cured meats and sausages of a specific cuisine. Another key factor that has brought these jobs back into the limelight is a growing interest in foods that are raised and produced locally using techniques that do not rely on large-scale food processing.

Garde manger The garde manger is often the spot where chefs begin to work. They are responsible for cold appetizers, cold salads, and sandwiches offered on the menu. The preparation, decoration, and presentation of platters and plates served at buffets and receptions are also part of the garde manger's responsibilities. In larger operations, the garde manger chef may direct a team to prepare and execute the cold foods at large events. They may prepare ice carvings, develop

food and sauce combinations, and typically work closely with the banquet chef or banquet manager.

Charcutière A chef who prepares a variety of smoked and cured meats such as ham or bacon, sausages, pâtés, and terrines is known as a charcutière. Some large operations may have a person on staff who is responsible for house-made charcuterie specialties. Smaller operations may also produce these specialty items, but typically it is part of the chef's general job description, rather than being a separate position. Many talented charcutières either have retail shops or are purveyors that supply restaurants or markets.

Butcher Butchers may work in a number of different situations. Grocery chains have butchers on staff to cut larger pieces into smaller cuts; for instance, they may cut a whole pork loin into chops. They prepare special-order items, such as crown roasts or steaks of a specific thickness. Restaurants that use locally sourced meats may have the entire carcass delivered to the restaurant, and then their in-house butcher cuts the meat into various roasts, steaks, cutlets, chops, and other cuts. Because the entire animal is purchased, rather than specific cuts, the butcher must also prepare lesser-known cuts to be cooked into dishes that appeal to the guests.

Entry-Level Requirements

Garde manger may be an entry-level position in many professional kitchens. There are no particular requirements for education or training.

Helpful for Advancement

A degree in the culinary arts and/or professional certification is helpful in order to advance from entry-level positions to management positions. Successful garde manger chefs typically participate in culinary competitions, or they may spend time as an apprentice with a butcher or charcutière.

A charcutière often prepares sausages

MARK ELIA

Chef Mark Elia is the founder, owner, and operator of Elia's Catering Company and House of Sausage in the Hudson Valley, New York. Prior to establishing his own company, he was the Assistant Manager and Meat Processor for Edward's Food Warehouse in Poughkeepsie, New York and Vaccaro's Meat Market in Highland, New York. In addition to running his catering company, Chef Elia teaches Meat Identification and Fabrication at The Culinary Institute of America. In his class, students learn the fundamentals of ordering, receiving, and fabricating meat for professional kitchens.

Mark Elia

Chef Elia is well known for his Texas-style BBQ, and in 2006, he won the Peoples' Choice Award at the Hudson Valley Ribfest. He is an expert in making smoked meats and cold cuts and is working toward his USDA license for processing fresh and smoked sausage.

VITAL STATISTICS

Profession: Artisan, chef, culinary instructor

Interesting Items: Judge for the Kansas City Barbeque Society

Teaches sausage-making classes at his Hudson Valley shop

Specializes in Italian-American catering, in addition to his popular BBQs

CAREER PROFILES

Salary Ranges

Entry-level positions in garde manger, butchery, and charcuterie are typically hourly

Garde Manger Chefs: $35,000 to $80,000 or more, depending on the size of the operation and its location

Specialists and Shop Owners: Varies widely depending on location, experience, and number of years in business

Chapter 11

Sandwiches, Appetizers, and Hors d'Oeuvre

11.1 Sandwiches

11.2 Appetizers and Hors d'Oeuvre

READING PREVIEW

Key Concepts

- Understanding basic sandwich elements
- Understanding the mise en place for sandwich making
- Understanding the types of cold sandwiches
- Understanding the types of hot sandwiches

Vocabulary

- ciabatta
- closed sandwich
- club sandwich
- cubano
- finger sandwich
- grilled sandwich
- hero sandwich
- kaiser roll
- lavash
- open-faced sandwich
- panini
- pita bread
- pressed sandwich
- Pullman loaf
- tea sandwich
- tortilla
- wrap

Basic Sandwich Elements

Sandwiches have become so popular you can find them on dinner, lunch, and even breakfast menus. You can find them everywhere from diners to fast-food restaurants to fancy restaurants. Basically, the incredibly popular sandwich is a combination of four simple elements:

- Bread
- Spread
- Filling
- Garnish

These elements are the building blocks chefs use to create both classic sandwiches and new sandwich variations. You can adjust the various sandwich elements to produce bite-size versions for elegant receptions or big, robust sandwiches that serve as filling meals on their own.

Bread Different types of sandwiches require different types of breads. It is critically important that your bread be fresh and tasty for the best appearance and flavor in your sandwiches. Some sandwiches are best on crusty or dense breads like baguettes or rye, but a bread that is too crusty or hard makes a sandwich difficult to eat. Often the type of bread used depends on

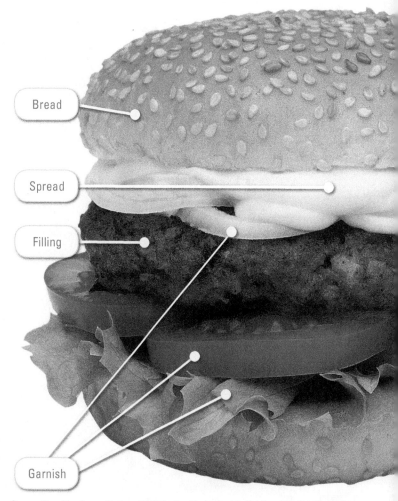

Bread

Spread

Filling

Garnish

Source: Dave King/Image Partners 2005/Dorling Kindersley Media Library/Dorling Kindersley

White, pumpernickel, and whole wheat bread
Source: Dave King/Image Partners 2005/
Dorling Kindersley Media Library/Dorling Kindersley

the type of filling used. The bread must hold the filling without falling apart. For example, a firm, thick slice of bread or a roll is best for a juicy steak sandwich. A softer, thinner slice of white bread is best for delicate tea and finger sandwiches.

Obviously, standard loaves of bread—wheat, white, rye, sourdough, to name only a few—often serve as the base for sandwiches. Some breads used for sandwiches are flavored with herbs, nuts, cheese, or fruit. However, any strong flavoring in the bread should complement the sandwich filling, without dominating or distracting from it.

Other types of types of breads often used in sandwiches are:

- **Pullman loaf.** Baked in a rectangular pan with a lid, a **Pullman loaf** is a long loaf. A slice from a Pullman loaf is square on all sides. The compact, fine-grain of a Pullman loaf makes it easier to slice off the crust or cut the bread into shapes. White and whole-wheat Pullman loaves are often used for cold sandwiches.

- **Kaiser roll.** A large, round, crusty roll, the **kaiser** (KIGH-zer) **roll** is also known as a *hard roll* or a *Vienna roll.*

- **Ciabatta.** A large, flat Italian bread, **ciabatta** (chee-ah-BOT-ah) is traditionally cut into squares, and then split to fill and garnish.

- **Pita bread.** A flat round or oval Middle Eastern bread, **pita** (PEE-tah) **bread** is also known as *pocket bread.* When it is cut in half, each half forms a pocket that can be filled as a sandwich.

- **Tortilla.** Mexico's unleavened bread, the **tortilla** (tohr-TEE-yuh) is a round, flat, bread made of corn or flour. A tortilla looks like a very thin pancake. The tortilla is often folded or wrapped around the filling.

FIGURE 11–1

Pita Bread

Pita bread has been cut to form a pocket, and the pocket has been filled to capacity.

PREDICTING *Which types of fillings would work best with pita bread pockets?*

Source: Brent Hofacker/Fotolia

- **Bagels.** Bagels have become increasingly popular for sandwiches, particularly breakfast sandwiches.

- **Croissants.** The flaky, buttery taste of a croissant helps create a rich-tasting sandwich.

- **Hot dog and hamburger rolls.** These specially created rolls are familiar to anyone who has ever had a backyard cookout.

Spread Spreads add additional flavor and texture to a sandwich. In some cases, they act as a moisture barrier for the bread, preventing the moisture from soaking into the bread. Spreads also keep a sandwich together while adding moisture to it and keeping loose fillings from falling off the bread. The spread is not always added separately; in some cases, it is an ingredient in fillings like tuna or egg salad.

One of the most common spreads is butter. Butter has a rich, smooth flavor and can be perked up by adding spices, peppers, garlic, or other flavorings. Butter spreads best when it is softened to room temperature so it doesn't tear the bread when it is spread.

Another common spread is mayonnaise. It adds a rich, tangy flavor to sandwiches, and it, too, can be perked up with spices, peppers, garlic, or other flavorings.

Vegetable-based purées made from avocados, olives, roasted peppers, or roasted eggplant can also be used as spreads. Although they reduce fat, purées do not usually provide a moisture barrier to the bread.

Filling The centerpiece of a sandwich is the filling. It can be hot or cold, meal-sized or just enough for a single bite. Attention to detail is what will make your sandwich a success. Salad and other greens should be carefully rinsed and dried, meat and poultry should be properly cooked, cheese should be fresh and not overpowering to other fillings. All slices should be evenly cut.

The filling will determine if you use a spread. The filling will also help you determine what kind of bread you should use. For example, tuna salad or any other mayonnaise-based filling will not require a spread and will require thin, dense bread that is sturdy enough to hold the filling. Sliced meat, particularly if it is dry, will require a generous amount of spread.

The following are some of the most common fillings:

- **Meat and poultry.** When used as the primary filling in a sandwich, meat and poultry can be roasted, griddled, fried, broiled, or simmered. They can be served either hot or cold. They can be served alone or in a combination, such as an Italian-style sub sandwich with a number of different meats. Meat and poultry can also be made into a mayonnaise-based sandwich salad, such as ham salad or chicken salad.

- **Seafood and fish.** Tuna and shrimp are commonly made into mayonnaise-based sandwich salads. Many varieties of seafood and fish are broiled or deep-fried for sandwiches and served with tartar sauce.

- **Vegetables.** The emphasis on healthy eating has increased the demand for vegetables in sandwiches. Lettuce, tomatoes, onions, and pickles have always been common on sandwiches. Today you might also use sprouts, peppers, radishes, and cucumbers. Vegetables such as portobello mushrooms are often the primary filling in a meatless sandwich. As a primary filling, vegetables can be grilled, roasted, or served raw. Often a vinaigrette adds flavor to vegetables when they are used as a primary filling.

- **Cheese.** Cheese can be a stand-alone filling, as in the classic grilled cheese sandwich. It is also a popular addition to many other

FOCUS ON Nutrition

Healthy Helpers

To cut calories, use a vegetable purée, such as roasted red peppers, rather than a fat-based spread. To increase nutritive value, select fiber-rich whole-grain bread. To decrease cholesterol, substitute grilled vegetables for some of the meat.

Source: juliedeshaies/Fotolia

Grilled cheese sandwich

sandwiches. The vast flavor and texture choices range from mild and spreadable to sharp and capable of being sliced. Choose a flavor and texture that complements the other flavors and textures in the sandwich. Low-fat cheeses can be used instead of full-fat versions in cold sandwiches, but they may not melt as well as regular cheeses in hot sandwiches.

- **Eggs.** Fried or scrambled eggs are often featured in breakfast sandwiches, along with bacon and cheese, but they can also be used in other types of sandwiches. For example, a French sandwich called a *croque madame* (CROKE ma-DAHM) includes ham, cheese, and a fried egg. Hard-cooked eggs can be made into mayonnaise-based salad sandwiches.

Garnish Garnishes are typically decorative, edible accompaniments on a plate with a sandwich. A garnish should complement the flavor of a sandwich, because the customer often incorporates the garnish into the sandwich itself. Lettuces, sprouts, pickles, relishes, tomatoes, onions, and olives are all potential internal garnishes that work well as part of the sandwich. Salad and other greens should be carefully rinsed and dried before they are used. Larger garnishes, such as whole vegetables, carrot or celery sticks, pickle spears, or slices of orange or melon, are considered external garnishes; they provide complementary flavors for the sandwich but are eaten separately.

READING CHECKPOINT *What are the four elements of a sandwich?*

Sandwich Mise en Place

Whether you are making many different individual sandwiches or a large amount of the same sort of sandwiches, you need to be organized and perform your mise en place. There are three steps to performing a mise en place for sandwiches:

- Gathering tools
- Selecting and preparing ingredients
- Organizing the job and the workspace

Gathering Tools Have the following tools on hand:

- Cutting board
- Tongs and spatulas

Pierre François de la Varenne

There is a bit of mystery surrounding the birth and early life of one of France's most influential chefs. Some have suggested that La Varenne may have learned his craft in the kitchens of Henry IV and Marie de Medici, Henry's second wife. By 1644, he was probably working for the Marquis d'Uxelles. There, he developed the mushroom preparation we know today as duxelles, made from minced mushrooms, shallots, and white wine. Béchamel, the milk-based grand sauce still made today, is also attributed to him.

La Varenne's famous motto, *"Santé, modération, et raffinement"* ("Health, moderation, and refinement"), marks him as an important reformer of the culinary arts. In the 17th century, when most chefs were still using heavy spices with all manner of savory foods, La Varenne urged cooks to choose flavorings that complemented the main foods and did not disguise them. He removed spices that we consider "sweet," such as cardamom, cinnamon, and nutmeg, from meat and fish dishes and saved them instead for desserts. Instead of using bread crumbs to thicken a dish, La Varenne used roux. He also included a great number of recipes for vegetables,

Henry IV, King of France
from 1589 to 1610

including some New World specialties such as Jerusalem artichokes, and a recipe for turkey.

Le Cuisinier François, first published in 1651, was among a handful of important books written for professionals. While other French chefs may have begun to make small changes, the publication of La Varenne's book marked a clean and decisive break with the old culinary traditions.

Vital Statistics

Born	1615 or 1618 in Châlon-sur-Saône, Burgundy, France
Died	1678 in Dijon, France
Profession	Chef to Marquis d'Uxelles
Credits	Creator of duxelles and béchamel sauce; author of *Le Cuisinier François* (and possibly others)

Research

Le Cuisinier François included many recipes that were new at the time. Find the names and descriptions of at least four dishes that La Varenne created and that are still prepared today. Explain how these dishes are different from the medieval dishes his new recipes replaced.

Beef Wellington, beef with pâté and duxelles, wrapped in puff pastry and baked

- Sharp knives, including a chef's knife, a bread knife, and a serrated knife. (Use a very sharp knife to cut sandwiches easily.)
- Scales or portioning scoops for portion control
- Palette knife or butter knife for spreads and mayonnaise-based sandwich salads

FOCUS ON Safety

Gloves

You need to wear gloves when handling any ready-to-eat foods.

Source: Gary Ombler/Dorling Kindersley Media Library/Dorling Kindersley

Palette knife

Chef's Tip

Sliced Bread

Bread dries out quickly after it is sliced. Keep sliced bread fresh in airtight containers. If bread must be toasted in advance, cover with a cloth and hold in a warm place.

- Toaster (if bread will be toasted)
- Food-handling gloves
- Frill picks and sandwich wrapping materials

Selecting and Preparing Ingredients In some situations, you will make just one sandwich, when it is ordered. Other times you could be making four, six, or even a hundred sandwiches at a time. No matter how many sandwiches you are making, you still must select the ingredients before service. Here are some tips for preparing sandwich ingredients:

- Slice bread and rolls as close to service as possible. If toasting is required, it's best to wait until assembly to toast.
- Have spreads ready and at a consistency that won't tear the bread. Use a palette knife to apply spreads, covering the entire surface.
- Prepare and portion the fillings in advance. Some sandwiches that will be grilled can be assembled in advance and grilled as they are needed.
- Wash and dry greens.
- Prepare garnishes in advance.

Organizing the Job and the Work Space As with any mise en place, you must break down the steps involved in making the sandwiches and make sure you rank the tasks in terms of their priority. For example, if you are serving a cold sandwich filled with sliced chicken breast, you need to allow sufficient time not only to cook the chicken, but also time to bring the chicken down to the correct temperature. If you are making sandwiches to order, you will organize your work space differently than if you are making large numbers of sandwiches at once. Here are some guidelines for organizing the job and your workspace:

- Make a list of the steps involved in your recipe, in the order they need to be done. (Remember to use the PRN—Preview, Read, Note—method for reading recipes discussed in Section 5.1.)
- Keep everything you need within reach to save time walking to it.
- Have everything move in one direction, starting with the bread on one side and the finished sandwiches on the other side. (Typically, right-handed people move from left to right, so the bread would be on your left and the finished sandwiches on your right.)
- When preparing large amounts of the same type of sandwich, increase efficiency by laying out multiple slices of bread, applying spread to all the sandwiches, adding filling, and then garnishing them all. Then cut and serve or wrap.

READING CHECKPOINT *What are three steps to performing mise en place for sandwiches?*

FIGURE 11–2

Efficient Assembly Line
Plates move in one direction.
When finished, they are stored on
racks.

SOLVING A PROBLEM *How does the
rack help increase efficiency?*
Source: Pearson Education/PH College

Cold Sandwiches

A wide diversity of cold sandwiches has developed to suit every taste and appetite. Cold sandwiches are often filled with sliced meats and cheese or mayonnaise-based sandwich salads such as egg salad, chicken salad, and tuna salad. Restaurants typically offer cold sandwiches as a lunch menu main course, often in combination with a soup or salad. The portability of cold sandwiches makes them a perfect take-out choice as well.

There are six main types of cold sandwiches:

- **Closed sandwich.** This is what everyone thinks of when they think of a sandwich. A **closed sandwich** is simply two pieces of bread, a bun, or a roll with a filling between them.

- **Open-faced sandwich.** When a sandwich is made with one slice of bread and topped with ingredients, it is called an **open-faced sandwich.**

- **Finger sandwich.** A simple, small sandwich, a **finger sandwich** (also called a **tea sandwich**) is usually made with firm, thinly sliced Pullman loaves. Finger sandwiches can be made both as closed sandwiches and as open-faced sandwiches. Because the bread is dense, sandwiches can be cut into small squares, diamonds, rectangles, rounds, and triangles. Pullman loaves can be sliced thinly, filled, and then cut into shapes to make quantity sandwich production more efficient.

- **Hero sandwich.** A large closed sandwich, the **hero sandwich** (or simply hero) uses a long thin loaf of bread (often called a *hero loaf*). Heroes are known by different names in different parts of the country. They can be called *submarines*, *grinders*, or *hoagies*. Whatever name you call it, this is a substantial sandwich often filled with thinly sliced meats, cheese, tomatoes, and lettuce, with a variety of garnishes.

Recipe Cards

45. Muffaletta Sandwich
46. Chicken Salad Sandwich

Chef's Tip

Tea Sandwiches

Fill open-faced tea sandwiches just before serving to prevent discoloration of the filling. Avoid covering open-faced sandwiches with plastic wrap as the wrap may stick to the filling.

Hero sandwich
Source: C Squared Studios/
Getty Images, Inc._ Photodisc

- **Club sandwich.** A double-decker closed sandwich, the **club sandwich** is made with three slices of bread (or toast). It is traditionally filled with chicken (or turkey, ham, or beef), bacon, lettuce, and tomato. These sandwiches are traditionally held together with sandwich picks and cut into four triangles, making them easier to eat.

- **Wraps and pita pockets.** A sandwich that is rolled up or otherwise enclosed in an edible wrapper is called a **wrap**. Tortillas or thin, flexible flat breads such as **lavash** (LAH-vohsh) are commonly used as the bread. Pita bread is used to make pita pockets. The advantage of a wrap or pita pocket is that they can hold many ingredients and the opening is only at the top. Be careful not to overstuff a wrap or use pieces of filling that are too chunky, as this can cause the wrap to come apart.

BASIC CULINARY SKILLS

Making a Club Sandwich

① **Toast the bread.** You will need three slices per sandwich.

② **Spread mayonnaise** on only one side of each slice of toast.

③ **Add the bottom filling.** Layer lettuce, tomato, and bacon.

Source: Pearson Education

④ **Add the second piece of toast,** mayonnaise side down.

⑤ **Spread mayonnaise** on top of the second piece of toast.

Source: Pearson Education

⑥ **Add the top filling.** Layer lettuce and turkey.

Source: Pearson Education

⑦ **Add the third piece of toast,** mayonnaise side down.

⑧ **Secure with sandwich picks.**

⑨ **Cut the sandwich into quarters.** Serve.

Source: Pearson Education

Recipe Card

47. Club Sandwich

Making a Wrap

1. **Warm a tortilla** in a hot skillet for about 15 seconds on each side.

2. **Spread puréed black beans** on half of the tortilla.

Source: Pearson Education

Source: Pearson Education

5. **Roll the tortilla closed tightly,** starting on the side with the filling.

Source: Pearson Education

3. **Add lettuce, tomatoes, and onions** on top of the puréed black beans.

4. **Add grilled chicken** on top of other filling.

6. **Secure with a sandwich pick.** Serve immediately.

READING CHECKPOINT *What are the six main types of cold sandwiches?*

Hot Sandwiches

There are four main types of hot sandwiches:

- **Sandwich with hot filling.** A closed sandwich, a hero sandwich, a club sandwich, and a wrap can all be served with a hot filling. Hamburgers and hot dogs are often served with room-temperature buns, for example. When vegetables such as lettuce or tomato are served with a hot filling, they are often served on the side until the customer assembles the sandwich. This prevents the hot filling from wilting the vegetable.

- **Grilled sandwich.** To make a **grilled sandwich**, the sandwich is first assembled and then the outside surface of the bread is spread with butter. The sandwich, also known as a *griddled sandwich*, is then cooked directly on the heat source, usually a griddle. Grilled

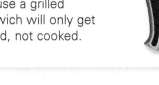

Chef's Tip

Grilled Meat Sandwiches

Be sure any meat in a grilled or pressed sandwich is precooked because a grilled sandwich will only get heated, not cooked.

Recipe Cards

48. Tuna Melt

49. Reuben Sandwich

Open-faced turkey sandwich

cheese and Reuben sandwiches are examples of grilled sandwiches.

- **Pressed sandwich.** A sandwich press is used to make a **pressed sandwich**. Sandwiches are toasted on a heavy, two-sided cooking press that compresses and grills them until they are hot and heated through on the inside. The Italian version of a pressed sandwich is called a **panini** (pa-NEE-nee). The Cuban version is called a **cubano** (ku-BAH-no).

- **Hot open-faced sandwich.** Hot open-faced sandwiches are often served on toasted bread, topped with gravy or sauce. In some parts of the country, mashed potatoes are added and the open-faced sandwich is called a *hot shot*. Eggs Benedict, a breakfast/brunch dish consisting of an English muffin, ham, a poached egg, and sauce, is actually a hot open-faced sandwich.

Source: Dorling Kindersley/Image Partners 2005/Dorling Kindersley Media Library/ Dorling Kindersley

Recipe Card
50. Open-Faced Turkey Sandwich

 **READING CHECKPOINT** *What are the four basic types of hot sandwiches?*

11.1 ASSESSMENT

Reviewing Concepts

1. What are the four elements of a sandwich?
2. What are three steps to performing mise en place for sandwiches?
3. What are the six main types of cold sandwiches?
4. What are the four main types of hot sandwiches?

Critical Thinking

5. **Predicting** What would happen if you served a hot turkey sandwich with gravy as a closed sandwich on thin slices from a Pullman loaf?
6. **Comparing/Contrasting** Is mayonnaise a better choice than a vegetable purée on a bacon, lettuce, and tomato sandwich on toast?
7. **Drawing Conclusions** Your tea sandwiches are dried up and hard. What went wrong and how could you have avoided it?

Test Kitchen

Divide into four teams. Each team will prepare a roast beef sandwich, using a different style of bread or wrap. Try to make them as different as possible. Use identical fillings, spreads, condiments, and garnishes. Evaluate the results.

LANGUAGE ARTS
Mouthwatering Adjectives

Create three flavored spreads for a roast beef sandwich. Write a mouthwatering menu description for each spread that will persuade customers to try it. Use at least three different adjectives in the description for each spread.

PROJECT 11 **Sandwich Basics** You are now ready to work on Project 11, "Sandwich Basics," which is available in "My Culinary Lab" or in your *Student's Lab Resources and Study Guide* manual.

11.2

Appetizers and Hors d'Oeuvre

READING PREVIEW

Key Concepts

- Identifying types of appetizers and hors d'Oeuvre
- Presenting appetizers and hors d'Oeuvre

Vocabulary

- antipasti
- appetizer
- bruschettas
- canapés
- carpaccio
- chef's tasting
- crostini
- crudités
- finger food
- hors d'Oeuvre
- hors d'Oeuvre variées
- kebobs
- pâtés
- seviche
- shrimp cocktail
- skewers
- tapas
- terrines

Types of Appetizers and Hors d'Oeuvre

A small, savory, flavorful dish, usually consumed in one or two bites, is called an **hors d'Oeuvre** (or-DERV), a French term that means "outside the meal." This term is used for both the singular ("an hors d'Oeuvre") and plural ("many hors d'Oeuvre"). The same dish, if it were served as the first course in a meal, would be called an **appetizer**. Although the same items may be served as either hors d'Oeuvre or appetizers, the appetizer portions tends to be slightly larger than the hors d'Oeuvre portion. As you can see, the main differences between an appetizer and an hors d'Oeuvre are both the context in which they are served (either outside the meal or part of the meal) and their size. There are hot and cold varieties of both hors d'Oeuvre and appetizers.

The purpose of both an hors d'Oeuvre and an appetizer is to stimulate the appetite and set a mood for the meal that will follow. A good menu includes appetizer offerings with a variety of flavors and textures that are complementary to the entrées but don't repeat them. For example, a ravioli appetizer might have the same basic flavor and texture as a lasagna, but a crisp texture is a good lead-in to a creamy pasta dish, while a stuffed mushroom would be a good lead in to a piece of grilled fish.

Hors d'Oeuvre are often served with a napkin and eaten with the fingers. When served this way, they are also called **finger food**. Hors d'Oeuvre rarely require a fork. Appetizers are usually served on a plate and are often eaten with a fork (although sometimes appetizers are also finger food).

Source: Kondor83/Fotolia

**Hors d'Oeuvre
or Appetizer?**

Meatballs served on a wooden stick become an hors d'Oeuvre.

RECOGNIZING PATTERNS *Why would large meatballs be served as an appetizer?*

Hot Appetizers and Hors d'Oeuvre There is an incredible diversity of hot appetizers and hors d'Oeuvre. In fact, virtually any type of savory food served in a small portion can be regarded as an appetizer. Any type of food that you can eat with your fingers or in bite-sized pieces could become an hors d'Oeuvre. The following are some common hot appetizers and hors d'Oeuvre:

- **Baked, sautéed, or grilled seafood.** Seafood, particularly scallops and shrimps, are quickly sautéed with herbs and served as an appetizer or hors d'Oeuvre.

- **Kebobs.** Meat, fish, poultry, or vegetables can be cooked on **skewers** (SKEW-ers), long, thin, pointed rods made of wood or metal. Small versions of these grilled or broiled skewers of food are called **kebobs** (kuh-BOBS). The food is usually marinated before cooking and is often served with a dipping sauce.

- **Fried food.** This includes batter-dipped fish, chicken, or vegetables, often served with some type of dipping sauce. Japanese tempura is an example.

- **Tartlets and turnovers.** Pie crusts lining small pans or molds can be stuffed with assorted savory fillings and baked. Fillings include custards, meat, poultry, vegetables, cheese, and seafood. The dough is sometimes folded around a filling to create a turnover. *Empanadas* are a Latin-American version of a turnover.

Pizza tarts

- **Meatballs.** Small meatballs or other highly seasoned ground-meat items are served with toothpicks as hors d'Oeuvre. Meatballs are often served in a sweet-sour sauce. Appetizer-sized meatballs are eaten with a fork. Hors d'Oeuvre-sized meatballs are often eaten on a skewer or sandwich pick.

- **Pasta.** Small portions of pasta can be served as an appetizer. Ravioli or other stuffed pastas can be served hot or cold, with a sauce or plain. In some cases, these pasta shapes are fried to make an appetizer.

- **Grilled, steamed, baked, or roasted vegetables.** Vegetables such as asparagus, artichokes, peppers, onions, garlic, zucchini, and carrots are cooked and often served with a dipping sauce or dressed with a vinaigrette. Mushroom caps are sometimes stuffed and baked.

- **Dumplings, egg rolls, and spring rolls.** These are the traditional hors d'Oeuvre and appetizers for Asian dinners.

Spring rolls

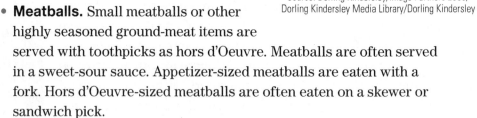

Vegetable Tempura

1. **Heat the oil** to 375°F.
2. **Blot the vegetables** dry and season.
3. **Coat the vegetables with batter.**

4. **Place the vegetables in the hot oil.**
5. **Deep-fry** until the batter is golden brown and puffy. Turn, if necessary, to brown and cook evenly.

6. **Remove the vegetables** from the fryer with tongs or a skimmer.

7. **Blot** briefly on absorbent toweling.
8. **Season,** if necessary, and serve at once. Serve with a dipping sauce.

 Recipe Cards

51. Vegetable Tempura

52. Shrimp Tempura

- **Crab cakes.** Crab meat is mixed with mayonnaise, herbs, and spices, formed into patties, and sautéed. Crab cakes are often served with a sauce.

Cold Appetizers and Hors d'Oeuvre It is possible to whet your guests' appetites with something as simple as a slice of smoked salmon on French bread. However, it is just as possible to whet their appetites with a much more elaborate offering, such as a bite-sized crab salad tartlet with mango chutney. The variety of possible cold appetizers and hors d'Oeuvre is endless. The only requirements are that the portion size is appropriate and the appetizer or hors d'Oeuvre is complementary to the main course offerings. A significant advantage of cold appetizers and hors d'Oeuvre is that you can prepare many of them well in advance. This can be extremely important in a fast-paced professional kitchen. The following are some common cold appetizers and hors d'Oeuvre:

- **Raw seafood.** This includes freshly shucked clams and oysters, served with a variety of sauces.
- **Smoked fish, meat, or poultry.** Often served with bread, condiments, and a sauce, smoked fish, meat, or poultry make an elegant appetizer or hors d'Oeuvre.

Crab cakes
Source: David Murray and Jules Selmes/
Image Partners 2005/ Dorling Kindersley
Media Library/Dorling Kindersley

 **Recipe Card**

53. Crab Cakes

Salmon canapes
Source: David Murray and Jules Selmes/Image Partners 2005/Dorling Kindersley Media Library/Dorling Kindersley

Bruschetta
Source: Philip Wilkins/Image Partners 2005/Dorling Kindersley Media Library/Dorling Kindersley

Pâté
Source: David Murray/Dorling Kindersley Media Library/Dorling Kindersley

- **Cold cooked seafood. Shrimp cocktail**, which is cold, steamed shrimp served with a spicy cocktail sauce, is a traditional cold appetizer. **Seviche** (seh-VEE-chee), also spelled *ceviche*, the Latin American dish of fish and seafood that is cooked in citrus juice and flavored with onions, chiles, and cilantro, is another traditional cold appetizer or hors d'Oeuvre.

- **Open-faced sandwiches.** Small, bite-sized, open-faced sandwiches are often used as hors d'Oeuvre. Crackers or hard breads are often used rather than soft breads. **Canapés** (KAN-uh-pays) are bite-sized pieces of bread or crackers with a savory topping. They are used as hors d'Oeuvre. Toppings can range from a simple piece of cheese to an elaborate spread. Larger pieces of bread are used for appetizers. **Bruschettas** (brew-SKEH-tahs) and **crostini** (kroh-STEE-nee) are a type of open-faced sandwich served as an appetizer. They consist of toasted bread drizzled with olive oil and topped with tomatoes, olives, cheese, or other ingredients.

- **Raw or cured meats.** This includes prosciutto and **carpaccio** (car-PAH-chee-oh). Carpaccio is raw beef sliced very thinly and dressed with a sauce. Cured meats are sometimes served with complementary fruits, such as melons or peaches.

- **Pickled vegetables.** Usually included as part of an antipasto plate, marinated or pickled vegetables complement other hors d'Oeuvre and appetizers.

- **Cold grilled or roasted vegetables.** Vegetables that have been grilled or roasted may be served cold (or at room temperature) with a variety of sauces and relishes.

- **Salads.** Small-portioned salads, including mayonnaise-based salads, are outstanding served as appetizers. They are sometimes referred to as composed salads, to distinguish them from mixed green salads and salads served as a side dish (see Section 10.2).

- **Cheese.** Cubes of cheese with sandwich picks make ideal hors d'Oeuvre.

- **Raw vegetables.** Vegetables that have been cut into bite-sized pieces are called **crudités** (kroo-de-TAYS). They are often served with dips.

Crudités
Source: Christina Richards/Shutterstock

- **Pâtés and terrines. Pâtés** (pah-TAYS) are a well-seasoned, baked mixtures of ground meat, fish, poultry, or vegetables. Although pâtés can be served hot, they are usually served cold. They have a texture that ranges from a creamy spread to a crumbly meat loaf. You can cook pâtés in molds, which are called **terrines** (teh-REENS). When pâté is served in its mold, the pâté is called a terrine.

READING CHECKPOINT *What is the difference between an appetizer and an hors d'Oeuvre?*

Presenting Appetizers and Hors d'Oeuvre

Presenting Appetizers Appetizers are presented to customers while they are seated, so it is acceptable to require the use of a fork, spoon, or even a knife.

Here are some general guidelines for presenting appetizers:

- **Serve small portions.** Appetizer portions should be small. They are supposed to stimulate the appetite, not satisfy it.

- **Use the correct balance of seasonings.** The correct balance of seasoning at the beginning of the meal affects the palate for the rest of the meal. If the flavor of the appetizer is overpowering, it takes away from the enjoyment of the courses that follow.

- **Make a good first impression.** Appetizers provide the customer's first impression of the food. Garnish should be minimal, yet add a touch of flavor and texture as well as color. The appetizer should be plated in an artistic and neat manner.

- **Consider a chef's tasting.** Appetizers are sometimes presented in a **chef's tasting**. This is a sampler plate with an assortment of different appetizers. The portions are often only one bite, just enough to sample the various appetizers.

READING CHECKPOINT *What are four guidelines to remember when presenting appetizers?*

FIGURE 11–4
Stuffed Mushrooms
Mushrooms stuffed with bread crumbs, garlic, and parsley.
RECOGNIZING PATTERNS *Why is this an appetizer and not an hors d'Oeuvre?*
Source: Martin Brigdale/Image Partners 2005/ Dorling Kindersley Media Library/Dorling Kindersley

••FOCUS ON ••Safety

Double-Dipping
When serving hors d'Oeuvre, consider ways to discourage guests from double-dipping (dipping a chewed portion of food in a communal dipping sauce) such as providing a spoon or serving dips in individual containers. Double-dipping increases the hazards of pathogens passed from the guests' hands and mouths to the food.

Presenting Hors d'Oeuvre Hors d'Oeuvre can be served buffet style, on platters, or on individual plates. Platters are usually used for events where guests are standing and the platters are circulated by the wait staff. (This type of service is referred to as *butler service*.) Because people often have glasses in their hands, only one hand is free. The best hors d'Oeuvre for these occasions are ones that do not require a plate or utensils. In addition to being served before a meal, hors d'Oeuvre may be the only food provided at parties and receptions. The same guidelines for service apply for both.

Here are some general guidelines for presenting hors d'Oeuvre:

- **Use fresh ingredients.** Ingredients must be at the peak of quality. Although trimmings or leftover ingredients can be used in hors d'Oeuvre, they should be perfectly fresh.

Spain

The cuisine of Spain is influenced by both its geography and its history. The country is bounded by both the Atlantic Ocean and the Mediterranean Sea. It is one of the most mountainous countries in Europe, with areas devoted to raising cattle, pigs, and sheep, as well as making cured meats such as the famous Serrano ham or sausages such as chorizo. Low-lying areas along rivers and near the shoreline produce a wide variety of goods, including the fruits and vegetables Spain is famous for. Also from these areas is the rice featured in one of Spain's most famous dishes, *paella* (pie-AY-yah), an elaborate dish of rice with a combination of vegetables, meats, and seafood.

Source: pavalena/Shutterstock

The use of certain spices (anise, cloves, coriander, cumin, paprika, and saffron) as well as almonds, honey, and olives tells the story of a time when Spain was under the influence of the Moors. The importance of bread and olive oil remains, even though Roman rule has been over for hundreds of years. In fact, Spain's famous cold soup, gazpacho, is traditionally a soup made from three ingredients: bread, ripe tomatoes, and olive oil.

Spanish foods often feature the flavors of preserved, salted, and dried foods. These foods were critical to sailors on long trips, who relied on the salted and dried foods while they harvested tuna, mackerel, mullet, eels, and other seafood. The rivers and lakes in Spain's interior are another traditional source of foods, which accounts for the popularity of fresh water specialties such as trout, frog's legs, and snails.

The Spanish have a popular tradition of small dishes of food served as snacks, or tapas, along with a glass of sherry. Originally, these dishes were served and meant to tide you over from lunch (which may be served as late as two o'clock) to dinner (never earlier than eight o'clock). Today, most regions in Spain have their own specialty tapas, and tapas bars are popular worldwide.

Research

1. Serrano ham is one of the most famous foods that Spain produces. Name at least three other foods that Spain is noted for and research the region that they come from and the way that the food is produced. Find two recipes for each ingredient that you research.

2. Research the Moors to find out more about the ways that they influenced the cuisine of Spain. Consider specific ingredients, cooking tools, and equipment. Find four recipes that demonstrate the impact of the Moors on Spanish cuisine.

Source: goodluz/Fotolia

Refrigerated display case containing tapas in Madrid, Spain

- **Make hors d'Oeuvre bite-sized.** One or two bites is the ideal size.
- **Complement other foods.** Hors d'Oeuvre should complement the other foods served, yet be different enough to avoid being repetitive.
- **Don't mix hot and cold items.** Hot and cold items should never be presented on the same plate or platter. Use multiple plates or platters if you are offering both hot and cold appetizers.
- **Serve a selection of hors d'Oeuvre.** Different cuisines feature different hors d'Oeuvre selections. The French serve **hors d'Oeuvre variées** (or-DERV vare-ee-AY), including pâtés, pickles, and marinated vegetables. The Spanish version is **tapas** (TAH-pahs), a collection of small bites featuring ingredients such as ham or eggs. The Italians serve **antipasti** (ahn-tee-PAHS-tee), a selection of sliced meats, cheeses, sausages, and olives served before the meal.

FIGURE 11–5

Hors d'Oeuvre Platter

This attractive platter contains a variety of cold hors d'Oeuvre.

APPLYING CONCEPTS *What rules of cold food presentation are shown in this hors d'Oeuvre platter?*

Source: Richard Embery/Pearson Education/ PH College

READING CHECKPOINT *What are two tips for presenting appetizers? What are two tips for presenting hors d'Oeuvre?*

11.2 ASSESSMENT

Reviewing Concepts

1. What is the difference between an appetizer and an hors d'Oeuvre?

2. What are two tips for presenting appetizers? What are two tips for presenting hors d'Oeuvre?

Critical Thinking

3. Comparing/Contrasting You are serving hors d'Oeuvre at a party where people will be standing. You are considering small seafood kabobs, chicken wings, or canapés. Which would you choose? Explain why.

4. Analyzing Information After a meal, a guest complained to the chef that the appetizer had too much garlic and basil. The main course was a gently poached chicken with a delicate sauce. Was the customer correct? Explain your answer.

Test Kitchen

Make a mayonnaise-based seafood salad for a cocktail party and divide it in half. Serve half as canapés and half as an appetizer salad. Taste the canapés while standing using one hand. Taste the appetizer salad while seated and using a fork. Which presentation method is preferable?

CULINARY MATH

Serving Hors d'Oeuvre

You are planning hors d'Oeuvre for a corporate party. Seventy-five people will be attending, and the client estimates that each person will eat ten hors d'Oeuvre. If there are five waiters, how many hors d'Oeuvre will each waiter eventually serve?

Reviewing Content

Choose the letter that best answers the question or completes the statement.

1. What is a Pullman loaf?
   a. a type of meat loaf
   b. a vegetable terrine
   c. a rectangular loaf of bread
   d. a sequenced arrangement of bread and meat

2. What is ciabatta?
   a. a large, flat Italian bread traditionally cut in squares and then split to fill
   b. seafood that is "cooked" in citrus juice
   c. a flat Middle Eastern bread that forms a pocket
   d. a type of warm hors d'Oeuvre made with cheese

3. What is finger food?
   a. food served with a napkin and eaten with the fingers
   b. long, thin sandwiches shaped like fingers
   c. large sandwiches with mayonnaise-based sandwich salads
   d. food that is prepared entirely by hand

4. Hors d'Oeuvre variées are hors d'Oeuvre that
   a. vary according to the day of the week.
   b. vary according to the daily specials.
   c. are a mixed variety on one plate.
   d. vary according to the season.

5. Canapés are
   a. bite-sized vegetables often served with dip.
   b. meat, fish, or vegetables cooked on a skewer.
   c. open-faced sandwiches consisting of toast, olive oil, and tomatoes.
   d. bite-sized pieces of bread or crackers with savory toppings.

6. Bruschettas are
   a. bite-sized vegetables often served with dip.
   b. meat, fish, or vegetables cooked on a skewer.
   c. open-faced sandwiches consisting of toast, olive oil, and tomatoes.
   d. bite-sized pieces of bread or crackers with savory toppings.

Understanding Concepts

7. What are the four elements of a sandwich?

8. What is the purpose of a spread in a sandwich?

9. What is a finger sandwich?

10. What is a pressed sandwich?

11. What is the difference between an appetizer and an hors d'Oeuvre?

12. What is a canapé?

13. What are crudités?

14. Why is correct portion size important for appetizers?

Critical Thinking

15. **APPLYING CONCEPTS** One dish has two small crackers with pâté on them and the other dish has a slice of pâté cut from a terrine. Which is more likely to be an appetizer? Why?

Culinary Math

16. **ANALYZING INFORMATION** You need 10 pounds of jumbo shrimp to make 100 canapés. It is estimated that each guest will eat 2 canapés. How many guests will 20 pounds of shrimp feed?

On the Job

17. **WRITING** Your boss wants to advertise free "finger food" that would be available for a 2-hour period in the bar. Write a simple, but appetizing, description of three types of finger food that could be featured. Because these will be free, they must be inexpensive items.

18. **DRAWING CONCLUSIONS** The spa menu at a health club features a low-fat wrap. You decide to omit all fat and fill the wrap with slices of tomato, cucumbers, peppers, and a portabella mushroom marinated in balsamic vinegar. Customers complain that the sandwich is too messy. What could be wrong?

Catering

Caterers provide a specialized service to their clients. When a client wishes to host a special event of some sort, whether a lunch break during a business meeting or a full-scale banquet for a wedding, caterers are responsible for menus, food preparation, and service throughout the event.

Owners and managers in the catering business may be focused primarily on business development, or they may perform many different functions including chef or maître d'. In addition to working directly with their clients to plan an event, they may also run a catering hall or house (or a banquet facility within a larger operation such as a hotel) as well as organizing and executing events off-site, either at the client's home or a public space such as a park or a museum.

Successful owners and managers have good business skills and the ability to work with others. They are detail-oriented and good at problem solving and managing others. People who choose catering as their career path must be both organized and adaptable.

Event planners are often part of the overall catering business. They usually work directly with the client, and then on behalf of the client, managing the staffing of an event, finding or planning its location, and attending to other details typically not related to food preparation or service.

Banquet chefs and cooks plan and cost the menu for an event, then make sure that foods are prepared and presented properly. They may be responsible for preparing a tasting menu for the client to sample during the menu planning stage.

The *banquet dining room manager* (*maître d'*) prepares the dining room, sets up buffets or stations, presets tables, and works with the event planner.

Servers bring food from the kitchen that is then served from trays, on buffets, or at the table.

The *catering manager*'s function is to develop business for a catering company. They bring new business to the company and maintain good relationships with existing clients. They may also be known as the *catering coordinator* or *sales staff*.

Entry-Level Requirements

At entry level, there are no specific degree requirements, although many companies require the completion of an in-house training program.

Helpful for Advancement

An associate's degree (or higher) in culinary arts, hospitality management, or event planning is helpful. Sales personnel should have at least a basic introduction to cooking and service to be effective, in addition to a two- or four-year degree.

Source: Culinary Institute of America

Caterers are responsible for menus, food preparation, and service—often at public spaces or restaurants chosen for their spectacular views and ambiance

ABIGAIL KIRSCH

When it comes to the influences in her life, Abigail Kirsch credits her grandmother for her cooking and baking skills, and her mother for leaving her at home alone to get dinner ready. After attending The Culinary Institute of America (at that time in New Haven) as well as the Cordon Bleu in France, she opened a cooking school in the basement of her home to advance her dreams of becoming a chef.

Abigail Kirsch

A few years later, when her classes outgrew the space she had available, she moved to a storefront. That was when a fateful call came from PepsiCo. The company was looking for a caterer to handle an event for 500. Abigail says she still can't explain why she said yes, but she did. From that event, her small business, serving mainly Westchester County, New York, and Fairfield County, Connecticut, suddenly expanded to include Manhattan and New Jersey as well. It was, and still is, a family business that includes Abigail's husband, who joined her as co-founder in 1973, and her son, Jim, who joined in 1984.

Today Abigail Kirsch, Catering Relationships is recognized for its excellence, which comes from the company's "obsessive commitment to perfection"—no matter the size and no matter the occasion.

VITAL STATISTICS

Graduated: The Culinary Institute of America and Le Cordon Bleu

Profession: Caterer, co-owner of Abigail Kirsch, Catering Relationships

Books: *The Bride and Groom's First Cookbook*

The Bride and Grooms' Menu Cookbook

Invitation to Dinner

CAREER PROFILE

Salary Ranges

Banquet Chef, Catering Manager, or Maître d': $36,500 to $60,000

Banquet Cooks: $16,000 to $22,500

Chapter 12

Fruit and Vegetables

12.1 Fruit

12.2 Vegetables

Key Concepts

- Identifying types of fruit
- Selecting and storing fruit
- Preparing fruit
- Cooking fruit
- Serving fruit

Vocabulary

- clingstone
- compote
- essential oils
- ethylene
- freestone
- fritters
- individually quick-frozen (IQF)
- maturation
- pith
- ripening
- stone

Types of Fruit

The fruit of a plant ensures the survival of the plant, because every fruit contains a seed (in some cases, hundreds of seeds) that can grow into a new plant. In the culinary sense, fruit is typically eaten as is or used to make sweets and desserts. But there are numerous exceptions to the rule. Fruit is also used in savory dishes, for instance.

Fruit grows on trees, bushes, or vines. Every fruit has a stem end, which is the place where the fruit was attached to the tree, bush, or vine it grew on. The blossom end is opposite the stem.

The seed is surrounded by the fruit's flesh. Melons and similar fruit have a lot of seeds located in a center pocket. Apples and pears have relatively few seeds, and those seeds are found in the center part of the fruit known as its core. Plums, peaches, and apricots have a single seed that is protected by a hard pit, sometimes known as a **stone**. Strawberries have seeds on the outside of the fruit.

The fruit's skin protects the flesh while the fruit grows and ripens. In some cases, the skin acts as a signal that the fruit is ripe and ready to eat. Ripe fruit has the most vivid colors; until a fruit ripens, it appears green.

You can eat the skin of some fruit, such as apples, pears, plums, and grapes. Other fruit has skin that is

Source: Serg64/Shutterstock

either too tough or too bitter to eat (bananas, oranges, and melons, for instance). The heavy outer skin of fruit such as watermelon and pineapple is sometimes referred to as the rind.

Apples Apples are one of the most widely available fruit. Some varieties, such as Red Delicious and Pink Lady, are very good when eaten fresh. Other varieties, such as McIntosh, are very good for cooking; they become very soft when cooked and are used for applesauce or apple butter. Rome Beauty apples hold their shape when cooked, making them a good choice for pie and pastry fillings. Many apple varieties are good for eating fresh, cooking, and baking. These are referred to as *general-purpose apples.*

Apples should be firm, with good color. There should be no bruises or soft spots, and the fruit should feel heavy for its size.

Berries Blueberries, strawberries, blackberries, and raspberries are probably what you think of first when you think about berries. They grow on bushes and have a short season. Look for good color, with no bruising or mold. If the packaging is stained with juice, the fruit has probably been damaged in delivery. If a few berries turn moldy, the rest of the container may go bad quickly. Keep berries as dry as possible until you are ready to serve or cook them.

Cranberries are firm, very tart berries that hold and freeze well. They are almost always cooked before they are served. In addition to these familiar berries, this category also includes gooseberries, boysenberries, and currants.

Citrus Fruit Citrus fruit includes oranges, grapefruits, lemons, and limes. Citrus fruit has a bright skin that contains its **essential oils**. These oils, which evaporate quickly, give the fruit its distinct aroma and flavor. Just below the outer skin is the white, bitter, and indigestible layer called the **pith**. Good-quality citrus fruit should have good color and aroma, no soft or bruised portions, and no signs of mold.

There are four basic types of oranges:

- Loose-skinned oranges with easy-to-peel skins, such as tangerines, Minneolas, and clementines

- Sweet oranges, which are large and easy to eat, with relatively few, if any, seeds, such as navel oranges

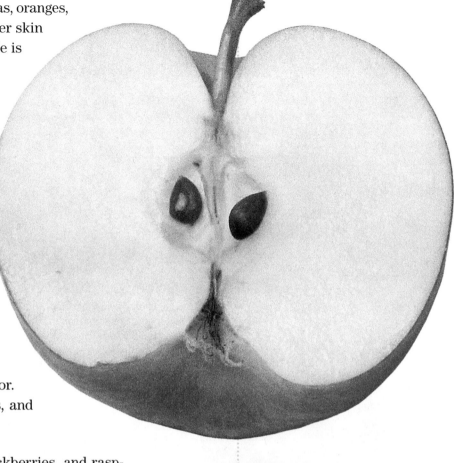

FIGURE 12–1

Fruit Anatomy

Here you can see all the parts of an apple.

INTERPRETING ILLUSTRATIONS

Can you identify all the parts of the apple?

Source: Andy Crawford/ Image Partners 2005/ Dorling Kindersley Media Library/Dorling Kindersley

Apples

Braeburn

Firm flesh, sweet-tart flavor. General-purpose. October to April.

Source: womue/Fotolia

Golden Delicious

Crisp flesh, sweet and juicy. Stays white after cutting longer than other varieties. General-purpose. September to May.

Source: Philip Dowell/Image Partners 2005/Dorling Kindersley Media Library/Dorling Kindersley

McIntosh

White flesh, juicy and tart. May be eaten fresh or used in sauces and cider. Can be frozen. September to June.

Source: Philip Dowell/Image Partners 2005/Dorling Kindersley Media Library/Dorling Kindersley

Red Delicious

Flesh is yellow-white, with firm texture and sweet taste. General-purpose. September to June.

Source: Pearson Education/PH College

Granny Smith

Crisp, finely textured, white or light-green flesh, tart. General-purpose. April to July.

Source: Tim Ridley/Image Partners 2005/Dorling Kindersley Media Library/Dorling Kindersley

Pink Lady

Crisp, sweet flesh. Eaten fresh. October to January.

Source: Alessio Cola/Fotolia

Jonathan

Tender flesh, semitart flavor. May be eaten fresh or used in pies and sauces. Can be frozen. September to January.

Source: VIP Design/Fotolia

Rome Beauty

Firm flesh, mild tart-sweet flavor. General-purpose. October to June.

Source: Ashok Rodrigues/Getty Images

Berries

Boysenberries
Similar in flavor and texture to red raspberry, but larger, with larger seeds, and a bit tarter. May be eaten fresh or used in jams and jellies, syrups. Spring.

Golden Raspberries
Similar in flavor and texture to red raspberry. May be eaten fresh or used in baking, syrups, sauces. Two seasons: early summer, late summer.

Blueberries
Sweet and juicy. May be eaten fresh and dried or used in baking. Late summer.

Strawberries
Juicy and sweet, with seeds on the exterior. May be eaten fresh and dried or used in baked goods, sauces, jams and jellies. Late spring into early summer.

Blackberries
Similar in flavor and texture to red raspberry, but larger, with larger seeds, and a bit sweeter. May be eaten fresh or used in jams, jellies, baked goods, sauces, syrups. Midsummer.

Red Currants
Red, black, or white flesh; red is the sweetest. Generally cooked in jams, jellies, and syrups, dried. Midsummer.

Source: Dorling Kindersley Limited

Red Raspberries
Sweet and juicy flesh with many seeds. May be eaten fresh or used in baking, sauces, syrups. Two seasons: early summer, late summer.

- Juicing oranges, which are also sweet, but have thin skin, lots of juice, and many seeds
- Bitter oranges, with heavy skins and a bitter taste, used to make marmalade

Grapes Grapes are juicy berries that grow in clusters on vines or shrubs. They are grown to produce table fruit, wine, and other products. Table fruit may be red, purple (or black), or green, with or without seeds. Concord grapes are used to produce juices, jellies, and preserves. Seedless grape varieties like Thompson or Sultana may be dried to produce raisins.

Grapes should be firmly attached to the stem with no shrinking or shriveling.

Pears Pears are similar to apples in many respects. They grow on trees and have sweet, cream-colored flesh and a core of multiple seeds. Their skin color can range from mottled brown to pale green to deep red. The skin of pears is edible, although some recipes call for peeling the fruit.

Green and red grapes
Source: Andrjuss/Shutterstock

Citrus Fruit

Orange

Sweet-tart flavor, juicy; some varieties are seedless. May be eaten fresh; used for juice, zest, or flavoring, or used in marmalade. Year-round.

Source: Dave King/Dorling Kindersley Limited

Grapefruit

Sweet-tart flavor, juicy; some varieties are seedless. Flesh can be pale yellow, pink, or deep red. May be eaten fresh or used for juice. Year-round.

Tangerine

Sweet-tart flavor, less tart than an orange; juicy, usually has many seeds. May be eaten fresh or used for juice. October to April.

Source: Valentyn Volkov/ Shutterstock

Lemon

Very tart flavor, juicy, with seeds. Used for juice, zest, and flavoring. Year-round.

Lime

Tart flavor, juicy, often seedless. Used for juice, zest, and flavoring. Year-round.

Clementine

Similar to an orange, but less tart, smaller, and seedless. Eaten fresh. November to February.

Source: Topseller/Shutterstock

Minneola

Tastes like a tangerine, very juicy, very few seeds. May be eaten fresh or used for juice. November to February.

Source: Peter Zijlstra/ Shutterstock

Ugli Fruit

Orange flesh, fewer seeds than a grapefruit, very juicy, has a smooth, sweet flavor. May be eaten fresh or used for juice. November to April.

Source: Roger Phillips/Image Partners 2005/Dorling Kindersley Media Library/Dorling Kindersley

Kumquat

Edible, sweet rind and sour flesh. May be eaten fresh (with rind) or used in marmalades. October to January.

Source: Ian O'Leary/Image Partners 2005/Dorling Kindersley Media Library/Dorling Kindersley

Pears

Seckel
Crisp flesh, with a delicate sweet, spicy flavor. May be eaten fresh (some consider it too crisp for eating fresh), poached, cooked, or canned. Fall.
Source: Culinary Institute of America

Anjou
Creamy white flesh that is slightly grainy, aromatic, juicy, sweet, and slightly acidic. May be eaten fresh, poached, or used in baked goods. Fall.
Source: seandnad/Fotolia

Red Bartlett
Aromatic and sweet, with a juicy, buttery texture. May be eaten fresh, poached, or canned. Fall.
Source: Chris Leachman/Fotolia

Bosc
Dense, crisp, smooth flesh, with a sweet-spicy flavor. May be eaten fresh, baked, or poached. Fall.
Source: chiyacat/Fotolia

Comice
Very sweet flavor, juicy, with silky smooth, soft flesh. Eaten fresh. Fall.
Source: funkyfood London - Paul Williams/Alamy

Asian
Fragrant and juicy, with a crisp, grainy texture. Eaten fresh. Fall.
Source: Vidady/Fotolia

Like apples, pears are a popular winter fruit because they can be held successfully in cold storage for several months without overripening or losing their quality.

Stone Fruit Cherries, apricots, plums, peaches, and nectarines are stone fruit. They all contain a hard pit that covers a central seed or kernel. Peaches and apricots have a fuzzy skin, which can be eaten fresh, but is typically removed before cooking. Plums are sold in many varieties. Purple or red plums are typically eaten as fresh fruit. Italian plums and Damson plums are best for cooking and baking.

Stone Fruit

Apricot

Soft flesh, juicy and fragrant, with a sweet-tart flavor. May be eaten fresh or used for baking, syrups, jams, sauces, and purées. Often dried, canned, or, frozen. Summer.

Source: David Murray/Image Partners 2005/Dorling Kindersley Media Library/Dorling Kindersley

Cherry

Juicy flesh; some varieties are more sour than sweet, others are sweeter. Skins and flesh may be red, black, or white. May be eaten fresh or used for baking, syrups, jams, or sauces. Often dried, canned, or, frozen. Early summer.

Source: David Murray/Image Partners 2005/Dorling Kindersley Media Library/Dorling Kindersley

Nectarine

Flesh similar to peaches with a smooth skin that may be red, pink, yellow, or white. May be eaten fresh or used for baking or jams. Summer.

Source: Philip Dowell/Image Partners 2005/Dorling Kindersley Media Library/Dorling Kindersley

Peach

Juicy, firm flesh that may be orange or a creamy white with a delicate aroma, varying degrees of tartness, and a sweet flavor. Peaches have a fuzzy skin that may be red, pink, yellow, or white. May be eaten fresh or used for baking or jams. Summer.

Source: Dave King/Image Partners 2005/Dorling Kindersley Media Library/ Dorling Kindersley

Santa Rosa Plum

Light-yellow soft, juicy flesh with a sweet-tart flavor. May be eaten fresh or used for jams and jellies. Summer.

Source: Philip Dowell/Image Partners 2005/Dorling Kindersley Media Library/Dorling Kindersley

Damson Plum

Fragrant, juicy yellow-green flesh with skins from dark blue to indigo and a very tart flavor. Used for jams and jellies or in baking. Late summer.

Source: Dave King/Image Partners 2005/Dorling Kindersley Media Library/Dorling Kindersley

Clingstone fruit is a type of fruit with flesh that clings tightly to the pit, making it difficult to cut the flesh away cleanly. **Freestone** fruit has flesh that separates easily from the pit. Peaches and nectarines come in both clingstone and freestone varieties.

Melons There are several varieties of melons, each differing in size, taste, color, and skin texture. Melons grow on vines and sit directly on the ground, giving one part of the rind a white, faded patch where it doesn't get any sun.

Melons

Cantaloupe

Smooth, orange, juicy flesh; very sweet, with a pleasant melon aroma. Eaten fresh. Summer.

Source: Ian O'Leary/Image Partners 2005/Dorling Kindersley Media Library/ Dorling Kindersley

Casaba

Light green-white flesh that is delicately sweet. Can be stored longer than most other melons. Eaten fresh. Early fall.

Source: Richard Embery/Pearson Education/ PH College

Watermelon

Very juicy, sweet red or yellow flesh; some seedless varieties. Eaten fresh. Mid- to late summer.

Source: Richard Embery/Pearson Education/PH College

Crenshaw

Dense, juicy, peach-colored flesh; sweet and slightly spicy. Two varieties: green and white. Eaten fresh. Early fall.

Source: Richard Embery/Pearson Education/PH College

Honeydew

Juicy flesh, usually pale green. Considered the sweetest of all melons. Eaten fresh. Summer.

Source: Roger Phillips/Image Partners 2005/Dorling Kindersley Media Library/ Dorling Kindersley

Some melons soften slightly at the stem end when they are ripe. Others have a smooth stem, showing that the melon ripened on the vine long enough to slip off the vine.

Good-quality melons should be firm and heavy for their size. Check for a sweet aroma.

Rhubarb Although technically not a fruit, rhubarb is often treated as one. Its red celery-like stalks are extremely tart and used primarily in jams and pies with a considerable amount of sweetener.

Tropical and Exotic Fruit Depending on availability, you can often find tropical and exotic fruit at the grocery and at specialty stores.

Rhubarb

Source: David Murray/Image Partners 2005/Dorling Kindersley Media Library/Dorling Kindersley

Tropical Fruit

Source: Roger Phillips/Image Partners 2005/Dorling Kindersley Media Library/Dorling Kindersley

Red bananas

Cavendish bananas

Source: Culinary Institute of America

Plantains

Source: Richard Embery/Pearson Education/PH College

Banana

Creamy white, soft flesh with sweet flavor. Varieties include yellow Cavendish, red bananas (shorter and typically sweeter than Cavendish), and baby or finger bananas. May be eaten fresh or used for baked goods. Plantains are related to bananas with starchy flesh that may be fried, boiled, or mashed. Year-round.

Date

Very sweet, sticky flesh with a thin, waxy skin and a long seed. May be eaten fresh or dried. Year-round.

Source: Dave King/Image Partners 2005/Dorling Kindersley Media Library/Dorling Kindersley

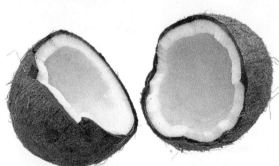

Coconut

Brilliant white flesh, rich and sweet, and somewhat starchy, surrounded by a hard brown shell. May be eaten fresh or used for baked goods and confections or in stews and curries. Often dried, canned as milk or cream, or frozen. Year-round.

Source: Dave King/Image Partners 2005/Dorling Kindersley Media Library/Dorling Kindersley

Fig

Sweet, soft flesh that may be pink, red, or amber, with many tiny seeds and purple, green, or brown skin. May be eaten fresh, poached, or used in baked goods. Often dried. Late spring through winter.

Source: Matthew Ward/Image Partners 2005/Dorling Kindersley Media Library/Dorling Kindersley

Tropical Fruit

Guava

Sweet, fragrant flesh that can be pale yellow to bright red with small edible seeds. The thick skin of the guava (GWAH-vah) ranges in color from yellow to deep purple. May be eaten fresh or puréed for juice or concentrate. Midsummer through winter.

Source: Barnabas Kindersley/Image Partners 2005/ Dorling Kindersley Media Library/Dorling Kindersley

Kiwi

Bright green, juicy flesh with a white core surrounded by minuscule black seeds and thin, brown, fuzzy skin. Eaten fresh. Year-round.

Source: Roger Phillips/Image Partners 2005/Dorling Kindersley Media Library/Dorling Kindersley

Mango

Deep yellow, sweet flesh that is aromatic with a large flat seed in the middle of the fruit and skins ranging from red to green. May be eaten fresh, poached, or canned. Year-round.

Source: Dorling Kindersley/Image Partners 2005/ Dorling Kindersley Media Library/Dorling Kindersley

Papaya

Juicy, sweet-tart, orange flesh with a core of glossy, dark gray edible seeds that have a peppery flavor. The papaya (puh-PI-yuh) is a pear-shaped fruit with yellowish-green skin. May be eaten fresh, poached, or used to make purées. Year-round.

Source: Dorling Kindersley/Image Partners 2005/Dorling Kindersley Media Library/Dorling Kindersley

Passion Fruit

Very fragrant, with tart, golden flesh and tiny edible black seeds with a tough red skin or shell that dimples when the fruit is ripe. Eaten fresh or used to make purées or concentrates. Early winter months.

Source: Ian O'Leary/PM, Getty Active, PS/Dorling Kindersley Media Library/Dorling Kindersley

Persimmon

Soft, creamy, orange-red flesh with a slightly tangy sweetness. The persimmon (puhr-SIM-muhn) has red-orange, smooth skin. May be eaten fresh, poached, or used in baked goods or jams. Late fall through early spring.

Source: Ian O'Leary/Image Partners 2005/Dorling Kindersley Media Library/Dorling Kindersley

Star Fruit

Translucent, juicy, golden flesh when ripe, with a sweet-tart flavor; dark, edible seeds; and a thin, waxy, edible skin that turns golden or yellow when ripe. Eaten fresh. Summer into early winter.

Source: Roger Phillips/Image Partners 2005/ Dorling Kindersley Media Library/ Dorling Kindersley

Pomegranate

Crunchy translucent red seeds surrounded by deep red, sweet, jellylike pulp. The pomegranate (POM-uh-gran-uht) has deep red, tough skin. Pockets of seeds are held in place by inedible white pith. May be eaten fresh or used for juice. Spring through early winter.

Source: Dave King/Image Partners 2005/Dorling Kindersley Media Library/Dorling Kindersley

Pineapple

Sweet-tart, extremely juicy, fibrous flesh with tough diamond-patterned skin and swordlike leaves. Fragrant and yielding when ripe. May be eaten fresh, poached, or grilled, or used in baked goods. Often canned. Year-round.

Source: Andy Crawford/PM, Getty Active, PS/mage Partners 2005/Dorling Kindersley Media Library/ Dorling Kindersley

Selecting and Storing Fruit

Fresh fruit can be purchased ripe or unripe, depending on how and when it will be used. It may be grown locally or be shipped from other parts of the world. Fruit is also available in a variety of forms.

Market Forms of Fruit Fruit is sold in a variety of forms. You can buy whole fresh fruit as individual pieces (a single lemon) or bunches (grapes or bananas). Fruit is also sold in containers of varying sizes and shapes: pint or quart baskets, pecks (one-quarter of a bushel), cartons, boxes, and crates.

The quality of most fruit is directly related to its growing season. A peach purchased in the dead of winter can't match the flavor, color, texture, aroma, and nutritional value of a peach you buy in the summer, at the peak of its growing season. Most fruit has a relatively short growing season, and some fruit is perishable, lasting only a few days even under ideal storage conditions.

Fresh fruit may also be processed before it is sold. Some examples are stemmed strawberries, sliced or cubed melon, or citrus segments.

Dried fruit has an extremely long shelf life and still contains most of the flavor and sweetness of the fresh form. Raisins (dried grapes), prunes (dried plums), dates, and figs are just some of the fruit sold in a dried form. Dried fruit may be sweetened to produce candied or crystallized fruit.

Frozen fruit may be **individually quick-frozen (IQF)**, which means that the fruit is frozen whole or in slices or chunks, without any added sugar or syrup. Frozen fruit is also sold as a purée (sweetened or unsweetened) or as a paste. Some frozen fruit is packed in syrup.

Canned fruit options include fruit cocktails (a combination of fruit that has been peeled, sliced or cut, cooked in syrup, and canned), whole or sliced fruit packed in syrup or juice, and fruit fillings, purées, and pastes.

The Ripening Process Chefs need to understand how fruit grows and ripens. This information helps them select and store fruit so that it is as delicious and nutritious as possible, and also to assure that as little fruit as possible is lost to spoilage.

Fruit that is left to grow on the vine, tree, or bush until it has reached its full size has reached **maturation**. A fully mature fruit has not necessarily finished ripening, however. **Ripening** means that the fruit has developed the brightest color and deepest flavor, sweetness, and aroma. That's why people sniff fresh melons and peaches. Some fruit also softens and gets juicier as it ripens. That's why people squeeze plums or apricots.

Chef's Tip

Quick-Freeze Berries

To freeze fresh berries or grapes, place them in a single layer on a sheet tray and freeze, uncovered, until solid. Then transfer to freezer containers.

The Vatel Society

Chefs, cooks, and other foodservice professionals around the world have formed organizations honoring François Vatel (FRAN-swah vah-TEL), the 17th-century chef to the Prince of Condé (con-DEH) in Chantilly, France.

In April 1671, the Prince of Condé was to have a three-day visit from the Sun King (Louis XIV). Etiquette demanded that the king and his followers should receive the finest hospitality, which would cost a huge amount of money. But the prince was bankrupt!

Vatel understood how crucial this visit was. He believed that if he managed the visit well, the prince might yet emerge from his financial troubles. So Vatel negotiated with the suppliers for ingredients and planned wonderful banquets and entertainment.

According to letters written at the time, the king was completely charmed. But there were a few problems. A fireworks display failed. There were not enough roasts for every table, so Vatel supplemented the meat with mushrooms. When there were problems with a custard sauce planned for dessert, Vatel substituted whipped cream. The cream was so popular, it became known as *Chantilly cream* and still is served to this day.

Vatel planned a final banquet that featured fish. On the morning of the banquet, he woke at four o'clock to discover that only two small deliveries of fish had been made. Vatel believed that his honor, and the honor of his prince, had been damaged beyond repair. He was found dead a few hours later when a servant came to tell him the rest of the fish had arrived.

Research

Research the history of François Vatel. How could Vatel's problem with his fish supplier have been corrected?

Source: Culinary Institute of America

Chantilly cream being applied to a cake

Depending on the type of fruit and the way it is to be processed, some fruit must ripen before being picked, such as apples and peaches. Other fruit is picked after maturing but before ripening. Bananas are a good example of a fruit that is picked mature but while it is still green. Kept at room temperature, bananas ripen to a golden yellow.

Fruit ripens because of a gas it gives off, known as **ethylene** (EH-thih-leen). Once the ethylene has ripened the fruit, it continues to affect the fruit. Ripe fruit continues to change and eventually becomes too soft and overripe. If left to ripen for too long, it will eventually turn rotten.

Chef's Tip

Ripening in a Brown Paper Bag

Place the unripe fruit in a paper bag, along with an apple or a banana. Twist the bag shut and keep at room temperature just until the fruit begins to soften.

FIGURE 12–2

Ripening Process
Bananas are green when picked and yellow when they ripen, and they begin to turn black as they overripen.

CLASSIFYING *Overripe bananas are most typically used for banana bread. Can you guess why?*

Source: Pearson Education

Grading Fruit After produce is harvested, it is graded by the USDA's Agricultural Marketing Service (AMS). Fresh fruit is judged on its size, shape, weight, and color and the presence or absence of defects such as splits in the skin. Fresh fruit is given the following grades:

- **U.S. Fancy.** Premium-quality produce.
- **U.S. No. 1.** Good-quality produce that is not quite as perfect as Fancy grade.
- **U.S. No. 2.** Medium-quality produce.
- **U.S. No. 3.** Standard-quality produce.

The grade of the fruit does not necessarily tell you anything about the fruit's flavor. U.S. No. 2 or 3 fruit does not look as nice as U.S. Fancy, but if you are planning to cut up the fruit to make a pie or a sauce, its appearance doesn't matter as much as its flavor. However, a dessert that features a whole pear or peach may demand the higher grades of either Fancy or No. 1.

Frozen fruit may receive slightly different grades:

- **U.S. Grade A.** Equivalent to U.S. Fancy for fresh produce.
- **U.S. Grade B.** Above-average quality (also known as *Choice*).
- **U.S. Grade C.** Medium quality (also known as *Standard*).

For more information on individual produce, go to the USDA Quality Standards website.

Storing Fruit You need to take the proper steps to preserve the ideal quality of your fruit for as long as possible.

Most fruit is stored under refrigeration. This slows down the ripening process slightly. Be sure that any produce is kept dry. Some fruit, especially apples and pears, gives off generous amounts of ethylene. Store apples and pears away from other fruit, because the ethylene can cause the other fruit to rot.

Some fruit can pick up odors from other foods. Other fruit produces strong odors that can affect foods stored nearby, especially dairy products. Try to keep fruit separated from other perishable goods, when possible.

Store frozen fruit in the freezer until you are ready to use it. Keep canned and dried fruit in the dry storage area of the kitchen. Once you open the packaging for dried fruit, close it tightly or transfer the fruit to a container with a tight-fitting lid to keep it from becoming overdry and also to keep bugs away.

READING CHECKPOINT *What happens to fruit when it ripens?*

Preparing Fruit

Whenever you are working with fresh fruit that is not going to be cooked before you serve it to your guests, remember to wear gloves. Cleaning is always the first step in preparing fruit. Once you have cleaned the fruit, you can perform other steps as needed and in the order that makes the most sense. For instance, you may peel a pineapple before you core it, but it may be easier to remove the pit from a mango before you cut away the skin.

Cleaning Even though fruit is not a potentially hazardous food, the skin can carry a number of pathogens. In addition, fruit is exposed to chemicals, dirt, animals, and pests while growing and while being prepared for sale. That makes cleaning fruit properly very important.

Use cold water and a gentle touch to avoid bruising fruit while handling it. Fruit with a heavy rind may need more vigorous cleaning; use a brush to scrub away any residue on the skin. Delicate fruit, such as raspberries, should be delicately rinsed at the last possible moment to be sure that the fruit doesn't become waterlogged.

Peeling, Seeding, and Trimming Some fruit has inedible skin or rind. Pull off the peel if it separates easily from the fruit, such as with bananas or oranges. Preparing fruit often involves removing skins, cores, seeds, stones, and stems.

- **Removing skins.** Use a peeler or paring knife to cut away the skins of apples or pears that have been treated with wax, skins that are too fuzzy or hairy to eat fresh (kiwi), or skins of fruit that you intend to cook. To remove heavy rinds from melons or pineapples, use a chef's knife. Cut between the rind and the flesh, making sure to leave as little flesh on the rind as you can. Pineapples have small "eyes" that should be cut completely away before cutting the fruit into pieces.
- **Removing cores.** To remove apple or pear cores, cut the fruit in half from the stem to the blossom end and use a melon baller to scoop out the core.
- **Removing seeds and stones.** To remove seeds from melons, cut the fruit in half and scoop out the seeds and membranes with

FOCUS ON Safety

Fruit and Cross-Contamination

It is important to clean fruit before you take it to your workstation to finish preparing it. Cross-contamination from the fruit to the cutting board, your knives, or your hands is a real possibility. Be particularly careful with melons, especially cantaloupe. Scrub the rind with a sanitized brush under running water before cutting.

FOCUS ON Safety

Keeping Fruit from Turning Brown

Some fruit begins to turn brown as soon as it is cut and exposed to air. This is known as *oxidization*. To keep fruit from oxidizing, sprinkle or cover the flesh with *acidulated water* (water to which you've added a little lemon or orange juice). Try using 3 Tbsp of lemon juice to 1 qt of water.

FIGURE 12–3

Peeling Apples

Use a paring knife or peeler to remove skin.

DRAWING CONCLUSIONS *What other parts of an apple can you trim by using a paring knife?*

Source: Culinary Institute of America

Making melon balls

Source: Culinary Institute of America

a serving spoon. Use the tip of a paring knife to remove seeds from citrus fruit. To remove the hard stone from cherries, use a cherry pitter. To pit plums, peaches, and nectarines, use a paring knife to cut around the fruit, through the skin and flesh, and up to the pit. Hold the piece of fruit with both hands and twist the halves in opposite directions.

- **Removing stems.** To remove the stems of strawberries, use the tip of your paring knife. Cut around the stem, angling your knife toward the center of the berry, to remove just the top and the white part around it.

- **Zesting.** The peel on citrus fruit can be grated or cut into thin strips to produce citrus zest. The zest is cut from just the bright colorful part of the peel, however. The white part of the skin (the pith) is bitter and should not be used. Zest is highly aromatic and can be used as a seasoning or as a garnish.

Cutting Fruit for Service Some fruit is cut into wedges, slices, chunks, or cubes for service. Be sure to use a sharp knife so that your cuts are clean. This not only helps the fruit's appearance, it also maintains the fruit's quality because you lose less juice.

One special way of cutting fruit is to make it into small rounds or balls. Use a Parisienne scoop or melon baller. Twist the scoop into the flesh to cut away a ball of the fruit. Make cuts evenly over the surface of the fruit. Cut away the layer of fruit that is left behind to make a clean layer and a second surface to cut into.

Juicing and Puréeing Fresh fruit can be juiced and puréed. Handheld juicers, including a special tool known as a reamer, can be used to juice citrus fruit. To make juice from fruit such as apples or pears, you need to use a juice extractor. A fruit purée is made by putting prepared fruit (peeled, trimmed, or seeded as necessary) into a blender or food processor. If the fruit is soft and juicy, you can make the purée without adding more liquid. If the fruit is hard or low in moisture, you may need to precook it or add more liquid as you purée.

Preparing Dried Fruit Dried fruit can be served as is, without any advance preparation. However, you may need to soften it before you add it to a dish or a baked item. The procedure for softening dried fruit is to put it in a bowl, cover it with a warm or hot liquid, and let it sit until it swells and

Trim Loss

In the food industry, people are concerned about how much usable product you get after you cut up your ingredients. The amount of scraps you produce when cutting something is called *trim*, and the percentage of trim for your whole product is called *trim loss*.

To calculate trim loss, follow these steps:

1. Weigh the initial product.

2. Trim or process your product per recipe instructions.

3. Weigh the trim.

4. Divide the trim weight by the total weight of the product.

5. Convert the number into a percentage.

Source: mareandmare/Fotolia

Example

> Product = 16 oz
>
> Trim = 2 oz
>
> 2 ÷ 16 = 0.125
>
> Converted to percentage: 0.125 × 100 = 12.5%

Computation

1. An apple weighs 6 oz and has a trim weight of 0.5 oz. What is the percentage of trim loss?

2. A watermelon weighs 25 lb and has a trim weight of 6 lb. What is the percentage of trim loss?

3. An average peach weighs 6 oz and has a trim weight of 0.5 oz. Your recipe calls for 40 oz of peach slices for a pie. How many peaches do you need for your pie?

---

softens slightly. Drain the fruit before serving. This process of restoring moisture to dried fruit is called either *plumping* or *rehydrating*.

 **READING CHECKPOINT** *What are the basic tasks involved in preparing fruit for service?*

Cooking Fruit

Fruit can be prepared by a variety of dry-heat and moist-heat methods. Dry-heat methods include grilling or broiling, sautéing, frying, and baking. Moist-heat options include poaching and stewing. Before you start, review your recipe to determine how you should prepare the fruit. Some methods are best for fruit that is fully ripe, and others are better with fruit that is not completely ripe.

- **Sautéing.** Sautéed fruit is typically peeled and cut into pieces, then cooked over medium to high heat in butter. Adding sugar produces a

••**FOCUS ON**
••**Safety**

Using Frozen Fruit

In some recipes, you can use frozen fruit without thawing. When you do need to thaw frozen fruit before using it, remember to follow safe food-handling procedures for thawing, as described in Section 1.2.

Recipe Card

55. Fruit Coulis

rich glaze on sautéed fruit. Bananas, pineapples, peaches, and plums are all good options. Sautéed fruit may be served on its own or as a filling for crepes, a topping for pancakes, or a kind of sauce for ice cream.

- **Frying.** Pieces of fruit can be coated in batter and then fried to make **fritters**. Instead of batter, you may apply a coating of cake crumbs, chopped nuts, or shredded coconut.

- **Baking.** Fruit can be baked in a number of different ways. A baked apple, for instance, may be simply cored and then baked until tender. To add more flavor, you can fill fruit before baking; chopped nuts and dried fruit are common options. Another way to make baked fruit more interesting is to top with a sauce or with whipped cream.

- **Poaching.** Poached fruit is cooked in a liquid, usually with some sugar and other flavorings until it is tender. The fruit should still hold its shape. You can serve poached fruit hot or cold, accompanied by the poaching liquid or not. Poaching can be the first step in preparing fruit to use as filling for pies or tarts.

- **Stewing.** Though similar to poaching, stewed fruit is often served with its cooking liquid. An example of a stewed fruit dish is a **compote**, which is made by slow-cooking fresh or dried fruit.

BASIC CULINARY SKILLS

Poaching Fruit

① **Prepare the fruit** by trimming, peeling, and cutting as necessary.

② **Simmer the liquid,** along with any flavoring ingredients called for in your recipe.

④ **Simmer** over low to moderate heat. Allow the liquid to come up to a simmer temperature of 170°F.

Source: David Murray/DK Images

Source: David Murray/Image Partners 2005/Dorling Kindersley Media Library/Dorling Kindersley

⑤ **Poach** the fruit until tender and flavorful.

⑥ **Cool** the fruit in the cooking liquid, drain, and serve or store.

③ **Place the fruit into the liquid.** Add more liquid, if necessary, to barely cover the fruit.

Recipe Card

56. Poached Pears

Puréeing Fruit

1. **Prepare the fruit** as necessary.

2. **Poach the fruit,** if your recipe says to do so, with sweeteners and flavorings, until it is very tender.

3. **Purée** using the appropriate tool (blender, food processor, or sieve) to the desired consistency and adjust the flavoring.

4. **Serve or store** the purée.

Recipe Card

57. Applesauce

Source: Dave King/Image Partners 2005/Dorling Kindersley Media Library/Dorling Kindersley

- **Puréeing cooked fruit.** Fruit purées can be made from poached or stewed fruit. Use a food processor or blender to make a smooth and light purée. Use a food mill for a more textured consistency. For the smoothest, most delicate texture, strain the purée through a fine-mesh sieve. Fruit purées are used as a sauce or as an ingredient in other dishes. Fruit soups are often nothing more complicated than purées that have been thinned with fruit juice or cream.

- **Grilling and broiling.** Fruit to be grilled can be cut into slices, left whole, or threaded on skewers. To protect tender or delicate fruit, you can brush it lightly with a little melted butter. To give fruit a rich glaze, sprinkle it with sugar or brush it with a little honey or maple syrup. Place the fruit directly on the grill. To broil fruit, arrange it on a sheet tray that you've either buttered lightly or lined with parchment. Broil or grill the fruit just until it has a rich aroma and caramel color.

 **READING CHECKPOINT** *What are the moist-heat and dry-heat methods for cooking fruit?*

Chef's Tip

Decorating with Fruit Purées

Put fruit purées of different flavors and colors into squirt bottles and use more than one sauce to decorate a dish.

Recipe Card

58. Broiled Pineapple

Serving Fruit

Fruit plates and salads are a popular way to serve fruit. Other dishes include fruit cocktails, a mixture of fruit served in syrup. Serve these dishes in chilled cups or bowls. Fresh fruit can be served as a garnish with entrées and desserts. Examples include fresh berries on a chocolate cake or a slice of melon with an omelet at breakfast or even sliced peaches on a bowl of cold cereal.

Fruit has the fullest flavor when served at room temperature, so if possible allow it time to lose the chill from the refrigerator by sitting at room temperature for a few minutes.

Fruit is sometimes paired with meats, fish, or poultry. Grapes, raisins, plums, prunes, apricots, and other fruit can be added as a filling or stuffing or added to a sauce. Fruit purées are also featured with savory dishes; cranberry sauce is served with turkey, applesauce with potato pancakes.

One popular fruit offering is a dessert fondue. Bite-size pieces of fresh fruit are dipped into a warm sauce, such as chocolate, caramel, or butterscotch sauce. Fresh fruit coated in a hard chocolate shell is served as a confection.

Chocolate fondue

Source: Simon Smith/Getty Active/Dorling Kindersley Media Library/Dorling Kindersley

READING CHECKPOINT *How might fruit appear on a dinner menu?*

12.1 ASSESSMENT

Reviewing Concepts

1. List the basic parts of a peach.
2. Describe the changes that occur when fruit ripens.
3. What should be the first step of every preparation involving fruit?
4. List the dry-heat methods you can use to cook fruit.
5. How can fruit be presented as an appetizer for dinner?

Critical Thinking

6. **Communication** Oranges are often gassed to produce a vivid orange color. Why do you think this is done?
7. **Drawing Conclusions** Why is fruit generally peeled before poaching?
8. **Classifying** Which fruit might be good for sautéing?

Test Kitchen

Divide into four teams. Each team will poach a different fruit. Prepare a single piece of fruit, of roughly the same size and weight (trim down the fruit if needed). Measure out equal amounts of poaching liquid (such as apple cider). Using the same size pans, place the fruit in the pan, and pour the liquid on top. Set the pan over moderate heat and poach the fruit. Carefully monitor the temperature so it stays at roughly 165°F to 170°F. Predict which will take the longest. Were you right or wrong? Suggest some reasons for the outcome.

LANGUAGE ARTS

Essay Writing

Review this section. Using at least one additional resource, write a one-page essay, about 350 words, discussing the definition of a fruit, the standard anatomy, and how a fruit develops from a flower to maturity.

Vegetables

Key Concepts

- Identifying types of vegetables
- Selecting and storing vegetables
- Preparing vegetables
- Cooking vegetables
- Serving vegetables

Vocabulary

- capsaicin
- heirloom plant
- tomato concassé
- tuber

Types of Vegetables

Vegetables are plants. We eat different parts of plants—from the bottom to the top—including the roots, stems, leaves, flowers, and seeds. Tomatoes and avocados, which are often thought of as vegetables, are technically fruits. However, in a culinary sense, they are used like vegetables, so they are included in this section. Some vegetables are eaten raw; some must be cooked. Vegetables can be served as a main dish or as an accompaniment to other foods, or they can be used as an ingredient in a dish.

Source: Image Source/Alamy

FIGURE 12–4
Avocados
A ripe avocado is firm but yields slightly to gentle pressure.
COMMUNICATING *How have you seen avocados prepared and served?*
Source: Simon Smith/Dorling Kindersley

Chef's Tip

Keeping Avocados Green

The cut surface of an avocado can be treated with lemon or lime juice. This keeps the flesh from turning brown and adds a complementary flavor.

Like fruit, vegetables are versatile, colorful, and available in many varieties. The need to prepare and serve good-tasting vegetables is increasing as more people focus on healthy eating.

Avocados Actually a fruit, avocados are one of the few produce items that contain substantial amounts of fat. The inedible skin can vary in color from brown, in the case of the ripe Hass avocado, to green, in the case of Florida varieties. The flesh is creamy and buttery. Once cut, the flesh begins to turn brown almost instantly. To counteract this, avocados are usually not cut until the last possible moment.

Cabbage Family The cabbage family provides a wide range of vegetables, including cabbages, Brussels sprouts, broccoli, and cauliflower.

Cabbage varieties include red and green cabbage, which should be heavy for their size, with tightly packed leaves. Savoy cabbage and Chinese cabbage (such as Napa cabbage and bok choy) have leaves that are more loosely packed than red or green cabbages.

When choosing vegetables from this family, look for good uniform color, stems that are not split, and leaves that are not dried out.

Gourds The gourd family includes cucumbers, eggplant, and the many varieties of summer squash and winter squash.

- **Summer squash.** Varieties include zucchini, yellow squash, and pattypan squash. Like cucumbers and eggplants, summer squash are picked when immature to take advantage of their tender flesh, seeds, and skins. Typically, all parts of these vegetables may be eaten, but you may opt to remove the seeds and skin if they are tougher than desired. The larger and older these vegetables grow, the thicker and tougher their skins, the dryer their flesh, and the larger their seeds.

- **Winter squash.** Varieties include acorn, butternut, and delicata squash. Their rinds are inedible and their large seeds are removed before serving. The seeds of some winter squash, such as pumpkins, are toasted and eaten like nuts. The flesh of winter squash is usually yellow to orange.

Cooking Greens Besides salad greens, which are discussed in Chapter 10, there are leafy greens that are typically used for cooking (although some, such as spinach, may be included in salads). These include

Cabbage Family

Broccoli

Look for tight flowers, with stem ends that are not split. Steamed or boiled. Summer, but available year-round through imports.

Source: Shebeko/Shutterstock

Bok Choy

Look for stem ends that are firm and fresh, with leaves that are firm and unwithered. Steamed, boiled, and stir-fried. Summer and fall, but available year-round through imports.

Source: Will Heap/Dorling Kindersley Limited

Brussels Sprouts

Look for stem ends that are firm and fresh, with leaves on individual sprouts firmly attached. Steamed or boiled. Late fall to winter, but available year-round from storage and through imports.

Source: Norman Chan/Shutterstock

Cauliflower

Look for white head, with no evidence of yellowing or browning, and tight flowers, with outside leaves firmly attached and unwilted. Steamed or boiled. Late summer to fall, but available year-round from storage and through imports.

Source: Steve Gorton/Image Partners 2005/Dorling Kindersley Media Library/Dorling Kindersley

Green and Red Cabbage

Look for stem ends that are firm and fresh. Outside leaves may be loose but should be firm and unwithered, free from browning or bore holes. Early varieties are less tight; winter or storage cabbages are tighter. May be eaten raw in salads, steamed, braised, or boiled; stuffed and baked, or pickled. Summer and fall, but available year-round from storage or through imports.

Source: Richard Embery/Pearson Education/PH College

Napa Cabbage

Look for stem ends that are firm and fresh. Outside leaves may be loose but should be firm and unwithered, free from browning or bore holes. May be eaten raw in salads, steamed, boiled, or stir-fried. Summer and fall.

Source: Pearson Education/PH College

Savoy Cabbage

Look for stem ends that are firm and fresh. Outside leaves may be loose but should be firm and unwithered, free from browning or bore holes. May be eaten raw in salads, steamed, braised, or boiled; stuffed and baked, or pickled. Summer and fall.

Source: Ian O'Leary/Dorling Kindersley

Gourds

Eggplant

Shiny and firm, with no bruising, softening, brownness. Skin is edible (if not waxed). May be stewed, braised, roasted, grilled, or stuffed and baked. Year-round.

Source: Richard Embery/Pearson Education/PH College

Kirby cucumber

Source: Lorenzo Vecchia/ Dorling Kindersley

Slicing cucumber

Source: Richard Embery/ Pearson Education/PH College

Cucumbers

Dark green, firm skin, with no discoloration. Skin is edible (if not waxed). Kirby cucumbers are used for eating fresh and pickles. Slicing cucumbers are used for salads, pickling, relishes, and uncooked sauces. English cucumbers are used for salads and crudités. Year-round.

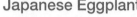

English cucumber

Japanese Eggplant

Shiny and firm, with no brownness. Skin is edible (if not waxed). May be stewed, braised, roasted, grilled, or stuffed and baked. Best in summer, available year-round.

Source: Pearson Education/PH College

Zucchini

Shiny and firm. Typically green, but there are yellow varieties. Skin is edible (if not waxed). May be stewed, braised, roasted, grilled, fried, stir-fried, stuffed and baked, or used in breads and fritters. Best in summer, available year-round.

Source: Philip Dowell/Image Partners 2005/Dorling Kindersley Media Library/Dorling Kindersley

Pattypan Squash

Shiny and firm. Skin is edible (if not waxed). May be steamed, sautéed, or pan-fried. Summer months.

Source: Dave King/Image Partners 2005/Dorling Kindersley Media Library/Dorling Kindersley

Acorn Squash

Firm. Some varieties may have an orange blush or be all orange. Baked, glazed with honey or maple syrup, puréed, simmered, or used in soups. Inedible rind. Best in late fall, available year-round.

Source: Roger Phillips/Image Partners 2005/Dorling Kindersley Media Library/Dorling Kindersley

Baby Yellow Squash

Shiny and firm. May have flower attached (which is edible, if fresh). Skin is edible (if not waxed). May be steamed, sautéed, pan-fried, or breaded and fried. Summer months.

Source: Richard Embery/Pearson Education/PH College

Butternut Squash

Firm. Tan, orange, or brown skin. Inedible rind. May be baked, glazed with honey or maple syrup, puréed, simmered, or used in soups. Best in late fall, available year-round.

Source: Philip Wilkins/Image Partners 2005/Dorling Kindersley Media Library/ Dorling Kindersley

Delicata Squash

Firm. Actually a summer squash, but more similar to a winter squash. Orange flesh. Rind is edible, although it is generally not included as part of a finished dish. Baked, glazed with honey or maple syrup, puréed, simmered, or used in soups. Best in late fall, available year-round.

Source: Alan & Linda Detrick/Photo Researchers, Inc.

Pumpkin

Firm. May be baked, glazed with honey or maple syrup, puréed, simmered or used in soups, pies, and breads. Seeds may be toasted. Inedible rind. Best in late fall, available year-round.

Source: Jo Foord/PM, Getty Active, PS/Dorling Kindersley Media Library/Dorling Kindersley

Cooking Greens

Spinach

Look for dark green, tender leaves; inedible stems. Steamed, sautéed (especially with garlic), served raw in salads. Year-round.

Source: Steve Gorton/Getty Active/Dorling Kindersley Media Library/Dorling Kindersley

Swiss Chard

Look for dark green leaves. Edible stems may be white (Swiss chard), red (ruby chard), or rainbow-colored (rainbow chard). Steamed, sautéed (especially with garlic), braised. Best in midsummer to late fall, available year-round.

Source: David Murray/Image Partners 2005/Dorling Kindersley Media Library/Dorling Kindersley

Turnip Greens

Look for medium-green leaves with ruffled edges. Inedible stems. Steamed, sautéed (especially with garlic), braised. Best in midsummer to late fall, available year-round.

Source: Richard Embery/Pearson Education/PH College

Collard Greens

Look for large, tender, green leaves. Inedible stems. Steamed, sautéed (especially with garlic), braised. Best in fall, available year-round.

Source: Roger Phillips/Image Partners 2005/Dorling Kindersley Media Library/Dorling Kindersley

Kale

Dark green to bluish-green leaves with curly edges. Inedible stems. Steamed, sautéed (especially with garlic), braised; used in soups. Best in midsummer to late fall, available year-round.

Source: Richard Embery/Pearson Education/PH College

Swiss chard, turnip greens, and two leafy members of the cabbage family, collards and kale. Cooking greens are often sautéed, steamed, or braised. Selection criteria and handling practices for cooking greens are similar to those for lettuce.

Mushrooms Mushrooms can vary significantly in size, shape, color, and flavor. For a long time, the only widely available mushrooms were white

Mushrooms

Porcini

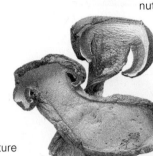

Wild. Smooth, creamy texture, with a nutty, slightly meaty flavor. Raw, cooked, marinated; used in sauces, soups, stews. May be dried. Summer and fall.

Source: Ian O'Leary/Image Partners 2005/Dorling Kindersley Media Library/Dorling Kindersley

Cremini

Commercially grown. Similar texture to button mushrooms, with a slightly more intense flavor. Raw, cooked; used in sauces. Year-round.

Source: Ian O'Leary/Image Partners 2005/Dorling Kindersley Media Library/Dorling Kindersley

Button/White

The most common type of cultivated mushroom. Firm, buttery texture and a pleasant mushroom flavor. Raw or cooked, marinated; used in sauces, soups, and stews. Year-round.

Source: Dorling Kindersley/Image Partners 2005/ Dorling Kindersley Media Library/ Dorling Kindersley

Oyster

Commercially grown. Delicate texture, with a sweet, fruity flavor. Sautéed, sauces. Year-round.

Source: Dorling Kindersley/Image Partners 2005/Dorling Kindersley Media Library/Dorling Kindersley

Chanterelle

Wild. Soft texture, with a fruity, earthy, spicy flavor (depending on variety). Raw, cooked, marinated; used in sauces, soups, stews. May be dried. Fall.

Source: Dorling Kindersley

Morel

Wild. Firm texture, with an intense earthy flavor. Must be thoroughly cooked. Sauces. May be dried. Early spring.

Source: David Murray/Image Partners 2005/Dorling Kindersley Media Library/Dorling Kindersley

Shiitake

Commercially grown. Firm and slightly chewy texture, with a meaty, earthy, smoky flavor. Sautéed, used in sauces. May be dried. Year-round.

Source: Philip Wilkins/Image Partners 2005/Dorling Kindersley Media Library/Dorling Kindersley

Portobello

Commercially grown. Texture that has been compared to fine beef filet mignon. Rich, robust mushroom flavor. Sautéed or grilled. Year-round.

Source: Richard Embery/Pearson Education/PH College

Truffle

Wild. Firm, meaty texture, very fragrant, with a pungent, meaty flavor. Expensive. Raw, sautéed; used in sauces, as flavoring for oil. Two varieties, black (fall) and white (spring and summer).

Source: Roger Phillips/Image Partners 2005/Dorling Kindersley Media Library/Dorling Kindersley

mushrooms (also sold as *button mushrooms* or *Parisian mushrooms*). Today, more varieties are being successfully farmed, which means many so-called wild varieties are actually farm-raised.

Cultivated mushroom varieties include white mushrooms, portobello, cremini (kray-MEE-nee), shiitake (shee-TAH-kay), and oyster mushrooms.

Wild mushroom varieties include porcini (pohr-CHEE-nee), chanterelles (shan-tuh-REHLS), morels (muh-REHLS), truffles, and many other varieties.

Select mushrooms that are firm, without soft spots, blemishes, or breaks in the cap or stem. Keep mushrooms under refrigeration. Cover with lightly dampened paper towels, not plastic wrap, to keep them fresher longer. Keep mushrooms as dry as possible until ready to cook.

Onions The onion family includes garlic, shallots, and two main categories of onions: green (fresh) and dry (cured).

- **Green onions.** Scallions and leeks are green onions. They have a tender white bulb. In some varieties, the green portion of the onion is edible (scallions, for instance), while in others it is discarded (leeks). Chives are also a type of green onion, although their main culinary application is as a fresh herb. The outer layers of green onions should be firm and not overly dry or torn. The roots should be firm and flexible. Rinse well and dry thoroughly immediately before cooking.

- **Dry onions.** These range in size from tiny pearl onions to large red or yellow onions. They have juicy flesh covered with layers of dry, papery skin that may be white, yellow, or red. Select dry onions, garlic, and shallots that are heavy for their size and have tight-fitting skins.

Peppers Look for firm peppers and chiles that feel slightly heavy for their size. The skin should be tight and glossy, with no puckering or wrinkling. The flesh should be relatively thick and crisp.

There are two basic types of peppers: sweet peppers and chiles.

- **Sweet peppers.** Sometimes called *bell peppers* because of their shape, all sweet peppers start out green, but some varieties ripen into other colors—green, red, and yellow being the most common. Sweet peppers of various colors have similar flavors, though red and yellow varieties tend to be sweeter.

Source: cloki/Shutterstock

Green pepper

Source: Givaga/Shutterstock

Yellow pepper

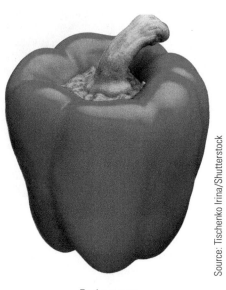

Source: Tischenko Irina/Shutterstock

Red pepper

Source: Culinary Institute of America

Orange pepper

Chapter 12 *Fruit and Vegetables*

Onion Family

Garlic

Avoid heads that are soft or cloves with green sprouts. Used as a flavoring ingredient. May be roasted into a purée. Year-round.

Source: Ian O'Leary/Image Partners 2005/Dorling Kindersley Media Library/Dorling Kindersley

Leek

Use white and light-green parts only. Used as main ingredient or flavoring. Grilled, steamed, braised; in soups, stews, sauces. Best in midsummer and fall; year-round.

Source: Pearson Education/PH College

White Onion

More pungent than red onion. Used as an aromatic or flavoring ingredient. Soups, stews. Year-round.

Source: Richard Embery/Pearson Education/PH College

Scallion

Also called *green onions*. Use entire plant, except roots. Raw as crudités, salads, uncooked sauces. Year-round.

Source: Richard Embery/Pearson Education/PH College

Red Onion

Flesh is red and white. Served raw in salads, grilled; used in sauces or as an aromatic or flavoring ingredient. Year-round.

Yellow Onion

More pungent than red onion. Used as an aromatic or flavoring ingredient. Soups, stews. Year-round.

Source: Richard Embery/Pearson Education/PH College

Pearl Onions

May be red or white. Boiled, pickled, brined. Often served in stews and braises. Year-round.

Shallots

More delicate flavor than onions. Flesh is white or lightly purple. Raw in salad dressings; used as an aromatic or flavoring ingredient. Year-round.

- **Chiles.** These are grown in various sizes, colors, and levels of spice or heat. **Capsaicin** (cap-SAY-ih-sin) is the compound that gives a chile its heat, and it is most potent on the white ribs inside the pepper. Generally, smaller chiles are hotter. In addition, you may work with canned, dried (whole, flaked, and ground), or smoked chiles. Some popular chile varieties, from mild to hot, are Anaheim, poblano, jalapeño, cayenne, Scotch bonnet, and habanero.

·:FOCUS ON
·· Safety

Beware of Heat!

Some chiles are extremely hot. The Scoville scale measures the heat units of a chile, based on how much capsaicin the chile contains. A sweet bell pepper, which has no capsaicin, has a zero rating. A habanero can rate as high as 350,000 units. Other chile ratings are Scotch bonnet, 325,000 units; cayenne, 50,000 units; jalapeño, 8,000 units; Anaheim, 2,500 units; poblano, 2,000 units.

Chiles

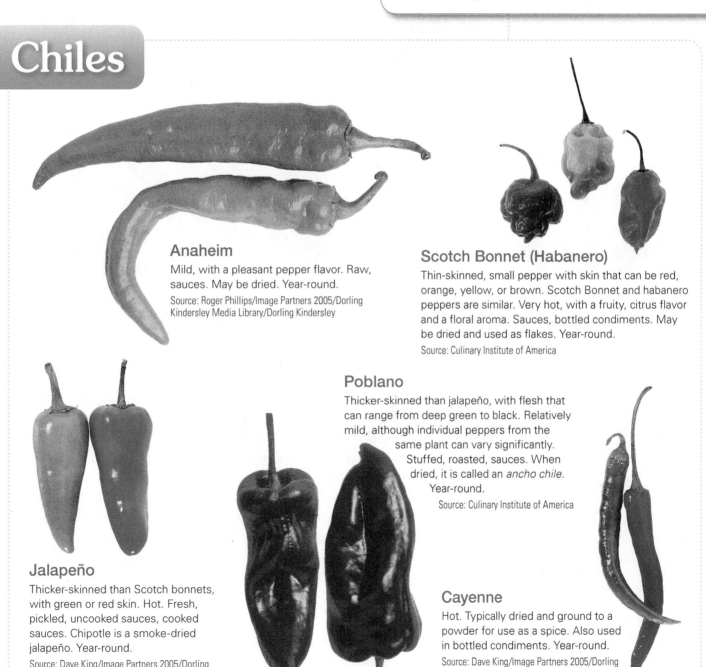

Anaheim
Mild, with a pleasant pepper flavor. Raw, sauces. May be dried. Year-round.

Source: Roger Phillips/Image Partners 2005/Dorling Kindersley Media Library/Dorling Kindersley

Scotch Bonnet (Habanero)
Thin-skinned, small pepper with skin that can be red, orange, yellow, or brown. Scotch Bonnet and habanero peppers are similar. Very hot, with a fruity, citrus flavor and a floral aroma. Sauces, bottled condiments. May be dried and used as flakes. Year-round.

Source: Culinary Institute of America

Poblano
Thicker-skinned than jalapeño, with flesh that can range from deep green to black. Relatively mild, although individual peppers from the same plant can vary significantly. Stuffed, roasted, sauces. When dried, it is called an *ancho chile*. Year-round.

Source: Culinary Institute of America

Jalapeño
Thicker-skinned than Scotch bonnets, with green or red skin. Hot. Fresh, pickled, uncooked sauces, cooked sauces. Chipotle is a smoke-dried jalapeño. Year-round.

Source: Dave King/Image Partners 2005/Dorling Kindersley Media Library/Dorling Kindersley

Cayenne
Hot. Typically dried and ground to a powder for use as a spice. Also used in bottled condiments. Year-round.

Source: Dave King/Image Partners 2005/Dorling Kindersley Media Library/Dorling Kindersley

Pods and Seeds

Wax Beans

Edible pod. Thinner skin, more subtle flavor than green bean. May be eaten raw, steamed, boiled, sautéed, baked, in soups or stir fries. May be pickled or frozen. Mid- to late summer.

Source: Dorling Kindersley/Image Partners 2005/Dorling Kindersley Media Library/Dorling Kindersley

Green Beans

Edible pod. Fresh, sweet flavor. May be eaten raw, steamed, boiled, sautéed, baked, in soups or stir fried. May be pickled or frozen. Mid- to late summer.

Source: Roger Phillips/Image Partners 2005/ Dorling Kindersley Media Library/ Dorling Kindersley

Bean Sprouts

Germinated beans that have begun to grow. Fresh, vegetal flavor. May be eaten raw, boiled, or stir-fried. Year-round.

Source: Andy Crawford/Getty Active/ Dorling Kindersley Media Library/Dorling Kindersley

Snow Peas

Edible pod. Crisp, with a sweet, fresh flavor. May be eaten raw, stir-fried, steamed, sautéed, boiled. May be frozen. Early spring to summer.

Source: Richard Embery/Pearson Education/PH College

Haricots Verts

Edible pod. Longer, thinner, and more tender than green beans, with a more complex flavor. May be steamed, boiled, sautéed, stir-fried. May be frozen. Mid- to late summer.

Source: Roger Philips/Image Partners 2005/ Dorling Kindersley Media Library/Dorling Kindersley

•••FOCUS ON •••Safety

Handling Chiles

Take appropriate precautions when handling chiles. Wear gloves while cutting chiles. Wash cutting surfaces and knives (including handles) immediately after you finish cutting chiles. Wash your hands well with soap and water. Avoid touching your eyes, lips, or other sensitive areas.

Pods and Seeds Pod and seed vegetables include peas, beans, and bean sprouts, as well as corn and okra. All varieties are best eaten young, when they are at their sweetest and most tender. Once picked, the natural sugars in the vegetable start to convert into starch. Many varieties of peas, beans, and corn are sold in their dried form as well, as discussed in Chapter 13.

Select fresh beans and pea pods with firm and crisp texture, bright color, and no wilting or puckering. Corn husks should be green and adhere tightly to the ear; the silk should be brown to black, but quite dry.

Some beans and peas have edible pods; some do not.

- **Edible pods.** Sugar snap peas, snow peas, green beans, and wax beans all have edible pods. The same is true for the French green bean, haricots verts (ar-ree-koh VEHR), and the Chinese long bean. They are all picked when the pod is still fleshy and tender enough to eat.

- **Inedible pods.** Green peas, fava (FAH-vah) beans, and lima beans are removed from their inedible pods before eating.

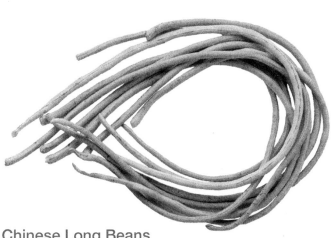

Chinese Long Beans

Edible pod. Similar to a green bean in flavor, but with a heartier, chewy texture. Stir-fried, sautéed. Mid- to late summer.

Source: Clive Streeter and Patrick McLeavy/Image Partners 2005/Dorling Kindersley Media Library/Dorling Kindersley

Sugar Snap Peas

Edible pod. Crisp texture, with a very sweet flavor. May be eaten raw, steamed, boiled, stir fried. Early spring to summer.

Source: Dorling Kindersley/Image Partners 2005/ Dorling Kindersley Media Library/Dorling Kindersley

Lima Beans

Inedible pod. Starchy, buttery texture, with a delicate, buttery flavor. Boiled, baked, steamed, puréed or used in soups. May be dried or frozen. Mid- to late summer.

Source: Roger Phillips/Image Partners 2005/Dorling Kindersley Media Library/Dorling Kindersley

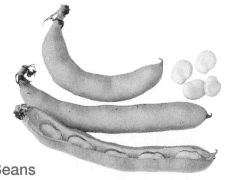

Green Peas

Inedible pod. Tender, with a fresh, sweet flavor. May be eaten raw, steamed, sautéed, boiled, stir-fried, or used in soups, stews. May be frozen or dried. Early spring to summer. Can be frozen or dried.

Source: Dorling Kindersley/Image Partners 2005/ Dorling Kindersley Media Library/Dorling Kindersley

Okra

Edible pod. Crisp texture, but slimy when cut. Delicate flavor. May be eaten raw, stir fried, sautéed, stewed, or used in soups. May be pickled or frozen. Summer to fall.

Source: Dorling Kindersley

Fava Beans

Inedible pod. Buttery texture, with a nutty, slightly bitter flavor. Steamed or used in soups, stews, purées. May be dried. Summer.

Source: Philip Wilkins/Image Partners 2005/Dorling Kindersley Media Library/Dorling Kindersley

Root Vegetables Root vegetables grow underground. They serve as nutrient and moisture reservoirs for the tops of the plant. They are rich in sugars, starches, vitamins, and minerals. Popular root vegetables include beets, carrots, parsnips, radishes, and turnips. Roots you may not be familiar with include celeriac (seh-LER-ee-AK), which tastes like celery, and the large Asian daikon (DI-kon) radish.

If root vegetables arrive in the kitchen with their green leafy tops still attached, check for a good color and texture in the leaves. The root end of the vegetable should be firm and dry. Root vegetables must be peeled before being eaten.

Shoots and Stalks Artichokes, asparagus, celery, fennel, and fiddleheads are examples of shoot and stalk vegetables. Fiddleheads are part of an edible fern.

Beets

Smooth, firm flesh that is red or golden, with a sweet, tangy flavor when cooked. Steamed, boiled; used in salads, soups. May be pickled or canned. Summer and fall.

Source: Richard Embery/Pearson Education/PH College

Turnip

Smooth, firm, flesh; usually white, but can be orange, yellow, or red, with a delicate, slightly cabbage flavor when cooked. Steamed, sautéed, baked, puréed; used in soups, stews. Late fall through winter (from storage).

Source: Dorling Kindersley/PM, Image Partners 2005 Active/Image Partners 2005/Dorling Kindersley Media Library/Dorling Kindersley

Daikon Radish

Firm white flesh, with a mild radish flavor. May be eaten raw, boiled, stir-fried; used in stews. May be pickled. Late summer and early fall, but available year-round from storage.

Source: Ian O'Leary/Image Partners 2005/Dorling Kindersley Media Library/Dorling Kindersley

Celeriac

Firm white flesh, with celery flavor. May be eaten raw, stewed, baked; used in soups. Fall and winter.

Source: David Murray/Image Partners 2005/Dorling Kindersley Media Library/ Dorling Kindersley

Parsnips

Similar to carrots, but paler, with a sweet, buttery, slightly spicy flavor when cooked. Boiled, baked; used in soups, stews. Fall to winter.

Source: Roger Phillips/Dorling Kindersley Limited

Carrots

Crisp, smooth texture. Flesh can be orange, yellow, red, purple, or white. Sweet flavor. May be eaten raw, stir-fried, steamed, sautéed, boiled; used in soups, stews, purées, juices, or baked goods and desserts. May be frozen. Year-round.

Source: Steve Shott/Image Partners 2005/Dorling Kindersley Media Library/Dorling Kindersley

Shoots and Stalks

Artichoke

The heart has a soft texture when cooked, with a nutty flavor. Steamed, boiled, sautéed, stewed. May be frozen. Year-round.

Source: Richard Embery/Pearson Education/PH College

Fennel

Crisp white-green flesh, with a strong anise flavor. Raw, sautéed, stewed, braised. Firm white flesh, with celery flavor. May be eaten raw, braised, or used in soups and stews. Year-round.

Source: Philip Dowell/Image Partners 2005/ Dorling Kindersley Media Library/Dorling Kindersley

Asparagus

Crisp, with delicate flavor. Raw, steamed, boiled, sautéed, stir-fried; used in soups and stews. Year-round. Can be frozen.

Source: Richard Embery/Pearson Education/PH College

Celery

Crisp. Unique taste. May be eaten raw, sautéed, stir-fried. Used in soups, stews, and sauces as a flavoring ingredient. Year-round.

Source: Dave King/Image Partners 2005/Dorling Kindersley Media Library/Dorling Kindersley

Fiddlehead Ferns

Soft when cooked, with a mild, nutty flavor a bit like asparagus. Steamed, boiled. Spring.

Source: Culinary Institute of America

Artichokes are green bulbs composed of many layers of leaves surrounding a mass of hairlike tendrils, called the *choke*. The heart of the artichoke is the part attached to the stem. Only the lower part of the leaves and the heart are eaten. Artichokes are actually undeveloped flowers. If left on the stalk, they bloom into beautiful, giant, purple flowers.

Asparagus is a member of the lily family. Look for firm, fleshy, full stalks, with no browning or wilting. The stalks should bend slightly; the small buds on the tip should be firmly closed.

Tomatoes Tomatoes are actually fruit and are grown in hundreds of varieties, varying in size, color, shape, flavor, and texture. All have juicy flesh, edible seeds, and smooth, shiny skin. Tomatoes grown commercially are picked unripe and allowed to ripen in transit, but most chefs prefer to find

Chef's Tip

White Asparagus

Look for white asparagus in the market. The stalks are thicker and the taste is milder than green asparagus. White asparagus is shielded from sunlight as it grows, so it does not develop the chlorophyll to turn it green.

Tomatoes

Beefsteak Tomato
Large and juicy. Slicing tomatoes. Fresh in salads and sandwiches. Late summer.

Plum Tomato
Relatively greater proportion of flesh. Used for sauces, purées, soups, and other cooked dishes. Late summer.

Pear Tomato
Yellow versions are low in acid. Fresh, salads, crudité platters. Mid- to late summer.

Tomatillo

Tomatillos (tohm-ah-TEE-ohs) are typically used in sauces and other cooked dishes. Tomatillos, which are green even when ripe, have a papery skin that is removed before use. Mid- to late summer.

Source: Richard Embery/Pearson Education/PH College

Source: Richard Embery/Pearson Education/PH College

Cherry Tomato
Yellow versions are low in acid. Fresh, salads, crudité platters. Can be added to pasta. Mid- to late summer.

locally grown vine-ripened varieties because of their rich flavor and juiciness.

Gaining popularity in the market these days are heirloom tomatoes. An **heirloom plant** (it can be a fruit or vegetable) is a variety that is grown from original seeds, before hybridized variations were developed to grow faster, extend shelf life, or extend the growing season. Most heirloom tomatoes are unique in look and flavor. Grown from heirloom seeds that have been saved by farmers who want to grow these original varieties, heirloom tomatoes are typically tender, sweet, and juicy.

FIGURE 12–5
Heirloom Tomatoes
Heirloom tomatoes come in all shapes, sizes, and colors.

PREDICTING *What might the benefits be of serving heirloom tomatoes?*

Source: Ted Stefanski/Cephas Picture Library/Alamy

Tubers A tuber (TOO-ber) is a fleshy portion of certain plants that usually grows underground. Potatoes are the most common type of tuber. Select tubers that are firm and the appropriate size and shape for their type. Most tubers fall into one of the following three categories:

- **High-starch/low-moisture potatoes.** This category includes rus-set potatoes (also called *Idaho*), which are used for baking. They are granular and dry after cooking, and they are preferred for baking, puréeing, and mashing. They are also excellent for frying because the low moisture content makes them less likely to splatter or absorb grease. Their natural tendency to absorb moisture makes them a good choice for scalloped or other casserole-style potato dishes.

- **Low-starch/high-moisture potatoes.** This category includes red-skinned potatoes, yellow potatoes (such as Yellow Finn and Yukon gold), all-purpose potatoes, boiling potatoes, and heirloom variet-ies such as purple potatoes and fingerlings. They are referred to as *waxy*, because they hold their shape even after they are cooked until tender. They are a good choice for boiling, steaming, sauté-ing, oven roasting, and braising or stewing, as well as in salads and soups. *New potatoes* (any potato that is harvested when less than 1½ inches in diameter) are also high in moisture. Their naturally sweet, fresh flavor is best showcased by simple techniques such as boiling, steaming, or oven roasting.

- **Yams and sweet potatoes.** Both varieties of tuber are similar and often confused with one another, but they are actually different plant species. Sweet potatoes have tapered ends, deep orange flesh, dense texture, sweet flavor, and thin, smooth skins. Use the same cooking techniques suggested for low-starch/high-moisture potatoes. True yams are starchier, drier, and less sweet than sweet potatoes. They have rough, scaly skin and are somewhat blocky in shape, with pale to deep yellow flesh. Use the same cooking techniques suggested for high-starch/low-moisture potatoes.

 **READING CHECKLIST** *How are roots and tubers different from all other vegetables?*

Chef's Tip

Potato Test

Check the starch content of different types of potatoes by preparing a brine (11 parts water to 1 part salt, by weight) and then placing the potatoes in the brine. Those that float contain less starch. Those that sink contain more starch.

Selecting and Storing Vegetables

Fresh vegetables are ready to eat or cook when purchased, with the excep-tion of avocados or tomatoes, which may need to ripen at room temperature. Vegetables must be selected and stored with care to ensure the best flavor and freshness. They are available in a variety of forms.

Market Forms Fresh vegetables are sold by weight and count, as well as in boxes, crates, and bags. Some fresh vegetables are peeled, trimmed, and cut before they are packaged and sold. In addition to fresh vegetables, you

Tubers

Yam

Starchier, dryer, and less sweet than sweet potatoes. Used for baking, puréeing, mashing, and frying, and in casseroles. Year-round.

Source: Philip Dowell/Image Partners 2005/Dorling Kindersley Media Library/Dorling Kindersley

Sweet Potato

Dense texture, sweeter than yams. Used for baking, puréeing, mashing, and frying, and in casseroles. Year-round.

Source: Dorling Kindersley/Image Partners 2005/Dorling Kindersley Media Library/Dorling Kindersley

Russet Potato

High starch/low moisture. Used for baking, mashing, and frying, and in casseroles. Year-round.

Source: Dorling Kindersley/Image Partners 2005/Dorling Kindersley Media Library/Dorling Kindersley

Red Potato

Low starch/high moisture. Used for boiling, steaming, sautéing, oven roasting, braising, and stewing, and in salads and soups. Year-round.

Source: David Murray/Image Partners 2005/Dorling Kindersley Media Library/Dorling Kindersley

New Potato

Low starch/high moisture. Used for boiling, steaming, oven roasting. Year-round.

Source: David Murray/Image Partners 2005/Dorling Kindersley Media Library/Dorling Kindersley

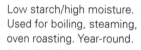

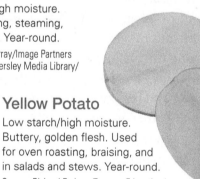

Yellow Potato

Low starch/high moisture. Buttery, golden flesh. Used for oven roasting, braising, and in salads and stews. Year-round.

Source: Richard Embery/Pearson Education/PH College

Fingerling Potato

Low starch/high moisture. Used for boiling, steaming, oven roasting. Year-round.

Source: Richard Embery/Pearson Education/PH College

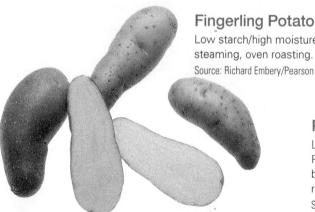

Purple Potato

Low starch/high moisture. Purple flesh. Used for boiling, steaming, oven roasting. Year-round.

Source: Richard Embery/Pearson Education/PH College

may also work with canned vegetables, such as canned tomatoes or corn, that are packed in salted water. Dried vegetables commonly used in the kitchen include tomatoes, mushrooms, and chiles.

Like fruit, vegetables are graded for quality by the USDA's Agricultural Marketing Service (AMS). The grade is awarded based on the appearance of the vegetable and its color, shape, and size. Grade designations are most often seen on packages of potatoes and onions. For example, U.S. No. 1 is the grade you will most often see. Potatoes are also assigned a letter (A, B, or C) to indicate their size: "A" indicates potatoes with a diameter ranging from $1\frac{7}{8}$ to $2\frac{1}{2}$ inches, "B" indicates $1\frac{1}{2}$ to $2\frac{1}{4}$ inches, and "C" indicates less than $1\frac{1}{4}$ inches.

Always try to select vegetables that feel firm and have good color and unblemished skin. And, also as with fruit, chefs should select vegetables according to the manner in which they are going to be used, as well as the price and quality of the produce. When fresh vegetables are out of season, chefs often rely on frozen vegetables instead of depending on more expensive, less flavorful imports.

Storing Vegetables Store vegetables properly to extend their life and maintain their quality.

All fresh vegetables, with the exception of potatoes, tomatoes, avocados, dry onions (including garlic and shallots), and winter squash, are considered perishable and should be kept under refrigeration. Wrap them loosely to keep them from getting too wet.

When fresh root vegetables such as carrots and beets have their leafy tops still attached, remove the tops to keep the vegetables from turning soft or shriveling too quickly. Trim any small roots before storage. To prevent moisture loss, keep roots dry and do not peel them. Store under refrigeration.

Keep unripened avocados at room temperature until they soften enough to use. Store tomatoes at room temperature, if they are still whole, to maintain their flavor.

Store all tubers in dry storage with good ventilation and away from direct light, heat, and moisture. If potatoes are stored in conditions that are not appropriate, they may soften, wither, develop green spots, or even sprout. Green spots and sprouts in potatoes can be poisonous—discard such potatoes.

Onions, garlic, and shallots should be stored in the same way as potatoes, but keep them separate to avoid flavor transfer. Store them in baskets, bags, or boxes that permit air to circulate.

Winter squash should also be stored in a cool, dark place and will last for several weeks without deteriorating in quality.

FIGURE 12–6
Receiving Fresh Vegetables
Vegetables and other produce are packed in boxes and crates for transportation.
INTERPRETING ILLUSTRATIONS
What might the chef be checking for?
Source: Culinary Institute of America

Travels of the Tomato

Probably no other plant has traveled as rocky a road to acceptance and universal appeal as the tomato. An ancestor of our current tomato grew wild in the Andes in South America, possibly as early as A.D. 700. Many years later, in the 1500s, Spanish explorers brought tomato seeds back to Spain. The seeds were eventually brought to Italy and France.

The tomato was not highly regarded in its early years, and some even considered it poison. In 1544, naturalist Petrus Matthiolus referred to the tomato as the *mala insana*, the "unhealthy apple." In his description, he says it is eaten like an eggplant, "fried in oil with salt and pepper." In 1585, Castore Durante offers a similar recipe in his botanical text, *Herbario Nuovo*, published in Rome. "They are eaten the same way as eggplants, with pepper, salt, and oil, but give little and bad nourishment." Pietro Antonio Michiel of Venice wrote, "If I should eat this fruit, cut in slices in a pan with butter and oil, it would be injurious and harmful to me." Early recipe books recommended cooking tomatoes for three hours to make them safe to eat.

The French appreciated the appearance of the early tomato, which looked like a small golden berry. They had no interest in it as food but enjoyed growing it. The Italians continued to experiment with it both in the garden and in the kitchen. As a result, by 1700, the marble-sized "golden apple" had evolved

Source: Dorling Kindersley

An early representation of a tomato plant showing an unlikely combination of golden and red tomatoes on the same plant.

into a red fruit closer in size and appearance to the plum tomato of today.

Despite the chill with which it was first received, the tomato is now a symbol of Italian cuisine and a basic cooking ingredient used around the world. And tomato lovers everywhere now take great pleasure in what was once considered unthinkable: eating tomatoes raw!

Research

Research the use of tomatoes in early America. Focus on Thomas Jefferson's interest in tomatoes.

Any vegetable that has been trimmed, peeled, or cut should be treated as a perishable food. Keep them refrigerated until you are ready to serve or cook them, and be sure to use them before they have a chance to go bad.

 **READING CHECKPOINT** *Which vegetables should be stored under refrigeration?*

Preparing Vegetables

Cleaning is always the first step in preparing vegetables. Once the vegetables are cleaned, you can cut and trim them as needed. Just as when working with fruit, always wear gloves when you prepare fresh vegetables that are not going to be cooked before you serve them.

Cleaning All fresh vegetables must be cleaned thoroughly, even if they will be peeled before cutting. Washing removes surface dirt as well as bacteria and other contaminants. Leafy vegetables can contain sand and dirt, and even bugs. Celery and leeks are always dirty at the root. They also trap

Trimming and Dicing Onions

① **Cut away a thin slice from the stem and root ends** of the bulb with a paring knife, making a flat surface on both ends.

② **Pull away the peel** by catching it between your thumb and the flat side of your blade. Trim away any brown spots from the underlying layers.

Source: Culinary Institute of America

③ **Cut the onion in half** from the root end to the stem end. Lay half the onion, cut side down, on the cutting board.

④ **Make evenly spaced cuts** (¼ inch for a small dice, ½ inch for a medium dice, ¾ inch for a large dice), running lengthwise, with the tip of a chef's knife. Leave the root end intact.

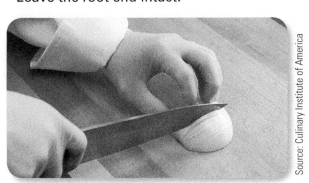

Source: Culinary Institute of America

⑤ **Make two or three horizontal cuts** parallel to the work surface, from the stem end to the root end, but do not cut all the way through.

Source: Culinary Institute of America

⑥ **Make even, crosswise cuts** working from stem end up to the root, cutting through all layers of the onion.

Source: Culinary Institute of America

dirt between the leaves and stalks. To clean vegetables, run them under cold water. As with fruit, special solutions are available for cleaning vegetables. Wash vegetables as close as possible to preparation time.

Trimming Remove the peels from vegetables if necessary with a swivel-bladed peeler, a paring knife, or a chef's knife. Remove woody stems from such vegetables as mushrooms, asparagus, artichokes, and broccoli.

Onions and garlic are key ingredients in many types of food preparations. It's important to master the techniques for preparing, trimming, and cutting them. They taste best when they are cut close to the time they are used.

BASIC CULINARY SKILLS

Trimming and Mincing Garlic

① **Separate the garlic cloves** by wrapping the entire head of garlic in a towel and pressing down on the top.

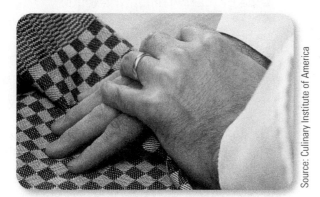

Source: Culinary Institute of America

③ **Peel off the skin** and remove the root end and any brown spots. If the clove has sprouted, split it in half and remove the sprout.

Source: Culinary Institute of America

② **Loosen the skin** from each clove by placing a clove on the cutting board, placing the flat side of the blade on top, and hitting the blade with a fist or the heel of your hand.

Source: Culinary Institute of America

④ **Crush** the cloves by laying them on the cutting board and using the same technique as for loosening the skin, but this time apply more force.

Source: Culinary Institute of America

⑤ **Mince** the cloves by using a rocking motion. To mash the garlic, hold the knife nearly flat against the cutting board and press down.

Tomato Concassé

① **Cut a small X in the bottom of the tomato** with the tip of a paring knife. Do not cut too deeply into the flesh.

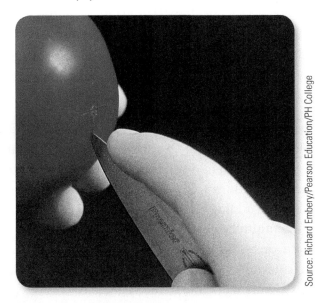

Source: Richard Embery/Pearson Education/PH College

② **Blanch** in boiling water for about 15 seconds (or slightly longer if the tomato is unripe). Place tomatoes into a bowl of ice water to stop the cooking.

③ **Pull away the skin** with a paring knife.

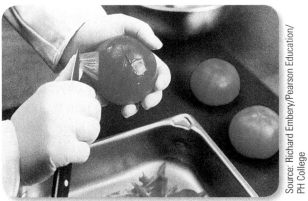

Source: Richard Embery/Pearson Education/PH College

④ **Cut the tomato in half** at its widest point.

⑤ **Squeeze or scoop out the seeds** gently.

⑥ **Dice** by making lengthwise cuts, horizontal cuts, and then crosswise cuts.

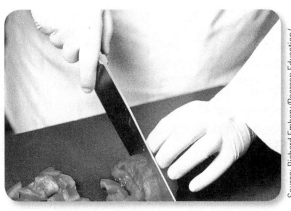

Source: Richard Embery/Pearson Education/PH College

Tomatoes are one of the most commonly used vegetables in the kitchen. They are often peeled, seeded, and then diced. This preparation is what chefs call **tomato concassé** (kon-kah-SAY).

READING CHECKPOINT *What is the first step in preparing fresh vegetables before cutting and trimming?*

Cooking Vegetables

There are distinct differences in how tender a vegetable should be when it is properly cooked. The proper doneness is determined by how you intend to serve or use the vegetable, the vegetable's characteristics, regional or ethnic preferences, and cooking technique.

There are four levels of doneness for vegetables:

- **Blanched.** Vegetables are blanched for 30 seconds to 1 minute. Blanching is appropriate for vegetables served cold or for those that will complete cooking in a separate process (braising, for instance).
- **Parcooked/parboiled.** Vegetables are cooked to partial doneness to prepare them to be finished by grilling, sautéing, or stewing.
- **Tender-crisp.** Vegetables are cooked until they can be bitten into easily but still offer a slight resistance and sense of texture.
- **Fully cooked.** Vegetables are quite tender, although they should retain their shape and color. If boiling vegetables to make a purée, boil them until they mash easily.

Boiling and Steaming Vegetables Properly steamed and boiled vegetables have vivid colors and identifiable, fresh flavors. Most vegetables are best when simmered, not cooked at a full boil. Add enough salt to develop a good flavor (a standard ratio is 1 tablespoon of salt for every gallon of water). Some chefs feel that adding a pinch of baking soda to turn the water alkaline will help maintain the color of boiled green vegetables.

To preserve the best flavor, texture, and nutritional value of vegetables, serve them as soon as possible after you cook them. Drain well so that any finishing or flavoring ingredients will cling to the vegetable.

Sometimes you will need to at least partially prepare vegetables ahead of time. To preserve the quality of vegetables, chefs use a technique known as *refreshing* or *shocking*. As soon as the vegetables are cooked, drain them in a colander and then immediately transfer them to a container filled with ice water. This stops the cooking process. Leave them there just long enough to chill; then drain once again. Store refreshed vegetables in the refrigerator until you are ready to use them.

To steam vegetables, use a large pot with a tight-fitting lid and a steamer insert, a tiered steamer, or a convection or pressure steamer for large quantities. The amount of liquid required depends on both the type of equipment you are using and how long the vegetable takes to cook: the shorter the cooking time, the less liquid needed.

Puréeing Vegetables Chefs use vegetable purées for a variety of purposes: to flavor and color another dish, to thicken a sauce, or as the basis for a sauce or soup. Vegetable purées can be made from any vegetable tender enough to chop fine enough for a soft, loose texture. Cook the vegetable by the desired technique until tender. (Very tender green vegetables should be briefly blanched to set their colors.) Drain them well before you start to purée them. Equipment options for purées include a food processor, blender, food mill, or sieve.

Taste and evaluate the purée. Some may require additional liquid for a good texture; others may benefit from simmering until they reduce slightly. A variety of ingredients may be added for additional flavor, richness, texture, or color: eggs, cream, butter, spices, herbs, or flavorful oils.

Glazing Vegetables (Classical Method)

① **Bring the liquids to a simmer** and season or flavor as the recipe instructs.

② **Add the vegetables to the cooking liquid.** Cook until they are just beginning to get tender.

③ **Sweat or smother any aromatics in a cooking fat.**

④ **Add the vegetables to the cooking fat** and aromatics (if desired).

⑤ **Pour or ladle just enough cooking liquid into the pan** to finish cooking the vegetables.

⑥ **Cover the pan** and cook until the vegetables are close to tender.

Source: Culinary Institute of America

⑦ **Remove the cover** and let the cooking liquid cook off to make the glaze.

Source: Culinary Institute of America

📁 Recipe Card

60. Glazed Carrots

Source: Culinary Institute of America

Glazing Vegetables Really a finishing technique, glazing vegetables generally incorporates aspects of boiling, steaming, and sautéing and potentially even roasting and baking. The classical method of glazing vegetables is to parcook your vegetables in water, then make the glaze in a separate pan, and finally toss your vegetables in the glaze and serve. You can, however, start the vegetables in the cooking liquid (stock works best), and once they are close to tender, add the butter (and sugar if desired) to form a glaze. Alternatively, you can place all the ingredients in a moderate-temperature oven and cook them until the vegetables are tender and the glaze has formed. The last method is a little tricky because your measurement and timing have to be exact to get it right.

Braising and Stewing Vegetables Vegetable stews and braises may include just one vegetable or a combination. Stewed or braised vegetables literally cook in their own juices. Stews and braises should be fork

Making Vegetable Braises or Stews

1 **Cook the aromatic vegetables** in a cooking fat, beginning with members of the onion family.

Source: Culinary Institute of America

2 **Add the remaining ingredients** based on the time they take to cook, stirring as necessary.

Source: Culinary Institute of America

3 **Adjust seasoning and consistency** of the dish as needed.

Source: Culinary Institute of America

4 **Stew or braise** the vegetables until flavorful, fully cooked, and fork tender.

5 **Serve** immediately or hold for later use.

Recipe Cards

61. Ratatouille

62. Braised Romaine

---

tender or, in some cases, meltingly soft. These dishes tend to hold well; some even improve after resting. The vegetables in a stew are customarily cut into small pieces. Vegetables for a braise may be parcooked or blanched to set their colors and improve the flavor or texture of the finished braise. (Review the basic braising and stewing techniques in Chapter 8.)

Grilling and Broiling Vegetables The intense heat of grills and broilers gives vegetables a rich, bold flavor. The basic procedures for grilling and broiling, including proper grill maintenance and applying sauces or glazes, apply to grilled and broiled vegetables. Grilled vegetables have a distinctive charred flavor and deeply browned exteriors.

High-moisture or tender vegetables (mushrooms, zucchini, or tomatoes) can be grilled from a raw state, but dense or starchy vegetables (squash, potatoes, or fennel) may require preliminary cooking to reach the proper

Recipe Card

63. Grilled Vegetables Provençal-Style

doneness on the grill. Soft and precooked hard vegetables may be marinated briefly before cooking. If a marinade has been used, it can be served as an accompanying sauce.

Roasting and Baking Vegetables Roasted vegetables have a deep flavor, the result of cooking in the dry environment of the oven. Even relatively dry or starchy vegetables cook properly with no added moisture. Roasting is often used to prepare squashes, yams, eggplant, or beets.

Preheat the oven to the right temperature. Some vegetables roast best at a low temperature for a long period of time; others are best for short periods at high temperatures.

Scrub and pierce vegetables you are baking whole. Piercing them allows steam to escape; otherwise, they can burst.

Add seasoning to cut or peeled vegetables before roasting. Marinades, butter, and oil are often used both to add flavor and to help brown the vegetables for a rich flavor. Stuffing mixtures (rice, bread, mushroom, forcemeat, or sausage, for example) can fill scooped-out vegetables (zucchini, mushrooms, eggplant, or tomatoes).

Frying and Sautéing Vegetables Sautéing and stir-frying are used both as the primary cooking technique for high-moisture vegetables (leafy greens, mushrooms, and soft-skinned squash, for instance) and as a finishing and reheating technique for vegetables parcooked by boiling, steaming, or baking. These techniques lend themselves to a layering of flavors and ingredients.

Match the cooking temperature to the vegetables you are cooking. To gently finish vegetables in cream or butter, use relatively low heat. To get some browning or to retain crispness, use high heat.

Choose a cooking fat that complements the flavor of the vegetable. Oils such as olive, peanut, canola, corn, or safflower can be used, as well as whole or clarified butter. Use seasonings and aromatics to heighten the vegetable's flavor. Use garnishes to add color or texture.

If you are sautéing or stir-frying a combination of vegetables, add those that require the longest cooking time first and end with those that require the least.

Pan-fried vegetables may be breaded or coated with flour or batter. Properly done pan-fried vegetables have a golden or brown, crisp exterior, with the interior tender to the bite and very hot. The coating, if any, is crisp and light. Sauces or other accompaniments add complementary or contrasting flavor and texture.

Perfectly fried vegetables include crisp chips, hearty croquettes, and tender vegetables with a light crunchy batter or breading.

Potato Purées The technique of preparing light and flavorful potato purées rests on three basic concepts: choosing the right potato (high-starch/low-moisture varieties are best), getting the potatoes dry before you purée

Chef's Tip
Baked Potato

To prepare a potato for baking, scrub, blot dry, rub with oil or salt, and pierce. Place in a 425° oven. Bake for 1 hour for a 6-oz potato. Use a fork to test for doneness. The skin should be crisp and the flesh tender.

Recipe Cards

64. Baked Acorn Squash with Cranberry-Orange Compote

65. Baked Potatoes

66. Potatoes au Gratin

Chef's Tip
Blanching French Fries

For crisp, light french fries, fry the potatoes at 325°F until they are just tender. Drain and reserve them. When you are ready to serve them, finish frying at 350°F until crisp and golden.

Recipe Card
67. Corn Fritters

Deep-Frying Vegetables

1 **Heat the oil** in a deep fryer or kettle.

2 **Add the vegetables** to the hot oil, using a basket or tongs.

Source: Culinary Institute of America

3 **Fry** the vegetables until fully cooked.

Source: Culinary Institute of America

4 **Remove** and drain; season if necessary.

Source: Culinary Institute of America

Recipe Card

68. French-Fried Potatoes

them, and having all the ingredients hot when you combine them into the finished purée.

One note about equipment. Use a potato masher, wooden spoon, sieve, potato ricer, or food mill to purée potatoes. A blender or food processor will overwork the potatoes, making them too loose and thin.

 **READING CHECKPOINT** *What are the techniques for cooking vegetables?*

Serving Vegetables

The technique you use to prepare and serve vegetables can produce dramatic differences in flavor, texture, color, and nutritive value. For example, although acorn squash is often roasted or puréed, it can also be gently stewed in cream, or grilled and served with a salsa. Cucumbers, most commonly considered a vegetable to be eaten raw, may be steamed, sautéed, or even

Puréeing Potatoes

① **Cook the potatoes** by steaming or boiling.

Source: Culinary Institute of America

② **Dry** the potatoes in a pot over low heat or in the oven on a sheet tray until no more steam rises.

③ **Purée** the hot potatoes until they are smooth.

Source: Culinary Institute of America

④ **Stir in finishing ingredients,** such as seasonings, warmed milk or cream, or whole butter.

Source: Culinary Institute of America

⑤ **Serve** as desired or reserve for later use.

Recipe Card
69. Whipped Potatoes

---

braised. You can prepare vegetables by all the basic cooking techniques outlined in Chapter 8, making them among the most versatile and interesting options on the menu.

Vegetables are more than just side dishes. They can be featured on their own as an appetizer or main course or served as an accompaniment to meat or fish. They are the foundation of many soups and sauces and an important ingredient in many other preparations. As more customers look for meatless or vegetarian options, your skills in vegetable cookery will ensure that vegetables need never be an afterthought.

READING CHECKPOINT *How can vegetables be used as more than a side dish?*

Reviewing Concepts

1. What is a tuber and how does it grow?
2. Which vegetables are stored at room temperature?
3. What is tomato concassé?
4. What level of doneness is required for puréed vegetables?
5. In addition to being a side dish, how else can vegetables be used?

Critical Thinking

6. **Predicting** Suggest a reason why onions should not be stored in a small refrigerator.
7. **Solving Problems** What's a good tool for pulling away the peel from onions and garlic?
8. **Classifying** Which types of peppers would be good for salads?

Test Kitchen

Split into three teams. Each team will boil the same amount of green beans in the same amount of water. Team 1 adds nothing to the water. Team 2 adds ¼ cup of salt per gallon of water. Team 3 adds 2 tsp of baking soda per gallon of water. Blanch for 2 minutes, and shock in ice water. Which has the brightest color? The best flavor? The best texture?

CULINARY MATH
Measuring Volume Yields of Cuts

Small-dice a carrot, medium-dice another, and large-dice a third. Weigh a 4-oz portion of each. Measure the volume of each portion. Evaluate the result.

PROJECT 12   **Cooking Potatoes** You are now ready to work on Project 12, "Cooking Potatoes," which is available in "My Culinary Lab" or in your *Student's Lab Resources and Study Guide* manual.

Reviewing Content

Choose the letter that best answers the question or completes the statement.

1. Every fruit contains:
   a. at least one seed.
   b. flesh.
   c. skin.
   d. all of the above

2. Which of the following vegetables should be stored at room temperature in a dark place?
   a. kale
   b. yams
   c. asparagus
   d. green leaf cabbage

3. In addition to cooking liquid, which of the following items are essential ingredients to form a glaze?
   a. bay leaf
   b. flour
   c. thickener
   d. cooking fat

4. Which of the following ingredients is not used in poaching fruit?
   a. cooking liquid
   b. sweetener
   c. flavoring
   d. cooking fat

5. What fruit are plantains related to?
   a. apples
   b. oranges
   c. bananas
   d. figs

6. What is a good flavor tip for boiling vegetables?
   a. add salt to the water
   b. add pepper to the water
   c. cook at a full boil
   d. all of the above

7. Which of the following should not be stored under refrigeration?
   a. tomatoes
   b. potatoes
   c. avocados
   d. all of the above

Understanding Concepts

8. Describe the difference between a mature piece of fruit and a ripe piece of fruit.

9. List the anatomy of a plant, using a different vegetable as an example of each anatomical feature.

10. Should apples be stored separately from other fruit? Why or why not?

11. How can fruit be used in savory dishes?

12. Explain the difference between a clingstone and a freestone fruit and give an example of each.

Critical Thinking

13. **PREDICTING** What might happen to a banana left over the weekend in a lunchbox with an apple?

14. **CLASSIFYING** Why are some fruits, such as tomatoes and avocados, referred to as vegetables?

15. **DRAWING CONCLUSIONS** Which potato would be best for oven roasting, a russet or a red-skin potato, and why?

Culinary Math

16. **SOLVING PROBLEMS** An 8-oz apple is peeled, cored, and sliced for a pie. The scraps weigh 1 oz. The recipe calls for 32 oz of sliced apples. How many whole apples are needed to make the pie?

17. **APPLYING CONCEPTS** Small-diced carrots take up half the space of large-diced carrots. If a 10-oz carrot, large-diced, yields a cup, how much would a 12½-oz carrot yield if small-diced?

On the Job

18. **SOLVING PROBLEMS** You are working the dessert station and have run out of pears for your poached dessert. You have oranges, apples, and pineapple in the walk-in cooler. Which is the best substitute?

19. **DRAWING CONCLUSIONS** A stewed dish you are preparing contains the following ingredients: onion, eggplant, zucchini, and corn. Which item would you add to the hot oil first?

Food Scientist

Food scientists have an increasing role in the foodservice industry. They may be responsible for developing new food products; researching ways to improve food-processing techniques, including food safety issues related to sanitation and outbreaks of food-borne illness; and conducting research on flavor preferences to better meet nutritional and dietary needs. They may work in various segments of the food-processing industry, for the government, or in schools and universities, both doing research and teaching.

Food scientists and technologists use their knowledge of chemistry, physics, engineering, microbiology, biotechnology, and other sciences to develop new or better ways of preserving, processing, packaging, storing, and delivering foods.

Some food scientists engage in basic research, discovering new food sources; analyzing food content; or searching for substitutes for harmful or undesirable additives, such as nitrites. Some research improvements in traditional food processing techniques, such as baking, blanching, canning, drying, evaporation, and pasteurization. Others enforce government regulations, inspecting food-processing areas and ensuring that sanitation, safety, quality, and waste management standards are met.

Food technologists generally work in product development, applying the findings from food science research to improve the selection, preservation, processing, packaging, and distribution of food.

Entry-Level Requirements

At entry level, a bachelor of science degree with coursework in food chemistry, analysis, engineering, and microbiology is needed. Although many individuals entering the area of food science predominantly have science backgrounds, an increasing number arrive with culinary arts degrees or experience, as well as degrees related specifically to food science and technology.

Helpful for Advancement

To move up into areas of research and development as a manager, you will need an advanced degree (either a master of science or a PhD in food science or related areas such as biology, chemistry, or nutrition).

Source: Waltraud Grubitzsch/EPA/Newscom

Food scientists often research food safety issues.

JENNIFER STACK

Jennifer Stack is a Registered Dietitian, Certified Diabetes Educator, and Chef. She is an Associate Professor at The Culinary Institute of America, teaching courses in nutrition and food safety, as well as a graduate. Stack also earned a Master of Science degree in Nutrition from New York University.

Stack practiced as a Registered Dietitian in New York City for 15 years, providing nutrition counseling for a range of patients. In addition, she has developed and managed weight management and compulsive eating therapy at NYU Medical Center.

Jennifer Stack

Stack is a member of both the Food and Culinary Professionals group and the American Association of Diabetes Educators.

An accomplished voice in food and nutrition, Stack has appeared on network television in addition to other local news stations. She has written for *Cooking Light* and *Woman's Day* magazines, with stories syndicated through the Associated Press. Using her broad depth of knowledge and expertise, Stack effectively develops and communicates food and nutrition information to both the public and culinary professionals.

VITAL STATISTICS

Graduated: MS in Nutrition from NYU; The Culinary Institute of America (CIA), 2003

Profession: Dietician, educator, chef

Interesting Items: Recipient of the Academie Brillat-Savarin Young Professional's Medal of Merit from the CIA

Created a healthy cooking program for children in the YMCA's After School Program

Authored *The Diabetes-Friendly Kitchen*, a specialized cookbook

CAREER PROFILE

Salary Ranges

Food Technologist: $30,000 to $60,000

Food Scientist: $60,000 to $80,500 (or more)

Grains, Legumes, and Pasta

13.1 Rice and Other Grains

13.2 Beans and Other Legumes

13.3 Pasta

Rice and Other Grains

Key Concepts

- Understanding grains and grain processing
- Selecting and storing grains
- Preparing grains
- Presenting grains

Vocabulary

- barley
- bran
- brown rice
- bulgur
- converted rice
- cornmeal
- cracked grain
- endosperm
- farinaceous
- germ
- grains
- grits
- hominy
- hominy grits
- hull
- husk
- instant oats
- kernel
- masa harina
- meal
- milling
- oat groats
- oatmeal
- parcooked grains
- pearl barley
- pearl grain
- pilaf
- polenta
- posole
- processed grains
- quick-cooking oats
- quinoa
- refined grains
- risotto
- rolled oats
- rye berries
- rye flakes
- Scotch barley
- wheat berry
- whole grain
- wild rice

Grains

Grains are the seeds of grasses that human beings have learned to cultivate for food. These particular grasses, known as *cereal grasses*, are prized for their ability to produce grain. In fact, grains are basic foods in almost any cuisine. Grains provide the majority of calories and nutrients in most diets. American food guidelines, and guidelines throughout the world, concentrate on grains as the foundation of a healthy diet.

Parts of a Grain Grains have several layers when they are first removed from the grasses on which they grow. Although each type of grain is different, most grains are composed of four basic parts: an outer **husk** or **hull**, the **bran**, the **germ**, and the **endosperm**. (See "Parts of a Grain," on the next page.)

Grains are not the only foods that are high in starch, of course. Beans and some vegetables, such as potatoes, are also starchy. Nutritionists and cooks sometimes refer to grains, along with these other starchy foods, as a food group called **farinaceous** (fare-eh-NAY-shus) foods.

Processed Grains We don't eat grain just as it comes from the grass. A grain undergoes a number of steps to make it into food. To

Source: Elenathewise (Elena Elisseeva)/Dreamstime LLC

Parts of a Grain

Husk or Hull

Tough protective outer seed coat. The edible seed, without its husk or hull, is typically referred to as the kernel.

Endosperm

Largest part of the grain. Made up almost entirely of carbohydrates, or starch.

Bran

Second layer. Contains dietary fiber, an important part of a balanced diet.

Germ

Contains most of the grain's oils, vitamins, and minerals. This is the part of the grian that sprouts to form a new plant.

The husk or hull is the tough protective outer seed coat. Since this portion of the grain is inedible, the husk or hull is removed in a process known as threshing. The edible seed that remains after the hull is removed is referred to as the grain **kernel**.

The bran layers protect the interior of the kernel. The bran may be left intact or only partially removed to produce what is referred to as a whole grain. In addition to protecting the kernel, the bran layers also contain several important vitamins and minerals as well as dietary fiber, an important part of a balanced diet. The fiber contained in the bran is mainly insoluble.

The endosperm is the largest part of a grain. It is made up almost entirely of carbohydrates, also referred to as *starch*. Most of the protein found in a grain is contained here, as well as B vitamins

and iron. The endosperm also contains some fiber, primarily soluble fiber.

The germ contains most of the grain's oils as well as some B vitamins and a small amount of protein. This is the part of the grain that sprouts to form a new plant. Removing the germ can improve shelf life, since the oils in the germ can turn rancid, but doing so does reduce the nutritional value of the grain.

Lab Activity

Prepare wheat berries, cracked wheat, and bulgur according to package directions. Time the preparation of each. Sample each finished product for taste and texture. Evaluate the results In terms of preparation time, taste, texture, and nutritional value (based on package nutritional information).

make grains easier to cook, digest, and store, some or all of the grain's protective layers (the hull and the bran) are removed. Removing these layers is the first step in processing grain into food.

- **Processed Grains.** Grains that have been prepared to use as food are called **processed grains**. Often grains are cut, crushed, rolled, or ground as part of the processing. This is referred to as **milling**. Some steps in processing are important to make the food digestible or able to store well. Some steps are performed to change the flavor, texture, color, or shelf life of the grain. The amount and type of processing determines whether we consider the grain whole or refined.

- **Whole Grains.** When just the husk or hull is removed from a grain, the grain is referred to as **whole grain** or *minimally processed grain*. Whole grains typically take longer to cook than grains that are more highly processed.

- **Parcooked Grains.** To make whole grains easier and quicker to cook, they can be partly or fully precooked during processing by boiling or steaming the grain. Grains treated this way are called **parcooked grains**. (*Parcooked* means partially cooked.) The parcooked grain may be rolled to make flakes and then dried, or it may be dried or toasted after parcooking and left whole or crushed or cracked into smaller pieces before packaging.

- **Pearl Grains and Other Refined Grains.** One of the parts of the grain that is often removed in the refining process is the bran. Removing the bran makes the grain lighter in color and quicker to cook. A grain that has been scrubbed of its bran is referred to as a **pearl grain**. Another part of the grain that is often removed is the germ. Removing a grain's germ removes oils, vitamins, and minerals but helps improve the grain's shelf life because the germ's oils tend to turn rancid quickly.

- **Cracked Grain.** Grain can be further processed by cutting or crushing the kernel into smaller pieces. Whole kernels that are cut into large pieces are known as **cracked grain** and have a coarse texture. Cracked wheat is an example of a cracked grain made from a minimally processed grain. Bulgur wheat is an example of a cracked grain made from a parcooked grain.

- **Refined Grains.** Highly processed grains are known as **refined grains**. The more the grain is processed, the more its layers are stripped away. Refined grains have less nutritional value than whole grains because they have fewer vitamins, minerals, and fiber.

- **Meals.** Processed grain can also be ground into fine particles by rolling the grain between steel drums or between stone wheels. Grains that are milled into fine particles this way are known as **meal**. An example of this is cornmeal. If grain has been partially cooked, it may be rolled to produce flakes instead of being ground. If the meal is ground very fine, the result is a flour. You can learn more about different flours in Chapter 17.

FIGURE 13–1
Farinaceous Foods
Grains, breads, pastas, and legumes are all farinaceous foods.
DRAWING CONCLUSIONS *How are all these foods alike?*
Source: Elena Schweitzer/Shutterstock

FIGURE 13–2
Processed Wheat
Each type of processing creates a different texture and taste.
INTERPRETING ILLUSTRATIONS *Which forms of wheat are familiar to you?*
Source: Culinary Institute of America

 **READING CHECKPOINT** *What are the four parts of a grain?*

Selecting and Storing Grains

Each type of grain has its own tastes and textures. However, the way a specific grain is processed also changes a grain's taste and texture. The following are three major types of grain:

- Rice
- Wheat
- Corn

Rice Rice is one of the most important grains in the world. Different varieties of rice produce grains with different lengths and shapes. When rice is harvested, the hull is removed by passing the rice through rollers. Once the hull is removed, the rice still retains the bran. Rice that retains some or all of its bran is called **brown rice**. Brown rice has a slightly nutty taste and takes longer to cook than white rice. If the milling process continues long enough to remove all of the bran, the result is *white rice*, sometimes

Types of Rice

Long-Grain Rice

Long-grain rice is four to five times longer than it is wide. Typically fluffy and dry when cooked, it separates easily and does not stick together. Examples: basmati (bahs-MAH-tee) and Thai jasmine.

Source: Roger Phillips/Image Partners 2005/Dorling Kindersley Media Library/Dorling Kindersley

Medium-Grain Rice

Medium-grain rice is shorter than long-grain rice. It is moister than long-grain rice after it is cooked and tends to stick together. Example: Calrose. This example of medium-grain rice is a brown rice (the bran remains on the rice).

Source: Philip Dowell/Image Partners 2005/Dorling Kindersley Media Library/ Dorling Kindersley

Short-Grain Rice

Short-grain rice is nearly round. This type of rice has a relatively high starch content and is quite sticky after it is cooked. Example: Arborio (ar-BOH-ree-oh) and sweet or glutinous rice.

Source: Philip Dowell/Image Partners 2005/Dorling Kindersley Media Library/Dorling Kindersley

Wild Rice

Wild rice is the seed of a marsh grass. Although it is not related to other rices, it is cooked like them. When wild rice is harvested, it is left to soak for a period of time; this is known as the *curing* process. After the grain is cured, it is toasted to dry it out. Toasting prepares the grain for storage and gives wild rice its toasty flavor. The last step of processing wild rice is removing the hull.

Source: David Murray/Image Partners 2005/Dorling Kindersley Media Library/Dorling Kindersley

referred to as *polished rice*. Each type of rice can be processed into either white rice (without its bran) or brown rice (with its bran).

Rice can also be partially cooked before the hull is removed. After the grain is softened in hot water, it is dried and then milled to produce either brown or white rice. Rice that is parcooked in this way before milling is known as **converted rice** and has a slightly different taste and texture.

Wheat   Wheat is an ancient grain that grows abundantly in parts of Europe, Asia, and North America. It was first cultivated thousands of years ago and has evolved into a number of different types. Like rice, wheat can be minimally processed, resulting in wheat berries or cracked wheat, or parcooked, to produce bulgur. It can also be ground very fine, to make flours used in baking. (The flours made from wheat and other grains are described in more detail in Chapter 17.)

Corn   Corn is the only grain that is eaten both fresh, as a vegetable, and dried, as a grain. Dried corn is processed into several different forms. Some types of dried corn products are made from kernels that are soaked in a solution of lye. The lye makes it easier for us to digest some of the important nutrients in the corn. Some varieties of corn produce white kernels, and others produce yellow kernels. The forms of corn in the following list may

Forms of Wheat

Cracked Wheat

Cracked wheat is made by crushing wheat berries into pieces.

Source: Roger Phillips/Image Partners 2005/Dorling Kindersley Media Library/Dorling Kindersley

Wheat Berries

The whole kernel of wheat, a **wheat berry** is not polished or steamed. Wheat berries are usually soaked overnight before being cooked to shorten their cooking time.

Source: Geoff Brightling/Image Partners 2005/Dorling Kindersley Media Library/Dorling Kindersley

Bulgur

Bulgur (BUHL-guhr) is made from steamed whole wheat berries that are then crushed into small pieces. Bulgur is often used to make a traditional Middle Eastern salad known as tabouli (tuh-BOO-lee).

Source: Philip Dowell/Image Partners 2005/Dorling Kindersley Media Library/Dorling Kindersley

Wheat Bran

Wheat bran is made from the bran surrounding the wheat kernel.

Source: Roger Phillips/Image Partners 2005/Dorling Kindersley Media Library/Dorling Kindersley

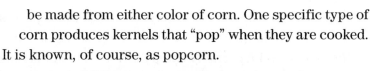

be made from either color of corn. One specific type of corn produces kernels that "pop" when they are cooked. It is known, of course, as popcorn.

- **Posole** (poh-SOH-leh) is the whole kernel with the germ and bran still intact and soaked in an alkaline solution to make the hull softer and easier to digest. *Pozole* is another common spelling for this type of corn.
- **Hominy** (HOM-uh-nee) is a whole dried corn kernel that has the hull and germ removed.
- **Cornmeal** is finely ground corn. When whole corn is ground into meal, it is called **grits** in America. Grits can be ground into coarse, medium, or fine particles. **Hominy grits** are grits made from hominy, so they do not contain the hull or germ. Cornmeal made from posole is known as **masa harina** (MAH-sah ah-REE-nah). **Polenta** (poh-LEHN-tah) is an Italian term for cornmeal.

Additional Grains Oats grow well in areas that are too cold for growing wheat, rice, or corn, or where the soil is poor. Oats are sold in many forms.

- **Oat groats** are the whole grain of the oat, with the hull removed.
- **Oatmeal** is coarsely ground oats that are cooked as a hot cereal or used in baking.
- **Rolled oats** are made by steaming groats and then rolling them into flat flakes. Rolled oats are also called *old-fashioned oats*. **Quick-cooking oats** are rolled oats cut into smaller pieces to reduce cooking time.
- **Instant oats** are rolled oats that have been partially cooked and then dried before being rolled again.

Barley is a grain that looks like a doubled grain of rice. It is most commonly sold as **pearl barley**, which means it has been milled several times to completely remove the outer husk and the bran. **Scotch barley**, which is also called *pot barley*, is also milled, although the bran is not completely removed.

Rye is sold as a whole grain known as **rye berries**. If the berries are put through a roller, the result is **rye flakes**.

Quinoa (KEEN-wah) is a high-protein grain that was originally grown in South America. It has a round kernel and becomes fluffy and light when you cook it. Before cooking quinoa, put it in a bowl of cold water and rub it between your palms for a few minutes. Repeat until the water is clear.

Storing Grains Grains are dry goods. They should be kept dry during storage. Hold them in containers with tight lids if they are removed from their packaging. Keep them above floor level in an area that is cool and dry.

FIGURE 13–3

Varieties of Corn

An ear of corn with its husk still attached, shown with corn kernels, grits, and cornmeal.

ANALYZING INFORMATION

Can you identify the grits?

Source: Dorling Kindersley/ Image Partners 2005/ Dorling Kindersley Media Library/Dorling Kindersley

Additional Grains

Oats

Oats are commonly available as groats, oatmeal, rolled or old-fashioned oats, quick-cooking oatmeal, instant oats, oat flour, and oat bran.

Source: Colin Walton/Image Partners 2005/Dorling Kindersley Media Library/Dorling Kindersley

Rye

Rye is commonly available as rye berries, rye flakes, and rye flour.

Source: Roger Phillips/ Dorling Kindersley

Barley

Barley is commonly available as pearl barley, Scotch or pot barley, and barley flour.

Source: Roger Phillips/ Image Partners 2005/ Dorling Kindersley Media Library/Dorling Kindersley

Quinoa

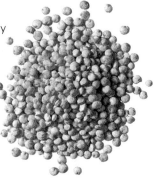

Quinoa is commonly available as whole kernels.

Source: Roger Phillips/Image Partners 2005/ Dorling Kindersley Media Library/Dorling Kindersley

---

CULINARY **HISTORY**

The Goddess of Grain

The word *cereal* doesn't just mean corn flakes, puffed rice, or oatmeal. It is a general term used to refer to all grains. Grains, and the ground meal made from grains, were very important to early civilizations—so important, in fact, that grain was sometimes used in place of money.

In early civilizations, many festivals and feasts were dedicated to grains. Most early cultures believed that a powerful god or goddess controlled the harvest of grains. That meant any grain-related festival was also usually dedicated to a god or goddess. Offerings were made to the god or goddess asking for good weather and growing conditions. Storytellers would tell how the god or goddess gave grain to humans in the long-distant past. In fact,

CERES (or Demeter, from Pompeii Wall Painting).

Source: Duncan Walker/Getty Images

the word *cereal* is based on the name of the Roman goddess of agriculture, Ceres.

Today we still observe some of the old customs associated with Ceres. Throwing grains of rice at a new bride dates back to ancient Roman times when people sprinkled grains of barley around the temples dedicated to Ceres.

Research

Research the relationship between a culture, nation, or people (past or present) and the grain associated with that culture, nation, or people. List and describe at least two dishes from that culture, nation, or people that prominently feature that specific grain. Make one of the dishes you have described.

FOCUS ON Nutrition

Unlocking Nutrients in Corn

Corn is a good source of many nutrients, including niacin. However, unless the corn is treated with an alkaline solution, our bodies cannot unlock the niacin from the corn. Treating the corn with lye (an alkaline solution) softens the hull and partially cooks the corn. It also makes the kernel swell. That is why lye-cured corn looks fatter than corn that is dried without this treatment.

Some whole grains, especially those that still contain some or all of the bran or germ, can lose their quality quickly. They should be stored in the refrigerator or freezer if they must be kept for more than a few weeks.

READING CHECKPOINT *Name the three major types of grain.*

Preparing Grains

There are several ways to prepare grains. Each involves a different method of adding liquid. The texture of cooked grains depends on the type of grain you are cooking as well as the way that the grain was processed. Some types of grain separate from each other easily after they cook. Other grains may become sticky and clump together. Fluffy grains are perfect for soaking up juices. Sticky grains are easy to eat with chopsticks. Another point to keep in mind is that different cooking

---

BASIC CULINARY SKILLS

Boiled or Steamed Grains

1. **Bring the liquid to a boil.**

2. **Add salt** and other seasonings as directed by your recipe.

3. **Add the grain** all at once. Stir to separate the grain.

4. **Reduce the heat.** Simmer until the grain is fully cooked and tender. Cover the pot if you are steaming the grain.

5. **Drain** the grain through a colander if you are boiling the grain.

6. **Fluff** the grain with a fork to test for doneness.

Source: Dave King/Image Partners 2005/Dorling Kindersley Media Library/Dorling Kindersley

Source: Dave King/Image Partners 2005/Dorling Kindersley Media Library/Dorling Kindersley

7. **Serve** grain while very hot.

Recipe Card
70. Boiled Rice

methods produce different textures as well. When grains are fully cooked by either steaming or boiling, they should be tender to the bite.

Boiling or Steaming Grains Boiled grains are made by simply stirring a measured amount of grain into a large pot of boiling salted water. The grains are simmered until tender.

Steamed grains are made by stirring a measured amount of grain into a measured amount of liquid. The amount of liquid is just enough for the grain to absorb. The pot is covered as the grain cooks. When steamed grains finish cooking, there should not be any liquid to drain away.

Preparing Cereals and Meals Cooked grain meal (such as cornmeal and oatmeal) is made by stirring the grain into a simmering liquid. Cereals and meals are stirred throughout their cooking time in order to develop a creamy, smooth texture. It is important to add the meal to the simmering liquid properly so the dish does not become lumpy. Add the grain meal in small amounts and stir constantly while you add the grain.

BASIC CULINARY SKILLS

Mush (Porridge)

1. **Bring the liquid to a boil.**

2. **Add salt** and other seasonings as directed by your recipe.

3. **Add the cereal or meal** in a thin stream, stirring constantly.

4. **Reduce the heat** to a simmer and cook, stirring as necessary, until done.

5. **Adjust the seasonings.** Add any additional ingredients suggested by your recipe.

6. **Serve** the cereal while very hot. (Or cool properly to serve later.)

Recipe Card
71. Polenta

Source: Dave King/Dorling Kindersley Limited

Some cooked meals are stiff enough to pull away from the sides of the pot and are relatively heavy in texture. Others remain liquid enough to pour easily.

Mush and *porridge* are general-purpose names for cooked grain meal. They may be made from almost any type of grain. Cooked meal is known by different names in different parts of the world. *Grits*, for example, is the name for the cornmeal porridge served in the United States, while *polenta* is the name of the cornmeal porridge enjoyed in Italy.

BASIC CULINARY SKILLS

Pilaf

1. **Heat the oil or butter** in a pan.

2. **Add onions** and sauté, stirring frequently, until softened.

3. **Add the grain** all at once and sauté, stirring frequently, until well coated with oil or butter.

Source: Culinary Institute of America

4. **Add the liquid** to the grain and bring to a simmer. Stir the grain to keep it from clumping together or sticking to the pan.

5. **Add any remaining flavorings,** such as bay leaf or thyme, according to your recipe.

Source: Culinary Institute of America

6. **Cover the pot and finish cooking** the pilaf either on the stovetop over low to moderate heat or in the oven. Do not stir the pilaf as it cooks.

7. **Test** a few grains for doneness. They should be tender, but not soft and mushy. If there's a hard white speck in the middle, it's undercooked. Grains should separate easily.

8. **Remove from the heat.** Let the pilaf rest, covered, for 5 minutes.

9. **Uncover** the pot. Use a fork to fluff the grain and release the steam.

Source: Culinary Institute of America

10. **Adjust the seasonings** and serve the pilaf while it is very hot.

Recipe Card

72. Rice Pilaf

Preparing Pilaf Originally from the Middle East, **pilaf** (PEE-lahf) is a grain dish in which the grain—usually rice—is first sautéed in a pan, usually with oil or butter, before adding a hot liquid. It is then covered and cooked over direct heat or in the oven.

In pilaf the grains remain separate and take on a nutty flavor from the initial sautéing of the grain. The grain has a slightly firmer texture than if it had been prepared by boiling.

Preparing Risotto Risotto (rih-ZOHT-toh) is an Italian rice dish typically made with Arborio rice, a special type of short-grain rice with a round shape that becomes creamy when cooked. Just as with a pilaf, the rice is sautéed. Then a small amount of liquid is added to the rice and stirred until it is absorbed. More liquid is added gradually and the rice is stirred constantly. This makes a creamy dish. A properly cooked risotto has a soft, almost pourable consistency.

Chef's Tip

Pilaf and Risotto

Pilafs and risottos call for large amounts of liquid. If you heat the liquid in a separate pot before you add it to the grain, the cooking time is reduced because the liquid is already at a simmer.

BASIC CULINARY SKILLS

Risotto

1. **Heat the oil or butter** in a pot.

2. **Add onions** and sauté, stirring frequently, until softened.

3. **Add the rice** all at once and sauté, stirring frequently, until well coated with oil or butter.

4. **Add one-fourth of the liquid** to the grain and bring to a simmer. Stir constantly until the rice has absorbed all the liquid.

Source: Culinary Institute of America

6. **Remove the pot from the heat** and stir in butter and any other ingredients called for in your recipe.

7. **Serve** the risotto at once.

Source: Culinary Institute of America

5. **Add the remaining liquid** in three more additions, stirring and simmering until the grain absorbs one addition of liquid before you add the next one.

Source: Culinary Institute of America

Recipe Card

73. Risotto

Cooking Grain

Type of Grain (1 cup)	Liquid	Simmer Time	Yield
Rice			
Long-grain white rice	1½–1¾ cups	18–20 minutes	3 cups
Long-grain brown rice	3 cups	40 minutes	4 cups
Short-grain white rice	1–1½ cups	20–30 minutes	3 cups
Short-grain brown rice	2½ cups	35–40 minutes	4 cups
Wild rice	3 cups	30–45 minutes	4 cups
Converted rice	2–2½ cups	20–25 minutes	3 cups
Wheat			
Wheat berries (soak overnight)	3 cups	1 hour	2 cups
Bulgur wheat (as pilaf)	2½ cups	15–20 minutes	2 cups
Cracked wheat	2 cups	20 minutes	3 cups
Grits			
Whole hominy (soak overnight)	2½ cups	2½–3 hours	3 cups
Hominy grits	4 cups	25 minutes	3 cups
Cornmeal, polenta, grits	3–3½ cups	35–45 minutes	3 cups
Oats			
Oat groats	2 cups	45–60 minutes	2 cups
Rolled oats, old-fashioned oats	1½ cups	15–20 minutes	1½ cups
Quick-cooking oats	1½ cups	5 minutes	1½ cups
Barley			
Pearl barley	2 cups	35–45 minutes	4 cups
Scotch barley	2½ cups	50–60 minutes	4 cups
Other			
Quinoa	1–1½ cups	10–12 minutes	3½–4 cups

 **READING CHECKPOINT** *What are the steps in preparing a pilaf?*

Presenting Grains

Grains are versatile. They can be served hot or cold, at any meal, as a side dish, an entrée, or an appetizer. The U.S. Department of Agriculture has established a serving size for grains of approximately ½ cup.

Hot Grain Dishes Many grain dishes are best when they are served as soon as possible after they are cooked. Serve hot grain dishes on heated plates so they will hold their heat. Grains can be seasoned, flavored, and garnished to make them more interesting and flavorful. Hot grain dishes can be served as an entrée, a side dish, or an appetizer.

Cold Grain Salads Many grains are served cold as a salad. Rice, barley, and cracked wheat are some examples of grains that can be served as a salad. Grains to be used in a salad must be fully cooked and tender. The cooked grains are then combined with a dressing or other sauce along with additional ingredients such as vegetables, fruits, or meats. Serve grain salads on chilled plates. Cold grain salads are typically served as a side dish or as an appetizer.

 **READING CHECKPOINT** *What is the correct way to serve a hot grain dish?*

FIGURE 13–4

Tabouli

A cold Middle Eastern salad that consists of bulgur, chopped tomatoes, parsley, mint, and scallions.

CLASSIFYING *Is this a warm-weather presentation or a cold-weather presentation?*

Source: Ian O'Leary/Dorling Kindersley

13.1 ASSESSMENT

Reviewing Concepts

1. What are the four common parts of a single seed of grain?
2. What are the three major types of grain?
3. What are the basic steps involved in boiling or steaming grains?
4. Why are grains regarded as being versatile?

Critical Thinking

5. **Comparing/Contrasting** What is the difference between masa harina, polenta, and hominy grits?
6. **Applying Concepts** Why do wheat berries take longer to cook than bulgur?
7. **Comparing/Contrasting** What is the difference between rolled oats and instant oats?

Test Kitchen

Prepare steel-cut oats, rolled oats, and instant oats. Time the preparation of each. Taste each finished cereal for taste and texture. Evaluate the results in terms of preparation time, taste, and texture.

SCIENCE

Parts of Grains

Research the individual seeds of rice, wheat, corn, oats, barley, rye, and quinoa. Draw and label the parts of each seed. For each grain, describe which component parts of the grain are removed by various types of processing.

 **PROJECT 13**

Preparing Rice You are now ready to work on Project 13, "Preparing Rice," which is available in "My Culinary Lab" or in your *Student's Lab Resources and Study Guide* manual.

Beans and Other Legumes

Key Concepts

- Identifying legumes
- Selecting and storing legumes
- Preparing legumes
- Presenting legumes

Vocabulary

- aflatoxin
- beans
- hummus
- legume
- lentils
- peas

Source: al62/Fotolia

Legumes

A **legume** (LEG-yoom) is a plant with a double-seamed pod containing a single row of seeds. As you know from Chapter 12, legumes eaten fresh, including green beans or green peas, are treated in the kitchen as vegetables. Depending on the variety of legume, people may eat only the seeds or the seeds together with the pods. This chapter deals with legume seeds that are removed from the pod and dried. After they are dried, the seeds can be stored for long periods and then cooked by boiling them in water until tender enough to chew and digest easily.

There are three types of legumes. Dried legumes that are longer than they are round are called **beans**. Examples are navy beans, kidney beans, and fava beans. Peanuts, although we think of them as a type of nut, are really a type of bean. Legumes that are round are called **peas**. Examples of peas are black-eyed peas, green peas, and chickpeas, which are also known as *garbanzo* (gar-BAHN-zoh) *beans* or *ceci* (cheh-chee). The third type of legume is called **lentils**. They are shaped like round disks.

READING CHECKPOINT *What are legumes?*

Selecting and Storing Legumes

Good-quality legumes have a uniform size and smooth skins. Most legumes are sorted and cleaned when they are packaged. A package should have a minimum of shriveled or crushed legumes.

Selecting Legumes Dried legumes are sold in bags, boxes, or packages. The packaging should be intact, with no rips or tears. You can buy legumes in packages of varying sizes.

Canned legumes have usually been cooked and should be soft and ready to eat. They should arrive in cans that are free of dents. The cans should not bulge, and there should be no signs that the contents of the can have started to leak. Beans come in various size cans.

Storing Legumes Buy dry legumes in quantities that will last for no more than one month. Legumes continue to age as they are held in storage. Very old legumes may have a musty flavor. Old legumes also take more time to soak, require more water to cook properly, and may take longer to cook.

Store legumes in airtight and moisture-proof containers. Keep the containers in a cool, dry storage area, at least 6 inches off the floor.

If dry legumes become damp during handling or storage, they can develop a dull or furry coating of mold. There is no way to get rid of the mold once it has formed, and the legumes must be discarded. Legumes that are infected with this mold may develop a dangerous toxic substance known as an **aflatoxin** (aff-la-TOX-in).

 **READING CHECKPOINT** *Why is it important to store legumes properly?*

Preparing Legumes

All dried legumes need to be sorted and rinsed before cooking. Most also need soaking time for softening.

Sorting and Rinsing Dry Legumes Sort and rinse legumes before cooking them. This step removes anything you don't want in the dish you are making, such as small stones. You must also get rid of any legumes that have shriveled or cracked. Never use a legume that is moldy.

Once you have sorted the legumes, put them in a large container. Add enough cold water to cover them completely. Stir them in the water to loosen any dirt. Legumes that are light enough to float to the top of the water either are very dry or may have been attacked by insects that eat out the inside of the bean. It's best to eliminate these.

Pour the legumes into a colander so water can drain away. Then rinse with fresh, cool water.

Legumes

Great Northern Beans

White beans used to make soups and stews as well as baked beans.

Source: Shaday365/Dreamstime LLC

Kidney Beans

Dark red beans, available in various sizes.

Source: Philip Dowell/Dorling Kindersley Limited

Chickpeas

Round legumes with a tan color, popular in Middle Eastern dishes.

Source: Madlen/Shutterstock

Fava Beans

Large, flat beans that are green when fresh and brown when dried. Also known as *broad beans*.

Source: eelnosiva/Fotolia

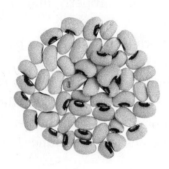

Black-Eyed Peas

Round, beige legume with a pronounced black dot, which is referred to as the *eye*.

Source: Stephen Oliver, Dorling Kindersley

Lentils

Can be brown, green, yellow, or red; popular in Indian cooking.

Source: Andrey Starostin/Shutterstock

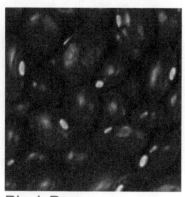

Black Beans

Shiny, small beans, sometimes known as turtle beans, used in Caribbean and South American dishes.

Source: Teresa Azevedo/Shutterstock

Split Peas

Can be green or yellow. Also known as *field pea*. Popular in soups.

Source: Elena Schweitzer/Shutterstock

Pinto Beans

Have a streaked red-and-white skin; are used in many Mexican dishes.

Source: Culinary Institute of America

Soaking Dry Legumes Beans and other legumes have a protective skin. Soaking legumes before cooking softens the skin so they will cook more quickly. Most legumes need to be soaked before cooking. Some, such as lentils and split peas, are ready to boil without soaking. If a recipe requires that you soak the legumes, use one of these techniques:

- **Quick-Soak Method.** Combine the sorted and rinsed beans in a large pot with enough cold water to cover them by about 2 inches. Bring to a boil, then remove the pot from the heat, cover tightly, and let the beans soak for about 1 hour. Drain the beans and rinse once more before cooking them.

Chef's Tip

Sorting Beans

An efficient way to sort beans is to spread them in an even layer in a shallow pan. Work from one end to the other in rows, pushing each row toward one end of the pan to keep them from mixing with the unsorted beans.

CULINARY **SCIENCE**

Dehydrating and Rehydrating Foods

When you let a food dry out, whether by accident or on purpose, the food shrinks and gets lighter. This happens because the food is losing moisture. And although this is good if you want to keep the food from spoiling, it is not so good if you want to eat the food. To make the food moist enough to chew and enjoy, you need to put moisture back into the food.

Dehydration (taking moisture out of foods) is a traditional method of preserving foods. It works especially well with grains and legumes, although it is also common for mushrooms, fruits, sausages, meats, and fish.

Sometimes your job as a cook is to turn dried foods into flavorful, moist, and tender dishes. Steaming, boiling, and simmering techniques all add water to foods, so these are the most appropriate cooking techniques. You may need to give these techniques a boost by soaking dried foods in cold water before you cook them. No matter how you put dried foods and water together, what you are doing is rehydrating them.

Dried food changes in three ways when you rehydrate it:

- Size (or volume)
- Weight
- Texture (dry versus moist and tender versus hard)

You know that dried foods are properly cooked when they are tender enough to bite into easily. More than just getting softer, some dried food also

Three types of dried beans
Source: Bill/Fotolia

gets bigger and plumps up. It weighs more than it did before you added water to it.

The difference in texture is obvious. When you bite into food, you are testing its texture.

Computation

Measure the volume and weight of a 1-pound batch of navy beans by using a measuring cup and a scale. Completely prepare the beans, using the long-soak method. After cooking the beans, measure the volume increase and the weight increase. Convert the increases to a percentage. By what percentage did the beans increase in volume? In weight?

- **Long-Soak Method.** Combine sorted and rinsed beans in a large container with enough cold water to cover them by about 3 inches. Refrigerate the beans as they soak. See the table below showing "Soaking and Cooking Times for Legumes." Drain the beans and rinse once more before cooking them.

Dried legumes can be stored at room temperature for quite a long time. However, once you cook them, legumes need to be handled like other potentially hazardous food. Cool cooked legumes quickly if you must store them. Keep them at a safe temperature during service so pathogens do not make the foods unsafe to eat.

Using Canned Legumes Canned legumes are already cooked. During the canning process, the legumes are combined with a liquid to keep them moist. Before using canned legumes in a recipe, pour them out of the can into a colander and rinse them well. Rinsing away the canning liquid reduces the legumes' sodium content.

READING CHECKPOINT *How do the quick-soak method and the long-soak method for preparing legumes differ?*

FIGURE 13–5
Soaking Beans
Put sorted and rinsed beans in a large container with enough cold water to cover them.

APPLYING CONCEPTS *Why should you put sorted beans in a large container before soaking them?*

Source: Dave King/Image Partners 2005/Dorling Kindersley Media Library/Dorling Kindersley

Soaking and Cooking Times for Legumes

Legume	Soaking Time (Long-Soak Method)	Cooking Time
Black beans	4 hours	1½ hours
Black-eyed peas	No soaking necessary	1 hour
Chickpeas	4 hours	2–2½ hours
Fava beans	12 hours	3 hours
Great Northern beans	4 hours	1 hour
Kidney beans (red or white)	4 hours	1 hour
Lentils	No soaking necessary	30–40 minutes
Peas, split	No soaking necessary	30 minutes
Peas, whole	4 hours	40 minutes
Pinto beans	4 hours	1–1½ hours

Cooking Dry Legumes

① **Sort and rinse** the legumes before preparing them.

Source: Culinary Institute of America

② **Soak the legumes,** if necessary, using either the long-soak or quick-soak method.

③ **Place in a pot** and add cold water to cover the legumes by about 2 inches.

④ **Bring to a boil.** Stir the legumes occasionally to keep them from sticking to the pan.

⑤ **Continue boiling** until the legumes are nearly tender.

⑥ **Skim the foam** to improve the flavor of the finished dish.

Source: Culinary Institute of America

⑦ **Add salt,** as well as any acidic ingredients (tomatoes, vinegar, or citrus juices, for instance) called for by your recipe, during the final third of cooking time.

⑧ **Cook lentils until they are tender** enough to mash easily. However, the skins should still be intact.

⑨ **Drain** fully cooked legumes or cool and hold them in their cooking liquid for later use.

 Recipe Card

74. Stewed White Beans

Presenting Legumes

Bean dishes are an interesting part of many cuisines. They may be served as a side dish, as a soup, as a main dish, or as an appetizer. Some bean dishes are served hot and others are served cold.

Legume Dishes You can serve legumes directly after they are simmered. They are also often cooked together with other ingredients to make a stew, soup, or chili.

Cooked legumes can be mashed or puréed after they are cooked. **Hummus** (HOOM-uhs), for example, is a popular Middle Eastern spread made from mashed or puréed chickpeas that are seasoned and served with pita bread, chips, or raw vegetables. Refried beans are made by mashing beans and cooking them with a fat such as lard or oil. Beans

 Recipe Card

75. Refried Beans

FIGURE 13–6

Beans and Rice

Red kidney beans, black-eyed peas, and green beans on a bed of rice.

INFERRING *Why are dishes such as this often described as a healthy alternative to meats?*

Source: Susanna Price/Dorling Kindersley Limited

can be added to soups as an ingredient or the soup can be made primarily from beans. Examples of bean soups include Senate bean soup, a Caribbean-style black bean soup, and split-pea soups.

Adding Cooked Legumes to Other Dishes Throughout the world, dishes that combine grains and legumes provide an important way of maintaining a healthy diet. Grain and legume combinations can be served as a main dish or as a side dish. Examples include red beans and rice and "Hoppin' John," a dish made with rice and black-eyed peas.

Combining legumes and grains is a good, inexpensive way to increase protein, fiber, and vitamins in your diet. A meal of rice and beans, for example, contains more fiber, vitamins, and minerals than meat. It contains less fat, especially saturated fat, than meat. And, far from adding cholesterol to your diet as meats do, rice and beans actually help your body clear out cholesterol.

Legume Salads After legumes are fully cooked and tender, they can be cooled and prepared as a salad. Legume salads are often served as a side dish or as part of an appetizer. To make a legume salad, combine the cooked and drained legumes with the desired dressing or sauce. Add additional ingredients such as herbs, chopped tomatoes, onions, and other vegetables. Serve legume salads on chilled plates.

FIGURE 13–7

Lentil Salad

A cold Greek salad made with green lentils, black olives, and lemon juice.

SOLVING PROBLEMS *Can you think of an additional ingredient that you might consider adding to this salad?*

Source: Clive Streeter/Image Partners 2005/ Dorling Kindersley Media Library/Dorling Kindersley

Most dressings added to legumes in a salad contain either vinegar or lemon juice. This toughens the skin of the legumes. To keep the texture of legumes in salads creamy and soft, do not add the dressing until you are ready to serve the salad.

 **READING CHECKPOINT** *Name several ways you might present cooked legumes.*

13.2 ASSESSMENT

Reviewing Concepts

1. What are legumes?
2. Identify three types of legumes. Briefly describe each.
3. How do you typically prepare legumes for cooking?
4. How can you use legumes in creating various dishes?

Critical Thinking

5. **Comparing/Contrasting** What are the major differences between the quick-soak method for preparing legumes and the long-soak method?
6. **Applying Concepts** If some stored beans have mold growing on them, would you feel safe in using other beans from the same storage container?
7. **Predicting** Restaurants sometimes hold a bean salad for days. Assuming that the salad is held at a safe temperature, is this a good idea? Explain your answer.

Test Kitchen

Prepare dried beans using the quick-soak method and the long-soak method. Compare them in terms of flavor and texture with a can of prepared beans that have been rinsed. Evaluate the results.

SOCIAL STUDIES ————————●
Wintertime Legume Dishes

Because legumes are inexpensive, easily stored, and highly nutritious, they are often used as an important part of the winter diet. Research hearty legume dishes suitable for a winter dinner. Describe the dish. Make sure to indicate the country or region in which the dish originated. If possible, make the dish.

READING PREVIEW

Key Concepts

- Identifying types of pasta
- Preparing pasta
- Presenting pasta

Vocabulary

- al dente
- dumplings
- extruded
- fettuccine
- gnocchi
- lasagna
- lo mein
- macaroni
- noodle
- pasta
- pierogi
- ravioli
- semolina flour
- spaetzle
- tagliatelle
- tortellini
- udon
- wontons
- wrappers

Types of Pasta

Pasta is Italian for "dough." The term is also used to describe the category of starchy foods made from shaped dough that includes flour and liquid. Pasta is typically cooked in boiling or simmering water. Almost every cuisine has some dish that is similar to pasta. The names of the dishes vary, but the concept—starchy foods made from shaped dough that includes flour and water—remains the same. The variety of names is just an imaginative way to dress up one of the world's simple staple foods.

The term *pasta* is most often associated with Italian cuisine. **Macaroni** is another common name used to refer to pasta in general. It, too, is associated with Italian cuisine. Wheat flour is commonly used in Italian pasta.

Noodle is another general term for pasta. Asian-style pastas are more often known as noodles, as are the pastas made in some parts of France and Germany. Asian-style noodles often use flours made from beans or rice.

Dumplings are made from dough that is soft enough to drop into a pot of boiling water. **Spaetzle** (SHPET-zuhl) is a popular Austrian and German dumpling. **Gnocchi** (NYOH-kee) is an Italian dumpling. **Pierogi** (peer-OH-gee) are Polish half-moon-shaped dumplings. They can have a sweet or a savory filling and can be fried or boiled.

Pasta is made in a wide variety of shapes and is available in two forms:

- Fresh pasta
- Dried pasta

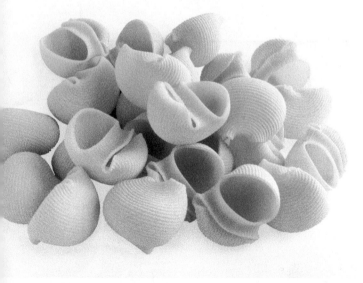

Source: Maria Brzostowska/Fotolia

Thailand

The cuisine of Thailand has recently been growing in popularity all over the world. Traditional Thai dishes and seasonings including curries; nam pla (nahm plah), which is a type of fish sauce; chiles; shrimp; and a host of dried and fermented foods. Most Thai dishes are served with rice or noodles. Contrasting the intense flavors of a curry or chili with the bland taste of rice or noodles is one way Thai cooks achieve a balance between what they call the four essences: hot, sour, salty, and sweet.

Rice grows extremely well throughout all of Southeast Asia. Thailand is at the center of the Southeast Asian peninsula. Throughout Thailand, rice is the central part of every meal. In fact, a common greeting is *"Kin khao!"* or "Eat rice!" The Thai people eat nearly ¾ pound of rice every day—nearly 40 times as much as the average person in the United States.

People in the northern part of Thailand favor sticky rice. In the south, they prefer long-grain fragrant rice, such as jasmine rice. Rice is always served very hot, and it may come to the table in covered woven baskets or lidded porcelain bowls. Thai cooks prepare rice without any added salt and cook it until it is quite dry so it can better absorb juices and flavors.

When dining at home, people may make small balls of rice with their fingertips to dip into the intensely spiced curries for which Thailand is famous. Thai curries come in different colors—each with a different level of spiciness. Green curry includes the hottest green chiles; red curry is also extremely hot, though not quite as fiery as green curry. Yellow curries get their color from turmeric, a spice that came to Thailand from Malaysia or Burma. Mussaman (MUSS-ah-mahn), or Muslim-style, curry features typically Middle Eastern spices such as clove, cumin, fennel seed, cinnamon, and cardamom. Most Thai curries include coconut milk, but some curries substitute tamarind paste, which is a paste made from a tart

fruit with a citrus flavor. Rice is an important part of enjoying a curry. Taking a bite of rice cools your mouth and tames the bite of the chiles in the curry.

Rice, along with wheat, beans, and buckwheat, is also made into noodles, another significant part of Thai cooking. Street vendors throughout the country sell pad thai (pahd tie), a dish of rice noodles served with bean sprouts, dried shrimp, eggs, chicken, pork, or onions. Mee krop (mee crop) is another popular dish, made of noodles that are puffed in oil and served with a sweet dressing.

Research

Research Thai noodles. What are the names of the noodles commonly used in Thai cooking? What grains or legumes are they made from? Research recipes for different styles of Thai noodle dishes. Based on your research, prepare a Thai noodle dish.

Pad thai is a traditional noodle dish found throughout Thailand
Source: GraficallyMinded/Alamy

FIGURE 13–8

Flavored Fresh Pasta
Adding vegetables, herbs, and spices to pasta changes its flavor and color.

SOLVING PROBLEMS *What ingredients do you think might give pasta the colors shown here?*

Source: Ian O'Leary/Image Partners 2005/Dorling Kindersley Media Library/Dorling Kindersley

Fresh Pasta Fresh pasta consists of dough made by blending flour with a liquid such as water or eggs. The dough is soft enough to knead by hand but stiff enough to hold a shape. Fresh pasta should feel smooth and supple. It should not appear dry or crumbly. It can be rolled into thin sheets and cut into shapes. After cooking, fresh pasta has a delicate texture.

Fresh pasta may be plain or it may be flavored with vegetables, fruits, spices, or herbs. These additional ingredients add both flavor and color to the pasta.

If your kitchen does not make its own dough, fresh pasta can usually be purchased. Fresh pasta is typically available commercially in sheets and in ribbon shapes such as **fettuccine** (feht-too-CHEE-nee) or **tagliatelle** (tag-lee-ah-TEHL-ee). Many Asian-style pastas, such as **udon** (oo-DOHN) or **lo mein** (low mane) noodles, can also be purchased fresh. **Wrappers** are another type of pasta used frequently in Asian cooking. Wrappers are sold in squares, rounds, and rectangles. They can be made from wheat or rice flour.

Fresh pasta or noodles are often dusted with cornstarch to keep the sheets or strands from sticking together. Keep fresh pasta in its packaging in the refrigerator or the freezer.

Dried Pasta Dried pasta is also made by blending flour with a liquid such as water or eggs to create dough. However, the dough is usually too stiff to shape by hand, so most dried pastas are made by machines. These pasta-making machines can create the same flat ribbon shapes found in fresh pastas. The dough can also be **extruded** (pushed through an opening in a pasta-making machine) to make special shapes, such as elbow macaroni, spaghetti, or penne. The shaped pasta is then dried until it is hard and brittle. Dried pasta should have an even color and break cleanly without bending.

Italian-style pasta is usually made with **semolina flour** (seh-muh-LEE-nuh), pale yellow flour made from durum (DUR-um) wheat. Durum is very hard wheat that has a high protein content and makes an elastic dough. Semolina flour gives pasta a pleasing, chewy texture after it is cooked.

Flours from other grains—including rice, chickpeas, buckwheat, quinoa, and millet—can be used to make dried pastas. These pastas have unique flavors and textures. They may be important to have on hand if you need to cook for people on a wheat- or gluten-free diet. As with fresh pasta, dried pastas can also be flavored with a number of different ingredients to give them a special color or flavor.

Global Pastas

Soba Noodles (Dried)

Soba noodles are made from buckwheat flour and have a brown color. They are popular in Japanese cooking.

Source: spe/Shutterstock

Wrappers (Fresh)

Wrappers can be made from wheat or rice flour. They are used to make a variety of Asian-style dishes.

Source: Paul Williams/Image Partners 2005/Dorling Kindersley Media Library/Dorling Kindersley

Flat Pasta (Dried)

Flat pasta is usually made from semolina flour and water. Flat pasta shapes include linguini (pictured here) and fettuccine. They may be sold as straight strands or in "nests."

Source: Culinary Institute of America

Rice Vermicelli (Dried)

This Asian pasta is made from rice instead of wheat. The noodles are very white after cooking.

Source: Elzbieta Sekowska/Fotolia

Egg Noodles (Fresh)

Egg noodles are made from wheat flour and eggs. They have a flat shape after they are cooked. They may have curly edges and are available in many sizes, from fine egg noodles to broad noodles.

Source: Philip Dowell/Image Partners 2005/Dorling Kindersley Media Library/Dorling Kindersley

Pasta is sold commercially in packages of various sizes, from 1-pound boxes to bulk packaging. Store dried pasta either in its original packaging or in airtight and moisture-proof containers in a cool, dry area. Keep pasta off the floor so pests cannot get into the packages. Do not let the packaging or the pasta become damp.

READING CHECKPOINT *In what forms is pasta available?*

Dried Pasta Shapes

Elbow Macaroni

Elbow macaroni is a popular pasta shape used for baked dishes and salads.

Source: Roger Phillips/Dorling Kindersley

Shells

Shells are produced in a range of sizes; small shells are used to garnish soups or for salads, and larger shells may be large enough to stuff and bake.

Source: David Murray/Dorling Kindersley Limited

Penne (PEN-nay)

Penne pasta may have ridges, as shown here, or it may be smooth.

Source: Noraluca013/Shutterstock

Manicotti (man-uh-KOT-tee)

Manicotti is a long, wide, ridged tube that is typically stuffed and then combined with a sauce and baked.

Source: John Scott/Getty Images

Rigatoni (ree-gah-TOE-nee)

Rigatoni is typically made with ridges, as shown, and is often combined with hearty sauces and then baked.

Source: Stephen Oliver/DK Images

Preparing Pasta

Preparing pasta involves first making the pasta dough and preparing the actual pasta. After that, the pasta is boiled before it is presented. Using commercially prepared pasta saves you the time and effort of making fresh pasta dough and then rolling out the dough to make pasta.

Spinach Fusilli (foo-SEEL-lee)

Dried pastas made with spinach have a green color. Fusilli is twisted to give it the appearance of a corkscrew.

Source: Stephen Oliver/Dorling Kindersley Limited

Farfalle (fah-FAHL-lay); Also Called Bowties

Farfalle is made by pinching a piece of pasta in the center to give it a bowtie shape.

Source: © David Murray/Shutterstock

Lasagna (luh-ZAHN-yuh)

Lasagna noodles are broad with a ruffled edge and are combined with a filling and sauce to make the baked pasta dish lasagna.

Source: EuToch/Shutterstock

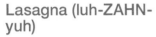

Orecchiette (ohr-RECK-ee-etty)

Orecchiette is a small, disk-shaped pasta good for pairing with hearty sauces.

Source: eelnosiva/Fotolia

Spaghetti

Spaghetti is sold in a range of thicknesses.

Source: Africa Studio/ Shutterstock

Capellini (kahp-payl-LEE-nee), Also Called Angel Hair

Capellini is an especially fine pasta, similar to spaghetti but much thinner.

Source: Philip Dowell/Image Partners 2005/Dorling Kindersley Media Library/Dorling Kindersley

Fresh Pasta Dough Fresh pasta dough is simple to prepare. Flour and eggs, along with either oil or water, are mixed and then kneaded to make a stiff dough. After making the dough, you need to let it rest before rolling it out with a pasta machine or a rolling pin.

Boiling Pasta Boiling pasta softens it so it is easy to eat. Fresh pasta is already moist when it goes into the pot, so it cooks very quickly. You can usually cook fresh pasta as you need it.

Fresh Egg Pasta

1. **Combine the flour and salt** in a bowl. Make a well in the center.

2. **Add the liquid** (usually eggs and water) in the well. If your recipe calls for oil, add it with the liquid ingredients.

3. **Pull the flour into the liquid**, stirring by hand until a loose mass forms. Work as rapidly as possible. Adjust consistency with additional flour or water as needed.

Source: Culinary Institute of America

Source: Culinary Institute of America

4. **Turn the dough** out onto a floured work surface.

5. **Knead** until the texture becomes smooth and elastic.

6. **Gather and smooth** the kneaded dough into a ball. If the ball is too large for your pasta machine, you can cut it.

Recipe Card

76. Fresh Egg Pasta

7. **Cover** the dough. Let it rest at room temperature for at least 1 hour.

8. **Roll the dough into thin sheets.** Cut into desired shapes by hand or by using a pasta machine.

Source: Culinary Institute of America

9. **Cook** the pasta. Or store in a refrigerator for up to 2 days.

Dried pasta, on the other hand, typically takes longer to cook, so you may need to prepare the pasta ahead of time and then reheat it in simmering water immediately before you serve it. To hold pasta for later service, rinse or submerge it in cold water until it is well chilled. After it is chilled, drain it thoroughly and mix it with a little oil. Transfer the pasta to a storage container, cover it, and keep it refrigerated until you are ready to reheat it for service.

Dried semolina pasta is traditionally cooked **al dente** (al DEN-tay). This Italian expression means "to the tooth," and it is used to describe pasta that

Boiling Pasta

1 **Bring a large pot of water to a boil** and add salt. Use at least 1 gallon of water for every pound of pasta. Add 1 ounce of salt (2 tablespoons) to every gallon of water.

Source: Culinary Institute of America

2 **Add the pasta** and stir until it is softened, submerged, and separated. Fresh and filled pasta is best when prepared in simmering, not boiling, water. Dried pasta is cooked at a boil throughout the entire cooking time.

Source: Culinary Institute of America

3 **Cook the pasta** until it is done, stirring occasionally. Pasta that is served immediately is cooked until fully tender. Pasta that will be baked, reheated, or held in a sauce should be slightly undercooked.

Source: Culinary Institute of America

4 **Drain** the pasta in a colander as soon as it is cooked.

5 **Serve** the pasta immediately with a sauce or toss the pasta with oil, chill, and store for later service.

Source: Culinary Institute of America

is cooked only until it gives a slight resistance when you bite it. The pasta should be neither too soft nor too hard.

READING CHECKPOINT *What are the steps in boiling pasta?*

Recipe Cards

77. Couscous with Lamb and Chicken Stew

78. Soba Noodles with Sesame

79. Pasta alla Carbonara

Presenting Pasta

Pasta is an extremely popular food. It can be served hot, as an appetizer, as the main course, or as a side dish. It can also be served cold in salads. Pasta is also added to other dishes, such as soups.

Adding Sauce to Pasta Combining pasta with a sauce is perhaps the most common way to present pasta. Different pasta shapes are traditionally paired with different types of sauces. A long, thin pasta such as spaghetti or linguini is traditionally served with a smooth, thin sauce such as a tomato or cream sauce that can cling to the pasta. Sometimes the sauce is as simple as good olive oil. Extruded tube-shaped pasta shapes such as rigatoni or penne are most often paired with chunkier sauces. Pasta shapes with wrinkles or ridges, such as fusilli, are also used with a chunky sauce.

To add a sauce to pasta, first drain the pasta well after cooking to remove any water that is still clinging to it or that is trapped inside tube-shaped pasta. Extra water dilutes the flavor of the sauce and may make it too thin to cling to the pasta properly.

There are two methods for combining cooked and drained pasta with a sauce:

- You can add the pasta directly to the sauce and then toss them together. This is typically done in a sauté pan over medium-high heat. This method of combining sauce and pasta guarantees that the pasta dish is very hot when you serve it.

- You can ladle the sauce over the drained pasta on a heated plate. You need to make sure that the pasta, the sauce, and the bowl or platter are very hot. Otherwise, the pasta will cool off too quickly.

FIGURE 13–9

Saucing Pasta

A pasta shape like orecchiette is a good match with a meat sauce.

APPLYING CONCEPTS *Why is this sauce a good choice to pair with this pasta shape?*

Source: Clive Streeter/Image Partners 2005/ Dorling Kindersley Media Library/Dorling Kindersley

Filled Pasta Dishes Pasta shells can be filled with various foods, including cheese, meats, seafood, and vegetables. Dried pasta is filled after the pasta is cooked. Fresh pasta is typically filled before it is cooked.

To add a filling to dried pasta, you first need to cook the pasta. Leave it slightly undercooked if you are planning to cook the pasta again after it is filled. Drain the pasta and cool it so you can handle it without burning yourself. Then spoon or pipe the filling into the pasta.

Ravioli and tortellini are two familiar Italian-style filled pastas made with fresh pasta. **Ravioli** (rav-ee-OH-lee) is Italian for "little wraps." Ravioli is made by layering a filling between two sheets of pasta and then cutting out filled squares, rounds, or rectangles. **Tortellini** (tohr-te-LEEN-ee) is Italian for "little twists." Tortellini is made by cutting out circles or squares of fresh pasta, adding a filling, and then folding and twisting the dough to get a specific shape.

Other cuisines also have a strong tradition of filled pastas. **Wontons** (WAHN-tahns) are a type of Chinese dumpling made with a fresh pasta wrapper. They are often served as appetizers or in soups.

To make filled pasta using fresh pasta, you can make your own dough or you can buy commercially prepared fresh pasta sheets or wrappers. After fresh pasta is filled, simmer it until the pasta is tender and the filling is very hot.

Serve filled pasta as is, with a sauce, or as a garnish for a soup. Filled pasta can be served immediately with a sauce or it can be baked with a sauce and then served.

Lasagna (luh-ZAHN-yuh) is a layered pasta dish. To assemble it, you put layers of sauce, pasta, and filling into an oiled dish. You may add a topping,

Chef's Tip

Using a Pastry Bag

Use a pastry bag to add a soft filling to pasta. The bag should not have a tip. Spoon the filling into the bag. Then twist the large end of the bag to force the filling into the pasta. Stop twisting to stop pressing out the filling.

Recipe Cards

80. Tortellini

81. Lasagna

FIGURE 13–10
Making Ravioli or Tortellini
Adding filling to fresh pasta rounds.

APPLYING CONCEPTS *How can this method be used to make either ravioli or tortellini?*

Source: Dorling Kindersley/Image Partners 2005/Dorling Kindersley Media Library/Dorling Kindersley

such as grated cheese or bread crumbs. The dish is baked until the pasta is fully cooked and tender. All the ingredients, including the sauce and fillings, should be very hot. If there is a topping, it should be golden brown.

Baked Pasta Dishes To assemble a simple baked pasta dish such as macaroni and cheese, you combine the pasta with the sauce and any other fillings. With any baked pasta dish, make sure to slightly undercook the pasta. The pasta will finish cooking as it bakes.

Recipe Card

82. Macaroni and Cheese

READING CHECKPOINT *What are the two ways to combine cooked pasta with sauce?*

13.3 ASSESSMENT

Reviewing Concepts

1. What is the difference between fresh and dried pasta?

2. How does cooking fresh pasta differ from cooking dried pasta?

3. What are the two methods for combining cooked and drained pasta with a sauce?

Critical Thinking

4. Comparing/Contrasting What are the advantages and disadvantages of using fresh versus dried pasta in a restaurant?

5. Recognizing Patterns What type of sauce would be best suited for farfalle pasta?

6. Drawing Conclusions Can you think of any disadvantages of adding pasta directly to the sauce before serving (as opposed to ladling the sauce over the cooked and drained pasta)?

Test Kitchen

Prepare a batch of fresh fettuccini and a batch of dried fettuccini. Compare the cooking time. Taste the finished pasta and evaluate the differences between the two pastas.

SOCIAL STUDIES ————●
Origin of Pasta

Research the history and origins of pasta. Describe your findings. Indicate which pasta dishes today resemble the most ancient pasta dishes.

Reviewing Content

Choose the letter that best answers the question or completes the statement.

1. The seed of grain without its husk is the
   a. germ.
   b. kernel.
   c. bran.
   d. endosperm.

2. Which of the following is not a legume?
   a. lentil
   b. chickpea
   c. oat
   d. pinto bean

3. Italian-style pasta is usually made with
   a. buckwheat flour.
   b. rice flour.
   c. semolina flour.
   d. corn flour.

4. A pearl grain is grain that
   a. is round.
   b. has been scrubbed of its bran.
   c. has been boiled.
   d. has been soaked in a solution of lime.

5. Using the long-soak method, you soak black beans for
   a. 12 hours.
   b. 4 hours.
   c. 1 hour.
   d. ½ hour.

6. Hominy is the whole dried kernel of what grain?
   a. wheat
   b. rice
   c. oats
   d. corn

7. Bulgur is
   a. made from corn that has been soaked in a solution of lime.
   b. made from parcooked rice.
   c. made from steamed whole wheat berries that are crushed.
   d. made from steamed groats that are rolled into flat flakes.

Understanding Concepts

8. What does the term *farinaceous* mean?

9. What is the difference between a legume and a grain?

10. What is fresh pasta?

11. What is a whole grain?

12. Is a lentil classed as a legume or a grain?

13. Which type of grain is more processed: a whole grain or a refined grain?

14. Why are legumes sorted before being rinsed?

Critical Thinking

15. **COMPARING/CONTRASTING** What is the difference between preparing grains by boiling them and preparing them by steaming them?

16. **PREDICTING** You are planning to make filled pasta using large, dried shell pasta. After filling, the pasta will be baked. To what degree of doneness will you cook the pasta before it is filled? Explain your answer.

Culinary Math

17. **SOLVING PROBLEMS** A 10-serving recipe for lasagna calls for 14 ounces of ricotta cheese. How much cheese is required to make 65 servings?

18. **APPLYING CONCEPTS** If a 10-serving recipe calls for 2½ pounds of spaghetti, how much pasta is a single serving?

On the Job

19. **APPLYING CONCEPTS** If you ran an Italian restaurant, which method of adding sauce to pasta would you prefer? Explain your answer.

20. **COMMUNICATING** A customer asks you the difference between rice pilaf and risotto. How would you answer? (Remember that the customer wants to know not only how they differ in preparation but also how they differ in flavor and texture.)

Specialty Bakers

Specialty bakers use their knowledge of foods, baking techniques, nutrition, and flavor development to develop menus and food products that meet the health and nutrition needs of their clients, while maintaining high standards for quality and creativity. While the pathway to becoming a specialty baker is similar to that for all bakers, the individual who chooses to make a specialty out of allergy-free, gluten-free, sugar-free, lactose-free, or low-sodium baking typically includes either coursework in special diets and dietetics or experience working in a kitchen or bakeshop that caters to people who have specific conditions, including celiac disease, diabetes, heart disease, or serious allergies.

Specialty bakers may work in a number of environments, such as wholesale or retail bakeries, hotels, food manufacturers, restaurants, volume and institutional settings, or contract feeding and school foodservice.

Baker's assistants are responsible for following recipes, measuring and mixing ingredients, operating baking equipment safely, and following all health and sanitation guidelines.

Bread bakers produce a wide range of breads. Some work in shops or outlets devoted exclusively to artisan breads; others work for larger retail operations. Bread bakers not only mix, shape, and bake a variety of yeast-raised breads, they are also responsible for developing specific formulations for products as diverse as yeast-free or gluten-free breads for their clients.

Entry-Level Requirements

Many specialty bakers attend culinary schools and earn an associate degree in baking and pastry. This period of formal education typically includes course work that lays some of the important groundwork for specialization: food safety and sanitation, business and management in the foodservice industry, nutrition, culinary science, and principles of flavor and texture development. However, you will still find that others have acquired their skills through on-the-job training and apprenticeships.

Helpful for Advancement

Certifications from organizations including the American Culinary Federation (ACF) and the Retail Bakers of America (RBA) can advance your career. These groups have established various criteria to evaluate your knowledge and skill. A degree in a health- or nutrition-related area, including food or culinary science, is another avenue to advance your career and achieve the goal of becoming a specialty baker.

Another effective way to advance your career in specialty baking is to join organizations and groups that can help you create a network.

Owning and operating a specialty baked goods wholesale or retail shop may be the ultimate goal for some. Learning more about business practices and management by attending classes or workshops is helpful in starting your own bakery.

GLUTEN FREE   EGG FREE   LACTOSE FREE   SUGAR FREE

RICHARD COPPEDGE, JR., CMB

Richard Coppedge is a Professor of Baking and Pastry arts at The Culinary Institute of America (CIA), where he teaches advanced baking principles to students pursuing their bachelor's and associate degrees from the CIA.

Before joining the college's faculty in 1992, Chef Coppedge held positions at such prestigious properties as the Ritz-Carlton Hotel Company and Walt Disney World. Chef Coppedge was also the bread baker for the Dunes Club in Providence, Rhode Island, and the Narragansett Bay Baking Company in Newport, Rhode Island. For 10 years he was an assistant professor in the baking program at Johnson and Wales University in Providence.

Richard Coppedge, Jr., CMB

Source: Courtesy of Richard Coppedge & Culinary Institute of America

He has been teaching students how to bake enticing alternatives for people with celiac disease or wheat allergies for many years. In this time he has not only educated his students by helping them to better understand their craft, he has also helped many an entrepreneur open a successful business selling wheat-free and gluten-free products, and enriched the lives of many people through his continuing-education classes by teaching them to make their own wheat-free or gluten-free baked goods.

VITAL STATISTICS

Graduated: BS, AS from Johnson and Wales University

Profession: Professor in Baking and Pastry Arts

Interesting Item: Authored a book on specialty baking: *Gluten Free Baking with The Culinary Institute of America* (Adams Media, 2008)

Member of Bread Bakers Guild and Retail Bakers of America

CAREER PROFILE

Salary Ranges

Baker's Assistant: $16,000 to $25,000

Bread Baker: $25,000 to $45,000

Assistant Pastry Chef: $25,000 to $50,000

Pastry Chef: $30,000 to $80,000

Executive Pastry Chef: $45,000 to $100,000

Stocks, Sauces, and Soups

14.1 Stocks

14.2 Sauces

14.3 Soups

Stocks

Key Concepts

- Identifying basic ingredients for stocks
- Identifying types of stocks
- Preparing and storing stocks
- Using stocks

Vocabulary

- brown stock
- double-strength stock
- fish fumet
- fonds de cuisine
- glaze
- neutral stock
- shellfish stock
- stock
- stock base
- vegetable stock
- white stock

Basic Ingredients for Stocks

A **stock** is a flavorful liquid used primarily to prepare soups, sauces, stews, and braises. The quality of a stock plays a major role in the quality of the soups and sauces you make with that stock. In fact, stocks are such an important part of classic French cooking that they are known as **fonds de cuisine** (FAHN duh kwee-ZEEN), which translates as "foundations of cooking."

Stocks are produced by simmering together the following basic types of ingredients:

- Bones, shells, or vegetables
- Mirepoix (and, often, additional aromatic ingredients)
- Spices and herbs
- A liquid (typically water)

Bones, Shells, or Vegetables The major ingredient in any stock determines its flavor, color, and body. A stock will use one of these major ingredients:

- **Beef and Veal Bones.** Use bones with some meat still clinging to them to give the stock a richer flavor.
- **Poultry Bones.** Use necks, wing tips, backs, or a cut-up chicken.
- **Fish Bones.** Use bones from flounder, sole, or any other lean white fish.
- **Shellfish Shells.** Use lobster, shrimp, or crayfish shells.
- **Vegetables.** Use a combination of vegetables for a rich, balanced flavor. Avoid starchy vegetables (potatoes or hard squash) to keep the stock from becoming cloudy. Also avoid vegetables that "bleed" such as beets.

Source: Marzia Giacobbe/Fotolia

Mirepoix Remember from Section 6.2 that most stocks include a mirepoix. Remember from Chapter 6 that a combination of onions, carrots, and celery is a *standard mirepoix*. A mirepoix in which parsnips replace the carrots (and often leeks replace some of the onions) is called a *white mirepoix*. Some stock recipes call for additional aromatic ingredients such as dry white wine, mushrooms, leeks, garlic, tomato paste, or even ham. Different types of stocks will call for different mirepoix and different combinations of aromatic ingredients.

Spices and Herbs Dried spices such as whole peppercorns give stocks a pungent aroma. Fresh or dried herbs such as bay leaf, thyme, or parsley stems also provide aroma to stocks. Individual recipes will list the specific spices and herbs a stock requires. Remember to tie dried herbs and spices up into a sachet d'épices. Fresh herbs are tied into a bouquet garni. (Sachet d'épices and bouquet garni are discussed in Section 6.2.)

Liquid Most stocks begin with cold water, never hot water. This prevents cloudiness. It also allows the flavor and nutrients to be gently and evenly extracted as the liquid moves from cold to the beginning of simmering.

 **READING CHECKLIST** *What are the four types of basic ingredients used in stocks?*

Types of Stock

A stock is named for its major ingredient (and in the case of brown and white stocks, how that major ingredient is prepared). There are five basic types of stock:

- A **brown stock** is made from bones that are roasted until they have a deep reddish-brown color. Using roasted bones causes the stock to have a dark brown color and a fuller "roasted meat" flavor. Brown veal stock, made from roasted veal bones, is the most common type of brown stock.
- A **white stock** is made from unroasted bones. Some chefs blanch the bones by simmering them in water before starting to make the stock. White beef stock is sometimes called **neutral stock** because it has a mild, unassertive flavor.
- A **fish fumet** (foo-MAY) is made by cooking fish bones in a little oil until they turn opaque (known as sweating) before adding water, mirepoix, spices, and herbs.
- A **shellfish stock** is made from shellfish shells that are sautéed in a little oil until they turn a deep vivid red before adding water, mirepoix, spices, and herbs.
- A **vegetable stock** contains a variety of vegetables that are cut or sliced before simmering.

FIGURE 14–1

Basic Ingredients for Stock
Ingredients for a chicken stock
APPLYING CONCEPTS *Is this a white stock or a brown stock?*
Source: Culinary Institute of America

Stock	Description	Ingredients for 1 Gallon of Stock
Brown stock	Roasted meat flavor, deep reddish-brown	8 lb roasted bones (meat or poultry) 1 lb mirepoix 4 to 6 oz tomato paste 1 sachet d'épices 6 qt cold water
White stock	Mild flavor, almost colorless when hot	8 lb unroasted bones (meat, poultry, or fish) 1 lb mirepoix 1 sachet d'épices 6 qt cold water
Fish fumet	Fish flavor, light color, translucent but not perfectly clear	11 lb fish bones (sweated) 1 lb white mirepoix 1 bouquet garni 4 qt cold water
Shellfish stock	Seafood flavor, red to orange-red color, translucent but not perfectly clear	11 lb shells (lobster, shrimp, or crayfish) 1 lb mirepoix 1 sachet d'épices 6 qt cold water
Vegetable stock	Varies according to vegetables selected	5 lb combined vegetables 1 lb mirepoix 1 sachet d'épices 5 qt cold water

 **READING CHECKPOINT** *What are the five basic types of stock?*

Preparing and Storing Stocks

As with most culinary efforts, much of the work of making a good stock is preparing the ingredients properly and choosing the right equipment to use. There are, however, three keys to success when simmering a stock:

- Keep the stock at a gentle simmer.
- Skim any foam or froth.
- Simmer long enough for a full flavor.

Preparing Bones Purchase beef or veal bones cut into short lengths. Pieces about 3 inches long are best. This releases more flavor into the stock.

White and brown stocks can be made from other types of bones. For lamb, venison, or pork bones, use the same simmering time as veal bones. For turkey, pheasant, or duck bones, use the same time as chicken bones.

FIGURE 14–2

Sweating Fish Bones
Cook bones and mirepoix until they soften and begin to release moisture.

DRAWING CONCLUSIONS *If you sweat the bones first, what type of stock are you making?*

Source: Culinary Institute of America

FIGURE 14–3

Cutting Mirepoix
Cut the mirepoix into a shape that best suits the stock's total simmering time.

RECOGNIZING PATTERNS *Why might a mirepoix be cut very fine?*

Source: Culinary Institute of America

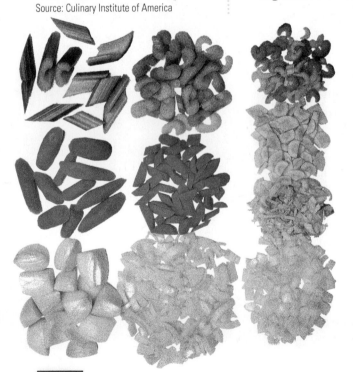

The following additional preparation steps also play an important part in developing the best color and flavor.

- **Browning Bones.** Place the bones in a hot roasting pan and roast at 375°F or higher until the meat clinging to the bones turns a deep brown. Remove the bones and pour off the extra fat. Dissolve any drippings that accumulate in the roasting pan in a little water and then add them back to the stock.

- **Blanching Bones.** The purpose of blanching bones is to keep the color of a stock very pale or clear. Place the bones in a large pot with enough cold water to cover them by about 3 inches. Bring the water to a simmer. Immediately drain and rinse the bones.

- **Sweating Bones.** The flavor of a fish fumet is intensified by sweating the bones in a small amount of fat. Sweating, as you remember from Section 8.1, involves moderate heat. The goal is to gently cook the fish bones along with the mirepoix until they soften and begin to release their moisture. The flesh clinging to the bones becomes opaque. You may also hear this step referred to as *smothering*, because the lid is left on the pot. Leave the bones in the pot and add the liquid and other ingredients.

Preparing Mirepoix Choose the ingredients for your mirepoix according to the type of stock you are making. A standard mirepoix (onions, carrots, and celery) is used for brown stocks. A white mirepoix (onions, leeks, celery, and parsnips) omits the carrots to keep white stocks pale in color.

Cut the mirepoix into a size and shape that best suits your stock's cooking time. For stocks that cook for more than 1 hour, cut the mirepoix into a medium or large dice. For stocks that simmer less than 1 hour, cut the mirepoix into a small dice or thin slices.

Preparing a Sachet d'Épices or a Bouquet Garni Wrap the ingredients for a sachet d'épices in a small piece of cheesecloth and tie the cheesecloth securely into a bundle with string. Gather together the ingredients for a bouquet garni into a bundle, wrap the bundle once or twice with string, and then tie the string securely.

Choosing Equipment The main piece of equipment for preparing a stock is a stockpot. Stockpots are taller than they are wide. This helps them concentrate flavors in the stock. The stockpot should hold all of the ingredients and the liquid with at least 3 inches of space at the top. Check the bottom of the pot and choose one with a flat surface. For very large quantities of stock, restaurants often use a steam-jacketed kettle. Restaurants often use a stockpot

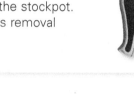

Chef's Tip

Easy Removal

Leave one end of the string on your sachet d'épices or bouquet garni long enough to tie it to the handle of the stockpot. This makes removal easier.

Recipe Card

83. Fish Fumet

with a spigot for draining the stock out of the pan without stirring up the other ingredients. If your pot does not have a spigot, you will need a large ladle to scoop the stock from the pot.

As stock simmers, you will need a skimmer or flat spoon to skim foam from the surface. Removing foam from the surface keeps the stock clear. To help keep the stock clear, try to disturb the bones as little as possible while you drain the stockpot or ladle out the stock.

When the stock is finished, you will need to strain it. To strain a stock, ladle or drain the stock carefully through a sieve or a cheesecloth-lined colander into containers suitable for cooling.

Preparing Fish Fumet Fish fumet has a more noticeable flavor than a white stock made with fish bones. This increase in flavor occurs because the bones and the mirepoix are allowed to sweat before the water is added. Adding other aromatic ingredients such as dry white wine or mushrooms can also add more flavor. Fish bones are delicate and release their flavor more quickly than animal or poultry bones. This means that the simmering time is shorter—45 minutes to 1 hour is enough for a good stock. When the cooking time is this short, you can add the sachet d'épices along with the cold water.

Preparing Shellfish Stock Lobster, shrimp, and crayfish shells turn a deep red when they are sautéed in oil. This deepens the stock's flavor. The mirepoix (often with the addition of tomatoes) is also sautéed long enough to produce a deep color. Like fish bones, shellfish shells require only 45 minutes to 1 hour of simmering time to flavor a stock. Therefore, you should add the sachet d'épices when you add the cold water.

Preparing Vegetable Stock Vegetable stocks cook in 30 to 60 minutes if the vegetables are cut into small dice or

Convection

Convection is one of the ways that heat travels through gases or liquids. A pot of stock simmering on the stove is a good example of using convection. As the stock pot sits on the burner, the pot gets warmer. Once the stock pot becomes hot, the liquid closest to the bottom heats up and begins to rise. Eventually, the warmed liquid rises to the top. Then, it starts to cool. As it cools, it falls. This constant rising and falling motion is known as *convection.*

You see convection beginning to take place when tiny bubbles form on the sides and bottom of a pot. After a while, the bubbles rise to the top of the pan. The hotter the liquid, the larger the bubbles, and the more action in the pot.

You can influence convection when you stir foods. This is known as *mechanical convection* and helps keep the heat more even for a more consistent temperature.

As liquid moves from the bottom of the pot to the top, it can trap impurities and grease, eventually

Source: Culinary Institute of America

taking them to the top of the pot. That is why you skim away the impurities to make a clear, clean stock.

Lab Activity

Bring a large amount of water to a boil using a glass pot or pan. Add a few drops of food coloring. Analyze the color pattern for convection as the food coloring travels through the pot of water.

Recipe Cards

84. Court Bouillon

85. Vegetable Stock

thin slices. This is long enough to extract the flavor from the vegetables, but short enough to avoid developing a strong or bitter flavor. There are two optional steps you can use to vary the flavor and color of a vegetable stock. The vegetables can be allowed to sweat over low heat, in the same way that you sweat fish bones for a fumet. Or, you can roast the vegetables until brown, as you would for a brown stock.

Brown Stock

1. **Prepare** the bones, mirepoix, and tomatoes.

2. **Roast** the bones, mirepoix, and tomatoes until they have a rich brown color.

3. **Combine** the roasted ingredients with cold water in a stockpot. Add water to dissolve drippings in the pan and add to the stockpot.

4. **Simmer** over medium heat for the recommended time.

5. **Skim** the surface to remove any foam.

6. **Add the sachet d'épices** during the last 30 to 45 minutes of simmering time.

7. **Strain** the stock.

8. **Cool** the stock to below 41°F. Store in the refrigerator.

Recipe Card

86. Brown Veal Stock

White Stock

1 **Prepare** the unroasted bones and mirepoix. If you are blanching the bones, blanch them now.

2 **Combine** the ingredients with cold water in a stockpot.

Source: Culinary Institute of America

3 **Simmer** over medium heat for the recommended time.

Source: Culinary Institute of America

4 **Skim** the surface to remove any foam.

Source: Culinary Institute of America

5 **Add the sachet d'épices** during the last 30 to 45 minutes of simmering time.

6 **Strain** the stock.

Source: Culinary Institute of America

7 **Cool** the stock to below 41°F. Store in the refrigerator.

Recipe Card
87. Chicken Stock

Using Prepared Stock Bases A stock base can be purchased in a highly concentrated form or as a powder or cube. These bases are made according to the manufacturer's instructions and brought to a simmer. You can use them instead of stocks or you can add them to a stock you made yourself to give a weak stock more flavor.

Good-quality stock bases from a manufacturer are made from the same basic ingredients as you would use to prepare your own stocks. However,

FIGURE 14–6

Stock Bases
Labels from two brands of prepared stock base.

ANALYZING INFORMATION *Which of these stock bases relies more on sodium for flavor?*

Source: Culinary Institute of America

Chef's Tip

More for Less

If you skim stock as it simmers, you remove most of the fat. Any remaining fat is easy to lift away once the stocks have chilled, making them virtually fat-free. Chefs trying to cut fat in dishes such as mashed potatoes, stuffings, or even vinaigrettes can substitute this fat-free stock for cream, butter, or oil. The result may even be more flavorful than the original dish, with less fat.

Chef's Tip

Testing Stock

Before using stock, check its quality. Add a cup of stock to a pan and bring to a boil. Determine whether the stock has good flavor, color, and body. If so, the stock can be used.

some lower-quality stock bases list high-sodium ingredients on the label, ahead of meats, poultry, or vegetables. Use the highest-quality stock base for the best results. For better results from a prepared stock base, simmer the base with meat and vegetable trimmings.

Storing Stocks Stocks that are not used immediately should be cooled and stored as quickly as possible after they are made. Cool stocks in an ice bath or with a chill wand. Once the stock is cool, transfer it to storage containers. Be sure to add a label with the stock's name and the date it was made. All stocks should be stored in the refrigerator or freezer.

READING CHECKPOINT *What are the three keys to success when making stocks?*

Using Stocks

Choosing the Right Stock Recipes often indicate the type of stock that should be used. A specific type of stock is selected to add the desired flavor, color, or texture to a dish.

- Use white or poultry stocks for dishes that should be a white or ivory color.

- Use a stock made from the same type of meat or fish featured in the recipe. For instance, use chicken stock for poached chicken breasts or fish fumet for poached fish.

- Use a brown stock for dishes that should be a dark color.

- Use a neutral stock to add body without adding a noticeable flavor. For instance, use white beef stock to make a vegetable soup or to cook beans.

Reducing Stock

1. **Test** the stock (see the Chef's Tip).

2. **Rapidly simmer** the stock. Transfer the stock to a smaller pot, if necessary, after it has reduced.

3. **Continue simmering until half the original amount of stock remains.** The stock has been reduced. It is now a double-strength stock.

4. **Strain** the double-strength stock.

5. **Cool** the double-strength stock to below 41°F. Store in the refrigerator.

Source: Culinary Institute of America

Reducing Stocks To concentrate a stock's flavor and give it more body, a stock can be reduced. To reduce a stock, you simmer the stock in order to cook away some of its liquid. If the stock is simmered until only half of the original water remains, it is a **double-strength stock**. If it is simmered until it has an intense flavor and a syrupy consistency, it is called a **glaze**.

Making a Glaze

1. **Rapidly simmer** the double-strength stock.

2. **Continue simmering** until the stock is reduced by half.

3. **Check the consistency** of the stock. A glaze is thick enough to cling to the front and back of a spoon and very syrupy. If the stock is not yet syrupy, continue to reduce it until it has the correct consistency.

4. **Cool** the glaze to below 41°F. Store in the refrigerator.

Source: Culinary Institute of America

READING CHECKPOINT *What is a double-strength stock?*

Reviewing Concepts

1. What are the four types of basic ingredients used to make stocks?
2. Identify the five basic types of stocks. Briefly describe each.
3. What are the basic steps involved in preparing a brown stock?
4. What is a glaze and how is it prepared?

Critical Thinking

5. **Drawing Conclusions** Why is it necessary to cool stocks and glazes below 41°F?
6. **Comparing/Contrasting** What is the difference between the preparation of a brown veal stock and a white beef stock?
7. **Predicting** How will the flavor, color, and aroma of a vegetable stock change if you use roasted vegetables in the stock?

Test Kitchen

Prepare chicken stock from unroasted bones, mirepoix, and a sachet d'épices. Make chicken stock from a purchased base. Taste the finished stocks and evaluate the results.

LANGUAGE ARTS
Descriptive Writing

Research five notable chefs' techniques for making stocks. Describe how each chef's technique is similar and how each is different. Assume that your audience is your fellow students and is familiar with the technique for making stock presented in this textbook. Focus on communicating specific details as clearly as possible so your audience can use the results of your research in their own cooking.

14.2

Sauces

READING PREVIEW

Key Concepts

- Identifying basic ingredients for sauces
- Preparing thickeners for sauces
- Identifying types of sauce
- Preparing and storing sauces
- Presenting sauces

Vocabulary

- béchamel sauce
- brown sauce
- chutney
- compound butter
- coulis
- demi-glace
- derivative sauces
- espagnol sauce
- grand sauces
- gravy
- hollandaise sauce
- jus de veau lié
- liaison
- nappé
- purée
- refined starch
- relish
- roux
- salsa
- sauce
- starch slurry
- tempering
- velouté

Basic Ingredients for Sauces

A **sauce** is a liquid served with foods to add more flavor, color, texture, and eye appeal to the food. Sauces are made from three basic types of ingredients:

- Liquids
- Aromatics and seasonings
- Thickeners

Liquids The main ingredient in a sauce is typically a flavorful liquid such as a stock. The flavor of the stock should match the flavor of the food you plan to serve with the finished sauce. For example, chicken stock is the best choice for a sauce to be used with a chicken dish. Shellfish stock is used in a sauce with seafood dishes. Sauces made with a stock get both their flavor and some of their color from the stock.

Other ingredients can be used in place of some or all the stock in a sauce. Milk or cream, for example, can be the main liquid ingredient in some sauces. They give sauces a creamy flavor and a white color. Sometimes egg yolks and butter are used in place of some of the stock. Some vegetables, such as tomatoes, mushrooms, and bell peppers, contain enough moisture to be used as the main liquid ingredient of a sauce without using any stock.

Aromatics and Seasonings Sauces need to be flavorful. In addition to the flavor from the liquid ingredient, other ingredients need to be added to the sauce as it cooks. Aromatic vegetables, including

Source: tawesit/Fotolia

FIGURE 14–7

Serving Sauces

Sauces can be served over food, under food, or on the side.

COMMUNICATING *How do you prefer sauces? Why?*

Source: Culinary Institute of America

shallots, onions, leeks, and mushrooms, are often added to a sauce as it cooks. Small amounts of aromatic liquids, such as wine or brandy, are sometimes added.

There are many seasoning options for sauces—the most basic are salt and pepper, but your sauce recipe may indicate others. Herbs, spices, and mustard are some of the most common types of seasonings found in sauces.

Thickeners Sauces must be thick enough to coat foods. Recipes often call for ingredients that will help thicken a sauce.

Roux (roo) is a cooked paste made from wheat flour and a fat. The starch in the flour thickens the sauce. However, in addition to starch, flour also contains proteins and other elements that do not help thicken the sauce and will need to be skimmed from the sauce as it simmers. The fat in the roux adds some flavor to the sauce, so it is common to use a flavorful fat, such as butter, when preparing a roux.

A **starch slurry** is a mixture of a refined starch and cold water. A **refined starch** is made from a starchy ingredient such as corn, rice, or potatoes that is processed to remove all elements except the starch. A refined starch is also known as *pure starch*. A starch slurry is a good choice as a thickener when you want to make a sauce that is very clear.

A **liaison** (lee-AY-zohn) is a mixture of cream and egg yolks that are added to a sauce at the end of cooking time. Liaisons add a creamy flavor, golden color, and a light thickness to a sauce.

A **purée** (pyur-AY) is a fine paste made by cooking a flavorful ingredient until it is soft and then straining it or using a food processor or blender to chop it fine. A purée is soft and smooth, with a liquid consistency. Sauces made from vegetable purees are sometimes described as self-thickening because the entire sauce, or a portion of the sauce, is blended until it achieves a sauce-like texture. They do not need an added thickener.

Molecular gastronomy uses a wide variety of thickeners in sauces. Many, such as the three listed here, are vegetarian and useful in gluten-free cooking.

- Xanthan (zan-THON) gum, a natural thickener made from fermented cane sugar, adds volume and viscosity to sauces.

- Gellen gum, made from algae, increases elasticity in sauces.

- Agar agar, a naturally occurring gelatinous substance derived from red algae, is a stabilizing and thickening agent.

 **READING CHECKPOINT** *What are the three basic types of ingredients used to make a sauce?*

Preparing Thickeners

Sauces are noted not only for their flavor and color, but also for their consistency. A good sauce is thick enough to coat foods. A sauce that has been thickened properly is described as **nappé** (nap-PAY), a French word that means "coating" or "covering." For your sauce to achieve the correct consistency, your sauce recipe may call for a roux, a starch slurry, a liaison, or some other type of thickener.

Roux Roux is made by cooking equal parts of fat and flour together. All-purpose flour is the most common choice for the flour in a roux. Clarified butter is the most common choice for the fat.

A roux is identified by its color. The longer a roux cooks, the darker its color will be. White roux is made with oil instead of butter and is cooked for a short time to give it a very white color. Pale or blond roux is made with clarified butter and is cooked longer than white roux for a golden color. Brown roux is made with clarified butter and oil. It is cooked long enough to give it a deep brown color. The lighter the roux, the more it thickens; the darker the roux, the less it thickens.

There are two ways to add roux to a sauce:

- Add a cooler liquid to the hot roux. Make the roux and, while it is still hot, gradually add a cooler liquid to it. Whisk the mixture as you add the liquid to smooth out any lumps that may form.

- Add a cooler roux to a hot liquid. Have the liquid at a simmer. Break cold roux into small pieces and put them in a bowl. Add enough hot liquid to dissolve the roux. Whisk well to completely dissolve the roux. Pour the dissolved roux into the simmering liquid.

FIGURE 14–8

Roux

Roux can be cooked to a variety of colors.

ANALYZING INFORMATION *Which color of roux would you choose for a light- or ivory-colored sauce?*

Source: David Murray and Jules Selmes/Dorling Kindersley

How Much Roux?

Consistency Desired		Description	Amount of Roux
	Light	Lightly coats a spoon. Pours easily. Used as the base for some soups.	10 to 12 oz per gallon (depending on type of roux)
	Medium	Clings to food and coats it evenly. Pours easily, but is not runny. Used for most sauces.	12 to 14 oz per gallon (depending on type of roux)
	Heavy	Stiff enough to mound when dropped from a spoon. Does not pour easily. Used to hold ingredients together (for example, a heavy sauce could bind a baked macaroni and cheese dish).	14 to 16 oz per gallon (depending on type of roux)

Source: Clive Streeter/Dorling Kindersley

Roux

1 **Measure** the ingredients.

2 **Heat the fat** in a heavy gauge skillet.

3 **Add the flour** all at once and stir to combine. There should be no lumps and the roux should not look greasy or be too stiff.

Source: Culinary Institute of America

4 **Cook the roux,** stirring constantly, until it has the correct color.

Source: Culinary Institute of America

5 **Use immediately** or store in a refrigerator.

Recipe Card
88. Roux

Sauces thickened with roux need to simmer at least 45 minutes to remove the starchy or pasty taste and gritty feel of the flour. You may hear this referred to as "cooking out the roux."

Use the right amount of roux to get the right consistency for the sauce. The less roux you add, the lighter the consistency. The more roux you add, the heavier the consistency.

Starch Slurries Starch slurries thicken liquids more quickly than roux. To make a starch slurry, stir the refined starch (typically cornstarch or arrowroot) together with a cold liquid until the starch is dissolved and the mixture has the consistency of heavy cream.

Add a starch slurry gradually to a simmering liquid. Continue to simmer after the starch slurry has been added, whisking or stirring until the liquid is thickened. Starch slurries typically thicken simmering liquids in 2 to 3 minutes.

Liaison To make a liaison, blend cream and egg yolks in a bowl until they are very smooth. The liaison will be added to a hot liquid, but before you can do that you need to use a special technique called **tempering** to warm the liaison. If you don't temper the liaison, the egg yolks could overcook or scramble when they first enter the hot liquid. To temper a liaison, gradually stir or whisk a few ladles of the hot liquid into the liaison. Add enough to bring the liaison close to the temperature of the simmering liquid. When the liaison is warmed enough, you can add it to the rest of the hot liquid. Continue to simmer very gently just long enough for the egg yolks to lightly thicken and form a sauce. Do not let the sauce come to a full boil.

READING CHECKPOINT *What are three added thickeners commonly used to prepare sauces?*

Types of Sauces

The Grand Sauces There are hundreds of different types of sauces. However, classic cookbooks written for chefs describe five **grand sauces** (also called *mother sauces* or *leading sauces*):

- Brown sauce
- Béchamel sauce
- Velouté sauce
- Tomato sauce
- Hollandaise sauce

A **brown sauce** has a rich brown color and is typically served with red meats and game. The three basic types of brown sauce are espagnol sauce, demi-glace, and jus de veau lié. **Espagnol sauce** (ess-spah-NYOL) is a brown sauce made by thickening a brown veal stock with a roux. **Demi-glace** (DEH-me-glahs) is made by simmering espagnol sauce with an equal amount of brown veal stock until the sauce is intensely flavored and thick enough to coat foods. **Jus de veau lié** (JHOO duh voh lee-AY) is made by simmering a brown stock with flavorings and aromatics and, in some cases, additional bones or meat trimmings to intensify the stock's flavor. Jus de veau lié is thickened with a starch slurry.

Béchamel sauce (BAY-shah-mell) is a white sauce made by thickening milk with a white roux. Béchamel is sometimes flavored with onions, cloves, and bay leaves. It is typically used on pastas, vegetables, veal, fish, and poultry.

Velouté (veh-loo-TAY) sauce is a white sauce made by thickening a poultry, fish, or shellfish stock with a blond roux. The type of stock you use determines the type of velouté you make: chicken stock for chicken velouté, fish stock for fish velouté, and so forth. It is commonly used on fish, shellfish, veal, and poultry.

The traditional tomato "mother sauce" was prepared in a French style that included stock and was thickened with roux. This type of sauce has lost favor over the years and has been replaced by Italian-style tomato sauces that do not include stock or roux. Typically chefs making this type of sauce

Chef's Tip

Tempering a Liaison

It is easier to temper a liaison with two people. One person can ladle the hot liquid while the other holds the bowl steady and whisks. If you are on your own, set the bowl on a dampened towel to keep it steady as you whisk.

Chef's Tip

"Spanish Sauce"

Some culinary historians say that espagnol sauce got its name, which translates from the French to "Spanish sauce," because it uses tomato paste or tomato purée toward the end of the cooking process. Spanish cooks adopted tomatoes into their cooking before French chefs did.

Recipe Cards

89. Jus de Veau Lié

90. Béchamel Sauce

Roux-Thickened Sauce

1️⃣ **Warm the liquid.** Add aromatics or seasonings if your recipe calls for it.

2️⃣ **Combine** the liquid and the roux.

Source: Culinary Institute of America

📁 Recipe Card

91. Velouté

3️⃣ **Whisk** until there are no lumps.

Source: Culinary Institute of America

4️⃣ **Simmer** for about 45 minutes.

5️⃣ **Strain** the sauce.

6️⃣ **Return to a simmer.**

7️⃣ **Add finishing ingredients,** if required by your recipe. Adjust seasonings.

Chef's Tip

Oily Hollandaise

If hollandaise sauce looks oily, you are adding butter too quickly. Stop adding butter. Whisk over barely simmering heat until the existing butter is absorbed into the yolks.

will create individual variations from scratch, using tomatoes and various flavoring agents. Tomato sauce is widely used on pastas, as well as with red meat, poultry, and fish.

Hollandaise sauce (HOLL-uhn-daze) is made by blending melted or clarified butter into slightly cooked egg yolks. Lemon juice and vinegar add flavor to the sauce. Hollandaise is a type of sauce that is sometimes referred to as a warm emulsion sauce. As you remember from Section 10.1, an emulsion is made when two ingredients that don't normally mix together are blended so that one of the ingredients is suspended evenly throughout the mixture.

Hollandaise sauce can be tricky to make. If it gets too hot, the eggs will begin to scramble. The first sign that eggs are beginning to scramble is that you may see very small clumps or threads in the sauce. If there aren't too many clumps, you can rescue the sauce by immediately taking it off the heat and adding a bit of cold water. Whisk the sauce until it looks smooth again, then continue to add the butter over gentle heat. If the sauce has a lot of clumps, you will need to strain it and then begin again with fresh egg yolks. This time, use the strained hollandaise to replace the warm clarified butter.

Hollandaise sauce is commonly used with eggs and vegetables but is also used on lighter fare such as poultry and fish.

France

Perhaps no country is more associated with food and cooking than France. In fact, there are two distinct types of French cooking: the high-level restaurant cooking known as *haute cuisine* (OHT kwee-ZEEN), which means "high cooking," and everyday cooking, which is often influenced by local ingredients and traditions.

Haute cuisine has its origins in restaurants of the 1850s, when elaborate meals of many courses were served to the aristocracy and upper classes. This type of cooking was very rigid. Dishes were prepared in specific ways and given specific names. That way, when customers ordered a dish in a restaurant they could know what they were ordering.

Sauces play a major role in haute cuisine. In fact, the concept of the grand sauces and their derivatives is from haute cuisine. Auguste Escoffier, in his important guide to haute cuisine, *Le Guide Culinaire*, first published in 1902, lists 221 types of sauces! In this groundbreaking guide, Escoffier rarely lists a preparation of meat without also listing a sauce, a garnish, and perhaps an accompanying dish or two.

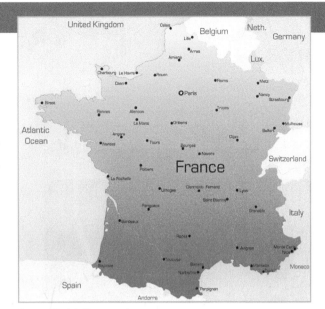

Source: Olinchuk/Shutterstock

French everyday cooking—or, as it's known in French, *cuisine bourgeoisie* (kwee-ZEEN bourshwa-ZEE)—is often influenced by the ingredients available within a specific region. For example, *bouillabaisse* (BOOL-yuh-BAYZ), a type of fish soup, comes from Provence in southern France, bordering on the Mediterranean. Alsace, famous for its cabbage and pigs, is also famous for *choucroute garnie* (shoo-KROOT GAR-nee), a dish made from sauerkraut, pork sausages, and ham.

These two styles have been blended in many restaurants, creating a cuisine that is simpler than haute cuisine but more complex than everyday cooking.

Research

Research four classic sauces that are not listed in this chapter. List the name of the sauce and indicate what grand sauce is used in making the sauce. Describe the flavoring ingredients used in making each of the sauces. Then name the foods each sauce is typically served with and the cooking method most often used to prepare these foods.

Bouillabaisse

Source: HLPhoto/Fotolia

Purée Sauce

1. **Prepare** the aromatic and main vegetables.

2. **Sauté the aromatic vegetables.**

3. **Add the main vegetables.** Add liquid, if necessary.

Source: Culinary Institute of America

4. **Simmer** until the vegetables are very tender.

Source: Culinary Institute of America

5. **Add additional seasonings or aromatics.**

6. **Remove the bouquet garni, sachet, or bay leaf.**

7. **Purée** to the appropriate smoothness.

Source: Culinary Institute of America

8. **Return to a simmer.**

9. **Add finishing ingredients,** if required by your recipe. Adjust seasonings.

Recipe Card

92. Tomato Sauce (Italian Style)

Derivative Sauces Grand sauces can be used as the main ingredient in another sauce. The grand sauce is combined with other seasonings or garnishes for a specific flavor, color, or texture. Sauces made this way are known as **derivative sauces** because they are derived from or based on a grand sauce. Other terms commonly used for derivative sauces include *small sauces* and *compound sauces*. The following tables show some of the classic derivative sauces.

Miscellaneous Sauces Today, chefs are making a great number of sauces that are not based on the grand sauces. These are often referred to

Warm Emulsion Sauce

① **Combine the egg yolks with the liquid.**

② **Cook** over barely simmering water in a stainless steel bowl, whisking constantly, until the yolks are thickened and warm.

③ **Add warm clarified butter** very gradually, still working over the barely simmering water. Whisk constantly as you add the butter.

④ **Add a small amount of warm water** when the sauce becomes stiff.

⑤ **Add lemon juice, salt, and pepper** after all the butter is blended into the yolks.

⑥ **Strain** the sauce. Keep warm for service.

 **Recipe Card**

93. Hollandaise Sauce

Brown Sauce Derivatives

	Name	Preparation	Serve With
	Red wine sauce	Simmer brown sauce with red wine, minced shallots, cracked peppercorns, thyme, and bay leaf. Strain and season before serving.	Grilled red meats (also with fish in contemporary cooking)
	◀ Mushroom sauce	Sauté sliced mushrooms in butter until tender, add brown sauce, and simmer until flavorful.	Beef, veal, poultry
	Robert sauce	Sauté minced onions in butter until tender, and add white wine. Simmer until wine cooks away. Add brown sauce and simmer until flavorful. Finish with a pinch of sugar and mustard.	Grilled pork

Source: Clive Streeter, Dorling Kindersley

Béchamel Sauce Derivatives

Name	Preparation	Serve With
◀ Cheddar sauce	Add grated Cheddar cheese to béchamel. Cook over low heat until the cheese melts.	Pasta, vegetables
Lobster sauce	Simmer béchamel sauce with cream until thickened and flavorful. Add diced lobster meat and season with cayenne pepper.	Lobster, fish
Mornay sauce	Add grated Gruyère and Parmesan cheeses to béchamel. Cook over low heat until the cheeses melt. Whisk in butter just before serving.	Veal, poultry, vegetables

Source: Monkey Business/Fotolia

Velouté Sauce Derivatives

Name	Preparation	Serve With
◀ Suprême sauce	Sauté sliced mushrooms in butter until tender. Add velouté and cream, simmer, and strain.	Poultry, fish
Aurore sauce	Simmer velouté with tomato purée.	Eggs, white meats, poultry
Shrimp sauce	Simmer velouté with cream. Add cooked shrimp and whisk in whole butter just before serving.	Fish, certain egg dishes

Source: Culinary Institute of America

as *miscellaneous sauces.* Some miscellaneous sauces are served hot; others are served cold.

- A **compound butter** is made by softening butter and blending it with ingredients such as minced herbs, shallots, ginger, citrus zest, or spices. To use a compound butter as a sauce, put slices of it on top of broiled or grilled meats. Compound butters can also be added to hot cooked pastas or vegetables. The food's heat melts the butter so it coats the food.

Tomato Sauce Variations

Source: CCat82/Fotolia

	Name	Preparation	Serve With
	Vodka sauce	Add vodka to tomato sauce and simmer. Add cream and Parmesan cheese.	Pasta (penne, penne rigate)
◀	Puttanesca sauce	Sauté onions, garlic, and anchovies (with possible additions of olives, peppers, and capers). Add tomato sauce and simmer.	Pasta (spaghetti, bucatini, penne, linguini)
	Arrabbiata sauce	Tomato sauce with the addition of a significant amount of red pepper flakes. The Italian translation of *arrabbiata* is "angry," so this is the "angry sauce."	Pasta penne, (penne rigate)

Hollandaise-Style Sauces

Source: Ian O'Leary, Dorling Kindersley

	Name	Preparation	Serve With
◀	Béarnaise sauce	Simmer tarragon vinegar, chopped tarragon, shallots, and peppercorns until liquid cooks away. Add water; then strain into the egg yolks and prepare as for a hollandaise. Finish with minced tarragon leaves.	Grilled meats
	Mousseline sauce	Fold whipped heavy cream into hollandaise sauce.	Boiled fish, asparagus
	Royal glaçage sauce	Fold together equal parts of velouté, hollandaise, and whipped heavy cream. Use as a coating, and then lightly broil the dish to brown before serving.	Poached white meats, fish

- A **coulis** (koo-LEE) is a thick puréed sauce, usually made from vegetables or fruits. Italian-style tomato sauces for pasta dishes are an example of a coulis-style sauce. For additional richness, coulis and purées may include a bit of cream just before they are served.

- A **gravy** is similar to the grand sauces but usually includes pan drippings produced by meats as they roast. These drippings are simmered with a stock or broth, and a thickener, such as roux or a starch slurry, is added to thicken the gravy. Gravies are often made in smaller batches than grand sauces.

- A **salsa** is a cold sauce made from a combination of vegetables, typically tomatoes, onions, peppers, and chilies. They are typically seasoned with salt, pepper, and lime juice. Salsas are often served as a dip with chips or vegetables but are also used as a topping or an ingredient in other dishes. They can be served with a wide range of foods, including meats, eggs, vegetables, grains, and legumes.

- A **relish** or a **chutney** is a sauce with a noticeably chunky texture that is typically served with meats, poultry, or fish. These sauces are typically made from fruits, vegetables, or a combination of fruits and vegetables. Relishes and chutneys are often seasoned with a combination of sweet and sour ingredients, such as vinegar and sugar. They may be made from raw or cooked ingredients. Some versions are sweet, others are savory, and some are very spicy.

- A wide range of sauces, including barbecue sauce, applesauce, cocktail sauce, and tartar sauce, fall under the category of *specialty sauces*. These sauces can be used as an ingredient in another dish or served as a topping or dip.

 **READING CHECKPOINT** *What are the five grand sauces?*

Preparing and Storing Basic Sauces

Preparing sauces requires patience and attention to detail. With all the work involved in making sauces, it makes sense to store an excess amount correctly for later use.

Equipment Used in Preparing Sauces? Using the correct equipment when making a sauce is important. Choose saucepans that hold the sauce comfortably with enough room to stir the sauce and skim it if necessary. Check the bottom of the pan to make sure it is very flat. Warped pans will develop hot spots that can burn or scorch the sauce. Avoid aluminum saucepans for white sauces because the sauce may become discolored. Additionally, aluminum pans react with sauces that contain acidic ingredients (such as tomatoes or lemons), creating a potential health hazard.

Sauces that need to be strained should be poured through a sieve. The smoother you want the finished sauce to be, the finer the sieve should be. Using cheesecloth in a sieve gives you the smoothest sauce.

The equipment you use to purée a sauce depends on the amount of sauce you are preparing and the texture you want in the finished sauce. A food mill will

FIGURE 14–9

Using Cheesecloth in a Sieve
Using cheesecloth in the sieve gives a velvety texture to a finished sauce.

DRAWING CONCLUSIONS *Why do you think fine restaurants emphasize the quality of their sauces?*

Source: Culinary Institute of America

produce an even but slightly coarse texture. Food processors and blenders make a finer purée.

Storing Sauces You can serve a sauce as soon as you have finished preparing it. To keep a sauce hot during a meal, transfer it to a holding container and keep it warm. Sauces that contain eggs should be kept warm but not too hot. If they overheat, the eggs will continue to cook and can give the sauce a lumpy or curdled appearance.

Some sauces can be stored for a few days, although sauces containing eggs cannot be stored. To cool and store a sauce, put it in a metal container and set it in an ice bath. Make sure the container is stable so you can stir the sauce. Remember that stirring a food as it cools helps it cool faster and keeps it safe. You can read more about the correct way to cool foods in Section 1.2.

 **READING CHECKPOINT** *When should aluminum saucepans be avoided?*

Chef's Tip

Holding Sauce

A sauce thickened with a starch slurry typically does not hold on a steam table as well as a roux-thickened sauce.

Presenting Sauces

Sauces add flavor, moisture, color, and sheen to other foods. When you pair the right sauce with a food, it enhances the dish by either making the flavor of the food more intense or adding a contrasting flavor. Here are some guidelines for presenting sauces:

- **Serve sauces at the right temperature.** Hot sauces should be at a simmer (around 180°F) when they are presented. Sauces thicken as they cool, and their flavors are not as pronounced as when they are hot. A cool sauce could also cool off the main item.

- **Reheat stored grand sauces properly.** Put the sauce in a heavy-bottomed saucepan and place the pan over low heat. Stir the sauce until it softens. Then increase the heat to high and bring the sauce to a full boil for 3 minutes.

- **Hold sauces properly.** Sauces that have been thickened with either a roux or a starch slurry can develop a skin on the surface when you hold them in a steam table. To prevent a skin from forming, put a thin layer of clarified butter on the surface, or cover the container tightly. Remove and discard any skin that does form. Warm emulsion sauces and sauces finished with a liaison should be warm but not hot enough to overcook or curdle. Keep them in a warm water bath.

FIGURE 14–10
Presenting Sauces
Serve enough sauce to flavor and moisten the dish.
INFERRING *Can there be too much sauce on a dish?*
Source: st-fotograf/Fotolia

Chef's Tip

Tasting Sauces

It's important to taste sauces both when they are made and when you reheat them. A food worker should never use a utensil more than once to taste food that is being sold or served.

• **Season sauces properly.** Be sure to taste sauces after you reheat them to check their flavor. Salt and pepper are the most common choices to season foods, but read your recipe to see if you need to adjust other ingredients as well, such as citrus juices, wine, or fresh herbs.

READING CHECKPOINT *At what temperature should a hot sauce be served?*

14.2 ASSESSMENT

Reviewing Concepts

1. What are three added thickeners commonly used to prepare sauces? Briefly describe each.
2. Describe the steps in making a roux.
3. What are the five grand sauces?
4. What types of sauces cannot be stored?
5. In what two ways can a sauce enhance a food?

Critical Thinking

6. **Predicting** What will happen to a béarnaise sauce if it gets too hot?
7. **Analyzing Information** What is the grand sauce used as the base for the light-colored sauce that uses Gruyère and Parmesan cheeses?
8. **Comparing/Contrasting** What is the difference between an espagnol sauce and a jus de veau lié?

Test Kitchen

Make three different batches of béchamel sauce. Use 10 oz of blond roux for the first batch. Use 12 oz of blond roux for the second batch. Use 16 oz of blond roux for the third batch. Evaluate each of the batches for thickness. Which do you think has the best consistency for a soup? Which would you choose for a sauce?

CULINARY MATH
Estimating Roux

1. A recipe for a chicken velouté sauce calls for 12 oz of roux for a 1-gal batch. How much roux do you need for 4 gal of sauce?
2. Your recipe for béchamel has a medium consistency and uses 12 oz of roux for a 1-gal batch. How much roux would you need to make a béchamel with a heavy consistency?

PROJECT 14

Preparing Tomato Sauce You are now ready to work on Project 14, "Preparing Tomato Sauce," which is available in "My Culinary Lab" or in your *Student's Lab Resources and Study Guide* manual.

480   Unit 3 *Culinary Applications*

Soups

Key Concepts

- Identifying basic types of soup
- Preparing soups
- Reheating and serving soups
- Garnishing soups

Vocabulary

- bisque
- bouillon
- broth
- clarification
- consommé
- cream soup
- crouton
- purée soup
- raft
- soup

Basic Types of Soup

Soups are liquid foods served in a bowl and eaten with a spoon. Serving a soup at the beginning of a meal provides an opportunity to make a good first impression on a guest. Preparing and serving soups will help you learn more about basic culinary techniques, seasoning, garnishing, and serving foods.

Soups are an effective way to use material that has been trimmed from other foods and can help reduce the overall food cost in the kitchen. Soups also allow you to feature seasonal foods. Most menus feature at least one selection of each of these two basic types of soup:

- Clear soups
- Hearty soups

Clear Soups Clear soups are richly flavored, aromatic liquids. The goal for any clear soup is to produce a clear liquid. The flavoring ingredients you add to the soup as it simmers are strained out and are not served. Typically, starchy ingredients are not used in clear soups because they make the soup cloudy. There are two basic types of clear soups: broths and consommés.

A **broth** is a clear, thin soup made by simmering a combination of meats, vegetables, aromatics, and water until you have a liquid with a good color and flavor. The flavoring ingredients are strained from the liquid and the result is a broth. The greater the care you take with a broth as it simmers, the clearer it will be. Almost all the fat is removed from a broth, although a few droplets of flavorful fat are common on a good broth. A broth is intended as a final product

Source: sarsmis/Shutterstock

Chef's Tip

Soup du Jour

Soup du jour (de ZHOOR) means "soup of the day." Many restaurants change their soups daily to adapt to changing weather, seasons, or special events—or simply to add variety.

to be consumed. While a broth can be used in preparing another type of soup, a stock is intended to be used in the preparation of a final product, and is not, itself, a final product. A stock may be used to add a depth of flavor to a broth, for example. **Bouillon** (BOOL-yohn) is the French term for a broth. You may be familiar with dehydrated bouillon cubes. These are a form of instant broth.

A **consommé** (KAHN-soh-may) is a clear soup that is completely fat-free. Consommés are a more refined broth, made by blending a good broth or a stock with a combination of ingredients, referred to as the **clarification**. The clarification adds flavor and color to enhance the broth, but the most important purpose of a clarification, and the reason for its name, is to clear the soup by trapping any fine particles in the broth or stock.

CULINARY **DIVERSITY**

Kosher Food

Kosher food is food prepared in accordance with Jewish dietary laws. *Kosher* means "fit" or "allowed to be eaten." At its most basic level, these laws govern which meats, dairy products, and produce are fit for consumption. For example, they prohibit eating pork, rabbit, shellfish, catfish, and sturgeon. All meat and poultry must be slaughtered in a specific way in order to meet these laws. Kosher laws also prohibit eating meat and dairy products together (so no cheeseburgers!). Mixing kosher food and nonkosher food results in food that is considered nonkosher. Food that contains neither fish nor dairy is considered *parve* and can be eaten with either meat or dairy.

As food production has become more complex, various certifying agencies have developed—both nationally and internationally—whose primary purpose is determining whether a food is kosher. Each agency uses a unique mark to indicate that the food is kosher. These marks are printed on the foods' labels and can help shoppers identify both that the food is kosher as well as the certifying agency.

There are two basic types of Jewish food, each one based on where the Jewish people originated. Sephardic Jews originated in countries bordering the Mediterranean (including the Middle East). Their foods include baba ghanoush (a mashed eggplant dip), hummus (a mashed chickpea dip), pita bread, and tabouli (a salad featuring bulgur, tomatoes, cucumbers, parsley, and mint, and seasoned with olive oil and lemon juice). Ashkenazi Jews originated in central and northern Europe. Their foods include such items as bagels, challah (a braided bread that includes eggs), pastrami, lox, and, of course, chicken soup (made with a kosher chicken). Often Jewish chicken soup is served with matzo balls, dumplings made from matzo (an unleavened bread that resembles a cracker) and eggs.

Research

Research a traditional Jewish recipe. Identify what makes the recipe kosher. Make the recipe using kosher ingredients, if possible.

Source: Brent Hofacker/Fotolia

Challah

Broths and consommés can be served on their own as a soup. You can add a simple garnish, such as herbs, diced cooked meats, or cooked noodles. Changing the aromatic ingredients and including a specific garnish can change these soups from a simple broth or consommé into a specialty soup. Specialty soups are soups that are associated with a specific country, region, or ethnic group. Some examples of clear specialty soups include wonton soup, hot and sour soup, and matzo ball soup.

Hearty Soups Hearty soups have a thickened broth. In hearty soups, the liquid called for in the recipe is an important part of the soup, but it is not the only important element. The main flavoring ingredients remain in the soup, sometimes left whole and sometimes puréed.

Hearty vegetable soups are soups with broth and a significant amount of vegetables (and often meats, pasta, and other ingredients). If you were preparing a broth, you would strain these ingredients out first. For a hearty vegetable soup, you leave them in the soup. The addition of starchy ingredients (rice, barley, potatoes, or pasta, for instance) thickens the soup slightly. The broth is typically not clear. A number of specialty soups fit the description of hearty vegetable soups. Minestrone (mee-ness-TROH-nay) is an example of a specialty soup that is a hearty vegetable soup from Italy. Borscht (BOHR-sht) from Russia or Poland and Manhattan clam chowder from the United States are other specialty soups that are hearty vegetable soups.

A **cream soup** is a noticeably thick soup with a velvety smooth texture. Cream soups are made by combining a broth or stock with the main flavoring ingredient (or a combination of flavoring ingredients). You may need to add a thickener such as roux, arrowroot, or cornstarch for a very smooth

FIGURE 14–11
Clear or Hearty?
A garnished clear soup and a hearty vegetable soup.

COMPARING/CONTRASTING
Compare how the vegetables in these two soups are cooked.

Sources: (left) Culinary Institute of America; (right) Ian O'Leary/Dorling Kindersley

Chef's Tip

Adding Cream to Soups

When making a large batch of cream soup, prepare the soup up to the point where you add cream. Cool the soup. Then reheat only as much soup as you need and add cream only to that amount.

FIGURE 14–12

Pumpkin Bisque
Soups allow you to feature seasonal foods.

DRAWING CONCLUSIONS *Why would a restaurant want to feature seasonal foods?*

Source: Culinary Institute of America

soup with an even texture. Some soups are made from ingredients that thicken the soup adequately by themselves; potatoes and some fruits are examples. Cream soups typically have the consistency of heavy cream and are opaque. Cold cream soup options include the classic vichyssoise (vee-shee-swahz) (a cold cream soup made from potatoes and leek) and fruit soups (such as apple soup or strawberry soup). New England clam chowder is a specialty soup that is a cream soup.

A **purée soup** is made by simmering a starchy ingredient (beans, dried peas, potatoes, or starchy vegetables) along with additional vegetables, meats, or aromatics in a broth or other liquid until they are tender enough to mash easily. The entire soup is puréed to the appropriate texture. Some purée soups are deliberately left chunky (for instance, black bean soup). Others are puréed until they are nearly as smooth as a cream soup (for example, split pea soup).

A **bisque** (bisk) is a type of purée soup that to which cream is typically added. Seafood bisques gets their color and flavor from lobster, shrimp, or crayfish shells. (A crayfish is a small freshwater, lobsterlike shellfish.) The shells are cooked until they are brightly colored. The soup is puréed, including the shells, then strained and finished with cream. Vegetable bisques are often made from tomatoes, pumpkin, or squash.

 **READING CHECKPOINT** *What are the two basic types of soup?*

Preparing Soups

You could spend months or years making nothing but soups and never repeat a recipe. Soups can feature a huge variety of ingredients, alone and in combination. However, making soup requires only a few basic skills. They are the same skills used in preparing stocks and sauces: selecting ingredients, careful simmering and skimming, puréeing, and thickening with a starch or a liaison.

Choosing Equipment for Soups A soup pot with a flat, heavy-gauge bottom is the basic piece of equipment for making most soups. In addition to a soup pot, you may need other equipment. Use wooden or metal spoons to stir soups and prevent scorching. Use sieves or colanders with cheesecloth to strain soups. If your soup needs to be puréed, use a food mill, a blender (either countertop or immersion-style), or a food processor.

Chef's Tip

 Wooden Spoons

A wooden spoon is the best tool to keep a soup from sticking to the pot. Try to feel the pot through the spoon. If you detect a heavy buildup, transfer the soup to a clean pot before it scorches.

Soups and Sops

The word *soup* comes from *sop*. A sop is a moistened piece of bread. Soups originally included slices of dry or stale bread because bread was too valuable to waste. Once it was too stale or dry to eat, the bread was used in other dishes. The bread might have been simmered in the soup as a thickener, or it might simply have been placed in the bottom of the bowl before broth was ladled over it.

The soups we enjoy today still bear the imprint of earlier soup-making techniques. One classic soup that follows this tradition is onion soup gratinée (grah-teen-nay). A toasted piece of bread, often topped with grated cheese, is floated on a rich broth chock-full of golden brown onions. The soup is baked until the bread and cheese forms a crust, known in French cooking as a gratinée.

Another soup that betrays its culinary history through its name is a bisque. Bisques can be thickened with cooked rice, potatoes, potato starch, or a roux. However, the first bisques were thickened by crumbling a type of stale biscuit into the soup to make it thicker and more substantial.

Today, many soups are thickened with ingredients other than bread, but the combination of soup and bread is still an important part of soup preparation and service. We often serve crackers or breadsticks with soups to offer texture and contrast.

Onion soup gratinée

Source: Culinary Institute of America

Research

Use a classic cookbook or the Internet to research the history of bisques. Describe how recipes for bisque have changed over time.

Making a Broth The goal for any clear soup, whether it is a broth or a consommé, is to produce a clear liquid. A selection of flavorful ingredients is the starting point for a good broth. Keeping a broth at a slow, even simmer helps extract the most flavor from the ingredients. Careful skimming removes the impurities that make a broth cloudy.

Making a Consommé Consommés differ from broths because they use a clarification to clear the broth. The ingredients for the clarification are selected according to the flavor and color you want in your finished consommé. Ground meat, poultry, or fish is blended with egg whites, finely chopped or ground vegetables, herbs, and an acid. Typical acids are tomatoes, lemon juice, or wine. This mixture is referred to as a clarification

Broth

① **Prepare the ingredients.**

② **Add cold liquid** to cover the main ingredient.

③ **Add the remaining ingredients.**

Recipe Card
94. Chicken Broth

④ **Bring to a simmer.**

⑤ **Maintain a slow, gentle simmer.** Skim to remove any foam that rises to the surface.

⑥ **Taste** the broth from time to time. Adjust the seasonings.

⑦ **Add aromatics** such as a bouquet garni or sachet d'épices during the final 30 to 45 minutes.

⑧ **Strain** the broth.

before it is cooked with a broth or stock. Once the consommé reaches a simmer, the clarification is referred to as a **raft**, because it floats on the top of the consommé like a raft on water.

Making a Hearty Soup Although a clear soup usually calls for all the ingredients to be added to the pot at the same time, hearty soups are made by adding ingredients in a particular order. Begin with the aromatic ingredients, such as onions, garlic, or leeks. Add the rest of the ingredients in order, starting with those that take the longest to cook and ending with those that take the least amount of time to cook.

Consommé

① **Prepare the clarification ingredients.**

② **Blend** the clarification ingredients together. They must be very cold.

Source: Culinary Institute of America

③ **Add cold stock** or broth to the cold clarification in a soup pot.

Source: Culinary Institute of America

④ **Bring to a simmer slowly,** stirring the consommé occasionally to keep the clarification from sticking and scorching.

⑤ **Stop stirring** the consommé when the clarification ingredients start to form a large soft mass (the raft).

⑥ **Break a small opening in the raft,** after it forms (if it hasn't broken open on its own).

Source: Culinary Institute of America

⑦ **Reduce the heat.** Very small bubbles will rise to the surface through the hole in the raft.

⑧ **Baste the raft** while the consommé simmers by gently ladling some of the consommé over the top of the raft.

Source: Culinary Institute of America

⑨ **Simmer the consommé** for the recommended time.

⑩ **Ladle the consommé out of the pot.** You can make a slightly larger opening in the raft, but don't break the raft apart.

Source: Culinary Institute of America

⑪ **Strain the consommé** through a fine sieve, cheesecloth, or filter.

⑫ **Skim or blot any fat on the surface** of the consommé.

 Recipe Card

95. Consommé

Hearty Soup

This is a general recipe for hearty soups, including cream soups, purée soups, and bisques.

1. **Prepare the ingredients.**

2. **Sauté the aromatic ingredients** (mirepoix, mushrooms, onions, bacon, garlic or similar ingredients).

Source: Culinary Institute of America

3. **Add a flavorful liquid.**

4. **Add roux,** if your recipe calls for it.

5. **Add the remaining ingredients** (including sachet d'épices or bouquet garni) in a sequence that ensures they will be cooked to the correct point of doneness.

Source: Culinary Institute of America

6. **Simmer** gently, stirring frequently so the soup doesn't stick to the pot.

7. **Skim** the surface to remove foam or fat.

8. **Taste** the soup as it cooks, adjusting seasonings and consistency as necessary.

9. **Continue simmering** until all the ingredients are fully cooked, tender, and flavorful.

10. **Remove the sachet d'épices or bouquet garni** and discard.

11. **Purée** the soup, if your recipe calls for it.

Source: Culinary Institute of America

12. **Add finishing ingredients or garnishes,** if your recipe calls for it.

Recipe Cards

96. Cream of Broccoli

97. Black Bean Soup, Caribbean-Style

98. Shrimp Bisque

99. Minestrone

READING CHECKPOINT *What is the difference between making a broth and making a consommé?*

Reheating and Serving Soups

When soups are served at the right temperature, they have the best possible flavor, texture, and color. If you've made enough soup to last for more than one day, you will need to reheat the soup. Then you will need to hold it at the right temperature until it is served to a customer.

Reheating Soups Reheat all soups over direct heat, not in the steam table. Use a heavy-gauge pot and place the pot on a burner. Clear soups can simply be brought to a boil over high heat.

To warm thinner hearty soups, put them into a pot over medium heat and stir frequently. Be careful. Most hearty soups have starchy ingredients; the starch can stick to the bottom of the pot and easily burn.

Thick hearty soups such as cream soups, purées, or bisques need extra care. For them, pour a thin layer of water or broth into the pot before you add the cold soup. Warm the soup over low heat until it is softened and warmed through. Once the soup is warm, you can increase the heat and bring it to a simmer, stirring frequently.

Serving Soups To serve a soup properly, you will need to hold it at the optimum temperature that not only keeps it safe but also maintains the right flavor, color, and texture.

- **Keep hot soups very hot.** For safety, all soups must be held at 165°F. Place them in containers in a steam table or a bain marie of hot water. Check the temperature of hot soups in the steam table periodically to be sure they are not getting cool.
- **Keep cold soups very cold.** Place cold soups in containers and hold them in a cold bain marie filled with ice.
- **Keep soups covered.** Covering the container prevents cross-contamination. A covered container of soup is also less likely to develop a skin. Covering the container helps keep hot soups hot and cold soups cold.

FIGURE 14–13

Reheating Soup
A thin initial layer of water or broth helps avoid scorching this cream of tomato soup as it reheats.

SOLVING PROBLEMS *Why are soups reheated over direct heat, not in a steam table?*

Source: Culinary Institute of America

FOCUS ON
Safety

Checking Soup's Temperature

Some restaurants use timers set for regular intervals to make sure that the temperature of hot soups that are being held is checked periodically.

READING CHECKPOINT *What are the differences when reheating clear soups and hearty soups?*

Garnishing Soups

A garnish adds an extra dimension to a soup. A fresh garnish such as herbs or grated citrus zest can add flavor or freshness. A garnish such as diced meats, grated cheese, or noodles can add substance to the soup. A garnish such as a dollop of cold sour cream on a hot soup or a crunchy crouton on a purée soup can add contrast. Even the crackers often served with soups are a type of garnish.

Clear Soups

Chicken Broth

Garnish: Chicken, pasta, carrot, celery

Source: David Murray and Jules Selmes/Dorling Kindersley

Fish Broth

Garnish: Sea bass, carrot, watercress, ginger

Source: David Murray and Jules Selmes/Dorling Kindersley

Beef Consommé

Garnish: Royale custard (cut into diamond shapes)

Source: Culinary Institute of America

Wonton Soup

Garnish: Wontons (dumplings), noodles, cilantro

Source: David Murray and Jules Selmes/Dorling Kindersley

Vegetable Broth

Garnish: Lettuce, cucumber, carrot, parsley

Source: David Murray and Jules Selmes/Dorling Kindersley

Hearty Soups

Carrot-Ginger Soup
Garnish: Heart-shaped croutons
Source: Dorling Kindersley Limited

New England Clam Chowder
Garnish: Oyster crackers
Source: Joshua Resnick/Fotolia

Soupe au Pistou (French Vegetable Soup)
Garnish: Pistou (basil sauce)
Source: Ian O'Leary/Dorling Kindersley

Lobster Bisque
Garnish: Lobster, tarragon
Source: David Murray and Jules Selmes/Dorling Kindersley

Cream of Mushroom Soup
Garnish: Mushrooms
Source: Oran Tantapakul/Fotolia

FIGURE 14–14

Holding Soups for Service
A soup should be brought to the table as soon as it is ready.

SOLVING PROBLEMS *What should you do if a soup is not hot enough to serve?*

Source: WavebreakmediaMicro/Fotolia

An item that is cooked in the soup is not considered a garnish but is a component of the soup. To be considered a garnish, a cooked item is added to the soup after it is cooked.

- Prepare garnishes properly and hold them at the appropriate temperature. All garnishes should be small enough to fit in a spoon so they are easy to eat.

- Garnishes such as fresh herbs, sour cream, and grated cheeses, do not need to be heated before adding them to the soup. Other garnishes may need to be hot when you add them to the soup so the garnish does not cool down the soup.

- Garnish soups right before they are served. Add garnishes and finishing ingredients to batches or individual portions as close to the time of service as possible.

- Serve crisp accompaniments on the side. Crackers, breadsticks, and similar crisp breads are often served with soups to offer a texture contrast.

Garnishes for Clear Soups Broths and consommés have a wide range of garnishes. If the garnish for a clear soup needs to be cooked, prepare it separately from the broth or consommé. Otherwise, the garnish will cloud the broth, particularly if the garnish contains a starch.

Garnishes for Hearty Soups A popular garnish for a hearty soup is a **crouton** (CREW-tahn), a small cube of bread that is toasted or fried until crisp and golden brown. There are many other options for garnishing hearty soups. Bisques often include diced cooked seafood. Cream soups are often garnished with small pieces of the main ingredient (for example, cooked broccoli for a cream of broccoli soup).

FIGURE 14–15

Gazpacho (Cold Tomato Soup) with Garnishes
These three garnishes provide substance, contrasting textures, and additional flavor to the soup.
APPLYING CONCEPTS *What other ways could you garnish this soup?*
Source: Clive Streeter/Dorling Kindersley

 **READING CHECKPOINT** *How are soups held for service?*

14.3 ASSESSMENT

Reviewing Concepts

1. Identify the two basic types of soup. Briefly describe each.

2. Explain the process of using a clarification in making a consommé.

3. Describe the differences when reheating clear soups and hearty soups.

4. Identify three things that a garnish can add to a soup.

Critical Thinking

5. Predicting What would happen to a clear broth if you simmered potatoes in it?

6. Comparing/Contrasting What is the difference between a purée soup and a cream soup?

7. Applying Concepts Describe five ways you could garnish your favorite soup.

Test Kitchen

Make three batches of cream of potato soup. For two batches, prepare the soup up to the point of adding the cream and then chill the soup. For the third batch, prepare the soup completely, adding the cream, and then chill it. The next day, reheat the soup that already includes the cream. Reheat one of the remaining batches and, when it is hot, add the cream. For the last batch, add the cream before you begin heating it. When all the soups are hot, taste and evaluate them.

LANGUAGE ARTS
Descriptive Writing

Research three different types of chowder. Write a description of each type of chowder, pointing out their similarities and differences.

Reviewing Content

Choose the letter that best answers the question or completes the statement.

Multiple Choice

1. White stock is made from
   a. carrots.
   b. unroasted bones.
   c. white rice.
   d. all of the above

2. Béchamel sauce is a
   a. brown sauce.
   b. derivative sauce.
   c. grand sauce.
   d. puréed sauce.

3. For safety, all hot soups must be held at
   a. 212°F.
   b. 100°F.
   c. 350°F.
   d. 165°F.

4. A sauce that has been thickened properly is described as
   a. nappé.
   b. slurry.
   c. roux.
   d. coulis.

5. In a roux, the balance of fat to flour is
   a. two parts fat to one part flour.
   b. four parts fat to one part flour.
   c. one part fat to one part flour.
   d. three parts fat to one part flour.

6. A bisque gets its color and flavor from
   a. lobster, crawfish, or shrimp shells.
   b. beets.
   c. black beans.
   d. split peas.

7. A liaison is a mixture of
   a. onions, parsnips, and celery.
   b. fat and flour.
   c. cream and egg yolks.
   d. refined starch and cold water.

Understanding Concepts

8. Describe the difference between a brown beef stock and a white beef stock.

9. Compare and contrast béchamel and velouté.

10. What is the difference between a broth and a consommé?

11. Describe the general process for making a roux-thickened sauce.

12. Describe the technique of tempering a liaison before you add it to a hot liquid.

Critical Thinking

13. **RECOGNIZING PATTERNS** Which stock would be darker: a vegetable stock made from fresh vegetables or a vegetable stock made from roasted vegetables? Explain your answer.

14. **PREDICTING** You have reheated a cream soup. Is it likely that you will need to adjust the seasonings? Explain your answer.

Culinary Math

15. **SOLVING PROBLEMS** A recipe for 1 gal of brown beef stock uses 8 lb of roasted bones, 1 lb of mirepoix, 4 to 6 oz of tomatoes, and 6 qt of water. How much of each of these ingredients is required to make 2½ gal of brown beef stock?

16. **APPLYING CONCEPTS** How much roux is required to make ½ gal of a sauce with a medium consistency?

On the Job

17. **APPLYING CONCEPTS** A customer who is allergic to dairy products orders a dish featuring Mornay sauce. Does the sauce present a problem for the customer? Explain your answer.

18. **INFERRING** What is the disadvantage for a restaurant in having a dish that features béarnaise sauce on its menu every day?

Owning a Food Business

Businesses large and small produce a wide array of food products. Some are large companies with multiple product lines; an example is Wolfgang Puck's company, which produces and sells soups, broths, stocks, pizzas, frozen entrées, and jarred sauces, in addition to cookware and equipment. Some businesses are quite small and may even operate out of a home, producing just one signature item. Food businesses supply products to restaurants, retail shops, grocery stores, and more.

Entrepreneurs often find a food business a good place to launch themselves. Someone who bakes great pies or cupcakes can start small, marketing his or her wares to local coffee shops, minimarts, or individuals. Restaurants occasionally package and sell their signature items such as sauces, dressings, or marinades. Some food busi-

Source: naypong/Fotolia

When considering what type of food business to enter, an entrepreneurial chef must decide what kinds of businesses best suit his or her talents

ness owners specialize in custom products for a single restaurant, while others are trying to create a brand that provides a number of related products. Some are looking for only a local market, while others have the goal of national or international distribution in mind.

Establishing and growing a food business often calls for long hours and hard work at tasks that take you out of the kitchen and into the larger world, no matter how large or small your business. You must have the appropriate business plan to keep your company growing as well as to find financial backing if you need or want to expand. Marketing, promotion, advertising, and media are also critical to your success. Sales and distribution are the keys to getting your product into your customers' hands. As your company grows, you will need to hire and train your staff.

Entry-Level Requirements

The initial requirement for any solid food business is a great product idea.

In order to produce and sell foods, you must meet appropriate zoning, health, and safety standards. All inspections must be current. Insurance may be required. All of these requirements may vary by community.

Helpful for Advancement

Owning a food business requires, above all, that you have great product ideas. You will need an established, loyal clientele who tell others about your business. You, or someone on your staff, will need to have good advertising and promotion skills. You will also need other business skills, including forecasting, cost control, and accounting—it is important for you to know how your business makes money and how it spends it.

KEN ARNONE

Chef Ken Arnone is a Certified Master Chef and Global Master Chef who has traveled the world mastering the culinary arts. A graduate of The Culinary Institute of America (CIA), Chef Arnone returned to the CIA in 1999 as a professor and oversaw the opening of two on-campus restaurants.

Ken Arnone

Since his time at the CIA, Chef Arnone has used his vast knowledge base as a culinary consultant, working with clients such as Colavita International, Yale University, and Panera Bread to develop recipes for retail food products. He is frequently invited to give lectures and to serve as a judge at culinary competitions.

Chef Arnone produces a product called Pesto Diavolo, a spicy spread and dip sold in retail markets. He is also cofounder of dcuisine, which delivers high-quality meals directly to the customer.

VITAL **STATISTICS**

Early Training: The Culinary Institute of America

Profession: Culinary consultant and entrepreneur

Interesting Items: Co-authored a food and wine pairing book in 2012, *Pairing with The Masters*

Has won four gold, eight silver, and two bronze medals in the Culinary Olympics

Has judged over 60 culinary competitions, including the Certified Master Chef Exam

CAREER **PROFILE**

Salary Ranges

Varies widely depending on the number of products, the size of the operation, and the location and the size of the business.

Fish and Shellfish

15.1 Fish

15.2 Shellfish

15.1

Fish

Key Concepts

- Identifying basic types of fish
- Selecting and storing fish
- Preparing fish
- Matching cooking methods to fish

Vocabulary

- anadromous fish
- belly bones
- cross cuts
- deep poaching
- drawn fish
- en papillote
- farm-raised fish
- fillet
- flat fish
- freshwater fish
- glazed fish
- goujonette
- headed and gutted fish
- lox
- pan-dressed fish
- paupiette
- pin bones
- PUFI mark
- quarter fillets
- round fish
- saltwater fish
- shallow poaching
- steaks (fish)
- tranche
- whole fish
- wild fish

Types of Fish

When you say *fish*, you could be referring to any of thousands of different types of fish. **Saltwater fish** live in oceans, seas, and the water of bays and gulfs. **Freshwater fish** live in freshwater ponds, lakes, rivers, and streams. Some fish live part of their lives in salt water and part in fresh water. This type of fish is known as **anadromous** (ann-AH-drom-us) **fish**. Fish are often identified according to the way that they are harvested or raised.

Farm-raised fish are raised in ponds or penned waters out in the ocean. They have the advantage of being more consistently available than **wild fish** (fish that are captured in nets or on fishing lines in open water). Some scientists also suggest that farm-raised fish reduce the demand for some wild fish that may be in danger of overfishing. On the other hand, there are some concerns about the impact that fish farming may have on the environment. Scientists are concerned about the possibility of pollution, disease, and parasites resulting from the living conditions of farm-raised fish. This may require administering drugs and medications to keep the fish healthy, and we may, in turn, ingest those drugs when we eat the farm-raised fish. But the numbers of wild fish are limited, and farm-raised fish do offer a solution to the consumer. Fishermen who fish for wild fish have to observe restrictions about when and where the fish can be harvested, as well as limits on the number of fish they can capture. Fish purveyors often indicate that fish was wild caught because some feel that it is a better indicator of quality and wholesomeness.

One of the biggest challenges in identifying fish is that a single fish can have many different names, depending on the part of the world you are in. However, what matters most to a chef is how the fish will taste when it is

Source: Julie Downing and Grahame Corbett/Dorling Kindersley

cooked. The most important factors in deciding how to cook a fish are its fat content and its body type.

Fat Content Fish don't have much fat, and the fat they do have is different from the fat found in animals that live on the land. The fat in fish gives each type of fish its distinctive flavor. The higher the fat content, the stronger the fish's flavor. Fish that swim constantly have more fat and darker-colored flesh than fish that stay in one place. In terms of fat content, there are three types of fish:

- **Lean Fish.** With light-colored flesh, a mild flavor, and a delicate texture, lean fish easily separates into flakes once it is cooked. Lean fish tend to stay relatively still, living and feeding at the bottom of the ocean (examples: Dover sole, halibut, and fluke).
- **Moderately Fatty Fish.** With a richer, more deeply flavored flesh than lean fish, moderately fatty fish have a texture that is somewhat firmer than lean fish. They also separate into flakes when they are cooked (examples: striped bass, red snapper, and grouper).
- **Fatty Fish.** Many fatty fish are saltwater fish, who swim over great distances. Their flesh is the most deeply flavored and colored (examples: Atlantic salmon, rainbow trout, and bluefin tuna).

Body Type From a chef's perspective, fish have three basic body types:

- **Round Fish.** With eyes on both sides of their heads, **round fish** swim in an upright position, belly down and back up. The skin on the belly is usually paler and the skin on the back and sides is darker (examples: mahi mahi, bluefish, brook trout).
- **Flat Fish.** With both eyes on the same side of their heads, **flat fish** swim close to the bottom. They are wider than they are thick (examples: gray sole, turbot, and halibut).
- **Nonbony and Other Fish.** Some of these fish have cartilage (CART-ti-ledj), a flexible material, rather than bones. Others are unusual fish that don't fit in other categories (examples: monkfish, tilapia, and American catfish).

Substitutions Sometimes a certain type of fish may be unavailable or there may be an oversupply of a particular type of fish, which results in lower prices for that fish. In these cases, chefs may find it necessary, or at least economical, to substitute one type of fish for another. A good rule of thumb is that you can substitute one type of round fish with a specific fat content for another round fish with the same fat content. You could substitute grouper for striped bass, for example. Both are moderately fatty round fish. This holds true for flat fish as well. There will, of course, be differences in taste. (This substitution rule doesn't apply to the unique category of nonbony and other fish.)

Advisory Lists A number of seafood advisory lists provide recommendations about seafood choices. Typically these lists show seafood ranging from "best choice" to "fish to avoid." Fish are placed in the "avoid" category if they are overfished or if they are fished or farmed in ways that hurt the

Lean Flat Fish

Dover Sole

Flesh is fattier and firmer than other members of the flat fish family. Baked, broiled, poached, sautéed, or steamed.

Source: David Murray/Dorling Kindersley

Lemon Sole

Also called *English sole, blackback flounder,* and *winter flounder.* Light, slightly sweet, delicate flesh. Baked, poached, or sautéed.

Source: Richard Embery/Pearson Education/PH College

Halibut

Dense, snow-white flesh, with a fine texture and mild taste. Halibut has the highest fat content of all low-fat fish. Baked, broiled, fried, grilled, poached, sautéed, or steamed.

Source: Roger Phillips/Dorling Kindersley

Turbot (TUR-bow)

Delicate flavor with a firm texture. Baked, broiled, fried, grilled, poached, steamed, or sautéed.

Source: Richard Embery/Pearson Education/PH College

Others

Fluke (Summer Flounder)
White, flaky flesh, with a delicate flavor and texture. Baked, poached, or sautéed.

Gray Sole (Witch Flounder)
Light, slightly sweet, delicate flesh. Baked or poached.

Rex Sole
Delicate, creamy white flesh, with a distinct flavor. Poached or sautéed.

Rock Sole
Firm and creamy white flesh. Baked, poached, or sautéed.

Lean Round Fish

Atlantic Cod

Thick, white flesh with a mild flavor. Roe, cheeks, and chins are delicacies. Shallow poached, baked, pan-fried, or deep-fried. Also smoked, cured, salted, or dried.

Source: Richard Embery/Pearson Education/PH College

Haddock

Firm texture, low fat, with a mild flavor. (The skin is left on fillets to distinguish them from Atlantic cod.) Poached, baked, sautéed, or pan-fried. Also salted or smoked.

Source: Philip Dowell/Dorling Kindersley

Alaskan Pollack

Also called *Pacific pollack* and *snow cod*. Light gray, flaky flesh with a mild flavor. Also smoked or processed to make surimi (soo-REE-mee), a Japanese product shaped, flavored, and colored to resemble various types of shellfish, such as crab and shrimp.

Source: Philip Dowell/Dorling Kindersley

Moderately Fatty Round Fish

Weakfish

Also called *sea trout*. Sweet, delicate flesh. Poached, baked, sautéed, grilled, broiled, or steamed.

Source: Culinary Institute of America

Black Sea Bass

Also called *rock sea bass*. White, firm flesh, with a delicate texture. Poached, baked, deep-fried, or sautéed. Also pickled. Commonly served whole, using tableside presentation.

Source: Culinary Institute of America

Striped Bass

Coarse texture, large flakes, with flavorful flesh. Broiled, grilled, poached, baked, deep-fried, or sautéed. Also pickled. Extremely versatile.

Source: Culinary Institute of America

Red Snapper

Also called *American snapper*. Firm texture. Poached, baked, sautéed, grilled, broiled, or steamed.

Source: Culinary Institute of America

Grouper

Varieties: yellowfin grouper, yellowmouth grouper, black grouper, and red grouper. Sweet, white flesh. Poached, baked, broiled, steamed, or deep-fried. Also used in chowders.

Source: Culinary Institute of America

Others

Walleyed Pike (Pike Perch)

Mild flavor, low fat content, with a firm texture. Broiled, sautéed, poached, steamed, baked, or stewed. Also used in soups.

Vermillion Snapper (Beeliner)

Often substituted for red snapper, though smaller; less flavorful. Poached, baked, sautéed, grilled, broiled, or steamed.

Tilefish

Firm yet tender flesh. Poached, baked, broiled, deep-fried, or pan-fried. Available whole or as fillets.

Fatty Round Fish

Rainbow Trout

Firm, off-white flesh with a mild flavor. Poached, baked, broiled, fried, grilled, or steamed. Often stuffed. Generally sold head-on.

Source: Frank Greenaway/Dorling Kindersley

Atlantic Salmon

Deep pink flesh; high fat content. Poached, baked, broiled, steamed, or grilled. Also smoked. Raw in sushi. Used in dips and soups.

Source: Culinary Institute of America

Coho Salmon

Also called *silver salmon*. Similar in taste and texture to Atlantic salmon. Poached, baked, broiled, steamed, or grilled. Also smoked. Used in dips and soups.

Source: Culinary Institute of America

Pompano (PAHM-pah-noh)

Also called *cobblerfish* and *palmenta*. Delicate, beige flesh that turns white when cooked, with a complex flavor and medium fat content. Poached, baked, broiled, grilled, fried, or steamed. Expensive.

Source: Culinary Institute of America

Bluefin Tuna

Dark red to reddish brown flesh, with a distinct flavor when cooked. Baked, broiled, grilled, or sautéed. The most sought-after fish for sushi and sashimi (with consistently high prices).

Source: Roger Phillips/Dorling Kindersley

King Mackerel

Also called *kingfish*. High fat content, finely textured and flavorful flesh. Baked, broiled, grilled, or sautéed. Also smoked.

Source: Picture Partners/Fotolia

Spanish Mackerel

Delicate flesh. Baked, broiled, grilled, or sautéed. Also smoked.

Source: Culinary Institute of America

Others

Albacore Tuna (AHL-ba-cor)

Light red to pink flesh that is off-white when cooked, with a mild flavor. Baked, broiled, grilled, or sautéed. Often canned and sold as "white tuna."

American Shad

White, sweet flesh, with a high fat content. Poached, baked, broiled, grilled, or sautéed. Also smoked. Eggs (roe) are considered a delicacy.

Arctic Char

Dark red to rose or white flesh. Poached, baked, broiled, fried, grilled, or steamed. Often stuffed.

Bluefish (Blue Runner)

Dark, oily, strongly flavored flesh, with a fine texture. Baked or broiled.

Brook Trout (Speckled Trout)

Delicate and buttery flesh. Poached, baked, broiled, fried, grilled, or steamed. Often stuffed.

Chinook Salmon (King Salmon)

Medium to dark red flesh. Smoked, poached, baked, broiled, steamed, or grilled. Used in dips and soups.

Dolphinfish (Mahi Mahi, Dorado)

Pink to tan flesh turns off-white when cooked; firm texture with a large flake; sweet, delicate flavor. Baked, broiled, grilled, pan-fried, or sautéed.

Sockeye Salmon (Red Salmon)

Dark red flesh. Poached, baked, sautéed, grilled, broiled, or steamed.

Nonbony and Other Fish

Monkfish

Also called *anglerfish, devilfish, frogfish,* and *goosefish.* Very firm, mild white flesh. Baked, broiled, grilled, fried, sautéed, or pan-fried. Commonly sold as tails and fillets. Low yield when sold head-on. Livers are popular in Japan.

Source: Culinary Institute of America

Eel

High-fat, firm flesh, with a rich, sweet flavor. Broiled, fried, or stewed. Also smoked.

Source: Culinary Institute of America

American Catfish

Firm flesh, with a mild, sweet flavor. Poached, baked, broiled, grilled, steamed, stewed, deep-fried, or pan-fried. Also smoked. Commonly sold headless and skinless.

Source: Culinary Institute of America

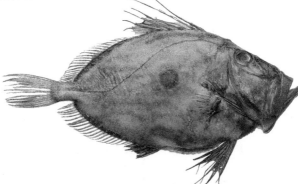

Anchovy

Silver skin; soft, flavorful flesh. Deep-fried or pan-fried whole. Also smoked or marinated. Sold canned (packed in oil or salt) and dried. Used as a flavoring additive and garnish. When whole, best less than 4 inches in length.

Source: Culinary Institute of America

John Dory

Also called *Saint Peter's fish.* Firm, bright white flesh, with a delicate flavor and fine flake. Poached, grilled, or sautéed.

Source: Ian O'Leary/Dorling Kindersley

Sardine

Silvery skin; delicate fatty flesh. Broiled, grilled, or deep-fried whole. Also marinated, salted, smoked, or canned. Available whole or dressed. When whole, best less than 7 inches in length.

Source: Clive Streeter/Dorling Kindersley

Others

Swordfish

Very firm, dense flesh, with a distinct flavor. Baked, broiled, grilled, or sautéed. Available skinless and headless, or as fillets or steaks.

Sturgeon

Firm, high-fat flesh, with a rich, delicate flavor. Baked, braised, broiled, grilled, or sautéed. Also smoked. Eggs used for caviar.

Mako Shark

Firm, pink to white flesh, with a sweet flavor. Poached, baked, broiled, grilled, fried, or sautéed.

Skate

Also called a *ray.* White firm flesh, with a sweet flavor. Poached, baked, fried, sautéed. Fins (called wings) produce two fillets. The upper fillet is generally thicker than the lower one.

Source: geniuscook_com/Shutterstock

Tilapia (til-AHP-ee-ah)

Also called *mudfish.* Off-white to pink flesh; flavor is very mild. Poached, baked, broiled, grilled, or steamed.

Source: Richard Embery/Pearson Education/PH College

Left- or Right-Eyed Fish?

When flat fish first hatch, they are shaped like round fish and are nearly transparent. They float on the water currents. Being transparent is most likely a way the fish have evolved to escape predator fish that might eat them.

The fish stay transparent as long as they are surviving on the food supplies in their yolk sacs. Once they begin to eat actual food, they start to change. Gradually, one eye starts to move across the fish's skull until eventually both eyes are on the same side of the head. The backbone and the skeleton also start to migrate, staying in line with the eyes.

Some fish have both eyes on the right side (right-eyed flat fish) and some have both eyes on the left (left-eyed flat fish). The skin on the side of the fish that has the eyes begins to darken and take on more color, usually a color that is similar to the bottom surface. The skin on the side of the fish opposite the eyes (the blind side)—that is, the side of the fish that faces down toward the bottom—stays light.

Source: Fuse/Getty Images

Rainbow flounder

Research

Research the life cycle of a flat fish such as halibut, Dover sole, turbot, or fluke. Write a report describing such things as the fish's habitat through its life cycle, what it eats, what eats it, its size and weight, its life span, how it is typically caught, and whether it is farmed. Make sure to discover whether it is a left-eyed or right-eyed fish. Report on its market form and market price. Finally, provide a recipe featuring the fish.

environment. These lists also provide health alerts for fish that have a high level of contaminants, such as mercury. One of the best known advisory lists is *Seafood Watch*, sponsored by the Monterey Bay Aquarium. Although *Seafood Watch* is updated regularly, consumers are regularly advised to limit consumption of the following fish because of concerns about mercury or other contaminants: Chilean sea bass, groupers, orange roughy, farmed salmon, sharks, sturgeon, swordfish, and tuna.

READING CHECKPOINT *Based on fat content, what are the three types of fish?*

Selecting and Storing Fish

Fish are extremely perishable. They need to be kept chilled and iced from the moment they are caught. Fish must be checked for quality when they arrive at the kitchen. Professional kitchens are required to keep any certificates and invoices for the fish they receive.

Inspection and Grading Fish (and shellfish) are inspected by the National Marine Fisheries Service (NMFS), a part of the National Oceanic and Atmospheric Administration (NOAA). The NMFS is charged with inspecting all fish that are processed for sale, including fish caught in the wild and fish that are farm-raised. The NMFS even inspects fishmeal that is intended for use as animal feed.

The NMFS has established three types of evaluation for fish:

- Type 1 is an evaluation for quality and wholesomeness.
- Type 2 is an evaluation of the accuracy of the labeling and weight.
- Type 3 is an evaluation of the sanitation of the processing facility itself.

If a facility passes a Type 1 inspection, it receives a mark from the United States Department of Commerce known as a **PUFI mark**, which stands for *packed under federal inspection*. (Processors of fish and shellfish often pay for inspections that ensure adherence with HACCP guidelines, cleanliness, and safety.)

Grades are assigned as part of a voluntary program. Only fish and shellfish that receive a PUFI mark are eligible for the highest grade, which is U.S. Grade A. These fish and shellfish are of the highest quality, with good shape, flavor, and aroma. Grade B is considered good quality, and fish graded C is considered fairly good quality. Grades B and C are used primarily for processed or canned products.

Fish can sometimes be contaminated with marine toxins. These naturally occurring chemicals can cause disease in humans when they eat a contaminated fish. Fish contaminated with these chemicals often look, smell, and taste normal. Cooking spoiled or toxic seafood doesn't destroy marine toxins.

Health departments sometimes test for marine toxins. State and federal regulatory agencies monitor reported outbreaks of diseases caused by these toxins and can prohibit fishing for specific types of fish from areas that may be the source of toxins.

Certain types of fish are more prone to carrying specific types of marine toxins:

- **Scombrotoxins** Tuna, mackerel, grouper, bonito, and mahi mahi can cause scombrotoxic fish poisoning caused by bacterial spoilage in the fish. Common symptoms include a rash, diarrhea, flushing, sweating, headache, and vomiting.
- **Ciguatoxins** Barracuda are often a source of ciguatera poisoning, especially those from the Caribbean, and should never be eaten. Sea bass, snapper, mullet, and other tropical reef fish are also sometimes associated with this marine toxin. Symptoms can include nausea, vomiting, diarrhea, cramps, sweating, headache, and muscle aches.

Although the toxins associated with fish and shellfish (see Section 15.2) are serious, it is important to realize that, with the millions of fish and

PUFI mark
Source: USDA

FIGURE 15–1

Cross Cuts

Cutting directly across the fish results in a cross cut. Often cross cuts include bones.

PREDICTING *As a customer, would you prefer a cross cut or a fillet?*

Source: Culinary Institute of America

••FOCUS ON •• Safety

Salt as a Preservative

When you add a large amount of salt to food, you draw out the moisture in the food. Even though the salmon used to make lox is never cooked, the salmon is safe to eat and is firm enough to slice paper thin.

shellfish eaten in the United States each year, only about 30 cases of poisoning by marine toxins are reported annually. And only one person every four years dies from seafood poisoning.

Market Forms In fish markets, fish is sold in a variety of forms:

- **Whole Fish.** The fish as it was caught, completely intact and still including the stomach, is referred to as a **whole fish.** Whole fish that has the stomach removed is referred to as a **drawn fish** (or a drawn whole fish). If the head is also cut off, the fish is referred to as **headed and gutted fish.** A **pan-dressed fish** has the fins removed, and sometimes the head and tail are also cut off. Pan-dressed fish are usually small enough to fit easily in a pan and make a single serving.

- **Cross Cuts or Steaks.** A large drawn fish can be cut into sections. Large sections are known as **cross cuts.** Small cross cuts, pieces portioned for a single serving, are known as **steaks.** Because they are a cross cut, steaks contain at least a portion of the spine and may contain other bones.

- **Fillets.** A boneless piece of fish is called a **fillet** (FILL-eh). The skin may be left on or it may be removed, depending on the type of fish.

- **Frozen Fish. Glazed fish** is a whole fish that has been dipped in water and then frozen several times to build up a layer of ice. Fish fillets and steaks are also sold already trimmed, cut into portions, and then packaged and frozen.

- **Canned Fish.** Canned fish is completely cooked and packed in cans. Tuna and salmon are two common types of canned fish.

- **Salted, Cured, and Smoked Fish.** Salt cod is made by filleting cod, soaking it in a salty brine, and letting it dry. Cured fish is also brined or coated with salt. The fish takes on a salty and savory flavor. **Lox** is cured salmon.

Selecting Fish Whole fish should pass the following five tests for freshness:

- **Smell the fish.** The fish should have a clean, sweet, sea-like smell. If the fish doesn't smell good, it has failed the most important of all the tests.

- **Check the temperature.** Whole fish should be received packed in ice. Fish portions, such as fillets or steaks, should be received at a temperature of no more than 41°F. The ideal temperature for shipping fresh fish is 30°F to 32°F.

- **Look at the fish.** Check for a good overall appearance: a clear shine, no cuts or bruising, and pliable fins. The scales (if there are any)

should tightly adhere to the fish. If the fish still has its head, look at the eyes. They should look full, not shrunken or dried out.

- **Press on the fish.** The flesh should rise quickly after being pressed. It should not hold on to the mark.

- **Open the gills and the belly.** The gills, located near the fish's head, are the way it breathes. If the gills have started to turn brown and have become slimy, the fish isn't fresh. If the guts have been removed, check inside the fish. The fish should be clinging to the bones, especially along the backbone.

Fish begin to lose moisture once they are cut. A small amount of liquid in the bottom of a container is hard to avoid, but there should not be a deep layer. Fish fillets and steaks should be packed in clean containers when you receive them.

If you are checking fillets or steaks for quality, look at the individual pieces. They should be neatly cut and of an even size. The fish should look moist and have few if any cracks. If the skin is still attached to the fish, it should look moist and have no tears or punctures.

Storing Fish Before you received any fish, its quality and wholesomeness was someone else's responsibility. From the moment you accept a fish, its quality and wholesomeness become your responsibility. The optimum storage temperature for fresh fish is 34°F to 38°F.

Fresh fish lasts only a few days, even under the best storage conditions. Fish needs to be kept very cold and moist, but not wet. Whole fish, including drawn or pan-dressed fish, need to be stored in a bed of shaved ice.

To store whole fish:

1. Put a layer of shaved ice in a perforated hotel pan or container, preferably made of stainless steel.

2. Pack some ice into the belly cavity of the fish, and then put the fish belly facing down on the bed of shaved ice in the perforated container. Fish are stored belly down because the gut and the gills have higher levels of bacteria than the back. By making sure the interior of the belly and gills are well iced, contamination and spoilage can be reduced.

FIGURE 15–2
Selecting Fish
Steps in checking for freshness: Press on the fish (left). Check the gills (middle). Check the belly (right).

APPLYING CONCEPTS *What would you do if you doubted the freshness of a fish you were about to serve?*

Source: Culinary Institute of America

Chef's Tip

Why Shaved Ice?

Shaved or flaked ice fits more tightly around the fish, reducing its contact with the air and keeping it cold. Make sure to permit melting ice to drain away from the fish.

Russia

Russia is a huge country, spanning Asia and Europe. It extends from the north Pacific Ocean—where it neighbors North Korea, China, and Japan—to eastern Europe, abutting Finland in the north and the Black Sea and the Caspian Sea in the south. Its cuisine reflects its geographic position, with a mixture of Asian and European influences.

Source: pavalena/Shutterstock

Borscht (BORSCH) is one of the most traditional dishes in Russian cuisine. It is a soup made with a broth based on beets (which give it a deep reddish-purple color). Borscht may include cabbage, potatoes, and meat, usually beef. It's usually served hot and may be served as a main dish or as an appetizer. Borscht is often garnished with a dollop of sour cream and chopped dill, and accompanied by thick, dark bread.

Reflecting its Asian-European heritage, Russian cuisine features a wide variety of dumplings. *Pelmeni* (PEL-muh-nee) are dumplings with a very thin dough made from flour and water, sometimes with a bit of egg added. They are filled with a savory raw meat filling and are boiled, after which they can be fried or baked. *Verenyky* (VER-ehn-ee-kee) are dumplings with a thicker dough that are filled with a precooked meat filling. Like pelmeni, they are first boiled, and then can be fried or baked. Unlike pelmeni, verenyky sometimes have a sweet filling

made from fruit, preserves, and, in some cases, cheese. These dumplings are similar to Chinese wontons, Polish pierogi, and, to some extent, Italian ravioli.

Shaslyk (shosh-LICK) is marinated meat on a skewer (like a shish kebob). The meat, often lamb, but sometimes beef or pork, is marinated in an acidic liquid such as wine, vinegar, or sour fruit juice. Herbs are added to the marinade as well. The skewers often contain meat alternating with vegetables such as peppers and onions. Shaslyk is not typically served in fine restaurants but is sold by street vendors who grill the skewers over wood, charcoal, or coal.

Some Russian dishes have become well known internationally. For example, beef stroganoff, sautéed pieces of beef served in a sour cream sauce, is served all over the world. Another Russian dish that has achieved international recognition is chicken Kiev, in which pounded, boneless chicken breast is rolled around cold garlic butter and then breaded and fried or baked.

Russia is also internationally famous for its smoked fish, caviar, and *blini* (the small, thin pancakes on which caviar is traditionally served).

Research

Research beef stroganoff recipes from Russia and from at least two other countries. Pick a recipe and make it. Then write a paper describing your experience creating the beef stroganoff and predicting how it would have been changed had you made the other variations. Remember to consider not only taste, but also smell, texture, and appearance.

Beef stroganoff

Source: Lilyana Vynogradova/Fotolia

Storing Fish
Perforated hotel pan (left) and fish stored on a bed of shaved ice (right).
DRAWING CONCLUSIONS *Why are fish stored with the belly facing down?*
Source: Culinary Institute of America

3. Mold the ice tightly around the fish.

4. Set the perforated container in a second container to allow water from melting ice to drain away.

5. Re-ice the fish daily.

To store fish fillets:

1. Place the fish in a storage container (stainless steel is preferable, although food-grade plastic is acceptable).

2. Set the container in an ice-filled hotel pan.

3. Keep fish fillets away from direct contact with the ice to keep as much flavor and texture in the fish as possible.

To store frozen fish:

1. Do not accept frozen fish with white frost on its edges. This indicates freezer burn, the result of improper packaging or thawing and refreezing of the product.

2. Store frozen fish at –20°F to 0°F until it is ready to be thawed and cooked.

READING CHECKPOINT *What are the five tests for freshness in a whole fish?*

Preparing Fish

Chefs use a variety of techniques to prepare fish before they cook it. They select the technique based on the kind of fish they are preparing.

Filleting Fish Round fish are filleted by using a different technique than is used for flat fish. Of course, many fish are sold already cut into fillets or even filleted and portioned. However, a kitchen may find it can control costs better, and improve the quality of the fish it serves, if it buys whole fish and asks chefs to fillet the fish themselves.

Round fish produce two fillets, one on each side of the backbone. Flat fish can be cut into two fillets or four fillets (which are sometimes known as **quarter fillets**).

Filleting Flat Fish (Quarter Fillets)

1 **Place the fish on the cutting board** with the head away from you and the tail toward you.

2 **Make a cut on one side of the backbone** from the head to the tail.

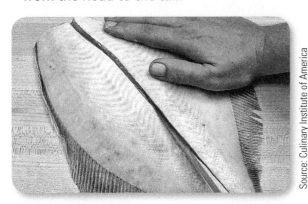

Source: Culinary Institute of America

3 **Cut along the bones,** working from the center to the edge. Keep the blade angled slightly so the cut is very close to the bones.

Source: Culinary Institute of America

4 **Remove the first quarter fillet** and lay it skin side down on the cutting board. Trim away any internal organs attached to the fillet.

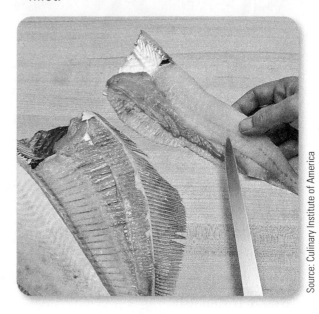

Source: Culinary Institute of America

5 **Turn the fish** around so the tail is toward you.

6 **Cut along the bones,** working from the center to the edge, to remove the second fillet.

7 **Turn the fish over.**

8 **Remove the bottom fillets,** using the same technique as for the first and second fillets.

Trimming a Fillet You can trim a fish fillet by removing any belly or pin bones. **Belly bones** are found along the thinner edge of the fillet. You can simply slice them away from the fillet. **Pin bones** are found in the middle of the fillet. To locate them, run your finger over the fillet from the head to the tail. Use needle-nose pliers or tweezers to pull out the bones. Pull them in the direction of the head to avoid ripping the flesh.

To remove the skin, lay the fillet parallel to the edge of the cutting surface. Hold the knife so the cutting edge is cutting against the skin and pull it taut with your guiding hand. Push the knife from one end to the other with a slight back-and-forth motion.

Filleting Round Fish

① **Place the fish on the cutting board** with the backbone parallel to the side of the cutting board and the head on the same side as your dominant hand (that is, on your right, if you are right-handed).

② **Cut behind the head and gill plates,** using a fish filleting knife. Angle the knife down and away from the body. Cut to the backbone only. Do not cut off the head.

Source: Culinary Institute of America

③ **Turn the knife,** without removing it, so the cutting edge points toward the tail.

④ **Run the blade down the length of the fish,** cutting against the backbone. Avoid sawing the knife back and forth.

Source: Culinary Institute of America

⑤ **Remove the fillet** and lay it skin side down on the cutting board.

Source: Culinary Institute of America

⑥ **Repeat** on the second side.

FIGURE 15–4

Removing Pin Bones

Use needle-nose pliers to pull out pin bones.

PREDICTION *As a customer, would you be upset if you discovered pin bones in your fillet?*

Source: Culinary Institute of America

Chapter 15 *Fish and Shellfish* **511**

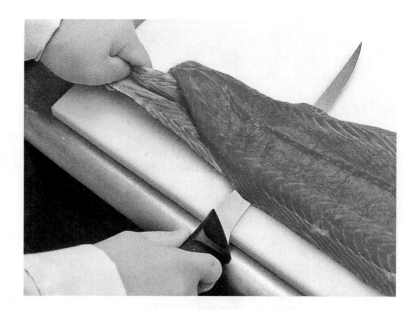

FIGURE 15–5
Removing Skin
The cutting edge of the knife should be against the skin.

DRAWING CONCLUSIONS *Why might a restaurant want to keep the skin on a fish?*

Source: Culinary Institute of America

Rolling Paupiettes A **paupiette** (poh-PYET) is a thin fillet that is rolled up before it is cooked. This gives the fish a neat appearance and helps it cook evenly. Paupiettes are generally made from lean fish, such as flounder or sole, although they may be made from some moderately fatty fish, such as trout or salmon. A paupiette is often filled with a stuffing.

Cutting Fillets Fillets can be cut into slices, using either an angled cut or a straight cut. By angling the blade as you cut, the cut slice, called a **tranche** (TRAHNSH), will have more surface area. A straight cut, called a **goujonette** (goo-zhohn-NET) or sometimes a *fish finger*, is usually about the width of a thumb.

FIGURE 15–6
Rolling Paupiettes
Roll the fillet from the head to the tail.

PREDICTING *As a customer, would you rather be presented with a stuffed paupiette or a thin fillet?*

Source: Culinary Institute of America

FIGURE 15–7
Cutting a Fillet
A slice from a fillet can be angled to create a tranche (left) or cut straight to create a goujonette (right).

PREDICTING *What cooking method might be best used with a tranche cut?*

Source: Culinary Institute of America

READING CHECKPOINT *How do you fillet a flat fish? A round fish?*

Matching Cooking Methods to Fish

The basic guideline for cooking fish is the leaner the fish, the more delicate the cooking method you should choose.

Determining Doneness in Fish No matter what type of fish you are preparing, fish is fully cooked when it reaches an internal temperature of 145°F. At that temperature, the fish will be more firm than when it was raw. The flesh, which is somewhat translucent when raw, will be opaque. Some types of fish may flake when they are done. The flakes should slide apart and appear very moist.

Some people may prefer fish cooked slightly less (especially salmon and tuna), but you should cook fish this way only if the customer specifically requests it or if the menu clearly states that you cook fish to a medium or medium-rare doneness.

Sautéing Sautéing works well for lean fish, including flounder, sole, halibut, and cod. Some moderately oily fish, such as trout, bass, and salmon, are also suitable for sautéing. Denser fish, such as tuna, shark, and swordfish, can also be successfully sautéed.

When sautéing, the more delicate the fish, the lower you should make the temperature. A fragile Dover sole fillet needs less intense heat than a piece of tuna. The small amount of fat used during sautéing keeps the fish moist and flavorful and helps prevent it from sticking to the pan and tearing.

Most fish sautés call for the fish to be dusted with flour to create a slight crust, as well as to keep the moisture in the fish from spattering too much when the fish is put into the hot oil. A classic presentation for fish is to dip it in flour, sauté it quickly, and then serve it with a sauce made of butter, lemon, and parsley. The name for this dish is *à la meunière* (ah la muhn-YEHR).

Sautéing Fish

1. **Heat the pan** and cooking fat over moderate heat.

2. **Dust** the fish with flour.

3. **Add the fish to the pan** carefully to avoid splashing.

4. **Sauté on the first side** until golden.

5. **Turn the fish** once and finish cooking on the second side.

6. **Remove the fish** from the pan and keep fish warm.

7. **Pour off the fat** from the pan, but do not wipe it out.

8. **Return the pan to the heat.**

9. **Add whole butter** and cook until the butter has a nutty smell.

10. **Add lemon juice and parsley.** Serve the fish very hot with the lemon-butter-parsley mixture.

Source: David Murray and Jules Selmes/Dorling Kindersley

Recipe Card

100. Sautéed Trout Meuniere

Recipe Card

101. Flounder à l'Orly

Grilled salmon

Source: Neil Mersh/Dorling Kindersley

Pan Frying and Deep Frying Frying is a good technique for most lean and some moderately fatty fish. Frying indicates that the fish will be given a coating of some kind, such as a batter or a coating of bread crumbs or cornmeal. Pan frying calls for more fat in the pan than sautéing does, usually enough to cover about one-third of the fish.

Deep-fried fish are cooked in enough hot oil to completely submerge them. Fish sticks, fish and chips (coated in cornmeal batter and fried), and a fisherman's platter that includes a variety of fish and shellfish are some common fried fish dishes.

Grilling and Broiling Grilling is suitable for virtually all fish, but the fish must be prepared properly for the grill. Moderately oily and oily fish such as mackerel, bluefish, and snapper usually require nothing more than seasonings. A marinade is also a common way to season and prepare moderately oily and oily fish for the grill. Their naturally firm and meaty texture holds up well to the intense heat of the grill. You do need to brush both the grill and the fish lightly with oil to keep the fish from sticking and tearing. Leaner fish can be grilled, but you need to use a hand rack. A hand rack is a cooking rack that opens, allowing fish to be inserted, and then closes. It is turned by hand. With a hand rack, you can lift and turn fish so they don't fall apart.

Broiling Fish

1. **Butter or oil a broiling pan** lightly.
2. **Add a bed of aromatic ingredients,** if desired.
3. **Season the prepared fish and brush with butter.**

the top is browned and the fish is cooked through.

6. **Serve** at once on heated plates.

Source: Culinary Institute of America

Source: Culinary Institute of America

4. **Add a bread crumb topping or sauce** to the fish.
5. **Broil** a few inches from the heat source, raising or lowering the broiler rack, until

Recipe Card

102. Broiled Lemon Sole on a Bed of Leeks

Broiled fish can be prepared in the same way as grilled fish. When broiling, the heat is located above the fish instead of below it, so the fish usually does not need to be turned. Because it is not turned, the fish can be coated with a sauce and then broiled. Fish prepared in this manner is known as *au gratin* (oh GRAH-ten). If the fish is brushed with butter and topped with bread crumbs before it is broiled, the dish is known as *à l'anglaise* (ah lahn-GLEZ).

Baking and Roasting Whole fish, fillets, and steaks can all be cooked in the oven. Whole fish are referred to as being roasted, while pieces are typically referred to as being baked. There is no significant difference between baking and roasting fish.

To keep the fish moist, it often has some sort of topping or crust. Other possibilities for roasted or baked fish include adding aromatics to the fish as it cooks or even stuffing the whole fish or fillets with a stuffing mixture.

Chef's Tip

Sizzler Platter

Some restaurants refer to the broiling pan as a *sizzler platter*.

Baked salmon

Recipe Cards

103. Tagine of Cod

104. Poached Trout Paupiettes with Vin Blanc Sauce

105. Poached Salmon with Asparagus and Basil Sauce

Steaming It is important to cook steamed fish just until it is done. Fish begins to dry out and lose flavor if it is overcooked. Asian cuisines have many classic preparations of whole steamed fish, but you can also steam smaller portions, such as fillets or steaks.

One special adaptation of the steaming technique calls for the fish to be wrapped, usually in parchment paper and often including aromatics and vegetables. Then the package is baked in the oven, causing the water in the vegetables and fish to steam the food. This is referred to as cooking the fish **en papillote** (ahn pap-ee-YOTE).

Poaching Fish is often poached. If you cook fish in enough liquid to completely cover it, you are **deep poaching** the fish. If you use just enough liquid to create some steam in the pan, you are **shallow poaching** the fish.

Deep poaching is typically used for fish steaks, whole fillets of larger fish such as salmon, or whole fish. Deep-poach fish until they are just cooked through. Keep the temperature of the liquid low so there are only a few small lazy bubbles breaking the surface. The poaching liquid can be reserved to use as a broth or as the base for a soup.

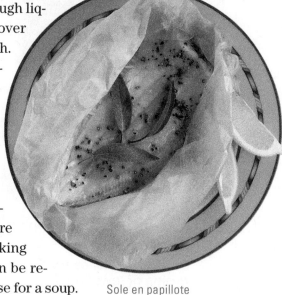

Sole en papillote

Poached trout

Shallow poaching cooks fish quickly. It is most often used for portion-sized fillets or fillets that have been rolled around a filling. The poaching liquid is almost always used to make a sauce that is served with the cooked fish.

READING CHECKPOINT *What is the safe internal temperature for fully cooked fish?*

15.1 ASSESSMENT

Reviewing Concepts

1. Based on fat content, what are the three types of fish?
2. What are the five tests for freshness in a whole fish?
3. How do you fillet a flat fish into quarter fillets?
4. What is the safe internal temperature for fully cooked fish?

Critical Thinking

5. **Classifying** Based on body type, what are the three types of fish?
6. **Drawing Conclusions** Explain why a PUFI mark is important in evaluating your supplier of fish.
7. **Recognizing Patterns** Can you see why the leaner the fish, the more delicate the cooking method you should choose for it? Explain.

Test Kitchen

Divide into six teams. Each team will cook the same cut and type of fish in a different way. The cooking options are sautéing, pan frying and deep frying, grilling and broiling, baking and roasting, steaming, and poaching. Each team must select its own recipe. Evaluate each team's results.

SCIENCE

NMFS

Research the National Marine Fisheries Service (NMFS). Write a report identifying two recent NMFS issues that could affect the quality of our seafood.

PROJECT 15 **Farm-Raised versus Wild** You are now ready to work on Project 15, "Farm-Raised versus Wild," which is available in "My Culinary Lab" or in your *Student's Lab Resources and Study Guide* manual.

READING PREVIEW

Key Concepts

- Identifying basic types of shellfish
- Receiving and storing shellfish
- Preparing shellfish
- Matching cooking methods to shellfish

Vocabulary

- calamari
- count (shrimp)
- crustaceans
- deveining (shrimp)
- drawn butter
- liquor (shellfish)
- mollusks
- shellfish
- shucked shellfish

Types of Shellfish

Shellfish are aquatic animals protected by some type of a shell. There are two types of shellfish:

- **Mollusks.** Shellfish that have soft bodies and no skeletons are **mollusks.** Many mollusks are protected by shells, and some have only a small amount of cartilage on the inside of their bodies. Abalones (a-buh-LOH-nee), clams, oysters, mussels, scallops, octopus, and squid are all mollusks. Squid is often called **calamari** (cahl-ah-MAHR-ee).

- **Crustaceans.** The second type of shellfish is **crustaceans** (crus-TAY-shuns), which have jointed exterior shells. Examples of crustaceans are lobsters, crabs, shrimp, and crayfish (also called *crawdads*).

Fresh and frozen shellfish are available in various forms.

- **Fresh Shellfish.** Fresh shellfish is available from suppliers in the following forms: live, shucked, tails, cocktail claws, and legs and claws.

- **Frozen Shellfish.** Frozen shellfish is available from suppliers in the following forms: shucked, tails, cocktail claws, and legs and claws.

Paella
Source: M. Studio/Fotolia

Mollusks

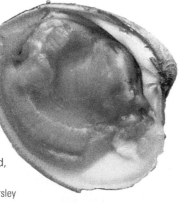

Clam

Easy to clean. Sometimes used uncooked in raw bars. Often fried, steamed, boiled, baked, or used in soups.

Source: Philip Dowell/Dorling Kindersley

Mussel

Mussels have a dark, shaggy beard that must be removed just before cooking. When removed, the mussel dies. Rarely served raw. Often steamed, boiled, poached, or used in soups and stews.

Source: Philip Dowell/Dorling Kindersley

Oyster

Easy to clean. Often used uncooked in raw bars. Also commonly fried, steamed, boiled, poached, or used in soups and stews.

Source: Andreas Einsiedel/Dorling Kindersley

Scallop

Easy to clean, but often purchased shucked. Often sautéed, stir-fried, grilled, baked, or used in soups and stews.

Source: Philip Dowell/Dorling Kindersley

Shucked shellfish means the seafood has been removed from its shell. When you purchase shucked shellfish, you receive the meat along with the shellfish's natural juices, known as its **liquor**.

Mollusks such as oysters, clams, and mussels may be available shucked. Scallops are nearly always sold shucked.

 **READING CHECKPOINT** *What are the two types of shellfish?*

Receiving and Storing Shellfish

For any restaurant specializing in shellfish, receiving and storing them is critically important. Few other foods spoil more quickly. It is important to purchase shellfish from reputable suppliers. As discussed in Section 10.4, you should buy only depurated mollusks. (Depurated mollusks have been placed in tanks of fresh water to purge them of their impurities.) Every foodservice establishment must keep full records of the fish and shellfish they purchase.

Crab

Source: Richard Embery/Pearson Education/PH College

To avoid spoilage, you must store live mollusks, such as oysters or mussels, at a temperature between 35° and 40°F. Do not hold them in fresh water or directly in ice; it will kill them. Mollusks need to be alive when served raw. If they are to be cooked, they must be alive at the beginning of the cooking process.

Live lobsters, crabs, shrimp, and crayfish should be packed in seaweed or damp paper on delivery. Look for signs of movement, indicating they are still alive. If a lobster tank is not available, lobsters can be stored directly in their shipping containers or in perforated pans under refrigeration until they are to be prepared.

Shrimp is the most popular of all shellfish. It is most commonly available previously frozen or frozen with the heads removed, although you occasionally will find fresh shrimp with their heads on. Shrimp is sold by the number of shrimp per pound. This is known as the **count**.

Clams, mussels, and oysters should have a sweet, sea-like aroma. Look for tightly closed shells. When purchased live in the shell, clams, mussels, or oysters should be delivered in a bag or sack. Store them directly in the bag in a perforated pan and keep the bag tightly closed and weighted to prevent it from opening. Any open shells should close immediately when they are tapped. Shells that do not close indicate the mollusk is dead and should be discarded, along with any that have broken shells. Store shellfish in their containers under refrigeration as you would fish fillets.

Just as with fish, shellfish are subject to marine toxins, which can lead to poisoning if a contaminated shellfish is consumed. The following are some of these types of poisoning:

- **Paralytic Shellfish Poisoning** Caused by a toxin with a reddish-brown color that form "red tides" in the colder coastal waters of the Pacific and the New England states, paralytic shellfish poisoning affects both mollusks and crustaceans. Symptoms are generally mild and include numbness or tingling of the face, arms, and legs, followed by headache, dizziness, nausea, and lack of muscular coordination. Some patients describe a floating sensation. Severe poisoning can result in paralysis and respiratory failure.

- **Neurotoxic Shellfish Poisoning** Neurotoxic shellfish poisoning is caused by a toxin that occasionally accumulates in oysters, clams, and mussels growing in the Gulf of Mexico and the southern Atlantic coast. Symptoms include numbness; tingling in the mouth, arms, and legs; lack of coordination; and gastrointestinal upset.

Shrimp Counts and Sizes

Count (Shrimp per Pound)	Common Name
10 or fewer	Colossal
11 to 15	Jumbo
16 to 20	Extra Large
21 to 30	Large
31 to 35	Medium
36 to 45	Small
About 100	Miniature

Shrimp
Source: Philip Dowell/Dorling Kindersley

Aquaculture

You may have read stories in the news about farm-raised fish, and you've probably seen farm-raised fish for sale in grocery stores. Aquaculture, the raising of fish and shellfish in a controlled environment, is actually very old practice. Ancient Chinese manuscripts describe the practice of raising fish. Ancient Egyptians may also have practiced aquaculture and passed their skills on to the Romans. The Romans raised oysters in beds, and as the Roman empire expanded throughout Europe, they carried this knowledge along with them.

Until the 18th century, fish or shellfish for aquaculture were captured when they were immature. They were transferred to ponds and allowed to grow to maturity. Modern aquaculture is different. Rather than capturing fish, the male and female fish are collected when they are ready to spawn. The fish eggs and sperm are pressed out of the fish and then mixed together so the eggs become fertilized. Once the eggs are fertilized, they are raised in carefully controlled conditions.

Initially, only luxury items such as shrimp and oysters were raised this way. Today, more and more species are being farm raised. Concerns have been raised about fish that have been genetically altered for quick growth. There are worries that the farmed fish may escape from their pens and drive out the wild species. Some chefs also feel that the taste

The Veta la Palma fish farm

Source: Kang Khoon Seang/Shutterstock

and texture of wild seafood is better than that of farmed seafood. With dwindling fish populations in the wild, the question remains: How can we farm fish in a way that is sustainable and healthy and produces high-quality fish?

Research

Research examples of sustainable aquaculture today (one example might be the Veta la Palma fish farm). Compare it to sustainable deep-sea aquaculture and more traditional methods of aquaculture. Write a paper describing the various methods of aquaculture.

- **Amnesiac Shellfish Poisoning** This rare toxin is made by a microscopic, red-brown plant. It can become concentrated in shellfish. Symptoms include gastrointestinal distress, dizziness, headache, disorientation, and permanent short-term memory loss. Severe poisoning can result in seizures, paralysis, and death.

When using local shellfish, make sure your provider continually checks with local health department advisories about algal blooms, "red tides," and other conditions that can indicate high concentrations of marine toxins. Some local health departments test shellfish within their jurisdiction for marine toxins. Based on their findings, they may prohibit recreational and commercial harvesting locally during times of risk. Additionally, state and federal regulatory agencies (including the Centers for Disease Control and Prevention) monitor reported cases of marine toxin poisoning and establish any necessary control measures.

••FOCUS ON
•• Safety

High-Risk Eating

Individuals with certain health conditions—such as liver disease, diabetes, cancer, stomach disorders, blood disorders, or immune disorders—who consume raw shellfish or other seafood are at a higher risk than others.

Preparing Shellfish

Thaw frozen shellfish safely by either placing it in the refrigerator until it thaws or putting the shellfish, still in its packaging, in a container and letting cool water run over it in a sink.

Lobster   Lobster is best when purchased alive. The first step in preparing a lobster to boil or steam is to kill it. Lobsters can be split before they are broiled or baked.

Once a lobster is cooked and cool enough to handle, you can remove the edible meat to produce a large tail portion and intact claw sections as well as smaller pieces from the knuckles and legs.

BASIC CULINARY SKILLS

Preparing Live Lobsters

1. **Leave the bands** on the lobster's claws.
2. **Place the lobster, stomach side down,** on a cutting board.
3. **Insert the tip of a chef's knife into the base of the head.**

Source: Culinary Institute of America

4. **Pull the knife down,** through the shell, splitting the head in half.

Source: Culinary Institute of America

5. **Reverse the direction of the lobster.**
6. **Split the tail** by starting at your initial cut and cutting through the shell of the tail section.

Source: Culinary Institute of America

📁 Recipe Card

106. Broiled Stuffed Lobster

Removing Meat from a Cooked Lobster

1 **Hold the tail section securely** in one hand while holding the body with the other.

2 **Twist your hands in opposite directions,** pulling the tail away from the body.

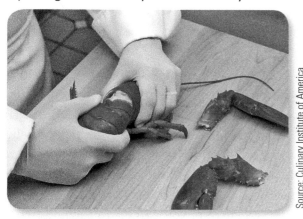

3 **Pull the tail meat out** of the shell. It should come away in one piece.

4 **Crack the claws,** using the heel of a chef's knife.

5 **Pry the shell away from the claw meat,** using your fingers. The meat should also come out in a single piece, retaining the shape of the claw.

6 **Cut through the knuckles.**

7 **Pull out the knuckle meat.**

Chapter 15 *Fish and Shellfish*   **523**

FIGURE 15–8

Raw Shrimp and Cooked Shrimp
When raw shrimp (left) is cooked (right), it turns pink.

RECOGNIZING PATTERNS *Can you name other foods that change color when they are fully cooked?*

Source: Culinary Institute of America

Shrimp There are two steps to cleaning shrimp. First, you remove the shell and then you remove the vein that runs along the back of the shrimp (this is actually the intestinal tract of the shrimp). Removing the vein from the shrimp is referred to as **deveining** (dee-VANE-ing). A special tool is available for deveining shrimp, but a paring knife works well too. For shrimp dishes that are grilled or sautéed, you need to clean the shrimp before cooking. When boiling or steaming shrimp, you can clean them either before or after cooking. Shrimp that have been boiled or steamed in the shell are moister and plumper than shrimp that were peeled and deveined before cooking. After cleaning, the shells can be reserved for other uses, such as making shrimp stock, bisque, or shellfish butters.

BASIC CULINARY SKILLS

Peeling and Deveining Shrimp

1. **Pull the shell away from the shrimp,** starting on the underside of the shrimp where the feathery legs are located.

2. **Place the shelled shrimp on a cutting board,** with the curved outer edge of the shrimp on the same side as your cutting hand.

3. **Make a shallow cut** on the curved outer edge by using a paring or utility knife.

4. **Scrape out the vein,** using the tip of the knife.

Source: Culinary Institute of America

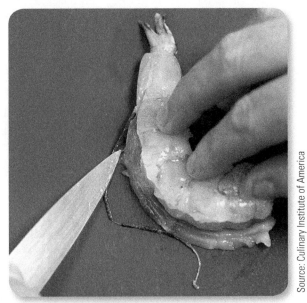

Source: Culinary Institute of America

Clams, Oysters, Mussels, and Scallops Mollusks such as clams, oysters, scallops, and mussels are sold already shucked. However, many restaurants purchase clams, oysters, and mussels live in their shells. These restaurants may use the oysters in a raw bar or they may have dishes that require clams, oysters, or mussels in their shells. It is important, in this sort of restaurant, to be able to open the clams and oysters with ease. Freshly shucked clams and oysters are often used for cooked dishes (shucked mussels are less commonly used). When opening oysters and clams, be sure to reserve any juices. They add great flavor to soups, stews, and stocks.

Before using any mollusks, you need to clean them. Clams and oysters are easy to clean. Scrub them well with a brush under cold running water. Discard any that remain open when tapped (this indicates that the clam or oyster has died and can't be eaten safely). If any closed shell feels unusually heavy or light, check it. Occasionally, you will find empty shells or shells filled with clay or sand.

Mussels are rarely served raw. The method for cleaning them before steaming or poaching is similar to the cleaning method used for clams and oysters. However, unlike clams and oysters, mussels have a dark, shaggy beard, which is removed just before cooking. Once the beard is pulled away, the mussel dies. To clean a mussel, hold it under cold running water. Use a brush with stiff bristles to thoroughly scrub the mussel and remove all the

Opening Clams

① **Wear a wire mesh glove** to hold the clam.

② **Place the clam in your hand** so the hinged side is tucked into the palm of your hand.

Source: Culinary Institute of America

③ **Work the side of a clam knife into the seam** between the upper and lower shells. You can use the fingers of your gloved hand to help guide the knife and give it extra force.

④ **Twist the blade slightly,** to pry open the shell.

⑤ **Slide the blade over the inside of the top shell** once it is open, to release the clam from the shell.

Source: Culinary Institute of America

⑥ **Slide the blade under the clam** to release it from the bottom shell.

Opening Oysters

1. **Wear a wire mesh glove** to hold the oyster.

2. **Place the oyster in your hand** or on a cutting board so the hinged side is facing outward.

3. **Work the tip of an oyster knife into the hinge** that holds the upper and lower shells together.

4. **Twist the blade,** like a key in a lock, to break open the hinge.

5. **Slide the blade over the inside of the top shell,** once it is open, to release the oyster from the shell.

Source: Culinary Institute of America

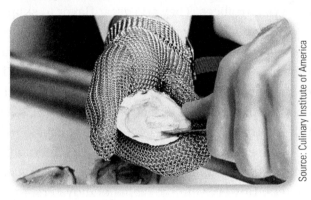

Source: Culinary Institute of America

6. **Slide the blade under the oyster** to release it from the bottom shell.

FIGURE 15–9

Removing the Beard

Pull the beard away from the shell.

DRAWING CONCLUSIONS *When preparing a dish with mussels, what are the implications for your mise en place?*

Source: Culinary Institute of America

sand, grit, and mud from the outer shell. Then, pull the beard away from the shell. Because removing the beard kills the mussel, do not clean the mussel and pull off the beard until you are ready to begin cooking the mussel.

READING CHECKPOINT *How do you prepare live lobsters?*

Matching Cooking Methods to Shellfish

As discussed in Chapter 10, oysters and clams are often served raw on a raw bar. The clams and oysters are served freshly shucked on the half shell. Aside from serving shellfish raw, you can use almost any of the basic cooking techniques when cooking shellfish.

Shellfish has a pronounced flavor, sometimes briny and slightly salty (shrimp and oysters) and sometimes slightly sweet (scallops, crabs, or lobsters). This flavor allows shellfish to pair well with strong flavors, including tomatoes, olives, capers, and ham. You can choose accompaniments for shellfish that contrast with these flavors. Or, you can use a rich cream sauce or even melted butter. Butter that is used as a sauce for shellfish is known as **drawn butter**. It is actually clarified butter. To make it, you melt butter and separate the melted butterfat (the clarified butter) from the milk solids and water.

Lemon wedges are a common garnish for seafood dishes, either added directly to the dish or served alongside the shellfish for the guest to add to taste.

Steaming and Boiling Shrimp, lobsters, crab, and crayfish are typically steamed or boiled. (For crabs, sometimes only the legs are steamed.) After being steamed or boiled, they may be eaten hot or cold. Adding aromatics, including herbs, spices, and vegetables, is a common practice that adds more flavor to the shellfish.

Mussels, clams, and oysters are often steamed. They can be steamed in a steamer, suspended over a simmering liquid. Another way to steam mussels, clams, and oysters is in the marinara style. In this style of steaming, the cleaned shellfish is placed in a pot along with a small amount of flavorful liquid such as a broth. Additional ingredients, including garlic, onions, tomatoes, olives, or even diced ham, are often added. The pot is covered and the liquid is brought to a simmer. The lid traps the steam and the shellfish is cooked in the steam until the shells open. The mussels, clams, and oysters become plump and their edges start to curl.

Frying Clams, oysters, shrimp, and squid can be coated with a batter or bread crumbs and fried until crisp on the outside. This technique provides a good contrast of flavors and textures for shellfish. Scallops are another type of shellfish that is often fried because the coating protects the sweet,

Steamed mussels
Source: Clive Streeter, Dorling Kindersley

Recipe Card
107. Mussels Marinara

Fried clam basket
Source: David Buffington/Getty Images

Caribbean

There are more than 7,000 Caribbean islands, including Cuba, Jamaica, Haiti, the Dominican Republic, Puerto Rico, and the Virgin Islands. The cuisine in these islands is actually a fusion of many cuisines, starting with the native people who originally lived on the islands, then Dutch, Spanish, French, and English explorers, and, finally, Africans who were brought to these islands as slaves.

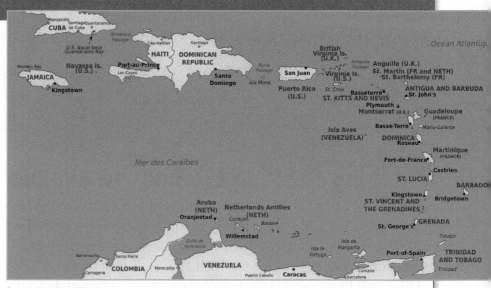

Source: Floki Fotos/Fotolia

One of the most famous examples of the Caribbean cooking style is called *jerk*. This preparation originated in Jamaica. Traditionally, chicken, pork, or goat is either dry-rubbed or marinated in Jamaican jerk spice, which contains two basic ingredients: allspice and Scotch bonnet peppers (one of the hottest types of peppers, 12 to 40 times as hot as a jalapeno pepper). Other spices, such as cloves, cinnamon, garlic, nutmeg, thyme, and salt are also added to the jerk spice blend. Every individual or restaurant has its own recipe. The jerked meat is then cooked over a charcoal or wood oven. Chefs today use the jerking method to cook a wide variety of meats.

Plantains (PLAN-tin) are a type of banana that must be cooked before they can be eaten. Found all across the islands, they are often sliced, cooked in a seasoned batter, and deep-fried for fritters. Ripe plantains taste like a cross between a sweet potato and a banana. They are used as a side dish.

Callaloo (cal-uh-LOO) is another popular Caribbean dish. Made from some type of leafy green vegetable, it has a dark green color when cooked. It seems that every island uses a different type of leafy green vegetable to make callaloo. Most recipes call for the addition of okra, coconut milk, crab, meat, chiles, and various aromatics such as onions and garlic. These are all steamed or heated until the mixture reaches a stewlike consistency. It is often served on a bed of rice as a side dish alongside a meat.

Conch (KONK) is an edible medium to large sea snail that can be eaten raw or cooked. The shells can reach a length of 13 inches. It is often added to callaloo. Today, it is illegal to harvest live conch from U.S. waters. However, it is available on many Caribbean islands, although it is becoming increasingly scarce and expensive. There is at least one commercial conch farm in the Caribbean, but because of their size and longevity (conch can live as long as 25 years), it takes quite a while to raise conchs to a size large enough for harvesting.

Jerked chicken

Source: Rohit Seth/Fotolia

Research

Research one of the larger Caribbean islands. Prepare a presentation about how the history of the various peoples who visited the island led to the island's current cuisine. Include information about the ingredients and cooking techniques that these different groups brought to the islands with them. Make a dish that you feel best represents your contention.

moist flesh of the shellfish while developing a golden, crunchy coating. Be sure to season shellfish before you dip them in batter or add a coating, so they are as flavorful as possible.

Grilled lobster tails

Source: evgenyb/Fotolia

Grilling and Broiling Scallops, shrimp, and lobsters are often prepared by grilling or broiling. Use skewers to hold small shellfish such as shrimp or scallops on the grill. Lobsters are typically halved before grilling or broiling.

Sautéing or Stir Frying Sautéed or stir-fried shrimp or scallops are popular. It is important to cook shrimp and scallops quickly at a fairly high temperature. Shrimp and scallops will often be soaked briefly in a marinade that has a blend of sweet and savory flavorings. The marinade often helps caramelize the cooked shrimp or scallops.

Stir-fried shrimp

Source: Clive Streeter and
Patrick McLeavy/
Dorling Kindersley

Baking and Roasting Lobster is sometimes baked. Squid and octopus are sometime stuffed and baked. Clams are often topped with a savory bread crumb mixture and baked. Shellfish are often added to stuffing for fish or poultry. For example, many Thanksgiving turkeys are filled with oyster stuffing.

Vietnamese stuffed squid

Source: Clive Streeter and Patrick
McLeavy/Dorling Kindersley

READING CHECKPOINT *Describe five ways that shellfish is cooked.*

15.2 ASSESSMENT

Reviewing Concepts

1. What are the two types of shellfish?
2. At what temperatures should live mollusks be stored?
3. How do you prepare live lobsters?
4. Describe some of the ways that shellfish can be cooked.

Critical Thinking

5. **Classifying** What type of shellfish are crayfish?
6. **Drawing Conclusions** Why is it important for a foodservice establishment to keep full records of the fish and shellfish they purchase?
7. **Recognizing Patterns** What relationship does the count have to the size of shrimp?

Test Kitchen

Divide into five teams. Each team will cook the same size shrimp in a different way. The cooking options are steaming and boiling, pan frying or deep frying, grilling and broiling, sautéing and stir frying, and baking and roasting. Each team must select its own recipe. Evaluate each team's results.

SCIENCE

Oysters

Research the life cycle of oysters in the wild. Compare this to the life cycle of farmed oysters. Based on your findings, write a report on oyster farming.

Reviewing Content

Choose the letter that best answers the question or completes the statement.

1. Shellfish are
   a. fish with shells.
   b. skates and rays.
   c. lobsters, but not clams, oysters, or mussels.
   d. clams, oysters, and mussels, but not lobsters.

2. An example of a mollusk is
   a. a lobster, but not a clam, oyster, or mussel.
   b. a clam, oyster, or mussel, but not a lobster.
   c. a shrimp, but not a lobster.
   d. an oyster, but not a scallop.

3. An anadromous fish is a
   a. freshwater fish.
   b. saltwater fish.
   c. farm-raised fish.
   d. fish that spends part of its life in salt water and part in fresh water.

4. An example of a lean flat fish is
   a. Atlantic salmon.
   b. lemon sole.
   c. Atlantic cod.
   d. striped bass.

5. An example of a fatty round fish is
   a. Atlantic salmon.
   b. lemon sole.
   c. Atlantic cod.
   d. striped bass.

6. A drawn fish is a
   a. whole fish.
   b. whole fish, with head, stomach, fins, and tail removed.
   c. whole fish, head and stomach removed.
   d. whole fish, stomach removed.

7. Store live mollusks between
   a. 0°F and 20°F
   b. 20°F and 30°F
   c. 30°F and 35°F
   d. 35°F and 40°F

Understanding Concepts

8. What do you do when you shuck shellfish?

9. What is the relationship between the count of shrimp and their size?

10. Which type of NMFS inspection is the most important for a foodservice establishment?

11. At what temperature is a fish fully cooked?

12. What is the difference between shallow poaching and deep poaching?

13. How can you tell whether a stored clam, mussel, or oyster is alive?

Critical Thinking

14. **APPLYING CONCEPTS** What effect would cooking mussels have on your mise en place?

15. **PREDICTING** What type of cooking method might you use for a tranche-cut of halibut?

16. **COMPARING/CONTRASTING** What is the difference between opening clams and opening oysters?

Culinary Math

17. **APPLYING CONCEPTS** You are making a recipe for broiled shrimp that requires 3½ lb of extra-large shrimp and serves 20. You need to expand the recipe to serve 60. How many pounds of shrimp do you require? About how many shrimp will that be? About how many shrimp is a portion?

On the Job

18. **APPLYING CONCEPTS** To increase efficiency, a cook debearded the mussels that will be used for steamed mussels early in the mise en place. The steamed mussels are prepared as they are ordered. Do you have any concerns?

19. **COMMUNICATING** A customer has received a salmon steak and sends the fish back because there are bones in it. What should you do?

Fish Cook (Poissonnier)

Fish and seafood have always been a major part of the human diet. People who lived near a source of fresh fish, including lakes, ponds, streams, rivers, and oceans could enjoy these foods fresh from the water. Some of the earliest efforts at food preservation, including smoked and cured salmon and dried and salted cod, made fish easier to keep and transport. In fact, explorers who traveled on ships from the Old World to the New World introduced salt cod and dishes made from it to Caribbean islands. But it was not until the arrival of refrigerators and freezers that people living far from water could enjoy fish that hadn't been either smoked or salted. Today, improved transportation methods means that fish is more widely distributed than ever before. Fish and seafood are universally acknowledged as healthy foods. Restaurants have increased the types of fish that they offer as well as the ways in which they are prepared, from classic French dishes such as coquilles St. Jacques (koh-KEEL sahn-ZHAHK) (a broiled scallop dish) to Japanese-style sushi and sashimi.

Chefs and cooks with a passion for fish cookery can be found in virtually any type of restaurant. Some restaurants have a specific position on the line that is devoted to fish cookery (sometimes called by the French term for fish cook, the "poissonnier"). Others integrate seafood dishes throughout the menu, and its preparation may be handled by various cooks on the line, depending on how it is being cooked.

Restaurants that specialize in seafood include fast-food chains such as Long John Silver's, family-style restaurants such as Red Lobster or Legal Seafoods, and upscale restaurants such as Le Bernadin.

Some people may find themselves working in areas other than restaurants. Supermarkets and grocery stores often have a department devoted to seafood. The responsibilities in this type of work are similar to those of chefs working in restaurants: Fish must be ordered, received, stored, presented to the customer, custom-cut into fillets or steaks, or made into ready-to-eat or ready-to-cook entrées and appetizers.

Fish farming has provided a vital source of food for humans throughout history. Today, fish farmers and hatcheries are at work to stock not just the cases at your local market but also ponds, streams, and rivers with fish meant for recreational fishers.

With all of the interest in fish and seafood on the part of chefs and consumers, the demand for fish has increased significantly. This has led to an increased emphasis on maintaining not only the safety of the fish we eat, but also the waters where the fish are harvested. Many chefs have become strong proponents of sustainable practices meant to avoid overfishing.

Entry-Level Requirements

At the entry level, the degree requirements are similar to those for any skilled cooking job. Culinary education that results in a certificate or a degree is desirable.

Helpful for Advancement

Specialized training, such as attending a sushi academy, attending workshops on sustainability, or learning fish-processing techniques such as smoking or freezing will be helpful, as well as training, certification, or degrees related to business, sales, and marketing.

Presenting an attractive fish dish

Source: © WavebreakMediaMicro/Fotolia

Chef Rick Moonen, a native New Yorker, has devoted his career to being the country's top culinary advocate for sustainable seafood. After graduating from The Culinary Institute of America, he apprenticed at L'Hostellerie Bressane. From there, he went to Manhattan's La Cote Basque, followed by two years at Le Cirque. Moonen then became executive chef and partner at Oceana. His next step was partnering to create Molyvos, a Greek fish house, the first Greek restaurant to earn three stars from *The New York Times*.

In 2005, he brought his sustainable seafood concept, Rick Moonen's RM Seafood, to the desert town of Las Vegas, Nevada. In 2008, Moonen published his cookbook *Fish without a Doubt*. That same year, on *The Oprah Winfrey Show* he served his Catfish Sloppy Joe, which earned the title of "Best Sandwich in America." He has appeared as a contestant on *Top Chef Masters* and as a judge on *Top Chef Las Vegas*. In 2013, he transformed rm upstairs into a steampunk-inspired restaurant, Rx Boiler Room, featuring a spin on classic comfort food with a creative and cutting-edge experience.

Moonen is passionate about ocean conservation and has testified for environmental and sustainability policy issues. He is a founding member of the Seafood Choices Alliances and an active member of Monterey Bay Aquarium's *Seafood Watch* and Seaweb. Second only to his passion for sustainability is his commitment to ending hunger; Moonen puts that commitment into action by serving on the chef's advisory board for the Las Vegas Three Square Food Bank.

Rick Moonen

VITAL STATISTICS

Graduated: A.O.S., The Culinary Institute of America, 1978 (first in his class)

Profession: Chef, restaurateur, and author

Interesting Item: Received three stars from the *New York Times* for both Oceana and RM Seafood

Opened RM Seafood in 2005 and Rx Boiler Room in 2013 in Mandalay Bay in Las Vegas

Named "Chef of the Year" in 2011 by Monterey Bay Aquarium

CAREER PROFILE

Salary Ranges

Fish Cook and Chef: $28,000 to $52,000

Sushi Chef: $22,000 to $72,500

Fish Processor (Frozen, Smoked, etc.), Entry Level: $20,000 to $40,000

Fish Processor (Frozen, Smoked, etc.), Manager Level: $50,000 to $90,000

Fish Purchaser (Supermarket, Specialty Shop, Hotels): $65,000 to $100,000

Meat and Poultry

16.1 Meat

16.2 Poultry

Key Concepts

- Understanding meat inspection and grading
- Identifying various types and cuts of meat
- Receiving and handling meat
- Preparing meat for cooking

Vocabulary

- aged (beef)
- boxed meat
- butterflied
- crown roast
- dry aging
- dry cured
- fabrication (of meat)
- forequarter
- foresaddle
- frenching
- game
- grain (of meat)
- hare
- haunch
- hindquarter
- hindsaddle
- lamb
- marbling
- mutton
- offal
- primal cuts
- quarters (of meat)
- retail cuts
- saddle
- seams (in meat)
- sides (of meat)
- silverskin
- subprimal cuts
- variety meat
- veal
- venison
- wet aging

Inspection and Grading of Meat

Meat is one of the costliest items on the menu—but also one of the most potentially profitable. To get the most value from the meat you buy, it is important to understand how to receive, store, and prepare it properly. However, before you can begin this process, you need to understand the inspection and grading process for meat.

Source: Susanna Price/Dorling Kindersley Limited

Meat Inspection Government inspection of all meat (including game and poultry) is required. In fact, inspections are required at various times—on the farm or ranch, at the slaughterhouse, and again after butchering. Most meat is inspected by federal inspectors. States that have their own meat inspections must meet or exceed federal standards. Both federal and state inspections are paid for with tax dollars.

Federal and state inspectors ensure that the following conditions exist:

- Animals are free from disease.
- Farms are operated according to appropriate standards for safety, cleanliness, and health.
- Meat is wholesome and fit for human consumption.

Quality Grading Quality grading, unlike inspection, is voluntary. The U.S. Department of Agriculture (USDA) has developed specific standards

Antoine Carême

One of the first celebrity chefs, Marie-Antoine Carême (1784–1833) was known as the "king of chefs and the chef of kings." However, he started off life in a less than regal way—he was abandoned by his parents when he was ten years old and had to work as a kitchen boy in a cheap restaurant to earn his room and board. He was later apprenticed and, through his hard work and ambition, eventually came to own his own patisserie (sweet shop). There, he made elaborate dessert for Parisian high society and catered their parties, which allowed him to learn to cook a full range of the dishes favored by his clientele.

His connections to wealthy Parisians led to employment by Tallyrand, a French diplomat who was an influential advisor to Napoleon. It is said that Tallyrand, a gourmet, spent an hour every day with Carême. Tallyrand gave Carême a famous test: To create a year's worth of menus, without repetition, and using seasonal ingredients. Of course, Carême passed! Through Tallyrand, Carême came to cook for Napoleon. When Napoleon fell out of power, Carême went to work for George IV, the king of England. He would go on to work briefly for Tsar Alexander of Russia and James Mayer Rothchild, a banker living in Paris.

Carême lightened and simplified the style of François Pierre la Varenne. Carême is seen as one of the first proponents of haute cuisine, known for its meticulous preparation and elegant presentation of food. He simplified sauces and published a classification of sauces based on four mother sauces. He is also credited with creating the standard chef's hat, the toque.

Source: Georgios Kollidas/Fotolia

Having served as chef for George IV (shown above) of England, as well as Napoleon and Tsar Alexander of Russia, Carême earned his reputation as "the king of chefs and the chef of kings."

Carême died in Paris at the young age of 48, perhaps due to years of inhaling the toxic charcoal fumes from the stoves.

Research

Form a small group to research the life and times of Antoine Carême. Focus on the relationship between the political upheavals of the time and the cuisine, particularly Carême's contributions to haute cuisine. If possible, locate a sauce or a dish created by Carême and recreate it in the kitchen. Evaluate it by contemporary standards.

that are used to assign grades to meat based on its quality. The USDA also trains graders, ensuring that quality standards are consistent across the country. Because quality grading is voluntary, the individual meat packer—not the taxpayer—absorbs the cost involved in grading meat. Packers may choose not to hire a USDA grader to assign a quality grade. Instead, packers may assign grades based on their own standards. However, those standards must meet or exceed federal standards.

FIGURE 16–1

Butchered Sides of Beef
The grade placed on a carcass is applied to all the cuts from that particular carcass.
DRAWING CONCLUSIONS *Why would a restaurant use retail cuts rather than fabricating cuts from a carcass?*
Source: Artem Merzlenko/Fotolia

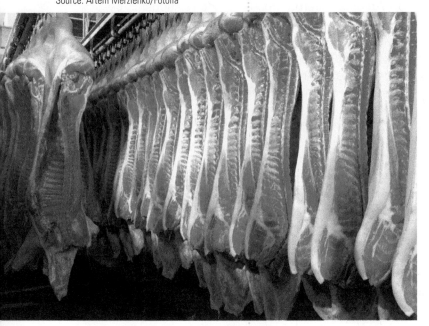

The grade placed on a particular carcass is applied to all the cuts from that particular carcass. Quality graders consider the following (adjusting the standards according to the type of meat being graded):

- The overall shape of the carcass
- The ratio of fat to lean meat
- The ratio of meat to bone
- The color of the meat
- The amount of fat present in the lean flesh (this is known as **marbling** in beef)

Butchering After slaughtering, inspection, and grading, a large animal carcass is butchered. It is first cut into manageable pieces. The exact standards for individual animal types govern where the cuts are made. There are typically two ways to cut up a carcass:

- **Sides and Quarters.** The first cuts made in this type of butchering divide the carcass into sides and then into quarters. **Sides** are prepared by making a cut down the length of the backbone. **Quarters** are made by cutting sides into two pieces and dividing them at specific points. The front quarter is called the **forequarter**. The rear quarter is called the **hindquarter**. Larger carcasses, such as those of beef and pork, are usually cut up this way.

- **Saddles.** This type of butchering divides the carcass into two portions by cutting across the belly. Each portion includes the left and right side of the carcass. Whenever a portion includes both the left and right side of the carcass, the portion is called a **saddle**. The front portion of the carcass is called the **foresaddle**. The rear portion is called the **hindsaddle**. Smaller carcasses, such as veal, are often cut up this way.

The next step is to cut the quarters or saddles into **primal cuts** (or, as they are sometimes referred to as *primals*). These are portions that meet uniform standards for beef, veal, pork, and lamb. Primal cuts are then broken down into **subprimal cuts** (or *subprimals*).

Subprimals can be trimmed, packed, and then sold to restaurants or butcher shops. A restaurant buying a subprimal would need to do additional butchering to break down the subprimal into portion-sized cuts of meat. This type of butchering is called **fabrication**. Increasingly, however, subprimals are broken down at the packing plant and sold in smaller pieces, referred to as **retail cuts**.

Most food-service establishments buy boxed meat. **Boxed meat** is meat that is fabricated to a

Common Cuts of Meat

Retail Cut	Description
Steak	Portion-sized cut, with or without the bone, that typically includes well-defined portions of lean meat and fat; typically requires dry-heat methods.
Roast	Large, multiportion cut intended for roasting or braising.
Chop	Portion-sized cut that often includes a portion of the rib; both dry heat and moist heat are used.
Cutlet	Thin, tender, boneless portion-sized cut, often taken from the leg or rib; typically requires dry-heat methods.
Medallion	Small, round or oval, portion-sized cut often from the rib or loin; typically requires dry-heat methods.
Noisette (nwah-ZEHT)	Small, tender, round portion-sized cut, usually from the rib or loin; typically requires dry-heat methods.
Émincé (EH man say)	Small, thin, portion-sized cut; typically requires dry-heat methods.
Stew Meat	Small chunks, typically ¾ to 1½ inch, of relatively lean meat cut from a variety of the primal cuts; used for stewing.
Ground Meat	Ground meat, including some percentage of fat, from various primals; also referred to as *hamburger* and *minced beef*.

specific point (such as primal, subprimal, or retail cuts) and then packed and boxed. At that point, as boxed meat, it is ready to ship for sale to restaurants, butchers, and retail outlets. Over the past few years, in-house butchering of various animals has become more common, however, as chefs practice a more sustainable approach to meat cookery that involves using the entire animal from head to tail. In addition to the advantage of being able to buy and use an entire animal, it also permits chefs to customize cuts to suit their menus and their customers' preferences.

 **READING CHECKPOINT** *What is a primal cut?*

Chef's Tip

Terms for Meat on the Menu

The names given to cuts of meat on the menu are different from those used to identify the meat you buy from a butcher or meat purveyor.

Types and Cuts of Meat

The flavor, color, and texture of any meat are influenced by several factors: the amount of exercise the muscle receives, the animal's age, the type of feed it received, and its breed.

Beef The animals used in the beef industry are typically young males (steers) and females (heifers). The older the animal, the less tender the meat.

Specialty beef is available from other countries, such as Kobe (KOH-bay) and Wagyu (WAG-yew) beef from Japan and Limousin (lee-MOO-zan) beef from France. Specialty beef from the United States includes Certified Angus, natural beef, and organic beef.

USDA grade shields

Beef may be **aged**, a process that gives meat a darker color, a more tender texture, and a fuller flavor. Boneless cuts such as steaks may be vacuum packaged and stored under refrigeration for several weeks, a process referred to as **wet aging**. **Dry aging** calls for the side, forequarter, or hindquarter to be hung in a climate-controlled area. Aged beef is expensive because of additional processing costs as well as the significant moisture and weight loss that reduce the ultimate yield.

There are eight USDA (US Department of Agriculture) grades of beef. From the highest to the lowest quality, they are Prime, Choice, Select, Standard, Commercial, Utility, Cutter, and Canner. The top three grades, Prime, Choice, and Select, come from younger beef. Grades lower than Select are generally used for processed meat, such as frankfurters, and are not used in the restaurant or retail industry. The grades most widely sold retail are Choice and Select.

- **USDA Prime.** Only a small percentage of beef is graded Prime. This grade is usually reserved for hotels, restaurants, and butcher shops. Prime beef is the most tender, juicy, and flavorful. It has abundant marbling, which enhances both flavor and juiciness. Prime roasts and steaks are excellent for dry cooking methods (roasting and broiling).
- **USDA Choice.** Choice is the most popular quality and the most widely sold grade in retail stores. Choice beef is very tender, juicy, and flavorful. It has less marbling than Prime.
- **USDA Select.** Uniform in quality, Select beef is gaining in consumer popularity because it is leaner than the higher grades (it has less marbling). Not as juicy or flavorful as Prime or Choice, Select beef is often marinated before cooking or cooked by using moist heat methods.

A beef forequarter contains four primal cuts: the chuck (shoulder), the rib, the brisket and foreshank, and the short plate. The hindquarter also contains four primal cuts: the loin, the sirloin, the flank, and the round (leg). These primal cuts may be sold individually, or, as is more often the case, they are broken down into subprimal cuts or retail cuts.

The following list summarizes the cooking methods and uses for the eight beef primal cuts.

- **Chuck (Shoulder).** Moist-heat and combination cooking methods are appropriate for cuts from the chuck primal, which usually need long, slow cooking. The meat is sold as roasts (bone-in or boneless) or cut into steaks. Chuck is often used for stew meat and ground beef.
- **Rib.** Roasting, grilling, broiling, and sautéing are the most common cooking methods for most cuts from the primal rib. The rib is often

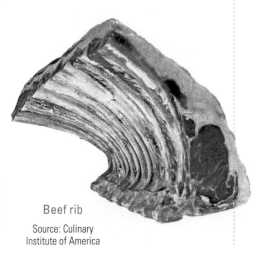

Beef rib
Source: Culinary
Institute of America

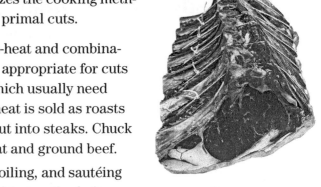

Rib roast
Source: Culinary Institute of America

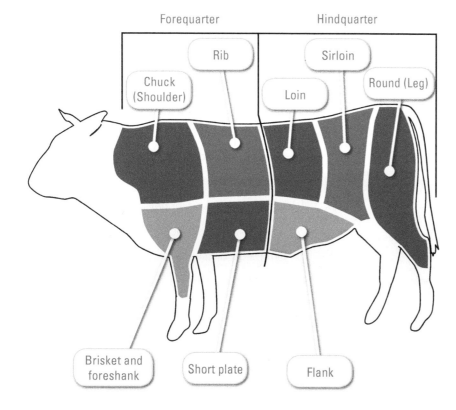

Forequarter　Hindquarter

Chuck (Shoulder)　Rib　Sirloin　Round (Leg)　Loin

Brisket and foreshank　Short plate　Flank

FIGURE 16–2

Beef Primal Cuts
Both the forequarter and the hindquarter are broken into four primal cuts each.

RELATING CONCEPTS *Have you ever seen one of these cuts in a butcher shop or grocery store?*

Beef rib eye roast
Source: Culinary Institute of America

Skirt steak
Source: Culinary Institute of America

sold whole. It is also sold in smaller roasts (bone-in and boneless), or cut into steaks such as rib eye steaks.

- **Brisket and Foreshank.** The brisket is typically braised. It is also used to make corned beef. When cured and smoked, it is used to make pastrami. The foreshank is typically braised or used in stews.

- **Short Plate.** This primal cut is under the primal ribs. Short ribs and skirt steak are fabricated from the short plate. Short ribs are often braised, while the skirt steak is cooked with dry-heat methods, such as grilling.

- **Loin (Short Loin).** The front portion of the loin contains some very tender meat. Most cuts are sold as whole roasts (which are roasted or braised) or steaks (which are grilled). The loin produces a variety of retail cuts, including T-bone steaks, strip loin steaks (also known as *Delmonico steaks* or *strip steaks*), filet mignon (FEE-lay me-NYON), tournedos (TOUR-nah-doughs), and tenderloin tips.

- **Sirloin.** The sirloin contains a portion of the tenderloin. Other than the tenderloin, sirloin meat is generally less tender than meat from the loin. Sirloin butt is a moderately tough retail cut. Roasting, grilling, broiling, and sautéing are the most common cooking methods for sirloin cuts.

Beef brisket
Source: Culinary Institute of America

Strip loin (top view)
Source: Richard Embery/Pearson Education/PH College

Tenderloin (top view)
Source: Culinary Institute of America

Chapter 16 *Meat and Poultry*

Beef Variety Meat

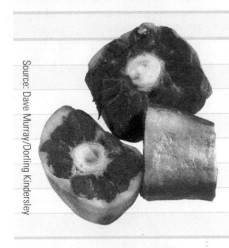

Variety Meat	Common Culinary Uses
Liver	Sautéed or ground to make pâté or sausages
Tripe (stomach lining)	Simmered or braised
Kidneys	Sautéed, stewed, or braised
Tongue	Simmered; also often pickled or smoked
◀ Oxtail	Simmered, stewed, or braised
Intestines	Used as large sausage casings
Heart	Simmered, braised, or stewed
Cheeks	Typically braised

Flank steak

Source: Culinary Institute of America

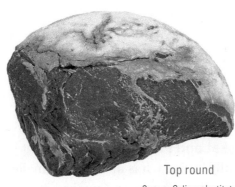

Top round

Source: Culinary Institute of America

Bottom round

Source: Culinary Institute of America

- **Flank.** Flank steak is below the loin and is almost always sold whole. Flank steak can be grilled, but it is also often braised, sometimes with a stuffing.

- **Round (Leg).** The most common cooking methods for cuts from the round are braising and stewing. Two portions of the round, the knuckle and the eye of the round, can be roasted. Cuts from the round are often made into cubes for stew meat or kebobs. Meat from the bottom round is often ground.

Kitchens also use cuts other than those from primal cuts. These cuts include organs, such as the liver, as well as some muscles—the tongue, for example. Overall, this type of meat is known as **variety meat**, or as **offal** (AW-full).

Veal Veal comes from a young calf, generally two to three months old. It has delicate, tender flesh that is pale pink in color. Milk-fed veal is no more than 12 weeks old at the time of processing. Veal of this age has received mother's milk or formula only. Formula-fed veal may be up to four months old, but the calf's diet contains no grass or feed.

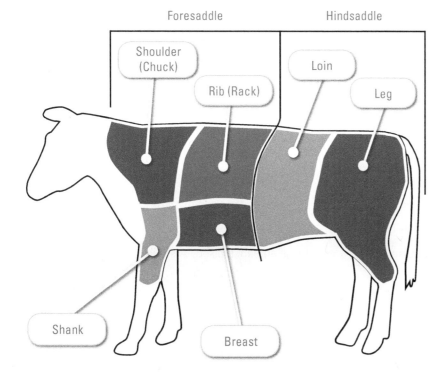

Foresaddle   Hindsaddle

Shoulder (Chuck)

Rib (Rack)

Loin

Leg

Shank

Breast

FIGURE 16–3

Veal Primal Cuts

The foresaddle is broken into four primal cuts, but the hindsaddle is broken into only two primal cuts.

COMPARING/CONTRASTING *How are veal primals different from beef primals?*

Veal shoulder roast
Source: Culinary Institute of America

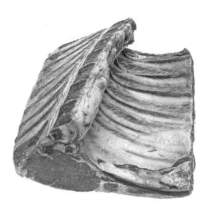

Veal rib
Source: Culinary Institute of America

Veal shank
Source: Culinary Institute of America

There are six USDA grades of veal: Prime, Choice, Good, Standard, Utility, and Cull. Only Prime and Choice are used in the restaurant industry or purchased retail. Prime has abundant marbling and is generally very juicy and tender. Choice is somewhat less juicy, less flavorful, and with less marbling.

Veal is usually cut into a foresaddle and a hindsaddle, but it can be split into two sides, similar to beef. The primal cuts for veal are the shoulder (also known as the *chuck*), shank, rack (or rib), breast, loin, and leg. Variety meat from veal is highly prized, especially the sweetbreads, liver, calf's head, and brains.

The following list summarizes the cooking methods and uses for the six veal primal cuts.

- **Shoulder (Chuck).** Moist-heat or combination cooking methods, such as stewing, simmering, and braising, are appropriate for roasts from the shoulder primal. Stew meat and ground meat are commonly made from less desirable cuts.

- **Rib (Rack).** Ribs can be roasted whole (both bone-in and boneless), or they may be broken down into individual chops and cooked by using dry-heat cooking methods. A **crown roast** is prepared by tying a rib roast into a crown shape.

- **Shank.** Meat from the shank is often braised. The meaty shank is used to prepare osso buco (AW-soh BOO-koh), an Italian method of braising veal shanks with aromatic vegetables.

- **Breast.** The breast (bone-in or boneless) is often stuffed and rolled, before being braised or slowly roasted.

Veal breast
Source: Culinary Institute of America

Veal Variety Meat

Variety Meat	Common Culinary Uses
Sweetbreads (pancreas or thymus gland)	Poached or sautéed
Tongue	Poached, simmered, or braised (and may be pickled or smoked)
Cheeks	Typically braised
Liver	Sautéed or used to make terrines and pâtés
Heart	Simmered or braised
◄ Kidneys	Sautéed, braised, or stewed
Feet	Simmered (feet are often used to give stocks body)

Source: Culinary Institute of America

Veal loin
Source: Culinary Institute of America

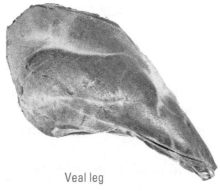

Veal leg
Source: Culinary Institute of America

Veal top round
Source: Culinary Institute of America

- **Loin.** Prized for its tender meat, the meat of the loin has an even texture. Cuts from the loin are very tender and are suitable for dry-heat techniques such as roasting, grilling, broiling, and sautéing. Whole roasts (bone-in), chops, and boneless portion-sized cuts are available. Bones for the roasts or chops are often scraped clean before they are cooked, a technique known as **frenching**.

- **Leg.** Veal legs may be purchased whole and then broken down into their smaller pieces. A subprimal cut from the leg is the top round. Veal from the top round has the best texture and cooks the most evenly.

Pork Pork, the meat of domesticated pigs, is some of the most popular meat sold in the United States. Pigs have been specifically bred over many generations to produce the leaner cuts of meat sold today. Pigs are commonly slaughtered when they are most tender, under the age of 12 months.

The USDA grades for pork reflect two quality levels: Acceptable and Utility. Within the Acceptable grade, there are four grades (grades 1 through 4)

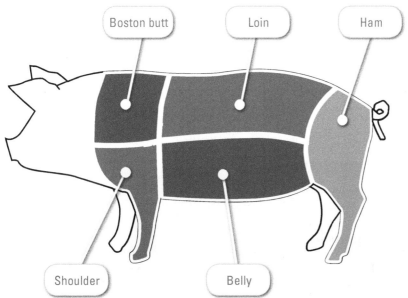

Boston butt

Loin

Ham

Shoulder

Belly

FIGURE 16–4

Pork Primal Cuts
The rib and loin are left together in one long primal loin.

COMPARING/CONTRASTING *How is the pork loin different from loins from other animals?*

based on yield. The higher the grade, the more meat compared to fat or bone. Generally, a bigger animal has more lean meat. Stores sell only USDA Acceptable, grade 1 or 2 pork. Lower-yield or utility grade is mainly used in processed products and is not available in supermarkets. The pork you buy may have quality grades assigned by a meat packer, rather than federal grades. The grading system used by an individual packer must be clearly defined and match or exceed federal standards.

The pork carcass is split into two halves along the backbone, like beef. However, then it is divided in a slightly different manner from most other meat. Instead of dividing the rib and loin into two portions, the rib and loin are left together in one long primal loin. Other primal cuts include the Boston butt, shoulder, belly, and ham.

The following list summarizes the cooking methods and uses for the five pork primal cuts.

- **Boston Butt.** This primal cut (bone-in or bone-out) often has regional names, such as *daisy ham* or *cottage butt*. Boston butt is used to prepare a specialty ham known as tasso (TA-soh). Common cooking methods for the Boston butt include roasting, sautéing, and stewing. It may also be cured or smoked. The smoked version is also known as *English bacon*.

- **Shoulder.** This primal pork cut is most suitable for stewing and braising (but may, because of the relatively high fat content, be roasted with some success). It is also used for ground pork. Because of the relatively high fat ratio, the shoulder is often used to make sausages. The shoulder is sometimes known as a *picnic ham*.

- **Loin.** Cuts from the pork loin are tender and suitable for dry-heat and quick-cooking methods such as roasting, grilling, broiling, sautéing, and pan frying. The meat is sold as whole roasts (bone-in and boneless), chops (bone-in or boneless), and cutlets. The loin may be

Pork, Boston butt
Source: Culinary Institute of America

Trimmed pork loin (above),
pork tenderloin (below)
Source: Culinary Institute of America

Pork Variety Meat

Variety Meat	Common Culinary Uses
Jowl bacon	Crumbly form of bacon from the jowl, used for flavoring rather than as slices
Fatback	Clear fat from the back that has no traces of lean meat; used in pâtés and terrines
Neck bones	Smoked; used for flavoring in soups, stews, and broths
Liver	Used for sausages, pâtés, and terrines
Heart	Simmered, braised, or stewed; used for sausages, pâtés, and terrines
Intestines	Used for sausage casings
Kidneys	Simmered, stewed, or braised

Slab bacon
Source: Culinary Institute of America

Ham, top view
Source: Culinary Institute of America

cured or smoked. When the loin is cured or smoked, it is known in the United States as *Canadian-style bacon.* Baby back ribs are also part of the loin. They are usually slow cooked by braising or barbecuing.

- **Belly.** Bacon is made by curing or smoking the belly. Dry-heat methods, including pan broiling, are appropriate for bacon. Spareribs are also cut from the belly. This popular cut is sold whole or cut into portions.

- **Ham (Leg).** Bone-in or boneless cuts from the ham may be whole roasts, steaks, or portion cuts. Top round is often prepared as thin boneless cuts and sautéed or pan-fried. The ham is typically roasted, baked (often with a glaze), or boiled. The shank can be simmered, stewed, or braised. These cuts are often smoked or cured. A ham can be fresh, cured, or smoked. Prosciutto is **dry cured** (cured by rubbing with salt and often seasonings) and then dried. Smithfield ham is dry cured and then smoked.

Spareribs
Source: Culinary Institute of America

Lamb and Mutton Lamb is the tender meat produced by young, domesticated sheep. The texture of lamb is a direct result of what the lamb consumes and the age at which it is slaughtered. Milk-fed lamb has the most delicate color and flavor. Grass-fed lamb has a more pronounced flavor and texture. Most lamb produced in the United States is finished on a grain diet and butchered at six to seven months old. The meat from sheep that is over 16 months old is called **mutton**. Mutton is tougher than lamb and has a strong, gamey taste.

Lamb for the restaurant industry and retail consumption is graded Prime or Choice, with Prime the most tender, juicy, and flavorful. Lower grades (Good, Utility, and Cull) are only used commercially.

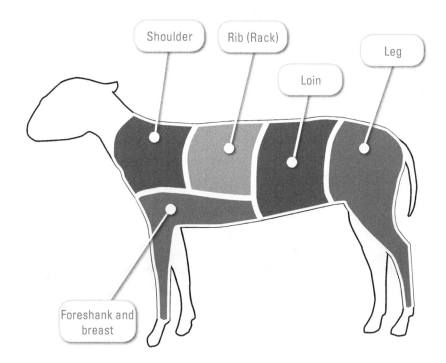

FIGURE 16–5

Lamb Primal Cuts
Lamb is cut into five primal cuts.

RELATING CONCEPTS *Which animal does lamb most resemble in terms of its primal cuts?*

Square-cut shoulder of lamb
Source: Culinary Institute of America

Like veal, lamb is usually cut into either a foresaddle and a hindsaddle or into sides. There are five primal lamb cuts: the shoulder, the foreshank and breast, the rib (known also as the *rack*), the loin, and the leg.

The following list summarizes the cooking methods and uses for the five lamb primal cuts.

- **Shoulder.** Common cooking methods include simmering, braising, and stewing. Cuts are sold as roasts and chops, as well as cubed and ground meat. Some boneless cuts may be roasted or grilled.

- **Foreshank and Breast.** The lamb foreshank is usually braised or simmered. The breast can be braised, simmered, broiled, or grilled.

Frenched rack with a single rib chop
Source: Culinary Institute of America

Full rack of lamb
Source: Culinary Institute of America

- **Rib (Rack).** The rib is typically roasted, as either a rack, a crown roast, or a bone-in roast. Chops from the ribs are sautéed, broiled, or grilled. Chops may be single- or double-boned. Bones may be frenched before cooking. The breast is usually braised or stewed. It may also be cut into small ribs (often called *riblets*) and barbecued.

- **Loin.** Meat from the loin is tender and best suited to quick-cooking dry-heat methods (sautéing, grilling, or broiling) to achieve the best flavor and texture. Whole cuts (bone-in or boneless) are usually roasted. English chops are bone-in and may be a single- or double-bone cut. Saratoga chops are boneless and may also be single- or double-bone cuts. The boneless cuts may be used for cutlets, émincé, medallions, or noisettes.

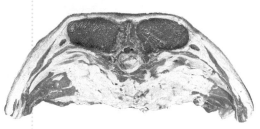

Lamb loin saddle
Source: Culinary Institute of America

Lamb Variety Meat

Variety Meat	Common Culinary Uses
Tongue	Simmered, often smoked
Liver	Sautéed; used in pâtés and terrines
Heart	Simmered, braised, or stewed
Kidneys	Simmered, braised, or stewed
Intestines	Used for sausage casings

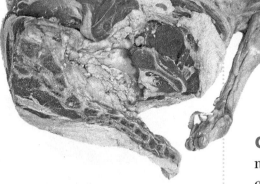

Leg of lamb with shank
Source: Culinary Institute of America

Venison haunch, outside
Source: Culinary Institute of America

- **Leg.** Some cuts from the leg are tender enough for dry-heat methods. Cuts from the leg (sirloin, top round, bottom round, and eye round) can be roasted or braised. The top round is also used to prepare steaks or cutlets. The lamb shank and heel are typically braised, stewed, or simmered. The leg may be **butterflied** (split down the middle and then spread open) and grilled or stuffed and braised.

Game Game is a general term for meat of wild mammals and birds. Although the term **venison** can be used as a general term for large game animals, in the United States venison typically refers to the meat from any member of the deer family, including antelope, caribou, elk, moose, reindeer, red-tailed deer, white-tailed deer, and mule deer. Meat from other popular large game, such as buffalo and wild boar, is usually identified as such in a restaurant.

The most popular small game animal is rabbit. It has mildly flavored, lean, tender meat with a fine texture. A **hare** is a type of large rabbit and is usually wild. They can weigh from 6 to 12 pounds. A mature rabbit that has been raised commercially for food typically weighs from 3 to 5 pounds, while a young rabbit weighs around 2½ pounds.

Game that is sold in restaurants is typically raised commercially for food. More game meat, and more varieties of game, is now being farm-raised. Most large game animals produce meat that is dark red and very lean. The flavor, color, and texture of the flesh are a direct result of its age and diet as well as the season.

The same general rules that determine how to cook red meat will typically work for venison and other large game:

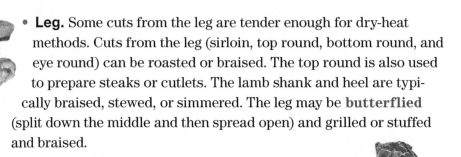

Venison shoulder, outside
Source: Culinary Institute of America

Rabbit, side view
Source: Culinary Institute of America

- Cuts from less-exercised portions such as the front of the loin and the rib may be prepared by any technique. Dry-heat methods such as grilling or roasting are frequently used.

- Well-exercised areas of the animal, such as the **haunch** (the hindquarters of a deer, consisting of the leg and the back of the loin), the shank, and the shoulder are best when cooked by moist-heat or combination methods. These cuts are also used for preparing pâtés and terrines.

 **READING CHECKPOINT** *What are the eight beef primal cuts?*

Receiving and Handling Meat

Meat is quite perishable. When you receive it, check its temperature by inserting a thermometer between packages, but do not puncture the packaging.

- Meat should be received below 41°F.

- Meat that has been subjected to previous temperature abuse will be dry or discolored.

- Look for packaging that is clean and intact.

- Check the temperature inside the storage area of the delivery truck.

At the proper temperature and under optimal conditions, meat holds for several days without noticeable loss of quality. Meat can also be frozen for longer storage. To keep meat properly chilled and prevent cross-contamination, follow these guidelines:

- Wrap and store meat under refrigeration, below 41°F.

- Hold meat in a separate unit, when possible, or in a separate part of the cooler.

- Place uncooked meat on trays to prevent it from dripping onto other food or onto the floor. Store on the bottom shelf.

- Keep different kinds of meat separated; for example, beef should not come into contact with pork.

- Store vacuum-packed meat directly in its packaging if the packaging has not been punctured or ripped.

- Once meat has been removed from its packaging, rewrap it in air-permeable paper, such as butcher's paper.

- For meat with a short shelf life (variety meat and uncured pork products), cook as soon as possible.

 **READING CHECKPOINT** *At what temperature should meat be stored?*

·•FOCUS ON
•• Sanitation

Airtight Containers

When storing fresh or thawed meats in the refrigerator, remember that airtight containers promote bacterial growth that can cause spoilage or contamination. Butcher's paper is capable of "breathing" and is a better choice.

Home on the Range

For most animals that are raised as food, home on the range means living on a factory farm. The high demand for meat, poultry, and dairy products means that these foods need to be mass-produced. For the animals, this means living conditions that are far removed from their natural state. And for the consumer, it can mean food products of poor nutritional value that may also, over time, pose health problems.

In recent years, many farmers and ranchers are trying something different. They are raising free-range animals. Instead of being confined to cages or pens, these animals are allowed to roam freely outdoors. Instead of eating commercially produced grain, they are able to graze on grass and plants in a pasture. Their diet is typically free of pesticides, antibiotics, and hormones.

Pesticides are toxic chemicals sprayed on crops. They are consumed by animals and then in turn consumed by us. Pesticides can impair the immune system and cause diseases. Antibiotics are given to factory-farmed animals to cut down on disease. Overuse of antibiotics can lead to strains of bacteria that are resistant to drugs. Some factory-farmed animals are also fed hormones to make them grow faster, and cows are sometimes given a hormone to produce more milk. There is growing concern that hormone residues in meat and dairy may be harmful to our health, potentially affecting our own hormone balance.

Free-range animals fed an organic diet are a quality food source. Research shows that free-range chickens have 21 percent less fat and 28 percent fewer calories than factory-raised chickens, and are often juicier and tastier. Their eggs have 34 percent less cholesterol. The meat from cattle raised on grass

Free-range cattle: a healthier alternative?
Source: Ingus Evertovskis/Fotolia

instead of grain has ¼ to ⅙ as much fat and more essential nutrients, such as omega-3 fatty acids, vitamin E, and beta-carotene.

Although it takes a lot of grass and a lot of land to raise animals naturally, animals that are truly home on the range offer a healthy alternative food source.

Lab Activity

Divide into two teams. One team will cook a cut of grass-fed beef; the other team will cook grain-fed beef of the same cut in the same size and using exactly the same cooking method and herbs and spices. Each team will taste both cuts of beef. Each team will prepare a report analyzing the texture, flavor, cost, and health benefits of their beef and supporting their beef in relation to the other type of beef.

Preparing Meat

Meat must be prepared before it is served. Some steps are performed before you cook the meat, and some are done after the meat is cooked, before you serve it to a guest.

Trimming Chefs refer to the **grain** of the meat. When chefs refer to the grain of the meat, they are talking about the direction in which the fibers in the meat run. Some meat preparation techniques call for meat to be cut across the grain. This means you slice the meat across the fibers. Other techniques call for the meat to be cut with the grain, that is, in the same direction as the fibers.

Some cuts of meat are actually several different muscles. These muscles are connected by a membrane. Chefs refer to these membranes that join the muscles as **seams**. Cutting along a seam helps separate a large cut into smaller pieces.

Many cuts of meat have fat you should cut away before cooking. Visible, or surface, fat is usually trimmed away. Sometimes, however, you may leave a thin layer of fat to provide natural basting, especially during long slow-cooking methods such as roasting or braising. For sautéing and other quick-cooking methods, you should usually remove the fat completely.

Silverskin is a tough membrane that surrounds some cuts of meat. It gets its name from its somewhat silvery color. Silverskin is likely to shrink when exposed to heat. When it shrinks, it can cause meat to buckle and cook unevenly. So before cooking you should remove any silverskin, along with any gristle or tendons (tough connective tissue that holds muscles onto the bones). As you trim meat and poultry, work carefully to be sure you don't cut away edible meat.

Cutting and Pounding Cutlets A cutlet may come from the loin, the tenderloin, or any other sufficiently tender cut of meat, such as the top

BASIC CULINARY SKILLS

Making Cutlets

① **Trim meat** completely. Remove all visible fat, tendons, gristle, and silverskin.

② **Cut pieces** of the same thickness and weight (generally ranging from 1 to 4 ounces).

Source: Culinary Institute of America

③ **Place the meat** between two layers of plastic wrap.

④ **Pound the meat.** Use a pounding and pushing motion to pound the cutlets to an even thickness over their entire surface. Do not tear or overstretch the meat.

Source: Culinary Institute of America

⑤ **Arrange the pounded cutlets** on a parchment-lined sheet pan. Keep well chilled until ready to cook.

Recipe Card

108. Pork Cutlet with Sauce Robert

round. Based on a restaurant's theme or style of menu, different types of restaurants will use different words for a cutlet. Some of the more common terms for a cutlet are *scallop*; *scaloppine* (skal-a-PEE-nee), typically used in Italian restaurants; and *escalope* (eh-SKAL-ope), used in French restaurants.

Cutlets are pounded to make sure they have an even thickness over their entire surface. This allows them to be rapidly sautéed or pan-fried. When you make cutlets, you need to adjust the weight of the mallet and strength of the blow to match the meat. Veal cutlets require a more delicate touch than pork cutlets, for example.

Preparing Meat for Stewing or Grinding It is usually best to cube meat that you intend to use for stewing or for grinding. This meat is usually tougher and fattier than other meat.

For both stew meat and meat you will be grinding, remove the surface fat and any large pockets of fat. Cut the meat along the seams. Remove silverskin, tendons, and gristle. Cut the meat into cubes of relatively even size and shape. To make the meat more tender in a stew, cut against the grain. To prepare meat you will be grinding, make sure your cubes are small enough to slide easily through the feed tube of a grinder.

Grinding Meat Grinding meat calls for scrupulous attention to safe food-handling practices. Observe the following procedures for best results:

- Clean the grinder well and put it together correctly. Make sure the blade is sitting flush against the die. In this position, the blade cuts the food neatly rather than tearing or shredding it.

- Chill all grinder parts that will come in contact with the meat by either chilling them in the refrigerator or putting them in an ice bath.

- Grind the meat into a stainless-steel bowl that is placed in a larger bowl of ice so the meat stays at a safe temperature throughout all steps of the grinding process.

- Do not force the meat through the feed tube. If the pieces are the correct size, they will be drawn through the tube easily.

- Be sure the blade is sharp. Meat should be cut cleanly, never mangled or mashed, as it passes through the grinder.

Recipe Cards

109. Beef Stroganoff

110. Estouffade of Beef

111. Chili

FIGURE 16–6

Grinding Meat

Start grinding meat with a die that has large openings.

RELATING CONCEPTS *Why would you put the bowl of ground meat in a bowl of ice?*

Source: Culinary Institute of America

- For all but very delicate meat (for example, some types of organ meat), begin with a die that has large openings. The ground meat will appear quite coarse. The lean meat and fat will be visible as separate components in the ground meat.
- Continue to grind through progressively smaller dies until the desired consistency is achieved. The coarse appearance of the meat starts to become finer as the lean meat and fat blend.

Tying a Roast Tying a roast with secure knots that have the right tension is one of the simplest and most frequently required types of meat fabrication. It ensures that the roast will be evenly cooked and that it will retain its shape after roasting.

Tying a Roast

① Cut lengths of string long enough to wrap completely around the meat twice.

② Pass one length of string around the meat and cross one end over the other end.

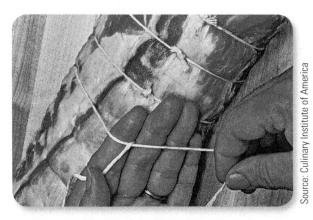

Source: Culinary Institute of America

③ Make a loop by passing one end around the index finger of one hand.

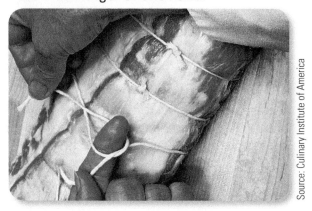

Source: Culinary Institute of America

④ Pass the string underneath itself.

⑤ Push the end of the string through the opening where your fingertip was.

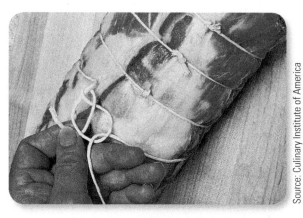

Source: Culinary Institute of America

⑥ Pull both ends of the string to tighten until the string is pressing firmly against the meat.

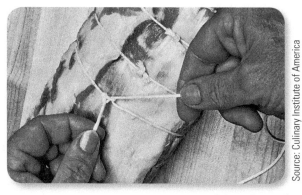

Source: Culinary Institute of America

(*Continued*)

Tying a Roast *Continued*

7 **Loop one end of the string** completely around your thumb and forefinger and pull the other end of the string through the loop.

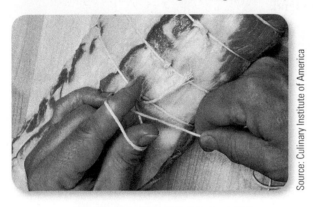

Source: Culinary Institute of America

8 **Pull both ends of the string to tighten** securely. Trim any long strings so the knots are neat.

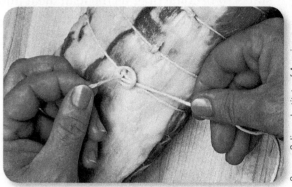

Source: Culinary Institute of America

Recipe Cards

112. Rib Roast au Jus

113. Roast Leg of Lamb

9 **Repeat.** Tie lengths of string at even intervals until the entire piece of meat is securely tied.

READING CHECKPOINT *How do you make cutlets?*

16.1 ASSESSMENT

Reviewing Concepts

1. What is a primal cut?

2. What are the eight beef primal cuts?

3. At what temperature should meat be stored?

4. How do you make cutlets?

Critical Thinking

5. Recognizing Patterns Which animal doesn't have a primal rib cut?

6. Drawing Conclusions What advantages does specifying the primal cuts offer to meat packagers, butchers, restaurants, and diners?

7. Comparing/Contrasting Compare the appropriate cooking methods for similar primals in two different animals (for example, compare the cooking methods used for beef and veal shoulders, or pork loin and lamb loin).

Test Kitchen

Divide into four teams. Each team will cook patties of a different ground meat, using only salt and pepper as seasonings. Grill or sauté patties to a safe temperature for the meat you are cooking (temperatures will vary). Evaluate the differences between the various types of meat.

SCIENCE

Mad Cow Disease

Research mad cow disease. Write a report on the disease, identifying its causes and the effect it has on humans. Discuss the efforts to keep mad cow disease out of national food chains.

Poultry

Key Concepts

- Understanding poultry inspection and grading
- Identifying various types and forms of poultry
- Preparing and serving poultry

Vocabulary

- disjointing
- giblet bag
- gizzard
- keel bone
- poultry
- ratites
- suprême
- trussing

Inspection and Grading

Poultry refers to any domesticated bird used for human consumption. Poultry must undergo a mandatory inspection for wholesomeness that is similar to the inspection process for meat. The USDA poultry grades are A, B, and C. Restaurants and retail outlets purchase Grade A poultry.

Raw poultry must be kept chilled to 40°F or below during processing. Some processing techniques may call for the poultry to be chilled to 26°F, which freezes the outer layers of the bird but does not freeze it all the way through. Poultry packed from 26°F to 40°F can be called *fresh*. Chicken packed from 1°F to 25°F may be labeled *chilled, chilled with ice,* or *chilled with dry ice.* Poultry chilled to 0°F or less must be labeled *frozen* or *previously frozen.*

READING CHECKPOINT *To what temperature must poultry be chilled during processing?*

Types of Poultry

Chicken is the most popular form of poultry, but poultry also includes turkey, ducks, geese, and a number of farm-raised game birds such as pheasant or quail. The chart on page 554 summarizes the types of poultry, their weight, their characteristics, and the appropriate cooking techniques used for them.

Recently, the family of flightless birds, referred to by their Latin name, **ratites** (RAT-ites), have become more popular. This family includes such birds as the ostrich, emu (E-moo), and rhea (RHEE-ah). Their meat is a rich red color, lean, and low in fat. Ratites have been subject to federal inspection

Source: tore2527/Fotolia

Common Types of Whole Poultry

Type of Poultry	Weight	Characteristics and Cooking Techniques
Chicken, broiler/fryer	2½–4½ lb	Younger than 10 weeks. Very tender; suitable for all cooking techniques.
Chicken, roaster	5–9 lb	Between 8 and 12 weeks old. Tender; suitable for all cooking techniques.
Chicken, stewing	4½–7 lb	Older than 10 months. Not tender; suitable for moist-heat and combination methods.
Chicken, capon (castrated male)	5–9 lb	Younger than 4 months old. Tender; usually roasted.
Duckling, broiler or fryer	2–4 lb	Young. Very tender; usually roasted but suitable for most techniques.
Duckling, roaster	4–6 lb	Older than broiler/fryer. Tender; usually roasted.
Goose, young or gosling	6–10 lb	Tender; usually roasted.
Guinea hen or fowl	¾ –1½ lb	Tender; suitable for most techniques.
Pheasant	1½ –2 lb	Tender; suitable for most techniques.
Rock Cornish game hen	Less than 2 lb	Younger than 5 weeks. Very tender; suitable for all cooking techniques.
Squab (domestic pigeon that has not begun to fly)	Under 1 lb	Light, tender meat; suitable for sautéing, roasting, grilling (as bird ages, meat darkens and toughens).
Turkey, young hen or tom	8–22 lb	Very tender; suitable for all cooking techniques.
Turkey, yearling	10–30 lb	Fully mature but still tender; usually roasted.

since April, 2002. The meat is sold as steaks, fillets, medallions, roasts, and ground meat. The tenderest meat is from the thigh. Meat is also produced from the forequarter.

Market Forms of Poultry Poultry is sold in a variety of forms. Whole birds have been cleaned and the head and feet removed. You may find a small bag in the cavity of a whole bird, known as the **giblet bag**, which includes the liver, stomach (or **gizzard**), heart, and neck.

The following are some other market forms for poultry:

- Whole chicken cut into individual pieces (typically breasts, drumsticks, thighs, and a back, but could be half chickens or quarter chickens, as well)

- Breasts (whole breast or half breast, with the skin and bones, boneless, or boneless and skinless)

- Whole legs (typically sold bone-in and with the skin)

- Thighs (sold bone-in or boneless, with or without the skin)

- Drumsticks (sold bone-in, with or without the skin)

Breast, thigh, drumstick, wing

Sources: Clive Streeter/Dorling Kindersley Limited

History of Turkeys

Everyone associates the turkey with America's first Thanksgiving. But where did that turkey come from? Most of us probably assume it was a wild turkey one of the colonists shot. However, the turkey on the Pilgrims' table probably came over on the same ship they did. In all likelihood, it was an English turkey.

To understand this, you need to know a little more about turkeys. Turkeys were originally native to North America and Mexico. They were domesticated in Mexico around 200 B.C.E. Returning conquistadors brought turkeys to Spain in 1510. A few years after that, turkeys were brought to English farmers. It

Wild turkey

Source: Angelika Elsebach/ Dorling Kindersley

was these turkeys, descended from the original Spanish turkeys, that the Pilgrims brought with them on the *Mayflower* in 1620. The Pilgrims eventually bred their domesticated turkeys with wild turkeys, developing new, hardier, meatier, and better-tasting turkeys. On Thanksgiving, as you eat your turkey, think of the long journey on which turkeys traveled to arrive on the first Thanksgiving table!

Research

Research the breeds of turkey today. Compare heirloom, heritage, or legacy breeds with the breeds produced for factory farming. Determine what kinds of turkeys are available in your area.

- Wings (typically sold bone-in, with the skin)
- Ground poultry
- Processed poultry (made into such processed items as patties, sausages, or bacon)

Choosing Quality Poultry Poultry should have plump breasts and meaty thighs. The skin should be intact with no tears or punctures. Poultry must be purchased from reputable purveyors and, for optimum quality, kept chilled to below 40°F during storage. Put poultry in drip pans before storing it in the refrigerator so it does not contaminate food stored below it.

 **READING CHECKPOINT** *What types of whole chickens are commonly available?*

Preparing and Serving Poultry

Poultry is one of the most popular of all menu offerings. Basic poultry fabrication techniques can be applied to virtually all types of poultry, not only chicken but also squab, ducks, or turkey. You will, however, need to make some adjustments. Smaller birds require more delicate, precise cuts and a smaller blade. Larger or older birds call for a heavier blade and greater pressure to break through tough joints.

Chef's Tip

Knife Selection and Care

Select the right knife for the task and use a steel before and during work. With a sharp knife, you are less likely to waste poultry. Cuts will also be neat and straight for better-looking dishes.

Trussing Poultry One of the most important skills required for cooking poultry is trussing whole birds. The object of **trussing**, or tying, a bird is to give it a smooth, compact shape so it cooks evenly and retains moisture. There are several methods for trussing poultry. Some involve special trussing needles; some require only string. The method demonstrated demonstrated in the box on page 557 uses only string.

Disjointing Poultry Before or after cooking, poultry can be cut into halves, quarters, or eighths. Overall, this process is referred to as **disjointing**. When you divide a bird in half, you need to cut through breast. The two halves of the breast are joined by some cartilage as well as a bone known as the **keel bone** because it is shaped like the bottom (or keel) of a boat.

Cutting into halves is an especially important technique for use on smaller birds, such as Cornish game hens and broiler chickens, that will be grilled. These birds are small enough to cook through before the skin becomes scorched or charred. One half of the bird is usually enough for a single portion.

Disjointing Poultry

1. **Remove the backbone** by cutting along both sides of it.

2. **Remove the keel bone** by pulling it away from the chicken.

3. **Cut the chicken into halves** by making a cut down the center of the breast to divide the bird in half.

Source: Culinary Institute of America

5. **Cut at the joints to separate the leg and thigh, and the wing and breast,** if desired. Otherwise, leave in quarters (as shown).

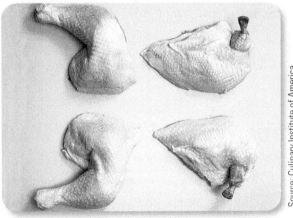

Source: Culinary Institute of America

Source: Culinary Institute of America

4. **Separate the leg and thigh from the breast** and wing by cutting through the skin just above where the breast and thigh meet.

Trussing Poultry

1. **Remove the giblets** (if any).

2. **Cut off the first wing joints.** Also cut away any pockets of fat from the bird's cavity.

3. **Stretch the skin to cover the breast meat.**

4. **Pass the middle of a long piece of string underneath the joints at the end of the drumstick.** Cross the ends of the string to make an X.

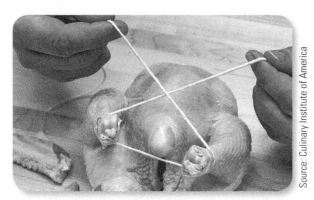

Source: Culinary Institute of America

5. **Pull the string toward the tail** and begin to pull the string back along the body on both sides.

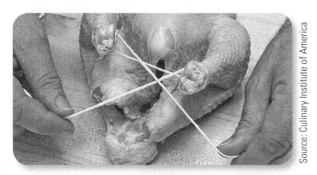

Source: Culinary Institute of America

6. **Pull the string tightly across the joint connecting the drumstick and thigh.** Then pull it along the body toward the bird's back, catching the wing underneath the string.

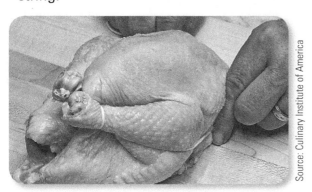

Source: Culinary Institute of America

7. **Pull one end of the string underneath the backbone** at the neck opening.

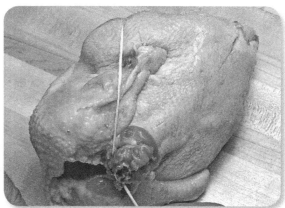

Source: Culinary Institute of America

8. **Tie the two ends of the string** securely.

Source: Culinary Institute of America

9. **The properly trussed bird is ready to cook.**

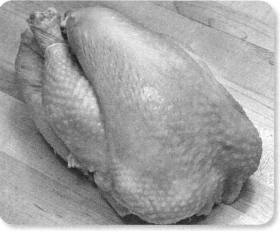

Source: Culinary Institute of America

China

China is a vast land with many individual cuisines. These are based on the geography, climate, resources, cooking styles, and lifestyles of particular regions. For instance, the landlocked Szechuan province in southwestern China has subtropical areas in the southeast and cold mountainous regions in the northwest. Szechuan cuisine is known for its bold flavors featuring chili peppers, garlic, and ginger.

Fujian cuisine, from the Fujian province on the southwest cost of China, is very different. It focuses on retaining the original flavors of the main ingredients, which are typically fish and seafood or, in inland areas, peanuts, bamboo shoots, and other woodland delicacies. But perhaps no dish from any Chinese cuisine is more internationally famous than Peking duck.

Roast duck can be traced back as far as 1330 in China. When the Ming Dynasty capital was shifted from Nanjing to Beijing in the early 15th century, roast duck was one of the favorites of the imperial court. According to local history, the Bianyfang restaurant in Beijing, which opened in the mid-16th century, was the earliest roast duck restaurant. By the 18th century, Beijing-style roast duck had become a favorite of the upper classes. (Peking duck gained its name from *Peking*, an alternate spelling of *Beijing*. Peking duck is now often called Beijing duck.) Eventually a special breed of duck was reared exclusively for the dish.

What makes Peking duck so good? It starts with an air pump! The carcass is inflated, separating the skin from the body. After some seasoning and drying, the duck is roasted in a hot oven. The duck's fat melts away and the skin becomes crispy.

The traditional way of serving Peking duck is as a three-course meal. First the crispy skin is served with small steamed pancakes, raw scallions, hoisin (HOY-sinh) sauce (a thick, brown, sweet-and-spicy sauce made from soybeans, garlic, chiles, and spices), and plum sauce (a spicy, fruity sauce made from plums, chiles, vinegar, and sugar). For the next course, the duck meat is chopped up, stir-fried, and eaten wrapped in fresh lettuce. For the final course, the bones are used for broth.

Lab Activity

Divide the class into small groups. Each group will select a different Chinese dish to research. Explain how your dish is a representative of a particular style of Chinese cooking. Focus on the geography, climate, resources, cooking style, and lifestyle of the region from which your dish originates. If possible, cook your dish and compare to the dishes of the other groups.

Source: Olinchuk/Shutterstock

Peking duck in a pancake
Source: Clive Streeter and Patrick McLeavy/Dorling Kindersley

Large birds can be further broken down into quarters for portion-sized pieces or into eighths for smaller pieces. If the bones are left in during cooking, they provide some protection against scorching and shrinking. Save the wing tips and backbone for use in the preparation of stock.

Fabricating Skinless, Boneless Breasts The same technique used to make boneless, skinless chicken breast portions can be used for pheasant, partridge, turkey, or duck. If one wing joint, often frenched, is left attached to the breast meat, it may be referred to as a **suprême** (soo-PREM).

Determining Doneness Cooking poultry properly is important. Guests are as aware of food-borne illnesses, and as concerned by them, as chefs are. Fully cooking poultry is an important way to be sure it is safe when you serve it to a guest. When poultry is fully cooked, its juices should be clear, with no trace of pink. When a chicken is properly roasted, you can move the leg easily. You can also test whole poached chickens this way. Of course, the final test is always a thermometer. The safe internal food temperature for poultry is 165°F taken at the thickest point of the cut, or in the thigh near the body for whole birds. In some restaurants, and for some types of poultry such as duck breast, guests may ask for a specific degree of doneness.

••FOCUS ON
•• Safety

Be Safe
The safe internal temperature for poultry is 165°F.

BASIC CULINARY SKILLS

Boneless Breast Portions

① **Cut along either side of the keel bone,** with the breast bone facing up. Use your guiding hand to steady the bird.

③ **Free the meat from the bones,** using the tip of the knife. Run the tip of the knife along the bones.

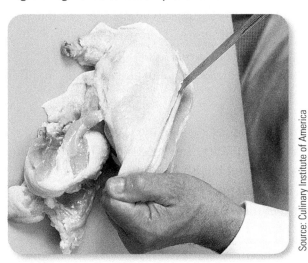

Source: Culinary Institute of America

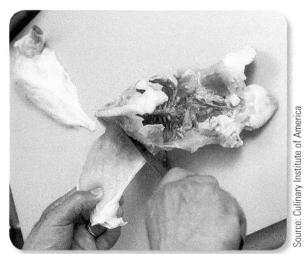

Source: Culinary Institute of America

② **Remove the breast meat from the rib cage** with delicate cuts.

④ **Boneless breast portions can be pounded into cutlets,** if desired.

FIGURE 16-7

Testing for Doneness
The chef checks the internal temperature of a roast chicken.

COMMUNICATING *What would you serve with this roast chicken?*

Source: Richard Embery/Pearson Education/ PH College

Recipe Cards

114. Sateh of Chicken

115. Chicken Fajitas

116. Roast Turkey

117. Southern Fried Chicken with Country-Style Gravy

Recipe Card

118. Chicken Pot Pie

Dry-Heat Methods Roast whole chicken, baked chicken parts, grilled or barbecued chicken, and fried chicken are all popular chicken dishes made by dry-heat cooking methods. All but a few types of poultry are excellent for these methods. Most of the poultry you will find for sale in supermarkets is young, tender, and meaty—perfect for dry-heat methods.

When you are roasting whole birds, such as turkey, chickens, ducks, or geese, it can sometimes be difficult to get the dark meat of the legs and thighs fully cooked without overcooking the leaner white meat portions. So, if you are preparing portions, start the dark meat portions before the white meat portions so both types of meat are finished at the same time.

Moist-Heat Methods Any moist-heat method or combination method is suitable for poultry, including steaming, poaching, simmering, stewing, and braising. Steaming and poaching are often used for lean, tender portions. Shallow poaching is popular for breast portions because the cooking liquid can serve as the basis for a sauce that can add moisture and flavor to the breast when it is served.

Serving Poultry Poultry is, perhaps, the most popular menu choice in restaurants today. Guests enjoy poultry because of its flavor, but they also choose it because of its perceived health benefits. It is lower in saturated fat and cholesterol than most red meat. Poultry is a versatile food that pairs well with most cooking techniques and is a good vehicle for flavors from around the globe.

READING CHECKPOINT *What is the safe internal temperature for cooking poultry?*

FIGURE 16–8

Variety of Poultry Dishes
Duck with sesame seeds (left), chicken stir-fry with mango (right), turkey tortillas.

COMMUNICATING *Which of these poultry dishes looks the most appealing to you?*

Source: Edward Allwright/Dorling Kindersley

16.2 ASSESSMENT

Reviewing Concepts

1. To what temperature must poultry be chilled during processing?

2. What types of whole chickens are commonly available?

3. What is the safe internal temperature for cooking poultry?

Critical Thinking

4. Comparing/Contrasting Compare the smallest and largest types of commonly available whole chickens in terms of their size and cooking techniques.

5. Inferring Why might it be helpful for a restaurant to purchase whole chickens and disjoint them in the kitchen?

6. Inferring Do you think cooking ostrich meat would be more like cooking turkey or more like cooking beef? Why?

Test Kitchen

Divide into four teams. Each team is responsible for locating a simple recipe that uses skinless, boneless breast of chicken. Each team will make its recipe and share the dish with the other teams. Evaluate the differences, focusing on the role that chicken plays in the dish.

SCIENCE

Chicken Breeds

Research the history of three particular breeds of chicken that are used as a food. Write a report on the breeds, including where they originated, how long they have been bred, and any comments on the amount, flavor, color, or texture of their meat.

PROJECT 16
Trussed or Untrussed You are now ready to work on Project 16, "Trussed or Untrussed," which is available in "My Culinary Lab" or in your *Student's Lab Resources and Study Guide* manual.

Reviewing Content

Choose the letter that best answers the question or completes the statement.

1. The quality grading of meat is
   a. required by the USDA.
   b. required at the state level.
   c. required by local governments.
   d. voluntary.

2. The front portion of a side of beef is called the
   a. foresaddle.
   b. forequarters.
   c. hindsaddle.
   d. hindquarters.

3. A medallion is
   a. a small round or oval portion-sized cut.
   b. a large multiportion cut intended for roasting or braising.
   c. stew meat, cut to ¾ to 1½ inch.
   d. none of the above

4. Which of the following is not a primal cut for pork?
   a. Boston butt
   b. shoulder
   c. sirloin
   d. belly

5. Meat should be received at a temperature below
   a. 49°F.
   b. 41°F.
   c. 32°F.
   d. 26°F.

6. Raw poultry must be chilled to what temperature during processing?
   a. 49°F or below
   b. 40°F or below
   c. 32°F or below
   d. 26°F or below

7. For optimum quality, poultry should be stored to below
   a. 49°F.
   b. 40°F.
   c. 32°F.
   d. 26°F.

8. In poultry, *gizzard* is another name for
   a. the liver.
   b. the stomach.
   c. the neck.
   d. the kidney.

Understanding Concepts

9. In terms of poultry, what does disjointing mean?

10. In terms of butchering meat, what is a primal cut?

11. In terms of butchering meat, what is a subprimal cut?

12. What grades of beef are most widely sold in retail outlets?

13. Why are cutlets pounded?

Critical Thinking

14. **APPLYING CONCEPTS** Why do you chill the parts of a grinder when you are grinding meat?

15. **PREDICTING** What would happen if you didn't truss poultry before roasting it?

Culinary Math

16. **APPLYING CONCEPTS** You are making a recipe for a dish that requires 40 oz of lamb stew meat for 10 servings. You are cutting the stew meat yourself from pieces of a lamb shoulder but have experienced 15 percent waste due to trimming. About how much shoulder will you need for 50 servings?

On the Job

17. **APPLYING CONCEPTS** The chef has just asked you to sauté some baby back pork ribs. What should you do?

18. **COMMUNICATING** A customer has asked for a rare duck breast. You know that this means the duck breast will not be at a safe internal food temperature. What should you do?

Banquet Manager

Many operations, including hotels, casinos, restaurants, conventions centers, and civic centers, count on conventions, meetings, and special events such as weddings, bar mitzvahs, and receptions to generate a large part of their revenue. The banquet manager is crucial to the success or failure of this part of an operation.

Banquet coordinators are responsible for coordinating all aspects of multiple functions held in the banquet facility, including scheduling, staffing, and acquiring service items such as tables, chairs, linens, and glassware. In a large hotel, several events may take place on the same day, even at the same time.

Banquet managers are responsible for developing menus that can be adjusted to meet the guests' requirements, typically working together with the banquet or catering chef. Menus must be carefully priced so customers perceive them as a value yet the business generates the greatest possible profit. It is generally easier to make a specific profit margin when you know in advance how many people will be dining, at exactly what time, and on exactly which evening. Banquet managers must be able to organize an incredible number of details. The advance preparation, cooking, and service require concentration, endurance, and skill. Banquet managers and chefs work in public view, which presents its own set of physical and emotional demands. Managers are often responsible for hiring and training service staff. They are

often perfectionists who find great reward in their ability to bring off an event perfectly.

Assistant banquet managers work under the direction of the coordinator or the manager to handle a variety of tasks such as organizing and overseeing the set up of the banquet facility, managing the staff during a function, or coordinating with the host.

Banquet beverage managers handle all aspects of beverage service for a variety of functions. They may be responsible for coordinating "beverage breaks" for large meetings, or they may organize full-service bars as well as all drinks served during the course of a meal. They must purchase the appropriate quantities of beverage, make sure that all service items are on hand, and train and oversee bartenders and other servers.

Banquet servers are responsible for serving all foods and drinks to the guests. They are usually expected to set up tables and chairs, buffet lines, and tray stands for service. Depending on the type of banquet, in some cases, this includes tray service of hors d'Oeuvre and drinks. They may be responsible for keeping buffet lines filled with foods and even for the actual service of buffet items to the guest. Seated service indicates that the servers will bring the food on plates to the table and then serve them to the guest.

Banquets require large quantities, efficient service, and attention to details.

Entry-Level Requirements

Banquet servers rarely need special training and are often trained on the job. Skills include ability to carry heavy items, interpersonal skills, and cleanliness.

Helpful for Advancement

Banquet managers and assistant banquet managers often have at least a two-year degree in culinary arts and hospitality. Many have a four-year degree in business administration and management. They often have two or more years of experience working in banquets and many have completed a manager-in-training (MIT) program.

Source: Johnny Greig UK/Alamy

Hotels count on conventions to generate a large part of their revenue

EZRA EICHELBERGER

Imagine coordinating a graduation event every three weeks with a full-service four-course meal for nearly 100 graduates and their nearly 400 guests. That is just one of the responsibilities that Ezra Eichelberger faces as an instructor for table service and banquets at The Culinary Institute of America (CIA). His experience before coming to the CIA prepared him for the work, and his genuine concern for the well-being of his guests is what makes him so good at what he does, both as a banquet manager and as a professor. He has worked at several well-known establishments in New York City: as dining room manager/maître d'hôtel at the Greene Street Cafe, general manager for 65 Irving Place, maître d'hôtel for the Island Grill, and general manager/maître d'hôtel for Andiamo. Before that, he was general manager at The Studio in Nashville, Tennessee. Among other positions in the hospitality industry, he has waited tables at T.G.I. Friday's and at Ruby Tuesday before it became a successful chain.

Ezra Eichelberger

VITAL STATISTICS

Graduated: BS, Southern Illinois University

Profession: Professor of Hospitality and Service Management

Interesting Item: Writer and consultant for *Remarkable Service*, a textbook

Author of *Remarkable Banquet Service*, a textbook

Consultant for front-of-the-house management and banquet services

Associate dean of curriculum and instruction at The Culinary Institute of America

CAREER PROFILES

Salary Ranges

Banquet Server: $10 to $20 per hour

Assistant Banquet Manager: $26,000 to $42,000 (or more; varies depending on location and size of establishment)

Banquet Manager or Coordinator: $36,000 to $72,000 with commissions (percentage of banquet sales) of $2,000 to $30,000 per year (or more; varies depending on location and size of establishment)

Chapter **17**

Yeast Breads, Rolls, and Pastries

17.1 Introduction to Baking

17.2 Yeast Dough

17.3 Breads, Rolls, and Pastries

17.1

Introduction to Baking

Key Concepts

- Identifying bakeshop ingredients and their functions
- Identifying and using bakeshop equipment
- Understanding formulas used in the bakeshop

Vocabulary

- all-purpose flour
- baking stones
- bench scraper
- blooming (gelatin)
- bread flour
- cake comb
- cake flour
- chemical leavener
- confectioner's sugar
- corn syrup
- denaturing
- dough divider
- dough sheeter
- egg wash
- formulas
- gelatin
- gluten
- granulated sugar
- knead
- leavener
- loaf pans
- organic leavener
- parchment paper
- pastry bag
- pastry blender
- pastry brush
- pastry wheel
- pectin
- peel
- physical leavener
- proofer
- retarder
- SilPad
- springform pans
- superfine sugar
- tapioca
- tart pans
- tube pans
- turntable

Bakeshop Ingredients

Although they share certain similarities, cooking and baking (and making desserts) are fundamentally different. Although a soup, stew, or even a sauté can be changed at virtually any stage of preparation, most breads, cookies, muffins, cakes, or custards need to be put together exactly as the recipe describes before you bake, chill, or freeze them. Once a batter is ladled into the pan, for example, it is usually too late to adjust the amount of salt or change the texture.

Another important distinction between cooking and baking or dessert-making is that most baked goods and desserts require more advance planning. Cakes need to cool and be frosted, custards and puddings need to chill and firm up in the refrigerator, and yeast breads need plenty of time to rise.

Approach baking and dessert-making in a systematic way. Before you begin baking, gather all the equipment and measure out the ingredients called for in your recipe. Read the recipe carefully; you may need to sift dry ingredients together, melt and cool some ingredients, or permit others to warm slightly to room temperature. Plan ahead so your frozen dessert is perfectly chilled when you want to serve it, your pastry dough is ready to roll out when your filling is complete, and a cake is cooled before you start to frost and decorate it.

Source: Culinary Institute of America

Ingredients function in specific ways to help determine the final texture, flavor, and color of baked goods and desserts. Good bakers know how each ingredient affects the outcome.

Flour Perhaps no ingredient is as important to a baker as flour. The amount of protein and starch in a particular type of flour determines how it will behave in a recipe.

Wheat flour is the most common type of flour used in the bakeshop. It contains the right amounts and types of certain proteins, such as glutenin (GLU-teh-nin) and gliadin (glee-AH-din), which give structure to yeast-raised dough. You should first moisten a wheat flour and then **knead** (NEED) it, working it by hand or in a mixer to distribute the ingredients. Kneading develops **gluten** (GLOO-tihn), a network of long, stretchy strands that trap the carbon dioxide given off by yeast in the dough. This is what causes yeast-based dough to rise.

Flour also contains starch that thickens when it is heated and absorbs liquids. Different flours contain different types of starch. That is why the results you get when you cook or bake with different types of flour differ greatly. For example, a cornstarch-thickened pudding has a different look and feel than a flour-thickened pudding.

Because of these differences in the proteins and starches in different types of flours, it is important to follow a recipe precisely when selecting flour. The following are some of the more common types of wheat flour used in baking recipes:

- **All-Purpose Flour.** A blend of half "soft" (low-protein) and half "hard" (high-protein) wheat, **all-purpose flour** is probably the most common type of flour used in the bakeshop.

- **Bread Flour.** Considered "harder" or "stronger" than all-purpose flour because it has more protein in it, **bread flour** is most appropriate for use in most yeast-bread recipes.

- **Cake Flour.** With less protein than either bread or all-purpose flour, **cake flour** is "softer" than the other two flours. It is used in most cake recipes and many cookie and muffin recipes because it provides a less chewy, more tender texture.

- **Whole-Grain and Stone-Ground Flour.** Whole-grain flour is milled to leave some of the bran intact. Stone-ground flour is milled by using stone mill wheels and is usually produced in small batches. Both whole-grain flour and stone-ground flour usually retain more oil and are more flavorful.

To store opened packages of flour, transfer the contents to an airtight container or a large resealable plastic bag to keep out moisture, dirt, and pests.

FIGURE 17–1

Approach Baking in a Systematic Way
Baking requires that you follow a recipe and measure ingredients precisely.

DRAWING CONCLUSIONS *Why might professional bakers be less willing than other types of chefs to share their recipes?*

Source: Pearson Education

Chef's Tip

Perishable Flour

Whole-grain and stone-ground flours are more perishable than other types of flour. They are best stored in the refrigerator after opening so their oils don't turn rancid.

Classes of Wheat

In the United States, wheat has two growing seasons. Winter wheat is planted in the fall and harvested in the spring or summer. It accounts for 70 to 80 percent of the wheat grown in the United States. Spring wheat is planted in the spring and harvested in late summer or early fall.

Although many varieties of wheat are grown in the United States, all of it falls into six classes, as shown in the table below.

Typically, white wheat has a lighter color and a milder, sweeter flavor than red wheat. The protein levels of flour vary within a class based on environmental conditions such as soil or weather. For example, a drought causes wheat to contain more protein. So flour produced from that wheat will behave differently than flour of the same type of wheat that comes from a crop that didn't experience a drought.

Lab Activity

Pick a bread recipe. Research to locate and purchase wheat flour made exclusively from a single class of flour. (You may have to search online for this.) Divide into as many groups as you have classes of flour. Each group will make soft rolls (Recipe Card 122) using a different class of wheat flour, but keeping all other ingredients and recipe steps the same. Evaluate the results. (This can be done in conjunction with Project 17, "Differences in Flour.")

Classes of Wheat	Level of Protein	Where Grown	Uses
Hard red spring	Highest	Montana, Dakotas, Minnesota	Bread
Durum (spring)	High	North Dakota	Pasta
Hard red winter	Medium to high	Great Plains, between the Mississippi and Rockies	Bread, rolls, all-purpose flour
Hard white winter	Similar to hard red winter	Previously the Pacific Northwest, but increasing in the Great Plains	Bread, rolls, bulgur, tortillas, Asian noodles
Soft red winter	Low to medium	East of the Mississippi	Cakes, pastries, flatbreads, crackers
Soft white winter	Low	Primarily Pacific Northwest	Cakes, crackers, cookies, pastries, quick breads, muffins, snack foods

Unopened packages of white flour keep for up to two years in a cool, dry location. Once opened, they should be used within eight months. Store other types of standard-ground flour (such as potato, rice, rye, oat, or corn flour) in a cool, dry location and use them within two or three months after opening. You could also keep them in the refrigerator for up to six months.

Eggs Eggs contribute proteins, fat, and moisture to baked items. They also provide structure and texture. As eggs are stirred, whipped, or heated, their protein strands unfold and recombine. This creates a network that traps liquids or air, resulting in a texture that can range from a soft foam, such as a meringue, to a sliceable custard, such as a quiche. Other ingredients in the recipe, as well as the way you mix and cook egg-rich dishes, can give a variety of results.

Egg substitutes (powdered or liquid) may be substituted for fresh eggs in some cases. When you use substitutes, you will find some differences in the flavor, color, and texture of the baked goods. Egg substitutes can be refrigerated in unopened containers for up to ten days. Once they are opened, they should be used within three days.

Here are some examples of how eggs are used in the bakeshop:

- When eggs are stirred over direct heat, as when making a custard, the stirring keeps the protein strands short enough to prevent a solid network from forming. This produces a product with a smooth, spoonable consistency.

- When a custard is baked in the oven, the mixture is not stirred as it cooks. This allows longer strands of protein to form, which settle into a firm structure that holds its shape.

- When eggs are whisked, they trap enough air to make a foam, giving lightness to soufflés and similar dishes.

- Adding eggs to dough provides the dough with moisture, helping it stick together. Eggs also provide additional protein to the dough for a firmer and drier product after baking. The water in eggs expands when you bake cakes and muffins, helping them to rise.

- Adding egg yolks to dough adds a rich golden color to the final item, such as a sponge cake, bread, or a vanilla sauce.

- Brushing the tops of breads and pastries with an **egg wash**—a mixture of egg and water or milk—before baking gives a glossy sheen. Egg washes that include only the whites become very shiny, and those that include the yolks give a brilliant golden hue.

Eggs
Source: Viktor Lugovskoy/Fotolia

FIGURE 17–2

Brushing with an Egg Wash
Brushing the top of dough with an egg wash before baking gives the product a glossy sheen when baked.

COMMUNICATING *What does a glossy sheen add to the final baked product?*

Source: Ian O'Leary, Dorling Kindersley

FIGURE 17–3

Yeast Increases the Volume of Dough

Yeast produces carbon dioxide that increases the volume of the dough.

INTERPRETING ILLUSTRATIONS
Can you see the carbon dioxide bubbles in this rising dough?

Source: Dave King © Dorling Kindersley

Eggs are an enormously versatile ingredient, but they are also a potential source of pathogens such as Salmonella. Controlling the temperature of eggs as you cook, cool, and store them is one of the most important ways to keep eggs wholesome. Shell eggs should be refrigerated at a temperature between 33°F and 38°F. Cooking egg dishes to a safe temperature of 160°F also helps prevent illness by killing any pathogens. Cool egg-based dough quickly to keep it from sitting too long in the temperature danger zone (between 41°F and 135°F).

Leaveners A **leavener** (LEV-en-er) increases the volume of a dough or batter by adding air or other gas. Bakers rely on three basic types of leaveners—organic leaveners, chemical leaveners, and physical leaveners—to raise breads, cakes, and cookies.

- **Organic Leaveners.** Yeast, a tiny single-celled organism, is an **organic leavener**. It must be living to do its work. Like any living organism, yeast needs the right environment in order to live. When the conditions are right, yeast cells grow and reproduce, giving off carbon dioxide and alcohol in the process. Carbon dioxide increases the volume of dough when the yeast is first added to the dough and then again when the dough is exposed to the heat of the oven. This is what gives bread its spongy texture. To grow and reproduce, yeast requires moisture, warmth, and food (in the form of sugar, whether added to the dough or naturally present in the flour). Yeast grows most rapidly between 60°F and 90°F. Cooler temperatures slow the yeast down, although they don't kill it. Yeast is destroyed when the temperature of a baked good reaches temperatures between 130°F and 140°F.

- **Chemical Leaveners.** Baking powder is a **chemical leavener**. It reacts rapidly to leaven a baked good when it is combined with moisture and heat. When we say that a baked good has been leavened, we mean that the volume of the batter has been increased by the addition of air or gas. Baking soda is similar to baking powder, but it also requires an acidic ingredient. When these leaveners are blended with liquid in a batter, a chemical reaction produces gas that forms bubbles. As the batter settles into a firm structure during baking, these bubbles give the baked item a spongy, springy texture, sometimes known as its *crumb*. If baking soda and baking powder are not properly blended into the batter, the bubbles may be too large, resulting in tunnels or big air pockets. Recipes often call for chemical leaveners to be sifted with the flour and other dry ingredients to break up any clumps and make sure they are mixed well.

- **Physical Leaveners.** Steam and air are **physical leaveners**. When moisture from butter, eggs, or other liquid is heated in a batter, it turns to steam. The steam takes up more space than water. Air also expands when it is heated, thereby leavening a batter. Creaming butter or whipping egg whites incorporates air into a batter, and as items such as cakes or soufflés bake in the oven, the pockets of air are trapped while the batter dries enough to take on a relatively firm structure. The trapped pockets give baked goods height as well as a soft, spongy crumb.

Fat Fat is critical to the success of most baked goods. Fats contribute to a baked good's flavor, texture, and freshness.

- **Flavor.** Some fats, such as butter, lard, and nut oils, contribute their own flavor to baked goods. Other fats, such as vegetable oil, margarine, and shortening, are chosen because they lack flavor. Flavorless fats allow the flavors of other ingredients to come to the front. The fat in a batter or dough also encourages browning on crusts and edges; this provides extra flavor for the baked good.

- **Texture.** Fats determine the texture of baked goods. Depending on the type of fat you use in a baked good and the way it is worked into a batter or dough, the resulting texture may range from meltingly smooth to flaky and brittle. The more fat in the recipe, the softer the batter or dough. Baked goods that are made from soft batters or doughs have a tendency to spread out while they bake. The way batter spreads is important, for example, in making cookies of the right size. Fats also produce a texture contrast, as the outer edges become crisper than the middle of the baked good.

- **Freshness.** Fat extends the life of a baked good by holding in moisture, so the baked good stays fresh longer.

FIGURE 17–4

Flaky Pie Crust
The flavor and flakiness of a pie crust depends on the type of fat used.

INTERPRETING ILLUSTRATIONS
Does this pie crust look flaky to you?
Source: Brent Hofacker/Fotolia

Solid Fats

Fat	Description	Flavor and Use
Butter	Made from cream	Adds flavor and flakiness to pastry or biscuits.
Lard	Made from refined pork fat	Has a unique flavor. Makes a very flaky pastry. Substitute it in equal amounts for the shortening or butter in pie dough. Especially good in pastry for savory dishes.
Shortening	Made from vegetable oil that has been processed (hydrogenated) to make it solid at room temperature	Lacks flavor. Used like butter or lard, but adds extraordinary flakiness.
Margarine	Production process is similar to that of shortening	Lacks flavor (unless flavoring is added). Used as a substitute for butter.

Liquid Fats

Fat	Description	Flavor
Neutral oil	Canola, corn, safflower oils	Lacks flavor.
Vegetable oil	Blend of neutral oils	Lacks flavor.
Oil from nuts and seeds	Nut oils (walnut, peanut, sesame, almond) and olive oil	Has a distinctive flavor.

FOCUS ON Nutrition

Hydrogenation

Many shortenings and margarines contain trans fatty acids, by-products of hydrogenation, which turns liquid fats into solid fats. Some people are concerned about the health risks of trans fatty acids and search for products without trans fatty acids.

Chef's Tip

Superfine Sugar

In a pinch, you can make superfine sugar by grinding regular sugar in a food processor or blender.

Fats can be divided into two basic types: solid fats, which are firm at room temperature, and liquid fats, which are liquid at room temperature. The texture of solid fats permits them to be worked into the dough or batter. If you melt a solid fat, such as butter or shortening, you can use it in a recipe as a liquid fat. An oil is a pure liquid fat.

The mixing method used for a batter or dough often dictates the form a fat must take. Some recipes for cakes and breads require a fat in liquid form—oil, melted butter, or melted shortening. Some recipes call for butter or shortening to be room temperature, and other recipes require the solid fat to be firm, even chilled, before you add it to other ingredients.

Sweeteners A variety of sweeteners are used in the bakeshop. Different sweeteners behave differently when they are mixed and baked, so it is important to use the type specified in a recipe.

The following are the most commonly used sweeteners.

- **Granulated Sugar.** Refined from sugarcane or sugar beets, **granulated sugar** is ordinary white sugar.
- **Superfine Sugar.** Granulated sugar that is more finely ground so it dissolves more easily is called **superfine sugar** (also referred to as *baker's sugar* and *castor sugar*).

- **Confectioner's Sugar.** Sugar that has been ground into a fine, white, easily dissolvable powder is called **confectioner's sugar** (also referred to as *powdered sugar*).

- **Brown Sugar.** Thick, dark molasses is combined with white sugar to make flavorful and moist light or dark brown sugar.

- **Molasses.** A by-product of sugar refining, molasses is a thick, sweet, brownish-black syrup that has a distinctive, slightly bitter flavor.

- **Honey.** Ranging in color from very light to almost as dark as molasses, honey is often identified by the flowers from which the bees gathered nectar.

- **Maple Syrup.** The boiled-down sap of maple trees, maple syrup is graded according to color, body, and flavor. Grade B is richer in flavor than grade A and is suggested for baking.

- **Corn Syrup.** Made from cornstarch, **corn syrup** is a thick, sweet syrup that is available light or dark; the dark has added caramel flavor and color.

Brown sugar

Source: C Squared Studios/Getty Images

Sweeteners provide baked goods with more than sweetness and flavor. They also provide texture. In some cases, they help baked products rise. Sweeteners attract moisture, making baked goods softer and longer-lasting than those with little or no sugar. Because of caramelization, sweeteners develop a rich brown color when heated. This adds appealing color, as well as flavor.

Sugar interacts with other ingredients on a chemical level. When combined with liquids, sugar raises the temperature at which the liquid will boil. Adding sugar makes eggs less prone to overcook, even over direct heat.

Adding liquids to hot sugar can cause the sugar to splatter or foam up. To lessen the chances of burning yourself, take the pan away from the heat before you add liquid. Wear oven mitts to protect your hands when you add a liquid, and keep your face partially turned away. Even if the mixture doesn't splatter, the steam can scald you.

Acids Citrus and other fruit juices, wine, vinegar, yogurt, and buttermilk are some of the acids used in baked goods. Acids change the structure of proteins, an effect known as **denaturing**. When an acid is added to a protein, the strands that compose the protein either tighten or loosen, depending on the specific proteins the food contains. By changing the amount and type of acid in a recipe, you can create different textures. For example, adding lemon juice to a cream-cheese tart filling breaks down the texture of the cream cheese so it becomes lighter and spreadable.

Fermenting yeast cells give off alcohol—an acid—to produce a good flavor and texture in breads. The alcohol relaxes the gluten strands so they can stretch while the dough increases in volume and bakes. Acidic ingredients are also added to batters leavened with baking soda to start the leavening action.

Chef's Tip

Salvaging Honey

If honey (and molasses) crystallizes or becomes solid, you can liquefy it by warming it briefly in a microwave.

Lemon juice

Source: Ian O'Leary/ Dorling Kindersley

In baking, coarse salt and sea salt are used primarily as toppings. The larger crystals add both flavor and texture to breads and rolls.

FIGURE 17–5

Blooming Gelatin

Dissolving gelatin in water is referred to as blooming the gelatin.

APPLYING CONCEPTS *Would vegetarians eat a product that was thickened with gelatin?*

Source: Dorling Kindersley

Salt Salt is a powerful flavor enhancer and seasoning, even for sweet dishes. In small amounts as a seasoning, salt does not actually add an identifiable flavor to a dish. Instead, it balances other flavors and makes them more vivid. As you add salt in larger quantities, it begins to contribute its own distinctive flavor.

Salt is important in baking because of the way it reacts with other ingredients. Salt controls the activity of yeast, keeping it from overfermenting and thereby ensuring a good texture. If the yeast is not controlled, the bread may rise rapidly at first, only to deflate.

Thickeners Bakeshops often use thickeners to give body to liquid mixtures. The following are some of the most common thickeners:

- **Cornstarch and Arrowroot.** After being blended with cold liquid, cornstarch and arrowroot are added as thickeners to such dishes as a simmering pudding or pie filling. (You can substitute an equal amount of arrowroot for cornstarch in most recipes.) Both of these thickeners last for up to eight months on the shelf.

- **Gelatin.** A protein processed from the bones, skin, and connective tissue of animals, **gelatin** is used as a gelling agent to thicken and stabilize foams or liquids. Gelatin is widely available in granulated or powdered form, in tins or individual packets (1 package equals 2¼ tsp and weighs ¼ oz). When substituting the less widely available gelatin sheets, use the same weight as powdered gelatin (refer to the package information; different types of gelatin sheets may have different weights). Packages of powdered gelatin desserts contain flavorings and sweeteners in addition to gelatin and cannot be used in place of unflavored powdered gelatin in a recipe. Dissolving gelatin in water is referred to as **blooming** the gelatin.

- **Pectin.** Working like gelatin to thicken a liquid, **pectin** is a substance naturally found in high concentration in certain fruits, especially apples and citrus fruit. Unlike gelatin, pectin does not usually require chilling to reach its full thickening potential, making it well suited for fruit preserves and confections. Also unlike gelatin, pectin requires the presence of both a liquid and the correct amount of acid to thicken properly.

- **Tapioca.** Quick-cooking or instant **tapioca** (tap-ee-OH-kah) is made from the cassava root, a starchy tropical tuber. Because tapioca contributes no flavor of its own and imparts transparent gloss to fruit, it is often used to thicken fruit pie fillings and to make pudding.

- **Other Thickeners.** Molecular gastronomy (see Section 14.2) has introduced a variety of thickeners—such as xanthan gum, gellen gum, and agar agar—that can be used in place of gelatin, pectin, and tapioca. They have different attributes and uses but are commonly used as vegetarian alternatives to gelatin.

READING CHECKPOINT *What are the three types of leaveners?*

Bakeshop Equipment

The quality of the equipment you use for baking has a distinct effect on the quality of your baked goods.

Tools for Measuring Scales, thermometers, measuring cups, and measuring spoons are necessary to make accurate measurements in the bakeshop. You can review the various types of measuring tools and the right way to use them in Section 4.2. In addition to these tools, bakers and pastry chefs also use some other measuring tools.

- Wooden dowels of various thicknesses make rolling dough to the proper thickness easier.

- Rulers or tape measures make rolling dough to the proper thickness and dimensions easier. They are also useful when you need to determine the dimensions of a baking pan or mold.

- Timers keep track of time as you bake. The classic dial-type timer works by counting down the time, but some digital timers give you the option of counting time down or up. Some timers allow you to keep track of the baking times for as many as four different items, which is a helpful feature when you are making multiple batches or a variety of baked goods. Many digital timers have a cord or clip so you can carry them with you if you leave the kitchen.

FIGURE 17–6

Tools for Measuring
Bakeshop measuring tools include a ruler, a timer, and a candy thermometer.

INFERRING *How might a bakeshop's specialty influence the types of measuring tools it uses?*
Source: Culinary Institute of America

CULINARY **MATH**

A Pint's a Pound?

There's a famous expression, "A pint's a pound the world around," which means that 1 pint by volume (that is, 2 cups) of anything weighs 1 pound by weight (that is, 16 ounces). But is this really true?

Lab Activity

Weigh 2 cups of flour and 2 cups of sugar. Is a pint a pound? Now try it with water.

Marble Work Surface
Fudge cooling on a marble work surface.

DRAWING CONCLUSIONS *Why is a marble work surface better than a wooden work surface for this use?*

Source: Myrleen Ferguson Cate/PhotoEdit, Inc.

Work Surfaces Two work surfaces are commonly seen in a bakeshop: wood surfaces are required when you want to keep the item you are making warm, and marble surfaces are used when you want to keep the item from getting warm.

Wood surfaces are excellent for kneading bread dough. A wooden surface has a texture that grabs the dough, making it easier to stretch the dough. It is also relatively warm, compared to marble, metal, or even plastic materials.

Marble, on the other hand, is a cool, smooth stone with no texture. It is useful for making items such as chocolates, fudge, or caramels when you don't need to stretch dough and want to keep the item cool as you work it. Marble is very good for rolling out delicate pastry dough and cookies; you can work them more easily with less chance of their warming up and getting too soft.

Tools for Cutting Bakers and pastry chefs use many of the same cutting tools that are used throughout the kitchen, including a basic set of knives. Serrated knives are especially good for slicing breads and cakes without tearing them. Some tools, however, are more common in the bakeshop:

Source: Gleason Group, Pam Ross

Bench scraper

Pastry blender

- **Bench Scrapers.** With a rectangular steel blade and capped with a wooden or plastic handle, a **bench scraper** (also called a *bench knife*) is usually six inches wide. The steel blade has a dull edge but is thin enough to cut through dough. You can use a bench scraper like a knife to cut soft ingredients such as butter or soft cheese or to lift and turn soft or wet dough as you knead it, as well as to transfer ingredients such as chopped nuts from your work surface to the mixing bowl. Bench scrapers also make short work of cleaning off a work surface.

- **Pastry Blenders.** With a crescent-shaped loop of thin wires attached to a handle, a **pastry blender** is used to mix fat into flour when you make a pastry dough. If you don't have one, substitute two table knives to cut the fat into the flour.

- **Biscuit and Cookie Cutters.** Made of thin metal sheets or molded plastic, biscuit cutters and cookie cutters have edges that are sharp enough to cut through pastry or cookie dough cleanly. Biscuit cutters may have straight or scalloped edges; 3-inch cutters are a good basic size. Cookie cutters are sold in a variety of shapes and sizes; a 3-inch-diameter round cutter is common for rolled and cutout cookies.

FIGURE 17–8
Pastry Blender
A pastry blender is a specialized hand tool for mixing fat into flour.
DRAWING CONCLUSIONS *How does a pastry blender help a chef avoid overmixing?*
Source: Dave Murray, Dorling Kindersley

Bread-Baking Equipment Bakers use special bread-baking equipment, such as the following:

- **Baking Stones.** Unglazed ceramic pieces used to line an oven rack are called **baking stones**. These stones or tiles help develop a crisp crust on breads and pizza by holding and transferring the oven's heat evenly. The stones need to pre-heat along with the oven for best results.

- **Peels.** A large flat wooden or metal paddle used to slide bread onto baking stones and to retrieve them when they are done is called a **peel**. If you don't have a peel, you can use a cookie sheet that has no sides.

FIGURE 17–9
Peel
The peel is also used to slide pizzas into and out of ovens.
INFERRING *How much practice do you think it would take to use a peel effectively?*
Source: David Levinson/Fotolia

Appliances Mixers make baking tasks easier and more efficient. As you may recall from Section 3.3, bakeshops tend to use free-standing mixers, which are capable of mixing and kneading heavy yeast dough. Mixers, food processors, blenders, and other large equipment share space in the bakeshop with other specialized equipment such as the following:

- **Proofers.** A **proofer** is a special box that holds dough as it rises. Most models have thermostats to control heat and are able to generate steam.

- **Dough Sheeters.** A **dough sheeter** rolls large batches of dough into sheets. Some dough sheeters also roll dough into loaves and cut out doughnuts or croissants.

- **Dough Dividers.** A **dough divider** (also called a *dough press*) cuts a quantity of dough into equal pieces so they can be shaped into rolls.

- **Retarder.** To control fermentation by slowing it down, bakers use a refrigerated cabinet called a **retarder**.

··**FOCUS ON**
·• **Safety**

First Aid for Bakers
Burns are the most common baking hazard. If you are burned, immediately flush the affected area with cool water. Keep a cool compress on the area until it feels more comfortable, and then apply a bandage.

Baking Pans and Molds The surface of a pan has an effect on how items bake. Darker pans produce baked goods with a deep crust color, and those with shiny or light surfaces tend to produce goods with a lighter color. Lining pans properly makes it easier for you to get baked goods out without sticking or tearing.

Bakers use parchment paper to line pans. **Parchment paper** is a grease-resistant, nonstick, heatproof paper. The paper is coated with silicone on one side, allowing baked goods to spread properly and release from the paper easily. It comes in rolls, or precut for use as pan liners.

Bakers also use a special liner made of silicone, sometimes known as a **SilPad**, that can be used over and over again. Silicone can withstand temperatures up to 600°F. Flexible silicone mats, sold in several sizes, give baking pans a nonstick surface and provide a heat-resistant surface for candy making. Baking pans and molds made of the same material are available in a variety of sizes.

The following are some more common baking pans and molds:

Loaf pan
Source: Dave King/Dorling Kindersley

- **Loaf Pans.** Rectangular pans used for simple cakes and quick breads are called **loaf pans**. Mini loaf pans are available for making small loaves. You can buy loaf pans in metal, glass, and ceramic, with or without a nonstick coating.

- **Pie Pans.** Pie pans have sloped sides and are made from aluminum, glass, or earthenware. The sides of the pan may be up to 3 inches tall. The deeper the pan, the more filling you will need. One of the most common sizes is a 9-inch pie pan with sides that are $1\frac{1}{2}$ inches tall. If you prefer to use glass pie pans, reduce the oven temperature by about 25°F and the baking time by 5 to 10 minutes. Glass conducts heat efficiently, so the edges and bottom of your pie may brown too rapidly if you use the recipe's temperature and baking time.

Tart pan
Source: Philip Watkins/Dorling Kindersley

- **Tart Pans.** Made of tinned steel or ceramic, **tart pans** have short, often scalloped sides and usually have a removable bottom. They may be round, square, or rectangular. Some pans have a nonstick coating. Tartlet pans are simply small tart pans, sized to make individual pastries.

- **Cake Pans.** Cake pans are manufactured of tinned steel, aluminum, glass, or silicone. They may have a nonstick coating. Common cake pans range in size from 6 inches to 18 inches.

- **Springform Pans.** Consisting of a hinged ring that clamps around a removable base, **springform pans** are used for baking delicate cakes that might otherwise be difficult to unmold, such as a cheese cake.

Tube pan
Source: Martin Cameron/Dorling Kindersley

- **Tube Pans.** With a center tube of metal that conducts heat through the center of the batter, **tube pans** bake heavy batters evenly, without overbrowning the outside of the cake. A tube pan (also called

FIGURE 17–10

Springform Pan
Removing the frame of a springform pan from a cake.

PREDICTING *What advantages would a springform pan offer?*

Source: Dave King/Dorling Kindersley

an *angel food cake pan* or a *Bundt pan*) works well for batters that need to bake quickly. Tube pans are typically made of thin metal, with or without a nonstick coating. They come in a range of sizes, and the sides may be fluted, molded, or straight.

- **Soufflé Dishes and Custard Cups.** Soufflé dishes, custard cups, and pudding molds are ovenproof ceramic, glass, or earthenware dishes used to bake a variety of dishes. Soufflé dishes have straight, smooth sides that are typically as high as the dish is wide and come in a range of sizes, from 2 ounces to 2 quarts. Custard cups have straight or sloped sides and come in a variety of sizes. Petits pots are custard cups that may have lids. Gratin dishes may be oval or round and have relatively short sides. Pudding molds may have smooth or patterned sides for a special appearance when the pudding is unmolded.

Rolling pin

Source: C Squared Studios/Getty Image

Tools for Pastry Bakers use special tools for working with pastry, such as the following:

- **Rolling Pins.** Rolling pins stretch dough into thin sheets. Ball-bearing rolling pins have a steel rod extending through the pin and fixed to the handles. Ball bearings on each end of the rod make it easy to roll the pin. Rolling pins may be made of wood, marble, metal, or a synthetic material. Straight (or French) rolling pins are just round rods that are often 16 inches long. They have no handles. Tapered rolling pins are good for rolling dough into circles. Marble rolling pins stay cool, which is helpful to a pie baker or pastry maker. Specialty rolling pins may have grooves or patterns to imprint in the dough as you roll.

Chef's Tip

Rolling Pin Care

Wooden rolling pins should never be soaked in water because they will absorb moisture and could warp. Soap should never be used on them. Wipe wooden rolling pins well with a moist towel and air-dry thoroughly.

Pastry brush

Pastry wheel

FIGURE 17–11

Pastry Bag

Applying whipping cream using a pastry bag.

RELATING CONCEPTS *As a customer, would you rather have whipped cream applied this way or spread on the pie with a palette knife?*

- **Pastry Brushes.** Used to apply egg wash and to butter pans and muffin tins, a **pastry brush** is made of soft, flexible nylon, silicone, or unbleached hog bristles. Unlike brushes used for paint, pastry brushes have no reservoir in the handle, so they are easy to clean completely after each use. Soak the brush briefly if dried food needs to be loosened, but avoid prolonged soaking. Let the brush air-dry as soon as it is clean. A 1- to 1½-inch wide brush is suitable for most uses. Brushes used for pastry work should be kept separate from those used to apply barbecue sauces, marinades, and other savory ingredients.

- **Pastry Wheels.** A round blade mounted on a handle is called a **pastry wheel.** As you roll the blade over pastry dough, it makes a single, clean cut. The blade may be straight or scalloped to make a decorative edge. You can also use a sharp paring knife or scissors to cut pastry.

- **Pastry Bags and Tips.** A **pastry bag** is a cone-shaped bag with two open ends. On the smaller, pointed end, you apply a decorative tip. Into the larger opening you add dough, fillings, or whipped cream. You squeeze the bag to force the contents through the tip, allowing you to add fillings to pastries, make delicate cookies, and apply decorative finishes to cakes and pastries. Tips that are round or star-shaped are the most versatile, but you can buy specialty tips to make leaves, flowers, and other shapes. Pastry bags are typically made of nylon or plastic. Some bags are designed for only a single use. If your bag is reusable, wash it well in warm soapy water inside and out, rinse it thoroughly, and air-dry completely before storing.

- **Metal Spatulas and Palette Knives.** The bakeshop often uses metal spatulas and palette knives with long metal blades and blunt edges. The handle may be offset (angled) to make it easier to lift baked goods from the pan. Palette knives are long and narrow, with a rounded, blunt end. They are good for spreading fillings, icings, and glazes; decorating cakes and pastries; and spreading batter or dough into an even layer before baking. Some palette knives have a serrated edge for slicing cakes into layers.

- **Cake Combs.** Used to create a decorative edge on iced cakes or to give texture to a chocolate coating, a **cake comb** is a triangular or rectangular piece of metal or plastic with serrated edges. The teeth vary in their size and shape, giving you a choice of three or four different effects.

- **Turntables.** Although not essential, a **turntable** makes it easier to decorate cakes. You can easily turn the cake with one hand while the other is free to use the palette knife or cake comb.

READING CHECKPOINT *What are at least five of the most common types of baking pans and molds found in the bakeshop?*

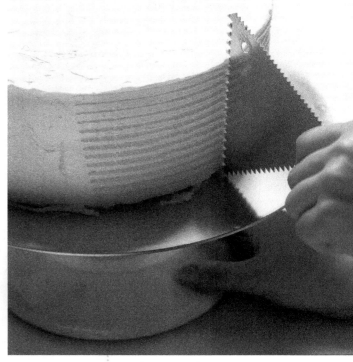

FIGURE 17–12
Cake on a Turntable
Turning the cake with one hand while using a cake comb to create a pattern with the other hand.
APPLYING CONCEPTS *Why is it usually more efficient to use a turntable than to move around the cake yourself?*
Source: Richard Embery/Pearson Education/ PH College

Formulas

Bakers and pastry chefs often call their recipes **formulas**. This distinction helps point out the importance of accuracy in all aspects of baking, from measuring ingredients to having them at the right temperature. For success, ingredients must be prepared correctly and combined in the right order, using the right technique.

Bakers' Percentages Baking formulas often include percentages as a type of measurement for ingredients. Any recipe that has been written in percentages shows the baker how each ingredient compares to the total amount of flour. In a formula written in percentages, the flour called for in the formula is considered to be 100 percent.

If your formula calls for 2 pounds of flour and 1 pound of sugar, the flour is 100 percent and the sugar is 50 percent. If the formula calls for 2 pounds of flour and 3 pounds of sugar, the flour is still 100 percent, but now the sugar is 150 percent. Knowing how the ingredients relate to each other as a percentage makes it easy for bakers to accurately increase or decrease recipes.

Dry Ingredients Flour, granulated or powdered sugar, baking soda, baking powder, cocoa powder, and similar powdery ingredients are generally referred to as dry ingredients. These ingredients may need to be sifted together, sometimes two or three times, to remove any clumps and to incorporate some air. Sifting also distributes ingredients such as salt and chemical leaveners evenly throughout the baked item.

Wet Ingredients Milk, water, eggs, oil, melted butter, honey, and vanilla extract are all examples of wet ingredients. Be sure you check the formula carefully. Sometimes liquid ingredients are combined and then added to dry ingredients all at once. At other times, they are added in sequence. You may also be asked to add wet ingredients in parts, adding some of the wet ingredients, then some of the dry ingredients, and then some more of the wet ingredients, and so on.

FIGURE 17–13

Sifting Dry Ingredients
Some recipes call for dry
ingredients to be sifted.
DRAWING CONCLUSIONS *Why
might it be necessary to sift dry
ingredients more than once?*
Source: Richard Embery/Pearson Education/
PH College

 **READING
CHECKPOINT** *What is a baking formula?*

17.1 ASSESSMENT

Reviewing Concepts

1. What are the three types of leaveners?

2. What are five of the most common types of baking pans and molds found in the bakeshop?

3. What is a baking formula?

Critical Thinking

4. Comparing/Contrasting What is the difference between a pie pan and a tart pan?

5. Inferring In a bakeshop, when would you want to use a fat that lacked flavor?

6. Classifying If you were working with chocolates, fudge, or caramel, which type of work surface would you use?

Test Kitchen

Divide into four teams. Each team will locate a baking recipe that is not written as a baking formula. Every team will share a copy of its baking recipe with the other three teams (so each team will have the same four recipes). Each team will then convert the recipes to baking formulas. Compare the results.

SCIENCE
Maple Sugar

Research the history and process of making maple sugar. Discuss how the various grades are made.

READING PREVIEW

Key Concepts

- Identifying basic types of yeast dough
- Understanding the straight dough-mixing method
- Modifying the straight dough-mixing method

Vocabulary

- biga
- brioche
- challah
- chlorine dioxide
- dough starter
- enriched dough
- fermentation
- gluten window test
- hard dough
- hot cross bun
- kuchen
- kugelhopf
- laminated yeast dough
- lean dough
- medium dough
- modified straight dough-mixing method
- pan de muertos
- pâte fermentée
- pickup
- poolish
- pre-ferment
- rolled-in yeast dough
- scaling
- soft dough
- sourdough
- sponge
- stollen
- straight dough-mixing method
- sweet rich dough
- yeast hydration

Basic Types of Yeast Dough

Yeast dough is the blank canvas of baking. You can make it plain or add different ingredients to create a variety of products such as bread and cakes. Master the art of basic yeast dough techniques and the sky's the limit.

Lean Dough **Lean dough** (also called **hard dough**) is the most basic type of yeast dough. Only the bare essentials—flour, yeast, salt, and water—are used to make it. Spices, herbs, dried nuts, and fruit may be added, but very little (if any) sugar and fat is included.

Pizza crust, hard rolls, Italian-style bread, and the slender French baguette, with its chewy texture and hard crust, are classic examples of products made with lean dough. Whole-wheat, rye, pumpernickel, and sourdough breads are also variations of lean dough. The coarse flour used in these breads makes for a denser texture.

Lean dough can be difficult to handle because little or no fat is used. Commercial bakeries sometimes use chemical dough conditioners such as **chlorine dioxide** (klor-EEN die-OX-ide) to produce a more stable dough, increase loaf volume, and prevent the loss of leavening.

A pizza crust is made from a lean dough that is stretched or rolled until it is thin. There are several options for shaping

Source: Culinary Institute of America

FIGURE 17–14
Lean Dough
French baguettes, pumpernickel, and rolls.

CLASSIFYING *What percentage of the yeast bread and pastry you eat is made from lean dough?*

Source: © 1506965/Fotolia

Chef's Tip

Sweet Nothing

Added fat and sugar make enriched dough moist and soft. Be very sparing with extra flour on the work surface or in shaping the dough because too much flour can toughen the finished product.

the dough once it is properly fermented. You may simply stretch it out by pulling on the edges of the dough. Or you can use a rolling pin to stretch it out. The most entertaining approach calls for the dough to be draped over your fist and repeatedly spun off your fists and into the air. Each time you toss and catch the dough, it stretches a bit more.

Soft Dough The soft slices of Pullman bread, which is typically used for sandwiches, are made with **soft dough** (also called **medium dough**). It is lean dough with sugar and fat added. The amounts of fat and sugar vary from 6 percent to 9 percent.

As you know from Section 11.1, Pullman slices get their square shape from the covered loaf pans in which the loaves are baked. You can also use soft dough to make soft rolls that you can shape into knots or cloverleaf balls. Fat and sugar help make soft dough tender when it's baked and give it a soft crust.

Enriched Dough When lean dough is enriched with butter, oil, sugar, eggs, or milk products, it becomes **enriched dough** (also called **sweet rich dough**). Enriched dough has fat and sugar amounts up to 25 percent, making the dough sweet and rich. The addition of fat and other ingredients changes the texture of the dough, making it softer and a bit more difficult to handle. It also slows down the yeast activity and requires more time for the dough to ferment.

Eggs and butter not only tenderize, but they also create a soft crust and a golden color. The percentage of eggs is important because too many eggs will result in heavy dough. The finished product should have a cakelike texture.

Enriched dough is used around the world to create some of the best-loved yeast breads, cakes, and rolls, including the following:

- **Cinnamon Buns.** Sugar and cinnamon are spread on sweet dough that is rolled and then sliced before baking to make cinnamon buns. Raisins are sometimes added to the dough. Drizzled with icing and served warm, these comforting confections have become an American standard.

- **Hot Cross Buns.** A signature cross made of icing tops a **hot cross bun**. These sweet yeast buns originated in England and were traditionally served on Good Friday. They are popular for Easter breakfast, too.

- **Braided Easter Egg Bread.** Sweet bread is braided around colored Easter eggs for this holiday bread.

- **Pan de Muertos.** A Mexican holiday bread, **pan de muertos** (PAHN de MOO-er-tohs, bread of the dead) is a sweet bread, flavored with orange zest, orange juice, and anise seeds, that is traditionally baked around the Day of the Dead. The bread is often decorated with bone-shaped pieces of dough.

FIGURE 17–15
Uses of Enriched Dough
All of these baked goods were made using enriched dough.
APPLYING CONCEPTS *How would you use these compared to breads made from lean dough?*
Source: Jag_cz/Fotolia

- **Brioche.** A rich French bread, **brioche** (BREE-ohsh) often has a knotted top and is made in individual molds with a fluted base. It can also be made into round loaves or rolls. Brioche dough is used as a crust to wrap cheese, sausage, and other food.

- **Challah.** A sweet and airy bread made with lots of eggs, **challah** (HAL-la) is a Jewish bread that is usually braided. Traditionally served on the Sabbath and holidays, this bread is a treat on any occasion.

- **Stollen.** The traditional Christmas bread of Germany, **stollen** (STOH-len) is a sweet, loaf-shaped yeast bread that is filled with dried fruit and topped with icing and cherries.

- **Kuchen.** Another German original, the popular **kuchen** (KOO-ken), a sweet, yeast-raised cake filled with fruit or cheese, has spread throughout Europe and the United States. Kuchen can be served for breakfast, teatime, or dessert.

- **Kugelhopf.** A light yeast cake filled with candied fruit, nuts, and raisins, **kugelhopf** (KOO-guhl-hof) is usually baked in a fluted ring mold. A tradition of Austria, kugelhopf is also associated with Poland, Alsace, and Germany.

Brioche
Source: Neil Mersh/Dorling Kindersley

 **READING CHECKPOINT** *What are the basic types of yeast dough?*

Straight Dough-Mixing Method

The simplest and most common way of mixing yeast dough is called the **straight dough-mixing method**. In this method, you mix all the ingredients for the dough together at the same time. When the ingredients are mixed, either by hand or in a mixer, the yeast starts to develop immediately. Although the process is not difficult, you must pay attention to the following details.

Scaling Ingredients The most accurate way to measure ingredients is to weigh them. When liquids and solids are weighed, it is called **scaling**. (Some recipes may instruct you to measure liquids, such as milk and water, with a volume measure.)

Precise measurement is important, because ingredients interact together. Inaccurate measurements in baking alter the balance of ingredients and affect the finished product. For example, the amount of yeast in a recipe is the exact amount needed to raise the dough. Adding too much egg, flour, or other ingredients to the dough interferes with the yeast development. Baker's formulas—in which basic ingredients are listed as percentages, or parts, based on the weight of the flour—are often used for yeast dough.

CULINARY SCIENCE

The 240 Factor

The temperature of the air can warm an icy beverage. The friction created by rubbing your knee on a rug can feel like a burn. In the same way, the temperature of the air around dough, as well as friction created by mixing it, affects the dough's temperature.

The temperature of ingredients used to make dough has a direct impact on the temperature of the dough. For example, if you drop a handful of room-temperature raspberries into a chilled glass of lemonade, they will warm the lemonade a bit. Likewise, if you use cold eggs or warm flour, it will affect the desired dough temperature (or DDT, for short). The DDT for yeast dough is typically around 80°F.

The faster you mix dough, the greater the friction created by the beaters and the warmer it makes the dough. It is difficult to control the heat generated by beating. It is also difficult to control the room temperature and the temperature of some of the ingredients. But you *can* control the temperature of the water you use.

There is a simple, three-step scientific formula, sometimes called *the 240 factor*, for producing the DDT of a yeast dough, based exclusively on

controlling the temperature of the water used in the dough:

1. Multiply the desired dough temperature by 3. (Remember, the DDT = 80°F.)

$$80 \times 3 = 240$$

2. Then, add together the current temperature of the flour, the room, and friction (with average friction = 30°F).

Flour = 50°F, room = 68°F, and friction = 30°F
Total = 148°F

3. Subtract the total from 240. The answer is the ideal water temperature.

$$240 - 148 = 92$$

The ideal water temperature is 92°F.

Computation

Based on your kitchen's temperature and the temperature of flour in your kitchen, calculate the temperature of the water you should use in making a bread dough.

Straight Dough-Mixing Method

1. **Scaling the ingredients.** The ingredients are precisely weighed.

Source: Culinary Institute of America

2. **Hydrating the yeast.** The yeast is activated when combined with water.

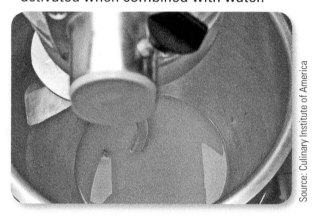

Source: Culinary Institute of America

3. **Pickup stage.** All other ingredients are added at once with the mixer on a slow speed.

Source: Culinary Institute of America

4. **Gluten development and kneading.** Increase the mixer speed to medium until the dough begins to catch on the dough hook. Properly kneaded dough is satiny and

forms a ball in the mixing bowl. If a small piece is stretched thin, it holds together without breaking (gluten window test).

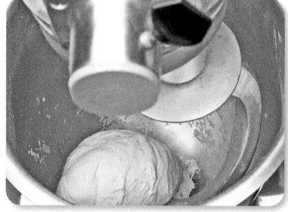

Source: Culinary Institute of America

5. **Bulk fermentation.** The dough will double or triple in size as the yeast ferments.

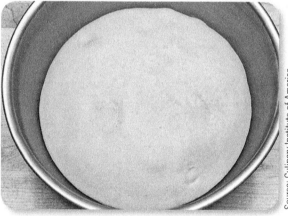

Source: Culinary Institute of America

6. **Folding the dough.** Folding and pushing down the dough releases its carbon dioxide.

Source: Culinary Institute of America

Yeast Hydration Yeast is an organic leavener, which means it is alive but resting or dormant until it is moistened. The soaking process that activates yeast is called **yeast hydration**. When mixed with a liquid, the cells start to work.

Pickup The first stage of mixing ingredients is called **pickup**. Set the mixer at a low speed to combine the yeast and water. Oil, if it is being used, is added next, followed by the dry ingredients. Shortening, if it is used, goes in last. After everything is combined, increase the mixer speed to medium.

Gluten Development Gluten is one of the proteins in flour. Kneading dough causes a web of gluten strands to stretch and expand. The network of elastic strands that form during gluten development is important because it enables dough to hold in the gas bubbles that are formed by the yeast without breaking through the dough. The gas bubbles cause the dough to rise.

Dough that has been properly kneaded is shiny and elastic. To test the strength of the gluten and be sure it is properly developed, you can pinch off a piece of the dough and pull it. It should be stretchy without tearing, and when you hold it up to the light, it should be thin enough for some light to come through. This is called the **gluten window test**.

Bulk Fermentation The organisms in hydrated yeast produce carbon dioxide and alcohol as a by-product when they have moisture and a food source and are at the right temperature. This is called **fermentation** and it makes the dough rise until double or triple in size. Bread made from underfermented dough that hasn't risen enough will be flat, while bread made from overfermented dough will have a yeasty, sour taste.

The surface of the dough should be oiled so it won't dry out during fermentation. The container should also be oiled so the dough won't stick to the sides. Cover the dough with plastic wrap or a clean cloth and leave it to rise in a warm area until the rising is completed.

Folding Dough After the rising is complete, the dough is folded over and turned onto a floured work surface. The dough is continuously folded over on itself to get rid of any more gases. Each piece is gently pushed down a few times to release the carbon dioxide that formed during fermentation. This process helps distribute the yeast evenly. In addition, folding helps create a uniform overall temperature by folding the cooler, outside dough into the warmer center.

The dough is then scaled into pieces for size consistency and baked.

FIGURE 17–16

Bulk Fermentation
The dough doubles or triples in size during bulk fermentation.
APPLYING CONCEPTS *Would the dough rise as much if the temperature were lower?*
Source: Culinary Institute of America

READING CHECKPOINT *Describe the straight mixing method for yeast dough.*

Pizza Dough

1. **Hydrate** the yeast in water.

2. **Add the flour and salt and mix** at a low speed until the dough is evenly moistened. (This is the pickup stage.)

3. **Mix and knead the dough** by hand on a floured surface or on medium speed in a mixer until the dough is very smooth and springy to the touch.

4. **Make a gluten window** to test the dough.

5. **Transfer the dough to an oiled bowl,** oil the surface lightly, and cover.

6. **Bulk-ferment the dough** until it doubles in size and the dough retains an imprint when pressed with a gloved fingertip.

7. **Fold the dough over on itself in several places.** The dough is ready to shape into pizza crust at this point.

Recipe Card

119. Pizza Dough

Modifying the Basic Method

Rather than adding all the ingredients at once, the **modified straight dough-mixing method** adds ingredients in steps. This method provides better distribution for fat and sugar and is particularly useful for enriched dough.

Enriched Yeast Dough Enriched yeast dough may call for modifications to the basic straight dough-mixing method. One simple change is to use milk in place of the water used in a lean dough. Once the dough is mixed, it may be softer and stickier than regular lean dough.

Very rich dough may need to be kept cool, even during bulk fermentation, so the extra butter stays in the dough rather than melting and separating out of the dough. This requires that ingredients are mixed in a specific order:

1. Hydrate the yeast and add the flour.

2. Add liquid ingredients (milk, cream, eggs, oils, or melted butter) and sweeteners (honey, sugar, or maple syrup).

3. Mix the dough until all the flour is evenly moistened.

4. Add additional butter (room temperature or softened) gradually (if the formula calls for it) until evenly blended.

5. Continue to mix and knead the dough until it is properly developed.

Sponge Mixing Method The sponge method combines one-third to one-half of the formula's total liquid with all the yeast and enough flour to make a very loose dough. This dough is called a **sponge**. A sponge is usually mixed in the same bowl you will use to prepare the entire batch of dough. When the sponge has doubled in size, the remaining ingredients are added to the sponge and mixed to make a dough. Breads made with a sponge have a richer, deeper flavor and an improved texture.

FIGURE 17–17

Sponge

An overhead view of a developed sponge in the mixing bowl.

ANALYZING INFORMATION *How can you tell when sponge dough is developed?*

Source: Culinary Institute of America

Sourdough bread

Source: emf_images/Fotolia

Danish

Source: Miro/Fotolia

Pre-Ferments A pre-ferment, also called a **dough starter**, is similar to a sponge. Some or all the yeast is mixed with water and some flour to create the pre-ferment. This is allowed to ferment for a specific time and is then added to the dough before its final mixing. The pre-ferment increases the fermentation time, which increases the strength of the gluten in the dough. This adds depth and complexity to the flavor while also extending the shelf life of the bread.

If you want to make a pre-ferment for a dough that does not specify one in the formula, you need to subtract the amount of flour, water, and yeast in the pre-ferment from the total flour, water, and yeast in the formula.

There are several types of pre-ferments. Each has a different flavor and is used for different breads. The following are some common examples:

- **Poolish.** Combining equal parts of flour and water (by weight) with some yeast, a **poolish** (poo-LEESH) is then allowed to ferment. The actual amount of yeast varies, depending on how long the poolish will be allowed to ferment. Use less yeast for a long, slow fermentation. A poolish is fermented at room temperature until it doubles in volume and then begins to get smaller (anywhere from 3 to 15 hours). The poolish is added to the rest of the ingredients during mixing.

- **Biga.** The process for making a **biga** (BEE-gah), an Italian pre-ferment, is similar to that for making a poolish, but a biga is stiffer because it contains less water. A biga usually calls for about one-third to one-half the total amount of yeast called for in the formula. Bigas, like poolish, are allowed to ferment from 3 to 15 hours at room temperature. Before you can add the biga to the rest of the dough, however, you need to loosen it by adding the additional water required by the formula.

- **Sourdough.** With a tangy, slightly sour flavor, **sourdough** pre-ferment is made from wild yeast. The difference between sourdough and most other pre-ferments is that sourdough starter can be kept alive a long time, sometimes hundreds of years.

- **Pâte Fermentée.** A French term that literally means "old dough," **pâte fermentée** (PAHT fer-mahn-TAY) is a piece of dough saved from one batch and added to a new batch along with the flour, yeast, and liquid. Wrap the pâte fermentée airtight and you can save it in the refrigerator for 48 hours or in the freezer up to 3 months.

Rolled-In Dough Fat can be used to add flavor to any type of yeast dough. When fat is rolled in or folded into dough (as opposed to being mixed into the dough itself), it adds flakiness. Buttery yeast pastries, such as the classic Danish and croissants, get their feathery flakiness from folding the dough into many thin layers with butter layers in between. The process of rolling in and folding in fat creates layers of dough called **rolled-in yeast dough**. It is also known as **laminated yeast dough** because it is made up of alternating layers of dough and fat (and under a microscope would look like plywood, with all its layers).

The fat layers produce steam in the oven, creating lightness by puffing up the thin dough layers. The dough is rolled into a rectangle, layered with chilled butter, and folded into thirds, like a letter. The process is then repeated. The added handling of rolling and folding means that you should not knead the dough as much as regular yeast dough. Overhandling a laminated yeast dough can ruin the finished product, making it tough and chewy.

The final rolled-in dough is then refrigerated to chill the fat again. This dough keeps well in the refrigerator for several days.

Yeast-Bread Garnishes Yeast-bread garnishes are ingredients that stay separate from the dough's structure while maintaining a distinctive flavor. Some garnishes are mixed into the dough before the dough rises. For example, black olives and cranberries are added to bread dough before it rises. Blueberries and chocolate chips are garnishes added to pastries before the dough rises. Other garnishes are added after the dough has risen, as with filled croissants. The dough is folded or rolled around the garnish.

Garnishes can add crunch and flavor to dough, but they can also add extra weight. More yeast may be required, depending on the quantity of filling that will be added. It is important to consult your recipe for the precise ratio of garnish to the flour in the recipe.

READING CHECKPOINT *What is a pre-ferment?*

Recipe Card
120. Focaccia

Chef's Tip

Sweet Something

When fruit is added to yeast dough, it releases some sugar into the dough. This could slow the bread's rise. The finer the fruit is chopped, the more likely it is to release sugar, altering the dough's sugar ratio.

17.2 ASSESSMENT

Reviewing Concepts

1. What are the basic types of yeast dough?
2. What are the basic steps in the straight dough-mixing method?
3. What is a pre-ferment?

Critical Thinking

4. **Comparing/Contrasting** What do both soft dough and enriched dough have that lean dough doesn't?
5. **Predicting** Why is the final product of enriched dough often yellow, whereas lean dough is never yellow?
6. **Comparing/Contrasting** What is the difference between the modified straight dough-mixing method and the basic straight dough-mixing method?

Test Kitchen

Divide into two teams. One team will prepare a bread recipe, using active dry yeast. The other team will prepare the same recipe, using instant yeast. All other ingredients should be identical and the measured amounts should be identical. Compare the results.

CULINARY MATH

Substituting Yeast

To substitute instant yeast for active dry yeast, use ⅔ the weight of the active dry yeast for the instant yeast. For example, 1 teaspoon of active dry yeast = ⅔ teaspoon of instant yeast. If a recipe calls for 3 teaspoons of active dry yeast, how much instant yeast would you substitute for it?

Breads, Rolls, and Pastries

Key Concepts

- Dividing and preshaping the dough
- Shaping breads, rolls, and pastries
- Baking breads, rolls, and pastries
- Evaluating the quality of yeast breads, rolls, and pastries

Vocabulary

- baguette
- bench boxes
- bench proofing
- boule
- free-form loaf
- injera
- oven spring
- pan loaf
- pan proofing
- scoring

Dividing and Preshaping Dough

For large-scale baking, the dough must be divided into equal parts for uniform sizes. Once the dough is divided, it is preshaped and allowed to relax.

Cutting and Scaling Dividing dough into pieces that are of uniform size is important for quality control. Scale each piece, using the bench scraper to add pieces of dough or remove excess to get the exact weight. The dough is fermenting while you work, so the sooner you finish, the better. The divided pieces are smaller and will ferment more quickly than the undivided dough.

It's always easier to use the right tool for a job. Bakers use a bench scraper to divide dough for superior results. Pulling or tearing the dough weakens the gluten.

Preshaping After the dough is cut and scaled, you preshape the divided dough on a lightly floured surface by covering it with your hands and gently shaping it into tight rounds. The purpose of preshaping is to get the dough close to the final shape. You should also use the bench scraper to move and lift the round balls of dough for minimal handling.

Bench Proofing After the dough has been rounded, cover the rounds and let the dough rest until you can stretch it carefully without tearing—usually about 20 minutes. This is called **bench proofing**, a brief resting period that allows the gluten to relax and makes the dough easier to shape.

Source: Ian O'Leary/Dorling Kindersley

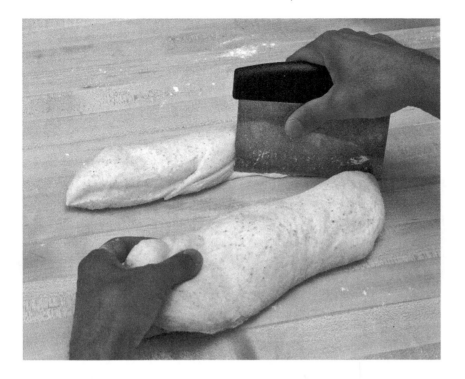

FIGURE 17–18

Cutting Dough
Use a bench scraper to cut dough.

PREDICTING *How might the shape of your initial cut be affected by the type of product you are going to make?*

Source: Culinary Institute of America

Bench proofing can be done directly on the workbench or in bowls covered with cloth or plastic wrap or in covered containers called **bench boxes**. During bench proofing, the dough forms a skin that holds in the carbon dioxide.

READING CHECKPOINT *What is the purpose of bench proofing?*

FIGURE 17–19

Bench Proofing
Dough can be proofed in a linen-lined mold or in a basket.

INFERRING *Why is it important that the skin on dough holds in carbon dioxide?*

Source: Ian O'Leary/Dorling Kindersley

Preshaping Dough into Rounds

1. **Bring the edges of the dough together in the middle.**

2. **Turn over.** Tuck any loose dough into the bottom.

3. **Cover with your hands** and round out the edges.

4. **Press edges toward the middle** to tighten the ball.

Source: Culinary Institute of America

Shaping Breads, Rolls, and Pastries

The shapes of bread, rolls, and pastries are as distinctive as a person's signature. The shape identifies what they are, from the oval of a rye bread to the long and narrow loaf of French bread. Bread can be shaped by the pan it is baked in, such as a loaf pan, or by hand, as with pizza. Another important aspect is that specific shapes complement specific dough qualities. For example, braiding challah dough keeps the egg-rich dough from spreading out as the bread bakes. Some of the shapes look complicated, but once you learn the basic techniques, you'll enjoy perfecting them.

Begin shaping with little or no flour on the work surface. You want the dough to stay in place, and too much flour will make it slip around. Try to work without interruptions, because the fermentation process is still going on. If you are working with several pieces of pre-shaped dough, complete the shaping technique in the same order that you completed the pre-shaping step.

Flatbread

Source: Dave King/Dorling Kindersley

Flatbreads Many cultures throughout the world have a variation of flatbread in their cuisine. The shape of flatbread lends itself to being a carrier for other food, much as we use sliced bread to make sandwiches. For example, in some African countries, such as Ethiopia, a flatbread called **injera** (in-JAY-rah) is traditionally used, instead of utensils, to pick up food and as part of the meal.

Flatbreads can be crisp, soft, puffy, or flat as a cracker. Some examples of flatbreads are pita and focaccia. Another example is pizza. Pizza is an Italian word for "pie." When you think about it, a pizza is just a flatbread covered with tomato sauce, mozzarella cheese, or other ingredients. A pizza can be round or rectangular, thick or thin, crispy or chewy. Too much topping on a pizza weighs down the crust, interfering with its ability to bake properly.

The Middle East

The Middle East is a region including western Asia and northern Africa. It is composed of, among other countries, Iran, Iraq, Israel, Saudi Arabia, Egypt, Syria, Turkey, and Yemen. It was here that wheat was first cultivated and that humans first learned about fermentation and leavening bread. Today bread is very important to Middle Eastern cuisine.

The typical bread used in the Middle East is *pita bread*. It's a slightly leavened round or oblong flatbread. Pitas are typically baked at high temperatures, which causes the dough to puff up. When the pitas are removed from the oven, they deflate but still leave a pocket inside the bread. When the bread is cut, the pocket is revealed and can be stuffed.

In Palestinian and Israeli cuisine, almost everything is eaten in the pocket of a pita. In Turkey, pita bread is called *pide* and does not have a pocket. Instead, meat or other foods are placed on top of the pide. In other areas of the Middle East, where people take their food from a common plate in the center, pitas are used to scoop up food. In some cultures only the right hand is used for scooping food with a pita because the left hand is reserved for bodily hygiene and is therefore considered unclean.

One of the items most commonly found in or on a pita is *kebob*. In the United States, when we think of kebob, we think of *shish kebob*, meat cooked on skewers. In Middle Eastern cuisine, kebob refers to grilled, roasted, or stewed, or even ground, meat—traditionally lamb—served on plates, in bowls, or with pita. There are many types of kebobs. *Döner kebob* (also called *shawarma*) is lamb (or chicken or beef) that is sliced, assembled on a large vertical rotating spit, and roasted. Strips are then cut off and, typically, served with salad in a pita bread. A *kebob koobideh* is an Iranian kebob of minced lamb or beef mixed with spices and onions and grilled like a hamburger.

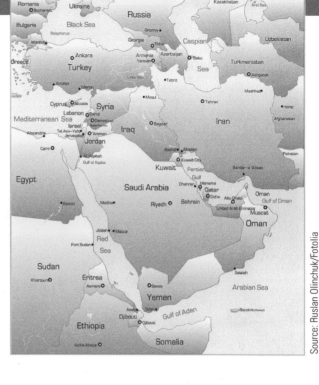

Source: Ruslan Olinchuk/Fotolia

Chickpeas play an important role in Middle Eastern cuisine. *Hummus*, made from cooked, mashed chickpeas mixed with *tahini* (a paste of ground sesame seeds), lemon juice, garlic, and olive oil, is typically scooped up with pita bread. *Falafel*, a deep-fried ball or patty of ground chickpeas. is placed in a pita bread along with a salad and a tahini-based sauce.

Herbs and spices common to Middle Eastern cuisine include parsley, mint, cumin, turmeric, cloves, allspice, and sumac (the small red fruit of a shrub or small tree that is dried and ground; sumac provides a tangy, lemony taste to salads and meats).

Lab Activity

Divide into three teams. Team 1 will locate and make a recipe for pita bread. Team 2 will locate and make a kebob recipe. Team 3 will locate and make a chickpea recipe. Both Teams 2 and 3 will use Team 1's pitas to serve their dish. Evaluate the results of each team's product.

Döner kebob
Source: uwimages/Fotolia

Baguettes

1. **Scale the dough** into pieces of the correct size.

2. **Reshape** the pieces into rounds.

3. **Bench proof the dough.**

4. **Press the dough into a puffy rectangle.**

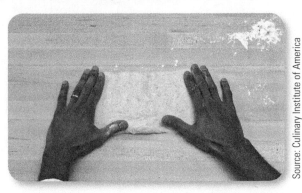

Source: Culinary Institute of America

5. **Lift the ends of the dough** and allow its own weight to stretch it out.

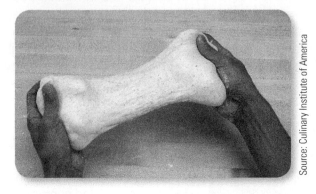

Source: Culinary Institute of America

6. **Roll the stretched dough into a long cylinder,** pressing the seams shut for the best finished loaf.

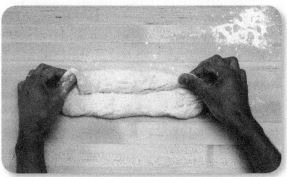

Source: Culinary Institute of America

7. **Transfer the shaped dough to a baking sheet** or a floured cloth.

8. **Proof** (in a proofer with steam, if possible) until nearly doubled in size.

9. **Score** (cut) the loaf lightly. Brush or mist lightly with water.

10. **Bake** the dough until a good crust develops and the loaf sounds hollow when you tap the bottom.

11. **Cool** the loaf on a cooling rack before slicing or serving.

 Recipe Card

121. Baguettes

Baguettes A **baguette** (bag-EHT) is a long, narrow French bread with a crispy, golden brown crust and a light, chewy crumb dotted with holes. The skinny, cylindrical shape of a baguette provides a maximum amount of crunchy crust.

Free-Form Loaves A **free-form loaf** is not pressed into a mold or a pan. It is shaped by hand into an oval, round ball, or other shape. The French word for ball, **boule** (BOOL), is used to describe a round loaf of bread. You make the shape by pressing dough into a round patty, folding the edges into the center, and pinching them together. You then press the edges of the dough together with your cupped hands, rotating in a circular fashion until a neat ball is formed.

Boule

Source: Ian O'Leary/Dorling Kindersley

Pan Loaves A pan loaf is made by pressing dough into a mold or a pan. The first step to making a loaf shape is pressing dough into a wide rectangle. Then, fold the right side just past the middle and slightly overlap the left side onto the right. Roll down the top edges of the dough and push it away from you with your thumbs. Roll it back and forth into a rectangular loaf shape just a bit longer than the pan. Tuck the ends in before placing the dough in the loaf pan.

Braided Loaves Three tapered ropes of dough are often used to make a braided loaf (although four ropes can also be used). Braided loaves are often made with rich dough. The braids help the bread keep its structure so the bread doesn't flatten. The dough must be firm enough to hold the shape, and the ropes must be of uniform size to make an even braid. Divide the dough into thirds and shape them in the same way as the baguette.

Starting with an outside rope, cross the outside rope over the center rope. Now the center rope is an outside rope and the outside rope is the center rope. Do the same thing with the other outside rope. Repeat until you have used all the bread. Pinch the finished braid ends together and tuck underneath the loaf, toward the center.

Rolls and Pastries The first step in making rolls and pastries is to cut and scale. Then you round off the dough. Eventually you can use any of the shaping techniques for breads to create free-form shapes or shapes that are a result of a mold or small-sized pan, or even use the braiding technique to create knots and twists. Aside from all the other shaping techniques, some pastries are rolled and sliced.

The sight of pastries, with their distinctive shapes, is enough to turn a breakfast buffet, teatime, or coffee break into a special occasion. The techniques for shaping individual pastries are a bit labor-intensive, but the results are well worth it. The distinctive shapes help customers distinguish between different types of pastries.

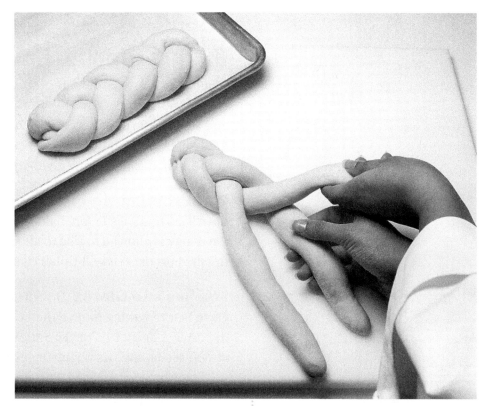

FIGURE 17–20
Braiding Challah Dough
This loaf of challah bread uses three ropes of dough.

INTERPRETING ILLUSTRATIONS
Can you see how the outside rope becomes the center rope?
Source: Richard Embery/Pearson Education/ PH College

 **READING CHECKPOINT** *Why is the shape of a bread, roll, or pastry important?*

Baking Breads, Rolls, and Pastries

When making yeast dough products, there is a great deal of preparation before you are actually able to bake the product. After you have created and shaped the dough, you have a series of final steps before you are able to bake. Understanding the purpose of these final steps and what happens in the oven during baking gives you better control of the outcome.

Pan Proofing After the dough is shaped, it is allowed to rise one last time. This final rise before baking is called **pan proofing**. During this stage, the dough is allowed to rise to about three-quarters the size of the expected finished product. It will finish rising in the oven.

Washes and Glazes Dough is sometimes covered with an egg wash or glaze before baking to give the crust a shiny appearance. Egg washes give the crust a deeper color. The stickiness of egg washes is used like glue to attach seeds, such as poppy or sesame seeds, to breads.

Some bread is sprayed with water before baking or steamed during baking to create a crispy crust. When bread is given this treatment, an egg wash is not used (because it would just be washed off).

Toppings such as melted butter or warmed, strained fruit preserves can be used as glazes. Sticky buns, for example, have a specific glaze made from the sugary liquid in which the raisins used in the sticky buns are soaked. These glazes are brushed on in the pan just before the product is baked in the oven.

Scoring The top of dough is sometimes cut with slashes to release steam that builds up during baking. This is called **scoring**, and it is done to control the tearing that could otherwise occur at the seam on the loaf. The sharp, thin blade of a knife or single-edge razor produces the best results when scoring. Cuts should be between ¼ and ½ inch deep.

FIGURE 17–21

Scoring
Loaves of bread with different scoring.

CLASSIFYING *Why do customers prefer that specific types of bread are always scored in the same way?*
Source: felix/Fotolia

Recipe Card

122. Soft Rolls

Chef's Tip

Clean Cut

You will get the straightest line if you work fast when you score bread. Slow-motion scoring can drag the dough and create an uneven line.

Baking Stages A series of chain reactions begins to take place as soon as dough is placed in an oven. Oven spring and crust formation are the most important of these reactions. The final step in the process is determining doneness.

- **Oven Spring.** The last stage of rising that occurs in the oven is called **oven spring**. This occurs when the heat expands the carbon dioxide gas in the dough and stretches the gluten into a network of strands that trap steam and carbon dioxide. This ultimately gives the dough its final shape and allows it to reach full size.

- **Crust Formation.** The crust starts forming as the dough's outer surface dries out. Once the crust is formed, the dough can no longer expand. Steam ovens and a water spray are sometimes used to keep the dough surface moist and delay the formation of crust so full development can occur. This moisture during baking also creates better browning.

- **Determining Doneness.** A golden color and good aroma are both indicators of doneness. Another indicator is a hollow sound when you thump the bread. In general, you should regard the recipe's recommended baking time as a guideline and use actual indicators to evaluate doneness.

FIGURE 17–22
Cooling Bread
Loaves of fresh-baked bread cool on racks in a bakery.
APPLYING CONCEPTS *Why is fresh-baked bread cooled on racks and not on shelves?*
Source: Nolte Lourens/Shutterstock

Cooling and Slicing Breads Remove breads, rolls, and pastries from their baking pans immediately. Cool bread on a rack before slicing. Hot bread continues to bake until it is cooled, often evaporating excess moisture. Slice bread with a serrated knife after it has cooled. Use a gentle, sawing motion to cut even slices.

 **READING CHECKPOINT** *What is pan proofing?*

Evaluating Quality

The final, postbaking stage is when you assess the quality of your product. An evaluation is like detective work in which you look for clues to help you understand what happened. Evaluating helps you improve your technique by showing the cause-and-effect relationships of your product's appearance, crumb, and flavor.

- **Appearance.** The golden-brown color of a well-developed crust is the first indication that proper baking has occurred. Special flours, such as rye or oat, will influence color. If the finished product is pale, it has been baked at too low a temperature or it isn't completely done. Dough that has been brushed with an egg wash has a more tender and golden crust than others.

- **Crumb.** Yeast breads should be fairly elastic but easy to bite into. The more eggs, fat, and milk used in the product, the more tender the crumb will be. The more times the dough is allowed to rise, the finer and more even the crumb will be.

- **Flavor.** If there is a strong taste of alcohol, either too much yeast was used or insufficient time was spent proofing before baking. A strong alcohol odor and bland flavor indicate not enough salt was used.

 **READING CHECKPOINT** *What is the purpose of evaluating your finished product?*

17.3 ASSESSMENT

Reviewing Concepts

1. What is the purpose of bench proofing?

2. Why is the shape of a bread, roll, or pastry important?

3. What is pan proofing?

4. What makes yeast bread taste like alcohol?

Critical Thinking

5. Predicting What would happen if you made a baked product without scaling the dough?

6. Applying Concepts Is it a good idea to change the traditional shape of a bread, roll, or pastry? Explain your answer.

7. Analyzing Information Your pizza is soggy and didn't rise properly. What might have happened?

Test Kitchen

Divide into three teams. Each team will make a batch of yeast rolls. Team 1 will use an egg wash consisting of egg yolks. Team 2 will use an egg wash of egg whites. Team 3 will not use an egg wash. Bake the rolls and evaluate the results.

SOCIAL STUDIES ──────●
Versatile Flatbreads

Flatbreads are used in many cultures and in different ways. Research two more examples of flatbreads. Indicate the country where the flatbread originated and the food with which it is served.

PROJECT 17

Differences in Flour You are now ready to work on Project 17, "Differences in Flour," which is available in "My Culinary Lab" or in your *Student's Lab Resources and Study Guide* manual.

Reviewing Content

Choose the letter that best answers the question or completes the statement.

1. The difference between lean dough and enriched dough is
   a. texture.
   b. color.
   c. sweetness.
   d. all of the above

2. Another word describing rolled-in dough is
   a. layered.
   b. rounded.
   c. laminated.
   d. flattened.

3. When ingredients are weighed, it is called
   a. measuring.
   b. dividing.
   c. the method.
   d. scaling.

4. In the modified straight dough-mixing method,
   a. ingredients are all mixed at the same time.
   b. yeast is not used.
   c. ingredients are added in steps.
   d. dissolved yeast and flour are added last.

5. In baking, a sponge is
   a. made with half the yeast and all the liquid.
   b. a thick yeast mixture developed separately.
   c. a type of sweet roll.
   d. a sweet dessert dough.

6. Dough starters start fermentation
   a. before yeast is added.
   b. while the oven is preheating.
   c. before the final mixing of the dough.
   d. before the yeast is packaged.

7. Dough garnishes are
   a. decorative designs on the bread.
   b. decorations made of dough.
   c. part of the dough structure.
   d. ingredients that stay separate from the dough structure.

Understanding Concepts

8. Why are enriched dough products more tender than lean dough products?

9. What is rolled into laminated dough and how does it contribute to lightness?

10. What does the gluten window test show?

11. What is the difference between bench proofing and pan proofing?

12. What happens when the crust forms during the baking process?

Critical Thinking

13. **COMPARING/CONTRASTING** What is the difference between the straight dough-mixing method and the modified straight dough-mixing method?

14. **APPLYING CONCEPTS** Your first bread had a strong smell of alcohol. What went wrong?

Culinary Math

15. **SOLVING PROBLEMS** If it takes you 2 hours to shape 48 baguettes, how many can you do in half an hour? Based on that figure, approximately how long does it take to shape each baguette?

16. **APPLYING CONCEPTS** You are having 66 guests for breakfast. The serving size per person is three mini-Danishes. You are making six different fillings. You want to divide the total amount of mini-Danishes by six to determine how many of each flavor you will make.

On the Job

17. **APPLYING CONCEPTS** You are working in a nursing home, and the elderly residents want more whole grains in their diet. You add barley and oats to their favorite bread. What other ingredient(s) in the formula may have to be adjusted? Why?

18. **COMMUNICATING** Students in your high school cafeteria are concerned about their weight. You have developed a tasty and healthy pizza with low-fat cheese and fresh vegetables for them. Write a brief and playful description of your pizza for the menu board.

Pastry Chefs and Bakers

Pastry chefs and bakers prepare food items that are cooked in ovens, such as breads, cakes, cookies, and other pastries. They often develop their own recipes, experimenting with ingredients to change the taste and consistency of their baked goods.

The most successful pastry chefs or bakers combine their ability to follow written or verbal directions, attentiveness to detail, basic mathematics, and measurement skills with a healthy dose of creativity and passion. For decorating cakes and other pastries, they also need hand-eye coordination, manual dexterity, and artistic talent.

They work in a number of locations, including restaurants, coffee shops, grocery stores, and specialty bakeries. Professionals in the field often work early mornings or late nights in order to have items made when a store or business opens.

Baker's assistants are responsible for following recipes, measuring and mixing ingredients, operating baking equipment safely, and following all health and sanitation guidelines.

Bread bakers produce a wide range of breads. Some work in shops or outlets devoted exclusively to artisanal breads, and others work for larger retail operations. Bread bakers not only mix, shape, and bake a variety of yeast-raised breads, they are also responsible for developing specific formulations for yeast-free or gluten-free breads for their clients.

Entry-Level Requirements

Many bakers attend culinary schools and earn an associate degree in baking and pastry. This period of formal education typically includes coursework that lays some of the important groundwork for specializing: food safety and sanitation, business and management in the foodservice industry, nutrition, culinary science, and principles of flavor and texture development. However, you will still find that others have acquired their skills through on-the-job training and apprenticeships.

Helpful for Advancement

Certifications from organizations including the American Culinary Federation (ACF) and the Retail Bakers of America (RBA) can advance your career. These groups have established various criteria to evaluate your knowledge and skill. Joining these organizations and other groups can help you create a network and is an effective way to advance your career in baking and pastry.

A degree in a health- or nutrition-related area is another avenue to advance your career and achieve the goal of becoming a specialty baker.

Bakers often work late nights and early mornings to have baked items when the store opens

Source: Carole Castelli/Shutterstock

HANS WELKER

Hans Welker

Chef Hans Welker grew up in Germany, where at age 14 he apprenticed in a local pastry shop, Café Brenner. For three years, he worked long hours to prepare for a two-day practical, after which he could seek employment as a pastry chef. He passed his practical and set off to work in pastry shops across Germany, then in Switzerland and Sierra Leone.

Chef Welker returned to Germany, where he studied to earn his Master in Pastry Arts degree before moving to the United States in 1986. It was when he moved to the United States that he began transitioning from pastry work to bread baking, especially the hearty rye breads that are popular in Germany.

Chef Welker opened Alpine Bakery & Café in upstate New York, but after 10 years, he struggled to find good employees. This motivated him to teach others his craft, and he joined the faculty at the French Culinary Institute as the Director of the Bread Program. He is now an Associate Professor of Baking and Pastry at The Culinary Institute of America.

VITAL STATISTICS

Education: Master in Pastry Arts, F.U.U. Gemeinnuetzige Fortbildung Schule, Heidelberg, Germany

Profession: Baker and Instructor

Interesting Items: Completed the Certified Master Chef exam in 2008

Five-time recipient of Best in Show at the Salon of Culinary Art Competition in New York City

Appeared on the Food Network's competition show, *Throwdown with Bobby Flay*, giving a lesson in donut-making

CAREER PROFILE

Salary Ranges

Baker's Assistant: $18,000 to $25,000

Bread Baker: $25,000 to $45,000

Assistant Pastry Chef: $25,000 to $50,000

Pastry Chef: $35,000 to $80,000

Executive Pastry Chef: $45,000 to $100,000

Chapter 18

Quick Breads

18.1 Muffins and Quick Breads

18.2 Biscuits and Scones

18.1

Muffins and Quick Breads

Key Concepts

- Identifying basic ingredients
- Identifying methods of mixing and baking
- Garnishing muffins and quick breads

Vocabulary

- creaming method
- crumb topping
- quick bread
- stir-ins
- streusel
- sugar glaze
- well method

Basic Ingredients

A **quick bread** is a type of bread that is quick to make because baking soda or baking powder, rather than yeast, is used for leavening. The result is a batter rather than a dough. The batter can be baked immediately after the ingredients are mixed because there is no need to wait for fermentation to occur. Quick breads are usually baked in loaf pans. Muffins can be made from the same batter and baked in individual cup-shaped tins.

Quick breads and muffins may be sweet or savory and can be served throughout the day. They are equally appropriate at simple coffee shops or fancy restaurants. Quick breads freeze well and can be kept in the refrigerator up to a week when tightly wrapped. Muffins are best when served freshly baked and still warm from the oven. They freeze well and should be wrapped in aluminum foil when reheated.

The basic ingredients for muffins and quick breads are as follows:

- **Flour.** All-purpose flour is considered standard for muffins and quick breads. Other types of flour, such as whole-wheat, oat, graham, and pastry flour, or cornmeal may be substituted entirely or in part for the all-purpose flour.

- **Sugar.** White sugar, brown sugar, honey, and molasses are typical sweeteners.

- **Fat.** Fat provides moisture and tenderness. Either oil or butter may be used.

- **Liquid.** Milk, buttermilk, and water are all used to give moisture to muffins and quick breads.

Source: Stephanie Frey/Fotolia

Baking Powder and Baking Soda

As you know from Section 17.1, baking powder and baking soda are chemical leaveners. When baking soda is combined with a dry acid and a liquid, it creates a chemical reaction that produces carbon dioxide, which makes batter rise.

Baking powder is simply baking soda that is already combined with at least one dry acid, cream of tartar, and some cornstarch. The cornstarch is there to absorb moisture so the chemical reaction doesn't happen before baking begins.

There are usually two acids in baking powder, one that reacts at room temperature to produce carbon dioxide, and one that produces carbon dioxide with heat. This is known as *double-acting baking powder.*

Baking soda does not contain any acid. It must be mixed with a liquid and an acidic ingredient such as buttermilk, lemon juice, or sour cream to begin releasing carbon dioxide.

Lab Activity

Make two loaves of quick bread using the same recipe, except in one, use baking soda and a liquid acid (such as lemon juice, buttermilk, or sour cream). In the other, use double-acting baking powder. Before you begin, write down a hypothesis about which will rise more, including a percentage increase in rising. When you have baked the two breads, compare the amount they rose. Calculate the difference as a percentage. Were you correct? Describe any other differences in taste and texture.

Chef's Tip

Warming Eggs

Refrigerated eggs can be brought to room temperature quickly by submerging them in a bowl of warm water.

FOCUS ON Nutrition

Half the Fat

Applesauce and fruit purée work especially well as fat substitutes when making quick breads and muffins. The fruit fibers hold moisture and the natural sugars promote browning. Substitute purée for up to half the fat.

- **Eggs.** Eggs should be at room temperature because this makes them easier to mix into the batter. Be careful not to leave eggs out of the refrigerator for more than two hours. Eggs may be called for as either whole, yolks, or whites.

- **Salt.** Salt is a seasoning and should not be eliminated.

- **Leavening Agent.** Either baking soda or baking powder can be used in making muffins and quick breads. Both are chemical leavening agents, creating carbon dioxide to make the batter rise. Baking powder starts to lose its ability to leaven within six months and should be tested to make sure it is still active. Mix 2 tsp of baking powder with 1 cup of warm water. It should fizz.

 **READING CHECKPOINT** *Why is quick bread quicker to make than yeast bread?*

Methods of Mixing and Baking

Two basic methods are used for mixing muffins and quick breads: the well method, which is simpler and more frequently used, and the creaming method. A liquid fat such as melted butter or oil is used for the well method. A solid fat such as softened butter or shortening is used for the creaming method.

As you know from Sections 17.1, gluten, an elastic protein, develops when flour is combined with liquids. Gluten helps ingredients stick together. However, when too much gluten forms, as it does when batter is overmixed, the batter becomes elastic and cannot rise well. The result will be heavy, misshapen loaves or muffins, dotted with air holes.

Well Method In the **well method**, liquids are blended in one bowl and dry ingredients are sifted in another. Next, a depression (often called a *well*) is made in the dry ingredients and the liquids are poured into the well. The batter is then mixed just enough to moisten the dry ingredients. Even if the batter looks lumpy, do only a minimal amount of mixing to avoid overmixing.

Creaming Method In the **creaming method**, sugar and fat are combined vigorously, usually with a paddle attachment, to incorporate air. Beating granulated sugar into the fat fills the batter with tiny air bubbles that expand in baking and produce lightness in the final texture. This gives muffins and quick breads that use the creaming method a finer texture than products that use the well method. See the Basic Culinary Skill on page 609.

Eggs are then beaten in, one at a time. It's important that the eggs are at room temperature or they will cause the butter to become firm and reduce creaminess.

As the final step, dry ingredients are sifted together and added to the mixture, alternating with any liquid ingredients.

Preparing and Filling Pans Pans and muffin tins need to be greased, that is, coated with a fat such as butter or a sprayed vegetable oil. This promotes browning and makes muffins and quick breads easier to remove.

Use a portion scooper to ensure a uniform muffin size. Muffin tins should be filled only halfway, because the batter will double in volume and form a dome-shaped top. Overfilling can cause batter to spill over the sides and result in a flat top.

Baking Muffins and quick breads should be baked until the edges begin to shrink from the sides and the top springs back when lightly pressed. A wooden skewer inserted in the middle should come out clean.

Cool loaf breads on a rack before removing the loaves from the pan. Muffins should be removed immediately because steam may become trapped and make them soggy.

READING CHECKPOINT *What is the difference between the well method and the creaming method of making muffins and quick breads?*

FIGURE 18–1
Picture Perfect
To make a perfect muffin, you must avoid overmixing.

PREDICTING *As a consumer, how would you feel if you purchased a misshapen muffin that was filled with air holes?*

Source: Ian O'Leary/Image Partners 2005/Dorling Kindersley Media Library/Dorling Kindersley

Chef's Tip

Breakdown

If the creamed fat-and-sugar mixture breaks down after the addition of the eggs, continue to beat until the mixture becomes smooth and creamy again.

FIGURE 18–2

Before and After
Muffin tins are filled only halfway.
The finished muffins expand to
full size.

PREDICTING *What would happen if
you overfilled the muffin tin?*

Source: Richard Menga/Fundamental
Photographs

Recipe Cards

123. Corn Muffins

124. Zucchini Bread

Chef's Tip

Better Berries

Use frozen blueberries
to make muffins or quick
breads. Do not thaw them.
Blueberries contain yellow
pigment that can bleed,
sometimes turning batter
green. Thawed berries also
tend to get gummy when
mixed with flour.

FIGURE 18–3

Cranberry Bread
Cranberries have been added as a
stir-in to a sweet quick bread.

COMMUNICATING *Do you have a
favorite type of quick-bread or muffin
stir-in?*

Source: Andrea Skjold/Shutterstock

Garnishes and Serving Accompaniments

Muffins and quick breads can easily be enhanced with the addition of simple
toppings and fillings.

Stir-Ins A wide variety of ingredients can be added to muffins and quick
breads to transform a basic recipe into a special treat. Known as **stir-ins**,
these ingredients can range from savory to sweet. Shredded vegetables, fresh
fruit, nuts, whole grains, meat, cheese, and chocolate are all popular stir-ins.

Stir-ins should be chopped in proportion to the size of the product being
made. If they are too large, they may interfere with the batter's ability to
hold together. The quantity of stir-ins should be limited for the same reason.
One cup of additions per cup of flour is the maximum you should use. Stir-
ins should be mixed in just enough to distribute them without
overmixing.

Chop or shred any fruit, vegetables, nuts, or other ingredients before you begin mixing your recipe. Muffins and quick-
bread batters should be baked immediately after they are mixed
so the leavening is still active.

Sugar Glazes A **sugar glaze** is a thin liquid made by dissolving sugar in water. It becomes smooth and glossy after
setting. Glazes can be flavored with the addition of other ingredients, such as lemon juice or vanilla.

Confectioner's sugar or superfine granulated sugars are
commonly used for glazes. In addition to the added sweetness,
sugar glazes seal the top and help prevent baked goods from
drying out. Glazes are applied with a pastry brush.

Creaming Method for Blueberry Muffins

① Sift the flour and baking powder together.

② Cream the butter, sugar, and salt together with a paddle attachment in the bowl of an electric mixer.

Source: Pearson Education/PH College

③ Add the eggs, one at a time, at low speed. Scrape the sides of the bowl each time.

④ Alternate adding milk with the dry ingredients, one-third each time.

⑤ Remove from the mixer.

⑥ Fold in the blueberries with a rubber spatula.

Source: Culinary Institute of America

⑦ Portion equal amounts of batter into greased muffin tins.

Source: Pearson Education/PH College

⑧ Bake at 400°F for 20 minutes or until lightly browned on top.

⑨ Remove the muffins from the tins. Serve warm.

Source: Pearson Education/PH College

Recipe Card

125. Blueberry Muffins

Crumb Toppings and Streusels A **crumb topping** is a crumbly mixture of fat, sugar, and flour. A **streusel** (STRU-sel) is a crumb topping that may also include spices and nuts. A careful balance of these ingredients produces a crispy quick-bread and muffin topping.

FIGURE 18–4

Adding a Streusel Topping

A streusel topping adds additional salty, sweet flavor and a special texture to a muffin or quick bread.

DRAWING CONCLUSIONS *Would you rather have a muffin/quick bread with or without a streusel topping?*

Source: A_Lein/Fotolia

Chef's Tip

A Sticky Situation

To prevent dates and other sticky stir-ins from adhering to your knife when cutting, first spray the knife with cooking oil.

READING CHECKPOINT *What is a stir-in for a muffin or a quick bread?*

18.1 ASSESSMENT

Reviewing Concepts

1. Why is a quick bread quicker to make than a yeast bread?
2. How does the well method differ from the creaming method?
3. What is a stir-in for a muffin or a quick bread?

Critical Thinking

4. **Applying Concepts** You are creating a new muffin recipe and you want it to be light and fluffy. Would you use the well method or the creaming method?
5. **Analyzing Information** In an emergency could you substitute baking powder for baking soda? Baking soda for baking powder? Would you need to change the recipe?
6. **Drawing Conclusions** A muffin made by using the well method did not rise well and was heavy, misshapen, and filled with air holes. What might have happened?

Test Kitchen

Divide into two teams. Using the same recipe, make muffins. One team will use the well method and the other will use the creaming method. Evaluate the differences, focusing on the differences in texture and flavor.

CULINARY MATH

Converting Loaf Yield into Muffin Yield

Measure the volume capacity of a loaf pan by filling it three-fourths full of water. Then measure the capacity of an individual muffin in a muffin tin that makes 12 muffins by filling it half full of water.

1. Calculate how much muffin batter is required for the muffin tin.
2. How many muffin tins will the batter for a loaf pan fill?

PROJECT 18

Blueberry Muffins You are now ready to work on Project 18, "Blueberry Muffins," which is available in "My Culinary Lab" or in your *Student's Lab Resources and Study Guide* manual.

Biscuits and Scones

Key Concepts

- Identifying biscuits, scones, and soda bread
- Identifying methods of mixing and baking
- Serving biscuits and scones

Vocabulary

- biscuits
- rubbed-dough method
- shortcake
- soda bread

Biscuits, Scones, and Soda Bread

Biscuits, scones, and soda bread are all flaky quick breads. They are made from dough that uses flour and a solid fat.

Biscuits Biscuits are small quick breads with little or no sugar. There are three main types of biscuits. However, it seems that every region has its own biscuit variation.

- **Rolled and Cut Biscuits.** Biscuit dough is patted out by hand or rolled out and then cut into circular shapes.
- **Drop Biscuits.** The dough for drop biscuits has more liquid and can be dropped from a spoon onto the baking sheet.
- **Beaten Biscuits.** Beaten biscuits are a southern tradition that dates back to the 1800s. Unlike regular biscuits, where light mixing creates a flaky dough, beaten biscuits are beaten for a long period and the resulting dough is hard and stiff. According to some old recipes, the dough was put on a tree stump and beaten at length with a rolling pin, mallet, or heavy object.

Scones Scones are sweet, biscuitlike, individual quick breads. The main difference between a biscuit and a scone

Source: Culinary Institute of America

George Auguste Escoffier

George Auguste Escoffier (es-kaw-FYEY) started his culinary career as an apprentice in his uncle's restaurant at age 13. From there he went on to work in a number of restaurants, mostly in Paris, and eventually opened his own restaurant in 1871. Seven years later, Escoffier was given the management of the Maison Chevet, a fashionable restaurant, particularly for big dinners and official banquets. He went on to become the director of cuisine for two prestigious hotels—the Ritz Hotel in Paris (opened in 1898) and the Carlton Hotel in London (opened in 1899).

Always aware that the hotels were businesses and needed to show a profit, Escoffier was expected to serve excellent meals to diners who had little time to spare. It was not unusual, for example, to serve up to five hundred diners in an evening. With a team of 60 chefs at the Carlton, Escoffier's organization had to be excellent. He developed the kitchen brigade, with individual *chefs de partie*, as a way to make sure that each chef had a particular responsibility and that there were no redundancies in their responsibilities. More than any other chef before him, Escoffier demonstrated that cooking was an honorable, and potentially prestigious, profession.

It had been typical for French meals to be served with many dishes served all at once. However, Escoffier simplified the menu and served them *à la carte*. This meant writing down the dishes, allowing diners to choose from the menu, and serving the dishes in the order in which they appeared on the menu.

Escoffier had to create new menus every day. Often he created a dish in honor of his guests. Many of these dishes were set down in Escoffier's *Le Guide Culinaire*, first published in 1903. He went on to publish three more editions over the years, with the last edition published in 1921.

The Ritz Hotel in Paris
Source: TMAX/Fotolia

Research

Research some of the dishes that Escoffier developed for guests. Write a report about one of the dishes and prepare it based on the recipe in Escoffier's *Le Guide Culinaire* (translated as *Escoffier: The Complete Guide to Modern Cookery*.) Describe your experience in your report.

Source: © akg_images

Vital Statistics

Born	October 28, 1846 in Villeneuve-Loubet, Provence, France
Died	February 12, 1935, Monte Carlo, Monaco
Profession	Chef, restaurant director, culinary writer
Credits	Developed the kitchen brigade system of kitchen organization; showed that being a chef was an honorable profession
	Simplified the menu, began serving meals à la carte
	Wrote a comprehensive guide to cooking

FIGURE 18–5

Scones
These scones were made with cream rather than water.

PREDICTING *How would the use of cream rather than water affect the flavor of the scone?*

Source: Culinary Institute of America

is that a biscuit is not sweetened and a scone typically is. Scones can also have fruit or nuts added to the dough. Cream scones are richer scones because cream is substituted for the water.

Scone dough is shaped into wedges, diamonds, squares, or rounds. Scones, originally made with oatmeal and cooked on a griddle in a way similar to pancakes, are a Scottish tradition. They are named after the Stone of Destiny (Scone), the place were Scottish kings were once crowned.

Soda Bread **Soda bread** is named for the baking soda that is used to leaven it. An acid ingredient is also added to the mixture, such as buttermilk. The dough is similar to that of biscuits and scones and is shaped into a round loaf marked with an X made by cutting through the top layer before it is baked. Some versions of soda bread are sweetened and include either raisins or currants and are flavored with caraway seed. Other versions are left unsweetened and do not include any ingredients that add fat, such as eggs or butter.

Rubbed-Dough Method Biscuits, scones, and soda bread are made by using the **rubbed-dough method.** Rather than blending butter or some other fat with flour to form a batter, the fat in the rubbed-dough method is cut into chunks and then rubbed into the flour. The fat must be cold when it is combined with the flour. This process promotes flakiness because it prevents the fat from fully combining with the flour.

FOCUS ON
Nutrition

Healthy Substitution
Create a healthy biscuit or scone by substituting whole-grain flour, such as wheat, for some of the white flour. Whole grains may reduce the risk of heart disease and cancer. They also provide fiber that may be an important component to a healthy diet.

Chef's Tip

Cold Case

Scone dough can be prepared in advance and refrigerated up to 24 hours before baking. Resting the dough in the refrigerator makes scones tender because it settles the gluten.

Rubbed-Dough Method

① **Combine the dry ingredients** in a bowl and sift or blend.

② **Rub the cold butter** or other fat into dry ingredients with your fingertips until the mixture looks like coarse oatmeal.

Source: Culinary Institute of America

Source: Culinary Institute of America

④ **Gather the dough into a ball** on a floured work surface and gently pat or lightly roll it into the appropriate thickness, about ½ inch thick for biscuits.

Source: Culinary Institute of America

③ **Make a well** in the center of the dry ingredients and pour in the blended liquids. Combine the wet and dry ingredients quickly, mixing them just enough to be able to press the dough together.

READING CHECKPOINT *What is the rubbed-dough method?*

Chef's Tip

Keep It Cool

When using the rubbed-dough method, use only your fingertips to combine the flour and chilled butter. If you use your whole hand, you bring more heat to the dough, softening the butter.

Methods of Mixing and Baking

Baking techniques can change the attractiveness of a biscuit or scone dramatically. It's important to know how the result is affected by temperature, basic shaping, and egg washes.

Temperature Chilling butter or fat is important in the rubbed-dough method because the coldness keeps the butter or other fat from blending in too much with the flour. Chilled fat contributes to the final product's flakiness because it serves as a temporary barrier between thin layers of the dough. The layer of fat usually stays intact just long enough for the layers of dough to begin to set. The chilled fat melting during baking and the moisture from the dough turning into steam both act to push the layers apart, allowing the development of a light, flaky structure.

Chilling biscuits and scones in the freezer for half an hour or more once they are shaped allows the fat to firm up again, for a better texture in the finished baked item.

A high temperature in the oven is as important as using chilled fat in the dough. High temperatures help produce the steam that you want to trap

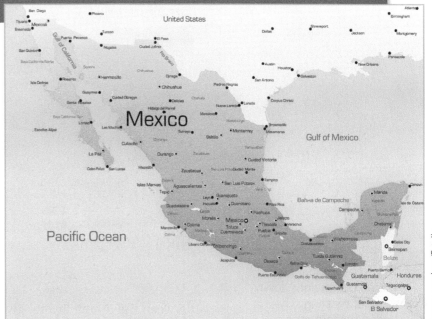

FIGURE 18–6

Cutting Biscuits
Use a sharp tool when cutting biscuit dough.

APPLYING CONCEPTS *How has waste been minimized when cutting out these biscuits?*

Source: Culinary Institute of America

Chef's Tip

High Risers

If you are using a biscuit cutter, cut straight down without twisting. The added movement of turning the cutter makes the edges of the dough stick together, inhibiting its ability to rise.

Recipe Card

126. Cream Scones

between the dough layers, giving additional rise and flakiness to biscuits and scones.

Basic Shaping The softness of biscuit dough requires that the work surface, dough, and cutter are all floured generously. However, be careful not to add too much flour or overwork the dough. It will make the biscuits heavy and thick, rather than light and fluffy.

Use long, smooth movements when rolling the dough, lifting the rolling pin before reaching the edges so the dough doesn't get too thin. You will get a greater yield if edges are rolled out straight.

Dough must be cut with a sharp tool, such as a biscuit cutter or a knife. Using a cup or anything else with dull edges squeezes the outside of the dough together, interfering with its ability to rise properly. When cutting out biscuits, try to avoid waste. The added handling of rerolling the scraps will toughen the dough.

Sometimes an optional step of folding the dough into thirds, like a letter, or fourths, like a book, is added. This is a type of laminating process (similar to the laminated yeast dough described in Section 17.2) that results in multiple layers. Laminating makes it easier for steam, which is produced during baking, to stay trapped in the dough and to promote flakiness.

After the dough is shaped, you can brush it with an egg wash. This coating is brushed on baked goods to add gloss and color for a more appealing look.

Making Laminated Biscuits

① **Roll** the dough out to half the desired thickness.

② **Fold** it into thirds or fourths.

Source: Pearson Education/PH College

Source: Pearson Education/PH College

 **Recipe Card**

127. Buttermilk Biscuits

③ **Turn** it so the long side is parallel to the edge of the work surface.

④ **Roll** the dough out again, this time to the desired thickness for baking.

⑤ **Repeat** the process of folding, turning, and rolling the dough one more time.

READING CHECKPOINT *How do you make laminated biscuit dough?*

Serving Biscuits and Scones

Biscuits are usually served warm with a meal. Scones are served throughout the day with coffee and tea. Biscuits and scones are both popular for breakfast. In addition, there are occasions with which each is specifically associated.

Afternoon Tea The custom of taking an afternoon tea break provides an opportunity to slow down and enjoy one of the simple pleasures of life. Afternoon tea served with scones, small sandwiches, and cakes helps boost sagging energy and spirits. In the last decade, the popularity of afternoon tea has led to a booming new business. Tea shops are opening across the nation, and scones are quite popular. Scones are served with butter, jam, or thick cream.

FIGURE 18–7
Shortcake
Mixed berries are used for this shortcake.
RECOGNIZING PATTERNS *What other type of fruit could have been used for a shortcake?*
Source: Michael Lamotte/Cole Group/Photodisc/ Getty Images

Recipe Card

128. Strawberry Shortcake

Shortcakes Biscuits are the foundation for a dessert called a **shortcake**. Uncooked fruit and some of its juices are spooned between a split biscuit and crowned with a mound of whipped cream to make a shortcake. Soft fruit such as strawberries is ideal for a shortcake.

READING CHECKPOINT *What is a shortcake?*

18.2 ASSESSMENT

Reviewing Concepts

1. What is the rubbed-dough method for making biscuits and scones?
2. How do you make laminated biscuits?
3. What is a shortcake?

Critical Thinking

4. **Drawing Conclusions** You order "fluffy buttermilk biscuits" from a menu, but hard, flat disks are served instead. What might have gone wrong with the biscuits?
5. **Applying Concepts** Two job candidates are asked to make biscuits. Why does the one who uses the laminating process get hired?
6. **Analyzing Information** The edges of your cut biscuits didn't rise properly. What might have gone wrong?

Test Kitchen

Divide into two teams. Both teams will make biscuits, using the same recipe. One team will roll out the dough once and make nonlaminated rolled and cut biscuits. The other team will make laminated rolled and cut biscuits. Evaluate the results.

CULINARY MATH
Scones for a Tea

You are planning an afternoon tea for 24 people. Each guest will be served 2 scones. There's enough dough for eight disks, from which you are cutting wedge-shaped scones.

1. How many wedges must each disk yield?
2. At the last minute, eight more guests are added. You can increase the yield by making smaller scones. How many must each disk yield now?

Reviewing Content

Choose the letter that best answers the question or completes the statement.

1. Quick breads are
   a. made without yeast.
   b. quick to make.
   c. made with chemical leaveners.
   d. all of the above

2. In the creaming method, which of the following ingredients are creamed together?
   a. eggs and flour
   b. butter and flour
   c. butter and sugar
   d. cream and eggs

3. In the well method,
   a. a special mixer blade is used.
   b. the edges of the dough are given a special treatment.
   c. liquids and dry ingredients are mixed separately and then combined.
   d. all ingredients are mixed together at the same time.

4. The purpose of the creaming method is to
   a. save time.
   b. beat in air bubbles.
   c. use less milk.
   d. none of the above

5. Scones are usually served with
   a. cold cuts.
   b. butter, jam, and thick cream.
   c. maple syrup.
   d. olive spread.

6. Streusel is
   a. a mini-loaf pan.
   b. a German word for pastries.
   c. a crumb topping.
   d. none of the above

7. Biscuits are baked at
   a. low temperature.
   b. high temperature.
   c. moderate temperature.
   d. a combination of high and low.

Understanding Concepts

8. How do baking soda and baking powder differ?

9. Why is the well method used more often than the creaming method?

10. How does the rubbed-dough method contribute to flakiness?

11. How do biscuits and scones differ?

12. Why do you use cold butter to make biscuits and scones?

Critical Thinking

13. **APPLYING CONCEPTS** Why might you be able to substitute baking powder for baking soda in quick breads, but not baking soda for baking powder?

14. **COMPARING/CONTRASTING** What is the difference between the rubbed-dough method of making biscuits and the creaming method of making muffins and quick breads?

15. **PREDICTING** Which are more likely to be flakier, rolled and cut biscuits or drop biscuits? Explain why.

Culinary Math

16. **SOLVING PROBLEMS** If a quick bread recipe yields 6 cups of batter and a muffin requires ¼ cup of batter, how many muffins will the quick bread recipe yield?

17. **ANALYZING INFORMATION** You are serving hot biscuits for a 7:30 breakfast meeting. The biscuits require 20 minutes for preparation and 20 minutes for baking. What is the latest you need to be in the kitchen?

On the Job

18. **ANALYZING INFORMATION** You have opened a bakery. Two tea shops have opened in nearby towns. They're crowded. Do they give you any ideas to help your bakery?

19. **COMMUNICATING** You have created a new muffin for the many health-conscious customers you serve. Write a sign for the window.

Hospitality Managers

Owning and operating a small inn or bed-and-breakfast (often referred to as a B&B) is a goal for many people in the foodservice industry. This career choice is not just for those who want to run their own business, however. Hotels, motels, resorts, cruise ships, and camps often employ people who work as managers to make sure that all aspects of a guest's stay are properly planned and executed.

Hospitality managers Hotels and motels may be part of larger chains. These large organizations typically have a career path for the hospitality and lodging professionals they employ. You may start out working the desk, which may mean that you are responsible for handling reservations, greeting and registering guests, and handling any questions or problems that guests have during their stay. You will also be handling the billing of guests and checking them out when they depart. From there, you may advance to a management position. As a manager, you may also be responsible for the financial success of the unit (or in some cases, a group of properties within a region). Your tasks may include developing promotional and advertising strategies and coordinating with the kitchen to create menus for the restaurants and room service offered on the property.

Owner/operators Inns and bed-and-breakfasts are smaller than hotels and are typically owned and operated by individuals. Bed-and-breakfasts generally have between 3 and 6 rooms available. Inns may have between 6 and 20 rooms. Many people enjoy the more personal experience provided by inns and B&Bs. In these establishments, breakfast is an important part of what the guests are offered during their stay. You may also find inns that have a dining room that serves other meals. The dining rooms are typically small and may be open only to registered guests, but larger businesses may also be open to the public. The owner/operator of a bed-and-breakfast is likely to be a jack-of-all-trades, cooking and baking in the kitchen, serving in the dining room, and managing the guest rooms (cleaning, handling linens, interior decorating, and more).

It is important to be aware of the rules and regulations in the local area to be sure that the property is properly zoned and that all the appropriate inspections are up to date.

Entry-Level Requirements

While there are no absolute requirements concerning degrees or areas of study, the chances of advancement and for increased earnings is greater if you have a degree, either an associate or bachelor's degree, in hospitality management. Additional studies in business management and entrepreneurship are helpful for those who plan to operate their own establishment.

Helpful for Advancement

Working in a variety of establishments will give you exposure to the lodging industry.

Breakfast is an important part of what the guests are offered at a B&B

Source: zstock/Fotolia

PHIL CRISPO

Chef Phil Crispo is the owner and operator of the Norumbega Inn in Camden, Maine. As a trained chef with an extensive culinary background, Chef Crispo runs the inn's kitchen, providing gourmet meals for his guests.

Chef Crispo grew up in a quiet village in Scotland, where he cooked as a hobby. He later went on to earn an Advanced Culinary Diploma from the Craft Guild of Chefs in London, England, and a certification in pâtisserie and baking from Perth Technical College in Scotland. He's cooked in many restaurants, including his own in Scotland, as well as the original Cipriani in New York City.

Phil Crispo

Source: Courtesy of Phil Crispo

Before becoming an innkeeper, Chef Crispo was an instructor at The Culinary Institute of America, where he taught a variety of courses, as well as consulted with global food companies. He has appeared on many television cooking segments, and in 2012 he won the top prize on the Food Network's competition show, *Chopped*.

VITAL STATISTICS

Graduated: Advanced Culinary Diploma, Craft Guild of Chefs, London

Profession: Innkeeper and chef, Norumbega Inn, Camden, Maine

Interesting Items: Honored with the Societe Culinaire Philanthropiques' Grand Prize of Honor

Cooked a meal for the British Royal Family

Prepared dishes using ice cream cones and sports drinks to win the television competition show, *Chopped*

CAREER PROFILE

Salary Ranges

Hotel Desk Clerk: $25,000 to $35,000

Hospitality Manager: $30,000 to $60,500 (or more)

Innkeeper or Bed-and-Breakfast Owner: Varies widely depending on number of rooms, location, and season

In addition to a salary, hotels and resorts may provide housing or a bonus.

Desserts

19.1 Chocolate

19.2 Custards, Mousses, and Frozen Desserts

19.3 Cookies and Cakes

19.4 Pies, Tarts, Pastries, and Fruit Desserts

Source: Culinary Institute of America

Chocolate

Key Concepts

- Identifying various types of chocolate
- Working with chocolate
- Making ganache

Vocabulary

- baker's chocolate
- bittersweet chocolate
- chocolate liquor
- coating chocolate
- cocoa butter
- cocoa powder
- compound chocolate
- dark chocolate
- Dutch processed
- ganache
- milk chocolate
- nibs
- seeding method
- semisweet chocolate
- tabling method
- tempering
- unsweetened chocolate
- white chocolate

Identifying Various Types of Chocolate

There are three basic types of chocolate: dark chocolate (bittersweet or semisweet chocolate), milk chocolate, and white chocolate. However, seven variations of these basic types of chocolate are commonly used in baking.

- **Unsweetened Chocolate.** The actual chocolate-making process begins when the cleaned cocoa kernels, known as **nibs**, are milled into a thick paste. (See the Culinary Science feature in this section to find out where chocolate comes from.) This paste is called **unsweetened chocolate**, **chocolate liquor**, or **baker's chocolate**. Unsweetened chocolate is used primarily as a flavoring in recipes. By itself, chocolate is very bitter.

- **Cocoa Powder.** The unsweetened chocolate may be pressed to remove the cocoa butter, leaving dry **cocoa powder**. **Cocoa butter** is the cream-colored fat from the cocoa beans. It is used in the chocolate-making process. Most cocoa powder used in the kitchen is **Dutch processed** (also called *alkalized cocoa*). This involves reducing the acidity of the cocoa beans before they are ground. The process makes the cocoa powder milder, less acidic, and darker than untreated cocoa. Cocoa powder is commonly used in many baking preparations.

Source: Culinary Institute of America

- **Bittersweet and Semisweet Chocolate.** Cocoa butter, sugar, vanilla, and other flavorings are added to chocolate liquor to produce **bittersweet chocolate** and **semisweet chocolate** (both of which are commonly referred to as **dark chocolate**). Because there are no set standards, the amount of sugar in each varies. Bittersweet chocolate, with less sugar than semisweet chocolate, must contain at least 35 percent chocolate liquor, while semisweet can contain anywhere from 15 percent to 30 percent chocolate liquor.

- **Chocolate Chips or Morsels.** The chocolate used to make chocolate chips is a special blend of chocolate. Generally, chocolate chips contain less cocoa butter than other chocolates. This allows them to retain their shape when baked.

- **Milk Chocolate.** In Switzerland, the Nestlé Company developed **milk chocolate** by developing a milk powder and then adding it to dark chocolate. Today, milk chocolate must contain at least 12 percent milk solids and 10 percent chocolate liquor. Milk chocolate tends to be sweeter than dark chocolate. It is widely used in candies.

- **White Chocolate.** Although not a true chocolate, **white chocolate** is made from cocoa butter, sugar, milk powder, and flavorings. It does not contain any chocolate liquor. It is usually quite sweet.

- **Compound or Coating Chocolate.** Chocolate that is made with vegetable fat instead of cocoa butter is called **compound chocolate** or **coating chocolate**. Replacing the cocoa butter with other, cheaper fats saves the producer money. Compound chocolate is generally easier to use for dipping or glazing and does not require tempering.

READING CHECKPOINT *What are the seven variations of chocolate commonly used in baking?*

Working with Chocolate

Dark chocolate, milk chocolate, and white chocolate are available in several forms. The most common is a bar or large block that can be as small as a few ounces to larger than a few pounds. For convenience, many chocolate companies sell their chocolate in small drops, or coins. These cost slightly more than bars but are much easier to weigh and melt.

When chocolate is used to flavor desserts and pastry items, it can be melted and completely incorporated into the item, as in a chocolate cake. The chocolate can also be left intact, as in chocolate chip cookies. Or, it can be both incorporated and left intact, as in chocolate ice cream with chocolate chips in it.

Melting Chocolate Chocolate melts faster when you use small pieces. This also lessens the chance of burning the chocolate or making it too hot. When melting chocolate, you can use the coins or drops straight from the package; you don't need to cut them into smaller pieces. However, bars or blocks should be chopped into small, even pieces. Use a heavy knife to chop chocolate. Dark chocolate can be extremely hard and difficult to chop.

Place the small pieces of chocolate in a clean, dry bowl. When working with chocolate at any stage, keep the chocolate from contact with water or steam. Water reacts with the starch in cocoa and causes melted chocolate to become very thick. Even one drop of water can make a pound of chocolate unusable.

Place the bowl of chopped chocolate over a pan of simmering water. Stir the chocolate regularly as it is heated to speed the melting and prevent it from getting too hot. The milk solids in milk and white chocolate burn at very low temperatures, so be especially careful not to get them too hot. When melting milk or white chocolate, it is often safest to bring a pan of water to a boil and then turn off the heat. Place the bowl of chocolate in the pan and allow the residual heat to melt the chocolate. Alternatively, chocolate may be melted in a microwave. Place the chocolate in a clean, dry, microwave-safe bowl and microwave it for short periods of time at no more than 80 percent, stirring the chocolate between each heating. This method works well for small batches but is not practical in large-scale production.

Tempering Chocolate Tempering is the process of properly crystallizing chocolate. Tempering chocolate is necessary when the chocolate is to be used by itself and not incorporated into a recipe. Tempering gives chocolate a shiny appearance. It prevents the cocoa butter from separating out of the chocolate and causing white swirls or spots. It makes the chocolate stronger, giving it snap. Tempering also makes the chocolate contract as it cools and gives the chocolate a higher melting point. Although the process of tempering requires some skill and practice, the steps are simple and not difficult to master.

Three significant factors are involved in tempering chocolate:

- **Time.** There are no shortcuts in tempering. If the process is rushed, the chocolate will not crystallize properly.
- **Temperature.** Tempering involves both appropriate heating and appropriate cooling to ensure good crystallization.
- **Stirring.** Tempering requires continuous stirring or movement of the chocolate.

FIGURE 19–2
Melting Chocolate
Take care when melting chocolate not to let it get too hot.
APPLYING CONCEPTS *How does heating chocolate over water keep the chocolate from getting too hot?*
Source: Ian O'Leary/Dorling Kindersley

Chef's Tip

Correct Temperature

The specific working temperature for a chocolate is listed on the package.

FIGURE 19–3

Cooling Chocolate
With the tabling method, chocolate is spread around a marble surface.

APPLYING CONCEPTS *Why is a marble surface good for cooling chocolate?*

Source: Roger Phillips/Dorling Kindersley

Tempering begins by weighing out the total quantity of chocolate that you anticipate needing. If you are working with blocks of chocolate, you'll need to chop it into small pieces. Next, the chocolate is melted and heated to a specific temperature: 110°F for milk or white chocolate and 120°F for dark chocolate. Finally, the chocolate is cooled to a specific temperature: 83°F for milk or white chocolate and 85°F for dark chocolate.

One method for tempering chocolate is known as the **seeding method**. For this method, melt three-fourths of the chocolate you have measured out. Melt it to the correct temperature either over a water bath or in a microwave. Then, add the remaining one-fourth of the chocolate to the bowl of melted chocolate. Stir the chocolate until it cools to the correct temperature.

Another method professional chefs use to temper chocolate is called the **tabling method**. To use this method, pour two-thirds of the warm, melted chocolate from the bowl onto a marble slab. Then move the chocolate around the marble surface with a scraper and a palette knife. When the chocolate on the marble cools enough to thicken, it should still be fluid. Return it to the bowl and stir the chocolate vigorously until it cools to the appropriate temperature.

The next step, for both methods, is to test the chocolate for temper. The easiest way to test for temper is to dip a spoon in the chocolate. Properly tempered chocolate should become firm, or set, in three to five minutes. It should set smooth, with no swirls, streaks, or spots on the surface. If the test is successful, the chocolate is ready to be used. It is referred to as being *in temper*.

If the chocolate is not in temper (meaning that it did not set properly or had swirls, streaks, or spots), you can warm the chocolate again and then either add more chopped chocolate, if you are using the seeding method, or table one-third to one-half of the chocolate if you are using the tabling method. Once it is returned to the bowl, test the chocolate again for temper.

Where Does Chocolate Come From?

Did you ever wonder where chocolate comes from? It is made from the seeds of the cacao tree, which typically grows in tropical rain forests. The process of making chocolate begins with harvesting ripe cacao pods. These pods, similar in size to a small pineapple, contain about 50 seeds, which are also known as cocoa beans.

Most of the world's cocoa beans (about 80 percent) come from a variety of cacao tree called the Forastero, grown in Africa. The more expensive and rare beans, prized by chocolate makers, come from the Criollo, a cacao tree grown in Mexico, Central America, South America, and Indonesia. The Criollo bean was first used by the ancient Mayans. It is less bitter and more aromatic than other cocoa beans. Another variety of bean is the Trinitario, developed in Trinidad. It is a hybrid of the Forastero and the Criollo.

After the cocoa beans are harvested, the next step in the chocolate-making process is fermentation. The beans are piled together and allowed to sit for several days to ferment. This is a natural reaction that produces heat and begins to develop the chocolate flavor of the beans.

The fermented beans are then dried. They are spread in the sun for days or weeks to lower their moisture content. This allows them to be stored for long periods of time without spoiling.

The beans are then roasted in an oven to further develop the flavor of the chocolate. This is similar to roasting coffee beans. Roasting is a critical step—too light a roast will not generate a strong flavor and too dark a roast will give the chocolate a burned, bitter taste. Cocoa beans from different locations have different qualities and flavors, so chocolate makers often blend beans to produce a distinctive mix.

The roasted and cooled beans are cracked to help separate the hard shell on the outside of the beans. The shell is removed,

Cocoa beans shown in the pod and also dried

leaving the cocoa kernels, or nibs. These nibs, which are similar to coarsely ground coffee, are the raw material that manufacturers use to grind, blend, and mold into the product we call chocolate.

Research

Research how cacao trees are grown. Focus on how the growing methods affect the local environment.

Cocoa beans roasting in large, rotating ovens to release their flavor and aroma

FOCUS ON Nutrition

Heart-Healthy Chocolate?

Recent studies have shown that dark chocolate contains a large amount of antioxidants, which reduce the chance and severity of many types of heart disease. Although these studies show promising results, they are still in the early stages.

Keep tempered dark chocolate at around 90°F and tempered milk and white chocolate at around 86°F as you work with it to dip, coat, or glaze items.

Storing Chocolate Chocolate can be stored for up to a year, if it is held properly. Avoid the following four things when storing chocolate:

- **Heat.** Chocolate should be stored in a cool place. Heat can melt chocolate and cause the cocoa butter to separate out. The ideal temperature for storing chocolate is about 55°F.

- **Moisture.** Moisture will cause the chocolate to become very thick when it is melted. Although chocolate is usually packaged in a paper wrapper, it is a good idea to keep it wrapped in plastic or in an air-tight container to prevent moisture in the air from coming into contact with the chocolate.

- **Odors.** The cocoa butter in the chocolate absorbs odors easily. If the chocolate is stored near items that give off strong odors, the chocolate can absorb those odors and have an unpleasant taste.

- **Light.** Avoid storing chocolate in bright light. Light can break down the cocoa butter, causing it to go rancid. The covering of the chocolate should prevent contact with light.

READING CHECKPOINT *What is tempering?*

Making Ganache

Ganache (gahn-AHSH) is an emulsion made with chocolate and cream. It is used for fillings in candies and cakes and as a glaze for cakes and pastries. Heavy cream is heated to a boil before it is added to the chocolate. The ratio of chocolate to cream varies, depending on how the ganache will be used. For a firmer ganache, more chocolate is used, and for a lighter, looser ganache, more cream is used. When making a ganache, it is important to remember that it is an emulsion. If the mixture separates or the emulsion breaks, the final product will not have the desired creamy smooth texture.

A ganache can be flavored in a variety of ways. The cream used in the ganache can be flavored with vanilla, cinnamon, tea, or herbs. A fruit-flavored ganache is made by replacing a portion of the cream with a concentrated fruit purée. Extracts and alcohols can also be added. However, if more than a few drops of liquid are added to the cream, you will need to reduce the cream by that amount so you maintain the appropriate chocolate-to-liquid ratio for your ganache.

When two-thirds of the hot cream and chocolate are initially mixed, an emulsion forms. The mixture should be completely smooth, with no chunks

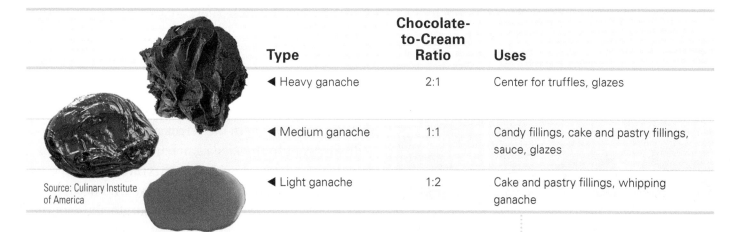

Type	Chocolate-to-Cream Ratio	Uses
◀ Heavy ganache	2:1	Center for truffles, glazes
◀ Medium ganache	1:1	Candy fillings, cake and pastry fillings, sauce, glazes
◀ Light ganache	1:2	Cake and pastry fillings, whipping ganache

Source: Culinary Institute of America

BASIC CULINARY SKILLS

Making a Ganache

① **Chop the chocolate** into small pieces of equal size and put it in a bowl.

Source: Culinary Institute of America

② **Bring the cream to a full boil** in a saucepan.

③ **Pour two-thirds of the cream** over the chopped chocolate.

Source: Culinary Institute of America

④ **Gently stir** the cream-and-chocolate mixture to dissolve the chocolate and create an emulsion.

Source: Culinary Institute of America

⑤ **Add the remaining cream,** a little at a time, to the mixture while stirring until all of the cream has been incorporated.

Recipe Cards

129. Chocolate Ganache

130. Chocolate Fondue

131. Chocolate Truffles

FIGURE 19–4

Truffles
These chocolate ganache truffles are coated with a tempered chocolate.

APPLYING CONCEPTS *Why is tempered chocolate used for the coating on these truffles?*

Source: Culinary Institute of America

of chocolate. It should have a shiny, elastic appearance. Once the initial mixture has come together, continue adding the cream a little at a time, stirring it in, to maintain the emulsion.

You can use the ganache immediately or allow it to cool and thicken before using it. For example, when using a ganache as a glaze, you would use it warm so it remains liquid. For truffles, on the other hand, the ganache should be allowed to thicken in the refrigerator overnight.

If you want to thicken a ganache, allow it to cool at room temperature, stirring the mixture from time to time to ensure that it cools and sets evenly. For light ganache that will be whipped to incorporate air, cool the ganache to room temperature first, stirring occasionally, and then chill the ganache in the refrigerator overnight before whipping.

 **READING CHECKPOINT** *What is a ganache?*

19.1 ASSESSMENT

Reviewing Concepts

1. What are the seven variations of chocolate commonly used in baking?

2. What is tempering chocolate?

3. What is a ganache?

Critical Thinking

4. Predicting What would happen if you used regular dark chocolate as the chocolate chips in chocolate chip cookies?

5. Solving Problems If chocolate that had been stored for a long time was melted and it was too thick, what might have happened to it during storage?

Test Kitchen

Divide into four teams. Each team will make a heavy ganache. Team 1 will use cream. Team 2 will use milk. Team 3 will use water. Team 4 will use orange juice. Compare the texture and flavor of the ganaches.

SOCIAL STUDIES ●———————●
Chocolate for Everyone

Research how chocolate has moved from being a food reserved for royalty and the elite to become a treat for everyone.

19.2

Custards, Mousses, and Frozen Desserts

Key Concepts
- Making custards
- Making mousses and other aerated desserts
- Making frozen desserts

Vocabulary
- aerating
- Bavarian cream
- crème anglaise
- custard
- frozen soufflé
- granité
- meringue
- mousse
- parfait
- pastry cream
- sabayon
- sherbet
- sorbet
- soufflé
- sugar syrup

Custard

A **custard** is a liquid that is thickened with eggs. As a custard is cooked, proteins in the eggs bond together, giving the liquid more body or thickness. Generally the liquid used is a dairy product—milk, cream, or a combination of the two. Great care must be taken when preparing custard recipes. You need to cook the eggs until they bind the custard, but you also have to avoid overcooking them.

There are three basic types of custards.

- Baked custards
- Stirred custards
- Boiled custards

Baked Custards This is probably the most common type of custard. Cheesecake and pumpkin pie, as well as *crème caramel* (CREM KAIR-ah-mehl) and *crème brûlée* (CREM broo-LAY), are examples of baked custards.

Baked custards are made by preparing a mixture of liquid, eggs, and flavoring. The liquid can be dairy or nondairy, such as pumpkin purée. The eggs are added along with flavorings. The flavorings could be sugar, vanilla, spices, chocolate, herbs, or fruits. Flavorings can be added to the liquid before the eggs or added after the eggs are mixed.

In the recipe, you add hot milk to the eggs. If you added all the hot milk to the eggs at once, the eggs would cook. To avoid cooking the eggs, you add only one-third of the hot milk to the eggs while whisking. This increases their temperature without

Source: Culinary Institute of America

Chapter 19 *Desserts*   631

FIGURE 19–5

Crème Brûlée
A crème brûlée is a custard topped with a crust of caramelized sugar.

PREDICTING *Describe the texture of this topping.*

Source: Edward Allwright/Dorling Kindersley Limited

cooking them. You can then add the remaining milk to the egg mixture without cooking the eggs. This is referred to as *tempering* the eggs, slowly increasing their temperature to avoid cooking them.

BASIC CULINARY SKILLS

Baked Custard

① **Preheat the oven** to 350°F.

② **Heat the milk** with half the sugar over medium or high heat.

③ **Combine the remaining sugar** with the eggs in a bowl.

Source: Culinary Institute of America

④ **Add one-third of the hot milk** to the eggs and whisk together.

⑤ **Add the remaining milk.**

⑥ **Strain** the mixture through a fine strainer.

⑦ **Pour the custard** into ovenproof containers and place the containers into a hotel pan.

⑧ **Place the hotel pan in the oven.** Pour warm water into the hotel pan to provide a water bath.

Source: David Murray/Dorling Kindersley

⑨ **Bake** until just set. When moved, the custard should jiggle and not look liquid.

⑩ **Remove containers** from the water bath, transfer to a sheet pan, and refrigerate.

Recipe Card

132. Bread and Butter Pudding

Stirred Custard

1 **Heat the milk** with half the sugar over medium to high heat.

2 **Combine the remaining sugar** with the eggs in a bowl.

3 **Add one-third of the hot milk** to the eggs and whisk together.

Source: Culinary Institute of America

4 **Add the remaining milk.**

5 **Place the pan over low to medium heat.** Stir the mixture thoroughly with a wooden spoon.

6 **Test** the consistency of the custard. The custard is finished cooking when it coats the back of a wooden spoon.

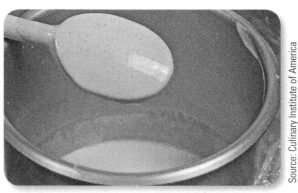

Source: Culinary Institute of America

7 **Remove the pan from the heat** immediately and strain the custard through a fine strainer.

8 **Place the custard in an ice bath** and stir it occasionally to ensure that it cools quickly and evenly. Refrigerate after cooling.

Recipe Card

133. Crème Anglaise

Stirred Custards Stirred custards contain ingredients almost identical to those in baked custards. The difference between the two is how they are cooked. Instead of being baked in the oven, stirred custards are cooked over low heat on the stove. Controlling the cooking and the maximum temperature is extremely important.

With baked custard, temperature is controlled by keeping the oven temperature low and by cooking the custard in a water bath. With stirred custard, you need to stir the custard continuously as it is heated and to stop the cooking at the right moment. As the mixture cooks, the consistency will change from very liquid or watery to slightly thicker (like heavy cream). When the custard coats the back of a wooden spoon, it is finished cooking. Stop the cooking immediately by placing the cooked custard over an ice bath.

Crème anglaise (CREM on-GLAZE), a classic stirred custard, is used as a base for ice cream and mousses. It is also used as a dessert sauce on its own, poured over cake or fruits.

Boiled Custard Boiled custards have the same basic ingredients as baked and stirred custards, but they also include a starch. When a thickener such as flour or cornstarch is added to a custard, it is known as a

Chef's Tip

Infusing

Herbs, spices, and nuts can be used to flavor custards by infusing the milk. To do this, put the flavoring in the milk. Leave it submerged in the refrigerator overnight. Strain the milk and use it for the custard.

Korea

Korea is an Asian country entirely occupying a peninsula jutting out from mainland China toward Japan. Since the 1950s, Korea has been divided at the 38th parallel into North Korea and South Korea. While Korean cuisine has some culinary ties to both China and Japan, it has a unique cuisine all its own.

Perhaps the best-known Korean food is *kimchi* (kim-CHEE), which is made from fermented vegetables with a variety of seasonings. The vegetables typically include cabbage but may also include radishes, scallions, and cucumbers. The seasonings may include chiles, ginger, garlic, and fermented fish or shrimp sauce. Kimchi is often used as an ingredient in stews, soups, and rice. Koreans typically eat kimchi as a side dish to accompany a meal and many do not consider a meal complete without kimchi.

A Korean main dish is usually accompanied by side dishes or *banchan* (BAHNCH-ahn). The most popular banchan is, of course, kimchi. There are typically between two to eleven additional banchan—and several types of kimchi could be served as banchan at one meal. Other types of banchan include steamed, stir-fried, or marinated vegetables; beef simmered in a seasonal broth; pan-fried, thin savory pancakes; steamed eggs; and stir-fried baby octopus in a spicy sauce. Small portions of banchan are placed in the middle of the table to be shared throughout the meal. They are replenished if needed. The more formal the meal, the more banchan there will be.

Bibimbap (BEE-bimbop) is a signature Korean dish. It means "mixed rice" and is a bowl of hot rice with sautéed vegetables and chile paste on top. Often a raw egg or a slice of beef is served on top of the vegetables. To eat the dish you mix everything together (cooking the egg in the process). Additional chile paste is offered on the side if you want to increase the heat level of the bibimbap.

Another signature Korean dish is *bulgogi* (bull-ga-GEE), a kind of barbecued beef. The beef is sliced and marinated before being grilled. The cooked beef is served with lettuce leaves and a thick chile/garlic sauce. You place a slice of beef, some of the sauce, and perhaps some kimchi or other banchan on the lettuce leaf, then roll up the lettuce leaf to eat.

Research

Research the varieties and health benefits of kimchi. Locate a source of kimchi and taste it as part of your research. If you can find ingredients, consider making a version of kimchi.

Source: uckyo/Fotolia

Bibimbap

Source: Ruslan Olinchuk/Fotolia

China

North Korea

Sea of Japan

Korean Peninsula

Yellow Sea

South Korea

Boiled Custard

1 **Heat the milk** with half the sugar over medium to high heat.

2 **Combine the remaining sugar and cornstarch** with the eggs in a bowl.

3 **Add one-third of the boiling milk** to the eggs and whisk together.

4 **Add the egg mixture** to the pan of milk and stir.

5 **Heat the mixture,** stirring continuously, until it comes to a boil.

6 **Continue boiling** the custard for one minute, stirring continuously.

7 **Pour** the custard into a shallow container.

8 **Cover the surface** of the custard with plastic wrap and refrigerate.

Source: Culinary Institute of America

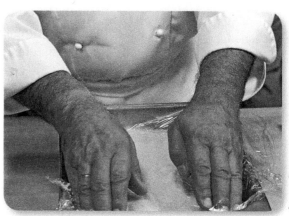

Source: Culinary Institute of America

Custards

Custard Type	Basic Ingredients	Thickening Agent	Cooking Method	Uses
Stirred	Milk, sugar, eggs	Eggs	Cooked slowly on stove	Sauce anglaise, ice cream base, Bavarian cream base, mousse base
Baked	Milk, sugar, eggs	Eggs	Baked in a water bath	Crème brûlée, crème caramel, custard pies
Boiled	Milk, sugar, cornstarch, eggs	Eggs, cornstarch	Cooked on stove	Pastry cream, cream pie fillings, soufflés

pastry cream. By incorporating starch, you make the custard thicker than the other types of custards. The starch also allows you to cook the custard to a higher temperature. In fact, the addition of starch requires that you bring the custard to a full boil and cook it for one minute to completely activate the starch and to remove any starchy taste. The boiled custard method is used in cream pie fillings.

READING CHECKPOINT *What are the three types of custards and how are they made?*

**Storing Custards
and Mousses**
Because custards and
mousses contain eggs and
dairy products, they should
be kept in the refrigerator at
all times. In general, custards
should be used within three
days after they're made.
You may freeze mousses to
prolong their shelf life.

FIGURE 19–6
Light as Air
Mousse is prized for being light
and airy.

INFERRING *Is there such a thing as a
mousse that is too airy?*

Source: David Murray/Dorling Kindersley Limited

Mousses

A **mousse** (MOOSE) is made by adding air to flavored bases, such as chocolate or fruit purées. The term *mousse* comes from a French word that means "fluffy." Adding air to food is referred to as **aerating** (AIR-ate-ing) the food. *Aeration* (air-AY-shun) makes mousses very light and delicate.

Mousses are used by themselves, as well as for fillings for cakes and other pastries. A mousse is just one type of aerated (AIR-ate-ed) dessert. Other types of aerated desserts include most types of frozen desserts, such as ice cream and sorbet.

Mousses and other aerated desserts are made from four basic components: a flavored base, an egg foam, gelatin, and whipped cream. By varying the type or amount of these components, you can achieve different flavors and consistencies.

- **Bases.** The base is what gives mousses and other aerated desserts their flavor. Fruit mousses are based on fruit purée. Chocolate mousses use melted chocolate or sometimes cocoa powder. A stirred custard can also be used as a base for a mousse. The custard can be flavored with a fruit purée, chocolate, spices, or nuts.

- **Egg Foam.** Mousses use an egg foam to provide their airy texture. The foam can be based on either egg yolks or egg whites. The egg foam is heated to 140°F to ensure that it is safe. Use egg yolks to create a sabayon. A **sabayon** (sah-by-YON) is made by whipping egg yolks as they are heated with sugar. Use an egg-white foam to create a **meringue** (mehr-ANG), a mixture of stiffly beaten egg whites and sugar. Because more air can be incorporated into egg whites than into egg yolks, a mousse made with a meringue will be lighter than one made with an egg-yolk foam. Some recipes, such as that for chocolate mousse, use both an egg-yolk foam and one based on egg whites.

- **Gelatin.** Most mousse recipes require gelatin to stabilize the mousse and allow it to hold its shape. The gelatin is soaked in cold water and then melted before adding it to the mousse. The gelatin is usually added to the base, before adding the egg foam.

- **Whipped Cream.** As the last step in making a mousse, whipped cream is folded into the mousse. The cream should be whipped to the soft-peak stage and gently incorporated to avoid overworking it, possibly causing the cream to separate.

Four other types of aerated desserts are quite common:

- **Fruit Mousse.** A fruit mousse is prepared by incorporating gelatin and flavoring with fruit purée and then folding in an egg foam and whipped cream.

- **Chocolate Mousse.** A chocolate mousse is made by folding egg foam and whipped cream into melted chocolate. It typically does not use gelatin because the cocoa butter in the chocolate acts as a stabilizer.

- **Soufflé.** Made by folding egg foam into pastry cream, a **soufflé** (soo-FLAY) rises significantly when baked. Soufflés can be sweet (chocolate, orange, lemon, and raspberry are common flavors) or savory (often adding cheese). Soufflés fall quickly after they leave the oven, so they are best served immediately after they come out of the oven.

- **Bavarian Cream.** Similar to a mousse except that it is made without any egg foam, a **Bavarian** (bah-VAIR-ee-uhn) **cream** is made from a base of stirred custard (vanilla sauce), fruit purée, or a combination of the two. Gelatin is added to the base and whipped cream is carefully folded in. Bavarian cream is simpler to make but is denser and less airy than a mousse.

 **READING CHECKPOINT** *What are the four basic components of a mousse?*

Frozen Desserts

Frozen desserts include a wide variety of items that, similar to mousses, are aerated to give them a special texture. The texture is also achieved by the ingredients used in the frozen dessert. The following are five of the most common types of frozen desserts:

- **Granité.** Made from a flavored water base, a **granité** (grah-nee-TAY) is made by either stirring the base as it begins to freeze or by scraping the frozen base into a sort of shaved ice. Granités have very large ice crystals. They may be fruit-based or made by flavoring a **sugar syrup** (a concentrated solution of sugar and water). *Granité* is the French name for this frozen dessert. *Granita* (grah-NEE-tah) is the Italian name.

- **Sorbet.** Made from flavored bases frozen and aerated in an ice cream maker, a **sorbet** (sor-BAY) is generally fruit-based and does not contain dairy or eggs. As the base begins to freeze, the air is trapped inside the base, creating a smooth, creamy texture. Both granités and sorbets are often served between courses in a multi-course meal to cleanse the palate. They may also be served as a component in a plated dessert.

- **Sherbet.** A variation of a sorbet, a **sherbet** (SHUR-bit) is made similarly but has a meringue folded into it to further aerate it.

FIGURE 19–7

Sorbet
Fruit sorbets garnished with fresh fruit and mint.
PREDICTING *Why would you garnish a fruit sorbet with the same fruit from which it was made?*
Source: Simon Smith/Dorling Kindersley Limited

- **Ice Cream.** Ice cream is made by aerating a dairy base in an ice cream maker. Because it uses dairy in the base, ice cream tends to be heavier and richer than granités, sorbets, and sherbets. Ice cream can be made from a crème anglaise or from sweetened milk or cream. Aside from being served in scoops or cones, it can also be sandwiched between cookies or molded into cakes or other shapes. Shakes and ice cream sodas are other ways to use ice cream.

- **Parfait and Frozen Soufflé.** When a mousse is frozen, it is referred to as a **parfait** (par-FAY) or **frozen soufflé**. Both parfaits and frozen soufflés rely on egg foams and whipped cream to aerate them.

The texture of frozen desserts—their hardness, softness, smoothness, or creaminess—is important. The hardness of a frozen dessert is affected by two main factors:

- **Sugar Content.** One important factor—perhaps the most important factor affecting the hardness of a frozen dessert—is its sugar content. Sugar lowers the freezing point of water. The more sugar a

---

BASIC CULINARY SKILLS

Frozen Soufflé

① **Make a paper collar** that circles a ramekin.

Source: Dorling Kindersley

② **Whip the cream** to a soft peak.

③ **Combine the sugar and water** in a saucepan. Wash sugar crystals off the sides of the pot.

④ **Boil** the sugar-and-water solution over high heat.

⑤ **Place the egg whites in a mixing bowl** and whip.

⑥ **Pour the whipped egg whites** over the sugar solution when the solution reaches 240°F.

⑦ **Whip** the mixture until it is room temperature. It forms a meringue.

⑧ **Fold in the fruit purée.**

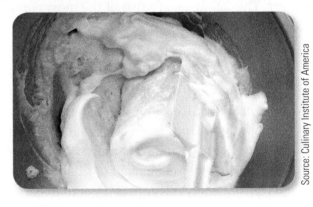

Source: Culinary Institute of America

⑨ **Fold in the whipped cream.**

⑩ **Fill** the prepared ramekin with the mixture.

⑪ **Freeze overnight.**

⑫ **Serve.** Remove the paper collar and dust the top with powdered sugar.

Recipe Card

137. Frozen Lemon Soufflé

recipe has, the softer the frozen dessert will be at 32°F. For example, if you made a sorbet and it came out very hard and brittle, you could melt it, increase the sugar, and reprocess it in the ice cream maker. On the other hand, if the sorbet was very soft, you could melt it, increase the amount of fruit purée (or simply add water) and reprocess. The added water dilutes the sugar in the recipe and allows the sorbet to freeze at a higher temperature.

- **Amount of Aeration.** Another major factor affecting the texture of a frozen dessert is the amount of aeration it receives. The airier the dessert, the lighter and softer it will feel in the mouth. An ice cream maker that spins very rapidly will aerate ice cream or sorbet more than one that is turned very slowly. Granités that are made by stirring by hand will have a much denser and coarser texture than a granité made with the same ingredients but processed in an ice cream machine.

READING CHECKPOINT *What are the two major factors affecting the texture of frozen desserts?*

19.2 ASSESSMENT

Reviewing Concepts

1. What are the three types of custard?

2. What are the four basic components of a mousse?

3. What are the two major factors affecting the texture of frozen desserts?

Critical Thinking

4. Applying Concepts What is the purpose of tempering the eggs when making a custard?

5. Comparing/Contrasting What is the difference between a sabayon and a meringue?

6. Comparing/Contrasting What is the difference between a granité and a sorbet?

7. Comparing/Contrasting What is the difference between a sorbet and a sherbet?

Test Kitchen

Divide into three teams. Choose a basic baked custard recipe. Team 1 will make the custard using egg yolks only. Team 2 will use egg whites only. Team 3 will use whole eggs. All teams will use the same amount of eggs. Compare the texture and taste of the custards.

SCIENCE

Ice Cream

Research how early hand-turned ice cream makers worked. Report on how they got the liquid cold enough to form ice cream and how they aerated it. Compare them to modern electric home ice cream makers.

19.3

Cookies and Cakes

READING PREVIEW

Key Concepts

- Identifying the basic ingredients of cookies and cakes
- Identifying various types of cookies
- Making cookies
- Making cakes
- Building, icing, and finishing cakes

Vocabulary

- American buttercream
- bar cookies
- buttercream
- cut-out cookies
- double-panning
- drop cookies
- French buttercream
- German buttercream
- icebox cookies
- Italian buttercream
- molded cookies
- piped cookies
- rolled cookies
- simple syrup
- stabilizing
- stenciled cookies
- torte
- twice-baked cookies

Basic Ingredients of Cookies and Cakes

The characteristics of a cookie or cake are determined to some degree by their ingredients. Each ingredient contributes to the flavor and texture. Four basic ingredients are used for both cookies and cakes:

- **Flour.** The gluten found in flour gives cookies structure. It also adds some flavor and nutritional value. Most cake recipes call for cake flour, which is lower in protein content. This prevents gluten development in the cake, which would make it tougher.

- **Eggs.** Eggs provide structure and moisture.

- **Sugar.** Sugar is predominantly a flavoring agent, but it is also responsible for browning during baking. It helps cookies expand during baking.

- **Fat.** Fat adds moisture and contributes to tenderness and mouth-feel.

The following ingredients are often found in many types of cookies and cakes:

- **Leaveners.** Chemical leaveners for cookie and cake production include baking soda and baking powder.

- **Flavorings.** Flavor agents used in cookies and cakes are almost limitless. Extracts are an easy way to impart flavor without altering a recipe. Citrus zest can be added to give a lemon or orange flavor. You can also use nuts, spices, chocolate chips, and fruit as flavorings.

Source: Clive Streeter/
Dorling Kindersley

Julia Child

Anyone who cares about cooking and eating probably knows about Julia Child. With two French co-authors she wrote *Mastering the Art of French Cooking*, which introduced mainstream America to French cooking. She followed that up with a television show, *The French Chef*, which started in 1963 and was an instant success. She continued writing cookbooks and teaching cooking in various shows through the 1990s.

What people may not know about Julia Child is that she might never have mastered French cooking or starred in television shows if she hadn't been six feet, two inches tall!

Julia Child was born in 1912. She was in her late twenties when World War II started. She wanted to volunteer with the Women's Army Corps (WACs) or the U.S. Navy's WAVEs—but she was too tall for both of them. Instead, she joined the Office of Strategic Services (OSS), the U.S. intelligence agency that had just been formed. (The OSS was the precursor to the CIA.) Because of her education, experience, and intelligence, she quickly assumed a high level of responsibility as a top-secret

Julia and Paul Child

researcher. She was posted in Ceylon, where she met Paul Child, who would become her husband.

Paul Child had lived in Paris and was known for his sophisticated palate. After his marriage to Julia, Paul was assigned to Paris and introduced Julia to French food. And Julia Child discovered that she loved French food! She wanted to make French food, any food, for Paul, but she didn't know how to cook. To remedy that, she enrolled in Le Cordon Bleu, a famous French cooking school. Soon she was teaching American women in Paris how to cook French food. That led to joining a women's cooking club where she met two French women, Simone Beck and Louisette Bertholle, who were writing a book to teach American women how to cook French food. They were looking for an American to help them make the book appealing to Americans. And the rest is history!

All because she was six feet, two inches tall!

Research

Form a group and choose a recipe from *Mastering the Art of French Cooking*. Compare a recipe for the same dish in another cookbook. Cook both recipes. Discuss the differences in the dishes and in the recipes. Which dish did you prefer? Which recipe did you prefer?

Julia Child in *The French Chef*

- **Garnishes.** Garnishes add additional flavor, texture, and eye appeal to cakes and cookies. You can add them to cookie dough or batter before baking or apply them after baking as decorative touches. Garnishes include chocolate chips, nuts, candy pieces, dried fruit, citrus zest, icing, and melted or tempered chocolate.

READING CHECKPOINT *What are the four basic ingredients used for both cookies and cakes?*

Types of Cookies

The three main types of cookies are drop cookies, bar cookies, and rolled cookies.

Drop Cookies The most common type of cookie is the drop cookie. **Drop cookies** are made from a firm dough or batter that holds its shape on a sheet pan. Form drop cookies by scooping out a portion of dough and dropping it onto a sheet pan. Most recipes for this type of cookie contain a high percentage of fat. The fat melts during baking to give the cookie its finished shape. A drop cookie can be crispy or chewy, depending on its ingredients and how long it is baked. Two common types of drop cookies are chocolate chip cookies and oatmeal cookies.

There are three special types of drop cookies: icebox cookies, piped cookies, and stenciled cookies.

- **Icebox Cookies.** Often called *refrigerator cookies*, **icebox cookies** are formed into a cylinder, chilled, and then sliced and baked. This type of cookie is ideal for high-volume production demands. If cylinders have a similar weight and circumference and the slices are the same thickness, each cookie is guaranteed to be the same portion and to bake evenly. Cylinders of chilled cookie dough are quick to slice and place on sheet pans. If properly wrapped, the dough can be held in the freezer for two to three months.

- **Piped Cookies.** Made of soft dough that can be piped through a pastry bag, **piped cookies** can be made into many decorative shapes if you use different pastry tips. The size of the pastry tip is often determined by the consistency of the dough. The thinner the dough, the smaller the tip. Uniform piping is crucial to the success of this cookie's production. Spritz cookies, ladyfingers, and macaroons (mac-uh-ROONS) are among the many types of piped cookies.

- **Stenciled Cookies.** Delicate, wafer-like **stenciled** (STEN-sild) **cookies** are made with batter that can be spread very thin and baked without losing its detailed shape. You form these cookies either by spreading the batter onto sheet pans into stencils to make perfect designs or by spreading the batter freehand, without any

Chocolate chip cookie
Source: Vlad Ivantcov/Fotolia

Spritz cookie
Source: Dave King/Dorling Kindersley

FIGURE 19–8
Chocolate Tuiles
Tuiles, a type of stenciled cookie, are rolled into shape while still warm.
APPLYING CONCEPTS *How might you fill this cookie?*
Source: Ian O'Leary/Dorling Kindersley Limited

stencil. Ingredients for this type of cookie vary, but recipes often contain a high percentage of sugar and eggs, with very little flour. Stenciled cookies bake quickly and, when you remove them from the oven, they can be rolled, curled, or draped over an object while still warm to form different shapes. A popular stenciled cookie is the *tuile* (TWEEL). It is frequently used as an edible container or accompaniment to frozen desserts, mousses, and custards.

Bar Cookies Bar cookies are made from a soft batter that is spread into a pan before baking. Once baked, bar cookies are cut into individual cookies. Some types, such as lemon bars, are layered with different components. Although bar cookies generally have a shorter shelf life than other cookies (their sliced edges turn stale quickly), they are good for production because they can be portioned into different sizes and shapes.

Twice-baked cookies are a special type of bar cookie. They are made of dough that is formed into a large log-shaped cookie and baked. Once baked, the cookies are cut into slices and baked a second time to attain a very crisp texture. This type of cookie has a long shelf life because of its low fat content. Italian *biscotti* (bee-SKAWT-tee) are the most common twice-baked cookies. They are very crunchy and are often dipped in chocolate for added flavor.

Rolled Cookies Rolled cookies (also called **cut-out cookies**) are made of stiff dough that is rolled flat and then cut into decorative shapes, often using cookie cutters. You can also create them freehand with the tip

Bar cookies
Source: Clive Streeter/Dorling Kindersley

Biscotti
Source: Elena Elisseeva/Fotolia

of a sharp knife. Cut-out cookies have great eye appeal because of their unique shapes and their garnishing possibilities. However, they are among the most challenging cookies to make because the cookies need to retain their shapes during baking. Cut-out cookies are generally crisp, although some varieties have chewy or soft textures.

Molded cookies are a variation of rolled cookies. They are made with stiff dough that is shaped by hand. The dough can also be stamped, pressed, or piped into carved molds. When making this type of cookie, the dough must be firm enough to hold its shape when baking. Cookie molds come in a variety of shapes and sizes and are commonly made of wood. Many molded cookies are of international origin, such as the German *springerle* (SPRING-uhr-lee) and English shortbread. Bakeries and pastry shops customarily offer these traditional varieties for special holidays.

 READING CHECKPOINT *What are the three main types of cookies?*

Making Cookies

Unless otherwise stated in the recipe, cookie ingredients should be at room temperature (70°F–75°F) before mixing. Cold ingredients (such as butter, eggs, and milk) should be brought to room temperature before adding them to the dough. When added during the mixing process, cold ingredients can cause the dough to separate and lose its uniform consistency.

Accurately measured ingredients are necessary to ensure dependable baking results. A scale provides the most precise measurements. If in doubt, measure a second time. It is easier to correct a potential baking problem at this point. Once cookies go into the oven, it is too late to correct any problems.

Preparing Cookie Pans Cookies that are evenly baked and uniform in size require the use of specific pans that are properly prepared. Most bakers prepare their cookie pans *before* mixing their dough.

- **Selecting a Pan.** Flat, standard-sized sheet pans are suitable for most cookies. Cookies with a high fat content tend to brown easily, so it is good practice to use two stacked sheet pans. This is called **double-panning.** Double-panning creates insulation for cookies, allowing for gentle heating of the bottoms. When preparing bar cookies, use the pan size specified in the recipe. Using a pan with the correct dimensions ensures that bars bake evenly and reach the desired thickness.

- **Preparing the Pan.** Pans are typically lined with either parchment paper or silicone baking mats. Silicone baking mats are ideal

Cut-out cookie
Source: Dave King/Dorling Kindersley

for baking cookies. They provide a nonstick surface, can withstand oven temperatures up to 500°F, and are cost-effective because they are reusable. Stenciled cookies, in particular, bake best on silicone mats. For bar cookies, line the pan with parchment paper and leave an overhang on two sides of the pan to act as handles. When properly cooled, the entire bar can be removed from the pan easily and without breakage. If the recipe calls for a greased pan, either spray the surface lightly with a nonstick cooking spray or use clean paper toweling to apply a light coating of fat. (Greasing pans is not recommended for all types of cookies; the fat may cause some types to spread excessively and brown more on the bottoms.)

FIGURE 19–9
Using a Silicone Mat
Cookies are easy to remove from this type of pan liner.
ANALYZING INFORMATION *How is the chef forming the shape of these cookies?*
Source: Pearson Education/PH College

- **Temperature of Pan.** Never portion cookie dough onto hot sheet pans or baking pans. Pans should be at room temperature before they are prepared or filled. If the pans are hot, the cookie dough will start to melt before it goes into the oven. This will result in excessive spreading.

Two Methods of Mixing Dough The texture, shape, and structure of a finished cookie rely heavily on the way it is mixed. The following are the two most common mixing methods for cookies:

- Creaming method
- Foaming method

Creaming Method Many cookies are made by using the creaming method. As you know from Section 18.1, to cream means to blend a combination of ingredients together until their consistency is smooth and uniform. Unlike baked products that require a long creaming time to allow for the incorporation of air (such as some sorts of cakes), the mixing time for cookies is short, eliminating the addition of too much air. (Longer creaming times cause increased leavening, which results in light and airy, cakelike cookies.)

A short creaming time prevents cookies from spreading too much during baking. If the dough becomes too warm as it is creamed and shaped, the cookies may spread too much and run into each other on the baking sheet. However, if the dough remains cool until it goes into the oven, cookies will spread at the proper rate. Avoid over mixing. This causes gluten to develop and the cookies will not be as tender, nor will they spread properly. Cookies that are intended to spread during baking will normally contain a significant amount of butter to help encourage their expansion.

Chef's Tip

Cleaning Silicone Mats

Silicone baking mats must be properly washed after each use to maintain a sanitary surface. Once the mats are clean and dry, store them flat to prevent splitting.

Creaming Method for Cookies

1. **Place the sugar and fat into the bowl of a mixer.**

2. **Cream** the ingredients on medium speed with a paddle attachment until the mixture is smooth.

Source: Culinary Institute of America

3. **Add the eggs** in several additions and beat well after each addition.

4. **Scrape the bowl** with a rubber spatula, when needed, to blend ingredients.

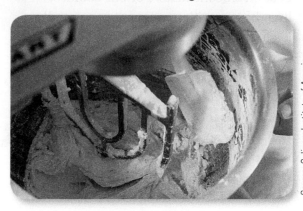

Source: Culinary Institute of America

5. **Add the dry ingredients** all at once and mix on low speed until just incorporated.

6. **Add garnishes.**

7. **Blend** until evenly combined. Do not overmix.

Recipe Card

138. Oatmeal Raisin Cookies

Foaming Method   The foaming method is used to make several varieties of cookies, including meringues, macaroons, and madeleines. The foam in this method is made by whipping eggs and sugar until thick and light in texture. Cookies made with this mixing method tend to use less flour and have a more resilient texture than those made with the creaming method.

Foaming Method for Cookies

1. **Place the sugar and eggs in the bowl of a mixer.**

2. **Whip the ingredients** on high speed, using a whisk attachment, until thick and light.

3. **Add the dry ingredients** and mix on low speed until just incorporated.

4. **Add fat,** if required by your recipe, and mix on low speed until just incorporated.

5. **Scrape the bowl** with a rubber spatula, when needed, to blend ingredients.

6. **Add garnishes,** if required by your recipe.

7. **Blend** until evenly combined. Do not overmix.

Shaping Cookies Techniques vary for shaping different types of cookies. With the exception of bar cookies, the manner in which cookies are portioned, shaped, and placed onto the baking sheet will determine how they bake.

- **Drop Cookies.** To portion drop cookies, fill a scoop of the proper size with dough and level it off. Release the dough onto the prepared sheet pan. If stated in the recipe, flatten the mounded dough for a more even spread. Leave 1 to 2 inches of space between the mounds of dough. This gives the cookies enough space to spread during baking. Also, portion the dough into even rows so space is used efficiently.

- **Icebox Cookies.** Chill the dough for about 10 minutes. Divide it into manageable portions. Mound each portion onto a separate piece of parchment paper, leaving 2 to 3 inches at each end. Roll the paper around the dough and smooth it into an even cylinder. When the paper is wrapped tightly around the dough, gather the ends of the paper and twist to compact the dough into a log. If the roll becomes flat on one side, round it by gently rolling it again. After the dough is rolled into a cylinder, chill it until it is very firm. Most frozen dough can be sliced directly from the freezer. Use a sharp knife for clean and uniform slices. The thickness of the slices determines the character of the baked cookie. Thin slices will result in a crisp texture; thicker slices will be softer. Place the slices on a prepared sheet pan in even rows, spacing the cookies about 2 to 3 inches apart to allow for spread. Icebox cookie dough can be stored in the refrigerator for up to one week. For longer storage, wrap properly, label the packaging, and freeze until needed.

- **Piped Cookies.** Place the dough in a pastry bag fitted with the appropriate tip. When the pastry bag is one-half to two-thirds full, twist the top of the bag to seal it. Squeeze the bag to release any air in the tip. Hold the twisted end firmly in one hand. Use the other hand to lightly guide the tip. Apply even pressure to dispense cookies in even rows onto a prepared sheet pan. Maintain consistent pressure while keeping the tip at a constant level to produce uniform cookies. The shape of the cookie determines the angle of the bag. Hold the bag upright for stars and swirls. Hold the bag at an angle for straight lines. To finish each cookie, release the pressure, push down slightly, and then quickly lift the tip away. If the tip is lifted away before the pressure is released, the dough will form a "tail" on the top of the cookie that is likely to become too dark during baking. Use a template to

Piped cookies
Source: Chris Leachman/Fotolia

maintain even spacing when you are piping cookies. You can create a template by marking a pattern on the back of parchment paper. Pipe the cookie dough onto the front of the paper to avoid contamination from ink.

- **Stenciled Cookies.** Place the stencil on a silicone-lined sheet pan. Spoon a small amount of chilled batter into the center of the design and use a small offset spatula to spread it evenly to the edges of the stencil. This makes the cookies bake uniformly. Carefully lift the stencil from the sheet pan, scrape off any excess batter, and repeat the process. Spacing depends on the size of the stencil. If you are shaping the cookies freehand, place the batter on the prepared sheet pan and use an offset spatula to shape. Stenciled cookies are often baked in small batches because they must be wrapped or shaped while hot from the oven.

- **Bar Cookies.** Begin with a properly lined baking pan of the correct size. Use a rubber or offset spatula to spread the batter evenly. Hold the spatula nearly parallel to the surface of the batter while spreading. Spread the dough to an even thickness. The corners and edges will dry out during baking if they aren't as thick as the center.

- **Twice-Baked Cookies.** Place the dough on a prepared sheet pan and form into a log according to the dimensions of the recipe. Gently even out the sides of the log with lightly floured hands. Bake the log until it is a light golden brown and then remove it from the oven and cool for 10 to 15 minutes. The center of the log will be soft when removed from the oven. If indicated in the recipe, lower the oven temperature while the log cools. Using a wide offset spatula, transfer the log to a clean work surface and cut it with a serrated knife crosswise on the diagonal into slices of the desired thickness. Return the slices to the sheet pan and position each slice cut side down, ½ inch apart in even rows. Return them to the oven and bake to the desired crispness.

- **Cut-Out Cookies.** When rolling cookie dough, always work with chilled dough. Prepare the sheet pans before rolling so you can transfer the cookies directly to the pan. Divide the dough into manageable portions. Work with one portion at a time and keep the remaining dough tightly wrapped and refrigerated. When rolling out the dough, if it is soft and delicate, place it between two sheets of parchment paper for easier rolling. If the dough becomes warm while rolling, place it in the refrigerator to chill. When cutting the cookies, press firmly to make clean cuts through the dough; twisting the cutter can cause the cookies to lose their shape. You can place cut-out cookies relatively close together on the sheet pan because cut-outs do not generally spread much. When using cutters of varying sizes and shapes, bake cookies of like sizes together to ensure even baking.

- **Molded Cookies.** If the dough is too soft to hold its shape, refrigerate until it is firm enough to work with. To shape by hand, roll dough

Source: Culinary Institute of America

Biscotti are twice-baked cookies

Recipe Card

139. Biscotti

Cut-Out Cookies

Source: Pearson Education/PH College

1. **Dust** the dough and the work surface lightly with flour. Do not use more flour than needed.

2. **Place the dough on the board.**

3. **Roll out the dough** from the center to the outer edge. Turn the dough often while rolling to keep it an even thickness. Most cookie dough should be rolled ⅛ to ¼ inch thick.

4. **Cut cookie shapes** freehand or use cookie cutters. Dip the cutting edge of the knife or cutter into flour to keep it from sticking to the dough. To minimize trimmings, place the cutter close to the cut-out holes.

5. **Transfer cookies** to the prepared sheet pan. Maintain even rows for consistency.

into smooth balls of a uniform size. Place the balls of dough on a prepared sheet pan in even rows, spacing the cookies about 2 to 3 inches apart. To make stamped cookies, roll the dough according to the cut-out cookie directions, press the prepared stamp into each cookie, and remove quickly. Use a sharp knife to cut the dough into individual portions. Place cookies on a prepared sheet pan in even rows 1 inch apart. To make cookies with a cookie mold, pack the dough into the prepared mold and run a rolling pin over the surface a few times to fill the mold completely. Molds should be very clean so the cookies are clearly imprinted with the design and unmold easily.

Baking Cookies Cookies need to be properly baked to attain their desired shape, size, flavor, and texture. Consider the following factors before placing the cookie dough in the oven:

- **Oven Temperature.** Preheat the oven to the correct temperature before baking cookies. A preheated oven ensures that the cookies bake at the proper rate, spread to the preferred size, and achieve the expected texture, flavor, and color. Preheating an oven normally takes about 15 minutes.

- **Position of Oven Racks.** Generally, when baking only one pan of cookies at a time, center the rack so the cookies are in the middle of the oven for even browning and baking. When baking multiple sheet pans, leave at least 2 inches around each sheet to allow for even heat circulation.

- **Baking.** Halfway through the recommended baking time, rotate the sheet pans so the part that had been in the back of the oven is now

Source: nickola_che/Fotolia

Fully-baked biscotti

FIGURE 19–11
Elaborate Icing
This gingerbread heart was first iced with a red frosting, which was allowed to dry. Then an elaborate design was piped on the frosting.

INFERRING *With the amount of work required to prepare this cookie after baking, would you expect it to be expensive?*

Source: cristi180884/Fotolia

in the front of the oven. This helps achieve even browning and baking. When baking more than one sheet pan at a time, change their positions on the oven racks as well as rotating them. Because most cookies are smaller than other baked goods and often contain a high percentage of sugar, they burn easily. Check for doneness several minutes before the recipe indicates.

- **Determining Doneness.** Because many types of cookies remain on the hot sheet pan for several minutes before transferring to wire cooling racks, they will continue to bake when they are removed from the oven. To account for the carryover baking, you can remove cookies from the oven when they appear slightly underbaked. Most cookies are done when they are light golden brown on the bottom and along the edges. Consult the recipe for specific indications of doneness.

- **Cooling Cookies.** Instructions for cooling vary among recipes. Generally, you should remove cookies from the sheet pan as quickly as possible after baking to prevent further browning. Some cookies, however, are too soft to be removed immediately. When necessary, allow the cookies to cool briefly on the baking pan just until they have set enough to be transferred to a wire cooling rack. Stenciled cookies should be shaped as soon as they are removed from the oven.

Finishing Cookies Finished cookies provide versatility to any foodservice establishment. From big, chunky drop cookies to expertly garnished cut-outs, cookies are a part of many catered events, receptions, banquets, buffets, and plated desserts. Many cookies are ready to be served as soon as they cool. However, bar cookies need to be cut and stenciled cookies need to be shaped (if desired). You can also ice or glaze cookies or create sandwich cookies.

- **Cutting Bar Cookies.** Cool bar cookies completely and remove the entire bar from the pan, using the handles of the parchment paper. Place on a clean cutting surface. If glazing or icing, apply the desired amount and chill the bar to firm the glazing or icing before cutting. Use a thin, sharp knife for clean, straight cuts. Wipe the blade of the knife clean between cuts.

- **Glazing or Icing Cookies.** There are several ways to apply glazes and icings to cookies after baking. To eliminate mess and waste, arrange cookies closely together on wire racks placed over sheet pans. Pipe icing or glaze over the surface of the cookies to create a design, or simply drizzle the icing or glaze free-form. Another technique involves spreading icing or ganache on the surface of a cookie with a small offset spatula. You can also dip cookies into melted chocolate or warm ganache. When dipping, allow the excess chocolate or ganache to drain into the bowl. Scrape any extra from the bottom of the cookie and place the coated cookies on wire racks to set until firm.

- **Shaping Stenciled Cookies.** Shape warm stenciled cookies by draping them over various objects to create different shapes. To make a container, for example, you could drape the cookie over an inverted cup. The cookie must be warm and pliable enough to shape without cracking.

- **Sandwiching Cookies.** Making sandwich cookies involves joining two cookies together with a thin layer of filling or ice cream. The cookies used for sandwiching should be uniform in shape and thickness. Apply just enough filling to hold the cookies together. Using a small offset spatula, spread the filling so it doesn't quite reach the edge of the cookies; the filling will spread when the cookies are pressed together.

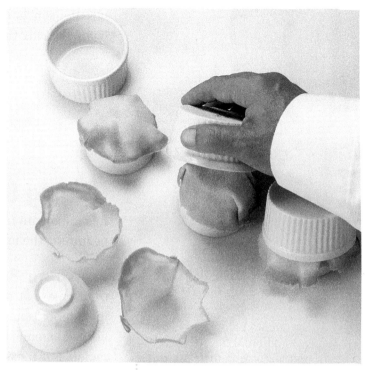

FIGURE 19–12
Shaping Stenciled Cookies
The baked cookies are draped over cups while they are still pliable.
PREDICTING *Why is it important to work fairly quickly when shaping a stenciled cookie?*
Source: Pearson Education/PH College

Serving and Storing Cookies Although cookies have always been served with hot beverages and cold milk, they also provide the perfect accompaniment to frozen desserts, mousses, and custards. Their crisp texture is a nice contrast to the creaminess of the dessert. Cookies are an important element of plated desserts. As a combination of various items, such as cool ice cream, warm chocolate sauce, light-as-air whipped cream, and crunchy cookies, plated desserts offer chefs the freedom to create signature desserts. Even with contrasting flavors, textures, and temperatures, the components of a plated dessert are meant to complement one another. Ice cream, chocolate sauce, whipped cream, and a cookie may sound like ingredients found in a common sundae, but when presented in a unique and decorative manner, the dessert becomes a one-of-a-kind creation.

The most important step in storing cookies is to cool them completely on wire racks before putting them away. Because cookies contain a significant amount of sugar, and sugar attracts moisture from the air, cookies can turn soggy or stick together if they're not stored in airtight containers at room temperature. To prevent fragile cookies from breaking, store them between layers of parchment paper. Precut bar cookies should be wrapped individually. Most cookies can be frozen for up to 2 to 3 months. They should be wrapped well in plastic, freezer bags, or plastic containers with airtight

Chef's Tip

Cool Cookies

If stenciled cookies become cool and brittle while shaping, return the pan of baked cookies to the oven to warm briefly.

Ice cream with biscotti
Source: Getty Images

Chef's Tip

Mixed Cookies

Do not store cookies with different flavors and textures in the same container. If stored together, their flavors will mix and crisp cookies will become soft.

FIGURE 19–13

Preparing Cake Pans

This springform pan is first greased (left) and then coated with flour (right).

PREDICTING *Why does a springform pan make it even easier to remove a cake without damaging it?*

Sources: (left) Dave King/Dorling Kindersley; (right) Dave King/Dorling Kindersley Limited

lids. Remember to date and label the cookies on the outside of the packaging before storing them in the freezer.

READING CHECKPOINT *What are the two most common mixing methods for cookies?*

Making Cakes

It is important to have all ingredients for a cake properly scaled out before beginning the mixing process.

Preparing Pans Most bakers prepare their cake pans before mixing their cake batter. Cakes are baked in a wide variety of pans. Pan types include loaf pans, tube pans, Bundt pans, round pans, and square pans, as well as pans that use new materials such as silicone and special paper molds. For most types of cakes, pan preparation is vital. If the pan is not properly prepared, you will not be able to remove the baked cake without damaging it.

Most cake pans are prepared by greasing and flouring them. Brush soft butter or shortening into the pan, being careful to completely cover the pan. After greasing, put a small amount of flour in the pan and move it around to ensure that the flour completely coats the inside. For some cake pans, you can use paper liners.

Mixing Methods For any type of cake, it is important to sift all the dry ingredients. Sifting the dry ingredients together helps to mix and combine them. More important, it breaks up any lumps in the flour.

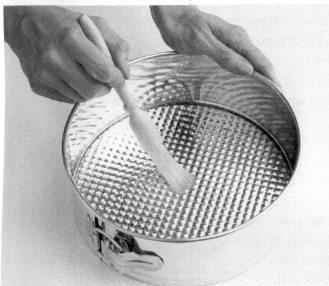

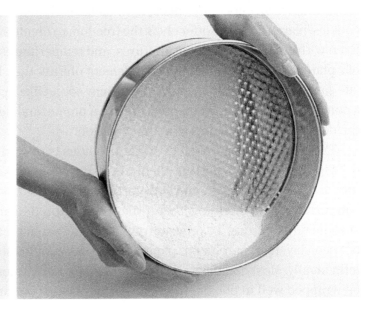

The mixing methods used for different cakes greatly affect their texture and density. The method used also affects the specific ingredients called for by the recipe. The following are the three most common mixing methods for cakes:

- Creaming method
- Warm foaming method
- Cold foaming method

Creaming Method The creaming method is one of the simplest ways to make a cake batter and is similar to the creaming method for making cookies. Pound cake is a classic example of a cake made by using the creaming method. Creaming-method cakes tend to be denser and heavier than cakes made by using other mixing methods. The air that is trapped in the fat by creaming creates small pockets of air in the baked cake. The trapped air expands slightly during baking, helping to leaven the cake. In a classic pound cake, for example, the trapped air is the only leavener, so it is important to add as much air as possible during the creaming process.

In the creaming method, you mix the sugar and fat (butter) together until they are very light and fluffy. After the sugar and fat are creamed, add the eggs a little at a time to prevent the mixture from separating and breaking the emulsion.

The eggs should not be straight from the refrigerator, because they will cool the creamed fat and sugar, increasing the time it takes to cream them. Once all the eggs are incorporated, add the flour and mix just to incorporate it. Do not overmix the batter.

Chef's Tip

Warm Butter

Creaming time is decreased if you slightly warm the fat to room temperature before beginning to cream it with the sugar.

Recipe Card

140. Marbleized Pound Cake

FIGURE 19–14

Emulsifying the Batter
When adding the eggs or other liquids to the fat and sugar in a creaming-method cake, be sure to add them slowly to avoid separating the mixture.

INFERRING *How would a cake turn out if the sugar and fat do not emulsify with the eggs?*

Source: Culinary Institute of America

Warm Foaming Method Sponge cakes are a wide category of cakes that are typically made with a warm egg-foam base. (Angel food cake is made by using the cold foaming method.) The lighter, airier texture is due to the air beaten into the eggs before other ingredients are added. Because eggs are capable of trapping very large quantities of air, cakes made by using the warm foaming method are much less dense than cakes made by using the creaming method.

Heating the egg-and-sugar mixture dissolves the sugar and loosens the proteins in the eggs, which allows them to accept and hold more air throughout the mixing and baking. When the warm egg-and-sugar mixture is whipped in a mixer on high speed, it will quadruple in volume, become very pale in color, and have a much firmer texture. This is the egg foam that is so important for this method of mixing.

After the egg foam has reached maximum volume, slow down the mixer to a medium speed and allow to mix for another 15 minutes. This step is called **stabilizing**. After the initial high-speed whipping, the air in the foam is in both large and small bubbles. In the stabilizing step, the continued mixing breaks the large bubbles into smaller ones. This provides a better final texture.

After the egg mixture has stabilized, the dry ingredients are incorporated by hand, folding in several small additions. You must do this very carefully to prevent the tiny air pockets from being broken. A small amount of liquid fat is gently folded in last. The fat will speed up the breaking down of the foam, so it should always be added last.

Cold Foaming Method Angel food cake is made by using the cold foaming method. Angel food cake is a meringue-based cake batter. Its light, airy texture results from the large amount of air that can be beaten into the meringue. Angel food cakes tend to be very sweet because a high sugar content helps stabilize the meringue.

To make an angel food cake, begin whipping the egg whites and slowly add sugar as if you were making a meringue. After whipping the meringue to the soft-peak stage, fold in cake flour and more sugar. One important step that sets these cakes apart from other types of cakes is that the pans are not greased. The delicate batter needs to adhere to the sides of the pan as it cools or it will collapse. After filling the pan with the batter, run a knife or spatula around the inside of the pan to get rid of any large air pockets. After baking, the cakes are cooled upside down to prevent collapse.

Baking Cakes No matter which mixing method you use to make a cake, baking is the last step. All types of cakes are delicate mixtures that have trapped air in them. If the cake is not baked immediately after mixing, the air can easily escape before the batter sets. This makes the crumb irregular.

Always preheat the oven to the desired temperature before beginning a cake recipe. Most cakes bake between 350°F and 400°F, although thin sheet cakes are sometimes baked at a slightly higher temperature. After the

Recipe Cards

141. Common Meringue

142. Angel Food Cake

Angel food cake

Source: Culinary Institute of America

Warm Foaming Method

① **Prepare the pans** and preheat the oven.

② **Sift** the dry ingredients.

③ **Combine the eggs and sugar** in a bowl.

④ **Place the egg mixture over a pan of simmering water.**

⑤ **Stir** the egg mixture while it heats.

Source: Culinary Institute of America

⑥ **Remove from the heat** when the mixture reaches 110°F.

⑦ **Whip** the mixture with an electric mixer on high speed for 5 minutes.

Source: Culinary Institute of America

⑧ **Continue whipping** the mixture on medium speed for 10 to 15 minutes.

Source: Culinary Institute of America

⑨ **Add the dry ingredients** in several batches, carefully folding them in.

Source: Culinary Institute of America

⑩ **Combine a small portion of the batter with the fat** and then fold it into the rest of the batter.

Source: Culinary Institute of America

⑪ **Pour the batter into the prepared pans** and put them in the oven.

⑫ **Turn cakes out** of their pans and onto a cooling rack when they are baked.

Recipe Cards

143. Vanilla Sponge Cake

144. Cheesecake

FIGURE 19–15

Testing Doneness
A sponge cake should spring back when gently touched with a finger.

INFERRING *Why would it be better to test a sponge cake by touching it gently rather than sticking a skewer in it?*

Source: Culinary Institute of America

cake is put in the oven, avoid opening the door to the oven until the cake is about half baked. The change in temperature from hot air escaping can cause the cake to fall.

There are several tests to tell when a cake is done. The first and easiest is to look for even browning on the surface. Because most cakes have a large amount of sugar, they get very brown as the sugar caramelizes. As the cake bakes, it will also pull away from the sides of the pan, leaving a small gap. (The exception to this is angel food cakes, which stick to the pan.) If both of these tests are positive, gently touch the top of the cake with the tip of a finger. The small dent should spring back immediately. If the dent remains, the cake needs more time. The last test is to insert a skewer or paring knife into the center of the cake. The tester should come out completely clean, with no moist batter sticking to it.

Once the cake is baked, it should be unmolded. Turn the pan upside down over a cooling rack. If the pan was properly prepared, the cake will drop out of the pan. If the cake is left to cool in the pan, it may become soggy from steam and is likely to stick. If the cake is stuck in the pan, gently run a paring knife around the edge of the pan. After the cake is completely cooled, it can be filled and served. It can also wrapped and frozen for later use.

READING CHECKPOINT *What are the three mixing methods used for cakes?*

Building, Icing, and Finishing Cakes

Almost any type of cake can be used to make a filled cake. After the cake is baked and allowed to cool, it may be cut horizontally into several thin layers if desired. A filling is spread or piped between the layers. The cake is then reassembled. At this point it is ready to be iced. In general, a spreadable icing is used for cakes, but pourable icings such as a liquid glaze, or even rolled icings such as marzipan, may be used. After the cake is covered with icing, it is garnished or decorated and is ready to be served.

Building Slice the cake, using a long serrated knife, if necessary. Try to keep the layers level and even in thickness. If you are using a sponge cake, you can brush the layers with flavored simple syrup. **Simple syrup** is a mixture of equal amounts of sugar and water that has been brought to a boil to dissolve the sugar crystals. The syrup adds both moisture and flavor to the finished cake. Spread a layer of the filling to be used (jam, buttercream, ganache, mousse, or another filling). Repeat these steps with all the layers of the cake. Do not put filling on the top layer. At this stage, the cake can be finished, wrapped and refrigerated, or frozen for finishing at a later time.

A **torte** (TORT) is typically a type of layered cake or pastry that originated in central Europe. The cake portion of a torte is sometimes made with little or no flour, using instead ground nuts, sugar, eggs, and flavorings. Tortes are often filled with buttercream, mousse, jam, or fruits. One of the most well-known types of tortes is the Austrian sachertorte, traditionally made with chocolate sponge cake, a layer of apricot preserves, and chocolate icing on the top and sides. The German linzertorte, another famous torte, features a crumbly dough made with flour, butter, egg yolks, lemon zest, cinnamon, and ground nuts, usually hazelnuts. The pastry dough is typically covered with raspberry or red currant jam, and a pastry lattice is placed on top of the jam layer.

Icing Icings on cakes serve four primary functions. Icing obviously makes the cake look attractive, but it also protects the cake from drying out, adds additional flavor to the cake, and adds a different texture to the cake. Icings used as a filling between layers in a layer cake can introduce new and unexpected flavors and textures to a cake.

Buttercream is a type of icing that is made by aerating butter, shortening, or a combination of the two with powdered sugar. Buttercream is used to ice and decorate cakes. It is also used as a filling in cakes and pastries. Buttercream is very rich, and the amount per serving should be kept small. Most buttercreams have a long shelf life if properly stored. If you use buttercream that was made ahead of time and stored in the refrigerator, it must be warmed and then rewhipped or it will be very stiff and dense.

The most common types of buttercream are American, Italian, French, and German.

- **American Buttercream.** The easiest type of buttercream to make is **American buttercream**. It is just butter that is creamed with powdered sugar. It is denser and richer than the other types of buttercreams. It is usually used on traditional layer or butter cakes.

- **Italian Buttercream.** **Italian buttercream** is made by adding butter to a meringue. After the meringue is made, softened butter is added to it. Italian buttercream is very white, which makes it appropriate for use on wedding cakes.

- **French Buttercream.** **French buttercream** is made from egg yolks that are whipped. Sugar is added to the whipped yolks and

FIGURE 19–16
Sachertorte
This sachertorte has flakes of very thin, tasteless edible gold sheet on top.
INFERRING *What do the flecks of gold on the top of the torte contribute to the value of the torte? The taste of the torte?*
Source: StefanieB/Fotolia

Recipe Card
145. Layer Cake

Recipe Card
146. Italian Buttercream

Icing a Cake

1 **Cool** the cake completely.

2 **Eliminate any crumbs.**

3 **Place the cake on a cake turntable,** if one is available.

4 **Apply a thin coat of icing** on all surfaces using a palette knife. This is called the *crumb coat* because it keeps crumbs from appearing in the next coating.

5 **Apply a thicker layer of icing** to finish the cake. Try to get it as smooth as possible.

6 **Finish the cake** as desired.

then softened butter is added. Because French buttercream is made with yolks, it has a yellow color. It is often flavored with coffee or chocolate. Keep any cake filled or frosted with French buttercream refrigerated.

- **German Buttercream.** German buttercream is made from a base of whipped pastry cream. When the pastry cream is cool, butter is added to it. German buttercream is very rich but a good choice for a cake filling. Because German buttercream is dairy-based, it has a short shelf life and should be made and used in several days. Keep any cake filled or frosted with German buttercream refrigerated.

You can flavor buttercreams in a number of ways. The simplest way is to add an extract or flavor paste when you finish making the buttercream. For example, you can add melted chocolate to make a chocolate buttercream. Because buttercream uses a large amount of sugar, unsweetened chocolate is often the best choice to flavor it. Alcohols, fruit purées, and fruit juices can all be added to a buttercream to flavor it, but take care not to add too much or the mixture is likely to separate.

Cakes can also be glazed. Glazes for cakes are typically made with butter, powdered sugar, and milk (or cream, for a richer glaze). Flavor extracts, fruit juice, or liquor can be added to the glaze to flavor it. The glaze can be drizzled on or brushed on with a pastry brush. Before applying the glaze you can use a fork to make pinpricks in the cake so the glaze penetrates into the interior of the cake. Depending on the glaze, nuts or other garnishes can be sprinkled on the glaze while it is still wet.

Finishing/Decorating After icing, you can add decorations for visual appeal. Decorations can be very simple, such as combing the sides of the cake with a cake comb. Or, you can get more elaborate. For example, you could make intricate piped designs.

Decorations on the top can include a decoration placed on top of each slice. You could also decorate the top with a large design, such as writing

FIGURE 19–17

Piped Designs with Buttercream

Buttercream is a perfect medium to pipe decorations on cakes, but it needs to be the proper consistency to look its best.

COMMUNICATION *Do you like the basket-weave pattern that the pastry chef is applying to this wedding cake?*

Source: Culinary Institute of America

Happy Birthday. In general, it is more appealing to keep decorations small in relation to the size of the cake. If the decorations are large, they tend to overwhelm the cake and make it look top-heavy.

READING CHECKPOINT *What are the four types of buttercream icing?*

19.3 ASSESSMENT

Reviewing Concepts

1. What are the four basic ingredients used for both cookies and cakes?
2. What are the three main types of cookies?
3. What are the two most common mixing methods for cookies?
4. What are the three most common mixing methods for cakes?
5. What are the four types of buttercream icing?

Critical Thinking

6. **Applying Concepts** Why is it necessary to cream cookie ingredients for only a short period of time?
7. **Drawing Conclusions** Why is simple syrup often brushed onto a sponge cake before it is filled?

Test Kitchen

Divide into two teams. Team 1 will make a drop cookie from scratch. Team 2 will make the same variety of drop cookie but use either a cookie mix or a prepared cookie dough. Compare the flavor, texture, and color of the finished cookies.

SOCIAL STUDIES ———•
Wedding Cakes

Many cultures have a specific tradition for wedding cakes. Research traditional wedding cake styles for France, England, and the United States. Compare and contrast the different traditions.

Pies, Tarts, Pastries, and Fruit Desserts

Key Concepts

- Making pie and tart dough
- Assembling pies and tarts
- Making pastries with other types of dough
- Making fruit desserts
- Plating desserts

Vocabulary

- blind-baked
- choux paste
- éclairs
- fluting
- lattices
- phyllo dough
- puff pastry
- rubbed-dough method
- streusel
- top crust

Pie and Tart Dough

Source: Clive Streeter/Dorling Kindersley

The pastry shell is a major component of a pie or tart. It has a large effect on the texture of the final product. Pies and tarts are both made by filling a pastry shell with a fruit, nut, or cream filling. Pies are made in a pan that has tall sides that flare out. Tarts are made in pans that have shorter sides and tend to be vertical. Tart pans may have either straight sides or fluted sides.

Three types of pastry dough are used for both pies and tarts: flaky dough, cookie dough, and crumbly dough. They are defined by their ingredients and how they are made.

Flaky Dough Flaky dough is generally used for pies. It is made with flour, water, and butter or shortening. The fat is cut into the dry ingredients and left in small pieces before adding the water. This method is called the **rubbed-dough method** because when you make it by hand, you rub the fat into the dry ingredients with your hands. The spaces left by the melted fat when the dough is baked give it a flaky texture. For flavoring, you usually add a small amount of salt and sometimes a small amount of sugar. Flaky dough tends to be pale or white when baked.

Cookie Dough Cookie-textured dough is a sugar cookie–type dough made from flour, sugar, fat, and eggs using the creaming method.

FIGURE 19–18

Pie vs. Tart
The apple pie (left) has tall sides that flare out. The pear tart (right) has shorter sides that are typically vertical.

DRAWING CONCLUSIONS *Which do you think would have a greater ratio of filling to dough, a pie or a tart?*

Sources: (left) M.Studio/Fotolia; (right) Scruggelgreen/Shutterstock

The complete incorporation of the fat is what gives the dough the texture of a cookie. This type of dough is most often used for tarts. The addition of eggs gives this type of dough a golden-brown color when baked. This is also known as *short dough* or *tart dough*.

Crumbly Dough Crumbly dough is very rich in both fat and sugar. It is typically made from flour, sugar, fat, and eggs. Crumbly dough is very delicate to work with. It can be made by using either the rubbed-dough method or the creaming method. When using the rubbed-dough method, you work

BASIC CULINARY SKILLS

Rubbed-Dough Method Pie Dough

1. **Sift** together the dry ingredients.

2. **Chill the shortening or butter** until very firm.

3. **Cut the fat** into cubes ½ inch square.

Source: Culinary Institute of America

4. **Place the fat in the mixing bowl** with the dry ingredients.

5. **Break the fat into smaller pieces** by rubbing the mixture with your fingers in the bowl.

6. **Add the liquid** to the bowl when the pieces of fat are the size of split peas. The liquid should be cold to avoid melting the fat.

7. **Mix** the liquid carefully with the dry ingredients and fat. Mix just until the mixture comes together and forms a ball.

8. **Wrap** the dough in plastic wrap.

9. **Chill** the dough for several hours before using.

Recipe Card

147. Pie Crust

FIGURE 19–19

Assorted Pies

The texture of the pie crust is determined mostly by the incorporation of the fat.

COMMUNICATING *How important to you is a flaky pie crust?*

Source: Zigzag Mountain Art/Shutterstock

the fat completely into the dry ingredients rather than leaving large pieces of fat before incorporating the liquid.

 **READING CHECKPOINT** *What are the three types of dough used in pies and tarts?*

Assembling Pies and Tarts

After the dough is made, a pie or tart must be assembled. This involves making a filling, rolling out the dough, filling the pie shell, and, in some cases, topping the pie or tart.

Fillings There are four types of filling for pies: raw fruit filling, cooked fruit filling, cream filling, and custard filling.

- **Raw Fruit Filling.** Raw fruit fillings are made by mixing cut-up fruit with sugar, other flavorings, and either flour or cornstarch. The fruit and other ingredients are tossed together and then placed into an unbaked shell. As the filling bakes, the fruit releases juices that are thickened by the flour or cornstarch. This is one of the simplest methods and is often used for apple pies, peach pies, and berry pies. Raw fruit pies must be prepared and baked as soon as the filling is made or the fruit will begin to break down.

- **Cooked Fruit Filling.** For a cooked fruit filling, the cut fruit is cooked on the stove with sugar and other flavorings. You thicken the liquid released by the fruit by using a cornstarch slurry. Once the filling has cooled, it is placed in an unbaked pie shell. Cooked fruit fillings are used for apple pies, cherry pies, and blueberry pies. Cooked fruit fillings have the advantage of being able to be prepared in advance and stored in the refrigerator for several days before you fill and bake the pie.

 Recipe Card

148. Apple Pie

Blueberry filling

Source: Janis Christie/Getty Images

- **Cream Fillings.** Cream fillings are made by preparing a boiled custard and filling a prebaked shell after it has cooled. Classic cream-filled pies include Boston cream pies and lemon meringue pies, as well as chocolate, coconut, and banana cream pies. Because the filling must go into the previously baked shell as soon as it is cooled, pies with cream fillings cannot be made in advance and stored in the refrigerator waiting to be baked.

- **Custard Fillings.** For a custard filling, a liquid is combined with eggs to form a custard, and the raw custard is poured into the shell and baked until set. The shell may either be raw or prebaked, depending on how long the custard will take to fully set. Pecan pies, pumpkin pies, and quiches are examples of custard fillings. Custard fillings may be made a day or two before baking but should not be stored longer because they contain raw eggs that can quickly spoil.

Rolling Dough No matter which type of dough you use, it should be rested and well chilled before you use it to make a pie or tart. Some tarts are made by pressing the dough evenly into a tart pan. Most pies are made by rolling the dough and placing it into a pie pan.

Roll the pie dough, using plenty of flour to prevent it from sticking to the bench and to the rolling pin. The dough should be rolled to approximately ⅛ inch thick. Roll the dough larger than the pan so there will be enough dough to go up the side of the pan.

Before moving the dough into the pan, brush the excess flour off with a soft brush. Fold the dough in half and then in half again. Gently lift the dough up and place it in the pan. Unfold the dough. Gently work the dough into the pan, being sure to cover all the surface area of the pan. You can then trim off the excess dough with a small knife or by pressing the dough against the edge of the pan to pinch it off.

Pie crusts are usually given a decorative edge, called a **fluting**. This fluting makes the pie more attractive. In the case of double-crusted pies, it

Chocolate custard filling

Chef's Tip

Need Dough?

As a general rule, one ounce of dough is needed for each inch of the pan's diameter.

FIGURE 19–20

Fluting

Fluting can be done by hand or by using special tools.

DRAWING CONCLUSIONS *Why would a professional bakery or restaurant want its pies to have perfectly fluted crusts?*

Lined shell weighted with beans
Source: Dave King/Dorling Kindersley

Recipe Card

149. Fruit Tart

FIGURE 19–21

Lattice Effect
Strips of dough are evenly spaced and woven together on top of the filling.

DRAWING CONCLUSIONS *How might you seal the edges of the strips when the lattice work is finished?*

Source: Richard Embery/Pearson Education/ PH College

also helps to seal the bottom and top crusts together. You can flute a crust by gently squeezing the dough between your fingers or by using a special tool.

Blind Baking A pie shell either is filled and then baked or it is baked before filling. A prebaked pie shell is also called a **blind-baked** pie shell. Blind-baked pie shells are used either when the filling is not baked at all or when the pie will be in the oven for a shorter time than it would take to bake the dough.

To blind-bake a pie shell, line the shell with parchment paper and fill the paper with weights. The weights may be dried beans, uncooked rice, or special pie weights made from metal or ceramic. Bake the weighted shell in the oven until the dough is baked. The weights keep the pie shell from bubbling.

Assembling After the pan has been lined with dough (and, in some cases, blind-baked), it can be filled with the pie filling. Mound the pie so that the center is higher than sides of the pan for both raw fruit and cooked fruit fillings. Both of these fillings will tend to shrink when baked. Custard pie fillings should come nearly to the upper edge of the pie crust. Filling custard pies is best done as close to the oven as possible because it is difficult to carry the pie filled with the liquid filling. Cream pie fillings should also completely fill the crust; they are usually topped with meringue or whipped cream to make them look very full.

Toppings Both pies and tarts can have a variety of toppings, either before baking or after baking. Toppings include a top crust, streusel or crumbs, a lattice, fresh fruit, meringue, or whipped cream.

- **Top Crust.** A large piece of pastry dough that is rolled out and placed on top of the filled shell before baking is called a **top crust**. The rim of the bottom crust needs to be brushed with water before placing the top crust on it. The top crust may be egg-washed to give it color and a shiny appearance. Small slits should be cut in several places in the top crust to allow steam from the filling to escape.

- **Lattice.** Made with the same dough as you use to line the shell, **lattices** are rolled-out dough that is cut into strips. The strips are laid across the top of the filling to create a crosshatch, or lattice, effect. Lattices may be egg-washed for color and shine before baking. A lattice adds an interesting visual effect and allows some of the filling to be visible after the item is baked.

- **Streusel or Crumbs.** Streusel is a mixture of flour, sugar, nuts, oatmeal, or other dry ingredients and butter to create large chunks or crumbs (which is why streusel is often referred to as a *crumb topping*).

These chunks or crumbs are sprinkled over the pie or tart filling to completely cover it before baking. Crumb toppings provide flavor as well as an interesting texture to the pie or tart.

- **Fresh Fruit.** Fresh fruit can make an attractive addition to a pie or tart. After the pie has been baked and cooled, slice the fruit and arrange it in a decorative fashion on top.

- **Meringue and Whipped Cream.** Cream pies are often covered with either meringue or whipped cream. To cover a cream-filled pie or tart with meringue, prepare the pie or tart. Make a meringue and spread it on completely, covering the filling. Then lightly brown the meringue in a very hot oven, in a broiler, or by using a propane torch. For whipped cream, the sweetened cream is usually piped on the cooled pie in a decorative way.

Streusel topping on apple-cranberry pie
Source: Richard Embery/Pearson Education/PH College

 **READING CHECKPOINT** *What are the four types of pie fillings?*

Pastries Made with Other Types of Dough

Three other types of dough are commonly used in making pastries: choux paste, phyllo dough, and puff pastry.

Choux Paste Widely used by pastry chefs and bakers, **choux** (SHOO) **paste**, also called *pâté à choux* (PAHT AH SHOO), is a versatile dough or batter. It can be used to create both sweet and savory items. Probably the most widely known pastries made with choux paste are **éclairs** (EE-clahrs) and cream puffs. Éclairs are long, straight pastries that are filled with cream and glazed on top.

Choux paste is made from basic ingredients—liquid, fat, flour, and eggs. The liquid used is usually water, milk, or a combination of the two. Almost any fat can be used, but you should consider the taste of the fat. For example, if you were making a savory item with the choux paste, lard or bacon drippings might be appropriate as the fat, but they would not be appropriate for a sweet item. Flour is used to give the choux its structure and allows it to trap steam during baking, pushing the choux up and creating the hollow space inside for fillings. Eggs add flavor and moisture.

Choux paste is usually piped out and baked, but it can also be fried and served like a doughnut. Choux paste can easily be used for savory items, such as hors d'Oeuvre or appetizers, because the paste has little or no sugar in it.

After making the choux paste, use it to fill a pastry bag fitted with a large round tip. Pipe out the desired shapes on a parchment-lined sheet pan. You could egg-wash the items to give them more shine and color. Bake the items in a preheated oven until they are completely browned. As they bake, the liquid in the paste turns to steam and pushes the dough apart, creating a hollow in the center. This is where you can put a filling after baking.

Meringue topping on lemon pie
Source: David Murray and Jules Selmes/Dorling Kindersley

Choux Paste

1. **Scale** the ingredients.
2. **Pour the liquid** into a saucepan.
3. **Cut the fat** into small cubes.
4. **Add the cubed fat** to the liquid.
5. **Heat the mixture** over medium to high heat.
6. **Remove the mixture from the heat** when it comes to a full boil.
7. **Add the flour** all at once and stir it in.
8. **Cook the mixture,** while stirring, for about 30 seconds.

Source: Culinary Institute of America

9. **Put the dough in a mixing bowl** and stir for a minute to cool it slightly.

10. **Add eggs one at a time,** allowing them to incorporate after each addition.

Source: Culinary Institute of America

11. **The paste is done when all the eggs are incorporated.** You can then pipe the choux paste into the desired shape.

Source: Culinary Institute of America

Recipe Card

150. Profiteroles

After the choux is baked and cooled, you can fill it. For sweet items you will usually use a cream-based filling. The most traditional filling is a flavored pastry cream. You can lighten the pastry cream by folding in whipped cream. You can also use mousses and even ice cream. The cleanest way to fill the choux is to poke a small hole in the bottom and pipe the cream inside, being sure to completely fill it. For some items it may be more appropriate to slice the choux and pipe the filling in.

Choux paste items are usually finished with a glaze or other garnish on top. They may also be finished by dipping the tops in caramel or chocolate or by simply lightly dusting them with powdered sugar.

Phyllo Dough Used in Middle Eastern and Greek cuisine, **phyllo** (FEE-low) **dough** is unleavened dough made from flour, water and a small amount of oil. It is rolled and stretched into paper-thin sheets. It is usually layered and then it can be folded or rolled. When sheets are layered, melted butter is spread between the layers with a pastry brush. As the dough is cooked, the butter keeps the layers separated. As the butter in the dough bakes, the steam released by the dough and the butter is trapped in the layers. This causes the phyllo dough to expand and rise as it bakes and produces a number of layers that are flaky and crisp.

Phyllo dough is labor intensive to make. You can purchase frozen phyllo dough in commercially prepared sheets. The Greek pastry baklava (BACH-la-vah) is phyllo dough layered with chopped nuts and syrup or honey. Spanakopita is another Greek specialty made from phyllo that is filled with spinach and feta cheese.

Puff Pastry Somewhat similar to phyllo dough, **puff pastry** starts with a dough made from flour, water, and melted butter. This dough is rolled out and a layer of solid butter is placed on top of the dough. (In some cases, lard or vegetable shortening may used for savory pastries.) The dough is folded around the butter. Then it is rolled out again and folded in thirds (like a letter) or fourths (like a book). This process is repeated three or four times. To produce the most layers, the dough and the butter must be cool enough so that the butter is firm. If the butter (or other fat) becomes warm, then it is allowed rest in the refrigerator in between folding and rolling out the dough. This creates a dough that is actually many, many layers (often more than a hundred and sometimes more than five hundred layers, depending on how many times it was folded over onto itself).

Baklava
Source: © Constantinos/Fotolia

Just as with phyllo dough, the butter between the layers of dough keeps them separated and creates steam, which evaporates, leaving air pockets and causing the dough to puff up. Because puff pastry is also labor-intensive, commercially prepared frozen sheets of puff pastry are available. Puff pastry is used for making pastries such as *palmiers* (PAHLM-ee-yay), also known as *elephant ears*. The puff pastry is rolled out, and then each side is rolled to meet in the middle. The rolled dough is cut into ¼-inch-thick

FIGURE 19–22

Choux + Filling + Glaze = Dessert

Many pastries can be made using different combinations of choux paste shapes, fillings, and glazes.

APPLYING CONCEPTS *What different choux paste desserts are you familiar with?*

Source: Edward Allwright/Dorling Kindersley Limited

Palmier
Source: © Brad Pict/Fotolia

slices, coated with sugar, and baked. Puff pastry is also folded over savory or sweet fillings to create turnovers. Because puff pastry can be easily molded to a shape and rises when it is baked, it is often used as a base or container for savory or sweet fillings.

READING CHECKPOINT *What are the steps in making choux paste?*

Fruit Desserts

Fruit is used in pies, cakes, cookies, and pastries, but it can also be used to create sweet, flavorful fruit sauces to accompany these desserts. The simplest fruit sauce is one made from puréed berries, sugar, and water. If the berries have seeds, strain the purée before adding the sugar and water. To add complexity, you can substitute a citrus juice (such as orange juice) for some of the water. For a more syrupy sauce, you can add a cornstarch slurry to the fruit sauce and heat it until it thickens. Whole berries or diced fruit can be added to the finished sauce to give it additional texture.

Fruit can be baked or roasted as a dessert. Apples are often cored, filled with nuts, brown sugar, cinnamon, and butter, and then baked. Softer fruits like plums, pears, and peaches are often cut and roasted, sometimes with a little butter, sugar, and orange juice.

Bananas Foster

Source: © sarsmis/Fotolia

Fruit can also be sautéed and poured over ice cream, pancakes, waffles, French toast, biscuits, or cakes. Bananas Foster, a famous New Orleans dessert, starts with bananas sautéed in butter, brown sugar, cinnamon, and banana liquor. Rum is added to the mixture and it is flambéed, then spooned over vanilla ice cream.

Another way to serve fruit as dessert is to poach it. While any firm fruit such as apples, apricots, prunes, and figs can be poached, the most common poached fruits are peaches and pears. The pears or peaches are sometimes peeled and cored or pitted before poaching, but they may also be poached whole with the skin and the core or pit and then peeled and cored or pitted after they have finished poaching. Wine is often used as the poaching liquid, with aromatic spices such as cinnamon, cloves, or vanilla beans added to it. The fruit is poached in the liquid until the fruit becomes soft. Then it is removed and the liquid may be reduced until it becomes syrupy and then served as a sauce with the fruit. One of the most famous poached fruit desserts is Peach Melba, invented by Auguste Escoffier (see Section 18.2) in 1892 for the Australian opera singer Nellie Melba. Poached pears are served on top of vanilla ice cream, and raspberry sauce is drizzled over it. When Escoffier created the first Peach Melba, he displayed it in an ice sculpture of a swan.

Peach Melba

Source: © unpict/Fotolia

READING CHECKPOINT *How do you poach fruit?*

Plating Desserts

Plating desserts is often thought of as the showplace for a chef's skill in pastry and dessert making. Plates can range from simple arrangements, such as a slice of cake or a tart on a plate, to multicomponent designs that coordinate a number of flavors, textures, and temperatures. In fact, those three elements—flavor, texture, and temperature—need to be considered when you create a plated dessert.

When thinking about a plated dessert, you also should consider everything added to the plate as adding to the pleasure of eating the dessert. Nothing on the plate should be placed there simply for visual purposes or just because it looks good.

A plated dessert starts with the major component of the dessert. This could be a tart, pastry, cake, or some other sweet. The main component should look attractive and interesting.

Try to work with small molds or to cut from a large item in a way that does not look just like a wedge.

After the main component, everything else added to the plate needs to complement and contrast the flavor, texture, and temperature of the main component. You can add a sauce, or several sauces, to the plate to increase flavor. You could use a simple fruit sauce made from a purée and sugar or use a cream sauce, such as crème anglaise.

Frozen components are often added to provide a major change in temperature. If the main component is warm or room temperature, adding an ice cream or sorbet provides contrast. Using a frozen component can also give the chef an opportunity to add another flavor to the plate. For example, an individual apple tart could be paired with caramel ice cream. The caramel will work well with the apple flavor and is not a part of the tart itself.

For textural contrast, a small cookie or tuile may be added to the plated dessert. The distinct crunch of a properly made cookie adds to the overall enjoyment of the dessert. This textural change can be especially important if the main component in the dessert has only one texture. This could happen with a mousse or baked custard.

When deciding how to plate a dessert and what other items to put with a main

FIGURE 19–23

More Than Just a Chocolate Tart

The components of this plated dessert offer contrasting flavors, textures, and temperatures.

DRAWING CONCLUSIONS *Is there anything you would add to or subtract from this arrangement?*

Source: Maksim Shebeko/Fotolia

component, think about flavor combinations and experiment with several options to come up with the best combination. It is also a good idea to try the plate as your client or customer would and sit at a table to eat it. That way, you can discover which desserts are hard to eat or which flavors and textural combinations just do not work well.

 **READING CHECKPOINT** *What are the three elements of a plated dessert?*

19.4 ASSESSMENT

Reviewing Concepts

1. What are the three types of dough used for pies and tarts?

2. What are the four types of pie fillings?

3. What are the steps in making choux paste?

4. How do you poach fruit?

5. What are the three elements of a plated dessert?

Critical Thinking

6. Compare and Contrast What is the difference between a pie and a tart?

7. Compare and Contrast What is the difference between a cream filling and a custard filling?

8. Applying Concepts If your major component is a brownie, what might you do to make a memorable plated dessert?

Test Kitchen

Divide into three teams. Decide on a pie filling. Each team will make a different version of a pie shell and fill it with the same filling. Team 1 will make the pie using a flaky dough. Team 2 will use a cookie dough. Team 3 will use a crumbly dough. Evaluate the pies.

LANGUAGE ARTS

Gather Information

Discuss with four chefs and/or bakers their methods for making flaky pie dough. Compare and contrast their different approaches and tricks for achieving a flaky crust.

PROJECT 19 **Chocolate, Chocolate, Chocolate** You are now ready to work on Project 19, "Chocolate, Chocolate, Chocolate," which is available in "My Culinary Lab" or in your *Student's Lab Resources and Study Guide* manual.

Reviewing Content

Choose the letter that best answers the question or completes the statement.

1. The chocolate made from cocoa butter, sugar, milk powder, and flavorings is
   a. unsweetened chocolate.
   b. semisweet chocolate.
   c. white chocolate.
   d. coating chocolate.

2. Boiled custard is
   a. thickened by eggs.
   b. thickened by starch.
   c. cooked on the stove.
   d. all of the above

3. If a cookie recipe spreads too much when it is baked, it may have
   a. had a long creaming period.
   b. too much yeast.
   c. been kept too cold.
   d. an inadequate amount of butter.

4. Sponge cakes are an example of
   a. the creaming method.
   b. the angel food method.
   c. the foaming method.
   d. the rubbed-dough method.

5. Choux paste gets its structure from
   a. eggs.
   b. butter.
   c. flour.
   d. cream.

6. Granité is a type of
   a. mousse.
   b. custard.
   c. cake.
   d. frozen dessert.

7. An oatmeal cookie is a type of
   a. stenciled cookie.
   b. piped cookie.
   c. drop cookie.
   d. bar cookie.

Understanding Concepts

8. What is a ganache?

9. What is a sabayon?

10. What type of cookie is made by using the foaming method?

11. What is the base for an angel food cake?

12. In relation to the pie shell, what makes a cream pie different from other types of pies?

13. What is the most widely known pastry made from choux paste?

Critical Thinking

14. **RECOGNIZING PATTERNS** Would a ganache made with white chocolate have a stronger or weaker chocolate flavor than a ganache made with milk chocolate? Explain your answer.

15. **ANALYZING INFORMATION** What is the difference between a stirred custard and a baked custard?

16. **COMPARING/CONTRASTING** How are bar cookies and twice-baked cookies similar? How are they different?

Culinary Math

17. **APPLYING CONCEPTS** How much cream is required to make 6 pounds of light ganache?

18. **SOLVING PROBLEMS** If a recipe of choux paste makes 42 éclairs and a recipe of pastry cream makes enough to fill 24 éclairs, how much of each recipe will be needed to fill an order for 84 éclairs?

On the Job

19. **CLASSIFYING** A customer has given you a recipe for shoo-fly pie that is made with 1 quart of molasses, 2 cups of sugar, 8 whole eggs, and 4 egg yolks. What type of filling is this likely to be?

Pastry Chefs

Pastry chefs in fine dining restaurants play a crucial role in the success of the restaurant. Like their counterparts, the executive chefs who manage the main kitchen, pastry chefs are responsible for the operations of an entire section of the kitchen. Depending on the size of the operation, an executive pastry chef may be charged with overseeing an entire brigade, with each person in the brigade filling a specific role or practicing a specific skill.

Pastry chefs are responsible for developing dessert menus, generating new offerings, managing costs, overseeing purchasing, and producing dessert items. They are generally expected to take an active part in selecting and maintaining specialized pastry equipment, writing recipes, and training their staff. Executive pastry chefs may work for restaurants, chains, or large companies that produce desserts or dessert components that are then sold to other restaurants or directly to consumers through retail shops.

Candy makers and chocolatiers produce a wide range of confections. The name for this position in the classic brigade system is *confiseur* (kawn-FEE-zeur). Some work in shops or outlets devoted exclusively to artisan chocolates, and others work for larger companies that manufacture chocolates and candies.

The *décorateur* (deh-core-a-TOUR) creates showpieces and special cakes, notably wedding cakes. This involves a high degree of artistic and technical skill. The popularity of specialty cakes continues to grow, making chefs' skills with such techniques as piping and sugar work a valuable asset in their careers.

Entry-Level Requirements

Many pastry chefs attend culinary schools and earn an associate degree in baking and pastry. This period of formal education typically includes coursework that lays some of the important groundwork for specializing: food safety and sanitation, business and management in the foodservice industry, nutrition, culinary science, and principles of flavor and texture development. However, you will still find that others have acquired their skills through on-the-job training and apprenticeships.

Helpful for Advancement

Certifications from organizations including the American Culinary Federation (ACF) and the Retail Bakers of America (RBA) can advance your career. These groups have established various criteria to evaluate your knowledge and skill.

Some pastry chefs have added to their practical knowledge related to chocolate and sugar work by taking courses or pursuing degrees in food science. Workshops and seminars are another way for them to gain valuable training and education.

Another effective way to advance your career in baking and pastry is to join organizations and groups that can help you create a network.

Owning and operating a retail shop or a larger wholesale operation may be the ultimate goal for some. Learning more about business practices and management by attending classes or workshops is helpful.

Source: Culinary Institute of America

Pastry chefs in fine-dining restaurants play a crucial role in the success of the restaurant

STÉPHANE WEBER

Stéphane Weber is the Pastry Chef and Instructor at Bocuse Restaurant of The Culinary Institute of America (CIA), where he is responsible for the dessert menu and bakery items. He joined the CIA faculty in 2002, after working in many prestigious kitchens.

Chef Weber was the Executive Pastry Chef at Osteria del Circo in New York City, and was the chef pâtissier at Le Meridien Hotel in Chicago and the Parker Meridien in New York City. He has also held pastry positions in London and Paris.

Stéphane Weber

Chef Weber holds a Certificat, Aptitude Professionnelle from Jean-Ferandi in Paris and completed his apprenticeship with Jean Jeudon in Paris. Chef Weber has also won many awards, such as Best Dessert Menu at the 2001 Food Online food show and First Place in the 1995 Domain Cameros Wedding Cake Competition.

VITAL **STATISTICS**

Graduated: Certificat, Aptitude Professionnelle from Jean-Ferandi, Paris

Profession: Pastry Chef and Instructor, Bocuse Restaurant at the CIA

Interesting Items: Taught pastry courses at the French Culinary Institute in New York City

Was voted CIA Faculty Member of the Year in 2012

In 1993, won third place in the Godiva Liqueur Cup and the Kahlua Liqueur Competition

CAREER **PROFILE**

Salary Ranges

Assistant Pastry Chef: $25,000 to $50,000

Pastry Chef: $35,000 to $80,000

Executive Pastry Chef: $45,000 to $100,000

Business Owner: Varies widely

Working in a Restaurant

20.1 Restaurant Personnel

20.2 Service Tools, Utensils, and Equipment

20.3 Serving the Meal

20.4 Handling Complaints and Problems

20.1

Restaurant Personnel

READING PREVIEW

Key Concepts

- Identifying types of restaurants
- Identifying restaurant personnel
- Working the front door
- Greeting and seating diners

Vocabulary

- back of the house
- back waiter
- brigade
- bus person
- captain
- carver
- chef de cuisine
- continuous seating plan
- dining room attendant
- dining room manager
- entremetier
- executive chef
- expediter
- external clients
- fish station chef
- fixed seating plan
- front of the house
- front waiter
- grill station chef
- grillardin
- internal clients
- line chef
- maître d'
- maître d'hotel
- no-reservation policy
- pastry chef
- pâtissier
- poissonier
- prep chef
- receptionist
- reservation policy
- roast station chef
- rôtisseur
- roundsman
- runner
- saucier
- sauté station chef
- second chef
- server
- sommelier
- soup and vegetables station chef
- soup station chef
- sous-chef
- station chef
- swing chef
- tournant
- trancheur
- vegetable station chef
- wine steward

Types of Restaurants

Restaurants can be formal or casual, expensive or inexpensive. Some restaurants that offer their guests a limited and simple menu make their reputations on the basis of serving convenient foods that are prepared and served quickly over a counter or drive-up window. Others prefer to offer their guests a more elaborate menu with a greater number of options along with table service. Some dining operations are meant to serve large numbers of people very quickly; others invest more time and money in creating a customized experience for the guest. What all types of restaurants and dining rooms have in common is the need to serve the guest the right food at the right temperature, in a friendly and welcoming environment. There are a number of aspects that go into the success of a restaurant, no matter what its basic style.

There are four basic styles of restaurant (the restaurant or dining room may be a freestanding unit or it may be part of a larger chain):

- Fast-food and quick-service restaurants
- Institutional dining

Source: auremar/Fotolia

- Casual and family-style restaurants
- Fine-dining restaurants

Fast-Food and Quick-Service Restaurants Fast-food and quick-service restaurants with drive-up windows and counter service are a mainstay in the foodservice industry. The menu may be limited and often specializes in a specific type of food that is easy to eat. Customers expect the same food, prepared the same way, and of the same basic quality every time they come. They also expect that there will be no more than a few minutes of time between placing their order and receiving it. Guests can either drive up to a window where their order is taken, or they may come into the restaurant and give their order to someone working behind the counter. The entire meal is ordered at once: drinks, main items, side dishes, and desserts. Servers take the order and then package the entire order once the kitchen has cooked the food. The server hands the food to the guest, who then takes it to a dining area. Guests clear their own trays and trash in a central area. The important characteristic of good service in fast-food and quick-service restaurants is prompt delivery of food.

Institutional Dining School cafeterias, hospital dining rooms, and mess halls in the military serve a large number of people in a relatively short amount of time. Servers in this type of dining room may have very limited contact with the customer. The options are clearly posted or easy to see, guests often walk through a line to make their selections, and a cashier may be on hand to tally the order and handle the money.

Casual and Family-Style Restaurants Service in casual and family-style restaurants calls for more guest interaction than at a quick-serve restaurant. Guests are seated at tables and order from menus. The servers take the order and deliver it to the kitchen. Customers expect that the service staff will be knowledgeable about the food and drinks offered by the establishment, that servers will help them to make selections, and that servers will ensure that special requests are filled in the kitchen. The service staff bring food and drink to the table and clear away empty dishes and glassware. The meal is typically served in courses, starting with appetizers and ending with dessert. Often, this type of restaurant may include some type of self-service, such as a buffet or salad bar. The server's job is to keep these areas well stocked and clean, in addition to taking orders and serving food and drink that does not come from the buffet.

Fine-Dining Restaurants The guest's expectations for service are much higher in a fine-dining restaurant. The menu generally offers more expensive and elaborate preparations. The dining room setting may call for more upscale china, flatware, and glassware. Interior decoration, lighting, and music are important aspects of the dining experience. Servers must be adept at reading their guests, making appropriate suggestions and recommendations regarding food and drinks when asked, and have good communication skills. They must be able to identify and use a wide array of dining room equipment, ranging from espresso machines to fingerbowls. They are expected to be able to answer questions about the ingredients and techniques used to prepare dishes. They may also be expected to do table-side cooking and presentation of foods.

READING CHECKPOINT *What are four basic types of restaurants?*

Restaurant Personnel

How does everything get done properly in a restaurant? The answer is: Restaurants break down a big task into smaller manageable parts, each carried out by well-trained staff. Typically, the system of staffing a restaurant is referred to as a brigade system. A **brigade** (bri-GADE) is a group of workers assigned a specific set of tasks. The tasks might be related by cooking method, type of food, or equipment used.

Restaurants typically use the brigade system in both the dining room, which is often referred to as the **front of the house**, and in the kitchen, which is referred to as the **back of the house**.

No matter whether you work in the kitchen or the dining room, you are responsible for delivering great service to all of your clients. Some of your clients are external. You may think immediately of the guests who come to your restaurant, but your **external clients** also include purveyors, consultants, salespeople, delivery agents, and others. An external client is anyone who does business at your restaurant and is not employed by the restaurant itself. You should also recognize that you will be interacting with **internal clients**. These internal clients may include different departments in your organization; for instance, if you work in the dining room, your internal clients could include the kitchen staff, the cleaning crew, and the catering staff. The specific interactions will vary, but in all cases, it is critical that you provide service that is prompt, responsive, and effective.

The skills necessary in the front and the back of the house depend on the style of the food establishment. Most restaurants use standard names for personnel within their brigades. These often are based on a classic French brigade system. The specific terms used in a restaurant may vary, based on the size of the restaurant and the type of food and service offered by the restaurant.

Front-of-the-House Brigade The front-of-the-house brigade is typically the first contact a guest has with a restaurant. Surveys of restaurant-goers reveal that for most people, the quality of the service that they receive is at least as important, if not more important, as the food. That puts a lot of responsibility on the dining room staff. The attitude, appearance, and actions of every member of the team have an effect on the customer's experience.

Guests expect servers to be friendly and helpful, of course. They also expect that servers will know about the menu and be able to answer questions about it. Servers dressed in a clean, fresh uniform, with clean nails and controlled hair, make guests feel more comfortable in the restaurant. Your guests will evaluate how long it takes for someone to take their order and deliver their meal. They may not notice or comment on the fact that the glassware is sparkling and that the silverware is spotless, but they will notice and comment if their tablecloth is dirty or the plates are smudged. There are many details that go into good service, from a welcoming smile to a friendly thank you as your guests depart. Smart restaurant owners and employees know that their guests are the key to their restaurant's success, and the way to keep them coming back and bringing new guests with them is to meet and exceed their expectations.

Your guests are more likely to remember that they were served by friendly, helpful, knowledgeable staff than they are to remember the specific menu items they ordered. They are more likely to return, and become regular customers, when the service they receive is good. They are also more likely to recommend a restaurant to their friends and colleagues if they have received good service. This all plays an important role in the restaurant's success.

A formal restaurant may require some or all of the following professionals in the front-of-the-house brigade. An informal restaurant may require only a few of these professionals. The most common term for each position is listed here first, but common variations (both English and French) are also indicated when appropriate.

FIGURE 20–1

Maître d' and Chef
The maître d' works with the chef to design the menu.

INFERRING *What kind of personality characteristics do you think a maître d' should possess?*

Source: Ken Fisher/Getty Images

- **Maître d'.** The person responsible for running the front of the house is the **maître d'** (MAY-truh DEE), which is short for **maître d'hôtel** (MAY-truh doh-TELL). The maître d' is also called the **dining room manager**. The maître d' is responsible for training service personnel, working with the chef to design the menu, arranging guest seating, taking reservations, and engaging in good public relations with guests.

- **Receptionist.** In formal restaurants, the **receptionist** assists the maître d' in greeting guests, answering the telephone at the front desk, and taking telephone reservations. In more casual restaurants, the receptionist may replace the maître d' and be referred to as the host or hostess.

- **Captain.** At fine-dining restaurants, the **captain** is responsible for explaining the menu to guests and taking their orders. The captain is also responsible for the smooth-running service in a specific group of tables. The captain may help serve the food. The captain is always available to the tables in his or her charge and never leaves the dining room.

- **Carver.** In classic service, the person in charge of carving and serving meats or fish and their accompaniments from the meat cart is called the **carver** or the **trancheur** (tran-SHUR). In modern dining rooms, the captain often replaces the carver.

- **Wine Steward.** It is the responsibility of the **wine steward**, who is also called the **sommelier** (suhm-uhl-YAY), to manage the buying and storing of wines, maintain proper wine inventory, counsel guests about wine choices, and serve wine properly at the table.

- **Server.** Second in line of responsibility after the captain, the **server**, sometimes called the **front waiter**, often helps the captain take orders. The server is responsible for making sure the table is set appropriately for each course, that food is delivered properly to the correct tables, and that the diners' needs are met. The server can take an order to the kitchen, if necessary.

- **Runner.** Depending on the size and formality of the restaurant, the **runner** may deliver food and drinks to the front waiter, clear plates, and refill bread and water. The runner, often called the **back waiter**, provides overall assistance to the server.

- **Bus Person.** In large or formal restaurants where the back waiter assists the front waiter, a separate worker, the **bus person** (sometimes called the **dining room attendant**), is responsible for clearing and cleaning tables.

Back-of-the-House Brigade A formal restaurant may require some or all of the following professionals in the back-of-the-house brigade. Many formal restaurants use French terms to describe their back-of-the-house cooking positions. A chef who has responsibility for a particular type of food is often referred to as a **station chef** or a **line chef**.

- **Executive Chef.** The head chef is called the **executive chef**, or **chef de cuisine** (shef de kwih-ZEEN). The executive chef commands the kitchen, designs the menu and oversees its execution, and is responsible for managing food costs. The executive chef also coordinates the style of service with the maître d' and devises a system for the service staff to communicate orders to the kitchen.

- **Sous-Chef.** The French term **sous-chef** (SU-chef) means underchef. The sous-chef, also known as the **second chef**, is the executive chef's principal assistant, and is responsible for scheduling personnel and temporarily replacing the executive chef or other chefs as necessary. The sous-chef sometimes acts as the expediter.

- **Expediter.** The **expediter** accepts orders from the dining room and relays them to the various station chefs. The expediter also reviews the dishes before service to make sure they are correct.

FIGURE 20–2

Bus Person
The bus person is a vital component in a smoothly running dining establishment.

COMMUNICATION *What does the performance of the bus person communicate about a restaurant?*

Source: Ryan McVay/Getty Images

- **Grill Station Chef.** The chef responsible for all the grilled items is the **grill station chef**, also called the **grillardin** (gree-yar-DAHN).
- **Roast Station Chef.** The chef responsible for all the roasted items is the **roast station chef**, also called the **rôtisseur** (roh-tess-UHR).
- **Fish Station Chef.** The chef responsible for preparing and cooking fish and seafood is the **fish station chef**, also called the **poissonier** (pwah-sun-YAY).
- **Sauté Station Chef.** The chef responsible for sautéed dishes and accompanying sauces is the **sauté station chef**, also called the **saucier** (saw-see-YAY).
- **Garde Manger.** As you know from Section 10.1, the garde manger or pantry chef is the chef responsible for cold food preparations, including salads and salad dressings and cold appetizers.
- **Soups and Vegetables Station Chef.** The chef responsible for hot appetizers, pasta courses, and vegetable dishes is the **soup and vegetables station chef**, also called the **entremetier** (ehn-tray-meh-tee-AY). In larger kitchens, this position is broken into the **soup station chef**, who is responsible for stocks and soups, and the **vegetable station chef**, who is responsible for vegetables and starches.
- **Roundsman.** Working wherever needed, the **roundsman** is a roving chef who may fill in for absent chefs or assist chefs in other stations. This position is also known as a **swing chef** or **tournant** (toor-NAHN).
- **Pastry Chef.** The chef responsible for making pastry and many other desserts is the **pastry chef**, also called the **pâtissier** (Pah-tees-SYAY).
- **Prep Chef.** The chef responsible for preparing ingredients that will be used by other chefs is the **prep chef**. A prep chef washes and peels vegetables and fruits, cuts meat, and does any other work necessary for supporting other chefs.

The positions just described are often referred to as the classic brigade. This system was established at a time when most professional cooking was centered on fine-dining establishments. Today, there are a greater number of styles for foodservice establishments. To effectively organize and manage the personnel for a number of different restaurant styles, managers often modify the classic brigade to customize it for the specific situation, such as fast-food restaurants and institutional catering. These contemporary brigades take into account the way that foods are purchased, the operation's menu, and the skill levels of the available staff, as can be seen in the following charts.

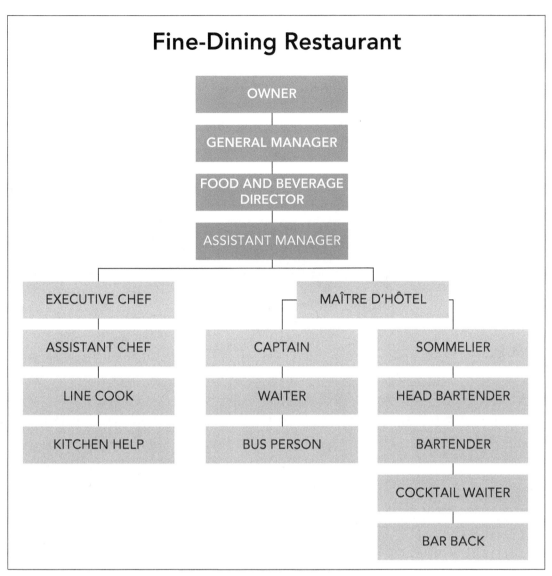

Fine-Dining Restaurant

OWNER

GENERAL MANAGER

FOOD AND BEVERAGE DIRECTOR

ASSISTANT MANAGER

EXECUTIVE CHEF

MAÎTRE D'HÔTEL

ASSISTANT CHEF

CAPTAIN

SOMMELIER

LINE COOK

WAITER

HEAD BARTENDER

KITCHEN HELP

BUS PERSON

BARTENDER

COCKTAIL WAITER

BAR BACK

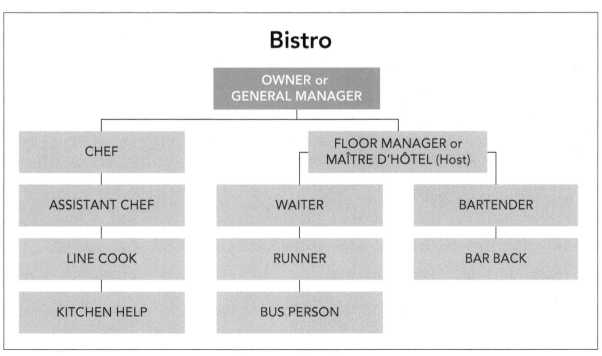

Bistro

OWNER or GENERAL MANAGER

CHEF

FLOOR MANAGER or MAÎTRE D'HÔTEL (Host)

ASSISTANT CHEF

WAITER

BARTENDER

LINE COOK

RUNNER

BAR BACK

KITCHEN HELP

BUS PERSON

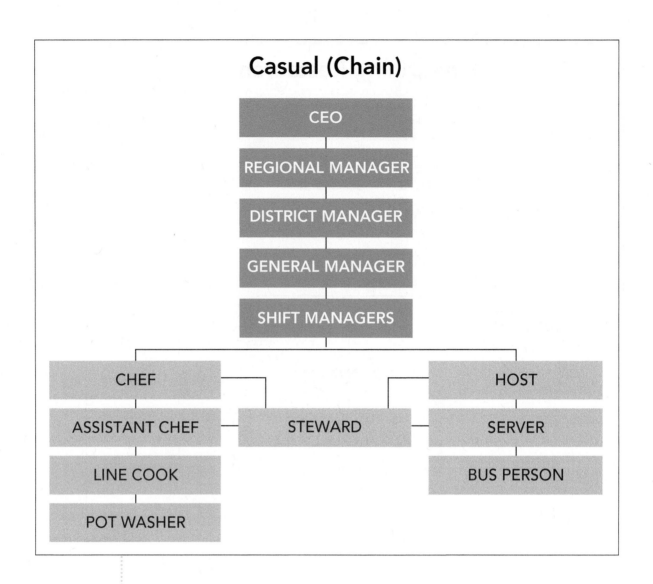

Casual (Chain)

CEO

REGIONAL MANAGER

DISTRICT MANAGER

GENERAL MANAGER

SHIFT MANAGERS

CHEF		HOST
ASSISTANT CHEF	STEWARD	SERVER
LINE COOK		BUS PERSON
POT WASHER		

 **READING CHECKPOINT** *In a fine-dining restaurant, what position is the head of the front-of-the-house brigade? Of the back-of-the-house brigade?*

Working the Front Door

The first opportunity a restaurant has to make a good impression is at its front door. The guest's first contact with the restaurant is with the maître d' or the receptionist. Whether that first contact with the customer is made on the telephone or in person at the door, the person making the contact plays an important role. Naturally, a warm telephone conversation or personal reception at the front door makes guests feel welcome and promises a good dining experience before they are even seated at their table.

Telephone Etiquette In the foodservice business, you sometimes communicate with people as much by telephone as in person. It can be difficult for a customer to get through to the restaurant or to understand what the restaurant representative is saying. If the person answering the phone is uncooperative or not well informed, the customer is not likely to form a good impression. Callers can become so discouraged that they do not make a dinner reservation. The person assigned to answer the telephone should be trained to keep the following telephone etiquette in mind:

- As much as possible, answer the telephone at the first ring and no later than the third ring.

- Develop an appropriate and brief telephone greeting. For example, "Hello, this is Oliver's Restaurant, Vanessa speaking. May I help you?" Have the greeting written down and placed next to the telephone where it can easily be seen by anyone answering the phone.

- Speak slowly and clearly. Very often people answering the phone speak so fast that callers cannot understand what they say.

- Know the restaurant's hours and location.

- Focus on the person being spoken to until you satisfy his or her question. Be pleasant and courteous.

- Avoid speaking to anyone else while you are on the phone.

- Avoid putting customers on hold for long. If unable to give your complete attention, ask callers for their telephone number. If they do not give you a number, ask them to call back soon, making sure to give them your name. It is better to call back than not to give your full attention.

- When a caller asks to speak to someone, reply with, "May I ask who is calling?"

FIGURE 20–6

Answering the Telephone

Be pleasant and courteous when answering the phone.

PREDICTING *How would you feel if you were treated discourteously in your first contact with a restaurant?*

Source: Culinary Institute of America

Reservations Restaurant kitchens need to anticipate how much food to buy and prepare. Dining room managers need to know how many guests to set up for and how many servers will be necessary. Reservations provide information about how many customers to expect and when they will arrive, making it easier for a restaurant to plan. Advance knowledge of how many guests to expect is particularly necessary for busy mealtimes when there might otherwise be too many people for a dining room to handle and not enough food, or too many servers and too much food.

Upscale restaurants usually take reservations because their dining service is often more elaborate and lengthy, their customers do not dine casually, and the customers often travel from a distance to get to the restaurant. When a restaurant takes reservations, it is said to have a **reservation policy**.

Some restaurants don't take reservations. This is referred to as a **no-reservation policy**. They serve customers on a first-come-first-served basis. Most restaurants that do this expect a steady volume of diners or a quick turnover. However, some popular upscale restaurants that have a steady following don't take reservations, which leads to lines of customers waiting to get into the restaurant. Some restaurants view this as a way of generating an image of desirability.

Many formal restaurants that use reservations will accept guests without reservations when the restaurant is slow. On the other hand, casual

Analyzing the Decision to Take Reservations

Using a Reservation Policy

Advantages	Disadvantages
• Guests can make definite plans for dining in the restaurant.	• Taking and confirming reservations is more labor intensive initially.
• Restaurant management can plan ahead.	• Customers who don't show up for their reservations can throw off planning for both the kitchen and the dining room.
• Guest traffic flow and table sittings can be staggered, improving traffic flow in the dining room.	• The policy may discourage diners from spontaneously patronizing a restaurant if the expectation is that reservations are required.
• Food orders can be staggered, enabling kitchen staff to produce dishes with greater attention to detail and consequently higher quality.	
• Less rush and stress in the dining room and kitchen encourages smooth relations between guests and service staff.	
• Service staff has greater opportunity to provide better service to diners.	
• Service staff can more easily handle requests for special diets, menu exceptions, birthdays, and so on.	

restaurants that don't usually take reservations may require them for groups over eight.

The Reception Desk The front desk (also called the *reception desk*) provides any information necessary to a guest or the dining room for smooth operation. Here you might find the reservation book or computer station, a seating plan for the dining room, copies of the menu and wine list, a logbook or history of daily dining room records, telephone and telephone directory, an answering machine, an employee directory, a credit card machine, maps, emergency numbers, paper supplies, pens, pencils, and other administrative necessities.

Menus should undergo quality control at the reception desk. Menus that are dog-eared, stained, or otherwise unsightly or outdated should be replaced.

Taking Reservations An efficient system for taking and recording reservations should be in place. One way to organize the procedure is to use a preprinted form that can be filled in at the time the reservation is made.

Reservations should include the following:

- Date when the reservation was taken
- Name of the person taking the reservation
- Date and time for the reservation
- Name and telephone number of the guest
- Number in the party
- Any special seating requests

Chef's Tip

Messy Menus

Sloppy menus are unappealing and signal sloppy service or careless management.

Chef's Tip

Holiday Reservations

Because holidays such as Mother's Day, Easter, Thanksgiving, New Year's Day, and Valentine's Day are especially hectic for restaurants, take special care when taking reservations for these days.

Analyzing the Decision to Take Reservations

Using a No-Reservation Policy

Advantages	Disadvantages
• Eliminates the cost of staff to take and manage reservations. • Encourages turnover of tables. • Tables are not tied up by customers who don't show up for their reservations. • Revenue is increased through bar sales to guests waiting to be seated.	• The wait for a table can discourage potential customers. • Diners may become rushed by service staff who are feeling pressured by people waiting to be seated. • Extended waiting can result in disgruntled customers and bad publicity. • Creates crowding at the entrance.

Source: Pavel Losevsky/Fotolia

- Any special server requests
- Any handicapped seating requests
- Any other special requests (birthday or other occasion, accommodating children or others with special needs, and so on)

READING CHECKPOINT *What are the advantages and disadvantages of a reservation policy?*

Greeting and Seating Guests

The maître d' or receptionist is typically the first person guests see. This important person sets in motion the entire restaurant experience.

Greeting Guests The maître d' or receptionist should greet guests with a warm smile and a professional demeanor. Regular customers will feel appreciated if the person at the front door knows them and refers to them respectfully by name. After the greeting, guests should be asked if they have a reservation and accommodated as soon as possible. The maître d' or receptionist should offer to check coats and wraps before customers are seated.

Seating The maître d' should lead guests to their tables rather than permit them to make their own way. This gives management control over the traffic flow and establishes a relationship between the maître d' or receptionist and the guests.

There are many advantages to a preplanned dining room seating plan. Placement of tables should take into account the flow of server traffic through the room, exit doors, and paths for leading guests to their seats. It should allow for an even distribution of customers, as well as the safe and attractive placement of tables and seats. Diners should be distributed to the wait staff evenly to prevent overload for any one server and to provide an equal opportunity to everyone on duty.

A seating plan should create an impression that the room is filled. This is done by seating guests strategically, first at window seats and then in the central area of the room. The plan should allow for servers to move about to set tables, serve food and drinks, and clear dishes without disturbing guests at nearby tables.

There are typically two ways to organize seating:

- **Fixed Seating Plan.** By staggering set mealtimes (such as at 6 p.m., 8 p.m., and 10 p.m.), a **fixed seating plan** enables the kitchen to work at a steady, reliable pace.

FIGURE 20–7
Greeting Guests
All guests feel appreciated if they are greeted warmly.
DRAWING CONCLUSIONS *Why would restaurants use databases to keep track of their regular customers' preferences?*
Source: Myrleen Pearson/PhotoEdit

- **Continuous Seating Plan.** As long as there are empty tables that turn over regularly, a **continuous seating plan** allows the wait staff to pace themselves and the restaurant to have a steady volume of business, even if checks are not large.

No-Shows and Late Arrivals Customers who don't show up for their reservations, or who show up very late, cause big problems for restaurant management. These customers cause restaurants to lose money and disappoint customers who have had to wait for tables—only to see empty tables in the dining room.

One way of minimizing the likelihood of no-shows or late arrivals is to call the day before to confirm reservations. A restaurant may decide that a policy of giving away a table if guests are more than a half hour late might be better than not filling a table at all, and losing revenue. Of course, you could always allow for bad weather or for regular customers, who should always receive special consideration.

READING CHECKPOINT *What are the two ways to organize seating in a restaurant?*

20.1 ASSESSMENT

Reviewing Concepts

1. What are the four basic types of restaurants?

2. In a fine-dining restaurant, what position is the head of the front-of-the-house brigade? Of the back-of-the-house brigade?

3. What are the advantages and disadvantages of taking reservations?

4. What are the two ways to organize seating in a restaurant?

Critical Thinking

5. Drawing Conclusions Most upscale restaurants require reservations. Why would the service staff hold tables for guests even if they don't arrive on time? What do you think are the best measures a restaurant can take to protect itself from no-shows without discouraging their repeat business?

6. Comparing/Contrasting Compare a fixed seating plan with a continuous seating plan.

7. Predicting How will a no-reservations policy in a fine-dining restaurant affect customers? Service staff? Kitchen staff?

8. Comparing/Contrasting Compare a guest's expectations at a family-style restaurant and a college cafeteria.

Test Kitchen

Divide into groups of 10. Each group will be a kitchen brigade, with each individual assuming the role of a specific type of chef at the appropriate location in the kitchen. Using a menu from a local upscale restaurant, your teacher or classmates will order 10 meals from the menu. An expediter will relay the meal orders to the various chefs, who will describe what they must do to prepare each dish.

LANGUAGE ARTS
Descriptive Writing

Research the reservation policies of five different types of restaurants by calling them during their downtime. Describe the advantages and disadvantages of each of the policies of the particular establishments you have researched.

20.2

Service Tools, Utensils, and Equipment

Key Concepts

- Identifying service ware
- Setting covers properly for service
- Cleaning and polishing service utensils

Vocabulary

- airpot brewers
- automatic brewers
- china
- coffee percolators
- coffee urns
- cover
- crumber
- espresso makers
- flatware
- glassware
- hollowware
- pour-over brewers
- service station
- service ware
- side stand
- tableware
- water boiler

Source: Gary Gold/Mira.com

Service Ware

The dishware, utensils, and service equipment used in the dining room, whether they are placed on the table or found elsewhere in the dining room, are called **service ware**. The service ware that is used by customers is sometimes called **tableware**.

Service ware includes all the dishes and silverware, as well as such things as carving knives, serving spoons, and ladles. Service ware is often broken into the following four categories:

- **China.** Everything designed to contain food is regarded as **china**. This includes such things as plates, bowls, dishes, cups, saucers, and individual creamers.
- **Flatware.** All utensils used at the table or for serving are considered **flatware**. This includes all knives, forks, and spoons used at the table or for serving.
- **Glassware.** All glass containers for containing liquids are regarded as **glassware**. This includes water glasses, wine glasses, champagne goblets, cocktail or liquor glasses, beer mugs, pitchers, and carafes.
- **Hollowware.** Serving pieces such as tea pots, large cream pitchers, sugar bowls, caddies for sweeteners and condiments, plate covers, and sauceboats are known as **hollowware**. These pieces are used to serve foods; the guest does not eat directly from them.

China The plates, bowls, cups, and saucers used in a restaurant play a part in the overall ambience of any foodservice operation. They are made in a variety of materials, including china, plastic, or paper. In

China

Fine-Dining
Fine-dining china is usually thin and delicate and often has an elegant design or an innovative shape.
Source: Eugenio Chelli/Fotolia

Casual-Dining
Casual-dining china often uses color to seem welcoming.
Source: getanov/Fotolia

Institutional
Hospital china is usually heavy and durable to stand up to high-temperature washing and sterilization.
Source: dvarg/Fotolia

Fast-Food
China at a fast-food restaurant is often paper or plastic (as this plate is). Plates are used only one time before being thrown away.
Source: dp3010/Fotolia

restaurants that provide quick service or fast foods, you are likely to find paper or plastic goods. High-end restaurants may look for a special design, shape, or color to suit their décor.

Flatware Flatware, like china, is selected according to the overall style of the operation. Disposable flatware is common in fast-food operations.

Flatware

Fine-Dining
Fine-dining flatware may be silver plated, as this set is.

Source: Dleindec/Fotolia

Casual-Dining
Family-style dining flatware needs to be attractive and easy to clean, but also needs to be sturdy.

Source: brontazavra/Fotolia

Institutional
Institutional flatware may not have to be particularly attractive, but it definitely needs to be sturdy and not need replacing often.

Source: exopixel/Fotolia

Fast-Food
Fast-food flatware is often plastic and disposable.

Source: Brooke Becker/Fotolia

Forks & Spaghetti

During the 18th and 19th centuries, poor people ate spaghetti and other pasta with their hands. Needless to say, this was messy and napkins were required at the end of eating. For this reason, the rich just didn't eat pasta—it wasn't dignified! All this changed around the 1830s when, upon the explicit request of the Bourbon King Ferdinand II ("Ferdinand II of the Two Sicilies," 1831–1859), the royal majordomo Gennaro Spadaccini introduced a short fork with four tines, replacing the longer one with three. While it was practically impossible to wrap the spaghetti around a three-tined fork without losing the sauce, the task became fairly easy with a four-tined one. Pasta could now be twirled around the fork and eaten in a dignified way. Pasta began being served to Italian aristocrats and the court. Soon pasta, and the four-tined fork, began to be seen in the hands of aristocrats in other countries. Pasta and the fork were made for each other.

Today, according to Italian rules of etiquette, pasta and sauce should be served on flat dinner plates, not in a bowl. The proper utensil with which to eat pasta is a fork. A spoon is typically not offered with pasta, unless the sauce is very thin (such as is the case with some seafood sauces). The goal in eating pasta is to twirl a moderate amount of pasta around the prongs of the fork, using the curve of the plate to help twirl the pasta onto the fork.

Not every new invention for eating spaghetti was as successful as the fork. A "spaghetti fork" was developed that had a little handle at the top that passed through a hollow tube and was connected to the tines at the bottom. You would twirl the little

Ferdinand of the Two Sicilies, 1831–1859

Source: PRISMA ARCHIVO/Alamy

handle to twirl the fork at the bottom, twirling the spaghetti onto the fork. This two-handed utensil for eating spaghetti never caught on. A battery-powered, single-handed "spaghetti fork" was also developed, but it too failed to catch on.

Research

Research the history of the fork. Explain how people ate before the fork was invented. List a few different kinds of forks and their purposes. Describe how the invention of the fork changed table manners.

Casual restaurants may opt for flatware that is inexpensive and easy to clean; stainless steel is the most common material for this type of flatware. The heavier the flatware, the more expensive it is likely to be. Stainless steel flatware is available in a variety of quality levels and prices. Higher-end flatware may have special designs. Some restaurants may prefer to use silver-plated flatware. This material requires special care and handling and can be expensive to buy and to maintain.

Glassware Your glassware is selected to serve the types of beverages your restaurant offers. If you serve just water and soft drinks, you may only

Glassware

Fine-Dining

Fine-dining glassware includes many types of glasses.

Source: mihalec/Fotolia

Casual-Dining

Typically, casual-style dining uses fewer types of glassware, often just a red wine glass, a white wine glass, and a water glass.

Source: lithian/Fotolia

Fast-Food

Fast-food glassware is often plastic and disposable, comes with a lid, and is often used with a straw. It often comes in different sizes.

Source: Fotofermer/Fotolia

Institutional

Institutional dining would typically use even fewer types of glassware than casual-style dining, with only one sturdy wine glass for both red and white wine.

Source: Africa Studio/Fotolia

need one or two sizes. If you serve a variety of beverages, such as cocktails, wine, beer, or fountain drinks, you will need a greater variety.

Hollowware The specific hollowware that a restaurant needs depends on the menu and the style of service. Fine-dining establishments may need a wide array of items to present and serve various menu items. Casual restaurants may not require much, if any, hollowware. Hollowware can be made from stainless steel or be silver plated. It is also produced from glass or china; some restaurants choose hollowware that has the same pattern as their china. The more elaborate the decoration on the hollowware, the more expensive it tends to be, and the more care and upkeep it may require.

Service staff also use many tools and utensils in the course of a shift. The restaurant management often posts a list of these items to help personnel remember what they are responsible for. These typically include candles or table lights, chairs, china, coffee-making equipment, condiments, creamers, side tables, linens, menus, and side stands.

The wait staff must have the tools of their trade with them at all times when they are on duty. Their essential tools include two working pens, a **crumber** (a device for cleaning crumbs from the table), order forms (for recording customers' orders), a small calculator, and a small notebook.

Some types of equipment found in restaurants are the specific responsibility of the dining room staff. These items include equipment for making hot beverages such as coffee and tea, cold beverages such as iced tea and lemonade, and specialty beverages such as espresso and cappuccino, as well as bread or soup warmers. This equipment may be located in the dining room, at the waiter's stand, or in a section of the kitchen. Regardless of where the equipment is located, the front-of-the-house staff is generally responsible for operating and cleaning these items.

Both coffee and tea are popular beverages at all types of restaurants. The volume of service in a restaurant can help determine which style and size coffee maker a restaurant should have. There are several different options available:

- **Airpot brewers** are generally used in low-volume settings. There is a basket to hold the filter and ground coffee. Water is added to a well, and then as the water is heated, it runs through the coffee. The brewed coffee flows into an insulated carafe that can keep the coffee warm for a few hours.

- **Pour-over brewers** are similar to airpot brewers, except that the coffee flows into a pot or carafe that sits on a heating element. This style of coffee maker brews coffee quickly. Many have more than one heating

FIGURE 20–8
Hollowware
Hollowware includes silver candlesticks, cake stands, platters, and coffee pots.

PREDICTING *In what type of restaurant would you see hollowware like this?*
Source: Culinary Institute of America

FIGURE 20–9
Cleaning a Table
Wait staff using a crumber to remove crumbs from the table.

PREDICTING *Why would wait staff clean the table when guests are still at the table?*
Source: Culinary Institute of America

element to keep several pots of coffee, regular or decaffeinated, ready to serve.

- **Automatic brewers** are good in high-volume settings. Because the entire unit has been plumbed so that water is supplied directly to the well, there is no need for servers to add water. Instead, the ground coffee is added to a filter held in a basket, the carafe is placed under the basket, and a button is pushed to start the brewing process. Some units have a hot water faucet that dispenses water to brew tea.

- **Coffee percolators** and **coffee urns** produce a large batch of coffee. The basket, holding ground coffee, sits on a stem inside the coffee pot. Cold water is added to the pot and the unit is plugged in or turned on. As the water heats up, it rises (percolates) up and out of the stem onto the coffee. After the coffee is brewed, the percolator or urn keeps the coffee warm. These large units have faucets to dispense coffee.

- **Espresso makers** are a specialized type of coffee machine. Instead of letting hot water flow over the ground coffee, an espresso maker forces hot water under pressure through finely ground coffee. Often, these machines are equipped with steam nozzles that are used to froth milk for espresso drinks such as lattes, cappuccinos, macchiatos, mochas, and americanos.

No matter what style of coffee maker you are using, it is important to clean the unit thoroughly. If your restaurant has hard water, the units can become clogged with calcium and other minerals. It may be necessary to use a special cleaning product designed to remove scale, although white vinegar may be another cheaper alternative. Clean coffee pots and thoroughly rinse them to remove any traces of the cleaning product.

Hot tea that sits in a pot and on a warmer can turn bitter very fast. In some restaurants, the server may present a small pot of hot water with the teabag or simply a cup of boiling water; the guest adds the tea to the pot or cup and lets it steep as long as desired. The customer can then remove the bag once the steeping is done. Many fine-dining restaurants have a more elaborate tea service. They bring two pots filled with boiling water along with any accompaniments, such as milk, sugar, honey, or lemon. Then, they present a variety of teas to the guest to make a selection. The guest adds the tea to one pot of boiling water to brew. The second pot is used to adjust the strength of the brewed tea once it is poured into the cup.

Restaurants, cafes, bakeshops, or other establishments that want to provide individual servings of hot tea use a **water boiler** that holds boiling water and dispenses it from a spigot to brew tea by either the cup or the pot. The capacity requirements depend on how much boiling water you want to have on hand all day long.

At least once a day, you should empty all of the water out of the boiler and wipe down the inside to help reduce calcium and lime buildup inside the unit.

A **service station**, sometimes called the pantry, is the mise en place station for the dining room. A well-organized and fully stocked service station makes it easier to provide good service to your guests. The service station or pantry typically includes equipment such as coffee makers, water boilers, and bread warmers, as well as glassware, pitchers and carafes for serving water or hot beverages, flatware, china, hollowware, trays and tray stands, and linens. Often, cleaning supplies for the dining room are stored here as well. There may be a single member of the dining room staff responsible for setting up this area before service with all necessary items, making sure that coffee is brewed and tea water is ready, bread is sliced, and butter is prepared for the entire dining room throughout service.

A **side stand** hold items necessary for setting the table. There is usually one side stand for each station in the dining room. Waiters typically stock the side stand before service. The side stand should be cleaned and well stocked with all necessary materials before service, including additional service items (glasses, flatware, plates, napkins, serving spoons) and food items (salt and pepper shakers, sugar, mustard, oil, vinegar, pepper grinders, and ketchup).

Food items also include bread, butter, sweeteners, condiments, and creamers. These food items should be handled properly to keep them safe and ready for use, as follows:

- Remove storeroom prices.
- Store condiments on a clean rack or tray.
- Clean the cover, rim, and body of all jars and containers.
- Refrigerate opened bottles overnight.

 **READING CHECKPOINT** *What are the four basic types of service ware used in the dining room?*

FIGURE 20–10
Service Station
A service station usually includees coffee makers.

COMPARE/CONTRAST *What are the advantages of having a single person be responsible for making all the coffee? What are the disadvantages?*

Source: CandyBox Images/Fotolia

Covers

In restaurant terms, a **cover** is a complete place setting for one person. It includes china, glassware, and flatware. Follow these general guidelines when setting covers on tables for the most visual appeal and comfort:

- Place settings should face each other across the table, whenever possible.
- Every place setting should be set identically to achieve a consistent look.
- The width of each place setting should be about 18 inches.

Different types of restaurants require different types of covers or place settings. Fast-food operations do not normally set a cover on a table. Instead, the server may be required to add such service items as napkins, flatware, straws, and condiments to take-out orders. For orders that are eaten in the restaurant, guests simply stop by a central location to get their own service items and condiments. It is generally a server's job to be certain that these areas are clean and fully stocked before and during service.

Casual and fine-dining restaurants typically set a cover on tables or counters. Sometimes this is done before guests arrive, or it is done when the guests are seated. Very casual spots, including diners and family restaurants, may set a cover with paper napkins and placemats, a fork, and a knife. Condiments such as sugar, ketchup, mustard, salt, and pepper are often left on the table for the entire service period. Decorations such as fresh flowers or candles and menus for specials, drinks, or desserts may also be placed on the table before guests arrive.

For a preset cover, silverware may be set either directly on a tablecloth or placemat, or it may be set on top of a napkin. Some restaurants include a large plate, known as a *charger*, that is set on the table between the flatware. The charger is an oversized plate. No food is served on the charger; its function is purely decorative. In some situations, the charger plate may be removed as soon as the guests are seated. In others, the charger is left in place until the main item is served.

Fine-dining restaurants may preset the dining room with only a few pieces. In a banquet setting, the cover includes all the service ware a guest might need, from the first course through the dessert course.

In fine-dining establishments and for banquets, the cover must be arranged in a specific way:

- On square or rectangular tables, the bottom of the plate, napkin, and flatware should be placed in a straight line, 1 inch from the edge of the table.

- On round tables, the bottom of the charger (if used) and flatware should be arranged in a straight line with the outermost edges of the cover 1 inch from the edge on either side.

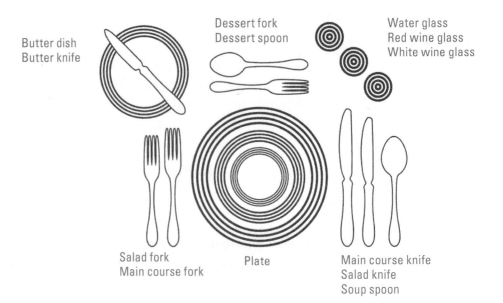

Butter dish
Butter knife

Dessert fork
Dessert spoon

Water glass
Red wine glass
White wine glass

Salad fork
Main course fork

Plate

Main course knife
Salad knife
Soup spoon

- Cloth napkins can be placed to the left side of the place setting under the flatware on the left side. If the napkin is folded, it can be placed in the middle of the cover between the flatware or in the middle of the charger.

- For banquets, each cover should be set with all of the flatware, glassware, and china that is required for the entire meal, from butter knives and soupspoons to coffee cups and water glasses.

- Some fine restaurants set only a fork and knife as the cover because it is expected that the server will bring the exact flatware that each guest needs just before the food arrives from the kitchen.

- Flatware should be arranged in order of use; the pieces needed first are placed on the outside.

- Forks are set on the left side of the cover, with the tines facing up. The one exception to this general rule is for seafood cocktail forks; they are placed on the right side of the cover.

- Knives should be placed with the cutting edge toward the rim of the plate.

- Spoons are placed on the right side of the knife, facing up. For a full banquet cover, you may place the teaspoon, along with the dessert fork, just above the plate.

- The butter plate should be placed on the left of the cover.

- The cup and saucer should be placed on the right of the cover, above the flatware. The handle should face to the right, angled slightly forward, toward the diner, and be positioned to easily slip into the diner's finger.

- Glassware should be placed on the right side of the cover. The first glass is arranged to line up with the tip of the dinner knife. Additional glasses are lined up behind the first glass on an angle.

READING CHECKPOINT *What is a cover?*

Cleaning Service Utensils

Proper cleaning of service utensils prevents spreading of germs and bacteria, which can thrive in restaurant settings where food is ever present and attention to detail can lose its priority in the hectic pace of kitchens and dining rooms. Government regulations concerning hygiene are rigorous for restaurants. All personnel should be well informed about them, and should comply with them.

Proper cleaning is also important when considering customers. Nothing turns customers away and spreads bad publicity faster than dirty conditions.

Dining room floors, walls, windows, and doors should be kept spotless, as should all furniture and tableware. This includes condiment dishes, sugar bowls, cruets, breadbaskets, ashtrays, and candleholders.

Washing Tableware Restaurants must comply with local health department regulations for dishwasher water temperature and other standards designed to ensure sanitary cleaning conditions.

The high water temperature of any dishwasher is enough to kill bacteria, but the process doesn't automatically guarantee spotless glassware and dishes unless dirty tableware is handled properly before being loaded. Enough detergent should be used and chemical desanitizers can be added during the rinse cycle. At the end of the day, dishwashing areas, spray devices, and rinse pipes should be dismantled and cleaned thoroughly with hot water. Keep the following guidelines in mind when washing tableware:

- **China.** China should be scraped and rinsed by hand before it is loaded in the dishwasher. This should be followed by a prewash rinsing cycle in the dishwasher. For the best circulation of detergent and water, avoid overloading the dishwasher. China with any chips or cracks should be thrown out and replaced.

- **Glassware.** Before machine-washing, it is important to spot-wash glassware by hand to eliminate lipstick marks or any other resistant traces of use. Glassware should be checked again when it is unloaded for any remaining marks.

- **Flatware.** Rinse and presoak flatware before spreading it out and washing it on a wire rack in the dishwasher. Bunching flatware together in rack sections may prevent water from entirely surrounding each piece and adequately disinfecting and washing it. After washing, flatware should be air-dried and stored to avoid prolonged contact with any airborne contaminants.

FIGURE 20–12
Checking Glassware
Wait staff need to check glassware for any remaining marks.

PREDICTING *How would you feel if you received a glass with a lipstick mark in an upscale restaurant?*

Source: John A. Rizzo/Getty Images

Polishing Automatic dishwashing can clean glasses and flatware, but it may leave behind a film, residue, or spots. Rinse aids added to the machine along with detergent will help reduce the amount of film, but only hand polishing removes resistant water spots from glassware and tarnish from silverware.

- **Glassware.** If local regulations permit, clean glassware can be exposed to steam and wiped with a clean wiping cloth to polish. The steam can be applied with a steam wand, or racks of clean glassware can be set over chafing dishes filled with steaming water.

- **Flatware.** Stainless steel utensils should be dipped in hot water and wiped dry with a clean wiping cloth to polish. Place the polished utensils on clean linen napkins and store in closed drawers.

- **Silverware.** Silver-plated flatware and hollowware can turn dull gray or even black. This coating is known as tarnish. It develops when silver is exposed to air and certain chemicals. Tarnish-removing agents are the best method for removing tarnish and polishing silver. However, if these agents are used, the silverware must be thoroughly washed afterward to remove any trace of chemicals. The silverware should then be wiped with a clean wiping cloth. To store for daily use, place silverware on linen napkins in closed drawers. If silver is not used every day, it should be placed in bags specifically designed for silverware or in airtight containers.

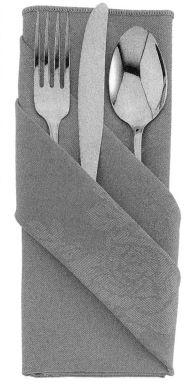

Source: Digital Vision/Getty Images

Silverware stored in napkin ready for casual-dining service

 **READING CHECKPOINT** *Why do you need to spot-wash glassware?*

20.2 ASSESSMENT

Reviewing Concepts

1. What are the four basic types of service ware used in the dining room?

2. What is a cover?

3. Why do you need to spot-wash glassware?

Critical Thinking

4. Predicting What would happen if flatware were not presoaked before washing?

5. Comparing/Contrasting How does a banquet cover differ from the cover of a fine restaurant?

6. Applying Concepts On which side of the plate is the fork?

7. Applying Concepts On which side of the plate is the butter plate?

8. Applying Concepts Where is glassware placed in relation to the plate and the flatware?

Test Kitchen

Working in teams of three, and without viewing other teams, set covers for a family-style restaurant, a four-course banquet, and a fine restaurant. Each team member is responsible for setting one of the covers. Compare each team's covers.

SOCIAL STUDIES ———●
Table Settings

Research the history of table settings in a specific nation at a specific time. Focus on the connection between the way the table was set, the types of dinners enjoyed by that particular society, and what this says about society as a whole.

Serving the Meal

Key Concepts

- Identifying styles of service
- Serving guests

Vocabulary

- American service
- buffet service
- butler service
- cafeteria service
- counter service
- dupes
- English service
- family service
- French service
- platter service
- Russian service
- service style
- table service
- tableside service
- take-out service

Service Styles

In the culinary world, when we talk about **service style** or **table service**, we are concerned with how food and drink are delivered to the guest.

Common International Service Styles Before the French Revolution, French inns and taverns served simple food, often consisting of only one dish, usually a stew or plain roasted or boiled meats without sauces. Elaborate dining was the privilege of the wealthy, who retained skilled cooks and servants to cater to them in their homes.

In the 1800s, after the French Revolution, cooks who once worked for noble households brought their skills to restaurants and began to experiment with sauces and to offer more types of food. As the food in restaurants became more refined, so did the service. Where once waiters were low-paid servants for the aristocracy, restaurant service became a paid profession. Elegant French service influenced the style of service in other countries, including the United States. For example, the sequence of whose orders are taken first at the table and whose orders are served first, etiquette about which side to serve from, and how to treat guests in general all began with the French tradition.

Some of the more common international service styles are seen in a variety of U.S. restaurants. For example, a casual restaurant might offer family-style service with foods served on platters or in bowls, so that the guests can help themselves. A fine restaurant might offer a streamlined version of tableside service; for instance, salads might be dressed, tossed, and served from a cart or table in the dining room. It helps to be aware of all the varieties of service styles.

Source: Culinary Institute of America

- **French Service.** Established in the court of Louis XIV in about 1680, **French service** is an elaborate style of service based on serving a meal in three courses: the first, the second, and the dessert. The first course, or the entrée, was timed for the entrance of guests into the dining room. (The French word "entrée" is derived from "enter.") For both of the first two courses, hot dishes were brought into the dining room on silver platters and placed on a side table. Many dishes were prepared or finished off by a specialized server at the table. After each course, the guests left the table while it was cleared, cleaned, and reset for the following course. Servers served courses at the right side of the place setting. The system is based on a clear division of labor, with detailed tasks assigned to carefully trained servers. The first two courses were made up of as many as 40 dishes—including soup, meat, and fish. French service is elegant and leisurely, but it requires costly equipment and a large number of highly trained servers.

- **Tableside Service.** With **tableside service**, dishes are prepared, finished, or plated in the dining room in view of the guests. This style of service requires a mobile cart, a burner or heat source for cooking, and a large silver dome for covering food to keep it warm. This special type of French service is theatrical and elegant but labor intensive and time consuming. Classic tableside preparations include dishes such as crêpes suzette (thin crêpes sautéed with butter, sugar, and an orange liqueur), Caesar salad, and steak Diane (a sautéed steak served with a sauce made from pan juices, cognac, shallots, and cream). Large cuts of meat, such as rib roasts, hams, and turkeys, may be sliced at a cart in the dining room. Fish may be prepared whole in the kitchen and then filleted in the dining room so the guest can see the process. Desserts may be arranged on a cart and rolled to the table so guests can choose from the selection. The server slices, fillets, carves, or cuts the food as appropriate, arranges it on a plate, and adds the appropriate sauces or garnishes before serving it to the guest. Contemporary tableside preparations may be more rustic, such as guacamole prepared at the table, or quite dramatic, such as sorbets and ice creams frozen in liquid nitrogen. Once the dish is finished and plated, the server places it in front of the guest from the guest's right side with the server's right hand.

- **Russian Service.** Typically used for banquets, **Russian service** is less elaborate than French service, but is elegant and requires skill from the waitstaff. The server places the empty plates on the table in front of the guest, with the right hand from the guest's right side. The kitchen staff puts the food on large platters that servers bring to the table and present to the guests, standing on the guests' left. The guests indicates which item or items they want and the server transfers it to the guests' plates with the right hand using a spoon and fork

When steak Diane is prepared using a tableside cart, the congnac is often flambéed

Source: Monkey Business/Fotolia

Russian service

Source: Jeff Greenberg, PhotoEdit

to pick up and move the food. Any sauces, side dishes, or condiments are served in the same manner. This method delivers completely prepared hot food immediately from the kitchen quickly, but with some ceremony. Serving guests freshly cooked dishes directly at the table without the ritual of plating at the side table saves time without sacrificing quality. This is in contrast to other styles of service where dishes are served at the right side of the guest. This style of service is also called **platter service**.

- **English Service.** Usually offered in restaurants, **English service** is for special groups or private dinners. The table is fully preset and food is delivered on platters to the dining room. The serving dishes are placed on the table or on a table nearby. A server or the host serves soup from a tureen, carves meat, and serves food from the platter to the guests.

- **Family Service.** Probably the most efficient form of table service, **family service** is similar to English service except that all foods are placed on the table in serving dishes and guests help themselves. Some casual restaurants feature family service to create a homey atmosphere.

- **Butler Service.** Similar to Russian service, **butler service** also has the server bring the platter to the table. However, unlike Russian service, butler service means that guests serve themselves from the platter. The server stands at the left of each guest, holding the platter with both hands, moving from guest to guest.

FIGURE 20–13

Butler Service

Guests make their own selections from a platter.

DRAWING CONCLUSIONS *What type of food might be difficult to serve this way?*

Source: Culinary Institute of America

Common Service Styles in the United States There are many styles for table service. Sometimes a combination of styles is used. Some are more formal than others. The four most common types of table service in the United States are American service, buffet service, counter service, and take-out service.

- **American Service.** The predominant service style in American restaurants, including casual restaurants and banquets, is **American service**. In this style, food is fully prepared and plated on individual serving plates in the kitchen and brought to the dining room. Tables are fully preset. Dishes are served by the right hand at the right side of the guest. This leaves the server's left hand free to carry other plates. American service allows for quick distribution of food by relatively few servers.

- **Buffet Service.** Practical for serving a large number of people over a period of time, **buffet service** features servers who stand behind long tables spread with dishes. Servers may serve guests, or guests may serve themselves. This style of service allows for a great variety

Chef's Tip

Special Occasions

Special occasions, such as banquets or private parties, may require a restaurant to use a style that is different from its normal style.

of dishes. The buffet is a good solution for feeding groups of people meeting in conference rooms or catered dining rooms because it offers a great deal of choice, while permitting guests to mingle. Service requirements are limited, making this method of service economical in terms of labor costs. On the other hand, because guests pay a set price for all they can eat, food cost can be very high. Waste and excess can be controlled if servers, rather than guests, dish out portions. Another possible disadvantage of this system can be the compromised quality of the food if it is left out for a long time. Foods can dry out when exposed to the heat of a chafing dish or steam table. Care must be taken to offer foods that won't spoil or lose their freshness easily when left on the buffet table. A style of service similar to buffet service is **cafeteria service**, which allows diners to select foods from an array of items. Instead of serving themselves as they would in buffet service, servers dish out controlled portions and hand them to the guests. Guests then carry their dishes on trays to their tables, eliminating the need for any servers in the dining room. The cafeteria method of service requires service staff to keep the dining area clean, even if customers bring their dishes to a cleanup station or throw out disposables themselves.

FIGURE 20–14
Buffet Service
Buffets offer diners a wide variety of foods to sample.

COMPARING/CONTRASTING *What are the pros and cons of a buffet service?*
Source: .shock/Fotolia

FIGURE 20–15
An American Classic
Counter service at a diner is an American tradition.

COMPARING/CONTRASTING *What are the pros and cons of diner service?*
Source: Dave King/Dorling Kindersley Limited

- **Counter Service.** The purpose of **counter service** is to provide fast and easy dining away from home. A profitable alternative to table dining, counter service provides fast and easy turnover of guests. As long as condiments are within easy reach of counter stools, diners can easily help themselves. Servers require fewer steps to take and deliver orders, making it easy to serve customers. However, a counter filled with diners can create a hectic situation as servers try to take, place, pick up, and deliver orders in a hurry. Some upscale restaurants have counters where guests can sit casually and have beverages and appetizers before dinner—or even eat dinner at the counter.

- **Take-Out Service.** Italy, France, and other European countries have had popular, high-quality **take-out service** traditions for years, where people buy prepared food as an alternative to cooking at home. Take-out has become wildly popular in the United States in recent decades.

Many people prefer to purchase food to take to their offices or to bring home, rather than eating in a restaurant setting. Where once only the take-out restaurants or casual restaurants offered take-out, now even upscale restaurants sometimes provide take-out menus and options such as food delivery and Internet ordering. Take-out service is sometimes referred to as home-meal replacement service.

 **READING CHECKPOINT** *Describe four service styles common in the United States.*

Serving Guests

In Italy and in France, restaurant service is considered a profession, not just a job. The server should always be professional, no matter what style of restaurant. This means learning the skills of the restaurant service trade and practicing them until confidence is acquired. A server becomes a seamless connection between the dining room and the kitchen.

The interactions between the guest and the server are based upon proper etiquette. Etiquette calls for specific actions and behaviors. Servers make guests feel welcome and comfortable. They anticipate guests' needs while keeping a respectful distance. They make eye contact when speaking to someone, they listen carefully, and they answer questions honestly and completely. Policies for service staff differ from restaurant to restaurant, but the guidelines presented here apply to most restaurants.

An important aspect of treating guests properly is making accommodations for the disabled. The restaurant itself is required to provide access to the restaurant for patrons who may be in wheelchairs. The bathrooms should also be handicapped accessible. The server should be alert to the needs of handicapped patrons. For instance, seat them where they will not be bumped into by servers or runners passing by with food and drink. Bring braille or large-type menus for individuals with difficulty seeing.

Starting the Meal

- Pull out chairs for guests when they are being seated. If they have to leave the table, pull out the chairs again when they return to the table.
- Greet guests with a smile once they are seated and attend to them as soon as possible.
- Acknowledge children and bring them bread or other designated food at once; a contented child makes a contented parent.

Writing the Order Each restaurant has its own system of numbered guest checks and **dupes** (duplicates orders) for passing orders from the dining room to the back of the house. There may be separate dupes for

appetizer and dessert stations or for drinks from the bar. Guest checks need to be very clear, because many people will see them, including the waiter, the person entering the order, the kitchen staff, the guest, the cashier, the manager, and the bookkeeper. Guest checks are typically numbered. Servers are responsible for all of the checks that they have issued. This helps assure that there is no loss or theft and that food sales are properly recorded.

Each guest check should also include the server's name or initials, the number of the table (already assigned by the host or manager), the number of guests, and the date. Servers should fill this information in before they arrive at the table to take the order. A complete and properly written dupe means that, if necessary, another server or the manager could step in and deliver orders to the right person at the right table, without needing to ask the guests what they ordered.

To take the order, you should walk to the table and ask the guests if they are ready to order. You may take orders first for drinks, then for the meal, and again for dessert and after-dinner beverages.

- Unless some guests volunteer their orders while others are still deciding, start with the ladies, older first, then older gentlemen, followed by other gentlemen, and children last.

- Write down the order for each person in the order in which it will be served. Go over each order with every guest before leaving the table to be sure you have made no mistakes.

- Certain abbreviations are usually specified by the restaurant for food and beverages. It is the server's responsibility to learn these abbreviations and use them properly.

- Include all of the information about each order. For example, if a guest orders steak, you should ask him or her what degree of doneness is preferred. If there is a choice of dressing for the salad or bread for a sandwich, that must be recorded as well. This is especially important for special requests that have to do with food allergies.

- In most restaurants, only one check is written for each table unless guests request otherwise.

- If an order is continued on a second guest check, the first check should be subtotaled and stapled to the second.

Once the order is written, it must be communicated to the kitchen or the bar. Some restaurants have their servers bring the dupe to the kitchen. In others, the server may use a point-of-sale (POS) system. In that case, the server uses a computer to enter the order and all of the appropriate details and then the information is printed out on a ticket in the kitchen. A POS system also generates the final check. Accuracy is important no matter what system you use.

Source: Feng Yu/Fotolia

Guest check

FIGURE 20–16

Point of Sale (POS) System
Wait staff uses a POS system to submit orders to the kitchen.

COMPARING/CONTRASTING *What advantages does a POS system offer over bringing the dupe into the kitchen? What disadvantages?*

Source: CandyBox Images/Fotolia

Serving water

Source: Culinary Institute of America

Serving Water and Bread

- Ask guests if they want water immediately after they sit down.

- Fill water glasses as soon as they are half empty.

- If a glass becomes greasy or otherwise soiled from a guest handling it during the course of the meal, replace it with a fresh one.

- Bring bread as soon as possible according to the restaurant's established procedures. Some restaurants serve a basket of bread along with butter or dipping oils. Others serve the bread from a basket to the guest's bread-and-butter plate. Serve from the guest's left onto the plate at the left side of the place setting. Lift the bread with tongs or a serving fork on the bottom and a spoon on top.

Presenting the Menu

- Hand guests their menus from the right side, with the right hand, after any beverages are brought. The host may give menus to the guests when they are seated, or the server may do this, before or after taking the drink orders.

- Servers should name and describe any specials of the day and inform guests about any dishes on the menu that are not available. This prevents disappointment later.

- Be informed about the menu and any specials of the day so you can answer any questions and make appropriate recommendations. Guests may want to know if they can split an order or share it with the table. They may need information about ingredients, especially seafood, nuts, eggs, wheat, and dairy. They may need you to describe the cooking method.

- Use descriptive language to help your guests decide what to order and to steer them toward specific items. Letting them know that soups are made fresh daily, that vegetables are locally grown, or that meats are from free-range or grass-fed animals can make the difference to many guests. This added information often encourages them to order a specific dish.

- Be prepared to make vegetarian recommendations and to answer any questions about how the kitchen can prepare dishes for people with special diets. To do this successfully, you need to know how the menu item is prepared in the kitchen. Leaving the garlic out of a dish that is prepared to order is simple, but taking the chicken broth out of a whole pot of soup is impossible.

- Be diplomatic but straightforward if asked for suggestions or opinions. Guests appreciate honesty.

FIGURE 20–17

Discussing the Menu
Be informed about the menu and offer suggestions if asked.

COMMUNICATING *When you eat out, do you ever ask wait staff questions about what to order?*

Source: Andres Rodriguez/Fotolia

Serving Food

- Anticipate guests' needs. Check the table before you go to the kitchen to pick up the order for a table to see if the right flatware is on the table.

- Serve orders without delay to make guests feel they are being taken care of and to present the food at its best. If foods have to wait in the kitchen under a heat lamp, they can overcook and dry out. If there is no heat lamp, they will be cold.

- Serve women first and children last.

- Serve guests from their right, with the right hand, unless the restaurant or style of service requires a different approach.

- Check tables after serving courses to see if anything more is needed.

- Keep the table clear of empty plates, glassware, and unused flatware. Leave the bread-and-butter plates on the table until after the main course has been cleared and dessert ordered.

- Pay attention to tables even when you are not serving them directly.

- Be available as a server, but keep a professional distance when speaking to guests. This means not standing closer than 3 feet and making no personal conversation.

- Be a team player; everything runs more smoothly in a cooperative environment, especially in a hectic dining room.

Course Sequence

- The order in which various courses are served varies based on the type of food, the restaurant, and the country. The classic sequence in the United States is as follows: appetizer (or soup), salad, main course, and dessert. In Europe, the salad course may be after the main course. More elaborate menus could include additional courses such as an intermezzo or a cheese course.

- Often the course sequence will be determined by guests' preferences. Guests may order two appetizers, for example, with one being used as their main course. Others may choose to have a salad after the meal, whereas other guests want the salad before the main course.

- Regardless of course sequence, clear empty and soiled dishes and flatware after each course.

- Based on each guest's order, replace soiled dishes and flatware with appropriate dishes and flatware for the next course.

- If there are crumbs on the table, use a crumber to clean the table. Crumbing is done starting on the left side of the place setting, moving to the right side from guest to guest, moving clockwise.

- Separate dessert menus are usually passed out before the last course.

Learn to carry multiple orders, but remember to serve with the right hand

Source: John A. Rizzo/Getty Images

Chef's Tip

Serving Order

Traditionally, the woman sitting at the left of the host is served first. If there is no host, the server selects any woman at the table to begin with. Service then proceeds clockwise. This is repeated for clearing plates.

After-Dinner Beverages

- Take orders for tea, coffee, and other after-dinner beverages only after the table is cleared entirely and decrumbed.
- Bring appropriate cups, saucers, and utensils before serving any beverages.
- Be sure creamers are full to the top when delivered to the table and check them for refilling if guests linger.
- Be sure water for tea is boiling hot so tea will steep properly.
- Pour or serve all beverages from the right.

Basic Math Skills for Preparing the Check

- Adding up the charges for all of the food and drink ordered by the guests at a table is the most basic math skill you will need. You may add the charges by hand or using a calculator.
- The ability to do a rough estimate of charges will help you avoid errors that are the result of entering the figures into the calculator incorrectly. If it seems like way too much or not enough, redo the calculations.
- Typically, you will add together all the charges for food. Next, add together all the charges for alcoholic drinks. This makes it easier to calculate the tax properly. Your restaurant may only charge a tax on the sale of food items, and not on alcoholic beverages.
- The tax is a percentage of the total sales. The percentage varies from place to place, so be sure to use the correct tax for your location. You may use a table or chart that shows you the dollar amount for taxes. Or, you may use a calculator as follows: Convert the tax percent to a decimal (an 8 percent sales tax converts to .08, for example). Multiply the total for all taxable items by the decimal. Record the tax on the guest check.
- Add the total food charges, the total for alcoholic beverages, and the tax. This is the total amount.

Presenting the Check

- Tally the check only after asking guests if they desire anything more.
- Know which credit cards your restaurant accepts, if any, and whether or not personal checks are accepted.
- When guests are ready for the check, deliver it in the way specified by the restaurant. Many restaurants have a special folder for this, with a clear pocket inside to accommodate a credit card.
- Always include a pen when returning the check with a credit card form.

Pouring coffee from the right

Source: Culinary Institute of America

FIGURE 20–18

Presenting the Check
At this restaurant, the check is delivered in a leather folder with complimentary chocolates.

PREDICTING *What are the effects of bringing a check too soon or making guests wait too long for it?*
Source: Culinary Institute of America

BASIC CULINARY SKILLS

Service Sequence for Maître d' (Md), Server (S), and Runner (R)

1. **Welcome guests** warmly. (Md)
2. **Hand out menus.** (Md)
3. **Greet guests** cheerfully. (S)
4. **Fill water** glasses. (R)
5. **Take beverage order.** (S)
6. **Enter beverage order.** (S)
7. **Serve** beverages. (S)
8. **Bring bread** and butter or oil. (R)
9. **Take food order** and bring it to kitchen or order station. (S)
10. **Deliver dupe** to dupe board or station or enter into POS system. (S)
11. **Place flatware** for first course, if it is not already on the table. (S)
12. **Serve** first course. (S)
13. **Check** to see if guests need anything else or have any requests. (S)
14. **Clear** first course. (R)
15. **Reset tableware** for next course. (R)
16. **Deliver** next course. (S)
17. **Check** to see if guests need anything else or have any requests. (S)
18. **Clear** second course. (R)
19. **Crumb,** and remove salt and pepper. (R)
20. **Present dessert menus.** (S)
21. **Take order** for dessert and after-dinner beverages. (S)
22. **Enter dessert order.** (S)
23. **Reset tableware** for dessert. (R)
24. **Serve after-dinner beverages.** (S)
25. **Serve** desserts. (S)
26. **Refill** hot beverages. (S)
27. **Print check.** (S)
28. **Clear** desserts. (R)
29. **Present check.** (S)
30. **Pick up payment** from table and process payment. (S)
31. **Return receipt** or change to table. (S)
32. **Thank guests** and show them out. (S)

Brazil

It's Wednesday in Brazil, so what's for lunch? If it's a Brazilian restaurant, it's likely that you will have feijoada (fey-zhoo-AH-da), a dish that many Brazilians regard as their national dish. Feijoada is a stew typically made from black beans, onions, and garlic, with pieces of pork and beef. Often the meat is salted or smoked and the flavor is salty, rich, and hearty. Typically, feijoada is served on a bed of rice, with side dishes of cooked collard greens and peeled orange segments. Hot pepper sauce is often added to the feijoada. Because feijoada is a heavy dish, it is usually served at lunch. And because it takes a long time to prepare, restaurants serve it on only a few days of the week—traditionally on Wednesdays and Saturdays.

Brazilian feijoada reflects the strong influence that Portugal has had on Brazil. The Brazilian feijoada is similar to Portuguese feijoada, except that the Portuguese version uses white beans. This strong influence is because Brazil was a colony of Portugal until 1822. Portuguese is still the primary language of Brazil. However, being the largest country in South America, and the fifth largest in the world, both in geographic area and in population, Brazil has had many other influences on its cuisine.

Of course, before Brazil was made a Portuguese colony, the native population of Brazil made use of

Source: Ruslan Olinchuk/Fotolia

root vegetables, such as yams, cassava (a starchy root vegetable somewhat similar to a yam), and peanuts. They used the fruits growing in Brazil—mango, guava, pineapple, papaya, and oranges.

Coastal Brazil was also influenced by the cuisine of the African slaves brought to the area by Europeans. Acaraje (ak-air-AH-jhe) is a popular street food in Brazil's northeastern state, Bahia, which had been the center of the slave trade in Brazil. Acaraje is made from peeled black-eyed peas that are crushed, formed into a ball, and deep-fried in dendê (palm oil). To serve, the fried dough is split in half and stuffed with a salad of tomatoes, fried shrimp, vatapá (vah-TAH-pa), and/or caruru (car-RU-ru). Vatapá is a creamy paste made from bread, shrimp, coconut oil, peanuts, and palm oil. Caruru is a condiment made with okra, onion, shrimp, ground nuts, and palm oil.

Research

Research feijoada (both Brazilian and Portuguese) and bean dishes like it. Locate recipes for the bean dishes. Identify what gives each bean dish its distinctive characteristics. Divide into teams and cook some of the bean dishes. Compare the taste of each. Consider, when you compare them, how each dish was shaped by cultural influences.

Feijoada

Source: uckyo/Fotolia

Parting Company

- Service staff should make a point of thanking guests and offering a warm good-bye such as, "Thank you for coming, we hope we'll see you again soon."

- Servers should take care not to make guests feel rushed to leave by anything that is said or done, directly or indirectly.

- However, there are times when the front of the house needs to seat guests who have been waiting for a table and seated parties have long since finished their meal or when tables linger long after it is time for the service staff to go home. Notifying guests who have finished their meal that the restaurant is backed up is a delicate matter that is usually best left to the maître d'. Restaurant policy differs, depending on the type of establishment and what the customers are paying for a meal. Regular customers may become offended by being asked to leave, no matter how long they have lingered. More casual restaurants that depend on volume for profit are less likely to allow guests to linger if others are waiting to be seated.

 **READING CHECKPOINT** *Why should service staff be careful not to give the impression to guests that other customers are waiting for a table?*

20.3 ASSESSMENT

Reviewing Concepts

1. Describe four service styles common in the United States.

2. Why should service staff be careful not to give the impression to guests that other customers are waiting for a table?

Critical Thinking

3. Predicting What would happen if service staff waited until asked by guests to refill water glasses or bread baskets?

4. Comparing/Contrasting What is a dupe?

5. Applying Concepts Which should come first, taking the order or serving water?

6. Applying Concepts From which side should you pass the menu?

7. Applying Concepts Unless a guest volunteers an order, in what sequence should you typically take orders?

Test Kitchen

Working in teams of three, make a simple hot dish. When it is prepared, one team member acts as a runner, carrying the dish to a stand that is at least 100 feet away. Another team member acts as the server, serving the dish to a third team member, who acts as the customer. Evaluate the correctness of the service.

SOCIAL STUDIES ———————

Descriptive Writing

Research the order in which courses are served in three traditions: Indian, Chinese, and French. Write a description of the way the meal is brought to the table. Compare the traditions.

20.4

Handling Complaints and Problems

READING PREVIEW

Key Concepts

- Handling customer complaints
- Handling problems

Vocabulary

- accident report
- walkout

Source: Mona Daly/Getty Images

Handling Customer Complaints

Handling problems in a restaurant almost always involves communicating in an appropriate way. It doesn't matter if the customer has a problem with the restaurant or the restaurant has a problem with the customer—the way to handle the problem is by communicating effectively.

Effective communication can avoid problems in the first place. If the server can provide information about how dishes are prepared or which items are currently not available, the guest will not feel disappointed. If guests are in a hurry or celebrating a special event, the server can communicate that to the kitchen so they can adapt to the guests' needs.

The style of communication between the guest and the server can make the difference between a good experience for the guest and an unpleasant one. Servers should speak clearly and be able to pronounce menu items correctly, of course. In addition, they should speak to guests with respect and courtesy. Honesty is an important part of effective communication. If guests have a question that you cannot answer, assure them that you will find the answer and bring it to them as soon as you can. Avoid using slang. Some of the terminology in a restaurant makes perfect sense to the staff, but not to the guest.

Take the time to read the table and adjust your style and tone to meet your guests' needs. Reading the table means that you are observing clues that can tell you when a guest is impatient, unhappy with an item, or ready to have the check. Classic signs that guests are in need of your assistance include looking around the dining room, trying to catch someone's eye, looking out the window, tapping their fingers on the table, crossing their arms, pushing their chairs away from the table, or pushing their plates away.

Customer complaints are inevitable in any service business, but the restaurant business is probably the ultimate service business. Not only does a food-service establishment concern itself with providing tasty and nourishing food, it also promises to deliver it from kitchen to table with efficiency and style. There are two important steps in handling any potential customer complaints:

- Anticipating problems
- Addressing complaints quickly

Anticipating Problems The best way to avoid complaints that may arise is to prevent them before they happen. Just as a good driver practices defensive behavior behind the wheel to prevent accidents, so does the server practice good professional habits to assure customer satisfaction. Here are some techniques the professional server should keep in mind:

- Keep water glasses and bread baskets full.
- Communicate with guests. Ask if they need anything more after the food is delivered and then retreat to a place that is inconspicuous but from which you can still observe activity in the dining room.
- Keep an eye on your tables even after they have been served. Watch for any signs that your tables are having problems.
- If a guest gestures to speak with you, go to the table immediately. If you are not able to help a guest immediately, ask another server to go in your place or say that you will return quickly (and then do so).

FIGURE 20–19
Keep an Eye on Your Tables
Communicate with your guests and be aware of their needs.
INFERRING *What kinds of problems can be avoided by being attentive to the needs of guests?*
Source: Bruce Ayres/Getty Images

Addressing Complaints Quickly When something goes wrong, a professional server does two things:

- Acknowledges the problem and apologizes
- Resolves the problem as quickly as possible

Guests in a restaurant are entitled to satisfactory food and good service. Customers often don't feel comfortable complaining about unsatisfactory food, beverages, or service. They often remain silent and dissatisfied, but silent guests will usually not return to the restaurant. Again, communication is the key.

When guests do complain, apologize for their inconvenience or discomfort and show that you are genuinely interested in seeing to it that the situation is remedied. By communicating in this way, you have a much better chance that the guest will ultimately be satisfied and consider returning.

Here are some common complaints that may arise, and the ways in which a professional server is expected to remedy them. Of course, remedies are always carried out based on the restaurant's policy, but restaurants are in business to please customers. Most restaurants would rather appease guests than risk losing customers.

- **Miscooked Food.** Undercooked, overcooked, or improperly cooked food should be returned to the kitchen to be cooked further or replaced with properly cooked food. Depending on the restaurant's policies, the server may ask if the guest would prefer to select a different dish from the menu.

- **Foreign Object in the Food.** Incidents such as a fly or a hair in the food are not pleasant, but they sometimes happen despite routine precautions. In such a case, the server should apologize at once and offer to bring a new or different dish without drawing attention to the table.

FIGURE 20–20
Potential Problem
A customer might have trouble reading the menu in a dimly lit restaurant.

SOLVING PROBLEMS *What do you do if a customer complains about the lighting or décor in a restaurant?*

Source: Michael S. Yamashita/Corbis Images

- **Food Temperature.** Food that is served at the wrong temperature should be redone or replaced.

- **Dining Room Temperature.** If guests feel the room temperature is too hot, too cold, or too drafty, ask management if an adjustment can be made. If this is not possible, ask the guests if they would prefer moving to a table in a different part of the room where they might be more comfortable.

- **Lighting.** Lighting is an important part of the design plan of any restaurant because the quality and amount of light affects the mood of customers. Sometimes the lighting in restaurants is not sufficient to enable customers to read menus or see their food properly. In such a case, table lamps or candlesticks should be provided.

 **READING CHECKPOINT** *What are the two things a professional server should do when something goes wrong?*

Handling Problems

Cleaning Spills Any spills at the table should be cleaned up immediately. Minor spills should be absorbed with a clean cloth and covered with a clean table napkin. Large spills may require replacing the soiled tablecloth with a fresh one. In this case, the server should get help from other service staff to get the table back to order as quickly as possible.

To replace a tablecloth after a large spill, transfer all the objects that were on the soiled part of the tablecloth to the other side. Roll up the soiled half of the tablecloth and then place half of the fresh one in its place. Move all the objects on the table to the new tablecloth and remove the soiled tablecloth completely. Then finish spreading out the clean tablecloth. Finally, replace all the china, glassware, and flatware to their proper places.

A server responsible for spills on a customer's clothing should offer a sincere apology immediately and offer to pay for dry cleaning costs. The maître d' should discuss details for the dry cleaning.

Emergencies The maître d' should be trained to calmly and competently handle a serious health problem or physical injury to a customer. The most important thing is to attend to the immediate needs of the guest, calling for emergency help if necessary. You may need to file an **accident report**, which is a written description of what took place, including the name of the guest, any server involved, the date, and the time.

"The show must go on" is an expression from show business. In many ways the restaurant business is like show business. The kitchen is the

FIGURE 20–21
Handling Spills
Replace a tablecloth after a large spill.
PREDICTING *How would it make guests feel if you quickly and professionally replaced the tablecloth after one of the guests spilled something?*
Source: Steve Cole/Getty Images

Guidelines for Communicating Before, During, and After a Crisis

- Know your restaurant's procedures for evacuating the building or safe places in the restaurant to wait out an emergency.

- Know the location of first-aid kits and fire extinguishers.

- Stay calm and ask everyone around you to stay calm as well.

- Call for help if needed, or ask someone to call. Emergency numbers should be clearly posted near the phone at the host's desk and in the kitchen.

- If it is necessary to ask guests to leave the building or move to a different area, speak clearly and loudly enough for everyone to hear you, but don't yell.

- Provide accurate information if you have it. This might include letting guests know that authorities have been contacted or that emergency service providers are on the way. Do not pass along rumors, however.

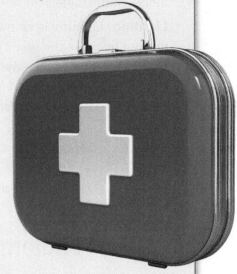

Source: Sashkin/Shutterstock

equivalent to backstage and the performance takes place in the dining room.

Natural events can cause electricity failure, or the sickness of a chef or other critical kitchen personnel can create chaos in the smooth running of business. Many personnel depend on the restaurant for their livelihood, so it isn't appropriate to close the restaurant unless absolutely necessary. In addition, closing the restaurant very often can cause a restaurant to lose customers permanently. Restaurants should try to construct contingency plans for such events, unlikely as they may be, so they will be prepared if an emergency happens.

Internal emergencies include situations such as a fire, a sudden illness, accidents, flooding from leaking sinks or toilets, or even a case of foodborne poisoning. Sometimes, an external crisis such as tornadoes, blizzards, high winds, or power outages will have a direct impact on the restaurant.

Managing a crisis situation calls for appropriate planning in order to deal with the crisis. What and how you communicate both internally and externally can make the difference between a successful outcome and a disaster.

Noisy Guests A restaurant is a naturally convivial place where people gather to enjoy themselves. It is also a place where people go to relax and, sometimes, to have privacy. But what if some guests want to have a noisy

FIGURE 20–22
Quiet Children
Coloring books and crayons are a good distraction for children until the food arrives.

APPLYING CONCEPTS *Are certain types of restaurants better options for families with children?*

Source: Culinary Institute of America

party while others want peace and quiet? Sometimes guests become so loud that others can't enjoy themselves.

If customers complain about the behavior of other guests, service professionals should be prepared to handle the situation without making either party angry. Thoughtless guests who disturb others should be tactfully asked to quiet down. If they continue to be loud, they should be calmly—but firmly—asked to leave before the situation gets out of hand.

Children and babies can raise the sound level in an otherwise quiet restaurant. Children's toys that beep and buzz can also be a distraction to other guests. The front desk should be stocked with coloring books and crayons or other such playthings for children that will keep them occupied quietly.

Cell Phones and Other Electronic Devices Today many people carry cell phones and other electronic devices. The public is accustomed to hearing them, but in a restaurant setting, they can be disturbing to other guests. However, doctors, emergency workers, and certain other professionals must answer their devices.

If the ring of an electronic device or a loud conversation over the phone is disturbing other guests at nearby tables, the service staff should tactfully ask the customer to take the call in the lobby or some other part of the restaurant where it will not disturb others. When a guest persists in violating other customers' rights to tranquility, only after repeated requests to change the behavior should the maître d' ask the guest to leave.

Nonpayment Problems Wait staff is responsible for recording orders, tallying checks properly, and making sure checks get paid. If a customer has had a problem with the food and refuses to pay, the maître d' should handle the situation, not the server.

Chef's Tip

Child Food

If a noisy toy is turned off and a child fusses, ask parents if they would like you to bring something for the child while the rest of the table is waiting for their food order to arrive.

Cash or Credit Card Problems What happens if the server brings the check to the table, only to learn that the guest is not able to pay it? A restaurant has a similar problem if a customer's credit card is declined. These are difficult situations for restaurants. Wait staff should notify the maître d' immediately. Restaurants typically have policies in place about such problems and the maître d' will resolve the issue accordingly.

Walkouts Customers have been known to leave their tables without paying their bills. If a restaurant is very hectic, an unpaid bill at an abandoned table may go unnoticed until it is too late. In the restaurant business, this unfortunate occurrence is called a **walkout**. This problem can be prevented. The dining room staff needs to be alert to this potential problem at all times. If someone starts to walk out without paying, wait staff should not try to approach the guest alone to avoid an unpleasant or even dangerous reaction by the guest. The maître d' should be notified and any decision to call the police should be made by management.

Customer Theft Thefts of flatware, china, and other objects is a problem with which most restaurants struggle. Guests who are seen pocketing or otherwise stealing restaurant property should be reported to the maître d, who will make the decision of whether to confront the perpetrator.

Robbery No establishment can anticipate a robbery. In such an event, it is crucial to remain calm and to avoid eye contact with the perpetrator. Do not make any heroic attempts to intervene. If such an attempt backfired, it could endanger the lives of guests and restaurant personnel. Do your best to remember any details about the robbers and the robbery that can later help police in solving the crime. Restaurants typically protect themselves from crime losses by taking out insurance.

FIGURE 20–23

Credit Card Problems
A customer's credit card may be declined.

PROBLEM SOLVING *What might a maître d' do in such a situation?*

Source: Xavier Bonghi/Getty Images

 **READING CHECKPOINT** *What is a walkout?*

Reviewing Concepts

1. What are the two things a professional server should do when something goes wrong?

2. What is a walkout?

Critical Thinking

3. Drawing Conclusions Why should a server avoid drawing attention to a table that has found a foreign object in the food?

4. Applying Concepts What should a server do if a diner says that the food she received was improperly cooked?

5. Predicting What could happen if service staff tried to take charge and protect restaurant patrons during a robbery?

6. Drawing Conclusions Why is it necessary to apologize for a complaint, even if you have acknowledged it?

7. Solving Problems What should you do if a guest asks you to resolve a problem in a way that is contrary to the restaurant's policies?

Test Kitchen

Divide into teams of four. Each team member will pick a role: chef, server, maître d', and customer. The chef will select and cook a dish that is served by the server to the customer. The customer will find a reason to complain. The server will bring in the maître d' to resolve the issue. The server will return the dish to the chef, who will make the correction. The server will then present the dish to the customer again and the maître d' will check that everything is acceptable to the customer. Evaluate the interaction.

SOCIAL STUDIES ———•
Restaurant Etiquette

Use the Internet to research sites about restaurant etiquette. Describe some of the most common mistakes restaurant personnel make and explain how to correctly respond to each situation.

PROJECT 20

You are now ready to work on Project 20, "Restaurant Role Play," which is available in "My Culinary Lab" or in your *Student's Lab Resources and Study Guide* manual.

Reviewing Content

Choose the letter that best answers the question or completes the statement.

1. The mâitre d' is the person responsible for
   a. explaining the menu to guests.
   b. running the restaurant.
   c. running the back of the house.
   d. running the front of the house.

2. The captain is the person responsible for
   a. explaining the menu to guests and taking orders.
   b. running the restaurant.
   c. running the back of the house.
   d. running the front of the house.

3. The front waiter
   a. is another name for the bus person.
   b. is another name for the runner.
   c. is another name for the server.
   d. answers the telephone.

4. A sous-chef
   a. runs the back of the house.
   b. is the executive's principal assistant.
   c. runs the front of the house.
   d. is responsible for sautéed dishes.

5. A fixed seating plan
   a. has no more than six chairs per table.
   b. requires payment prior to seating.
   c. allows customers to be seated at any time.
   d. has set mealtimes (such as at 6 p.m., 8 p.m., and 10 p.m.).

6. In the restaurant business, a cover is a(n)
   a. complete place setting for one person.
   b. extra bus person.
   c. extra chef.
   d. extra server.

7. A walkout is
   a. another name for a bus person.
   b. another name for a server.
   c. a customer who leaves without paying.
   d. another name for the hostess.

Understanding Concepts

8. When something goes wrong, what should a professional server do?

9. From which direction should a server typically serve guests?

10. In most U.S. restaurants, moving from left to right, how would you set the following silverware: knife, regular fork, salad fork, and spoon?

11. In the restaurant trade, what is the front of the house?

12. In the restaurant trade, what does it mean when you say a restaurant has a reservation policy?

Critical Thinking

13. **RECOGNIZING PATTERNS** What is the rule for arranging flatware for a cover where, for example, there will be multiple types of forks?

14. **COMPARING/CONTRASTING** What is the difference between a roundsman and a sous-chef?

Culinary Math

15. **APPLYING CONCEPTS** You estimate that a fixed seating plan, with three seatings, averages 48 covers in an average night, with an average cover costing $42. You estimate that a continuous seating plan will average about 60 covers a night, with an average cost of $30. Which seating plan produces higher sales?

On the Job

16. **COMMUNICATING** What would you say to a group of noisy guests in your first discussion with them about their noise?

17. **APPLYING CONCEPTS** You see that your customers are upset at the length of time it has taken to receive their check and are preparing to walk out without paying. What should you do?

Restaurant Managers

There are many managers in the culinary profession. An **executive chef**, for instance, is a manager. So is a **banquet manager** or a **caterer**. Lower-level managers are also needed for specific areas within a foodservice business.

Food and beverage managers in a foodservice business have to fill many shoes in the course of a day. They must have a strong background in math and accounting because they are generally held accountable for the profitability of the dining rooms they oversee. They must manage physical resources such as the furnishings in the dining room as well as human resources such as the dining room staff. They should be widely read in management topics that relate to a restaurant and its operation, and must be up to date on health and safety regulations.

Food and beverage managers may be responsible for a single dining room, a number of dining rooms in a single operation (such as the multiple dining rooms in a large hotel), or all dining room operations for a large region or the entire company.

They must be able to handle and resolve custom issues or complaints regarding the quality of the food or the service. This involves a significant amount of interpersonal skills and may require tact and diplomacy.

They should be familiar with kitchen operations and capabilities. They hold staff meetings to educate the wait staff about the menu, special offerings, and wines and other beverages sold at the restaurant.

Dining room managers are in charge of a single dining room. They are responsible for the organization of the dining room into stations and assigning wait staff to handle the stations. They generate work lists for the staff, oversee the preparation of the dining room for service, and oversee the dining room's maintenance throughout service. They may work directly with the owner, or they may report to the food and beverage manager.

Shift managers are assigned to manage a specific shift in the dining room. They typically report to the dining room manager or the food and beverage manager.

Entry-Level Requirements

There are examples of food and beverage managers who have risen through the ranks with little or no advanced education. Most, however, have some training in food and beverage management.

Helpful for Advancement

To rise through the ranks of food and beverage management, you should consider specific types of education or training. An associate, bachelor, or master's degree in management is a good idea. Large corporations often have a manager-in-training program for promising candidates.

Source: Wavebreakmedia Ltd/Getty Images

Chefs must also be managers

GIANNI SCAPPIN

Chef Gianni Scappin was born in northern Italy, where his parents owned the trattoria that gave him his first taste of the industry. He studied at the Recoaro Terme Culinary Institute for four years. After receiving his degree, he cooked his way around the world, eventually finding himself in New York City as the Executive Chef at Castellano and later, Le Madri.

Chef Scappin worked as a consultant during the opening of The Colavita Center at The Culinary Institute of America, and stayed on as an instructor. In the Hudson Valley, Chef Scappin partnered with actor Stanley Tucci to open Finch Tavern, and in 2001, he opened Gigi Trattoria. Most recently, Chef Scappin went back to his Italian roots, opening two new restaurants, Cucina in Woodstock, New York and Market Street in Rhinebeck, New York.

Gianni Scappin

VITAL STATISTICS

Graduated: Recoaro Terme Culinary Institute

Profession: Chef and restaurant owner, instructor at the CIA

Interesting Items: Co-authored four cookbooks, including *Cucina and Famigilia*, and The Culinary Institute of America's *Pasta*.

Consulted on the award-winning film *Big Night* with Stanley Tucci

Returned to Italy to reopen and run his father's trattoria

CAREER PROFILE

Salary Ranges

Shift Manager/Dining Room Manager: $25,000 to $40,500 (or more)

Food and Beverage Manager: $34,000 to $65,000 (some managers receive bonuses and commissions on sales as part of their salary)

Regional Manager: $50,000 to $95,000

Chapter 21

Menus

21.1 Planning the Menu

21.2 Pricing Menu Items

Source: Pixel & Création/Fotolia

Planning the Menu

READING PREVIEW

Key Concepts

- Understanding the purpose of a menu
- Identifying types of menus
- Planning the menu
- Organizing and designing a menu

Vocabulary

- à la carte menu
- California menu
- cyclical menu
- du jour menu
- entrée
- fixed menu
- limited menu
- market research
- menu
- menu conversion
- menu modification
- mission statement
- modified à la carte menu
- prix fixe menu
- table d'hôte menu
- table tent menus

Source: Candy Box Images/Fotolia

Purpose of a Menu

A **menu** is a list of food and drink choices available in a restaurant. A menu does much more than tell customers that steaks are flame-broiled or the chocolate cake is homemade. Menus are actually tools with two primary functions: planning and communication.

In most foodservice operations, management plans the menu. However, in a hotel, the executive chef typically works with management to plan the menu. For chain restaurants, central management plans the menu. Generally, it is only in individual restaurants that are not part of a chain where a chef has the opportunity to plan a menu.

Menus as Planning Tools A menu is an important planning tool for a foodservice operation because it affects every aspect of the operation's business. Typically, eight factors influence the choice of foods on a menu:

- **Customers' Needs and Expectations.** A menu should reflect the market for which it is intended. For example, a coffee shop in a neighborhood of office buildings will have a menu that offers sandwiches for people with little time for lunch. The menu for a restaurant at a beach resort will feature fresh seafood for tourists who expect seafood on the menu. The same idea of meeting a customer's needs applies to cafeterias. A hospital cafeteria will offer simple yet nutritious choices that appeal to the staff as well as the patients.

- **Prices.** Customers expect to pay according to the type of food and service they receive. Office workers who stop at a coffee shop usually want filling food and quick service without spending too much money. On the other hand, tourists on a vacation expect to splurge on a memorable meal, and they pay the check willingly.

- **Mission Statement.** A **mission statement** is a statement of an organization's goal. The mission statement of a restaurant or other foodservice establishment must be clear before menu planning can begin. The mission statement must reflect customers' needs and expectations, as well as the price they would be willing to pay for their food. The mission of a Mexican restaurant might be to offer authentic foods of a particular region, whereas the mission of the snack bar at a health spa might be to offer only low-fat, healthy choices.

- **Type of Food Served.** The type of food on a menu is a direct reflection of the mission statement.

- **Service Style.** Fancy dishes or dishes that require special preparation at the table require a much different level of service than simpler food. Items on the menu determine what style of service will be required. In a cafeteria, for example, which requires minimal service, either the food is on display for easy self-service or it is plated by a minimal number of employees. Contrast that with an expensive restaurant, where several waiters sometimes work together on just one table.

- **Workers' Skills.** The food on a menu determines how many workers will be needed to prepare and serve the food. A French restaurant may require French chefs (or chefs who have trained in French cooking) and a wait staff able to speak French. A fast-food restaurant will require minimal training for staff.

- **Required Equipment.** The food on a menu determines what sort of equipment is required in the kitchen. A high-end steak restaurant may need an open-flame grill capable of using hickory wood, whereas a health spa snack bar might only need a couple of blenders to make shakes. Whenever menus are modified or updated, you also need to take the availability of equipment into consideration.

FIGURE 21–1

Lunch Counter

Lunch counter menus are different from upscale restaurant menus.

COMMUNICATING *What would be an appropriate mission statement for this foodservice establishment?*

Source: Laura Stone/Shutterstock

Chef's Tip

Quiet Time

Take your time when creating a menu. Work in a quiet place where you can focus without interruptions. Test your concepts by asking for feedback from coworkers or colleagues.

- **Competitors.** Before planning a menu, it is important to visit competing foodservice operations that have the same mission as your business. You need to see what they are doing because you will inevitably be compared to them.

Menus as Communication Tools The menu is like a letter written directly to customers. It often provides such information as the location of your food establishment, the prices for food, the hours of operation, and sometimes even a history of the establishment. Menus offer an opportunity to go into detail about a new food item or a special cooking technique. Menus come in all sizes, but in terms of advertising, even the smallest menu can be as effective as a billboard for telling the public what you want them to know. Menus are essentially tools for communicating. A well-designed menu communicates in the following ways:

- **Informing Customers about Food Choices.** On its most basic level, a menu lists the food your establishment offers. Customers want to know exactly what kind of food to expect. In a high-end restaurant with unusual ingredients or cooking methods, this might require a great deal of detail for each specific item. In a different sort of restaurant, you might not need to be very descriptive at all—just the name of the item will do. Not all descriptions need to be written. You could use a symbol to indicate a dish's degree of spiciness or whether a dish is vegetarian. It's helpful to think of your mission statement when describing individual food choices. You can even take some space on the menu to describe your mission in terms the customer will understand and appreciate.

- **Influencing Customer Choices.** A menu can influence customer choices in many ways. You can use the menu descriptions to tell

FIGURE 21–2

Informing Customers

Customers study a menu to decide on their food choices.

RECOGNIZING PATTERNS *Have you ever felt that a menu has influenced your choice of food?*

Source: Steve Mason/Getty Images

customers about your establishment's most popular items. You can use the menu to list the day's special or featured items. Some restaurants use the menu to tell customers that a dish is recommended by the chef. Some menus use symbols, such as four stars, to indicate particularly popular dishes. Overall, the menu is a valuable selling tool when used effectively. It acts as not only a communication tool but also as a marketing tool. A menu influences what items customers choose, and ultimately affects their dining experience (as well as their decision to return or become a regular customer).

- **Creating an Impression.** First impressions matter. The menu is your chance to project an image for the restaurant. Decisions about the cover, the quality of paper, the use of artwork, and how the menu items are positioned all communicate a message to the customer. For example, a leather menu cover identifies a restaurant that wishes to be perceived as a higher-end, more formal location. A menu that is printed on a paper placemat indicates that the dining experience will be more casual and probably much less expensive. A handwritten menu on a chalkboard with balloons attached indicates an informal setting where families might feel welcome, as does an oversized, plastic-covered menu with playfully named dishes.

Chef's Tip

Keep Menus Clean

Replace menus when they start to show signs of wear and tear. No one wants to handle a menu if it has stains on it or the pages are bent. A soiled or damaged menu communicates a negative message.

READING CHECKPOINT *What are the two primary functions of a menu?*

Types of Menus

The type of menu chosen for a food establishment is based on a number of factors, including pricing considerations, location, type of customer, and hours of operation. There are many styles of menus. Seven of the most popular types of menu are:

- À la carte and modified à la carte menus
- California menus
- Du jour menus
- Table d'hôte and prix fixe menus
- Fixed menus
- Cyclical menus
- Limited menus

À la Carte and Modified à la Carte Menus An **à la carte** (ah-lah-CART) **menu** is a menu on which each food item or beverage is priced and served separately. Typically, an à la carte menu is for a specific meal, such as lunch or dinner. This type of menu is popular because customers can choose exactly what they want as main courses, side dishes, appetizers,

Today's Specials
Friday, June 7

Appetizers

Louisiana Duck & Okra Gumbo	7.00
Oven-Roasted Shrimp with Rosemary White Beans	8.00

Entrees

Grilled Filet Mignon Medallions with Mushroom Sauce served with Roasted Garlic Mashed Potatoes	21.50
Seared Wild Salmon with Crispy Polenta, Goat Cheese and Glazed Baby Carrots	18.00

Desserts

Glazed Baked Apple on Puff Pastry with Vanilla Ice Cream	6.50
Hot Molten Chocolate Cake with Cherry Compote	7.00

FIGURE 21–3
Du Jour Menu
A restaurant's specials of the day.
DRAWING CONCLUSIONS *What is the best way to present a du jour menu, from both the restaurant's and the customer's point of view?*

salads, or desserts. The à la carte menu offers the freedom to mix and match according to individual taste. A customer may choose two appetizers and a salad rather than choosing a main course, for example. Hotels and upscale restaurants often use à la carte menus.

On a **modified à la carte menu**, appetizers and desserts are usually priced and served separately. Often the main course will include a soup or salad as well as a starch, vegetable, and possibly a beverage. This type of menu is often found in family-style restaurants.

California Menu A **California menu** is a single menu listing breakfast, lunch, and dinner foods. It offers customers the freedom to choose any item at any time of day. California menus are especially popular with foodservice establishments that are open 24 hours. They are also used for hotel room service.

Du Jour Menu A **du jour menu** (DOO ZHOOR) lists food that is served only on that particular day. The next day, a different du jour menu will be offered. The words *du jour* are French for "of the day." Sometimes a restaurant has only one or two daily specials that are made just for that day. A soup du jour, for example, is a soup made just for that day. These restaurants will have a du jour menu in addition to their standard à la carte menu.

Table d'Hôte and Prix Fixe Menus A **table d'hôte** (TAH-blah DOHT) **menu** offers a complete meal—from an appetizer to a dessert and often including a beverage—for a set price. Banquets often feature a table d'hôte menu. For example, diners might choose in advance from four meals: beef, chicken, fish, or vegetarian. Each meal would include an appetizer, a salad, rolls, a main course, a dessert, and coffee or tea. Individual meals might be priced separately.

For a specific event or banquet, a table d'hôte menu might feature a single meal with a specific theme. For instance, the appetizer, salad, main course, and dessert might all be French or Italian menu items. Or all the items might be centered around seafood or "farm-to-table" selections (featuring organic produce and meat).

A **prix fixe** (PREE FEEKS) **menu** is similar to the table d'hôte menu. A prix fixe menu typically offers a complete meal, often including a beverage, for a set price. Sometimes diners are offered a choice for one or more of the courses, and sometimes diners can choose, for a supplemental charge, a luxury item such as lobster or caviar. In some instances, the price of a prix fixe menu is relatively low because it reduces production costs by allowing the kitchen to operate at a set pace and flow. If the same dishes were

Chef's Tip
Collect Your Thoughts

Whenever you have a menu idea, write it down and keep it in a file folder for future reference. Put any copies of menus that inspire you in the same file.

ordered à la carte, the bill would be much higher. Both casual restaurants and upscale restaurants use prix fixe menus.

Fixed Menu A fixed menu offers the same items every day. Some customers like fixed menus because they continue to return to a restaurant for a favorite dish and would be disappointed if the dish weren't offered. For this reason, many neighborhood and ethnic restaurants use a fixed menu, although they often supplement the menu with du jour offerings.

Cyclical Menu A cyclical (SICK-li-cal) menu is written for a certain period of time and then it repeats itself. For example, a cyclical menu (also called a *cycle menu*) might repeat after three weeks, although the time between cycles may vary based on seasonal availability of ingredients and other factors. Some cyclical menus change four times a year, according to the seasons. Some change every week, so the same food is offered every Monday, different food is offered every Tuesday, and so on. Longer-term cyclical menus are particularly suited for institutions such as hospitals, schools, and cafeterias where the same people are being served each day. Weekly cyclical menus are particularly suited to family, casual, and neighborhood restaurants.

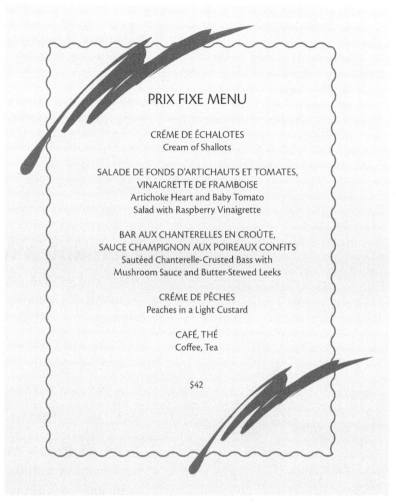

PRIX FIXE MENU

CRÉME DE ÉCHALOTES
Cream of Shallots

SALADE DE FONDS D'ARTICHAUTS ET TOMATES,
VINAIGRETTE DE FRAMBOISE
Artichoke Heart and Baby Tomato
Salad with Raspberry Vinaigrette

BAR AUX CHANTERELLES EN CROÛTE,
SAUCE CHAMPIGNON AUX POIREAUX CONFITS
Sautéed Chanterelle-Crusted Bass with
Mushroom Sauce and Butter-Stewed Leeks

CRÉME DE PÊCHES
Peaches in a Light Custard

CAFÉ, THÉ
Coffee, Tea

$42

Prix fixe menu

FIGURE 21–4
Cyclical Menu
Colleges and institutions often have menus that are cyclical.
DRAWING CONCLUSIONS *What period of time would you use as a cycle in your school cafeteria?*
Source: CandyBox Images

Limited A **limited menu** offers a limited range of choices to the customer. For example, a restaurant might offer a limited menu of four sandwiches, two soups, and a salad for lunch. A fast-food menu is an example of a limited menu. Limited menus make it easy to keep track of costs because there are typically fewer ingredients.

READING CHECKPOINT *What are seven common types of menus?*

Planning a Menu

When you write a menu, the goal is to please the customer as well as the owner. It is possible, with careful planning, to do both. Keep these four important considerations in mind when planning a menu:

- Type of place and customers
- Facility, staff, and equipment limitations
- Balance and variety
- Truthfulness

Type of Place and Customers It's important to understand your customers in relation to your type of foodservice establishment. You need to include specific menu items that are appropriate for both your type of place and your type of customer. For example, if you have a family seafood restaurant, consider that some nonseafood items will make the menu more interesting and will offer an alternative for family members or other guests who may not want seafood. Likewise, if you are running the foodservice for a senior center, consider that they might welcome something entirely new on the menu. Seniors may not have an opportunity to eat anywhere else, and variations on the menu will add variety to their lives. A menu with a theme has specific characteristics. You could introduce a Mexican or other themed meal as a special surprise from time to time.

Understanding your place and your customer involves five additional factors:

- **Geography and Culture.** People have food preferences. Preferences are often connected to geography and culture. In an area of Minnesota populated by people with a Swedish heritage, hearty soups with root vegetables might be a winter preference. The same item in Florida might be unappealing.

- **Economics.** People need to feel they are getting their money's worth when they go out to eat. The prices on a menu should reflect the value expected. If an expensive restaurant delivers a sense that exotic ingredients were used, the customer will be satisfied. If a budget meal is advertised at another place, the price needs to match the customers' expectations.

- **Population Density.** The number of people living in an area determines the potential number of customers. If you are in a remote rural area, it would be unrealistic to plan a menu with several pages of choices, because much of your food would be wasted. If, however, you are in the heart of a large city, such a menu might be appropriate.

- **Industry Guidelines and Governmental Regulations.** Institutions, such as schools and assisted living residences for seniors, must comply with industry guidelines and governmental regulations. Federal programs such as the National School Lunch and School Breakfast programs outline the types of food and the portion size for schools wishing to receive funding. For many institutional settings, the calorie count of each menu item must be shown and the overall caloric intake of people eating at the institution is set.

- **Age.** Special menus or sections within a menu may be required for certain age groups. A family restaurant may require a special children's menu with limited offerings in smaller portions at lower prices. Senior citizens also provide a special menu situation. Elderly people tend to eat less and often have flexibility in their schedules to dine outside the regular hours. They may also need food choices that are easy to chew.

FIGURE 21–5

Influences on the Menu

This restaurant has a special children's menu.

DRAWING CONCLUSIONS *Why might a restaurant have a children's menu?*

Source: Magnus Rew/Dorling Kindersley

Facility, Staff, and Equipment Limitations How many people a dining facility can serve is influenced by its menu and the service it requires. If a dining facility is used as a cafeteria or for buffet-style dining, it can serve more people than if it is used for fine-dining with many different courses served at a leisurely pace. If space becomes a problem, a menu change could help accommodate more people.

Every business needs to make money to stay in operation. As you plan a menu, you also need to keep in mind the limits of your equipment and your staff. For example, you may want to feature French onion soup on your menu, but if you don't have individual ovenproof bowls or the extra staff required to apply the finishing touches, it could be too costly for your restaurant. You may want to add pizza to the menu, but that requires an expensive pizza oven, a large amount of space in the kitchen, and additional staff. If you were cooking steaks on a flattop range, but wanted to change to a grill, you would obviously need new equipment, but you would also need to retrain your staff (or hire new staff who were familiar with cooking on the grill). Ultimately, every menu item requires specific types of food, equipment, supplies, and staff.

Chef's Tip

Play It Up

A playful children's menu with colorful pictures and drawings will make children feel special. Activities on the menu may keep children busy and quiet while they wait for their food.

FIGURE 21–6

Equipment Limitations
A small kitchen cannot easily
increase space or equipment.

PREDICTING *If you were a chef in a
small kitchen, would you focus on dishes
that are easy to prepare and don't use
many pans?*

Source: Kim Steele/Getty Images

The cost of labor is one of the biggest expenses in the food business. The
best way to maximize labor is to know the existing skills of all your workers and write a menu that uses those skills well. You could teach workers
new skills to suit a new menu, but training costs time and money. On the
other hand, underusing workers' time and skills is inefficient for business.
The workers don't feel challenged, which leads to boredom, dissatisfaction,
and job turnover.

Balance and Variety The specific items on your menu need to be appropriate for your type of place, your customers, your staff, and your equipment. They also need to be balanced and have variety. Typically, a balanced
menu is one that has been written with the following considerations in mind:

- **Variety.** People appreciate variety. It makes dining more interesting
  and encourages return visits to a restaurant. You can add variety to
  a menu in a number of ways. You can use different cooking methods.
  For example, offer some fried, baked, or sautéed dishes and serve
  them with side dishes that are also prepared in a variety of different
  ways, such as pureed, steamed, or stir-fried. You can use different
  tastes and textures. Vary taste by varying spices. Make some foods
  crunchy and others soft. Finally, use color. Remember the saying,
  "We eat with our eyes."

- **Balance.** A menu needs to accommodate different tastes. You need
  to offer a balance of choices. Each food section should be considered
  for balance. For example, appetizers might be hot or cold, cooked or
  raw. Main course choices could include fish, poultry, meat, and vegetarian options.

- **Special Needs.** Some customers have special needs that could be
  addressed on the menu. You could indicate a dish's suitability for dia-
  betics, vegetarians, or someone with food allergies. You might also
  indicate that a dish could be adjusted to make it more appropriate

Chef's Tip

Inventory Control

When increasing your
number of menu offerings,
choose recipes that use
the same cut of meat,
poultry, or seafood so you
will have better control of
your inventory.

for someone with special needs. For example, you could adjust a dish to make it suitable for someone with low-fat or low-calorie requirements.

- **Religion.** Many religious faiths have dietary restrictions. For example, some people have a tradition of sacrificing desserts or not eating meat at certain times of the year. Other people do not eat pork. Sensitivity to these considerations broadens the appeal of a menu.

- **Regional Cuisine.** People are proud of the region where they live and the food specialties found there. Maine is known for steamed lobster, and Texas has a reputation for barbecued meat. People enjoy seeing these things on a menu when they visit those regions and are more likely to patronize a restaurant that offers them.

- **Trends.** Collecting information to find out what customers like or dislike is called **market research**. Questionnaires, phone interviews, and observations are all studied to spot trends. Use these reports to find out what your potential customers favor so you can include those items as menu choices.

- **Various Price Levels.** You will need to have some dishes that are at the high end of your customers' affordability scale and other dishes that are less expensive. All your prices need to be within your customers' range.

- **Product Availability.** Before listing anything on the menu, be certain that you can get a sufficient supply of it. If you want to avoid reprinting the menu, you can put "in season" for items that may have limited availability, such as summer fruit or seasonal fish. The quality of most food depends on the seasons. Food that is in season will be at the peak of its flavor, texture, and color. For example, peaches are better in the summer, but cranberries are freshest in the fall and winter.

Truthfulness. Many laws are designed to protect consumers from fraudulent claims related to foods and menus. Collectively, these laws are called the *Truth-in-Menu laws.* They are administered by dozens of agencies, but all focus on the accurate labeling of food. The laws are constantly being revised, so it is important in planning a menu to be honest—both in regard to the price that is charged and the food that is served.

FIGURE 21–7

Regional Cuisine
Different regions have different cuisines.
APPLYING CONCEPTS *Why would a restaurant want to serve regional specialties?*
Source: Jeff Greenberg/PhotoEdit

Peach pie
Source: David Murray/Dorling Kindersley

Truth-in-Menu Laws

Claim	Description
Quantity	Amounts and weights must be accurate. For example, if the weight shown is before the item is cooked, the menu must say so.
Quality	The stated quality must be accurate. "Prime" meat must actually be "Prime." It cannot be "Choice."
Price	The price must be accurate and not misleading. If six oysters are sold at a specific price, then six oysters should be delivered on the plate.
Brand Names	Brand names, such as Tabasco Sauce® or Godiva Chocolates®, must be represented accurately.
Product Identification	The product listed in the menu must be the product in the dish. If lobster was supposed to be included in a chowder, you cannot substitute monkfish.
Point of Origin	The location of ingredients must be accurate. Vermont maple syrup actually has to be from Vermont.
Merchandising Terms	Terms used to encourage customers to purchase menu items must be completely accurate. If the menu says that salad comes with the main course, be sure a salad comes with all main courses.
Means of Preservation	The method by which food on the menu was preserved must be accurate. This means, for example, that frozen fish can't be used if the menu says the fish is fresh.
Methods of Preparation	The method of preparation must be accurate. If the menu says the cod was broiled, it cannot be baked.
Verbal and Visual Presentation	Pictures and descriptions of food on the menu must be accurate in every detail.
Dietary and Nutritional Information	It is critically important that any dietary or nutritional information be completely correct. All dietary and nutritional data must be supported with statistical data.

READING CHECKPOINT *What are four important considerations to keep in mind when planning a menu?*

Organizing and Designing a Menu

Three important aspects of creating a menu are organizing the menu, designing the actual menu that will be put in your customers' hands, and writing the menu descriptions.

Organizing a Menu Food is organized into categories on a menu. Usually the categories are listed in the sequence in which they are to be eaten. For example, on a lunch or dinner menu, appetizers are usually the first category and hot beverages are the last. Menus are also organized within each of these categories. For example, if the main-course category has two poultry dishes and three beef dishes, the poultry would typically be listed together, as would the beef.

You should have a balanced number of categories and within those categories a balanced number of choices. A lunch menu might offer fewer choices in each category than a dinner menu. If eight main courses are listed, there might be two beef, two poultry, one fish, two vegetables, and one pasta option. Within the categories, there should also be a variety of cooking styles, such as grilling, frying, baking, and roasting.

Ethnic menus may have a unique organization, and there are many variations even among relatively similar restaurants. However, as a general guideline, for nonethnic restaurants, menu categories are typically shown on a menu in the following sequence:

- **Hors d'Oeuvres.** You would list hors d'Oeuvres on a menu only in a formal situation or perhaps at a banquet.

- **Appetizers.** Appetizers (also called *starters*) might be further broken down as cold and hot appetizers. Soups are sometimes included in the appetizers category.

Chef's Tip

Entrées

In the United States, an entrée is the main course. In some European countries, an entrée is the first course.

FIGURE 21–8
Lunch Menu
Notice that salads and starters have been combined under one category.

ANALYZING INFORMATION *Why do you think this menu has a separate category for wood-fired pizzas?*

ST. ANDREW'S CAFÉ
Lunch Menu

Soups

Cuban Style Black Bean Soup 4.
with Smoked Jalapeño Peppers and Croutons

Curried Apple and Roasted Butternut Squash Soup 4.
with Cilantro and Toasted Coconut

St. Andrew's Café Soup Sampler 5.

Starters and Salads

Warm Risotto Cake with Fresh Mozzarella 8.
with Shaved Prosciutto and Grilled Vegetables

Grilled Jumbo Shrimp with Pesto 9.
with Couscous and Arugula Salad

St. Andrew's Caesar Salad 6.
with Parmesan Croutons

Autumn Pear and Roquefort Garden Salad 6.
with Grapes, Hazelnuts and Verjus Vinaigrette

Warm Spinach Salad 7.
with Smoked Bacon Dressing and Pickled Red Onions

Wood-Fired Pizzas

Thai-Style Barbecue Chicken Pizza 10.
Aged Jack Cheese and Tomatillo Salsa on top

Pizza Margherita 10.
Tomatoes, Basil and Mozzarella

Entrées & Specialty Sandwiches

Grilled Steak Caesar Entrée Salad 15.
with Parmesan Croutons

Japanese Udon Noodles and Jumbo Shrimp and Scallops 16.
Served with Vegetables, Mushrooms and Ponzu Sauce

Sautéed Pork Loin 14.
Served with Prune Chutney, Herbed Spaetzle and Braised Cabbage

Vegetable Pita Sandwich 8.
Grilled Vegetables, Basil and Sun Dried Tomatoes Served on Warm Pita with Taboulleh Salad

Smoked Ham & Fresh Mozzarella Panini Sandwich 10.
with Tomatoes and Basil

Desserts

St. Andrew's Dessert Sampler 6.
A special sampling of our Pastry Chef's delicacies of the day

Seasonal Fruit Crisp 5.
A variety of Assorted Fresh Berries with Dark Chocolate Served with Oatmeal-Walnut Crisp Topping and Ice Cream

Sorbet of the Day 5.
Made daily with fresh fruit

White Chocolate and Honey Cheesecake 6.
with Strawberries

Indicates a Vegetarian Selection   Indicates Nuts in Selection

- **Soups.** Soups may be further broken down as cold or hot soups. Soups may also be included in the appetizers category.

- **Salads.** American-style restaurants would tend to place salads before the main course. European-style restaurants might place the salad after the main course.

- **Sandwiches.** On a lunch menu or a casual dinner menu, you might find sandwiches listed as a separate category. Sandwiches might be further broken down as hot or cold sandwiches.

- **Main Courses.** The main course is usually broken down as hot or cold and then further broken down by type of meat or other similar feature. A main course is also referred to as an **entrée** (AHN-tray) in the United States.

- **Side Dishes.** Vegetables and starches that accompany the main course are usually listed as side dishes.

- **Desserts.** Sometimes restaurants that want to emphasize their dessert offerings will provide a separate dessert menu.

- **Hot Beverages.** Hot beverages that are served with dessert are usually listed last on the menu. Cold beverages, including alcoholic drinks, are often listed on a separate menu or list. If both cold and hot beverages are listed on the menu, they will typically be broken down as hot or cold.

Designing a Menu Because the menu is a communication tool between you and the customer, you need to be concerned about just what you communicate with your menu.

The three most common menu formats are:

- **Printed Menu.** The printed menu is presented to customers to look at. This is the most common type of menu. It often has a cover and back, with the actual menu printed inside on heavy paper. These are permanent menus. When specials are offered, an insert or clip-on is attached to the menu. Some establishments place folded cards, known as **table tent menus**, directly on the tables to tell customers about specials.

- **Spoken Menu.** Some restaurants have their servers memorize the menu and then repeat it to the customers. This is called a spoken menu. It usually has a limited number of choices. The spoken menu creates a more intimate feeling in a restaurant, but some people find it demanding because they can't linger over the menu and study the choices.

- **Menu Board.** The menu board is on display, usually on the wall or an easel, for everyone to see. Menu items are either handwritten or printed. The menu board is associated with casual dining.

On written menus, design details such as materials, colors, and images communicate your message just as strongly as words do. Your pictures,

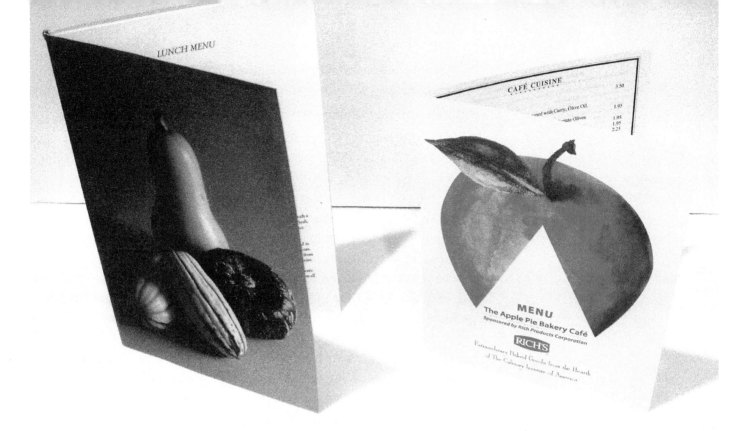

FIGURE 21–9
Menu Design
Two contrasting menu covers.
COMPARING/CONTRASTING *What message do these menus communicate?*
Source: Culinary Institute of America

colors, words, and materials set a tone. They tell your customers what to expect in their dining experience. You need to make the menu send a clear written and visual message about your place of business and the food being served.

Follow these guidelines in designing a printed menu:

- Make sure the menu contains your restaurant's vitals (name, address, and phone, at least).
- Design the shape and size of the menu so it is in keeping with your restaurant's concept.
- Avoid photos inside the menu.
- Emphasize the items on the menu, not their prices.
- Use graphics sparingly.
- Use print, not a hard-to-read script.
- Use numbers for the prices; do not spell them out.

Writing a Menu When writing the descriptions of your menu items, keep these guidelines in mind:

- Keep your descriptions free from misspellings and grammatical errors.
- Make sure the language reflects the restaurant's concept and style.
- Make the food sound attractive.
- Eliminate all unnecessary words.
- Do not use restaurant jargon.

Mexican restaurant menu
Source: Prentice Hall School Division

- Provide customers with a road map for their dining experience, one for which they will not require further directions.
- Make sure the menu is easy to read.
- Use words that are in keeping with current food and restaurant trends.
- Be positive.

Changing a Menu There are many reasons to change a menu. You may notice that certain menu items are not ordered very often. Diners may leave a particular menu item uneaten on their plate. It isn't unusual for diners to provide feedback to the chef directly or through the wait staff. It is a very good idea for a restaurant to provide some means for diners to provide feedback to the restaurant. Often this will be done through an anonymous survey provided to diners along with their check at the end of the meal. A restaurant may have an item that everyone loves, but it may use an ingredient that is no longer in season or that has gone up in price, so the price for the item is no longer acceptable. Some restaurants change their menu very often, others change to reflect the seasons, and others change only occasionally.

Restaurants also use sales information to analyze how menu items are selling. Owners and managers will often analyze the daily and weekly sales patterns to determine which items on the menu are selling. They use this information to decide to make menu modifications or, in extreme cases, to perform a menu conversion.

Based on diner feedback, availability of ingredients, sales information, and profitability, a restaurant may decide to modify its menu. As you know, restaurants often modify dishes on an individual basis. For example, if a customer is lactose-intolerant, the chef could make a sauce without cream. But a **menu modification** is a decision by the restaurant to add, change, or delete one or more menu items. A restaurant could decide to use only organic produce in its menu items. Or, a restaurant could decide to permanently reduce the amount of cream in its sauces. A restaurant could change the recipe for its pasta sauce to make it more appealing to diners. Based on the popularity of salads at a particular restaurant, it may decide to add more salads and reduce its meat dishes.

A restaurant may decide that its basic menu is not appealing to customers in the region for some reason. For example, a Thai restaurant may discover that the market doesn't understand Thai food. So the restaurant may decide to broaden its appeal by focusing on Asian food, which includes not only Thai, but also Japanese, and Chinese items. An Italian restaurant might find that there are too many Italian restaurants in the area, which is reducing the amount of daily diners (and thus diminishing its profits). So it decides to do a **menu conversion**, changing the menu radically from one type of food to another. The restaurant closes down and re-opens with a focus on American cuisine. This often requires a change in the décor, the equipment, and even the staff. A full-scale menu conversion is a dramatic decision that should be undertaken only when it is absolutely necessary. A restaurant may lose its current customers in an effort to appeal to new customers.

READING CHECKPOINT *What is the typical order of menu categories for a nonethnic restaurant?*

21.1 ASSESSMENT

Reviewing Concepts

1. What are the two primary functions of a menu?

2. What are seven common types of menus?

3. What are four important considerations to keep in mind when planning a menu?

4. What is the typical order of menu categories for a nonethnic restaurant?

Critical Thinking

5. Drawing Conclusions Equipment availability is important to remember when planning a menu. How could too many soup choices on the menu create a problem?

6. Applying Concepts A vegetarian diet book tops the best-seller list for two months in a row. How could that affect the choices of foods on your menu?

7. Analyzing Information Every entrée on a menu is deep-fried and all the sides are white. What is wrong with the menu balance, and how could you correct it?

Test Kitchen

Divide into four teams. Each team will develop a semi à la carte dinner menu for a restaurant. Before writing the menu, each team will develop a mission statement for the restaurant. Teams will then produce one item, their signature item, from their appetizer category and one from their main-course category. Evaluate each team's results.

LANGUAGE ARTS
Descriptive Writing

Write descriptions for three du jour menu items. Tempt the customers by appealing to their senses of taste, touch, smell, and sight.

21.2

Pricing Menu Items

Key Concepts

- Identifying factors that influence menu prices
- Understanding menu-pricing methods
- Making a menu-pricing decision

Vocabulary

- actual cost method
- base price method
- copycat method
- factor method
- forced food method
- gross profit method
- pricing factor
- pricing system comparison chart
- prime cost
- prime cost method
- psychological factors
- raw food cost

Factors Influencing Menu Prices

You understand the purpose of your menu. You've decided on the type of menu you will be using. You have planned a balanced menu that would seem to be perfect for your restaurant. You have organized the menu, designed it, and written truthful and attractive descriptions of your menu items. One thing still remains, however. You now must assign prices to the menu items, prices that will appeal to customers while being profitable for you.

The following six factors will influence your decision about menu prices:

- **Type of Restaurant.** Your mission statement determines the type of restaurant, and the type of restaurant determines, in part, the amount you can charge for your menu items. For example, a hamburger in a fast-food restaurant will probably be less expensive than one in a family dining restaurant, which will be less expensive than a hamburger in a high-end restaurant.

- **Meal Occasion.** The time of day that customers eat determines, in part, what they are willing to pay for the food they are consuming. For example, customers typically expect to pay more for dinner than for breakfast.

- **Style and Elaborateness of Service.** Because of the increased labor costs, the more elaborate the service, the more expensive the items on the menu will need to be.

- **Competition.** Your restaurant cannot charge more for a menu item than your competitors do unless there is a significant

Source: Tim Knox/Dorling Kindersley

FIGURE 21–10
Customer Mix
A restaurant's customer mix involves many factors.

COMMUNICATING *How would you describe this restaurant's customer mix?*
Source: zech/Fotolia

reason for the increased price. If your family-style restaurant charges $2.00 more for an item than another family-style restaurant in your area, customers will tend to go to your competitor's restaurant. Competitor pricing is extremely important in determining menu prices.

- **Customer Mix.** Your customer mix involves many factors, including the male-to-female ratio, the number of businesspeople eating in the restaurant, the number of families with children, and the ages of your customers.

- **Profit Objective.** You may decide that your most popular menu items can be priced slightly higher, increasing your profit on those items. Or you may decide that you can decrease your profit on an item because you will make up for the decreased profit per item by increasing the volume.

READING CHECKLIST *What are six factors influencing menu prices?*

Menu-Pricing Methods

There are actually many ways to price menu items. Only the restaurant owner or manager can actually decide which method is best for a particular restaurant. The best method is often an adaptation or combination of the following seven methods.

Copycat Method The simplest way to determine your prices is to go to a nearby restaurant that has the same menu items and copy its prices. This is the **copycat method** of menu pricing (also called the *nonstructured*

Raw Food Cost
The raw food cost includes the cost of all the raw ingredients used in a dish.

PREDICTING *How might you take into account costs of such food as condiments, salt, pepper, bread, and butter?*

Source: Culinary Institute of America

method). Although simple, this is not a very wise method of determining your prices. Every restaurant's situation is different. For example, your competitor might own the building in which her restaurant is located, so she does not need to pay rent. You may need to take your rent into account when pricing items. Although checking competitors' pricing is important, it should not be used as the sole basis for making menu-pricing decisions.

Factor Method The **factor method** is one of the oldest, and simplest, methods for pricing menu items. To determine the price of a menu item, you multiply the **raw food cost** (that is, the cost of all the ingredients that went into a single serving of the dish) by an established **pricing factor**. This means that you mark up every item on your menu by the same amount.

To use the factor method, you first have to establish the raw food cost you would like to have. For example, many restaurants try to keep their raw food cost at 37 percent of the menu price. This means that 63 percent of the cost of the menu item is for overhead (all nonfood costs associated with the restaurant except for labor), labor, and profit.

- **Determine the Pricing Factor.** Divide 100 by the actual or desired raw food cost. In our example, that means you divide 100 by 37 to get a pricing factor of 2.7.

- **Determine the Price for a Menu Item.** Multiply the raw food cost by the pricing factor. For example, if the raw food cost for a hamburger is $1.70, the menu price for that hamburger will be $4.59.

Beverages are often priced using the factor method. For example, a restaurant may purchase a bottle of wine for $15 and mark it up to $45, so the "raw beverage cost" is one-third of the price for the bottle of wine on the wine list. If the restaurant sells wines by the glass and charges $8 to $14 per glass, it will recover the price of the wine on the second glass it sells. Carbonated beverages are also typically priced using the factor method.

Prime Cost Method The **prime cost method** was developed for use in cafeteria operations. It is very similar to the factor method but also calculates the cost of preparing the menu item. With the prime cost method, you start with the raw food cost, just as you did in the factor method. Let's use the raw food cost of $1.70 for a hamburger again. The next step is to figure out the cost of the labor that went directly into producing that menu item. This would include all mise en place associated with the preparation of the item, but wouldn't include work such as cleaning the dishes or serving customers.

Raw Food Cost

To calculate the raw food cost based on a standard-ized menu:

1. Determine the cost of each of the ingredients that went into the dish. For example, if the dish requires a breast of chicken, you have to determine how much a breast of chicken costs.

2. Add the cost of all the ingredients in the dish.

3. Divide by the number of portions the recipe yields.

Computation

Calculate the raw food cost for a dish with which you are familiar. Calculate the menu price by using a pricing factor of 2.7. In a restaurant, would you order this menu item at the price you calculated?

- **Determine Direct Labor Cost.** There are many ways to determine the cost of the labor that is directly involved in making a dish. Perhaps the easiest way is to record the time involved in making the dish, multiply by the hourly wage of the chefs making the dish, and divide by the number of portions in the recipe. Figured in this way, the chef making a hamburger might spend only a couple of minutes actually making a hamburger. If a chef makes approximately $0.50 a minute and spends only four minutes actually cooking the hamburger (assuming that the chef is doing other things while the hamburger is actually on the grill), you would add $2.00 (4 minutes $\times$ .50 per minute) to the raw food cost to arrive at the prime cost of $3.70 ($2.00 + $1.70 = $3.70).

- **Add Direct Labor to the Raw Food Price.** Based on their experience, many restaurants use 9 percent as their direct labor cost. They add 9 percent to the 37 percent raw food cost to calculate an amount that includes the cost of all ingredients plus the cost of the labor involved in making a portion of the dish. This amount is referred to as the **prime cost**. In our example, this is 46 percent.

- **Determine the Prime Cost Factor.** Divide 100 by the prime cost. In our example, you divide 100 by 46 to get a prime cost factor of 2.17.

- **Determine the Price for a Menu Item.** Multiply the prime cost by the prime cost factor. For example, if the prime cost for a hamburger is $3.70, the menu price for that hamburger will be $8.03.

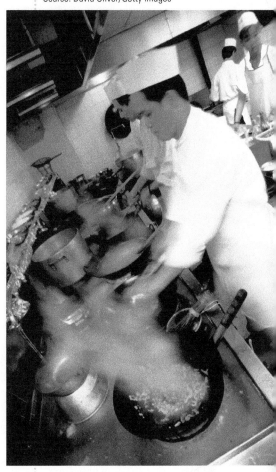

FIGURE 21–12

Cost of Labor
The prime cost method includes the price of labor.

DRAWING CONCLUSIONS *When might a prime cost method be more useful than a factor method of determining menu price?*

Source: David Oliver/Getty Images

Actual Cost Method In the **actual cost method**, the actual cost for the raw food, labor, other expenses, and profit are all added together to determine a menu price. The raw food cost and labor are calculated in actual dollars. In addition, they are also calculated as a percentage of the menu price. This allows a restaurant to use percentages (based on the restaurant's total sales) for other expenses and profits.

For example, if the raw food cost and labor for a dish equals $2.00 and the restaurant calculates that this is 40 percent of the menu price, the menu price will be $5.00. If the actual percentage for profit is 10 percent, the amount of profit on this item will be $0.50.

Gross Profit Method The **gross profit method** is designed to determine a specific amount of profit that should be made from each customer who comes into the restaurant. It is a method that is used primarily in well-established restaurants, because it requires analysis of past financial statements, counts of customers over a specific amount of time (often one year), and analysis of what each customer ordered.

This method of calculating the cost of menu items guarantees the owner or manager that a predetermined amount of profit will be made on every customer. It tends to benefit the customer choosing from the more expensive items and penalize the customer ordering less expensive items. This is because the restaurant expects to make the same amount of profit from each of them, no matter what they order. It is often used in banquets or catered events when there are a known amount of customers at a specific event.

Base Price Method (Example)

Customer's Expected Meal Cost	$10.00	100%
Profit	1.00	10%
Overhead	2.70	27%
Labor	2.60	26%
Raw Food Cost	$3.70	37%

Base Price Method The **base price method** starts by analyzing what customers want to spend per meal. It works backward from there to come up with menu items, their prices, and a built-in level of profit. Similar to the gross profit method, the base price method requires data about customers' eating habits in the restaurant over a long period. Without such data, a new restaurant would be forced to make assumptions about the spending patterns of its customers. A new restaurant's mission statement needs to be clear and the restaurant needs to be certain of its market.

In the example shown to the left, you know that your customers are comfortable spending $10.00 per meal, and you know that you want a profit of 10 percent, your overhead is 27 percent, and your total labor is 26 percent, accounting for a total of 63 percent. This means that so long as you spend less than 37 percent ($3.70) on a menu item priced at $10.00, you will cover your actual costs and receive a 10 percent profit.

Forced Food Method The **forced food method** is determined by the market—that is, by the choices your customers actually make in your restaurant. It takes into account loss and spoilage and assumes that food that is at a high risk of loss or spoilage should have a higher price. It also includes volume in the calculation. The lower the volume, the higher the price (and vice versa). Every item on the menu is analyzed in terms of its volume and price.

Each type of menu item is then given a specific profit margin based on its volume/risk category. Taking the basic volume/risk category and the type of menu item into consideration, you then calculate menu prices, using the restaurant's overhead cost, labor cost, and a predetermined profit—all as a percentage of the total cost. Subtracting this as a percentage gives you a

Four Basic Volume/ Risk Categories

Low Volume & High Cost	High Volume & High Cost
Low Volume & Low Cost	High Volume & Low Cost

percentage for the raw food cost. So, for example, if your total overhead, labor, and profit equal 68 percent, you know that your raw food cost should be 32 percent ($100 - 68 = 32$) of the menu price. If your actual raw food price for a hamburger is $2.70 and that is 32 percent of the menu price, the menu price will be $8.43 (calculated as ($2.70 \times 100)/32$).

 **READING CHECKPOINT** *What are the seven menu-pricing methods?*

Deciding on Menu Prices

Once you have decided on a menu-pricing option and have done all your calculations, you are ready to decide on your menu prices. However, there are a few additional considerations.

Comparison Charts A **pricing system comparison chart** is a valuable aid in making pricing decisions. It shows a comparison of the prices from various pricing methods (the example shows the factor method, the gross profit method, and the forced food cost method). It also shows two competitors' prices along with your final decision for the menu price, as well as your value judgments—basically any nonscientific judgment you make concerning the price you have assigned. For example, you may see that your hamburger's price using the factor method is lower than either of your competitors. Because you plan to focus on hamburger sales you expect a high volume of hamburger sales, so the forced food method pricing is also showing a very competitive price. However, you decide that you can increase your price to be slightly higher than the lower-priced competitor because you want to be seen as having a higher quality product. By using the pricing system comparison chart, you guaranteed that your hamburger would be profitable and well positioned competitively.

Typical Profit Margins

Appetizers	20–50%
Salads	10–40%
Main Courses	10–25%
Vegetables	25–50%
Beverages and Bread	10–20%
Desserts	15–35%

FIGURE 21–13

Pricing System Comparison Chart

Use a pricing system comparison chart to arrive at your final menu prices.

COMMUNICATING *What kind of remarks would go in the value judgments column?*

Source: Culinary Institute of America

Menu Item	Factor	Gross Profit	Forced Food Cost	Competitor A	Competitor B	Final Menu Price	Value Judgment	

The Q Quotient

Have you ever wondered how restaurants account for the cost of seasonings such as salt and pepper? Some restaurants add the cost of salt, pepper, condiments, bread, rolls, butter, and oil that are served at the table to the selling price of an item, typically the main-course item.

This is referred to as the Q quotient. Restaurants might add the following to the cost of each main-course menu item:

Calculating the Q Quotient

Salt & Pepper	$0.02
Bread & Rolls	$0.10
Butter & Oil	$0.08
Condiments	$0.05
Total Q Quotient	$0.25

Computation

Contact 10 restaurants to see how they deal with Q-quotient items. How do the restaurants add this cost to the menu items?

Psychological Factors After you have determined the menu price by using one of the menu-pricing methods, you may need to consider **psychological factors**. Psychological factors take into account how a customer perceives specific menu items. For example, customers might associate high-end menu items, such as lobster, caviar, or truffles, with a higher price. They may also associate specific ingredients with a higher or lower

Customers may be willing to pay more for high-end menu items

Source: Ali Safarov/Fotolia

5 and 9 Magic Numbers?

Did you ever wonder why prices on menus often end with a 9 or a 5? Scientific evidence has proven that certain prices—those ending in a 9 or a 5—are more enticing to customers than other numbers. For instance, $7.95 is more enticing and seems much less expensive than $8.00 would for a given menu item. These numbers are sometimes referred to as "magic numbers" and the type of pricing is referred to as "odd cents" pricing. No matter what it is called, this pricing seems to have some sort of special appeal to consumers. Odd cents pricing has been used for years by the food-service industry to affect customers psychologically and maximize profits. Scientists have tried to explain odd cents pricing as creating an illusion of a discount that thereby reduces customers' resistance to purchasing.

Research

Gather menus from 20 local restaurants and look for odd cents pricing. If possible, talk to the owners about the odd cents pricing strategy to see if they have any actual evidence that it works.

price. For example, customers who are willing to pay $6.00 for a normal hamburger may be willing to pay $9.00 for a hamburger if you add blue cheese.

Price Increases Most of the time, restaurant owners wait too long to raise their prices. Once a menu price is decided on, managers tend to leave it at that price. In many cases, this can be a problem for the restaurant because it fails to take into account rising prices.

When a price increase is necessary, make it as bearable as possible. You could, for example, slightly reduce the size of the portions so you make up the difference in the profit margin. Or, you could add something to the plate to create a new dish for which a higher price is appropriate.

Avoid rapid increases over a short period of time. Timing is critical in increasing prices. It is important to make sure that you maintain quality standards when you raise prices. Otherwise, customers will sense that both value and quality have declined. Above all, avoid across-the-board increases of menu prices.

READING CHECKPOINT *What is a pricing system comparison chart?*

21.2 ASSESSMENT

Reviewing Concepts

1. What are the seven menu-pricing methods?

2. What is a pricing system comparison chart?

Critical Thinking

3. Applying Concepts Why is competition such an important factor influencing menu prices?

4. Analyzing Information Describe a situation in which using the copycat method of menu pricing could lead to problems.

5. Comparing/Contrasting Compare the factor method and the prime cost method of pricing in terms of their ease of use on a day-to-day basis.

6. Inferring Describe a situation, either imaginary or from your experience, in which a local restaurant may have used psychological factors to increase the price of a menu item.

Test Kitchen

Choose a recipe for a dish that is commonly offered by restaurants in your area. Divide into four teams. Each team will decide on a menu price for the dish. Team 1 will use the copycat method based on two local restaurants. Team 2 will use the factor method. Team 3 will use the prime cost method. Team 4 will use the base price method. Teams 2, 3, and 4 will calculate the raw food price and use the percentages shown in the text.

CULINARY MATH

Prime Cost Method

The raw food cost for a main course is $3.25. Using a pricing factor of 2.7, what is the menu price for the factor method? Using a prime pricing factor of 2.3, what is the menu price for the prime cost method?

PROJECT 21 You are now ready to work on Project 21, "Menu Pricing," which is available in "My Culinary Lab" or in your *Student's Lab Resources and Study Guide* manual.

Chapter

21 Review and Assessment

CREPES   €
Sucre   3.90
beurre, sucre   4.50
chocolat   5.20
confiture ou miel 5.20
Sucre, citron   5.20
crème de marron 5.20
                5.20
                5.70
            co 5.70
                5.70

Reviewing Content

Choose the letter that best answers the question or completes the statement.

1. The mission statement is a statement of
   a. a bill.
   b. a financial report.
   c. an organization's goal.
   d. job assignments.

2. An à la carte menu offers
   a. items priced separately.
   b. the same items everyday.
   c. breakfast, lunch, and dinner any time.
   d. a complete meal for a set price.

3. A table d'hôte menu offers
   a. items priced separately.
   b. the same items everyday.
   c. breakfast, lunch, and dinner any time.
   d. a complete meal for a set price.

4. A California menu offers
   a. items priced separately.
   b. the same items everyday.
   c. breakfast, lunch, and dinner anytime.
   d. a complete meal for a set price.

5. The raw food cost is the cost of
   a. a salad.
   b. all of the ingredients that went into a single portion of a dish.
   c. all of the ingredients that are used by a restaurant in one day's dinners.
   d. ingredients used in a salad bar.

6. In the factor method, the
   a. direct labor cost and the raw food cost are multiplied by a factor.
   b. raw food price multiplied by pricing factor.
   c. menu price is determined by how much a customer spends per meal.
   d. menu price is determined by how much the customer wants to spend.

Understanding Concepts

7. What is the difference between a table d'hôte menu and a prix fixe menu?

8. What is the difference between the raw food cost and the prime cost?

9. How would you determine a menu price by using the actual cost method?

10. Using the forced food method of menu pricing, by which two factors would you analyze each item on the menu?

11. What is the difference between a fixed menu and a limited menu?

Critical Thinking

12. **APPLYING CONCEPTS** You write truthfully in your menu that one of your dishes is your most popular dish. In what way are you using the menu as a communication tool?

13. **COMPARING/CONTRASTING** Compare the gross profit method and the base price method of pricing menu items.

Culinary Math

14. **SOLVING PROBLEMS** The raw food cost of a dish is $2.37. You are using the factor method for pricing menu items and want the raw food price to be 34 percent of the menu price. What is the price of this dish?

15. **APPLYING CONCEPTS** Your customers expect to spend $24.00 for a meal at your restaurant. Using the base price method of menu pricing, you calculate that your raw food cost should be no more than 34 percent of what your customer expects to spend for a meal. What is your maximum raw food price per customer?

On the Job

16. **APPLYING CONCEPTS** Your menu says that a chocolate cake is "homemade" but you actually buy it from a bakery. Do you think this represents a truth-in-menu problem?

Purchasing Agents

Purchasing managers, buyers, and purchasing agents buy farm products, supplies, services, durable and nondurable goods (including equipment), and software for organizations and institutions. They try to get the best deal for their organization—the highest-quality goods and services at the lowest cost. They do this by studying sales records and inventory levels of current stock, identifying suppliers, and keeping up to date with changes affecting the supply and demand for products and materials.

Purchasing agents and buyers consider price, quality, availability, reliability, and technical support when choosing suppliers and merchandise. To be effective, purchasing agents and buyers must have a working technical knowledge of the goods or services to be bought. That is one reason that the most effective food purchasing agents or managers have at least some experience and training in the culinary arts. They should also fully understand how to prepare appropriate specifications ("specs") that are used to assure that the foods that are purchased have the desired quality for their intended use. In other words, all of the apples they buy should be of good quality, but the apples used to make applesauce may not need to be the same quality grade as those purchased to feature in a fruit basket on a buffet.

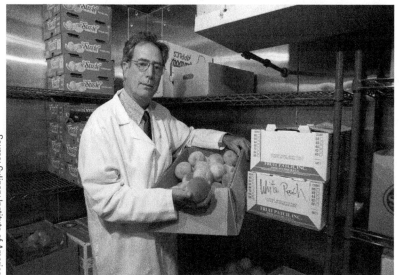

Purchasing agents purchase all the food and other food-related items required by the organization

Source: Culinary Institute of America

Most purchasing managers, buyers, and purchasing agents work full time. Many work more than 40 hours per week. They typically work in an office, but may also need to travel or attend various conferences and trade shows to make new contacts and learn about new products and services, to interview vendors, or negotiate prices and contracts.

Purchasing managers or agents for hotels purchase goods and other items such as china, linen, glassware, and cooking equipment used throughout the foodservice operation of a large hotel. Some agents are responsible for more than one location.

Purchasing agents and buyers for institutions buy foods and other products for a particular institution. They may need to adhere to specific standards. For example, a purchasing agent for a school district must buy foods that meet certain cost requirements and also meet nutrition standards set by the federal government.

Purchasing managers plan and coordinate the work of buyers and purchasing agents, and they usually handle more complicated purchases.

Entry-Level Requirements

Buyers and purchasing agents need a high school diploma and on-the-job training. Purchasing managers need a bachelor's degree and work experience as a buyer or purchasing agent.

Helpful for Advancement

Educational requirements usually vary with the size of the organization. A high school diploma is enough at many organizations for entry into the purchasing agent occupation, although large stores and distributors may prefer applicants who have completed a bachelor's degree program and have taken some business or accounting classes. Many manufacturing firms put an even greater emphasis on formal training, preferring applicants who have a bachelor's or master's degree in engineering, business, economics, or one of the applied sciences.

Purchasing managers usually have at least a bachelor's degree and some work experience in the field. A master's degree may be required for advancement to some top-level purchasing manager jobs.

There are several recognized credentials for purchasing agents and purchasing managers. These certifications involve oral or written exams and have education and work experience requirements.

The Certified Professional in Supply Management (CPSM) credential covers a wide scope of duties that purchasing professionals do. The exam requires applicants to have a bachelor's degree and three years of supply management experience.

DAVE SHEPPARD

Dave Sheppard

Dave Sheppard is a native Texan, and has lived in the Dallas area for over 50 years. His grandfather owned restaurants in the 1970s and 1980s, where Dave would work as a busboy and dishwasher during the summers. Sheppard found the restaurant business exciting, and he loved to see the journey a dish took from the development process to a diner's table.

Sheppard studied business in college, and in 1984, he began working in restaurant management. In his early restaurant days, Sheppard worked toward a position in sales, but soon realized that purchasing was his true passion. He took his first entry-level purchasing job at Brinker Test Kitchen, where he worked for 15 years, before becoming the Purchasing Director for M-CROWD Restaurant Group. In this role, he was responsible for purchasing, negotiating contracts, and sourcing vendors. He enjoys the challenges of purchasing and finds it rewarding to see how he can positively impact a restaurant's profits.

VITAL STATISTICS

Graduated: Richland College, 1983

Profession: Food service professional—purchasing, restaurant operations, sales

Interesting Items: Worked in the front-of-house positions at several white-tablecloth restaurants while working toward his degree

Serves as the National Accounts Manager for Food Source, LP

CAREER PROFILE

Salary Ranges

Purchasing Agent, Entry Level: $29,000 to $34,000

Purchasing Agent: $34,000 to $52,000

Purchasing Manager for a Multi-Institution Entity: $52,000 to $85,000+

Nutrition

22.1 Nutrition Basics

22.2 Making Menus More Nutritious

Nutrition Basics

Key Concepts

- Understanding the importance of nutrition
- Learning the language of nutrition
- Understanding nutrition information

Vocabulary

- amino acids
- antioxidants
- calories
- carbohydrates
- cholesterol
- complex carbohydrates
- daily values
- Dietary Guidelines
- Dietary Reference Intakes (DRIs)
- fat-soluble vitamins
- fatty acids
- glucose
- hydrogenation
- insoluble fiber
- monounsaturated fats
- mutual supplementation
- MyPlate
- nutrients
- omega-3 fatty acids
- polyunsaturated fats
- protein
- Recommended Dietary Allowance (RDA)
- saturated fats
- simple carbohydrates
- soluble fiber
- trans fats
- water-soluble vitamins

The Importance of Nutrition

Nutrition is a field of study that is concerned with the foods we eat and the way those foods affect our bodies and our health. Nutritionists are trying to find out which foods are the most likely to keep us healthy by learning more about how **nutrients**, the parts of food our bodies use, can help or hurt us.

The science of nutrition is still uncovering new information. Many of us have difficulty making sense of this information. Yet with so many people interested in eating a healthy diet, it is the chef's job to learn the basics of nutrition. Once you've learned these basics, you can incorporate nutrition into your cooking.

Poor Nutrition At different times in history, getting enough food was a serious everyday concern. Lack of food is still a major concern in many parts of the world. People who don't get enough to eat are not just hungry. They don't have enough energy to function well. Their appearance may change, and they are usually not able to fight off disease easily because they aren't getting certain nutrients.

Good Nutrition Good nutrition means not only getting enough food to eat but also getting enough of the right foods. When nutritionists talk about a good diet or a healthy diet, they are talking about diets that include a variety of foods and appropriate portions. A healthy diet is sometimes referred to as a balanced diet.

Even people who get enough food to eat can suffer from poor nutrition. They may gain weight if they eat too much. Gaining weight can have some serious health consequences, including diabetes, heart disease, and even cancer. People who aren't eating the right foods needed for a good supply of nutrients could develop certain diseases as well.

 **READING CHECKPOINT** *What does "good nutrition" mean?*

The Language of Nutrition

Food is one of the basic requirements for life. Some people compare food to the gasoline we put in a car: it is the fuel that keeps our bodies running. Choosing the right foods makes it easier for your body to function properly.

When we talk about nutrition and food, we are talking about the following basic nutrients: proteins, carbohydrates, fats, vitamins, minerals, and water. In addition to providing us with the nutrients we need, foods also provide us with the fuel, or energy, we need to stay warm, walk, talk, and do our work. This energy is measured in units known as **calories**. Too little of any nutrient can result in a deficiency that leads to a disease. Getting more than you need, or an excess of a vitamin, means that you have built up too much of that vitamin in your body. This excess can result in potentially serious health conditions.

Proteins Protein is a nutrient our bodies need so they can grow, replace worn-out tissues and cells, and help us recover from injuries and illnesses.

The basic building blocks of protein are known as **amino** (ah-MEEN-oh) **acids**. The proteins found in the cells of our skin, hair, teeth, bones, fingernails, muscles, and tendons are made up of 22 amino acids. Our bodies produce some of these amino acids on their own. However, there are nine amino acids adult humans cannot produce. They are known as essential amino acids because we must eat foods that contain them.

A food that provides all the essential amino acids is known as a complete protein. Meats, poultry, fish, and other animal products (including eggs and cheese) are complete proteins.

Grains, dried legumes, and nuts are also rich in protein; however, these foods may not contain all the essential amino acids, or they may have only small amounts of some of the essential amino acids. This does not mean that the protein they do provide is not of good quality. It simply means you need to eat other foods as a supplement to the amino acids in that food. This is sometimes referred to as **mutual supplementation**. Some traditional dishes that combine beans and grains, such as the red beans and rice

A healthy diet includes a variety of foods
Source: adisa/Fotolia

"Enriched with Essential Vitamins and Minerals"

The above phrase has been a common sight on packages of cold cereals for so long that many of us do not think twice about how enriched foods first came about. The story of their origin begins in 1936, when a survey revealed that growing numbers of people were suffering from deficiency diseases. These diseases were understood to be the direct result of diets that were lacking important nutrients.

Until that time, whole-wheat bread was far more common than white bread. Bread made with whole-grain flour supplied the majority of daily requirements of iron, thiamin, niacin, riboflavin, magnesium, zinc, vitamin B_6, folacin, and dietary fiber.

But as milling machinery improved, it was easier to make a whiter, smoother flour that produced a softer white bread. This highly refined white bread became cheap, readily available, and far more popular than the coarser, peasant-style whole-grain breads. As soon as the demand for whole-grain breads dropped, nutritional deficiency diseases increased.

It became obvious that something needed to be done to boost people's nutrient supplies.

The Enrichment Act of 1942, still in effect, required manufacturers to enrich all grain products sold across state lines, including cereals, pastas, and breads. Iron, thiamin, niacin, and riboflavin levels have to be close to what they had been in the whole-grain versions.

In 1998, an amendment to the law also required that folic acid, a B vitamin shown to prevent birth defects, must also be added. Other nutrients are typically added as part of the enrichment process, but they don't have to match the original nutritional value of the grain before it was refined. And there is no requirement for replacing dietary fiber.

Enriched products are certainly a better nutritional bargain than unenriched, bleached, and refined ones. However, they are no match for whole grains. Replacing some nutrients doesn't make the product nutritionally complete, even if the label claims that a cereal offers 100 percent of 8 or 10 essential nutrients. The body's ability to fully absorb and process these enriched foods is still being researched as scientists uncover more about the special roles played by the nearly 50 known essential nutrients.

Real-World Skills

Locate labels for three different refined, enriched products—for example, white bread, sweetened cereal, and pasta. Try to find whole-grain versions of each of these products and compare the nutritional values to those of the refined products.

served in New Orleans or the Italian soup pasta e fagioli made from pasta and beans, provide all of the essential amino acids.

If your body is growing or if it has been injured in some way (for example, a cut, a burn, or a broken bone), getting enough protein-rich foods in your diet is very important. In most developed countries, getting enough protein is not a big concern. Instead, we are more likely to be eating more protein-rich foods than our bodies need.

An excess of protein can lead to such conditions as osteoporosis (a condition where bones become brittle or porous), kidney failure, and gout

FIGURE 22–1
Animal and Vegetable
Protein is found in both animal foods and vegetable foods.
INFERRING *Which foods would you choose for a vegetarian entrée?*
Source: © a4stockphotos/Fotolia

(a condition characterized by painful joint inflammation, especially in the hands and feet). An inadequate amount of protein in the diet can lead to conditions such as slowed growth, especially in children, and an increase in secondary infections.

Carbohydrates Carbohydrates are an important source of energy for our bodies. Just as proteins are made up of smaller units, carbohydrates are also made up of smaller units, known as sugars. When we eat carbohydrate-rich foods, our bodies turn them into a specific type of sugar known as **glucose** (GLOO-kohs). This is the fuel our bodies need to keep us warm and keep our muscles, brains, and nervous systems working properly. There are two types of carbohydrates:

- **Simple carbohydrates** contain one or two sugars. They are found in fruit, milk, and the refined sugars used in the kitchen or bakeshop: white sugar, brown sugar, molasses, and honey. Simple carbohydrates are digested and absorbed quickly. They provide a short burst of energy.

- **Complex carbohydrates** contain long chains that include many sugars. They are found in plant-based foods such as grains, legumes, and vegetables. Before we can use the nutrients in complex carbohydrates, our bodies have to break them down into simple sugars. Complex carbohydrates are sometimes referred to as "starches." They provide a long-lasting source of energy.

Carbohydrate-rich foods such as fruits, vegetables, grains, and legumes can provide us with something else we need for good health—fiber. There are two types of fiber:

Soluble fiber dissolves in water. When we eat foods that contain soluble fiber, we feel full for a longer time. Soluble fiber also slows down

Chef's Tip

A Sweet Taste

You can usually tell if a food contains simple carbohydrates simply by tasting it. Simple carbohydrates taste sweet.

FIGURE 22–2

Whole Fruit or Juice
Whole oranges and orange juice.
APPLYING CONCEPTS *Which of these foods contains more fiber?*
Source: Sergii Moscaliuk/Fotolia

the release of sugar into the blood and helps lower cholesterol levels in the blood. Good sources of soluble fiber include beans, fruits, vegetables, and whole grains such as oats and barley.

Insoluble fiber does not dissolve in water. It was once referred to as roughage. It acts like a stiff broom to clean and scrub the digestive tract so we can eliminate wastes from our systems more easily. Good sources include most fruits and vegetables, wheat bran, nuts, and whole-grain flours.

Sometimes, fiber is removed from food before we eat it. Carbohydrate-rich foods such as wheat or barley are sometimes processed to remove the fiber. White flour, fruit juices, and table sugar are all examples of refined and processed foods that contain very little, if any, fiber. The end result of too many empty calories in the form of refined carbohydrates is weight gain, but not enough carbohydrates in your diet can result in a condition known as *ketosis*, which means that your body is attempting to get the energy it needs by breaking down fats or proteins.

Fats and Cholesterol Fats such as butter, cream, and oils play an important part in making foods taste good or giving them a specific texture. In our bodies, fats are important for other reasons. They provide energy and fulfill several important roles in keeping our bodies functioning. Fat also slows digestion, giving our bodies time to absorb the nutrients contained in the foods we eat. By slowing digestion, fats help send a signal to our brains so we stop eating before we overeat. Diets that do not include enough of the right kinds of fats may lead to eczema, a skin condition; lowered resistance to infection; and even hair loss. However, too much fat in the diet can increase the risk of heart disease, certain cancers, and obesity. Being obese means being dangerously overweight and prone to many health risks.

A fat such as olive oil or butter is actually a chain made up of many smaller units known as **fatty acids**. These fatty acids are made from atoms of carbon, hydrogen, and oxygen linked together. Fatty acids are grouped into three main categories according to their structure: saturated, polyunsaturated, and monounsaturated.

- **Saturated fats** are usually solid at room temperature. They come from animal sources, with the exception of coconut oil and palm oil, which come from plants.
- **Polyunsaturated fats** come from plants and are liquid at room temperature. They sometimes undergo the process of **hydrogenation** (hie-DROJ-en-ay-shun), which changes a liquid polyunsaturated fat, such as corn oil, into a solid fat, such as margarine. Hydrogenation

FOCUS ON Nutrition

Health Risk
Saturated fats and products made from hydrogenated or partially hydrogenated oils (which contain trans fats) have been linked to some forms of cancer, increased cholesterol levels, and heart disease. Avoid consuming too many foods that are rich in saturated and trans fats.

Fats in Foods

Saturated Fats

Butter, cheese, cream, lard, coconut oil, palm oil, margarine, and fatty meat are high in saturated fat.

Source: Culinary Institute of America

Monounsaturated Fats

Olives, olive oil, avocados, most nuts and nut oils, canola oil, and peanut oil are foods high in monounsaturated fat.

Source: Culinary Institute of America

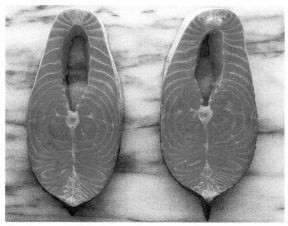

Omega-3 Fatty Acids

Food rich in omega-3 fatty acids include salmon, mackerel, dark-green leafy vegetables, walnuts, and canola oil.

Source: Dave King/Dorling Kindersley Limited

Polyunsaturated Fats

Corn, sesame seeds and sesame oil, and walnuts and walnut oil are high in polyunsaturated fat.

Source: Culinary Institute of America

Cholesterol

Sources of cholesterol include eggs, organ meats, and other meats, which are also high in saturated fats.

Source: Culinary Institute of America

Trans Fats

Trans fats are found in processed foods made with hydrogenated or partially hydrogenated vegetable oils.

Source: perlphoto/Fotolia

creates **trans fats** (also called *trans fatty acids*), a potentially harmful type of fat that has been linked to heart disease.

- **Monounsaturated fats** are considered the healthier fats; they come from plants and are liquid at room temperature. They help balance cholesterol levels in the blood, reducing the risk of heart disease.

Omega-3 fatty acids are a type of polyunsaturated fat that is linked to reducing the risk of stroke and heart attack and improving brain growth and development. They are found in some plants and in all fish.

Cholesterol (koh-LESS-ter-all) is a fatty substance that the body needs to perform various functions. The body makes its own supply of cholesterol. Cholesterol in foods is known as dietary cholesterol, which occurs only in animal foods, never in plant foods. Cholesterol in the body is known as serum cholesterol. When doctors check a person's cholesterol levels, they are trying to determine how much serum cholesterol is found in that person's blood.

The blood test for cholesterol looks at the levels of two types of protein in the blood: low-density lipoproteins (LDLs) and high-density lipoproteins (HDLs). Too much LDL, or "bad" cholesterol, is a health risk. It could indicate a buildup of cholesterol on the walls of arteries, reducing blood flow to the heart. The doctor will suggest changes in diet, exercise, or even medication to help reduce LDL levels. Having high levels of HDL is good news. HDL clears cholesterol out of the circulatory system.

Vitamins Vitamins are similar to the major nutrients because we need them in our diets every day to keep our bodies healthy. They differ from the major nutrients in that they do not contain any calories. They are sometimes referred to as noncaloric nutrients. Vitamins may be water soluble or fat soluble.

- **Water-Soluble Vitamins.** The B vitamins and vitamin C are **water-soluble vitamins**. They dissolve in water and are easily transported throughout the body in the bloodstream. We can store a small amount of these vitamins in our lean tissue, such as muscles and organs, but not enough to last more than a day or two. If we get more of these vitamins than our bodies can use, the excess is flushed from our bodies.

- **Fat-Soluble Vitamins.** Vitamins A, D, E, and K are fat soluble, which means they dissolve in fat. **Fat-soluble vitamins** are stored in our body fat. Any excess that we consume cannot be easily flushed from the body once ingested. If we take in too much of a particular vitamin or mineral, the level can become so high that it is toxic to our bodies.

Minerals Minerals play an important role, along with vitamins, in regulating our bodies and keeping our teeth and bones strong. The nervous system depends on minerals to function properly as well. Some minerals, such as calcium, magnesium, and phosphorus, are needed in large amounts. Other minerals, such as iodine, iron, selenium, and zinc, are needed in very small amounts.

Vitamin-Rich Foods

Vitamin A

The form of vitamin A found in animal foods is known as retinol. Vitamin A itself is not found in plant foods, but a substance known as beta-carotene, which the body uses to produce vitamin A, is contained in orange, deep-yellow, and dark-green leafy vegetables. Vitamin A is an antioxidant.

Source: Richard Embery/Pearson Education/PH College

B Vitamins

Meats are a good source of B vitamins, as are whole and enriched grains, legumes, leafy greens, avocados, yogurt, and fish such as tuna and salmon. The B-complex vitamins, which include thiamin (THY-uh-mihn), riboflavin (RYE-bo-flay-vihn), niacin (NYE-uh-cihn), folic (FO-lihk) acid, biotin (BY-oh-tihn), pantothenic (PANT-uh-THEN-ik) acid, B_6, and B_{12} are water soluble. They are critical to proper digestion of various nutrients and are part of nearly every cell in the body.

Source: atoss/Fotolia

Vitamin C

Vitamin C, found in fruit (such as citrus, papaya, and strawberries) and vegetables (such as parsley, peppers, and broccoli), helps the body absorb iron and promotes the production of the proteins necessary to maintain, grow, and repair connective tissues. It is an antioxidant that boosts the immune system and may help reduce serum cholesterol levels.

Source: Photographee.eu/Fotolia

Vitamin D

Vitamin D is responsible in part for the proper formation of bones. A lack of vitamin D results in the disease called rickets, in which bones grow abnormally. People with limited exposure to sunlight, which is needed to produce vitamin D, may need to eat foods fortified with vitamin D, such as milk and cereals.

Source: Susanna Price/Dorling Kindersley Limited

Vitamin E

Vitamin E, like vitamin C, is an antioxidant that may have cancer-fighting potential. It is found in a variety of foods and is not difficult to obtain from dietary sources. Vegetable oils, sunflower seeds, wheat germ, and green leafy vegetables contain significant amounts of vitamin E.

Source: Colin Walton/Dorling Kindersley Limited

Vitamin K

Vitamin K is essential for normal blood clotting. It is produced by bacteria found in the intestines. A person eating a varied and healthy diet also obtains vitamin K from foods, particularly dark-green vegetables such as spinach, broccoli, and kale.

Several vitamins act as **antioxidants**—substances that prevent tissue damage in the body that can lead to premature aging, heart disease, or cancer.

Source: Richard Embery/Pearson Education/PH College

Vitamins

Vitamin	Functions	Sources	Deficiency	Excess
A	Supports vision, healing of wounds, growth, and normal immune function	Egg yolk, dark-green and deep-yellow vegetables, fruits	Night blindness, dry eyes, poor bone growth, lowered resistance to infection	Fatigue, night sweats, vertigo, headache, dry or cracked skin, jaundice, vomiting
B_1 (Thiamin)	Supports growth and repair of brain, nerves, and muscles, metabolism of other nutrients and alcohol	Pork, liver, whole grains, bread, cereal, nuts, eggs, milk, legumes	Cardiomyopathy, numbness of extremities (beriberi), heart failure, mental confusion	
B_2 (Riboflavin)	Assists in breaking down food for energy	Liver, kidney, milk, cheese, eggs, legumes, breads, cereal	Cracked lips, sore tongue, skin disorders, impaired vision	
Niacin	Assists in breaking down food for energy	Fish, meat, poultry, whole grain, breads, cereals, eggs, peanuts	Pellagra, digestive irritation, diarrhea, anxiety or dementia	Flushing of the skin
B_6 (Pyridoxine)	Assists in breaking down food for energy	Pork, liver, whole grains, bread, cereal, nuts, eggs, milk, legumes	Skin irritation, dry lips, depression, nausea, seizures	Neuropathy (degeneration of the nervous system)
B_{12}	Red blood cell production; healthy nerves	Liver, other animal products	Pernicious anemia, confusion, ataxia	
Folic Acid	Red blood cell production	Liver, vegetables, wheat, eggs, legumes	Anemia, poor growth	Can mask symptoms of pernicious anemia or vitamin B_{12} deficiency
C (Ascorbic Acid)	Growth, health of cells, infection response, stress	Citrus fruits, vegetables	Bleeding gums (scurvy), stiff limbs	Nausea, cramping, possible formation of kidney stones
D	Good bone structure and teeth; helps in calcium and phosphorus absorption	Liver, fish oils, eggs, milk, butter, sunlight	Rickets in children; osteomalacia in adults; bone fracture in the elderly	Abnormally high blood calcium levels, retarded growth, vomiting
E	Damage and degeneration protection for cells	In most foods: wheat germ, green leafy vegetables, eggs, nuts	Rare but may affect premature and newborn infants, causing spinocerebellar and retinal degeneration	May interfere with vitamin K, affecting blood clotting, suppresses normal response to iron
K	Blood clotting	Green leafy vegetables, vegetable oils, liver	External and internal bleeding; especially likely to affect baby during pregnancy	Hemolytic anemia, jaundice

Mineral-Rich Foods

Calcium

Calcium is the body's most abundant mineral. Ninety-nine percent of the calcium needed by the body is used in the development of bones and teeth. A calcium deficiency results in stunted growth and loss of bone density. Good sources of calcium include dairy products such as yogurt and milk, broccoli, leafy greens, and beans.
Source: Simon Smith/Dorling Kindersley Limited

Iodine

Iodine is essential for the normal functioning of the thyroid gland and also helps regulate energy metabolism, cellular oxidation, and growth. Iodine deficiency was common in the early 1900s but has since been corrected by adding iodine to table salt (iodized salt). Other sources of iodine include sea vegetables, yogurt, milk, eggs, and strawberries.
Source: Culinary Institute of America

Magnesium

Magnesium (mag-NEE-zee-uhm) plays an important part in the structure and function of the body, including bones, muscle contraction, nerve transmission, and bowel function. A lack of magnesium can cause possible growth failure, headaches, depression, muscle spasms, and weakness. Good food sources of magnesium include nuts, legumes, whole grains, and leafy green vegetables, such as Swiss chard.
Source: Culinary Institute of America

Iron

Iron is a critical component of *hemoglobin* (HE-mo-glo-bin), the part of the red blood cell that carries oxygen from the lungs and distributes it throughout the body. People suffering from iron deficiency are considered *anemic* (a-NEE-mik). They may appear pale, feel weak, and have impaired immune systems. Good sources of iron are liver and other red meat, but iron is also found in beans, fish, leafy green vegetables, whole grains, and dried fruit such as raisins.
Source: Reich/Fotolia

Potassium

Potassium (puh-TA-see-uhm) is essential for the body's growth and maintenance. It helps maintain the body's normal fluid balance and plays a part in nerve and muscle functions. Symptoms of potassium deficiency include muscle weakness, confusion, irritability, and fatigue. The richest sources of potassium are fruits and vegetables.
Source: Zbyszek Nowak/ Fotolia

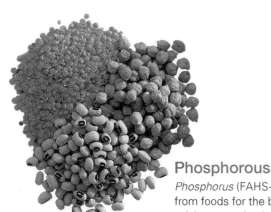

Phosphorous

Phosphorus (FAHS-fuh-ruhs) plays a role in releasing energy from foods for the body to use. It also works in conjunction with calcium to maintain bone and tooth structure. A deficiency of phosphorus is rare because it is found in most foods, including meats, fish, dairy products, nuts, cereals, and legumes.
Source: Ranald MacKechnie/Dorling Kindersley Limited

Mineral-Rich Foods

Sodium

Salt is the major source of sodium in our diet. Although sodium helps regulate body functions, many people get far more sodium than they need, which can cause high blood pressure and other health problems. Sodium levels can be quite high in processed foods, such as soups, salad dressings, smoked fish and meats, pickled foods, and snack foods. Many people make a point of avoiding high-sodium foods.

Source: Jiri Hera/Fotolia

Selenium

Selenium (sih-LEE-nee-uhm) is essential in very small amounts. It functions as an antioxidant that works with vitamin E. It also supports thyroid function. Lack of selenium has been associated with a type of heart disease called Keshan disease. Sources of selenium include nuts, particularly Brazil nuts, meats, whole grains, fish, and shellfish.

Source: Ian O'Leary/Dorling Kindersley Limited

Zinc

Zinc supports the immune system, as well as our senses (sight, taste, and smell) and memory. Lack of zinc can result in loss of taste or smell, depression, lack of appetite, growth failure in children, and frequent colds and infections. Oysters, red meat, poultry, eggs, legumes, whole grains, nuts, pumpkin seeds, and sunflower seeds are all sources of zinc.

Source: Colin Walton/Dorling Kindersley Limited

Chart of Minerals

Mineral	Function	Sources	Deficiency	Excess
Calcium	Strengthens the bones and teeth, helps regulate heartbeat, muscle, and nerve functions	Milk, dairy products, green leafy vegetables, salmon, sardines, turnips, tofu, almonds, broccoli	Minor deficit can affect bone and teeth formation	Vomiting, lethargy, excess calcification of bones and other tissues
Chromium	Required for the proper metabolism of sugar in the blood	Beans, cheese, whole-grain foods, peas, meat	Can affect the potency of insulin in regulating sugar balance	
Copper	Supports nerve function and red blood cell formation, maintains energy levels through iron absorption, also supports healthy bones and the immune system	Beans, raisins, chocolate, nuts, meat, shellfish	Anemia, hair loss, dry skin, vitamin C deficiency	Reduced neurological function

Mineral	Function	Sources	Deficiency	Excess
Fluorine	Strengthens bones and teeth; improves resistance to cavities (dental caries)	Gelatin desserts, saltwater fish (salmon), tea, fluoridated water	Weak teeth and bones	Mottled or discolored teeth, increased bone density
Iodine	Helps thyroid glands work to regulate the rate of physiological functions	Seafood, seaweed, dairy products, iodized salt	Goiter, depressed thyroid function, cretinism	Enlargement of the thyroid gland
Iron	Helps the blood and muscles carry oxygen to the body	Liver, red meat, egg yolk, legumes, whole/enriched grains, dark-green vegetables	Tiredness and lethargy, feelings of weakness, insomnia, palpitations	Blood conditions (hemochromatosis, hemosiderosis)
Magnesium	Helps muscles work, aids metabolism and aids bone growth	Whole grains, nuts, legumes, apricots, bananas, soybeans, green leafy vegetables, spinach	Fatigue, numbness, poor memory, muscle twitching and irritability, tingling, rapid heartbeat	Diarrhea
Manganese	Essential for metabolism of protein and energy	Whole grains, fruits, vegetables, tea, egg yolk	Rare, but may result in slowed or diminished hair and nail growth, scaly dermatitis, weight loss, impaired blood clotting	In extremely high doses, severe psychiatric and neurological disorders
Molybdenum	Helps cells and nerves to function	Dark-green vegetables, peas, milk, beans, grains	Very rare, but may result in rapid heart and respiratory rates, headache, night blindness	Gout-like symptoms (pain and swelling in joints)
Potassium	Essential for nerve function, muscle contraction, and maintenance of fluid and blood pressure in the body	Oranges, bananas, peanuts, beans, potatoes, spinach	Rare, but may result in depression, fatigue, hypertension, decreased heart rate	
Selenium	Helps to prevent damage to cells and aids in the functioning of the thyroid gland; also an antioxidant for the body	Brazil nuts, tuna, eggs, grains, chicken, shellfish, fish	Poor heart function, osteoarthropathy, mental retardation, muscle tenderness, degeneration of pancreas	
Sodium	Helps to regulate water in the body's blood and tissue	Salts, dairy products, smoked and cured meats such as sausage or bacon	Fatigue, apathy, and nausea, as well as cramps in the muscles of the extremities	
Zinc	Helps wounds to heal and aids taste and smell sensory perception	Whole-wheat foods, peanuts, poultry, eggs, legumes, beef, shellfish	Growth retardation, hair loss, diarrhea, delayed sexual maturation and impotence, eye and skin lesions, loss of appetite	

Colors and Nutrients

When we talk about vegetables, we can describe them by their color: green, white, red, orange, or yellow. Vegetables have different colors because they contain different types of coloring compounds, known as pigments.

Choosing vegetables that have different colors is one of the ways you can make a menu healthier. In fact, the Dietary Guidelines for Americans make some very specific suggestions about how many servings of different-colored vegetables you should eat each week.

The colors in vegetables can give you a hint about the types of vitamins they contain. Choosing vegetables with bright, vivid colors is a good technique.

When you cook vegetables, the color can change, because the pigments react with other ingredients. Acids such as lemon juice or vinegar turn green vegetables a dull olive color, but they help white vegetables stay white and keep red vegetables

such as red cabbage from turning purple. The amount of time a vegetable spends cooking in hot water can also change its color.

When vegetables have a gray or dull appearance, it means that the pigments have been destroyed. It also may mean that certain vitamins have been destroyed.

Lab Activity

Rinse and trim green beans. Divide the green beans into two equal-sized batches. Fill two pans with enough water to hold the green beans. Add 2 teaspoons of salt to one pan, and 2 tablespoons of vinegar to another pan; bring the water to a boil. Add a batch of green beans to each pan. Cook the beans until they are tender. Do they differ in color? Do they differ in texture? Do they differ in taste?

Assorted vegatables

Source: Serghei Velusceac/Fotolia

Water Water contains no calories, but humans need it to live. It is in all of our cells and our blood, bones, teeth, hair, and skin. We must replenish water daily by drinking fluids and eating foods that contain water.

Water is critical to the body's chemical reactions. It dissolves minerals and other compounds so they can travel through the bloodstream. It removes impurities from the bloodstream and the body.

Water cushions joints, organs, and sensitive tissues, such as the spinal cord. Water maintains pressure on the optic nerves so we can see properly. It also stabilizes blood pressure and helps regulate body temperature.

When our bodies get too hot, because we exert ourselves or our environment is hot, the water in our bodies turns to sweat to cool us off. The human body generally loses about a quart of water daily through the cleansing and cooling processes. It's a good idea to replace at least this amount of lost water throughout the day. Some sources recommend drinking double this amount—eight 8-oz glasses a day. You might need more or less, depending on how active you are and how many other fluids you consume as part of your regular diet.

Calories Eating foods unlocks nutrients so we can use them for growth, regeneration, and repair in the body. Energy from foods fuels our daily activities. No matter how little we exercise, we still need energy for basic functions such as breathing and keeping our hearts beating. We measure a food's energy value in calories.

Calories come from four sources: carbohydrates, proteins, fats, and alcohol. Not all foods that contain calories contain good amounts of other nutrients. In fact, high-calorie foods such as a soft drink or a candy bar or an alcoholic beverage may contain very few nutrients, if any. These foods are said to have empty calories. Foods that contain a lot of nutrients in relation to the number of calories they contain are described as nutrient-dense foods.

Calorie Needs by Age, Gender, and Activity Level

Age and Gender	Low Activity	High Activity
Children		
2–3	1000	1400
Females		
4–8	1200	1800
9–13	1600	2200
14–18	1800	2400
19–30	2000	2400
31–50	1800	2200
51 plus	1600	2200
Males		
4–8	1400	2000
9–13	1800	2600
14–18	2200	3200
19–30	2400	3000
31–50	2200	3000
51 plus	2200	2800

Source: U.S. Department of Agriculture, Center for Nutrition Policy and Promotion

The number of calories that is right for an individual depends on:

- **Weight.** The more you weigh, the more calories you need to maintain your body at its current weight.

- **Activity Level.** The more active you are, the more calories you need. The less active you are, the fewer calories you need.

- **Age/Life Cycle.** Anyone who is still growing or who is in a developmental stage in the life cycle needs more calories. This includes infants and children, adolescents, and pregnant or nursing women. People with a lifestyle low in activity, with lots of sitting and little physical exercise, need fewer calories. On the other hand, people with a lifestyle of high activity, getting lots of exercise, need more calories. As people age, they require fewer calories.

- **Gender.** Men tend to require more calories than women because they typically have leaner body mass than women do.

The number of calories people consume each day plays an important role in determining whether their weight stays the same, increases, or decreases. When the calories you eat match the calories you use, your current weight is maintained. When you eat more calories than you use, you gain weight. When you eat fewer calories than you use, you lose weight.

 **READING CHECKPOINT** *How do the calories in your diet affect your weight?*

Nutrition Information

Nutrition information is designed to tell us how much of a certain nutrient a food or a dish contains in a single serving, and the number of calories in the serving. We get nutrition information from a variety of sources. One of these sources is the U.S. government, which provides dietary guidelines and recommendations for healthy eating, whether you need to plan a menu for yourself or for someone else.

Nutrition Labels and Information Sheets Food manufacturers have included nutrition information on their labels since 1973. As cooks, we use nutrition labels to choose foods that give us the best nutritional value possible.

Foods that don't come with a nutrition label on the package, such as fresh produce, seafood, or meats, still have nutrition information. You can get this information from many sources, including the large database of nutrition information prepared and managed by the U.S. Food and Drug Administration (FDA).

Serving Size Read the information about serving size carefully. The nutrition information on the label is true for the serving size the label indicates.

The serving size is usually listed as a weight (grams or ounces); it may also give a volume measure (½ cup, for instance). Doubling the size of a serving doubles the calories in that serving, along with the saturated fat, cholesterol, sodium, and other nutrients.

Calorie Content The calories in foods come from protein, fats, carbohydrates, or alcohol. If you know how much of each of these nutrients is in the food by weight (gram is the most common unit), you can convert the grams into calories. Then you can add up the calories from each nutrient to get the total calories for a serving.

Calorie content is one of the most basic pieces of information nutrition labels or nutrition software can provide. You can use these numbers to help make wise choices that keep both calories and fats within the suggested limits, such as substituting a food that is lower in saturated fats, cutting back on the salt or sugar you add to a dish, or making portion sizes slightly smaller or larger.

Recommended Dietary Allowance The **Recommended Dietary Allowance (RDA)** was developed by the U.S. National Academy of Science during World War II in order to investigate issues that, in the U.S. N.A.S's words, might "affect national defense." A committee was formed to create a set of recommendations regarding the standard daily allowance for each type of nutrient that could be used for the armed forces, for civilians, and for groups overseas in need of food relief. The final set of guidelines, called RDAs for "Recommended Dietary Allowances," were accepted in 1941. The allowances included a "margin of safety" as well as taking into account food rationing during the war. The RDAs were reviewed and revised every 5 to 10 years. In the early 1950s, nutritionists within the U.S. Department of Agriculture made a new set of guidelines that also included the number of servings of each food group in order to make it easier for people to receive their RDAs of each nutrient.

Dietary Reference Intake The **Dietary Reference Intake (DRI)** is a system of nutrition recommendations from the Institute of Medicine (IOM) of the U.S. National Academy of Sciences. The DRI system is used by both the United States and Canada and is intended for the general public and health professionals to guide them in creating diets for schools, prisons, hospitals, or nursing homes; to monitor industries developing new food products; and to assist health-care policymakers and public health officials.

The DRI was introduced in 1997 in order to broaden the RDAs. The DRI values are not currently used in nutrition labeling, where the older Reference Daily Intakes are still used.

Percent of Daily Value The U.S. Food and Drug Administration (FDA) has established the amount of carbohydrates, fiber, vitamin C, sodium, calcium, and other nutrients your body needs each day. These amounts, known

Sources of Calories

Nutrient	Calories
Protein	4 calories per gram
Fat	9 calories per gram
Carbohydrates	4 calories per gram
Alcohol	7 calories per gram

Nutrition Facts

Serving Size 2/3 cup (55g)
Servings Per Container about 8

Amount Per Serving	Oats & Honey Granola	with 1/2 cup skim milk
Calories	230	270
Calories from Fat	50	50
	% Daily Value**	
Total Fat 6g*	9%	9%
Saturated Fat 1g	4%	5%
Trans Fat 0g		
Polyunsaturated Fat 0.5g		
Monounsaturated Fat 3.5g		
Cholesterol 0mg	0%	1%
Sodium 110mg	5%	7%
Potassium 140mg	4%	10%
Total Carbohydrate 42g	14%	16%
Dietary Fiber 3g	12%	12%
Sugars 14g		
Other Carbohydrate 25g		
Protein 5g		
Vitamin A	0%	4%
Vitamin C	0%	2%
Calcium	2%	15%
Iron	8%	8%
Thiamin	4%	8%
Riboflavin	2%	15%
Niacin	2%	2%
Vitamin B6	2%	4%
Phosphorus	15%	25%
Magnesium	10%	15%
Zinc	6%	10%

*Amount in cereal. A serving of cereal plus skim milk provides 6g total fat, less than 5mg cholesterol, 170mg sodium, 340mg potassium, 48g total carbohydrate (20g sugars) and 9g protein.
** Percent Daily Values are based on a 2,000 calorie diet. Your daily values may be higher or lower depending on your calorie needs:

	Calories	2,000	2,500
Total Fat	Less than	65g	80g
Saturated Fat	Less than	20g	25g
Cholesterol	Less than	300mg	300mg
Sodium	Less than	2,400mg	2,400mg
Potassium		3,500mg	3,500mg
Total Carbohydrate		300g	375g
Dietary Fiber		25g	30g

FIGURE 22–3

Cereal Nutrition Label

The daily values are shown as percentages.

ANALYZING INFORMATION *How do the daily values change when the cereal is served with milk?*

Source: iQoncept/Fotolia

as **daily values**, are listed on nutrition labels as a metric weight (in milligrams or grams) and also as a percent value, shown as "% of daily value" or "%DV."

The %DV shows what percentage of the daily requirement for that nutrient you are getting in a single serving, based on a 2000-calorie diet. Even if you eat more or less than 2000 calories each day, this information can show you which foods are good choices to meet your requirements. Anything that has a value of 20 percent or more is considered a good source of that nutrient.

MyPlate The U.S. Department of Agriculture (USDA) has developed a graphic representation of a healthy diet, known as **MyPlate**. This graphic is part of a system that can be personalized to help you find a balance between food and physical activity. The MyPlate graphic represents five basic food groups and shows them in relationship to one another on a plate, to show clearly that about half of the plate should be devoted to fruits and vegetables, with the remainder split between protein-rich foods and carbohydrate-rich foods. A serving of a dairy food also appears next to the plate.

The motivation behind this graphic representation of a healthy diet is to simplify and clarify the choices that people should make in order to get the nutrients they need. The difficulty with such an image, according to many experts, is that is fails to recommend specific foods that are known to be a healthier choice (whole grains, such as brown rice, versus processed grains, such as white rice, for instance). This makes the graphic difficult to apply for some individuals. Another concern is that some foods have been included that may not be healthy choices for certain individuals. The recommendations regarding dairy have often come under fire, as some health experts do not consider dairy essential to a healthy diet. In fact, some individuals are unable to eat dairy for either health, religious, or ethical reasons. Vegetarians may need further guidance in order to create healthy meals and diets. The same is true of other groups, such as those who follow a specific ethnic diet that differs from the "typical" American diet. As a result, you will find a number of other graphic representations of diets.

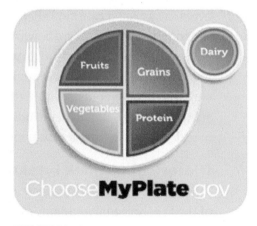

FIGURE 22–4

MyPlate.gov

INFERRING? *Why aren't sweets represented on the plate?*

Source: USDA

Dietary Guidelines Another tool developed by the federal government to help people create a healthy and well-balanced diet is the Dietary Guidelines for Americans. With an emphasis on reducing risk for major diseases through diet and physical activity, the **Dietary Guidelines** are revised every five years and published by the U.S. Department of Health and

Human Services and the USDA. These guidelines expand upon MyPlate by providing a specific number of servings that should come from the basic foods groups, as well as providing guidance concerning physical activity, alcoholic beverages, and food safety. The following recommendations are in the 2010 Dietary Guidelines:

2010 Dietary Guidelines

- ☑ Aim for a healthy weight.
- ☑ Be physically active each day.
- ☑ Let MyPlate guide your food choices.
- ☑ Choose a variety of grains daily, especially whole grains.
- ☑ Choose a variety of fruits and vegetables daily.
- ☑ Keep food safe to eat.
- ☑ Choose a diet that is low in saturated fat and cholesterol and moderate in total fat.
- ☑ Choose beverages and foods to moderate your intake of sugars.
- ☑ Choose and prepare foods with less salt.
- ☑ If you drink alcoholic beverages, do so in moderation.

The number of servings you need from each of the five groups is based on your age, sex, and activity level. If you go to the website for ChooseMyPlate, you can find out exactly what is recommended for your individual needs. The five basic food groups and recommended number of servings are as follows:

- **Grains.** The number of recommended servings varies depending on age and gender, ranging from 2 oz equivalents for children to 8 oz equivalents for teenage boys and men. The average recommendation is 6 oz of grains a day, with at least half of the servings made up of whole or minimally processed grains. Examples of 1 oz equivalents for grains include ½ cup cooked grain, hot cereal, or pasta; ½ bagel; 1 slice whole-grain bread; or 1 cup ready-to-eat (cold) cereal.

- **Vegetables.** Young children should consume 2 to 2½ cups of vegetables each day. Boys and girls aged 13 to 18 need 2½ to 3 cups each day. Women should have 2 to 2½ cups each day, whereas 2½ to 3 cups are suggested for men. There are further recommendations regarding the number of servings of different subgroups of vegetables that should be eaten each week. You can find more information about these subgroups at the ChooseMyPlate website.

- **Fruit.** Suggested servings for fruits range from 1 cup for young children to 1½ cups for teenagers and women and up to 2 cups for men. Examples of a ½-cup serving of fruit include about 18 grapes; 1 small banana, apple, or orange; ½ cup of applesauce; and ¼ cup of dried fruits. Choose a variety of fruits and opt for whole fruits instead of fruit juices.

- **Milk Products.** Children up to the age of 4 should have 2 cups of milk products each day; those aged 4 to 8 should have 2½ cups each day. Teenagers and adults should aim for 3 cups each day. Look for low-fat versions of milk, cheese, and yogurt whenever possible. Soy and nut milk products can be substituted for those with lactose intolerance.

- **Meat, Fish, Eggs, Beans, and Nuts.** Like grains, the number of servings for these protein-rich foods is expressed in terms of ounce equivalents. Children under the age of 8 should have 2 to 4 ounce equivalents daily; girls ages 9 through 18 should have 5 ounce equivalents. Boys ages 9 through 13 need 5 ounce equivalents as well, and those ages 14 through 18 should have 6. Women need 5 to 5½ ounce equivalents and men need 6 to 6½. One small chicken breast is equal to 3 ounce equivalents. One medium egg is a 1 ounce equivalent, as are 1 tablespoon of peanut butter, ¼ cup of cooked beans or lentils, or 2 tablespoons of hummus. Choose meats and poultry that are low in fat or lean, and trim any visible surface fat.

- **Oils.** Fats and oils are naturally present in many foods, including meats, dairy, nuts, and eggs. This means that you should think of oils in terms of what you can be allowed instead of how much you need. Children up to the age of 4 may have up to 1 tablespoon; those aged 4 to 8 may have 4 to 5 teaspoons. Teenagers and adults should limit their added fats and oils to about 2 tablespoons.

The Impact of Food Processing and Preservation Techniques on Foods

The foods we find in grocery stores and in restaurants are often processed in some fashion. Cooking foods is one way that foods are processed, even though we don't always think of cooking as processing foods. Cooking foods can have a direct impact on their overall nutritional value. Some nutrients are sensitive to heat, water, and air. The vitamins found in fruits and vegetables that are dissolved by water can be removed from those foods when they are cooked in water. Cutting foods exposes them to the air; if they are then cooked in water or steam, even more nutrients can be lost. Foods that are cooked at temperatures that are too high or cooked for too long also lose valuable nutrients. That is why most healthy cooking techniques suggest that you cook foods for the shortest amount of time possible, leaving them whole whenever possible, and that you serve them as soon after they are cooked as possible.

Other food-processing techniques can also reduce the quantity of valuable nutrients in the food. Milling grains, for example, strips away the bran and germ and the nutrients that they contain. The heat from milling also cuts down on the vitamins in the grain. Foods that are canned or jarred are often combined with salts. This increases the sodium level in those foods.

Some traditional food-preservation techniques include salting, curing, smoking, and drying. These techniques remove the moisture from foods to keep them safe from spoilage. This is accomplished by adding significant amounts of salt to the food to draw out the moisture. Some water-soluble nutrients are lost during this process, and the level of sodium in the food can jump significantly.

Some foods are preserved by combining them with sugar. Sugar also helps keep foods from spoiling by trapping the moisture in the food and preventing microorganisms from growing. Adding sugar or high-fructose corn syrup to foods ranging from tomato sauce to fruits helps to preserve the foods, but also increases the amount of sugar that they include.

Freezing foods can be an effective way to process them. Fruits and vegetables may retain more nutrients than other processed foods, and they may even have higher nutrient levels than the same food in its fresh form. That is because while foods are traveling from the point of harvest to the store, the food changes and often loses nutrients. Freezing them in the field or on a ship can stop that loss before it becomes significant. To maintain color, texture, and flavor, frozen foods may be treated with salt, sugar, or other preservatives, however. The challenge for consumers and chefs is recognizing when foods contain more sodium or simple sugars. The only way to be sure is to read the list of ingredients on the label as well as the nutrition information included on the label.

READING CHECKPOINT *What are the five basic food groups?*

22.1 ASSESSMENT

Reviewing Concepts

1. What does "good nutrition" mean?

2. How do the calories in your diet affect your weight?

3. What are the five basic food groups?

Critical Thinking

4. Predicting How can a small amount of fat in a meal prevent you from overeating?

5. Comparing/Contrasting Why is it safer to consume excess B vitamins than excess vitamin A?

6. Classifying Which minerals and foods are important for anyone in a growth cycle?

Test Kitchen

Go to the kitchen pantry. Look for foods that show on their nutritional labels that they contain saturated fats, trans fats, and high levels of sodium. Knowing that these ingredients are a potential health risk, how do you feel about consuming these foods or serving them to others? How might you limit their use or use other foods as substitutes?

SCIENCE
Dietary Fiber

Research the health benefits of fiber. Describe its role in promoting health and reducing the risk of disease. Make a list of foods that are rich in soluble fiber, and make another list of foods that are rich in insoluble fiber.

Making Menus More Nutritious

Key Concepts

- Planning healthy menus
- Using healthy food preparation techniques
- Using portioning and presentation techniques

Vocabulary

- batch cooking
- nutritional balance
- ovo-lacto vegetarian
- portion control
- vegan
- vegetarian

Planning Healthy Menus

Healthy menus have **nutritional balance**, which means they provide enough calories to meet energy needs and enough specific nutrients to promote health.

Some menus are planned to meet certain objectives, such as controlling weight, blood pressure, or diabetes. For specialized diets, medical professionals such as doctors or nutritionists often make recommendations about foods to eat or avoid, appropriate calorie intake, and daily values for a given vitamin, mineral, or other nutrient. Other menus must take into account food allergies to ingredients such as nuts, seafood, eggs, or wheat. Some are developed in order to help manage other diet-related conditions such as gluten or lactose intolerance.

Menus are more than just a list of foods to buy, dishes to prepare, and serving sizes to observe, however. Whether you are creating a menu for a restaurant or a menu to meet your own health and wellness objectives, the challenge is planning menus that meet both nutritional and culinary objectives. In other words, a balanced and healthy menu that isn't interesting, attractive, and delicious may not get eaten. If no one eats the food, then no one gets the benefit of its nutritional value.

A successful restaurant is able to meet its guests' special needs and still provide delicious, appealing menu options. Today's chef must be aware of the many ways that menu items, recipes, and cooking techniques can be modified and adapted to keep foods safe for those with allergies to ingredients such as peanuts or seafood or with intolerances to milk (lactose) and wheat (gluten). Chefs must be able to make food appropriate for guests with conditions such as diabetes or hypertension (high

Source: © iQoncept/Fotolia

blood pressure), or for patrons who want to eat healthier foods that are lower in calories as part of a weight-loss plan.

Choosing Healthy Ingredients The ingredients you choose play a significant role in creating healthy menus. Dietary recommendations and healthy eating plans suggest adding more fresh fruit, vegetables, and whole grains to the diet and keeping refined carbohydrates and sugars at a minimum. In addition, it is important to be aware of added sodium. Ingredients added to foods during processing (for instance, canning or freezing) can increase calories and sodium, so reading labels carefully is very important. If food allergies are a concern, you should also read the label to be sure those ingredients you are allergic to are not added, and that the food was not processed in a plant that also processes foods to which you are allergic. Guidelines for healthy choices include the following:

Whole-wheat pizza
Source: Clive Streeter/
Dorling Kindersley Limited

- **Produce.** Foods that are in season and locally available have several advantages for healthy cooking. They have the best flavor and texture, so they will appeal to your guests. Produce that doesn't undergo a great deal of handling or processing offers the best nutritional value. When foods are not in season in your region, choosing frozen foods may be a better option in term of nutrition and flavor, as well as cost. Some foods are frozen within hours of being harvested, and that means that their overall nutritional value can be higher than that of "fresh" foods that have to travel a significant distance over a period of days or weeks before they reach the market.

- **Whole Grains.** Nutritionists recommend whole grains as a healthy source of carbohydrates in a balanced diet. Whole grains are minimally processed. That means that some or all of the outer layers that contain many important oils, vitamins, minerals, and fiber were not removed, even if the grain has been ground into a meal or flour. Choose whole grains whenever you can. For instance, choose brown rice instead of white rice to make a pilaf. Replace some or all of the white flour in baked goods with whole-wheat flour. If you aren't sure whether a product contains whole grains, read the ingredients on the label to find out.

FIGURE 22–5
Using Lean Meat
Trimming the fat from a beef tenderloin.
RELATING CONCEPTS *What are the problems associated with saturated fat?*
Source: Pearson Education/PH College

- **Lean Meat and Poultry.** To keep fat, calories, and cholesterol under control, choose meats that are naturally lean, especially the tenderloin and some parts of the leg or shoulder. Trim surface fat away either before you start to cook the food or before you serve it. For instance, you might want to leave the skin on a chicken while you roast it to protect the meat, but it is easy to remove before you carve the bird and serve it to your guests.

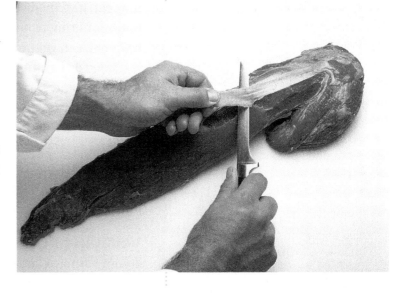

Chef's Tip

Visible and Invisible Fats

You can see fat in such foods as sausage and steak. Foods such as nuts and avocados "hide" the fat they contain. Consider not only the amount of fat in a food, but the type of fat it contains.

FOCUS ON Safety

Food Allergy Precautions

Even a tiny amount of a food can set off an allergic reaction in a person suffering from a food allergy. That means that if a customer is allergic to walnuts, simply scraping off a walnut garnish is not enough to prevent an allergic reaction. Food for allergy sufferers should be prepared without any contact with the problem food. This also applies to the prep table and utensils used to prepare the food.

- **Fish.** Like poultry, fish is much lower in saturated fats than meats such as beef, veal, lamb, and pork. Fish has the added advantage of being a source of omega-3 fatty acids. Seafood is low in saturated fats, too, although some varieties may still contain enough cholesterol to be of concern for certain individuals.

- **Reduced Salt.** Consider the total amount of salt in a dish when you choose ingredients. If your recipe calls for ingredients such as soy sauce, capers, olives, anchovies, or cheeses that are already high in sodium, remember to cut back on the amount of salt you add to the dish while it cooks. Foods that are packed in a brine can be rinsed in cool water to remove some of the sodium without removing all of the flavor. Substitute other ingredients for salt, such as spices, herbs, plain and flavored vinegars, and chiles. Lemon and lime juice can also add flavor without adding salt.

- **Reduced Sugar.** Adding sugar to a dish makes it taste sweet. It also adds calories, without adding any additional nutrients. Adding fresh or dried fruit to a dish also makes it taste sweet. An important advantage to using dried fruit as sweeteners is that you also add more nutritional value to the dish. You may also add color and texture. Adding fruit to a dish means you can sometimes cut back on the amount of sugar you need to add.

Food Allergies Certain ingredients, although considered healthy by most people, pose problems for people with specific food allergies. Foods such as shellfish, milk, eggs, wheat, soy, peanuts, and other nuts have been known to cause allergic reactions. Allergic reactions can begin very quickly. Some people will develop hives and the eyes, nose, and throat may be extremely itchy. The face, hands, and throat may start to swell. Severe reactions are potentially life threatening, as the throat may swell to such an extent that the person may not be able to breath. Many people who are aware of their food allergies will carry an epi-pen, which contains a medication that they can give themselves right away. If someone in your restaurant appears to be suffering from an allergic reaction, call for help immediately so that he or she can get proper medical care.

Menu descriptions should list any foods that are known to cause allergic reactions, and service staff should be able to describe menu items upon request. A dish with a peanut sauce, for example, could then be avoided by a person with an allergy to peanuts. A foodservice establishment should consider substitutions when planning a dish with ingredients that can cause allergic reactions. The establishment should also be careful about cross-contaminating foods with foods that can cause allergic reactions. That may mean keeping some areas of the kitchen free from those foods.

Vegetarian Options Entire food groups are off limits for people who do not eat meat or other animal products. A **vegetarian** is a person who, for religious, ethical, economic, or nutritional reasons, does not eat meat,

Greece

Greek cooking features intense flavors: lemon, mint, rosemary, oregano, and lamb. Olives and olive oil from the trees that grow throughout the country are woven into nearly every dish. The country is mountainous and suited for herding sheep and goats. The Greeks make many delicious yogurts and cheeses from the milk of sheep and goats.

No part of Greece is more than 85 miles from the sea, and nearly 15 percent of the country is small islands, so it isn't surprising that fish and seafood are an important part of Greek cuisine.

Greece has a mild climate, so vegetables can grow year-round. Eggplant, tomatoes, lettuces, and spinach are just some of the ingredients you'll find in many famous Greek dishes. Fruits, especially melons, peaches, grapes, and cherries, are also available fresh year-round.

Source: Ruslan Olinchuk/Fotolia

Source: Christian Jung/Fotolia

Olives and olive oil are important in the Greek diet

An important study, done between 1958 and 1975 by Dr. Ansel Keyes, found that men living on the Greek island of Crete had diets that included 43 percent fat, a rate much higher than is typically suggested as healthy. However, they had extremely low rates of heart attacks. It was discovered that the type of fat they ate most—the monounsaturated fat found in olive oil—has important nutritional benefits.

The health-giving properties of the Greek diet are numerous: olive oil, fresh milk products, fresh fish and seafood, and locally grown produce. Meats are served less often than in the United States and in smaller portions. Dishes that feature whole grains, beans, lentils, and nuts are an important source of protein in the Greek diet.

There is one more aspect of the Greek diet that has important health benefits. A meal in Greece is often an opportunity for family and friends to gather together. No one is in a hurry to get away from the table. The social aspect of Greek dining and its relaxed pace are as beneficial as the diet itself.

Research

Locate Crete on a map of Greece. Describe the geography and climate. Research the typical diet of a person living on Crete in the 1950s. What meals were common? What would be a typical menu for each meal?

poultry, and fish. There are several types of vegetarians in the world today. An **ovo-lacto vegetarian** does not eat meat, poultry, and fish but does eat eggs and dairy products. A **vegan** eats no animal products whatsoever and consumes only plant-based foods—vegetables, fruits, grains, legumes, nuts, and seeds. A "semi-vegetarian" might eat no red meat but include poultry and fish in the diet.

Growing numbers of people dining out today are seeking balanced and nutritious vegetarian meals. Dishes that offer complete protein are important menu items. To create such dishes, simply use one of these basic food group combinations:

- Grains and legumes
- Grains and dairy products
- Legumes and seeds/nuts
- Legumes and dairy products
- Seeds/nuts and dairy products

Examples include peanut butter sandwiches, baked beans on toast, peas and rice, refried beans and tortillas, split pea soup and crackers, minestrone soup, hummus on pita bread, pasta and cheese, and rice pudding.

Most foodservice establishments provide vegetarian options for those who have made vegetarianism their lifestyle and for those who simply want a healthy menu choice.

Options for Weight Loss

Americans are getting fatter. Nearly one-third of us are obese, which makes healthy weight loss a high priority for everyone. Restaurants often take the blame for some of the nation's ballooning weight, even though it can be argued that no one is making us choose rich desserts or huge servings of french fries. The question is, how can the foodservice industry be part of the solution instead of being viewed as a stumbling block in the nation's quest to get healthier by losing weight?

Americans have been "dieting" for decades. There have been a number of fad diets, including the grapefruit diet, the cabbage soup diet, and even diets that cut out entire food groups, such as grains. Some of these diets work well for a short time, but successful weight loss that can be maintained remains a challenge, even though the formula for weight loss is quite simple: Consume fewer calories and exercise more.

Many popular diets are very strict concerning the types of foods that can be eaten, how they can be combined, and when they should be eaten. Diets such as the South Beach, Atkins, or Dukan diet ask you to essentially eliminate an entire group of foods (starches) and instead, they suggest you eat a diet that is made up mainly of protein-rich meats and fish. When these diets were at their most popular, many restaurants found themselves serving burgers without buns and cutting way back on the quantity of baked goods they offered.

Some diets restrict the number of calories that can be eaten in the course of a day. In fact, some diets even recommend consuming far fewer calories than is reasonable. Dieters often complain that they are too hungry to stick

FIGURE 22–6
Minestrone
Because minestrone has a combination of grains and legumes, it offers complete protein.

ANALYZING INFORMATION *What form of grain is used in minestrone? What legume?*

Source: Dorling Kindersley/Dorling Kindersley Limited

Nouvelle Cuisine

Nouvelle cuisine, or new cuisine, is the name given to a internationally popular style of cooking that was developed during the 1960s and 1970s. It stressed freshness, lightness, and clarity of flavor. It can be viewed as a reaction to some of the richer and more calorie-laden extravagances of classic French haute cuisine. Instead, nouvelle cuisine emphasized the natural flavors, textures, and colors of foods. This style of cuisine was a response to what was clearly an unhealthy cooking style that was heavy in fats, sugars, refined starches, and salt. Nouvelle cuisine was also influenced by the Japanese style of food presentation, in an effort to replace heavy, buttery, starch-laden sauces and stuffings by means of simplifying the recipes and allowing the food to be its own garnish. The phrase *nouvelle cuisine* was coined by the French food critics Christian Millau and Henri Gault to describe the styles created by a group of French chefs, notably Paul Bocuse, Jean and Pierre Troisgros, Michel Guérard, Roger Verge, and Paul Haeberlin.

Nouvelle cuisine was based around 10 characteristics meant to improve and advance the work being done in restaurants to meet the needs of their clients and their concerns about health and wellness, innovation, cultural exploration, and quality. The characteristics of nouvelle cuisine are:

- A rejection of overly complicated dishes.
- Cooking times for most fish, seafood, game birds, veal, green vegetables, and pâtés were greatly reduced in an attempt to preserve the natural flavors. Steaming food became a new trend.
- Use of the freshest possible ingredients.
- Large menus with a wide array of selections abandoned in favor of shorter menus.
- Strong marinades that mask the true flavors of meat and game were abandoned.
- Eliminating heavy sauces thickened with flour-based roux, in favor of fresh herbs, high-quality butter, lemon juice, and vinegar.
- Inspiration taken from traditional and regional dishes.
- Technology is embraced, along with new techniques and modern equipment. (Paul Bocuse, said to be one of the founders of nouvelle cuisine and named the Chef of the Century, even used microwave ovens in his restaurant.)
- Attention given to meet the dietary needs of guests with revised menu offerings.
- Inventive and creative new combinations and pairings of foods and flavors.

Research

Find three or four images of menu items from restaurants or hotels from the years 1920 to 1950. Next, find two or three photographs featuring menu items from restaurants where nouvelle cuisine was practiced in the 1970s. What differences can you find? Which one appeals to you more? How has the presentation and portioning of the food changed from classic to nouvelle cuisine?

Plating is important in nouvelle cuisine

Source: © Kondor83/Fotolia

to the plan. Low- or restricted-calorie plans can account for the popularity of "diet" foods that are artificially sweetened. Dieters who are counting calories often ask for sauces to be served on the side or to have foods baked or broiled instead of sautéed or fried. Butter, cream, and cheese are typically eliminated from their meals because they are so high in calories.

Ultimately, a healthy diet is one that includes a variety of foods over the course of a day, so you can be certain to get the full range of nutrients you need. That means you should be consuming all of the "macro-nutrients," including proteins, carbohydrates, and fat. The key when it comes to weight loss is controlling how much you serve yourself or others and making smart choices. Proper portioning helps you determine easily whether you are on track to meet appropriate goals for weight loss.

 **READING CHECKPOINT** *What is nutritional balance?*

Using Healthy Food Preparation Techniques

When we cook foods, we change their nutritional value. Sometimes the change is minor but sometimes it is quite significant. Healthy menus call for techniques that keep as many nutrients as possible and don't add too many calories or too much fat, sodium, or cholesterol to the dish. The way a dish looks when you serve it to your guest plays a big part in the success of a healthy menu.

Techniques to Emphasize If the start of a healthy dish is choosing and handling ingredients carefully, the next step is the way you choose to cook it. Grilling, broiling, roasting, and baking are all examples of dry-heat methods that have the advantage of not calling for adding fats. Moist-heat methods are also almost always appropriate: steaming, poaching, simmering, boiling, stewing, and braising.

Foods that are prepared ahead of time and held for a long time in a steam table may lose most of their nutrients, especially the water-soluble vitamins B and C. Similarly, if vegetables soak in water for very long before or after cooking, the vitamins dissolve into the water. A general guideline is to try not to leave vegetables in water for longer than necessary and to cook foods as close as possible to the time you want to serve them. There are situations in a foodservice setting where foods have to be made in advance, but you can take steps to minimize any loss of flavor and nutrition.

You can prepare certain foods in larger amounts, such as vegetables, pasta, rice, soups, stocks, and sauce. Once you have cooked or parcooked them, you can cool them down safely to below 41°F and keep them in the refrigerator.

FIGURE 22–7
Grilled Vegetables
Grilling helps retain nutrients and color in vegetables.
RELATING CONCEPTS *How can you add flavor to grilled foods without adding fat?*
Source: Edward Allwright/Dorling Kindersley Limited

Batch Cooking for Vegetables

1. **Rinse, trim, and peel vegetables** properly.

2. **Cut** vegetables into even pieces, as directed in your recipe.

3. **Blanch or parcook** vegetables by boiling or steaming them.

4. **Cool** vegetables quickly in ice water.

5. **Drain** vegetables thoroughly.

6. **Refrigerate** blanched or parcooked vegetables until you are ready to prepare a batch.

7. **Reheat small batches** of vegetables in simmering water.

When you need to get the food ready to serve, you can prepare just the amount you need—in other words, a small batch. **Batch cooking** is the process of reheating or finishing a small batch of food, as needed, or preparing a small amount of food several times during a service period so a fresh supply of cooked items is always available. This process improves the nutritional value, flavor, color, and texture of the food.

Techniques to Limit Any cooking technique that calls for large amounts of oil, butter, or shortening is one that you will want to limit on a healthy menu. Frying is an obvious example, but other cooking techniques might also encourage adding too many calories, fat, or sodium to a dish.

Thickeners such as roux (made from flour and butter) and liaison (made from heavy cream and egg yolks) give dishes a good texture but may not be appropriate as healthy menu offerings.

Saucing techniques vary, depending on how you want the dish to taste as well as how you want the dish to look. If a sauce gets the majority of its shine or body from heavy cream or butter, you may need to serve the sauce in a slightly different way so you can offer a smaller portion, or you may want to simply find a different sauce to replace sauces that are too high in calories or fat.

Chef's Tip

Sauces

Choose vegetable sauces or stews such as marinara sauce, salsas, or ratatouille to replace sauces that call for lots of butter or cream. Vegetable sauces and stews add flavor, color, texture, and fiber to a dish.

Replacing Oil with Stock in Vinaigrette

1. **Measure the stock,** using the same amount of stock as you would use oil.

2. **Simmer** the stock.

3. **Blend cornstarch or arrowroot** with cold water to make a slurry.

4. **Add the slurry** to the stock, whisking constantly.

5. **Simmer** long enough to thicken the stock, usually two or three minutes.

6. **Cool** the thickened stock.

7. **Add vinegar and seasonings** to the stock and use as a salad dressing, dip, or marinade.

FIGURE 22–8

Coatings for Crunch
Add a crispy coating and bake foods instead of frying.

PREDICTING *What would happen to your crunchy coating if you covered the pan while the chicken baked?*

Source: Culinary Institute of America

•FOCUS ON
•• Safety

Keep Fruit and Vegetables Safe

Nutritious foods such as fruit and vegetables aren't good for you if they can make you sick. Remember to scrub all produce well and keep potentially hazardous foods refrigerated to keep them safe.

Substituting or Modifying Techniques One of the reasons we like fried foods is their crunchy crust. Fried foods are often heavily salted, another reason we enjoy them so much. But they add too many calories and too much fat and sodium to most diets. Eating many fried foods, which are not nutrient rich, means you need to eat more calories than you should to meet your basic nutritional requirements.

Your challenge as a chef is finding ways to give foods that crisp crunch and salty savor without using a frying technique. Some options you can try include adding a coating such as breadcrumbs, crushed cornflakes, or shredded potatoes to a baked dish. When you bake foods coated this way, the coating gets crunchy and crisp. You can add fresh herbs, a little cheese, or chopped toasted nuts to add flavor.

Fried potatoes are also easy to modify. Instead of cooking them in enough oil to cover them, you can brush or spray potatoes with a little oil and then roast them at a high temperature. Adding chopped garlic, herbs, pepper, and spices is a good way to cut back on the amount of salt you might otherwise want to add.

You can almost always use a little less oil when you sauté. Using nonstick and cast-iron pans also makes it easier to cook with less oil. When possible, substitute oils high in monounsaturated fats (olive, canola, and peanut) for oils high in polyunsaturated fats (corn, cottonseed, safflower, sesame seed, sunflower, and vegetable).

Many baked goods will turn out properly if you reduce the amount of added sugar by 20 or 30 percent, but you should always make a trial batch of any baked goods you want to modify. Sometimes sugar is used just to add a sweet flavor, but other times it is a major factor in making sure you get the right texture in baked goods.

READING CHECKPOINT *Which cooking techniques are the healthiest?*

Using Portioning and Presentation Techniques

Serving a variety of fresh vegetables, fruit, dry legumes, and whole grains as part of a menu item means that you can create an appealing and nutritious presentation. You can present a balanced dish that makes it a pleasure rather than a chore to get a variety of important nutrients. You can serve small portions of foods that are high in fat, sodium, cholesterol, or calories. You can use these foods more as seasonings than as a main element on the plate.

Portions One of the most important ways you can make a dish healthier is to use **portion control**, which means controlling the quantity of particular foods by using appropriately sized servings. The information included with MyPlate and in the Dietary Guidelines for Americans can tell you what a standard serving is for various foods. In some cases, the portion size might strike you or your guests as either very large or too small. For example, if you ate a whole English muffin, that might sound like just one serving, but it actually counts as two.

Many Americans have become accustomed to extremely large servings of meats, mainly because restaurants feature large cuts as a way to bring in

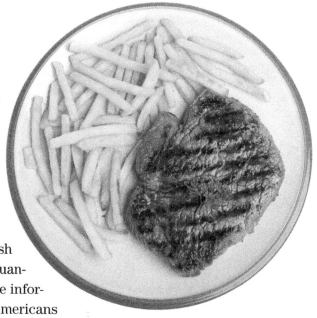

FIGURE 22-9

Portion Control

A nutritionally balanced meal calls for 2 to 3 oz of cooked meat, ½ to 1 cup of vegetables, 2 servings of a whole grain, and 1 serving of fruit.

 ANALYZING INFORMATION
What is wrong with the servings shown on this plate, and how could you improve this dish?

Source: Joe Gough/Fotolia

Serving Sizes

Food Group	Examples of a Single Serving
Grains	1 slice of bread ½ cup of cooked rice or pasta or hot cereal 1 tortilla 5 whole-wheat crackers or 7 saltine crackers 1 cup of cold cereal ½ bagel or English muffin or hamburger bun
Vegetables	1 cup of raw leafy green vegetables 1 cup of orange vegetables ½ cup of other raw or cooked vegetables ½ cup of vegetable juice
Fruit	1 whole medium-sized fruit (about 1 cup) ½ cup of cooked or canned fruit ¼ cup dried fruit ½ cup of fruit juice
Milk Products	1 cup of milk or yogurt ½ cup cottage cheese 2 slices cheese (1 ounce)
Meat, Fish, Eggs, Beans, and Nuts	2 oz cooked lean meat, poultry, or fish 1 egg ½ cup cooked dry beans 1 tablespoon peanut butter 1 ounce nuts or seeds

customers. They often see these super-sized portions as a sign of a good deal. A typical burger might weigh anywhere between 4 and 6 ounces, whereas specialty burgers are sometimes over ½ pound. That means that a single burger from a restaurant might be more calories, saturated fat, cholesterol, and protein than is suggested for an entire day. We've become so used to these portion sizes that scaling back to a more reasonable portion leaves some patrons feeling cheated. Restaurants that feature all-you-can-eat buffets or outrageously large portions of steak, entire chicken halves, or huge cuts of prime rib weighing a pound or more certainly have the right to do so, but patrons, as well as owners and chefs, are starting to question why they are serving portions that are large enough to pose a health risk.

Learn what the accepted portion size is for various foods in each of the five basic food groups. Once you know more about portion sizes and what a portion looks like, you can make adjustments to the way a portion looks on the plates or in the cups and bowls you use in your establishment.

Presentation Techniques You can use the wonderful colors, textures, and shapes of foods to entice your guests to eat nutritional menu items. This strategy is in line with the recommendations of MyPlate, which calls for us to fill plates up halfway with fruits and vegetables and then split the remainder of the plate between lean meats, chicken, fish, or beans and a reasonable portion of a whole grain. It makes the plate look bountiful. Cutting or slicing meats to give them more surface area can make an appropriately sized portion look more bountiful. Another technique calls for

FIGURE 22–10
Colorful Presentation
Broiled cod steak topped with a brightly colored tomato and pepper salsa, garnished with lemon zest, and served on green beans.

RELATING CONCEPTS *Which food from the grain family food group might be a nice accompaniment to this meal?*

Source: Ian O'Leary/Dorling Kindersley Limited

adding high-protein foods such as beef or chicken as a condiment or garnish to stir-frys and main-course salads.

Combining a variety of vibrant colors on a plate is more exciting and appealing than sticking to foods that are mainly beige or brown. Fruit, vegetables, and herbs are a good way to add color. Moist-heat techniques can help "set" the bright vivid colors of some foods. Dry-heat techniques can intensify or darken a food's color.

You can control the texture of foods by cutting or cooking them in particular ways. Moist-heat techniques result in tender, soft foods. Dry-heat techniques result in foods with exteriors that are firm or crunchy.

You can introduce whole-grain foods and dry legumes by serving them as a side dish or as an ingredient in a dish. You can also choose to feature them as the main part of the dish, leaving you free to serve smaller portions of meat, poultry, or fish, or perhaps omit them entirely.

READING CHECKPOINT *What can you do to entice your guests to try healthy menu items?*

22.2 ASSESSMENT

Reviewing Concepts

1. What is nutritional balance?

2. Which cooking techniques are the healthiest?

3. What can you do to entice your guests to try healthy menu items?

Critical Thinking

4. Drawing Conclusions Why is batch cooking a healthy cooking method?

5. Compare and Contrast Why serve a colorful healthy meal versus a mostly beige and brown healthy meal?

6. Predicting How would adding butter to a baked potato change it from a health standpoint?

7. Applying Concepts What is the healthiest way to sauté?

Test Kitchen

Divide into four teams. Each team will sauté the same item, trying to do it in as healthy a way as possible. Evaluate the other teams' efforts. Compare appearance, taste, and texture. Decide which method produced the best result.

SOCIAL STUDIES ——————●
Vegetarianism

Research the history of vegetarianism. Explore some of the early beliefs that led to this diet and how they have carried over into the present. Describe some of the world cultures that follow a vegetarian diet, and list some historical figures who were vegetarians.

PROJECT 22 You are now ready to work on Project 22, "Reducing Calories and Fat in Brownies," which is available in "My Culinary Lab" or in your *Student's Lab Resources and Study Guide* manual.

Reviewing Content

Choose the letter that best answers the question or completes the statement.

1. Energy from food is measured in units known as
   a. nutrients.
   b. calories.
   c. amino acids.
   d. antioxidants.

2. Which of the following is a water-soluble vitamin?
   a. Vitamin C
   b. Vitamin A
   c. Calcium
   d. Glucose

3. A meal that provides mutual supplementation is
   a. fish and vegetables.
   b. meat and potatoes.
   c. rice and beans.
   d. rice and salad.

4. Healthy eating plans generally recommend adding more of which food groups?
   a. Meat, fish, and eggs
   b. Milk products
   c. Fresh fruit, vegetables, and whole grains
   d. Dairy, meat, and other protein foods

5. A vegan is someone who does not eat
   a. meat, poultry, and fish.
   b. dairy products.
   c. red meat and eggs.
   d. any animal products.

6. Which food group does the MyPlate graphic indicate should make up half the plate?
   a. Meats and dairy
   b. Sweets and oils
   c. Fruits and grains
   d. Fruits and vegetables

7. Which of the following cooking methods should *not* be emphasized for healthy cooking?
   a. Grilling
   b. Sautéing
   c. Broiling
   d. Roasting

Understanding Concepts

8. Describe the health benefits of grilling over frying.

9. Which foods contain complete proteins?

10. What is glucose, and how does it work in our bodies?

11. What type of fiber scrubs the digestive tract, and what are some sources of it?

12. What is the physical characteristic of oils that are high in saturated fat? Give two examples.

Critical Thinking

13. **RECOGNIZING PATTERNS** You want to find the most healthful way to cook broccoli, using a moist-heat method. Which method do you choose? Explain your answer.

14. **PREDICTING** Which would be a more satisfying fruit serving, one whole fresh fruit or ½ cup of fruit juice? Why?

Culinary Math

15. **SOLVING PROBLEMS** A one-cup serving of pasta provides 10% of the daily value of carbohydrates, based on a 2000-calories per day diet. If you eat 2500 calories per day, how much pasta would you need to achieve the same 10% of daily value?

16. **APPLYING CONCEPTS** You need to create a meal plan that includes 2½ cups of fruit. One serving will be a whole apple. You want to divide the remaining amount of fruit into 4 equal servings. How large will each of those servings be?

On the Job

17. **APPLYING CONCEPTS** Your 2-oz serving of fish, with a cream sauce, looks skimpy on the plate next to the ½ cup of rice. How can you use other food groups to fill out the plate and still present a balanced, healthy meal?

18. **INFERRING** Why should your menu always specify if dishes are made with milk products, shellfish, or nuts?

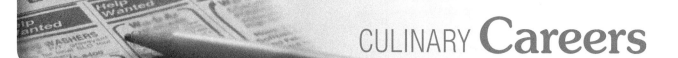

Dietitians and Nutritionists

Dietitians and nutritionists are experts in food and nutrition. They advise people on what to eat in order to lead a healthy lifestyle or achieve a specific health-related goal. Dietitians and nutritionists work in many settings, including hospitals, cafeterias, nursing homes, and schools. Some are self-employed with their own practice. Most dietitians and nutritionists have a bachelor's degree and have participated in supervised training. Also, many states require dietitians and nutritionists to be licensed.

Some dietitians and nutritionists provide customized information for specific individuals. For example, a dietitian or nutritionist might teach a patient with high blood pressure how to use less salt when preparing meals. Others work with groups of people who have similar needs. A dietitian or nutritionist might, for example, plan a diet with reduced fat and sugar to help overweight people lose weight.

Clinical dietitians provide medical nutrition therapy. They work in hospitals, long-term care facilities, and other institutions. They create both individualized and group nutritional programs based on the health needs of patients or residents. Clinical dietitians may further specialize, such as working only with patients with kidney diseases. They may work with other health-care professionals.

Management dietitians plan meal programs. They work in foodservice settings such as cafeterias, hospitals, and food corporations. They may be responsible for buying food and for carrying out other business-related tasks. Management dietitians may oversee kitchen staff or other dietitians.

Community dietitians educate the public on topics related to food and nutrition. They often work with specific groups of people, such as pregnant women. They work in public health clinics, government and nonprofit agencies, health maintenance organizations (HMOs), and other settings.

Entry-Level Requirements

Bachelor's degree in nutrition or food science. License is required by most states.

Helpful for Advancement

Earn Registered Dietitian (RD) certification, as well as master's degree or PhD. Become a member of the American Dietetic Association.

Source: Culinary Institute of America

Dieticians work in many institution settings, including schools

CATHARINE POWERS, MS, RD, LD

Catharine Powers is an innovative communicator and engaging trainer, works with clients to leverage nutrition in marketing, menu development, and sales. Cathy has extensive experience developing cutting-edge training and curricular materials for chefs, dietitians and others in the foodservice industry. In 2007 she became a founding partner in Culinary Nutrition Associates, a consulting firm with a unique expertise in assisting their clients in navigating the nutrition maze and translating scientific information into tasty bites.

Catharine Powers

She spent nearly 15 years at the world's most prominent culinary education facility, The Culinary Institute of America (CIA), where she was instrumental in developing the Institute's cutting-edge nutrition program, which served as model for culinary schools across the country. Cathy was project manager for the National Food Service Management Institute's (NFSMI) award-winning training program, *Cooks for Kids*. She was project coordinator on the development of their online course, *Culinary Techniques for Healthy School Meals*.

She is an in-demand keynoter at state dietetic association, child nutrition program, and college conferences. She is also a popular presenter at the Academy of Nutrition and Dietetics (AND) Food and Nutrition Conference and Exhibition.She spearheaded the development of many other educational materials, including videos and software. Today, she continues to provide training to foodservice operators across the country so that they can put healthful cooking principles into practice.

VITAL **STATISTICS**

Graduated: Bachelor's degree from Indiana University of Pennsylvania, 1982

Master's degree from Purdue University, 1984

Profession: Registered Dietitian, nutrition consultant, industry training, policy

Interesting Items: Major contributor to the CIA's internationally recognized text, *Techniques of Healthy Cooking*

Founding chair-elect of the Academy of Nutrition and Dietetics Food & Culinary Professionals Dietetic Practice Group

Recipient of Medallion award from Academy of Nutrition and Dietetics

Co-author *Essentials of Nutrition for Chefs,* the IACP 2011 cookbook winner for the Health and Special Diet category

CAREER **PROFILE**

Salary Ranges

Entry Level: $35,000 to $48,000

Mid-level: $52,000 to $65,500 (or more)

Senior: $75,000 and up

23.1 Owning Your Own Restaurant

23.2 Purchasing and Inventorying

23.3 Managing a Restaurant

Owning Your Own Restaurant

Key Concepts

- Creating a business plan
- Establishing a client base
- Marketing and promoting a restaurant
- Reading income statements

Vocabulary

- ambience
- assets
- bottom line
- brand
- budget
- business plan
- client base
- cost control
- expenses
- fixed cost
- income statement
- liabilities
- logo
- marketing plan
- P&L
- product/service mix
- profit
- profit and loss statement
- promotion
- public relations
- revenue
- sales
- theme
- variable cost

Creating a Business Plan

Owning a restaurant is a dream for many individuals in the foodservice industry, but there are no guarantees of success. The National Restaurant Association estimates that out of every five restaurants that open, only one will still be in operation after five years. Even if you are not ready to open up your own place, it is important that you understand how the business operates so you can contribute toward keeping the restaurant in which you work open by working in a business-like, professional manner.

Before embarking on the business journey, every good business owner comes up with a business plan. A **business plan** helps you take a few steps back from your dream and turn an objective eye on the advantages and disadvantages of opening and operating the business. A good business plan makes a clear statement about the restaurant. It typically includes a mission statement, specific goals that support the mission of the business, sample menus, preliminary operating budgets, and staffing needs.

You can go about creating a business plan in different ways. Perhaps you will begin with your menu, or perhaps you have a market or type of customer you want to attract. You may already know where you want your business to be or the hours that you expect to be in operation.

Source: Friedberg/Fotolia

No matter where you start, you will need to make decisions about the **product/service mix**. This is the relationship between the products a restaurant offers (the menu and the price of items on the menu) and the services it offers (which include the location/type of restaurant, the type of service, the staff, and the hours of operation). It is, of course, possible to open a business without a written business plan. The details of opening a business, however—borrowing money, getting loans or other assistance, securing permits—make a written plan extremely helpful. It becomes a way for you to explain to potential lenders, partners, or governmental agencies how your business will be run.

Type of Restaurant You will need to determine exactly what type of restaurant you are planning. Is it a fast-food restaurant or a high-end restaurant? Will it be open for all meals or just for dinner? Will it focus on one type of cuisine or many types? Will it offer a buffet service or a sit-down service? These and many other questions need to be explicitly addressed in a business plan.

Two essential aspects of a restaurant are its theme and ambience. A restaurant's **theme** is very important. The theme will tie everything—including the decorations, the lighting, the food, and the prices—together in one package. One aspect of the theme is the **ambience** (AM-bee-ahnce), or the feeling or mood of the restaurant. Think about any restaurant you have visited. Were there candles or fresh flowers on the table? Was the lighting

Our mission is to be a respected leader in the food service and hospitality industries. We guarantee our customers quality products that provide real value, with the service they expect, in clean, pleasant surroundings. We dedicate ourselves to sound management practices and effective human relations, while returning maximum earnings to our stockholders.

FIGURE 23–1
Mission Statement
A mission statement is the business plan boiled down to a few sentences.
ANALYZING INFORMATION *How does a mission statement affect restaurant staff?*

FIGURE 23–2
Creating an Ambience
An upscale dining room.
COMMUNICATING *Describe the ambience of this dining room.*
Source: Dorling Kindersley/Dorling Kindersley Limited

bright, or was it soft and somewhat dark? All of these factors contribute to the ambience of the restaurant.

The decisions you make about the theme and ambience of the restaurant will affect how the business operates. One of the ways that you can give a potential lender or partner insight into the restaurant's feel is by including sample menus. The type of dishes you serve and the price you might charge affect the furnishings for the restaurant, the type of uniforms you might use for wait staff, and even the number of people you need to hire in the kitchen and the dining room.

Budget Each restaurant needs a **budget**, a list of planned income and expenses. Every item in the restaurant, including food items, silverware, and cleaning products, is listed in the budget. The owner tries to anticipate every expense the business might face over the course of a year to produce an annual budget. At the same time, the owner tries to anticipate the potential income the restaurant will generate.

The annual budget is used to create budgets for shorter periods of time. Budgets become an important way to measure how effectively your business is operating. They can help you determine whether the business is meeting its goals. The sooner you know that you are over-budget in an area, the sooner you can make an adjustment. For instance, if the amount you spend on salaries is too high, you can reconsider how you are scheduling your staff.

Staffing Needs Because salaries are an important part of the cost of operating a restaurant, it is important to plan the number of employees you need. Having too many people on staff means that you are spending a great deal on salaries. If you don't have enough staff, you may have difficulty providing the kind of quality food and service that will keep your customers coming back.

Salaries are a big part of the expenses in any restaurant. In addition to having a clear idea of how many people you need, you also need to decide what kind of staff you need. You may not need highly skilled individuals for some work. However, you should also understand when a skilled worker could actually help you make more money. For instance, for specialized work such as cutting meats or fish, having experienced staff can save you money.

Hours of Operation To make a good plan, you need to know when your restaurant is going to be open for service. The more hours your restaurant is open, the more staff you need and the more food you may need. After you have been open for a period of time, you can begin to see which days are busy and which days are slow.

FIGURE 23–3
Restaurant Staff
A primary concern for a restaurant is the number of people needed and their skill levels.

RELATING CONCEPTS *How does the dining room staff impact a restaurant's budget?*

Source: Chris Ryan/Getty Images

Basic Forecasting Technique

Once a restaurant has a track record, it can forecast it's overall sales for the coming weeks and months, even for a year, in order to make predictions about income from sales. To see how this might work, let's assume that your French restaurant is open only on weekend nights (Friday, Saturday, and Sunday). Your records show that your restaurant typically serves 80 diners each weekend evening (Friday, Saturday, and Sunday). On a percentage basis, the bills for the diners are broken down as shown in the table.

Weekend Bills for Various Types of Diners

Type A (50% of Diners)
Appetizer ($6), entrée ($17), dessert ($9), beverages ($10). Total bill: $42.

Type B (30% of Diners)
Appetizer ($6), entrée ($17), beverages ($10). Total bill: $33.

Type C (20% of Diners)
Entrée ($17), beverages ($10). Total bill: $27.

To calculate the total average sales on a weekend night's dinner service, you would calculate the percentage of total diners who had one type of order multiplied by the bill for that type of order.

For example:

Type A: 50% of 80 diners = 40 diners; 40 × $42 =	$1,680
Type B: 30% of 80 diners = 24 diners; 24 × $33 =	792
Type C: 20% of 80 diners = 16 diners; 16 × $27 =	432
Total sales: Weekend dinner service =	$2,904

Computation

1. Calculate the weeknight sales (Monday through Thursday) if there are typically 40 diners per night Monday through Thursday and if the percentage breakdown is the same as the weekend breakdown.

2. Based on question 1 (for weekday dinner service) and on the weekend service (calculated above), calculate the total weekly sales for this restaurant.

3. As a very rough forecast, calculate the total sales for the restaurant if it were open every week in the year. (This is obviously a very rough estimate because sales will probably vary from season to season, holidays may increase sales, etc.)

Normal hours of operation should be part of your plan, but you should also try to include additional activities. For instance, a catered event may be scheduled for a day when your restaurant is usually closed.

READING CHECKPOINT *What does a business plan typically include?*

Establishing a Client Base

Your **client base** is the group of customers who come to your restaurant to dine. Your client base may be a little difficult to identify when you are planning your business or in the early stages of its operation. Before you start your restaurant and in the early stages of running it, you need to find out as much as you can about your location, your market, and your early customers' reactions to your food and service. You can use the information to make good choices when it comes to advertising and promoting your restaurant.

Location Sometimes your location determines who your client base will be. A restaurant located near a college campus is likely to count on a young clientele with limited money to spend on fancy meals. If you know that, you can tailor your business to that client base. On the other hand, if you are located near office businesses, you may have somewhat wealthier clients who don't have much leisure and who all want to eat at about the same time; you may have a great breakfast and lunch business but practically no one for dinner.

FIGURE 23–4
Your Client Base
Get to know your customers through opinion surveys.
SOLVING PROBLEMS *What might you do to attract customers who are under 30 years of age?*
Source: ARENA Creative/Shutterstock

Market When large companies want to introduce a new product, they do market research. They try to find out as much as they can about the market—who wants (or might want) the product, how often they might use it, and what they are willing to pay for it. To ensure your restaurant's success, you must know who your target customers are. This means you need to conduct market research to determine the likely age, income, and other related information about typical customers. Will your restaurant serve mostly families? Will it be a restaurant geared toward a younger, single crowd? An upscale restaurant has pricey menu items, and the customers tend to dress up more. A casual restaurant has less expensive menu items, with customers who are casually dressed. Knowing your potential customer helps you determine what kind of restaurant you should open.

Customers' Reactions Feedback is when people give you their opinions about how things are going. Getting feedback from your customers is a great way to conduct ongoing market research in the early stages of running a restaurant. Owners can use different ways to gather information about who is visiting the restaurant and whether customers are happy. This can lead to changes in the way you do business, or it can reinforce concepts and practices that keep the customer happy. Once a customer has dined at your restaurant, it is important that you find ways to keep that customer coming back. This repeat clientele means that you have achieved a high rate of customer satisfaction.

There are many ways to make sure your customers are satisfied. Have you ever visited a restaurant where a person other than the waiter came up to the table and asked how the meal was? Often, a restaurant manager visits the tables and inquires about the quality of the food and the service. Have you noticed suggestion cards and questionnaires on the tables at some restaurants? This is because they want to learn what the customers think. For many restaurants, even those that have been in business for years, obtaining feedback from customers is one of the most important aspects of determining a restaurant's direction.

 **READING CHECKPOINT** *What are three things you need to find out about early in the process of planning and running a restaurant?*

Marketing and Promoting a Restaurant

Restaurant owners have many means at their disposal to entice guests to visit their restaurant. Some obvious ways include advertisements and signs. Some less obvious ways include participating in charity events or serving on committees. Choosing the right way to market and promote your restaurant depends on your goals and your budget.

Your Brand Many people talk about a business's **brand**. What they mean is the public image of your business. It's an accumulation of all the things that come to mind when someone mentions your business, including your name, your logo, and sometimes even a slogan.

Your restaurant's name affects how you market your restaurant. The name gives guests a clue about your food or the kind of experience they might have. Your **logo**—a drawing, picture, or other symbol that identifies your restaurant—should be instantly recognizable.

FIGURE 23–5

Brand Recognition
A seafood restaurant with a lobster logo.

CLASSIFYING *Name some restaurants that have distinctive logos.*

Source: Gunter Marx/Dorling Kindersley Limited

Advertising Advertisements are the way you tell a potential customer about your business. Printed materials you might use to market or promote your restaurant run from advertisements in local papers, magazines, and entertainment guides to listings in phone directories. Some restaurants use flyers as a way to attract guests. Posting your menu outside the restaurant where walkers can read it is another example of advertising. You may also decide you need other items, such as bumper stickers or hats, with your logo or name.

Newspaper and magazine articles are another way to advertise your restaurant. You may be featured in an article as an expert, someone the reporter turned to for answers to questions or for a professional opinion. You may actually write an article. Or you may prepare a press release for a magazine or newspaper about your restaurant that provides details or information about events or other happenings at your restaurant. Websites are also an effective way to give your customers information about your restaurant and a good way to advertise.

Outdoor Advertising
A prominent sign is another way to attract customers.

COMMUNICATING *What are the different types of outdoor advertising you have seen for restaurants?*
Source: Joey Kotfica/Getty Images

In any ad, you should include information about how to get in touch with the restaurant. You may not always have space in the ad to list the hours of operation, your menu, or directions, but you need to let people know how to find out more information about your restaurant.

Word-of-mouth is a type of informal advertising. You can't really pay for it, but most restaurants depend on it. When your guests leave your operation happy with their experience, they will tell other people they know to come for a meal. Word-of-mouth advertising is not automatically positive, but it is almost always one of the most powerful types of advertising. Restaurant reviews are a type of word-of-mouth advertising.

A restaurant's website is a form of advertising. It can educate potential customers, providing a history of the restaurant, photographs of the interior, directions, information about the chef, the restaurant's philosophy, and its menu. It can also provide information about upcoming events and allow online reservations.

Most restaurants today have a social media plan. This might include a Facebook page, a blog, and tweets from the chef or a representative of the restaurant. Special promotions might be announced on the Facebook page as a way to encourage people to visit it frequently.

Promoting Sometimes, you need to do more than just advertising to get people interested in your restaurant. These extra steps aimed at filling up the dining room are known as **promotion** and are often quite innovative. One example of promoting a restaurant might be to have a booth or stall at the county fair. Another way might be to include money-off coupons in your advertising. Or, you might decide to participate in a charity event. Promotional efforts can be as simple as having a special deal every Tuesday evening, such as "buy one main course and get a second one free." Promotional events can also be original and community-minded, such as having the entire kitchen staff volunteer to work at a local soup kitchen. This type of promotional effort is often referred to as **public relations**, which is the effort to maintain a positive opinion of the restaurant in the public's view.

Marketing Plan Many restaurants prepare a **marketing plan**, a plan of the restaurant's overall marketing and promotion efforts. A restaurant's initial marketing plan is typically incorporated in the business plan. Once

Marketing Plan

1. **Market Description**
   a. **Market Demographics:** Describes the restaurant's customers, including the number of customers and percentage of families, couples, and individuals; this also includes geographic information about customers.
   b. **Customers' Needs and Wants:** What type of restaurant is it? Why do customers come to the restaurant (for business, leisure, price, family meals, breakfast, lunch, dinner, 24-hour service, special dietary concerns, etc.)?
   c. **Market Trends:** What kinds of local, regional, and larger trends are likely to influence customers' dining choices?
   d. **Competitors:** Describes competitors (local and national), including prices, ambience, service, marketing, etc.
   e. **SWOT Analysis:** The restaurant performs a SWOT analysis in which it analyzes its **S**trengths, **W**eaknesses, **O**pportunities, and **T**hreats.

2. **Marketing Strategy**
   a. **Mission:** What is the mission of the restaurant? This is usually stated in one sentence.
   b. **Marketing Objectives:** What will the restaurant's marketing accomplish in terms of customers, both new and existing?
   c. **Financial Objectives:** What are the objectives of the restaurant in terms of its revenue and profits?
   d. **Target Markets:** What markets will the restaurant target? Most restaurants target more than one market. (These target markets are sometimes referred to as *market segments*.)
   e. **Positioning:** How will the restaurant position itself in relation to the competition (both in terms of products—the actual food it serves—and in terms of its service)?

   f. **Marketing Mix:** How will the restaurant reach its target market(s)? What kinds of advertising does it intend to use? What kinds of promotion? What kinds of social media will it use (Facebook, website, Twitter, blog, etc.)?
   g. **Marketing Calendar:** A marketing calendar shows the intended marketing and promotional events, when the event is scheduled, and the cost of the effort. Often the calendar will also show the contact names for the marketing effort and the significant dates involved in its implementation.
   h. **Market Research:** Typically, a restaurant will perform some sort of market research (if only to ask customers their opinion of their meal).

3. **Financials**
   a. **Sales Forecast:** An existing restaurant can forecast its sales based on its previous sales. Sales forecasts are often broken out by meals (breakfast, lunch, dinner, if applicable) and by month. In addition to using the records of sales over the past year, a restaurant might adjust its sales forecast based on planned changes to the operation. For example, a restaurant that increased its marketing and promotions efforts might expect its sales to increase by a specific percentage. A new dining area might also be a good reason to adjust the sales forecast.
   b. **Marketing Expenses:** Although the marketing calendar shows the cost of each marketing and promotional effort, the marketing expenses are often shown on a month-by-month basis. There may be a direct relation between a particular marketing effort and the sales forecast.

the restaurant is in business, a marketing plan is often generated annually. It outlines how the restaurant plans to market and promote itself over the course of the year and sets up a budget to accomplish that plan.

READING CHECKPOINT *What is a brand?*

Reading Income Statements

Running a business properly means keeping track of your sales and expenses. A record of your profit and loss is known as an **income statement**, or you may hear it referred to as a **profit and loss statement** (often referred to simply as a **P&L**). This statement collects information about the money coming into the restaurant (its **sales**) and the money being spent by the restaurant (its **expenses**). The P&L then calculates whether the business is making money or losing money.

You will often hear business owners refer to the **bottom line**. What they are talking about is this: the amount of money they have left after they have paid all the bills—that is, after they have subtracted the expenses from their sales. A restaurant has many different expenses. Some of them, such as the cost of food and beverages, are obvious. Others, such as the cost of having garbage hauled away or having to do some repairs to the air conditioning in the dining room, for example, are not so obvious.

In a business, the **assets** are things the business owns. These include raw ingredients, of course, but also such things as cash on hand, chairs, large equipment, signs, carpets, appliances, and even china. **Liabilities** (lie-a-BILL-i-ties) are losses that occur when a restaurant business uses up assets without making a profit..

A restaurant's sales represent the money spent in the restaurant by customers. This is also referred to as the restaurant's **revenue**. You calculate **profit** by subtracting expenses (such as the cost of raw ingredients or labor) from the sales (money received from customers). An income statement shows this basic equation:

$$\text{Sales} - \text{Expenses} = \text{Profit}$$

If there are too many expenses and not enough sales, the restaurant will eventually fail. A successful restaurant, on the other hand, is able to successfully minimize expenses and maximize profits.

The food you buy to prepare is one of a restaurant's expenses. Anything you need to spend money on to run the business is an expense. Your chef might mention the kitchen's raw food cost to you. Remember from Section 21.2 that the raw food cost is the cost of all the ingredients that go into a dish. So the raw food cost for the entire restaurant is the cost of all the ingredients that go into all of the dishes on the menu.

The raw food cost is a measurement of how much you are spending on food, compared to the amount of money your customers are spending in the restaurant. The raw food cost is usually expressed as a percentage. Some owners use a menu pricing method that indicates what an acceptable raw food cost percentage is. They may even include this percentage in their business plan. Most restaurant managers certainly watch this percentage and try to control it. Knowing what your raw food costs are is important if you want to make improvements in the bottom line.

Dropping from a 40 percent raw food cost to a 35 percent raw food cost will improve profits.

Food costs are a type of expense that can vary from one day, week, month, or year to the next. They are an example of a **variable cost** (also called a *variable expense*). That means that the amount you spend changes from time to time. A **fixed cost** (also called a *fixed expense*), on the other hand, is the same from one month to the next. Your lease or insurance payment is an example of a fixed cost.

A restaurant manager should always try to control variable costs. This means the manager will ask the staff to try to get the most they can from everything the restaurant pays for. For example, the manager will make sure that food isn't left out to spoil or that new food deliveries are put away behind the older items so you don't have to throw out food that has become too old to serve. (Remember from Section 1.2 that this is called the *"First In, First Out,"* or *"FIFO,"* system.) Turning ovens on when you need them rather than simply turning them on in the morning and letting them run until you turn out the lights at night is another way you can keep variable expenses in check. This is also known as **cost control**.

In addition to variable expenses, a restaurant owner or manager must keep an eye on fixed costs. For example, the owner or manager needs to account for such things as the cost of owning, renting, or leasing the property, as well as services that may be required (such as a linen service that delivers uniforms and table linens or a pest management service).

Just as there are fixed and variable costs at a restaurant, there are potentially other sources of income as well. Of course, the sale of food and beverages to customers typically generates the biggest income for a restaurant. However, some restaurants find other ways to add income opportunities. For example, restaurants sometimes offer an on- or off-premises catering service. These other sources of income can sometimes be good ways to add to the profit at a restaurant.

Requirements for a Catering Business

- Enough equipment, kitchen staff, and wait staff so catering doesn't interfere with the regular business of the restaurant
- State and/or local catering licenses
- Appropriate insurance for catering events
- Mention of the catering business in the restaurant's advertising (or separate ads for the catering business)
- Computerized record system so manager can easily access past catering jobs and repeat an event that occurs on a regular basis
- Dedicated catering/events planning manager

FIGURE 23–7

Catering for Added Income

A restaurant can cater parties or host special events to increase income.

SOLVING PROBLEMS *What types of parties or events might a restaurant cater or host?*

Source: Dave Bartruff/Corbis Images

 **READING CHECKPOINT** *What basic equation does an income statement show?*

23.1 ASSESSMENT

Reviewing Concepts

1. What does a business plan typically include?
2. What are three things you need to find out about early in the process of planning and running a restaurant?
3. What is a brand?
4. What basic equation does an income statement show?

Critical Thinking

5. **Comparing/Contrasting** What is the difference between a variable cost and a fixed cost? Provide examples.
6. **Comparing/Contrasting** What is the difference between profit and sales?
7. **Applying Concepts** If your sales in a month were $150,000 and your expenses were $124,500, what would be your profit?

Test Kitchen

Divide into four teams. Each team will create a mission statement for a new restaurant and cook a signature main course that fits the mission statement. Evaluate the results as if you were a banker deciding whether to give a loan to a new restaurant business.

CULINARY MATH

Business Plans

Using the Internet, research the ready-to-use business plans that are based on such software programs as Microsoft Excel or Quick-Books. Report on two of these. If you were a small-restaurant owner, would you feel comfortable using this sort of program?

PROJECT 23 You are now ready to work on Project 23, "Creating a Business Plan," which is available in "My Culinary Lab" or in your Student's Lab Resources and Study Guide manual.

Purchasing and Inventorying

Key Concepts

- Using basic purchasing principles
- Preparing inventories

Vocabulary

- bid
- continuous inventory
- farm-to-table restaurant
- formal buying process
- informal buying process
- intermediary source
- inventory
- market quote
- order
- par-stock list
- perpetual inventory
- physical inventory
- primary source
- producer
- product specifications
- production record
- purveyor
- supplier
- vendor

Basic Purchasing Principles

Purchasing the items a restaurant needs is a big job. It is much more than simply placing an order or picking up a product at the store.

Restaurants purchase the items they need to stay in business in different ways. They can buy the same product from different places. They can buy in bulk or buy just what they need for a day or two. The challenge is determining which vendor has the quality the restaurant requires, at the best price, and who can deliver it on time.

Basic Steps of Purchasing The buyer at a restaurant needs to understand the basic steps in the purchasing process. The typical purchasing process involves five steps (summarized on the next page). After items are ordered, the vendor sends them to the restaurant, where they are formally received and stored properly.

Step 1: Creating a Par-Stock List A par-stock list is a list of the quantity of supplies you need to have on hand in the restaurant to make every item on your menu for a specified amount of time. For example, if you had deliveries once a week, your par-stock amount would be the amount you needed to make every item on your menu for that week.

Usually, a small extra amount is added to the par-stock list as a type of cushion, or protection, against unexpected needs for items. The size of this extra amount depends on a number of factors: how busy the restaurant is, any special events that might change the level of business, or

Source: B. and E. Dudzinscy/Fotolia

Basic Steps in the Purchasing Process

1. Create a par-stock list (a list of required goods).

2. Write the purchase specifications for each item, including the quantity and the acceptable conditions for the item.

3. Select one or more suppliers.

4. Obtain the price quotes or bids from different suppliers.

5. Place the order with one or more suppliers. Ordering can be done verbally, in writing, or on the Internet.

the time between deliveries. The more information you have about how well a dish sells and how many customers you usually have, the more accurate your par-stock lists will be.

To help with purchasing decisions, large kitchens, especially those at schools and other state- or federally funded institutions, use a **production record**. This is a record of all the food served at every meal in the institution. It includes an indication of the recipe of an item (if appropriate), the serving size, the portions planned, the total prepared, the time the product was completed, its temperature, the temperature at serving, any corrective action required, amount of leftovers, and comments (such as how well the item was liked). A production record also helps managers plan day to day, as well as in communicating plans to the staff.

Step 2: Writing Purchase Specifications Buying exactly what you need is one of the ways you can improve quality as well as profits. If you are the person doing the purchasing for the restaurant, you must write out an exact description of each product the restaurant needs. To let the vendor know the specific product the restaurant wants, you use **product specifications**. Many factors affect food prices. These specifications precisely describe the product you expect. Each specification can affect the price of the product. It might include only a product's brand name or it might include many details, as shown in the table at the top of page 801.

Specifying the intended use is considered the most important product specification. For instance, you may need chicken for two different dishes. The first dish might require boneless, skinless chicken breast portions to make a chicken piccata main course. The second dish might require a whole stewing chicken for your chicken soup.

Some product specifications are not as obvious. For example, product specifications may detail how the product is supposed to be delivered.

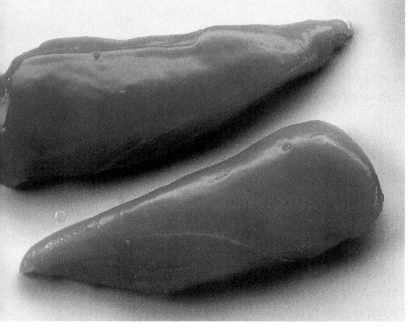

FIGURE 23–8

Purchase Specifications
Boneless, skinless chicken breasts can be the most expensive cut of chicken.

PREDICTING *What might happen to your food costs if you receive boneless skinless chicken breasts instead of bone-in chicken thighs with the skin on?*

Source: Clive Streeter, Dorling Kindersley Limited

800 Unit 5 *Culinary Management*

Writing Product Specifications: Possible Details

- Intended use of the product
- Exact name of the product
- Product's brand name
- U.S. quality grade
- Point of origin (where did it come from?)
- Color (example: red, green, or yellow bell peppers)
- Size information
- Acceptable waste (maximum amount of waste you will tolerate)
- Degree of ripeness
- Production standards (examples: farm-raised vs. wild-caught, organic vs. conventional)
- Preservation and/or processing method

- Expiration date
- Package size
- Type of packaging
- Packaging procedure (example: wrapped individually vs. being tossed into the container)
- Cost limitations (if above a certain price, the product is not acceptable)
- Approved substitutes (if the desired product is not available or priced too high)
- General instructions (delivery method, credit terms, allowable number of returns or stock outages)
- Bidding procedures (if being submitted for a bid)
- Inspection procedures (how the product will be inspected when it is received)

You might specify that frozen goods must be delivered in good condition and at a temperature that maintains quality and safety.

The type of product specification you use will depend on your suppliers and how long you have been specifying a particular product. However, the more detail in your product specifications, the better. You may have your own unique specifications related to quality, color, size, or ripeness. There are also specifications associated with many goods that get quality grades from the U.S. Department of Agriculture (USDA), such as those shown in the following Sample Product Specifications table.

Sample Product Specifications

Product	Specification
◀ Peach	Fresh peach. 84 count, small 2⅛" diameter. Fruit shall be firm, not hard, with a yellowish cast rather than distinctly green.
Polish Dill Pickles	U.S. grade 8 or better. Whole pickles. Uniform in size and shape. Size of each medium pickle is 2¾" to 3½". Firm, crisp texture. No soft or hollow centers. Free from objectionable odors.
Beef Patty	U.S. Grade Beef Good or better. Not to exceed 25 percent fat. 2.67 oz. patty, with 6 patties per pound. No soy, meat by-products, binders, or extenders. Meat shall be free from bone. Meets Institutional Meat Purchase Specification #1136.
White Bread	Loaf. Pullman sandwich sliced, with 16 slices per pound. From enriched flour. Must contain 62 percent total solids. Weight of each slice must be 28 grams or 1 ounce.

Source: bajinda/Fotolia

The Influence of Dieter Schorner

Chef Dieter Schorner grew up in a small mining town in Germany. He and his three siblings were raised by their mother, after their father died in World War II, and they lived with little money and few material possessions. He saw that his classmates had things that he could only dream of, and in hopes of buying a pair of skis or ice skates, he took a job salting pretzels in a local bakery. The owner of the bakery convinced Chef Schorner's mother to send him for an apprenticeship away from home, where he worked long, hard hours.

When Chef Schorner's grandmother died, she left him money that he used to move to Basel, Switzerland. As a young boy, he had been given Hershey's chocolates by American soldiers, and these memories inspired him to attend school for chocolate. After five years, he returned to Germany to work in The Konig Café, which he still holds high as the best café he has ever encountered.

Chef Schorner eventually found himself in London, as the Pastry Chef at the famous Savoy Hotel. After four years in London and a brief stay in Washington, D.C., he began working for Sirius Maccioni, the legendary restaurant owner, at Le Cirque in New York City. It was at this time that Chef Schorner was credited with introducing the iconic dessert *crème*

brûlée to the United States. He worked at Le Cirque for three years, then spent another year working at Tavern on the Green. Chef Schorner has a wealth of stories from his days at these restaurants, like preparing Salvadore Dali's favorite dessert (*Brûléed* grapefruit) or cooking for the Queen of England.

Back in Washington, D.C., Chef Schorner opened Patisserie Café Didier, which became hugely successful and well-respected among the capitol elite. Unfortunately, such great success lead to a higher cost of running the business, and the café eventually closed. In 1996, Chef Schorner became the Chairman of the Pastry Department at the French Culinary Insitute, and three years later joined the faculty of The Culinary Institute of America, where he remains to this day.

Chef Schorner says that he envies students who have the opportunity study for a world class education, and he inspires his students to work hard and learn as much as possible. Even with more than 50 years of experience, he considers his students to be among his greatest influences, and says that one of the greatest things he can imagine is for his students to be even better chefs than he is himself.

Dieter Schorner

Source: Courtesy of Dieter Shorner & Culinary Institute of America

Step 3: Selecting Suppliers A restaurant can buy food from many sources. The person or business selling you something may be known by one of the following terms: **supplier**, **vendor**, **purveyor** (puhr-VAY-er), or **producer**. Some suppliers offer a large number of items. Others specialize in a specific type of product.

Many restaurants have begun buying food from a **primary source**, the farm that produces the product, eliminating an **intermediary source** and retailors, who process or distribute an original food product before it gets to the restaurant. A restaurant that buys food directly from farms producing food (vegetables, meat, etc.) is sometimes called a **farm-to-table restaurant**.

You can find suppliers for a particular product by asking other restaurant owners where they buy their goods. You can also search on the Internet. Some vendors are best for large quantities or items you want to purchase in bulk. Others are best for items that are difficult to find.

A supplier will give the restaurant a product list and a delivery schedule. Review the product lists and delivery schedules carefully. If you know that you want organic, free-range chicken, for example, and the supplier doesn't carry that sort of chicken, you will need to locate another supplier. Or, if a supplier delivers only on Mondays and your restaurant is closed that day, you may need to find someone else.

Some restaurants find it easier to deal with a small number of suppliers. They try to find suppliers that offer a wide range of products, from produce to paper goods. However, many restaurants develop primary and secondary suppliers. Restaurants order most of a particular product from their primary supplier, but order some of the product from their secondary supplier. This allows the restaurant to have an established business relationship to turn

FIGURE 23–9
Farm-to-Table
Many restaurants are choosing to become farm-to-table restaurants, buying produce and meat directly from farms.
PREDICTING *Why do you think restaurants might choose a farm-to-table orientation?*
Source: Alexander Raths/Fotolia

Chef's Tip

Grocery Stores

Retail prices for foods at grocery stores are typically higher than those from a supplier. It makes good business sense to buy items at a grocery store only in an emergency.

Questions to Ask Potential Suppliers

- Are deliveries made when you need them (specific days, weekends)?
- What are their credit terms?
- What is their minimum order?
- What is the lead time for placing an order?
- Will they call in advance to notify about shortages?
- Will deliveries be disrupted if there are labor disputes?
- Do they place items in the walk-in coolers or freezers?
- Do they break cases (or do you have to buy full cases)?
- Do they honor competitor's prices?
- What are the return policies?

to for a product if one supplier has an issue (food safety issue, equipment problems, fire, hurricane or storms, labor issues, etc.). Most restaurants that develop primary and secondary suppliers ask the suppliers to agree not to buy or pack their products at each other's facilities or supply each other with raw material. Otherwise, if there were an issue at one, it affects both the primary and the secondary supplier.

Step 4: Obtaining Market Quotes and Bids

Once you have written your par-stock list and your purchase specifications, you can ask suppliers to give you market quotes. A **market quote** is a statement of the product's selling price and an indication of the length of time that the price will be effective. The length of time the market quote is in effect depends on the product. Some foods have prices that change a great deal from week to week. Most fresh produce, meat, and poultry falls into this category. Some products, such as canned and paper goods, have the same price week in and week out. Be sure to take note of the effective dates on the market quote.

A **bid** is essentially a proposal from the supplier, telling you the price the supplier will charge you if you accept the supplier's proposal. A bid can be affected by business factors. For example, if your restaurant buys in bulk, a supplier may give you a bid at a lower price per pound than would be charged for a smaller amount. Suppliers you have not used before might offer lower bids than usual in an attempt to persuade you to try their products. In an **informal buying process**, the person in charge of buying evaluates the various proposals and makes the choice of which to buy.

Schools, hospitals, and other governmental or nonprofit institutions often must use a **formal buying process** for large purchases. This involves sending out a formal Invitation to Bid and making sure that the bidding process is conducted in a way that provides full and open competition. Potential suppliers submit sealed bids, which are opened in public at the same time. The contract is awarded to the supplier who can meet the conditions of the bid at the lowest price.

Step 5: Placing Orders

An **order** is a communication between a buyer (the restaurant) and a seller (the supplier). The restaurant tells the supplier the name of the product the restaurant wants (based on the restaurant's purchase specifications and the supplier's product list) and the amount of that product that the restaurant needs.

To fill out an order properly, you need to know the unit for the product. Some foods are sold by the piece, so you may simply give a number. For example, you might order 5 legs of lamb.

Other foods are sold in cases, cartons, crates, bags, or boxes. Be sure to review the description of the packaging in the supplier's product list. Different suppliers may sell the same item in different units. A case of lettuce from one supplier may weigh 50 pounds, whereas a case of lettuce from another supplier may weigh 20 pounds. Both

FIGURE 23–10

Units of Carrots

Carrots from this supplier come in large bags that weigh many pounds.

DRAWING CONCLUSIONS *How many pounds would you guess are in these bags?*

Source: Culinary Institute of America

would be listed in the supplier's product list as a case, but you would need to notice that each of the individual cases has a different weight.

Ordering food and other items for a restaurant can be time consuming. In very large operations, ordering may be the job of a single individual or even a group of individuals. To be certain you do the job effectively and are following good business practices, you should have the following information to place your order:

- Par-stock list
- Product specifications
- Inventory
- Suppliers and their product lists
- Suppliers' market quotes or bids

One of the ways that restaurants manage the purchasing process more efficiently is by using software and the Internet. Some software links inventory, par-stock lists, and menus so that parts of the work are done automatically.

Purchasing managers need to be aware of ethical issues related to purchasing. In the United States, gratuities are not ethical, and, in a formal bidding process, could be illegal. However, for those restaurants that might purchase goods from international vendors, some form of gratuity might be expected. It is important to be aware of these expectations and explicitly indicate what your company's position is in relation to your international vendors' expectations.

 **READING CHECKPOINT** *What are the five basic steps in the purchasing process?*

FIGURE 23–11
Managing Orders and Inventory
Using a computer program to track orders and inventory.
DRAWING CONCLUSIONS *How could purchase and inventory software help improve the ordering process?*
Source: Benjamin Haas/Fotolia

Inventories

An **inventory** is a list of all the assets in the restaurant, usually organized by category. The par-stock list is a list of what you think you should have on hand. An inventory is an exact count of what is actually on hand. You calculate the amount of stock you need to order by subtracting the current inventory from the amount shown on the par-stock list.

Par-Stock List – Inventory = Amount to Order

Taking a **physical inventory** means actually counting up what you have. For instance, you need to count all the cans of tomato sauce, all the boxes of pasta, all the cases of paper towels, and all the 3-ounce ladles in the restaurant. This is a time-consuming but very important part of running a restaurant. Without an accurate inventory, you won't know when you are low on something or when you have so much that you are wasting space to store it. A very exact physical inventory is taken as often as necessary. Some restaurants may take a physical inventory on a weekly basis and some may do it monthly.

For a small restaurant, inventory-taking usually means people with clipboards count cans, boxes, bags, and individual items. A larger restaurant's inventory may be managed completely on a computer, especially if every product has a barcode. For its financial records, a restaurant sometimes must calculate the dollar value of its inventory. If the inventory is managed on a computer, this is relatively easy and can be accomplished by using the inventory program. In a small restaurant this can be a more time-consuming job. For each inventory item you would need to multiply the price of a single item by the number of items in the inventory.

Many large restaurants today use a **perpetual** or **continuous inventory** system in which information about inventory quantity and availability is computerized and updated on a continuous basis. The inventory system is connected to the order-entry system and the production record.

Even though they may be computerized, any inventory system can be vulnerable to overstatements (phantom inventory) and understatements (missing inventory) that can result from theft, breakage, or scanning errors. Both overstatements and understatements can lead to errors in replenishing the inventory. Additionally, if consistent understatements are occurring, the restaurant may be suffering from systematic pilfering, which is both an ethical concern and a drain on the restaurant's profits.

 **READING CHECKPOINT** *What is a physical inventory?*

23.2 ASSESSMENT

Reviewing Concepts

1. What are the five basic steps in the purchasing process?

2. What is a physical inventory?

Critical Thinking

3. Compare and Contrast What is the difference between a par-stock list and an inventory?

4. Drawing Conclusions Why is a par-stock list important for a restaurant?

5. Inferring Why would a supplier indicate the length of time for which a market quote is effective?

6. Inferring What type of event might require that you add a small extra amount of items to your par-stock list?

7. Drawing Conclusions Why would you obtain market quotes from multiple suppliers?

Test Kitchen

Divide into four teams. Each team will choose three main courses and three appetizers to put on a menu for a small restaurant. Assume that the restaurant serves only these dishes to only 30 people a night, with the dishes evenly balanced. Construct a par-stock list, assuming that there are three days between deliveries. Ask another team to evaluate your list.

SCIENCE

Restaurant Suppliers

Using the Internet, research three restaurant suppliers for a specific hard-to-find food. Identify what each supplier's specialty is. Check to see if they have an online product list or list of their delivery schedules.

Managing a Restaurant

Key Concepts

- Understanding facility layout and design
- Managing a restaurant
- Managing people

Vocabulary

- Fair Labor Standards Act (FLSA)
- job description
- orientation
- performance evaluation
- sexual harassment
- termination
- training
- verbal warning
- written warning

Facility Layout and Design

The layout of a restaurant depends on factors related to safety and cleanliness. A restaurant manager starts thinking about sanitation during the design layout process. For example, there must be enough space to effectively clean each of the restaurant's areas. The materials used in the building should be easy to clean and maintain. Any equipment, such as blenders or mixers, should be easy to clean and easy to take apart for cleaning.

The health codes that affect the operation of a foodservice establishment are found at all levels of government, including federal and state laws as well as local and city ordinances. Restaurant owners and managers must be familiar with all the legal requirements that apply to a restaurant. The manager also has to ensure that the staff know and understand the rules as well.

All areas in a restaurant have to meet sanitary standards and health regulations. If the restaurant does not meet these standards, the restaurant could be fined.

Kitchen The kitchen usually takes up about one-third of the restaurant's entire floor space. For any commercial kitchen, there are laws about cleanliness. Any surfaces that come into contact with food must be smooth, nontoxic, nonabsorbent, free from crevices, and free from sharp corners and edges.

As you know from Section 3.1, the floor plan of the kitchen should allow for good work flow. People need to move around easily between work areas. You may need areas reserved for baking and pastry work or an area where fish and meat are

Source: Bruce Ayres/Getty Images

FIGURE 23–12

Managing the Facility
Properly disposing of garbage is part of keeping the operation running smoothly and safely.

COGNITIVE SKILLS/ INTERACTIONS *Apart from appearance, why should dumpsters have lids?*

Source: Pearson Education/PH College

butchered. These areas may require special refrigeration, baking, or cooking equipment. The area should be selected with an eye to the amount of work being done and the skills of the staff.

Food Storage Areas Food storage typically includes a walk-in refrigerator, a walk-in freezer, and a dry storage area. It is important to make sure that the walk-in refrigerator and freezer are relatively new and functioning properly because a refrigeration failure can lead to significant losses. In areas where the loss of electricity is common, many restaurants use a generator that automatically powers on if the electricity goes off. Storage space is usually in a corner or a far wall of the kitchen, often near the manager's office. This makes it more secure and less prone to theft. There also has to be enough room near the food storage area so kitchen staff can receive and inspect incoming products. Some larger kitchens have a special receiving area with a door and an outside dock allowing easy access for deliveries.

Waste Management The waste management system is a critically important part of the kitchen. A lot of trash is created during the food preparation process. Trash containers should be leak-free, pest-proof, and easy to clean and sanitize. The trash containers should be covered when not in use and should be cleaned frequently (inside and out). Of course, you must regularly get rid of the trash, using a public or private hauler.

Office The manager's office is usually as small as possible, while still being large enough to seat the manager and a visitor or two, when necessary. It should be in a secure place in the building, away from the employee area, the dining room, and the major noise of the kitchen.

Employee Area Somewhere near the kitchen, an area is usually reserved for employees to change into uniforms, congregate, keep their personal items, and hang their coats. This is also the area where important information, such as work schedules and managerial policies, is communicated to the staff. The employee area is usually located near the kitchen. It may also include storage areas for cleaning products as well as for all the linens for the tables.

Dining Room A restaurant manager faces many decisions when designing a restaurant. Will the restaurant use tables or booths? Will it be tightly packed, holding as many customers as possible, or more open, which could potentially reduce profitability by limiting the number of patrons the room can hold? What will the color scheme be? Will it have a classic look or be more contemporary? Answering these questions (and hundreds more) will determine your customers' dining experience and your restaurant's profitability.

Balancing the Cash Register

Typically, at the end of the day the restaurant owner or manager balances the cash register. This involves accounting for starting cash on-hand and tracking that day's sales. Then, the next day's starting cash on-hand is put back in the cash drawer and stored for the next day's service. Additional cash is deposited at a bank, along with checks (if the restaurant takes checks; many don't).

Many restaurants use a form such as the one shown below to track the day's sales. Credit card slips, cash register receipts, and any other significant accounts of the day's sales or transactions are stapled to the form. The forms, with all their attachments, are then filed by date.

Date: _____

Preparer: _____

Deposit

Cash	$ 564.67
Checks	$ 0.00
AMEX	$ 1,006.58
Visa	$ 594.45
MasterCard	$ 870.21
Discover	$ 68.79
Store Credit	$ 0.00
Other	$ 0.00
Starting Cash On-Hand (Subtract This)	($ 200.00)
Deposit Total	$ _____

Cash Paid Out

Returns	$ 0.00
Voids	$ 64.69
Paid Out	$ 132.00
Other	$ 0.00
Total Cash Paid Out	$ _____

Total Sales
(Add Deposit Total
& Total Cash Paid Out) $ _____

Sales Tax Collected
(Sales Tax Percent (07%)
× Total Sales) $ _____

Register Reading $ 3,117.50

Difference
(+ Is Over/− Is Short) $ _____

Computation

Compute the five blank totals and write them on a separate sheet of paper. Note that this restaurant is in a locality with a 7 percent sales tax.

Having more customers typically means more profit. However, the dining room cannot be completely full of tables. Not only would that be unpleasant for diners, it is also illegal. There are capacity limits that restrict how many people a room will hold. The restaurant manager must be aware of those limits, which are usually laid out in the fire code for the building. Enclosed spaces and partitions can create private areas in the dining room that can allow large parties and banquets. In most cases, a combination of booths, tables, and private spaces offers the best chance to maximize revenue.

The dining room will need to allow adequate space for the wait staff, who must navigate through the dining room with ease and speed. If the tables are arranged too closely together, or if there is not a clear path to the

FIGURE 23–13

Dining Rooms

Clear paths around the tables and through the dining room improve service.

PREDICTING *How might a restaurant's theme influence the number of tables and their positions in a dining room?*

Source: Steve Mason/Getty Images

kitchen, your wait staff will have difficulty performing their jobs. A dining room should have a natural flow.

Finally, all public accommodations, from seating arrangements to restrooms, must meet the standards of the Americans with Disabilities Act. This means providing adequate space and accessibility for people with special needs (for example, wheelchair-accessible restrooms). It is illegal for public establishments to deny service to customers with disabilities.

Bar Not all restaurants have a bar, but many restaurants find that a bar fits into the concept of the restaurant and enhances profitability. If a restaurant has a bar with seating for patrons, then the bar must be capable of standing alone as a destination for any dining experience your restaurant offers. This means that the bar staff must be trained to serve meals in the bar. A bar must be visually inviting and clean, and its arrangement should highlight the products the bar is selling.

Entrance The entrance is the first, and the last, impression a customer will have of your restaurant. It needs to represent the essence of your restaurant. It has to be large enough for people to congregate if there's a wait, but it shouldn't take too much space away from the profit-making areas of the restaurant. There is often a coat room near the entrance. Above all else, your entrance area needs to be inviting. It should offer a glimpse of the excitement in the restaurant and encourage guests to enter.

Restrooms It is easy to overlook the importance of the restrooms. Your guests are very likely to visit the restroom. The overall experience must provide a feeling of cleanliness and reflect the overall restaurant experience. It should be large enough to accommodate multiple guests.

Restaurants are required by law to have working hand-washing stations in both the public restrooms and the employees' restrooms. This means there must be hot and cold running water, soap, something for drying hands, and a waste container. The public restrooms must be clearly marked and be in a convenient location within the restaurant.

READING CHECKPOINT *Name at least three areas in a restaurant besides the kitchen and dining room.*

Managing a Restaurant

Being the manager of a restaurant is a demanding job. You work long hours, often late at night and on weekends and holidays. You must deal with stressful situations and manage people under time pressure. It's definitely not a job for everyone, but it can be rewarding when everything goes well and your guests are happy with the meals your restaurant serves them.

Each of the 10 qualities of an effective restaurant manager listed on the right are discussed at length below.

Responsible Restaurant managers are responsible for *every* aspect of a restaurant. If the restaurant is short-handed, a restaurant manager must roll up his or her sleeves and work alongside the employees. This means you may have to wash dishes or take out the garbage—you need to do whatever needs to be done to make your restaurant a success!

Ultimately, if anything goes wrong in the restaurant, it is the restaurant manager's responsibility. You must be willing to assume full responsibility for the mistakes and shortcomings of your staff. If someone makes a mistake or demonstrates incompetence, you must consider that your failure and take responsibility for the problem. Then you need to take steps to make sure the problem is corrected and not repeated.

Good Communicator One of the critical factors in the success of a restaurant involves communication between the manager and the employees. A good manager knows each member of the staff and communicates with each person individually. The manager communicates the expectations for each worker and offers the chance for each worker to check in periodically to talk about how the job is going.

Managers need to be aware not only of how they communicate with employees, but also how employees communicate with each other and with the customers. Everyone works better when they feel that they are being treated professionally and with dignity. Failure to communicate properly can also have legal implications. Using profanity, ethnic slurs, or any type of abusive language is a serious concern. Managers need to be aware of what is appropriate and let their employees know what are considered the best practices for the restaurant. One important aspect of communication skills is the ability to listen to your employees and to your customers.

Managers must also be able to write effectively. They often need to write letters, menus, e-mails, catering or event proposals, advertisements, newsletters, training materials, and other business documents. It is important that they understand grammar and use it effectively.

Decisive Managers often need to make a decision quickly and then follow through on that decision immediately, directing their staff quickly and efficiently. Managers who waver when making a decision show that

10 Qualities of an Effective Restaurant Manager

- Responsible
- Good Communicator
- Decisive
- Detail Oriented
- Customer Focused
- Cost Aware
- Adaptable
- Calm
- Consistent
- Knowledgeable
- Self-Motivated

FIGURE 23–14

Communicating
The manager and chef must keep lines of communication open.
COMMUNICATION SKILLS/ INTERACTIONS *Why is it important that the chef and manager communicate about the menu?*
Source: Culinary Institute of America

they are not sure of themselves. This can undermine their ability to lead their staff. Decisiveness and leadership are strongly linked because restaurant managers lead by example. Every decision they make, every action they take, should be a demonstration of the qualities they want to see in their staff. One aspect of being a decisive leader is being able to delegate work effectively and to supervise staff appropriately.

Detail Oriented Nothing should escape the notice of a restaurant manager. You must be able to see the restaurant through the guests' eyes, as well as through the staff's eyes. This means that every detail of the restaurant—food, kitchen staff, service, ambiance, pricing—demands the attention of the restaurant manager. You constantly need to seek ways to improve your guests' experiences and to improve the effectiveness of your staff.

One aspect of being detail oriented is the ability to plan effectively. A successful restaurant manager must be able to plan his or her work well in advance and then work that plan, realizing, however, that at any moment he or she may need to change directions based on new circumstances. A restaurant manager must be involved with maintaining stock and supplies before they are needed to make sure that the items on the menu are available for every service period.

Customer Focused Restaurant managers often say "we serve people, not food." Research has indicated that one of the major reasons people return to a restaurant is because of the service. A restaurant manager's attitude toward guests should serve as an example for the staff.

If a customer has a problem, a restaurant manager treats it as a genuine concern. You and your staff should meet every request with a smile, no matter how difficult or picky the customer may be. A restaurant manager needs to be an expert in conflict resolution, trying to make sure that every guest leaves the restaurant feeling happy and well taken care of.

Another aspect of being customer focused is the concern for your guests' safety. The restaurant manager must pay attention to the safety of the food, maintenance of regulatory requirements, the upkeep of the restaurant building, the front sidewalk, any outside lighting, and even the parking lot. All of this contributes to the customer's good experience.

FIGURE 23–15

Customer Focused
Restaurant managers often say "we serve people, not food."
APPLYING CONCEPTS *What does this slogan mean to you?*
Source: michaeljung/Fotolia

Cost Aware Restaurant managers must be aware of the cost of the food, the staff, and the other costs associated with the restaurant. They need to be sure that the restaurant makes a profit. They need to have a strong knowledge of accounting and maintain accurate records for employees, cash flow, cost of menu items, inventory, and regulatory compliance. They must check to make sure that the cashier has balanced the register correctly, and they have to find the time to do the banking in hours when the restaurant is not open or not busy.

Adaptable A restaurant manager must be able to quickly adjust to changing circumstances, understanding the implications of the change and adjusting goals and strategies accordingly. A restaurant manager cannot afford to hold on to the way it should be; he or she must realize what is happening in the moment, what the current reality is, and act accordingly. The manager's adaptability will serve as an example to the staff.

Calm A restaurant manager cannot become frazzled, no matter what happens. He or she must remain calm and determine the best course of action in every situation. The entire restaurant's state of mind depends on the manager. If he or she doesn't stay calm, even in a very difficult situation, the staff will receive the message that it is acceptable to lose patience, shout, and blame others.

Consistent If a manager is inconsistent, it will be difficult for the staff to take individual action. They simply won't know what to do. In a business as fluid as the restaurant business, it is important to establish as many consistent procedures as possible. That way, they will know exactly what to do without being told in normal circumstances; the staff will also understand that when change does happen, it is a deviation from the normal way of doing things.

It is important for a restaurant manager to treat individuals at the same level on the staff in a consistent way. Obviously, every employee is different and must, to some extent, be treated in a way that recognizes his or her individuality. However, in terms of a manager's formal expectations for staff at the same level, failing to be consistent will be seen as a type of favoritism and will eventually demoralize the staff. A restaurant manager must be fair, consistent, and understanding with staff. You need to motivate staff, praising them when work is done well and training them to do a better job if there is a problem.

Knowledgeable It is critically important for the restaurant manager to know all aspects of his or her restaurant. This includes not only knowing the menu and the prices of items, but also being able to recognize when a dish is properly or improperly made, knowing how each dish tastes, and being able to describe the differences in dishes.

For example, if a manager personally doesn't like raw oysters, he or she should still be able to discuss with a customer the differences between the various oysters offered by the restaurant, recognize when the oysters have been shucked properly, and notice if the oysters are accompanied by the sauce chosen by the customer. If the oyster shucker has called in sick that night and no one is available to shuck oysters, the manager might be required to show another staff member how to shuck the oysters (especially because live oysters are very perishable and are fairly expensive), so it is important that the manager have the skills necessary to perform the task and to teach it to someone else if need be.

Oyster
Source: Lev/Fotolia

The more a manager knows about each staff job, the more he or she can appreciate what each member of the staff does. Managers need to know the staff's schedules, important customers, and all aspects of the building and its maintenance. Ultimately, the more a manager knows, the better he or she will be able to perform the job.

Self-Motivated Finally, restaurant managers must be self-motivated. They may report to an owner or to an executive in charge of the overall hotel or restaurant facility, but there is typically no one telling the manager what to do on a day-to-day basis. A restaurant manager can't motivate others if he or she isn't motivated.

READING CHECKPOINT *What are the 10 qualities of an effective restaurant manager?*

Managing People

A restaurant manager needs to be able to hire, train, supervise, motivate, promote, and, if necessary, fire employees.

Hiring The manager will typically hire, train, and supervise most of the restaurant staff. A restaurant business typically has a high turnover rate. This means that often people do not stay with the establishment for long periods of time. For this reason, the restaurant manager is frequently hiring new employees.

To locate prospective new employees, the manager can choose to place help-wanted ads in the restaurant windows, in local newspapers, or on the Internet. The manager could also rely on word of mouth—letting current workers know that a position is available and then interviewing candidates recommended by them.

If the manager feels that a job applicant may be right for the restaurant, the manager will invite the applicant for an interview. Managers look for three basic things when making most hiring decisions:

- Is the candidate qualified for the job? Does this candidate have the right amount of experience?
- Does the candidate meet the skill standards for the position?
- Is the candidate dependable?

In the hiring process at any business, the manager must always be aware of potential discrimination. Although you do not have to hire unqualified people, you cannot discriminate on the basis of

FIGURE 23–16
Hiring Staff
Offering an applicant the job.
COMMUNICATION SKILLS/ INTERACTIONS *List several questions you think the employer should ask an applicant.*
Source: Culinary Institute of America

race, color, religion, sex, nationality, age, marital status, or disability. For this reason, interview questions related to these areas are strictly off-limits and should never be asked. These sorts of questions can be used as evidence of discrimination, even if the interviewer did not intend them as such. Many mid-size and large restaurants have a written human resources policy that identifies the rights and responsibilities of employers and employees.

A restaurant manager must be knowledgeable about the provisions and requirements of the **Fair Labor Standards Act (FLSA)**. This federal law establishes the minimum wage, overtime pay, and child-labor laws for full- and part-time employees. It also describes when certain types of deductions from wages are appropriate and the method for compensating tipped workers.

Training Each employee should know the **job description** for his or her position. A job description includes the duties to be performed and responsibilities involved, as well as the level of education and training the worker should possess. A job description can even be used during the hiring process when the manager is seeking to fill a position at the restaurant. These are all ways to keep the lines of communication open and to keep workers happy. At many restaurants, managers provide a training manual to each new hire. The manual describes the general policies and procedures of the restaurant.

Any employee hired at a restaurant must undergo orientation and training. During **orientation**, it is important for the employee to learn about the restaurant, including the menu items and the layout. This process teaches new employees about their roles in the organization and about the organization as a whole.

The **training** process allows employees time to learn the job and practice it, usually by on-the-job training through shadowing someone who has the same or a similar position. Additionally, a good manager will have a system for ongoing training so employees can always be involved in the learning process. This lets employees grow and develop new skills and contributes to the overall success of the restaurant.

Supervising As a restaurant manager, you supervise the work of your staff and are ultimately responsible for their work. You set the standards that each employee is expected to maintain. Some standards can be quantifiable—for example, the number of tables to be set or the amount of food to be prepared. Some standards are not as easily quantifiable, such as maintaining good relations with a customer or making sure the kitchen staff treats each other with respect.

To be a good supervisor it is essential that you give clear work instructions, demand good work, and hold your staff accountable. You will need to praise them when work is done correctly and train them if they have problems performing the work.

FIGURE 23–17
Training Staff
Teaching a newly hired waiter
how to use the coffee maker.
APPLYING CONCEPTS *What's the
relationship between job training and job
satisfaction?*
Source: Pearson Education/PH College

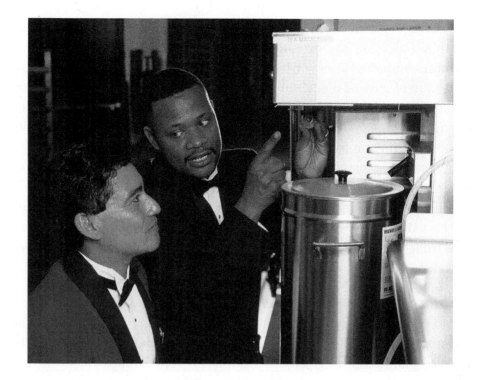

It is important for restaurant managers to be aware of any sort of harassment or violence in the workplace. **Sexual harassment** is the persistent request for sexual favors, unprovoked and unwanted sexual advances, or any verbal or physical harassment of a sexual nature. It can also include offensive comments about a person's sex. Sexual harassment, or any type of disrespectful or violent behavior, can create a hostile or offensive work environment and will be detrimental to the overall functioning of the restaurant. Sexual harassment is also illegal and could lead to fines if the restaurant is found guilty of it over an extended period.

Periodically, the manager will sit down with each employee and conduct a **performance evaluation**. In this meeting, the manager and the employee talk about whether or not the employee has met expectations, based on the job description. It is not uncommon for people to be promoted to more responsible or demanding jobs after they prove themselves capable of performing the job for which they were initially hired.

Disciplining There will come a time when every manager needs to discipline an employee. This usually happens when an employee does not act according to the rules or is not performing up to expectations. Some ways of disciplining an employee include:

- **Verbal Warning.** The manager can give an employee a **verbal warning**. This means that the employee is told about the need for improvement in a particular area.

- **Written Warning.** The manager can give an employee a **written warning**. This means that the manager sits down with the employee to inform the employee of the need for improvement, and this is documented in a letter that is given to the employee and placed in the employee's file.

- **Termination.** If the employee still does not improve, the manager moves to fire the employee. This is often referred to as the **termination** of the employee.

A manager usually allows for a sequence or process of disciplinary measures. For example, an employee who breaks a rule or is not performing may receive a verbal warning for the first offense and a written warning for a second offense, before being terminated.

READING CHECKPOINT *What is sexual harassment?*

23.3 ASSESSMENT

Reviewing Concepts

1. Name at least three areas in a restaurant besides the kitchen and dining room.
2. What are the 10 qualities of an effective restaurant manager?
3. What is sexual harassment?

Critical Thinking

4. **Inferring** Do you think shadowing someone in the same or a similar position would be a good training method? Why?
5. **Drawing Conclusions** Why is orientation important for new employees?
6. **Drawing Conclusions** Why do you think restaurants might have a high turnover rate?
7. **Forming a Model** What qualities do you think are most important for a restaurant manager? Explain your reasoning.
8. **Inferring** Why might using a word-of-mouth method of locating prospective new employees work well?

Test Kitchen

Partner with a class member. Partner 1 plays the role of an experienced employee; partner 2 plays the role of a new employee. Partner 1 will prepare an easy recipe without showing the recipe to partner 2, who will shadow partner 1, asking questions and taking notes as needed. After the dish is completed, partner 2 will describe step-by-step how to make the dish. Compare partner 2's recipe with the actual recipe.

LANGUAGE ARTS
Describing Jobs

Research restaurant employment ads in your local paper or on the Internet. Are similar jobs described in similar ways? Are some jobs made to sound more exciting than other, very similar jobs? Compare 10 ads for similar positions.

Reviewing Content

Choose the letter that best answers the question or completes the statement.

1. The ambience of a restaurant is its
   a. location.
   b. name.
   c. feeling or mood.
   d. type of food.

2. Another name for an income statement is a(n)
   a. assets statement.
   b. profitability statement.
   c. sales statement.
   d. profit and loss statement.

3. The money customers spend in the restaurant is referred to as the restaurant's
   a. sales.
   b. profits.
   c. assets.
   d. bottom line.

4. A variable cost is a cost that
   a. relates only to the cost of ingredients.
   b. changes over time.
   c. relates only to the cost of labor.
   d. does not change over time.

5. A listing of the quantity of supplies you need to have on hand in the restaurant to make every item on the menu is
   a. an inventory.
   b. a physical inventory.
   c. a par-stock list.
   d. the mise en place.

6. A statement of a product's selling price and an indication of the length of time that the price is effective is the
   a. market quote.
   b. par-stock list.
   c. product specifications.
   d. product list.

7. When restaurant owners talk about the bottom line, they are talking about
   a. sales.
   b. expenses.
   c. profit.
   d. inventory.

Understanding Concepts

8. What basic equation does an income statement show?

9. What is the difference between a variable cost and a fixed cost?

10. What does a business plan typically include?

11. What are the basic steps in the purchasing process?

12. What is the typical sequence of disciplinary measures?

Critical Thinking

13. **COMPARING/CONTRASTING** What is the difference between profit and sales?

14. **COMPARING/CONTRASTING** What is the difference between a par-stock list and an inventory?

Culinary Math

15. **SOLVING PROBLEMS** Your par-stock list indicates 280 boneless, skinless chicken breasts. Your inventory shows 30 boneless, skinless chicken breasts. You are ordering chicken today. How much chicken should you order?

16. **APPLYING CONCEPTS** The monthly income for a restaurant was $124,000. The monthly expenses equaled $105,000. What was the restaurant's profit for that month? Show the profit both as a dollar amount and as a percentage of the restaurant's monthly income.

On the Job

17. **COMMUNICATING** Write a mission statement for a restaurant you would like to open.

18. **APPLYING CONCEPTS** If you were planning to open a restaurant in your area, where would you locate it to achieve the highest possible sales? Why?

Managers

There are many managers in the culinary profession. An executive chef, for instance, is a manager. So is a banquet manager or a caterer. Lower-level managers are also needed for specific areas within a foodservice business.

Managers in a foodservice business usually serve in a specific function. For example, a large hotel restaurant might employ a purchasing agent or a storeroom supervisor. These managers must have a strong background in math and accounting. They also typically need strong computer skills and some specific management training (often related to safety and sanitation) for their position.

A manager must be able to organize work that is done by others. The ability to communicate effectively, including providing positive and negative feedback to workers, is a critical job skill. In some situations, being multilingual is an advantage if employees speak languages other than English.

Management is sometimes required to work long hours to accomplish tasks specified by upper-level management. Managers need to be very competent in their particular area. The general thought is that a manager should be able to perform any job function performed by his or her subordinates.

Small business owners are actually managers, as well. They must make all of their own decisions, and the success or failure of their businesses depends on their decisions.

Small business owners need to have a full complement of skills that will allow them to both perform specific tasks and to manage others who may be performing those tasks. As a small business owner, whether you own a deli, a bakery, a pizzeria, or a bed-and-breakfast, you must be able to perform any and all tasks that need to be accomplished by your business. If you aren't able to do them, who else will?

Entry-Level Requirements

Although a culinary or hospitality/restaurant management degree may be helpful, it is more important to understand the specific aspects of the area that you are managing.

Helpful for Advancement

Completing a manager-in-training program or taking coursework in the following areas: business management, supervision, accounting, safety, and sanitation courses.

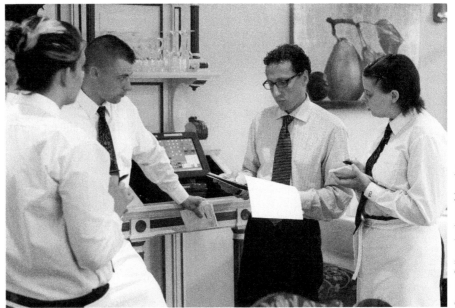

A manager must be able to organize work that is done by others

SUSAN WYSOCKI

Susan Wysocki is the owner of Babycakes Café and Soul Dog Café, in Poughkeepsie, New York. A graduate of The Culinary Institute of America, Wysocki has had success as a chef, working under Paul Prudhomme and Larry Forgione.

Susan Wysocki

Before the start of her culinary career, Wysocki, who holds a Finance degree, worked in the banking industry, with dreams of someday starting a catering company or restaurant. With her experience in finance and an entrepreneurial spirit, she was finally able to take a risk and purchase a pre-existing restaurant in the Hudson Valley. Wysocki took control of her restaurant's finances and believes that her background is a vital to the success of her businesses.

Wysocki takes great pride in being a part of her restaurants' community. As a business owner, she feels a responsibility to give back, and is active in local charities and community organizations.

VITAL **STATISTICS**

Education: The Culinary Institute of America, 1989; Bachelor of Science, Babson College

Profession: Restaurant owner

Interesting Items: Her restaurants are well-known for their gluten free menu options

Worked as a Culinary Institute of America (CIA) faculty member for 13 years

CAREER **PROFILE**

Salary Ranges

Entry Level: $26,000 to $48,000

Mid-Level: $45,000 to $60,500 (or more)

Senior: 45,000 to $60,500 (or more)

Owner/Operator: Varies widely depending on size of operation and geographic location of business

Appendix

Starting Your Career in Food Service

READING PREVIEW

Key Concepts

- Setting your goals
- Preparing your résumé
- Locating job opportunities
- Applying for a job
- Working

Setting Your Goals

Looking for a job? Now is the perfect time to assess or reassess your personal goals. You will be the only one evaluating the goals and dreams that you write down. Get out pen and paper, make sure there are no distractions, and decide how you want to live the rest of your life. Sounds hard? It's simpler than you think.

Organizing Your Long-Term Dreams First, record any dream or hope you have for the future. Do you want to make enough money to build your dream house? Do you want to write cookbooks? Do you want to travel the world teaching nutrition and basic cooking skills to mothers? No matter how abstract or unobtainable the goal might seem to be, write it down.

Second, put the list aside for a few days. When you're ready, pare down the list and rank the goals. For example: 1) Work my way through culinary school; 2) Make enough money to start a family; 3) Become an established chef; 4) Learn to speak Italian; 5) Write a cookbook; 6) Market own line of hot sauce.

You now have a picture of a promising future.

Developing Goals Your goals should point you toward your long-term dreams. Making this plan takes a little research. Discover schools and intern programs that offer training in your areas of interest. How long would you study? How much would it cost?

Then find out what jobs you are qualified for right now. What wages might you expect? Working in your chosen field will give you information, insight, experience, and cash.

Next, draft a timeline. In the first column, put time periods. In the second column, list what you want to be doing. Examine the Early Career Timeline below. Notice that work and study activities can overlap.

As you search for a job, and after you land one, refer to your timeline to keep yourself on track. You should change it and extend it as you go, but don't ignore it. A plan keeps you aware of what you want to do next.

EARLY CAREER TIMELINE

When	What
June–July	Informational interviews, job hunt
August–December	Entry-level job in a bakery
September–December	Pastry-making course
January–June	Job as assistant pastry chef

Preparing Your Résumé

To start any job search, you need a résumé. A résumé is a summary of your job abilities. It tells prospective employers what you can do, where you have worked, and a little bit about you. The main purpose of a résumé is to get you an interview. Employers will refer to the résumé during the interview, and you can add more details then.

People with years of work experience usually prepare a chronological résumé. This is a list of their jobs (most recent first), with details of their accomplishments in each position. After you have worked for a while, look for information on the format and content of chronological résumés to prepare your own.

People like you, who are just starting out, usually prepare a functional résumé. A functional résumé focuses on the things you can do—your skills. It also lists education, work experience, professional activities, awards, and personal interests. The sample résumé on page 825 is an example of a functional résumé.

Contact Information Start your résumé with your name and contact information. Your goal is to be contacted for an interview, so you want to be sure an employer can reach you.

Objective Your objective is the job you want. If you are responding to a specific opening, describe the job being offered as the one you want! That will help you pass the employer's first test.

You may want to send the same résumé to several employers, however, as a way of introducing yourself. In that case, you should list the related jobs you might do. The sample résumé takes this approach.

Some applicants try to match their objective to the business objectives of their prospective employers. For instance, if a job ad invites you to "join our team," your objective might be "To help your restaurant succeed by becoming part of the food preparation team as a cook or assistant cook." If the slogan of an eating place is "Every Visit a Delight," your objective might be "To delight your customers by helping prepare delicious meals as a cook or cook's assistant."

Whatever approach you take, be sure the objective clearly tells employers what you can do for them.

Education List your formal training, including degrees and certificates earned. Use the same format for each item. Include the years of study or completion, the school name, and the location.

Skills List the skills you want to highlight and give examples of your performance. You'll want to use the achievements that match the needs of the job you are shooting for. If the job description lists skill qualifications, try to use those as headings. Again, you want to organize your information so employers can easily find the details they are looking for.

When describing your skills, begin with an active verb that tells what you did, such as "supervised," "achieved," "prepared," "cooked," "assisted," "assembled." Using the same format for each point shows you are well organized.

Work Experience People hiring for entry-level jobs want to be sure their new employees can function well in a business. Your work experience can show that you are ready to do what a job requires. It can also show a pattern of productive employment. Even if some of your jobs are not related to food-service, they show that you took the initiative to get the job and did the work for the times you listed. You want to list all jobs that reflect positively on you. (Don't include any jobs that started and ended on the same day!)

List your most recent job experiences first. Include the employer's name, the location, the job title, and the dates you worked. Follow the same format for each job.

Professional Involvement and Awards This section lets you show off your contribution to the food-service profession and the formal recognition you have achieved.

Use a heading that matches your accomplishments. For example, if you wrote a restaurant review or published a recipe in the school paper, you could list it under the heading "Professional Involvement and Publications." You can leave out this heading if you don't have supporting experience yet.

Personal Interests People like to work with interesting coworkers. This optional category lets the employer get a sense of you as a person. List the activities you can discuss to show your enthusiasm and your interests beyond work.

References The sample résumé ends with the notice, "References Available on Request." A reference is a person who will describe your character or job abilities.

An employer wants to be reassured that you will be productive, honest, and dependable. That means you should choose references who:

- Know you well
- Think well of you and your work
- Can verify your résumé claims
- Can impress an employer on your behalf

Former employers are ideal references. Heads of volunteer organizations and teachers also make good references.

- **Letters of Reference.** When your involvement in an organization is coming to an end, consider asking a trusted leader for a letter that you can show to future employers. Letters of reference often begin "To Whom It May Concern," and they explain how the writer knows you and his or her opinion of your work and character. Examples of accomplishments that match those on your résumé are also helpful. If the reference is willing to talk to future employers, be sure the letter includes the reference's contact information.
- **Reference List.** You should also prepare a reference list, so employers can quickly call the people who have agreed to speak for you. The table below shows a simple format. You will want to include three to five references.

REFERENCE LIST

Contact Information	Best Reached	Relationship
Emma Smith (602) 555-1234 name@place.com	Business hours Weekdays	Sponsor of community Emergency Food Service where I volunteered

Important: Be sure to ask permission *before* you list anyone as a reference. Also, let your references know when you are job hunting so they might expect calls. You can describe promising opportunities to your references so they are ready to reinforce your qualifications for the specific job.

SAMPLE FUNCTIONAL RÉSUMÉ

Identifying Information

Jackie Jones
Street Address
City, State Zip
E-Mail (if any)
Telephone

The Job You Want

Objective

To work as a chef, chef's assistant, or kitchen assistant.

Formal Training

Education

- Diploma, Certificate in Culinary Arts, 2014
- Mytown Vocational High School, Mytown, NH
- Environmental Sanitation in Food-service, 3 credits, 2014
- New Hampshire Community Technical College, Mytown, NH

Job Skills and Examples

Skills

Sanitation and Safety

- Supervised culinary lab cleanup including four workstations, using custom checklist
- Achieved certification in safe food-handling procedures

Cold Preparation

- Prepared mise en place for short-order restaurant
- Prepared sandwiches and salads for church soup kitchen

Hot Preparation

- Prepared grill items for private parties
- Cooked breakfast and lunch for day camp
- Assisted in soup and chili preparation for caterer

Plating and Presentation

- Assembled and plated meals for awards banquet
- Worked service line at soup kitchen

Work Experience

Work Experience

- Pleasant Valley Day Camp, Mytown, NH, cook, summer 2014
- Lunchbox Café, Mytown, NH, kitchen assistant, 2013–2014
- Emergency Food Service, Mytown, NH, volunteer food preparation and line service, Sundays 2011–2013

Professional Involvement and Awards

Professional Involvement and Awards

Student Government Food Committee, Best Quiche Award, MVHS, 2014

Personal Interests

Collecting kitchen tools, listening to jazz, swimming

Personal Interests

References Available on Request

Locating Job Opportunities

There are several methods and many available resources for finding job opportunities. Be organized when conducting your job search.

Managing the Details When you begin a job search, be sure to keep records. You will be talking to many people at many businesses, and it is easy to get confused.

- **Master List.** Keep a master list like the one below, listing all your prospects. Use the "Next" and "Due" columns to organize your job searching.

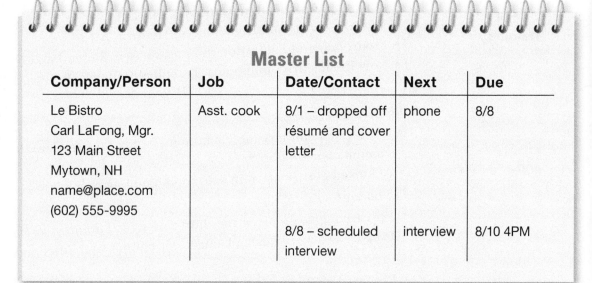

Master List

Company/Person	Job	Date/Contact	Next	Due
Le Bistro Carl LaFong, Mgr. 123 Main Street Mytown, NH name@place.com (602) 555-9995	Asst. cook	8/1 – dropped off résumé and cover letter	phone	8/8
		8/8 – scheduled interview	interview	8/10 4PM

- **Folders.** Start a folder for each interview. Include two copies of the résumé and cover letter that you sent (one for you and one for the interviewer, who may have lost the one you sent). Add your research notes about the company and questions you will ask. In the interview, be sure to get contact information and the correct names of all interviewers. Add any notes you have taken during the interview. Add copies of the thank-you notes you sent after the interview.

Prospecting Prospecting means exploring for opportunities. You can find job openings in several ways:

- **General Mailings and Phone Calls.** Send your résumé to all businesses you want to consider. Ask about job openings in your cover letter. Try to address your inquiry to the right contact person. You can get this name from the business itself, its website, or a friend. After the résumé arrives, call your contact and ask about the company's job openings.
- **Apply in Person.** Pounding the pavement is a legitimate job-search method in the hospitality industry. Dress professionally, have copies

of your résumé, and be polite with everyone. You can offer to demonstrate your skills or to begin work "on trial."

- **Internet Advertisements.** Companies advertise openings on their websites. Go to a hotel or restaurant website and look for a Careers or Jobs link. You can try culinary websites such as escoffier.com, starchefs.com, and foodservice.com. Also try general job websites such as careerbuilder.com, myjobsearch.com, and monster.com, where you can post a résumé and get notices of jobs that fit your interests.

- **Classified Ads.** Read the hometown newspapers and check their online editions. The Want Ads often list hospitality openings. Also read trade publications such as *Nation's Restaurant News.* This weekly paper for the food industry has a section of employment ads in every issue.

- **Employment Agencies.** Job agencies work for employers, so you should act professionally in all your dealings with them. You should not have to pay a fee. Agencies screen applicants to save employers time, and the employer pays the agency when you are hired. Some agencies will take inexperienced applicants.

- **Networking.** The best way to find a job is through networking. Your network includes your personal contacts—and the contacts they refer you to. Write a 15- to 30-second speech about the job you want, and tell it to everyone. Find out what people do and how you might help them. Exchange contact information. Pass on leads to people you know. They will do the same for you. To expand your network, you might get involved with clubs, activities, and other professional organizations. Also, if an employer does not need anyone at the moment, ask about other places that need help.

Informational Interviewing An informational interview is a chance for you to learn about a company or a career from a professional on the inside. You are not seeking a job from this person. The professional is doing you the favor of sharing information about work.

To get an informational interview, you have to know someone. That means networking. Ask your contact for a chance to meet for a short time, and make clear the kind of information you want: how the professional developed his or her career, what is most rewarding and most challenging, what skills and traits the person wants in the people he or she hires, what it is like to work in a certain company.

- **You're the Leader.** Because this is your meeting, you have to come prepared to lead the discussion. Dress for an interview. Be ready to tell a little about yourself, and bring a résumé for the professional's information. Research the job and company before the interview, and prepare a list of questions or topics. Give a copy to the professional, and use it as an agenda. Keep the meeting short, 15 to 20 minutes. The professional's time is valuable.

- **Be Friendly and Positive.** During the interview, show interest. A little flattery never hurts. You might say, "Henry gave me your name and told me you're the best pastry chef in town. How did you get started?"

- **Get Names.** Ask for other contacts with whom you might speak. Even if no names are suggested, be grateful for any help provided.

- **Follow Up.** Thank the person before leaving, but don't forget to also send a letter stating your gratitude for the time given. Contact every referral you receive. Every person you speak with brings you closer to your new career. Stay in touch by phone or e-mail, and let the person know how the information helped.

Applying for a Job

After doing your research, you're ready to state your interest in a particular job.

Job Applications Most employers will ask you to complete a job application form. The information you put on the application should be consistent with your résumé. If you cannot complete this form at home, bring documents to the interview that include the details you may need: social security number, past employer addresses, list of references, and résumé.

Cover Letters and Other Introductions The purpose of the cover letter is to draw attention to your résumé. Start by identifying the job and where you learned about it. If someone recommended you, get permission to use that person's name. You can also point out your skills and experiences that match the job requirements. The prospective employer may be sorting through many résumés. A short letter that makes your qualifications clear can help get you noticed.

Dear _____: [or To Whom It May Concern:]

I am applying for the position of assistant cook that I read about in Saturday's *Morning News*. My résumé is attached.

As you can see, I have the experience you need. I am trained in hot and cold preparation, plating and presentation, and health and safety procedures. I have cooked and assisted in several local establishments.

I will call to set up an interview and demonstration.

Sincerely,

Cover letters and résumés can be sent by mail or e-mail, or you can deliver one by hand with a job application.

Phone Calls If a job ad asks you to respond by phone, write a cover letter and use it as a script for your conversation. Ask for an interview, and be sure to thank the employer.

Interviewing and Demonstrating An interview is a chance for you and the employer to get to know each other. Bring your résumé and reference list, and be prepared to tell about yourself professionally. Write out a one-minute introduction and practice it. Be ready to provide positive details about every item on your résumé. Think of questions you might be asked and practice interviewing with a friend. Develop answers that are short and positive.

Generally, the interviewer will give you information about the job and the establishment. Taking notes shows your interest. Be prepared to ask a few questions about the employer's needs: "What is your greatest challenge, and how can I help with it?" "When would the job begin?" "What other information can I give you?" Before you leave, remember to find out the next step in the hiring process.

You may be asked to prepare a dish. Knowing what they want to see in advance will let you practice before the demonstration. In any case, use the opportunity to show your basic skills, including safety and sanitation.

Follow Up Always write a thank-you note immediately after an interview. It should be short and polite, thanking your hosts for showing you their establishment and taking the time to get to know you. You might say you hope you can work together.

If you call to follow up, be cheerful. Actually smile while you're on the phone—your voice will sound positive. Identify yourself and the job, and ask about the status of your application. If they hired someone else, stay positive. You might say, "Oh, too bad. You would be great people to work with! I hope you can keep my application on file. By the way, do you know of anyone else who is hiring?" By demonstrating your skills and making a personal connection, you can add to your network of culinary professionals, no matter what the outcome of a single job application.

Apprentice Programs Apprentice programs or internships are generally unpaid opportunities to gain experience in a professional kitchen. Ask your instructor or guidance counselor about companies that will train promising students. They often hire the people they successfully train!

Developing a Career Portfolio As you gather experience, you will want to assemble a portfolio, a set of exhibits of your work for future employers. Start collecting proof of your success as you develop your career:

- Diplomas and certificates
- Letters of reference
- Letters of commendation, awards, and prizes
- Written job reviews by employers

- Your special recipes
- Photos of your creations
- Reviews of restaurants where you cooked
- Restaurant reviews and recipes you published

Working

After you have located job opportunities and applied for jobs, you will receive job offers and eventually go to work for a restaurant or another culinary-oriented business. But in the culinary field, it isn't always that easy! In lower-level positions there is often high employee turnover, and changing jobs is often the best way to advance your career. Ultimately, the people most likely to succeed in the culinary field are those who take the individual responsibility and initiative to continually hone their skills and develop new ones.

Getting the Offer After all your efforts, an employer makes you an offer. What do you do then? How do you evaluate the offer? You have many things to consider. Here are just a few:

- **Salary.** Is it competitive with similar positions at other companies?
- **Benefits.** Does the company offer health insurance, child care, a pension plan, or other similar benefits? If so, you will not have to pay for those items yourself. Also, compare the benefits offered by other companies for similar positions. Many culinary employers do not offer benefits to lower-level employees because of the high job turnover.
- **Hours.** Will you be required to work at night only? Are the working hours long? What days would you have off? Many restaurants are very busy on holidays. Are you prepared to work on holidays?
- **Overtime.** If you work on holidays or a long shift, do you receive additional compensation (such as double-time or time-and-a-half pay)?
- **Substitutions.** What is the policy for sick days or personal time? Do you need to find a substitute?
- **Uniform.** Is a uniform required? If so, is there a uniform allowance?
- **Working Conditions.** What do the working conditions seem like to you? Is there high stress in the workplace? Is there any way you can talk to an employee privately before making your decision?
- **Advancement.** What kinds of possibilities for advancement are there?

Working, Advancing, and Changing Jobs The first day you report to work you will probably have to fill out an I-9 form ("Employment Eligibility Verification") and a W-4 form ("Employee's Withholding Allowance Certificate"). Make sure to use your first few days and weeks of employment to learn all of the job's aspects. Don't be afraid to ask questions!

As time goes on, you will learn your job and become more skillful in completing your tasks—if your performance is good, you might be offered a chance for advancement. This could take years, however, depending on the size of the business. If you feel that there may be better options elsewhere, begin discreetly asking friends about other possibilities. Respond to ads, just as you did when you first were looking for a job. However, it is not good business etiquette (and not a good idea overall) to let your current company know that you are looking for another job.

Life-Long Learning Finally, remember that you must keep your skills current. Take classes, learn about new equipment, and experiment with new cooking or preparation methods. A long culinary career in our rapidly changing global economy requires life-long learning!

Glossary

Numbers behind definitions refer to the chapter and section of the book where the term is discussed.

A

à la carte (ah-lah-CART) **menu** Menu on which each food item or beverage is priced and served separately. (21.1)

accident report Standard form used to report accidents to OSHA; must be filed within eight hours. (2.2) Also used to describe an event related to a serious health problem or physical injury to a customer; should include the customer name, any server involved, the date, and the time it occurred. (20.4)

actual cost method Menu-pricing method in which the actual cost for the raw food, labor, other expenses, and profit are all added together to determine a menu price. (21.2)

aerating (AIR-ate-ing) Adding air to food. (19.2)

aflatoxin (aff-la-TOX-in) Toxin produced by molds, sometimes found on legumes. (13.2)

aged (beef) Beef that undergoes a process that gives it a darker color, a more tender texture, and a fuller flavor. (16.1)

airpot brewers Coffee makers used in low-volume settings. Water is added to a well by hand, as the water is heated it runs over coffee in a basket. (20.2)

al dente (al DEN-tay) Italian expression meaning "to the tooth"; used to describe pasta that is cooked only until it gives a slight resistance when you bite it. (13.3)

albumen (al-BYOO-men) White part of an egg, composed of water and protein. (9.1)

all-purpose flour Blend of "soft" (low-protein) and "hard" (high-protein) wheat; the most common type of flour used in the bakeshop. (17.1)

ambience (AM-bee-ahnce) Feeling or mood of the restaurant. (23.1)

American buttercream Dense and rich buttercream icing that is just butter creamed with powdered sugar. (19.3)

American service Service style in which food is fully prepared and plated on individual serving plates in the kitchen, brought to the dining room, and served by the right hand at the right side of the guest, leaving the server's left hand free to carry other plates. (20.3)

amino (ah-MEEN-oh) **acids** Basic building blocks of protein, some of which our bodies make. Others, the essential amino acids, we must get from food. (22.1)

anadromous (ann-AH-drom-us) **fish** Fish that live part of their lives in saltwater and part in freshwater. (15.1)

anaphylactic (an-ah-fil-ACK-tic) **shock** The result of a severe allergy. Symptoms such as hives, fainting, and nausea develop rapidly. The most significant symptom is swelling of the throat severe enough to block the airway. Requires immediate medical attention. (2.2)

anti-griddle Similar to a regular griddle except that instead of heating the surface of the food, it freezes the surface instantly. (3.3)

antioxidants Substances, such as certain vitamins, that prevent tissue damage in the body. (22.1)

antipasti (ahn-tee-PAHS-tee) A selection of Italian sliced meats, cheeses, sausages, and olives served before a meal. (11.2)

antipasto (an-tee-PAHS-toh) **platter** Assortment of cured meats (such as prosciutto and salami), cheeses, and pickled vegetables served on a platter. (10.4)

appetizer Dish that is served as the first course in a meal. (11.2)

appetizer salad Salad designed to whet the appetite before the main course. (10.2)

aromatic (air-o-MAT-ic) Strong smelling; foods with especially strong smells are referred to as aromatic. (6.1)

arson The act of deliberately setting a fire; the opposite of an accidental fire. (2.1)

aspic A bound salad held together by mixing the ingredients into a gelatin-thickened liquid. (10.2)

assembly points Meeting points at a predetermined spot at a safe distance from the building where everyone should gather after a fire. (2.1)

assets Items a business owns, such as furnishings and appliances. (23.1)

assignment In terms of mise en place, the food for which you will be responsible. (7.1)

asymmetrical (AY-sym-met-rih-cull) In terms of plate presentation, unequal numbers of items on either side of the plate. (7.3)

automated external defibrillator (AED) Device that shocks the heart into starting again. (2.2)

automatic brewers Coffee makers used in high-volume settings. The entire unit is plumbed, so water is supplied directly to the well. (20.2)

automatic fire control systems Extinguishers, sprinklers, and alarms triggered by the heat of a fire. (2.1)

B

baba ghanoush (BAH-bah gha-NOOSH) Vegetable-based dip made from roasted eggplant that has been pureed and seasoned with olive oil, tahini, lemon juice, and garlic. (10.1)

back of the house In a restaurant, the kitchen area. (20.1)

back waiter Provides overall assistance to the front waiter; may deliver food and drinks to the front waiter, clear plates, and refill bread and water. (20.1)

bacteria Single-celled organisms that can live in food or water and also on our skin or clothing; some are a potential biological hazard, capable of producing food-borne illness. (1.1)

baguette (bag-EHT) Long, narrow French bread with a crispy, golden-brown crust and light, chewy crumb dotted with holes. (17.3)

bain marie (BANE ma-REE) Another name for a double boiler. (4.2)

baker's chocolate Chocolate that has no sugar added. Also called *unsweetened chocolate* or *chocolate liquor*. (19.1)

baking Dry-heat method of cooking in which food is cooked by hot air trapped inside an oven. Baking typically means you are preparing smaller pieces of food than when roasting. (8.1)

baking stones Unglazed ceramic pieces used to line an oven rack; they help develop a crisp crust on breads and pizza by holding and transferring the oven's heat evenly. (17.1)

balance scale Scale typically used for weighing baking ingredients. Ingredients are placed on one side; weights are placed on the other side. When the sides balance, the ingredients weigh the same as the weights. (4.2)

balsamic (bal-SAH-mihk) **vinegar** Commercial balsamic vinegar is dark brown and has a sweet-sour taste. (10.1)

bar cookies Cookies made from a soft batter that is spread into a pan before baking and then cut into individual cookies. (19.3)

barley Grain that looks like a doubled grain of rice. (13.1)

base price method Menu-pricing method that analyzes what customers want to spend per meal and then works backward to come up with menu items, their prices, and a built-in level of profit. Requires data about customers' eating habits in the restaurant over a long period. (21.2)

basic vinaigrette A temporary emulsion, typically of some type of oil and some type of vinegar. Ingredients are stirred or mixed vigorously to mix ingredients. Over time, the ingredients will separate. (10.1)

batch cooking Process of preparing a small amount of food several times during a service period so that a fresh supply of cooked items is always available. (22.2)

bâtonnet (bah-tow-NAY) Long, rectangular cut that is 1/4 inch wide by 1/4 thick and 2 to 2 1/2 inches long. (4.1)

batter Coating option on foods made by blending a type of flour and a liquid. (8.1) Wet form of dough made from flour, oil or melted butter, eggs, milk or other liquids, salt, and usually baking powder. Used to create waffles, cakes, and other items. (9.2)

battuto (bah-TOOT-oh) Aromatic combination used in Italian soups, sauces, stews, and meat dishes; consists of cooking fat, garlic, onions, parsley, carrots, and celery. (6.2)

bavarian (bah-VAIR-ee-uhn) **cream** Aerated dessert similar to a mousse but without an egg foam. (19.2)

beans Legumes that are longer than they are round. (13.2)

béchamel sauce (BAY-shah-mell) One of the grand sauces; a white sauce made by thickening milk with a white roux. (14.2)

belly bones Fish bones found along the thinner edge of the fillet. (15.1)

bench boxes Covered containers in which dough is bench proofed; a skin forms on the dough that holds in the carbon dioxide. (17.3)

bench proofing Brief resting period that allows gluten to relax after dough has been pre-shaped. (17.3)

bench scraper Tool with a rectangular steel blade, usually 6 inches wide, that is capped with a wooden or plastic handle. Used like a knife to cut soft ingredients such as butter or soft cheese, to lift and turn soft or wet dough, or to transfer ingredients from a work surface to a mixing bowl. (17.1)

bid Proposal from a supplier that states the price to be charged for an item. (23.2)

biga (BEE-gah) In baking, an Italian dough starter developed overnight or longer; can be wet or dry. (17.2)

bimetallic-coil thermometer Thermometer that uses a metal coil in the probe to measure temperature. Oven-safe version can stay in food while cooking and gives a reading in 1 to 2 minutes. Instant-read version is not oven-safe and gives a reading in 15 to 20 seconds. (4.2)

biological hazards Living organisms such as bacteria, viruses, fungi, and parasites that can make us sick. (1.1)

biscuits Small quick breads that have little or no sugar. (18.2)

bisque (bisk) A special type of puree soup that is thickened by pureeing the soup after the main flavoring ingredients and rice are simmered together until the rice is soft enough to fall apart. (14.3)

bittersweet chocolate Dark chocolate with less sugar than semisweet chocolate. (19.1)

black pepper Dried, unripe berries of the pepper vine; used as a seasoning. (6.4)

blanching Moist-heat method of cooking that involves cooking in a liquid or with steam just long enough to cook the outer portion of the food. The food is immediately placed in ice water to stop *carryover cooking*. (8.2)

blast-chill refrigerator Refrigerator that quickly cools prepared food through the danger zone down to the safe storage temperature. Also called a *quick-chill refrigerator*. (3.2)

blender Electrical mixing device used for combining ingredients by means of a rotating blade. (3.3)

blending Type of mixing in which the ingredients are chopped so the overall mixture has a uniform consistency. (3.3)

blind-baked Prebaked pie shell. (19.4)

blinis (BLEE-nees) Very thin Russian crêpes. (10.4)

blooming (gelatin) The process of dissolving gelatin in water. (17.1)

blue-vein cheeses Cheeses in which needles are injected into the cheese to form holes in which mold spores multiply. The cheese is salted and ripened in a cave. (10.3)

boiling Moist-heat method of cooking in which food is cooked at 212°F. (8.2)

bolster Point at the heel of a knife blade where the blade and handle come together. Gives the blade greater strength and durability. (4.1)

boning knife Knife about 6 inches long with a narrow blade, used to separate meat from the bone. (4.1)

bottom line Money left in a business after subtracting expenses from earnings. (23.1)

bouillon (BOOL-yohn) French term for broth. (14.3)

boule (BOOL) Round loaf of white bread named for the French word for "ball." (17.3)

bound salad Salad made from a combination of ingredients that are held together, typically by a thick, creamy dressing such as mayonnaise. (10.2)

bouquet garni (boo-KAY GAR-nee) Combination of fresh herbs and other aromatic ingredients used to flavor dishes. (6.2)

box grater Hand tool used for grating; has four sides each with a different-sized grate. (4.2)

boxed meat Meat that is fabricated to a specific point (such as primal, subprimal, or retail cuts) and then packed, boxed, and sold to foodservice establishments. (16.1)

braesola (bray-SO-lah) Italian-style dried beef. (10.4)

braising (BRAYZ-ing) Combination cooking method in which food is first seared and then gently cooked in flavorful liquid. Braising usually indicates that the food is left whole or in large pieces. (8.2)

braising (BRAYZ-ing) **pan** Pan with medium-high walls and a lid to keep moisture in. (4.2)

bran Coating found on kernels of grain, located just beneath the hull. (13.1)

brand Public image of a business, including the business name, logo, and sometimes a slogan. (23.1)

bread flour Flour that contains more protein than all-purpose flour; it is used in most yeast-bread recipes. (17.1)

brigade (bri-GADE) Group of workers assigned a specific set of tasks. (20.1)

brioche (BREE-ohsh) French version of sweet bread with a knotted top made in individual molds with a fluted base; it can also be made into a round loaf or rolls. (17.2)

broiler Cooking unit with a radiant heat source located above the food. Some units have adjustable racks that can be raised or lowered to control cooking speed. (3.3)

broiling Dry-heat method of cooking that is similar to a grill except the heat source is above the food. (8.1)

broth Clear, thin soup made by simmering a combination of meat, fish, poultry, or vegetables in a liquid with aromatics. (14.3)

brown rice Rice with some or all of the bran still intact. (13.1)

brown sauce One of the grand sauces; a sauce with a rich brown color made from brown stock. See *Espagnol sauce, Demiglaçe,* and *Jus de veau lié.* (14.2)

brown stock Type of stock made from roasted animal or poultry bones. Brown stock has a deep reddish-brown color and a roasted-meat flavor. (14.1)

brunoise (brewn-WHAZ) Smallest dice cut, about 1/8 inch square. Means "to brown" in French. (4.1)

bruschettas (brew-SKEH-tahs) Type of open-faced sandwich served as an appetizer. It consists of toasted bread drizzled with olive oil and topped with tomatoes, olives, cheese, or other ingredients. See *crostini.* (11.2)

budget List of planned income and expenses. (23.1)

buffalo chopper Machine that holds food in a rotating bowl that passes under a hood where blades chop the food. Some units have hoppers or feed tubes and interchangeable disks for slicing and grating. Also called a *food chopper.* (3.3)

buffet service Serving style practical for serving a large number of people a wide variety of dishes over a period of time; servers behind the buffet table may serve guests or guests may serve themselves. (20.3)

bulgur (BUHL-guhr) Steamed whole wheat berries that are dried and crushed into small pieces. (13.1)

bus person Person responsible for clearing and cleaning tables. Also called *dining room attendant*. (20.1)

business plan Written plan that a business owner develops to launch a new business, such as a restaurant. Includes a mission statement, goals that support the mission statement, sample menus, preliminary operating budgets, and staffing needs. (23.1)

butler service Serving style in which the server brings a platter to the table and provides a serving spoon and fork, and guests serve themselves. (20.3)

buttercream Icing made by aerating butter, shortening, or a combination of the two; used to decorate cakes and as a cake and pastry filling. (19.3)

butterfat Fat content of dairy products, measured by the weight of the fat compared to the total weight of the product. Same as *milkfat*. (9.1)

butterflied Split down the middle and then spread open, as with boneless meat. (16.1)

C

cafeteria service Self-service where diners choose their own foods from behind a counter or barrier. Servers dish out controlled portions from the other side and diners carry their dishes on trays to their tables. (20.3)

caffeine Chemical found in coffee, tea, chocolate, and sodas; it stimulates your body and mind. (9.2)

Cajun (CAGE-uhn) **trinity** Aromatic combination used in Creole and Cajun cooking; consists of onion, celery, and green pepper. (6.2)

cake comb Triangular or rectangular piece of metal or plastic with serrated edges, used to create a decorative edge on iced cakes or to give texture to a chocolate coating. (17.1)

cake flour Flour that has less protein than bread or all-purpose flour; it is used in most cake recipes and many cookie and muffin recipes. (17.1)

calamari (cahl-ah-MAHR-ee) Another name for squid. (15.2)

California menu Single menu listing breakfast, lunch, and dinner foods; it offers customers the freedom to order any item at any time of day. (21.1)

calories Measured units, derived from food, that provide energy. (22.1)

Canadian bacon Leaner than regular bacon and similar to ham. (9.2)

canapés (KAN-up-pays) Bite-sized pieces of bread or crackers with a savory topping, used as an hors d'Oeuvre. (11.2)

capers (KAY-pers) The dried flower bud of a bush native to the Mediterranean and parts of Asia. Typically pickled in a vinegar-and-salt solution; used to add a pungent taste to dishes. (6.2)

capsaicin (cap-SAY-ih-sin) Compound that gives a chile its heat; it is most potent on the white ribs inside the pepper. (12.2)

captain At fine dining restaurants, the person responsible for explaining the menu to guests and taking their orders; the captain is also responsible for the smooth-running service in a specific group of tables. (20.1)

caramelize (CAR-muh-lyze) Change that takes place in food that contains sugar when it is heated. The surface of the food starts to turn brown. (8.1)

carbohydrates Energy sources for the body, made up of smaller units known as sugars. (22.1)

carcinogenic (car-sin-oh-JEN-ik) Causing cancer, such as a toxic chemical exposure. (2.2)

cardiopulmonary resuscitation (CARD-ee-oh-PULL-mohn-ayr-ee ree-suss-ih-TAY-shun) **(CPR)** Technique used to restore a person's breathing and heartbeat. (2.2)

carpaccio (car-PAH-chee-oh) Raw beef, sliced very thinly and dressed with a sauce. (11.2)

carryover cooking Cooking that takes place in a food after it is removed from a source of heat. (8.1)

carver Person in charge of carving and serving meats or fish and their accompaniments from the meat cart. Also called *trancheur*. (20.1)

casserole Pan with medium-high walls and a lid to keep moisture in. (4.2)

caviar Type of salted fish eggs; in France and the United States, only sturgeon eggs are classified as caviar. (10.4)

centrifuge A machine used to separate substances of different densities. Often used in molecular gastronomy. (3.3)

chafing (CHAYF-ing) **dish** Metal holding pan mounted above a heat source and used to keep food warm. The pan is usually contained within a larger unit that holds water. When the water is heated, the steam heats the food evenly. (3.4)

challah (HAL-la) Sweet, airy, braided bread made with a lot of eggs; it is a Jewish bread traditionally served on the Sabbath and on holidays. (17.2)

channel knife Tool used to cut grooves lengthwise in a vegetable such as a cucumber or carrot. A rondelle cut from the grooved vegetable has decorative edges that resemble a flower. (4.2)

charcuterie (shahr-KOO-tuhr-ee) French term used in professional kitchens to refer to cured meats, sausages, pâtés, and terrines. (10.4)

cheese board Flat platter on which cheese is served. (10.3)

cheese cart Cart that is wheeled to the guests' table to give them an opportunity to choose cheeses of different kinds. (10.3)

chef de cuisine (shef de kwih-ZEEN) Head chef who commands the kitchen, designs

the menu, and oversees food costs. Also called *executive chef*. (20.1)

chef's knife All-purpose knife used for peeling, trimming, slicing, chopping, and dicing. Blade is usually 8 to 12 inches long. Also known as a French knife. (4.1)

chef's tasting Method of presenting appetizers; it is a sampler plate with an assortment of different appetizers. The portions are often only one bite, just enough to sample the various appetizers. (11.2)

chemical hazards Human-made toxins such as cleaning compounds, bug sprays, food additives, or fertilizers found in food or water. (1.1)

chemical leavener Baking powder or baking soda, which increases the volume of a batter by the addition of air or gas. (17.1)

ciabatta (chee-ah-BOT-ah) A large, flat Italian bread, traditionally cut into squares and then split to fill and garnish. (11.1)

chicken-fried steak Thin steak dipped into a mixture of egg, milk, and seasonings and then fried like chicken until crisp; popular in the South and Midwest. (9.2)

chiffonade (shiff-en-ODD) Cut used for cutting herbs and leafy greens into fine shreds. (4.1)

china Everything designed to contain food is regarded as china. This includes such things as plates, bowls, dishes, cups, saucers, and individual creamers. (20.2)

chlorine dioxide (klor-EEN die-OX-ide) Chemical dough conditioner to facilitate handing of lean dough. (17.2)

chocolate liquor Chocolate that has no sugar added. Also called *unsweetened chocolate* or *baker's chocolate*. (19.1)

cholesterol (koh-LESS-ter-all) Fatty substance the body needs to perform various functions; it becomes a health risk when certain protein levels appear as elevated in the blood, indicating a possible build-up of cholesterol on the walls of arteries, reducing blood flow to the heart. (22.1)

choux (SHOO) **paste** Versatile pastry dough made from liquid, fat, flour, and eggs; used for both sweet and savory baked goods. Also called *pâté à choux*. (19.4)

chutney Sauce with a chunky texture, typically fruit- or vegetable-based and made with a sweet and sour flavoring. (14.2)

clarification Mixture of ingredients including ground meat, aromatic vegetables, and an acid such as tomatoes or lemon juice used to add flavor and clear a broth to make a consommé. (14.3)

clarified butter Butter with all water and particles removed, leaving pure fat for cooking at high temperatures. (9.1)

client base Group of customers who come to a restaurant. (23.1)

clingstone Describes fruit that clings tightly to its pit, making it difficult to cut the flesh away cleanly. (12.1)

closed sandwich Two pieces of bread with a filling between them. (11.1)

club sandwich Double-decker closed sandwich, made with three slices of bread (or toast) and traditionally filled with chicken (or turkey, ham, or beef) bacon, lettuce, and tomato. (11.1)

coating chocolate Chocolate made with vegetable fat instead of cocoa butter. Also called *compound chocolate.* (19.1)

cocktail sauce Dipping sauce of ketchup, horseradish, and possibly Tabasco sauce; used with shellfish. (10.4)

cocoa butter Cream-colored fat from cocoa beans; used in the chocolate-making process. (19.1)

cocoa powder Unsweetened chocolate with the fat removed and then ground into a powder. (19.1)

coddled eggs Eggs cooked in their shells for 30 seconds, leaving the whites warm and thickened and the yolks warm but still runny. (9.1)

coffee percolators Produce a large batch of coffee. Water is heated and rises through a hollow stem onto the coffee. Also called *coffee urns.* (20.2)

coffee urns Produce a large batch of coffee. Water is heated and rises through a hollow stem onto the coffee. Also called *coffee percolators.* (20.2)

colander (COL-un-der) Large, perforated stainless steel or aluminum bowl used to strain or drain foods. (4.2)

cold food presentation Collection of cold foods presented in an artful manner, often in a buffet setting. (10.4)

cold storage area Kitchen area where walk-in refrigerators, reach-in refrigerators, and other large refrigeration equipment is located. (3.2)

collaborate (ko-LA-bo-rate) To work together, with your team members, for the good of the kitchen. (7.2)

combination steamer/oven Oven powered by either gas or electricity. It can cook like a convection oven, a steamer, or both. (3.3)

complex carbohydrates Carbohydrates that contain long chains of many sugars; found in plant-based foods such as grains, legumes, and vegetables. (22.1)

composed salad Salad with any combination of ingredients (greens, vegetables, proteins, starches, fruits, or garnishes) that are arranged carefully and artfully on a plate or in a bowl. (10.2)

compote Dish of fresh or dried fruit that is slow-cooked in stewing liquid. (12.1)

compound butter Flavored butter made by blending aromatics or garnishes with softened butter, typically served with grilled meats. (14.2)

compound chocolate Chocolate made with vegetable fat instead of cocoa butter. Also called *coating chocolate.* (19.1)

condiments (CON-di-ments) Prepared mixtures that are used to season and flavor foods. Condiments are served on the side and added by the individual diner. (6.3)

conditioning the pan Process of letting the pan heat up before adding any oil or food, when sautéing. (8.1)

confectioner's sugar Sugar that has been ground into a fine, white, easily dissolvable powder. (17.1)

conical (CON-i-cal) **sieve** Made of very fine mesh and shaped like a cone. Also called a *chinois,* a *china cap,* or a *bouillon strainer.* Used to strain or purée foods. (4.2)

consommé (KAHN-soh-may) Very clear broth made by simmering a broth or stock with a clarification. A consommé should be fat-free. (14.3)

continental breakfast Light breakfast of baked goods served with coffee or tea, and juice. (9.2)

continuous inventory An inventory system in which information about inventory quantity and availability is computerized and updated on a continuous basis. (23.2)

continuous seating plan Seating plan that allows use of tables according to the flow of business. (20.1)

convection oven Oven with fans that force hot air to circulate around the food, cooking it evenly and quickly. Some convection ovens have the capacity to introduce moisture. Special features may include infrared and/or microwave oven functions. (3.3)

convection steamer Cooking unit that generates steam in a boiler and then pipes it to the cooking chamber, where it is vented over the food. It is continuously exhausted, so the door may be opened at any time without danger of scalding or burning. However, you need to wait for the steam to clear away before reaching into the convection oven, otherwise a serious burn could occur. (3.3)

converted rice Rice that is parcooked before it is milled to shorten the cooking time. (13.1)

conveyor belt dishwasher Large piece of dishwashing equipment that can process a high volume of dishes as a continuous flow. (4.2)

cook-chill technique Cooking process that quickly cools prepared food through the danger zone down to the safe storage temperature using a quick-chill refrigerator (also called a *blast-chill refrigerator*). (3.2)

cookware Utensils used for cooking, such as pots and pans. (4.2)

copycat method Simple menu-pricing method that involves going to a nearby restaurant that has the same menu items and copying its prices. (21.2)

corer Tool used to remove the core of an apple or pear in one long, round piece; corers are available in various sizes to

use with small fruits like apples or larger fruits like pineapples. (4.2)

corn syrup Thick, sweet syrup made from cornstarch. It is available light or dark. (17.1)

cornmeal Finely ground corn. Can be ground into coarse, medium, or fine particles. Called *grits* in America. (13.1)

corrective action Steps a foodservice establishment takes to correct a problem or situation, such as food held too long at an unsafe temperature. (1.3)

corrosive (core-OH-siv) Having the ability to irritate or even eat away other materials. (2.2)

cost control Keeping variable expenses in check, such as avoiding waste or conserving electricity. (23.1)

coulis (koo-LEE) Thick puréed sauce, usually made from vegetables or fruit. (14.2)

count (shrimp) Number of shrimp per pound. (15.2)

counter scale Scale that sits on a counter and weighs moderate-sized packages. (3.2)

counter service Alternative to table dining; guests sit at a counter, often on stools. (20.3)

countertop blender Blender with the motor and blades at the base and a glass, metal, or plastic container on top to hold ingredients. Also called a *bar blender.* (3.3)

countertop mixer Mixer used on top of a counter in small to moderate-size kitchens. It can stand about 2 feet high and weigh 100 pounds. (3.3)

cover Complete place setting for one person; includes china, glassware, and flatware. (20.2)

cracked grain Whole kernels of grain that are cut into large pieces. (13.1)

cream soup Soup made with cream that is noticeably thick with a velvety smooth texture. (14.3)

creaming method In baking, a mixing method in which fat and sugar are combined vigorously to incorporate air. (18.1)

crème anglaise (CREM on-GLAZE) Classic dessert sauce made with the stirred custard method; often used as a base for ice cream and mousses. (19.2)

crème fraîche (krehm fraysh) Cultured dairy product similar to sour cream but with more butterfat. French for "fresh cream." (9.1)

crêpe (KRAYP) Thin, French-style pancake made with very thin batter that contains no baking powder; often folded or rolled and spread with a sweet mixture or filled with savory ingredients. (9.2)

crêpe (KRAYP) **pan** Shallow skillet with very short, sloping sides; often has a non-stick coating. (4.2)

critical control points (CCPs) Specific points in the process of food handling where you can prevent, eliminate, or reduce a hazard. (1.3)

critical limits (CLs) Measurements indicating when foods are at unsafe temperatures based on time and temperature. (1.3)

croissants (kwah-SAHNTs) Buttery-rich crescent-shaped yeast rolls. (9.2)

cross cuts Large cuts of a large drawn fish that contain a portion of the spine. (15.1)

cross-contamination Contamination of food that occurs when safe food comes in contact with biological, physical, or chemical contaminants while it is being prepared, cooked, or served. (1.1)

crostini (kroh-STEE-nee) Type of open-faced sandwich served as an appetizer. It consists of toasted bread drizzled with olive oil and topped with tomatoes, olives, cheese, or other ingredients. See *bruschetta*. (11.2)

crouton (CREW-tahn) Small cube of bread that is toasted or fried until crisp and golden brown; a popular garnish for hearty soups. (14.3)

crown roast Roast prepared by tying a rib roast into a crown shape. (16.1)

crudités (kroo-deh-TAYS) Vegetables that have been cut into bite-size pieces; often served with dips. (11.2)

crumb topping Crumbly mixture of fat, sugar, and flour; often applied to muffins or quick breads. (18.1)

crumber A device for cleaning crumbs from the table. (20.2)

crustaceans (crus-TAY-shuns) Shellfish that have jointed exterior shells. (15.2)

cubano The Cuban version of a pressed sandwich. (11.1)

cube Large dice that is 3/4 inch or greater. (4.1)

cuisine (kwih-ZEEN) The characteristic style of foods, flavors, and cooking practices associated with a specific area; the areas considered for cuisine can vary widely. (6.4)

cultured dairy products Describes dairy products such as buttermilk, sour cream, and yogurt that are made by adding a specific type of beneficial bacteria to milk or cream to achieve a desired texture, taste, and aroma. (9.1)

cured foods Foods that are preserved by drying, salting, pickling, or smoking. Examples are ham, bacon, and salted anchovies. (6.2)

custard Liquid, such as milk or cream, thickened with egg and then baked. (9.1, 19.2)

custard cup Baking dish that is round and straight-edged; comes in various sizes. (4.2)

cut-out cookies Cookies made of stiff dough that is rolled flat and then cut into decorative shapes, often using cookie cutters. (19.3)

cyclical (SIC-li-cal) **menu** Menu that is written for a certain period of time and then repeats itself. Some cyclical menus change four times a year, according to the seasons. Some change every week. (21.1)

D

daily values Daily requirements for nutrients, as established by the FDA; amounts are listed on nutrition labels as a metric weight and also as a percent value and are based on a 2000-calorie diet. (22.1)

dark chocolate Bittersweet or semisweet chocolate; it is less sweet than milk chocolate. (19.1)

deadline In terms of the mise en place timeline, your completion time; when the dish you are preparing must be ready to serve. (7.1)

deck ovens Ovens stacked like shelves, one above the other, like pizza ovens. Food is placed directly on the deck instead of on a wire rack. (3.3)

deep-fat fryers Freestanding or countertop units that hold frying oil in a stainless-steel reservoir. A heating element, controlled by a thermostat, raises the oil to the desired temperature and maintains it. Stainless-steel wire baskets are used to lower foods into the hot oil and lift them out. (3.3)

deep-frying and dry-heat method Dry heat method of cooking in which foods are cooked in hot oil that completely covers the food. (8.1)

deep poaching Moist cooking method in which food is cooked in enough liquid to completely cover it. (15.1)

demi-glace (DEH-me-glahs) Type of brown sauce; made by simmering equal amounts of Espagnol sauce and brown veal stock until the sauce is intensely flavored and thick enough to coat foods. (14.2)

denaturing Altering the chemical structure of a protein, as with acid. (17.1)

denominator Bottom number in a fraction. (The top number is the *numerator*). (5.2)

depurated (DEP-yew-rate-ed) Shellfish that have been placed in tanks of fresh water to purge them of their impurities and sand. (10.4)

derivative sauces Sauces that use a grand sauce as the main ingredient. The grand sauce is combined with other seasonings or garnishes for a specific flavor, color, or texture. (14.2)

dessert salad Salad served as dessert often features fruits, gelatin, and nuts; usually served with a sweetened dressing, a citrus-based dressing, or whipped cream. (10.2)

deveining (dee-VANE-ing) Process of removing the vein that runs along the back of the shrimp; the vein is the intestinal tract of the shrimp. (15.2)

diagonal cut Variation of a rondelle, cutting diagonally instead of straight down, to expose a greater surface area of the vegetable. (4.1)

dice Cut that produces a cube-shaped piece of food. (4.1)

dietary guidelines Developed by the USDA as a method for helping people create a healthy and well-balanced diet; emphasis is on reducing risk for major diseases through diet and physical activity. (22.1)

dietary reference intake (DRI) A system of nutrition recommendations from the Institute of Medicine (IOM) of the U.S. National Academy of Sciences. Used by the United States and Canada. (22.1)

dining room attendant Person responsible for clearing and cleaning tables. Also called *bus person*. (20.1)

dining room manager Person running the dining room portion of the restaurant; also responsible for training service personnel, working with the chef on the menu, arranging seating, and taking reservations. Also called *maître d'hôtel* or *maître d'*. (20.1)

dip Sauce or condiment served with raw vegetables, crackers, bread, potato chips, or other snack food. (10.1)

direct contamination Contamination caused by introducing disease-causing substances directly to a food. (1.1)

disjointing Cutting poultry into halves, quarters, or eighths, before or after cooking. (16.2)

double boiler Cookware that is actually a pair of nesting pots. The bottom pot is filled with water and heated, providing steady, even heat for the top pot. (4.2)

double-panning Using two stacked sheet pans to gently heat the bottom of cookies and avoid overbrowning. (19.3)

double-strength stock Stock that is simmered long enough to cook away half of the water. (14.1)

dough divider Baking equipment that cuts a quantity of dough into equal pieces so they can be shaped in rolls. (17.1)

dough sheeter Baking equipment used to roll large batches of dough out into sheets. (17.1)

dough starter In baking, a dough mixture that starts the fermentation process before the final mixing of all the ingredients. The longer fermentation gives the dough time to develop more gluten strength and depth of flavor. Also called a *pre-ferment*. (17.2)

drawn butter Butter that is melted to use as a sauce for shellfish; also called *clarified butter*. (15.2)

drawn fish Whole fish that has the stomach removed. (15.1)

drop cookies Cookies made from a firm dough or batter that is dropped onto a sheet pan. (19.3)

drum sieve (SIV) Screen stretched on an aluminum or wood frame; used to sift dry ingredients or purée very soft foods. (4.2)

dry aging Process of storing meat by hanging it in a climate-controlled area to make it more tender and flavorful. (16.1)

dry cured Method of preserving food by rubbing it with salt and seasonings. (16.1)

dry goods Foods such as flour, tea, sugar, rice, or pasta. (1.2)

dry-sautéing Dry heat method used for foods high in fat. Similar to pan-broiling. (8.1)

dry storage area Kitchen area where goods such as flour, dry pasta, canned goods, and supplies are stored on shelves at room temperature. (3.2)

du jour (DOO ZHOOR) **menu** Menu that lists food served only on that particular day. "Du jour" means "of the day" in French. (21.1)

dumplings Type of pasta; made from dough that is soft enough to drop into boiling water. (13.3)

dupes Duplicates of guest checks, passed from the dining room to the back of the house. (20.3)

dutch processed Process used for cocoa powder to make it less acidic. (19.1)

E

éclairs (EE-clahrs) Long, straight pastries filled with cream and glazed on top. (19.4)

edible quantity The amount that you use in a recipe and serve to guests (vs. the purchase quantity, the amount you need to purchase for a recipe). (5.2)

effective criticism Criticism that not only points out what went wrong or where things could be better, but also indicates how you can improve. (7.2)

egg wash Mixture of egg and water or milk; brushed onto the tops of breads and pastries to give a glossy sheen. (17.1)

emulsified vinaigrette A vinaigrette that is permanently emulsified as a result of adding an emulsifier. (10.1)

emulsifier (e-MULL-si-fy-er) Ingredient added to an emulsion that makes an emulsion permanent. (10.1)

emulsion (e-MULL-shon) Mixture of two ingredients that would otherwise not combine so that one of the ingredients is suspended evenly throughout the mixture; an emulsion has a uniform consistency. (10.1)

en papillote (ahn pap-ee-YOTE) Fish or shellfish baked in a wrapped package, usually made of parchment paper. Often the fish or shellfish is wrapped with aromatics and vegetables. (15.1)

endosperm Largest part of a grain; it contains the food necessary to support a new plant and is made up almost entirely of carbohydrates, or starch. (13.1)

English service Service style for special groups or private dinners in which the table is fully preset, food is delivered on platters to the dining room, serving dishes are placed on the table or on a table nearby, and a server serves the food to the guests. (20.3)

enriched dough Lean dough that has added butter, oil, sugar, eggs, or milk products. Also called *sweet rich dough*. (17.2)

entrée (AHN-tray) The main course of a meal. (21.1)

entremetier (ehn-tray-meh-tee-AY) Chef responsible for hot appetizers, pasta courses, and vegetable dishes. Also called *soup and vegetables station chef*. (20.1)

environmental protection agency (EPA) Federal agency that plays a part in regulating workplace safety along with OSHA by requiring food service operations to track any chemicals that pose a risk to health. (2.2)

espagnol (ess-spah-NYOL) **sauce** Type of brown sauce; made by thickening a brown veal stock with a roux. (14.2)

espresso makers Specialized types of coffee machines. They force hot water under pressure over finely ground coffee. Often these machines are equipped with steam nozzles used to froth milk for espresso drinks such as lattes and cappuccinos. (20.2)

essential oils Quickly evaporating oils that occur in plants and their fruit and that give the plant or fruit its characteristic odor and/or flavor. (12.1)

ethylene (EH-thih-leen) Gas that accelerates the ripening and rotting process in fruit and vegetables. (12.1)

evacuation routes Escape routes that give everyone in the building at least two ways to get out of the building. (2.1)

even-thaw refrigerator Refrigerator used to thaw large amounts of food quickly and safely. It adds small amounts of heat to rapidly circulating cold air and never exceeds 41°F. (3.2)

executive chef Head chef who commands the kitchen, designs the menu, and oversees food costs. Also called *chef de cuisine*. (20.1)

expediter Person who accepts orders from the dining room, relays them to the various station chefs, and reviews the dishes before service to make sure they are correct. (20.1)

expenses Money being spent by a restaurant. (23.1)

external clients Anyone who does business at a restaurant and is not employed by the restaurant itself. (20.1)

extra-virgin olive oil Finest grade of olive oil, produced by pressing olives once without using any heat. It has a fruity, grassy, or peppery taste with a pale yellow to bright green color and a very low acid content. (10.1)

extruded Act of pushing material through an opening. Pasta machines extrude dough to make special shapes, such as elbow macaroni, spaghetti, and penne. (13.3)

F

fabrication (of meat) Additional butchering done by a restaurant to break down a subprimal cut of meat into portion-sized cuts of meat. (16.1)

factor method One of the oldest, simplest methods for pricing menu items; it involves multiplying the raw food cost by an established pricing factor. (21.2)

Fair Labor Standards Act (FLSA) Federal law that establishes the minimum wage, overtime pay, and child-labor laws for full- and part-time employees, among other things. (23.3)

family service Table service in which food is placed on the table in serving dishes and guests help themselves. (20.3)

farinaceous (fare-eh-NAY-shus) A term nutritionists used to refer to grains and other starchy foods. (13.1)

farm-raised fish Fish raised in ponds or in penned waters. (15.1)

farm-to-table restaurant A restaurant that buys food (vegetables, meats, etc.) directly from the farms producing the food. (23.2)

fat-soluble vitamins Vitamins A, D, E, and K; they dissolve in fat; are stored in body fat, cannot be easily flushed out once ingested, and so should not be taken in excess. (22.1)

fatty acids Small units, made of carbon, hydrogen, and oxygen atoms linked together, that are contained in a fat such as olive oil or butter. (22.1)

FDA food code Frequently updated document by the Food and Drug Administration providing recommendations about keeping food safe. (1.3)

fermentation Chemical reaction that is triggered when hydrated yeast is mixed with food; it makes dough rise until double or triple in size. Produces carbon dioxide and alcohol as byproducts. (17.2)

fermière (FURM-ee-air) Rustic cut that produces 1/8- to 1/2-inch pieces. Means "farmer" in French. (4.1)

fettuccine (feht-too-CHEE-nee) Flat, ribbon-style pasta; may be fresh or dried. (13.3)

fillet (FILL-eh) Boneless piece of fish. (15.1)

filleting (fill-AY-ing) **knife** Knife with flexible blade; used for filleting fish. (4.1)

finger food Hors d'Oeuvre that is served on a napkin and eaten with the fingers. (11.2)

finger sandwich Simple, small sandwich usually made with firm, thinly sliced Pullman loaves. Can be made both as closed sandwiches and as open-faced sandwiches. Also called *tea sandwich*. (11.1)

fire detectors Devices that warn you about a fire so you can get out of a building safely; the two basic types of fire detectors are smoke detectors and heat detectors. (2.1)

fire emergency plan Established plan of action in case of a fire. (2.1)

fire extinguishers Handheld devices used to put out a small fire; specific types of extinguishers are designed to handle specific types of fires. (2.1)

first in, first out (FIFO) system A stock rotation technique in which freshly delivered food is stored behind food already on hand so the oldest food gets used first. (1.2)

fish fumet (foo-MAY) Type of stock made from fish bones that are sweated until they change color and release some of their moisture. (14.1)

fish poacher Long, narrow, metal pan with a perforated rack used to raise or lower the fish so it doesn't break apart. (4.2)

fish station chef Chef responsible for preparing and cooking fish and seafood in a restaurant. Also called *poissonier*. (20.1)

fixed cost Business expense that is the same from one month to the next, such as rent. (23.1)

fixed menu Menu that offers the same items every day. (21.1)

fixed seating plan Seating plan that uses set, staggered meal times (such as 6 p.m., 8 p.m., and 10 p.m.), enabling the kitchen to work at a steady, reliable pace. (20.1)

flat edge A type of cutting edge in which the angle is on only one side of the knife's blade; typical of many Japanese style knives. (4.1)

flat fish Fish with both eyes on the same side of their heads. (15.1)

flat omelette Omelette that is not stirred. It is cooked slowly for a firm texture and is not rolled or folded. It is often baked and cut in wedges. (9.1)

flattop range Cooking unit with a thick solid plate of cast iron or steel set over the heat source; provides an indirect, less intense heat than an open burner. Pots and pans are set directly on the flattop, which is ideal for items that require long, slow cooking. (3.3)

flatware Utensils used at the table or for serving; includes knives, forks, and spoons. (20.2)

flavor The way a food tastes, as well as its texture, appearance, doneness, and temperature. (6.1)

flight of cheeses Offering a number of different cheeses at the same time. (10.3)

floor scale Device at floor level at a receiving area, used for weighing bulky and heavy packages. (3.2)

flow of food Route food takes from the time a kitchen receives it to the time it is served to the customer. (1.2)

fluting Giving pie crusts a decorative edge; it is done by squeezing the dough between your fingers or using a special tool. (19.4)

fonds de cuisine (FAHN duh kwee-ZEEN) French term for stocks; translates as "foundations of cooking." (14.1)

food-borne illness An illness that results from eating contaminated foods. (1.1)

food-borne infection Infection caused by eating a food that contains a pathogen, which grows and reproduces internally, causing a food-borne illness. (1.1)

food-borne intoxication The result of consuming poisons produced by a pathogen and found in food. (1.1)

food chopper Machine that holds food in a rotating bowl that passes under a hood where blades chop the food. Some units have hoppers or feed tubes and interchangeable disks for slicing and grating. Also called a *buffalo chopper*. (3.3)

food contamination Food made unsafe by being contaminated by biological or environmental materials. (1.1)

food dehydrator Equipment that dries food so it can be stored for later use either directly from the dry state or partially rehydrated. Often used in raw food restaurants. (3.3)

food mill Tool used to strain and purée at the same time. Has a flat, curving blade that is rotated over a disk by a hand-operated crank to purée foods. (4.2)

food processor Machine used to grind, mix, blend, crush, and knead foods; it houses the motor separate from the bowl, blades, and lid. (3.3)

food safety Activities, standards, and procedures necessary to keep foods from being contaminated. (1.1)

food-safety audit Inspection of a foodservice establishment by a representative of the local health department. (1.3)

food-safety system System of precautionary steps that take into account all the ways food can be exposed to biological, chemical, or physical hazards. (1.3)

food security The availability of sufficient food on a regular basis to maintain health; also refers to preventing intentional contamination. (1.1)

forced food method Menu-pricing method that is determined by the market; the choices your customers actually make in a restaurant. It takes into account loss and spoilage and assumes that food that is at a high risk of loss or spoilage should have a higher price. It also includes volume in the calculation. The lower the volume, the higher the price (and vice versa). (21.2)

forequarter Front quarter of an animal carcass, such as beef. (16.1)

foresaddle Front portion of the saddle of an animal carcass, such as veal. (16.1)

forged blade Knife blade made from a single piece of heated metal; it is dropped into a mold and then the metal is cut free and hammered into the correct shape. (4.1)

fork-tender Describes foods that are fully cooked and allow a knife or fork to slide all the way into the food easily. (8.2)

formal buying process A buying process that involves sending out a formal invitation to bid and making sure that the bidding process is conducted in a way that provides a full and open competition. (23.2)

formulas Term that bakers and pastry chefs often use for recipes; it points out the importance of accuracy in all aspects of baking. (17.1)

free-form loaf Loaf of bread that is not pressed into a mold or a pan but is shaped by hand into an oval, a round ball, or another shape. (17.3)

freestanding mixer Mixer that sit on the floor and is typically used in commercial bakeries; it can stand about 5 feet high and weigh 3,000 pounds. (3.3)

freestone Describes fruit that has flesh that separates easily from its pit. (12.1)

French buttercream Yellow buttercream icing made by adding sugar and butter to whipped egg yolks. (19.3)

French service Elaborate style of service based on serving a meal in three courses: the first course, or entrée, the second course, and the dessert. (20.3)

French toast Piece of bread dipped in a mixture of milk and eggs, fried until golden brown on both sides, and then served with syrup, fruit, or other toppings. (9.2)

frenching Technique of scraping clean the bones for roasts or chops before they are cooked. (16.1)

fresh cheeses Moist, soft cheeses that typically have not ripened or significantly aged. (10.3)

freshwater fish Fish that live in freshwater ponds, lakes, rivers, and streams. (15.1)

frittata (free-TAH-ta) Type of flat omelette made by pouring eggs mixed with other ingredients into a pan, cooking the mixture, and then finishing it in a hot oven. It is typically cut in wedges. (9.1)

fritters Small deep-fried pieces made by dipping food items, such as fruit, in a batter or other coating and then frying. (12.1)

front of the house In a restaurant, the dining room area. (20.1)

front waiter Person second in line of responsibility after the captain. Helps the captain take orders, makes sure tables are set properly for each course and that food is delivered properly to the correct tables. (20.1)

frozen soufflé Frozen mousse; also called a *parfait.* (19.2)

fully cooked Describes food that is cooked all the way through or to the doneness requested by a customer. (8.2)

fungi Single-celled or multicelled organisms (plural of fungus). May be beneficial, such as a mold used to produce cheese; may be a biological hazard, such as a fungus that causes a food-borne illness. (1.1)

G

game General term for meat of wild mammals and birds. (16.1)

ganache (gahn-AHSH) Emulsion made from chocolate and a liquid, typically heavy cream. (19.1)

garde manger (GAHRD mohn-ZHAY) Person or persons responsible for cold food preparation. Also known as the *pantry chef.* (10.1)

garni French term for any garnished food or plate. (10.4)

garniture French term for an item used to garnish. (10.4)

gaufrette (go-FRET) Cut typically made by a mandoline. Means "waffle" in French. (4.1)

gauge (GAGE) Thickness of the material of which cookware is made. (4.2)

gelatin Protein processed from the bones, skin, and connective tissue of animals; it is used as a gelling agent to thicken and stabilize foams or liquids. (17.1)

general safety audit Review of the level of safety in an establishment. (2.2)

germ Smallest part of a grain; the germ can produce a new plant and contains most of the grain's oils and many vitamins and minerals. (13.1)

German buttercream Rich buttercream icing made by adding butter to pastry cream. (19.3)

giblet bag Small bag in the cavity of a whole bird; includes the liver, stomach, and neck of the bird. (16.2)

gizzard Stomach of a bird, such as a chicken gizzard. (16.2)

glassware Glass containers used to contain liquids, including water glasses, wine glasses, champagne goblets, cocktail or liquor glasses, beer mugs, pitchers, and carafes. (20.2)

glaze Stock that is simmered long enough to produce an intense flavor and a syrupy consistency. (14.1)

glazed fish Whole fish that has been dipped in water and then frozen several times to build up a layer of ice. (15.1)

glucose (GLOO-kohs) What our bodies turn carbohydrates into to use as fuel for warmth and for muscle, brain, and nervous system function. (22.1)

gluten (GLOO-tihn) Network of long, stretchy strands that trap the carbon dioxide given off by yeast when kneading dough. (17.1)

gluten window test Test to check the strength of the gluten in dough—pinch off a piece of dough to see if it stretches without tearing and if it is thin enough for some light to come through. (17.2)

gnocchi (NYOH-kee) Italian dumpling. (13.3)

goujonette (goo-zhohn-NET) Straight cut of fish, sometimes called a *fish finger,* usually about the width of a thumb. (15.1)

grain (of meat) Direction that the fibers in the meat are running. (16.1)

grains Seeds of grasses that human beings have learned to cultivate for food. (13.1)

grand sauces The five basic sauces in classic cookbooks. They are: brown sauce, velouté sauce, béchamel sauce, tomato sauce, and hollandaise. Also called *mother sauces* or *leading sauces.* (14.2)

granité (grah-nee-TAY) Frozen dessert made from a flavored water base; it has large ice crystals, similar to shaved ice. (19.2)

granton (GRAN-ton) **edge** Knife edge that has a series of ovals ground along the edge of the blade to prevent moist foods from sticking to the blade while slicing. (4.1)

granulated sugar Ordinary white sugar that is refined from sugar cane or sugar beets. (17.1)

gratin dish Shallow baking dish made of ceramic, enameled cast iron, or enameled steel. (4.2)

grating cheeses Solid, dry cheeses that have a grainy consistency; they are grated or shaved on food rather than cut into slices because of their crumbly texture. (10.3)

gravy Similar to the grand sauces, but usually has pan drippings produced by meats as they roast. Often made in smaller batches than grand sauces. (14.2)

griddle Thick cast iron or steel plate used as a cooking surface heated from below. Foods are cooked directly on this surface, which is usually designed with edges to contain foods and a drain to collect used oil and waste. (3.3)

grill station chef Chef responsible for all the grilled items made in a restaurant. Also called *grillardin.* (20.1)

grillardin (gree-yar-DAHN) Chef responsible for all the grilled items made in a restaurant. Also called *grill station chef.* (20.1)

grilled sandwich Sandwich that is assembled, the outside surface of the bread spread with butter, and then cooked directly on a heat source, usually a griddle. Also known as a *griddled sandwich.* (11.1)

grilling Dry-heat method of cooking that uses a grill to cook food, with the heat source below the grill. (8.1)

grit Degree of coarseness or fineness of a sharpening stone. (4.1)

grits The American name for cornmeal. (13.1)

gross profit method Menu-pricing method that determines a specific amount of money that should be made from each customer who comes into the restaurant. (21.2)

grosse pièce (GROHSS pee-YES) Method of serving a main item in a presentation or buffet in which a large part of the main item is left unsliced. (10.4)

guacamole (gwah-kah-MOH-lee) Mexican dip made from mashed avocado, seasoned with lime or lemon juice, tomatoes, cilantro, onions, and chiles. (10.1)

H

HACCP (Hazard Analysis Critical Control Plan, pronounced "HASS-ip") Scientific system for maintaining food safety; originally developed for astronauts. (1.3)

hanging scale Scale that weighs large items that can be lifted on a hook, like a side of beef. (3.2)

hard cheeses Cheeses with a drier texture than semisoft cheeses and a firmer consistency. They slice and grate easily. (10.3)

hard dough Basic yeast dough made with the bare essentials – flour, yeast, salt, and water. Also called *lean dough.* (17.2)

hare Type of larger rabbit; it is usually wild. (16.1)

hash Breakfast mixture of pan-fried chopped meat (typically corned beef), potatoes, and seasonings. (9.2)

hash browns Finely chopped or grated potatoes, pressed down in a pan or on a griddle to brown on one side and then flipped to brown on the other side. (9.2)

haunch Hindquarters of a game animal, such as a deer, consisting of the leg and the back of the loin. (16.1)

hazard analysis An examination of the flow of food from the moment you receive it until you serve it. (1.3)

hazard communication program Part of an effective safety program; it includes several important documents that can be used as evidence that reasonable care was taken if someone is injured. (2.2)

hazard communication standard (HCS) Also known as Right-to-Know or HAZCOM; a health regulation that makes sure an employer tells all employees about any chemical hazards present on the job. (2.2)

headed and gutted fish Drawn fish with the head cut off. (15.1)

heat lamp Light with a special bulb placed directly above an area where food is held to keep it hot. (3.4)

heat transfer How efficiently heat passes from cookware to the food inside it. (4.2)

heel Widest, thickest part of the knife blade closest to the handle; used for cutting tasks that require some force, such as chopping through the joints of a chicken. (4.1)

Heimlich (HIME-lick) maneuver Emergency procedure performed to remove an obstruction from the throat of a choking victim. Also called the *obstructed airway maneuver*. (2.2)

heirloom plant Variety of fruit or vegetable that existed many years ago, before produce was grown for mass-market consumption. Grown from heirloom seeds that have been saved by farmers. (12.2)

herbs Leaves and stems of certain plants; used either fresh or in a dried form to flavor dishes. (6.2)

herbes de Provence (AIRBS duh pro-VAWNS) Dried herb mixture associated with France's Provence region. Includes basil, thyme, marjoram, rosemary, sage, fennel seeds, and lavender. (10.1)

hero sandwich Large, closed sandwich that uses a long thin loaf of bread (often called a *hero loaf*). Hero sandwiches (or *heroes*) are known by different names in different parts of the country. Also called *submarines, grinders, po' boys*, or *hoagies*. (11.1)

high-sodium food Food that has a strong salty taste and that contains a significant amount of sodium. (6.4)

hindquarter Rear quarter of an animal carcass. (16.1)

hindsaddle Back portion of the saddle of an animal carcass, such as veal. (16.1)

holding The process of keeping prepared food hot in steam tables or cold in the refrigerator until you are ready to serve it. (1.2)

holding cabinets Metal containers on wheels that can hold large quantities of food or plates on trays, ready to serve. (3.4)

hollandaise (HOLL-uhn-daze) sauce One of the grand sauces; made by blending melted or clarified butter into slightly cooked egg yolks. (14.2)

hollow-ground edge The cutting edge of a knife in which more metal has been removed than in a taper-ground edge, resulting in a thinner, sharper blade that is less durable than the taper-ground blade. (4.1)

hollowware Large objects, decorative or utilitarian, including silver platters, candlesticks, large tea or coffee pots, sauceboats, fondue sets, and cake stands. (20.2)

home fries Sliced potatoes that are pan-fried, often with chopped peppers and onions. (9.2)

hominy (HOM-uh-nee) Whole dried corn kernels that have the hull and germ removed. (13.1)

hominy grits Meal made from hominy so they do not contain the hull or germ. (13.1)

homogenized Process that evenly distributes and emulsifies the fat particles in milk. (9.1)

honing Straightening a knife's edge on a steel to sharpen the knife. (4.1)

hood suppression systems Fire protection systems installed in the ventilation hood over ranges, griddles, broilers, and deep fat fryers; instead of water, they release chemicals, carbon dioxide, or gases that can smother and put out a fire. (2.1)

hors d'Oeuvre (or-DERV) Small, savory, flavorful dish, usually consumed in one or two bites. Means "outside the meal" in French. (11.2)

hors d'Oeuvre variées (or-DERV vare-ee-AY) Method of presenting hors d'Oeuvre. A variety plate for one person with a combination of hors d'Oeuvre on it, usually fewer than ten small offerings. (11.2)

hot cross bun Sweet yeast bun with an icing cross drizzled on top; they originated in England and were traditionally served on Good Friday and Easter. (17.2)

hot plate Device with an electrical heating element typically used to warm coffee and water. (3.4)

hotel pans Stainless-steel or plastic containers used for cooking, holding, and storage. Available in standard sizes that fit in steam tables and other serving equipment. (3.4)

household units Measurements such as teaspoons (tsp), tablespoons (Tbsp), and cups (c). (5.1)

hull Inedible outer layer of a grain; provides a tough protective coat. Also called the *husk*. (13.1)

hummus (HOOM-uhs) Popular Middle Eastern spread made from mashed or pureed chickpeas that are seasoned and served with pita bread, chips, or raw vegetables. (13.2)

husk Inedible outer layer of a grain; provides a tough protective coat. Also called the *hull*. (13.1)

hydrogenation (hy-DROJ-en-ay-shun) Process that changes a liquid polyunsaturated fat, such as corn oil, into a solid fat, such as margarine. (22.1)

I

icebox cookies Drop cookies made from a batter that is formed into a cylinder, chilled, and then sliced and baked. (19.3)

ice-cream freezer Freezer used for ice cream. It operates at colder temperatures than normal freezers, typically around 15°F. (3.2)

immersion blender Long hand held machine that houses a motor at one end and a blade on the other end; it is placed directly in the container of the food to be blended. (3.3)

income statement Record of earnings (or income), losses, and profits of a business. Also called a *profit and loss statement* or a *P&L*. (23.1)

individually quick-frozen (IQF) Describes fruit that has been frozen whole or in slices or chunks, without any added sugar or syrup. (12.1)

informal buying process A buying process in which the person in charge of buying evaluates the various proposals and makes the choice of which to buy. (23.2)

infrared thermometer Device for reading the surface temperature of food without touching the food by measuring invisible infrared radiation. Often used in kitchens to check holding temperatures. (3.2)

initiative (i-NISH-ee-ah-tiv) To perform work without prompting or direction from someone else. (7.2)

injera (in-JAY-rah) Spongy, sourdough-tasting flatbread used as a utensil to scoop up meat and vegetables in Ethiopia. (17.3)

insoluble fiber Fiber that does not dissolve in water. Also called *roughage*, it cleans our digestive tracts, assisting in waste elimination. (22.1)

instant oats Rolled oats that have been partially cooked and then dried before being rolled again. (13.1)

intermediary source Companies that process or distribute an original food product before it gets to the restaurant. (23.2)

internal clients The people who work within the restaurant and whom you come in contact with. (20.1)

inventory List of all the assets in a restaurant, usually organized by category. (23.2)

iodized (EYE-oh-dized) **salt** Table salt to which iodine has been added. (6.4)

Italian buttercream White buttercream icing made by adding butter to meringue. (19.3)

J

job description Duties to be performed and responsibilities involved for a particular job, as well as the level of education and training needed for the job. (23.3)

julienne (ju-lee-EHN) Long, rectangular cut measuring 1/8 inch wide × 1/8 inch thick and 1 to 2 inches in length. (4.1)

jus de veau lié (JHOO duh voh lee-AY) Type of brown sauce; made by simmering brown stock with flavorings and aromatics and, in some cases, additional bones or meat trimmings. (14.2)

K

kaiser (KIGH-zer) roll Large, round, crusty roll used for sandwiches. Also known as a *hard roll* or a *Vienna roll*. (11.1)

kebobs (kuh-BOBS) Small portions of grilled or broiled meat, poultry, or vegetables cooked on a skewer. (11.2)

keel bone Bone that joins the two halves of a breast of poultry. (16.2)

kernel The edible seed of grain that remains after the hull is removed. (13.1)

kitchen shears Scissors used for kitchen chores such as cutting string and butcher's twine, trimming artichoke leaves, cutting grapes into clusters, and trimming herbs. (4.2)

knead (NEED) Work dough by hand or in a mixer to distribute ingredients. (17.1)

kosher salt (KOH-shure) Salt made without any additives; sold in coarse or fine grain styles. Typically flakier than table salt. (6.4)

kuchen (KOO-ken) Sweet, yeast-raised cake filled with fruit or cheese; originally from Germany. (17.2)

kugelhopf (KOO-guhl-hof) Light yeast cake, filled with candied fruit, nuts and raisins, traditionally baked in a fluted ring mold; a tradition in Austria as well as Poland, Alsace, and Germany. (17.2)

L

lamb Tender meat produced by young, domesticated sheep. (16.1)

laminated yeast dough Yeast dough that has fat rolled and folded into it, creating alternating layers of fat and dough, adding flavor and flakiness to the finished product. Also called *rolled-in yeast dough*. (17.2)

lasagna (luh-ZAHN-yuh) Layered baked pasta dish. (13.3)

lattices Strips of pie dough laid across the top of the filling to create a cross-hatch effect. (19.4)

lavash (LAH-vohsh) Thin, flexible flat bread, sometimes used to make a wrap. (11.1)

lean dough Basic yeast dough made with the bare essentials—flour, yeast, salt and water. Also called *hard dough*. (17.2)

leavener (LEV-en-er) Baking ingredient that increases the volume of a dough or batter by adding air or other gas. (17.1)

lecithin (LES-i-thin) Substance found in egg yolks that serves as a natural emulsifier. (9.1)

legume (LEG-yoom) Plant that has a double-seamed pod containing a single row of seeds. Some varieties have edible seeds; some have edible seeds and pods. Seeds are often removed from the pod and dried. (13.2)

lentils Legume shaped like a round disk. (13.2)

liabilities (lie-a-BILL-i-ties) Losses that occur when a restaurant business uses up assets without making a profit. (23.1)

liaison (lee-AY-zohn) Mixture of egg yolks and cream used to lightly thicken and enrich a sauce. (14.2)

limited menu Menu that offers a limited range of choices to the customer, such as four sandwiches, two soups, and a salad for lunch. (21.1)

line chef Chef responsible for a particular type of food. Also called *station chef*. (20.1)

liquid-filled thermometer Thermometer that has either a glass or metal stem filled with a colored liquid. Designed to stay in the food while cooking. (4.2)

liquor (shellfish) Natural juices of a shellfish. (15.2)

lo mein (low mane) Asian-style noodle, often purchased fresh. (13.3)

loaf pans Rectangular pans used for simple cakes and quick breads. (17.1)

logo Drawing, picture, or other symbol that identifies your restaurant. It should be instantly recognizable. (23.1)

low boy Undercounter reach-in refrigerator unit for storing a small amount of ingredients within easy reach at a workstation. (3.2)

lox Cured salmon. (15.1)

lozenge (LOZ-enj) **cut** Diamond-shaped cut measuring 1/2 inch long, 1/2 inch wide, and 1/4 inch thick; most often used in garnishes. (4.1)

M

macaroni Common name used to refer to pasta in general. (13.3)

maillard (MY-yard) **reaction** Color change seen in food that contains protein when it is heated. The food turns brown. (8.1)

main-course salad Salad that is the main course. (10.2)

maître d' (MAY-truh DEE) Person running the dining room portion of the restaurant; also responsible for training service personnel, working with the chef on the menu, arranging seating, and taking reservations. Also called *maître d'hôtel* or *dining room manager*. (20.1)

maître d' hotel (MAY-truh doh-TELL) Person running the dining room portion of the restaurant; also responsible for training service personnel, working with the chef on the menu, arranging seating, and taking reservations. Also called *maître d'* or *dining room manager*. (20.1)

mandoline (MAHN-duh-lihn) Special slicing tool used for precise slicing. It has extremely sharp blades that can be adjusted to achieve precise cuts and thicknesses. (4.1)

marbling Amount of fat present in lean meat. (16.1)

market quote Statement from a supplier of a product's selling price and an indication of the length of time that the price will be effective. (23.2)

market research Information collected to find out what customers like or dislike. (21.1)

marketing plan A plan of the restaurant's overall marketing and promotion efforts. (23.1)

masa harina (MAH-sah ah-REE-nah) Cornmeal made from posole. (13.1)

material safety data sheet (MSDS) A product identification sheet, provided by a chemical manufacturer or supplier, that describes the specific hazards posed by a chemical. (2.2)

matignon (mah-tee-YOHN) Aromatic combination of onions, carrots, celery, and ham used to flavor dishes. (6.2)

maturation Process of reaching the full potential size and weight, as with fruit. (12.1)

mayonnaise (MAY-oh-nayz) Thick, creamy emulsion of oil and egg yolks. (10.1)

meal Grains that are milled into fine particles by rolling the grain between steel drums or stone wheels. (13.1)

meat cleaver Cleaver with a very heavy blade; used to chop through sinews and bones. Also called a *butcher's cleaver*. (4.1)

meat grinder Freestanding machine, or an attachment for a mixer, that grinds meat dropped through a feed tube. The meat is pushed through the machine, cut by blades, and forced out. (3.3)

meat slicer Slicing tool with a circular blade on a horizontally titled frame across which food is passed by means of a carriage. Used to slice foods to even thicknesses. (3.3)

medium dough Lean dough with some sugar and fat added. Pullman loaves, the soft sliced bread used for sandwich making, are made from medium dough. Also called *soft dough*. (17.2)

melon baller Tool used to scoop smooth balls from melons, cheese, and butter. (4.2)

menu List of food and drink choices available in a restaurant. (21.1)

menu conversion Changing the menu radically from one type of food to another. Typically, the restaurant will close down and re-open with a new focus. (21.1)

menu modification Decision by the restaurant to add, change, or delete one or more menu items. (21.1)

meringue (mehr-ANG) Mixture of stiffly beaten egg whites and sugar. (19.2)

mesclun (MEHS-kluhn) French-style salad mix that often includes baby red romaine, endive, mâche, radicchio, and arugula. (10.2)

microplane General-purpose tool used for grating food, such as grating the skin of a lemon to produce fine lemon zest. (4.2)

milk chocolate Chocolate made with milk powder; it is sweeter than dark chocolate. (19.1)

milkfat Fat content of dairy products, measured by the weight of the fat compared to the total weight of the product. Same as *butterfat*. (9.1)

milling Cutting, crushing, rolling, or grinding grain; part of the processing of grain. (13.1)

mirepoix (MEER-uh-pwah) Combination of vegetables used as an aromatic flavoring ingredient in many dishes. Common varieties are *standard, white, Cajun trinity, matignon*, and *battuto*. (6.2)

mise en place (MEEZ uhn PLAHS) French term meaning to "put in place." It includes gathering all the raw materials required for your station and making sure you have all the required equipment and tools for your culinary operation. (3.1) (7.1)

mission statement Statement of the goal of an organization, such as a restaurant. (21.1)

mixer Machine consisting of a bowl and mixing tool for combining ingredients, primarily for batter and dough. (3.3)

mixing Process of combining ingredients so they are evenly spread throughout the mixture. (3.3)

modified à la carte menu Menu on which appetizers and desserts will be priced and served separately. Often the main course includes a soup or salad, a starch, a vegetable, and possibly a beverage. Found in family-style restaurants. (21.1)

modified straight dough-mixing method Baking method in which ingredients are added in steps, providing better distribution for fat and sugar. Useful for enriched dough. (17.2)

molded cookies Made with stiff dough that is shaped by hand; it can also be stamped, pressed, or piped into carved molds. (19.3)

molded salad Another term for aspic, a salad bound with gelatin-thickened liquid. (10.2)

molecular gastronomy (mo-LECK-u-lar gas-TRON-o-mee) A specialized type of food preparation that focuses on the physical and chemical processes that can occur in food preparation. (3.3)

mollusks Shellfish that have soft bodies and no skeletons. (15.2)

monosodium glutamate (MSG) (mon-oh-SO-dee-um GLUTE-ah-mate) Used in much the same way as salt. Provides the umami taste rather than the salty taste and is often associated with Chinese or Japanese food. Enhances the meaty or brothy flavor in meat, poultry, fish, and vegetables. The source of MSG is seaweed. (6.4)

monounsaturated fats Fats that come from plants and are liquid at room temperature. Considered healthy fats, they help balance cholesterol levels in the blood. (22.1)

mousse (MOOSE) Aerated dessert made with a flavored base, gelatin, egg foam, and whipped cream. (19.2)

muesli (MYOOS-lee) Swiss version of granola; a mixture of cereal (such as oats and wheat), dried fruit, nuts, bran, and sugar; eaten with milk or yogurt. (9.2)

mutton Meat from sheep that is over 16 months old; it is tougher than lamb and has a strong, gamey taste. (16.1)

mutual supplementation Combining foods, such as rice and beans, to create a complete protein with all the essential amino acids. (22.1)

MyPlate A graphic representation of a healthy diet developed by the U.S. Department of Agriculture (USDA). It represents five basic food groups and shows them in relationship to one another on a plate. (22.1)

N

nappé (nap-PAY) French term used to describe a sauce that has been properly thickened (thick enough to lightly coat foods). (14.2)

national cuisine The cuisine shared by a nation. Examples are French and Chinese cuisines. (6.4)

neutral stock Another name for white beef stock; it has a very mild flavor and a light color. (14.1)

nibs Cleaned cocoa kernels, removed from their hard outer shell. (19.1)

nonverbal feedback Form of feedback that is written, not spoken. (7.2)

noodle A general term for pasta. (13.3)

no-reservation policy Restaurant policy of not accepting reservations but instead serving customers on a first-come-first-served basis. (20.1)

numerator Top number in a fraction. (The bottom number is the *denominator*). (5.2)

nutrients Parts of food our bodies use. (22.1)

nutritional balance Providing enough calories to meet energy needs and enough specific nutrients to promote health. (22.2)

nutritional value All the benefits a food might have for our bodies; nutritive value. (8.1)

nutritive (NEW-tri-tiv) **value** All the benefits a food might have for our bodies; nutritional value. (8.1)

nuts Dried fruit of a tree. (6.3)

O

oat groats Whole grain of the oat, with the hull removed. (13.1)

oatmeal Coarsely ground oats; cooked as a hot cereal or used in baking. (13.1)

oblique (ob-LEEK) **cut** Cut for vegetables where sides are neither parallel nor perpendicular but cut on an angle, with the vegetable rolled after each cut. Used for long, cylindrical vegetables such as parsnips, carrots, and celery. Also called a *roll cut*. (4.1)

obstructed airway maneuver (Heimlich maneuver) Emergency procedure performed to remove an obstruction from the throat of a choking victim. (2.2)

Occupation Safety and Health Administration (OSHA) Federal agency charged with making sure workers have a safe and healthful working environment. (2.2)

offal (AW-full) Organs and other portions of an animal, including the liver, heart, kidneys, and tongue. Also known as *variety meat*. (16.1)

omega-3 fatty acids Type of polyunsaturated fat found in some plants and in all fish; they are linked to reducing the risk of stroke and heart attack and improving brain growth and development. (22.1)

omelette Blended eggs cooked in a sauté pan with or without other ingredients. It can be folded, rolled, or finished in an oven and served flat. (9.1)

omelete pan Shallow skillet with very short, sloping sides; often has a nonstick coating. (4.2)

on the half shell Method of serving shellfish in which they are opened and served on one of their shells. (10.4)

one-stage cooling method Safely cooling foods to below 41°F within four hours to avoid food-borne illness. (1.2)

opaque (o-PAKE) Indicates that light will not pass through an object. (6.1)

open-burner range Electric or gas-fueled cooking unit with a set of adjustable open burners. Pots and pans are set directly on an electric element or on a grid over a gas flame. (3.3)

open-faced sandwich Sandwich made with one slice of bread and topped with ingredients. (11.1)

order A communication between a buyer (the restaurant) and a seller (the supplier). The restaurant tells the suppliers the product it wants and the amount of the product it wants. (23.2)

organic leavener Yeast, a living organism, which is used to increase the volume of dough. (17.1)

orientation Period of time during which new employees learn about the business and their roles in it. (23.3)

oven spring In baking, last stage of rising that determines volume; it occurs in the oven when gluten strands expand rapidly and trap steam, allowing full size to be reached. (17.3)

over egg Fried egg cooked and then flipped once during frying. (9.1)

ovo-lacto vegetarian Person who does not eat meat, poultry, and fish but does eat eggs and dairy products. (22.2)

P

P&L Record of the money coming into the restaurant (its sales) and the money being spent by the restaurant (its expenses).

Also called a *profit and loss statement* or an *income statement*. (23.1)

palette (PAL-et) knife Tool with a long, flexible blade and a rounded end; used for turning cooked or grilled foods and spreading fillings or glazes. Sometimes used in baking. Also called a *straight spatula* or a *flat spatula*. (4.2)

pan-broiling and dry-heat method Dry-heat method of cooking very much like sautéing, except no fat is used. (8.1)

pan de muertos (PAHN de MOO-er-tohs) Mexican holiday sweet bread, flavored with orange zest, orange juice, and anise seeds; traditionally baked around the Day of the Dead.

pan-dressed fish Fish with the fins removed, and sometimes the head and tail cut off; usually small enough to fit easily in a pan and make a single serving. (15.1)

pan-frying and dry-heat method Dry-heat method of cooking in which food is cooked in hot oil in a pan. (8.1)

pan loaf Loaf of bread made by pressing dough into a mold or a pan. (17.3)

pan proofing Allowing dough to rise one last time outside of the oven before baking. (17.3)

panini (Pa-NEE-nee) Italian version of a pressed sandwich. (11.1)

parasites Large multicelled organisms that reproduce on their own and need a host. Examples: round worms and tapeworms. (1.1)

parboiled Moist-heat method of cooking in which food is cooked at 212°F. (8.2)

parchment paper Grease-resistant, nonstick, heatproof paper; often used to line pans. (17.1)

parcooked Stands for "partially cooked." Method of cooking in which the food is not cooked fully. (8.2)

parcooked grains Grains that are processed by partially cooking them. (13.1)

parfait (par-FAY) Frozen mousse, also called a *frozen soufflé*. (19.2)

paring (PAIR-ing) knife Small knife with 2- to 4-inch blade; used mainly for trimming and peeling fruits and vegetables. (4.1)

Parisienne (pah-REE-see-ehn) scoop Melon baller with a scoop at each end, one larger than the other. (4.2)

par-stock list Listing of the quantity of supplies you need to have on hand in a restaurant to make every item on the menu. (23.2)

pasta Italian for dough; used to describe the category of starchy foods made from shaped dough that includes flour and liquid. Typically cooked in boiling or simmering water. (13.3)

pasteurized Heated at high temperature to kill harmful bacteria and other pathogens. (9.1)

pastry bag Cone-shaped bag with two open ends. Fill the bag with dough or whipped cream, apply a decorative tip to the pointed end, and then squeeze the bag to add fillings to pastries, make delicate cookies, and apply decorative finishes to cakes and pastries. (17.1)

pastry blender Tool with a crescent-shaped loop of thin wires attached to a handle; it is used to mix fat into flour when you make a pastry dough. (17.1)

pastry brush Brush used to apply egg wash and to butter pans and muffin tins; made of soft, flexible nylon, silicone, or unbleached hog bristles. (17.1)

pastry chef Chef responsible for making pastry and other desserts. Also called *pâtissier*. (20.1)

pastry cream Custard with an added thickener such as flour or cornstarch. (19.2)

pastry wheel Cutting tool with a round blade mounted on a handle; roll the blade over pastry dough to make a single, clean cut. Blade may be straight or scalloped to make a decorative edge. (17.1)

pâté fermentée (PAHT fer-mahn-TAY) In baking, a piece of dough saved from one batch and added at the end of mixing to the next batch. French term for "old dough." (17.2)

pâté (pa-TAY) mold Oven cookware that is deep, rectangular, and made of metal, sometimes with hinged sides. (4.2)

pâtés (pah-TAYS) Well-seasoned ground meat, fish, poultry, or vegetables mixture that has been baked. Usually served cold. (10.4, 11.2)

pathogens Disease-causing organisms, such as bacteria, viruses, parasites, or fungi. (1.1)

pâtissier (Pah-tees-SYAY) Chef responsible for making pastry and other desserts. Also called *pastry chef*. (20.1)

paupiette (poh-PYET) Thin fish fillet that is rolled up before it is cooked. (15.1)

paysanne (pahy-SAHN) Rustic type of cut that produces 1/2-inch-square by 1/8-inch-thick pieces. Means "peasant" in French. (4.1)

pearl barley Barley that has been polished to remove the bran. (13.1)

pearl grain Grain that has the bran completely removed. (13.1)

peas Legumes that are round. (13.2)

pectin Substance naturally found in certain fruits; it is used to thicken a liquid. (17.1)

peel Large, flat wooden or metal paddle used to slide bread onto baking stones and to retrieve loaves when they are done. (17.1)

performance evaluation Meeting where a manager and an employee talk about whether or not the employee has met expectations, based on the job description. (23.3)

perishable goods Foods, such as meats and milk, that must be properly wrapped or kept cold until they can be stored in a refrigerator or freezer. (1.2)

perpetual inventory Inventory system in which information about inventory quantity and availability is computerized and updated on a continuous basis. Also called *continuous inventory*. (23.2)

pest infestation Large numbers of a species that is harmful to human health. Examples: rodents or cockroaches. (1.1)

pest management A process involving restricting access of pests, disposing of waste properly, and using pesticides to eliminate pests. (1.1)

phyllo (FEE-low) dough Unleavened dough made from flour, water and a small amount of oil. Folded and layered, with butter between layers, it rises as it bakes and is flaky and crisp. (19.4)

physical hazards Foreign objects found in food that can cause injury or illness. (1.1)

physical inventory Counting the actual assets in a restaurant, such as the number of cans or boxes on a shelf. (23.2)

physical leavener Steam or air incorporated into a batter, causing it to increase in volume. (17.1)

pickup In baking, the first stage of mixing ingredients. (17.1)

pierogi (peer-OH-gee) Polish half-moon-shaped dumplings with a sweet or savory filling. (13.3)

pilaf (PEE-lahf) Grain dish in which the grain—typically rice—is first sautéed in a pan, usually with oil or butter, before adding a hot liquid and being cooked over direct heat or in the oven. (13.1)

pin bones Fish bones found in the middle of the fillet. (15.1)

piped cookies Drop cookies made of soft dough that can be piped through a pastry bag to form decorative shapes. (19.3)

pita (PEE-tah) bread Flat round or oval Middle Eastern bread; also known as pocket bread. When cut in half, each half forms a pocket that can be filled as a sandwich. (11.1)

pith The white, bitter, and indigestible layer that is just below the outer skin of a citrus fruit. (12.1)

planetary mixer Mixer with a stationary bowl and a mixing tool that moves within it, like a planet orbiting the sun. Three standard attachments are a paddle, a whip, and a dough hook. (3.3)

plate cover Metal cover placed over a plate of food to keep the food warm on its way to the customer. (3.4)

plate presentation The way you put food into a dish or on a plate. (7.3)

platform scale Scale on the receiving platform that weighs bulky or heavy packages. (3.2)

platter service Serving style typically used for banquets in which completely prepared hot food is delivered from the kitchen in large platters to a table and then servers present the food to the guests who choose an item. The server then transfers the item to the guests' plate. Also called *Russian service*. (20.3)

poaching Moist-heat method of cooking in which food is cooked at 160°F to 170°F. (8.2)

poissonier (pwah-sun-YAY) Chef responsible for preparing and cooking fish and seafood in a restaurant. Also called *fish station chef*. (20.1)

polenta (poh-LEHN-tah) The Italian term for cornmeal. (13.1)

polyunsaturated fats Fats that come from plants; they are liquid at room temperature. (22.1)

poolish (poo-LEESH) In baking, a wet dough starter with a consistency like pancake batter. (17.2)

portable refrigeration cart Movable refrigerator units for temporary refrigeration or off-site catering. (3.2)

portion Serving size for one person, expressed in pieces, weight, or volume. (5.1)

portion control Controlling the quantity of particular foods by using appropriately sized servings. (22.2)

portion scale Scale that measures the weight of a small amount of food or ingredient (typically a portion). Can be reset to zero to allow for the weight of a container or weigh more than one ingredient at a time. Also known as a *spring scale*. (4.2)

portioning foods Serving the correct amount of a particular food. (7.3)

posole (poh-SOH-leh) The whole kernel of corn that is soaked in an alkaline solution to make the hull softer and easier to digest. Also spelled *pozole*. (13.1)

potentially hazardous foods Foods that offer a friendly environment for disease-producing organisms. (1.1)

poultry Refers to any domesticated bird used for human consumption. (16.2)

pour-over brewers Coffee makers that are similar to airpot brewers except that coffee flows into a pot or carafe that sits on a heating element. Brews coffee quickly. (20.2)

pre-ferment In baking, a dough mixture that starts the fermentation process before the final mixing of all the ingredients, giving the dough time to develop more gluten strength and depth of flavor. Also called a *dough starter*. (17.2)

prep chef Chef responsible for washing and peeling vegetables and fruits, cutting meat, and preparing any other ingredients that will be used by other chefs. (20.1)

presentation side The most attractive side of a food item. (7.3)

pressed sandwich Sandwich that is toasted on a heavy, two-sided cooking press that compresses and grills it until it is hot and heated through on the inside. (11.1)

pressure steamer Cooking unit that heats water under pressure in a sealed compartment, allowing it to reach temperatures above the boiling point. Cooking time is controlled by automatic timers that open the exhaust valves, releasing steam pressure so the unit can be opened safely. (3.3)

pricing factor Factor by which a raw food cost is multiplied to arrive at the price of a menu item. (21.2)

pricing system comparison chart Aids in making pricing decisions; it shows a comparison of the prices from various pricing methods, two competitors' prices, the final decision for the menu price, and your value judgments. (21.2)

primal cuts Cuts made to saddles or quarters of meat that meet uniform standards for beef, veal, pork, and lamb. (16.1)

primary source The farm that produces the food product. (23.2)

prime cost Raw food cost plus the direct cost of labor involved in preparing a menu item. (21.2)

prime cost method Used in cafeteria operations; it prices menu items and also calculates the cost of preparing the menu item. (21.2)

prix fixe (PREE FEEKS) **menu** Menu that offers a complete meal, often including a beverage, for a specific price, allowing a diner to choose one selection from each course. Similar to table d'hôte menu. (21.1)

processed cheese Cheese made from one or more cheeses that have been finely ground, mixed together with other non-dairy ingredients, heated, and poured into a mold. (10.3)

processed grains Grains that have been prepared to use as foods. (13.1)

producer Person or business selling items to a restaurant. Also called *vendor, purveyor*, or *supplier*. (23.2)

product/service mix The relationship between the products a restaurant offers (the menu and the price of menu items) and the services it offers (location/type of restaurant, staff, hours). (23.1)

product specifications Description of a product, including its size, quality, grade, packaging, color, weight, or count. (23.2)

production record Record of all the food served at every meal in the institution. It includes the recipe, the serving size, total prepared, and additional information. Used by large kitchens, especially those at schools and other state- or federally funded institutions. (23.2)

profit The amount left over after expenses are subtracted from sales. (23.1)

profit and loss statement Record of money coming into the restaurant (its sales) and the money being spent by the restaurant (its expenses). (23.1)

promotion Extra effort taken, in addition to advertising, to make a restaurant

business known and get people interested in coming to it. (23.1)

proofer Special box used in baking that holds dough as it rises. Some models have thermostats to control heat and are able to generate steam. (17.1)

prosciutto (pro-SHU-tow) Italian country-style ham. (10.4)

protein Nutrient our bodies need to grow and to replace worn-out tissues and cells; it comes from foods such as meat, fish, eggs, milk, and legumes. (22.1)

psychological factors Factors that take into account how a customer perceives a specific menu item. Customers may psychologically associate high-end menu items, such as lobster, caviar, or truffles, with a higher price. (21.2)

public relations An effort to maintain a positive opinion of the restaurant in the public's view. (23.1)

puff pastry Similar to phyllo dough, a dough made from flour, water, and melted butter. It is rolled out and a layer of butter is added on top the dough. This is folded out again and again, resulting in a multi-layered flaky, crispy dough.

PUFI mark Mark from the U.S. Department of Commerce that indicates a facility has passed a Type 1 inspection. (15.1)

Pullman loaf Long loaf of bread that is baked in a rectangular pan with a lid. A slice from a Pullman loaf is square on all sides. (11.1)

purchase quantity The amount you need to purchase for a recipe (vs. the edible quantity, the amount you use in a recipe and serve to guests). (5.2)

purchase unit The way an ingredient is sold, whether in pounds, bunches, cans, or cases. (5.2)

purée (pyur-AY) To process food until it has a soft, smooth consistency. (4.2) Very fine paste made by cooking a flavorful ingredient until it is very soft and then straining it or using a food processor or blender to chop it very fine. (14.2)

purée soup Hearty soup made by simmering a starchy ingredient such as dried beans or potatoes along with additional vegetables, meats, or aromatics in a broth or other liquid and then puréeing it to the appropriate texture. (14.3)

purveyor (puhr-VAY-er) Person or business selling items to a restaurant. Also called *vendor, supplier*, or *producer*. (23.2)

Q

quarter fillets Common name for the four fillets cut from a flat fish. (15.1)

quarters (of meat) Four pieces of an animal carcass that are made by dividing two sides. (16.1)

quiche (KEESH) Baked egg dish made by blending eggs with cream or milk and other ingredients and baking in a pie shell. (9.1)

quick bread Type of bread that is quick to make because baking soda or baking powder, instead of yeast, is used for leavening, resulting in a ready-to-use batter rather than a dough that needs fermentation time. (18.1)

quick-chill refrigerator Refrigerator that quickly cools prepared food through the danger zone down to the safe storage temperature. Also called a *blast-chill refrigerator*. (3.2)

quick-cooking oats Rolled oats cut into smaller pieces to reduce cooking time. (13.1)

quinoa (KEEN-wah) Grain originally grown in South America; it has a round kernel and becomes fluffy and light when you cook it. (13.1)

R

radiant (RAY-dee-uhnt) **heat** Heat transferred by rays that come from a glowing, or red-hot, heat source such as burning coals, flames, or a hot electric element. (8.1)

raft Name for a clarification that has cooked enough to form a mass and rise to the surface of a simmering consommé. See *clarification*. (14.3)

ramekin (RAM-i-kin) Baking dish that is round and straight-edged; comes in various sizes. (4.2)

range Similar to a stovetop on a home oven; used to heat food in pots and pans. (3.3)

ratites (RAT-ites) Family of flightless birds, such as the ostrich, emu, and rhea. Their meat is a rich red color, lean, and low in fat. (16.2)

ravioli (rav-ee-OH-lee) Italian for "little wraps"; made by layering a filling between two sheets of pasta and then cutting out filled squares, rounds, or rectangles. (13.3)

raw bar Bar or counter at which raw shellfish is served. (10.4)

raw food cost Cost of all the ingredients purchased for a recipe; can also be applied to the cost of all the ingredients that went into a single serving of a dish. (5.2, 21.2)

reach-in Full-size refrigerator with a door that opens and shelves for storing food. May be a single unit or part of a bank of units. (3.2)

receptionist In formal restaurants, the person who assists the maître d' in greeting guests and taking telephone reservations. Referred to as the host or hostess in casual restaurants. (20.1)

recipe Written record of the ingredients and preparation steps needed to make a particular dish. (5.1)

recipe conversion factor (RCF) Amount you multiply a recipe's ingredients or yield to scale it up or down. (5.2)

recommended dietary allowance (RDA) Developed during World War II to investigate issues of nutrition that might "affect national defense." It created a set of recommendations regarding the standard daily allowance of each type of nutrient. (22.1)

recovery time Time it takes for a pan to heat up again after food is added. (8.1)

refined grains Grains that have been processed to remove some or all of the bran and germ; this process removes fiber, vitamins, and minerals from the grain. (13.1)

refined starch Starch (corn, rice, or potatoes) that has been processed enough to remove all but the starch itself; examples include cornstarch and arrowroot. (14.2)

refrigerated drawer Small undercounter refrigerator drawer within easy reach at a workstation. (3.2)

regional cuisine The cuisine shared by a specific region. These regions can be quite large and include many nations. Examples are Mediterranean, Latin, and Asian cuisines. (6.4)

relish Sauce with a chunky texture, typically fruit- or vegetable-based and made with a sweet-and-sour flavoring. (14.2)

reservation policy Restaurant policy of accepting reservations. (20.1)

retail cuts Cuts made to subprimal pieces of meat to prepare smaller pieces, such as steaks, chops, roasts, stews, or ground meat. (16.1)

retarder Refrigerated cabinet used by bakers to slow down fermentation. (17.1)

revenue The money spent in the restaurant by customers; a restaurant's sales. (23.1)

ricer Device in which cooked food, typically potatoes, is pushed through a pierced container, resulting in rice-like pieces. (4.2)

rind (RYND) Surface of a cheese. (10.3)

ring-top range Cooking unit similar to a flattop range, but with thick concentric plates or rings of cast iron or steel set over the heat source. Removing one or more rings provides more intense direct heat. (3.3)

ripening Process when a mature fruit develops its brightest color and deepest flavor, sweetness, and aroma. Some fruit also softens and gets juicier as it ripens. (12.1)

risotto (rih-ZOHT-toh) Creamy rice dish typically made with arborio rice, a short-grain rice. (13.1)

rivets Pieces of metal used to attach the handle of the knife to the blade; lie flush with the surface of the handle. (4.1)

roast station chef Chef responsible for all the roasted items cooked in a restaurant. Also called *rôtisseur*. (20.1)

roasting Dry-heat method of cooking in which food is cooked by hot air trapped inside an oven. Roasting typically means you are preparing larger pieces of food than for baking. (8.1)

roasting pan Pan used for roasting and baking; has low sides and comes in various sizes. Roasting racks are placed inside the pan to hold foods as they cook so the bottom, sides, and top of the food all are cooked evenly. (4.2)

rock salt Salt that is less refined than table salt; not generally consumed. (6.4)

rolled oats Made by steaming oat groats and then rolling them into flat flakes; also called *old-fashioned oats*. (13.1)

rolled cookies Cookies made from a stiff dough that is rolled flat and then cut into decorative shapes, often using cookie cutters. (19.3)

rolled omelette Type of omelette made by stirring the eggs as they cook to make them tender enough to roll or fold. (9.1)

rolled-in yeast dough Yeast dough that has fat rolled and folded into it, creating alternating layers of fat and dough, adding flavor and flakiness to the finished product. Also called *laminated yeast dough*. (17.2)

rolling boil Description of liquid that is rapidly boiling. (8.2)

rondelles (rahn-DELLS) Round shapes produced by cutting through any cylindrical vegetable, such as a carrot or cucumber. Means "rounds" in French. (4.1)

rôtisseur (roh-tess-UHR) Chef responsible for all the roasted items cooked in a restaurant. Also called *roast station chef*. (20.1)

round fish Fish with eyes on both sides of their heads. (15.1)

roundsman Roving chef who fills in for absent chefs or assists chefs in other stations. Also called *swing chef or tournant*. (20.1)

roux (ROO) Cooked paste of wheat flour and a fat used to thicken simmering liquids, producing a sauce. (14.2)

rubbed-dough method In baking, process of cutting fat into chunks, chilling it, and then rubbing it into flour. This prevents the fat from fully combining with the flour and promotes flakiness. (18.2, 19.4)

rubber spatula (SPAT-chew-la) Scraping tool with a broad, flexible rubber or plastic tip. Used to scrape food from the inside of bowls and pans and also to mix in whipped cream or egg whites. (4.2)

runner The front-of-the-house person who delivers food and drinks to the front waiter. The runner, also called the *back waiter*, provides overall assistance to the server. (20.1)

Russian service Serving style typically used for banquets in which completely prepared hot food is delivered from the kitchen in large platters to a table and presented to guests, who indicate their choice. The wait staff then transfers the item to guests' plates. Also called *platter service*. (20.3)

rye berries Whole kernel of rye. (13.1)

rye flakes Rye berries that are put through a roller. (13.1)

S

sabayon (sah-by-YON) Egg foam made by whipping egg yolks and sugar over heat. (19.2)

sachet d'épices (SAH-shay day-PEES) A mixture of fresh and dried herbs and dried spices tied up in a piece of cheesecloth; used to flavor a dish. (6.2)

saddle Half of an animal carcass, such as veal; it includes the right and left sides. (16.1)

safe foods Foods that won't make you sick or hurt you when you eat them. (1.1)

salad Combination of raw or cooked ingredients, served cold or warm, and coated with a salad dressing. (10.2)

salad dressing Use to flavor salads and sometimes to hold a salad together. (10.1)

salamander Small broiler used primarily to brown or melt foods. (3.3)

sales Money coming into a restaurant; also known as *earnings* or *income*. (23.1)

salsa Cold sauce or dip made from a combination of vegetables, typically tomatoes, onions, chilies, peppers, and other ingredients, and often seasoned with salt, pepper, and lime juice. (10.1, 14.2)

saltwater fish Fish that live in oceans, seas, and the water of bays and gulfs. (15.1)

sanitizing Using either heat or chemicals to reduce the number of pathogens on a surface to a safe level. (1.1)

sanitizing solution A solution made by mixing water and a chemical sanitizer. (1.1)

santoku (san-TOE-koo) **knife** A general-purpose knife that originated in Japan; has a blade that curves down toward the tip. It is used for slicing, chopping, and mincing food. (4.1)

saturated fats Fats that come from animal sources (except for coconut oil and palm oil); they are usually solid at room temperature. (22.1)

sauce A liquid served with food to add more flavor, color, texture, and eye appeal to the food. Sauces are made from three types of ingredients: liquids, aromatics and seasonings, and thickeners. (14.2)

saucepan Pan that has straight or slightly flared sides and a single long handle. (4.2)

saucepot Pot that is similar in shape to a stockpot but not as large. Has straight sides and two loop-style handles to ease lifting. (4.2)

saucier (saw-see-YAY) Chef responsible for sautéed dishes and accompanying sauces prepared in a restaurant. Also called *sauté station chef.* (20.1)

sauté pan Shallow, general-purpose pan. (4.2)

sauté station chef Chef responsible for sautéed dishes and accompanying sauces prepared in a restaurant. Also called *saucier.* (20.1)

sautéing (SAW-tay-ing) Dry-heat method of cooking in which food is cooked quickly, often uncovered, in a very small amount of fat in a pan over high heat. (8.1)

sauteuse (SAW-toose) Sauté pan that is wide and shallow with sloping sides and a single long handle. (4.2)

sautoir (SAW-twahr) Sauté pan that has straight sides and a long handle; often referred to as a skillet. (4.2)

savory (SAY-va-ree) Meaty or brothy flavor; the umami flavor. (6.1)

scale (a recipe) To change the amount of recipe ingredients to get the yield you need. Scale up to increase the yield or scale down to decrease it. (5.2)

scaling In baking, weighing liquid and solid ingredients to get precise measurements. (17.2)

scimitar Knife with a long curved blade, used for portioning raw meats. (4.1)

scone Rich biscuit that sometimes contains raisins and is served with butter, jam, or thick cream. (9.2)

scoring Slashes cut on the top of dough to release steam that builds up during baking. (17.3)

scotch barley Barley that retains some of its bran; also called *pot barley.* (13.1)

scrambled eggs Blended eggs that are stirred as they cook in a sauté pan or double boiler over low to medium heat. (9.1)

sea salt Salt made by evaporating seawater; not significantly refined. (6.4)

seams (in meat) Membranes that connect muscles in cuts of meat. (16.1)

searing (SERE-ing) Dry-heat method of cooking in which food is cooked, usually uncovered, in a small amount of fat just long enough to color the outside of the food. (8.1)

seasonings Ingredients you add to a food to improve its flavor. (6.4)

second chef Executive chef's principal assistant, responsible for scheduling personnel and temporarily replacing the executive chef or other chefs as needed. Also called *sous-chef.* (20.1)

seed Portion of a plant capable of producing a new plant. (6.3)

seeding method Method for tempering chocolate in which three-quarters of the chocolate is heated to the correct temperature at which point the remaining one-quarter is added to it to cool it. (19.1)

semisoft cheeses Cheeses that are more solid than soft cheeses and retain their shape. They may be mild or strongly flavored as a result of the process used to make them. (10.3)

semisweet chocolate Dark chocolate that has more sugar than bittersweet chocolate. (19.1)

semolina (seh-muh-LEE-nuh) **flour** Pale yellow flour made from durum wheat. Semolina flour has a high protein content and makes an elastic dough; it is widely used for pasta. (13.3)

separate-course salad Salads that refresh the appetite and provide a break before dessert; usually a light, green salad with a simple vinaigrette or a single vegetable such as asparagus. (10.2)

sequencing Arranging slices to overlap one another in the order they were cut. (10.4)

serrated (SER-ay-ted) **edge** Knife edge that has a row of teeth; works well for slicing foods with a crust or firm skin. (4.1)

server Second in line in responsibility after the captain. The server is responsible for making sure the table is set correctly, food is delivered properly, plates are cleared, and all the diner's needs are met. (20.1)

service carts Carts used in a dining area to carry food and provide a work surface for carving, plating, assembling, and preparing dishes beside a table. Specialized carts are used to flame-finish (flambé) dishes, display pastry, warm food in a chafing dish, and prepare salads. (3.4)

service station The mise en place station for the dining room. Sometimes called the *pantry.* (20.2)

service style How food and drink is delivered to a guest. Also called *table service.* (20.3)

service ware Dishware and utensils used in the dining room, on or off the table. (20.2)

setting priorities In terms of mise en place, deciding which tasks are most important. (7.1)

seviche (seh-VEE-chee) Latin American dish of fish and seafood that is cooked in citrus juice and flavored with onions, chiles, and cilantro. A traditional cold appetizer or hors d'Oeuvre. Also spelled *ceviche.* (11.2)

sexual harassment The persistent request for sexual favors, unprovoked and unwanted sexual advances, or any verbal or physical harassment of a sexual nature. (23.3)

shallow poaching Moist cooking method in which food is cooked in just enough liquid to create some steam in the pan. (15.1)

sheet pan All-purpose baking pan; it is shallow and rectangular, with sides generally no higher than 1 inch. They may be full, half, or quarter size. (4.2)

shellfish Aquatic animals protected by some type of shell. Can be one of two types: mollusks and crustaceans. (15.2)

shellfish stock Type of stock made by sautéing shellfish shells (lobster, shrimp, or crayfish) until bright red. (14.1)

sherbet (SHUR-bit) Frozen desert that is similar to a sorbet but has meringue incorporated to make it lighter. (19.2)

shirred (SHURD) **eggs** Eggs topped with cream and baked in a small dish until they set. (9.1)

shortcake Dessert made with a foundation of biscuits topped with fruit and whipped cream, such as strawberry shortcake. (18.2)

shrimp cocktail Cold, steamed shrimp served with a spicy cocktail sauce; a traditional cold appetizer. (11.2)

shucked shellfish Seafood that has been removed from its shell. (15.2)

side salad Salad served to accompany the main dish. (10.2)

side stand Holds items necessary for setting the table. There is usually one side stand for each station in the dining room. (20.2)

sides (of meat) Two halves of an animal carcass that are made by cutting down the length of the backbone. (16.1)

silpad Flexible pan liner made of silicone that provides a nonstick, heat-resistant surface. Can be used repeatedly. (17.1)

silverskin Tough membrane that surrounds some cuts of meat; it is somewhat silver in color and is generally removed before cooking. (16.1)

simmering Moist-heat method of cooking in which food is cooked at 170°F to 185°F. (8.2)

simple carbohydrates Carbohydrates that contain one sugar or two sugars. Found in fruit, milk, and refined sugars and are digested quickly. (22.1)

simple syrup Mixture of equal amounts of sugar and water, brought to a boil to dissolve the sugar crystals. (19.3)

single-rack dishwasher Dishwasher that processes small loads of dishes quickly. (4.2)

skewers (SKEW-ers) Long, thin, pointed rods made of wood or metal, used to cook meat, fish, poultry, or vegetables. (11.2)

skimmer Tool with a perforated surface used to skim impurities from liquids; also used to remove cooked food or pasta from hot liquid. Sometimes referred to as a *spider*. (4.2)

slicer Knife with a long thin blade used to make smooth slices in a single stroke. (4.1)

smallware Hand tools, pots, and pans used for cooking. (4.2)

smoker Used for smoking and slow-cooking foods, which are placed on racks or hooks, allowing foods to smoke evenly. Some units can be operated at either cool or hot temperatures. (3.3)

smoothie Cold drink made by mixing fresh fruit (such as bananas and strawberries),

juice, and ice in a blender until thick and smooth; can also contain milk or yogurt. (9.2)

smothering Dry-heat method of cooking that is a variation of *sweating*; food, typically vegetables, is cooked covered over a low heat in a small amount of fat until food softens and releases moisture. (8.1)

sneeze guards See-through barriers that protect foods in a service station from cross-contamination caused by a sneeze. People can see and reach food under the guard. (3.4)

soda bread Quick bread leavened with baking soda and an acid ingredient, usually buttermilk, and shaped into a round loaf. (18.2)

sodium chloride Chemical name for salt. (6.4)

soft dough Lean dough with some sugar and fat added. Pullman loaves, the soft sliced bread used for sandwich making, are made from soft dough. Also called *medium dough*. (17.2)

soft, rind-ripened cheeses Soft cheeses that have been ripened by being exposed to a spray or dusting of "friendly" mold. (10.3)

soluble fiber Fiber that dissolves in water; foods that contain it help us feel full and help lower cholesterol levels in the blood. (22.1)

sommelier (suhm-uhl-YAY) Person responsible for buying and storing wines, maintaining proper wine inventory, counseling guests about wine choices, and serving wine properly at the table. Also called *wine steward*. (20.1)

sorbet (sor-BAY) Frozen dessert made from a flavored base that is frozen and aerated in an ice cream maker. (19.2)

soufflé (soo-FLAY) Light, puffed, baked egg dish. (9.1, 19.2)

soufflé (soo-FLAY) **dish** Baking dish that is round and straight-edged; comes in various sizes. (4.2)

soup Liquid foods served in a bowl and eaten with a spoon. (14.3)

soup and vegetables station chef Chef responsible for hot appetizers, pasta courses, and vegetable dishes. Also called *entremetier*. (20.1)

soup station chef Chef responsible for stocks and soups. (20.1)

sourdough In baking, a tangy, slightly sour dough starter made from wild yeast. Can be kept alive for a long time. (17.2)

sous-chef (SU-chef) Executive chef's principal assistant, responsible for scheduling personnel and temporarily replacing the executive chef or other chefs as needed. Also called *second chef*. (20.1)

sous vide (SU veed) **machine** A cooking device that cooks food in a sealed airtight plastic bag in a water bath, often for a long

time. The temperature of the water is precisely controlled. (3.3)

spaetzle (SHPET-zuhl) Popular Austrian and German dumpling. (13.3)

spice blends Combination of spices (and in some cases, herbs) used to flavor a dish. (6.2)

spices Aromatic dried seeds, flowers, buds, bark, roots, or stems of various plants used to flavor food. (6.2)

spine Noncutting edge of a knife blade. (4.1)

spiral mixer Mixer used for bread dough in which the bowl turns instead of the mixing tool, which is a spiral-shaped hook. (3.3)

sponge In baking, a thick, batter-like mixture created when yeast is combined with water and some flour. (17.2)

spring scale Scale used to measure the weight of a small amount of food or an ingredient; can typically be reset to zero so you can allow for the weight of a container. Also known as a *portion scale*. (4.2)

springform pans Baking pans consisting of a hinged ring that clamps around a removable base; used for cakes that might otherwise be difficult to unmold. (17.1)

stabilizing In mixing, the step after which the mixed ingredients reach maximum volume and the mixer is slowed down to break the large air bubbles into smaller ones, providing better texture. (19.3)

stamped blade Knife blade made by cutting blade-shaped pieces from sheets of previously milled steel. (4.1)

standard breading Process of coating food prior to cooking it (typically by pan-frying or deep-frying). Involves dusting the food with flour, dipping it in beaten eggs, and then covering it in breadcrumbs. (8.1)

standard mirepoix Type of mirepoix consisting of 2 parts onion, 1 part carrot, and 1 part celery; used to flavor a dish. (6.2)

standardized ingredients Ingredients that have been processed, graded, or packaged according to established standards (eggs, shrimp, and butter, for instance). (5.1)

standardized recipe Recipe tailored to suit the needs of an individual kitchen. (5.1)

starch slurry Mixture of a refined starch and cold water used to thicken simmering liquids, producing a sauce. (14.2)

station chef Chef responsible for a particular type of food. Also called *line chef*. (20.1)

steaks (fish) Small cross cut pieces of fish portioned for a single serving. (15.1)

steam table Large freestanding unit that keeps food hot while it is being served. It holds several inserts or hotel pans, under which is steaming hot water. Large steam tables have a thermostat to control the heating elements that maintain the desired temperature. (3.4)

steamer Set of stacked pots or bamboo baskets with a tight-fitting lid. The upper pots or baskets have perforated bottoms so steam can gently cook or warm the contents of the pots or baskets. In a metal steamer, water is placed in the bottom pot and it is placed on the range. Bamboo steamers are generally placed over water in a wok. (4.2)

steaming Moist-heat method of cooking in which food is in a closed pot or steamer and the steam trapped in the pot or steamer circulates around the food. (8.2)

steam-jacketed kettle Freestanding or tabletop cooking unit that circulates steam through the walls, providing even heat for cooking stocks, soups, and sauces. Units may tilt or have spigots or lids. (3.3)

steel Tool used to maintain a knife's edge between sharpenings; it is a rod made of textured steel or ceramic. (4.1)

stenciled (STEN-sild) **cookies** Delicate drop cookies made with batter that is spread very thin, sometimes onto sheet pans into stencils to make a perfect shape. They are often rolled or curled while still warm. (19.3)

stewing Combination cooking method in which food is first seared and then gently cooked in flavorful liquid. Stewing indicates that food is cut into smaller pieces and then cooked in enough liquid to completely cover the ingredients. (8.2)

stir-frying Dry-heat method of cooking that is a variation of *sweating*; food is typically cooked in a wok quickly and evenly while you constantly stir and toss it. (8.1)

stir-ins Savory or sweet ingredients that can be chopped up and added to muffins and quick breads; examples are vegetables, fruit, nuts, cheese, and chocolate. (18.1)

stock Flavorful liquid used primarily to prepare soups, sauces, stews, and braises. Made by simmering bones, shells, or vegetables, mirepoix, herbs, and spices in a liquid (typically water). (14.1)

stock base Highly concentrated liquid or a dry powder that is mixed with water to make a stock. (14.1)

stockpot Large pot that is taller than it is wide and has straight sides. Used to cook large quantities of liquid, such as stocks or soups. Some stockpots have a spigot at the base so the liquid can be drained off without lifting the heavy pot. (4.2)

stollen (STOH-len) Sweet, loaf-shaped yeast bread filled with dried fruit and topped with icing and cherries; it is the traditional Christmas bread of Germany. (17.2)

stone Hard pit that covers a seed, such as the pit in a peach or apricot. (12.1)

straight dough-mixing method Method most commonly used for mixing yeast dough, in which all the ingredients are mixed together at the same time. (17.2)

strategies Skills and techniques you will use to get a job done. (7.1)

streusel (STRU-sel) Crumbly mixture of fat, sugar, and flour that may include spices and nuts; often applied to muffins or quick breads. (18.1, 19.4)

sturgeon (STURH-jen) Large fish whose eggs are made into caviar. (10.4)

subprimal cuts Next level of cuts made to meat after cutting primals from saddles or quarters. Subprimal cuts can be trimmed, packed, and sold to restaurants or butcher shops. (16.1)

sugar glaze Thin liquid made by dissolving sugar in water, applied to baked goods. (18.1)

sugar syrup Concentrated solution of sugar and water. (19.2)

sunny-side-up egg Fried egg cooked without turning, keeping the yolk intact. (9.1)

superfine sugar Granulated sugar that is more finely ground than ordinary sugar so it dissolves more easily. (17.1)

supplier Person or business selling items to a restaurant. Also called *vendor, purveyor,* or *producer.* (23.2)

suprême (soo-PREM) Boneless, skinless breast of poultry with one wing joint, often frenched, still attached. (16.2)

sweating Dry-heat method of cooking in which food, typically vegetables, is cooked uncovered over a low heat in a small amount of fat until food softens and releases moisture. (8.1)

sweet rich dough Lean dough that has added butter, oil, sugar, eggs, or milk products. Also called *enriched dough.* (17.2)

swing chef Roving chef who fills in for absent chefs or assists chefs in other stations. Also called *roundsman* or *tournant.* (20.1)

swiss brasier Large shallow freestanding cooking unit, used to cook large quantities of meats or vegetables at one time. Most units have lids that allow the unit to function as a steamer. (3.3)

symmetrical (sym-MET-rih-cull) In terms of plate presentation, equal numbers of items on either side of the plate. (7.3)

T

table d'hôte (TAH-blah DOHT) **menu** Menu that offers a complete meal—from an appetizer to a dessert, and often including a beverage—for a set price. (21.1)

table salt Salt that is refined to remove other minerals and processed to give it a fine, even grain. (6.4)

table service How food and drink is delivered to a guest. Also called *service style.* (20.3)

tableside service Service in which dishes are prepared, finished, or plated in the dining room in view of the guests. (20.3)

table tent menus Folded cards placed directly on restaurant tables to tell customers about specials. (21.1)

tableware Dishware and utensils used by customers. (20.2)

tabling method Method of cooling melted chocolate by moving it around on a marble slab. (19.1)

tagliatelle (tag-lee-ah-TEHL-ee) Thin, ribbon-shaped pasta. (13.3)

tahini (ta-HEE-nee) Sesame paste. (6.3)

take-out service Buying prepared food and taking it home or to work, as an alternative to cooking at home or eating in a restaurant. (20.3)

tamarind (TAM-uh-rihnd) Fruit used in the Middle East, Asia, and India to provide a sour-sweet taste. (6.2)

tang Section of knife blade that extends into the handle. Tangs can be full or partial. (4.1)

tapas (TAH-pahs) Spanish hors d'Oeuvre selection; small bites featuring ingredients such as ham or eggs. (11.2)

tapenade (top-en-ODD) Dip made from black olives, capers, anchovies, garlic, herbs, lemon juice, and olive oil; originally from France's Provence region. (10.1)

taper-ground edge Knife edge in which both sides of the blade taper smoothly to a narrow V shape. The most common type of cutting edge for general use. (4.1)

tapioca (tap-ee-OH-kah) Thickener made from the cassava root, a starchy tropical tuber; often used to thicken fruit pie fillings and to make pudding. (17.1)

tare weight Weight of the container holding food on a scale. To account for the tare, reset the scale to zero while weighing the empty container. If the scale cannot be reset, subtract the tare from the total weight. (4.2, 5.1)

tart pans Baking pans made of tinned steel or ceramic, with short, often scalloped sides and usually a removable bottom. May be round, square, or rectangular. (17.1)

tasks In terms of mise en place, smaller jobs that lead to the completion of an assignment. (7.1)

taste One of the senses; the taste and aroma of a food. (6.1)

tea sandwich Simple, small sandwich usually made with firm, thinly sliced Pullman loaves. Can be made both as closed sandwiches and as open-faced sandwiches. Also called *finger sandwich.* (11.1)

temperature danger zone Temperature range from 41°F to 135°F in which pathogens can grow. (1.1)

tempering Heating and cooling a blade several times to ensure that the blade will be properly hardened and will not be brittle (4.1) Warming a liaison (a mixture of cream and egg yolks) so the yolks will not overcook or scramble when added to a simmering sauce or other liquid. (14.2) Process of correctly crystallizing chocolate. (19.1)

termination Firing of an employee. (23.3)

terrine (teh-REEN) **mold** Oven cookware usually made of pottery but can also be metal, enameled cast iron, or ceramic. Produced in a wide range of sizes and shapes; some have lids. (4.2)

terrines (teh-REENS). Mold for pâtés. When pâté is served in its mold, it is called a terrine. (10.4, 11.2)

theme In a restaurant, the decorations, lighting, food, and prices, all of which tie the restaurant concept together. (23.1)

thermistor (therm-IS-tor) **thermometer** Thermometer that uses a resistor (electronic semiconductor) to measure temperature. Gives a fast reading, can measure temperature in thin and thick foods, and is not designed to stay in food while cooking. (4.2)

thermocouple (THER-mo-cup-ul) **thermometer** Thermometer that uses two fine wires within the probe to measure temperature. Gives the fastest reading, can measure the temperature in thin and thick foods, and is not designed to stay in food while cooking. (4.2)

timeline In terms of the mise en place, a schedule that tells you when certain tasks have to be completed. (7.1)

time-temperature-abused food Food that has been held in the temperature danger zone for more than two hours. (1.2)

tomato concassé (kon-kah-SAY) Tomatoes that have been peeled, seeded, and diced. (12.2)

tongs Tool used for picking up hot items such as meat or large vegetables. Can also be used for sanitary serving of such items as cookies or ice cubes. (4.2)

top crust Large piece of pastry dough rolled out and placed on top of a filled shell before baking. (19.4)

toque (toke) Tall chef's hat that is open at the top. It prevents hair from falling into the food. (2.2)

torte (TORT) Typically a type of layered cake or pastry that originated in central Europe. The cake or pastry is sometimes made with little or no flour, using instead ground nuts, sugar, eggs, and flavorings. (19.3)

tortellini (tohr-te-LEEN-ee) Italian for "little twists"; made by cutting out circles or squares of fresh pasta, adding a filling, and then folding and twisting the dough to get a specific shape. (13.3)

tortilla (tohr-TEE-yuh) Mexico's unleavened bread; it is round, flat, and made of corn or flour. (11.1)

tossed salad Salad in which all the ingredients are combined with dressing. (10.2)

tournant (toor-NAHN) Roving chef who fills in for absent chefs or assists chefs in other stations. Also called *swing chef* or *roundsman*. (20.1)

tournée (TOUR-nay) **knife** Paring knife with a curved blade. Also called a *bird's-beak knife*. (4.1)

toxin-mediated Infection An infection caused by eating food containing harmful bacteria. The bacteria reside in the intestinal tract and produce toxins that make an individual sick. (1.1)

training Period of time during which new employees learn the job and practice it. (23.3)

tranche (TRAHNSH) Portion of a fish fillet that has been cut on an angle. (15.1)

trancheur (tran-SHUR) Person in charge of carving and serving meats or fish and their accompaniments. Also called *carver*. (20.1)

trans fats Also called *trans fatty acids*, a potentially harmful type of fat created from the process of hydrogenation; has been linked to heart disease. (22.1)

translucent (trans-LU-cent) Indicates that some light will pass through an object. (6.1)

tray stands Used by serving staff to place a tray holding multiple dishes close to the table where they will be served. (3.4)

trueing Process of straightening a knife's edge using a steel. (4.1)

trussing Tying or securing poultry or other food so it maintains its shape while cooking. (16.2)

tube pans Baking pans with a center tube of metal that conducts heat through the center of the batter; they bake heavy batters evenly and quickly, without over-browning the outside of the cake. Typically made of thin metal with or without a nonstick coating. (17.1)

tuber (TOO-ber) Fleshy portion of certain plants; usually grows underground. Potatoes are the most common type of tuber. (12.2)

turner Tool with a broad blade and a short handle that is bent to keep the user's hands off hot surfaces. Used to turn or lift hot foods from hot cookware, grills, broilers, and griddles. Also called an *offset spatula* or a *flipper*. (4.2)

turntable Used to decorate cakes; you turn the cake on the turntable with one hand while the other is free to use a palette knife or cake comb. (17.1)

twice-baked cookies Cookies made of dough formed into a large log-shaped cookie and baked, and then cut into slices and baked a second time for a very crisp texture. (19.3)

two-stage cooling method Safely cooling foods to 70°F within two hours and to below 41°F within an additional four hours, for a total cooling time of six hours, to avoid food-borne illness. (1.2)

udon (oo-DOHN) Asian-style noodle, often purchased fresh. (13.3)

umami (OO-mam-ee) Meaty or brothy flavor; also called *savory*. (6.1)

undercounter dishwasher Dishwasher that holds portable dish racks to allow for easy transfer of clean and dirty dishes. (4.2)

undercounter reach-in Refrigerator unit under a workstation counter used for storing a small amount of ingredients within easy reach. Also called a *low boy*. (3.2)

unsweetened chocolate Chocolate that has no sugar added. Also called *baker's chocolate* or *chocolate liquor*. (19.1)

utility knife Smaller, lighter version of the chef's knife, with a 5- to 7-inch blade. (4.1)

variable cost Business expense that can vary from one day, week, month, or year to the next, such as the cost of food. (23.1)

variety meat Organs and other portions of an animal, including the liver, heart, kidneys, and tongue. Also known as *offal*. (16.1)

veal Meat that comes from a young calf, generally two to three months old. It has delicate, tender flesh that is pale pink. (16.1)

vegan Person who eats no animal products whatsoever and consumes only plant-based foods. (22.2)

vegetable cleaver A cleaver with a rectangular blade and straight sides; often used in the same applications as a chef's knife. (4.1)

vegetable station chef Chef responsible for vegetables and starches. (20.1)

vegetable stock Type of stock made from a combination of vegetables. (14.1)

vegetarian Person who, for religious, ethical, economic, or nutritional reasons, does not eat meat, poultry, and fish. (22.2)

velouté (veh-loo-TAY) One of the grand sauces; a white sauce made by thickening a poultry, fish, or shellfish stock with a blond roux. (14.2)

vendor Person or business selling items to a restaurant. Also called *supplier, purveyor,* or *producer*. (23.2)

venison Meat from any member of the deer family, including antelope, caribou, elk, and moose. (16.1)

verbal feedback Form of feedback that is spoken. (7.2)

verbal warning When a manager tells an employee about the need for improvement in a particular area. (23.3)

vertical chopping machine (VCM) Machine used to grind, whip, blend, or crush large quantities of foods. A motor at the base is permanently attached to a bowl with blades; the hinged lid must be locked in place before the unit will operate. (3.3)

vinaigrette (vin-eh-GRETT) Salad dressing made by combining oil and vinegar into an emulsion. (10.1)

viruses Biological hazards that can cause illness when they invade a cell and trick the cell into making more viruses. (1.1)

volume Measurement of the space occupied by a solid, liquid, or gas. (5.1)

W

walk-in Large refrigeration or freezing unit that usually has shelves arranged around the walls of the unit. (3.2)

walkout Customer who leaves the table without paying the bill. (20.4)

warewashing station Area for rinsing, washing, and holding tools, pots and pans, and dishes. Also includes trashcans, sinks, garbage disposals, and dishwashing equipment. (4.2)

water activity (Aw) Measurement of the amount of moisture available in a food; the scale runs from 0 to 1.0, with water at 1.0 and potentially hazardous foods at .85 or higher. (1.1)

water bath Method of baking in which a container of food is put into a pan of water in the oven to control the heat. A water bath is often used when a chef wants the finished item to have a creamy, smooth consistency. (8.1)

water boiler Holds boiling water and dispenses it from a spigot. Used to provide hot water for tea by the cup or pot. (20.2)

water-soluble vitamins The B and C vitamins; they dissolve in water and are transported throughout the body in the bloodstream. They must be replenished often because they cannot be stored for very long in the body. (22.1)

well method Quick-bread mixing method in which liquid ingredients are added to a depression in the dry ingredients and mixed minimally to avoid overmixing. (18.1)

wet aging Process of storing meat in vacuum packaging under refrigeration to make it more tender and flavorful. (16.1)

wheat berry Whole kernel of wheat. (13.1)

whetstone Hard, fine grained stone for sharpening knives and other tools. (4.1)

whip Hand mixing tool similar to a whisk but narrower and with thicker wires; used to blend sauces or batters without adding too much air. (4.2)

whisk Hand mixing tool with thin wires in a sphere or an oval shape used to incorporate air for making foams. Very round whisks incorporate a large amount of air and are sometimes called *balloon whisks*. (4.2)

white chocolate Chocolate made from cocoa butter, sugar, and milk powder; it contains no chocolate liquor. (19.1)

white mirepoix Type of *mirepoix* consisting of onions, parsnips, celery, and, in some cases, leeks; used to flavor white stocks and soups. (6.2)

white pepper Ripe berries from the pepper vine that have been allowed to dry and have had the husks removed; used as a seasoning. (6.4)

white stock Type of stock made from unroasted bones. The bones may be blanched before simmering. Often called *neutral stock*. (14.1)

whole fish A fish that is sold as it was caught, completely intact and still including the stomach. (15.1)

whole grain Grain with just the husk or hull removed; also referred to as *minimally processed*. (13.1)

wild fish Fish that are caught in nets or on fishing lines in open water. (15.1)

wild rice Seed of a marsh grass. Not related to other rice, but cooked like them. (13.1)

wine steward Person responsible for buying and storing wines, maintaining proper wine inventory, counseling guests about wine choices, and serving wine properly at the table. Also called *sommelier*. (20.1)

wok Cookware for fast stovetop cooking, such as stir-frying; has tall, sloped sides. Once one ingredient cooks, you can push it up the sides, leaving the hot center free for another ingredient. (4.2)

wontons (WAHN-tahns) Type of Chinese dumpling made with a fresh pasta wrapper; often served as an appetizer or with soup. (13.3)

work flow Planned movement of food and kitchen staff as food is prepared. (3.1) In terms of mise en place, putting ingredients, tools, and equipment in a logical order for accomplishing your task. (7.1)

work lines Geometric arrangements of workstation equipment and storage areas, designed to fit the available kitchen space and improve efficiency of staff. Examples include straight-line, L-shaped, U-shaped, back-to-back, and parallel. (3.1)

work sections Combination of workstations in a kitchen. (3.1)

work sequencing In terms of mise en place, doing the right thing at the right time. (7.1)

work simplification In terms of mise en place, getting things done in the fewest steps, the shortest time, and with the least amount of waste. (7.1)

worker's compensation Program run by each state that provides help for employees who are hurt or who become sick because of an accident on the job. (2.2)

workstation Work area containing equipment and tools for accomplishing a specific set of culinary tasks. (3.1)

wrap Sandwich that is rolled up, or otherwise enclosed in an edible wrapper, such as a tortilla. (11.1)

wrappers Type of pasta used in Asian cooking. Sold in squares, rounds, or rectangles; can be made from wheat or rice flour. (13.3)

written warning When a manager documents in writing to an employee that there is need for improvement in a particular area. (23.3)

Y

yeast hydration In baking, the soaking process that activates yeast. (17.2)

yield Measured output of a recipe, expressed in total weight, total volume, or total number of servings of a given portion. (5.1)

yield percentage The adjustment made to certain recipe ingredients, especially fruits, vegetables, meats, fish, and poultry, that have to be trimmed, boned, skinned, cored, or peeled before they can be used in a recipe. (5.2)

Z

zest Colored outer layer of citrus fruit peel. (4.2)

zester Tool that cuts away thin strips of citrus fruit peel. (4.2)

Index

1999 Model Food Code, 25

A

à l'anglaise, 515
à la carte, 727–728
à la meuniére, 513
abrasion, 48
abrasive cleaner, 17
acaraje, 710
accident log, 62
accident report, 62, 715
accidents, 48–49
    preventing, 50–54
Achatz, Grant, 265
acid cleaner, 17
acidity, 10
acids, 199
    baking ingredients, 573
    salad dressing, 299
acidulated water, 383
advertising, 793–794
aeration, 636
    frozen desserts, 639
aflatoxin, 435
afternoon tea, 617
agar agar, 468
aged, beef, 538
Agricultural Marketing Service
    (AMS), 382, 405
aïoli, 302
airpot brewers, 693
al dente, 448–449
albumen, 267
alkalinity, 10
alkalized cocoa, 623
all-purpose flour, 567
all-purpose knives, 108
allergies, 14, 56–57, 774
allspice, 181
almond, 193
aluminum cookware, 135
ambience, 789
American buttercream, 657
American Culinary Federation
    (AFC), 225
American omelette, 277–278
American service, 702
amino acids, 753
amnesiac shellfish poisoning, 521
AMS; See Agricultural Marketing
    Service
anadromous fish, 498
anaphylactic shock, 56
angel food cake pan, 579
Anisakiasis, 9
Anisakidae (roundworms), 9
anise, 176
anodized aluminum cookware,
    135
anti-griddle, 89
antipasti, 365
antipasto platter, 332–333
appearance,
    bread quality, 600
    doneness, 262
    ganache, 630
appetizer,
    cheese, 329
    salad, 305
    types of, 359–362

apples, 371–372
appliance thermometer, 22
appliances, 577
applications,
    job, 828
applying,
    for a job, 828–830
apprentices, 264
    programs, 829
apron, 50
aquaculture, 521
Armentrout, Jennifer, 167
Arnone, Ken, 496
aromatic, 170
    combinations, 188–190
    fruits, 184–185
    liquids, 185
    pepper, 199
    sauce, 467–468
    vegetables, 184–185
arrangement, 231
    asymmetrical, 232
    cold food presentation,
        337–339
arrowroot, 574
arson, 39
arugula, 309
Asian cuisine, 200, 201
    stir-frying, 245
aspic, 306
assembling,
    pies, 662–665
    tarts, 662–665
assembly line,
    sandwiches, 355
assembly points, 46
assets, 796
assignments, 210
assistant banquet coordinators,
    563
asymmetrical arrangement,
    232
attendance, 220
au gratin, fish, 515
automated external defibrillator
    (AED), 56
automatic brewers, 694
automatic fire control systems,
    41–42
avocados, 390
avulsion, 49
Aw (water activity), 11

B

baba ghanoush, 304
Bacillus cereus, 8
back-to-back work line, 70–71
bacon, 288
    Canadian-style, 288, 544
bacteria, 5–6
bagels, 350
baguettes, 596
bain marie, 133
baked custard, 631–632
baked pasta, 452
baker's assistants, 602
baker's chocolate, 623
baker's sugar, 572
bakers, 36, 602
bakers' percentage, 581

bakeshop,
    ingredients, 566–574
    uses of eggs, 569
    work surfaces, 576
baking formulas, 581
baking powder,
    quick breads, 606
baking soda,
    and grease fires, 40
    quick breads, 606
baking stones, 577
baking, 240–243
    biscuits, 614–617
    bread equipment, 577
    breads, 598–599
    cakes, 654–656
        oven temperature,
            654–656
    cookies, 649–650
    fish, 515
    fruit, 386
    molds, 578–579
    muffins, 607
    pans, 578–579
    pastries, 598–599
    quick breads, 606–607
    rolls, 598–599
    shellfish, 529
    stages of bread, 599
    types of chocolate, 623–624
    vegetables, 413
    water bath, 243
baklava, 667
balance scale, 129
balloon whisks, 127
balsamic vinegar, 299
bananas foster, 668
banchan, 634
banquet beverage manager, 563
banquet chefs, 367
banquet cooks, 367
banquet coordinators, 563
banquet dining room manager,
    367
banquet hall,
    holding equipment, 95–96
banquet manager, 563
banquet servers, 563
banquet,
    cover, 696
bar blender, 84
bar cookies, 643, 648
bar, 810
barbequed ribs, 202
basic vinaigrette, 297
basil, 176
batch cooking,
    vegetables, 779
bâtonnet, 115, 118
batter, 246, 284
    drop cookie, 642
    quick bread, 605
battuto, 189
Bavarian cream, 637
bay leaf, 176
beans, 434
    Dietary Guidelines, 770
    in salads, 315
    sorting, 437
beaten biscuits, 611
béchamel sauce, 471

beef,
    cuts of, 537–540
    primal cuts, 538–539
    recommended temperature, 25
    variety meat, 540
belgian endive, 309
belly bones, 510
belly, pork, 544
bench boxes, 593
bench knife, 576
bench proofing, 592
bench scraper, 576, 592
benificial organisms, 4–5
berries, 371, 373
beverages,
    breakfast, 289–290
    milk, 280
bibb lettuce, 308
bibimbap, 634
bid, 804, 805
biga, 590
bimetallic-coil thermometer, 130
biological hazards, 5–6, 8–9
biscotti, 643
biscuit cutters, 576
biscuits,
    baking, 614–617
    cutting, 616
    laminating process, 616
    mixing, 614–617
    serving, 617–618
    shaping, 616
    temperature of dough,
        614–616
    types of, 611
bisque, 484
bitter greens, 307, 309
bitter, 169
bittersweet chocolate, 624
black pepper, 199
blades, knife, 105–106
blanching, 239, 261
    bones, 460
    vegetables, 410
blast chiller, 26
blast-chill refrigerator, 77
blender, 84
    bar, 84
    countertop, 84
    hand, 84
    immersion, 84
    stick, 84
blending, 83
    equipment, 82–83
blind-baked, 664
blinis, 335–336
blooming the gelatin, 574
blueberries,
    in quick breads, 608
blueberry muffins, 609
    recipe, 147
Blumenthal, Heston, 103
boards, cutting, 122–123
body type,
    of fish, 499
boiling point, 11
boiling, 253, 255
    grains, 428–429
    pasta, 447–449
    shellfish, 527
    vegetables, 410

bolster (of blade), 106
Bon Appétit, 145
bones,
    preparing for stock, 459–460
    for stock, 457
boning knife, 108
borscht, 508
Boston butt, 543
boston lettuce, 308
bottom line, 796
Botulism, 8
bouillabaisse, 473
bouillon strainer, 128
bouillon, 482
boule, 596
bound salad, 305–306
bouquet garni, 190, 458
    preparing for stock, 458
bowls,
    mixing, 127
box grater, 125
boxed meat, 536–537
bracsola, 336
braided Easter egg bread, 584
braided loaves, 597
braising pan, 134
braising, 258–260
    vegetables, 411–412
bran, 421–422
brand, 793
brasier, swiss, 86
Brazilian cuisine, 710
bread bakers, 602
bread flour, 567
bread,
    baking equipment, 577
    breakfast, 286–288
    cooling, 599
    doneness, 599
    evaluating quality, 599–600
    in salads, 314
    sandwich, 349–350
    shaping, 594–597
    slicing, 599
breading, standard, 246
breakfast,
    beverages, 289–290
    breads, 286–288
    cereals, 286–288
    meats, 288–289
    potatoes, 288–289
    Vietnamese, 287
breast,
    lamb, 545
    veal, 541
brioche, 585
brisket, 539
broiler, 88
broiling, 240–241
    fish, 514–515
    fruit, 387
    shellfish, 529
    vegetables, 412–413
broth, 481–483
    making, 485–486
brown rice, 424–425
brown sauce, 471
    derivatives, 475
brown stock, 458–459, 462
brown sugar, 199, 573
browning,
    bones, 460
brunoise, 116–118
bruschettas, 362
budget, 790
buffalo chopper, 82

buffet service, 702–703
    holding equipment, 95–96
buffet table,
    design, 339
building,
    cakes, 656–657
bulgogi, 634
bulk fermentation, 588
Bundt pan, 579
burns, 48–49, 91, 246, 577
    first aid, 55
    preventing, 51
burr mixer, 84
business plan, 788–791
butcher's cleaver, 109
butcher's steel, 120
butchering, 536–537
butchers, 36
butler service, 363, 702
butter, 281–282
    baking, 571
    biscuit dough, 614
    drawn, 527
    sandwiches, 351
    softening, 644
buttercream icing, 657
butterfat, 280
butterflied, leg of lamb, 546
butterfly cut,
    holding the knife, 111
butterhead lettuce, 308
buying; *See* purchasing

C

cabbage family, 390–391
cadmium, 6
cafeteria service, 703
cafeteria,
    holding equipment, 95–96
caffeine, 289–290
Cajun trinity, 188
cake combs, 580–581
cake flour, 567
cake pans, 578
    preparing, 652
cakes,
    baking, 654–656
    building, 656–657
    cooling, 656
    decorating, 658–659
    doneness, 656
    finishing, 658–659
    glazes, 658
    icing, 657–658
calamari, 518
California menu, 728
callaloo, 528
calories, 753, 765–766
Campylobacter jejuni, 8
Canadian bacon, 288, 544
canapés, 362
canned,
    fish, 506
    legumes, 438
capers, 187
capsaicin, 397
caramelize, 238
caraway seeds, 181
carbohydrates, 755–756
cardamom, 181
Cardamone, Victor, 67
cardiopulmonary resuscitation
    (CPR), 55–56
careers; *See* culinary careers
Carême, Antoine, 535

Caribbean cuisine, 528
carpaccio, 362
carryover cooking, 250–251
    blanching, 261
carts, 70
carving,
    holding the knife, 111
cash register, 809
cashew, 193
casserole, 134
cast iron cookware, 132
castor sugar, 572
casual restaurants, 676
catering coordinator, 367
catering manager, 367
catering, 797–798
caviar presentation, 334–336
CCPs, 31–32, 148
centerpieces, 340–341
centrifuge, 85
cereals, 427
    breakfast, 286–288
Certified Executive Chef (CEC),
    264
Certified Professional in Supply
    Management (CPSM), 750
ceviche, 362
chafer cart, 100
chafing dish, 96
challah, 585
channel knife, 126
Chantilly cream, 381
charcuterie, 336
charger, 696
cheese board, 329–330
cheese cart, 329
cheese makers, 36
cheese,
    blue-vein, 322, 325
    buying, 326–327
    cooking with, 330–331
    fresh, 320
    grating, 125, 322, 326
    handling, 326–328
    hard, 322, 325
    making, 327
    processed, 320, 326
    sandwich filling, 351–352
    semisoft, 322, 324
    serving, 329–330
    soft, rind-ripened, 321, 324
    storing, 326–328
    types of, 320–326
cheesecloth, 478
chef's knife, 108
chef's tasting, 363
chefs, 264
    pantry, 296
ChefSteps.com, 103
chemical hazards, 5–6
    mercury in fish, 16
chemical leaveners, 570
chemicals,
    carcinogenic, 60
    corrosive, 60
    MSDS, 60–61
chervil, 176
chestnut, 193
chicken-fried steak, 289
chiffonade, 114–115
Child, Julia, 641
chiles, 397
chili powder, 184
chill wand, 26
china cap, 128
china, 688–689

Chinese cuisine, 200, 558
Chinese parsley, 177
chinois, 128
chives, 176
chlorine dioxide,
    in lean dough, 583
chlorine, 17
chocolate chips, 624
chocolate liquor, 623
chocolate,
    making of, 627
    melting, 625
    mousse, 637
    storing, 628
    tempering, 625–628
    types of, 623–624
    working with, 624–628
Choice, 538
choking, 55
cholesterol, 270
chopping, 113
choucroute garnie, 473
choux paste, 665–666
chuck, 538–539
    veal, 541
chutney, 478
ciabatta, 350
ciguatoxins, 505
cilantro, 177
cinnamon buns, 584
cinnamon, 181
citrus friut, 371–374
clams, 525
clarifying,
    butter, 281–282
    soups, 482
cleaning, 16–18
    coffee makers, 694
    cooking equipment, 89–93
    cookware, 135–138
    crumber, 693
    cutting boards, 123
    food preparation equipment, 85
    freezers, 77–78
    fruit, 383, 780
    holding equipment, 99
    knives, 121
    mollusks, 525
    mushrooms, 395
    OSHA procedures, 85
    pastry tools, 579–581
    pest control, 19–20
    plate presentation, 228
    refrigerators, 77–78
    service equipment, 100
    service utensils, 697–699
    shelves, 80
    silicone mats, 645
    smallware, 135–138
    spills, 715
    storage containers, 80
    vegetables, 407, 780
    water boiler, 694
cleansing agents, 17
clear soups, 481–483
clear,
    describing flavor, 173
cleaver,
    meat, 109
    vegetable, 109
client base, 791–793
clingstone fruit, 376
closed sandwich, 355
Clostridium botulinum, 8
Clostridium perfringens, 8
cloves, 181

CLs, 31–32
club sandwich, 356
coating chocolate, 624
cocktail sauce, 333
cocoa butter, 623
cocoa powder, 623
cocoa,
    Dutch processed, 623
coddled eggs, 271
coffee, 289–290, 708
    airpot brewers, 693
    automatic brewers, 694
    espresso makers, 694
    percolators, 694
    pour-over brewers, 693–694
    urns, 694
colander, 128
cold food presentation,
    centerpieces, 340–344
    elements in, 336–340
    garnishes, 340–344
    types of, 332–336
cold storage area, 78
collaboration, 224–225
color, 231
    blanching, 261
    cold food presentation, 337
    composed salads, 318
    describing flavor, 173
    garnishes, 342
    moist heat affects, 252
    and nutrients, 764
    nutritional value, 253
    olive oil, 299
    roux, 469
combi oven, 88
combination cooking methods,
    258
combination steamer/oven, 88
come out of temper, 106
commercial kitchen consultant, 66
commercial kitchen designer, 66
communication, 217–220
    customer complaints, 712–715
    in emergencies, 716
    menus, 726–727
    restaurant manager, 811
    telephone etiquette, 683
    work flow, 74
complaints, 219
    addressing quickly, 713
    anticipating problems, 713
    handling, 712–715
complex carbohydrates, 755
compliments, 219
composed salads, 316–317
    examples, 318
compote, 386
compound butter, 476
compound chocolate, 624
compound sauces, 474
compressing, 152
conch, 528
Condé Nast, 145
condiments, 191–192
conditioning the pan, 245
confectioner's sugar, 573
conflict resolution, 812
conflicts, 218, 220
conical sieve, 128
consommé, 482
    making, 485–487
containers,
    bench boxes, 593
    for legumes, 435
    storing chocolate, 628

contamination,
    biological, 5–6
    cross-, 12
    direct, 11–12
    food, 4
    fungi, 5–6
    indirect, 12
    parasites, 5–6
    sources, 11–12
    viruses, 5–6
continental breakfast, 287–288
continuous inventory, 806
continuous seating plan, 687
convection oven, 88, 243
convection steamer, 86
convection, 462
convenience foods, 238–239, 253
conventional oven, 88
converted rice, 425
conveyor belt dishwasher, 137
cook-chill technique, 77
Cook's Warehouse, 235
cookbooks, 143
cooked dips, 303
cooked dressings, 303
cookie cutters, 576
cookie dough crust, 660–661
cookies,
    baking, 649–650
    finishing, 650–651
    glaze, 650–651
    icing, 650–651
    making, 644–652
    types of, 642–644
cooking contests, 144
cooking equipment,
    broiler, 88
    cleaning, 89–93
    convection steamer, 86
    deep-fat fryer, 89
    griddle, 89
    grill, 89
    kettles, 86
    microwave, 88–90
    ovens, 88
    pressure steamer, 86
    ranges, 87
    selection, 89
    smoker, 88
    sous vide machine, 86
cooking methods,
    changes to food, 237–238, 252
    combination, 258
    moist-heat, 253–257
cooking time,
    scaling recipes, 160–161
cooking,
    beef, 538–540
    carryover, 250–251
    cereals, 429–430
    with cheeses, 330–331
    cold food presentation, 337
    crêpes, 286
    eggs, 270–280
    fish, 513–517
    fruit, 385–387
    game, 546–547
    grain, 432
    greens, 390–393
    lamb, 545–546
    meals, 429–430
    mixing, 127
    pancakes, 285
    pork, 543–544
    poultry, 560
    resting food, 251

safely, 23–27
    shellfish, 527–529
    and taste, 172
    tools, 127
    veal, 541–542
    vegetables, 409–414
    waffles, 285
cooks, 264
cookware, 132–135
    gauge, 132
    heat transfer, 132
    materials made of, 132, 135
    oven, 134
    stovetop, 133
    warping, 132
cool foaming method,
    cake batter, 654
cooling method,
    one-stage, 25
    two-stage, 25
cooling,
    bread, 599
    cakes, 656
    chocolate, 626
    cookies, 650
    food safely, 25–26
Coppedge, Richard, Jr., 455
copper cookware, 132
corer, 126
coriander, 181
corn salad, 308
corn syrup, 199, 573
corn, 425–426
cornmeal, 426
cornstarch, 574
corrective action, 33
corrosive materials, 60
cos lettuce, 308
cost control, 797
cost of labor, 743
cost of single portion, 162
cottage butt, 543
coulis, 477
count,
    measurement conventions,
    150
    shrimp, 520
counter scale, 76
counter service, 703
countertop blender, 84
countertop mixer, 83
courtesy, 224
cover letters, 828
cover, 695–697
covered racks, 96
CPR, first aid, 55
crab cakes, 361
cracked grain, 423
cream fillings,
    tarts, 662–663
cream soup, 483–484
cream, 281
    adding to soup, 483
creaming method, 607
    cakes, 653
    cookie dough, 645–646
creativity, 221–222
crème anglaise, 633
    ice cream, 638
crème brûlée, 631
crème caramel, 631
crème fraîche, 281
Creole/Cajun cuisine, 203
crêpe pan, 133
crêpes, 285–286
Crispo, Phil, 621

critical control points (CCPs),
    31–32
critical limits (CLs), 31–32
criticism, 218–220
croissants, 287, 350
cross cuts, 506
cross-contamination, 12
    cleaning to prevent, 16
    cutting boards, 123
    fruit and, 383
    measuring tools, 152
    meat, 547
    and preparing foods safely, 23–24
    sneeze guards, 95
    soups, 489
crostini, 362
croutons, 313, 492
crown roast, 541
crudités, 362
crumb topping, 609
    pies, 664–665
crumb, 570
    bread quality, 600
crumber, 693
crumbly dough crust, 661–662
crust formation, 599
crustaceans, 518
cubano, 358
cube, large dice, 117
cuisine bourgeoisie, 473
cuisine, 200–203
    African, 187
    Asian, 200
    Brazilian, 186, 710
    Caribbean, 187, 528
    Chilean, 186
    Chinese, 186, 558
    Eastern European, 187
    French, 186, 473
    German, 802
    Greek, 186, 775
    haute, 310
    Indian, 186
    Italian, 187, 254
    Japanese, 186
    Korean, 634
    Latin American, 186, 200
    medieval, 242
    Mediterranean, 200
    Mexican, 186, 615
    Middle Eastern, 187, 595
    modernist, 206
    Moroccan, 187
    Russian, 508
    Scandinavian, 187
    Spanish, 187, 364
    Thai, 186, 443
    Vietnamese, 186
Culinarian's Code, 225
culinary careers, 36–37, 66–67
    applying for a job, 828–830
    apprentice programs, 829
    assistant banquet coordinators,
    563
    baker, 602
    baker's assistants, 454, 602
    banquet beverage manager, 563
    banquet coordinators, 563
    banquet manager, 563, 721
    banquet servers, 563
    bread bakers, 454, 602
    butcher, 346
    candy makers, 672
    caterer, 721
    catering, 367
    charcutiére, 346

culinary careers (continued)
  chef, 264
  chocolatiers, 672
  clinical dietitians, 785
  community dietitians, 785
  confiseur, 672
  cook, 264
  cover letters, 828
  culinary instructor, 234
  décorateur, 672
  demonstrating for an interview, 829
  demonstrators, 234
  dietitians, 785
  dining room managers, 721
  event planners, 367
  executive chef, 721
  fish cook, 531
  food and beverage managers, 721
  food communications, 166
  food flavorist, 206
  food scientist, 418
  food technologist, 418
  foodservice equipment developers, 102
  foodservice equipment manufacturers, 102
  goal setting, 821–822
  hospitality managers, 620
  informational interviewing, 827–828
  instructor, 234
  job offers, 830
  job opportunities, 826–828
  letters of reference, 824
  management dietitians, 785
  nutritionists, 785
  owner/operators, 620
  owning a food business, 495
  pastry chef, 602, 672
  personal chef, 293
  poissonnier, 531
  portfolio, 829–830
  preparing a résumé, 822–825
  private chef, 293
  prospecting, 826–827
  purchasing agents, 749
  restaurant managers, 721
  shift managers, 721
  specialty bakers, 454
  taster, 206
culinary diversity,
  Brazil, 710
  Caribbean cuisine, 528
  China, 558
  France, 473
  Greece, 775
  India, 201
  Korea, 634
  kosher food, 482
  Mexico, 615
  Middle East, 595
  Russia, 508
  Spain, 364
  Thailand, 443
culinary history,
  Carême, Antoine, 535
  cereal, 427
  Child, Julia, 641
  early ovens and stoves, 59
  Escoffier, George Auguste, 612
  the first cookbook, 271
  forks and spaghetti, 691
  knives, 116
  Medici, Caterina de, 310

  nouvelle cuisine, 777
  before the refrigerator, 28
  Schorner, Dieter, 802
  soups and sops, 485
  spice routes, 180
  tomato, 406
  Vatel, Francois, 381
culinary math,
  cash register, 809
  converting fractions, 156
  forecasting, 791
  measuring angles, 120
  multiplying fractions, 157
  preparing the check, 708
culinary science,
  the 240 factor, 586
  aquaculture, 521
  chocolate, 627
  colors and nutrients, 764
  convection, 462
  eggs, 275
  fish, 504
  osmosis, 198
  raising meat, 548
  turkeys, 555
  vitamins and minerals, 754
culinary skills,
  service sequence, 709
culinology, 102
cultured dairy products, 281
cumin, 181
cured fish, 506
cured foods, 185–187
curly endive, 309
curry leaf, 177
curry powder, 184
custard cups, 134, 579
custard, 569, 631–635
  baked, 631–632
  boiled, 633–635
  egg, 279
  stirred, 633
  tart filling, 662–663
customers,
  planning menus, 724–726, 730
cut biscuits, 611
cut-out cookies, 643–644, 648–649
cutlets,
  making, 549–550
  pounding, 549–550
cuts, 48–49
  first aid, 55
cutters,
  biscuit, 576
  cookie, 576
cutting boards, 122–123
  colored, 23
cutting edge (of blade), 106
cutting gloves, 51
cutting tools,
  bakeshop, 576–577
  safe handling, 50
cutting,
  bar cookies, 650
  biscuits, 616
  dough, 592
  fruit, 383–384
  meat, 548–552
  richness, 197
cyclical menu, 729

D

daily values, 767–768
dairy management degree, 36

dairy,
  dressings, 302–303
  ice cream, 638
  storage, 23, 280–283
daisy ham, 543
dandelion greens, 309
deadline, 212
death cap, 5
decision making, 221
deck, oven, 88
decorating,
  cakes, 658–659
  fruit purées, 387
decorative cuts, 119
deep frying, 247–250
  fish, 514
deep poaching,
  fish, 516
deep-fat fryer, 89
degreaser, 17
dehydrating, 437
demi-glace sauce, 471
demonstrating,
  for an interview, 829
demonstrators, culinary, 234
denaturing, 573
denominator, 156
depurated,
  mollusks, 519
  shellfish, 333
derivative sauces, 474
  béchamel, 476
  brown, 475
  velouté, 476
design,
  bar, 810
  dining room, 808–810
  employee area, 808
  entrance, 810
  food storage areas, 808
  kitchen, 807–808
  office, 808
  restaurant, 807–810
  restrooms, 810
  waste management, 808
designing,
  menus, 734–737
dessert salad, 307
desserts,
  cakes, 652–656
  cookies, 642–644
  frozen, 637–639
  fruit, 665–668
  pastries, 665–668
  pie, 660–665
  plating, 669–670
  tarts, 660–665
detergent, 17
deveining, shrimp, 524
diagonal cut, rondelle, 113
dicing, 116–117
  onions, 407
Dietary Guidelines, 768–770
Dietary Reference Intake (DRI), 767
dietitians, 785
digital scale, 129
dijon mustard, 299
dill, 177
dining room, 808–810
dips, 297–304
  cocktail sauce, 333
  dairy-based, 302–303
  vegetable, 304
direct contamination, 11–12
disabled accomodations, 704

disciplining, 816–817
dish carts, 135
dishwashing machines, 18, 136–138
disjointing,
  holding the knife, 111
  poultry, 556, 559
display holding unit, 97
disposable gloves, 14
diversity, 224
dividing,
  dough, 592–594
doneness, 250–251
  al dente, 448–449
  baking cookies, 650
  bread, 599
  cakes, 656
  eggs, 272
  fish, 513
  fried eggs, 275
  moist-heat, 260–262
  pasta, 448–449
  poultry, 559
  quick breads, 607
  roux, 469–470
  vegetables, 410
double boiler, 133
double-breasted jacket, 50
double-panning, 644
double-strength stock, 465
dough, 567
  bench proofing, 592
  choux paste, 665–666
  cookie dough crust, 660–661
  crumbly dough crust, 661–662
  dividers, 577
  dividing, 592–594
  drop cookie, 642
  flaky, 660
  glazes, 598
  hook, 84
  phyllo, 667
  pie, 660–662
  preshaping, 592–594
  press, 577
  puff pastry, 667–668
  rolled-in, 590–591
  rolling pie, 663–664
  rubbed-dough method, 660–661
  sheeter, 577
  starter, 590
  tart, 660–662
  types of yeast, 583–585
  washes, 598
draining tools, 128–129
drawn butter, 527
drawn fish, 506
dressing for safety, 50
dressings,
  composed salad, 317
  dairy-based, 302–303
  salad, 297–304
  vegetable, 304
dried fruit, 380, 384–385
drop biscuits, 611
drop cookies, 642, 647
drum sieve, 128–129
dry aging, 538
dry cured ham, 544
dry goods, 22
dry storage area, 78
dry volume, 152
dry-heat method,
  poultry, 560
dry-rind semisoft cheese, 322
dry-sautéing, 245
du jour menus, 728

dumplings, 360, 442
dupes, 704
durum wheat, 254, 444
Dutch processed cocoa, 623

E

E. coli, 8, 542
echoing, 74, 218
éclairs, 665
edible flowers, 310
edible paper, 102
edible quantity, 162
editors, food, 166
Educational Foundation of the
        National Restaurant
        Association, 7
effective criticism, 218–219
egg foam, 636
egg pasta, 448
egg rolls, 360
egg substitutes, 569
egg wash, 569
    biscuits, 616
    pie crust, 664
eggs, 267–280, 568–570
    in cakes, 640
    in cookies, 640
    in custard, 631
    Dietary Guidelines, 770
    ideal storage temperature, 23
    meringue, 636
    in quick breads, 606
    sabayon, 636
    safety, 302
    sandwich filling, 351–352
    temperature, 606
    tempering, 631–632
Eichelberger, Ezra, 564
Electrolux, 102
Elia, Mark, 347
emergencies, 715–716
    preparing for, 57–58
empanadas, 360
employee area, 808
employment,
    applying for, 828–830
employment; See culinary careers,
emulsified vinaigrette, 297
emulsifier, 297
emulsifying,
    cake batter, 653
emulsion, 297, 472
    ganache, 628
en papillote, 516
endosperm, 421–422
English bacon, 543
English service, 702
enhancing taste, 196
enriched dough, 584
enriched yeast dough, 589
Enrichment Act, the, 754
entrance, 810
entrées, 735
Environmental Protection Agency
        (EPA),
    mercury in fish, 16
    workplace safety, 58
EPA; See Environmental
        Protection Agency
epazote, 177
Epicurious, 145
equipment, 146
    bakeshop, 575–581
    blending, 82–83
    bread-baking, 577

chopping, 82
cooking, 86–93
food preparation, 81–85
grinding, 82
holding, 94–99
mixing, 82–83
other food preparation, 85
planning a menu, 731
planning menus, 725
preparing sauces, 478–479
receiving, 75–76
refrigeration, 76–78
selection, 89
service, 99–100
slicing, 82
for soups, 484
stock pot, 460
storage, 78–80
escape routes, 44
escarole, 309
Escherichia coli (E. coli), 8
Escoffier, George Auguste, 473, 612
espagnol sauce, 471
espresso makers, 694
essential oils, 371
ethics, 224
ethylene, 381
evacuation routes, 44
even-thaw refrigerator, 77
event planners, 367
executive chef, 264
exit sign, 46
exotic fruit, 378–379
expenses, 796
extra-virgin olive oil, 298–299
extruded pasta dough, 444

F

fabrication, 536
    breast of chicken, 559
    poultry, 555
face-to-face work line, 70, 72
facility design, 807–810
facility layout, 807–810
Fair Labor Standards Act (FLSA),
        815
falls, 49, 52
family service, 702
family-style restaurants, 676
fan cut, 119
    garnishes, 342–343
farinaceous foods, 421
farm-raised fish, 498
farm-to-table restaurant, 803
fast-food restaurants, 676
    holding equipment, 94–95
Fat Duck Experimental Kitchen,
        103
FAT TOM, 10–11
fat-soluble vitamins, 758
fat,
    in cakes, 640
    in cookies, 640
fats, 756–758
    baking ingredient, 571–572
    in fish, 499
    menu planning, 774
    in quick breads, 605
fattoush, 314
fatty acids, 756
FDA Food Code, 30
    critical limits, 32
FDA,
    Food Code, 30
    HACCP, 31

mercury in fish, 16
nutrition labels and information
        sheets, 766
    sanitation standards, 30
    two-stage cooling method, 25
feedback, 219–220, 792
feijoada, 710
fennel, 182
fenugreek, 182
fermentation,
    bulk, 588
fermiére, 117, 118
fettuccine, 444
FIFO; See First In, First Out
        system
filled pasta, 451
filleting knife, 108
fillets, fish, 506, 509–513
fillings,
    cake, 657
    choux paste, 665–666
    cookie, 651
    ganache, 628
    pans for quick breads, 607
    pies, 662–663
    sandwich, 351
    tarts, 662–663
Fine Cooking, 167
fine-dining restaurants,
        676–677
finger food, 359
finger sandwich, 355
finishing,
    cakes, 658–659
    cookies, 650–651
fire control, 41–44
fire detectors, 41
fire drills, 47
fire emergency plan, 44
    assembly points, 46
    escape routes, 44
    evacuation routes, 44
fire extinguishers, 42–44, 87
    classes of fires, 43
    PASS system, 43–44
    types of, 43
fire hazards, 39–41
fire-safety plan, 39
fire,
    classes of, 43
    color of flames, 45
    drills, 47
    emergency plans, 44–47
    small, 42
first aid, 54–58
    anaphylactic shock, 56
    automated external
            defibrillator (AED), 56
    broken bones, 55
    burns, 55
    choking, 55
    CPR, 55
    cuts, 55
    sprains, 55
    stitches, 55
    strains, 55
First In, First Out (FIFO) system,
        22–23, 797
    storage containers, 80
first-aid kit, 54
fish cooks, 264, 531
fish farming, 531
fish finger, 512
fish fumet, 458–459
fish poacher, 133
fish scaler, 126

fish,
    body type, 499
    cooking methods, 513–517
    Dietary Guidelines, 770
    doneness, 513
    fat content, 499
    ideal storage temperature, 23
    menu planning, 774
    mercury in, 16
    preparing, 509–513
    recommended temperature, 25
    sandwich filling, 351
    seafood advisory lists, 499, 504
    selecting, 504–507
    storage, 507–509
    substitutions, 499
    types of, 498–504
five senses, 169–171
fixed cost, 797
fixed expense, 797
fixed menu, 729
fixed seating plan, 686
flaky dough, 660
flambé cart, 99
flank steak, 540
flat edge (of blade), 106
flat fish, 499
flat omelette, 276
flat spatula, 127
flatbreads, 594
flattop range, 87
flatware, 689–691
flavor, 171
    bread quality, 600
    buttercream, 658
    caviar, 334–336
    chocolate, 623–624
    composed salads, 318
    condiments, 191–192
    describing, 172–174
    fats in baking, 571
    food flavorist, 206
    ganache, 628
    garnishes, 342
    layering, 200
    mousse, 636
    seasonings, 196–197
    steaming, 253–255
    of stock, 458
    sugar syrup, 637
flavorings, 200
    in cakes, 640
    in cookies, 640
    custard, 631
    sugar, 199
flavorist, 206
flight of cheeses, 329
flipper, 127
floor scale, 76
Florentine, 310
flour, 567–568
    in cakes, 640
    in cookies, 640
    in quick breads, 605
    shaping enriched dough, 584
    storage, 567–568
flow of food, 21
    holding, 27
    receiving equipment, 75–76
    receiving, 21–22
    storing, 22–23
fluted cut, 119
fluting,
    pie crusts, 663–664
foaming method,
    cookie dough, 646

folding,
  dough, 588
fonds de cuisine, 457
food allergies, 4
Food and Drug Administration;
  See FDA
food batchmakers, 36
food choices,
  menus, 726
food chopper, 82
food contamination, 4
  bacteria, 5–6
  fungi, 5–6
  parasites, 5–6
  sources, 11–12
  symptoms, 6
  viruses, 5–6
food dehydrator, 85
food manufacturers, 36
food mill, 128–129
food photographers, 166
food preparation equipment, 81–85
food preservation,
  nutrition, 770–771
food processors, 36, 82
  slicing, 112
food recall, 12
food safety, 3
  sanitation certification, 7
food safety; *See* safety
food science degree, 36
food security, 3
food source, 4
food spoilage, 5
food storage areas, 808
food stylists, 166
food temperature,
  monitoring, 24–25
food writers, 166
food-borne illness, 4
  cooling food safely, 25–26
  reheating, 27–28
food-borne infection, 5
food-borne intoxication, 5
food-processing,
  nutrition, 770–771
food-safety audit, 30
food-safety system, 30–31
forecasting, 791
forequarter, of meat, 536
foresaddle, of meat, 536
foreshank, 539
  lamb, 545
forged blade, 105–106
fork-tender, 261–262
formal buying process, 804
formulas, 581
France, 473
free-form loaf, 596
free-range animals, 548
freestanding mixer, 83
freestone fruit, 376
freezing point, 11
  water in frozen desserts, 638
freezing,
  cookies, 651
  fruit, 380
French buttercream, 657–658
French cuisine, 200
french fork spiral mixer, 84
french fries, 115
  blanching, 413
French knife, 108
French Laundry, 265
French omelette, 276–278
French service, 701

French toast, 284–286
French-top range, 87
frenching, 542
freshness,
  fats in baking, 571
  spices, 180
freshwater fish, 498
fried eggs, 274–275
frisée, 309
frittata, 278
fritters, 386
frozen desserts,
  aeration, 639
  sugar content, 638–639
  temperature, 639
frozen soufflé, 638
frozen,
  fish, 506
fruit mousse, 636
fruits,
  aromatic, 184–185
  cleaning, 780
  desserts, 668
  Dietary Guidelines, 769–770
  pie topping, 665
  safety, 780
  in salads, 316
  types of, 370–379
  yeast dough, 591
fry station, 69
frying,
  fruit, 386
  shellfish, 527–529
  vegetables, 413
fully cooked, 261
  vegetables, 410
functional résumé, 825
fungi (fungus), 5–6
funnel, 128

G

game,
  cuts of, 546–547
  recommended temperature,
    25
ganache, 628–630
  types of, 629
garde manger, 296, 680
  cheese, 320
  cold food presentation, 332
garlic,
  mincing, 408
  trimming, 408
garni, 341
garnishes, 148
  in cakes, 642
  cheese, 331
  choux paste, 665–666
  cold food presentation, 341–344
  composed salads, 317
  in cookies, 642
  hard-cooked eggs, 272
  quick breads, 608–610
  salad, 312
  sandwich, 352
  shellfish, 527
  for soup, 483
  soups, 489–493
  yeast bread, 591
garniture, 341
gas,
  fire hazard, 39
gaufrette cuts, 113
gauge (cookware), 132
gazpacho, 493

gelatin, 574, 636
gellen gum, 468
general safety audit, 62–63
German buttercream, 658
German cuisine, 802
ghee, 201
Giardia lamblia (protozoa), 9
Giardiasis, 9
giblet bag, 554
Gigliotti, Lynn, 235
ginger, 182
  grating, 125
gizzard, 554
glassware, 691–693
glazed fish, 506
glazes, 465
  cakes, 658
  choux paste, 665–666
  cookies, 650–651
  dough, 598
  ganache, 628–630
  vegetables, 411
gliadin, 567
global flavor profiles, 186–187
gloves,
  disposable, 14
  making sandwiches, 354
glucose, 755
gluten development, 588
gluten window test, 588
gluten, 567, 592
  quick breads, 607
glutenin, 567
gnocchi, 442
goal setting, 821–822
goujonette, 512
gourds, 390, 392
Gourmet, 145
graders, meat, 535
grading,
  eggs, 268
  fish, 505
  fruit, 382
  of meat, 534–537
  poultry, 553
grain of meat, 548–549
grains,
  Dietary Guidelines, 769
  parts of, 421–422
  in salads, 314
Grana Padano, 321
grand sauces, 471
granita, 637
granité, 637
granton edge, 109
granulated sugar, 572
grapes, 373
Grappa, 235
gratin dish, 134
grating,
  box grater, 125
  microplane, 125
graviax, 338
gravy, 477
grease fire, 40
Greek cuisine, 775
green goddess, 302
green salads, 307–312
greens,
  cooking, 390–393
  preparing, 311
  salad, 307–310
  shredding, 119
griddle, 89
griddled, 239
  sandwich, 357–358

grill cooks, 264
grill marks, 240
grill station, 69
grill, 89
grilled, 239
  sandwich, 357–358
grilling, 239–241
  fish, 514
  fruit, 387
  shellfish, 529
  vegetables, 412–413
grinders, 355
grinding,
  meat, 550–551
grit, sharpening stone's, 119
grits, 426, 430
grooming, 13–16
grosse piéce,
  cold food presentation, 340
guacamole, 304
guéridon, 99–100
Guide Culinaire, Le (Escoffier),
  473

H

HACCP, 30–34, 147–148
  documentation, 33
  fish, 505
  log book, 32
  monitoring procedures, 32–33
  procedures, 33
  seven steps, 31–33
hairnets, 15
ham, 544
  recommended temperature,
    25
hand blender, 84
hand rack,
  grilling fish, 514
hand tools, 124–131
  plate presentation, 228
hand washing, 13–14
handle, 107
handling,
  caviar, 335
  cheese, 328
  meat, 547
handwashing cookware, 135
hanging scale, 76
hard dough, 583–584
hard-boiled eggs, 272
hard-cooked eggs, 272
hare, 546
hash, 289
hash browns, 289
hatcheries, fish, 531
haunch, game, 547
haute cuisine, 310, 473
Hawaiian cuisine, 203
Hazard Analysis Critical Control
  Point; *See* HACCP
hazard analysis, 31–32
hazard communication program,
  60–61
Hazard Communication Standard
  (HCS), 60
  HAZCOM, 60
  Right-to-Know, 60
hazards,
  biological, 5–6, 8–9
  chemical, 5–6
  mercury in fish, 16
  physical, 5–6
HAZCOM, 60
hazelnut, 193

HCS, *See* Hazaard Communication Standard
head chef, 264
headed and gutted fish, 506
health department,
    food-safety audit, 30
health inspection report, 31
health inspection, 30
hearing, 171
hearty soup, 483–484
    making, 486, 488
heat detectors, 41
heat lamp, 96
heat transfer, 132, 252
    methods of, 237
heel (of blade), 106
height,
    cold food presentation, 337–338
    composed salads, 318
Heimlich Maneuver, 55–56
heirloom plant, 402
Hepatitus A, 9
herbes de Provence, 299–300
herbs, 175–179
    salad, 310
    selecting, 175–179
    for stock, 458
    storing, 175–176
    for vinaigrettes, 299–300
hero loaf, 355
hero sandwich, 355
high school teacher, 234
high-sodium food, 197
hindquarter, 536
hindsaddle, 536
hiring, 814–815
hoagies, 355
holding, 27
    cabinets, 96
    equipment, 94–99
    pasta, 448
    reading recipes, 149
    sauces, 479
    soups, 492
    warewashing station, 136–137
hollandaise sauce, 472
hollandaise-style, 477
hollow-ground edge, 106
hollowware, 693–695
    crumber, 693
home fries, 289
hominy, 426
homogenized,
    milk, 280
honey, 199, 573
honing knives, 120–121, 122
hood suppression systems, 41–42
hors d'Oeuvre variées, 365
hors d'Oeuvre,
    types of, 359–362
hospitality managers, 620
hot cross bun, 584
hot plate, 96
hot shot sandwich, 358
hotel pans, 97–99
hotels,
    purchasing managers, 749
hours of operation, 790–791
household units, 150–151
hull, 421–422
hummus, 439, 595
husk, 421–422
hydrogenated oils, 756
hydrogenation, 572
hygiene, 13–16
    hand washing, 13–14

I

ice cream freezer, 77
ice cream, 638
ice sculpture, 341
iceberg lettuce, 308
icebox cookies, 642, 647
icing,
    cakes, 657–658
    cookies, 650–651
immersion blender, 84
in temper,
    chocolate, 626
income statements, 796–797
Indian cooking, 201
indirect contamination, 12
individually quick-frozen (IQF), 380
informal buying process, 804
infrared thermometer, 75–76
infusing,
    custard, 633
ingredients, 149
    aromatic, 184–185
    bakeshop, 566–574
    baking formula, 581
    cakes, 640–642
    choosing healthy, 773–774
    choux paste, 665–666
    composed salads, 317
    condiments, 191–192
    cookies, 640–642, 644
    custard, 631–633, 635
    edible quantity, 162
    layering flavors, 200
    list, 146
    mousse, 636
    purchase quanitity, 162
    purchase unit, 162
    quick bread, 605–606
    raw food cost, 162
    sandwich, 354
    sauces, 467–468
    scaling, 159–160, 586
    seasonings, 197–199
    stir-ins, 608
    yield percentage, 162
initiative, 221–222
injera, 594
injuries, 48–49
    preventing, 50–54
insoluble fiber, 756
inspecting, 22
    eggs, 268
    fish, 505
    meat, 534–537
    poultry, 553
instant oats, 426
instant-read thermometer, 229
institutions,
    purchasing managers, 749
institutional dining, 676
instructor, culinary, 234
intermediary source, 803
internet,
    organizing recipes, 145
    source of recipes, 144
interviewing, 829
    informational, 827–828
inventory, 210, 805–806
    First In, First Out system, 22–23
    menu planning, 732
    physical, 805
iodine, 17
iodized salt, 204

IQF; *See* individually quick-frozen
Italian buttercream, 657
Italy, 254

J

jamaican pepper, 181
James Beard Foundation, 103
jerk, 528
jewelry, 15
job description, 815
job offers, 830
job opportunities, 826–828
juicing, 384
julienne, 115, 118
juniper berries, 182
jus de veau lié, 471

K

Kaimel, Maya
    Savoring the Spice Coast of India: Fresh Flavors from Kerala, 37
Kaimel, Maya,
    Curried Favors: Family Recipes of South India, 37
kaiser roll, 350
kebobs, 360, 595
keel bone, 556
kernal, 422
kettles, 86
Keyes, Ansel, 775
kimchi, 28, 634
Kirsch, Abigail, 368
kitchen fork, 127
kitchen shears, 126
kitchen, 807–808
knead, 567
knife guards, 122
knife kits, 121–122, 123
knives,
    bench, 576
    cleaning, 121
    cutting bar cookies, 650
    the guiding hand, 111
    holding, 110
    honing, 120
    maintaining, 119–123
    methods of holding, 110
    palette, 127, 580
    parts of, 105–107
    safe handling, 50
    safety, 112
    sample cuts, 118
    sanitizing, 121
    selection for poultry, 555
    sharpening, 119
    sticky stir-ins, 610
    storing, 121–122
    trueing, 120–121
    types of cuts, 112–119
    types of, 108
    using properly, 110–111
Korean cuisine, 634
kosher salt, 198
kuchen, 585
kugelhopf, 585

L

l-shaped work line, 70–71
laceration, 48
ladders safety, 53
ladle, 130

lamb,
    cuts of, 544–546
    recommended temperature, 25
lamb's lettuce, 308
laminated yeast dough, 590
laminating process,
    biscuits, 616
language, 219, 226
lasagna, 451
latex allergy, 14
Latin American cuisine, 200
lattices,
    pie crust, 664
lavash, 356
layering flavors, 200
leadership, 225
leading sauces, 471
leaf lettuce, 308
lean dough, 583–584
leaveners, 570–571
    in cakes, 640
    in cookies, 640
    in quick breads, 606
lecithin, 267
leg,
    of beef, 540
    of lamb, 546
    of pork, 544
    of veal, 542
legumes, 434
    cooking, 438
    preparing, 435
    presenting, 439–441
    selecting, 434
    soaking and cooking times, 438
    storing, 435
lemon, 199
lemongrass, 177
lentils, 434
letters of reference, 824
liabilities, 796
liaison, 468, 779
    preparing, 470–471
lifting safely, 52
light-flavored sweeteners, 199
limestone lettuce, 308
limited menu, 730
liquid fats, 572
liquid nitrogen, 102
liquid-filled thermometer, 130
liquids,
    aromatic, 185
    measuring tools, 130
    measuring volume, 152
    in quick breads, 605
    sauce, 467
    for stock, 458
    sugar glaze, 608
    temperature, 256
liquor, shellfish, 519
Listeria monocytogenes, 8
Listeriosis, 8
lo mein, 444
loaf pans, 578
lobster, 522–523
location, 792
logo, 793
loin,
    of beef, 539
    of lamb, 545
    of pork, 543–544
    of veal, 542
long-soak method, 438
Loss, Chris, 207

low boy, 77
lox, 506
lozenge cut, 117, 118

M

macadamia, 193
macaroni, 442
mace, 182
mâche, 308
Maillard reaction, 238
main-course salad, 306
maître d', 367
  service sequence, 709
  working the front of house,
    678
making,
  broth, 485–486
  cakes, 652–656
  consommé, 485–487
  cookies, 644–652
  ganache, 629
  hearty soup, 486, 488
management,
  people, 814–817
  restaurant, 810–814
  stress, 222–223
manager, 819
  purchasing, 749
manager, catering, 367
managing,
  inventory, 805–806
  orders, 805
mandoline, 112
manufacturers,
  source of recipes, 143
maple syrup, 199, 573
marbling, 536
margarine, 281–282
marjoram, 177
market forms,
  fish, 506
  poultry, 554–555
market quote, 804, 805
market research, 733
market, 792
marketing plan, 794–795
marketing, 793–795
marrying condiments, 192
masa harina, 426
masalas, 201
master list, 826
Material Safety Data Sheet
  (MSDS), 60
matignon, 189
maturation, fruit, 380–381
mayonnaise, 300–302
  sandwiches, 351
meal, grain, 423
measurement conventions,
  150
measurement systems, 150–152
measurements,
  blueberry muffin recipe, 148
  changing for yield, 161
  volume, 151
  weight, 151
measuring techniques, 152–153
  scaling, 586
measuring tools, 129–131
  bakeshop, 575
  cup, 130
    reading, 150
  spoons, 130
measuring,
  cookie ingredients, 644

meat,
  breakfast, 288–289
  cleaver, 109
  cuts of, 537–547
  cutting, 548–552
  Dietary Guidelines, 770
  grading, 534–537
  grain of, 548–549
  grinder, 82–83
  grinding, 550–551
  ideal storage temperature, 23
  inspections, 534–537
  menu planning, 773
  pounding cutlets, 549–550
  preparing, 548–552
  sandwich filling, 351
  slicer, 82, 112
  stewing, 550
  terms for, 537
  trimming, 548–549
  tying a roast, 551–552
  types of, 537–547
meatballs, 360
mechanical convection, 462
Medici, Caterina de, 310
medieval cuisine, 242
Mediterranean cuisine, 200
medium dough, 584
melon baller, 126, 384
melons, 376–378
melting point,
  chocolate, 625
melting,
  chocolate, 625
mentor, 220
menu conversion, 738
menu modification, 738
menu planning,
  balance, 732
  food allergies, 774
  preparing healthy food, 778–780
  price levels, 733
  product availability, 733
  regional cuisine, 733
  religion, 733
  special needs, 732–733
  trends, 733
  variety, 732
  vegetarian, 774–776
  weight loss, 776–778
menu prices,
  actual cost method, 743–744
  base price method, 744
  changing, 747
  comparison charts, 745
  competition, 740–741
  copycat method, 741–742
  customer mix, 741
  deciding on, 745–747
  force food method, 744–745
  gross profit method, 744
  meal occasion, 740
  nonstructured method, 741–742
  pricing system comparison
    chart, 745
  prime cost method, 742
  profit objective, 741
  psychological factors, 746–747
  Q quotient, the, 746
  style of service, 740
  type of restaurant, 740
menus, 685, 724
  à la carte, 727–728
  California, 728
  changing, 738
  condition of, 727

cyclical, 729
designing, 734–737
  menu board, 736
  printed, 736
  spoken, 736
du jour, 728
fixed, 729
limited, 730
modified à la carte, 727–728
organizing, 734–736
  appetizers, 735
  desserts, 736
  hors d'oeuvres, 735
  hot beverages, 736
  main courses, 736
  salads, 736
  sandwiches, 736
  side dishes, 736
  soups, 736
  starters, 735
planning, 730–734, 772–778
presenting to guests, 706
prix fixe, 728–729
table d'hôte, 728–729
types of, 727–730
writing, 737–738
mercury, 6
  in fish, 16
meringue, 636
  pie topping, 665
mesclun, 307
metal spatula, 580
methods, 148, 149
  dry-heat, 248–249
Mexico, 615
microplane, 125
microwave oven, 88–90, 243
  food temperature, 25
  reheating, 28
  thawing foods safely, 26
Middle East cuisine, 595
Midwestern cuisine, 203
mild greens, 307–308
milk chocolate, 624
milk products,
  Dietary Guidelines, 770
milk, 280
milkfat, 280
milling, 422
mincing, 113
  garlic, 408
minerals, 758, 761–763
minestrone, 776
minimally processed grain,
  423
mint, 177
mirepoix, 188, 458
  preparing for stock, 460
miscellaneous sauces, 474–478
Mise Design Group, LLC, 67
mise en place, 73, 209–210
  mayonnaise, 300
  plate presentation, 227–228
  sandwich, 352–354
  service station, 695
  service, 227–228
  vinaigrette, 297
mission statement, 725, 789
mixers, 83
  burr, 84
  cake batter, 654
  countertop, 83
  freestanding, 83
  french fork spiral, 84
  oblique, 84
  planetary, 83–84, 87

spiral, 84
vertical, 84
mixing methods,
  cakes, 652–654
mixing, 82–83
  batter, 572
  biscuits, 614–617
  bowls, 127
  cookie dough, 645–646
  creaming method, 607
  methods of dough, 585–591
  quick breads, 606–607
  straight dough-mixing method,
    585–588
  well method, 607
mizuna, 309
modernist cuisine, 206
*Modernist Cuisine: The Art
  and Science of Cooking,*
  (Young), 103
modified à la carte, 727–728
modified straight dough-mixing
  method, 589–591
modifying,
  healthy food, 780
moist-heat method,
  poultry, 560
moisture,
  carryover cooking, 250–251
  maintaining in food, 238
  resting food, 251
  storing chocolate, 628
molasses, 573
molded cookies, 644, 648–649
molded salad, 306
molds, 231
  cookie, 644
  pâté, 336
  pudding, 579
  terrines, 336
moldy food, 5, 6
mole, 615
molecular gastronomy, 85, 206,
  468
  Achatz, Grant, 265
  baking thickeners, 574–575
mollusks, 518–519
monosodium glutamate (MSG),
  169
monounsaturated fats, 758
Moonen, Rick, 532
mother sauces, 471
mousses, 636–637
MSDS, 60–61
MSG *See* monosodium glutamate
muesli, 288
mush, 429–430
mushrooms, 393–395
  fluted, 119
  poisonous, 5
mussels,
  preparing, 525
mustard greens, 309
mustard, 182, 299
mutton, 544
mutual supplementation, 753
mycotoxins, 9
MyPlate, 768

N

nappé, 469
national cuisine, 200
National Fire Protection Agency
  (NFPA),
  hood suppression systems, 41

National Marine Fisheries Service (NMFS), 505
National Oceanic and Atmospheric Administration (NOAA), 505
National Sanitation Foundation, 95
    professional tool certification, 125
neurotoxic shellfish poisoning, 520
neutral stock, 458–459
New England cuisine, 203
NFPA; *See* National Fire Protection Agency
nibs, 623
nonbony fish, 499
nonfood items, 22
nonverbal feedback, 219–220
noodle, 442
Norwalk virus, 9
nostick coatings, 135
nouvelle cuisine, 777
numerator, 156
Nutley, Sean, 141
nutmeg, 182
    grating, 125
nutrients, 752
    and colors, 764
nutrition information,
    calorie content, 767
    Dietary Reference Intake (DRI), 767
    information sheets, 766
    labels, 766
    MyPlate, 768
    percent of daily value, 767–768
    Recommended Dietary Allowance, 767
    serving size, 766–767
nutrition,
    amino acids, 753
    calories, 753, 765–766
    carbohydrates, 755–756
    chocolate, 628
    cholesterol, 756–758
    cooking vegetables, 410
    corn, 428
    Dietary Guidelines, 768–770
    eggs, 270
    fat substitutes, 606
    fats, 756–758
    food preservation, 770–771
    food processing, 770–771
    glucose, 755
    good, 752–753
    healthy greens, 307
    importance of, 752–753
    information, 766–771
    insoluble fiber, 756
    language of, 753–766
    meat, 536
    menu planning, 772–778
    minerals, 758, 761–763
    mutual supplementation, 753
    nitrates, 289
    nitrites, 289
    planning menus, 726
    poor, 752
    portion control, 781
    prepared stock base, 464
    preparing healthy food, 778–780
    proteins, 753
    reducing fat, 594
    salad, 313
    soluble fiber, 755–756
    substituting flour in biscuits, 613

vinaigrette, 298
vitamins, 758–760
water, 764–765
nutritional balance, 772
nutritional value, 238, 253
    cheese, 321
    dry heat and, 238
nutritionists, 785
nuts, 192–195
    Dietary Guidelines, 770
    in salads, 316

O

oat groats, 426
oatmeal, 426
oblique cut, 117, 118
oblique mixer, 84
obstructed airway maneuver, 55–56
Occupational Safety and Health Administration (OSHA), 58
    accident log, 62
    procedures for cleaning equipment, 85
offal, 540
office, 808
offset spatula, 127
oils, 299
    Dietary Guidelines, 770
    replacing with stock, 779
olive oil, 298
olive pitter, 126
omega-3 fatty acids, 758
omelet pan, 133
omelettes, 276–278
on the half shell, 333
one-stage cooling method, 25
onion soup gratinée, 485
onions, 395–396
opaque, 173
open-burner range, 87
open-faced sandwich, 355
orange juice, 199
order, 804–805
oregano, 178
organic foods, 4
organic leaveners, 570
organisms,
    beneficial, 4–5
organization,
    long-term dreams, 821
    menu ideas, 728
    menus, 734–736
    sandwiches, 354
    skills, 221
    work, 210–214
orientation, 815
OSHA; *See* Occupational Safety and Health Administration
osmosis, 198
osso buco, 541
oven racks,
    baking cookies, 649
oven,
    combi, 88
    combination steamer, 88
    spring, 599
over egg, 274–275
ovo-lacto vegetarian, 776
owner/operators,
    bed and breakfasts, 620
    catering, 367
    of a food business, 495
oxidization, fruit, 383
oysters, 525–526

P

P&L, 796
packing,
    measuring dry ingredients, 152
paddle, 84
palette knife, 127, 580
    tempering chocolate, 626
Palladin, Jean-Louis, 235
pan de muertos, 584
pan loaf, 597
pan proofing, 598
pan-broiling, 245
pan-dressed fish, 506
pan-frying, 246–250
    fish, 514
pancakes, 284–286
paneer, 201
panini, 358
pans,
    baking, 578–579
    cake, 652
    conditioning, 245
    cookie, 644–645
    for quick breads, 607
    roasting, 134
    sheet, 134
    size when scaling recipes, 161
    steamer, 255
    tilting fry, 86
pantry chef, 296
pants, houndstooth, 50
panzanella, 314
par-stock list, 799–800, 805
parallel work line, 70, 72
paralytic shellfish poisoning, 520
parasites, 5–6
parboiled, 261
    vegetables, 410
parchment paper, 578
    cookie pans, 644–645
    pie crusts, 664
parcooked, 261–262
    grains, 423
    vegetables, 410
parfait, 638
paring knife, 108
Parisienne scoop, 126, 384
parmesan cheese, 254
parroting, 218
parsley, 178
partially cooked foods, 238–239, 253
PASS system, 43–44
pasta,
    dried, 446
    fresh egg, 448
    global, 445, 447
    in salads, 314
    types of, 442–446
pastes, nut and seed, 195
pasteurized,
    eggs, 270, 570
pastries, 597
    shaping, 594–597
pastry bag,
    piped cookies, 647–648
pastry chef, 680
pastry cream, 635
pastry,
    bags, 451, 580
    blenders, 576–577
    brushes, 580
    cart, 100
    chef, 602

tips, 580
tools, 579–581
wheel, 126, 580
pâté à choux, 665
pâte fermentée, 590
pâté, 336, 362
    mold, 134
pathogens, 5, 10–11
    acidity, 10
    food source, 10
    moisture, 10–11
    oxygen, 10–11
    temperature danger zone, 11
    temperature, 10
    time, 10–11
paupiette, 512
paysanne, 117
Peach Melba, 668
peanut, 193
pearl barley, 426
pearl grains, 423
pears, 373, 375
peas, 434
pecan, 193
pectin, 574
peeler, 126
peeling,
    fruit, 383–384
    holding the knife, 111
peels, bread, 577
Peking duck, 558
pelmeni, 508
pepper, 199
    salad dressing, 300
peppercorns, 183
peppermint, 177
peppers, 183, 395
percent of daily value, 767–768
percolators, coffee, 694
performance evaluation, 816
periodicals,
    recipes in, 143
perishable goods, 21–22
perpetual inventory, 806
personal hygiene, 15
personal integrity, 220–221
personnel,
    planning menus, 725
pest control, 19–20
pest infestation, 20
pest management, 20
pH scale, 10
pho, 287
phyllo dough, 667
physical hazards, 5–6
physical inventory, 805
physical leaveners, 571
pickling, 28
pickup,
    mixing dough, 588
picnic ham, 543
pie crusts,
    blind-baked, 664
    cookie dough crust, 660–661
    crumbly dough crust, 661–662
    dough, 660–662
    fluting, 663–664
    lattices, 664
    rolling dough, 663–664
    rubbed-dough method, 660–661
    streusel, 664–665
    toppings, 664–665
pie pans, 578
pierogi, 442

pies,
  assembling, 662–665
  fillings, 662–663
  top crust, 664
pilaf, 430–431
pin bones, 510–511
pinch, size of, 196
pine nut, 194
piped cookies, 642, 647–648
pistachio, 194
pita bread, 350, 595
pita pockets, 356
pith, 371
pizza cutter, 126
planetary mixer, 83–84, 87
planning, 214
  dessert-making, 566
  menus, 724–726, 730–734
plantains, 528
plate covers, 99
plate presentation, 227
plates, 230
  charger, 696
  color on, 231
platform scale, 76
plating,
  desserts, 669–670
  resting food, 251
platter service, 702
platters,
  cold food presentation, 332–333
  hors d'Oeuvre, 365
poached eggs, 272–274
poaching, 255
  fish, 516–517
  fruit desserts, 668
  fruit, 386
pocket bread, 350
pods, 398–399
point of sale (POS) system, 705
poissonnier, 531
polenta, 426, 430
polishing,
  tableware, 699
polyunsaturated fats, 756–758
poolish, 590
poppy seeds, 194
pork,
  cuts of, 542–544
  recommended temperature, 25
  roundworms, 6
porridge, 429–430
portable refrigeration cart, 77
portfolio, 829–830
portion control, 781
portioning, 228–229
portions, 146, 228, 781–782
  condiments, 192
  cost of single, 162
  scale, 129
  scaling recipes, 157–158
  scooper, 607
posole, 426
potato purées, 413–414
potatoes, 403–404
  baked, 413
potentially hazardous foods, 10–11
poultry,
  grading, 553
  ideal storage temperature, 23
  inspecting, 553
  knife selection, 555
  menu planning, 773
  preparing, 555–561
  recommended temperature, 25
  sandwich filling, 351

serving, 555–561
shears, 126
types of, 553–555
pour-over brewers, 693–694
powdered sugar, 573
Powers, Catharine, 786
pre-ferment, 590
precision cuts, 113–118
preheat,
  baking cakes, 654
prep cooks, 264
prep tools, 125, 126
preparation,
  bouquet garni for stock, 458
  cake pans, 652
  composed salads, 317–318
  cookie pans, 644
  fish fumet, 461
  fish, 509–513
  foods safely, 23–24
  grains, 428–432
  healthy food, 778–780
  legumes, 435–439
  liaison, 470–471
  meat, 548–552
  mirepoix, 460
  pans for quick breads, 607
  pasta, 446–449
  poultry, 555–561
  résumé, 822–825
  roux, 469–470
  sachet d'épices for stock, 460
  shellfish stock, 461
  shellfish, 522–527
  soups, 484–488
  starch slurries, 470
  stock, 459–464
  and taste, 172
  thickeners, 469–471
  vegetable stock, 461–462
  vegetables, 406–409
prepared foods, 238–239, 253
presentation side, 231
presentation, 227–228
  appetizers, 363–365
  caviar, 334–336
  cold food presentation, 332–344
  grain, 432–433
  hors d'Oeuvre, 363–365
  nutritional menu, 782–783
  pasta, 450–452
  resting food, 251
  sauces, 479–480
  smoked fish, 336
preservation,
  nutrition, 770–771
preserved food, 28
preshaping,
  dough, 592–594
pressed sandwich, 358
pressure steamer, 86
prices,
  planning menus, 725
  supplier, 803
pricing factor,
  menu pricing, 742
pricing system comparison chart, 745
primal cuts, 536
  lamb, 545–546
  pork, 543–544
  veal, 540–542
primals, 536
primary source, 803
prime cost, 743
Prime, 538

priorities, setting, 213–214
prix fixe menus, 728–729
PRN method, 148–150, 210
problem solving, 221
processed grains, 421–423
processing tools, 128–129
processing,
  frozen dessert, 639
  nutrition, 770–771
produce,
  ideal storage temperature, 23
  menu planning, 773
producer, 803
product specifications, 800, 805
product/service mix, 789
production record, 800
productivity, 221
professional tool certification,
  National Sanitation Foundation, 125
professionalism, 223–225
profit and loss statement, 796
profit, 796
progressive cuisine,
  Achatz, Grant, 265
promotion, 793–795
proofer, 577
prosciutto, 336, 362
prospecting, 826–827
protein sources,
  in salads, 315–316
proteins, 753
protozoa, 9
public relations, 794
pudding molds, 579
puff pastry, 667–668
PUFI mark, 505
Pullman bread, 584
Pullman loaf, 350
pumpkin pie spice, 184
punctuality, 220
puncture, 49
purchase quantity, 162
purchase unit, 162
purchasing agents, 749
purchasing manager, 805
purchasing,
  basic steps, 799–805
  bid, 804
  cheese, 326–327
  eggs, 267–270
  formal buying process, 804
  fruit, 380–383
  informal buying process, 804
  market quote, 804
  par-stock list, 799–800
  placing orders, 804–805
  product specifications, 800–801
  production record, 800
  selecting suppliers, 803–804
  shellfish, 333–334
  specifications, 800–801
pure starch, 468
purée, 468, 474
  fruit mousse, 636
  soup, 484
puréeing,
  fruit, 384, 387
  vegetables, 410
purveyor, 803

Q

Q quotient, the, 746
quality grading, meat, 534–536

quality,
  of bread, 599–600
  of fruit, 380
quarter fillets, 509
quarters, of meat, 536
quaternary ammonium
    compounds, 17
Quelly, Jewels, 294
quiches, 279
quick breads,
  crumb topping, 609
  garnishes, 608–610
  ingredients, 605–606
  stir-ins, 608
  streusel, 609–610
quick-chill refrigerator, 77
quick-cooking oats, 426
quick-service restaurants, 676
quick-soak method, 437
quinoa, 426

R

rabbit, 546
rack, lamb, 545
radiant heat, 237
radicchio, 309
raft, 486
rainbow of foods, 170
ramekin, 134
ranges, 87–89
rat-tail tang, 107
ratites, 553
ravioli, 451
raw bar, 333–334
raw food,
  cost of, 162–163
  meat, 12
  vegetables, 12
raw food costs, 796
  menu pricing, 742
RCF; See recipe conversion factor
reach-in, 77
receiving foods, 21–22
  equipment, 75–76
  infrared thermometer, 75–76
  meat, 547
  scales, 76
  shellfish, 519–521
  vegetables, 405
reception desk, the, 685
recipe category, 146
recipe conversion factor (RCF), 154
recipes,
  bakers formulas, 581
  baking, 566
  blueberry muffins, 147
  boiled white rice, 155
  finding, 143–144
  modifying, 163–164
  organizing, 144–145
  reading, 148–150
  scaling, 154–156
  sources, 143–144
  standardized, 145–148
Recommended Dietary Allowance, 767
recovery time, 245
recycling, 18–19
reducing stock, 465
reference list, 824
refined grains, 423
refined starch, 468
refreshing vegetables, 410
refrigerated drawer, 77
refrigerated holding unit, 97

refrigeration equipment, 76–78
refrigerator cookies, 642
refrigerator,
    blast-chill, 77
    cleaning, 77–78
    cooling food safely, 25
    even-thaw, 77
    quick-chill, 77
    reach-in, 77
    storing fruit, 382
    walk-in, 76
regional cuisine, 200–204
regulations,
    OSHA, 58
reheating, 27–28
    soups, 488–489
rehydrating, 437
relish, 478
reports,
    accident/illness, 62
reservation policy, 684
    holiday reservations, 685
    taking reservations, 685–686
reservations, 684–685
restaurant critics, 166
restaurant manager,
    people management, 814–817
    qualities of, 810–814
restaurant personnel, 677–682
    back waiter, 679
    brigade, 677
        back of the house, 679–682
        front of the house, 677
    bus person, 679
    captain, 678
    carver, 679
    chef de cuisine, 679
    dining room attendant, 679
    dining room manager, 678
    entremetier, 680
    executive chef, 679
    expediter, 679
    external clients, 677
    fish station chef, 680
    front waiter, 679
    garde manger, 680
    grill station chef, 680
    grillardin, 680
    internal clients, 677
    line chef, 679
    maître d' hotel, 678
    maître d', 678
    pantry chef, 680
    pastry chef, 680
    pâtissier, 680
    poissonier, 680
    prep chef, 680
    receptionist, 678
    roast station chef, 680
    rôtisseur, 680
    roundsman, 680
    runner, 679
    saucier, 680
    sauté station chef, 680
    second chef, 679
    server, 679
    servers, 678
    sommelier, 679
    soup station chef, 680
    sous-chef, 679
    station chef, 679
    swing chef, 680
    tournant, 680
    trancheur, 679
    vegetable station chef, 680
    wine steward, 679

restaurant personnel; See culinary
        careers
restaurant,
    advertising, 793–794
    ambience, 789
    bar, 810
    brand, 793
    business plan, 788–791
    cash register, 809
    cell phones, 717
    client base, 791–793
    customer theft, 718
    design, 807–810
    dining room, 808–810
    emergencies, 715–716
    employee area, 808
    entrance, 810
    facility layout, 807–810
    farm-to-table, 803
    feedback, 792
    food storage areas, 808
    forecasting, 791
    greeting guests, 686
    handling complaints, 712–715
    handling problems, 715–718
    hours of operation, 790–791
    income statements, 796–797
    kitchen, 807–808
    location, 792
    logo, 793
    managing a, 810–814
    market, 792
    marketing plan, 794–795
    marketing, 793–795
    mission statement, 789
    no-reservation policy, 684
    noisy guests, 716–717
    nonpayment, 717
    office, 808
    payment problems, 718
    product/service mix, 789
    promoting, 793–795
    promotion, 794
    public relations, 794
    reservation policy, 684
    reservations, 684–685
    restrooms, 810
    robbery, 718
    seating guests, 686–687
        continuous seating plan,
            687
        fixed seating plan, 686
    service style, 700–704
    staffing, 790
    type of, 789
    types of, 675–677
    waste management, 808
resting food, 251
restrooms, 810
résumé,
    awards, 823
    contact information, 822
    education, 823
    objective, 822–823
    personal interests, 823
    preparing, 822–825
    professional involvement,
        823
    references, 824
    skills, 823
    work experience, 823
retail cuts, 536–537
retarder, 577
revenue, 796
rhubarb, 378

rib,
    beef, 538–539
    lamb, 545
    veal, 541
riblets, lamb, 545
rice, 424–425
ricer, 128
Right-to-Know, 60
rind-ripened semisoft cheese, 322
rind, 321
ring-top range, 87–88
rinsing area, 136–137
ripening, fruit, 380–381
ripple, 113
rising,
    bulk fermentation, 588
risotto, 254, 431
rivets, 107
roast,
    tying, 551–552
roasted nuts and seeds, 195
roasting pan, 134
roasting, 240–243
    fish, 515
    shellfish, 529
    vegetables, 413
rock salt, 198
rocket, 309
roll cut, 117
rolled biscuits, 611
rolled cookies, 643–644
rolled oats, 426
rolled omelette, 276
rolled-in dough, 590–591
rolled-in yeast dough, 590
rolling boil, 255
rolling pins, 579
rolls, 597
    shaping, 594–597
romaine lettuce, 308
rondelles, 113, 114, 118
root vegetables, 399–400
rosemary, 178
rotary evaporator, 102
round fish, 499
round, beef, 540
roundworms, 6, 9
roux, 468, 779
    in hearty soup, 483
    preparing, 469–470
rubbed-dough method, 613–614,
    660–661
rubber spatula, 127
runner, 709
russian dressing, 302
Russian service, 701–702
rye berries, 426
rye flakes, 426

S

sabayon, 636
sachertorte, 657
sachet d'épices, 189, 458
    preparing for stock, 460
saddles, of meat, 536
safe foods, 4
safety,
    booster chairs, 704
    burns, 92, 246, 577
    certified pork, 542
    chiles, 397–398
    cooked poultry temperature,
        559
    critical control points, 148
    cutting board, 122

double-dipping, 363
dressing for, 50
driving, 54
egg, 277
food allergies, 774
food preparation equipment,
    81–82
frozen fruit, 385
fruit, 383, 780
knife, 112
knives,
    washing, 121
ladders, 53
ongoing process, 58–63
pasteurized eggs, 302
professional tool certification,
    National Sanitation
    Foundation, 125
raw bar, 333
raw shellfish, 521
restaurant manager and, 812
restaurant seating plan, 687
salt as a preservative, 506
sandwich, 354
slicing, 112
soups, 489
storing custard and mousses, 636
vegetables, 780
washing knives, 121
saffron, 183
sage, 178
salad cart, 100
salad dressing, 297–304
    acids used for, 299
salads, 305
    cold grain, 433
    legume, 440–441
salamander, 87, 88
sales staff, 367
sales, 796
salmon, 336
salmonella, 8, 542
    eggs and, 570
Salmonellosis, 8
salsa, 304, 477–478
salt, 197–198, 200
    baking ingredient, 574
    menu planning, 774
    in quick breads, 606
    salad dressing, 300
salted,
    fish, 506
saltwater fish, 498
salty, 169
sandwich,
    cookies, 651
sandwiches,
    cold, 355–356
    hot, 357–358
sanitation, 16–18
    certification, 7
    clearing tables, 708
    cookware, 135–138
    facility layout, 807
    FDA standards, 30
    knives, 121
    marrying, 192
    measuring tools, 152
    meat handling, 549
    meat, 547
    pest control, 19–20
    silicone mats, 645
    smallware, 138
    washing tableware, 698
sanitizers, 17
    and preparing foods safely, 24

sanitizing, 16–18
sanitizing solution, 17
santoku knife, 108
saturated fats, 756
saucepan, 133
saucepot, 133
sauces,
    créme anglaise, 633
    healthy, 779
    hollandaise-style, 477
    ingredients, 467–468
    mole, 615
    with pasta, 450
    purée, 474
    tomato, 477
    types of, 471–478
sauté cooks, 264
sauté pan, 133
sautéing, 241, 244–245
    fish, 513–514
    fruit, 385–386
    shellfish, 529
    vegetables, 413
sauteuse, 133
sautoir, 133
*Savoring the Spice Coast of
India: Fresh Flavors from
Kerala* (Kaimel), 37
savory, 169, 178
scales, 76, 129, 152
    portioning, 229
scaling,
    cookie ingredients, 644
    dough, 592
    down a recipe, 155
    ingredients, 586
    recipe, 154
    recipes,
        limits on, 162
    up a recipe, 155
scallops,
    preparing, 525
Scappin, Gianni, 722
scarf, 50
Schorner, Dieter, 802
scimitar, 109
scombrotoxins, 505
scones, 288, 611–613
    serving, 617–618
scoring, dough, 598
Scotch barley, 426
Scoville scale, 397
scrambled eggs, 276
scraper,
    tempering chocolate, 626
scullery, 136
sea salt, 197–198
Seafood Watch, 504, 532
seafood,
    advisory lists, 499, 504
    appetizers, 360, 361
    hors d'Oeuvres, 360–361
    sandwich filling, 351
    shellfish on the half shell, 333
seams, of meat, 549
searing, 241, 245
seasoned flour, 246
seasonings, 196–197, 200
    pepper, 199
    sauce, 467–468
    scaling recipes, 162
seeding method,
    tempering chocolate, 626
seeding,
    fruit, 383–384
seeds, 192–195, 398–399
Seeger, Gunther, 235

Select, 538
selecting,
    condiments, 192
    cookie pans, 644
    fish, 504–507
    fruit, 380–383
    grains, 424–428
    legumes, 435
    vegetables, 403–405
self-rising flour, 571
semisweet chocolate, 624
semolina flour, 444
separate-course salad, 306
sequencing,
    cold food presentation, 340
    work, 214–215
serrated edge knife, 109
servers, 367
    service sequence, 709
service carts, 99–100
service equipment, 99–100
service station, 695
service style, 700–704
    American service, 702
    buffet service, 702–703
    butler service, 702
    cafeteria service, 703
    counter service, 703
    English service, 702
    family service, 702
    French service, 701
    planning menus, 725
    platter service, 702
    Russian service, 701–702
    tableside service, 701
    take-out service, 703–704
service ware, 688–695
    china, 688–689
    flatware, 688, 689–691
    glassware, 688, 691–693
    holloware, 688, 693–695
service,
    butler, 363
    mise en place, 227–228
    in a recipe, 148
    sequence, 709
serving size, 766–767, 781
serving, 228
    biscuits, 617–618
    caviar, 335
    cheese, 329–330
    cold food presentation, 340
    cookies, 651–652
    foods safely, 27–29
    fruit, 387–388
    guests, 704–711
        after dinner beverages, 708
        course sequence, 707
        parting company, 711
        preparing the check, 708
        presenting the check,
          708–709
        presenting the menu, 706
        serving food, 707
        serving water and bread, 706
        starting the meal, 704
        writing the order, 704–705
    order, 707
    poultry, 555–561
    reading recipes, 149
    scones, 617–618
    soups, 489
    tools,
        cold food presentation, 340
    vegetables, 414–415
ServSafe Essentials, 7
sesame seeds, 194

setting priorities, 213–214
seviche, 362
sexual harassment, 816
shallow poaching, 516
shank, veal, 541
shapes, 231
    cold food presentation,
        337–338
shaping,
    biscuits, 616
    cookies, 647–649
    stenciled cookies, 651
sharpening knives, 119
sharpening stones, 119
shaslyk, 508
shears, 126
sheet pan, 134
shellfish,
    on the half shell, 333
    ideal storage temperature, 23
    mercury, 16
    preparing, 522–527
    raw bar, 333
    stock, 458–459
    types of, 518–519
shells, for stock, 457
shelves, 78–79
Sheppard, Dave, 750
sherbet, 637
Shigella, 8
Shigellosis, 8
shirred eggs, 278–279
shocking vegetables, 410
shoes, protective, 50
shoot vegetables, 399, 401
short dough, 661
short loin, beef, 539
short plate, beef, 539
shortbread, 644
shortcakes, 618
shoulder,
    beef, 538–539
    lamb, 545
    pork, 543
    veal, 541
shredding tools, 125
shrimp,
    cocktail, 362
    count, 520
    preparing, 524
shucked shellfish, 519
side salad, 305
side stand, 695
sides, of meat, 536
sifting, 582
sight, 170
silicone,
    baking mats, 644–645
SilPad, 578
silverskin, 549
simmering, 255
simple carbohydrates, 755
simple syrup, 656
single-rack dishwasher, 137
sink,
    "fill-to" line, 16
    four-compartment, 18
    three-compartment, 18
sirloin, 539
sizzler platter, 515
skewers, 360
skillet, tilting, 86
skimmer, 127
slicer, knife, 109
slicing, 112
    bread, 599
    cold food presentation, 340

small business owners, 819
small fire, 42
small sauces, 474
small tools,
    salad greens, 311
    for stock, 461
smallware, 124–131
smell, 170
    describing, 173
smoke detectors, 41
smoke point, 250
smoked fish, 336, 506
smoker, 88
smoothie, 290
smothering, 246
    bones, 460
sneeze guards, 95
soaking legumes, 437–438
soda bread, 613
sodium chloride, 197
soft dough, 584
soft-boiled eggs, 271
soft-cooked eggs, 271
solanine, 5
solid fats,
    baking, 572
soluble fiber, 755–756
sorbet, 637
sorting beans, 437
soufflé dish, 134, 579
soufflés, 279–280, 637
soup du jour, 482
soups,
    garnish, 489–493
    preparing, 484–488
    reheating, 488–489
    serving, 489
    types of, 481–484
sour, 169
sourdough, 590
sous chefs, 264
sous vide machine, 86
Southern cuisine, 203
Southwestern cuisine, 203
spaetzle, 442
Spain, 364
spatula,
    filling cookies, 651
spatulas,
    flat, 127
    offset, 127
    pastry, 580
    rubber, 127
spearmint, 177
specialty beef, 537
specialty sauces, 478
spice blends, 184
spices, 180–184
    for stock, 458
spicy greens, 307, 309
spiders (skimmers), 127
spills, 52, 715
spinach, 308
spine (of blade), 106
spiral mixer, 84
sponge dough, 589
sponge mixing method, 589
spoons, 127
sprains, 49
    first aid, 55
spreads, 350–351
spring rolls, 360
spring scale, 129
springerle, 644
springform pans, 578–579
squash, 390, 392
stabilizing,

cake batter, 654
Stack, Jennifer, 419
staffing, 790
    hiring, 814–815
    planning a menu, 731
    supervising, 815–816
    training, 815
stainless steel cookware, 135
stalk vegetables, 399, 401
stamped blade, 105–106
standard breading, 246
standard mirepoix, 188, 458
standardized ingredients, 150
standardized recipe, 145–148
    purpose, 146
    sections, 146–148
Staphylococcus aureus
        (staph), 9
star anise, 183
starch slurries, 468
    preparing, 470
starch test, potatoes, 403
StarChefs, 145
starches,
    in salads, 314–315
stations, 69–70
    garde manger, 296
steaks,
    fish, 506
steam table, 97
    monitoring temperature, 33
steam-jacketed kettle, 86,
        460–461
steamer, 133, 253, 255
    combination oven, 88
    convection, 86
    pressure, 86
steaming, 253–255
    fish, 516
    grains, 428–429
    shellfish, 527
    vegetables, 410
steel cookware, 135
steel, butcher's, 120
stenciled cookies, 642–643, 648
    shaping, 651
stewing, 258–260
    fruit, 386
    meat, 550
    vegetables, 411–412
stick blender, 84
stir-frying, 245
    shellfish, 529
stir-ins, 608
stirring,
    tempering chocolate, 625
stitches,
    first aid, 55
stock base, 463–464
stock, 457
    hearty soup, 483
    reducing, 465
    types of, 458–459
    using, 464
stockpot, 133, 460
stollen, 585
stone fruit, 375–376
stone-ground flour, 567
stone, of fruit, 370
storage area,
    fire hazard, 41
storage,
    buttercream icing, 657
    cheese, 328
    chocolate, 628
    cold, 78
    condiments, 192

containers, 79–80
cookies, 651–652
dairy products, 280–283
dry, 78
dry goods, 23
eggs, 267–270
equipment, 78–80
fish, 507–509
flour, 567–568
foods, 22–23
fruit, 380–383
grains, 426, 428
hotel pans, 97–99
icebox cookies, 647
ideal temperature, 22–23
knives, 121–122
legumes, 435
meat, 547
nuts, 192–195
olive oil, 299
pasta, 445
salad dressings, 297
salad greens, 311
salt, 197
sauces, 479
scone dough, 613
seeds, 192–195
shellfish, 519–521
shelves, 78–79
silicone mats, 645
sliced bread, 354
stocks, 464
tableware, 699
vegetables, 403–405
stoves, 87–89
straight dough-mixing method,
        585–588
straight spatula, 127
straight-line, 70–71
straightening steel, 120
straining tools, 128–129
strains, 49
    first aid, 55
strategies, 214
Streptococcus pyogenes, 9
stress, 222–223
streusel, 609–610, 664–665
sturgeon,
    caviar, 334–336
submarines, 355
subprimal cuts, 536
subprimals, 536
subrecipes, 164
substituting,
    healthy food, 780
sugar glaze, 608
sugar syrup, 637
sugar, 199
    baking, 572–573
    in cakes, 640
    in cookies, 640
    in frozen desserts, 638–639
    menu planning, 774
    in quick breads, 605
    salad dressing, 300
sumac, 183
sunny-side-up egg, 274–275
superfine sugar, 572
suppliers, 803
    selecting, 803–804
supply, food, 4
suprême, 559
sweating, 246
    bones, 460
Sweden, 338
sweet rich dough, 584
sweet, 169

sweeteners, 199
    baking ingredients, 572–573
sweetness,
    chocolate, 623–624
swiss brasier, 86
symmetrical arrangement, 232
syrup, simple, 656

T

table d'hôte menu, 728–729
table salt, 197–198
table service, 700
table service; See also service
        style
table setting, 696–697
table tent menus, 736
tableside service, 701
tableware, 688
tabouli, 314, 433
tagliatelle, 444
tahini, 192–195
Taillevent, 271
take-out service, 703–704
tamarind, 185
tamis, 128
tandoors, 201
tang, 107
tapas, 365
tapenade, 304
taper-ground edge, 106
tapioca, 574
tare weight, 131, 152
tarragon, 178
tart dough, 660–662
tart pans, 578
tarter sauce, 302
tartlets, 360
tarts,
    assembling, 662–665
    fillings, 662–663
tasks, 210–211
tasso, 543
taste, 169–170, 171
    balancing, 196
    condiments, 191–192
    sauces, 480
    seasonings, 196–197
    storing chocolate, 628
tasters, 206
tea,
    serving, 694
tea sandwich, 355
teamwork, 224
technical skills, 224
temperature, 229–230
    the 240 factor, 586
    baking cookies, 649
    baking with eggs, 570
    biscuit dough, 614–616
    boiling, 255
    caviar, 335
    cheese, 329
    cooked legumes, 438
    cooked poultry, 559
    cookie ingredients, 644
    cookie pans, 645
    cooking vegetables, 413
    corrective action, 33
    critical limits, 32
    dairy products, 283
    danger zone, 11, 24
        cooling foods safely, 25–26
    deep-frying, 249
    egg foam, 636
    eggs, 270, 606
    frozen desserts, 639

ganache, 630
holding equipment, 95–96
holding food, 27
ideal storage, 22–23
liquids, 256
melting cheese, 330
moist-heat methods, 252
monitoring food, 24–25
oven,
    baking cakes, 654, 656
poached eggs, 272
poaching, 255
receiving meat, 547
recommended, 25
salad dressing storage, 297
sauces, 479
scaling recipes, 160
selecting fish, 506
silicone, 578
simmering, 255
soups, 489
stirred custard, 633
storing chocolate, 628
storing cookies, 651
storing fish, 507
storing poultry, 553
storing shellfish, 520
and taste, 172
tempering chocolate, 625
washing tableware, 698
yeast, 570
tempering, 470–471
    chocolate, 625–628
    eggs, 631–632
    seeding method, 626
    tabling method, 626
tempering, knives, 106
tempura, 361
tender-crisp vegetables, 410
termination, 817
terrine mold, 134
terrines, 336, 362
Tex-Mex, 203
texture, 171, 230–231
    braising, 259–260
    cake batter, 654
    caviar, 334–336
    cheese rind, 331
    cold food presentation, 337
    composed salads, 318
    denaturing, 573
    describing, 173–174
    dried foods, 437
    fats in baking, 571
    frozen desserts, 637, 639
    garnishes, 342
    grains, 428–429
    moist heat affects, 252
    mousse, 636
    stewing, 259–260
Thailand, 443
thawing foods safely, 26
the 240 factor, 586
theme, restaurant, 789
thermistor thermometer, 130
thermocouple thermometer, 130
thermometer, 255
    appliance, 22
    bimetallic-coil, 130
    callibrating, 131
    infrared, 75–76
    instant-read, 27, 229
    liquid-filled, 130
    pan-frying, 246
    sanitizing, 24
    thermistor, 130
    thermocouple, 130

thickeners,
    baking ingredient, 574–575
    preparing, 469–471
    sauce, 468
three-compartment sink,
    handwashing smallware,
        135–136
thyme, 178
tilting fry pan, 86
tilting skillet, 86
time-temperature-abused food, 27
time,
    tempering chocolate, 625
timeline, 212–213
    career, 822
timing, 149
tip (of blade), 106
Tirel, Guillaume, 271
title of recipe, 146
toasting,
    nuts, seed, and spices, 194
tomato concassé, 409
tomato sauce, 477
tomatoes, 401–402
tongs, 127
tongue, 170
tools,
    bakeshop cutting, 576–577
    bakeshop, 575–577
    cooking, 125, 127
    draining, 128–129
    garnishes, 343
    grating, 125
    measuring, 129–131
    mixing, 125, 127
    pastry, 579–581
    portioning, 229
    prep, 125, 126
    processing, 128–129
    sandwich, 352–354
    shredding, 125
    straining, 128–129
    trimming, 125, 126
Top Chef, 144, 225
top crust, 664
toppings,
    pie, 664–665
toque, 50
torte, 657
tortellini, 451
tortilla, 350, 356
tossed salad, 307
total raw food cost, 162
touch, 170–171
tournée knife, 108
tourner, 119
toxic metals, 6
toxin-mediated infection, 5
toxins, 5
    mercury, 16
toxoplasmosis, 542
training, 815
tranche, 512
trans fats, 758
trans fatty acids, 758
translucent,
    describing flavor, 173
transparent,
    describing flavor, 173
tray stands, 99
trays, 99
    cold food presentation, 333
Triana, Gregory, 141
Trichinella spiralis (roundworm),
    6, 9
trichinosis, 9, 542

trim,
    fruit, 385
    loss, 385
trimming,
    fish fillets, 510–512
    fruit, 383–384
    garlic, 408
    holding the knife, 111
    meat, 548–549
    onions, 407
    tools, 125, 126
    vegetables, 408–409
tropical fruit, 378–379
trueing knives, 120–121
truffles,
    chocolate, 630
trussing poultry, 556–557
Truth-in-Menu laws, 733–734
tube pans, 578–579
tubers, 403–404
tuile, 643
turkey, history of, 555
turmeric, 183
turned cut, 119
turners, 127
turnovers, 360
turntables, 581
twice-baked cookies, 643, 648
two-stage cooling method, 25

 U

u-shaped work line, 70, 72
U.S. Department of Agriculture
    (USDA),
    grading of meat, 534–536,
        538
U.S. Department of Agriculture;
    See also USDA
udon, 444
umami, 169
undercounter dishwasher, 137
undercounter reach-in, 77
Unichef, 145
uniform, 14, 50
unsafe foods, 4
unsweetened chocolate, 623
urns, coffee, 694
USDA grade shields, 538
USDA grades,
    lamb, 544
    pork, 542–543
    poultry, 553
    veal, 541
USDA Select, 538
USDA,
    Agricultural Marketing Service,
        382, 405
    eggs, 268
    grading of meat, 534–536, 538
    grains, 432
    HACCP, 31
    MyPlate, 768
utility knife, 108

 V

Varenne, Pierre François de la,
    353
variable cost, 797
variable expense, 797
variety meat,
    beef, 540
    lamb, 546
    pork, 544
    veal, 542

Vatel, Francois, 381
VCM, 82
veal,
    cuts of, 540–542
    recommended temperature, 25
vegan, 776
vegetable cleaver, 109
vegetable dips, 304
vegetable dressings, 304
vegetable stock, 458–459
vegetables,
    aromatic, 184–185
    batch cooking, 779
    cleaning, 780
    color and nutrition, 764
    cooking, 409–414
    Dietary Guidelines, 769
    safety, 780
    in salads, 313–314
    sandwich filling, 351
    for stock, 457
    types of, 389–403
vegetarian, 774–776
velouté, 471
vendor, 803
venison, 546–547
ventilation hood, 41–42
verbal feedback, 219–220
verbal warning, 816
verenyky, 508
vertical chopping machine (VCM),
    82
vertical cutter/mixer, 82
vertical mixers, 84
vichyssoise, 484
Vietnamese breakfasts, 287
vinaigrette, 297–300, 779
    uses for, 300
vinegar, 199, 299
    poaching eggs, 273
viruses, 5–6
vitamins, 758–760
vocational teacher, 234
volume, 148, 150
    measuring, 130–131
    measuring dry, 152

 W

waffles, 284–286
walk-in, 76
walnut, 194
warewashing station, 136
warm emulsion sauce, 472, 475
warm foaming method,
    cake batter, 654–655
washes, dough, 598
washing area, 136–137
waste disposal, 18–19
waste management, 808
water activity (Aw), 11
water bath, 243
water boiler, 694
water cress, 309
water-soluble vitamins, 758
waxed-rind semisoft cheese,
    322
Weber, Stéphane, 673
weight loss, 776–778
weight, 148, 150
    eggs, 269
    measuring tools, 129
    measuring, 152
Welker, Hans, 603
well method, 607
wet aging, 538

wheat berry, 425
wheat flour, 567–568
wheat, 425
    classes of, 568
whetstone, 119
whip, 84
whipped cream,
    mousse, 636
    pie topping, 665
whisk, 127
white chocolate, 624
white mirepoix, 188, 458
white pepper, 199
white stock, 458–459, 463
whole fish, 506
whole grains, 423
    menu planning, 773
whole-grain,
    flour, 567
wild fish, 498
wild game,
    roundworms, 6
wine, 199
woks, 133, 245
wontons, 451
wooden spoon, 484
work flow, 70, 215–216
    communication, 74
    garde manger, 296
    mise en place, 73
    planning, 73
    timing, 73–74
work habits, 220–222
    cheese, 328
work lines, 70–72
work sections, 70
work sequencing, 214–215
work simplification, 215
work space,
    sandwiches, 354
work surfaces,
    bakeshop, 576
worker's compensation, 62
workstation, 69–70, 215–216
    plate presentation, 228
wrappers, 444
wraps, 356
written warning, 816
Wysocki, Susan, 820

X

xanthan gum, 468

Y

yeast dough,
    laminated, 590–591
    rolled-in, 590–591
    types of, 583–585
yeast hydration, 588
yeast, 570
yield of recipe, 146
yield percentage, 162
yield, 149
    scaling recipes, 157–160
Young, Chris, 103
    ChefSteps.com, 103
    Modernist Cuisine: The Art
        and Science of Cooking,
        103

Z

zest, 126
zester, 125, 126